S. Dressler

Elsevier's Wörterbuch Medizin

Elsevier's Dictionary of Medicine

Stephan Dressler

Elsevier's Wörterbuch Medizin

Englisch–Deutsch/Deutsch–Englisch

Elsevier's Dictionary of Medicine

English–German/German–English

Ein Praxiswörterbuch mit englischen Definitionen der wichtigsten Stichwörter

ELSEVIER
URBAN & FISCHER

URBAN & FISCHER
München · Jena

Zuschriften bitte an:
Elsevier GmbH, Urban & Fischer Verlag, Lexikonredaktion, Karlstraße 45, 80333 München. Nachschlagewerke@elsevier.de

Wichtiger Hinweis für Benutzer
Die Erkenntnisse in der Medizin unterliegen laufendem Wandel durch Forschung und klinische Erfahrungen. Herausgeber und Autoren dieses Werkes haben große Sorgfalt darauf verwendet, dass die in diesem Werk gemachten therapeutischen Angaben (insbesondere hinsichtlich Indikation, Dosierung und unerwünschter Wirkungen) dem derzeitigen Wissensstand entsprechen. Das entbindet den Nutzer dieses Werkes aber nicht von der Verpflichtung, anhand der Beipackzettel zu verschreibender Präparate zu überprüfen, ob die dort gemachten Angaben von denen in diesem Buch abweichen und seine Verordnung in eigener Verantwortung zu treffen.

Wie allgemein üblich wurden Warenzeichen bzw. Namen (z.B. bei Pharmapräparaten) nicht besonders gekennzeichnet.

Bibliografische Information der Deutschen Nationalbibliothek
Die Deutsche Nationalbibliothek verzeichnet diese Publikation in der Deutschen Nationalbibliografie; detaillierte bibliografische Daten sind im Internet über http://dnb.d-nb.de abrufbar.

1. Auflage 2007

Der Urban & Fischer Verlag ist ein Imprint der Elsevier GmbH.
Gemeinschaftsausgabe mit dem Langenscheidt Fachverlag GmbH, Berlin und München

07 08 09 10 11 5 4 3 2 1

Planung und Lektorat: Dr. med. Norbert Boss
Herstellung: Petra Laurer
Satz: Mitterweger & Partner, Plankstadt
Covergestaltung: Spieszdesign, Büro für Gestaltung, Neu-Ulm
Druck und Bindung: Krips b.v., Meppel, Niederlande

ISBN 978-3-437-15200-9

Aktuelle Informationen finden Sie im Internet unter www.elsevier.de und www.elsevier.com

Vorwort

Aufgabe des vorliegenden Wörterbuchs ist es, zuverlässige Übersetzungen der aktuellen medizinischen Fachausdrücke zu geben, verbunden mit Kurzdefinitionen der wichtigsten englischsprachigen Stichwörter, um damit dem Benutzer den Umgang sowohl mit der englischen als auch mit der deutschen Fachsprache der Medizin zu erleichtern. Ein zweisprachiges Wörterbuch ist keine Enzyklopädie der Medizin und kann einschlägige einsprachige Lexika nicht ersetzen.

Berlin, im April 2007 Stephan Dressler

Preface

This dictionary provides translations of current medical terms, short English definitions of clinically relevant entries, and is thus intended to be an aid for the user who seeks information on German as well as on English medical terminology. However, a bilingual dictionary is not an encyclopedia of medicine. Much useful information which many English or German monolingual medical dictionaries can provide had to be omitted.

Berlin, April 2007 Stephan Dressler

Hinweise zur Benutzung dieses Wörterbuchs

I. Auswahl der Stichwörter

Das Wörterbuch enthält als Kernbestand Stichwörter aus dem Gebiet der klinischen und praktischen Medizin. Bei der weiteren Auswahl wurden allgemeinmedizinisch relevante Stichwörter aus Grundlagenfächern wie Chemie, Physik, Biochemie oder Biologie und aus Nachbargebieten wie Pharmakologie und Biotechnologie berücksichtigt. Bei Medikamenten sind die internationalen Freinamen (INN), nicht jedoch Handelsnamen aufgeführt.

Nicht aufgenommen wurden allgemeinsprachliche Wörter; anderssprachige, z.B. lateinische oder griechische Stichwörter wurden nicht aufgenommen, wenn sie sowohl in der englischen als auch in der deutschen medizinischen Fachsprache identisch verwendet werden. Die (international einheitlichen) Nomina Anatomica bleiben ebenso wie akademische Titel, Berufsbezeichnungen, Abkürzungen und Namen von Gesellschaften in der Regel unberücksichtigt.

II. Anordnung der Stichwörter

Die Stichwörter sind alphabetisch angeordnet. Die Umlaute ä, ö und ü werden wie ae, oe und ue, ß wird wie ss behandelt. Vorsilben griechischer Herkunft sind ausgeschrieben, wenn sie fester Bestandteil des Stichworts sind. Bei Eigennamen gelten Namensbestandteile wie Da, Le oder Mc als untrennbare Bestandteile des Namens.

Die Stichwörter sind normalerweise im Nominativ Singular bzw. bei Sammelbezeichnungen und nicht im Singular gebrauchten Wörtern im Nominativ Plural angesetzt. Verben werden im Infinitiv, Adjektive in der unflektierten Form angesetzt.

Für zusammengesetzte oder mehrteilige Stichwörter gilt: sind zwei Bestandteile durch einen Bindestrich verbunden, wird nach dem ersten Bestandteil alphabetisch geordnet. So steht z.B. after-loading unter A. Dasselbe gilt für unverbunden nebeneinander stehende Substantive, die zusammen ein Stichwort bilden. Besteht das Stichwort aus einem Adjektiv und einem Substantiv, so ist das Adjektiv maßgebend für die alphabetische Einordnung, d.h. man findet *alcoholic fatty liver* unter A oder *urinary tract* unter U:

urinary tract: Harntrakt *m*.
urinary tract infection: infection of the urinary tract, typically caused by bacteria, which may affect the urethra, the bladder, the ureters, and the kidneys. Initial symptoms include urination disorders like dysuria or pollakiuria. Harnweginfektion *f*.
urination/*n*: Miktion *f*, Wasserlassen *n*.
urine/*n*: Urin *m*, Harn *m*.
uriniferous/*adj*: harnleitend.
urinometry/*n*: Urometrie *f*.
urobilin/*n*: Urobilin *n*.
urobilinogen/*n*: Urobilinogen *n*.

Bei deutschsprachigen Stichwörtern, die aus einem identischen Substantiv und aus einem oder mehreren jeweils wechselnden Adjektiven bestehen, werden Wortnester gebildet. Dabei ersetzt innerhalb des Wortnests eine Tilde (≈) jeweils das Hauptstichwort:

Tachykardie *f*: tachycardia, tachyrhythmia; **digitalisinduzierte** ≈ digitalis-induced tachycardia; **ektope** ≈ ectopic tachycardia; **heterotope** ≈ supranodal tachycardia; **orthostatische** ≈ orthostatic tachycardia; **paroxysmale** ≈ paroxysmal tachycardia, Bouveret's disease; **supraventrikuläre** ≈ supraventricular tachycardia; **ventrikuläre** ≈ ventricular tachycardia.
Tacrin *n*: tacrine.
Tacrolimus *m*: tacrolimus.
Tadalafil *n*: tadalafil.
täglich: daily, quotidian.
Tänie *f*: taenia.
Tätowierung *f*: tattoo, tattooing.
Täuschung *f*: delusion, illusion; **optische** ≈ optical illusion.

III. Schreibweise der Stichwörter

Englischsprachige Stichwörter werden mit Ausnahme von Eigennamen prinzipiell klein geschrieben. Berücksichtigt wird in der Regel nur die amerikanische Schreibweise (z. B. *hematology* statt *haematology*; *center* statt *centre*).
Die Schreibweise der deutschsprachigen Übersetzungen und Einträge richtet sich in der Regel nach dem *Roche Lexikon Medizin* 5. Auflage 2003.

IV. Angaben zu den einzelnen Stichwörtern

Bei englischsprachigen Stichwörtern finden sich folgende Angaben:

<abbr> = abbreviation (Abkürzung)
/n = noun (Substantiv)
/adj = adjective (Adjektiv)
/vb = verb (Verb)

Klinisch besonders relevanten englischsprachigen Stichwörtern wurde eine englischsprachige Kurzdefinition beigegeben.

Bei den deutschsprachigen Äquivalenten englischer Stichwörter und bei den deutschen Stichwörtern finden sich bei Substantiven als Genusangaben:

m = masculinum (männlich)
f = femininum (weiblich)
n = neutrum (sächlich)

Englisch – Deutsch

A

A

a <*abbr*> **1. absorbent; 2. accommodation; 3. acid; 4. actin; 5. adenine; 6. allergy; 7. artery**: 1. Absorbens *n*; 2. Akkomodation *f*, A; 3. Säure *f*; 4. Aktin *n*; 5. Adenin *n*, A; 6. Allergie *f*; 7. Arterie *f*, Arteria *f*, A.
abacavir/*n*: Abacavir *n*.
abarelix/*n*: Abarelix *n*.
abdomen/*n*: Bauch *m*, Abdomen *n*.
abdominal/*adj*: abdominal.
abdominal aneurysm: an aneurysm of the abdominal aorta, usually located below the renal arteries. abdominales Aortenaneurysma *n*.
abdominal bandage: Leibbinde *f*.
abdominal breathing: Bauchatmung *f*.
abdominal canal: Leistenkanal *m*.
abdominal cavity: Bauchhöhle *f*.
abdominal colic: Abdominalkolik *f*.
abdominal cutaneous reflex: Bauchhautreflex *m*, BHR.
abdominal epilepsy: abdominale Epilepsie *f*, Moore-Syndrom *n*.
abdominal fistula: Bauchdeckenfistel *f*.
abdominal hernia: protrusion of internal organs or abdominal structures through the abdominal wall, for example median abdominal hernia localized in the linea alba, or extramedian abdominal hernia in the linea semilunaris. Bauchwandbruch *m*.
abdominal pad: Bauchtupfer *m*.
abdominal pain: Bauchschmerz *m*.
abdominal percussion: Perkussion des Abdomens *f*.
abdominal position: Bauchlage *f*.
abdominal pregnancy: Bauchhöhlenschwangerschaft *f*.
abdominal pressure: Bauchpresse *f*.
abdominal pulse: abdomineller Aortenpuls *m*.
abdominal puncture: Bauchhöhlenpunktion *f*, Aszitespunktion *f*.
abdominal reflex: Bauchmuskelreflex *m*.
abdominal region: Bauchregion *f*.
abdominal respiration: Bauchatmung *f*.
abdominal retractor: Bauchdeckenhaken *m*.
abdominal section: Laparotomie *f*.
abdominal surgery: Bauchchirurgie *f*.
abdominal testis: Abdominalhoden *m*, Bauchhoden *m*.
abdominal trauma: Bauchtrauma *n*.
abdominal typhus: Typhus abdominalis *m*.
abdominal version: äußere Wendung *f*.
abdominal zone: Bauchregion *f*.
abducens paralysis: uni- or bilateral paralysis of the abducent nerve, resulting in paralysis of external eye muscles and impairment of eye abduction. Abduzenslähmung *f*.
abducent/*adj*: abduzierend.
abduct/*vb*: abduzieren.
abduction/*n*: Abduktion *f*.
aberrant/*adj*: aberrant, abweichend.
aberrant bundle: aberrierendes Bündel *n*.
aberrant conduction: abnorme Reizüberleitung *f*.
aberrant goiter: Nebenstruma *f*.
aberrant ureter: fehlmündender Harnleiter *m*.
aberration/*n*: Aberration *m*.
abeyance/*n*: Unentschiedenheit *f*.
abietic acid: Abietinsäure *f*.
ability/*n*: Fähigkeit *f*.
abnormal/*adj*: abnorm, anormal.

abnormal development: Entwicklungsstörung *f*.
abnormality/*n*: Abnormalität *f*.
abnormal position: Lageanomalie *f*.
abnormal reflex: pathologischer Reflex *m*.
AB0 system: ABNull-System *n*.
abortion/*n*: termination of pregnancy before the embryo or fetus has reached the period of viability. Accidental abortion or miscarriage may be due to abnormalities of the ovum or the infant, endocrine or nutritional disorders, as well as other diseases like infections. Abort *m*, Schwangerschaftsabbruch *m*.
abortive epilepsy: Petit-mal-Epilepsie *f*.
abrade/*vb*: abkratzen, abschürfen.
abraded wound: Abrasionsverletzung *f*.
abrupt pulse: schnellender Puls *m*.
abscess/*n*: collection of pus enclosed in a tissue, an organ, or newly formed sac, resulting from inflammation and formed when foreign organisms like bacteria destroy tissue. Abszess *m*.
abscessed tonsil: Tonsillenabszess *m*.
absent state: Absence *f*.
absinthe/*n*: Absinth *m*.
absolute/*adj*: absolut.
absolute agraphia: vollständige Agraphie *f*.
absolute alcohol: absoluter Alkohol *m*.
absolute dullness: absolute Dämpfung *f*.
absolute near point: absoluter Nahpunkt *m*.
absolute polycythemia: Polycythaemia vera *f*.
absolute refractory period: absolute Refraktärperiode *f*.
absorbable suture: resorbierbares Nahtmaterial *n*.
abstinence symptom: any sign or symptom an alcohol, drug or narcotics addict experiences when the use of the substance is stopped abruptly. Entzugssymptom *n*.
abstract/*n*: Zusammenfassung *f*.
abuse/*n, vb*: 1. wrong use and misuse, or excessive use, of something. The term is frequently used in connection with alcohol and psychoactive substance abuse, such as in drug abuse, and to characterize a dependence. Missbrauch *m*, Abusus *m*; 2. missbrauchen.
acalculia/*n*: Akalkulie *f*.
acamprosate/*n*: Acamprosat *n*.
acanthoma/*n*: Akanthom *n*.
acanthosis/*n*: Akanthose *f*.
acapnia/*n*: Akapnie *f*.
acapnial alkalosis: respiratorische Alkalose *f*.
acarbose/*n*: Acarbose *n*.
acariasis/*n*: Acariasis *f*.
acaricide/*n*: Akarizid *n*.
acatalasia/*n*: an autosomal recessive disorder which is characterized by a deficiency of the enzyme catalase. Usually asymptomatic, it may, however, manifest in some patients with oral ulcerations and gangrene. Akatalasie *f*, Takahara-Krankheit *f*.
acathisia/*n*: Akathisie *f*, Bewegungsunruhe *f*.
accelerated conduction: beschleunigte Reizüberleitung *f*.
accelerated idioventricular rhythm: beschleunigter Kammereigenrhythmus *m*.
acceptor/*n*: Akzeptor *m*.
access/*n*: Zugang *m*.
accessory/*adj*: akzessorisch.
accessory bone: akzessorischer Knochen *m*.
accessory mamma: mammary gland present in excess to the normal number of two, usually found along the embryonic milk line. akzessorische Mamma *f*.
accessory nucleus: Nebenkern *m*.
accessory pathway: Nebenstoffwechselweg *m*.
accessory placenta: Placenta accessoria *f*, Nebenplazenta *f*.
accessory sign: Nebensymptom *n*.
accessory thymus: Nebenthymus *m*.
accident/*n*: Unfall *m*, Zufall *m*.
accidental/*adj*: zufällig, akzidentell.
accidental albuminuria: akzidentelle

Albuminurie *f*.
accidental death: Unfalltod *m*.
accidental neurosis: Unfallneurose *f*.
acclimatization/*n*: Akklimatisierung *f*.
accommodation/*n*: Akkommodation *f*, Anpassung *f*.
accommodative convergence: Akkommodationskonvergenz *f*.
accommodative strabismus: disorder with deviation of the eye, resulting from excessive or deficient accommodative effort. Akkommodationsschielen *n*.
accompanying effect: Begleiteffekt *m*.
accompanying illness: Begleiterkrankung *f*.
accretion/*n*: Anlagerung *f*.
accretionary growth: Akkretionswachstum *n*.
accuminate papular syphilid: makulopapulöses Syphilid *n*.
accumulated dose: Kumulativdosis *f*.
accumulative effect: kumulative Wirkung *f*.
accuracy/*n*: Akkuratheit *f*, Genauigkeit *f*.
acebutolol/*n*: Acebutolol *n*.
acecarbromal/*n*: Acecarbromal *n*.
aceclidine/*n*: Aceclidin *n*.
aceclofenac/*n*: Aceclofenac *n*.
acefylline piperazine: Acefyllinpiperazin *n*.
ACE inhibitor: ACE-Hemmer *m*.
acemetacin/*n*: Acemetacin *n*.
acenocoumarol/*n*: Acenocoumarol *n*.
acentric occlusion: Okklusionsstörung *f*.
acephalic/*adj*: azephal, kopflos
acephaly/*n*: Azephalie *f*.
acetabular/*adj*: acetabulus, azetabulär, Pfannen-.
acetaminophen/*n*: Acetaminophen *n*, Paracetamol *n*.
acetanilid/*n*: Acetanilid *n*.
acetazolamide/*n*: Acetazolamid *n*.
acetic acid: Essigsäure *f*.
acetoacetic acid: Acetessigsäure *f*.
acetone/*n*: Aceton *n*.
acetonemia/*n*: Acetonämie *f*.
acetonuria/*n*: Acetonurie *f*.
acetrizoic acid: Acetricoesäure *f*.
acetylcholine/*n*: Acetylcholin *n*.
acetylcysteine/*n*: Acetylcystein *n*.
acetylproprionic acid: Lävulinsäure *f*.
acetylsalicylic/*adj*: acetylsalicylsauer.
acetylsalicylic acid: Acetylsalicylsäure *f*, ASS.
achalasia/*n*: inability of a muscular sphincter or the smooth muscles of a hollow organ to relax, for example achalasia of the esophagus. Causes include disturbances in innervation, or lesions of ganglions. Achalasie *f*.
ache/*n, vb*: 1. Schmerz *m*; 2. schmerzen.
Achilles tendon: Achillessehne *f*, Tendo calcaneus *m*.
Achilles tendon reflex: Achillessehnenreflex *m*.
aching/*adj*: schmerzhaft.
achlorhydria/*n*: Achlorhydrie *f*.
achlorhydric anemia: Chloranämie *f*, Faber-Syndrom *n*.
acholia/*n*: Acholie *f*.
achondroplasia/*n*: a hereditary chondrodysplasia with inadequate enchondral bone formation in which the trunk is of normal size, but the extremities are too short, resulting in dwarfism. Achondroplasie *f*.
achondroplastic pelvis: achondroplastisches Becken *n*.
achrestic anemia: achrestische Anämie *f*.
achromatic/*adj*: achromatisch, farblos.
achromatic lens: achromatische Linse *f*.
achromatic vision: totale Farbenblindheit *f*.
achromatopsia/*n*: Achromatopsie *f*, komplette Farbenblindheit *f*.
achylia gastrica: Achylia gastrica *f*, Magensaftmangel *m*.
achylic anemia: severe form of an iron deficiency anemia resulting from insufficient iron uptake in achlorhydric conditions which are characterized by the absence of hydrochloric acid from gastric secretions. Symptoms include xerodermia, oral fissures, changes of the nails,

coarseness, dysphagia, and glossitis. Chloranämie *f*, Faber-Syndrom *n*.
aciclovir/*n*: Aciclovir *n*.
acid/*n, adj*: 1. Säure *f*; 2. sauer.
acid-base balance: Säure-Basen-Haushalt *m*, Säure-Basen-Gleichgewicht *n*.
acidemia/*n*: Azidämie *f*, Azidose *f*.
acid-fast: säurefest.
acid-inhibiting agent: Antazidum *n*.
aciditiy/*n*: Azidität *f*.
acidomycin/*n*: Acidomycin *n*.
acidophilic adenoma: eosinophiles Adenom *n*.
acidophilic cell: Eosinophiler *m*.
acidosis/*n*: a condition which is characterized by increased acid levels in the blood. Causes include disease or failure of the lungs or kidneys. Acidosis can also be caused by dehydration, metabolic disorders, intoxications, and acid poisoning. Azidose *f*.
acid resistance: Säurebeständigkeit *f*.
acid susceptibility: Säureempfindlichkeit *f*.
aciduria/*n*: Azidurie *f*.
acinar cell: Azinuszelle *f*.
acinar cell carcinoma: Azinuszellkarzinom *n*.
acinic cell: Azinuszelle *f*.
acitretin/*n*: Acitretin *n*.
acknowledgment/*n*: Anerkennung *f*.
aclarubicin/*n*: Aclarubicin *n*.
acme/*n*: Akme *f*, Höhepunkt *m*.
acne/*n*: a skin condition in which sebaceous glands become infected, and which is characterized by comedos and small skin elevations with or without pus. Found usually in adolescents, acne will normally subside when puberty is completed. Akne *f*, Hautfinnenausschlag *m*.
acne rosacea: Acne rosacea *f*.
aconite/*n*: Akonit *n*, Eisenhut *m*.
aconitic acid: Akonitsäure *f*.
aconitine/*n*: Akonitin *n*.
aconuresis/*n*: Harninkontinenz *f*.
acorea/*n*: Akorie *f*.
acoustic/*n, adj*: 1. Akustik *f*; 2. akustisch.
acoustic agnosia: akustische Agnosie *f*, Lautagnosie *f*.
acoustic neurinoma: a usually benign tumor growing from the acoustic nerve within the auditory canal. Symptoms vary with size and localization of the tumor and may include hearing loss, headache, disturbances of balance, pain, and tinnitus. Akustikusneurinom *n*.
acoustic labyrinth: akustisches Labyrinth *n*.
acoustics/*n*: Akustik *f*.
acoustic trauma: Lärmtrauma *n*.
acquired/*adj*: erworben.
acquired cerebellar syndrome: a condition resulting from cerebellar lesion, for example cerebellar hemorrhage or tumor. Symptoms include ataxia, disturbances of diadochokinesis and muscle tonus, and movement disorders. erworbenes Kleinhirnsyndrom *n*, Goldstein-Reichmann-Krankheit *f*.
acquired epilepsy: symptomatische Epilepsie *f*.
acquired immunodeficiency syndrome: a chronic infectious disease caused by the human immunodeficiency virus, HIV. HIV attacks certain cells of the immune system, which results in immune deficiency and the occurrence of opportunistic infections and cancers. erworbenes Immundefektsyndrom *n*, AIDS.
acquired reflex: konditionierter Reflex *m*.
acquired sideroachrestic anemia: therapierefraktäre sideroachrestische Anämie *f*.
acral lentiginous melanoma: akrolentiginöses Melanom *n*.
acrid/*adj*: ätzend, scharf.
acrocephaly/*n*: Akrozephalie *f*.
acrocyanosis/*n*: Akrozyanose *f*.
acrodermatitis/*n*: Akrodermatitis *f*.
acrodynia/*n*: Akrodynie *f*, Feer-Krankheit *f*.
acrokeratosis/*n*: Akrokeratose *f*.
acromegalic gigantism: akromegaler Riesenwuchs *m*.
acromegaly/*n*: state of excessive growth of the nose, chin, ears, hands, and feet, and sometimes the

entire body with gigantism, caused by overactivity of the pituitary gland, usually due to a pituitary adenoma. Akromegalie *f*, Marie-Krankheit *f*.

acromioclavicular/*adj*: akromioklavikular.

acronym/*n*: Akronym *n*.

acropathy/*n*: Extremitätenerkrankung *f*.

acrosomal cone: Akrosomenkörperchen *n*.

acrosomal granule: Akrosomengranulum *n*.

acrotic/*adj*: pulslos.

acrotism/*n*: Pulslosigkeit *f*.

acrylic acid: Akrylsäure *f*.

acting out: Agieren *n*.

actinic/*adj*: aktinisch.

actinic conjunctivitis: Conjunctivitis actinica *f*.

actinic dermatitis: inflammatory reaction of the skin, caused by exposure to radiation, or sun rays. The term is also used to describe chronic, inflammatory skin changes resulting from sun exposition. Aktinodermatitis *f*, Strahlendermatitis *f*.

actinic keratosis: aktinische Keratose *f*.

actinic retinitis: aktinische Retinopathie *f*.

actinomycin/*n*: Actinomycin *n*.

action/*n*: Aktion *f*, Wirkmechanismus *m*.

activated clotting factor: aktivierter Gerinnungsfaktor *m*.

activated partial thromboplastin time: aktivierte partielle Thromboplastinzeit *f*, APTT.

activated reticular cell: aktivierte Retikulumzelle *f*.

activating agent: Aktivator *m*.

active/*adj*: aktiv.

active carrier: aktiver Träger *m*.

active component: Wirkkomponente *f*.

active gene: aktives Gen *n*.

active labor: Eröffnungsperiode *f*.

active movement: Willkürbewegung *f*.

active phase: Eröffnungsperiode *f*.

active renal tubular transport: aktiver Tubulustransport *m*.

active site: aktive Region *f*.

activity/*n*: Aktivität *f*, Wirksamkeit *f*.

actomyosin/*n*: Aktomyosin *n*.

actual/*adj*: wirklich, gegenwärtig.

actual neurosis: Aktualneurose *f*.

acuity/*n*: Schärfe *f*.

acuminate wart: spitzes Kondylom *n*.

acupressure/*n*: Akupressur *f*.

acupuncture/*n*: Akupunktur *f*.

acute/*adj*: akut.

acute abdomen: condition with rapid onset of abdominal pain, vomiting, meteorism, and muscular defense, requiring emergency diagnostics. An acute abdomen typically indicates a disease requiring surgical intervention. akutes Abdomen *n*.

acute ascending paralysis: Paralysis acuta ascendens spinalis *f*, Landry-Paralyse *f*.

acute benign lymphocytic meningitis: lymphozytäre Choriomeningitis *f*.

acute bronchitis: akute Bronchitis *f*.

acute bulbar polioencephalitis: Bulbärpoliomyelitis *f*.

acute care: Akutpflege *f*.

acute catarrhal rhinitis: Erkältung *f*.

acute chorea: Chorea minor *f*, Sydenham-Chorea *f*.

acute congestive glaucoma: sudden increase in intraocular pressure, caused by closure of the anterior angle of the eye, due to iris block with pupillary block, iris block without pupillary block, or ciliary block. Symptoms include headache, vision disorder, hardening of the eyeball, and unequal pupils. akutes Engwinkelglaukom *n*.

acute contagious conjunctivitis: Koch-Weeks-Konjunktivitis *f*.

acute cystitis: akute Zystitis *f*.

acute diffuse familial infantile cerebral sclerosis: Krabbe-Syndrom *n*, Globoidzellen-Leukodystrophie *f*.

acute exudative pericarditis: akute exsudative Perikarditis *f*.

acute febrile neutrophilic dermatosis: akute febrile neutrophile Dermatose *f*, Sweet-Syndrom *n*.

acute fulminating meningococcal septicemia: akute fulminante Meningokokkensepsis *f*, Waterhouse-Friderichsen-Syndrom *n*.

acute gastritis: akute Gastritis *f*.

acute heart failure: akutes Herzversagen *n*.

acute hemorrhagic pancreatitis: akute hämorrhagische Pankreatitis *f*.

acute hepatitis: acute inflammatory reaction of the liver, usually caused by viruses, bacteria, protozoa, or other pathogenic microorganisms, or by toxic substances. Symptoms include elevated liver function tests, endocrine disturbances, enlargement of the liver, and eventually pain and jaundice. akute Hepatitis *f*.

acute infantile encephalopathy: Brown-Symmers-Krankheit *f*.

acute infantile hemiplegia: Strümpell-Leichtenstern-Krankheit *f*.

acute infantile spinal muscular atrophy: Werdnig-Hoffmann-Krankheit *f*.

acute infectious gastroenteritis: akute infektiöse Gastroenteritis *f*.

acute infectious jaundice: an infectious disease caused by the bacterium Leptospira interrogans. Symptoms include high fever, chills, muscle and joint pain, enlargement of the liver, and icterus. ikterohämorrhagische Leptospirose *f*, Weil-Krankheit *f*.

acute infectious paralysis: Poliomyelitis anterior acuta *f*.

acute infective polyneuritis: a neurologic disorder of unknown etiology, possibly due to an autoimmune disorder following viral or bacterial infection. Symptoms include polyneuritis, ascending motor neuron paralysis and muscular weakness, initial paralysis of the legs, ascending to the arms and trunk. akute infektiöse Polyneuritis *f*, Guillain-Barré-Syndrom *n*.

acute intermittent porphyria: akute intermittierende Porphyrie *f*.

acute lymphatic leukemia: leukemia which is characterized by the increase of circulating malignant lymphoblasts, primarily affecting infants. Symptoms include anemia, thrombocytopenia, enlargement of lymph nodes, and splenomegaly. akute lymphatische Leukämie *f*.

acute lymphonodular pharyngitis: Coxsackie-Pharyngitis *f*.

acute miliary tuberculosis: akute Miliartuberkulose *f*.

acute myeloid leukemia: leukemia which is characterized by the predominance of myeloblastic cells, primarily affecting middle-aged and elder people. Symptoms include anemia, weight loss, thrombocytopenia, and granulocytopenia and consecutive bacterial infections. akute myeloische Leukämie *f*, AML.

acute necrotizing gingivitis: akute nekrotisierende Gingivitis *f*.

acute necrotizing stomatitis: akute nekrotisierende Stomatitis *f*, Noma *f*.

acuteness/*n*: Spitze *f*, Schärfe *f*.

acute nonsuppurative thyroiditis: Quervain-Thyreoiditis *f*.

acute pain: akuter Schmerz *m*.

acute paranoid disorder: akute paranoide Störung *f*.

acute pharyngitis: akute Pharyngitis *f*.

acute postinfectious polyneuropathy: a neurologic disorder of unknown etiology, possibly due to an autoimmune disorder following viral or bacterial infection. Symptoms include polyneuritis, ascending motor neuron paralysis and muscular weakness, initial paralysis of the legs, ascending to the arms and trunk. akute infektiöse Polyneuritis *f*, Guillain-Barré-Syndrom *n*.

acute pyelitis: akute Pyelitis *f*.

acute rejection: akute Abstoßungsreaktion *f*.

acute renal failure: akutes Nierenversagen *n*.

acute rheumatic carditis: akute rheumatische Karditis *f*.

acute rhinitis: Rhinitis acuta *f*, Schnupfen *m*.

acute sleeping sickness: afrikanische Trypanosomiasis *f*, Schlafkrankheit *f*.
acute spinal pachymeningitis: Pachydermitis spinalis externa *f*.
acute suppurative thyroiditis: akute eitrige Thyreoiditis *f*.
acute trypanosomiasis: afrikanische Trypanosomiasis *f*, Schlafkrankheit *f*.
acute vascular purpura: a condition which is characterized by the presence of small hemorrhages, probably due to an inflammation of blood vessels. It is most frequently observed in children and may affect also the joints, the intestine, and the kidneys. The platelet count is normal. Schoenlein-Henoch-Purpura *f*.
acute yellow atrophy: akute gelbe Leberatrophie *f*.
acyesis/*n*: weibliche Sterilität *f*.
adactylia/*n*: Adaktylie *f*.
Adam's apple: Adamsapfel *m*.
adapalene/*n*: Adapalen *n*.
adaptation/*n*: Anpassung *f*, Adaptation *f*.
adapted milk: adaptierte Milch *f*.
adaptive behavior: Anpassungsverhalten *n*.
adaptive hypertrophy: Anpassungshypertrophie *f*.
add/*vb*: addieren, hinzufügen.
addict/*n, vb*: 1. Abhängiger *m*; 2. abhängig sein.
addiction/*n*: Abhängigkeit *f*.
addisonian anemia: Addison-Anämie *f*, perniziöse Anämie *m*.
addisonian crisis: Addison-Krise *f*.
addisonian dermal pigmentation: Addison-Bronzehaut *f*.
Addison's disease: a condition which is characterized by insufficent activity of the adrenal glands. Symptoms include fatigue, weakness, weight loss, dehydration, hyperpigmentation of the skin, hypotonia, and reduced levels of blood glucose. Addison-Krankheit *f*, Nebennierenrindeninsuffizienz *f*.
additional sound: zusätzlicher Herzton *m*.
additive effect: additive Wirkung *f*.
adduction/*n*: Adduktion *f*.
adductor/*n*: Adduktor *m*.
adefovir/*n*: Adefovir *n*.
adendritic/*adj*: adendritisch.
adenectomy/*n*: Drüsenexstirpation *f*.
adenitis/*n*: Adenitis *f*, Drüsenentzündung *f*.
adenocarcinoma/*n*: a malignant neoplasm originating from glandular structures. Forms include tumors with tubular, acinar, cystic, papillary, and trabecular growth. Adenokarzinom *n*.
adenofibroma/*n*: Adenofibrom *n*.
adenohypophysial hormone: Hypophysenvorderlappenhormon *n*.
adenohypophysis/*n*: Adenohypophyse *f*, Hypophysenvorderlappen *m*, HVL.
adenoid/*n, adj*: 1. Rachenmandel *f*; 2. adenoid.
adenoid cystic carcinoma: Zylindrom *n*.
adenoidectomy/*n*: Adenotomie *f*.
adenoid face: Facies adenoidea *f*.
adenoiditis/*n*: Rachenmandelentzündung *f*.
adenoid vegetation: hypertrophic enlargement of the pharyngeal adenoids, most usually found in children. Symptoms may include recurrent infections of the upper respiratory tract, and impaired respiration. adenoide Vegetation *f*, Rachenmandelhyperplasie *f*.
adenolipoma/*n*: Lipoadenom *n*.
adenolymphoma/*n*: Adenolymphom *n*, Warthin-Tumor *m*.
adenoma/*n*: Adenom *n*.
adenomatosis/*n*: Adenomatose *f*.
adenomatous polyposis: adenomatöse Polypose *f*.
adenomatous struma: Knotenstruma *f*.
adenomyoma/*n*: Adenomyom *n*.
adenomyosis/*n*: Adenomyosis *f*, Endometriosis interna *f*.
adenopathy/*n*: Lymphadenopathie *f*.
adenosine/*n*: Adenosin *n*.
adenosine 3',5'-cyclic phosphate: zyklisches Adenosinphosphat *n*, AMP.

adenosine diphosphate: Adenosindiphosphat *n*, ADP.
adenosine monophosphate: Adenosinmonophosphat *n*, AMP.
adenosine triphosphate: Adenosintriphosphat *n*, ATP.
adenosine triphosphatase: Adenosintriphosphatase *f*, ATPase.
adenosquamous carcinoma: Adenoepitheliom *n*.
adenotonsillectomy/*n*: Adenotomie *f*.
adenovirus/*n*: Adenovirus *n*.
adenylic acid: Adenylsäure *f*.
adequate/*adj*: adäquat, angemessen.
adequate stimulus: adäquater Reiz *m*.
adherence/*n*: Adhärenz *f*.
adherent placenta: Placenta adhaerens *f*, festhaftende Plazenta *f*.
adhesion/*n*: Adhäsion *f*.
adhesive adsorbent dressing: Adhäsionsverband *m*.
adhesive bandage: Heftpflasterverband *m*.
adhesive pericarditis: fusion of the parietal and visceral layers of the pericardium and obliteration of the pericardial cavity. Causes include direct or indirect injury of the pericardium, infections, metabolic disorders, and autoimmune diseases. adhäsive Perikarditis *f*, Perikardsynechie *f*.
adhesive peritonitis: adhäsive Peritonitis *f*.
adhesive plaster: Heftpflaster *n*.
adhesive pleurisy: adhäsive Pleuritis *f*.
adhesive tape: Heftpflaster *n*.
adipose/*adj*: adipös, fett.
adipose body: Bichat-Fettpfropf *m*.
adipose cell: Adipozyt *m*, Fettzelle *f*.
adipose degeneration: fettige Degeneration *f*.
adiposity/*n*: a condition which is characterized by an excess of fat tissue in relation to other body components, and an increase of twentyfive percent or more over normal weight. Adiposity or obesity is typically resulting from a persistent caloric intake that exceeds the energy needs of the body. Causative factors may include constitutional and/or metabolic or endocrine factors, but frequently emotional, cultural, or dietary influences, and lack of physical exercise are the main causes. Adipositas *f*, Fettsucht *f*, Übergewicht *n*.
adiposogenital syndrome: an endocrine disorder resulting from lesions of hypothalamic nuclei and reduced hormonal production. Symptoms include rapidly developing adiposity, in children associated with reduced growth and delayed onset of puberty with sexual retardation. adiposogenitales Syndrom *n*, Fröhlich-Syndrom *n*.
adjusting cone: Einstellungstubus *m*.
adjustment/*n*: Anpassung *f*.
adjuvant/*n, adj*: 1. Adjuvans *n*; 2. adjuvant.
adjuvant medication: Begleitmedikation *f*.
administration/*n*: Darreichung *f*, Applikation *f*.
admission/*n*: Aufnahme *f*, Zulassung *f*.
adnexectomy/*n*: Adnexektomie *f*.
adolescent acne: juvenile Akne *f*.
adolescent osteochondritis: juvenile Osteochondritis *f*.
adoption/*n*: Adoption *f*.
adrenal/*adj*: Nebennieren-.
adrenal apoplexy: Nebennierenapoplexie *f*, Nebennierenrindeninfarkt *m*.
adrenal cortex: Nebennierenrinde *f*, NNR.
adrenal cyst: Nebennierenzyste *f*.
adrenalectomy/*n*: Adrenalektomie *f*, Nebennierenentfernung *f*.
adrenal gland: Nebenniere *f*.
adrenal hyperplasia: Nebennierenrindenhyperplasie *f*.
adrenaline/*n*: Adrenalin *n*, Epinephrin *n*.
adrenal steroid: Nebennierensteroid *n*.
adrenergic/*adj*: adrenerg.
adrenergic amine: Katecholamin *n*.
adrenergic fiber: adrenerge Nervenfaser *f*.

adrenergic receptor: adrenerger Rezeptor *m*.
adrenocortical/*adj*: adrenokortikal.
adrenocortical adenoma: a benign tumor of the cortex of the adrenal gland. Symptoms depend on the endocrine activity of the tumor and may include feminization or virilization, and Cushing's syndrome. Nebennierenrindenadenom *n*.
adrenocortical crisis: Addison-Krise *f*.
adrenocortical insufficiency: a condition which is characterized by insufficent activity of the adrenal glands. Symptoms include fatigue, weakness, weight loss, dehydration, hyperpigmentation of the skin, hypotonia, and reduced levels of blood glucose. Nebennierenrindeninsuffizienz *f*, Addison-Krankheit *f*.
adrenocorticotropic/*adj*: adrenokortikotrop.
adrenocorticotropic hormone: adrenokortikotropes Hormon *n*, ACTH.
adrenogenital syndrome: a group of syndromes which are characterized by inappropriate virilism or feminization, caused by dysfunction of the adrenal glands which also affect the gonadal steroidogenesis. adrenogenitales Syndrom *n*, AGS.
adrenolytic/*n, adj*: 1. Adrenolytikum *n*; 2. adrenolytisch, sympatholytisch.
adult/*n, adj*: 1. Erwachsener *m*; 2. adult, erwachsen.
adult diabetes: diabetes mellitus type II with a gradual onset in adults around the age of fifty and in which basal insulin secretion is maintained at normal or reduced levels, but is delayed or reduced in relation to the blood glucose levels. Erwachsenendiabetes *m*, Altersdiabetes *m*.
adulterant/*n*: Streckmittel *n*.
adult-onset diabetes: Erwachsenendiabetes *m*.
adult respiratory distress syndrome: a condition of pulmonary insufficiency which is characterized by insufficient oxygenation. Common causes include generalized shock, septicemia, multiple trauma, and embolism. posttraumatische pulmonale Insuffizienz *f*, Schocklunge *f*, ARDS.
advance/*n, vb*: 1. Fortschritt *m*, Verbesserung *f*; 2. fortschreiten, fördern.
advanced/*adj*: fortgeschritten.
advanced stage: fortgeschrittenes Stadium *n*.
adventitial cell: Adventitiazelle *f*, Perizyt *m*.
adverse/*adj*: nachteilig, gegensätzlich.
adverse effect: nachteiliger Effekt *m*, Nebenwirkung *f*.
adverse reaction: Unverträglichkeitsreaktion *f*.
adversive/*adj*: adversiv.
adversive attack: Adversivanfall *m*.
adversive epilepsy: Adversivepilepsie *f*.
adversive movement: Adversivbewegung *f*.
advice/*n*: Rat *m*, Ratschlag *m*.
advisable/*adj*: ratsam, empfehlenswert.
advise/*vb*: beraten, empfehlen.
adynamic fever: adynamisches Fieber *n*
aerial fistula: Luftfistel *f*.
aerobe/*n, adj*: 1. Aerobier *m*; 2. aerob.
aerobic/*adj*: aerob.
aerobic bacteria: Aerobier *m*.
aerobic respiration: aerobe Atmung *f*.
aerocele/*n*: Aerozele *f*.
aerodontalgia/*n*: Aerodontalgie *f*.
aerogenic/*n, adj*: 1. Gasbildner *m*; 2. gasbildend.
aerophagia/*n*: air-swallowing, usually involuntary, and if not accompanied by belching, sometimes associated with accumulation of air in the stomach, gastric dilatation, and flatulence. Aerophagie *f*, Luftschlucken *n*.
afebrile/*adj*: afebril.
affect/*n, vb*: 1. Affekt *m*; 2. affizieren.
affection/*n*: Affekt *m*, Affektion *f*, Erkrankung *f*.
affective amnesia: elektive Amnesie *f*.

affective discharge: Affektabfuhr *f.*
affective disorder: affektive Störung *f*, Affektstörung *f.*
affective psychosis: affektive Psychose *f*, Affektpsychose *f.*
afferent/*adj*: afferent, zuführend.
afferent fiber: afferente Faser *f.*
afferent loop: zuführende Schlinge *f.*
afferent vessel: afferentes Gefäß *n.*
affinity/*n*: Affinität *f*, Verwandtschaft *f.*
afibrinogenemia/*n*: Afibrinogenämie *f.*
aflatoxin/*n*: Aflatoxin *n.*
African hemorrhagic fever: Ebola-Viruskrankheit *f.*
African Kaposi sarcoma: afrikanisches Kaposi-Sarkom *n.*
African lymphoma: Burkitt-Lymphom *n.*
afterbirth/*n*: Nachgeburt *f.*
aftercare/*n*: Nachsorge *f.*
aftereffect: Nachwirkung *f*, Nacheffekt *m.*
afterimage/*n*: Nachbild *n.*
afterload/*n*: Afterload, Nachlast *f.*
afterloading technique: Afterloading-Verfahren *n.*
afterpains: Nachwehen.
aftertaste/*n*: Nachgeschmack *m.*
agalactia/*n*: Agalaktie *f.*
agalsidase/*n*: Agalsidase *n.*
agammaglobulinemia/*n*: Agammaglobulinämie *f.*
agar/*n*: Agar *m.*
agaricic acid: Agaricinsäure *f.*
age/*n, vb*: 1. Alter *n*; 2. altern.
age distribution: Altersverteilung *f.*
ageing/*n*: Altern *n*, Alterung *f.*
agenesis/*n*: Agenesie *f.*
agent/*n*: Agens *n*, Substanz *f*, Keim *m.*
agglutinating antibody: agglutinierender Antikörper *m.*
agglutination/*n*: Agglutination *f.*
agglutinin/*n*: Agglutinin *n.*
aggravation/*n*: Aggravation *f*, Verschlimmerung *f.*
aggregate/*n, vb*: 1. Aggregat *n*; 2. ansammeln.
aggressin/*n*: Aggressin *n.*
aggression/*n*: Aggression *f.*
aggressive personality: aggressiver Charakter *m.*
aging/*n, adj*: 1. Altern *n*; 2. alternd.
aging-lung emphysema: Altersemphysem *n.*
agitated depression: agitierte Depression *f.*
aglepristone/*n*: Aglepriston *n.*
agnathia/*n*: Agnathie *f.*
agnosia/*n*: Agnosie *f.*
agonist/*n*: Agonist *m.*
agonistic muscle: Agonist *m.*
agony/*n*: Agonie *f.*
agoraphobia/*n*: extreme fear of large, empty places. The term is also used to describe a neurotic anxiety of crowds, sometimes associated with fear to leave home. It may be accompanied by panic attacks and can result in severe restrictions of daily activities. Agoraphobie *f.*
agranular cell: ungekörnte Zelle *f.*
agranulocytosis/*n*: a condition which is characterized by an almost complete absence of granulocytes in the peripheral blood. Symptoms include angina, and generalized infections. Agranulozytose *f.*
agraphia/*n*: Agraphie *f.*
agreement/*n*: Übereinkommen *n*, Vereinbarung *f.*
ague/*n*: Wechselfieber *n*, Schüttelfrost *m.*
aid/*n*: Hilfe *f.*
AIDS *<abbr>* **Acquired Immune Deficiency Syndrome**: a chronic infectious disease caused by the human immunodeficiency virus, HIV. HIV attacks certain cells of the immune system, which results in immune deficiency and the occurrence of opportunistic infections and cancers. AIDS, erworbenes Immundefektsyndrom *n.*
AIDS-defining disease: AIDS-definierende Erkrankung *f.*
ailment/*n*: Unpässlichkeit *f*, Leiden *n.*
air/*n, vb*: 1. Luft *f*; 2. belüften.
air-borne infection: aerogene Infektion *f.*
air cell: pneumatische Zelle *f*, Alveole *f.*
air embolism: Luftembolie *f.*

air hunger: a form of respiration which is characterized by excessively rapid, deep, and noisy breathing characteristic especially of acidosis. Lufthunger *m*, Schnappatmung *f*, Kussmaul-Atmung *f*.
air sickness: Luftkrankheit *f*.
air splint: aufblasbare Schiene *f*.
airway obstruction: a hindrance or complete blockage of the normal air flow in the upper respiratory tract and the trachea. Causes include foreign body aspiration, acute swelling of mucous membranes, or tumors. Atemwegsobstruktion *f*.
airway resistance: Atemwegswiderstand *m*.
airways: Atemwege, Luftwege.
akathisia/*n*: Akathisie *f*, Bewegungsunruhe *f*.
akinesia/*n*: Akinesie *f*.
akinetic-abulic syndrome: akinetisch-abulisches Syndrom *n*.
akinetic apraxia: gliedkinetische Apraxie *f*.
akinetic attack: myostatischer Anfall *m*.
akinetic crisis: akinetische Krise *f*.
alar scapula: Scapula alata *f*.
alatrofloxacin/*n*: Alatrofloxacin *n*.
albendazole/*n*: Albendazol *n*.
albinism/*n*: Albinismus *m*.
albumin/*n*: Albumin *n*.
albuminuria/*n*: Albuminurie *f*.
alclometasone/*n*: Alclometason *n*.
alcohol/*n*: Alkohol *m*.
alcohol abuse: Alkoholmissbrauch *m*, Alkoholabusus *m*.
alcohol addiction: the condition of being physically and/or psychologically dependent on alcohol, characterized by craving for alcohol and its effects. Repeated, chronic ingestion of excessive amounts of alcohol may result in psychological problems such as mood disorders, neurologic disorders such as polyneuropathy or encephalopathy, and organ damage such as gastritis and liver cirrhosis. Alkoholabhängigkeit *f*.
alcohol consumption: Alkoholkonsum *m*.
alcohol dehydrogenase: Alkoholdehydrogenase *f*.
alcoholic/*n, adj*: 1. Alkoholiker *m*; 2. alkoholisch.
alcoholic ataxia: alkoholbedingte Ataxie *f*.
alcoholic delirium: Alkoholdelir *n*.
alcoholic dementia: Alkoholdemenz *f*.
alcoholic encephalopathy: any disease or generative condition of the brain which is due to alcohol ingestion, including the short-term disturbances associated with acute intoxication such as delirium, and irreversible changes such as those of Wernicke's disease. Alkoholenzephalopathie *f*.
alcoholic extract: alkoholischer Extrakt *m*.
alcoholic fatty liver: alkoholische Fettleber *f*.
alcoholic hepatitis: Alkoholhepatitis *f*.
alcoholic intoxication: acute alcoholism or drunkenness due to excessive ingestion of alcohol. Symptoms include muscular dyscoordination, mental confusion, and disorders of the consciousness. Alkoholintoxikation *f*.
alcoholic paralysis: Alkoholneuropathie *f*.
alcoholic paranoia: Alkoholparanoia *f*.
alcoholic polyneuritic psychosis: Wernicke-Korsakoff-Syndrom *n*.
alcoholic polyneuropathy: Alkoholneuropathie *f*.
alcoholic psychosis: Alkoholpsychose *f*.
alcoholism/*n*: Alkoholismus *m*, Alkoholkrankheit *f*.
alcohol withdrawal delirium: Alkoholentzugsdelir *n*, Delirium tremens *n*.
alcuronium/*n*: Alcuronium *n*.
alcuronium chloride: Alcuroniumchlorid *n*.
aldehyde/*n*: Aldehyd *m*.
aldesleukin/*n*: Aldesleukin *n*.
aldobionic acid: Aldobionsäure *f*.

aldosterone/*n*: Aldosteron *n*.
aldosteronism/*n*: Aldosteronismus *m*, Hyperaldosteronismus *m*.
alemtuzumab/*n*: Alemtuzumab *n*.
alendronic acid: Alendronsäure *f*.
alert/*adj*: wachsam.
alertness/*n*: Wachsamkeit *f*, Vigilanz *f*.
aleukemic leukemia: aleukämische Leukämie *f*.
alexia/*n*: acquired inability to read and understand written language, usually due to cerebral lesions, and in the absence of any vision disorder. Causes include acquired cerebral lesions, generally involving the dominant parietal lobe. Developmental alexia or congenital word blindness is often familial and sometimes inherited. Alexie *f*, Leseunfähigkeit *f*.
alfacalcidol/*n*: Alfacalcidol *n*.
alfatradiol/*n*: Alfatradiol *n*.
alfentanil/*n*: Alfentanil *n*.
alfuzosin/*n*: Alfuzosin *n*.
alginic acid: Alginsäure *f*.
algogenic/*adj*: schmerzerzeugend.
algorithm/*n*: Algorithmus *m*.
alienation/*n*: Entfremdung *f*, Alienation *f*.
alignment/*n*: Abgleichung *f*, Einrichten *n*.
alimentary/*adj*: alimentär.
alimentary allergy: Nahrungsmittelallergie *f*.
alimentary edema: Hungerödem *n*.
alimentary obesity: alimentäre Fettsucht *f*.
alimentary osteopathy: alimentäre Osteopathie *f*, Hungerosteopathie *f*.
alimentary therapy: Diätbehandlung *f*.
alimentation/*n*: Alimentation *f*, Ernährung *f*.
aliphatic acid: aliphatische Säure *f*.
alitretinoin/*n*: Alitretinoin *n*.
alive/*adj*: lebendig.
alizapride/*n*: Alizaprid *n*.
alkali/*n*: Alkali *n*, Laugensalz *n*.
alkaline/*adj*: alkalisch, basisch.
alkaline phosphatase: alkalische Phosphatase *f*, AP.
alkalinity/*n*: alkalische Beschaffenheit *f*.
alkalinuria/*n*: Alkaliurie *f*.
alkali reserve: Alkalireserve *f*.
alkaloid/*n*: Alkaloid *n*.
alkalosis/*n*: a condition which is characterized by increased levels of alkaline in the blood. Causes include disorders of the lungs or kidneys. It can also be caused by dehydration, metabolic disorders, and excessive alkali ingestion. Alkalose *f*.
alkaptonuria/*n*: Alkaptonurie *f*.
alkylate/*vb*: alkylieren.
alkylating agent: Alkylantium *n*.
allantoic placenta: Allantoisplazenta *f*.
allantois/*n*: Allantois *f*.
allele/*n*: Allel *n*.
allelic gene: alleles Gen *n*.
allelomorph/*adj*: allelomorph.
allergen/*n*: Allergen *n*.
allergen testing: Allergentestung *f*.
allergic/*adj*: allergisch.
allergic alveolitis: allergische Alveolitis *f*.
allergic angiitis: an autoimmune disease which is characterized by inflammation and necrotic changes of small blood vessels. Symptoms depend on the localization of the angiitis and include bronchitis, asthma, pneumonia, as well as generalized symptoms like fever, weakness, weight loss. allergische granulomatöse Angiitis *f*, Churg-Strauss-Syndrom *n*.
allergic asthma: allergisches Asthma *n*.
allergic dermatitis: allergische Dermatitis *f*.
allergic eczema: allergisches Ekzem *n*.
allergic purpura: allergische Purpura *f*, Schoenlein-Henoch-Purpura *f*.
allergic reaction: allergische Reaktion *f*, Überempfindlichkeitsreaktion *f*.
allergic rhinitis: allergische Rhinopathie *f*.
allergy/*n*: acquired hypersensitivity of the body against a foreign substance. These substances or aller-

gens can include nutrients like milk or fish proteins, environmental agents such as pollen, hairs of animals, chemical substances, drugs, or microorganisms. Manifestations include a variety of immune reactions of the immediate type like urticaria, catarrhal inflammation, or asthma. Allergie *f*.
alleviate/*vb*: erleichtern, lindern.
alloantibody/*n*: Alloantikörper *m*.
alloantigen/*n*: Alloantigen *n*.
allocation/*n*: Allokation *f*, Verteilung *f*.
allochiria/*n*: Allochirie *f*.
allogenic/*adj*: allogen, homolog.
allogenic antigen: Alloantigen *n*.
allogenic graft: allogenes Transplantat *n*, Allograft *n*.
allograft/*n*: Allograft *n*, allogenes Transplantat *n*.
allopathy/*n*: Allopathie *f*.
allophanic acid: Allophansäure *f*.
alloplast graft: alloplastisches Transplantat *n*.
alloplasty/*n*: Alloplastik *f*, Alloplastie *f*.
allopurinol/*n*: Allopurinol *n*.
all-or-none law: Alles-oder-Nichts-Gesetz *n*.
alloxan diabetes: Alloxan-Diabetes *m*.
alloy/*n*: Legierung *f*.
almotriptan/*n*: Almotriptan *n*.
alopecia/*n*: loss of hair which affects circumscribed areas or the entire body. Causes include infections, iron deficiency, metabolic or endocrine disorders, radiation, chemical substances or pharmaceutical drugs, or mechanical causes like trichotillomania. Alopezie *f*, Haarausfall *m*.
alpha-aminobetahydroxypropionic acid: α-Amino-β-hydroxypropionsäure *f*, Serin *n*.
alpha-aminoisocaproic acid: Leucin *n*.
alpha blocker: Alphablocker *m*.
alpha fetoprotein: Alphafetoprotein *n*.
alpha-hydroxypropionic acid: Milchsäure *f*.
alpha ray: Alphastrahl *m*.
alpha wave: Alphawelle *f*.
alprazolam/*n*: Alprazolam *n*.
alprenolol/*n*: Alprenolol *n*.
alprostadil/*n*: Alprostadil *n*.
alteplase/*n*: Alteplase *f*.
altered consciousness: Bewusstseinsveränderung *f*.
alternate hemianesthesia: alternierende Hemianästhesie *f*.
alternate hemiplegia: Hemiplegia alternans *f*.
alteration/*n*: Abänderung *f*, Veränderung *f*.
alternating/*adj*: alternierend, wechselnd.
alternating current: Wechselstrom *m*.
alternating oculomotor hemiplegia: a neurologic syndrome usually due to infarction of one cerebral peduncle. Symptoms include palsy of the oculomotor nerve on the side of the lesion and a contralateral hemiplegia. Weber-Syndrom *n*.
alternating paralysis: alternierende Lähmung *f*.
alternating psychosis: bipolare Psychose *f*.
alternative/*adj*: alternativ.
alternative medicine: Alternativmedizin *f*.
altitude sickness: Höhenkrankheit *f*.
altretamine/*n*: Altretamin *n*.
alveolar/*adj*: alveolär.
alveolar air: Alveolarluft *f*.
alveolar-capillary block: alveolokapillärer Block *m*.
alveolar-capillary diffusion: alveoläre Kapillardiffusion *f*.
alveolar cell: Alveolarepithelzelle *f*, Pneumozyt *m*.
alveolar cell carcinoma: Alveolarzellkarzinom *n*.
alveolar cleft: Alveolarspalte *f*.
alveolar dead space: alveolärer Totraum *m*.
alveolar fistula: Zahnfistel *f*.
alveolar gas: Alveolarluft *f*.
alveolar macrophage: Alveolarmakrophage *m*.
alveolar phagocyte: Alveolarmakrophage *m*.

alveolar point: Alveolarpunkt *m*.
alveolar pressure: Alveolardruck *m*.
alveolar sac: Lungenalveole *f*.
alveolar tumor: bronchoalveolärer Tumor *m*.
alveolar volume: Lungenvolumen *n*.
alveolitis/*n*: 1. inflammation of a dental alveolus, particularly following dental extraction. 2. inflammation of the pulmonary alveoli, for example extrinsic allergic alveolitis as a respiratory hypersensitivity reaction to repeated inspiration of organic substances. Alveolitis *f*.
Alzheimer's disease: a neurologic disease which is characterized by a degenerative brain disease and progressive mental deterioration, occurring in persons of middle age. Initial symptoms include loss of short-term memory, disorientation, confusion, and result in progressive dementia which is often accompanied by dysphasia and/or apraxia, and mood disorders such as depression. Alzheimer-Demenz *f*, präsenile Demenz *f*.
amacrine cell: amakrine Zelle *f*.
amalgam/*n*: Amalgam *n*.
amantadine/*n*: Amantadin *n*.
amarillic typhus: Gelbfieber *n*.
amastia/*n*: Amastie *f*.
amaurosis/*n*: Amaurose *f*.
amaurotic/*adj*: amaurotisch.
amaurotic familial idiocy: a condition which is characterized by an abnormal accumulation of gangliosides, due to an autosomal recessive defect in the enzyme hexosaminidase. Symptoms include an early onset in the first year of life with psychomotor retardation, paralysis, seizures, and progressive vision loss. amaurotische familiäre Idiotie *f*, Tay-Sachs-Krankheit *f*, G_{M2}-Gangliosidose Typ I *f*.
ambenonium chloride: Ambenoniumchlorid *n*.
ambidextrous/*adj*: beidhändig.
ambient air: Umgebungsluft *f*.
ambiguoaccessorius-hypoglossal paralysis: Jackson-Syndrom *n*.
ambiguospinothalamic paralysis: Avellis-Syndrom *n*.
ambivalence/*n*: Ambivalenz *f*.
amblyopia/*n*: a congenital or acquired condition of reduced or dim vision in an eye, usually without any detectable organic disease. Amblyopie *f*, Sehschwäche *f*.
ambroxol/*n*: Ambroxol *n*.
ambulance/*n*: Krankenwagen *m*.
ambulanceman/*n*: Rettungssanitäter *m*.
ambulant/*adj*: ambulant.
ambulant clinic: Poliklinik *f*.
ambulatory/*adj*: ambulant, beweglich.
ambulatory care: ambulante Versorgung *f*.
ambulatory surgery: ambulante Chirurgie *f*.
Ambu resuscitator bag: Ambu-Beatmungsbeutel *m*.
ambutonium bromide: Ambutoniumbromid *n*.
amcinonide/*n*: Amcinonid *n*.
ameba/*n*: Amöbe *f*.
amebiasis/*n*: an infectious disease caused by the bacterium Entamoeba histolytica. Amebiasis typically affects the intestine, but also other organs like the liver can be involved. Symptoms include diarrhea and dysentery, and eventually formation of abscesses. Amöbiasis *f*, Amöbenruhr *f*.
amebic balanitis: Amöbenbalanitis *f*.
amebic colitis: Amöbenkolitis *f*.
amebic cyst: Amöbenzyste *f*.
amebic diarrhea: Amöbenruhr *f*.
amebic dysentery: Amöbendysenterie *f*, Amöbenruhr *f*.
amebic granuloma: Amöbengranulom *n*.
amebic hepatitis: Amöbenhepatitis *f*.
amebicide/*n*: amöbizide Substanz *f*.
ameboma/*n*: Amebom *n*.
amelanotic melanoma: amelanotisches Melanom *n*.
amelia/*n*: Amelie *f*.
ameloblastic adenomatoid tumor: Adenoameloblastom *n*.
ameloblastic fibroma: Ameloblasten-

fibrom *n*.

ameloblastic odontoma: Ameloblastenodontom *n*.

ameloblastic sarcoma: Ameloblastosarkom *n*.

amenorrhea/*n*: absence of menstrual bleeding, physiologically occurring in pregnancy, or as traumatic amenorrhea a symptom of psychological or physical stress. Amenorrhö *f*.

amentia/*n*: Amentia *f*, Intelligenzdefekt *m*.

American encephalitis: St.-Louis-Enzephalitis *f*.

American trypanosomiasis: amerikanische Trypanosomiasis *f*, Chagas-Krankheit *f*.

ametria/*n*: Uterusagenesie *f*.

ametropia/*n*: Ametropie *f*, Fehlsichtigkeit *f*.

amezinium metilsulfate: Ameziniummetilsulfat *n*.

amfepramone/*n*: Amfepramon *n*.

amfetaminil/*n*: Amfetaminil *n*.

amide/*n*: Amid *n*.

amifostine/*n*: Amifostin *n*.

amikacin/*n*: Amikacin *n*.

amilomer/*n*: Amilomer *n*.

amiloride/*n*: Amilorid *n*.

amine/*n*: Amin *n*.

aminoacetic acid: Aminoessigsäure *f*, Glycin *n*.

amino acid: Aminosäure *f*.

aminoaciduria/*n*: Aminoazidurie *f*.

aminobenzoate/*n*: Aminobenzoat *n*.

aminobenzoic acid: Paraaminobenzoesäure *f*.

aminobutyric acid: Aminobuttersäure *f*.

aminocaproic acid: Aminocapronsäure *f*.

aminoglutethimide/*n*: Aminoglutethimid *n*.

aminohippuric acid: Aminohippursäure *f*.

2-amino-3-indole propionic acid: L-2-Amino-3-(3-indolyl)-propionsäure *f*, Tryptophan *n*.

2-aminoisovaleric acid: α-Aminoisovaleriansäure *f*, Valin *n*.

δ-aminolevulinic acid: Delta-Aminolävulinsäure *f*.

2-aminopropionic acid: Aminopropionsäure *f*, Alanin *n*.

aminopterin/*n*: Aminopterin *n*.

aminosalicylic acid: Aminosalizylsäure *f*.

amiodarone/*n*: Amiodaron *n*.

amiphenazole/*n*: Amiphenazol *n*.

amisulpride/*n*: Amisulprid *n*.

amitosis/*n*: Amitose *f*.

amitriptyline/*n*: Amitriptylin *n*.

amitriptylinoxide/*n*: Amitriptylinoxid *n*.

amlodipine/*n*: Amlodipin *n*.

ammonia/*n*: Ammoniak *n*.

ammonium chloride/*n*: Ammoniumchlorid *n*, Salmiak *m*.

amnesia/*n*: Amnesie *f*.

amnesic aphasia: amnestische Aphasie *f*.

amnestic-confabulatory syndrome: an organic disorder of the nervous system which is characterized by severe memory disorders with specific impairment of short-term memory and by confabulation. It is usually associated with chronic alcoholism. Korsakoff-Psychose *f*.

amniocele/*n*: Amniozele *f*.

amniocentesis/*n*: Amniozentese *f*.

amniography/*n*: Amniographie *f*.

amnion/*n*: Amnion *n*.

amnioscopy/*n*: Amnioskopie *f*, Fruchtwasserspiegelung *f*.

amniotic/*adj*: amniotisch.

amniotic amputation: Amnionschnürfurche *f*.

amniotic bag: Amnionhöhle *f*, Fruchtblase *f*.

amniotic band: Amnionstrang *m*.

amniotic cavity: Amnionhöhle *f*.

amniotic constriction: constriction of a limb or amputation caused by bandlike formations of the placental membranes which surround the umbilical cord or a fetal extremity. Amnionschnürfurche *f*.

amniotic fluid: Amnionflüssigkeit *f*, Fruchtwasser *n*.

amniotic fluid test: Fruchtwasserdiagnostik *f*.

amniotic fold: Amnionfalte *f*.

amniotic sac: Amnion *n*.

amodiaquine/*n*: Amodiaquin *n*.
amorphic gene: amorphes Gen *n*.
amorphous/*adj*: amorph, formlos.
amount/*n*: Menge *f*, Quantität *f*.
amoxicillin/*n*: Amoxicillin *n*.
amp <*abbr*> **1. ampere; 2. ampule**: 1. Ampere *n*; 2. Ampulle *f*.
amphetamine/*n*: Amphetamin *n*.
amphophilic granule: amphophiles Granulum *n*.
amphoric rale: amphorisches Atemgeräusch *n*.
amphoric resonance: amphorischer Schall *m*.
amphoteric/*adj*: amphoterisch.
amphotericin B/*n*: Amphotericin B *n*.
ampicillin/*n*: Ampicillin *n*.
amprenavir/*n*: Amprenavir *n*.
ampulla/*n*: Ampulle *f*.
ampullar pregnancy: an ectopic pregnancy located in the ampulla of the fallopian tube. Tubal pregnancy accounts for the majority of ectopic pregnancies in humans. Symptoms include spotting, abdominal pain, and eventually the signs of tubal rupture. Eileiterschwangerschaft *f*.
ampullary aneurysm: sackförmiges Aneurysma *n*.
amputating saw: Amputationssäge *f*.
amputation/*n*: Amputation *f*.
amrinone/*n*: Amrinon *n*.
amsacrine/*n*: Amsacrin *n*.
amylase/*n*: Amylase *f*.
amyl nitrite/*n*: Amylnitrit *n*.
amyloid body: Amyloidkörperchen *n*.
amyloid disease: Amyloidose *f*.
amyloid kidney: Amyloidniere *f*.
amyloidosis/*n*: a generalized condition of unknown cause which is characterized by the accumulation of amyloid fibrils in tissues and organs. Organs most frequently affected include the liver, kidney, spleen, heart, and the gastrointestinal tract. Amyloidose *f*.
amyloid spleen: Amyloidmilz *f*.
amyotonia/*n*: Amyotonie *f*.
amyotrophic/*adj*: amyotroph.
amyotrophic lateral sclerosis: a chronic progressive, neurologic disease of unknown cause which is characterized by degeneration of the lateral columns of the spinal cord. Symptoms include progressive paralysis. amyotrophe Lateralsklerose *f*, AML.
amyotrophy/*n*: Amyotrophie *f*, Muskelatrophie *f*.
anabolic/*n, adj*: 1. Anabolikum *n*; 2. anabol.
anabolic pathway: anaboler Stoffwechselweg *m*.
anabolic steroid: anaboles Steroid *n*.
anabolism/*n*: Anabolismus *m*.
anaclitic depression: anaklitische Depression *f*.
anacrotic/*adj*: anakrot.
anacrotic wave: anakrote Welle *f*.
anadicrotic pulse: anadikrotischer Puls *m*.
anaerobe/*n*: Anaerobier *m*.
anaerobic respiration: anaerobe Atmung *f*.
anakinra/*n*: Anakinra *n*.
analbuminemia/*n*: Analbuminämie *f*.
anal atresia: Analatresie *f*.
anal cleft: Crena ani *f*, Afterfurche *f*.
analeptic/*n*: Analeptikum *n*.
anal fissure: a tear of the lining and/or the skin in the anal region. Symptoms include pain, and ulcerative skin lesions. Analfissur *f*.
anal fistula: an abnormal passage with one end opening onto the mucosal epithelium of the anal region, for example anorectal fistula communicating with the rectum. Causes include inflammations, infections, or gastrointestinal diseases, for example regional enteritis. Analfistel *f*.
analgesia/*n*: Analgesie *f*.
analgesic/*n*: Analgetikum *n*, Schmerzmittel *n*.
analgesic ladder: Stufenleiter der Analgetika *f*.
analgesic nephropathy: Analgetikanephropathie *f*.
analgesic therapy: Schmerztherapie *f*.
analgetic/*n, adj*: 1. Analgetikum *n*; 2. analgetisch.
analogous/*adj*: analog, ähnlich.
analogue/*n*: Analogon *n*, Analogstoff.

anal papilla: Analpapille *f*, Morgagni-Papille *f*.
anal prolapse: downward displacement of the anal mucosa into the external environment, eventually associated with hemorrhoids or rectal prolapse. Analprolaps *m*.
anal reflex: Analreflex *m*.
anal region: Analregion *f*.
anal stricture: Analstriktur *f*.
analysis/*n*: Analyse *f*, Untersuchung *f*, Psychoanalyse *f*.
anamnestic response: anamnestische Reaktion *f*.
anancastic personality: anankastischer Charakter *m*, Zwangscharakter *m*.
anaphase/*n*: Anaphase *f*.
anaphoresis/*n*: Anhidrose *f*.
anaphylactic reaction: anaphylaktische Reaktion *f*.
anaphylactic shock: anaphylaktischer Schock *m*.
anaphylaxis/*n*: Anaphylaxie *f*.
anaplasia/*n*: Anaplasie *f*, Entdifferenzierung *f*.
anaplastic carcinoma: entdifferenziertes Karzinom *n*.
anastomosis/*n*: Anastomose *f*.
anastomotic operation: Anastomosenoperation *f*.
anastomotic ulcer: Anastomosenulkus *n*.
anastrozole/*n*: Anastrozol *n*.
anatomical/*adj*: anatomisch.
anatomical position: anatomische Lage *f*.
anatomy/*n*: Anatomie *f*.
ancrod/*n*: Ancrod *n*.
ancylostomiasis/*n*: an infectious disease caused by nematodes or so-called hookworms. Mild infections may be asymptomatic. Symptoms of heavy, chronic infection include anemia, weight loss, hypoalbuminemia, and edema. Cutaneous ancylostomiasis is associated with dermatitis, erythema and pruritus. Ankylostomiasis *f*, Hakenwurmbefall *m*.
androgen/*n*: Androgen *n*.
androgenetic acne: androgenetische Akne *f*.
androgenetic alopecia: Alopecia androgenetica *f*.
androgenic hormone: Androgen *n*.
android/*adj*: android.
android pelvis: männliche Beckenform *f*.
androstanolone/*n*: Androstanolon *n*.
androstenedione/*n*: Androstendion *n*.
androstenone/*n*: Androstenon *n*.
androsterone/*n*: Androsteron *n*.
anemia/*n*: a condition which is characterized by a decrease of red blood cells, concentration of hemoglobin, or hematocrit. Causes include insufficient production, or increased loss or destruction of erythrocytes. Symptoms include pallor, weakness, and dyspnea. Anämie *f*, Blutarmut *f*.
anemia of pregnancy: Schwangerschaftsanämie *f*.
anemic murmur: Anämiegeräusch *n*.
anemic polyneuritis: Vitamin-B-Mangel-Neuropathie *f*.
anencephaly/*n*: Anenzephalie *f*.
anesthesia/*n*: Narkose *f*, Anästhesie *f*, Gefühllosigkeit *f*.
anesthesist/*n*: Narkosearzt *m*, Anästhesist *m*.
anesthetic/*n, adj*: 1. Narkotikum *n*, Anästhetikum *n*; 2. narkotisch, anästhetisch.
anesthetic block: Leitungsanästhesie *f*.
anesthetic risk: Narkoserisiko *n*.
anethole/*n*: Anethol *n*.
aneurysm/*n*: a saccular or fusiform dilatation of a blood vessel arising from the stretching of a weak place in the vessel wall. A true aneurysm is characterized by the dilatation of the wall of the blood vessel, while in a false aneurysm the entire vessel wall is injured and the blood is contained by the surrounding tissues. Aneurysma *n*.
aneurysmal hematoma: falsches Aneurysma *n*.
aneurysmal sac: Aneurysmawandaussackung *f*.
aneurysmal thrill: Aneurysmaschwirren *n*.

angiectasia/*n*: Angiektasie *f*.
angiitis/*n*: inflammation of a vessel, for example arteritis with inflammation of an artery, phlebitis with inflammation of a vein, or lymphangitis with inflammation of lymphatic vessels. Angiitis *f*, Gefäßentzündung *f*.
angina of effort: Belastungsangina *f*.
angina pectoris: severe attacks of chest pain, often radiating to the left arm, occurring as a symptom of a cardiovascular disease, for example coronary artery disease or aortic stenosis. Angina pectoris *f*.
angioblastic cyst: Angiozyste *f*.
angiocardiography/*n*: Angiokardiographie *f*.
angiogram/*n*: Angiogramm *n*.
angiography/*n*: Angiographie *f*.
angioma/*n*: Angiom *n*.
angiomatosis/*n*: Angiomatose *f*.
angioneurotic/*adj*: angioneurotisch.
angioneurotic edema: a chronic condition which is characterized by circumscribed subcutaneous edema, laryngeal edema, and abdominal pain. Causes include deficiency of C1 esterase inhibitor. angioneurotisches Ödem *n*, Quincke-Ödem *n*.
angiopathy/*n*: any disease of a vessel, for example microangiopathy affecting small blood vessels, or arteriopathy with pathological affection of arteries. Angiopathie *f*, Gefäßkrankheit *f*.
angioplasty/*n*: Angioplastie *f*.
angiosarcoma/*n*: Angiosarkom *n*.
angiospasm/*n*: Angiospasmus *m*, Vasospasmus *m*.
angiospastic vertigo: arteriosklerotischer Schwindel *m*.
angiotensin/*n*: Angiotensin *n*.
angiotensinamide/*n*: Angiotensinamid *n*.
angiotensin-converting enzyme: angiotensin converting enzyme, ACE, Angiotensin umwandelndes Enzym *n*.
angiotensin-converting enzyme inhibitor: ACE-Hemmer *m*.
angle/*n*: Winkel *m*.
angle tumor: Kleinhirnbrückenwinkeltumor *m*.
angular stomatitis: inflammatory disease of the lips resulting in chronic fissures. Causes include bacterial and fungal infections, malnutrition, and iron deficiency. Cheilitis angularis *f*, Angulus infectiosus *m*.
anhidrosis/*n*: Anhidrose *f*.
anhidrotic ectodermal dysplasia: anhidrotische Ektodermaldysplasie *f*, Anhidrosis hypotrichotica polydysplastica *f*, Christ-Siemens-Syndrom *n*.
anhydrous/*adj*: wasserfrei.
anicteric hepatitis: anikterische Hepatitis *f*.
animal model: Tiermodell *n*.
animal parasite: Zooparasit *m*.
animal protein: tierisches Eiweiß *n*.
animal toxin: tierisches Gift *n*.
anion/*n*: Anion *n*.
anion exchanger: Anionenaustauscher *m*.
aniseikonia/*n*: Aniseikonie *f*.
anisic acid: Anissäure *f*.
anisochromia/*n*: Anisochromie *f*.
anisocoria/*n*: Anisokorie *f*.
anisocytosis/*n*: Anisozytose *f*.
anisogamy/*n*: Anisogamie *f*.
anisometropia/*n*: Anisometropie *f*.
ankle/*n*: Fußknöchel *m*, Sprunggelenk *n*.
ankle bone: Sprungbein *n*, Talus *m*.
ankle clonus: Fußklonus *m*.
ankle edema: Knöchelödem *n*.
ankle jerk: Achillessehnenreflex *m*.
ankyloblepharon/*n*: Ankyloblepharon *n*.
ankyloglossia/*n*: Ankyloglosson *n*.
ankylosing/*adj*: ankylosierend.
ankylosing spondylitis: chronic inflammatory disease of the vertebra which is characterized by impaired movement or immobility of the vertebrae. Spondylitis ankylosans *f*, Bechterew-Syndrom *n*.
ankylosis/*n*: Ankylose *f*, Gelenkversteifung *f*.
annular/*adj*: ringförmig.
annular hernia: indirekte Leistenhernie *f*.

annular pancreas: Pancreas anulare *n*.
annular placenta: ringförmige Plazenta *f*.
annular scleroderma: Morphaea *f*.
annular scotoma: Ringskotom *n*.
annular stricture: Ringstriktur *f*.
annular thrombus: Ringthrombus *m*.
anode/*n*: Anode *f*.
anodyne/*n, adj*: 1. schmerzstillendes Mittel *n*; 2. schmerzstillend.
anomalous/*adj*: anomal.
anomalous conduction: Überleitungsstörung *f*.
anomaly/*n*: Anomalie *f*.
anomia/*n*: Anomie *f*, Wortfindungsstörung *f*.
anonychia/*n*: Anonychie *f*.
anonymous/*adj*: anonym.
anoperineal/*adj*: anoperineal.
anorchism/*n*: Anorchie *f*, Anorchidie *f*.
anorectal/*adj*: anorektal.
anorectal ring: Levatorschlinge *f*.
anorexia/*n*: loss or complete lack of appetite or desire for food. Causes include nervous conditions, organic diseases, intoxications, or adverse effects of drugs. Anorexie *f*.
anorexia nervosa: Anorexia nervosa *f*.
anorgasmy/*n*: Anorgasmie *f*.
anosmia/*n*: Anosmie *f*.
anovulation/*n*: Ausbleiben der Ovulation.
anovulatory/*adj*: anovulatorisch.
anovulatory cycle: anovulatorischer Zyklus *m*.
anoxemia/*n*: Anoxämie *f*.
anoxia/*n*: Anoxie *f*.
ansamycin/*n*: Ansamycin *n*.
anserine/*n*: Anserin *n*.
answer/*n, vb*: 1. Antwort *f*; 2. antworten.
antacid/*n, adj*: 1. Antazidum *n*; 2. antazid.
antagonism/*n*: Antagonismus *m*.
antagonist/*n*: Antagonist *m*.
antagonistic muscle: Antagonist *m*.
antecedent sign: Vorzeichen *n*.
antecolic gastrectomy: antekolische Gastrektomie *f*.
antenatal/*adj*: pränatal.
anterior asynclitism: Vorderscheitelbeineinstellung *f*.
anterior curvature: Kyphose *f*.
anterior horn cell: Vorderhornzelle *f*.
anterior internuclear ophthalmoplegia: a neurologic syndrome which is characterized by a paralysis of ocular muscles due to a lesion of the medial longitudinal fasciculus, caused for example by tumors, multiple sclerosis, an abscess, or cerebral hemorrhage. internukleäre vordere Ophthalmoplegie *f*, Lhermitte-Augenmuskellähmung *f*.
anterior pituitary insufficiency: Hypophysenvorderlappeninsuffizienz *f*, Hypopituitarismus *m*.
anterior rhizotomy: vordere Rhizotomie *f*.
anterior root: Vorderwurzel *f*.
anterior sagittal diameter: vorderer gerader Durchmesser *m*.
anterior spinal paralysis: Poliomyelitis anterior acuta *f*.
anterior tibial sign: Tibialisphänomen *n*, Strümpell-Zeichen *n*.
anterior tibial syndrome: a syndrome which is characterized by swelling of tibial muscles within their compartments, and pain. It is caused by overuse of the anterior tibial muscles. Tibia-Kompartment-Syndrom *n*.
anterograde/*adj*: anterograd.
anterograde amnesia: anterograde Amnesie *f*.
anterograde block: anterograder Block *m*.
anterolateral syndrome: a neurologic syndrome which is characterized by a degeneration of the anterior horns and the lateral columns of the spinal cord. Symptoms include dissociated sensibility disorders. Vorderseitenstrang-Syndrom *n*.
anterolateral tract: Vorderseitenstrang *m*.
anteversion/*n*: Anteversion *f*.
anthelminthic/*n, adj*: 1. Anthelminthikum *n*; 2. antihelminthisch.
anthracosis/*n*: pneumoconiosis due to inhalation of carbon dust, for ex-

ample as occupational disease in coal mine workers. Forms include noncollagenous pulmonary anthracosis, and anthracosis with progressive massive fibrosis. Anthrakose *f*, Kohlenstaublunge *f*.

anthracycline/*n*: Anthrazyklin *n*.

anthramycin/*n*: Anthramycin *n*.

anthraquinone/*n*: Anthrachinon *n*.

anthrax/*n*: acute infectious disease which occurs in ruminants, especially cattle, sheep, and goats, as a result of ingestion of spores of Bacillus anthracis and which may be transmitted to human by direct contact with spores from the infected animal or from products containing material from infected animals. Symptoms include erythematous papular skin lesions, upper respiratory tract infection and respiratory distress, fever, abdominal pain, and bloody diarrhea. Anthrax *m*, Milzbrand *m*.

anthrax pneumonia: Lungenmilzbrand *m*.

anthropoid/*n, adj*: 1. Menschenaffe *m*; 2. menschenähnlich.

anthropology/*n*: Anthropologie *f*.

antiarrhythmic drug: Antiarrhythmikum *n*.

antibacterial agent: Antibiotikum *n*.

antibiotic/*n, adj*: 1. Antibiotikum *n*; 2. antibiotisch.

antibiotic cream: antibiotikahaltige Creme *f*.

antibiotic enterocolitis: Antibiotika-Enterokolitis *f*.

antibiotic resistance: Antibiotikaresistenz *f*.

antibiotic spectrum: antibiotisches Wirkspektrum *n*.

antibody/*n*: Antikörper *m*, Ak.

anticholinergic/*adj*: anticholinerg.

anticoagulant/*n*: Antikoagulans *n*, gerinnungshemmendes Mittel *n*.

anticoagulant therapy: Antikoagulanzientherapie *f*.

anticodon/*n*: Antikodon *n*.

anticonvulsant/*n, adj*: 1. Antikonvulsivum *n*, Antiepileptikum *n*; 2. antikonvulsiv.

antidepressant/*n, adj*: 1. Antidepressivum *n*; 2. antidepressiv.

antidiabetic/*n, adj*: 1. Antidiabetikum *n*; 2. antidiabetisch.

antidiuretic/*n, adj*: 1. Antidiuretikum *n*; 2. antidiuretisch.

antidiuretic hormone: antidiuretisches Hormon *n*, ADH, Adiuretin *n*.

antidote/*n*: Antitoxin *n*, Antidot *n*.

antiepileptic/*n, adj*: 1. Antiepileptikum *n*; 2. antiepileptisch.

antiestrogen/*n*: Antiöstrogen *n*.

antigen/*n*: Antigen *n*, Ag.

antigen drift: Antigen-Drift *f*, langsame Antigenveränderung *f*.

antigenic site: antigener Bereich *m*.

antigenic variation: Antigenvariation *f*.

antigen-presenting cell: antigenpräsentierende Zelle *f*.

antigen shift: Antigen-Shift *m*, schnelle Antigenveränderung *f*.

antiglobulin/*n*: Antiglobulin *n*.

antiglobulin test: Antiglobulintest *m*, Coombs-Test *m*.

antiglomerular basement membrane antibody glomerulonephritis: Antibasalmembran-Antikörper-Glomerulonephritis *f*.

antihistamine/*n*: Antihistaminikum *n*.

antihuman globulin: Antihumanglobulin *n*.

antihypertensive drug: blutdrucksenkendes Medikament *n*.

anti-immune body: Antiantikörper *m*.

anti-inflammatory/*n, adj*: 1. Antiphlogistikum *n*; 2. antiinflammatorisch, antiphlogistisch, entzündungshemmend.

antilipemic agent: Lipidsenker *m*.

antilymphocyte globulin: Antilymphozytenglobulin *n*.

antimalarial/*n, adj*: 1. Malariamittel *n*; 2. gegen Malaria.

antimetabolite/*n*: Antimetabolit *m*.

antimitochondrial antibody: antimitochondrialer Antikörper *m*.

antimitotic/*n, adj*: 1. Antimitotikum *n*; 2. antimitotisch.

antimonic acid: Antimonsäure *f*.

antimony/*n*: Antimon *n*, Stibium *n*, Sb.
antimycotic/*n, adj*: 1. Antimykotikum *n*; 2. antimykotisch.
antinuclear/*adj*: antinukleär.
antinuclear antibody: antinukleärer Antikörper *m*.
antiperistaltic/*adj*: antiperistaltisch.
antiperistaltic anastomosis: antiperistaltische Anastomose *f*.
antipsychotic/*n, adj*: 1. Antipsychotikum *n*; 2. antipsychotisch.
antipyretic/*n, adj*: 1. Antipyretikum *n*, fiebersenkendes Mittel *n*; 2. antipyretisch, fiebersenkend.
antirabies serum: Tollwutserum *n*.
antirabies vaccination: Tollwutschutzimpfung *f*.
antirabies vaccine: Tollwutimpfstoff *m*.
antirachitic/*n, adj*: 1. antirachitische Substanz *f*; 2. antirachitisch.
antiretroviral/*n, adj*: 1. antiretrovirales Medikament *n*; 2. antiretroviral.
antiseptic/*n, adj*: 1. Antiseptikum *n*; 2. antiseptisch.
antiseptic solution: antiseptische Lösung *f*.
antiserum/*n*: Antiserum *n*.
antisocial personality: antisoziale Persönlichkeit *f*.
antispasmodic/*n, adj*: 1. Antispasmodikum *n*, Spasmolytikum *n*; 2. spasmolytisch.
antithrombin/*n*: Antithrombin *n*.
antithyroid/*adj*: thyreostatisch.
antitoxic serum: Antitoxin *n*.
antitoxin/*n*: Antitoxin *n*.
antitubercular agent: Tuberkulostatikum *n*.
antivenin/*n*: Antivenin *n*.
antiviral/*n, adj*: 1. antivirale Substanz *f*; 2. antiviral.
antral cyst: Antrumzyste *f*.
antral gastritis: Antrumgastritis *f*.
antroscopy/*n*: Antroskopie *f*.
antrotomy/*n*: Antrotomie *f*, Antrumdrainage *f*.
antrum/*n*: Antrum *n*.
anuria/*n*: Anurie *f*.
anus/*n*: Anus *m*, After *m*.
anxiety/*n*: Angst *f*, Beklemmung *f*.
anxiety attack: Angstattacke *f*.
anxiety neurosis: in psychoanalysis, an actual neurosis which is characterized by anxious expectation and excessive free-floating anxiety, and fear of common dangers. Angstneurose *f*.
anxious/*adj*: ängstlich, besorgt.
aorta/*n*: Aorta *f*.
aortic/*adj*: aortal.
aortic aneurysm: Aortenaneurysma *n*.
aortic arch: Aortenbogen *m*.
aortic arch angiography: Aortenbogenangiographie *f*.
aortic calcification: Aortenverkalkung *f*.
aortic insufficiency: a condition in which there is an improper closing of the valve between the aorta and the lower left ventricle of the heart, and a backflow of blood into the ventricle. Aorteninsuffizienz *f*.
aortic murmur: Aortenmurmeln *n*.
aorticopulmonary anastomosis: aortopulmonale Anastomose *f*.
aorticopulmonary septal defect: aortopulmonales Fenster *n*.
aortic overload: linksventrikuläre Überlastung *f*.
aortic pressure: Aortendruck *m*.
aortic regurgitation: Aortenklappeninsuffizienz *f*.
aortic rupture: Aortenruptur *f*.
aortic sclerosis: Aortensklerose *f*.
aortic stenosis: Aortenstenose *f*.
aortic valve: Aortenklappe *f*.
aortic valve prolapse: Aortenklappenprolaps *m*.
aortic valvular stenosis: a condition in which there is an improper opening of the valve between the aorta and the left ventricle of the heart. Aortenklappenstenose *f*.
aortitis/*n*: Aortitis *f*.
aortocaval fistula: aortokavale Fistel *f*.
aortocoronary bypass: aortokoronarer Bypass *m*.
aortoiliac occlusive disease: partial or complete obstruction of the abdominal aorta, usually due to arteriosclerosis and thrombosis. Symptoms

include pallor of the legs, muscular atrophy, pain in the legs, and sexual dysfunction. aortoiliakale Verschlusskrankheit *f*, Aortenbifurkationssyndrom *n*, Leriche-Syndrom *n*.
aortoplasty/*n*: Aortenplastik *f*.
aortopulmonary/*adj*: aortopulmonal.
apalcillin/*n*: Apalcillin *n*.
apathy/*n*: Apathie *f*.
aperient/*n, adj*: 1. Abführmittel *n*; 2. abführend.
aperiodic/*adj*: unregelmäßig, unperiodisch.
aperiosteal amputation: aperiostale Amputation *f*, Bunge-Amputation *f*.
aperistalsis/*n*: Aperistaltik *f*, Aperistalsis *f*.
aperture/*n*: Apertur *f*, Öffnung *f*.
apex beat: Herzspitzenstoß *m*.
apex of the heart: Herzspitze *f*.
apex of the lung: Lungenspitze *f*.
Apgar scale <*abbr*> **Appearance pulse grimace attitude respiration scale**: APGAR-Schema *n*, Atmung Puls Grundtonus Aussehen Reflexe.
aphagia/*n*: Aphagie *f*.
aphakia/*n*: Aphakie *f*, Linsenlosigkeit *f*.
aphasia/*n*: inability to form or to understand words in written or spoken language. Forms include motor aphasia which is characterized by loss of the ability to express language, and sensory aphasia which is characterized by an inability to understand spoken and written language, and sometimes gestures. Aphasie *f*.
aphasic agraphia: aphasische Agraphie *f*.
aphasic alexia: aphasische Alexie *f*.
aphonia/*n*: Aphonie *f*, Stimmlosigkeit *f*.
aphrodisiac/*n*: Aphrodisiakum *n*.
aphtha/*n*: Aphthe *f*.
aphthous/*adj*: aphthös.
aphthous fever: an infectious disease of animals caused by a picornavirus, which can be transmitted to humans by direct contact. Symptoms include fever, malaise, headache, and vesiculation of the mouth and fingertips. Maul- und Klauenseuche *f*.
aphthous stomatitis: aphthöse Stomatitis *f*.
aphthous ulcer: inflammatory alteration and small, often painful ulcers on the surface of a mucous membrane, for example of the mouth, gastrointestinal tract, or sexual organs. Causes include generalized diseases, infectious diseases, or autoimmune disorders. Aphthe *f*.
apical abscess: Alveolarabszess *m*.
apical body: Apikalkörper *m*.
apical impulse: Herzspitzenstoß *m*.
apical osteitis: Zahnspitzenostitis *f*.
apicectomy/*n*: Apikoektomie *f*, Lungenspitzenresektion *f*.
aplanatic lens: Aplanatlinse *f*.
aplasia/*n*: Aplasie *f*.
aplastic/*adj*: aplastisch.
aplastic anemia: aplastische Anämie *f*.
aplastic stem cell: aplastische Stammzelle *f*.
aplaviroc/*n*: Aplaviroc *n*.
apnea/*n*: Apnoe *f*, Atemstillstand *m*.
apocrine/*adj*: apokrin.
apocrine acne: Hidradenitis suppurativa *f*.
apocrine gland: apokrine Drüse *f*.
apomorphine/*n*: Apomorphin *n*.
aponeurosis/*n*: Aponeurose *f*.
aponeurotic reflex: Fußsohlenreflex *m*.
apophyseal fracture: Apophysenfraktur *f*, Apophysenlösung *f*.
apophysis/*n*: Apophyse *f*.
apoplectic coma: apoplektisches Koma *n*, zerebrales Koma *n*.
apoplectic retinopathy: Zentralvenenthrombose *f*, Apoplexia retinalis *f*.
apoplectic stroke: Apoplexie *f*.
apoplectiform attack: apoplektiformer Anfall *m*.
apoplexy/*n*: a neurologic condition characterized by sudden onset and a variety of symptoms due to acute brain hemorrhage or infarction. Apoplexie *f*, Schlaganfall *m*.
apostolic hand: Predigerhand *f*.
apparatus/*n*: Apparat *m*, Gerät *n*.
apparent death: Scheintod *m*.

appearance/*n*: Erscheinung *f*, Aspekt *m*.
appendectomy/*n*: Appendektomie *f*.
appendiceal abscess: appendizitischer Abszess *m*.
appendiceal phlegmon: Appendixphlegmone *f*.
appendicitis/*n*: inflammation of the vermiform appendix. Symptoms include abdominal pain, with typical pain at McBurney's point elicited by pressure in the left lower quadrant, accompanied by nausea, vomiting, and fever, and tenderness of the abdomen. Appendizitis *f*, Blinddarmentzündung *f*.
appendicular colic: Blinddarmkolik *f*.
appendicular lobe: Riedel-Lappen *m*.
appendix/*n*: Appendix *f*, Blinddarm *m*.
apperception/*n*: Apperzeption *f*.
apperceptive blindness: optische Agnosie *f*.
appetite/*n*: Appetit *m*.
appetite suppressant: Appetitzügler *m*.
appliance/*n*: Apparat *m*, Anwendung *f*.
application/*n*: Applikation *f*, Anwendung *f*.
applicator/*n*: Applikator *m*.
applied anatomy: angewandte Anatomie *f*.
appointment/*n*: Termin *m*, Vereinbarung *f*.
appositional growth: appositionelles Wachstum *n*.
apprehension/*n*: Apprehension *f*, Auffassung *f*.
approach/*n, vb*: 1. Annäherung *f*, Zugang *m*, Vorgehen *n*; 2. sich nähern.
approval/*n*: Zulassung *f*, Zustimmung *f*.
apraclonidine/*n*: Apraclonidin *n*.
apramycin/*n*: Apramycin *n*.
apraxia/*n*: Apraxie *f*.
apraxic agnosia: pragmatische Agnosie *f*, Pragmatagnosie *f*.
apraxic agraphia: apraktische Agraphie *f*.
aprepitant/*n*: Aprepitant *n*.
aprindine/*n*: Aprindin *n*.
apron/*n*: Schürze *f*.
apt/*adj*: geeignet, geneigt.
aptitude/*n*: Eigenschaft *f*, Eignung *f*.
aptyalism/*n*: Aptyalismus *m*, Asialie *f*.
apyrexia/*n*: Fieberfreiheit *f*.
aqueduct/*n*: Aquädukt *m*.
aqueous/*adj*: wässrig, wasserhaltig.
aqueous chamber: vordere Augenkammer *f*.
aqueous solution: wässrige Lösung *f*.
aqueous tincture: wässrige Tinktur *f*.
arabin/*n*: Arabin *n*.
arachic acid: Arachinsäure *f*.
arachidonic acid: Arachidonsäure *f*.
arachnodactyly/*n*: dysplasia of fingers and toes, resulting in long, thin digits, occurring for example as a sign of Marfan syndrome, an autosomal dominant inherited disorder of connective tissue. Arachnodaktylie *f*, Marfan-Syndrom *n*.
arachnoid/*n*: Arachnoidea *f*.
arachnoid pulse: fadenförmiger Puls *m*.
arborization/*n*: Arborisation *f*.
arborization block: Arborisationsblock *m*, Verzweigungsblock *m*.
arbovirus/*n*: Arbovirus *n*.
arch/*n*: Bogen *m*.
arcuate uterus: Uterus arcuatus *m*.
ARDS <*abbr*> **adult respiratory distress syndrome**: a condition of pulmonary insufficiency which is characterized by insufficient oxygenation. Common causes include generalized shock, septicemia, multiple trauma, and embolism. posttraumatische pulmonale Insuffizienz *f*, Schocklunge *f*, ARDS.
area/*n*: Areal *n*, Bereich *m*, Feld *n*.
arecoline/*n*: Arecolin *n*.
areola/*n*: Areola *f*, kleiner Hof *m*.
argentaffin carcinoma: argentaffines Karzinom *n*.
argentaffin cell: argentaffine Zelle *f*, argyrophile Zelle *f*.
Argentinian hemorrhagic fever: Junin-Fieber *n*.
arginine/*n*: Arginin *n*, Arg.
argininosuccinic acid: Argininbernsteinsäure *f*.

argininosuccinicaciduria/*n*: Argininosukzinurie *f*, Argininbernsteinsäurekrankheit *f*.
argatroban/*n*: Argatroban *n*.
argyria/*n*: Argyrie *f*.
argyrophilic fiber: argyrophile Faser *f*.
aripiprazol/*n*: Aripiprazol *n*.
arm/*n*: Arm *m*.
arm circumference: Armumfang *m*.
armored heart: Panzerherz *n*.
armpit/*n*: Achselhöhle *f*.
arm presentation: in obstetrics, the position of the fetus in which the arm appears first in the uterine cervix. Armvorfall *m*.
arm sling: Armschlinge *f*.
aromatic acid: aromatische Säure *f*.
aromatic amino acid: aromatische Aminosäure *f*.
aromatic oil: aromatisches Öl *n*.
aromatic tincture: aromatische Tinktur *f*.
arousal effect: Arousal-Effekt *m*, Weck-Effekt *m*.
arrangement/*n*: Anordnung *f*.
array/*n, vb*: 1. Ordnung *f*, Anordnung *f*; 2. ordnen.
arrest/*n, vb*: 1. Stillstand *m*; 2. zum Stillstand bringen.
arrhenoblastoma/*n*: Arrhenoblastom *n*, Androblastom *n*.
arrhythmia/*n*: disturbance of normal, regular rhythm, for example cardiac arrhythmia with an irregular rate of heart beats, or irregular breathing. Arrhythmie *f*.
arsenic/*n*: Arsen *n*, As.
arsenic acid: Arsensäure *f*.
arsenic amblyopia: Arsenamblyopie *f*.
arsenic cancer: Arsenkrebs *m*.
arsenic neuropathy: Arsenneuropathie *f*.
arsenic pigmentation: Arsenpigmentierung *f*.
arsinic acid: Arsinsäure *f*.
arsonic acid: Arsonsäure *f*.
arterial/*adj*: arteriell.
arterial blood: arterielles Blut *n*.
arterial blood pressure: Arteriendruck *m*, arterieller Blutdruck *m*.
arterial calcification: Arterienverkalkung *f*.
arterial embolism: arterielle Embolie *f*.
arterial hemorrhage: arterielle Blutung *f*.
arterial insufficiency: arterielle Insuffizienz *f*.
arterial murmur: Arteriengeräusch *n*, Arterienrauschen *n*.
arterial obstruction: Arterienverschluss *m*.
arterial pulse: Arterienpuls *m*.
arterial sclerosis: Arteriosklerose *f*.
arterial spasm: Arterienspasmus *m*.
arterial stenosis: Arterienverengung *f*.
arterial thrill: arterielles Schwirren *n*.
arterial thrombosis: Arterienthrombose *f*.
arterial vessel: arterielles Gefäß *n*.
arteriography/*n*: Arteriographie *f*.
arteriolar nephrosclerosis: Nierenarteriolosklerose *f*.
arteriolar sclerosis: Arteriolosklerose *f*.
arteriole/*n*: Arteriole *f*.
arteriopathy/*n*: Arteriopathie *f*.
arterioplasty/*n*: Arterioplastie *f*.
arteriosclerosis/*n*: a condition in which artery walls become thickened and inelastic. The most frequently and most seriously affected arteries are the aorta, the coronary arteries, and cerebral and kidney arteries. Arteriosklerose *f*.
arteriosclerotic dementia: Multiinfarktdemenz *f*.
arteriosclerotic nephritis: Arterionephrosklerose *f*.
arteriosclerotic retinopathy: Netzhautarteriosklerose *f*.
arteriotomy/*n*: Arteriotomie *f*.
arteriovenous/*adj*: arteriovenös.
arteriovenous anastomosis: arteriovenöse Anastomose *f*.
arteriovenous aneurysm: arteriovenöses Aneurysma *n*.
arteriovenous angioma: arteriovenöses Angiom *n*.
arteriovenous communication: arteriovenöser Shunt *m*.

arteriovenous fistula: arteriovenöse Fistel *f*, AV-Fistel *f*.
arteriovenous shunt: arteriovenöser Shunt *m*.
arteriovenous thrill: arteriovenöses Schwirren *n*.
arteritis/*n*: inflammation of an artery, usually associated with infections, septicemia, autoimmune disorders, or reactions to toxic chemicals or drugs. Arteriitis *f*, Arterienentzündung *f*.
artery/*n*: Arterie *f*.
arthralgia/*n*: pain in a joint which may be associated with heat, redness, impaired function, and swelling. Causes include arthritis and trauma. Arthralgie *f*, Gelenkschmerz *m*.
arthrectomy/*n*: Gelenkresektion *f*.
arthritic/*adj*: arthritisch.
arthritic pain: Gelenkschmerz *m*.
arthritis/*n*: inflammation of one or several joints, occurring for example in rheumatic fever, infections, or autoimmune disorder. Arthritis *f*, Gelenkentzündung *f*.
arthrodesis/*n*: Arthrodese *f*.
arthrography/*n*: Arthrographie *f*.
arthrolith/*n*: Arthrolith *m*, Gelenkkörper *m*.
arthropathy/*n*: Arthropathie *f*, Gelenkerkrankung *f*.
arthroplasty/*n*: Arthroplastik *f*.
arthropod/*n*: Arthropode *m*.
arthroscopic surgery: arthroskopischer Eingriff *m*.
arthroscopy/*n*: Arthroskopie *f*.
arthrosis/*n*: any degenerative disease of a joint, usually affecting the joint cartilage. Symptoms include pain, aches, and impairment of function. Arthrose *f*.
arthrosis of the hip: Hüftgelenkarthrose *f*, Koxarthrose *f*.
arthrotomy/*n*: Arthrotomie *f*, Gelenkeröffnung *f*.
articaine/*n*: Articain *n*.
articular/*adj*: artikulär.
articular block: Gelenksperre *f*.
articular calculus: Arthrolith *m*, Gelenkkörper *m*.
articular capsule: Gelenkkapsel *f*.
articular cartilage: Gelenkknorpel *m*.
articular facet: Gelenkfacette *f*.
articular fracture: intraartikuläre Fraktur *f*.
articular head: Gelenkkopf *m*.
articular process: Gelenkfortsatz *m*.
articular sensation: Gelenksensibilität *f*.
articulation/*n*: Gelenkverbindung *f*, Artikulation *f*.
artifact/*n*: Artefakt *n*.
artificial/*adj*: artifiziell, künstlich.
artificial alimentation: künstliche Ernährung *f*.
artificial ankylosis: Arthrodese *f*.
artificial anus: künstlicher After *m*, künstlicher Darmausgang *m*.
artificial blood: künstliches Blut *n*, Blutersatz *m*.
artificial eye: Augenprothese *f*.
artificial fever: künstliches Fieber *n*.
artificial heart: Kunstherz *n*.
artificial insemination: künstliche Insemination *f*.
artificial kidney: künstliche Niere *f*.
artificial labor: künstlich eingeleitete Wehen
artificial leech: Schröpfkopf *m*.
artificial limb: Prothese *f*.
artificial respiration: künstliche Beatmung *f*.
artificial rupture of the membranes: künstliche Blasensprengung *f*, Amniotomie *f*.
artificial sphincter: künstlicher Sphinkter *m*.
artificial ventilation: künstliche Beatmung *f*.
artificial vessel: Gefäßprothese *f*.
arytenoid/*adj*: arytänoid.
asbestosis/*n*: disease of the lung with bilateral, diffuse fibrosis, occurring in persons who inhaled asbestos or asbestos-like material with a delayed onset after years. Asbestose *f*.
ascariasis/*n*: an infectious disease resulting from invasion of the body by ascarid worms, the so-called roundworms. Symptoms include diarrhea, loss of appetite, and during lung passage, pneumonia. Askariasis *f*.

ascaridol/*n*: Ascaridol *n*.
ascending/*adj*: aszendierend, aufsteigend.
ascending neuritis: aszendierende Polyneuritis *f*, Guillain-Barré-Syndrom *n*.
ascending neuropathy: aszendierende Neuropathie *f*.
ascending paralysis: aszendierende Lähmung *f*.
ascending polyneuritis: a neurologic disorder of unknown etiology, possibly due to an autoimmune disorder following viral or bacterial infection. Symptoms include polyneuritis, ascending motor neuron paralysis and muscular weakness, initial paralysis of the legs, ascending to the arms and trunk. aszendierende Polyneuritis *f*, Guillain-Barré-Syndrom *n*.
ascending pyelonephritis: aszendierende Pyelonephritis *f*.
ascending reticular activating system: aufsteigendes retikuläres aktivierendes System *n*, ARAS.
ascending urography: retrograde Urographie *f*.
ascertain/*vb*: feststellen, ermitteln.
Aschheim-Zondek test: Aschheim-Zondek-Schwangerschaftstest *m*.
ascites/*n*: abnormal accumulation of free body fluid in the abdomen, occurring for example as a complication of liver cirrhosis, metastatic cancer, or obstruction of the thoracic duct. Aszites *m*.
ascitic fluid: Aszites *m*.
ascorbic acid: Ascorbinsäure *f*, Vitamin C *n*.
asepsis/*n*: Asepsis *f*.
aseptic/*adj*: aseptisch, keimfrei.
aseptic fever: aseptisches Fieber *n*.
aseptic surgery: aseptische Chirurgie *f*.
aseptic technique: Asepsis *f*.
asexual/*adj*: asexuell, ungeschlechtlich.
asexual reproduction: ungeschlechtliche Fortpflanzung *f*.
Asian influenza: asiatische Grippe *f*.
Asiatic schistosomiasis: Schistosomiasis japonica *f*.
asiderotic anemia: Eisenmangelanämie *f*.
asleep/*adj*: schlafend.
asomnia/*n*: Asomnie *f*, Schlaflosigkeit *f*.
asparaginase/*n*: Asparaginase *f*.
aspartic acid: Asparaginsäure *f*.
aspergillic acid: Aspergillsäure *f*.
aspergillosis/*n*: an infectious disease caused by a fungus of Aspergillus species. Forms include pulmonary aspergillosis with infection of the lung, predominantly occurring in immunocompromised persons, and aural aspergillosis with infection of the external ear. Aspergillose *f*.
aspermia/*n*: Aspermie *f*.
asphyxating thoracic dystrophy: asphyxierende Thoraxdystrophie *f*, Jeune-Krankheit *f*.
asphyxia/*n*: Asphyxie *f*.
aspiration/*n*: Aspiration *f*.
aspirator/*n*: Absauggerät *n*.
assay/*n*: Probe *f*.
assessment/*n*: Prüfung *f*, Beurteilung *f*.
assist/*vb*: assistieren, unterstützen.
assistance/*n*: Assistenz *f*, Hilfeleistung *f*.
assistant/*n*: Assistent *m*, Hilfsperson *f*.
assisted breathing: assistierte Beatmung *f*.
assisted circulation: unterstützter Kreislauf *m*.
assisted ventilation: assistierte Beatmung *f*.
associated affect: Begleiteffekt *m*.
associated disease: Begleiterkrankung *f*.
associated movement: Mitbewegung *f*.
assumption/*n*: Annahme *f*, Vermutung *f*.
asteatosis/*n*: Asteatose *f*.
astemizole/*n*: Astemizol *n*.
astereognosis/*n*: Astereognosie *f*, Tastblindheit *f*.
asthenia/*n*: Asthenie *f*, Effort-Syndrom *n*.
asthenic bulbar paralysis: a neurologic disorder which is considered to

be caused by an autoimmune reaction against muscular receptors of acetylcholine. It is characterized by severe muscle weakness following movements or exercise, affecting all voluntary muscles, including eye muscles and respiratory muscles. Myasthenia gravis *f*.

asthenopia/*n*: Asthenopie *f*, Sehschwäche *f*.

asthma/*n*: a condition which is characterized by a decrease in diameter of some air passages, resulting in dyspneic episodes. Asthma may result from allergic reaction to an inhaled substance or occur in individuals who are constitutionally predisposed. Asthma *n*.

asthmatic cough: Asthmahusten *m*.

astigmatism/*n*: Astigmatismus *m*.

astringent/*n*: Adstringens *n*.

astroblastoma/*n*: Astroblastom *n*.

astrocytic glioma: Astrozytom *n*.

astrocytoma/*n*: Astrozytom *n*.

astroglia/*n*: Astroglia *f*.

astronautic diet: Astronautenkost *f*.

asymmetrical pelvis: asymmetrisches Becken *n*.

asymmetry/*n*: Asymmetrie *f*.

asymptomatic/*adj*: asymptomatisch.

asymptomatic gastritis: asymptomatische Gastritis *f*.

asymptomatic proteinuria: asymptomatische Proteinurie *f*.

asynchronous pacemaker: Festfrequenzschrittmacher *m*.

asynclitism/*n*: Asynklitismus *m*, Scheitelbeineinstellung *f*.

atavism/*n*: Atavismus *m*.

ataxia/*n*: loss of coordinated movement and unsteadiness, usually caused either by a disease of the nervous system and loss of the normal cerebellar control over motor activity, or caused by impairment of proprioception and deep sensibility. Ataxie *f*.

ataxic gait: ataktischer Gang *m*.

ataxic paraplegia: ataktische Paraplegie *f*.

atazanavir/*n*: Atazanavir *n*.

atelectasis/*n*: Atelektase *f*.

atelectatic rale: Atelektaseknistern *n*.

atenolol/*n*: Atenolol *n*.

atevirdine/*n*: Atevirdin *n*.

atherogenic/*adj*: atherogen.

atheroma/*n*: Atherom *n*.

atheromatous plaque: atheromatöse Plaque *f*.

atherosclerosis/*n*: Atherosklerose *f*.

athetoid spasm: Athetose *f*.

athetosis/*n*: a neurologic disorder which is characterized by repetitive, involuntary movements, usually occurring uni- or bilateral in the extremeties. Causes include cerebral hemiplegia, lesions in the corpus striatum, hepaticolenticular degeneration, and various forms of leukodystrophy. Athetose *f*.

athlete's foot: Fußpilz *m*, Tinea pedis *f*.

athletic heart: Sportlerherz *n*.

athletic proteinuria: Belastungsproteinurie *f*.

atlanto-occipital joint: Atlas-Axisgelenk *n*.

atmospheric pressure: Atmosphärendruck *m*.

atomizer/*n*: Vernebler *m*.

atonic-astatic encephalopathy: Diplegia atonica congenita *f*, Atonie-Astasie-Syndrom *n*, Foerster-Krankheit *f*.

atonic diplegia: Diplegia atonica congenita *f*, Atonie-Astasie-Syndrom *n*, Foerster-Krankheit *f*.

atonic seizure: atonischer Anfall *m*.

atony/*n*: Atonie *f*, Erschlaffung *f*.

atopic allergy: Atopie *f*.

atopic conjunctivitis: allergische Konjunktivitis *f*.

atopic dermatitis: atopisches Ekzem *n*, Neurodermitis atopica *f*.

atopic disease: atopische Erkrankung *f*.

atopic eczema: a skin disease which is characterized by an inflammatory skin reaction in association with atopy. Onset is usually in early infancy, and atopic dermatitis or eczema may persist into childhood. The face and the flexures are usually among the body regions that are affected first.

A

atopisches Ekzem *n*, atopische Dermatitis *f*.
atopic neurodermatitis: atopisches Ekzem *n*, atopische Dermatitis *f*.
atorvastatin/*n*: Atorvastatin *n*.
atosiban/*n*: Atosiban *n*.
atovaquone/*n*: Atovaquon *n*.
atracurium besilate: Atracuriumbesilat *n*.
atraumatic suture: atraumatische Naht *f*.
atresia/*n*: Atresie *f*.
atrial/*adj*: atrial.
atrial beat: Vorhofkontraktion *f*, Vorhofwelle *f*.
atrial bigeminy: Vorhofbigeminie *f*.
atrial complex: Vorhofkomplex *m*.
atrial dissociation: Vorhofdissoziation *f*.
atrial fibrillation: a cardiac arrhythmia which is characterized by atrial impulses that are conducted randomly to the ventricles, resulting in highly irregular activity of ventricles. Vorhofflimmern *n*.
atrial flutter: a cardiac arrhythmia which is characterized by atrial activation at a rate between 250 and 300(-350) per minute. Only some of atrial impulses are conducted to the ventricles, usually as a 3:1 or 2:1 block. Vorhofflattern *n*.
atrial heart septal defect: Vorhofseptumdefekt *m*.
atrial myxoma: Vorhofmyxom *n*.
atrial natriuretic factor: atrialer natriuretischer Faktor *m*, atriales natriuretisches Hormon *n*.
atrial pacing: Vorhofstimulation *f*.
atrial septal defect: Vorhofseptumdefekt *m*.
atrial septum: Vorhofseptum *n*, Vorhofscheidewand *f*.
atrial sound: Vorhofgeräusch *n*.
atrial standstill: Vorhofstillstand *m*.
atrial systole: Vorhofsystole *f*.
atrial tachycardia: Vorhoftachykardie *f*.
atrial thrombosis: Vorhofthrombose *f*.
atrial venous pulse: atriovenöser Puls *m*.
atriodigital dysplasia: a congenital, autosomal dominant inherited syndrome which is characterized by hypoplasia of the thumbs and a short forearm, in association with an atrial or ventricular septal defect of the heart. atriodigitale Dysmelie *f*, Hand-Fuß-Syndrom *n*, Holt-Oram-Syndrom *n*.
atriosystolic murmur: atriosystolisches Geräusch *n*, Vorhofsystolikum *n*.
atrioventricular/*adj*: atrioventrikulär.
atrioventricular block: atrioventrikulärer Block *m*, AV-Block *m*.
atrioventricular bundle: Atrioventrikularbündel *n*, His-Bündel *n*.
atrioventricular canal: Atrioventrikularkanal *m*.
atrioventricular conduction: atrioventrikuläre Überleitung *f*.
atrioventricular dissociation: atrioventrikuläre Dissoziation *f*.
atrioventricular escape: AV-Knoten-Ersatzrhythmus *m*.
atrioventricular junction: Atrioventrikularbündel *n*, AV-Bündel *n*, His-Bündel *n*.
atrioventricular junctional tachycardia: AV-Knoten-Tachykardie *f*.
atrioventricular node: Atrioventrikulärknoten *m*, AV-Knoten *m*, Aschoff-Tawara-Knoten *m*.
atrioventricular rhythm: AV-Rhythmus *m*, Atrioventrikularrhythmus *m*.
atrioventricular septal defect: a defect in the heart septum which is localized in the atrioventricular septum and potentially permits a communication between all atrial and ventricular chambers. Vorhofkammerseptumdefekt *m*.
atrioventricular valve: Atrioventrikularklappe *f*.
atrium/*n*: Vorhof *m*.
atrophic/*adj*: atrophisch.
atrophic alopecia: atrophische Alopezie *f*.
atrophic anemia: aplastische Anämie *f*.

atrophic emphysema: Altersemphysem *n*.
atrophic gastritis: atrophische Gastritis *f*.
atrophic heart: Herzatrophie *f*.
atrophic kidney: Schrumpfniere *f*.
atrophic pharyngitis: chronic inflammation of the pharynx which is characterized by an atrophy of the pharyngeal mucosa and of the mucous glands, usually due to atrophic rhinitis. Pharyngitis atrophicans *f*.
atrophic rhinitis: chronic-atrophic inflammation of the lining of the nose, frequently associated with Klebsiella ozaenae. Symptoms include the production of a mucopurulent, foul-smelling discharge. atrophische Rhinitis *f*, Ozäna *f*.
atrophic skin: Hautatrophie *f*.
atrophy/*n, vb*: 1. Atrophie *f*, Schwund *m*; 2. atrophieren.
atropine/*n*: Atropin *n*.
attachment/*n*: Bindung *f*, Anhänglichkeit *f*.
attack/*n, vb*: 1. Attacke *f*, Anfall *m*, Angriff *m*; 2. angreifen, befallen.
attempt/*n, vb*: 1. Versuch *m*; 2. versuchen.
attempted suicide: Suizidversuch *m*.
attend/*vb*: pflegen, aufwarten.
attention deficit disorder: Aufmerksamkeits-Hyperaktivitätsstörung *f*, ADHS.
attenuated vaccine: attenuierter Impfstoff *m*.
attitude/*n*: Einstellung *f*, Haltung *f*.
attitudinal reflex: Haltungsreflex *m*, Haltereflex *m*.
attribution/*n*: Attribution *f*, Zuschreibung *f*.
atypical/*adj*: atypisch, untypisch.
atypical bacterial endocarditis: Libman-Sacks-Endokarditis *f*.
atypical facial pain: atypische Gesichtsneuralgie *f*.
atypical pneumonia: atypische Pneumonie *f*.
atypical psychosis: atypische Psychose *f*.
atypical schizophrenia: undifferenzierte Schizophrenie *f*.
audiogram/*n*: Audiogramm *n*.
audiology/*n*: Audiologie *f*.
audiometer/*n*: Audiometer *n*.
audiometric curve: Hörkurve *f*.
audiometric threshold: audiometrische Schwelle *f*.
auditory/*adj*: akustisch.
auditory acuity: Hörschärfe *f*.
auditory agnosia: akustische Agnosie *f*, Lautagnosie *f*.
auditory amnesia: auditorische Amnesie *f*.
auditory aphasia: sensorische Aphasie *f*, Wernicke-Aphasie *f*.
auditory area: Hörzentrum *n*.
auditory aura: akustische Aura *f*.
auditory cell: Hörzelle *f*.
auditory center: Hörzentrum *n*.
auditory cortex: akustischer Kortex *m*.
auditory evoked potential: akustisch evoziertes Potential *n*.
auditory flutter: auditorisches Flimmern *n*.
auditory hair: Hörhaar *n*.
auditory hallucination: akustische Halluzination *f*.
auditory image: Wortklangbild *n*.
auditory ossicle: Gehörknöchelchen *n*.
auditory perception: akustische Wahrnehmung *f*.
auditory test: Hörtest *m*.
auditory threshold: Hörschwelle *f*.
auditory vertigo: a disease of the organs of balance in the inner ear. Symptoms include deafness and sudden attacks of extreme giddiness, vomiting, and loss of balance. Menière-Schwindel *m*.
augmentation mammoplasty: Mammavergrößerung *f*.
aura/*n*: Aura *f*.
auranofin/*n*: Auranofin *n*.
auricle/*n*: Ohrmuschel *f*, Vorhof *m*.
auricular/*adj*: aurikulär.
auriculotemporal/*adj*: aurikolotemporal.
auriculotemporal syndrome: a syndrome which is characterized by profuse sweating over one side of the face, provoked by eating and someti-

mes by emotion. This gustatory sweating syndrome may be caused by aberrant growth of the facial nerve after injury. aurikulotemporales Syndrom *n*, gustatorisches Schwitzen *n*.

auriculoventricular/*adj*: atrioventrikulär.

aurothioglucose/*n*: Aurothioglukose *f*, Goldthioglukose *f*.

auscultate/*vb*: auskultieren, abhören.

auscultation/*n*: Auskultation *f*.

auscultatory/*adj*: auskultatorisch.

auscultatory gap: auskultatorische Lücke *f*.

auscultatory sound: auskultatorisches Geräusch *n*.

autism/*n*: Autismus *m*.

autistic/*adj*: autistisch.

autistic thinking: autistisches Denken *n*.

autoagglutination/*n*: Autoagglutination *f*.

autoallergic eczema: autoallergisches Ekzem *n*.

autoantibody/*n*: Autoantikörper *m*.

autoantigen/*n*: Autoantigen *n*.

autocatalysis/*n*: Autokatalyse *f*.

autochthonous parasite: autochthoner Parasit *m*.

autoclave/*n, vb*: 1. Autoklav *m*; 2. autoklavieren.

autodigestion/*n*: Autolyse *f*.

autogenous/*adj*: autogen, körpereigen.

autogenous graft: autogenes Transplantat *n*.

autograft/*n*: Autotransplantat *n*.

autoimmune/*adj*: autoimmun.

autoimmune antibody: Autoantikörper *m*.

autoimmune disease: Autoimmunkrankheit *f*.

autoimmune glomerulonephritis: Autoimmunglomerulonephritis *f*.

autoimmune hemolytic anemia: an acquired hemolytic anemia in which antibodies to the patient's erythrocytes can be detected which may bind to red blood cells in warm or cold environment. autoimmunhämolytische Anämie *f*.

autoimmune response: Autoimmunantwort *f*.

autoimmune thyroiditis: a chronic, autoimmune disorder which is characterized by an inflammatory reaction of the thyroid gland resulting from antibodies directed against thyroid tissue. Autoimmune thyroiditis or Hashimoto's disease may present as thyroid gland enlargement or hypothyroidism with myxedema. Autoimmunthyreoiditis *f*, Hashimoto-Thyreoiditis *f*.

autoimmunity/*n*: Autoimmunität *f*.

autoimmunization/*n*: Autoimmunisierung *f*.

autoinfection/*n*: Autoinfektion *f*.

autointoxication/*n*: Autointoxikation *f*.

autologous blood transfusion: autologe Transfusion *f*, Eigenbluttransfusion *f*.

autologous graft: Autograft *n*.

autologous serum: Eigenserum *n*.

autologous transplantation: autologe Transplantation *f*.

autolysis/*n*: Autolyse *f*.

automatic action: Automatismus *m*.

automatic beat: Herzautomatismus *m*.

automatic behavior: Automatismus *m*.

automatic bladder: automatische Blase *f*.

automatic movement: Bewegungsautomatismus *m*.

automatism/*n*: Automatismus *m*.

autonomic disorder: Erkrankung des autonomen Nervensystems *f*.

autonomic nervous system: autonomes Nervensystem *n*.

autonomous bladder: a reaction of the urinary bladder to injury of the vesicospinal centers, characterized by frequent urinary excretion due to contractions of muscle fibres. Blasenautonomie *f*, autonome Blase *f*.

autonomous breathing: autonome Atmung *f*.

autoplasty/*n*: Autoplastik *f*.

autopsy/*n*: Autopsie *f*, Obduktion *f*.

autopsy record: Sektionsbericht *m*.
autoradiography/*n*: Autoradiographie *f*.
autosomal/*adj*: autosomal.
autosomal gene: autosomales Gen *n*.
autosuggestion/*n*: Autosuggestion *f*.
autotransfusion/*n*: Autotransfusion *f*.
autotransplant/*n*: Autotransplantat *n*.
autumnal catarrh: Autumnalkatarrh *m*, Heuschnupfen *m*.
auxiliary enzyme: Hilfsenzym *n*.
auxiliary fiber: akzessorische Faser *f*.
auxiliary nurse: Hilfsschwester *f*.
availability/*n*: Verfügbarkeit *f*.
available conjugate: kleinster Beckeneingangsdurchmesser *m*.
avascular/*adj*: avaskulär, gefäßfrei.
average/*n, adj*: 1. Durchschnitt *m*; 2. durchschnittlich.
aversion/*n*: Aversion *f*.
aversion therapy/*n*: Aversionstherapie *f*.
aversive stimulus: Aversivreiz *m*.
avian/*adj*: aviär.
avian influenza: a cosmopolitan infectious disease caused by influenza virus in poultry, especially chicken, which can be transmitted to humans. Symptoms include acute respiratory disease, and fever. aviäre Influenza *f*, Vogelgrippe *f*.
avirulent/*adj*: avirulent.
avitaminosis/*n*: Avitaminose *f*.
avoidable/*adj*: vermeidbar.
avoidance/*n*: Vermeidung *f*.
avoidance behavior: Vermeidungsverhalten *n*.
avoidant disorder: Angstsyndrom mit Vermeidungsverhalten.
avulsed wound: Avulsion *f*.
awake/*vb*: aufwachen, erwachen.
aware/*adj*: bewusst.
awareness/*n*: Bewusstsein *n*.
axial ametropia: Achsenametropie *f*.
axial cataract: Kernstar *m*.
axial hyperopia: Achsenhyperopie *f*.
axial symptom: Achsensymptom *n*.
axiliary cataract: Zentralstar *m*.
axillary/*adj*: axillär.
axillary line: Axillarlinie *f*, Linea axillaris *f*.
axillary lymph node: Achsellymphknoten *m*.
axillary paralysis: Axillarislähmung *f*.
axillary space: Achselhöhle *f*.
axis/*n*: Achse *f*, Axis *m*, Epistropheus *m*.
axis deviation: Achsenabweichung *f*.
axis of the body: Körperachse *f*.
axon/*n*: Axon *n*, Achsenzylinder *m*.
axonal degeneration: axonale Degeneration *f*.
axon hillock: Axonhügel *m*.
axonotmesis/*n*: Axonotmesis *f*.
azamethonium/*n*: Azamethonium *n*.
azamethonium bromide: Azamethoniumbromid *n*.
azapropazone/*n*: Azapropazon *n*.
azatadine/*n*: Azatadin *n*.
azathioprine/*n*: Azathioprin *n*.
azelaic acid: Azelainsäure *f*.
azelastine/*n*: Azelastin *n*.
azidamfenicol/*n*: Azidamfenicol *n*.
azidocillin/*n*: Azidocillin *n*.
azidothymidine/*n*: Azidothymidin *n*.
azithromycin/*n*: Azithromycin *n*.
azlocillin/*n*: Azlocillin *n*.
azoospermia/*n*: absence of mature, motile sperm in the semen, while precursor forms are detectable. Azoospermie *m*.
azosemide/*n*: Azosemid *n*.
azotemia/*n*: Azotämie *f*.
azotemic encephalopathy: urämische Enzephalopathie *f*.
azoturia/*n*: Azoturie *f*.
aztreonam/*n*: Aztreonam *n*.
azurophil granule: azurophiles Granulum *n*, Azurgranulum *n*.

A

B

B <*abbr*> **boron**: Bor *n*, B.
Babes-Ernst corpuscle: Babes-Ernst-Polkörperchen *n*.
Babinski sign: Babinski-Zeichen *n*.
baby/*n*: Baby *n*, Säugling *m*.
baby food: Säuglingsnahrung *f*.
baby scale: Babywaage *f*.
bacampicillin/*n*: Bacampicillin *n*.
bacillary/*adj*: bazillär.
bacillary dysentery: an infectious disease caused by bacteria of the Shigella species and characterized by bloody diarrhea which results from irritation of the bowel. Dysenterie *f*, Bakterienruhr *f*, Shigellose *f*.
bacilliform/*adj*: bazilliform.
bacillin/*n*: Bacillin *n*.
bacilluria/*n*: Bazillurie *f*, Bakteriurie *f*.
bacillus/*n*: Bazillus *m*.
bacitracin/*n*: Bacitracin *n*.
bacitrin/*n*: Bacitrin *n*.
back/*n*: Rücken *m*.
backache/*n*: Rückenschmerzen *f*.
backbone/*n*: Wirbelsäule *f*.
backflow/*n*: Rückfluss *m*, Reflux *m*.
background/*n*: Hintergrund *m*.
backrest/*n*: Rückenstütze *f*.
back-tooth/*n*: Backenzahn *m*.
backward curvature: Lordose *f*.
backward heart failure: Rückwärtsversagen *n*.
baclofen/*n*: Baclofen *n*.
bacteria/*n*: Bakterie *f*.
bacterial/*adj*: bakteriell.
bacterial allergy: Bakterienallergie *f*.
bacterial cast: Bakterienzylinder *m*.
bacterial embolism: Bakterienembolie *f*.
bacterial endocarditis: acute or chronic infection of the inner layer of the heart resulting from bacterial infection, usually a complication of a systemic infectious disease, an injury, or a surgical intervention. Frequently, the lining of the cardiac valves is affected. bakterielle Endokarditis *f*.
bacterial filter: Bakterienfilter *m*.
bacterial infection: bakterielle Infektion *f*.
bacterial nephritis: Pyelonephritis *f*.
bacterial sepsis: Septikämie *f*.
bacterial strain: Bakterienstamm *m*.
bacterial toxin: Bakterientoxin *n*.
bactericidal/*adj*: bakterizid.
bacteriemia/*n*: Bakteriämie *f*.
bacteriology/*n*: Bakteriologie *f*.
bacteriolytic/*adj*: bakteriolytisch.
bacteriophage/*n*: Bakteriophage *m*, Phage *m*.
bacterium/*n*: Bakterium *n*.
bacteriuria/*n*: Bakteriurie *f*.
bad breath: Mundgeruch *m*, Foetor ex ore *m*.
bag/*n*: Beutel *f*, Hülle *f*, Sack *m*.
bagassosis/*n*: Bagassose *f*.
bag of waters: Amnionhöhle *f*, Fruchtblase *f*.
balance/*n*: Gleichgewicht *n*.
balanced diet: ausgeglichene Ernährung *f*.
balanitis/*n*: inflammation of the glans of the penis or clitoris, caused for example by bacterial infections, or autoimmune disorders. Balanitis *f*.
balanorrhea/*n*: Balanoblennorrhö *f*.
bald-headed/*adj*: kahlköpfig, glatzköpfig.
baldness/*n*: Kahlköpfigkeit *f*, Glatzköpfigkeit *f*.
Balint group: Balint-Gruppe *f*.
balloon angioplasty: Ballonangioplastie *f*, perkutane transluminale Angioplastie *f*.

ballooning/*n*: Auftreibung *f*, Ballondilatation *f*.
ballooning degeneration: Schwellungsdegeneration *f*.
ballott/*vb*: ballottieren.
ballottement/*n*: Ballottement *n*.
ball-valve thrombosis: Kugelventilthrombus *m*.
balm/*n*: Balsam *m*.
balneology/*n*: Balneologie *f*.
bambuterol/*n*: Bambuterol *n*.
band/*n*: Band *n*, Bandenspektrum *n*, Ligamentum *n*.
bandage/*n, vb*: 1. Bandage *f*, Verband *m*, Binde *f*; 2. bandagieren.
banding/*n*: Banding *n*, Bändelung *f*.
bandwidth/*n*: Bandbreite *f*.
banked blood: Blutkonserve *f*.
bar/*n*: 1. Stange *f*, Schranke *f*; 2. Bar, bar.
barber's itch: infection of the beard area, including fungal infections like ringworm, bacterial folliculitis like sycosis barbae, or pseudofolliculitis. Bartflechte *f*.
barbiturate/*n*: Barbiturat *n*.
barbituric acid: Barbitursäure *f*.
bare/*adj*: nackt, kahl.
barium contrast medium: bariumhaltiges Kontrastmittel *n*.
barium enema: Bariumkontrasteinlauf *m*.
barking cough: Bellhusten *m*.
baroceptor/*n*: Barorezeptor *m*, Druckrezeptor *m*.
barotraumatic otitis: Barootitis *f*.
barotraumatic sinusitis: Barosinusitis *f*.
barrel chest: Fassthorax *m*.
barrier/*n*: Barriere *f*, Schranke *f*.
bartholinian abscess: Bartholini-Abszess *m*.
bartholinitis/*n*: inflammation of the Bartholin's glands, the greater vestibular glands, usually due to bacterial infection, for example with gonococcus or coli bacteria. Bartholinitis *f*.
basal/*adj*: basal.
basal body: Basalkörperchen *n*.
basal body temperature: Basaltemperatur *f*.
basal cell: Basalzelle *f*.
basal cell carcinoma: a tumor originating in the basal cells of the epidermis or from follicles of sebaceous glands. Most frequent localizations include body ares exposed to sunlight like face, neck, ears, or lower legs. Basaliom *n*, Basalzellkarzinom *n*.
basal-cell nevus syndrome: an autosomal dominant inherited condition which is characterized by multiple basal cell nevi, basalioma, skeletal deformation, and cerebral lesions. Basalzellnävussyndrom *n*, Gorlin-Goltz-Syndrom *n*.
basal ganglion: Basalganglion *n*.
basal granule: Basalkörperchen *n*.
basal layer: Basalzellenschicht *f*, Basalis *f*.
basal membrane: Basalmembran *f*.
basal metabolic rate: Grundumsatz *m*.
basal pleurisy: basale Pleuritis *f*.
basal requirement: Grundbedarf *m*.
basal skull fracture: breaking of the bony floor of the skull. Symptoms may include rhinorrhea, accumulation of blood behind the tympanic membrane, otorrhea, or an ecchymosis with skin discoloration behind the ear. Schädelbasisfraktur *f*.
basal temperature: Basaltemperatur *f*.
base/*n*: Basis *f*, Grundlage *f*, Base *f*.
base excess: Basenüberschuss *m*.
baseline/*n*: Grundlinie *f*.
base pairing: Basenpaarung *f*.
basic amino acid: basische Aminosäure *f*.
basic immunization: Grundimmunisierung *f*.
basic life support: Herz-Lungen-Wiederbelebung *f*, HLW.
basilar/*adj*: basilär, basilaris.
basilar insufficiency: Arteria-basilaris-Insuffizienz *f*, Basilarisinsuffizienz *f*.
basilar invagination: Platybasie *f*.
basilar membrane: Basilarmembran *f*.
basin/*n*: Becken *n*, Schüssel *f*.
basis/*n*: Grundlage *f*, Basis *f*.

basophil/*n, adj*: 1. basophiler Granulozyt *m*; 2. basophil.
basophil adenoma: basophiles Adenom *n*.
basophilia/*n*: Basophilie *f*.
basophilic cell: Basophiler *m*.
basophilic leukemia: Basophilenleukämie *f*.
basophilic leukocyte: Basophiler *m*.
bath/*n, vb*: 1. Bad *n*; 2. baden.
batroxobin/*n*: Batroxobin *n*.
battering/*n*: Kindesmisshandlung *f*.
battery/*n*: Batterie *f*, Serie *f*, Misshandlung *f*.
bead/*n*: Kügelchen *n*, Perle *f*, Tröpfchen *n*.
beak/*n*: Schnabel *m*.
beaked pelvis: Schnabelbecken *n*.
beam/*n*: Balken *m*, Strahl *m*, Lichtstrahl *m*.
bear/*vb*: gebären, tragen.
beat/*n, vb*: 1. Schlag *m*, Herzschlag *m*; 2. schlagen, klopfen.
becaplermin/*n*: Becaplermin *n*.
beclamide/*n*: Beclamid *n*.
beclometasone/*n*: Beclometason *n*.
bed/*n*: Bett *n*.
bedbug/*n*: Bettwanze *f*, Cimex *m*.
bed capacity: Bettenkapazität *f*.
bedfast/*adj*: bettlägerig.
bedpan/*n*: Bettpfanne *f*, Steckbecken *n*.
bed rest: Bettruhe *f*.
bedridden/*adj*: bettlägerig.
bedside teaching: Bedside-Teaching *n*, Unterricht am Krankenbett *m*.
bedsore/*n*: lesion over prominant areas on the body of a bedridden person, caused by prolonged pressure. Initial symptoms include reddening of the skin, and formation of blisters, leading to necrotic alterations and lesions including lower layers of the tissue, muscle, and sometimes skeletal bones. Dekubitus *m*, Druckgeschwür *n*.
bedwetting/*n*: Bettnässen *n*.
beer heart: Bierherz *n*.
bee sting: Bienenstich *m*.
behavior/*n*: Verhalten *n*.
behavior disorder: Verhaltensstörung *f*.
behaviorism/*n*: Behaviorismus *m*.
behavior modification: Verhaltensänderung *f*.
belch/*n, vb*: 1. Eruktation *f*, Aufstoßen *n*; 2. aufstoßen.
belladonna/*n*: Atropa belladonna *f*, Tollkirsche *f*.
bell-metal resonance: Münzenklirren *n*.
belly/*n*: Bauch *m*, Magen *m*, Muskelbauch *m*.
bemegride/*n*: Bemegrid *n*.
bemetizide/*n*: Bemetizid *n*.
benactyzine/*n*: Benactyzin *n*.
benazepril/*n*: Benazepril *n*.
bencyclane/*n*: Bencyclan *n*.
bend/*n, vb*: 1. Krümmung *f*, Flexur *f*; 2. biegen, krümmen.
bendamustine/*n*: Bendamustin *n*.
bending fracture: Biegungsbruch *m*, Grünholzfraktur *f*.
bendroflumethiazide/*n*: Bendroflumethiazid *n*.
beneficial effect: positive Wirkung *f*.
benefit/*n*: Vorteil *m*, Nutzen *m*.
benfotiamine/*n*: Benfotiamin *n*.
benign/*adj*: benigne, gutartig.
benign dry pleurisy: gutartige trockene Pleuritis *f*.
benign familial icterus: hereditäre Hyperbilirubinämie *f*, Gilbert-Meulengracht-Syndrom *n*.
benign familial pemphigus: Pemphigus chronicus benignus familiaris *m*, Hailey-Hailey-Krankheit *f*.
benign intracranial hypertension: benigne intrakranielle Drucksteigerung *f*, Pseudotumor cerebri *m*.
benign lymphocytic reticulosis: Lymphadenosis cutis benigna *f*, Bäfverstedt-Syndrom *n*.
benign mucosal pemphigoid: Schleimhautpemphigoid *n*.
benign prostatic hypertrophy: hyperplasia of the prostate of unknown origin. Symptoms include pollakiuria, nycturia, residual urine, and in some cases complete obstruction of urethra. benigne Prostatahyperplasie *f*, BPH.
benign proteinuria: benigne Proteinurie *f*.

benign reticulosis: Katzenkratzkrankheit *f*.
benign tertian malaria: Malaria tertiana *f*.
benign tumor: benigner Tumor *m*.
benign typhus: Brill-Zinsser-Krankheit *f*.
benorterone/*n*: Benorteron *n*.
benperidol/*n*: Benperidol *n*.
benproperine/*n*: Benproperin *n*.
benserazide/*n*: Benserazid *n*.
bent catheter: gekrümmter Katheter *m*.
bentiromide/*n*: Bentiromid *n*.
benzaldehyde/*n*: Benzaldehyd *n*.
benzalkonium chloride: Benzalkoniumchlorid *n*.
benzathine/*n*: Benzathin *n*.
benzathine benzylpenicillin: Benzathin-Benzylpenicillin *n*.
benzathine penicillin: Benzathin-Penicillin *n*.
benzatropine/*n*: Benzatropin *n*.
benzbromarone/*n*: Benzbromaron *n*.
benzilonium bromide: Benzilonbromid *n*.
benzocaine/*n*: Benzocain *n*.
benzoctamine/*n*: Benzoctamin *n*.
benzodepa/*n*: Benzodepa *n*.
benzodiazepine/*n*: Benzodiazepin *n*.
benzoic acid: Benzoesäure *f*.
benzothiadiazide/*n*: Benzothiazidinderivat *n*.
benzoylaminoacetic acid: Benzoylaminoessigsäure *f*, Hippursäure *f*.
benzoylglucuronic acid: Benzoylglukuronsäure *f*.
benzydamine/*n*: Benzydamin *n*.
benzydiamine/*n*: Benzydiamin *n*.
benzydroflumethiazide/*n*: Bendroflumethiazid *n*.
benzylpenicillin/*n*: Benzylpenicillin *n*, Penicillin G *n*.
berry aneurysm: beerenförmiges Aneurysma *n*.
berylliosis/*n*: acute or chronic inflammation of the lungs, occurring for example as an occupational disease resulting from inhalation of beryllium oxide dust. Berylliumkrankheit *f*.
bestiality/*n*: Bestialität *f*, Zoophilie *f*.
beta-acetylpropionic acid: Lävulinsäure *f*.
beta blocker: Betablocker *m*, Betarezeptorenblocker *m*.
betahistine/*n*: Betahistin *n*.
beta-hydroxybutyric acid: β-Hydroxybuttersäure *f*.
beta-ketobutyric acid: Acetessigsäure *f*.
betamethasone/*n*: Betamethason *n*.
betamethasone acetate: Betamethasonacetat *n*.
betamethasone sodium phosphate: Betamethasonnatriumphosphat *n*.
beta-naphtholsulfonic acid: β-Naphthalensulfonsäure *f*.
beta-oxybutyric acid: β-Oxybuttersäure *f*.
beta wave: Betawelle *f*.
betaxolol/*n*: Betaxolol *n*.
betulinic acid: Betulinsäure *f*.
bewilderment/*n*: Verwirrtheit *f*.
bexarotene/*n*: Bexaroten *n*.
bezafibrate/*n*: Bezafibrat *n*.
bezoar/*n*: Bezoar *m*, Haarball *m*.
bias/*n, adj*: 1. Bias, Verzerrung *f*, Tendenz *f*; 2. schräg, quer.
bicalutamide/*n*: Bicalutamid *n*.
biceps reflex: Bizepssehnenreflex *m*, BSR.
bichloracetic acid: Dichloressigsäure *f*.
biconcave lens: Bikonkavlinse *f*.
biconvex lens: Bikonvexlinse *f*.
bicornate/*adj*: zweihörnig, bicornis.
bicornate uterus: Uterus bicornis *m*.
bicuspid/*adj*: bicuspidalis, zweizipflig.
bicuspid valve: Bikuspidalklappe *f*.
bifacial paralysis: beidseitige Fazialislähmung *f*.
bifid foot: Spaltfuß *m*.
bifocal glasses: Bifokalbrille *f*, Zweistärkenbrille *f*.
bifocal lens: bifokale Linse *f*.
bifonazole/*n*: Bifonazol *n*.
bifurcate/*vb, adj*: 1. gabeln, sich aufteilen; 2. gegabelt, zweigeteilt.
bigeminal pregnancy: Zwillingsschwangerschaft *f*.
bigeminal pulse: Bigeminie *f*.
bigeminy/*n*: Bigeminie *f*.

biguanide/*n*: Biguanid *n*.
bilateral/*adj*: bilateral, beidseitig.
bilateral athetosis: Athétose double *f*, Hammond-Krankheit *f*.
bilateral hearing loss: beidseitiger Hörverlust *m*.
bilateral hemianopia: bilaterale Hemianopsie *f*.
bilateral periocular hematoma: Brillenhämatom *n*.
bilateral strabismus: alternierendes Schielen *n*, Strabismus alternans *m*.
bilateral transfer: gegenseitige Übertragung *f*.
bile/*n*: Galle *f*.
bile acid: Gallensäure *f*.
bile duct: Gallengang *m*.
bile duct atresia: Gallengangatresie *f*.
bile pigment: Gallenfarbstoff *m*.
bile reflux: Gallereflux *m*.
bile salt: Gallensäuresalz *n*.
bilharzia/*n*: Bilharzia *f*, Schistosoma *f*.
bilianic acid: Biliansäure *f*.
biliary/*adj*: biliär, gallig.
biliary atresia: Gallengangatresie *f*.
biliary calculus: a calculus or stone-like object in the gall bladder or its drainage system, composed primarily of calcium. Symptoms include attacks of severe pain when the stone moves which may spread to both sides, in the back, and throughout the abdomen. If a gallstone causes obstruction to the bile duct, jaundice may occur. Gallenstein *m*.
biliary cirrhosis: biliäre Zirrhose *f*.
biliary colic: Gallenkolik *f*.
biliary encephalopathy: hepatische Enzephalopathie *f*.
biliary hypercholesterolemic xanthomatosis: biliäre hypercholesterinämische Xanthomatose *f*.
biliary liver cirrhosis: biliäre Zirrhose *f*.
biliary obstruction: Gallengangsverschluss *m*.
biliary peritonitis: gallige Peritonitis *f*.
biliary stasis: Cholestase *f*.
biliary system: Gallentrakt *m*.
biliary tract: Gallensystem *n*.
bilious/*adj*: biliär, gallig.
bilious colic: Gallenkolik *f*.
bilirubin/*n*: Bilirubin *n*.
bilirubinemia/*n*: Bilirubinämie *f*.
bilirubinic acid: Bilirubin *n*.
biliuria/*n*: Bilirubinurie *f*.
biliverdin/*n*: Biliverdin *n*.
bilobate placenta: zweigelappte Plazenta *f*.
bilocular stomach: Uhrglasmagen *m*.
bimanual/*adj*: bimanuell, beidhändig.
bimanual compression: bimanuelle Kompression *f*.
bimanual examination: bimanuelle Untersuchung *f*.
bimanual percussion: bimanuelle Perkussion *f*.
bimanual version: bimanuelle Wendung *f*.
bimatoprost/*n*: Bimatoprost *n*.
binary/*adj*: binär.
binasal hemianopia: binasale Hemianopsie *f*.
binaural/*adj*: binaural, beidohrig.
binaural fusion: binaurale Fusion *f*.
binding/*n*: Bindung *f*.
binding capacity: Bindungskapazität *f*.
binding site: Bindungsstelle *f*.
binocular/*adj*: binokulär.
binocular fixation: binokuläre Fixierung *f*.
binocular fusion: binokuläre Fusion *f*.
binocular hemianopia: bilaterale Hemianopsie *f*.
binocular vision: Binokularsehen *n*.
binovular/*adj*: zweieiig.
binovular twins: zweieiige Zwillinge.
bioassay/*n*: biologische Prüfung *f*.
bioavailability/*n*: Bioverfügbarkeit *f*.
biochemical test: biochemische Funktionsprobe *f*.
biochemistry/*n*: Biochemie *f*.
biocompatibility/*n*: Biokompatibilität *f*.
bioethics/*n*: Bioethik *f*.
biofeedback/*n*: Biofeedback *n*, Biorückkoppelung *f*.
biogenesis/*n*: Biogenese *f*.
biogenetic law: biogenetisches Grundgesetz *n*.

biogenic amine: biogenes Amin *n*.
biologic availability: Bioverfügbarkeit *f*.
biologic behavior: biologisches Verhalten *n*.
biologic rhythm: Biorhythmus *m*.
biology/*n*: Biologie *f*.
biomedical engineering: Biotechnologie *f*.
biometry/*n*: Biometrie *f*.
biophysics/*n*: Biophysik *f*.
biopsy/*n*: Biopsie *f*.
biopsychology/*n*: Psychobiologie *f*.
biosafety/*n*: biologische Sicherheit *f*.
biosynthesis/*n*: Biosynthese *f*.
biosynthetic pathway: anaboler Stoffwechselweg *m*.
biotin/*n*: Biotin *n*.
biparietal diameter: biparietaler Durchmesser *m*.
bipartite uterus: Uterus septus *m*.
bipedicle flap: Brückenlappen *m*, Visierlappenplastik *f*.
biperiden/*n*: Biperiden *n*.
biphasic cycle: biphasischer Zyklus *m*, biphasischer Menstruationszyklus *m*
bipolar/*adj*: bipolar.
bipolar affective psychosis: psychiatric disorder of unknown cause which is characterized by alternating periods of mania-like excitement and depression. bipolare affektive Psychose *f*, manisch-depressive Psychose *f*.
bipolar depression: bipolare Depression *f*.
bipolar disorder: bipolare Störung *f*.
bipolar leads: bipolare Ableitungen.
bipolar version: kombinierte Wendung *f*, Braxton-Hicks-Wendung *f*.
bird flu: a cosmopolitan infectious disease caused by influenza virus in poultry, especially chicken, which can be transmitted to humans. Symptoms include acute respiratory disease, and fever. Vogelgrippe *f*, aviäre Influenza *f*.
birdlike face: Vogelgesicht *n*.
birth/*n*: Geburt *f*.
birth certificate: Geburtsurkunde *f*.
birth control: Geburtenkontrolle *f*, Geburtenregelung *f*.
birth defect: angeborene Fehlbildung *f*, Geburtsschaden *m*.
birthing room: Kreißsaal *m*.
birth injury: any injury to an infant during the birth process. The most frequently occurring birth injuries include fractures of the skull, extremities, scapula, and tearing of the shoulder joint with brachial palsy. Geburtsverletzung *f*.
birth rate: Geburtenziffer *f*.
bisexual/*adj*: bisexuell.
bismuth/*n*: Bismut *n*, Bi, Wismut *n*.
bisoprolol/*n*: Bisoprolol *n*.
bistoury/*n*: Bistouri *n*.
bite/*n, vb*: 1. Biss *m*, Okklusion *f*, Bisswunde *f*; 2. beißen.
bitemporal/*adj*: bitemporal.
bitemporal diameter: bitemporaler Durchmesser *m*.
bitemporal hemianopia: bitemporale Hemianopsie *f*, Scheuklappenhemianopsie *f*.
bithionol/*n*: Bithionol *n*.
bivalirudin/*n*: Bivalirudin *n*.
biventricular failure: biventrikuläres Herzversagen *n*.
black death: schwarzer Tod *m*, Beulenpest *f*.
black fever: Kala-Azar *f*, viszerale Leishmaniase *f*.
black hairy tongue: schwarze Haarzunge *f*.
blackhead/*n*: Komedo *m*, Mitesser *m*.
blackout/*n*: Blackout *m*, Bewusstlosigkeit *f*.
black plague: schwarzer Tod *m*, Beulenpest *f*.
black sickness: schwarze Krankheit *f*, Kala-Azar *f*, viszerale Leishmaniase *f*.
black smallpox: schwarze Blattern, Variola haemorrhagica *f*.
blackwater fever: Schwarzwasserfieber *n*.
bladder/*n*: Blase *f*.
bladder cancer: malignant tumor of the urinary bladder. Symptoms include hematuria, pollakiuria, dysuria, and cystitis-like signs. Blasenkarzinom *n*.

bladder exstrophy: Blasenekstrophie *f*.
bladder instillation: Blaseninstillation *f*.
bladder reflex: Blasenreflex *m*.
bladder training: Blasentraining *n*.
blade/*n*: Blatt *n*, Klinge *f*.
bland/*adj*: mild, sanft, blande.
blank/*n, adj*: 1. Leerwert *m*; 2. leer.
blast cell leukemia: Stammzellenleukämie *f*.
blast injury: Detonationstrauma *n*.
blastodermic layer: Keimblatt *n*.
blastomycin/*n*: Blastomycin *n*.
blastomycosis/*n*: Blastomykose *f*.
bleacher/*n*: Bleichmittel *n*.
bleeder's disease: X-linked, hereditary bleeding disorders which are characterized by a defect in blood coagulation, due to a lack of certain coagulation factors. Major forms include hemophilia A, or classical hemophilia with a deficiency of factor VIII, and hemophilia B or Christmas disease with a deficiency of factor IX. Bluterkrankheit *f*, Hämophilie *f*.
bleeding/*n*: extravasation of blood. The term bleeding is usually used to indicate bleeding from capillaries when blood trickles or oozes from a small cut or wound. In contrast to hemorrhage, bleeding will usually clot of its own accord. Blutung *f*, Hämorrhagie *f*.
bleeding time: Blutungszeit *f*, BZ.
blennorhea/*n*: Blennorrhö *f*.
bleomycin/*n*: Bleomycin *n*.
blepharitis/*n*: acute or chronic inflammation of the eyelids, characterized by redness, crusting, swelling, and infection of the eyelashes, sometimes associated with the presence of scaly and greasy flakes deposited along the palpebra margins. Blepharitis *f*.
blepharospasm/*n*: Blepharospasmus *m*, Spasmus nictitans *m*, Lidkrampf *m*.
blind/*n, adj*: 1. Blende *f*, Schirm *m*; 2. blind.
blind fistula: inkomplette Fistel *f*.
blind gut: Blinddarm *m*, Zäkum *n*.
blind-loop syndrome: a condition which is characterized by the stagnation of intestinal contents, often in a blind loop created by side-to-side intestinal anastomosis. Symptoms include gastrointestinal signs, irritation of mucous membranes, diarrhea, malabsorption of nutrients and vitamins like vitamin B_{12}, resulting in megalocytic anemia. Blind-Loop-Syndrom *n*, Syndrom der blinden Schlinge *n*.
blindness/*n*: Blindheit *f*.
blind passage: Blindpassage *f*.
blind pouch: Blindsack *m*.
blind spot: blinder Fleck *m*.
blink/*n, vb*: 1. Blinzeln *n*, Lidschlag *m*; 2. blinzeln.
blinking reflex: Blinzelreflex *m*.
blinking tic: Blinzeltic *m*.
blister/*n*: Bläschen *n*, Hautblase *f*.
bloated/*adj*: geschwollen, aufgedunsen.
block/*n, vb*: 1. Block *m*, Unterbrechung *f*; 2. blockieren.
blockade/*n*: Blockade *f*.
blocking operation: Verblockungsoperation *f*.
blood/*n*: Blut *n*.
blood alcohol concentration: Blutalkoholkonzentration *f*.
blood bank: Blutbank *f*.
blood-brain barrier: Blut-Hirn-Schranke *f*.
blood cell: Blutzelle *f*, Blutkörperchen *n*.
blood cell count: Blutzellzählung *f*.
blood circulation: Blutkreislauf *m*.
blood clot: Blutgerinnsel *n*, Koagulum *n*.
blood disease: hämatologische Erkrankung *f*.
blood examination: Blutuntersuchung *f*.
blood flow disorder: Durchblutungsstörung *f*.
blood gas analysis: Blutgasanalyse *f*, BGA.
blood glucose: Blutzucker *m*, Blutglukose *f*.
blood grouping: Blutgruppenbestimmung *f*.

bloodletting/*n*: Aderlass *m*.
blood pressure: Blutdruck *m*, RR.
blood sample: Blutprobe *f*.
blood sedimentation rate: Blutkörperchensenkungsgeschwindigkeit *f*, BSG.
blood smear: Blutausstrich *m*.
bloodstream/*n*: Blutfluss *m*.
blood test: Blutuntersuchung *f*.
blood-tinged sputum: blutig tingiertes Sputum *n*.
blood transfusion: Bluttransfusion *f*.
blood type: Blutgruppe *f*.
blood urea clearance: Harnstoff-Clearance *f*.
blood volume: Blutvolumen *n*.
bloody/*adj*: blutig.
bloody ascites: hämorrhagischer Aszites *m*.
blot/*vb*: blotten.
blowing sound: fauchendes Geräusch *n*.
blue baby: a child which shows at birth a blue color of the skin, usually due to cyanosis resulting from a cardiac defect, for example Fallot's tetralogy. Blue Baby *n*, zyanotischer Säugling *m*.
blue blindness: Blaublindheit *f*.
blue navel: blauer Nabel *m*, Cullen-Zeichen *n*.
blue phlebitis: Phlegmasia coerulea dolens *f*.
blue rubber-bleb nevus: Blue-rubber-bleb-Nävus *m*, Bean-Syndrom *n*
blunt/*adj*: stumpf, abgestumpft, unempfindlich.
blunt dissection: stumpfe Auftrennung *f*.
blunt hook: stumpfer Haken *m*.
blunt injury: stumpfes Trauma *n*.
blunt probe: stumpfe Sonde *f*.
blurred/*adj*: unscharf, verwischt.
blush/*n, vb*: 1. Erröten *n*, Flush *m*; 2. erröten.
boat-shaped heart: Aortenherz *n*.
body/*n*: Körper *m*, Corpus *n*.
body cell: Körperzelle *f*.
body control: Körperbeherrschung *f*.
body image: Körperschema *n*.
body-righting reflex: Körperstellreflex *m*.
body scheme: Körperschema *n*.
body surface: Körperoberfläche *f*.
body temperature: Körpertemperatur *f*.
body weight: Körpergewicht *n*.
boil/*n, vb*: 1. Furunkel *n*, Beule *f*; 2. kochen, sieden.
bolus/*n*: Bolus *m*.
bond/*n*: Band *n*, Bindung *f*.
bone/*n*: Knochen *m*.
bone age: Knochenalter *n*.
bone biopsy: Knochenbiopsie *f*.
bone conduction: Knochenleitung *f*.
bone-cutting forceps: Knochenzange *f*.
bone cyst: Knochenzyste *f*.
bone graft: Knochentransplantat *n*.
bone marrow/*n*: Knochenmark *n*, Medulla ossium *f*.
bone marrow aplasia: incomplete development and impaired function of the bone marrow. Symptoms include a pancytopenia with reduction of all peripheral blood cells, and anemia. Knochenmarkaplasie *f*.
bone marrow puncture: Knochenmarkpunktion *f*.
bone pain: Knochenschmerz *m*.
bone reflex: Periostreflex *m*.
bone scan: Knochenscan *m*.
bonesetter/*n*: Knocheneinrichter *m*.
bony ankylosis: knöcherne Ankylose *f*.
bony face: knöcherner Gesichtsschädel *m*.
bony labyrinth: knöchernes Labyrinth *n*.
bony pelvis: knöchernes Becken *n*.
bony process: knöcherner Fortsatz *m*.
bony thorax: knöcherner Thorax *m*.
boost/*vb*: verstärken, boostern.
booster injection: Boostern *n*, Wiederholungsimpfung *f*.
bopindolol/*n*: Bopindolol *n*.
border/*n*: Rand *m*, Grenze *f*.
borderline/*n*: Borderline *f*, Grenzlinie *f*.
borderline personality disorder: Borderline-Persönlichkeitsstörung *f*.
boric acid: Borsäure *f*.
born/*adj*: geboren.
bornaprine/*n*: Bornaprin *n*.

borne/*adj*: übertragen.
borrowing-lending hemodynamic phenomenon: Borrowing-lending-Phänomen *n*.
bortezomib/*n*: Bortezomib *n*.
bosentan/*n*: Bosentan *n*.
botryoid sarcoma: Sarcoma botryoides *n*.
bottle-feeding/*n*: Flaschenernährung *f*.
bottom/*n*: Boden *m*, Grund *m*, Bodensatz *m*.
botulinum toxin/*n*: Botulinustoxin *n*, Botulin *n*.
botulism/*n*: Botulismus *m*.
bougie/*n*: Bougie *m*, Dehnsonde *f*.
bound fat: gebundenes Fett *n*.
bounding pupil: springende Pupille *f*, Hippus *m*.
bout/*n*: Anfall *m*.
bovine albumin: Rinderalbumin *n*.
bovine heart: Cor bovinum *n*.
bovine insulin: Rinderinsulin *n*.
bovine lymph: Kuhpockenlymphe *f*.
bovine spongiform encephalopathy: an infectious disease of cattle, caused by prions. Symptoms include encephalopathy with destruction of brain tissue. Bovine spongiform encephalopathy or BSE may be transmitted to humans by ingestion of prion-containing meat and is associated with a neurologic disease similar to Creutzfeldt-Jakob's disease. bovine spongiforme Enzephalopathie *f*, BSE, Rinderwahnsinn *m*.
bovine tuberculosis: Rindertuberkulose *f*.
bowel/*n*: Darm *m*, Eingeweide.
bowel disease: Darmerkrankung *f*.
bowel movement: Stuhlgang *m*.
bowel preparation: Darmreinigung *f*.
bowing spasm: Nickkrampf *m*.
bowing tic: Spasmus nutans *m*, Nickkrampf *m*.
bowleg/*n*: outward curved leg with the knees being abnormally divergent and the ankles abnormally approximated. O-Bein *n*, Genu varum *n*.
brace/*n*: Gurt *m*, Stützkorsett *n*.
brachial/*adj*: brachial.
brachial block: Plexusblockade *f*.
brachial palsy: paralysis of one or more of the nerves of the brachial plexus, resulting in paralysis of various muscles of the upper extremity. Most common forms include Erb's paralysis or Klumpke's paralysis resulting from birth injury; in later life, accidents are the most common cause. Armplexuslähmung *f*, Brachialislähmung *f*.
brachial plexus: Armplexus *m*.
brachiofacial paralysis: brachiofaziale Lähmung *f*.
brachycephaly/*n*: Brachyzephalie *f*, Kurzschädel *m*.
bracing/*n*: Verankerung *f*.
bradycardia/*n*: Bradykardie *f*.
bradykinin/*n*: Bradykinin *n*.
brain/*n*: Gehirn *n*, Enzephalon *n*.
brain biopsy: Hirnbiopsie *f*.
brain concussion: a sudden and violent shaking of the brain, resulting from a blow on the head. Symptoms include a temporary impairment of brain function and usually a momentary or brief loss of consciousness with amnesia for the injury. Gehirnerschütterung *f*.
brain death: Hirntod *m*.
brain dysfunction: zerebrale Dysfunktion *f*.
brain injury: Hirnverletzung *f*.
brain stem/*n*: Hirnstamm *m*, Stammhirn *n*.
brain tumor: benign or malignant neoplasm originating from, or localized in the brain. Forms of primary brain tumors include ectodermal tumors like craniopharyngioma, adenoma of the pituitary gland, neuroepithelial tumors like medulloblastoma, glioma, or ganglioneuroma, and mesodermal tumors like menigioma, angioblastoma, fibroma. Secondary brain tumors are metastatic tumors, most frequently from bronchial carcinoma, and malignant melanoma. Signs and clinical symptoms depend on size and localization. Hirntumor *m*.
brain waves: Hirnstromwellen.
branched-chain amino acid: ver-

zweigtkettige Aminosäure *f*.
branchial/*adj*: kiemenförmig.
branchial arch: Branchialbogen *m*, Kiemenbogen *m*.
branchial cleft: Kiemenbogenspalte *f*.
branchial cyst: Kiemengangzyste *f*.
branchial fissure: Kiemenspalte *f*.
branchial fistula: Kiemengangfistel *f*.
branchiogenic carcinoma: branchiogenes Karzinom *n*.
brassy cough: metallischer Husten *m*.
Brazilian spotted fever: Rocky-Mountain-Fieber *n*.
bread-crumbling tremor: Krumendrehertremor *m*, Pillendrehertremor *m*.
breadth/*n*: Breite *f*, Ausdehnung *f*.
break/*n, vb*: 1. Bruch *m*, Lücke *f*, Riss *m*; 2. brechen, platzen, zersprengen.
breakdown/*n*: Aufspaltung *f*, Zusammenbruch *m*.
breast/*n*: Brust *f*, Mamma *f*.
breast augmentation: Brustvergrößerung *f*.
breast cancer: malignant neoplasm of the mammary gland. The cause is unknown, an association with certain gene patterns and endocrine factors is discussed. Symptoms may include palpable nodules, secretion, swelling, retraction of the nipple, skin alterations, inflammation, and enlargement of lymph nodes. Brustkrebs *m*, Mammakarzinom *n*.
breast-feeding/*n*: Brusternährung *f*, Stillen *n*.
breast implant: Brustimplantat *n*.
breast pump: Milchpumpe *f*.
breast self-examination: Selbstuntersuchung der Brust *f*.
breath/*n*: Atem *m*, Atemzug *m*.
breath analyzer/*n*: Atemprüfgerät *n*.
breathe/*vb*: atmen.
breath-holding/*n*: respiratorischer Affektkrampf *m*.
breathing/*n*: Atmung *f*, Respiration *f*.
breathing bag: Beatmungsbeutel *m*.
breathing reserve: Atemreserve *f*.
breathless/*adj*: atemlos.
breath sounds: Atemgeräusche.
breech/*n*: Gesäß *n*.
breech presentation: in obstetrics, the position of the fetus in which the buttocks or feet are presented and appear first in the uterine cervix. Steißlage *f*.
breed/*vb*: züchten, brüten.
bregma/*n*: Bregma *n*.
brephoplastic graft: Brephoplastik *f*.
bretylium/*n*: Bretylium *n*.
bridle/*n*: Band *n*.
bridle scar: Narbenstriktur *f*.
brief reactive psychosis: kurze reaktive Psychose *f*.
brimonidine/*n*: Brimonidin *n*.
brinzolamide/*n*: Brinzolamid *n*.
brittle/*adj*: spröde, zerbrechlich.
brittle diabetes: Brittle-Diabetes *m*.
brivudine/*n*: Brivudin *n*.
broad/*adj*: breit.
broad foot: Spreizfuß *m*.
bromidrosis/*n*: Bromhidrose *f*.
bromindione/*n*: Bromindion *n*.
bromism/*n*: Bromismus *m*.
bromisoval/*n*: Bromisoval *n*.
bromocriptine/*n*: Bromocriptin *n*.
5-bromodeoxyuridine/*n*: 5-Bromodesoxyuridin *n*.
bromopride/*n*: Bromoprid *n*.
bromouracil/*n*: Bromuracil *n*.
bromperidol/*n*: Bromperidol *n*.
brompheniramine/*n*: Brompheniramin *n*.
bronchial/*adj*: bronchial.
bronchial adenoma: Bronchialadenom *n*.
bronchial allergy: Bronchialallergie *f*.
bronchial asthma: a condition which is characterized by a variable decrease in diameter of bronchi, resulting in dyspneic episodes. Asthma may result from allergic reaction to an inhaled substance or occur in individuals who are constitutionally predisposed. Asthma bronchiale *n*, Bronchialasthma *n*.
bronchial breathing: Bronchialatmung *f*.
bronchial fistula: Bronchusfistel *f*.
bronchial fremitus: Bronchialfremitus *m*.
bronchial lavage: Bronchiallavage *f*.
bronchial obstruction: Bronchusverlegung *f*.

bronchial pneumonia: Bronchopneumonie *f*.
bronchial respiration: Bronchialatmung *n*.
bronchial spasm: Bronchospasmus *m*.
bronchial stenosis: Bronchostenose *f*.
bronchiectasis/*n*: a condition in which the lung tissue around the bronchi is characterized by dilatation and the formation of sac-like cavities which show a tendency to become infected. Bronchiektasie *f*.
bronchoalveolar carcinoma: malignant neoplasm of the lung, a non-small cell lunger cancer with tumor cells located along the alveolar septa. bronchoalveoläres Karzinom *n*.
bronchiole/*n*: Bronchiole *f*.
bronchiolitis/*n*: Bronchiolitis *f*.
bronchitis/*n*: acute or chronic inflammation of mucous membranes of the bronchial tubes. Causes include infections like virus infections or tuberculosis, inhalation of allergens, tobacco smoke, and chemical or physical irritation. Chronic forms may result in respiratory insufficiency. Bronchitis *f*.
bronchoalveolar lavage: bronchoalveoläre Lavage *f*, BAL.
bronchoesophageal fistula: bronchoösophageale Fistel *f*.
bronchogenic/*adj*: bronchogen.
bronchogenic cyst: bronchogene Zyste *f*.
bronchography/*n*: Bronchographie *f*.
broncholith/*n*: Broncholith *m*.
bronchopleural fistula: bronchopleurale Fistel *f*.
bronchopneumonia/*n*: Bronchopneumonie *f*.
bronchopulmonary segment: Lungensegment *n*.
bronchoscope/*n*: Bronchoskop *n*.
bronchoscopy/*n*: Bronchoskopie *f*.
bronchospasm/*n*: Bronchospasmus *m*.
bronchus/*n*: Bronchus *m*.
bronze diabetes: Bronzediabetes *m*.
bronzed skin: Bronzehaut *f*.
broth/*n*: Bouillon *f*, Fleischbrühe *f*.
brotizolam/*n*: Brotizolam *n*.
brow/*n*: Augenbraue *f*, Stirn *f*.
brown adipose tissue: braunes Fettgewebe *n*.
brown atrophy: braune Atrophie *f*.
brow presentation: in obstetrics, the position of the fetus in which the forehead is presented and appears first in the uterine cervix. Stirnlage *f*.
brucellar meningitis: Brucellosemeningitis *f*.
brucellosis/*n*: Brucellose *f*, Bang-Krankheit *f*.
brucine/*n*: Brucin *n*, Dimethoxystrychnin *n*.
bruise/*n, vb*: 1. Kontusion *f*, Prellung *f*; 2. quetschen.
bruit/*n*: Geräusch *n*.
brush/*n, vb*: 1. Bürste *f*, Pinsel *m*; 2. bürsten.
BSE <*abbr*> **bovine spongiform encephalopathy**: an infectious disease of cattle, caused by prions. Symptoms include encephalopathy with destruction of brain tissue. BSE may be transmitted to humans by ingestion of prion-containing meat and is associated with a neurologic disease similar to Creutzfeldt-Jakob's disease. bovine spongiforme Enzephalopathie *f*, BSE.
bubble/*n, vb*: 1. Blase *f*, Bläschen *n*; 2. lallen, sprudeln.
bubo/*n*: Bubo *m*.
bubonic/*adj*: inguinal, Leisten-.
bubonic plague: Bubonenpest *f*, Beulenpest *f*.
buccal/*adj*: bukkal.
buccal cavity: Mundhöhle *f*.
buccal flap: Wangenlappen *m*.
buccal smear: Wangenschleimhautabstrich *m*.
bucket-handle fracture: Korbhenkelriss *m*.
buclizine/*n*: Buclizin *n*.
buclosamide/*n*: Buclosamid *n*.
bud/*n, vb*: 1. Keim *m*, Knospe *f*; 2. knospen.
budesonide/*n*: Budesonid *n*.
budipine/*n*: Budipin *n*.
buffer/*n*: Puffer *m*.
buffy coat: buffy coat *m*, Leukozytenmanschette *f*.

buflomedil/*n*: Buflomedil *n*.
bug/*n*: Wanze *f*, Bettwanze *f*.
bulb/*n*: Zwiebel *f*, Knolle *f*, Bulbus *m*.
bulbar/*adj*: bulbär.
bulbar apoplexy: Bulbärapoplexie *f*.
bulbar encephalitis: Bulbärenzephalitis *f*.
bulbar hemianesthesia: bulbäre Hemianästhesie *f*.
bulbar palsy: Bulbärparalyse *f*.
bulbar paralysis: Bulbärparalyse *f*.
bulbar respiratory center: medulläres Atemzentrum *n*.
bulbomimic reflex: bulbomimischer Reflex *m*, Mondonesi-Reflex *m*.
bulbourethral gland: Bulbourethraldrüse *f*.
bulbous probe: Knopfsonde *f*.
bulimia/*n*: an eating disorder which is characterized by hyperphagia with an insatiable appetite and excessive food intake in a short period of time, eventually followed by self-induced vomiting. Bulimie *f*, Esssucht *f*.
bulk/*n*: Masse *f*, Menge *f*.
bulking agent: Ballastmittel *n*.
bullous eczema: bullöses Ekzem *n*
bullous emphysema: bullöses Lungenemphysem *n*.
bullous ichthyosiform hyperkeratosis: bullöse Erythrodermie *f*.
bullous papuloalboid epidermolysis: Epidermolysis bullosa albupapoloidea *f*, Pasini-Syndrom *n*.
bullous pemphigoid: bullöses Pemphigoid *n*.
bumadizone/*n*: Bumadizon *n*.
bumetanide/*n*: Bumetanid *n*.
bump/*n*: Beule *f*, Höcker *m*, Stoß *m*.
bunazosin/*n*: Bunazosin *n*.
bundle/*n*: Bündel *n*, Faszikel *m*.
bundle branch block: Schenkelblock *m*.
bunitrolol/*n*: Bunitrolol *n*.
bupivacaine/*n*: Bupivacain *n*.
bupranolol/*n*: Bupranolol *n*.
buprenorphine/*n*: Buprenorphin *n*.
bupropion/*n*: Bupropion *n*.
burn/*n, vb*: 1. an injury to the body caused by high temperature. Burns are classified in several ways: by the extent of the burned surface, by the depth of the burn, and by the cause of the burn. The extent of body surface burned is the most important factor in determining the seriousness of the burn. Brandwunde *f*, Verbrennung *f*; 2. verbrennen, brennen.
burn blister: Brandblase *f*.
burn center: Verbrennungszentrum *n*.
burning pain: brennender Schmerz *m*.
bursal cyst: Schleimbeutelzyste *f*.
bursitis/*n*: acute or chronic inflammation of the bursal sac of a joint, characterized by cystic swellings, and sometimes pain. Bursitis *f*, Schleimbeutelentzündung *f*.
burst/*n, vb*: 1. Durchbruch *m*, Ausbruch *m*, Entladung *f*; 2. platzen, sprengen.
burst abdomen: Platzbauch *m*.
bursting fracture: Berstungsbruch *m*.
buserelin/*n*: Buserelin *n*.
buspirone/*n*: Buspiron *n*.
bust/*n*: Busen *m*, Mamma *f*.
busulfan/*n*: Busulfan *n*.
butalamine/*n*: Butalamin *n*.
butamirate/*n*: Butamirat *n*.
butane/*n*: Butan *n*.
butanol/*n*: Butanol *n*.
butenafine/*n*: Butenafin *n*.
butinoline/*n*: Butinolin *n*.
butizide/*n*: Butizid *n*.
buttocks/*n*: Gesäß *n*.
button/*n*: Knopf *m*, Beule *f*.
buttonhole deformity: Knopflochdeformität *f*.
butyl/*n*: Butylradikal *n*.
butylcarboxylic acid: Valeriansäure *f*.
butylparaben/*n*: Butylparaben *n*.
butylscopolamine/*n*: Butylscopolamin *n*.
butyric acid: Buttersäure *f*.
butyrometer/*n*: Butyrometer *n*.
butyrophenone/*n*: Butyrophenon *n*.
buzzing/*n*: Ohrensausen *n*, Summen *n*, Schwirren *n*.
bypass/*n, vb*: 1. Bypass *m*, Umgehung *f*; 2. umgehen, entlasten.
bypass surgery: Bypass-Operation *f*.

by-product/*n*: Nebenprodukt *n*.

byssinosis/*n*: irritation and allergic inflammation of the upper respiratory tract, the trachea, and the bronchial tubes due to the inhalation of cotton dust, occurring as occupational disease in cotton farmers. Byssinose *f*.

C

C *<abbr>* **1. calorie; 2. contraction**: 1. Kalorie *f*; 2. Kontraktion *f*.
cabergoline/*n*: Cabergolin *n*.
cachectic/*adj*: kachektisch.
cachectic fever: Kala-Azar *f*, viszerale Leishmaniase *f*.
cachet/*n*: Kachet *n*.
cachexia/*n*: Kachexie *f*.
cactinomycin/*n*: Cactinomycin *n*.
cadaver/*n*: Leiche *f*.
cadaveric position: Kadaverstellung *f*.
cadaveric rigidity: Totenstarre *f*.
caduceus/*n*: Äskulapstab *m*.
cafaminol/*n*: Cafaminol *n*.
caffeine/*n*: Koffein *n*.
caffetannic acid: Kaffeegerbsäure *f*.
caisson disease: a condition caused by a rapid decrease in atmospheric pressure which results in the formation of nitrogen bubbles in the blood and body tissues. It occurs for example in divers who return rapidly from below sea level. Symptoms include pain in the legs, joints and thorax, skin irritation, numbness and paralysis of the limbs, and vertigo. Caissonkrankheit *f*, Dekompressionskrankheit *f*, Druckfallkrankheit *f*.
caked breast: Kindbettmastitis *f*.
Calabar bean: Kalabarbohne *f*.
Calabar swellings: Kalabarschwellung *f*, Loa loa *f*, Kamerunbeulen.
calcaneal/*adj*: Kalkaneus-.
calcaneal fracture: breaking of the heel bone which may involve the ankle joint, and tearing of the Achilles tendon. Kalkaneusfraktur *f*.
calcaneal osteochondritis: Achillobursitis *f*, Sever-Krankheit *f*.
calcareous/*adj*: kalkhaltig.
calcifediol/*n*: Calcifediol *n*.
calciferol/*n*: Calciferol *n*.
calcification/*n*: Kalzifikation *f*.
calcific deposit: Kalkeinlagerung *f*.
calcified fibroma: verkalktes Fibrom *n*.
calcifying giant-cell tumor: kalzifizierende Riesenzellgeschwulst *f*.
calcinosis/*n*: Kalzinose *f*.
calcipotriol/*n*: Calcipotriol *n*.
calcitonin/*n*: Calcitonin *n*.
calcitriol/*n*: Calcitriol *n*.
calcium/*n*: Calcium *n*, Ca, Kalzium *n*.
calcium channel blocker: Kalziumkanalblocker *m*.
calcium oxide: Kalziumoxid *n*.
calcium pantothenate: Calciumpantothenat *n*.
calciuria/*n*: Kalziurie *f*.
calculus/*n*: Stein *m*, Konkrement *n*.
calf bone: Wadenbein *n*, Fibula *f*.
calibrate/*vb*: kalibrieren.
calibration/*n*: Kalibrierung *f*.
caliceal diverticulum: Kelchdivertikel *n*.
caliper/*n*: Schiene *f*.
call/*n, vb*: 1. Rufbereitschaft *f*; 2. rufen.
callosal demyelinating encephalopathy: Corpus-callosum-Demyelinisierung *f*, Marchiafava-Bignami-Syndrom *n*.
callosal syndrome: a condition which results from lesions of the corpus callosum, usually caused by a brain tumor or trauma. Symptoms include amnesia, seizures, confusion, inattention, and eventually apraxia or ataxia. Corpus-callosum-Syndrom *n*, Balken-Syndrom *n*.
callosity/*n*: Hornschwiele *f*, Callositas *f*.

callus/*n*: Kallus *m*.
calor/*n*: Wärme *f*.
caloric/*adj*: kalorisch.
caloric equivalent: kalorisches Äquivalent *n*.
caloric intake: Kalorienaufnahme *f*.
caloric requirement: Kalorienbedarf *m*.
caloric test: kalorische Prüfung *f*.
caloric value: Brennwert *m*.
calorigenic/*adj*: wärmeproduzierend.
calorimeter/*n*: Kalorimeter *n*.
calvaria/*n*: Schädeldach *n*.
camazepam/*n*: Camazepam *n*.
camphorated oil: Kampferliniment *n*.
camphor oil: Kampferöl *n*.
camptomelic dysplasia: Kamptomelie *f*.
canal/*n*: Kanal *m*.
canalized thrombus: kanalisierter Thrombus *m*.
cancer/*n*: any malignant tumor. Major forms include carcinomas, which develop in the lining and covering of organs, and sarcomas, which develop in the connective and supportive tissues and bones. Krebs *m*.
cancer cell: Krebszelle *f*.
cancer gene: Onkogen *n*.
cancerophobia/*n*: Krebsangst *f*.
cancer register: Krebsregister *n*.
cancroid/*n*: Kankroid *n*.
candidal vaginitis: Candida-Vaginitis *f*, Soorkolpitis *f*.
candidiasis/*n*: infection with the Candida fungus Monilia, manifesting for example as cutaneous candidiasis, oral candidiasis or thrush, endocarditis, and vulvovaginitis. Candidiasis *f*, Kandidamykose *f*.
candidulin/*n*: Candidulin *n*.
canine/*n, adj*: 1. Eckzahn *m*; 2. Hund-.
canine laugh: Risus sardonicus *m*.
canker/*n, vb*: 1. Geschwür *n*; 2. zerfressen.
cannabis/*n*: Kannabis *m*.
cannula/*n*: Kanüle *f*.
canrenoic acid: Canrenoinsäure *f*.
cantharides/*n*: Cantharides, Blasenkäfer *m*.
cantharidic acid: Cantharidinsäure *f*.
cantharidin/*n*: Cantharidin *n*.
cap/*n*: Zahnkrone *f*, Kappe *f*.
capacity/*n*: Kapazität *f*.
capecitabine/*n*: Capecitabin *n*.
capillary/*n, adj*: 1. Kapillare *f*; 2. kapillär.
capillary bed: Kapillarbett *n*.
capillary ectasia: Kapillarektasie *f*.
capillary embolism: Kapillarembolie *f*.
capillary fragility: Kapillarfragilität *f*.
capillary hemangioma: Kapillarhämangiom *n*.
capillary loop: Kapillarschenkel *m*.
capillary permeability: Kapillarpermeabilität *f*.
capillary pressure: Kapillardruck *m*.
capillary pulse: Kapillarpuls *m*.
capillary resistance: Kapillarwiderstand *m*.
capitate/*adj*: kopfförmig.
capreomycin/*n*: Capreomycin *n*.
caproic acid: Capronsäure *f*.
caprylic acid: Caprylsäure *f*.
capsular antigen: Kapselantigen *n*.
capsular cataract: Kapselstar *m*.
capsular hemiplegia: Kapsellähmung *f*.
capsular hemorrhage: Kapselblutung.
capsular phlegmon: Kapselphlegmone *f*.
capsule/*n*: Kapsel *f*.
capsulitis/*n*: Kapselentzündung *f*.
capsulolenticular cataract: Kapselpolstar *m*.
capsulotomy/*n*: Kapseleröffnung *f*.
captodiamine/*n*: Captodiamin *n*.
captopril/*n*: Captopril *n*.
caramiphen/*n*: Caramiphen *n*.
carazolol/*n*: Carazolol *n*.
carbachol/*n*: Carbachol *n*.
carbamazepine/*n*: Carbamazepin *n*.
carbamic acid: Carbaminsäure *f*.
carbamoylphosphate/*n*: Carbamylphosphat *n*.
carbenicillin/*n*: Carbenicillin *n*.
carbenoxolone/*n*: Carbenoxolon *n*.
carbidopa/*n*: Carbidopa *n*.
carbimazole/*n*: Carbimazol *n*.
carbocisteine/*n*: Carbocistein *n*.
carbohydrate/*n*: Kohlenhydrat *n*.
carbolic acid: Karbolsäure *f*, Phenol *n*.

carbon/*n*: Kohlenstoff *m*, Kohle *f*.
carbonated water: kohlensäurehaltiges Wasser *n*.
carbon dioxide: Kohlendioxid *n*.
carbonic acid: Kohlensäure *f*, Carbonsäure *f*.
carbon monoxide poisoning: poisoning with carbon monoxide, a colorless, odorless, tasteless gas that binds to hemoglobin and forms carboxyhemoglobin which results in a reduction of the oxygen-carrying capacity of the blood. Symptoms include severe headache, vertigo, vision disorders, nausea, vomiting, impaired cognitive functions, and loss of consciousness. Kohlenmonoxidvergiftung *f*.
carbon tetrachloride: Tetrachlorkohlenstoff *m*.
carboxyhemoglobin/*n*: Carboxyhämoglobin *n*, Kohlenmonoxidhämoglobin *n*.
carbromal/*n*: Carbromal *n*.
carbuncle/*n*: Karbunkel *m*.
carbuncular fever: Anthrax *m*, Milzbrand *m*.
carbuterol/*n*: Carbuterol *n*.
carcinoembryonic antigen: carcinoembryonales Antigen *n*.
carcinogenic/*adj*: karzinogen.
carcinoid/*n*: a malignant neoplasm of the diffuse endocrine system which is characterized by a strong affinity of the tumor cells for silver staining. Most frequent localizations of these tumors include the appendix, the small intestine, and cecum. Karzinoid *n*.
carcinoma/*n*: a malignant neoplasm of the epithelium which develops in the lining and covering of organs. Carcinomas represent the most frequent form of cancer. Among the most frequently occurring carcinomas are cervix carcinomas, carcinomas of the breast, bronchial carcinomas, and carcinomas of the gastrointestinal tract. Karzinom *n*.
carcinomatosis/*n*: Karzinomatose *f*.
carcinomatous dermatitis: paraneoplastische Dermatitis *f*.
carcinomatous myopathy: paraneoplastische Myopathie *f*.
carcinomatous pericarditis: Pericarditis carcinomatosa *f*.
carcinomatous polyneuropathy: paraneoplastische Polyneuropathie *f*.
cardia/*n*: Kardia *f*.
cardiac/*n, adj*: 1. Herzmittel *n*; 2. kardial.
cardiac aneurysm: Herzaneurysma *n*.
cardiac arrest: complete stop of heart action and asystolia, most commonly due to ventricular fibrillation, but also occurring in coronary artery disease, cardiac compression, or accidental passage of electricity. Herzstillstand *m*.
cardiac asthma: Herzasthma *n*.
cardiac atrophy: Herzatrophie *f*.
cardiac cachexia: kardiale Kachexie *f*.
cardiac calculus: Herzkonkrement *n*.
cardiac chamber: Herzkammer *f*.
cardiac cirrhosis: Cirrhose cardiaque *f*, kardiale Leberzirrhose *f*.
cardiac compression: Herzkompression *f*, Herzmassage *f*.
cardiac conduction: Herzreizleitung *f*.
cardiac cycle: Herzzyklus *m*.
cardiac defect: Herzfehler *m*.
cardiac dropsy: kardiales Ödem *n*.
cardiac edema: kardiales Ödem *n*.
cardiac failure: Herzversagen *n*.
cardiac index: Herzindex *m*.
cardiac infarction: damaging and necrosis of a part of the heart muscle, resulting from insufficient blood supply, usually caused by occlusion of coronary arteries in coronary artery disease. Symptoms include sudden severe pain in the chest, often radiating to the left arm. Myocardial infarction is among the most common causes of sudden death. Herzinfarkt *m*.
cardiac insufficiency: Herzinsuffizienz *f*.
cardiac lung: Stauungslunge *f*.
cardiac massage: Herzmassage *f*.
cardiac murmur: Herzgeräusch *n*.
cardiac neurasthenia: neurozirkulatorische Asthenie *f*.

C

cardiac neurosis: Herzneurose *f*.
cardiac output: Auswurfvolumen des Herzens *n*, Herzminutenvolumen *n*.
cardiac pacemaker: Herzschrittmacher *m*.
cardiac pacing: Herzfrequenzsteuerung *f*.
cardiac rate: Herzfrequenz *f*.
cardiac reserve: Reservekraft des Herzens.
cardiac resuscitation: kardiale Reanimation *f*.
cardiac rhythm: Herzrhythmus *m*.
cardiac rupture: Herzruptur *f*.
cardiac sound: Herzgeräusch *n*.
cardiac standstill: Herzstillstand *m*.
cardiac stimulant: Kardiotonikum *n*.
cardiac surgery: Herzchirurgie *f*.
cardiac syncope: kardiale Synkope *f*.
cardiac tamponade: Herztamponade *f*.
cardiac transplantation: Herztransplantation *f*.
cardiac valve: Herzklappe *f*.
cardinal symptom: Leitsymptom *n*.
cardioauditory syndrome: autosomal recessive disorder with sensorineural deafness, ventricular tachycardia and/or ventricular fibrillation. kardioauditives Syndrom *n*, Jervell-Lange-Nielsen-Syndrom *n*.
cardiogenic shock: kardiogener Schock *m*.
cardiograph/*n*: Kardiograph *m*.
cardiology/*n*: Kardiologie *f*.
cardiomyopathy/*n*: a disease of the heart muscle. Forms include idiopathic disease of the myocardium, and secondary cardiomyopathy resulting from arteriosclerosis, hypertension, valvular heart disease, or cor pulmonale. Symptoms include cardiac insufficency, thoracic and epigastric pain, cardiac arrhythmia, and sudden cardiac death. Kardiomyopathie *f*.
cardiopathy/*n*: Kardiopathie *f*, Krankheit des Herzens *f*.
cardiopulmonary murmur: atemabhängiges Herzgeräusch *n*.
cardiopulmonary resuscitation: kardiopulmonale Reanimation *f*.
cardiospasm/*n*: inability of the cardia of the esophagus to relax and to open, caused by disturbances in innervation, or lesions of ganglions. Symptoms include dysphagia, regurgitation, and eventually substernal pain. Kardiospasmus *m*, Kardiaachalasie *f*.
cardiothoracic ratio: Herz-Thorax-Verhältnis *n*.
cardiotomy/*n*: Kardiotomie *f*.
cardiovascular/*adj*: kardiovaskulär.
cardiovascular agent: Kreislaufmittel *n*.
cardiovascular collapse: Herz-Kreislauf-Kollaps *m*.
cardiovascular disease: any disease that affects the heart and the blood vessels, for example arteriosclerosis. kardiovaskuläre Erkrankung *f*, Herz-Kreislauf-Erkrankung *f*.
cardiovascular surgery: Herz- und Gefäßchirurgie *f*.
cardiovascular system: Herz-Kreislauf-System *n*.
carditis/*n*: Karditis *f*.
care/*n, vb*: 1. Betreuung *f*, Pflege *f*; 2. betreuen, pflegen.
caregiving/*n*: Pflege *f*.
carglumic acid: Carglumsäure *f*.
caries/*n*: Karies *f*.
carinate/*adj*: kielförmig.
carinate abdomen: Kielbauch *m*.
carisoprodol/*n*: Carisoprodol *n*.
carminic acid: Karminsäure *f*.
carmustine/*n*: Carmustin *n*.
carneous/*adj*: fleischig.
carnitine/*n*: Carnitin *n*.
carotene/*n*: Carotin *n*.
carotid/*n*: Karotis *f*, Arteria carotis *f*.
carotid angiography: Karotisangiographie *f*.
carotid arteriography: Karotisangiographie *f*.
carotid body: Karotiskörper *m*, Glomus caroticum *n*.
carotid sinus syndrome: a condition which is characterized by bradycardia and hypotension, following slight pressure on one or both carotid sinuses. Karotissinussyndrom *n*.
carpal/*adj*: karpal.

carpal tunnel syndrome: nerve compression syndrome with compression of the median nerve through surrounding tissue of the carpal tunnel. Symptoms include local pain, paresthesia in the hands and the fingers, and impairment of sensorial and motor nerve functions, including atrophy of the lateral half of the thenar. Karpaltunnelsyndrom *n*.
carpometacarpal/*adj*: karpometakarpal.
carpometacarpal reflex: Karpometakarpalreflex *m*.
carpopedal spasm: Karpopedalspasmus *m*.
carpophalangeal reflex: Karpophalangealreflex *m*.
carprofen/*n*: Carprofen *n*.
carpus/*n*: Karpus *m*, Handwurzel *f*.
carrier/*n*: Träger *m*.
carry/*vb*: übertragen, tragen.
carteolol/*n*: Carteolol *n*.
cartilage/*n*: Knorpel *m*.
cartilaginous tissue: Knorpelgewebe *n*.
caruncle/*n*: Karunkel *f*.
carvedilol/*n*: Carvedilol *n*.
cascade reaction: Kaskadenreaktion *f*.
case/*n*: Fall *m*, Krankheitsfall *m*.
case-control study: Fall-Kontroll-Studie *f*.
case history: Krankengeschichte *f*, Anamnese *f*.
casein/*n*: Casein *n*, Kasein *n*.
caseous necrosis: verkäsende Nekrose *f*.
caseous osteitis: Knochentuberkulose *f*.
case report: Kasuistik *f*.
case study: Fallstudie *f*.
Casoni skin test: Casoni-Intrakutantest *m*.
caspofungin/*n*: Caspofungin *n*.
cast/*n, vb*: 1. Gips *m*, Abdruck *m*, Zylinder *m*; 2. abformen.
casting/*n*: Abformen *n*.
castor oil: Castoröl *n*, Rizinusöl *n*.
castration/*n*: Kastration *f*.
casualty/*n*: Verletzter *m*, Unfallopfer *n*.
catabolism/*n*: Katabolismus *m*.
catacrotic wave: katakrote Welle *f*.
catadicrotic pulse: Katadikrotie *f*.
catalase/*n*: Catalase *f*, Katalase *f*.
catalepsy/*n*: Katalepsie *f*.
catalyst/*n*: Katalysator *m*.
catalytic activity: katalytische Aktivität *f*.
cataphylaxis/*n*: Kataphylaxie *f*.
cataplexy/*n*: Kataplexie *f*.
cataract/*n*: an ophthalmologic condition which is characterized by a partial or complete loss of transparency of the crystalline lens or its capsule. Cataracts occur with aging, or can be due to traumatic causes, and metabolic diseases. Katarakt *f*, Star *m*.
catarrh/*n*: any condition which is characterized by an inflammation of mucous membranes with a discharge of mucus, in particular inflammatory conditions of the upper respiratory tract. Katarrh *m*.
catarrhal otitis: Tuben-Mittelohrkatarrh *m*.
catathymic crisis: katathyme Krise *f*.
catatonia/*n*: a psychiatric disorder and form of schizophrenia which is characterized by alterations of muscle tone or motor reactivity, immobility and stupor. Katatonie *f*.
catatonic schizophrenia: katatone Schizophrenie *f*.
catechuic acid: Katechin *n*.
catharsis/*n*: Katharsis *f*.
cathartic/*n, adj*. 1. Abführmittel *n*, Kathartikum *n*; 2. kathartisch, abführend.
catheter/*n*: Katheter *m*.
catheterism/*n*: Katheterisierung *f*.
cation exchange resin: Kationenaustauscherharz *n*.
cat-scratch fever: Katzenkratzkrankheit *f*.
cauda equina syndrome: a neurologic condition resulting from a lesion of several lumbosacral nerve roots within the spinal canal. Symptoms depend on the localization of the lesions and may include paralysis of muscles, perineal anesthesia, abolition of the anal and bulbocavernous

reflexes, and sensory loss. Kaudasyndrom *n*.
caudal/*adj*: kaudal.
caudal anesthesia: Kaudalanästhesie *f*.
caudal block: Kaudalanästhesie *f*.
caudal dysplasia: Kaudadysplasie *f*, Syndrom der kaudalen Regression *n*.
caudate/*adj*: caudatus.
caul/*n*: Amnion *n*, Eihaut *f*.
causal/*adj*: kausal.
causal relationship: kausaler Zusammenhang *m*.
causal treatment: kausale Behandlung *f*.
causative/*adj*: ursächlich.
causative agent: auslösendes Agens *n*.
cause/*n, vb*: 1. Ursache *f*, Krankheitsursache *f*; 2. verursachen.
cause of death: Todesursache *f*.
cause of disease: Krankheitsursache *f*.
caustic/*n, adj*: 1. Kaustikum *n*; 2. kaustisch, ätzend.
cautery/*n*: Kauterisation *f*.
cautery knife: Kauter *m*.
caution/*n*: Vorsicht *f*.
caval umbrella: Kavaschirm *m*.
caval venography: Kavographie *f*.
cavernous/*adj*: kavernös.
cavernous body: Schwellkörper *m*.
cavernous hemangioma: kavernöses Hämangiom *n*.
cavity/*n*: Höhle *f*, Hohlraum *m*.
cecal sacculations: Haustra coli.
cecum/*n*: Zäkum *n*, Blinddarm *m*.
cefacetril/*n*: Cefacetril *n*.
cefaclor/*n*: Cefaclor *n*.
cefadroxil/*n*: Cefadroxil *n*.
cefalexin/*n*: Cefalexin *n*.
cefaloridine/*n*: Cefaloridin *n*.
cefalotin/*n*: Cefalotin *n*.
cefamandole/*n*: Cefamandol *n*.
cefazedone/*n*: Cefazedon *n*.
cefazolin/*n*: Cefazolin *n*.
cefepim/*n*: Cefepim *n*.
cefmenoxime/*n*: Cefmenoxim *n*.
cefoperazone/*n*: Cefoperazon *n*.
cefotaxime/*n*: Cefotaxim *n*.
cefotetan/*n*: Cefotetan *n*.
cefotiam/*n*: Cefotiam *n*.
cefoxitin/*n*: Cefoxitin *n*.
cefpodoxim/*n*: Cefpodoxim *n*.
cefradine/*n*: Cefradin *n*.
cefsulodin/*n*: Cefsulodin *n*.
ceftazidime/*n*: Ceftazidim *n*.
ceftizoxime/*n*: Ceftizoxim *n*.
ceftriaxone/*n*: Ceftriaxon *n*.
cefuroxime/*n*: Cefuroxim *n*.
celecoxib/*n*: Celecoxib *n*.
celiac/*adj*: zöliakal.
celiac arteriography: Zöliakographie *f*.
celiac crisis: Zöliakiekrise *f*.
celiac disease: a malabsorption syndrome caused by sensitivity to gluten-containing food. It is characterized by the presence of an excessive fat amount in the feces, and large, bulky stools. Zöliakie *f*, einheimische Sprue *f*, Heubner-Herter-Krankheit *f*.
celiac plexus: Plexus coeliacus *m*, Solarplexus *m*.
celiorrhaphy/*n*: Bauchnaht *f*.
celiprolol/*n*: Celiprolol *n*.
cell/*n*: Zelle *f*.
cell-bound antibody: zellständiger Antikörper *m*.
cell count: Zellzahl *f*, Zellzählung *f*.
cell culture: Zellkultur *f*.
cell-mediated allergy: zelluläre Allergie *f*.
cell-mediated immunity: zellvermittelte Immunität *f*.
cell membrane: Zellmembran *f*.
cell plasma: Zytoplasma *n*, Zellplasma *n*.
cellular/*adj*: zellulär.
cellular compartment: Zellkompartiment *n*.
cellular decay: Zelluntergang *m*.
cellular immunity: zelluläre Immunität *f*.
cellular pathology: Zellularpathologie *f*.
cellular therapeutics: Frischzellentherapie *f*.
cellulitis/*n*: Zellulitis *f*.
cellulose/*n*: Cellulose *f*, Zellstoff *m*.
cell wall: Zellwand *f*.
celsian operation: perineale Lithotomie *f*.

cenesthetic schizophrenia: zönästhetische Schizophrenie *f*.
center/*n*, *vb*: 1. Zentrum *n*; 2. zentrieren.
centigrade scale: Celsius-Skala *f*.
central/*adj*: zentral.
central amenorrhea: zentrale Amenorrhö *f*.
central anticholinergic syndrome: zentrales anticholinerges Syndrom *n*.
central blindness: zentrales Skotom *n*.
central body: Zentriole *f*.
central callus: Markkallus *m*.
central cell: Zentralzelle *f*.
central convulsion: zerebraler Krampf *m*.
central cyanosis: zentrale Zyanose *f*.
central deafness: zentrale Taubheit *f*, Rindentaubheit *f*.
Central European encephalitis: zentraleuropäische Zeckenenzephalitis *f*.
central excitatory state: zentralnervöser Erregungszustand *m*.
central giant cell reparative granuloma: Riesenzellgranulom *n*, Epulis gigantocellularis *f*.
central hearing loss: zentraler Hörverlust *m*.
centralization/*n*: Zentralisation *f*.
central nervous system: Zentralnervensystem *n*, ZNS.
central paralysis: zentrale Lähmung *f*.
central retinitis: zentrale Retinitis *f*.
central scotoma: Zentralskotom *n*.
central stimulant: zentralnervös wirksames Stimulans *n*.
central venous pressure: zentraler Venendruck *m*, ZVD.
centriacinar emphysema: zentroazinäres Emphysem *n*.
centric fusion: zentrische Fusion *f*.
centric occlusion: mittige Okklusion *f*.
centrifugal/*adj*: zentrifugal.
centrifuge/*n, vb*: 1. Zentrifuge *f*; 2. zentrifugieren.
centriole/*n*: Zentriole *f*.
centripetal/*adj*: zentripetal.
centroblastic-centrocytic lymphoma: zentroblastisch-zentrozytisches Lymphom *n*.
centroblastic lymphoma: Zentroblastom *n*.
centromere/*n*: Zentromer *n*.
cephalgia/*n*: acute or chronic pain affecting the head or parts of it, for example unilateral headache or hemicrania, or pain in the front or the back of the head. Symptoms may include steady or throbbing pain, barely noticeable pain, or completely prostrating sensations. Zephalgie *f*, Kopfschmerz *m*.
cephalic presentation: in obstetrics, the position of the fetus in which the head is presented and appears first in the uterine cervix. Schädellage *f*, Kopflage *f*.
cephalocele/*n*: a congenital herniation of the brain or its membranes into the orbit, for example a meningocele with herniation of meninges, or a meningoencephalocele with herniation of the meninges and the brain. Kephalozele *f*, Enzephalozele *f*.
cephalometry/*n*: Kephalometrie *f*.
cephalo-oculocutaneous telangiectasia: Sturge-Weber-Syndrom *n*.
cercaria/*n*: Zerkarie *f*.
cercarial dermatitis: Schistosomendermatitis *f*.
cerebellar ataxia: zerebelläre Ataxie *f*.
cerebellar atrophy: a condition which is characterized by an acquired wasting and shrinking of the cerebellar cortex or circumscribed areas of the cerebellum. Causes include hereditary or genetic factors, intoxications, or metabolic disorders. Kleinhirnatrophie *f*.
cerebellar degeneration: Kleinhirndegeneration *f*.
cerebellar diplegia: zerebelläre Diplegie *f*.
cerebellar dysarthria: zerebelläre Dysarthrie *f*.
cerebellar dysfunction: Kleinhirnfunktionsstörung *f*.

cerebellar epilepsy: Kleinhirnepilepsie *f*.
cerebellar fossa: Kleinhirngrube *f*.
cerebellar gait: zerebellärer Gang *m*.
cerebellar hemiplegia: Hemiataxie *f*, Halbseitenataxie *f*.
cerebellar hemisphere: Kleinhirnhemisphäre *f*.
cerebellar hemorrhage: Kleinhirnblutung *f*.
cerebellar infarct: Kleinhirninfarkt *m*.
cerebellar lobe: Kleinhirnlappen *m*.
cerebellar neoplasm: Kleinhirntumor *m*.
cerebellar tonsil: Kleinhirntonsille *f*.
cerebellar vertigo: Kleinhirnschwindel *m*.
cerebellopontine angle: Kleinhirnbrückenwinkel *m*.
cerebellum/*n*: Kleinhirn *n*.
cerebral/*adj*: zerebral.
cerebral abscess: Hirnabszess *m*.
cerebral aneurysm: Hirnarterienaneurysma *n*.
cerebral apoplexy: Apoplexie *f*, Schlaganfall *m*.
cerebral arteriography: zerebrale Arteriographie *f*.
cerebral arteriosclerosis: Hirnarteriensklerose *f*.
cerebral atrophy: a condition which is characterized by an acquired wasting and shrinking of the cerebral hemispheres or circumscribed brain areas. Causes include idiopathic degeneration, infections, intoxications, vascular disorders, or injuries. Hirnatrophie *f*.
cerebral compression: Hirndruck *m*, intrakranieller Druck *m*.
cerebral congestion: Hirnödem *n*.
cerebral cortex: Großhirnrinde *f*.
cerebral deafness: Rindentaubheit *f*, zentrale Taubheit *f*.
cerebral death: Hirntod *m*.
cerebral diffuse sclerosis: diffuse Hirnsklerose *f*.
cerebral diplegia: spastische Diplegie *f*, Little-Krankheit *f*.
cerebral edema: Hirnödem *n*.
cerebral embolism: Hirnembolie *f*.
cerebral function: Hirnfunktion *f*.
cerebral gigantism: Sotos-Syndrom *n*.
cerebral hemisphere: Großhirnhemisphäre *f*.
cerebral hemorrhage: Hirnblutung *f*.
cerebral infarction: Hirninfarkt *m*, ischämischer zerebraler Insult *m*.
cerebral neoplasm: Hirntumor *m*.
cerebral palsy: a chronic condition which is characterized by an impairment of motor functions and control, due to brain lesions, for example oxygen deficiency occurring at birth. zerebrale Lähmung *f*.
cerebral perfusion: Hirndurchblutung *f*.
cerebral seizure: fokaler Anfall *m*.
cerebral shock: zerebraler Schock *m*.
cerebral sinus: Hirnsinus *m*.
cerebral softening: Hirnerweichung *f*.
cerebral spastic infantile paralysis: zerebrale Kinderlähmung *f*.
cerebral stimulant: Weckamin *n*.
cerebral stroke: Schlaganfall *m*, Apoplexie *f*.
cerebration/*n*: Hirntätigkeit *f*.
cerebrocardiac syndrome: zerebrokardiales Syndrom *n*.
cerebrohepatorenal syndrome: an autosomal recessive syndrome which is characterized by craniofacial anomalies, renal cysts, liver enlargement, and elevated concentrations of fatty acids in the blood. zerebrohepatorenales Syndrom *n*, Zellweger-Syndrom *n*.
cerebronic acid: Cerebronsäure *f*.
cerebropupillary reflex: Haab-Reflex *m*.
cerebrospinal/*adj*: zerebrospinal.
cerebrospinal canal: Liquorraum *m*.
cerebrospinal fluid: Liquor cerebrospinalis *m*, L.
cerebrospinal-fluid block: Liquorblock *m*.
cerebrospinal pressure: Liquordruck *m*.
cerebrospinal syphilis: zerebrospinale Syphilis *f*.
cerebrotendinous xanthomatosis: zerebrotendinöse Xanthomatose *f*,

Bogaert-Scherer-Epstein-Syndrom *n.*
cerebrovascular/*adj*: zerebrovaskulär.
cerebrovascular accident: Schlaganfall *m.*
cerebrovascular aneurysm: Hirnarterienaneurysma *n.*
cerebrum/*n*: Großhirn *n.*
ceroid lipofuscin: Zeroidlipofuszin *n.*
ceroid lipofuscinosis: Zeroidlipofuszinose *f.*
certificate/*n*: Bescheinigung *f*, Attest *n.*
certoparin/*n*: Certoparin *n.*
certoparin sodium: Certoparinnatrium *n.*
ceruletide/*n*: Ceruletid *n.*
ceruloplasmin/*n*: Zäruloplasmin *n.*
cerumen/*n*: Zerumen *n.*
cervical/*adj*: zervikal.
cervical adenopathy: zervikale Lymphadenopathie *f.*
cervical canal: Zervikalkanal *m.*
cervical cancer: Zervixkarzinom *n.*
cervical cap: Portiokappe *f.*
cervical cyst: Halszyste *f.*
cervical dilatation: Zervixdilatation *f.*
cervical dystocia: Zervixdystokie *f.*
cervical ectopia: Zervixektopie *f.*
cervical factor: Zervixfaktor *m.*
cervical fissure: Halsfistel *f.*
cervical fistula: Halsfistel *f.*
cervical ganglion: Zervikalganglion *n.*
cervical intraepithelial neoplasia: zervikale intraepitheliale Neoplasie *f.*
cervical leukoplakia: Zervixleukoplakie *f.*
cervical migraine: Migraine cervicale *f*, Barré-Liéou-Syndrom *n.*
cervical polyp: Zervixpolyp *m.*
cervical radicular syndrome: compression of a cervical nerve root, usually due to protrusion of a cervical disk. Symptoms include radicular pain in the arm, eventually accompanied by numbness and muscle spasm. zervikales Wurzelsyndrom *n.*
cervical region: Halsregion *f.*
cervical smear: Zervixabstrich *m.*
cervical spine: Halswirbelsäule *f*, HWS.
cervical sympathetic paralysis: zervikale Sympathikuslähmung *f.*
cervicectomy/*n*: Zervixresektion *f.*
cervicitis/*n*: Zervizitis *f.*
cervicoaural fistula: Kiemengangfistel *f.*
cervicobrachial neuralgia: Zervikobrachialneuralgie *f.*
cervicobrachial syndrome: compression of a cervical nerve root, usually due to degenerative disorders of the cervical spine. Symptoms include sensory, motor, and trophic disorders in the neck region, the shoulder girdle, and the arms. Zervikobrachialsyndrom *n.*
cervix/*n*: Zervix *f*, Hals *m.*
cervix carcinoma: a malignant neoplasm of the neck of uterus. Early stages may not cause symptoms; in later stages, ulcerations, cervical bleeding, discharge, and pain may occur. Zervixkarzinom *n.*
cesarean section: Kaiserschnitt *m*, Schnittentbindung *f.*
cestode/*n*: Cestoda *f*, Bandwurm *m.*
cetrorelix/*n*: Cetrorelix *n.*
cetuximab/*n*: Cetuximab *n.*
cevitaminic acid: Ascorbinsäure *f*, Vitamin C *n.*
chain/*n*: Kette *f.*
challenge/*n, vb*: 1. Provokation *f*; 2. eine Reaktion hervorrufen.
chamber/*n*: Kammer *f.*
chance expectancy: Zufallserwartung *f.*
chancre/*n*: a sore that appears on the skin or mucous membrane caused by infection with certain types of sexually transmitted diseases, for example a syphilitic ulcer, or the soft chancre or chancroid caused by the bacterium Haemophilus ducreyi. Schanker *m.*
chancroid/*n*: Schankroid *n*, weicher Schanker *m.*
chancroidal bubo: schankröser Bubo *m.*

change/*n, vb*: 1. Wandel ***m***, Veränderung ***f***, Wechsel ***m***; 2. wechseln, ändern.
channel/*n*: Kanal ***m***, Rille ***f***.
chap/*n, vb*: 1. Hautschrunde ***f***; 2. aufreißen.
character disorder: Persönlichkeitsstörung ***f***.
characteristic symptom: charakteristisches Symptom ***n***.
Charcot sign: Charcot-Zeichen ***n***.
charge/*n, vb*: 1. Ladung ***f***, Gebühr ***f***; 2. laden, berechnen.
charity/*n*: gemeinnützige Stiftung ***f***, Almosen ***n***.
charlatan/*n*: Quacksalber ***m***.
chart/*n*: Tabelle ***f***, Diagramm ***n***.
check/*n, vb*: 1. Überprüfung ***f***, Kontrolle ***f***; 2. überprüfen.
checkup/*n*: Vorsorgeuntersuchung ***f***.
cheek/*n*: Backe ***f***, Wange ***f***.
cheekbone/*n*: Jochbein ***n***.
cheesy degeneration: käsige Nekrose ***f***.
cheesy nephritis: verkäsende Nierentuberkulose ***f***.
cheilitis/*n*: inflammation of the lips. Forms include for example solar cheilitis due to exposure to sunlight, or angular cheilitis which is a feature of several disorders including infectious diseases, or vitamin deficiency. Cheilitis ***f***, Lippenentzündung ***f***.
cheiloplasty/*n*: Cheiloplastik ***f***, Lippenplastik ***f***.
chelate complex: Chelatkomplex ***m***.
chelating agent: Chelatbildner ***m***.
chemical contraception: chemische Kontrazeption ***f***.
chemical dermatitis: chemische Dermatitis ***f***.
chemical gangrene: toxische Gangrän ***f***.
chemical litholysis: Chemolitholyse ***f***.
chemical peritonitis: Reizperitonitis ***f***.
chemical pneumonitis: chemische Pneumonitis ***f***.
chemistry/*n*: Chemie ***f***.
chemokine/*n*: Chemokin ***n***.
chemoreceptor/*n*: Chemorezeptor ***m***.
chemosis/*n*: Chemosis ***f***.
chemotaxis/*n*: Chemotaxis ***f***.
chemotherapeutic agent: Chemotherapeutikum ***n***.
chemotherapy/*n*: Chemotherapie ***f***.
chemotropism/*n*: Chemotropismus ***m***.
chenodeoxycholic acid: Chenodeoxycholsäure ***f***.
cherry-red spot: kirschrote Makula ***f***, Tay-Spot ***m***.
chest/*n*: Brustkorb ***m***, Thorax ***m***.
chest contusion: Thoraxkontusion ***f***.
chest film: Röntgenthoraxaufnahme ***f***.
chest wall: Brustwand ***f***.
chew/*vb*: kauen.
chewing force: Kaukraft ***f***.
chewing tablet: Kautablette ***f***.
chiasm/*n*: Chiasma ***n***.
chickenpox/*n*: highly contagious infectious disease caused by varicella-zoster virus. Symptoms include vesicular skin lesions with intensive pruritus, and mild constitutional symptoms. In adults, pneumonia and encephalitis can occur as complications. Windpocken, Varizellen.
chief nurse: Oberschwester ***f***.
chief physician: Chefarzt ***m***.
chigger/*n*: Trombiculalarve ***f***.
chigger-borne typhus: Tsutsugamushi-Krankheit ***f***.
chikungunya/*n*: Chikungunya-Fieber ***n***.
chilblain/*n*: Frostbeule ***f***, Pernio ***m***.
child/*n*: Kind ***n***.
child abuse: Kindesmisshandlung ***f***.
childbearing age: gebärfähiges Alter ***n***.
childbed fever: an infectious disease following birth or abortion, typically caused by the bacteria Streptococcus or Staphylococcus. Puerperal fever can affect the entire birth channel, the uterine cavity, and may eventually result in septic shock. Kindbettfieber ***n***, Puerperalfieber ***n***, Wochenbettfieber ***n***.
childbirth/*n*: Geburt ***f***.
childhood/*n*: Kindheit ***f***.

childproof/*adj*: kindersicher.
children's hospital: Kinderkrankenhaus *n*.
chill/*n*: Kältegefühl *n*, fiebrige Erkrankung *f*.
chimera/*n*: Chimäre *f*.
chin/*n*: Kinn *n*.
chin presentation: in obstetrics, the position of the fetus in which the chin is presented and appears first in the uterine cervix. Kinnlage *f*.
chip fracture: Absprengungsbruch *m*.
chiropody/*n*: Fußpflege *f*.
chiropractic/*n*: Chiropraktiker *m*, Chiropraxis *f*.
chi-squared test: Chi-Quadrat-Test *m*.
chlamydia infection: an infection with the bacterium Chlamydia. Serotypes A, B, and C of subgroup A cause trachoma, inclusion conjunctivitis is caused by serotypes D through K, and serotype L causes lymphogranuloma venereum. Serotypes of subgroup B cause psittacosis. Chlamydieninfektion *f*.
chlamydial salpingitis: Chlamydiensalpingitis *f*.
chloasma/*n*: Chloasma *n*.
chloracetic acid: Chloressigsäure *f*.
chlor acne: Chlorakne *f*.
chloral formamid: Chloralformamid *n*.
chloral hydrate: Chloralhydrat *n*.
chloralose/*n*: Chloralose *f*.
chlorambucil/*n*: Chlorambucil *n*.
chloramphenicol/*n*: Chloramphenicol *n*.
chlorazanil/*n*: Chlorazanil *n*.
chlorazol/*n*: Chlorazol *n*.
chlorbenzoxamine/*n*: Chlorbenzoxamin *n*.
chlorbetamide/*n*: Chlorbetamid *n*.
chlorhydric acid: Salzsäure *f*.
chloric acid: Chlorsäure *f*.
chloride/*n*: Chlorid *n*.
chlorisondamine/*n*: Chlorisondamin *n*.
chlormethine/*n*: Chlormethin *n*.
chlormezanone/*n*: Chlormezanon *n*.
chloroform/*n*: Chloroform *n*.
chloroform anesthesia: Chloroformnarkose *f*.
chloroma/*n*: Chlorom *n*.
chloroquine/*n*: Chloroquin *n*.
chlorothiazide/*n*: Chlorothiazid *n*.
chlorotrianisene/*n*: Chlorotrianisen *n*.
chlorous acid: chlorige Säure *f*.
chloroxylenol/*n*: Chloroxylenol *n*.
chlorphenamine/*n*: Chlorphenamin *n*.
chlorphenesin/*n*: Chlorphenesin *n*.
chlorpromazine/*n*: Chlorpromazin *n*.
chlorpropamide/*n*: Chlorpropamid *n*.
chlorprothixene/*n*: Chlorprothixen *n*.
chlorquinaldol/*n*: Chlorquinaldol *n*.
chlortalidone/*n*: Chlortalidon *n*.
chlortetracycline/*n*: Chlortetracyclin *n*.
choana/*n*: Choane *f*.
choanal atresia: Choanalatresie *f*.
choanal polyp: a polyp which is located in the nose or paranasal sinuses, usually due to chronic infections, allergic reactions, or analgesics intolerance. Symptoms include headache, impairment of nasal respiration, nasal resonance, and disturbances in the olfactory sense. Choanalpolyp *m*.
choanal stenosis: Choanalstenose *f*.
choice/*n*: Wahl *f*.
choke/*vb*: ersticken.
choked disk: edematous swelling of the optic nerve at the site where the nerve enters the eye. Papillenödem *n*, Stauungspapille *f*.
cholagogue/*n*: Cholagogum *n*.
cholangiography/*n*: Cholangiographie *f*.
cholangitic abscess: Gallengangsabszess *m*.
cholangitis/*n*: Cholangitis *f*.
cholanic acid: Cholansäure *f*.
cholecalciferol/*n*: Cholecalciferol *n*, Vitamin D_3 *n*.
cholecystectomy/*n*: Cholezystektomie *f*.
cholecystenterostomy/*n*: Cholezystenterostomie *f*.
cholecystitis/*n*: acute or chronic inflammation of the gallbladder, usually due to cholelithiasis. Symp-

toms include pain in the right upper quadrant of the abdomen, eventually colic, and vomiting and fever. Cholezystitis *f*.

cholecystography/*n*: Cholezystographie *f*.

cholecystolithiasis/*n*: Cholezystolithiasis *f*.

cholecystostomy/*n*: Cholezystostomie *f*.

choledochal cyst: Choledochuszyste *f*.

choledochal sphincter: Choledochussphinkter *m*.

choledocholithotomy/*n*: Choledocholithotomie *f*.

choledochotomy/*n*: Choledochotomie *f*.

choleic acid: Choleinsäure *f*.

cholelithiasis/*n*: presence of stones or calculi in the gallbladder or in the biliary tract. Symptoms include biliary colic, diffuse pain in the right upper quadrant of the abdomen, with radiation into the right shoulder. Cholelithiasis *f*.

cholemia/*n*: Cholämie *f*.

cholera/*n*: an infectious disease which is caused by the bacterium Vibrio cholerae. Symptoms result from the production of a toxin that alters the water and electrolyte balance in the upper intestinal tract and include watery diarrhea, dehydration, and electrolyte imbalance. Cholera *f*.

cholestatic hepatitis: cholestatische Hepatitis *f*.

cholestatic jaundice: cholestatischer Ikterus *m*.

cholesteatoma/*n*: Cholesteatom *n*.

cholesterol/*n*: Cholesterin *n*.

cholic acid: Cholsäure *f*.

cholinergic/*adj*: cholinerg.

cholinergic crisis: cholinerge Krise *f*.

cholinergic fiber: cholinerge Nervenfaser *f*.

cholinergic receptor: cholinerger Rezeptor *m*.

cholinergic urticaria: cholinergische Urtikaria *f*.

cholinesterase/*n*: Cholinesterase *f*.

cholinesterase inhibitor: Cholinesterasehemmer *m*.

choluria/*n*: Cholurie *f*.

chondral/*adj*: chondral.

chondrify/*vb*: verknorpeln.

chondritis/*n*: Chondritis *f*.

chondrocyte/*n*: Chondrozyt *m*.

chondrodysplasia/*n*: Chondrodysplasie *f*.

chondroectodermal dysplasia: chondroektodermale Dysplasie *f*, Ellis-Creveld-Syndrom *n*.

chondroitic acid: Chondroitinsäure *f*.

chondroitin sulfate: Chondroitinsulfat *n*.

chondroma/*n*: Chondrom *n*.

chondromalacia/*n*: Chondromalazie *f*.

chondromyxoid fibroma: Chondrofibromyxom *n*.

chondrosarcoma/*n*: Chondrosarkom *n*.

chordee/*n*: Gryposis penis *f*.

chorditis/*n*: Chorditis *f*.

chorea/*n*: Chorea *f*.

choreic convulsion: choreatiforme Zuckung *f*.

choreiform movement: choreatische Bewegung *f*.

chorioblastoma/*n*: Chorioblastom *n*.

choriogonadotropin/*n*: Choriongonadotropin *n*.

chorion/*n*: Chorion *n*.

chorionic/*adj*: Chorion-.

chorionic gonadotropin: Choriongonadotropin *n*.

chorionic villus: Chorionzotte *f*.

chorionic villus biopsy: Chorionzottenbiopsie *f*.

choroid/*n*: Aderhaut *f*, Choroidea *f*.

choroidal sclerosis: Aderhautsklerose *f*.

choroid fissure: Aderhautspalte *f*.

choroiditis/*n*: Chorioiditis *f*, Aderhautentzündung *f*.

chromaffin body: Zuckerkandl-Organ *n*, Paraganglion *n*.

chromatic aberration: chromatische Aberration *f*.

chromatic sensation: Farbsinn *m*.

chromatic vision: Farbensehen *n*.

chromatid/*n*: Chromatid *n*.

chromatin/*n*: Chromatin *n*.

chromatinic body: Chromatinkörperchen *n*.
chromatography/*n*: Chromatographie *f*.
chromic acid: Chromsäure *f*.
chromogenic body: Pigmentkörperchen *n*.
chromonucleic acid: Desoxyribonukleinsäure *f*, DNS.
chromophil/*adj*: chromophil.
chromophobe/*adj*: chromophob.
chromophobe adenoma: chromophobes Adenom *n*.
chromosomal aberration: Chromosomenaberration *f*.
chromosomal break: Chromosomenbruch *m*.
chromosomal fiber: chromosomale Spindelfaser *f*.
chromosomal sex: chromosomales Geschlecht *n*.
chromosome/*n*: Chromosom *n*.
chromosome analysis: Chromosomenanalyse *f*.
chromosome deletion: Chromosomendeletion *f*.
chromosome mapping: Chromosomenmapping *n*.
chronic/*adj*: chronisch.
chronic acholuric jaundice: chronischer hämolytischer Ikterus *m*.
chronic active hepatitis: chronisch-aggressive Hepatitis *f*.
chronic adrenocortical insufficiency: Nebennierenrindeninsuffizienz *f*, Addison-Krankheit *f*.
chronic aggressive hepatitis: chronisch-aggressive Hepatitis *f*.
chronic anemia: chronische Anämie *f*.
chronic atrophic gastritis: chronisch-atrophische Gastritis *f*.
chronic bacterial pyelonephritis: chronische bakterielle Nephritis *f*.
chronic bronchitis: chronische Bronchitis *f*.
chronic carrier: Dauerausscheider *m*.
chronic desquamative gingivitis: chronisch desquamative Gingivitis *f*.
chronic disease: chronische Krankheit *f*.
chronic endocarditis: chronische Endokarditis *f*.
chronic familial icterus: hereditäre Sphärozytose *f*.
chronic fatigue syndrome: a condition which is characterized by a state of weariness of body and mind which lasts for more than six months, without detectable organic basis. It is associated with impairment of cognitive functions, myalgia, arthralgia, headache, pharyngitis, and discomfort following physical exertion. chronisches Müdigkeitssyndrom *n*.
chronic fibrous thyroiditis: Riedel-Struma *f*.
chronic focal epilepsy: Epilepsia partialis continua *f*, Kozhevnikow-Epilepsie *f*.
chronic glomerulonephritis: chronische Glomerulonephritis *f*.
chronic hyperkeratotic esophagitis: chronische hyperkeratotische Ösophagitis *f*.
chronic idiopathic jaundice: Dubin-Johnson-Syndrom *n*.
chronic idiopathic xanthomatosis: Hand-Schüller-Christian-Krankheit *f*.
chronic interstitial cystitis: chronische transmurale Blasenentzündung *f*, Hunner-Zystitis *f*.
chronic interstitial salpingitis: chronische interstitielle Salpingitis *f*.
chronic myelocytic leukemia: chronische myeloische Leukämie *f*, CML.
chronic obstructive lung disease: chronisch-obstruktive Lungenerkrankung *f*, COLE.
chronic orthostatic hypotension: chronische orthostatische Hypotonie *f*, Shy-Drager-Syndrom *n*.
chronic pain: chronischer Schmerz *m*.
chronic pancreatitis: chronische Pankreatitis *f*.
chronic persistent hepatitis: chronisch persistierende Hepatitis *f*.
chronic pharyngitis: chronische Pharyngitis *f*.
chronic pleurisy: chronische Pleuraentzündung *f*.
chronic polyarthritis: chronische Polyarthritis *f*, primär-chronische Po-

lyarthritis *f*, PcP.
chronic progressive hereditary chorea: Chorea Huntington *f*.
chronic pyelitis: chronische Pyelonephritis *f*.
chronic rejection: chronische Abstoßungsreaktion *f*.
chronic renal insufficiency: chronische Niereninsuffizienz *f*.
chronic sinusitis: chronische Nasennebenhöhlenentzündung *f*.
chronic sleeping sickness: afrikanische Schlafkrankheit *f*.
chronic superficial gastritis: chronische Oberflächengastritis *f*.
chronic superficial scaly dermatitis: chronische oberflächlich-schuppige Dermatitis *f*.
chronobiology/*n*: Chronobiologie *f*.
chronological age: chronologisches Alter *n*.
chyle/*n*: Chylus *m*, Milchsaft *m*.
chylomicron/*n*: Chylomikron *n*.
chylous/*adj*: chylös.
chylous ascites: chylöser Aszites *m*.
chylous effusion: chylöser Erguss *m*.
chylous fistula: Chylusfistel *f*.
chyme/*n*: Chymus *m*.
chymopapain/*n*: Chymopapain *n*.
cicatricial/*adj*: narbig.
cicatricial contraction: Narbenkontraktion *f*.
cicatricial hypertrophy: Narbenhypertrophie *f*.
cicatricial tissue: Narbengewebe *n*.
cicatrix/*n*: Narbe *f*.
ciclacillin/*n*: Ciclacillin *n*.
ciclesonide/*n*: Ciclesonid *n*.
cicletanine/*n*: Cicletanin *n*.
ciclonium bromide: Cicloniumbromid *n*.
ciclopirox/*n*: Ciclopirox *n*.
cidofovir/*n*: Cidofovir *n*.
cilazapril/*n*: Cilazapril *n*.
cilexetil/*n*: Cilexetil *n*.
ciliar neuralgia: Erythroprosopalgie *f*.
ciliary/*adj*: ziliar.
ciliary action: Flimmerbewegung *f*.
ciliary body: Strahlenkörper *m*.
ciliary border: Ziliarrand *m*.
ciliary glands: Ziliardrüsen.
ciliary reflex: Ziliarisreflex *m*.
ciliate/*n, adj*: 1. Geißeltierchen *n*; 2. mit Zilien.
ciliated cell: Flimmerzelle *f*.
cimetidine/*n*: Cimetidin *n*.
cinacalcet/*n*: Cinacalcet *n*.
cinchocaine/*n*: Cinchocain *n*.
cinchona/*n*: Cinchona *f*, Chinarinde *f*.
cinchonism/*n*: Chininvergiftung *f*.
cinnarizine/*n*: Cinnarizin *n*.
cinoxacin/*n*: Cinoxacin *n*.
ciprofloxacin/*n*: Ciprofloxacin *n*.
circadian/*adj*: zirkadian.
circadian rhythm: zirkadianer Rhythmus *m*.
circinate/*adj*: zirzinär, kreisförmig.
circular amputation: Zirkelschnitt *m*.
circular suture: zirkuläre Naht *f*.
circulating immune-complex glomerulonephritis: Immunkomplexglomerulonephritis *f*.
circulation/*n*: Kreislauf *m*, Zirkulation *f*.
circulatory arrest: Kreislaufstillstand *m*.
circulatory center: Kreislaufzentrum *n*.
circulatory disorder: Kreislaufstörung *f*.
circulatory function: Kreislauffunktion *f*.
circulatory hormone: zirkulierendes Hormon *n*.
circulatory insufficiency: Kreislaufschwäche *f*.
circulatory overload: Kreislaufbelastung *f*.
circulatory resistance: Strömungswiderstand *m*.
circulatory system: Gefäßsystem *n*, Kreislauf *m*.
circumcision/*n*: Zirkumzision *f*, Beschneidung *f*.
circumferential wiring: Circumferential Wiring *n*, Drahtumschlingung *f*.
circumflex/*adj*: herumgebogen.
circumpapillary chorioretinal atrophy: zirkumpapilläre Chorioideaatrophie *f*.
circumscribed/*adj*: umschrieben, zirkumskript.

circumscribed amnesia: begrenzte Amnesie *f*.
circumscribed gangrene: umschriebene Gangrän *f*.
circumscribed scleroderma: zirkumskripte Sklerodermie *f*.
cirrhosis/*n*: a condition which is characterized by the transformation of tissue, resulting in induration and loss of normal organ structure. The process of cirrhosis formation includes chronic inflammation or necrosis, hypertrophy of connective tissue, and shrinkage with scar formation. The term is also used to refer to liver cirrhosis. Zirrhose *f*.
cirsoid/*adj*: traubenartig.
cirsoid aneurysm: rankenförmiges Aneurysma *n*, Traubenaneurysma *n*.
cirsoid hemangioma: Rankenhämangiom *n*.
cisapride/*n*: Cisaprid *n*.
cisatracurium besilate: Cisatracuriumbesilat *n*.
cisplatin/*n*: Cisplatin *n*.
cistern/*n*: Zisterne *f*.
cisternal puncture: Zisternenpunktion *f*.
cisternography/*n*: Zisternographie *f*.
citalopram/*n*: Citalopram *n*.
citrated blood: Zitratblut *n*.
citrate synthase: Zitratsynthase *f*.
citric acid: Zitronensäure *f*.
cladribine/*n*: Cladribin *n*.
claim for compensation: Schadenersatzanspruch *m*.
clamp/*n, vb*: 1. Klemme *f*, Klammer *f*; 2. klemmen, klammern.
clap/*n*: Tripper *m*, Gonorrhö *f*.
clapping/*n*: Klatschmassage *f*.
clarithromycin/*n*: Clarithromycin *n*.
clasp-knife phenomenon: Taschenmesserphänomen *n*.
class/*n*: Klasse *f*, Gattung *f*.
classical hemophilia: Hämophilie *f*.
classical renal tubular acidosis: renale tubuläre Azidose *f*.
classification/*n*: Klassifikation *f*.
classification of tumors: Tumorklassifikation *f*.
claudication/*n*: Claudicatio *f*, Hinken *n*.
claustrophobia/*n*: Klaustrophobie *f*.
clavicle/*n*: Schlüsselbein *n*, Klavikula *f*.
clavicle fracture: breaking of the collar bone, for example resulting from trauma or sports injury. Schlüsselbeinfraktur *f*.
clavicular deformity: Klavikuladefekt *m*.
clavulanic acid: Clavulansäure *f*.
clavus/*n*: hard or soft thickening of the skin with hyperkeratosis on the foot or a toe, resulting from friction and pressure. Klavus *m*, Hühnerauge *n*.
clawfoot: Klauenfuß *m*, Krallenfuß *m*.
clawhand: Klauenhand *f*, Krallenhand *f*.
clean/*adj, vb*: 1. rein, sauber; 2. reinigen.
clear/*adj, vb*: 1. klar, rein; 2. klären.
clearance/*n*: Clearance *f*, Klärung *f*.
clear cell acanthoma: Klarzellenakanthom *n*.
clear cell adenoma: Klarzellenadenom *n*.
clear cell tumor: Klarzelltumor *m*, Helle-Zellen-Tumor *m*.
cleavage/*n*: Teilung *f*, Furchung *f*, Spaltung *f*.
cleft/*n*: Spalte *f*, Spalt *m*.
cleft cheek: Wangenspalte *f*.
cleft palate: a congenital malformation along the midline of the palate which is characterized by a fissure of the soft palate and/or the hard palate, forming one cavity for the nose and the throat. Gaumenspalte *f*.
cleft uvula: Uvula bifida *f*.
cleidocranial dysplasia: kleidokraniale Dysostose *f*.
cleidotomy/*n*: Kleidotomie *f*.
clemastine/*n*: Clemastin *n*.
clemizole penicillin: Clemizolpenicillin *n*.
clenbuterol/*n*: Clenbuterol *n*.
click/*n*: Click *m*.
clidinium bromide: Clidiniumbromid *n*.
client-centered/*adj*: klientenzentriert.

C

climacteric/*n, adj*: 1. Klimakterium *n*; 2. klimakterisch.
climate/*n*: Klima *n*.
climatic bubo: Lymphogranuloma venereum *n*.
climatic factor: Klimafaktor *m*.
climax/*n*: Klimax *f*.
clindamycine/*n*: Clindamycin *n*.
clinic/*n*: Klinik *f*.
clinical/*adj*: klinisch.
clinical chemistry: klinische Chemie *f*.
clinical diagnosis: klinische Diagnose *f*.
clinical examination: klinische Untersuchung *f*.
clinical features: klinische Merkmale.
clinical finding: klinischer Befund *m*.
clinical picture: klinisches Bild *n*, Krankheitsbild *n*.
clinical presentation: klinisches Bild *n*, Krankheitsbild *n*.
clinical signs: klinische Symptomatik *f*.
clinical trial: klinische Studie *f*.
clinician/*n*: Kliniker *m*.
clip/*n, vb*: 1. Klemme *f*, Wundklemme *f*; 2. klemmen, klammern.
clip suture: Klammernaht *f*.
clitoris/*n*: Klitoris *f*.
cloacal membrane: Kloakenmembran *f*.
cloacal passage: Kloakengang *m*.
clobazam/*n*: Clobazam *n*.
clobetasol/*n*: Clobetasol *n*.
clobetasone/*n*: Clobetason *n*.
clock/*n*: Uhr *f*.
clockwise/*adj*: im Uhrzeigersinn.
clocortolone/*n*: Clocortolon *n*.
clofazimine/*n*: Clofazimin *n*.
clofenamic acid: Clofenamsäure *f*.
clofenamide/*n*: Clofenamid *n*.
clofezone/*n*: Clofezon *n*.
clofibrate/*n*: Clofibrat *n*.
clomethiazole/*n*: Clomethiazol *n*.
clomifene/*n*: Clomifen *n*.
clomipramine/*n*: Clomipramin *n*.
clone/*n, vb*: 1. Klon *m*; 2. klonen, klonieren.
clonic/*adj*: klonisch.
clonic convulsion: klonischer Krampf *m*, klonische Konvulsion *f*.
clonidine/*n*: Clonidin *n*.
clopamide/*n*: Clopamid *n*.
clopenthixol/*n*: Clopenthixol *n*.
clopidogrel/*n*: Clopidogrel *n*.
cloprednol/*n*: Cloprednol *n*.
clorazepate dipotassium: Dikaliumclorazepat *n*.
clorexolone/*n*: Clorexolon *n*.
clorophene/*n*: Clorofen *n*.
close/*vb, adj*: 1. schließen; 2. nahe, benachbart.
closed fracture: geschlossene Fraktur *f*.
closed pneumothorax: geschlossener Pneumothorax *m*.
closed reduction: geschlossene Reposition *f*.
clostebol/*n*: Clostebol *n*.
clostridium/*n*: Clostridium.
clot/*n, vb*: 1. Klumpen *m*, Blutgerinnsel *n*; 2. koagulieren.
clotrimazole/*n*: Clotrimazol *n*.
clotted blood: geronnenes Blut *n*, Blutkuchen *m*.
clotting time: Gerinnungszeit *f*.
cloudy swelling: trübe Schwellung *f*.
cloudy urine: flockiger Urin *m*.
cloxacillin/*n*: Cloxacillin *n*.
cloxiquine/*n*: Cloxiquin *n*.
clozapine/*n*: Clozapin *n*.
clubbing of the fingers: fingers with a short, broad tip and overhanging nail, resembling a drumstick. Forms include idiopathic clubbing of the fingers, present at birth, or secondary forms associated with chronic liver disease, bacterial endocarditis, cyanotic heart disease, or chronic suppuration. Trommelschlägelfinger.
club foot: congenital or acquired foot deformity with abnormal position or form of the foot, resulting from malformations of the tendons, and frequently associated with bone malformations. According to the malformation, different forms are distinguished, for example talipes equinus, talipes valgus, talipes varus. Klumpfuß *m*.
clumping/*n*: Verklumpung *f*.
cluster/*n*: Cluster *m*.

cluster headache: Clusterkopfschmerz *m*, Horton-Syndrom *n*.
CMV <*abbr*> **cytomegalovirus/*n***: Zytomegalievirus *n*.
cnemial/*adj*: tibial.
coagulation/*n*: Koagulation *f*, Gerinnung *f*.
coarctation/*n*: Koarktation *f*.
coat/*n, vb*: 1. Hülle *f*, Belag *m*; 2. einhüllen, ummanteln.
coated tongue: belegte Zunge *f*.
coaxial catheter: Koaxialkatheter *m*.
cobalt/*n*: Kobalt *n*, Co.
cocaine/*n*: Kokain *n*.
cocarcinogen/*n*: Kokarzinogen *n*.
coccidiomycosis/*n*: Kokzidioidomykose *f*.
coccus/*n*: Coccus *m*, Kokke *f*.
coccydynia/*n*: Kokzygodynie *f*.
coccygeal bone: Steißbein *n*.
coccygeal vertebra: Steißwirbel *m*.
coccyx/*n*: Steißbein *n*.
cochlea/*n*: Cochlea *f*, Schnecke *f*.
cochlear/*adj*: kochleär.
cochlear deafness: kochleäre Taubheit *f*.
cochlear implant: Cochlear Implant *n*.
cochlear otosclerosis: Innenohrotosklerose *f*.
cochleopupillary reflex: Kochleopupillarreflex *m*.
code/*n, vb*: 1. Kode *m*, Code *m*; 2. kodieren.
codeine/*n*: Codein *n*.
coding/*n*: Kodierung *f*.
cod liver oil: Lebertran *m*, Oleum Jecoris aselli *n*.
codominance/*n*: Kodominanz *f*.
codon/*n*: Kodon *n*.
coefficient of regression: Regressionskoeffizient *m*.
coenzyme/*n*: Koenzym *n*.
cofactor/*n*: Kofaktor *m*.
coffeine/*n*: Koffein *n*.
cognition/*n*: Kognition *f*.
cognitive/*adj*: kognitiv.
cognitive development: kognitive Entwicklung *f*.
cogwheel sign: Zahnradphänomen *n*.
cohort study: Kohortenstudie *f*.
coil/*n, vb*: 1. Spule *f*, Spindel *f*, Knäuel *n*; 2. spiralisieren.
coinfection/*n*: Koinfektion *f*.
coin lesion: Rundherd *m*, Rundschatten *m*.
coitus/*n*: Koitus *m*.
colchicine/*n*: Colchicin *n*.
cold/*n, adj*: 1. Erkältung *f*, Kälte *f*; 2. kalt.
cold abscess: kalter Abszess *m*.
cold agglutination: Kälteagglutination *f*.
cold agglutinin: Kälteagglutinin *n*.
cold allergy: Kälteallergie *f*.
cold compress: kalter Wickel *m*.
cold gangrene: trockene Gangrän *f*.
cold hemagglutinin: Kältehämagglutination *f*.
cold hemolysin: Kältehämolysin *n*, Donath-Landsteiner-Antikörper *m*.
cold sensation: Kälteempfindung *f*.
coldsore/*n*: clusters of vesicular lesions of the skin or mucosa, due to herpes simplex. The small blisters are typically localized around the lips. Herpes labialis *m*.
colecalciferol/*n*: Colecalciferol *n*.
colectomy/*n*: Kolektomie *f*.
colesevelam/*n*: Colesevelam *n*.
colestipol/*n*: Colestipol *n*.
colestyramine/*n*: Colestyramin *n*.
colic/*n, adj*: 1. Kolik *f*; 2. kolonisch.
colic pain: krampfartiger Schmerz *m*.
coliform/*adj*: koliform.
colistin/*n*: Colistin *n*.
colitis/*n*: inflammation of the large intestine, usually due to infections, autoimmune diseases, ischemia, or following antibiotic therapy which allows the growth of Clostridia that release a toxin which causes colonic damage. Kolitis *f*.
collagen/*n*: Kollagen *n*.
collagen fiber: Kollagenfaser *f*.
collapse/*n, vb*: 1. Kollaps *m*; 2. kollabieren.
collapsing pulse: Pulsus celer et altus *m*, Corrigan-Puls *m*.
collar bone: Schlüsselbein *n*.
collateral/*n, adj*: 1. Kollaterale *f*; 2. kollateral.
collateral circulation: Kollateralkreislauf *m*.

collateral hemiplegia: kollaterale Hemiplegie *f*, homolaterale Hemiplegie *f*.
collateral vessel: Kollateralgefäß *n*.
collective/*n*: Kollektiv *n*.
collective dose: Kollektivdosis *f*.
collective neurosis: Massenneurose *f*.
collective suicide: erweiterter Suizid *m*.
colliquative necrosis: Kolliquationsnekrose *f*.
collodiaphyseal angle: Kollodiaphysenwinkel *m*, Centrum-Collum-Diaphysenwinkel *m*, CCD-Winkel *m*.
collodion/*n*: Kollodium *n*.
colloid/*n*: Kolloid *n*.
colloid body: hyalines Körperchen *n*.
colloid carcinoma: Gallertkrebs *m*.
colloid cyst: Kolloidzyste *f*.
colloid goiter: Kolloidstruma *f*.
colloid ovarian tumor: muzinöses Kystadenom *n*.
colloma/*n*: muzinöses Karzinom *n*.
coloboma/*n*: an ophthalmologic condition which is characterized by the presence of a gap, hole, or fissure in any ocular structure. Typical colobomas result from failure of fusion of the embryonic tissues. Kolobom *n*.
colon/*n*: Kolon *n*.
colonic bleeding: Kolonblutung *f*.
colonic diverticulitis: inflammation of small pouches or diverticulum in the large intestine. Symptoms include spasmodic pain, abdominal tenderness, constipation, meteorism, nausea, and vomiting. As complications obstruction, bleeding, or perforation may occur. Kolondivertikulitis *f*.
colonic diverticulum: Kolondivertikel *n*.
colonic fistula: Kolonfistel *f*.
colonic lavage: Kolonlavage *f*.
colonic polyp: presence of one or several polyps in the colon. Adenomatous polyposis coli is characterized by the presence of more than 100, sometimes up to 1000 polyps. Symptoms may include bleeding, diarrhea or constipation, abdominal pain, and malabsorption. Dickdarmpolyp *m*.
colonization/*n*: Besiedelung *f*.
colony/*n*: Kolonie *f*.
colony-stimulating factor: colony-stimulating factor *m*, koloniestimulierender Faktor *m*, CSF.
color/*n, vb*: 1. Farbe *f*; 2. färben.
color blindness: a congenital or acquired condition which is characterized by the inability to distinguish between particular colors, while ordinary vision remains normal. Causes include congenital absence or anomaly of cone pigments, or lesions of the optic nerve or the retina. Farbenblindheit *f*.
colorectal cancer: kolorektales Karzinom *n*.
colorectal neoplasm: kolorektaler Tumor *m*.
colored plate: Farbtafel *f*.
color index: Färbeindex *m*.
colostomy/*n*: Kolostomie *f*.
colostrum/*n*: Kolostrum *n*.
colotomy/*n*: Kolotomie *f*.
colpitis/*n*: inflammation of the vagina, typically resulting from bacterial or fungal infection. Symptoms include pain and purulent vaginal discharge. Kolpitis *f*, Vaginitis *f*, Scheidenentzündung *f*.
colpocele/*n*: Kolpozele *f*, Vaginozele *f*.
colpoplasty/*n*: Kolpoplastik *f*, Scheidenplastik *f*.
colporrhaphy/*n*: Kolporrhaphie *f*.
colposcope/*n*: Kolposkop *n*.
colposcopy/*n*: Kolposkopie *f*.
colpotomy/*n*: Kolpotomie *f*.
column/*n*: Säule *f*.
columnar cell: Säulenepithelzelle *f*.
coma/*n*: Koma *n*.
comatose/*adj*: komatös.
comb/*n*: Kamm *m*.
combination/*n*: Kombination *f*.
combination therapy: Kombinationstherapie *f*.
combined oral contraceptive pill: orales Kombinationskontrazeptivum *n*.
combined pelvimetry: kombinierte

Beckenmessung *f*.
combined vaccine: Kombinationsimpfstoff *m*.
combined version: kombinierte Wendung *f*.
combustion/*n*: Verbrennung *f*.
comedo/*n*: Komedo *m*.
comforter/*n*: Schnuller *m*.
command automatism: Befehlsautomatismus *m*.
commensal/*adj*: kommensal.
commercial preparation: Handelspräparat *n*.
comminuted fracture: Komminutivfraktur *f*.
commissural/*adj*: kommissural.
commissural fiber: Kommissurenfaser *f*.
common/*adj*: gemeinsam, üblich.
common acne: Acne vulgaris *f*.
common bedbug: Bettwanze *f*, Cimex lectularius *m*.
common cold: a common viral infection of the throat and nasal passages, causing symptoms of rhinitis, cough and feverish illness. Erkältungskrankheit *f*.
common cold virus: Schnupfenvirus *n*.
common everyday headache: gewöhnlicher Kopfschmerz *m*.
common human flea: Menschenfloh *m*, Pulex irritans *m*.
common male baldness: Calvities *f*, Alopezie *f*.
common salt: Kochsalz *n*, Natriumchlorid *n*.
common wart: circumscribed growth on the skin, sometimes caused by human papillomavirus. Warze *f*, Verruca vulgaris *f*.
communicable/*adj*: ansteckend, übertragbar.
communicable disease: übertragbare Krankheit *f*, Infektionskrankheit *f*.
communicating hydrocephalus: kommunizierender Hydrozephalus *m*.
communication/*n*: Kommunikation *f*, Verbindung *f*.
communication disorder: Kommunikationsstörung *f*.
community/*n*: Gemeinschaft *f*, Gemeinwesen *n*.
community psychiatry: Gemeindepsychiatrie *f*.
compact/*adj*: kompakt.
compact bone: Substantia compacta *f*.
compact osteoma: kompaktes Osteom *n*.
compact tissue: Kompakta *f*.
comparative anatomy: vergleichende Anatomie *f*.
comparative percussion: vergleichende Perkussion *f*.
compartment/*n*: Kompartiment *n*.
compatibility/*n*: Kompatibilität *f*.
compensated acidosis: kompensierte Azidose *f*.
compensated alkalosis: kompensierte Alkalose *f*.
compensation/*n*: Kompensation *f*, Entschädigung *f*.
compensation for pain and suffering: Schmerzensgeld *n*.
compensatory/*adj*: kompensatorisch.
compensatory atrophy: kompensatorische Atrophie *f*.
compensatory circulation: Kollateralkreislauf *m*.
compensatory emphysema: kompensatorisches Emphysem *n*.
compensatory hypertension: Erfordernishochdruck *m*.
compensatory polycythemia: kompensatorische Polyzythämie *f*.
competitive inhibition: kompetitive Hemmung *f*.
competitive renal tubular transport: kompetitiver Tubulustransport *m*.
complain/*vb*: sich beschweren, klagen.
complaint/*n*: Beschwerden.
complement/*n*: Komplement *n*.
complementary medicine: Komplementärmedizin *f*.
complementary therapy: Komplementärtherapie *f*.
complement fixation test: Komplementbindungsreaktion *f*, KBR.
complement-fixing antibody: komplementbindender Antikörper *m*.
complete/*vb, adj*: 1. vervollständigen; 2. vollständig.

complete abortion: vollständiger Abort *m*.
complete amelia: Tetraamelie *f*.
complete antibody: kompletter Antikörper *m*.
complete birth: vollständige Geburt *f*.
complete bundle branch block: kompletter Schenkelblock *m*.
complete fistula: kommunizierende Fistel *f*.
complete fracture: vollständige Fraktur *f*.
complete picture: Vollbild *n*.
complete recovery: vollständige Heilung *f*.
complex/*n*: Komplex *m*.
complex infection: Mischinfektion *f*.
complex partial seizure: komplexe Absence *f*.
compliance/*n*: Compliance *f*, Verordnungstreue *f*, Volumendehnbarkeit *f*.
complicated fracture: komplizierte Fraktur *f*.
complicated migraine: Migraine accompagnée *f*.
complication/*n*: Komplikation *f*.
comply/*vb*: befolgen.
component/*n*: Komponente *f*.
composite flap: Vollhautlappen *m*.
compound/*n*: Verbindung *f*, Präparat *n*.
compound cyst: mehrkammerige Zyste *f*.
compound fracture: offene Fraktur *f*.
comprehension test: Verständnistest *m*.
compress/*n, vb*: 1. Kompresse *f*; 2. komprimieren.
compression/*n*: Kompression *f*.
compression bandage: Kompressionsverband *m*.
compulsive action: an impulse to perform an action which cannot be suppressed voluntarily. Compulsions are a major feature in obsessive-compulsive neurosis. Zwangshandlung *f*.
compulsive crying: Zwangsweinen *n*.
compulsive idea: Zwangsidee *f*, Zwangsvorstellung *f*.
compulsive laughter: Zwangslachen.
compulsive tic: Gilles-de-la-Tourette-Syndrom *n*.
compulsory/*adj*: zwanghaft, zwangsweise.
compulsary vaccination: Pflichtimpfung *f*, Impfzwang *m*.
computerized tomography: Computertomographie *f*, CT.
computer tomography scan: Computertomogramm *n*.
concave lens: Konkavlinse *f*.
concavity/*n*: Konkavität *f*.
concentrate/*n, vb*: 1. Konzentrat *n*; 2. konzentrieren.
concentration/*n*: Konzentration *f*.
concentric/*adj*: konzentrisch.
concentric hypertrophy: konzentrische Hypertrophie *f*.
concentric sclerosis: konzentrische Sklerose *f*, Baló-Sklerose *f*.
conception/*n*: Konzeption *f*, Empfängnis *f*.
conchal cartilage: Muschelknorpel *m*.
concomitant/*adj*: konkomittierend, begleitend.
concomitant strabismus: Strabismus concomitans *m*, Begleitschielen *n*, Heterotropie *f*.
concomitant symptom: Begleitsymptom *n*.
concretion/*n*: Concretio *f*, Verwachsung *f*.
concussion/*n*: Kontusion *f*, Erschütterung *f*.
concussion injury: Kontusionsverletzung *f*.
condensation/*n*: Kondensation *f*, Kondensierung *f*.
condenser/*n*: Kondensator *m*.
condensing osteitis: Ostitis condensans *f*, Osteopoikilie *f*.
condition/*n, vb*: 1. Kondition *f*, Zustand *m*; 2. bedingen.
conditioned reflex: bedingter Reflex *m*.
conditioned response: konditionierte Reaktion *f*.
conditioning/*n*: Konditionierung *f*.
conditioning therapy: Verhaltenstherapie *f*.
condom/*n*: Kondom *n*.

conduct/*n, vb*: 1. Verhalten *n*; 2. leiten.
conductance/*n*: Leitfähigkeit *f*.
conduct disorder: Verhaltensstörung *f*.
conduction/*n*: Leitung *f*.
conductive deafness: Leitungsschwerhörigkeit *f*.
conductive hearing loss: Leitungsschwerhörigkeit *f*.
conductor/*n*: Konduktor *m*.
condylar fracture: Kondylenfraktur *f*.
condyle/*n*: Kondylus *m*.
condyloma/*n*: a wartlike growth on the skin or mucous membranes. Forms include condyloma latum or flat condyloma with flat papular lesions occurring in syphilis, and condyloma acuminatum or genital wart, a squamous cell papilloma, usually due to infection with human papillomavirus. Kondylom *n*.
cone/*n*: Horn *n*, Zapfen *m*.
confabulation/*n*: Konfabulation *f*.
confidence/*n*: Konfidenz *f*, Vertrauen *n*.
confidence interval: Vertrauensintervall *n*.
confinement/*n*: Bettlägerigkeit *f*.
confirmation test: Bestätigungstest *m*.
confirmatory trial: Bestätigungsstudie *f*.
conflict/*n*: Konflikt *m*.
confluence/*n*: Zusammenfluss *m*.
confluent growth: konfluierendes Wachstum *n*.
congenital/*adj*: kongenital.
congenital alopecia: kongenitale Alopezie *f*.
congenital alveolar dysplasia: kongenitale Alveolardysplasie *f*.
congenital amputation: Amnionschnürfurche *f*.
congenital aplastic anemia: Fanconi-Anämie *f*.
congenital cataract: kongenitale Katarakt *f*.
congenital chronic glomerulonephritis: kongenitale Glomerulosklerose *f*.
congenital defect: kongenitale Fehlbildung *f*.
congenital deformity: Defektfehlbildung *f*.
congenital dysplastic angiectasia: Klippel-Trénaunay-Weber-Syndrom *n*.
congenital dysplastic angiomatosis: kongenitale Angiomatose *f*.
congenital elephantiasis: kongenitales Lymphödem *n*.
congenital erythropoietic porphyria: kongenitale erythropoetische Porphyrie *f*.
congenital facial cleft: Gesichtsspalte *f*.
congenital facial palsy: angeborene Fazialislähmung *f*.
congenital fracture: Intrauterinfraktur *f*.
congenital gastrointestinal alkalosis: kongenitale Alkalose *f*.
congenital generalized lipodystrophy: kongenitale generalisierte Lipodystrophie *f*.
congenital goiter: kongenitale Struma *f*.
congenital hemolytic jaundice: kongenitaler hämolytischer Ikterus *m*.
congenital hydrocephalus: angeborener Hydrozephalus *m*.
congenital hyperbilirubinemia: idiopathische Hyperbilirubinämie *f*, Crigler-Najjar-Ikterus *m*.
congenital lymphedema: hereditäres Lymphödem *n*, Nonne-Milroy-Syndrom *n*.
congenital muscular dystrophy: kongenitale Muskeldystrophie *f*.
congenital oculofacial paralysis: Moebius-Syndrom *n*.
congenital ophthalmoplegia: angeborene Ophthalmoplegie *f*.
congenital spastic paraplegia: infantile spastische Paraplegie *f*.
congenital syphilis: angeborene Syphilis *f*.
congenital webbing of the neck: Pterygium colli *n*.
congestion/*n*: Kongestion *f*, Stauung *f*.
congestive/*adj*: kongestiv.

congestive abscess: Kongestionsabszess *m*.
congestive gastritis: inflammation of the mucosal lining of the stomach walls, resulting from right hear insufficiency and venous stasis. Symptoms include loss of appetite, meteorism, nausea, and vomiting. Staungsgastritis *f*.
congestive headache: Kongestionskopfschmerz *m*.
congestive splenomegaly: Banti-Krankheit *f*.
conic/*adj*: konisch.
coniine/*n*: Coniin *n*.
coning biopsy: Konusbiopsie *f*, Konisation *f*.
conization/*n*: Konisation *f*, Konusbiopsie *f*.
conjugate/*n, adj*: 1. Beckendurchmesser *m*, Conjugata *f*; 2. gekoppelt.
conjugated bilirubin: konjugiertes Bilirubin *n*.
conjugate of the outlet: Beckenausgangsdurchmesser *m*.
conjugate paralysis: konjugierte Augenmuskellähmung *f*, Blicklähmung *f*.
conjunctival reflex: Konjunktivalreflex *m*.
conjunctival sac: Bindehautsack *m*.
conjunctival test: Konjunktivaltest *m*.
conjunctivitis/*n*: inflammation of the conjunctiva, caused by viruses, bacteria, topical ocular medications, allergy, or physical damage. Konjunktivitis *f*, Bindehautentzündung *f*.
connate/*adj*: konnatal.
connection/*n*: Verbindung *f*.
connective tissue: Bindegewebe *n*.
connective tissue disease: Bindegewebserkrankung *f*.
connective-tissue fiber: Bindegewebsfaser *f*.
consanguinity/*n*: Konsanguinität *f*, Blutsverwandtschaft *f*.
conscious/*adj*: bewusst.
consciousness/*n*: Bewusstsein *n*.
consensual reaction: konsensueller Lichtreflex *m*.
conservative/*adj*: konservativ.
conservative surgery: erhaltende Chirurgie *f*.
conservative treatment: konservative Behandlung *f*.
consistent/*adj*: konsistent.
consolidation/*n*: Konsolidierung *f*.
consonating rale: klingendes Rasselgeräusch *n*.
constant/*n, adj*: 1. Konstante *f*; 2. konstant, gleichbleibend.
constipation/*n*: a condition which is characterized by a failure of bowels to excrete residue at proper intervals, resulting in retention of feces in the large intestine. Verstopfung *f*, Obstipation *f*.
constitution/*n*: Konstitution *f*.
constitutional disease: konstitutionell bedingte Erkrankung *f*.
constitutional gigantism: konstitutioneller Riesenwuchs *m*.
constitutional jaundice: Gilbert-Meulengracht-Syndrom *n*.
constitutional symptom: Allgemeinsymptom *n*.
constriction/*n*: Konstriktion *f*, Einschnürung *f*.
constrictive endocarditis: Löffler-Endokarditis *f*, fibroplastische Endokarditis *f*.
constrictive pericarditis: an inflammation of the outer sac of the heart that results in shrinking and thickening of the pericardium. Symptoms include impairment of normal heart muscle contraction and expansion. Pericarditis constrictiva *f*.
constructive agraphia: konstruktive Agraphie *f*.
constructive apraxia: konstruktive Apraxie *f*.
consultation/*n*: Konsultation *f*, Beratung *f*.
consulting room: Behandlungszimmer *n*.
consumer's protection: Verbraucherschutz *m*.
consumption/*n*: Verbrauch *m*, Konsum *m*.
consumption coagulopathy: Verbrauchskoagulopathie *f*, disseminierte intravasale Gerinnung *f*.

contact/*n, vb*: 1. Kontakt *m*, Berührung *f*; 2. berühren, kontaktieren.
contact disorder: Kontaktstörung *f*.
contact lens: Kontaktlinse *f*.
contact radiation: Kontaktbestrahlung *f*.
contact surface: Auflagefläche *f*.
contagiosity/*n*: Kontagiosität *f*, Infektiosität *f*.
contagious/*adj*: kontagiös, ansteckend.
contagious aphtha: Maul- und Klauenseuche *f*.
contagious disease: ansteckende Krankheit *f*.
contaminate/*vb*: kontaminieren, verunreinigen.
contamination/*n*: Kontamination *f*, Verunreinigung *f*.
continence/*n*: Kontinenz *f*.
continuous epilepsy: Status epilepticus *m*.
continuous fiber: Spindelfaser *f*.
continuous murmur: Kontinuum *n*.
continuous partial epilepsy: Epilepsia partialis continua *f*, Kozhevnikow-Epilepsie *f*.
continuous sound: Dauergeräusch *n*, Maschinengeräusch *n*.
continuous suture: fortlaufende Naht *f*.
contraception/*n*: Kontrazeption *f*, Empfängnisverhütung *f*.
contraceptive/*n, adj*: 1. Kontrazeptivum *n*; 2. kontrazeptiv.
contraceptive agent: Kontrazeptivum *n*.
contraceptive diaphragm: Diaphragmapessar *n*.
contraceptive pessary: Diaphragmapessar *n*.
contract/*vb*: kontrahieren, sich zuziehen.
contracted bladder: Schrumpfblase *f*.
contracted pelvis: enges Becken *n*.
contractile stricture: Kontraktionsstriktur *f*.
contraction/*n*: Kontraktion *f*.
contractions: Wehen.
contracture/*n*: Kontraktur *f*.
contraindication/*n*: Kontraindikation *f*, Gegenanzeige *f*.
contralateral/*adj*: kontralateral.
contralateral reflex: Kontralateralreflex *m*, Brudzinski-Zeichen *n*.
contrast/*n*: Kontrast *m*.
contrast enema: Kontrasteinlauf *m*.
contrast medium: Kontrastmittel *n*.
control/*n, vb*: 1. Kontrolle *f*, Steuerung *f*; 2. kontrollieren, steuern.
contused wound: Kontusionswunde *f*, Quetschwunde *f*.
contusion/*n*: an injury in which the skin is not broken, but underlying blood vessels are damaged or ruptured. Symptoms include swelling, and subdermal hematoma. Kontusion *f*.
convalescence/*n*: Rekonvaleszenz *f*, Genesung *f*.
convection/*n*: Konvektion *f*.
convergence/*n*: Konvergenz *f*.
convergent lens: Konvergenzlinse *f*.
convergent strabismus: Strabismus convergens *m*, Esotropie *f*, Einwärtsschielen *n*.
conversion/*n*: Konversion *f*, Umwandlung *f*, Somatisierung *f*.
convex/*adj*: konvex.
convex lens: Konvexlinse *f*.
convoluted gland: Knäueldrüse *f*.
convolution/*n*: Konvolut *n*, Knäuel *n*.
convulsant threshold: Krampfschwelle *f*.
convulsion/*n*: Konvulsion *f*
convulsive tic: Tic convulsif *m*.
cool/*adj, vb*: 1. kalt; 2. kühlen.
Coombs test: Coombs-Test *m*.
COPD <*abbr*> **chronic obstructive pulmonary disease**: chronisch-obstruktive Lungenerkrankung *f*, COLE.
cope/*vb*: bewältigen.
coping behavior: Copingverhalten *n*, Bewältigungsverhalten *n*.
copulation/*n*: Kopulation *f*, Koitus *m*.
copy/*n, vb*: 1. Kopie *f*; 2. kopieren.
coracoid/*n*: Korakoidfortsatz *m*.
cord/*n*: Schnur *f*, Strang *m*, Chorda *f*.
cordiform pelvis: Kartenherzbecken *n*.
cord presentation: in obstetrics, a prolapse of the umbilical cord into the vagina before delivery. Nabelschnurvorfall *m*.

core/*n*: Kern *m*, Zentrum *n*.
core temperature: Kerntemperatur *f*.
cork dust pneumoconiosis: Korkstaublunge *f*.
corn/*n*: hard or soft thickening of the skin with hyperkeratosis on the foot or a toe, resulting from friction and pressure. Hühnerauge *n*, Klavus *m*.
corneal/*adj*: korneal.
corneal astigmatism: Hornhautastigmatismus *m*.
corneal cleft: Hornhautfissur *f*.
corneal curvature: Hornhautkrümmung *f*.
corneal dystrophy: Hornhautdystrophie *f*.
corneal ectasia: Keratektasie *f*.
corneal opacity: Hornhauttrübung *f*.
corneal reflex: Kornealreflex *m*.
corneal scar: Hornhautnarbe *f*.
corneal transplantation: Hornhauttransplantation *f*.
corneal ulcer: Ulcus corneae *n*.
cornification/*n*: Verhornung *f*.
corn-plaster/*n*: Hühneraugenpflaster *n*.
coronal/*adj*: koronar.
coronal plane: Koronarebene *f*.
coronary angiography: Koronarangiographie *f*.
coronary angioplasty: Koronarangioplastie *f*.
coronary angiospasm: Koronarangiospasmus *m*.
coronary arteriography: Koronarangiographie *f*.
coronary arteriosclerosis: Koronararteriensklerose *f*.
coronary cataract: Kranzstar *m*.
coronary circulation: Koronarkreislauf *m*.
coronary embolism: Koronarembolie *f*.
coronary heart disease: a condition which is characterized by stenosis of the coronary arteries, usually due to arteriosclerosis. Symptoms result from insufficient blood supply of the cardiac muscles and include severe pain, sometimes irradiating into the left arm, and in case of complete obstruction of a coronary artery myocardial infarction. koronare Herzkrankheit *f*, KHK.
coronary reserve: Koronarreserve *f*.
coronary sclerosis: Koronarsklerose *f*.
coronary stenosis: Koronararterienstenose *f*.
coronary vessel: Herzkranzgefäß *n*.
coroner/*n*: Leichenbeschauer *m*.
coronoid/*n*: koronoid.
corpse/*n*: Leiche *f*, Leichnam *m*.
corpulency/*n*: Korpulenz *f*.
corpus/*n*: Körper *m*.
corpuscle/*n*: Korpuskel *n*, Körperchen *n*.
corpuscular volume: Blutkörperchenvolumen *n*.
corrective/*n, adj*: 1. Korrektiv *n*; 2. korrigierend.
corrective osteotomy: Korrekturosteotomie *f*.
correctness/*n*: Richtigkeit *f*.
correlation/*n*: Korrelation *f*.
correspondence/*n*: Übereinstimmung *f*, Korrespondenz *f*.
corrosive esophagitis: Ösophagusverätzung *f*.
corrosive gastritis: Ätzgastritis *f*.
cortex/*n*: Kortex *m*, Rinde *f*.
cortical/*adj*: kortikal.
cortical aphasia: kortikale Aphasie *f*.
cortical area: Rindenfeld *n*.
cortical atrophy: Rindenatrophie *f*.
cortical blindness: Rindenblindheit *f*.
cortical cataract: Rindenstar *m*.
cortical deafness: Rindentaubheit *f*.
cortical defect: Kortikalisdefekt *m*.
cortical epilepsy: Rindenepilepsie *f*.
cortical hormone: adrenokortikales Hormon *n*.
cortical osteitis: Periostitis *f*.
cortical paralysis: kortikale Lähmung *f*.
cortical psychic blindness: optische Agnosie *f*.
corticoadrenal/*adj*: adrenokortikal.
corticorelin/*n*: Corticorelin *n*.
corticosteroid/*n*: Kortikosteroid *n*.
corticosteroid-binding globulin: kortikosteroidbindendes Globulin *n*.
corticosteroid-induced myopathy: Steroidmyopathie *f*.

corticotrophic/*adj*: kortikotrop.
corticotropin/*n*: Corticotropin *n*, adrenokortikotropes Hormon *n*, ACTH.
cortisol/*n*: Cortisol *n*, Kortisol *n*.
cortisone/*n*: Cortison *n*, Kortison *n*.
coryza/*n*: Coryza *f*, Schnupfen *m*.
cosmetics/*n*: Kosmetik *f*.
cosmetic surgery: kosmetische Operation *f*, Schönheitsoperation *f*.
cost/*n*: 1. Rippe *f*; 2. Kosten.
costal/*adj*: kostal.
costal angle: Rippenwinkel *m*.
costal arch: Rippenbogen *m*, Arcus costalis *m*.
costal cartilage: Rippenknorpel *m*.
costal process: Rippenfortsatz *m*.
costal respiration: Kostalatmung *f*.
costochondral syndrome: Kostochondritis *f*.
costochondritis/*n*: inflammation of the cartilaginous parts of the ribs of unknown origin. Symptoms include pain and local tenderness over the anterior thoracic wall. Rippenknorpelentzündung *f*, Tietze-Syndrom *n*.
cot death: sudden death of an infant during the first year of life, characteristically during sleep, without detectable organic cause. The exact etiology is unknown, factors such as environmental temperature, abdominal position during sleep, and pre- or postnatal exposure to tobacco smoke are discussed. Krippentod *m*, plötzlicher Kindstod *m*.
cotton wool: Watte *f*.
cotton wool spots: an ophthalmologic condition which is characterized by bluish white lesions of the retina, usually due to ischemia of the nerve fiber layer. Cotton-Wool-Herde.
cough/*n, vb*: 1. sudden explosive expulsion of air from the lungs, or the attempt to expel voluntarily something causing irritation in the respiratory tract. Husten *m*; 2. husten.
coughing center: Hustenzentrum *n*.
cough reflex: Hustenreflex *m*.
coumaran/*n*: Cumaran *n*.
coumarin/*n*: Cumarin *n*.
counseling/*n*: Beratung *f*.
count/*n, vb*: 1. Zählung *f*, Zahl *f*; 2. zählen.
counter/*n*: Zähler *m*.
countercurrent/*adj*: gegen die Flussrichtung.
counterirritation/*n*: Gegenreizmassage *f*.
counting/*n*: Zählung *f*.
coupled beat: Bigeminie *f*.
coupled pulse: Bigeminie *f*.
couple therapy: Paartherapie *f*.
coupling/*n*: Kopplung *f*, Paarung *f*.
course/*n*: Verlauf *m*, Krankheitsverlauf *m*.
cover/*n, vb*: 1. Abdeckung *f*, Decke *f*; 2. bedecken.
cow milk allergy: Kuhmilchallergie *f*.
cowpox/*n*: Kuhpocken *f*.
cowpox virus: Vacciniavirus *n*.
coxalgia/*n*: Koxalgie *f*.
crab louse: Filzlaus *f*.
crack/*n*: Hautschrunde *f*, Rhagade *f*, Riss *m*.
cracked nipple: Mamillenfissur *f*.
cracked-pot sound: Geräusch des gesprungenen Topfes *n*, Bruit du pot fêlé, Münzenklirren *n*.
crackling rale: Knisterrasseln *n*.
cradle/*n*: Wiege *f*, Schiene *f*, Mulde *f*.
cramp/*n*: Krampf *m*.
cranial/*adj*: kranial.
cranial cavity: Schädelhöhle *f*.
cranial conduction: Knochenleitung *f*.
cranial nerve: Kranialnerv *m*, Hirnnerv *m*.
cranial polyneuritis: Polyneuritis cranialis *f*, Fisher-Syndrom *n*.
cranial polyneuropathy: Hirnnervenpolyneuritis *f*.
cranial region: Schädelregion *f*.
cranial synostosis: Schädelsynostose *f*.
craniobuccal cyst: Rathke-Tasche *f*.
craniocarpotarsal dysplasia: kraniokarpotarsale Dystrophie *f*, Freeman-Sheldon-Syndrom *n*.
craniocerebral trauma: any injury which involves the skull and the brain, for example open head injury

with injury to the brain associated with a fracture of the skull. Schädelhirntrauma *n*.

cranioclast/*n*: Kranioklast *m*.

craniofacial disjunction: LeFort-III-Fraktur *f*.

craniometaphyseal dysplasia: kraniometaphysäre Dysplasie *f*.

craniometric point: Schädelmesspunkt *m*.

craniometry/*n*: Kraniometrie *f*.

craniopharyngioma/*n*: a congenital intracranial tumor originating from embryonic remains of the craniopharyngeal duct. Symptoms depend on tumor size and may include vision disorders, papilledema, headache, vomiting, and behavioral changes. Kraniopharyngiom *n*, Erdheim-Tumor *m*.

craniostenosis/*n*: Kraniostenose *f*.

craniosynostosis/*n*: Kraniosynostose *f*.

craniotabes/*n*: Kraniotabes *f*.

craniotomy/*n*: Kraniotomie *f*.

cranium/*n*: Schädel *m*.

crater nipple: eingezogene Brustwarze *f*.

craving/*n*: Verlangen *n*, Sucht *f*.

C-reactive protein: C-reaktives Protein *n*.

cream/*n*: Creme *f*.

crease/*n*: Falte *f*.

creatine/*n*: Kreatin *n*.

creatine kinase: Kreatinkinase *f*.

creatinine/*n*: Kreatinin *n*.

creatinine clearance: Kreatininclearance *f*.

creep/*n, vb*: 1. Kriechdehnung *f*; 2. kriechen.

creeping/*adj*: schleichend, kriechend.

creeping eruption: Creeping Eruption *f*, schleichender Hautausschlag *m*.

creeping palsy: progressive Muskelatrophie *f*.

creeping ulcer: Ulcus serpens *n*.

cremasteric reflex: Kremasterreflex *m*.

crenated erythrocyte: Echinozyt *m*, Stechapfelform *f*.

crepitant rale: Knisterrasseln *n*.

crepitation/*n*: Krepitation *f*, Knisterrasseln *n*.

crescent/*n, adj*: 1. Halbmond *m*; 2. halbmondförmig.

crescent cell: Halbmondzelle *f*.

crest/*n*: Kamm *m*.

cretinism/*n*: Kretinismus *m*.

Creutzfeldt-Jakob disease: a neurologic condition which is characterized by a progressive brain degeneration, possibly caused by an infectious agent, a prion. Symptoms occur in middle and late life and include rapid impairment of cognitive functions and progressive dementia with myoclonus. Variant Creutzfeldt-Jakob disease or vCJD describes the presence of the syndrome in persons of less than thirty years, and is associated with bovine spongiform encephalopathy, BSE. Creutzfeldt-Jakob-Krankheit *f*.

crevice/*n*: kleiner Riss *m*.

cribriform/*adj*: kribriform, siebförmig.

cribriform compress: Lochkompresse *f*.

cricoid/*n, adj*: 1. Ringknorpel *m*; 2. ringförmig.

criminal abortion: krimineller Abort *m*.

cripple/*n, vb*: 1. Krüppel *m*; 2. lähmen.

crisis/*n*: Krise *f*.

crisis intervention: Krisenintervention *f*.

criterion/*n*: Kriterium *n*.

critical/*adj*: kritisch.

critical care: Intensivpflege *f*.

critical hemorrhage: lebensgefährliche Blutung *f*.

critical organ: kritisches Organ *n*.

crocodile tears syndrome: a syndrome which is characterized by lacrimation when eating. This syndrome is caused by aberrant growth of the chorda tympani after nerve injury. Krokodilstränenphänomen *n*, Phänomen der paroxysmalen Tränen *n*.

cromoglicic acid: Cromoglicinsäure *f*.

crossed/*adj*: gekreuzt.

crossed embolism: paradoxe Embolie *f*.

crossed hemianesthesia: gekreuzte Hemianästhesie *f*.
crossed hemianopia: gekreuzte Hemianopsie *f*.
crossed hemiplegia: gekreuzte Lähmung *f*.
crossed paralysis: gekreuzte Lähmung *f*.
cross-eye/*n*: Strabismus convergens *m*, Esotropie *f*, Einwärtsschielen *n*.
cross immunity: Kreuzimmunität *f*.
cross infection: Mischinfektion *f*.
crossing over: Crossover *n*.
cross-legged gait: Scherengang *m*.
cross linkage: Querverbindung *f*.
cross-matching/*n*: Blutprobenauskreuzung *f*, Kreuzprobe *f*.
cross-over/*n*: Crossover *n*.
cross-reacting antigen: kreuzreagierendes Antigen *n*.
cross-resistance/*n*: Kreuzresistenz *f*.
cross section/*n*: Querschnitt *m*.
cross-sectional anatomy: Schnittanatomie *f*.
cross-sectional study: Querschnittuntersuchung *f*.
cross-stitch/*n*: Kreuzstich *m*.
croton/*n*: Kroton *n*.
crotonic acid: Krotonsäure *f*.
croton oil: Krotonöl *n*.
croup/*n*: a syndrome which is characterized by brassy cough, inspiratory stridor, hoarseness, and laryngeal obstruction and which occurs in children with various respiratory illnesses. Kruppsyndrom *n*.
croupous bronchitis: kruppöse Bronchitis *f*.
croupous conjunctivitis: kruppöse Konjunktivitis *f*.
crown/*n*: Krone *f*.
crucial/*adj*: gekreuzt, kritisch.
cruciate ligament: Kreuzband *n*.
cruciform/*adj*: kreuzförmig.
crude/*adj*: roh, ungereinigt.
crunching sound: Knistergeräusch *n*.
crural/*adj*: krural.
crural canal: Femoralkanal *m*.
crural hernia: Schenkelhernie *f*.
crural paralysis: Femoralislähmung *f*.
crus/*n*: Schenkel *m*.
crush/*vb*: quetschen, zerquetschen.
crushed wound: Quetschwunde *f*.
crush fracture: Kompressionsfraktur *f*.
crushing clamp: Kompressionsklemme *f*.
crush injury: Quetschung *f*, Quetschwunde *f*.
crush syndrome: Crush-Syndrom *n*.
crust/*n*: Kruste *f*, Borke *f*, Schorf *m*.
crutch paralysis: Krückenlähmung *f*.
cryesthesia/*n*: Kryästhesie *f*, Kälteempfindung *f*.
cryoanesthesia/*n*: Kälteanästhesie *f*, Kryoanästhesie *f*.
cryogenic block: Kälteanästhesie *f*, Kryoanästhesie *f*.
cryosurgery/*n*: Kryochirurgie *f*, Kältechirurgie *f*.
cryotherapy/*n*: Kryotherapie *f*.
cryptitis/*n*: Kryptitis *f*.
cryptococcal meningitis: Kryptokokkenmeningitis *f*.
cryptorchism/*n*: Kryptorchismus *m*.
crystal/*n*: Kristall *n*.
crystal arthritis: kristallinduzierte Arthritis *f*.
crystalline penicillin: Kristallpenicillin *n*.
crystalloid/*n*: Kristalloid *n*.
crystalluria/*n*: Kristallurie *f*.
CT <*abbr*> **computerized tomography**: Computertomographie *f*, CT.
cubital/*adj*: kubital.
cubital fossa: Ellbogengrube *f*.
cubital paralysis: Ulnarislähmung *f*.
cuboidal cell: kubische Epithelzelle *f*.
cuff/*n*: Cuff *m*, Manschette *f*.
cuff suspension: Manschettenaufhängung *f*.
cuff tubus: Manschettentubus *m*.
culdoscopy/*n*: Kuldoskopie *f*.
culture/*n, vb*: 1. Kultur *f*; 2. kultivieren, anzüchten.
culture medium: Kulturmedium *n*, Nährboden *m*.
cumulation effect: kumulative Wirkung *f*.
cumulative/*adj*: kumulativ.
cumulative action: kumulative Wirkung *f*.
cumulative effect: kumulative Wirkung *f*.

cuneiform/*adj*: keilförmig.
cuneiform osteotomy: Keilosteotomie *f*.
cup/*n*: Becher *m*, Tasse *f*.
cupped disk: blinder Fleck *m*.
cupping glass: Schröpfbecher *m*.
curable/*adj*: heilbar.
curare/*n*: Curare *n*.
curative/*n, adj*: 1. Heilmittel *n*; 2. kurativ.
curative dose: kurative Dosis *f*.
curative ratio: therapeutische Breite *f*.
cure/*n, vb*: 1. Heilung *f*, Kur *f*; 2. heilen, kuren.
curettage/*n*: Kürettage *f*.
curette/*n, vb*: 1. Kürette *f*; 2. kürettieren, ausschaben.
curly/*adj*: gekräuselt.
current/*n, adj*: 1. Strom *m*, Fluss *m*; 2. aktuell.
curtain sign: Kulissenphänomen *n*.
curvature/*n*: Kurvatur *f*, Krümmung *f*.
curve/*n*: Kurve *f*, Krümmung *f*.
cushion/*n*: Kissen *n*, Polster *n*.
cushingoid face: a condition which is characterized by a round or moon face, a typical symptom of Cushing syndrome with hypersecretion of cortisol. Cushing-Gesicht *n*.
cusp/*n*: Spitze *f*, Stachel *m*, Segel *n*.
cut/*n, vb*: 1. Schnitt *m*, Schnittwunde *f*; 2. schneiden.
cutaneomucouveal syndrome: Behçet-Syndrom *n*.
cutaneous/*adj*: kutan.
cutaneous administration: perkutane Anwendung *f*.
cutaneous amyloidosis: Hautamyloidose *f*, Amyloidosis cutis *f*.
cutaneous anthrax: Hautmilzbrand *m*.
cutaneous candidiasis: Hautcandidiasis *f*.
cutaneous cyst: Epidermiszyste *f*.
cutaneous emphysema: Hautemphysem *n*.
cutaneous fibrous polyp: fibröser Hautpolyp *m*.
cutaneous fissure: Kutisfissur *f*.
cutaneous fungus: Hautpilz *m*, Dermatophyt *m*.
cutaneous gangrene: Hautgangrän *f*.
cutaneous hemorrhage: Hautblutung *f*.
cutaneous lesion: Hautläsion *f*.
cutaneous perception: Hautempfindung *f*.
cutaneous porphyria: Porphyria cutanea tarda *f*.
cutaneous reaction: Hautreaktion *f*.
cutaneous reflex: Hautreflex *m*.
cutaneous schistosomiasis: Schistosomendermatitis *f*.
cutaneous sensation: Hautsinn *m*.
cutaneous sign: Hautsymptom *n*.
cutaneous tuberculosis: Hauttuberkulose *f*.
cuticle/*n*: Oberhaut *f*, Nagelhaut *f*.
cuticular layer: Kutikularsaum *m*, Bürstensaum *m*.
cutis/*n*: Haut *f*.
cutting/*n*: Schneiden *n*.
cyanic acid: Zyansäure *f*.
cyanocobalamin/*n*: Cyanocobalamin *n*, Vitamin B_{12} *n*.
cyanosis/*n*: blueness of the lips or the skin, usually due to a lack of oxygen. Causes include an increase of reduced hemoglobin in the blood, stagnation of blood in capillaries, or the presence of methemoglobin. Zyanose *f*.
cyanuric acid: Zyanursäure *f*.
cyclamic acid: Cyclaminsäure *f*.
cycle/*n*: Zyklus *m*, Kreislauf *m*.
cyclic/*adj*: zyklisch.
cyclic fever: rekurrierendes Fieber *n*.
cyclitis/*n*: inflammation of the ciliary body. Symptoms include ciliary flush, eye tenderness, photophobia, lacrimation, and normal intraocular pressure. Zyklitis *f*, Ziliarkörperentzündung *f*.
cyclodialysis/*n*: Zyklodialyse *f*.
cyclofenil/*n*: Cyclofenil *n*.
cycloid psychosis: zykloide Randpsychose *f*.
cyclopean brain: Zyklozephalie *f*.
cyclopean eye: Zyklopie *f*.
cyclopentamine/*n*: Cyclopentamin *n*.
cyclopenthiazide/*n*: Cyclopenthiazid *n*.

cyclopentolate/*n*: Cyclopentolat *n*.
cyclophosphamide/*n*: Cyclophosphamid *n*.
cycloplegia/*n*: Zykloplegie *f*, Akkommodationslähmung *f*.
cycloserine/*n*: Cycloserin *n*.
cyclosporine/*n*: Ciclosporin *n*, Cyclosporin *n*.
cyclothiazide/*n*: Cyclothiazid *n*.
cyclothymia/*n*: Zyklothymie *f*.
cyclothymic disorder: zyklothyme Störung *f*.
cyclotomy/*n*: Zyklotomie *f*.
cylindrical carcinoma: Zylinderzellkarzinom *n*.
cylindric bronchiectasis: zylindrische Bronchiektasie *f*.
cylindric lens: Zylinderlinse *f*.
cylindromatous sarcoma: Zylinderzellsarkom *n*.
cyproheptadine/*n*: Cyproheptadin *n*.
cyproterone/*n*: Cyproteron *n*.
cyst/*n*: Zyste *f*, Blase *f*.
cystadenoma/*n*: Kystadenom *n*, Adenokystom *n*.
cystectomy/*n*: Zystektomie *f*.
cysteine/*n*: Cystein *n*, Zystein *n*.
cystic/*adj*: zystisch.
cystic adenoma: zystisches Adenom *n*.
cystic bile: Blasengalle *f*.
cystic bronchiectasis: zystische Bronchiektasie *f*.
cystic cataract: Milchstar *m*.
cystic colic: Blasenkolik *f*.
cystic degeneration: zystische Degeneration *f*.
cystic emphysema: bullöses Lungenemphysem *n*.
cysticercosis/*n*: Zystizerkose *f*.
cystic fibroma: Fibroma cysticum *n*.
cystic fibrosis: an autosomal recessive condition that affects the exocrine, or externally secreting, glands. Major symptoms include maldigestion due to decreased pancreatic exocrine function, and chronic bronchopneumonia due to decreased mucociliary transport. zystische Fibrose *f*, Mukoviszidose *f*.
cystic hematoma: zystisches Hämatom *n*.
cystic hyperplasia: glandulär-zystische Hyperplasie *f*.
cystic kidney: polyzystische Nephropathie *f*, Zystenniere *f*.
cystic mastopathy: zystische Mastopathie *f*.
cystine/*n*: Cystin *n*, Zystin *n*.
cystinosis/*n*: autosomal recessive disorder which is characterized by the accumulation of cystine. Symptoms of the infantile form include polyuria, glycosuria, polydipsia and renal failure with secondary rickets. Cystinose *f*.
cystinuria/*n*: Zystinurie *f*.
cystitis/*n*: inflammation of the urinary bladder, usually due to bacterial infection, for example Eschericha coli. Symptoms include pollakiuria, dysuria, nycturia, urinary incontinence, and retropubic pain on palpation. Zystitis *f*, Blasenentzündung *f*.
cystocele/*n*: Zystozele *f*, Blasenhernie *f*.
cystography/*n*: Zystographie *f*.
cystolithiasis/*n*: Zystolithiasis *f*.
cystometric curve: Zystometrogramm *n*.
cystometry/*n*: Zystometrie *f*.
cystoscope/*n*: Zystoskop *n*.
cystostomy/*n*: Zystostomie *f*.
cystotomy/*n*: Zystotomie *f*.
cytarabine/*n*: Cytarabin *n*.
cytidylic acid: Cytidylsäure *f*.
cytisine/*n*: Zytisin *n*.
cytobiology/*n*: Zellbiologie *f*.
cytochrome/*n*: Zytochrom *n*.
cytogenetics/*n*: Zytogenetik *f*.
cytoid body: zytoides Körperchen *n*.
cytokine/*n*: Zytokin *n*.
cytologic smear: zytologischer Abstrich *m*.
cytology/*n*: Zytologie *f*.
cytolysis/*n*: Zytolyse *f*.
cytolytic/*adj*: zytolytisch.
cytomegalovirus/*n*: Zytomegalievirus *n*.
cytopathic/*adj*: zytopathisch.
cytopathic effect: zytopathischer Effekt *m*.
cytophilic/*adj*: zytophil.
cytoplasma/*n*: Zytoplasma *n*.

cytoplasmic granule: zytoplasmatisches Granulum *n*.
cytotoxic/*adj*: zytotoxisch.
cytotoxic antibody: zytotoxischer Antikörper *m*.
cytotoxic reaction: zytotoxische Reaktion *f*.
cytotoxin/*n*: Zellgift *n*.
cytotrophoblast/*n*: Zytotrophoblast *m*.
cytotropic/*adj*: zytotrop.
cytotropic antibody: zytophiler Antikörper *m*.
cytozyme/*n*: Zytozym *n*.
cyturia/*n*: Zyturie *f*.
Czerny suture: Czerny-Naht *f*.

D

D *<abbr>* **1. deuterium; 2. dioptry**: 1. Deuterium *n*, D; 2. Dioptrie *f*, dpt.
dacarbazine/*n*: Dacarbazin *n*.
dacryoadenitis/*n*: Dakryoadenitis *f*.
dacryocystitis/*n*: acute or chronic inflammation of the lower lacrimal passages, including the lacrimal sac. Causes include infections, mainly with Pneumococcus, Streptococcus, or Staphylococcus, congenital anomalies, or stenosis of the lacrimal duct. Dakryozystitis *f*.
dacryocystorhinostomy/*n*: Dakryozystorhinostomie *f*.
dacryolith/*n*: Dakryolith *m*.
dactinomycin/*n*: Dactinomycin *n*.
dactyl/*n*: Finger *m*, Zehe *f*.
dactylitis/*n*: Daktylitis *f*.
dactylogy/*n*: Fingersprache *f*.
dactyloscopy/*n*: Daktyloskopie *f*.
daily dose: Tagesdosis *f*.
daily requirement: Tagesbedarf *m*.
daltonism/*n*: Daltonismus *m*, Rotgrünblindheit *f*.
damage/*n, vb*: 1. Schädigung *f*, Läsion *f*; 2. schädigen, schaden.
damage claim: Schadenersatzanspruch *m*.
damping/*n*: Dämpfung *f*.
danaparoid/*n*: Danaparoid *n*.
danazol/*n*: Danazol *n*.
dancing chorea: Choreomanie *f*, Chorea major *f*.
dandruff/*n*: a condition of the scalp which is characterized by the presence of dry scaling. Kopfgrind *m*, Kopfschuppen.
danofloxacin/*n*: Danofloxacin *n*.
dapiprazol/*n*: Dapiprazol *n*.
dapsone/*n*: Dapson *n*.
daptomycin/*n*: Daptomycin *n*.
darbepoetin alfa: Darbepoetin alfa *n*.
darifenacin/*n*: Darifenacin *n*.
dark adaptation: Dunkeladaptation *f*.
dark-adapted/*adj*: dunkeladaptiert.
dark-field examination: Dunkelfelduntersuchung *f*.
dark-field microscope: Dunkelfeldmikroskop *n*.
darunavir/*n*: Darunavir *n*.
Darwin's theory: Abstammungslehre *f*.
data analysis: Datenanalyse *f*.
database/*n*: Datenbank *f*.
data protection: Datenschutz *m*.
date/*n*: Datum *n*, Termin *m*.
date of birth: Geburtsdatum *n*
daughter cell: Tochterzelle *f*.
daunomycin/*n*: Daunomycin *n*.
daunorubicin/*n*: Daunorubicin *n*.
day care: Tagespflege *f*.
day nursery: Kindertagesstätte *f*.
dazzle reflex: Peiper-Reflex *m*.
dead/*adj*: tot.
dead birth: Totgeburt *f*.
dead body: Leichnam *m*, Leiche *f*.
dead finger: Digitus mortuus *m*, Reil-Finger *m*.
deadly/*adj*: tödlich.
dead space: Totraum *m*.
deaf/*adj*: taub, schwerhörig.
deaf-aid: Hörgerät *n*, Hörhilfe *f*.
deaf-and-dumb language: Taubstummensprache *f*.
deaf-mute/*n, adj*: 1. Taubstummer *m*; 2. taubstumm.
deafness/*n*: partial or complete hearing loss. Forms include conductive deafness with a cause located in the external ear or middle-ear structures, and central deafness with the cause located in the auditory nerve or the auditory centers of the brain. Taubheit *f*, Schwerhörigkeit *f*.

deamination/*n*: Desaminierung *f*.
deanol/*n*: Deanol *n*.
death/*n*: Tod *m*, Exitus *m*.
death certificate/*n*: Totenschein *m*.
death rate/*n*: Sterbeziffer *f*, Mortalität *f*.
debility/*n*: Debilität *f*, Schwäche *f*.
decapitate/*vb*: dekapitieren.
decapsulation/*n*: Dekapsulation *f*, Kapselentfernung *f*.
decay/*n, vb*: 1. Zerfall *m*, Fäulnis *f*; 2. zerfallen, verfaulen.
decerebrate position: Dezerebrationslage *f*.
decerebrate rigidity: Dezerebrationsstarre *f*, Enthirnungsstarre *f*.
decerebration/*n*: Dezerebration *f*.
decidua/*n*: Dezidua *f*.
decidual cell: Deziduazelle *f*.
decidual endometritis: Endometritis decidualis *f*, Deziduitis *f*.
deciduate placenta: Deziduaplazenta *f*.
deciduocellular sarcoma: Chorionkarzinom *n*.
deciduous/*adj*: vergänglich, vorübergehend.
decline/*n, vb*: 1. Verfall *m*, Abnahme *f*, Verminderung *f*; 2. verfallen, abnehmen, abfallen.
decompensation/*n*: Dekompensation *f*.
decomposition/*n*: Aufspaltung *f*, Zersetzung *f*.
decompression/*n*: Dekompression *f*.
decompression chamber: Dekompressionskammer *f*.
decompression sickness: a condition caused by a rapid decrease in atmospheric pressure which results in the formation of nitrogen bubbles in the blood and body tissues. It occurs for example in divers who return rapidly from below sea level. Symptoms include pain in the legs, joints and thorax, skin irritation, numbness and paralysis of the limbs, and vertigo. Dekompressionskrankheit *f*, Caissonkrankheit *f*, Druckfallkrankheit *f*.
deconditioning/*n*: Entkonditionierung *f*.
decrease/*n, vb*: 1. Abnahme *f*, Abfall *m*, Decrementum *n*; 2. nachlassen, absinken, abfallen.
decreased fremitus: abgeschwächter Fremitus *m*.
decreased function: Funktionsminderung *f*.
decreased secretion: verringerte Sekretion *f*, Hyposekretion *f*.
decrement/*n*: Dekrement *n*, Verminderung *f*, Rückgang *m*.
decubital gangrene: Dekubitus *m*.
decubital ulcer: Dekubitalulkus *n*, Druckgeschwür *n*.
decubitus/*n*: lesion over prominent areas on the body of a bedridden person, caused by prolonged pressure. Initial symptoms include reddening of the skin, and formation of blisters, leading to necrotic alterations, and lesions including lower layers of the tissue, muscle, and sometimes skeletal bones. Dekubitus *m*.
decussation/*n*: Kreuzung *f*.
deep/*adj*: tief.
deep coma: tiefes Koma *n*.
deep compartment: tiefes Kompartiment *n*.
deep reflex: Tiefenreflex *m*.
deep sensibility: Tiefensensibilität *f*.
deep sleep: Tiefschlaf *m*.
deep thrombophlebitis: Thrombophlebitis profunda *f*.
deep thrombosis: tiefe Thrombose *f*.
deep transverse arrest: tiefer Querstand *m*.
deep transverse presentation: tiefe Querlage *f*.
deep vein thrombosis: tiefe Venenthrombose *f*.
defecation reflex: Defäkationsreflex *m*.
defect/*n*: Defekt *m*, Mangel *m*.
defense mechanism: Abwehrmechanismus *m*.
defensive force: Abwehrkraft *f*.
defensive reflex: Schutzreflex *m*.
deferiprone/*n*: Deferipron *n*.
deferoxamine/*n*: Deferoxamin *n*.
defibrillator/*n*: Defibrillator *m*.
defibrinated/*adj*: fibrinfrei.
defibrinated blood: defibriniertes

Blut *n*.
deficiency/*n*: Defizienz *f*, Mangel *m*.
deficiency disease: Mangelkrankheit *f*.
deficit/*n*: Defizit *n*.
definitive callus: bleibender Kallus *m*.
deflazacort/*n*: Deflazacort *n*.
deflection/*n*: Deflexion *f*, Ablenkung *f*.
deflexed vertex presentation: Vorderhauptlage *f*.
deformed pelvis: Beckendeformität *f*.
deformed thorax: Thoraxdeformität *f*.
deformity/*n*: Deformität *f*.
degeneration/*n*: Degeneration *f*.
degenerative arthritis: Osteoarthritis *f*.
degenerative disease: degenerative Erkrankung *f*.
degenerative spondylosis: degenerative Spondylose *f*, degenerative Wirbelsäulengelenkerkrankung *f*.
deglutition/*n*: Deglutition *f*, Schluckakt *m*.
degradation/*n*: Abbau *m*.
dehydration/*n*: Dehydratation *f*.
dehydrocholic acid: Dehydrocholsäure *f*.
dehydroepiandrosterone/*n*: Dehydroepiandrosteron *n*, DHEA.
dehydrogenase/*n*: Dehydrogenase *f*.
dejection/*n*: Niedergeschlagenheit *f*.
delavirdine/*n*: Delavirdin *n*.
delay/*n, vb*: 1. Verzögerung *f*; 2. verzögern, hinziehen.
delayed-action preparation: Verzögerungspräparat *n*.
delayed allergy: verzögerte allergische Reaktion *f*.
delayed auditory feedback: verzögerte auditorische Rückkopplung *f*.
delayed conduction: Überleitungsverzögerung *f*.
delayed dentition: delayed teething or delayed eruption of a tooth, for example of the canine tooth. Delayed dentition may occur in association with growth retardation, congenital bone disorders, Nager's acrofacial dysostosis, rickets, and persistence of the thymus. Dentitio tarda *f*, verzögerte Dentition *f*.
delayed puberty: Pubertas tarda *f*.
delayed reaction: Reaktion vom verzögerten Typ *f*, Spätreaktion *f*.
delayed reflex: verzögerte Reflexantwort *m*.
delayed suture: aufgeschobene Naht *f*, verzögerte Naht *f*.
delay time: Verzögerungszeit *f*.
deletion/*n*: Deletion *f*.
delirious mania: delirante Manie *f*.
delirium/*n*: a condition which is characterized by confusion, mental disturbances, impairment of consciousness, orientation and memory, usually occurring in the course of some infectious diseases, high fever, or under the influence of alcohol, drugs, or toxic substances. Delirium *n*.
deliver/*vb*: entbinden.
delivery/*n*: Geburt *f*, Entbindung *f*.
delivery date rule: Naegele-Regel *f*.
delivery room: Kreißsaal *m*.
delta rhythm: Delta-Rhythmus *m*.
deltoid/*n*: Deltoideus *m*, Musculus deltoideus *m*.
delusion/*n*: Wahn *m*, Täuschung *f*.
delusional/*adj*: wahnhaft.
delusional idea: Wahnidee *f*.
delusion of persecution: Verfolgungswahn *m*.
demand/*n, vb*: 1. Anforderung *f*, Erfordernis *n*; 2. fragen, erfordern.
demand feeding: Stillen nach Bedarf.
demarcation/*n*: Demarkation *f*.
demeclocycline/*n*: Demeclocyclin *n*.
demelverine/*n*: Demelverin *n*.
demented/*adj*: dement.
dementia/*n*: a condition which is characterized by significant deterioration of intellectual and cognitive functions. Causes include cerebral arteriosclerosis and infarction, chronic intoxications or alcohol consumption, or head injury. However, in most cases of presenile or senile dementia, no organic cause for disturbance in brain functioning can be identified. Demenz *f*.
demilune body: Halbmond *m*.

demilune cell: Halbmondzelle *f*.
demographic development: Bevölkerungsentwicklung *f*.
demographic structure: Bevölkerungsstruktur *f*.
demography/*n*: Demographie *f*.
demyelinating disease: Entmarkungskrankheit *f*.
demyelinization/*n*: Demyelinisierung *f*, Entmarkung *f*.
denaturation/*n*: Denaturierung *f*.
denaverine/*n*: Denaverin *n*.
dendrite/*n*: Dendrit *m*.
dendritic/*adj*: dendritisch.
dendritic cell: dendritische Zelle *f*.
denervated bladder: autonome Blase *f*.
denervation potential: Denervationspotential *n*.
denial/*n*: Ablehnung *f*, Verleugnung *f*.
densitometry/*n*: Densitometrie *f*.
density/*n*: Dichte *f*.
dental/*adj*: dental.
dental abscess: Zahnabszess *m*.
dental amalgam: Zahnamalgam *n*.
dental calculus: Zahnstein *m*.
dental care: Zahnpflege *f*.
dental cast: Zahnabdruck *m*.
dental cyst: Zahnzyste *f*.
dental fistula: Zahnfleischfistel *f*.
dental formula: Gebissformel *f*, Zahnschema *n*.
dental granuloma: Zahngranulom *n*.
dental hygiene: Zahnpflege *f*.
dental implant: Zahnprothese *f*.
dental orthopedics: Kieferorthopädie *f*.
dental plaque: Zahnbelag *m*.
dental stone: Zahnstein *m*.
dental surgery: Kieferchirurgie *f*.
dental treatment: Zahnbehandlung *f*.
denticle/*n*: Dentikel *m*.
dentin/*n*: Dentin *n*.
dentinoma/*n*: Dentinom *n*.
dentist/*n*: Zahnarzt *m*.
dentistry/*n*: Zahnheilkunde *f*.
dentition/*n*: Dentition *f*, Zahnen *n*.
denture/*n*: Zahnersatz *m*, Gebiss *n*.
deny/*vb*: verweigern.
deodorant/*n*: Deodorant *n*.
deontology/*n*: Deontologie *f*.
deoxidant/*n*: Desoxidationsmittel *n*.
deoxyadenylic acid: Desoxyadenylsäure *f*.
deoxycholeic acid: Desoxycholsäure *f*.
deoxyribonuclease/*n*: Desoxyribonuklease *f*, DNase.
deoxyribonucleic acid: Desoxyribonukleinsäure *f*, DNS.
department/*n*: Abteilung *f*, Station *f*.
dependable/*adj*: zuverlässig.
dependency/*n*: Abhängigkeit *f*, Dependenz *f*.
dependent variable: abhängige Variable *f*.
depersonalization/*n*: Depersonalisation *f*.
depilation/*n*: Depilation *f*, Epilation *f*.
depilatory cream: Enthaarungscreme *f*.
depletion/*n*: Depletion *f*, Entleerung *f*.
deposit/*n, vb*: 1. Ablagerung *f*; 2. ablagern.
depot preparation/*n*: Depotpräparat *n*.
depravation/*n*: Depravation *f*.
depreotide/*n*: Depreotid *n*.
depressed/*adj*: deprimiert.
depressed fracture: Impressionsfraktur *f*.
depression/*n*: a psychiatric condition which is characterized by severe lowering of mood tone, a feeling of melancholy, hopelessness, and dejection. Depression *f*.
depression of pregnancy: Schwangerschaftsdepression *f*.
depressive disorder: depressives Syndrom *n*.
depressive psychosis: depressive Psychose *f*.
depressive reaction: depression or severe lowering of mood tone as a reaction to an external event or situation, for example loss of a closely related person. reaktive Depression *f*.
depressive stupor: depressiver Stupor *m*.
deprivation/*n*: Deprivation *f*.
depth/*n*: Tiefe *f*.
derealization/*n*: Derealisation *f*.

derivation/*n*: Ableitung *f*, Herkunft *f*.
derivative/*n*: Derivat *n*.
derma/*n*: Haut *f*.
dermal sensation: Hautsinn *m*.
dermal sinus: Dermalsinus *m*.
dermal suture: Hautnaht *f*.
dermal test: Hauttest *m*.
dermatitis/*n*: any inflammatory disease of the skin, for example actinic dermatitis which is provoked by exposure to sunlight, or contact dermatitis that is induced by contact with substances that damage the skin. Dermatitis *f*.
dermatofibrosarcoma/*n*: Dermatofibrosarkom *n*.
dermatoglyphics: Dermatoglyphen, Hautleisten.
dermatography/*n*: Dermographie *f*.
dermatologic agent: Dermatikum *n*.
dermatologic lesion: Hautläsion *f*.
dermatology/*n*: Dermatologie *f*.
dermatome/*n*: Dermatom *n*.
dermatomycosis/*n*: any fungal infection of the skin, for example tinea, trichophyton, candida, pityriasis versicolor, or onychomycosis. Systemic fungal diseases like cryptococcosis, blastomycosis or histoplasmosis may also show skin signs. Dermatomykose *f*.
dermatomyositis/*n*: Dermatomyositis *f*.
dermatophyte/*n*: Dermatophyt *m*, Hautpilz *m*.
dermatophytid reaction: Dermatophytid *n*, Id-Reaktion *f*.
dermatosis/*n*: any disorder or disease of the skin, for example dermatitis or eczema. Dermatose *f*.
dermis/*n*: Dermis *f*, Haut *f*.
dermographia/*n*: Dermographie *f*.
dermoid cyst: Dermoidzyste *f*.
descend/*vb*: abstammen, absteigen.
descending tract: absteigender Trakt *m*.
descending urography: Ausscheidungsurographie *f*.
descriptive anatomy: beschreibende Anatomie *f*.
desensitization/*n*: Desensibilisierung *f*.
desferrioxamine/*n*: Desferrioxamin *n*.
desflurane/*n*: Desfluran *n*.
desiccation/*n*: Desikkation *f*, Exsikkation *f*.
design/*n*: Entwurf *m*, Anordnung *f*.
design test: Zeichentest *m*.
desipramine/*n*: Desipramin *n*.
desirudin/*n*: Desirudin *n*.
desloratadine/*n*: Desloratadin *n*.
desmeninol/*n*: Desmeninol *n*.
desmoid/*n, adj*: 1. Desmoid *n*, Fibromatose *f*; 2. desmoid, desmal.
desmopressin/*n*: Desmopressin *n*.
desonide/*n*: Desonid *n*.
desoximetasone/*n*: Desoximetason *n*.
desoxycortone/*n*: Desoxycorton *n*.
desquamation/*n*: Desquamation *f*, Abschuppung *f*.
desquamative erythroderma: Erythrodermia desquamativa neonatorum *f*, Dermatitis exfoliativa Ritter von Rittershain *f*.
desynchronized sleep: desynchronisierter Schlaf *m*, REM-Schlaf *m*.
detached retina: partial or complete detachment of the retina, resulting from retinal lesions, or caused by accumulation of subretinal fluid. Symptoms include photopsia and scotoma. Netzhautablösung *f*.
detachment/*n*: Ablösung *f*, Lösung *f*.
detajmium bitartrate/*n*: Detajmiumbitartrat *n*.
detergent/*n, adj*: 1. Reinigungsmittel *n*, Detergens *n*; 2. oberflächenaktiv.
deterioration/*n*: Verschlechterung *f*.
determination/*n*: Determination *f*.
detoxification/*n*: Detoxikation *f*, Entgiftung *f*.
detrimental/*adj*: nachteilig, schädlich.
detritus/*n*: Detritus *m*.
detrusor/*n*: Detrusor *m*, Musculus detrusor *m*.
deuteranomaly/*n*: Deuteranomalie *f*.
development/*n*: Entwicklung *f*, Entstehung *f*.
developmental age: Entwicklungsalter *n*.
developmental arrest: Entwicklungsstillstand *m*.

developmental crisis: Entwicklungskrise *f*.
developmental defect: Entwicklungsschaden *m*.
developmental disorder: Entwicklungsstörung *f*.
developmental malformation: Entwicklungsfehlbildung *f*.
developmental period: Entwicklungsphase *f*.
development stage: Entwicklungsstadium *n*.
deviant behavior: abweichendes Verhalten *n*.
deviation/*n*: Deviation *f*, Abweichung *f*, Fehlstellung *f*.
deviation angle: Schielwinkel *m*.
device/*n*: Vorrichtung *f*, Hilfsmittel *n*.
dexamethasone/*n*: Dexamethason *n*.
dexibuprofen/*n*: Dexibuprofen *n*.
dexketoprofen/*n*: Dexketoprofen *n*.
dextran/*n*: Dextran *n*.
dextran sulfate: Dextransulfat *n*.
dextrocardia/*n*: Dextrokardie *f*.
dextrophobia/*n*: extreme or morbid fear of objects on the right side of the body, frequently associated with levophilia. Dextrophobie *f*.
dextroposed aorta: reitende Aorta *f*.
dextrothyroxine sodium: Dextrothyroxin-Natrium *n*.
dhobie itch: Dhobie-Itch *m*, Wäscherkrätze *f*.
diabetes/*n*: a disorder of carbohydrate metabolism which is characterized by excessive concentrations of glucose in the blood and urine, and a relative or absolute lack of insulin. Diabetes *m*, Diabetes mellitus *m*.
diabetes screening test: Diabetes-Suchtest *m*.
diabetic/*n, adj*: 1. Diabetiker *m*; 2. diabetisch.
diabetic acidosis: diabetische Ketoazidose *f*.
diabetic amyotrophy: diabetische Amyotrophie *f*.
diabetic cataract: diabetische Katarakt *f*.
diabetic coma: a condition which is characterized by a loss of consciousness, due to severe ketoacidosis in uncontrolled diabetes mellitus. diabetisches Koma *n*, ketoazidotisches Koma *n*.
diabetic gangrene: diabetische Gangrän *f*.
diabetic glycosuria: diabetische Glukosurie *f*.
diabetic nephropathy: any disease of the kidneys which is related to diabetes mellitus. Forms include diabetic glomerulosclerosis, arterionephrosclerosis, arteriolonephrosclerosis, and papillary necrosis and pyelonephritis. diabetische Nephropathie *f*.
diabetic polyneuritis: diabetische Polyneuropathie *f*.
diabetic polyneuropathy: diabetische Polyneuropathie *f*.
diabetic retinopathy: a condition of the retina of the eye which is related to diabetes mellitus and which is characterized by microvascular abnormalities, microaneurysms, and nonperfusion with consecutive retinal neovascularization. diabetische Retinopathie *f*.
diabetic xanthoma: diabetisches Xanthom *n*.
diabetogenic/*adj*: diabetogen.
diacetic acid: Acetessigsäure *f*.
diacetonuria/*n*: Ketonurie *f*, Acetonurie *f*.
diacetylnalorphine/*n*: Diacetylnalorphin *n*.
diagnosis/*n*: Diagnose *f*.
diagnostic/*adj*: diagnostisch.
diagnostic radiology: Röntgendiagnostik *f*.
diagnostics/*n*: Diagnostik *f*.
diagnostic sensitivity: diagnostische Sensitivität *f*.
diagnostic test: diagnostischer Test *m*.
diagonal conjugate: Conjugata diagonalis *f*.
diagonal diameter: schräger Beckendurchmesser *m*.
diagram/*n*: Diagramm *n*.
dialysis/*n*: Dialyse *f*.
dialysis membrane: Dialysemembran *f*.

diameter/*n*: Diameter *m*, Durchmesser *m*.
diaminodiphenyl sulfone: Diaminodiphenylsulfon *n*.
α,δ-diaminovaleric acid: α,δ-Diaminovaleriansäure *f*, Ornithin *n*.
diapedesis/*n*: Diapedese *f*.
diapedetic bleeding: Diapedeseblutung *f*.
diaper/*n*: Windel *f*.
diaper rash: an erythema of the skin in the diaper area of infants, caused by the chemical and physical action of urine and feces. As complications, chronic infections may occur. Windelerythem *n*.
diaphoretic/*n, adj*: 1. Diaphoretikum *n*; 2. schweißtreibend.
diaphragm/*n*: Diaphragma *n*, Zwerchfell *n*, Membran *f*, Blende *f*.
diaphragmatic breathing: Zwerchfellatmung *f*.
diaphragmatic flutter: Zwerchfellzuckung *f*.
diaphragmatic hernia: Zwerchfellhernie *f*, Morgagni-Hernie *f*.
diaphragmatic muscle: Zwerchfell *n*.
diaphragmatic paralysis: Zwerchfellähmung *f*.
diaphragmatic respiration: Zwerchfellatmung *f*.
diaphragm position: Blendeneinstellung *f*.
diaphyseal dysplasia: diaphysäre Dysplasie *f*, Camurati-Engelmann-Syndrom *n*.
diaphyseal-epiphyseal fusion: Knochenverschmelzung *f*.
diaphysis/*n*: Diaphyse *f*.
diaplacental infection: diaplazentare Infektion *f*.
diarrhea/*n*: Diarrhö *f*, Durchfall *m*.
diarthrosis/*n*: Diarthrose *f*.
diastase/*n*: Diastase *f*.
diastole/*n*: Diastole *f*.
diastolic/*adj*: diastolisch.
diastolic murmur: diastolisches Geräusch *n*, Diastolikum *n*.
diastolic pressure: diastolischer Blutdruck *m*.
diastolic sound: diastolisches Geräusch *n*, Diastolikum *n*.
diathermy/*n*: Diathermie *f*.
diatrizoic acid: Diatrizoesäure *f*.
diazepam/*n*: Diazepam *n*.
diazobenzenesulfonic acid: Diazobenzolsulfonsäure *f*.
diazoxide/*n*: Diazoxid *n*.
dibasic amino acid: dibasische Aminosäure *f*.
dibekacin/*n*: Dibekacin *n*.
dibenzepin/*n*: Dibenzepin *n*.
N,N'-dibenzylethylenediamine penicillin: Benzathin-Penicillin *n*.
dicarboxylic acid: Dicarbonsäure *f*.
dichlorethane/*n*: Dichlorethan *n*.
dichlorvos/*n*: Dichlorvos *n*.
diclazuril/*n*: Diclazuril *n*.
diclofenac/*n*: Diclofenac *n*.
diclofenamide/*n*: Diclofenamid *n*.
dicloxacillin/*n*: Dicloxacillin *n*.
dicoumarol/*n*: Dicoumarol *n*, Dicumarol *n*.
dicrotic/*adj*: dikrot.
dicrotic pulse: Dikrotie *f*.
dicrotic wave: dikrote Welle *f*.
didanosine/*n*: Didanosin s.
dideoxycytosine/*n*: Dideoxycytosin *n*.
die/*n, vb*: 1. Matrize *f*; 2. sterben.
dielectric/*adj*: dielektrisch.
diencephalic syndrome: a syndrome which is characterized by disorders of endocrine and autonomic functions, resulting from a lesion of the pathways which connect hypothalamus and pituitary gland. Zwischenhirnsyndrom *n*.
diet/*n, vb*: 1. Diät *f*, Ernährung *f*; 2. Diät leben.
dietary/*adj*: diätetisch.
dietary advice: Diätberatung *f*, Ernährungsberatung *f*.
dietary fat: Nahrungsfett *n*.
dietary fiber: Ballaststoff *m*.
dietary habit: Ernährungsgewohnheit *f*.
dietary protein: Nahrungseiweiß *n*.
dietary therapy: Diättherapie *f*.
dietetics/*n*: Diätlehre *f*.
diethylbarbituric acid: Diäthylbarbitursäure *f*, Barbital *n*.
diethylcarbamazine/*n*: Diäthylcarbamazin *n*.

diethylstilbestrol/*n*: Diäthylstilböstrol *n*.
diethylstilbestrol syndrome: a congenital anomaly of the cervix in the newborn which results from exposure of the mother during pregnancy toward diethylstilbestrol or DES. In later life, endometriosis and adenocarcinoma can develop. Stilböstrol-Syndrom *n*, DES-Syndrom *n*.
dietician/*n*: Diätassistent *m*.
difference/*n*: Differenz *f*, Unterschied *m*.
differential/*n, adj*: 1. Differential *n*; 2. differentiell.
differential diagnosis: Differentialdiagnose *f*, DD.
differentiate/*vb*: differenzieren.
difficult breathing: Atemnot *f*, Dyspnoe *f*.
diffraction/*n*: Diffraktion *f*.
diffuse antral gastritis: diffuse Antrumgastritis *f*.
diffuse arterial ectasia: rankenförmiges Aneurysma *n*.
diffuse cerebral sclerosis: diffuse Hirnsklerose *f*.
diffuse congenital hyperkeratosis: Ichthyosis congenita *f*.
diffuse cortical sclerosis: Alpers-Syndrom *n*.
diffuse corticomeningeal angiomatosis: Bogaert-Divry-Syndrom *n*.
diffuse epilepsy: diffuse Epilepsie *f*.
diffuse esophageal spasm: diffuser Ösophagospasmus *m*, Bársony-Teschendorf-Syndrom *n*.
diffuse interstitial pulmonary fibrosis: diffuse interstitielle Lungenfibrose *f*, Hamman-Rich-Syndrom *n*.
diffuse myelitis: disseminierte Myelitis *f*.
diffuse proliferative glomerulonephritis: diffuse proliferative Glomerulonephritis *f*.
diffuse scleroderma: diffuses Sklerodermn *n*.
diffuse sclerosing encephalitis: subakute sklerosierende Panenzephalitis *f*, SSPE.
diffusion/*n*: Diffusion *f*.
diflorasone/*n*: Diflorason *n*.
diflucortolone/*n*: Diflucortolon *n*.
diflunasil/*n*: Diflunasil *n*.
digallic acid: Tanninsäure *f*.
digest/*vb*: verdauen.
digestion/*n*: Digestion *f*, Verdauung *f*.
digestive enzyme: Verdauungsenzym *n*.
digestive fever: alimentäres Fieber *n*.
digestive organ: Verdauungsapparat *m*.
digestive system: Verdauungstrakt *m*, Magen-Darm-Trakt *m*.
digit/*n*: Finger *m*, Zahl *f*.
digital/*adj*: digital.
digital agnosia: Fingeragnosie *f*.
digital examination: digitale Untersuchung *f*.
digital gigantism: Makrodaktylie *f*.
digitalis/*n*: Digitalis *m*.
digitalis glycoside: Digitalisglykosid *n*.
digitalis-induced tachycardia: digitalisinduzierte Tachykardie *f*.
digital ray: Phalanx *f*, Fingerstrahl *m*.
digital reflex: Fingerreflex *m*.
digitoxin/*n*: Digitoxin *n*.
digoxin/*n*: Digoxin *n*.
dihydralazine/*n*: Dihydralazin *n*.
dihydrocodeine/*n*: Dihydrocodein *n*.
dihydrocortisone/*n*: Dihydrocortison *n*.
dihydroergocornine/*n*: Dihydroergocornin *n*.
dihydroergocristine/*n*: Dihydroergocristin *n*.
dihydroergocryptine/*n*: Dihydroergocryptin *n*.
dihydroergotamine/*n*: Dihydroergotamin *n*.
dihydrostreptomycin/*n*: Dihydrostreptomycin *n*.
dihydrotachysterol/*n*: Dihydrotachysterol *n*.
dihydroxybenzoic acid: Dioxybenzoesäure *f*.
2,5,-dihydroxyphenylacetic acid: Dihydroxyphenylessigsäure *f*, Homogentisinsäure *f*.
diiodotyrosine/*n*: Dijodtyrosin *n*.
dilatation/*n*: Dilatation *f*.

dilated stomach: Magendilatation *f*.
dilated ureter: Ureterdilatation *f*.
dilating pains: Eröffnungswehen.
dilator/*n*: Dilatator *m*, Dehnsonde *f*.
dilazep/*n*: Dilazep *n*.
diltiazem/*n*: Diltiazem *n*.
diluted solution: verdünnte Lösung *f*.
dilution/*n*: Dilution *f*, Verdünnung *f*.
dilution anemia: Verdünnungsanämie *f*.
dimenhydrinate/*n*: Dimenhydrinat *n*.
dimepranol/*n*: Dimepranol *n*.
dimercaprol/*n*: Dimercaprol *n*.
dimetacrine/*n*: Dimetacrin *n*.
dimethylacetic acid: Isobuttersäure *f*.
dimethylaminobenzaldehyde/*n*: Dimethylaminobenzaldehyd *m*, Ehrlich-Reagens *n*.
2-dimethylaminoethyl benzilate: Tropalpin *n*.
dimethyl sulfoxide/*n*: Dimethylsulfoxid *n*.
dimethyltryptamine/*n*: Dimethyltryptamin *n*.
diminution of contrast: Kontrastverminderung *f*.
dimple/*n*: Grübchen *n*.
dinoprost/*n*: Dinoprost *n*.
dinoprostone/*n*: Dinoproston *n*.
dioptometry/*n*: Dioptometrie *f*, Optometrie *f*.
dioptric power: Dioptriestärke *f*.
dioptry/*n*: Dioptrie *f*, dpt.
dioxin/*n*: Dioxin *n*.
diphenhydramine/*n*: Diphenhydramin *n*.
diphosphoglyceric acid: Diphosphoglyzerinsäure *f*.
diphtheria/*n*: an acute infection caused by the bacterium Corynebacterium diphtheriae. Symptoms include a dense gray membrane at the place of inoculation, usually the throat, larynx or trachea. Damage from endotoxins can result in myocarditis, and neuritis. Diphtherie *f*.
diphtheritic conjunctivitis: Conjunctivitis diphtherica *f*.
diphtheritic croup: diphtherischer Krupp *m*.
diphtheritic enteritis: diphtherische Enteritis *f*.
diphtheritic membrane: diphtherische Membran *f*.
diphtheritic neuritis: diphtherische Neuritis *f*.
diphtheritic tonsillitis: diphtherische Tonsillitis *f*.
dipivefrine/*n*: Dipivefrin *n*.
diplegia/*n*: Diplegie *f*.
diplococcus/*n*: Diplokokke *f*, Diplococcus *m*.
diploid/*adj*: diploid.
diplopia/*n*: Diplopie *f*.
dipotassium clorazepate: Dikaliumclorazepat *n*.
dipsomania/*n*: Dipsomanie *f*, periodische Trunksucht *f*.
dipstick/*n*: Teststreifen *m*, Urinstick *m*.
dipyridamole/*n*: Dipyridamol *n*.
direct auscultation/*n*: direkte Auskultation *f*.
direct bilirubin: direktes Bilirubin *n*.
directed movement: Zielbewegung *f*.
direct flap: Nahplastik *f*.
direct infection: Kontaktinfektion *f*.
direct light: Auflicht *n*.
direct percussion: direkte Perkussion *f*.
direct symptom: Leitsymptom *n*.
disability/*n*: Behinderung *f*, Unfähigkeit *f*.
disabled/*adj*: behindert.
disablement/*n*: Behinderung *f*, Invalidität *f*.
disaccharide/*n*: Disaccharid *n*.
disagreement/*n*: Diskrepanz *f*.
disappearance/*n*: Verschwinden *n*, Rückbildung *f*.
disarticulation/*n*: Exartikulation *f*.
discerning ability: Einsichtsfähigkeit *f*.
discharge/*n, vb*: 1. Absonderung *f*, Ausfluss *m*, Entladung *f*, Entlassung *f*; 2. ausscheiden, entlassen.
disciform macular degeneration: scheibenförmige Makuladegeneration *f*, Kuhnt-Junius-Krankheit *f*.
discomfort/*n*: Unwohlsein *n*.
discontinuity/*n*: Diskontinuität *f*.
discrepancy/*n*: Diskrepanz *f*.
discrete/*adj*: einzeln.
discretion/*n*: Diskretion *f*.

D

discrimination/*n*: Diskrimination *f*, Unterscheidung *f*.
discriminatory power: Unterscheidungsvermögen *n*.
disease/*n*: Erkrankung *f*, Krankheit *f*.
disease outbreak: Krankheitsausbruch *m*.
disease stage: Krankheitsstadium *n*.
dish/*n*: Schale *f*, Schüssel *f*.
disinfectant/*n, adj*: 1. Desinfektionsmittel *n*; 2. desinfizierend.
disinfestation/*n*: Entlausung *f*.
disjunction/*n*: Disjunktion *f*.
disk/*n*: Scheibe *f*, Bandscheibe *f*.
disk disease: Diskopathie *f*, Bandscheibenerkrankung *f*.
dislocation/*n*: Dislokation *f*, Luxation *f*.
dislocation fracture: Dislokationsfraktur *f*, Luxationsfraktur *f*.
disopyramide/*n*: Disopyramid *n*.
disorder/*n*: Störung *f*, Erkrankung *f*.
disorientation/*n*: Desorientiertheit *f*, Orientierungsstörung *f*.
dispensatory/*n*: Arzneimittelverordnungsbuch *n*.
dispersing lens: Zerstreuungslinse *f*.
dispersion/*n*: Dispersion *f*.
displacement/*n*: Verlagerung *f*, Verschiebung *f*.
display/*n, vb*: 1. Darstellung *f*, Entfaltung *f*; 2. entfalten, darstellen.
disposable/*n, adj*: 1. Einwegartikel *m*; 2. Einmal-.
disposable syringe: Einwegspritze *f*.
disproportion/*n*: Disproportion *f*.
disruption/*n*: Disruption *f*, Unterbrechung *f*.
dissecting/*adj*: dissezierend.
dissecting aneurysm: dissezierendes Aneurysma *n*.
dissecting forceps: Sezierpinzette *f*.
dissection/*n*: Dissektion *f*, Ausräumung *f*.
disseminated intravascular coagulation: disseminierte intravasale Gerinnung *f*, DIC, Verbrauchskoagulopathie *f*.
disseminated neuritis: Polyneuritis *f*.
disseminated sclerosis: a chronic, progressive disease of the central nervous system of unknown cause. The condition is characterized by multiple scarlike, demyelinating lesions and inflammatory changes on the brain and spinal cord. Symptoms depend on the localization of lesions and may include vision disorders, weakness, paralysis, and tremor. Encephalomyelitis disseminata *f*, multiple Sklerose *f*.
dissemination/*n*: Dissemination *f*.
dissociated affect: inadäquater Affekt *m*.
dissociated sensory loss: dissoziierte Sensibilitätsstörung *f*, Empfindungsdissoziation *f*.
dissociation/*n*: Dissoziation *f*.
dissolution/*n*: Zersetzung *f*, Auflösung *f*.
distal/*adj*: distal.
distal muscular dystrophy: distale Muskeldystrophie *f*.
distal renal tubular acidosis: renale tubuläre Azidose *f*.
distance/*n*: Distanz *f*, Entfernung *f*.
distant cardiac murmur: Distanzton *m*.
distant flap: Fernplastik *f*.
distant metastasis: Fernmetastase *f*.
distended/*adj*: gebläht.
distichiasis/*n*: Distichiasis *f*.
distigmine/*n*: Distigmin *n*.
distigmine bromide: Distigminbromid *n*.
distillation/*n*: Destillation *f*.
distilled water: destilliertes Wasser *n*.
distortion/*n*: Distorsion *f*.
distress/*n*: Leiden *n*, Qual *f*.
distribution/*n*: Verteilung *f*.
district general hospital: allgemeines Kreiskrankenhaus *n*.
disturbance/*n*: Störung *f*.
disulfiram/*n*: Disulfiram *n*.
disuse/*n*: Nichtgebrauch *m*.
dithranol/*n*: Dithranol *n*.
diuresis/*n*: Diurese *f*.
diuretic/*n, adj*: 1. Diuretikum *n*; 2. diuretisch.
diurnal/*adj*: am Tag, diurnus.
diurnal epilepsy: Wachepilepsie *f*.
diurnal rhythm: zirkadianer Rhythmus *m*.

diurnal variation: Tagesschwankung *f*.
divergent squint: Strabismus divergens *m*, Auswärtsschielen *n*, Exotropie *f*.
divers' ear: Taucherohr *n*.
diversity/*n*: Diversität *f*, Verschiedenheit *f*.
diverticulitis/*n*: inflammation of small pouches or diverticulum in the large intestine. Symptoms include spasmodic pain, abdominal tenderness, constipation, meteorism, nausea, and vomiting. As complications obstruction, bleeding, or perforation may occur. Divertikulitis *f*.
diverticulosis/*n*: Divertikulose *f*.
diverticulum/*n*: Divertikel *n*.
divided pancreas: Pancreas divisum *n*.
division/*n*: Teilung *f*.
dizygotic/*adj*: dizygot, zweieiig.
dizziness/*n*: Benommenheit *f*, Schwindel *m*, Vertigo *f*.
DNA <*abbr*> **deoxyribonucleic acid**: Desoxyribonukleinsäure *f*, DNS, DNA.
dobutamine/*n*: Dobutamin *n*.
docetaxel/*n*: Docetaxel *n*.
doctor/*n*: Doktor *m*, Arzt *m*.
documentation/*n*: Dokumentation *f*.
dofetilide/*n*: Dofetilid *n*.
dolasetron/*n*: Dolasetron *n*.
dolor/*n*: Schmerz *m*.
domestic accident: Haushaltsunfall *m*.
domestic plague: Rattenpest *f*.
dominant/*adj*: dominant.
dominant gene: dominantes Gen *n*.
dominant hemisphere: dominante Hemisphäre *f*.
domperidone/*n*: Domperidon *n*.
donepezil/*n*: Donepezil *n*.
donor/*n*: Spender *m*.
donor organ: Spenderorgan *n*.
dopa decarboxylase: DOPA-Decarboxylase *f*.
dopamine/*n*: Dopamin *n*.
dopaminergic receptor: dopaminerger Rezeptor *m*.
dopexamine/*n*: Dopexamin *n*.
doping/*n*: Doping *n*.
dormant/*adj*: ruhend.
dornase alfa: Dornase alfa *f*.
dorsal/*adj*: dorsal.
dorsal curve: Dorsalkrümmung *f*.
dorsal position: Rückenlage *f*.
dorsal root: Hinterwurzel *f*.
dorsiflexion/*n*: Dorsalflexion *f*.
dorsosacral position: Steinschnittlage *f*.
dorsum/*n*: Rücken *m*.
dorzolamide/*n*: Dorzolamid *n*.
dosage/*n*: Dosierung *f*, Dosis *f*.
dose/*n, vb*: 1. Dosis *f*; 2. dosieren.
dose-dependent/*adj*: dosisabhängig.
dose-finding study: Dosisfindungsstudie *f*.
dose unit: Dosiseinheit *f*.
dosulepin/*n*: Dosulepin *n*.
dot/*n, vb*: 1. Fleck *m*, Punkt *m*; 2. punktieren, tüpfeln.
double aorta: doppelte Aorta *f*.
double aortic arch: doppelter Aortenbogen *m*.
double athetosis: Athétose double *f*, Hammond-Krankheit *f*.
double-blind trial: Doppelblindstudie *f*.
double-button suture: Knopflochnaht *f*.
double cannula: Doppelkanüle *f*.
double combination: Zweifachkombination *f*.
double consciousness: Bewusstseinsspaltung *f*.
double contrast enema: Doppelkontrasteinlauf *m*.
double fracture: zweifache Fraktur *f*.
double helix: Doppelhelix *f*.
double image: Doppelbild *n*.
double-mouthed uterus: Uterus biforis *m*.
double pleurisy: beidseitige Pleuritis *f*.
double pneumonia: beidseitige Lungenentzündung *f*.
double-point threshold: Zweipunktediskriminationsschwelle *f*.
double-recurrent catheter: Doppellumenkatheter *m*.
double-stranded/*adj*: doppelsträngig.
double-stranded DNA: doppelsträngige DNA *f*.

double ureter: Ureter duplex *m*.
double uterus: Uterus duplex *m*, Uterus didelphys *m*.
double vaccination: Doppeltimpfung *f*.
double vision: Doppeltsehen *n*, Diplopie *f*.
double voice: Doppelstimme *f*, Diphonie *f*.
doubly armed suture: Doppelnadelnaht *f*.
douche/*n, vb*: 1. Spülung *f*; 2. spülen.
Douglas pouch: Douglas-Raum *m*, Excavatio rectouterina *f*.
downregulation/*n*: Downregulation *f*, Herunterregulation *f*.
doxapram/*n*: Doxapram *n*.
doxazosin/*n*: Doxazosin *n*.
doxepin/*n*: Doxepin *n*.
doxorubicin/*n*: Doxorubicin *n*.
doxycycline/*n*: Doxycyclin *n*.
draft/*n*: Arzneitrunk *m*.
dragon worm: Drachenwurm *m*, Dracunculus medinensis *m*.
drain/*n, vb*: 1. Drain *m*, Abfluss *m*; 2. drainieren, ableiten.
drainage/*n*: Drainage *f*.
drape/*n, vb*: 1. Operationsabdecktuch *n*; 2. abdecken.
drastic/*adj*: drastisch, durchgreifend.
drawer sign: Schubladenphänomen *n*.
drawing/*n*: Zeichnung *f*.
dream/*n*: Traum *m*.
dreamy state: Dreamy State, Traumzustand *m*.
drepanocyte/*n*: Drepanozyt *m*, Sichelzelle *f*.
drepanocytic anemia: Sichelzellenanämie *f*.
dressing/*n*: Verband *m*, Kleidung *f*.
Dressler syndrome: a condition occurring weeks or months after myocardial infarction which is characterized by fever, pleurisy, and pneumonia. Dressler-Syndrom *n*, Postmyokardinfarktsyndrom *n*.
dribble/*vb*: tröpfeln.
dried human plasma: humanes Trockenplasma *n*.
dried milk: Trockenmilch *f*.
drift/*n*: Treiben *n*, Drift *f*.
drill/*n*: Bohrer *m*.
drink/*n, vb*: 1. Getränk *n*, Trunk *m*; 2. trinken.
drinking behavior: Trinkverhalten *n*.
drip/*n, vb*: 1. Tropfen; 2. tröpfeln.
drip infusion: Infusion *f*, Tropf *m*.
drive/*n*: Trieb *m*, Antrieb *m*.
driving/*n*: Driving *n*, Steuerung *f*.
dromedary curve: Dromedarkurve *f*.
drop/*n, vb*: 1. Sturz *m*, Tropfen *m*; 2. stürzen, tropfen.
droperidol/*n*: Droperidol *n*.
drop finger: Hammerfinger *m*.
drop foot: Fallfuß *m*.
drop hand: Fallhand *f*.
drop heart: Tropfenherz *n*.
droplet infection: Tröpfcheninfektion *f*.
dropped beat: ausgefallene Systole *f*, Mobitz-Block *m*.
dropper/*n*: Pipette *f*.
dropsical nephritis: nephrotisches Syndrom *n*.
dropsy/*n*: Ödem *n*, Hydrops *m*.
drostanolone/*n*: Drostanolon *n*.
drowning/*n*: Ertrinken *n*.
drowsiness/*n*: Schläfrigkeit *f*, Somnolenz *f*.
drowsy/*adj*: schläfrig, somnolent.
drug/*n*: Medikament *n*, Arznei *f*, Droge *f*.
drug act: Arzneimittelgesetz *n*.
drug action: Arzneimittelwirkung *f*.
drug-drug interaction: Arzneimittelwechselwirkung *f*.
drug eruption: a visible cutaneous rash, following the administration of a drug or medicine, systematically or locally. A drug rash is a sign for intolerance against the drug. Arzneimittelexanthem *n*.
drug-fast/*adj*: arzneimittelresistent.
drug-induced/*adj*: medikamentös bedingt.
drug-induced pancreatitis: medikamenteninduzierte Pankreatitis *f*.
drug regulatory authority: Arzneimittelzulassungsbehörde *f*.
drug-resistant/*adj*: arzneimittelresistent.
drug use: Drogenkonsum *m*.
drum head: Trommelfell *n*.

drumming noise: Trommelgeräusch *n*.
drumstick finger: finger with a short, broad tip and overhanging nail, resembling a drumstick. Forms include idiopathic clubbing of the fingers, present at birth, or secondary forms associated with chronic liver disease, bacterial endocarditis, cyanotic heart disease, or chronic suppuration. Trommelschlägelfinger *m*.
drunken gait: schwankender Gang *m*.
drunkenness/*n*: Trunkenheit *f*.
dry/*vb, adj*: 1. trocknen; 2. trocken.
dry bronchiectasis: trockene Bronchiektasie *f*.
dry bronchitis: trockene Bronchitis *f*.
dry cough: trockener Husten *m*.
dry extract: Trockenextrakt *m*.
dry gangrene: trockene Gangrän *f*.
dry mouth: Mundtrockenheit *f*, Xerostomie *f*.
dry pleurisy: trockene Pleuritis *f*, Pleuritis sicca *f*.
dry rale: trockenes Rasselgeräusch *n*, Rhonchus *m*.
dry skin: trockene Haut *f*.
dry synovitis: Synovitis sicca *f*.
dual-chamber pacing: Zweikammerstimulation *f*.
duck-billed speculum: Sims-Spekulum *n*.
duck gait: Watschelgang *m*.
duct/*n*: Gang *m*.
ductal papillary carcinoma: Papillengangkarzinom *n*.
ductal papilloma: intraduktales Papillom *n*.
due date: errechneter Geburtstermin *m*.
dull/*adj*: stumpf, dumpf.
dullness/*n*: Dämpfung *f*, Stumpfheit *f*.
dull sound: dumpfes Geräusch *n*.
duloxetine/*n*: Duloxetin *n*.
dumb/*adj*: stumm, dumm.
dumb rabies: stille Lyssa *f*, paralytische Tollwut *f*.
dumping syndrome: a syndrome characterized by gastrointestinal and cardiovascular signs and symptoms like diarrhea, nausea, weakness, sweating, palpitation, headache etc. following food intake in persons who had gastrectomy. Dumpingsyndrom *n*, Postgastrektomiesyndrom *n*.
duodenal/*adj*: duodenal.
duodenal atresia: Duodenalatresie *f*.
duodenal diverticulum: Duodenaldivertikulose *f*.
duodenal obstruction: Duodenumverlegung *f*.
duodenal regurgitation: duodenaler Reflux *m*.
duodenal stenosis: Duodenalstenose *f*.
duodenal ulcer: an ulcer located in the duodenum, usually due to excessive presence of gastric acid. Symptoms include epigastric pain, especially after food intake, and fasting pain. Duodenalulkus *n*, Ulcus duodeni *n*.
duodenitis/*n*: Duodenitis *f*.
duodenogastric reflux: duodenaler Reflux *m*.
duodenojejunal angle: Flexura duodenojejunalis *f*.
duodenoplasty/*n*: Duodenoplastik *f*.
duplicated sound: verdoppelter Herzton *m*, Doppelton *m*.
duplication/*n*: Duplikation *f*.
dural forceps: Duralklemme *f*.
duration/*n*: Dauer *f*.
dust allergy: Hausstauballergie *f*.
dutasteride/*n*: Dutasterid *n*.
duty/*n*: Pflicht *f*, Dienst *m*.
dwarf/*n*: Zwerg *m*.
dye/*n, vb*: 1. Farblösung *f*, Färbung *f*; 2. färben.
dying/*n*: Sterben *n*.
dying-back neuropathy: Dying-back-Neuropathie *f*.
dynamic imaging: dynamische Bildgebung *f*.
dynamics/*n*: Dynamik *f*.
dysarthria/*n*: Dysarthrie *f*.
dyschezia/*n*: Dyschezie *f*.
dyschondroplasia/*n*: Dyschondroplasie *f*.
dyscoria/*n*: Dyskorie *f*.
dysdiadochokinesia/*n*: Dysdiadochokinese *f*.

D

dysentery/*n*: a condition which is characterized by diarrhea, associated with difficult bowel movements, resulting from irritation or infection of the gastrointestinal tract, for example in amebiasis or bacillary dysentery. Dysenterie *f*.
dysesthesia/*n*: Dysästhesie *f*.
dysfunction/*n*: Dysfunktion *f*, Funktionsstörung *f*.
dysfunctional uterine bleeding: dysfunktionelle Uterusblutung *f*.
dyshidrotic eczema: Pompholyx *m*.
dyskeratosis/*n*: Dyskeratose *f*, Verhornungsstörung *f*.
dyskeratotic eczema: dyskeratotisches Ekzem *n*.
dyskinesia/*n*: Dyskinesie *f*.
dyslalia/*n*: Dyslalie *f*.
dyslexia/*n*: Dyslexie *f*.
dysmenorrhea/*n*: menstruation which is associated with colic-like pain not related to the intensity of the bleeding. Causes include organic diseases, for example of the uterus, and mental factors; idiopathic dysmenorrhea occurs without detectable cause. Dysmenorrhö *f*, schmerzhafte Menstruation *f*.
dysmyelopoietic syndrome: myelodysplastisches Syndrom *n*.
dysostosis/*n*: Dysostose *f*.
dyspareunia/*n*: Dyspareunie *f*.
dyspepsia/*n*: a functional disturbance of the upper gastrointestinal tract, especially of the stomach, which is characterized by abdominal discomfort. Dyspepsie *f*.
dysphagia/*n*: Dysphagie *f*.
dysplasia/*n*: Dysplasie *f*.
dysplastic/*adj*: dysplastisch.
dyspnea/*n*: labored breathing or shortness of breath. Causes include physical effort, cardiac disease, or pulmonary diseases, for example pneumonia. Dyspnoe *f*.
dyspraxia/*n*: Dyspraxie *f*.
dysproteinemic purpura: Purpura hyperglobulinaemica *f*, Waldenström-Syndrom *n*.
dysthymic disorder: dysthyme Störung *f*.
dystocia/*n*: Dystokie *f*.
dystopic kidney: dystope Niere *f*.
dystrophic degeneration: dystrophische Degeneration *f*.
dystrophy/*n*: Dystrophie *f*.
dysuria/*n*: Dysurie *f*.

E

E. <*abbr*> **1. emmetropia; 2. eye**: 1. Emmetropie *f*; 2. Auge *n*.
ear/*n*: Ohr *n*.
earache/*n*: Ohrenschmerz *m*.
ear bones: Gehörknöchelchen.
ear deformity: Ohrfehlbildung *f*.
eardrum/*n*: Trommelfell *n*.
eardrum perforation: penetration of the membrana tympani, usually due to infections such as otitis media, or as therapeutic intervention with an incision of the tympanic membrane, so-called myringotomy. Trommelfellperforation *f*
early/*adj*: früh.
early abortion: Frühabort *m*.
early cancer: Frühkarzinom *n*.
early diagnosis: Frühdiagnose *f*.
early infantile autism: frühkindlicher Autismus *m*, Kanner-Syndrom *n*.
early manifestation: Frühform *f*.
early mobilization: Frühmobilisation *f*.
early neonatal period: Perinatalzeit *f*.
early-onset diabetes: diabetes mellitus type I with a sudden onset in the young around the age of twelve and in which basal insulin secretion is suddenly reduced or ceasing, possibly due to an autoimmune reaction. juveniler Diabetes *m*.
early operation: Frühoperation *f*.
early phase: Frühphase *f*.
early pregnancy: Frühschwangerschaft *f*.
early stage: Frühstadium *n*.
early symptom: Frühsymptom *n*.
early treatment: Frühbehandlung *f*.
ear malformation: Ohrfehlbildung *f*.
ear molds: Hörhilfe *f*.
ear noise: Ohrgeräusch *n*, Tinnitus *m*.
ear, nose and throat: Hals-, Nasen-, Ohren-, HNO.
earwax/*n*: Ohrenschmalz *m*, Zerumen *n*.
ease/*n, vb*: 1. Erleichterung *f*, Linderung *f*; 2. erleichtern.
East African trypanosomiasis: ostafrikanische Trypanosomiasis *f*.
Eastern schistosomiasis: Schistosomiasis japonica *f*.
eat/*vb*: essen.
eating behavior: Essgewohnheit *f*.
eating disorder: Essstörung *f*.
ebastin/*n*: Ebastin *n*.
Ebola virus: Ebola-Virus *n*.
ebriety/*n*: Trunkenheit *f*.
EBV <*abbr*> **Epstein-Barr virus**: Epstein-Barr-Virus *n*, EBV.
eccentric hypertrophy: exzentrische Hypertrophie *f*.
eccentric occlusion: exzentrische Okklusion *f*, Seitbiss *m*.
ecchondroma/*n*: Ekchondrom *n*.
ecchymosis/*n*: a discoloration of the skin caused by the extravasation of blood beneath skin. Ekchymose *f*.
eccrine/*adj*: ekkrin.
eccrine gland: ekkrine Drüse *f*.
ECG <*abbr*> **electrocardiography/*n***: Elektrokardiographie *f*, EKG.
echinococcosis/*n*: an infestation with echinococcus, a type of tapeworm. Symptoms include initially unspecific signs, in later stages, echinococcal cysts may cause compression of internal organs, infected cysts or perforation of cysts can cause severe general symptoms. Echinokokkose *f*.
echocardiogram/*n*: Echokardiogramm *n*.
echocardiography/*n*: Echokardiographie *f*.

E

echolalia/*n*: Echolalie *f*, Echophrasie *f*.
eclampsia/*n*: Eklampsie *f*.
eclamptic psychosis: eklamptische Psychose *f*.
ecology/*n*: Ökologie *f*.
econazole/*n*: Econazol *n*.
ectasia/*n*: Ektasie *f*.
ecthyma/*n*: Ekthym *n*.
ectoderm/*n*: Ektoderm *n*.
ectogenous/*adj*: ektogon, exogen.
ectopia/*n*: Ektopie *f*.
ectopic/*adj*: ektop.
ectopic beat: Extrasystole *f*.
ectopic hormone production: ektope Hormonbildung *f*.
ectopic pacemaker: ektoper Schrittmacher *m*.
ectopic rhythm: ektoper Rhythmus *m*.
ectopic tachycardia: ektope Tachykardie *f*.
ectopic testis: ektoper Hoden *m*.
ectozoic parasite: Ektozoon *n*, tierischer Ektoparasit *m*.
ectrodactyly/*n*: Ektrodaktylie *f*.
eculizumab/*n*: **Eculizumab** *n*.
eczema/*n*: an inflammatory disorder of the skin which is characterized by pruritus, erythema, papules or vesicles, hyperkeratosis, serous exudation, and crusting. Ekzem *n*.
eczematoid dermatitis: Ekzem *n*.
eczematoid seborrhea: seborrhoische Dermatitis *f*.
eczematous conjunctivitis: Conjunctivitis phlyctaenulosa *f*.
edema/*n*: Ödem *n*.
edematous/*adj*: ödematös.
edetic acid: Edetinsäure *f*, Ethylendiamintetraessigsäure *f*, EDTA.
edge/*n*: Kante *f*, Rand *m*.
education/*n*: Erziehung *f*, Ausbildung *f*.
EEG <*abbr*> **1. electroencephalogram; 2. electroencephalography**: 1. Elektroenzephalogramm *n*, EEG; 2. Elektroenzephalographie *f*, EEG.
efavirenz/*n*: Efavirenz *n*.
effect/*n, vb*: 1. Wirkung *f*, Effekt *m*; 2. bewirken.
effective/*adj*: wirksam, effektiv.
effective dose: Wirkdosis *f*, Effektivdosis *f*, ED.
effective fertility: effektive Fertilität *f*.
effector cell: Effektorzelle *f*.
efferent/*adj*: efferent.
efferent fiber: efferente Faser *f*.
efferent vessel: efferentes Gefäß *n*.
effervescent/*adj*: schäumend, sprudelnd.
efficacious/*adj*: wirkungsvoll, effektiv.
efficacy/*n*: Wirksamkeit *f*.
efficiency/*n*: Effizienz *f*.
effleurage/*n*: Effleurage *f*.
efflorescence/*n*: Effloreszenz *f*.
effort/*n*: Anstrengung *f*.
effort proteinuria: presence of excessive amounts of protein in the urine following physical stress or vigorous exercise. Belastungsproteinurie *f*.
effusion/*n*: Erguss *m*.
egg/*n*: Ei *n*.
egg cell: Ei *n*, Eizelle *f*.
egocentric/*adj*: egozentrisch, ichbezogen.
Egyptian ophthalmia: an infectious disease of the eye, caused the bacterium Chlamydia trachomatis. Symptoms include swelling of the conjunctiva and hypersecretion, followed by the formation of so-called trachoma inclusion bodies. Conjunctivitis trachomatosa *f*, Trachom *n*.
ejaculation/*n*: Ejakulation *f*.
ejection click: Ejektionsclick *m*, Austreibungston *m*.
elaidic acid: Elaidinsäure *f*.
elastic/*adj*: elastisch.
elastic bandage: elastische Binde *f*.
elastic cartilage: elastischer Knorpel *m*.
elastic fiber: elastische Faser *f*.
elastic garment: elastische Binde *f*.
elastic skin: Cutis elastica *f*.
elastic tissue: elastisches Bindegewebe *n*.
elastin/*n*: Elastin *n*.
elation/*n*: gehobene Stimmung *f*, Hochgefühl *n*.
elbow/*n*: Ellenbogen *m*.
elective/*adj*: elektiv.

elective surgery: elektiver Eingriff *m*.
electrical analgesia: Elektrostimulationsanalgesie *f*.
electrical cataract: Cataracta electrica *f*, Blitzstar *m*.
electric coagulation: Elektrokoagulation *f*.
electric cradle: Lichtkasten *m*.
electricity/*n*: Elektrizität *f*.
electric ophthalmia: aktinische Konjunktivitis *f*.
electric power: Strom *m*.
electric probe: Elektrosonde *f*.
electric stimulation: elektrische Stimulation *f*.
electrocardiogram/*n*: Elektrokardiogramm *n*, EKG.
electrocardiography/*n*: Elektrokardiographie *f*, EKG.
electroconvulsive therapy: Elektrokrampftherapie *f*, EKT.
electrocortical potential: kortikales EEG-Potential *n*.
electrode/*n*: Elektrode *f*.
electroencephalogram/*n*: Elektroenzephalogramm *n*.
electrolysis/*n*: Elektrolyse *f*.
electrolyte/*n*: Elektrolyt *n*.
electrolyte balance: Elektrolythaushalt *m*.
electromagnetic/*adj*: elektromagnetisch.
electromagnetic field: elektromagnetisches Feld *n*.
electromagnetic radiation: elektromagnetische Strahlung *f*.
electromyogram/*n*: Elektromyogramm *n*, EMG.
electron/*n*: Elektron *n*.
electron microscopy: Elektronenmikroskopie *f*.
electron spin resonance: Elektronenspinresonanz *f*.
electrophoresis/*n*: Elektrophorese *f*.
electroretinogram/*n*: Elektroretinogramm *n*.
electrotherapy/*n*: Elektrotherapie *f*.
element/*n*: Element *n*, Grundbestandteil *m*.
elementary body: Elementarkörperchen *n*.
elephantiasis/*n*: Elephantiasis *f*.
eletriptan/*n*: Eletriptan *n*.
elevated lesion: erhabene Läsion *f*.
elevation/*n*: Erhebung *f*, Anhebung *f*.
elevator/*n*: Heber *m*, Musculus levator *m*.
elimination/*n*: Elimination *f*.
elimination rate: Eliminationsrate *f*, Ausscheidungsrate *f*.
ELISA <*abbr*> **enzyme-linked immunosorbent assay**: enzymgekoppelter Immunoassay *m*, ELISA.
elixir/*n*: Elixir *n*.
elliptic amputation: ovaläre Amputation *f*, Ovalärschnitt *m*.
elliptocytic anemia: hereditäre Elliptozytose *f*.
elution/*n*: Elution *f*.
elvucitabine/*n*: Elvucitabin *n*.
embolectomy/*n*: Embolektomie *f*.
embolic abscess: embolischer Abszess *m*.
embolic gangrene: embolische Gangrän *f*.
embolic infarct: Infarktembolie *f*.
embolic thrombus: Thromboembolus *m*.
embolism/*n*: Embolie *f*.
embolus/*n*: an aggregate of blood cells, fat or tumor cells, a foreign body, or an air thrombus inside a blood vessel. Symptoms result from the obstruction of blood circulation. Embolus *m*.
embryo/*n*: Embryo *m*.
embryo development: Embryonalentwicklung *f*.
embryoid body: Embryoid *n*.
embryology/*n*: Embryologie *f*.
embryonal/*adj*: embryonal.
embryonal carcinoma: embryonales Karzinom *n*.
embryonal leukemia: Stammzellenleukämie *f*.
embryonal nuclear cataract: embryonale Kernkatarakt *f*.
embryonal sarcoma: embryonales Sarkom *n*.
embryonal tumor: embryonaler Tumor *m*.
embryonic circulation: Embryonalkreislauf *m*.
embryonic organ: Embryonalorgan *n*.

embryonic period: Embryonalperiode *f*.
embryopathy/*n*: Embryopathie *f*.
embryotomy/*n*: Embryotomie *f*.
embryo transfer: Embryonentransfer *m*.
emedastine/*n*: Emedastin *n*.
emepronium/*n*: Emepronium *n*.
emergence/*n*: Auftreten *n*, Ausbruch *m*.
emergency/*n*: Notfall *m*.
emergency admission: Notaufnahme *f*.
emergency care: Notfallversorgung *f*.
emergency medicine: Notfallmedizin *f*.
emesis/*n*: casting-up of the stomach or intestine content through the mouth. Causes include bodily disorders like inflammations of the gastrointestinal tract, central nervous diseases, or metabolic disorders. Emesis can be of psychic origin, or may be caused by external factors, for example intoxication, drug-induced vomiting. Emesis *f*, Erbrechen *n*.
emetic/*n*: Emetikum *n*, Brechmittel *n*.
emetine/*n*: Emetin *n*.
EMG *<abbr>* **electromyogram**/*n*: Elektromyogramm *n*, EMG.
eminence/*n*: Erhöhung *f*, Vorsprung *m*.
eminent/*adj*: erhaben.
emission spectrum: Emissionsspektrum *n*.
emmetropia/*n*: Emmetropie *f*, E.
emollient/*n*: Emolliens *n*.
emotion/*n*: Emotion *f*, Gefühl *n*.
emotional/*adj*: emotional.
emotional psychosis: Emotionspsychose *f*.
emotional stupor: Emotionsstupor *m*.
empathy/*n*: Empathie *f*.
emphysema/*n*: Emphysem *n*.
emphysematous chest: Emphysemthorax *m*.
emphysematous gangrene: gangrenous tissue lesion, usually resulting from infection in a wound with anaerobic bacteria like Clostridium, with putrefaction of tissue and the formation of gas. Gasgangrän *f*.
emphysematous thorax: Emphysemthorax *m*.
empiricism/*n*: Empirismus *m*.
empty/*vb, adj*: 1. leeren; 2. leer.
emptying/*n*: Entleerung *f*.
empyema/*n*: collection of pus in a cavity or a hollow organ, especially in the thoracic cavity and the lungs. Empyem *n*.
emtricitabine/*n*: Emtricitabin *n*.
emulsion/*n*: Emulsion *f*.
emylcamate/*n*: Emylcamat *n*.
enalapril/*n*: Enalapril *n*.
enalaprilat/*n*: Enalaprilat *n*.
enamel/*n*: Emaille *f*, Schmelz *m*.
enarthrosis/*n*: Enarthrose *f*.
encapsulated abscess: gekammerter Abszess *m*.
encephalic/*adj*: Enzephalon-.
encephalitis/*n*: diffuse or localized inflammation of the brain, usually due to infection with a virus, bacterium, or another pathogenic microorganism. Symptoms include febrile illness, impairment of consciousness, seizures, and meningoencephalitic signs. Enzephalitis *f*.
encephalocele/*n*: Enzephalozele *f*.
encephalofacial angiomatosis: enzephalofaziale Angiomatose *f*, Sturge-Weber-Krabbe-Syndrom *n*.
encephalogram/*n*: Enzephalogramm *n*.
encephalomalacia/*n*: Enzephalomalazie *f*.
encephalomeningitis/*n*: Enzephalomeningitis *f*, Meningoenzephalitis *f*.
encephalomyelitis/*n*: Enzephalomyelitis *f*.
encephalon/*n*: Encephalon *n*, Gehirn *n*.
encephalo-ophthalmic dysplasia: Dysplasia encephaloophthalmica *f*, Reese-Syndrom *n*.
encephalopathy/*n*: Enzephalopathie *f*.
enchondral ossification: enchondrale Ossifikation *f*.
enchondroma/*n*: Enchondrom *n*.
encopresis/*n*: involuntary defecation due to the inability to control the

anal sphincter, not resulting from an organic defect but associated with mental factors, regression, or insufficient toilet training. Enkopresis *f*, Einkoten *n*.

encyst/*vb*: einkapseln, enzystieren.

end/*n, vb*: 1. Ende *n*; 2. beenden, enden.

endangiitis/*n*: Endangiitis *f*.

endarteritis/*n*: Endarteriitis *f*.

end-diastolic ventricular volume: enddiastolisches Ventrikelvolumen *n*.

endemic/*n, adj*: 1. Endemie *f*; 2. endemisch.

endemic goiter: endemische Struma *f*.

endemic Kaposi sarcoma: endemisches Kaposi-Sarkom *n*.

endemic paralytic vertigo: Neuronitis vestibularis *f*.

endemic polyneuritis: Beriberi *f*.

end group: Endgruppe *f*.

ending/*n*: Endigung *f*, Endung *f*.

endocardial fibroelastosis: Endokardfibroelastose *f*.

endocardial pacing: endokardiale Schrittmacherstimulation *f*.

endocarditis/*n*: acute or chronic inflammation of the inner lining of the heart, especially of the heart valves, usually due to infection with a virus, bacterium, or fungus. Endokarditis *f*.

endocervicitis/*n*: Endometritis cervicis *f*.

endocrine/*adj*: endokrin.

endocrine ablative therapy: hormonelle Ablationstherapie *f*.

endocrine adenomatosis: multiple endokrine Neoplasie *f*, MEN.

endocrine gland: endokrine Drüse *f*.

endocrine obesity: endokrine Obesitas *f*.

endocrine ophthalmopathy: endokriner Exophthalmus *f*.

endocrine polyglandular syndrome: an autosomal dominant inherited syndrome which is characterized by the presence of benign or malignant neoplasms of more than one endocrine gland and neurocutaneous alterations. multiple endokrine Neoplasie *f*, MEN.

endocrine system: endokrines System *n*, Endokrinium *n*.

endocrinology/*n*: Endokrinologie *f*.

endoderm/*n*: Endoderm *n*, Entoderm *n*.

endogenous/*adj*: endogen.

endogenous depression: psychiatric disorder with severe lowering of mood, independent of events or external factors that could justify a depressive reaction. endogene Depression *f*.

endogenous toxin: Endotoxin *n*.

endolymph/*n*: Endolymphe *f*.

endolymphatic shunt: endolymphatische Fistel *f*.

endometrial biopsy: Endometriumbiopsie *f*.

endometrial cyst: Endometriumzyste *f*.

endometrial hyperplasia: Endometriumhyperplasie *f*.

endometrial stromal sarcoma: Endometriumsarkom *n*.

endometrioma/*n*: Endometriom *n*.

endometriosis/*n*: a condition which is characterized by the presence of endometrial tissue outside the uterus, for example the ovaries, broad ligaments, or rectovaginal septum. Symptoms include menstrual bleeding in the ectopic locations, dysmenorrhea, and pelvic pain. Endometriose *f*.

endometritis/*n*: Endometritis *f*.

endometrium/*n*: Endometrium *n*.

endomyocardial fibrosis: Endomyokardfibrose *f*.

endoneural fibroma: Neurofibrom *n*.

endoneurial sheath: Endoneuralscheide *f*.

endoneurium/*n*: Endoneurium *n*.

endophytic/*adj*: endophytisch.

endophytic papilloma: endophytisches Papillom *n*.

endoplasm/*n*: Endoplasma *n*.

endoplasmic/*adj*: endoplasmatisch.

end-organ/*n*: Endorgan *n*.

endorphin/*n*: Endorphin *n*.

endoscope/*n*: Endoskop *n*.

endoscopic biopsy: endoskopische Biopsie *f*.
endoscopic papillosphincterotomy: endoskopische Papillotomie *f*, EPT.
endoscopic retrograde cholangiography: endoskopische retrograde Cholangiographie *f*.
endoscopy/*n*: Endoskopie *f*.
endothelial cell: Endothelzelle *f*.
endothelioma/*n*: Endotheliom *n*.
endotoxin shock: Endotoxinschock *m*.
endotracheal/*adj*: endotracheal.
endotracheal tube: Endotrachealtubus *m*.
end point: Endpunkt *m*.
end-stage renal failure: terminale Niereninsuffizienz *f*.
end-systolic/*adj*: endsystolisch.
end-systolic volume: endsystolisches Volumen *n*.
end-to-end: End-zu-End-.
end-to-side: End-zu-Seit-.
end-to-side shunt: End-zu-Seit-Anastomose *f*.
enema/*n*: Klistier *n*.
energy/*n*: Energie *f*.
energy balance: kalorisches Gleichgewicht *n*.
energy quotient: Energiequotient *m*.
energy transfer: Energieübertragung *f*.
enervation/*n*: Denervierung *f*, Enervierung *f*.
enflurane/*n*: Enfluran *n*.
enfuvirtide/*n*: Enfuvirtid *n*.
engaged head: Kopfeinstellung *f*.
engorged kidney: Stauungsniere *f*.
engram/*n*: Engramm *n*.
enhancement/*n*: Verstärkung *f*.
enkephalin/*n*: Enkephalin *n*.
enlarged lymph node: vergrößerter Lymphknoten *m*.
enlarged spleen: Splenomegalie *f*.
enlargement/*n*: Erweiterung *f*, Vergrößerung *f*.
enophthalmos/*n*: Enophthalmus *m*.
enostosis/*n*: Enostose *f*.
enoxacin/*n*: Enoxacin *n*.
enriched culture medium: angereicherter Nährboden *m*.
enrichment/*n*: Anreicherung *f*.
enrofloxacin/*n*: Enrofloxacin *n*.
ensheathing callus: äußerer Kallus *m*.
ensiform/*adj*: ensiformis, schwertförmig.
ENT <*abbr*> **ear, nose and throat**: Hals-, Nasen-, Ohren-, HNO.
entacapone/*n*: Entacapon *n*.
entecavir/*n*: Entecavir *n*.
enteral/*adj*: enteral.
enteral nutrition: enterale Ernährung *f*.
enteric/*adj*: enteral.
enteric-coated tablet: gastrointestinales therapeutisches System *n*, GITS.
enteric fever: Salmonellose *f*.
enteritis/*n*: inflammation of the intestinal tract, usually due to viral or bacterial infection, irritating food, or infarction of intestinal tissue secondary to vascular occlusion. Enteritis *f*.
enteroanastomosis/*n*: Enteroanastomose *f*.
enterobiasis/*n*: Enterobiasis *f*.
enterocele/*n*: Enterozele *f*.
enterochromaffin cell: enterochromaffine Zelle *f*.
enterococcus/*n*: Enterokokke *f*.
enterocolitis/*n*: Enterokolitis *f*.
enterogastritis/*n*: inflammation of the stomach and intestine, usually caused by viral, bacterial, or parasitic infection. Symptoms include nausea and vomiting, diarrhea, and abdominal discomfort. Gastroenteritis *f*.
enterogenous cyanosis: Nitratzyanose *f*, Stokvis-Talma-Syndrom *n*.
enterohepatic/*adj*: enterohepatisch.
enterohepatic circulation: enterohepatischer Kreislauf *m*.
enterokinase/*n*: Enterokinase *f*.
enterolith/*n*: Enterolith *m*, Kotstein *m*.
enteropathic reactive arthritis: postenteritische Arthritis *f*, Begleitarthritis *f*.
enteropathy/*n*: Enteropathie *f*.
enteroptosis/*n*: Enteroptose *f*.
enterostenosis/*n*: Enterostenose *f*.
enterotomy/*n*: Enterotomie *f*.

enterovesical fistula: enterovesikale Fistel *f*.
enterovirus/*n*: Enterovirus *n*.
entoderm/*n*: Entoderm *n*, Endoderm *n*.
entozoic parasite: Darmparasit *m*.
entrance/*n*: Zugang *m*, Pforte *f*, Porta *f*.
entrance block: Eintrittsblock *m*.
entrance wound: Einschusswunde *f*.
entrapment/*n*: Einklemmung *f*, Einschluss *m*.
entrapment neuropathy: any neuropathy in which a peripheral nerve is injured by compression through surrounding tissue, for example carpal tunnel syndrome, Morton's neuralgia, or tarsal tunnel syndrome. Nervenkompressionssyndrom *n*.
enucleation/*n*: Enukleation *f*.
enuresis/*n*: inability to control urination in an age at which bladder control should be possible. Bedwetting may be a sign of emotional stress, or it may be associated with organic disorders such as neurologic diseases, malformation or infections of the lower urinary tract, or metabolic disorders. Enurese *f*, Einnässen *n*.
envelope protein: Hüllprotein *n*.
environment/*n*: Umwelt *f*, Umfeld *n*.
environmental disease: Umweltkrankheit *f*.
environmental factor: Umweltfaktor *m*.
environmental influence: Umwelteinfluss *m*.
environmental medicine: Umweltmedizin *f*.
environmental temperature: Umgebungstemperatur *f*.
enzyme/*n*: Enzym *n*, Ferment *n*.
enzyme deficiency: Enzymmangel *m*.
enzyme-linked immunosorbent assay: enzymgekoppelter Immunadsorbentassay *m*, ELISA.
enzyme-substrate complex: Enzym-Substrat-Komplex *m*.
eosinophil/*n, adj*: 1. Eosinophiler *m*; 2. eosinophil.
eosinophil adenoma: eosinophiles Adenom *n*.
eosinophil granules: eosinophile Granula.
eosinophilia/*n*: Eosinophilie *f*.
eosinophilic endomyocardial disease: Löffler-Endokarditis *f*.
eosinophilic esophagitis: eosinophile Ösophagitis *f*.
eosinophilic gastroenteritis: eosinophile Gastroenteritis *f*.
eosinophilic granuloma: eosinophiles Granulom *n*.
eosinophilic leukemia: Eosinophilenleukämie *f*.
eosinophilic leukocyte: Eosinophiler *m*.
eosinophilic lung: eosinophiles Lungeninfiltrat *n*, Löffler-Syndrom *n*.
eosinophilic pneumonitis: eosinophiles Lungeninfiltrat *n*, Löffler-Syndrom *n*.
eosinophilic pustular dermatosis: eosinophile pustulöse Dermatose *f*.
ependyma/*n*: Ependym *n*.
ependymal cell: Ependymzelle *f*.
ependymal cyst: Ependymzyste *f*.
ependymal glioma: Ependymom *n*.
ependymoma/*n*: Ependymom *n*.
ephedrine/*n*: Ephedrin *n*.
ephelides/*n*: Epheliden, Sommersprossen.
ephemeral fever: Eintagsfieber *n*.
EPH gestosis <*abbr*> **edema-proteinuria-hypertension gestosis**: EPH-Gestose *f*, Gestose mit Ödemen, Proteinurie und Hypertonus *f*.
epiblepharon/*n*: Epiblepharon *n*.
epicardium/*n*: Epikard *n*.
epicillin/*n*: Epicillin *n*.
epicondyle/*n*: Epikondylus *m*.
epicondylitis/*n*: a condition which is characterized by pain in the arm and inflammatory reaction of the epicondylus and the tendons, caused by excessive strain, particularly occurring when twisting inward. Epikondylitis *f*, Tennisellenbogen *m*.
epicrisis/*n*: Epikrise *f*.
epicritic sensibility: epikritische Sensibilität *f*.

epidemic/*n, adj*: 1. Epidemie *f*; 2. epidemisch.

epidemic benign dry pleurisy: an infectious disease caused by coxsackieviruses of group B. Symptoms include pain in the thoracic region and upper abdomen, and fever. A characteristic feature is a relapse occurring four to six days after the original attack. epidemische Pleurodynie *f*, Bornholmer Krankheit *f*.

epidemic conjunctivitis: Schwimmbadkonjunktivitis *f*.

epidemic dropsy: Epidemic Dropsy.

epidemic exfoliative dermatitis: Epidermolysis acuta toxica *f*, Lyell-Syndrom *n*.

epidemic hemorrhagic fever: epidemisches hämorrhagisches Fieber mit renalem Syndrom *n*, Nephropathia epidemica *f*.

epidemic hepatitis: epidemische Hepatitis *f*, Hepatitis A *f*.

epidemic infantile paralysis: Kinderlähmung *f*, Poliomyelitis anterior acuta *f*.

epidemic louse-borne typhus: Läusefleckfieber *n*, epidemisches Fleckfieber *n*.

epidemic myalgia: an infectious disease caused by coxsackieviruses of group B. Symptoms include pain in the thoracic region and upper abdomen, and fever. A characteristic feature is a relapse occurring four to six days after the original attack. Myalgia acuta epidemica *f*, Bornholmer Krankheit *f*.

epidemic nephropathy: Nephropathia epidemica *f*, epidemisches hämorrhagisches Fieber mit renalem Syndrom *n*.

epidemic parotitis: an infectious disease caused by a paramyxovirus. Symptoms include a characteristic swelling of the parotid glands, pain under the ears or under the chin, and fever. As complication, infections of the pancreas or, predominantly in adults, of the testis may occur. Parotitis epidemica *f*, Mumps *m*.

epidemics control: Seuchenbekämpfung *f*.

epidemiologic/*adj*: epidemiologisch.

epidemiology/*n*: Epidemiologie *f*.

epidermal/*adj*: epidermal.

epidermal cyst: Epidermiszyste *f*.

epidermal test: Epikutantest *m*.

epidermis/*n*: Epidermis *f*.

epidermolysis/*n*: Epidermolyse *f*.

epidermolytic hyperkeratosis: bullöse Ichthyosis *f*.

epidermophytosis/*n*: Epidermophytie *f*.

epidermous carcinoma: Plattenepithelkarzinom *n*.

epididymitis/*n*: inflammation of the epididymis which covers the upper end of the testicle. Causes include bacterial infection such as gonorrhea, unspecific prostatitis, and unsterile surgery of the prostate. Symptoms include pain radiating in the inguinal canal, redness of the scrotal skin, and fever. Epididymitis *f*.

epididymo-orchitis/*n*: Epididymoorchitis *f*.

epidural/*adj*: epidural.

epidural abscess: Epiduralabszess *m*, epiduraler Abszess *m*.

epidural anesthesia: Epiduralanästhesie *f*.

epidural ascending spinal paralysis: epidurale aszendierende Spinalparalyse *f*.

epidural block: Epiduralanästhesie *f*.

epidural cavity: Epiduralraum *m*.

epidural hematoma: accumulation of blood in the epidural space, usually due to a traumatic injury of the brain and rupture of the meningeal artery. Symptoms occur after an interval without any clinical signs and may include unconsciousness, focal neurologic signs, and pupillomotor disorders. Epiduralhämatom *n*.

epidural space: Epiduralraum *m*.

epigastric/*adj*: epigastrisch.

epigastric abdominal pain: Oberbauchschmerz *m*.

epigastric angle: epigastrischer Winkel *m*.

epigastric pulse: epigastrische Pulsation *f*.
epigastric region: Epigastrium *n*.
epiglottis/*n*: Epiglottis *f*, Kehldeckel *m*.
epilating forceps: Epilationspinzette *f*.
epilation/*n*: Epilation *f*, Enthaarung *f*.
epilepsy/*n*: a neurologic disorder which is characterized by the occurrence of seizures or convulsions. The condition may occur without obvious cause as idiopathic epilepsy, it can be due to brain disorders, or be associated with metabolic or infectious diseases affecting the brain. Major types of epilepsy include grand mal, petit mal, and focal seizures. Epilepsie *f*.
epileptic/*n, adj*: 1. Epileptiker *m*; 2. epileptisch.
epileptic attack: epileptischer Anfall *m*.
epileptic coma: epileptischer Nachschlaf *m*.
epileptic focus: epileptischer Herd *m*.
epileptic hallucination: epileptische Halluzination *f*.
epileptic myoclonus: Myoklonusepilepsie *f*.
epileptic state: Status epilepticus *m*.
epileptic threshold: Krampfschwelle *f*.
epileptic vertigo: epileptischer Schwindel *m*.
epileptiform/*adj*: epileptiform.
epileptogenic/*adj*: epileptogen.
epimenorrhea/*n*: Hypermenorrhö *f*.
epinephrine/*n*: Epinephrin *n*.
epineurium/*n*: Epineurium *n*.
epiphyseal cartilage: Epiphysenknorpel *m*.
epiphyseal detachment: Epiphysenlösung *f*.
epiphyseal fracture: Epiphysenfraktur *f*.
epiphysis/*n*: Epiphyse *f*.
epiphysitis/*n*: Epiphysitis *f*.
epiploon/*n*: großes Netz *n*, Omentum majus *n*.
epirubicin/*n*: Epirubicin *n*.
episcleral space: Episkleralraum *m*.
episcleritis/*n*: inflammation of the sclera, often bilateral, and frequently without detectable organic cause. Symptoms include localized pain and tenderness in the involved area. Episkleritis *f*.
episiotomy/*n*: Episiotomie *f*.
episode/*n*: Episode *f*.
epistaxis/*n*: hemorrhage from the nasal mucosa, mostly in the nasal septum. Causes include injury, arterial hypertension, blood coagulation disorders, leukemia, or acute infections; in many cases epistaxis occurs without evident cause as idiopathic nosebleed. Epistaxis *f*, Nasenbluten *n*.
epithelial/*adj*: epithelial.
epithelial body: Epithelkörperchen *n*, Nebenschilddrüse *f*.
epithelial border: Epithelgrenze *f*.
epithelial cast: Epithelzylinder *m*.
epithelial cell: Epithelzelle *f*.
epithelial cyst: Epithelzyste *f*.
epithelial layer: Epithelschicht *f*.
epithelial lining: Epithelauskleidung *f*.
epithelial sheath: Hertwig-Scheide *f*, Wurzelscheide *f*.
epithelial tissue: Epithelgewebe *n*.
epithelial tumor: Epitheltumor *m*.
epithelioma/*n*: Epitheliom *n*.
epithelium/*n*: Epithel *n*.
epitheloid cell: Epitheloidzelle *f*.
epitrochlea/*n*: Epitrochlea *f*.
epizoonosis/*n*: a skin disease that is caused by an animal parasite in or on the skin, for example infestation with pubic lice. Epizoonose *f*.
epizootic aphtha: an infectious disease of animals caused by a picornavirus, which can be transmitted to humans by direct contact. Symptoms include fever, malaise, headache, and vesiculation of the mouth and fingertips. Maul- und Klauenseuche *f*.
eplerenone/*n*: Eplerenon *n*.
epoetin/*n*: Epoetin *n*.
eponym/*n*: Eponym *n*.
eprazinone/*n*: Eprazinon *n*.
eprinomectin/*n*: Eprinomectin *n*.

eprosartan/*n*: Eprosartan *n*.
eptifibatide/*n*: Eptifibatid *n*.
equal/*adj*: gleich.
equational division: Äquationsteilung *f*.
equatorial plate: Äquatorialplatte *f*.
equianalgesic dose: analgetische Äquivalenzdosis *f*.
equilibration/*n*: Äquilibrierung *f*.
equilibratory disorder: Gleichgewichtsstörung *f*.
equilibrium/*n*: Äquilibrium *n*, Gleichgewicht *n*.
equine gait: Steppergang *m*.
equinovalgus/*n*: Spitzfuß *m*.
equipment/*n*: Gerät *n*, Ausstattung *f*.
erect/*vb, adj*: 1. aufrichten, erigieren; 2. aufrecht, erigiert.
erectile/*adj*: erektil.
erectile dysfunction: a condition which is characterized by disordered or missing erection, usually due to vascular diseases, nerve lesions, or environmental and mental factors. erektile Dysfunktion *f*, Erektionsstörung *f*.
erection/*n*: Erektion *f*.
ergocalciferol/*n*: Ergocalciferol *n*, Vitamin D_2 *n*.
ergograph/*n*: Ergometer *n*.
ergometer/*n*: Ergometer *n*.
ergonomics/*n*: Ergonomie *f*.
ergosterol/*n*: Ergosterin *n*, Ergosterol *n*.
ergot alkaloid: Ergotalkaloid *n*, Mutterkornalkaloid *n*.
ergotamine/*n*: Ergotamin *n*.
ergotherapy/*n*: Ergotherapie *f*, Beschäftigungstherapie *f*.
ergotism/*n*: Ergotismus *m*.
eritrityl tetranitrate: Eritrityltetranitrat *n*.
erlotinib/*n*: Erlotinib *n*.
erogenous zone: erogene Zone *f*.
erosion/*n*: Erosion *f*.
erosive balanitis: erosive Balanitis *f*.
erosive chancre: erosiver Primäraffekt *m*.
erosive gastritis: erosive Gastritis *f*.
erotic/*adj*: erotisch.
error/*n*: Fehler *m*.
ertapenem/*n*: Ertapenem *n*.
erucic acid: Erucasäure *f*.
eructation/*n*: Eruktation *f*.
eruption/*n*: Eruption *f*, Ausbruch *m*.
eruptive gingivitis: eruptive Gingivitis *f*.
eruptive xanthoma: eruptives Xanthom *n*.
erysipelas/*n*: an acute bacterial infection of the skin with hemolytic Streptococcus. Symptoms include a spreading, but well-demarcated inflammation of the skin with redness, fever, and pain. Erysipel *n*.
erysipeloid/*n, adj*: 1. Erysipeloid *n*, Rotlauf *m*; 2. erysipelartig.
erythema/*n*: redness of the skin, usually due to capillary dilatation. Causes include for example infections, autoimmune reactions, and hypersensitivity reactions. Erythem *n*.
erythema threshold: Erythemschwelle *f*.
erythematous/*adj*: erythematös.
erythroblastic anemia: Erythroblastenanämie *f*.
erythrocyanosis/*n*: Erythrozyanose *f*.
erythrocyte/*n*: Erythrozyt *m*.
erythrocyte sedimentation rate: Blutkörperchensenkungsgeschwindigkeit *f*, BSG.
erythrocytic phase: intraerythrozytäres Stadium *n*.
erythrocytolysis/*n*: Erythrozytolyse *f*.
erythrocytopenia/*n*: a decrease in the number of erythrocytes, resulting in anemia. Erythrozytopenie *f*.
erythrocytosis/*n*: Erythrozytose *f*.
erythrocyturia/*n*: Erythrozyturie *f*.
erythroderma/*n*: Erythrodermie *f*.
erythrodermic psoriasis: erythrodermale Psoriasis *f*.
erythromycin/*n*: Erythromycin *n*.
erythromycin estolate: Erythromycinestolat *n*.
erythromycin ethylsuccinate: Erythromycinethylsuccinat *n*.
erythromycin propionate: Erythromycinpropionat *n*.
erythropoietic porphyria: kongenitale erythropoetische Porphyrie *f*.
erythropoietin/*n*: Erythropoetin *n*,

EPO.
escape/*n, vb*: 1. Ausströmen *n*, Entweichen *n*; 2. ausströmen, entweichen.
escaped beat: Extrasystole *f*.
escape reflex: Fluchtreflex *m*.
eserine/*n*: Eserin *n*, Physostigmin *n*.
esketamine/*n*: Esketamin *n*.
esmolol/*n*: Esmolol *n*.
esomeprazole/*n*: Esomeprazol *n*.
esophageal/*adj*: ösophageal.
esophageal achalasia: inability of the cardia of the esophagus to relax and to open, caused by disturbances in innervation, or lesions of ganglions. Symptoms include dysphagia, regurgitation, and eventually substernal pain. Ösophagusachalasie *f*.
esophageal atresia: Ösophagusatresie *f*.
esophageal candidiasis: Ösophagussoor *m*.
esophageal diverticulum: a sac or pouch formed in the esophageal wall. Forms include pulsion diverticulum formed by hernial protrusion of the mucous membrane, and traction diverticulum of the esophagus, caused by adhesions resulting from lesions near the esophagus. Ösophagusdivertikel *n*.
esophageal electrocardiography: Ösophaguselektrokardiographie *f*.
esophageal leads: Ösophagus-EKG *n*.
esophageal paralysis: Ösophagusmotilitätsstörung *f*.
esophageal perforation: a perforation of the esophagus with a penetration or hole through the esophageal wall. Causes include trauma, lesions caused by foreign bodies, or injury due to endoscopic examination. Symptoms include severe substernal pain, dyspnea, cyanosis, cardiovascular shock, and acute abdomen. Ösophagusperforation *f*.
esophageal probe: Ösophagussonde *f*.
esophageal rupture: Ösophagusruptur *f*.
esophageal speech: Ösophagussprache *f*.
esophageal sphincter: Ösophagussphinkter *m*.
esophageal stricture: Ösophagusstriktur *f*.
esophageal tube: Ösophagussonde *f*.
esophagectomy/*n*: Ösophagektomie *f*.
esophagitis/*n*: inflammation of the esophagus, due to infections, iron deficiency, acid reflux from the stomach, or ingestion of strong chemicals. Ösophagitis *f*.
esophagobronchial fistula: bronchoösophageale Fistel *f*.
esophagogastric/*adj*: gastroösophageal.
esophagoscopy/*n*: Ösophagoskopie *f*.
esophagus/*n*: Ösophagus *m*, Speiseröhre *f*.
esoteric/*adj*: innen, esoterisch.
esotropia/*n*: Esotropie *f*, Strabismus convergens *m*.
essence/*n*: Essenz *f*.
essential/*adj*: wesentlich, essentiell, idiopathisch.
essential amino acid: essentielle Aminosäure *f*.
essential asthma: intrinsisches Asthma *n*.
essential fatty acid: essentielle Fettsäure *f*.
essential hypertension: essentielle Hypertonie *f*.
essential paralysis: idiopathische Lähmung *f*.
essential proteinuria: essentielle Proteinurie *f*.
esterase/*n*: Esterase *f*.
esthetic surgery: kosmetische Operation *f*, Schönheitsoperation *f*.
estivoautumnal fever: Ästivoautumnalfieber *n*, Malaria tropica *f*.
estradiol/*n*: Estradiol *n*, Östradiol *n*.
estramustine/*n*: Estramustin *n*.
estriol/*n*: Estriol *n*, Östriol *n*.
estrogen/*n*: Estrogen *n*, Östrogen *n*.
estrous cycle: Östrus *m*.
etacrynic acid: Etacrynsäure *f*.
etafenone/*n*: Etafenon *n*.
etamiphyllin/*n*: Etamiphyllin *n*.
etamivan/*n*: Etamivan *n*.
etanercept/*n*: Etanercept *n*.
ethambutol/*n*: Ethambutol *n*.

ethanoic acid: Essigsäure *f*.
ethanol/*n*: Ethanol *n*, Äthanol *n*, Äthylalkohol *m*.
ethereal oil: ätherisches Öl *n*.
ethereal tincture: ätherischer Auszug *m*.
ethical drug: verschreibungspflichtiges Medikament *n*.
ethics/*n*: Ethik *f*.
ethics committee: Ethikkommission *f*.
ethinyl estradiol/*n*: Ethinylestradiol *n*.
ethinyl testosterone/*n*: Ethinyltestosteron *n*.
ethionamide/*n*: Ethionamid *n*.
ethionic acid: Ethionsäure *f*.
ethisterone/*n*: Ethisteron *n*.
ethmoidal/*adj*: ethmoidal.
ethmoidal labyrinth: Labyrinthus ethmoidalis *m*, Siebbeinzellen.
ethmoidal sinusitis: Ethmoiditis *f*.
ethnology/*n*: Ethnologie *f*.
ethnomedicine/*n*: Ethnomedizin *f*.
ethnopsychiatry/*n*: Ethnopsychiatrie *f*.
ethosuximide/*n*: Ethosuximid *n*.
ethyl alcohol/*n*: Ethylalkohol *m*, Ethanol *n*.
ethylhydrogenfumarate/*n*: Ethylhydrogenfumarat *n*.
5-ethyl-5-isoamylbarbituric acid: Amobarbital *n*.
etidocaine/*n*: Etidocain *n*.
etidronate/*n*: Etidronat *n*.
etidronic acid: Etidronsäure *f*.
etilefrine/*n*: Etilefrin *n*.
etiology/*n*: Ätiologie *f*.
etiopathology/*n*: Pathogenese *f*.
etiroxate/*n*: Etiroxat *n*.
etodroxizine/*n*: Etodroxizin *n*.
etofenamate/*n*: Etofenamat *n*.
etofibrate/*n*: Etofibrat *n*.
etofylline/*n*: Etofyllin *n*.
etofylline clofibrate: Etofyllinclofibrat *n*.
etomidate/*n*: Etomidat *n*.
etonogestrel/*n*: Etonogestrel *n*.
etoposide/*n*: Etoposid *n*.
etoricoxib/*n*: Etoricoxib *n*.
etozolin/*n*: Etozolin *n*.
etretinate/*n*: Etretinat *n*.
eugenics/*n*: Eugenik *f*.
eugenol/*n*: Eugenol *n*.
eunuchoid/*adj*: eunuchoidal.
eunuchoidism/*n*: Eunuchoidismus *m*.
euphoria/*n*: Euphorie *f*.
euploidy/*n*: Euploidie *f*.
European blastomycosis: Kryptokokkose *f*.
European cholera: einheimische Cholera *f*, akute Gastroenteritis *f*.
European typhus: epidemisches Fleckfieber *n*, Läusefleckfieber *n*.
euroxenous parasite: euryxener Parasit *m*.
eurytrophic parasite: eurytropher Parasit *m*.
eustachian catheter: Tubenkatheter *m*.
eustachian tube: Eustachio-Röhre *f*, Tuba auditiva *f*.
euthanasia/*n*: Euthanasie *f*, Sterbehilfe *f*.
evacuation/*n*: Evakuierung *f*.
evagination/*n*: Evagination *f*.
evaporation/*n*: Evaporieren *n*.
even/*adj*: eben, flach, gleichmäßig.
event/*n*: Ereignis *n*, Reaktion *f*.
eventration/*n*: Eventration *f*.
everolimus/*n*: Everolimus *n*.
eversion/*n*: Eversion *f*.
evidence/*n*: Beweis *m*, Anzeichen *n*.
evidence-based medicine: evidenzbasierte Medizin *f*, EBM.
evident/*adj*: offensichtlich, nachweisbar.
evisceration/*n*: Eviszeration *f*.
evoked/*adj*: evoziert.
evoked contralateral pain: gekreuztes Lasègue-Zeichen *n*, Moutard-Martin-Zeichen *n*.
evoked potential: evoziertes Potential *n*.
evolution/*n*: Evolution *f*.
evulsion/*n*: Evulsion *f*.
exacerbation/*n*: Exazerbation *f*.
exaltation/*n*: Exaltation *f*.
exemestane/*n*: Exemestan *n*.
examination/*n*: Untersuchung *f*, Prüfung *f*.
examination technique: Untersuchungsverfahren *n*.
examine/*vb*: prüfen, untersuchen,

studieren.

exanthema/*n*: Exanthem *n*.

excavation/*n*: Exkavation *f*, Aushöhlung *f*.

excessive hairiness: Hypertrichose *f*.

excessive vomiting: Hyperemesis *f*.

excessive weight: Übergewicht *n*.

exchange transfusion: Austauschtransfusion *f*.

excipient/*n*: Arzneimittelträgersubstanz *f*.

excision/*n*: Exzision *f*, Ektomie *f*.

excisional biopsy: Exstirpationsbiopsie *f*.

excitability/*n*: Exzitabilität *f*, Erregbarkeit *f*.

excitation/*n*: Exzitation *f*, Erregung *f*.

excitatory process: Erregungsablauf *m*.

excited state: Exzitationsstadium *n*.

excitement phase: Erregungsphase *f*.

excoriation/*n*: rubbing away of superficial parts of the skin as a consequence of scratching, an injury or a disease, characterized by serous exudation and petechial bleeding. Exkoriation *f*, Abschürfung *f*.

excrement/*n*: Exkrement *n*.

excretion/*n*: Exkretion *f*.

excretion pyelography: Ausscheidungspyelographie *f*.

excretory organ: Ausscheidungsorgan *n*.

exenteration/*n*: Exenteration *f*.

exercise/*n, vb*: 1. Übung *f*, körperliche Bewegung *f*; 2. üben, trainieren.

exercise-induced asthma: Anstrengungsasthma *n*.

exercise test: Belastungstest *m*, Belastungs-EKG *n*.

exertional headache: Anspannungskopfschmerz *m*.

exfoliation/*n*: Abschuppung *f*, Exfoliation *f*.

exfoliative/*adj*: exfoliativ.

exfoliative cytology: Exfoliativzytologie *f*.

exhaustion/*n*: Erschöpfung *f*, Müdigkeit *f*.

exhibitionism/*n*: Exhibitionismus *m*.

exhumation/*n*: Exhumierung *f*.

exit block: Austrittsblock *m*.

exoerythrocytic stage: extraerythrozytäres Stadium *n*.

exogenous/*adj*: exogen.

exogenous depression: exogene Depression *f*.

exomphalos/*n*: Exomphalos *m*, Nabelschnurvorfall *m*.

exophthalmic goiter: Basedow-Struma *f*.

exophthalmic ophthalmoplegia: endokriner Exophthalmus *m*.

exophytic/*adj*: exophytisch.

exostosis/*n*: Exostose *f*.

exotoxin/*n*: Exotoxin *n*.

exotropia/*n*: Exotropie *f*, Strabismus externus *m*, Auswärtsschielen *n*.

expanding cast: Spreizgips *m*.

expansion/*n*: Expansion *f*.

expectation of life: Lebenserwartung *f*.

expectorant/*n*: Expektorans *n*.

expectoration/*n*: Expektoration *f*.

expenditure/*n*: Aufwand *m*.

expense/*n*: Kosten.

experiment/*n, vb*: 1. Versuch *m*, Experiment *n*; 2. experimentieren.

experimental/*adj*: experimentell.

experimental study: experimentelle Untersuchung *f*.

experimental therapy: experimentelle Therapie *f*.

expert/*n, adj*: 1. Experte *m*, Sachverständiger *m*; 2. erfahren.

expiratory dyspnea: exspiratorische Dyspnoe *f*.

expiratory murmur: exspiratorisches Geräusch *n*.

expiratory pressure: exspiratorischer Druck *m*.

expiratory resistance: exspiratorischer Widerstand *m*.

expiratory sound: exspiratorisches Geräusch *n*.

expiratory standstill: exspiratorischer Atemstillstand *m*.

expiratory stridor: exspiratorischer Stridor *m*.

exploration/*n*: Exploration *f*, Untersuchung *f*.

explorative laparotomy: Probelaparotomie *f*.

exploratory excision: Probeexzision *f*.

exploratory surgery: explorativer Eingriff *m*.
exposure/*n*: Exposition *f*, Belichtung *f*.
exposure dose: Strahlenbelastung *f*.
expression/*n*: Expression *f*, Ausdruck *m*.
expressive aphasia: motorische Aphasie *f*.
expulsion/*n*: Expulsion *f*, Austreibung *f*.
expulsion of placenta: Plazentaaustreibung *f*.
expulsive pains: Austreibungswehen.
expulsive stage: Austreibungsperiode *f*.
extended radical mastectomy: erweiterte radikale Mastektomie *f*.
extender/*n*: Streckmittel *n*, Plasmaexpander *m*.
extension/*n*: Extension *f*, Ausdehnung *f*.
extensor/*n*: Extensor *m*, Musculus extensor *m*.
external/*adj*: extern, äußerlich.
external acoustic canal: äußerer Gehörgang *m*.
external administration: äußere Anwendung *f*.
external conjugate diameter: Conjugata externa *f*, äußerer Beckendurchmesser *m*.
external ear: äußeres Ohr *n*.
external fistula: äußere Fistel *f*.
external genital organ: äußeres Geschlechtsorgan *n*.
external hemorrhage: äußere Blutung *f*.
external hydrocephalus: kommunizierender Hydrozephalus *m*.
external meningitis: Pachymeningitis *f*.
external ophthalmoplegia: Ophthalmoplegia externa *f*.
external pacemaker: externer Schrittmacher *m*.
external pelvimetry: äußere Beckenmessung *f*.
external rotation: Außenrotation *f*.
external strabismus: Strabismus externus *m*, Exotropie *f*.
external version: äußere Wendung *f*.
extirpation/*n*: Exstirpation *f*.
extra-anatomic bypass: extraanatomischer Bypass *m*.
extra-articular ankylosis: extraartikuläre Ankylose *f*, falsche Ankylose *f*.
extra-axial leptomeningeal cyst: Dandy-Walker-Zyste *f*.
extracapillary glomerulonephritis: extrakapilläre Glomerulonephritis *f*.
extracapsular/*adj*: extrakapsulär.
extracapsular ankylosis: extrakapsuläre Ankylose *f*.
extracapsular fracture: extrakapsuläre Fraktur *f*.
extracardiac murmur: extrakardiales Geräusch *n*.
extracellular/*adj*: extrazellulär.
extracellular fluid: Extrazellularflüssigkeit *f*.
extracellular space: Extrazellularraum *m*, EZR.
extracorporeal circulation: extrakorporaler Kreislauf *m*.
extracorporeal hepatic perfusion: extrakorporale Leberperfusion *f*.
extracorporeal oxygenation: extrakorporale Oxygenation *f*.
extract/*n, vb*: 1. Extrakt *m*, Auszug *m*; 2. extrahieren.
extracting forceps: Extraktionszange *f*.
extraction centrifuge: Extraktionszentrifuge *f*.
extradural abscess: extraduraler Abszess *m*, Epiduralabszess *m*.
extradural space: Epiduralraum *m*.
extrahepatic cholestatic jaundice: extrahepatischer cholestatischer Ikterus *m*.
extrapulmonary tuberculosis: extrapulmonale Tuberkulose *f*.
extrapyramidal/*adj*: extrapyramidal.
extrapyramidal syndrome: any neurologic disorder resulting from lesions of the extrapyramidal nuclei and pathways, for example Parkinson's syndrome, athetosis, or torsion dystonia. extrapyramidales Syndrom *n*.
extrapyramidal tract: extrapyramidales System *n*.
extrarenal azotemia: extrarenale

Azotämie *f.*

extrasystole/*n*: a cardiac impulse originating outside the sinuatrial node and resulting in a contraction of the heart that occurs prematurely and interrupts the normal rhythm. Forms are distinguished according to the site of origin, for example atrial extrasystole arising in the atrium, or supraventricular extrasystole deriving from above the ventricle. Extrasystole *f.*

extrauterine/*adj*: extrauterin.

extrauterine pregnancy: ectopic pregnancy with the implantation of the blastocyst outside the uterine cavity, mainly in the fallopian tubes. Symptoms depend on the localization and may include tubal rupture, and inflammations. Extrauteringravidität *f.*

extravasation/*n*: Extravasation *f.*

extravascular/*adj*: extravaskulär.

extravascular fluid: Extravasat *n.*

extremity/*n*: Extremität *f.*

extrinsic/*adj*: extrinsisch.

extrinsic allergic alveolitis: exogene allergische Alveolitis *f*, EEA.

extrinsic asthma: extrinsisches Asthma *n.*

extroversion/*n*: Extroversion *f.*

extubation/*n*: Extubation *f.*

exudate/*n, vb*: 1. Exsudat *n*; 2. ausscheiden.

exudation/*n*: Exsudation *f.*

exudation cyst: Exsudationszyste *f.*

exudative pleurisy: exsudative Pleuritis *f.*

exudative retinitis: Retinitis exsudativa *f.*

eye/*n*: Auge *n*, Gesichtssinn *m*, Öse *f.*

eyeball/*n*: Augapfel *m.*

eyebrow/*n*: Augenbraue *f.*

eyed probe: Schlitzsonde *f.*

eyedrops: Augentropfen.

eyeground/*n*: Augenhintergrund *m*, Fundus *m.*

eyelash/*n*: Wimper *f.*

eyelid/*n*: Augenlid *n.*

eye movement: Augenbewegung *f.*

eyesight/*n*: Sehkraft *f.*

ezetimibe/*n*: Ezetimib *n.*

E

F

F <*abbr*> **1. farad; 2. fluorine**: 1. Farad *n*; 2. Fluor *n*.
F. <*abbr*> **1. Fahrenheit; 2. formula**: 1. Fahrenheit; 2. Rezept *n*.
fabulation/*n*: Fabulieren *n*.
face/*n*: Gesicht *n*, Facies *f*.
face ache: Gesichtsschmerz *m*.
face presentation: in obstetrics, the position of the fetus in which the face appears first in the uterine cervix. Gesichtslage *f*.
facet/*n*: Facette *f*.
facial/*adj*: fazial.
facial center: Fazialiskern *m*.
facial cleft: a condition which is characterized by the persistence of fissures or grooves in the face, due to incomplete closure of embryonic fissures. Gesichtsspalte *f*.
facial diplegia: beidseitige Fazialislähmung *f*.
facial hemiatrophy: Hemiatrophia facialis progressiva *f*, Romberg-Syndrom *n*.
facial hemiplegia: einseitige Fazialisparese *f*.
facialis phenomenon: Fazialiszeichen *n*, Chvostek-Zeichen *n*.
facial neuralgia: any pain in the face caused by lesion or disease of a facial nerve. Forms include for example trigeminal neuralgia and supraorbital neuralgia. Fazialisneuralgie *f*, Gesichtsneuralgie *f*.
facial pain: Gesichtsschmerz *m*.
facial paralysis: partial or complete paralysis of the facial muscles, usually due to a lesion or disease of the facial nerve. Symptoms depend on the extent to which the nerve is affected and may include all muscles of facial expression, inadequate closure of the eyelids, speech disorders, and eventually hyperacusis. Fazialislähmung *f*.
facial reflex: bulbomimischer Reflex *m*, Mondonesi-Reflex *m*.
facial region: Gesichtsregion *f*.
facial spasm: Fazialiskrampf *m*, Bell-Spasmus *m*.
facies/*n*: Facies *f*.
facilitation of reflexes: Reflexbahnung *f*.
faciobrachial hemiplegia: faziobrachiale Hemiplegie *f*.
facioscapulohumeral atrophy: fazioskapulohumerale Muskeldystrophie *f*, Landouzy-Déjerine-Atrophie *f*.
factitious disorder: vorgetäuschte Störung *f*.
factor/*n*: Faktor *m*.
facultative/*adj*: fakultativ.
facultative anaerobe: fakultativer Anaerobier *m*.
facultative parasite: fakultativer Parasit *m*.
faculty/*n*: Vermögen *n*, Fähigkeit *f*, Fakultät *f*.
fade/*vb*: abklingen, verblassen.
fail/*vb*: versagen, ausfallen.
failure/*n*: Versagen *n*, Ausbleiben *n*.
failure rate: Versagerquote *f*.
faint/*vb, adj*: 1. bewusstlos werden, in Ohnmacht fallen, verblassen; 2. ohnmächtig, schwach.
faith healing: Gesundbeten *n*.
falciform body: Sporozoit *m*.
fall/*n, vb*: 1. Fall *m*, Sturz *m*; 2. fallen.
falling sickness: Epilepsie *f*.
fallopian tube: Tuba uterina *f*, Eileiter *m*.
false aneurysm: falsches Aneurysma *n*.
false articulation: Pseudarthrose *f*.

false cast: Pseudozylinder *m*.
false colonic obstruction: akute intestinale Pseudoobstruktion *f*, Ogilvie-Syndrom *n*.
false crisis: Pseudokrise *f*.
false croup: Laryngismus stridulus *m*, Pseudo-Krupp *m*.
false cyanosis: Pseudozyanose *f*.
false diverticulum: falsches Divertikel *n*, Pseudodivertikel *n*.
false ganglion: Pseudoganglion *n*.
false joint: Pseudarthrosis *f*.
false labor: Senkungswehen.
false-negative/*adj*: falsch-negativ.
false neuroma: Amputationsneurom *n*.
false pains: Vorwehen.
false paralysis: Pseudolähmung *f*.
false pelvis: großes Becken *n*.
false-positive/*adj*: falsch-positiv.
false pregnancy: Pseudoschwangerschaft *f*.
false proteinuria: Pseudoproteinurie *f*.
false tumor: Pseudotumor *m*.
false uterine contractions: Braxton-Hicks-Wehen.
falx/*n*: Falx *f*.
famciclovir/*n*: Famciclovir *n*.
familial/*adj*: familiär, hereditär.
familial ataxia: hereditäre Ataxie *f*.
familial erythroblastic anemia: Thalassaemia major *f*.
familial goiter: familiäre Struma *f*.
familial histiocytic reticulosis: familiäre histiozytäre Retikulose *f*.
familial hyperkalemic periodic paralysis: hereditäre hyperkaliämische periodische Lähmung *f*.
familial hypokalemic periodic paralysis: hereditäre hypokaliämische periodische Lähmung *f*.
familial hypophosphatemic rickets: familiäre hypophosphatämische Rachitis *f*.
familial hypotension: chronische orthostatische Hypotonie *f*, Shy-Drager-Syndrom *n*.
familial microcytic anemia: Thalassämie *f*.
familial nonhemolytic jaundice: Gilbert-Meulengracht-Syndrom *n*.
familial periodic paralysis: hereditäre hyperkaliämische periodische Lähmung *f*.
familial polyendocrine adenomatosis: an autosomal dominant inherited syndrome which is characterized by the presence of benign or malignant neoplasms of more than one endocrine gland and neurocutaneous alterations. pluriglanduläre Adenomatose *f*, multiple endokrine Neoplasie *f*, MEN.
familial polyposis: familiäre Polyposis coli *f*.
familial renal amyloidosis: familiäre Nierenamyloidose *f*.
familial spastic paraplegia: hereditäre spastische Paraplegie *f*.
familial xanthomatosis: Wolman-Krankheit *f*.
family/*n*: Familie *f*.
family doctor: Hausarzt *m*.
family history: Familienanamnese *f*.
family medicine: Familienmedizin *f*.
family planning: Familienplanung *f*.
family therapy: Familientherapie *f*.
famine edema: a condition which is characterized by the presence of generalized edema or dropsy, resulting from protein deficiency in chronically malnourished persons. Hungerödem *n*.
famotidine/*n*: Famotidin *n*.
famprofazone/*n*: Famprofazon *n*.
fantasy/*n*: Phantasie *f*.
faradic stimulation: faradische Stimulation *f*.
faradism/*n*: Faradisation *f*.
far-and-near suture: Faszienverschluss *m*.
Far Eastern hemorrhagic fever: fernöstliche hämorrhagische Nephrosonephritis *f*.
farmer's lung: Farmerlunge *f*.
far point: Fernpunkt *m*.
farsightedness/*n*: Weitsichtigkeit *f*, Hyperopie *f*.
fascia/*n*: Faszie *f*.
fascicle/*n*: Faszikel *m*.
fascicular/*adj*: faszikulär.
fascicular degeneration: faszikuläre Degeneration *f*.

F

fasciculated bladder: Balkenblase *f*.
fasciculation/*n*: Faszikulation *f*, faszikuläre Zuckung *f*.
fasciitis/*n*: acute or chronic inflammation of a fascia, usually due to a generalized inflammatory disease or rheumatoid disorder. Faszienentzündung *f*, Fasciitis *f*.
fast/*n, vb, adj*: 1. Fasten *n*; 2. fasten; 3. schnell, beständig.
fasten/*vb*: befestigen.
fasting/*n, adj*: 1. Fasten *n*; 2. nüchtern.
fasting value: Nüchternwert *m*.
fat/*n, adj*: 1. Fett *n*; 2. fett.
fatal/*adj*: fatal, letal.
fat atrophy: Fettatrophie *f*.
fat cell: Fettzelle *f*.
fat embolism: Fettembolie *f*.
father complex: Vaterkomplex *m*.
fatherhood/*n*: Vaterschaft *f*.
fatigue/*n, vb*: 1. Ermüdung *f*, Müdigkeit *f*; 2. ermüden.
fatigue fracture: Ermüdungsbruch *m*.
fat necrosis: Fettgewebsnekrose *f*.
fat-soluble/*adj*: fettlöslich.
fat tumor: Fettgeschwulst *f*.
fatty/*adj*: fettig.
fatty acid: Fettsäure *f*.
fatty atrophy: Fettatrophie *f*.
fatty body: Fettkörper *m*.
fatty cardiomyopathy: Herzverfettung *f*.
fatty cast: Fettzylinder *m*.
fatty change: Verfettung *f*.
fatty degeneration: fettige Degeneration *f*.
fatty heart: Fettherz *n*, Cor adiposum *n*.
fatty kidney: Fettniere *f*.
fatty liver: a hepatic condition which is characterized by an excessive amount of fat in the liver cells. Causes include chronic alcohol consumption or damage by chemical substances, and several systemic disorders such as diabetes mellitus. Fettleber *f*.
fatty tissue: Fettgewebe *n*.
faucial paralysis: Schlundlähmung *f*, Schlucklähmung *f*.
faucial reflex: Rachenreflex *m*.
faulty/*adj*: fehlerhaft.
faulty color discrimination: Farbenfehlsichtigkeit *f*.
favic alopecia: Favusalopezie *f*.
favism/*n*: Favismus *m*.
favorable response: gutes Ansprechen *n*.
favus/*n*: Favus *m*, Kopfgrind *m*.
fear/*n, vb*: 1. Furcht *f*, Angst *f*; 2. fürchten.
feasible/*adj*: geeignet, möglich.
feature/*n*: Charakteristikum *n*, Eigenschaft *f*.
febantel/*n*: Febantel *n*.
febrile/*adj*: febril.
febrile abortion: febriler Abort *m*.
febrile convulsion: Fieberkrampf *m*.
febrile crisis: Fieberkrise *f*.
febrile delirium: Fieberdelir *n*.
febrile illness: fieberhafte Erkrankung *f*.
febrile phase: Fieberphase *f*, Fieberstadium *n*.
febrile proteinuria: Fieberproteinurie *f*.
febrile pulse: Fieberpuls *m*.
febrile seizure: tonic-clonic convulsion occurring mostly in young infants in a situation when the body temperature rises, without any detectable organic defect of the central nervous system. Fieberkrampf *m*.
febuprol/*n*: Febuprol *n*.
fecal/*adj*: fäkal.
fecal abscess: Sterkoralabszess *m*.
fecal fat: Steatorrhö *f*.
fecal fistula: Kotfistel *f*.
fecal incontinence: inability to control the anal sphincter, for example due injury, lesions of the spinal cord, or mental factors. Symptoms include involuntary defecation. Stuhlinkontinenz *f*.
fecalith/*n*: Kotstein *m*.
fecal vomiting: Koterbrechen *n*.
feces/*n*: Fäzes *f*.
fecundation/*n*: Befruchtung *f*.
fecundity/*n*: Fruchtbarkeit *f*.
feeble/*adj*: schwach, kraftlos.
feeble pulse: schwacher Puls *m*.
feed/*vb*: füttern.
feedback/*n*: Feedback *n*, Rückkopplung *f*.

feedback control system: Regelkreis *m*.
feeding/*n*: Füttern *n*, Ernährung *f*.
feeding cup: Schnabeltasse *f*.
feeding tube: Ernährungssonde *f*.
feel/*vb*: fühlen, empfinden.
feeling/*n*: Gefühl *n*, Empfindung *f*.
felbamate/*n*: Felbamat *n*.
felodipine/*n*: Felodipin *n*.
felon/*n*: an infectious disease of the nail fold, mostly due to bacterial infection with Staphylococcus or Streptococcus, or resulting from herpes simplex infection. Symptoms include swelling, formation of a very painful abscess, and inflammation of lymphatic vessels. Nagelgeschwür *n*, Paronychie *f*, Umlauf *m*.
female/*n, adj*: 1. Frau *f*; 2. weiblich.
female hormone: weibliches Geschlechtshormon *n*.
feminization/*n*: Feminisierung *f*.
femoral/*adj*: femoral.
femoral fracture: breaking of the femoral bone. Fractures of the femoral neck typically occur in elderly persons as a result of falls. Femurfraktur *f*, Oberschenkelfraktur *f*.
femoral head: Femurkopf *m*.
femoral hernia: a prolapse of intestine into the femoral canal. Symptoms may include a palpable mass, pain, and incarceration of intestine, resulting in ileus and necrosis. Hernia femoralis *f*, Schenkelhernie *f*.
femoral pulse: Femoralispuls *m*.
femoral reflex: Femoralisreflex *m*.
femoral testis: Leistenhoden *m*.
femur head necrosis: Femurkopfnekrose *f*.
femur neck: Oberschenkelhals *m*.
fenbencillin/*n*: Fenbencillin *n*.
fenbendazole/*n*: Fenbendazol *n*.
fenbufen/*n*: Fenbufen *n*.
fenbutrazate/*n*: Fenbutrazat *n*.
fencarbamide/*n*: Fencarbamid *n*.
fenclofos/*n*: Fenclofos *n*.
fendiline/*n*: Fendilin *n*.
fenestra/*n*: Fenster *n*.
fenestrated bandage: Fensterverband *m*.
fenestrated clamp: Lochklemme *f*.
fenestrated compress: Fensterverband *m*.
fenestrated tenotomy: Fensterungstenotomie *f*.
fenfluramine/*n*: Fenfluramin *n*.
fennel tea: Fencheltee *m*.
fenofibrate/*n*: Fenofibrat *n*.
fenoprofen/*n*: Fenoprofen *n*.
fenoterol/*n*: Fenoterol *n*.
fenoxazoline/*n*: Fenoxazolin *n*.
fenpipramide/*n*: Fenpipramid *n*.
fenpiverinium bromide: Fenpiveriniumbromid *n*.
fenproporex/*n*: Fenproporex *n*.
fenprostalene/*n*: Fenprostalen *n*.
fentanyl/*n*: Fentanyl *n*.
fenthion/*n*: Fenthion *n*.
fenticonazole/*n*: Fenticonazol *n*.
fentonium bromide: Fentoniumbromid *n*.
fenyramidol/*n*: Fenyramidol *n*.
fermentation/*n*: Fermentation *f*.
fern test: Farnkrauttest *m*.
ferric hexacyanoferrate: Eisenhexacyanoferrat *n*.
ferric oxide: Eisenoxid *n*.
ferrocyanide/*n*: Ferrocyanid *n*.
ferrous/*adj*: eisenhaltig.
ferrous iodide: Eisenjodid *n*.
fertile period: fruchtbare Tage
fertility/*n*: Fertilität *f*, Fruchtbarkeit *f*.
fertility control: Geburtenkontrolle *f*.
fertilization/*n*: Befruchtung *f*.
fertirelin/*n*: Fertirelin *n*.
ferucarbotran/*n*: Ferucarbotran *n*.
fester/*n, vb*: 1. Eitergeschwür *n*; 2. eitern.
festinating gait: Trippelgang *m*.
fetal/*adj*: fetal, fötal.
fetal calf serum: fetales Kälberserum *n*, FKS.
fetal circulation: fetaler Kreislauf *m*.
fetal cleft: any fissure or groove which results from an incomplete closure of the normal fissures that appear during the embryonic period. Forms include for example branchial clefts, clefts of the face, or genital clefts. fetale Spaltbildung *f*.

fetal death: Fruchttod *m*.
fetal development: Embryonalentwicklung *f*.
fetal distress: Fetal distress *m*.
fetal heartbeat: kindliche Herztöne.
fetal hemoglobin: fetales Hämoglobin *n*, HbF.
fetal movement: Kindsbewegung *f*.
fetal parts: Kindsteile.
fetal period: Fetalperiode *f*.
fetal placenta: kindliche Plazenta *f*.
fetishism/*n*: Fetischismus *m*.
fetoprotein/*n*: Fetoprotein *n*.
fetor/*n*: Foetor *m*.
fetus/*n*: Fetus *m*, Fötus *m*.
fever/*n, vb*: 1. elevation of the body temperature above the normal of 38.3° degrees Celsius. Fever is mainly caused by infections, or may result from diseases of the central nervous system. It shows a characteristic course over the day with higher body temperature in the evening than in the morning. Fieber *n*; 2. fiebern.
fever blister: clusters of vesicular lesions of the skin or mucosa, due to herpes simplex. The small blisters are typically localized around the lips, or in the genital area. Fieberbläschen *n*, Herpesbläschen *n*.
fever curve: Fieberkurve *f*.
feverish/*adj*: fiebrig.
fever of undetermined origin: Fieber unbekannter Ursache *n*.
fexofenadine/*n*: Fexofenadin *n*.
fiber/*n*: Faser *f*.
fiberoptic bronchoscope: Fiberglasbronchoskop *n*.
fibrillar twitch: fibrilläre Zuckung *f*.
fibrillary wave: Flimmerwelle *f*.
fibrillation/*n*: Fibrillation *f*, Flimmern *n*.
fibrin/*n*: Fibrin *n*.
fibrin clot: Fibringerinnsel *n*.
fibrinogen/*n*: Fibrinogen *n*.
fibrinogen deficiency: Fibrinogenopenie *f*.
fibrinolysin/*n*: Fibrinolysin *n*.
fibrinolytic agent: Fibrinolytikum *n*.
fibrinous bronchitis: Bronchitis fibrinosa *f*.
fibrinous cast: Fibrinzylinder *m*.
fibrinous pericarditis: fibrinöse Perikarditis *f*.
fibrinous pleurisy: fibrinöse Pleuritis *f*.
fibroadenoma/*n*: Fibroadenom *n*.
fibroblast/*n*: Fibroblast *m*.
fibroid cataract: fibröse Pseudophakie *f*.
fibroplastic endocarditis: fibroplastische Endokarditis *f*, Löffler-Endokarditis *f*.
fibrocartilage/*n*: Fibrocartilago *f*, Faserknorpel *m*.
fibrochondritis/*n*: Faserknorpelentzündung *f*.
fibrocystic/*adj*: fibrozystisch.
fibrocystic osteitis: Ostitis fibrosa cystica *f*, Albright-Krankheit *f*.
fibrocyte/*n*: Fibrozyt *m*.
fibroelastosis/*n*: Fibroelastose *f*.
fibroepithelial papilloma: fibroepitheliales Papillom *n*.
fibroepithelial tumor: Fibroepitheliom *n*.
fibroid/*n*: Fibromyom *n*, Leiomyom *n*.
fibroid lung: Lungenfibrose *f*.
fibroma/*n*: a benign neoplasm composed of fibroblasts or fibrous tissue. Different forms are differentiated according to the site of origin, and other features, such as the presence of cysts or calcifications. Fibrom *n*.
fibromyoma/*n*: Fibromyom *n*, Leiomyom *n*.
fibrosarcoma/*n*: Fibrosarkom *n*.
fibrosing adenomatosis: Fibroadenomatose *f*.
fibrosing alveolitis: fibrosierende Alveolitis *f*.
fibrosis/*n*: a condition which is characterized by an increase of connective tissue in an organ, for example pulmonary fibrosis with abnormal quantities of fibrous tissue in the lung, or hepatic fibrosis. Fibrose *f*.
fibrositis/*n*: Fibrositis *f*.
fibrous/*adj*: fibrös.
fibrous ankylosis: fibröse Ankylose *f*.
fibrous cartilage: Fibrocartilago *f*, Faserknorpel *m*.

fibrous dysplasia: Fibrodysplasie *f*.
fibrous histiocytoma: Fibroxanthom *n*.
fibrous odontoma: odontogenes Fibrom *n*.
fibrous pericarditis: fibröse Perikarditis *f*.
fibrous tissue: Fasergewebe *n*.
fibrous tumor: Fibrom *n*.
fibular/*adj*: Fibula-, fibularis.
fibular bone: Fibula *f*, Wadenbein *n*.
field/*n*: Feld *n*, Gebiet *n*.
field block anesthesia: Feldblock *m*.
field of vision: Gesichtsfeld *n*.
field study: Feldstudie *f*.
fifth disease: a disease of unknown cause which is characterized by an initial butterfly-shaped erythema on the cheeks, followed by generalized rash. Occasionally occurring in epidemic form mainly in children and adolescents during spring and fall. Fünfte Krankheit *f*, Erythema infectiosum acutum *n*.
fight-or-flight reflex: Fluchtreflex *m*.
figure/*n*: Figur *f*, Form *f*, Zahl *f*, Abbildung *f*.
figure-of-eight suture: Achternaht *f*.
filament/*n*: Filament *n*.
filamentous hemagglutinin: filamentöses Hämagglutinin *n*.
filaria/*n*: Filarie *f*.
filarial elephantiasis: an infectious disease caused by filaria worms. Symptoms include swelling of the limbs or so-called elephantiasis, due to a blockage of lymph vessels. Filariose *f*.
filarial itch: kutane Onchozerkose *f*.
filgrastim/*n*: Filgrastim *n*.
filial generation: Filialgeneration *f*.
filiform/*adj*: filiform.
filiform pulse: fadenförmiger Puls *m*.
filiform-tipped catheter: Peitschenkatheter *m*.
filling/*n*: Füllung *f*.
filling defect: Füllungsdefekt *m*, Kontrastaussparung *f*.
filter/*n, vb*: 1. Filter *m*; 2. filtrieren, filtern.
filtration/*n*: Filtration *f*.
fimbriation/*n*: Fimbrienbildung *f*.
final illness: terminale Krankheit *f*.
final stage: Endstadium *n*.
finasteride/*n*: Finasterid *n*.
finding/*n*: Befund *m*.
fine/*adj*: fein.
fine tremor: feinschlägiger Tremor *m*.
finger/*n, vb*: 1. Finger *m*; 2. betasten.
fingerlike process: fingerförmiger Fortsatz *m*.
fingerprint/*n*: Fingerabdruck *m*, Daktylogramm *n*.
finger splint: Fingerschiene *f*.
fingerstall/*n*: Fingerling *m*.
fingertip: Fingerspitze *f*.
Finnish bath: Sauna *f*.
firing level: Firing Level *m*, Entladungsschwelle *f*.
firocoxib/*n*: Firocoxib *n*.
first aid: Erste Hilfe *f*.
first-aid kit: Verbandskasten *m*.
first-degree atrioventricular block: AV-Block I. Grades *m*.
first infection: Erstinfektion *f*.
first-order symptom: Symptom ersten Ranges *n*.
first parallel pelvic plane: obere Beckenapertur *f*.
first sign: Initialsymptom *n*.
first sound: erster Herzton *m*.
fissure/*n, vb*: 1. Fissur *f*, Furche *f*, Spalt *m*; 2. spalten, einreißen.
fist/*n*: Faust *f*.
fistula/*n*: an abnormal passage between two normally unconnected organs, for example rectovaginal fistula, or a communication leading from the surface of the body to an internal cavity, for example abdominal fistula. Fistel *f*.
fit/*n, adj, vb*: 1. Anfall *m*, Anpassung *f*; 2. passend, geeignet, fit; 3. passen, sitzen.
fitness/*n*: Eignung *f*, Gesundheit *f*.
fit to work: arbeitsfähig.
five-day fever: Fünftagefieber *n*, Wolhynisches Fieber *n*.
five-year survival rate: Fünf-Jahres-Überlebensrate *f*.
fixating eye: fixierendes Auge *n*.
fixation/*n*: Fixation *f*, Fixierung *f*.
fixed dressing: Fixierverband *m*.

F

fixed idea: Idée fixe *f*.
fixed phagocyte: fixierter Phagozyt *m*.
fixed pupil: Pupillenstarre *f*.
fixed-rate pacemaker: Festfrequenzschrittmacher *m*.
fixed scoliosis: fixierte Skoliose *f*.
fixing solution: Fixierlösung *f*.
flabby/*adj*: weich, schlaff.
flaccid/*adj*: weich, schlaff.
flaccid hemiplegia: schlaffe Hemiplegie *f*.
flaccid paraplegia: schlaffe Paraplegie *f*.
flagellation/*n*: Flagellation *f*.
flail/*adj*: abnorm beweglich.
flame photometer: Flammenphotometer *n*.
flap/*n*: Lappen *m*, Hautlappen *m*.
flapping tremor: Flügelschlagtremor *m*, Flattertremor *m*.
flare/*n, vb*: 1. Aufflackern *n*; 2. aufflackern.
flash/*n*: Flash *m*, Blitz *m*.
flask/*n*: Kolben *m*, Flasche *f*.
flask-shaped heart: Flaschenherz *n*.
flat/*adj*: flach, eben.
flat back: Flachrücken *m*.
flat chest: abgeflachter Thorax *m*.
flatfoot/*n*: Plattfuß *m*.
flat lesion: flache Läsion *f*.
flat papule: flache Papel *f*.
flat pelvis: flaches Becken *n*.
flatten/*vb*: abflachen.
flatulence/*n*: presence of excessive amounts of gas or air in the stomach or intestines. Causes include diseases and fermentation processes in the intestines, but most frequently air swallowing or aerophagia. Flatulenz *f*, Blähung *f*.
flatulent colic: Windkolik *f*.
flatworm/*n*: Plattwurm *m*, Plathelminthe *f*.
flavodic acid: Acriflaviniumchlorid *n*.
flavor/*n*: Geschmack *m*.
flaw/*n*: Fehler *m*, Riß *m*.
flea/*n*: Floh *m*.
fleabite/*n*: Flohstich *m*.
flea-borne typhus: Flohfleckfieber *n*, murines Fleckfieber *n*.
flecainide/*n*: Flecainid *n*.
fleroxacin/*n*: Fleroxacin *n*.
flesh/*n*: Fleisch *n*.
fleshy mole: Fleischmole *f*.
flexible catheter: flexibler Katheter *m*.
flexion/*n*: Flexion *f*, Beugung *f*.
flexor/*n*: Flexor *m*, Musculus flexor *m*.
flexure/*n*: Flexur *f*, Biegung *f*.
flexure line: Beugelinie *m*.
flight reflex: Fluchtreflex *m*.
flittering scotoma: Flimmerskotom *n*.
floating/*adj*: fluktuierend, schwimmend.
floating gallbladder: flottierende Gallenblase *f*, wandernde Gallenblase *f*.
floating head: frei beweglicher Kopf *m*.
floating kidney: Wanderniere *f*.
floating liver: Wanderleber *f*.
floating patella: tanzende Patella *f*.
flomoxef/*n*: Flomoxef *n*.
flooding/*n*: Flooding *n*, Überflutungstherapie *f*.
floor/*n*: Boden *m*, Grund *m*.
floppy/*adj*: schlaff.
floppy infant: Floppy-Infant-Syndrom *n*, Floppy Infant *n*.
floppy-valve syndrome: myxomatous deformation of a heart valve, mainly the mitral valve, resulting in valvular insuffiency and regurgitation. Floppy-Valve-Syndrom *n*.
florfenicol/*n*: Florfenicol *n*.
flow/*n, vb*: 1. Fluss *m*, Strömung *f*; 2. fließen.
flu/*n*: Influenza *f*, Grippe *f*.
fluanisone/*n*: Fluanison *n*.
flubendazole/*n*: Flubendazol *n*.
flucloxacillin/*n*: Flucloxaxillin *n*.
fluconazole/*n*: Fluconazol *n*.
fluctuation/*n*: Fluktuation *f*.
flucytosine/*n*: Flucytosin *n*.
fludarabine/*n*: Fludarabin *n*.
fludeoxyglucose/*n*: Fludeoxyglucose *n*.
fludrocortisone/*n*: Fludrocortison *n*.
fludrocortisone acetate: Fludrocortisonacetat *n*.
fludroxycortide/*n*: Fludroxycortid *n*.

flufenamic acid: Flufenaminsäure *f*.
fluffy/*adj*: flaumig, flockig.
fluid/*n, adj*: 1. Flüssigkeit *f*; 2. flüssig.
fluid balance: Flüssigkeitshaushalt *m*.
fluid cataract: Cataracta fluida *f*, Morgagni-Katarakt *f*.
fluid intake: Flüssigkeitsaufnahme *f*.
fluid lung: Fluid Lung *f*, Flüssigkeitslunge *f*.
fluke/*n*: Plattwurm *m*, Trematode *f*.
flumazenil/*n*: Flumazenil *n*.
flumetasone/*n*: Flumetason *n*.
flumethrin/*n*: Flumethrin *n*.
flunarizine/*n*: Flunarizin *n*.
flunisolide/*n*: Flunisolid *n*.
flunitrazepam/*n*: Flunitrazepam *n*.
flunixin/*n*: Flunixin *n*.
fluocinolone acetonide/*n*: Fluocinolonacetonid *n*.
fluocinonide/*n*: Fluocinonid *n*.
fluocortin butyl/*n*: Fluocortin-Butyl *n*.
fluocortolone/*n*: Fluocortolon *n*.
fluorescein/*n*: Fluorescein *n*.
fluorescence test: Fluoreszenztest *m*.
fluorescent/*adj*: fluoreszierend.
fluorescent radiation: Fluoreszenzstrahlung *f*.
fluoric acid: Flusssäure *f*.
fluoridation/*n*: Fluoridierung *f*.
fluoride/*n*: Fluorid *n*.
fluorine/*n*: Fluor *m*, F.
fluoroacetic acid: Fluoressigsäure *f*.
fluorometholone/*n*: Fluorometholon *n*.
fluoroscopy/*n*: Fluoroskopie *f*.
fluorouracil/*n*: Fluorouracil *n*.
fluoxetine/*n*: Fluoxetin *n*.
fluoxymesterone/*n*: Fluoxymesteron *n*.
flupentixol/*n*: Flupentixol *n*.
fluphenazine/*n*: Fluphenazin *n*.
flupirtine/*n*: Flupirtin *n*.
fluprednidene/*n*: Flupredniden *n*.
fluprednisolone/*n*: Fluprednisolon *n*.
flupropione/*n*: Flupropion *n*.
flurazepam/*n*: Flurazepam *n*.
flurbiprofen/*n*: Flurbiprofen *n*.
flush/*n, vb*: 1. Gesichtsröte *f*, Flush *m*; 2. erröten.
fluspirilene/*n*: Fluspirilen *n*.
flutamide/*n*: Flutamid *n*.
fluticasone/*n*: Fluticason *n*.
flutter/*n, vb*: 1. Flattern *n*; 2. flattern.
flutter-fibrillation: Flatterflimmern *n*, Flimmerflattern *n*.
fluvastatin/*n*: Fluvastatin *n*.
fluvoxamine/*n*: Fluvoxamin *n*.
flux/*n*: Ausfluss *m*, Fluss *m*.
fluxion/*n*: Ausfluss *m*, Fluss *m*.
fly/*n, vb*: 1. Fliege *f*, 2. fliegen.
flying fatigue: Jetlag *m*, zirkadiane Dysrhythmie *f*.
foam cell: Schaumzelle *f*, Xanthomzelle *f*.
foamy/*adj*: schaumig.
foamy liver: Schaumleber *f*.
focal/*adj*: fokal.
focal attack: fokaler Anfall *m*.
focal depth: Tiefenschärfe *f*.
focal embolic glomerulonephritis: fokal-eitrige Herdnephritis *f*.
focal emphysema: umschriebenes Emphysem *n*.
focal epilepsy: fokaler Anfall *m*, Fokalepilepsie *f*.
focal glomerulitis: fokale Glomerulitis *f*.
focal infection: Fokalinfektion *f*.
focal length: Brennweite *f*.
focal lesion: Herdläsion *f*.
focal necrosis: Herdnekrose *f*.
focal nephritis: Herdnephritis *f*.
focal reaction: Herdreaktion *f*.
focal sclerosing glomerulonephritis: fokale Glomerulosklerose *f*.
focal skin distance: Fokus-Haut-Abstand *m*.
focal symptom: Herdsymptom *n*.
focus/*n, vb*: 1. Fokus *m*, Brennpunkt *m*, Herd *m*; 2. fokussieren, einstellen.
fold/*n, vb*: 1. Falte *f*; 2. falten, umschlagen.
folic acid: Folsäure *f*.
folic acid deficiency anemia: Folsäuremangelanämie *f*.
folinic acid: Folinsäure *f*.
follicle/*n*: Follikel *m*.
follicle-stimulating hormone: follikelstimulierendes Hormon *n*, FSH.
follicular/*adj*: follikulär.
follicular adenocarcinoma: follikulä-

res Adenokarzinom *n*.
follicular adenoma: follikuläres Adenom *n*.
follicular atresia: Follikelatresie *f*.
follicular carcinoma: follikuläres Karzinom *n*.
follicular conjunctivitis: Follikularkatarrh *m*.
follicular cyst: Follikelzyste *f*.
follicular goiter: Kolloidstruma *f*.
follicular hormone: Follikelhormon *n*.
follicular hyperkeratosis: Hyperkeratosis follicularis *f*.
follicular hyperplasia: Follikelhyperplasie *f*.
follicular maturation: Follikelreifung *f*.
follicular tonsillitis: follikuläre Tonsillitis *f*, Tonsillitis lacunaris *f*.
follitropin/*n*: Follitropin *n*.
follow-up/*n*: Nachuntersuchung *f*, Verlaufskontrolle *f*.
fomepizole/*n*: Fomepizol *n*.
fominoben/*n*: Fominoben *n*.
fomivirsen/*n*: Fomivirsen *n*.
fomocaine/*n*: Fomocain *n*.
fondaparinux sodium/*n*: Fondaparinuxnatrium *n*.
fontanelle/*n*: Fontanelle *f*.
food/*n*: Nahrung *f*, Lebensmittel *n*.
food allergy: allergy caused by sensitivity to one or more nutrients. Symptoms which can appear shortly after the food intake, may include skin reactions, gastrointestinal complaints, nausea, vomiting, low blood pressure, and respiratory symptoms. Lebensmittelallergie *f*.
food intake: Nahrungsmittelaufnahme *f*.
food poisoning: Lebensmittelvergiftung *f*.
foodstuff/*n*: Nahrungsmittel *n*.
food value: Nährwert *m*.
foot/*n*: Fuß *m*.
foot-and-mouth disease: an infectious disease of animals caused by a picornavirus, which can be transmitted to humans by direct contact. Symptoms include fever, malaise, headache, and vesiculation of the mouth and fingertips. Maul- und Klauenseuche *f*.
foot deformity: Fußdeformität *f*.
footdrop gait: Steppergang *m*.
foramen/*n*: Loch *n*, Foramen *n*.
force/*n, vb*: 1. Kraft *f*, Zwang *m*; 2. zwingen.
forced alimentation: Zwangsernährung *f*.
forced delivery: Schnellentbindung *f*.
forced expiratory volume: forciertes exspiratorisches Volumen *n*, Sekundenkapazität *f*.
forced inversion: erzwungene Wendung *f*.
forced vital capacity: Sekundenkapazität *f*.
forced vomiting: Zwangserbrechen *n*.
forceps/*n*: Zange *f*, Geburtszange *f*, Forceps *f*.
forceps delivery: Zangengeburt *f*.
forearm/*n*: Unterarm *m*.
forearm sign: Léri-Zeichen *n*, Hand-Vorderarm-Zeichen *n*.
forebrain/*n*: Vorderhirn *n*, Prosencephalon *n*.
forecast/*n*: Vorhersage *f*.
forehead/*n*: Stirn *f*.
foreign body: Fremdkörper *m*.
foreign-body removal: Fremdkörperentfernung *f*.
foreign serum: Fremdserum *n*.
forensic/*adj*: forensisch.
forensic autopsy: gerichtliche Autopsie *f*.
forensic medicine: Gerichtsmedizin *f*.
foreskin/*n*: Vorhaut *f*, Präputium *n*.
forewaters/*n*: Vorwasser *n*.
fork/*n*: Gabel *f*.
form/*n, vb*: 1. Form *f*, Formblatt *n*; 2. formen, bilden.
formaldehyde/*n*: Formaldehyd *m*.
formestane/*n*: Formestan *n*.
formic acid: Ameisensäure *f*.
formication/*n*: Formicatio *f*, Ameisenlaufen *n*.
formiminoglutamic acid: Formiminoglutaminsäure *f*, FIGLU.
formocortal/*n*: Formocortal *n*.
formoterol/*n*: Formoterol *n*.
form perception: Formwahrnehmung *f*.

formula/*n*: Formel *f*, Arzneiformel *f*.
formulary/*n*: Medikamentenverzeichnis *n*, Formelnbuch *n*.
formulation/*n*: Zubereitungsform *f*.
forward heart failure: Vorwärtsversagen *n*.
fosamprenavir/*n*: Fosamprenavir *n*.
foscarnet/*n*: Foscarnet *n*.
fosfestrol/*n*: Fosfestrol *n*.
fosfomycin/*n*: Fosfomycin *n*.
fosinoprilat/*n*: Fosinopril *n*.
fossa/*n*: Grube *f*, Fossa *f*.
foster-family: Pflegefamilie *f*.
foudroyant/*adj*: foudroyant, fulminant.
foul breath: Mundgeruch *m*, Foetor ex ore *m*.
four-point gait: Vierpunktgang *m*.
fovea/*n*: Grube *f*.
fraction/*n*: Fraktion *f*.
fractionated curettage: fraktionierte Kürettage *f*.
fracture/*n, vb*: 1. complete or incomplete breaking of a bone. Main forms include simple fracture in which the injury is entirely internal without skin lesions, and compound fracture with an open wound in the soft tissues and the skin. Fraktur *f*, Bruch *m*; 2. brechen.
fracture-dislocation: Dislokationsfraktur *f*.
fragility/*n*: Fragilität *f*.
frambesia/*n*: Frambösie *f*.
frame/*n*: Rahmen *m*, Gerüst *n*.
framework/*n*: Stützgerüst *n*.
framycetin/*n*: Framycetin *n*.
freckle/*n*: Sommersprosse *f*, Epheliden.
free/*adj*: frei, ungebunden.
free fatty acid: freie Fettsäure *f*, FFS.
free flap: freier Lappen *m*.
free-floating/*adj*: frei flottierend, wandernd.
free graft: freies Transplantat *n*.
free hormone: ungebundenes Hormon *n*.
free phagocyte: freier Phagozyt *m*.
free radical: freies Radikal *n*.
freeze-dry/*vb*: gefriertrocknen.
freeze etching technique: Gefrierätztechnik *f*.
fremitus/*n*: Fremitus *m*.
frenal ulcer: Ulcus frenulum *n*, Riga-Fede-Geschwür *n*.
French flap: Verschiebelappen *m*.
frenulum/*n*: Frenulum *n*.
frequency/*n*: Frequenz *f*, Häufigkeit *f*.
frequent/*adj*: frequent, häufig.
frequent pulse: beschleunigter Puls *m*.
fresh/*adj*: frisch.
fresh blood: Frischblut *n*.
fresh frozen plasma: Fresh-frozen-Plasma *n*, FFP.
Freudian theory: Freud-Theorie *f*, Psychoanalyse *f*.
friction/*n*: Reibung *f*, Friktion *f*.
friction sound: Reibegeräusch *n*.
frigidity/*n*: Frigidität *f*.
frog test: Krötentest *m*, Galli-Mainini-Test *m*.
front/*n*: Front *f*, Stirn *f*.
frontal/*adj*: frontal.
frontal anterior position: vordere Vorderhauptlage *f*.
frontal ataxia: Frontallappenataxie *f*.
frontal lobe: Frontallappen *m*.
frontal plane: Frontalebene *f*.
frontal posterior position: vordere Hinterhauptlage *f*.
frontal sinus: Sinus frontalis *m*, Stirnhöhle *f*.
frontal sinusitis: Sinusitis frontalis *f*, Stirnhöhlenentzündung *f*.
front lens: Vorsatzlinse *f*.
frontotransverse position: vordere Querlage *f*.
frostbite/*n*: a condition caused by long exposure to severe cold temperatures with freezing of a part of the body, usually the nose, fingers, and toes. Symptoms include initial burning and stinging, and then numbness. In deep frostbites, tissue destruction extends beyond the skin and involves subcutaneous tissue, muscles, and eventually bones. Frostbeule *f*.
frothy/*adj*: schäumend.
frottage/*n*: Frottage *f*.
frovatriptan/*n*: Frovatriptan *n*.
fructosuria/*n*: Fruktosurie *f*.

F

fruity breath: Obstgeruch *m*, Acetongeruch *m*,.
fruity odor: Obstgeruch *m*, Acetongeruch *m*.
FTA-ABS test <*abbr*> **fluorescent treponemal antibody absorption test**: Fluoreszenz-Treponema-Antikörper-Absorptionstest *m*, FTA-ABS-Test *m*.
fugitive swelling: Kalabarbeule *f*.
fugitive wart: flüchtige Warze *f*.
fulgurant pain: blitzartig einschießender Schmerz *m*.
full agonist: reiner Agonist *m*.
full antagonist: reiner Antagonist *m*.
full-blood: Vollblut *n*.
full-blown/*adj*: voll ausgeprägt.
full pulse: Pulsus plenus *m*, voller Puls *m*.
fulminant hepatitis: fulminante Hepatitis *f*.
fulminant pancreatitis: fulminante Pankreatitis *f*.
fulminating/*adj*: fulminant.
fulvestrant/*n*: Fulvestrant *n*.
fumarate/*n*: Fumarat *n*.
fumaric acid: Fumarsäure *f*.
fume poisoning: Rauchvergiftung *f*.
fuming sulfuric acid: Schwefelmilch *f*.
function/*n, vb*: 1. Funktion *f*; 2. funktionieren.
functional/*adj*: funktionell.
functional ability: Funktionsfähigkeit *f*.
functional age: funktionelles Alter *n*.
functional amenorrhea: funktionelle Amenorrhö *f*.
functional bleeding: funktionelle Blutung *f*.
functional disorder: Funktionsstörung *f*.
functional hearing loss: funktioneller Hörverlust *m*.
functional illness: funktionelle Erkrankung *f*.
functional impairment: Funktionseinschränkung *f*.
functional murmur: funktionelles Herzgeräusch *n*.
functional paralysis: funktionelle Lähmung *f*.
functional proteinuria: physiologische Proteinurie *f*.
functional psychosis: Funktionspsychose *f*, funktionelle Psychose *f*.
functional rehabilitation: funktionelle Rehabilitation *f*.
functional residual capacity: funktionelle Residualkapazität *f*.
functional spasm: Beschäftigungskrampf *m*.
function test: Funktionsprobe *f*.
fundal placenta: fundusständige Plazenta *f*.
fundament/*n*: Fundament *n*, Grundlage *f*, Gesäß *n*.
fundamental function: Fundamentalfunktion *f*, Grundfunktion *f*.
fundoscopy/*n*: Fundoskopie *f*, Augenspiegelung *f*.
fundus/*n*: Grund *m*, Fundus *m*.
funduscopy/*n*: Fundoskopie *f*, Augenspiegelung *f*.
fungal eczema: Pilzflechte *f*.
fungal infection: Pilzinfektion *f*.
fungal toxin: Mykotoxin *n*.
fungating carcinoma: fungusartiges Karzinom *n*.
fungicide/*n*: Fungizid *n*.
fungus/*n*: Pilz *m*.
funic presentation: in obstetrics, a prolapse of the umbilical cord into the vagina before delivery. Nabelschnurvorfall *m*.
funicular hernia: Samenstranghernie *f*.
funicular myelitis: funikuläre Spinalerkrankung *f*, Lichtheim-Syndrom *n*.
funiculitis/*n*: Funikulitis *f*.
funis/*n*: Strang *m*, Nabelschnur *f*.
funnel chest: Trichterbrust *f*, Pectus excavatum *n*.
funnel pelvis: Trichterbecken *n*.
furacin/*n*: Furacin *n*.
furaltadone/*n*: Furaltadon *n*.
furazolidone/*n*: Furazolidon *n*.
furosemide/*n*: Furosemid *n*.
furrow/*n*: Furche *f*.
furuncle/*n*: inflammation of a hair follicle, usually due to infection with the bacterium Staphylococcus. Furuncles can be associated with

skin diseases, for example sycosis, or may result from spread of purulent material in other disorders. Furunkel *m*.
furuncular otitis: Gehörgangfurunkel *m*.
furunculosis/*n*: Furunkulose *f*.
fuse/*vb*: verschmelzen, einschmelzen.
fused kidney: Fusionsniere *f*.
fusidic acid: Fusidinsäure *f*.
fusiform/*adj*: spindelförmig.
fusiform bronchiectasis: spindelförmige Bronchiektasie *f*.
fusiform cataract: Spindelkatarakt *f*.
fusiform cell: Spindelzelle *f*.
fusimotor fiber: fusimotorische Muskelfaser *f*.
fusion/*n*: Fusion *f*, Vereinigung *f*.
fusional convergence: Fusionskonvergenz *f*.
fusion inhibitor: Fusionsinhibitor *m*.
fuzzy/*adj*: weich, flaumig.

G

G <*abbr*> **1. glycine; 2. guanosine**: 1. Glycin *n*; 2. Guanosin *n*.
gabapentin/*n*: Gabapentin *n*.
gag reflex: Rachenreflex *m*.
gain/*n, vb*: 1. Gewinn *m*, Zunahme *f*; 2. zunehmen.
gait/*n*: Gang *m*.
gait disorder: Gangstörung *f*.
galactagogue/*n, adj*: 1. Galaktagogum *n*, Laktagogum *n*; 2. milchtreibend.
galactocele/*n*: Galaktozele *f*.
galactorrhea/*n*: Galaktorrhö *f*, Laktorrhö *f*.
galactorrhea-amenorrhea syndrome: excessive nonpuerperal secretion of milk and simultaneous amenorrhea, usually caused by an adenoma of the pituitary gland. Galaktorrhö-Amenorrhö-Syndrom *n*, Forbes-Albright-Syndrom *n*.
galactose/*n*: Galaktose *f*, Gal.
galactosemia/*n*: Galaktosämie *f*.
galacturonic acid: Galakturonsäure *f*.
galantamine/*n*: Galantamin *n*.
gallamine/*n*: Gallamin *n*.
gallbladder/*n*: Gallenblase *f*.
gallic acid: Gallussäure *f*.
gallium scanning: Galliumszintigraphie *f*.
gallopamil/*n*: Gallopamil *n*.
gallop rhythm: an extra heart sound which can be clearly heard and that, when the heart rate is fast, resembles a horse's gallop. It may be a symptom in cardiac failure, but can also occur in healthy young people. Galopprhythmus *m*.
gallotannic acid: Gerbsäure *f*, Tannin *n*.
gallstone/*n*: a calculus or stone-like object in the gallbladder and its drainage system, composed primarily of calcium. Symptoms include attacks of severe pain when the stone moves which may spread to both sides, in the back, and throughout the abdomen. If a gallstone causes obstruction to the bile duct, jaundice may occur. Gallenstein *m*.
galvanism/*n*: Galvanismus *m*.
galvanometer/*n*: Galvanometer *n*.
Gambian fever: afrikanische Trypanosomiasis *f*, Schlafkrankheit *f*.
gamete/*n*: Gamet *m*.
gamete intrafallopian transfer: intratubarer Embryonentransfer *m*.
gamma-aminobutyric acid: Gamma-aminobuttersäure *f*, GABA.
gamma globulin: Gammaglobulin *n*.
ganciclovir/*n*: Ganciclovir *n*.
ganglion/*n*: Ganglion *n*.
ganglionectomy/*n*: Ganglionektomie *f*.
ganglionic block: Ganglienblock *m*.
ganglionic blocking agent: Ganglienblocker *m*.
ganglionic glioma: Gangliogliom *n*.
ganglionitis/*n*: Ganglionitis *f*.
gangliosidosis/*n*: inborn error of ganglioside metabolism which results in a storage of gangliosides in nervous tissue. Forms include general gangliosidosis with neuronal and somatic accumulation of gangliosides, and Tay-Sachs disease. Gangliosidose *f*.
gangrene/*n*: Gangrän *f*.
gangrenous/*adj*: gangränös.
gangrenous balanitis: gangränöse Balanitis *f*, Corbus-Krankheit *f*.
gangrenous cystitis: gangränöse Zystitis *f*.
gangrenous pharyngitis: gangränöse Pharyngitis *f*.

ganirelix/*n*: Ganirelix *n*.
gap/*n*: Lücke *f*, Öffnung *f*.
gap junction: Gap Junction *f*, offene Verbindung *f*.
gargle/*n, vb*: 1. Mundwasser *n*; 2. gurgeln.
gargoylism/*n*: autosomal recessive inborn error of mucopolysaccharide metabolism which is characterized by heavy facial features, impaired vision, mental retardation, and short stature. Gargoylismus *m*, Pfaundler-Hurler-Krankheit *f*, Mukopolysaccharidose I-H *f*.
garrot/*n*: Tourniquet-Presse *f*.
gas/*n, vb*: 1. Gas *n*; 2. vergasen.
gas bacillus: Gasbrandbazillus *m*, Clostridium perfringens *n*.
gas embolism: Luftembolie *f*.
gaseous/*adj*: gasförmig.
gaseous edema: Gasödem *n*.
gaseous gangrene: gangrenous tissue lesion, usually resulting from infection in a wound with anaerobic bacteria like Clostridium, with putrefaction of tissue and the formation of gas. Gasgangrän *f*.
gasometry/*n*: Gasvolumenbestimmung *f*.
gasp/*n, vb*: 1. Keuchen *n*, Ringen nach Luft *n*; 2. keuchen, schwer atmen.
gasping breathing: Schnappatmung *f*.
gasserian ganglion: Gasser-Ganglion *n*.
gasserian syndrome: a syndrome which is characterized by unilateral facial pain and paresthesia, loss of the corneal reflex, due to a lesion of the gasserian ganglion of the trigeminal nerve. Gasser-Syndrom *n*.
gastrectomy/*n*: Gastrektomie *f*.
gastric/*adj*: gastrisch.
gastric acid: Magensäure *f*.
gastric cancer: Magenkrebs *m*.
gastric carcinoma: malignant neoplasm of the stomach, caused by certain carcinogens, resulting from achlorhydria, or associated with certain genetic patterns. Symptoms depend on localization and size of the tumor and may include weight loss, loss of appetite, and gastric hemorrhage. Magenkarzinom *n*.
gastric diverticulum: Magendivertikel *n*.
gastric fistula: Magenfistel *f*.
gastric fold: Magenfalte *f*.
gastric hypersecretion: gesteigerte Magensaftsekretion *f*.
gastric irritation: Magenreizung *f*.
gastric juice: Magensaft *m*.
gastric lavage: Magenspülung *f*.
gastric lymphoma: Lymphom des Magens *n*.
gastric mucosal barrier: Magenschleimhautschranke *f*.
gastric operation: Magenoperation *f*.
gastric perforation: a hole in the gastric wall, usually occurring as a complication in gastric ulcer disease or gastric carcinoma, or sometimes resulting from medical interventions, for example gastroscopy. Magenperforation *f*.
gastric pit: Magengrube *f*.
gastric polyp: Magenpolyp *m*.
gastric regurgitation: gastroösophagealer Reflux *m*.
gastric resection: Magenresektion *f*.
gastric ulcer: ulceration of the mucosa of the stomach, usually due to peptic digestion. Symptoms include epigastric pain, especially after food intake, and fasting pain. Magenulkus *n*, Magengeschwür *n*.
gastric wall: Magenwand *f*.
gastrin/*n*: Gastrin *n*.
gastritic/*adj*: gastritisch.
gastritis/*n*: inflammation of the mucosal lining of the stomach walls, caused by gastric acid hypersecretion, infection, physical or chemical damage, or metabolic disorders. Symptoms depend on the severity of the disease and may include loss of appetite, and pain. Gastritis *f*, Magenschleimhautentzündung *f*.
gastrocele/*n*: Magenhernie *f*.
gastrocolic/*adj*: gastrokolisch.
gastrocolic fistula: gastrokolische Fistel *f*.
gastroduodenal ulcer: a peptic ulcer of the stomach and the duodenum. Symptoms depend on the severity of the disease and may include loss

of appetite, nausea, vomiting, and fasting pain. gastroduodenales Ulkus *n*.
gastroduodenoenterostomy/*n*: Gastroduodenoenterostomie *f*.
gastroenteritis/*n*: inflammation of the stomach and intestine, usually caused by viral, bacterial, or parasitic infection. Symptoms include nausea and vomiting, diarrhea, and abdominal discomfort. Gastroenteritis *f*.
gastroenteropathy/*n*: Gastroenteropathie *f*.
gastroenterostomy/*n*: Gastroenterostomie *f*.
gastroesophageal reflux: gastroösophagealer Reflux *m*.
gastroileal fistula: Magen-Ileum-Fistel *f*.
gastrointestinal/*adj*: gastrointestinal.
gastrointestinal examination: Magen-Darm-Passage *f*.
gastrointestinal hemorrhage: gastrointestinale Blutung *f*.
gastrointestinal hormone: gastrointestinales Hormon *n*.
gastrointestinal passage: Magen-Darm-Passage *f*.
gastrointestinal tract: Gastrointestinaltrakt *m*.
gastrojejunostomy/*n*: Gastrojejunostomie *f*.
gastrolysis/*n*: Gastrolyse *f*.
gastropexy/*n*: Gastropexie *f*.
gastroplasty/*n*: Magenplastik *f*
gastroptosis/*n*: Gastroptose *f*, Senkmagen *m*.
gastroscopy/*n*: Gastroskopie *f*, Magenspiegelung *f*.
gastrostomy/*n*: Gastrostomie *f*.
gastrulation/*n*: Gastrulation *f*.
gate/*n*: Tor *n*, Schleuse *f*.
gate-control theory: Gate-Control-Theorie *f*.
gathering/*n*: Eiteransammlung *f*.
gatifloxacin/*n*: Gatifloxacin *n*.
gauge/*n*: Maß *n*, Maßstab *m*.
gauze/*n*: Gaze *f*, Verbandmull *m*.
gavage/*n*: Sondenernährung *f*.
gaze/*n, vb*: 1. Blick *m*; 2. ansehen, anstarren.
gel/*n, vb*: 1. Gel *n*; 2. gelatinieren.
gelatin/*n*: Gelatine *f*.
gelatiniform carcinoma: Gallertkrebs *m*.
gelatinous ascites: gallertartiger Aszites *m*, Pseudomyxoma peritonei *n*.
gel diffusion test: Geldiffusionstest *m*.
gemcitabine/*n*: Gemcitabin *n*.
gemeprost/*n*: Gemeprost *n*.
gemfibrozil/*n*: Gemfibrozil *n*.
gender/*n*: Geschlecht *n*.
gender identity: Geschlechtsidentität *f*.
gene/*n*: Gen *n*.
gene activation: Genaktivierung *f*.
gene mapping: Genkartierung *f*.
gene product: Genprodukt *n*.
general/*adj*: generell, allgemein.
general anesthesia: Allgemeinnarkose *f*.
general anesthetic: Allgemeinanästhetikum *n*.
general atrophy: generalisierte Atrophie *f*.
general condition: Allgemeinzustand *m*, AZ.
general gangliosidosis: generalisierte Gangliosidose *f*.
generalization/*n*: Generalisierung *f*.
generalized anaphylaxis: generalisierte anaphylaktische Reaktion *f*.
generalized epilepsy: generalisierte Epilepsie *f*.
generalized epileptic somatic sensation: generalisierte epileptische somatische Aura *f*.
generalized seizure: generalisierter Anfall *m*.
generalized xanthoma: a condition which is characterized by the presence of multiple, disseminated xanthomas of the skin, mucosal membranes, and tendons, occurring as a symptom of hyperlipidemia or as idiopathic disorder with normal levels of cholesterol. generalisiertes Xanthom *n*, Xanthomatose *f*.
generally enlarged pelvis: weites, langes Becken *n*.
general pathology: allgemeine Pathologie *f*.

general practitioner: Arzt für Allgemeinmedizin.
general reaction: Allgemeinreaktion *f*.
general surgery: Allgemeinchirurgie *f*.
generation/*n*: Generation *f*, Fortpflanzung *f*.
generative power: Zeugungsfähigkeit *f*.
generic/*n, adj*: 1. Generikum *n*; 2. generisch.
generic name: Freiname *m*, generische Bezeichnung *f*.
gene therapy: Gentherapie *f*.
genetic/*adj*: genetisch.
genetic adaptation: genetische Anpassung *f*.
genetically significant dose: genetisch signifikante Dosis *f*.
genetic carrier: Heterozygot *m*.
genetic disease: genetische Erkrankung *f*.
genetic drift: Gendrift *f*.
genetic engineering: Gentechnologie *f*.
genetic immunity: natürliche Immunität *f*.
genetic locus: Genlokus *m*.
genetic recombination: genetische Rekombination *f*.
genetics: Genetik *f*
genetic screening: genetisches Screening *n*.
genetic sex: chromosomales Geschlecht *n*.
geniculate/*adj*: knieförmig.
geniculate neuralgia: Genikulatumneuralgie *f*.
geniculate otalgia: Genikulatumotalgie *f*.
genital/*adj*: genital.
genital cleft: Urogenitalspalte *f*.
genital tract: Genitaltrakt *m*.
genital tuberculosis: Genitaltuberkulose *f*.
genital wart: a squamous cell papilloma, usually due to infection with human papillomavirus. Genital warts or condylomata acuminata are mainly localized in the genital area and appear in clusters that may reach considerable size. Condyloma acuminatum *n*, Feigwarze *f*.
genital zone: Genitalbereich *m*.
genitourinary fistula: Urogenitalfistel *f*.
genitourinary tract: Urogenitaltrakt *m*.
genitourinary tuberculosis: Urogenitaltuberkulose *f*.
genome/*n*: Genom *n*.
genotype/*n*: Genotyp *m*.
genotypic resistance: genotypische Resistenz *f*.
gentamicin/*n*: Gentamicin *n*.
gentian violet: Gentianaviolett *n*.
gentisic acid: Gentisinsäure *f*.
genual/*adj*: knieförmig.
genucubital position: Knie-Ellbogen-Lage *f*.
genufacial position: Knie-Gesicht-Lage *f*.
genuine/*adj*: genuin.
genupectoral position: Knie-Brust-Lage *f*.
geomedicine/*n*: Geomedizin *f*.
gepefrine/*n*: Gepefrin *n*.
geriatric nurse: Altenpflegerin *f*.
geriatric psychiatry: Alterspsychiatrie *f*.
geriatrics: Geriatrie *f*.
germ/*n*: Keim *m*.
German measles: an acute infection which is caused by rubella virus. Symptoms include high fever, and a characteristic skin rash with exanthema and pink patches. Congenital rubella can be a fatal disease and is frequently associated with a wide range of severe congenital malformations, for example of the central nervous system. Rubella *f*, Röteln *f*.
germ cell: Keimzelle *f*.
germ-free: keimfrei, steril.
germicide/*n*: Germizid *n*, keimtötende Substanz *f*.
germinal disk: Keimscheibe *f*.
germinal factor: Keimfaktor *m*.
germinal tumor: Keimzelltumor *m*.
germinal vesicle: Keimbläschen *n*.
germinoblastic sarcoma: Germinoblastom *n*.
gerontology/*n*: Gerontologie *f*.

G

gestagen/*n*: Gestagen *n*.
gestalt psychology: Gestaltpsychologie *f*.
gestation/*n*: Gestation *f*, Schwangerschaft *f*.
gestational age: Gestationsalter *n*.
gestational diabetes: a diabetes mellitus that becomes evident during pregnancy only and is revealed by an abnormal glucose tolerance test. Schwangerschaftsdiabetes *m*.
gestational edema: Schwangerschaftsödem *n*.
gestational hypertension: Gestationshochdruck *m*.
gestational period: Schwangerschaftsdauer *f*, Tragzeit *f*.
gestational proteinuria: Schwangerschaftsproteinurie *f*.
gestational psychosis: Schwangerschaftspsychose *f*.
giant cell: Riesenzelle *f*.
giant-cell arteritis: Riesenzellarteriitis *f*, Arteriitis temporalis *f*, Horton-Arteriitis *f*.
giant-cell carcinoma: a malignant neoplasm which is characterized by the presence of numerous large, pleomorphic cells, most frequently located in the thyroid gland and the lung. Riesenzellkarzinom *n*.
giant-cell hepatitis: Riesenzellhepatitis *f*.
giant-cell pneumonia: Riesenzellpneumonie *f*.
giant-cell thyroiditis: Riesenzellthyreoiditis *f*, Quervain-Thyreoiditis *f*.
giant colon: Megakolon *n*.
giant condyloma: Riesenkondylom *n*.
giant fiber: Riesenaxon *n*.
giant follicular hyperplasia: gutartige hyalinisierende Lymphknotenhyperplasie *f*, Castleman-Tumor *m*.
giant follicular lymphoma: großfollikuläres Lymphoblastom *m*, Brill-Symmers-Krankheit *f*.
giant hypertrophic gastritis: Riesenfaltengastritis *f*, Ménétrier-Krankheit *f*.
giant osteoid osteoma: Osteoblastom *n*.
giardiasis/*n*: Giardiasis *f*, Lambliasis *f*.
giddiness/*n*: Schwindel *m*, Vertigo *f*.
GIFT <*abbr*> **gamete intrafallopian transfer**: intratubarer Embryonentransfer *m*.
gigantism/*n*: Gigantismus *m*, Hochwuchs *m*.
gingival/*adj*: gingival.
gingival border: Zahnfleischsaum *m*.
gingival fistula: Zahnfleischfistel *f*.
gingival hemorrhage: Zahnfleischblutung *f*.
gingival hyperplasia: Gingivahyperplasie *f*.
gingival line: Gingivasaum *m*.
gingivitis/*n*: Gingivitis *f*, Zahnfleischentzündung *f*.
ginglymoid joint: Ginglymus *m*, Scharniergelenk *n*.
ginglymus/*n*: Ginglymus *m*, Scharniergelenk *n*.
girdle/*n*: Gürtel *m*.
girth/*n*: Umfang *m*.
gitoformate/*n*: Gitoformat *n*.
glabella/*n*: Glatze *f*, Glabella *f*.
glabrous skin: glatte Haut *f*.
glafenine/*n*: Glafenin *n*.
gland/*n*: Drüse *f*, Glandula *f*.
glanders: Pferderotz *m*, Malleus *m*.
glandular/*adj*: glandulär.
glandular carcinoma: a malignant neoplasm originating from glandular structures. Forms include tumors with tubular, acinar, cystic, papillary, and trabecular growth. Adenokarzinom *n*.
glandular cell: Drüsenzelle *f*.
glandular-cystic hyperplasia: glandulär-zystische Hyperplasie *f*.
glandular fever: Pfeiffer-Drüsenfieber *n*, Mononucleosis infectiosa *f*.
glandular plague: Drüsenpest *f*, Beulenpest *f*.
glare/*n*: Blendung *f*.
glass/*n*: Glas *n*.
glasses: Brille *f*.
glass eye: Glasauge *n*.
glatiramer/*n*: Glatiramer *n*.
Glauber salt: Glaubersalz *n*.
glaucoma/*n*: an eye disease in which the pressure of the intraocular fluid increases. Prolonged high eye pressure may cause damage to optic ner-

ve fibers. Forms include for example acute congestive glaucoma, angle-closure glaucoma, congestive glaucoma, and obstructive glaucoma. Glaukom *n*, grüner Star *m*.
glaucomatous cataract: Glaukomkatarakt *f*.
glaucomatous ring: Halo glaucomatosus *m*.
glenoid/*adj*: glenoidal.
glia/*n*: Glia *f*, Neuroglia *f*.
glibenclamide/*n*: Glibenclamid *n*.
glibornuride/*n*: Glibornurid *n*.
glicazide/*n*: Glicazid *n*.
gliding articulation: Gleitgelenk *n*.
glimepiride/*n*: Glimepirid *n*.
glinide/*n*: Glinid *n*.
glioblastoma/*n*: Glioblastom *n*.
glioma/*n*: Gliom *n*.
glioneuroblastoma/*n*: Glioneuroblastom *n*, Ganglioneurom *n*.
gliosarcoma/*n*: Gliosarkom *n*.
glipizide/*n*: Glipizid *n*.
gliquidone/*n*: Gliquidon *n*.
glisoxepide/*n*: Glisoxepid *n*.
global aphasia: Globalaphasie *f*.
globe cell: Kugelzelle *f*, Sphärozyt *m*.
globoid leukodystrophy: Globoidzellen-Leukodystrophie *f*, Krabbe-Krankheit *f*.
globulin/*n*: Globulin *n*.
globus/*n*: Ball *m*, Kugel *f*, Globus *m*.
globus sensation: Globusgefühl *n*.
glomerular/*adj*: glomerulär.
glomerular cyst: Glomerulumzyste *f*.
glomerular fibrosis: Glomerulumfibrose *f*.
glomerular filtration rate: glomeruläre Filtrationsrate *f*, GFR.
glomerular nephritis: any glomerula disease which is characterized by acute or chronic inflammation. Acute glomerulonephritis is characterized by a syndrome of transient hematuria and proteinuria, and rarely accompanied by hypertension. Chronic glomerulonephritis usually begins with asymptomatic proteinuria and may result in the nephrotic syndrome, hypertension, and slowly developing renal failure. Glomerulonephritis *f*.
glomerular proteinuria: glomeruläre Proteinurie *f*.
glomerular sclerosis: Glomerulosklerose *f*.
glomerulitis/*n*: Glomerulitis *f*.
glomerulonephritis/*n*: Glomerulonephritis *f*.
glossa/*n*: Zunge *f*.
glossal/*adj*: Zungen-.
glossary reflex: Würgreflex *m*.
glossodynia/*n*: Glossodynie *f*.
glossopharyngeal/*adj*: glossopharyngeal.
glossopharyngeal neuralgia: Glossopharyngealneuralgie *f*, Sicard-Syndrom *n*.
glossoplegia/*n*: Glossoplegie *f*, Zungenlähmung *f*.
glossy/*adj*: glänzend.
glottic carcinoma: malignant neoplasm of the vocal apparatus of the larynx. Symptoms may include dysphagia, coughing, dyspnea, and hoarseness. Glottiskarzinom *n*.
glottic spasm: Laryngospasmus *m*, Stimmritzenkrampf *m*.
glottis/*n*: Stimmritze *f*.
glove/*n*: Handschuh *m*.
glucagon/*n*: Glukagon *n*.
glucagonoma/*n*: Glukagonom *n*.
glucametacin/*n*: Glucametacin *n*.
glucocorticoid/*n*: Glukokortikoid *n*.
glucogenesis/*n*: Glukogenese *f*.
gluconeogenesis/*n*: Glukoneogenese *f*.
gluconic acid: Glukonsäure *f*.
glucosamine/*n*: Glucosamin *n*, GlcN.
glucose/*n*: Glukose *f*.
glucose intolerance: Glukoseintoleranz *f*.
glucose tolerance test: Glukosetoleranztest *m*, GTT.
glucosuria/*n*: Glukosurie *f*.
glucuronic acid: Glukuronsäure *f*.
glue sniffing: Schnüffelsucht *f*, Trichloräthylensucht *f*.
glutamic acid: Glutaminsäure *f*.
glutamine/*n*: Glutamin *n*, Gln.
glutaric acid: Glutarsäure *f*.
gluteal/*adj*: gluteal.
gluteal cleft: Crena ani *f*, Afterfurche *f*.

G

gluteal gait: Hüfthinken *n*, Trendelenburg-Gang *m*.
gluteal reflex: Glutealreflex *m*.
gluten/*n*: Gluten *n*.
gluten enteropathy: Glutenenteropathie w, Zöliakie *f*.
gluten-free diet: glutenfreie Nahrung *f*.
glycemia/*n*: Glykämie *f*.
glyceric acid: Glycerinsäure *f*.
glyceric aciduria: Hyperoxalurie *f*.
glycerin/*n*: Glycerin *n*.
glycerinated tincture: Glycerintinktur *f*.
glyceroltrinitrat/*n*: Glyceroltrinitrat *n*.
glycine/*n*: Glycin *n*, Aminoessigsäure *f*.
glycocholic acid: Glykocholsäure *f*.
glycogen/*n*: Glykogen *n*.
glycogenesis/*n*: Glykogenese *f*.
glycogenolysis/*n*: Glykogenolyse *f*.
glycogen storage disease: Glykogenspeicherkrankheit *f*, Glykogenose *f*.
glycolic acid: Glykolsäure *f*.
glycolysis/*n*: Glykolyse *f*.
glycoprotein/*n*: Glykoprotein *n*, gp.
glycopyrronium bromide: Glycopyrroniumbromid *n*.
glycosuria/*n*: the presence of abnormal amounts of glucose in the urine, resulting either from excessively high plasma glucose levels, or from reduced kidney capacity to reabsorb glucose. Glukosurie *f*, Glykosurie *f*.
glycosuric acid: Glykosursäure *f*.
glycuronic acid: Glukuronsäure *f*.
glycosylated hemoglobin: glykosyliertes Hämoglobin *n*.
glymidine/*n*: Glymidin *n*.
glyoxylic acid: Glyoxalsäure *f*.
gnat/*n*: Stechmücke *f*, Schnake *f*.
gnathic/*adj*: Kiefer-.
gnostic disorder: gnostische Störung *f*.
gnostic sensibility: gnostische Sensibilität *f*, epikritische Sensibilität *f*.
GnRH <*abbr*> **gonadotropin-releasing hormone**: Gonadotropin-Releasing-Hormon *n*.
goblet cell: Becherzelle *f*.
goiter/*n*: a diffuse or nodular enlargement of the thyroid gland, often visible in the anterior neck region, usually caused by iodine deficiency, but sometimes associated with autosomal recessive genetic defects. Kropf *m*, Struma *f*.
gold/*n*: Gold *n*.
golden ointment: Unguentum hydrargyri flavum *n*.
gold standard: Goldstandard *m*.
gonad/*n*: Gonade *f*, Keimdrüse *f*.
gonadal agenesis: Gonadenagenesie *f*.
gonadal aplasia: Gonadenaplasie *f*.
gonadal dose: Gonadendosis *f*.
gonadal hormone: Keimdrüsenhormon *n*.
gonadal sex: Gonadengeschlecht *n*.
gonadorelin/*n*: Gonadorelin *n*.
gonadotrophic/*adj*: gonadotrop.
gonadotrophin/*n*: Gonadotropin *n*.
gonadotropic hormone: gonadotropes Hormon *n*, Gonadotropin *n*.
gonadotropin/*n*: Gonadotropin *n*.
gonadotropin-releasing hormone: Gonadotropin-Releasing-Hormon *n*.
gonial angle: Kieferwinkel *m*.
gonococcal conjunctivitis: Gonokokkenkonjunktivitis *f*, Gonoblennorrhö *f*.
gonococcal ophthalmia: Gonokokkenkonjunktivitis *f*, Gonoblennorrhö *f*.
gonococcal urethritis: gonorrhoische Urethritis.
gonococcal vaginitis: gonorrhoische Vaginitis *f*.
gonococcus/*n*: Gonokokke *f*, Neisseria gonorrhoeae *f*.
gonorrhea/*n*: sexually transmitted infection caused by the bacterium Gonococcus. Symptoms in the genitals include discharge, inflammation of the urethra, and ascending inflammations of the urinary tract; in neonates, congenital infection with gonococcus can result in gonorrheal eye infection. Gonorrhö *f*, Tripper *m*.
gonorrheal keratosis: Keratoderma blennorhagica *f*.
gonorrheal salpingitis: Gonokokken-

salpingitis *f*.
gonosome/*n*: Gonosom *n*.
gooseflesh: Gänsehaut *f*.
gosereline/*n*: Goserelin *n*.
gouge/*n*: Hohlmeißel *m*.
gout/*n*: a disease with impaired metabolism of uric acid, causing symptoms of joint pain similar to arthritis, due to the presence of monosodium urate crystals within the joint space. Gicht *f*.
gout attack: Gichtanfall *m*.
gouty arthritis: Arthritis urica *f*, Gicht *f*.
gouty nephropathy: Gichtniere *f*.
gouty node: Gichtknoten *m*.
gown/*n*: Operationskittel *m*.
GP <*abbr*> **general practitioner**: Arzt für Allgemeinmedizin.
graafian follicle: Graaf-Follikel *m*, Tertiärfollikel *m*.
grade/*n, vb*: 1. Grad *m*; 2. einstufen.
graded effect: dosisabhängige Wirkung *f*.
gradient/*n*: Gradient *m*, Steigung *f*.
grading/*n*: Grading *n*, Gradeinteilung *f*.
graduated/*adj*: skaliert.
graduated tenotomy: Z-förmige Tenotomie *f*.
graft/*n, vb*: 1. Transplantat *n*; 2. transplantieren.
grafting/*n*: Grafting *n*, Transplantieren *n*.
Gram staining: Gram-Färbung *f*.
granisetron/*n*: Granisetron *n*.
granular/*adj*: granulär, körnig.
granular cell carcinoma: Granulosazelltumor *m*.
granular conjunctivitis: an infectious disease of the eye, caused the bacterium Chlamydia trachomatis. Symptoms include swelling of the conjunctiva and hypersecretion, followed by the formation of so-called trachoma inclusion bodies. Conjunctivitis granulosa *f*, Trachom *n*.
granular corneal dystrophy: Groenouw-Syndrom *n*.
granular degeneration: körnige Degeneration *f*, trübe Schwellung *f*.
granular leukocyte: Granulozyt *m*.
granular vaginitis: Colpitis granularis *f*.
granulation/*n*: Granulation *f*.
granulation tissue: Granulationsgewebe *n*.
granule/*n*: Körnchen *n*, Granulum *n*.
granulocyte/*n*: Granulozyt *f*.
granuloma/*n*: Granulom *n*.
granulomatosis/*n*: Granulomatose *f*.
granulomatous angiitis: granulomatöse Angiitis *f*.
granulomatous arteritis: Arteriitis granulomatosa *f*, Riesenzellarteriitis *f*, Arteriitis temporalis *f*.
granulomatous gastritis: granulomatöse Gastritis *f*.
granulovacuolar degeneration: granulovakuoläre Degeneration *f*.
graph/*n*: Diagramm *n*.
grasp reflex: Greifreflex *m*.
gravel/*n*: Kies *m*, Harngrieß *m*.
Graves disease: Graves-Krankheit *f*, Basedow-Krankheit *f*.
gravid/*adj*: gravid, schwanger.
gravidity/*n*: Gravidität *f*, Schwangerschaft *f*.
gravity/*n*: Gravitation *f*, Schwerkraft *f*.
gray/*n, adj*: 1. Grau *n*; 2. grau.
gray cataract: grauer Star *m*.
gray substance: graue Substanz *f*, Substantia grisea *f*.
gray syndrome: a condition in preterm infants or newborns resulting from chloramphenicol treatment. Symptoms are due to the inability to metabolize chloramphenicol and include gray coloration of the skin, sudden drop of body temperature, vomiting, dyspnea, and shock. Grey-Syndrom *n*, Grausyndrom *n*.
greasy ointment: Fettsalbe *f*.
greater circulation: großer Kreislauf *m*, Körperkreislauf *m*.
greater pelvis: großes Becken *n*.
great toe: Großzehe *f*, Hallux *m*.
green cataract: grüner Star *m*, Glaukom *n*.
green sputum: grünliches Sputum *n*.
greenstick fracture: Grünholzfraktur *f*, Knickbruch *m*.
grepafloxacin/*n*: Grepafloxacin *n*.

G

grey/*n, adj*: 1. Grau *n*; 2. grau.
grid/*n*: Gitter *n*, Blende *f*, Raster *n*.
grief/*n*: Kummer *m*, Trauer *f*.
grief reaction: Trauerreaktion *f*.
grip/*n, vb*: 1. Griff *m*, Handgriff *m*, Grippe *f*, Influenza *f*; 2. greifen.
griping pain: kneifender Schmerz *m*.
grippe/*n*: Grippe *f*, Influenza *f*.
gripping reflex: Greifreflex *m*.
griseofulvin/*n*: Griseofulvin *n*.
Grocco sign: Grocco-Zeichen *n*, paravertebrale Dämpfung *f*.
grommet/*n*: Paukenröhrchen *n*.
groove/*n*: Furche *f*, Rinne *f*.
gross/*adj*: dick, aufgetrieben, grob.
gross motor activity: Grobmotorik *f*.
gross tremor: grober Tremor *m*.
ground/*n*: Grund *m*, Untergrund *m*.
ground state: Grundzustand *m*, Normalzustand *m*.
group/*n, vb*: 1. Gruppe *f*; 2. gruppieren.
group practice: Gemeinschaftspraxis *f*.
group-specific antigen: blutgruppenspezifisches Antigen *n*.
grow/*vb*: wachsen.
growth/*n*: Wachstum *n*, Größenzunahme *f*.
growth curve: Wachstumskurve *f*.
growth factor: Wachstumsfaktor *m*.
growth hormone: Wachstumshormon *n*, Somatotropin *n*.
growth rate: Wachstumsrate *f*.
growth retardation: Wachstumsverzögerung *f*.
guanabenz/*n*: Guanabenz *n*.
guanacline/*n*: Guanaclin *n*.
guanethidine/*n*: Guanethidin *n*.
guanfacine/*n*: Guanfacin *n*.
guanidine/*n*: Guanidin *n*.
guanoxan/*n*: Guanoxan *n*.
guanylic acid: Guanylsäure *f*, Guanosinmonophosphat *n*.
guardianship/*n*: Vormundschaft *f*.
guarding/*n*: Abwehrspannung *f*.
guideline/*n*: Richtlinie *f*, Empfehlung *f*, Leitlinie *f*.
guiding symptom: Leitsymptom *n*.
guinea pig: Meerschweinchen *n*.
guinea worm infection: Guinea-wurm-Infektion *f*, Drakunkulose *f*.
gullet/*n*: Schlund *m*, Speiseröhre *f*, Ösophagus *m*.
gulonic acid: Gulonsäure *f*.
gum/*n*: Gummi *m*, Kautschuk *m*, Zahnfleisch *n*.
gumboil/*n*: Zahnabszess *m*.
gumma/*n*: Gumma *n*.
gummatous meningitis: syphilitische Meningitis *f*.
gurgle/*vb*: gurgeln.
gustation/*n*: Geschmackssinn *m*.
gustatory/*adj*: gustatorisch.
gustatory bud: Geschmacksknospe *f*.
gustatory center: Geschmackszentrum *n*.
gustatory hair: Geschmackshaar *n*.
gustatory hyperhidrosis: a syndrome which is characterized by profuse sweating over one side of the face, provoked by eating and sometimes by emotion. This gustatory sweating syndrome may be caused by aberrant growth of the facial nerve after injury. gustatorisches Schwitzen *n*, aurikulotemporales Syndrom *n*.
gustatory sensation: Geschmackssinn *m*.
gut/*n*: Darm *m*.
gynatresia/*n*: Gynatresie *f*.
gynecoid pelvis: gynäkoides Becken *n*.
gynecology/*n*: Gynäkologie *f*, Frauenheilkunde *f*.
gynecomastia/*n*: enlargement of the mammary glands in males, occurring sometimes as a normal phenomenon of puberty, or resulting from various disorders such as genetic diseases, or endocrine disorders. Gynäkomastie *f*.
gyrase inhibitor: Gyrasehemmer *m*.
gyrus/*n*: Gyrus *m*, Windung *f*.

H

H <*abbr*> **1. hydrogen; 2. histidine**: 1. Wasserstoff *m*, H; 2. Histidin *n*.
habit/*n*: Gewohnheit *f*, Angewohnheit *f*.
habit disorder: Verhaltensstörung *f*.
habitual abortion: habitueller Abort *m*.
habitual dislocation: habituelle Luxation *f*.
hacking cough: Stakkatohusten *m*.
hair/*n*: Haar *n*.
hairball/*n*: an accumulation primarily of hair in the intestinal tract, usually found in the stomach. Haarball *m*, Trichobezoar *m*.
hair cell: Haarzelle *f*.
hair color: Haarfarbe *f*.
hair follicle: Haarfollikel *m*.
hairiness/*n*: Behaartheit *f*, Körperbehaarung *f*.
hair tongue: Haarzunge *f*, Trichoglossie *f*.
hairy-cell leukemia: Haarzellenleukämie *f*.
hairy heart: Zottenherz *n*, Cor villosum *n*.
hairy leukoplakia: Haarleukoplakie *f*.
hairy nevus: Tierfellnävus *m*.
hairy tongue: Haarzunge *f*, Glossotrichie *f*.
halcinonide/*n*: Halcinonid *n*.
half-glass spectacles: Halbbrille *f*.
half-life/*n*: Halbwertszeit *f*.
half-time/*n*: Halbwertszeit *f*.
half vision: Hemianopsie *f*.
hallucination/*n*: Halluzination *f*, Sinnestäuschung *f*.
hallucinatory image: Trugbild *n*.
hallucinogen/*n*: Halluzinogen *n*.
hallux/*n*: Großzehe *f*, Hallux *m*.
halofantrine/*n*: Halofantrin *n*.
halofuginone/*n*: Halofuginon *n*.
halogen/*n*: Halogen *n*.
halometasone/*n*: Halometason *n*.
haloperidol/*n*: Haloperidol *n*.
halothane/*n*: Halothan *n*.
haloxon/*n*: Haloxon *n*.
hamartoma/*n*: Hamartom *n*.
hamate/*adj*: hammerförmig.
hammer finger: Hammerfinger *m*.
hammer toe/*n*: Hammerzehe *f*.
hand/*n*: Hand *f*.
hand disinfection: Händedesinfektion *f*.
handgrip test: Faustschlussprobe *f*.
handicap/*n, vb*: 1. Behinderung *f*; 2. behindern.
handicap management: Behinderungsbewältigung *f*.
handle/*n, vb*: 1. Griff *m*; 2. hantieren, handhaben.
handpiece/*n*: Handstück *n*.
hand splint: Handschiene *f*.
hanging/*n*: Erhängen *n*.
hanging cast: Hängegips *m*.
hanging drop: hängender Tropfen *m*.
hanging heart: Tropfenherz *n*.
hangnail/*n*: partly detached piece of skin at the root of a fingernail, common in nail biters. Niednagel *m*.
hantavirus/*n*: Hantavirus *n*.
haploid/*adj*: haploid.
hapten/*n*: Hapten *n*.
haptic/*adj*: haptisch.
haptoglobin/*n*: Haptoglobin *n*.
hard-bodied tick: Schildzecke *f*.
hard chancre: harter Schanker *m*, Ulcus durum *n*.
harden/*vb*: härten, erhärten.
hard fibroma: Fibroma durum *n*.
hard pulse: Pulsus durus *m*.
hard radiation: harte Strahlen.
hard sore: harter Schanker *m*, Ulcus durum *n*.

harelip/*n*: Hasenscharte *f*, Lippenspalte *f*.
harm/*n, vb*: 1. Schaden *m*; 2. schaden.
harmful/*adj*: schädlich.
harmless/*adj*: harmlos, unschädlich.
harvest fever: Erntefieber *n*, Feldfieber *n*.
haustral segmentation: Haustrierung *f*.
HAV <*abbr*> **hepatitis A virus**: Hepatitis-A-Virus *n*, HAV.
haversian space: Havers-Kanal *m*.
hay fever: allergic rhinitis caused by specific airborne allergens like pollen. Typical symptoms include acute inflammatory reaction of the nasal mucosa and conjunctivitis. Heufieber *n*, Heuschnupfen *m*.
hazardous/*adj*: gefährlich.
Hb <*abbr*> **hemoglobin**/*n*: Hämoglobin *n*, Hb.
HBV <*abbr*> **hepatitis B virus**: Hepatitis-B-Virus *n*, HBV.
HCT <*abbr*> **hematocrit**/*n*: Hämatokrit *m*, HK, Hkt.
HCV <*abbr*> **hepatitis C virus**: Hepatitis-C-Virus *n*, HCV.
head/*n*: Kopf *m*.
headache/*n*: acute or chronic pain affecting the head or parts of it, for example unilateral headache or hemicrania, or pain in the front or the back of the head. Symptoms may include steady or throbbing pain, barely noticeable pain, or completely prostrating sensations. Kopfschmerz *m*, Kephalgie *f*.
head injury: Kopfverletzung *f*.
headless/*adj*: azephal.
head louse/*n*: Kopflaus *f*, Pediculus capitis *m*.
head presentation: in obstetrics, the position of the fetus in which the head is presented and appears first in the uterine cervix. Kopflage *f*.
heal/*vb*: heilen.
healer/*n*: Heiler *m*.
healing/*n*: Heilung *f*.
healing by first intention: Primärheilung *f*.
healing by second intention: Sekundärheilung *f*.
health/*n*: Gesundheit *f*.
health authorities: Gesundheitsbehörden.
health care: Gesundheitsversorgung *f*.
health care insurance: Krankenversicherung *f*.
health care system: Gesundheitssystem *n*.
health hazard: Gesundheitsrisiko *n*.
health information: Gesundheitsaufklärung *f*.
health insurance: Krankenversicherung *f*.
health office: Gesundheitsamt *n*.
health promotion: Gesundheitsförderung *f*.
health system: Gesundheitssystem *n*.
healthy/*adj*: gesund.
healthy carrier: gesunder Krankheitsüberträger *m*.
hear/*vb*: hören.
hearing aid: Hörhilfe *f*.
hearing disorder: Hörstörung *f*.
hearing loss: impairment or complete loss of hearing. Forms include conductive deafness with disturbances in the external meatus or in the middle ear, and perceptive or nerve deafness, resulting from a defect of the inner ear, the auditory nerve, or the cerebral auditory centers. Hörverlust *m*.
heart/*n*: Herz *n*.
heart attack: Herzanfall *m*, Angina pectoris *f*.
heartbeat/*n*: Herzschlag *m*.
heart block: a cardiac disorder in which the conduction of impulses is slowed down or unable to pass from the atrium of heart to the ventricles, resulting in independent beating of chambers. Herzblock *m*.
heartburn/*n*: burning pain in the stomach and gullet, associated with acid taste in the mouth, often associated with gastroesophageal reflux or dyspepsia. Sodbrennen *n*, Pyrosis *f*.
heart defect: Herzfehler *m*.
heart disease: Herzerkrankung *f*.
heart enlargement: Herzvergrößerung *f*.

heart failure: Herzversagen *n*, Herzinsuffizienz *f*.
heart-lung machine: Herz-Lungen-Maschine *f*.
heart murmur: Herzgeräusch *n*.
heart rate: Herzfrequenz *f*.
heart septal defect: Herzseptumdefekt *m*.
heat/*n, vb*: 1. Hitze *f*, Wärme *f*; 2. erhitzen, erwärmen.
heat collapse: Hitzekollaps *m*.
heat-labile antibody: hitzelabiler Antikörper *m*.
heat loss: Wärmeverlust *m*.
heatstroke/*n*: a condition which is due to direct exposure to high temperature, and characterized by high body temperature, thirst, dizziness, nausea, and confusion. Hitzschlag *m*.
heat-treated: hitzebehandelt.
heaving apex beat: hebender Herzspitzenstoß *m*.
heavy/*adj*: schwer, massiv.
hebephrenia/*n*: Hebephrenie *f*.
hebephrenic schizophrenia: hebephrene Schizophrenie *f*.
Heberden's nodes: Heberden-Knötchen.
hectic/*adj*: unruhig, hektisch.
hedonism/*n*: Hedonismus *m*.
heel/*n*: Absatz *m*, Ferse *f*.
heel bone/*n*: Fersenbein *n*.
heel-knee test: Knie-Hacken-Versuch *m*.
heel-to-crown measurement: Scheitel-Fersen-Länge *f*.
Hegar's dilator: Hegar-Stift *m*.
height/*n*: Höhe *f*.
Heinz body: Heinz-Ehrlich-Innenkörper *m*.
helicase/*n*: Helikase *f*.
heliotherapy/*n*: Heliotherapie *f*.
helix/*n*: Helix *f*, Spirale *f*.
helminth/*n*: Helminthe *f*.
helminthagogue/*n*: Anthelminthikum *n*.
helminthiasis/*n*: infestation of the body by parasitic worms, for exampla filariosis, echinococcosis, onchocerciasis, or trichinosis. Helminthiasis *f*.
helminthic dysentery: Helminthendysenterie *f*.
help/*n, vb*: 1. Hilfe *f*; 2. helfen.
helper/*n*: Helfer *m*.
helplessness/*n*: Hilflosigkeit *f*.
helvellic acid: Helvellasäure *f*.
hemadsorption/*n*: Hämadsorption *f*.
hemagglutinating virus: hämagglutinierendes Virus *n*.
hemagglutination/*n*: Hämagglutination *f*.
hemagglutinin/*n*: Hämagglutinin *n*.
hemangiectatic hypertrophy: angiektatischer Riesenwuchs *m*, Klippel-Trénaunay-Weber-Syndrom *n*.
hemangioma/*n*: a benign tumor composed of proliferated blood vessels, mainly localized in the skin and mucosal membranes. Forms include capillary, racemose, venous, or cavernous angioma. Hämangiom *n*, Blutschwamm *m*.
hemarthrosis/*n*: Hämarthrose *f*.
hematemesis/*n*: Hämatemesis *f*.
hematin/*n*: Hämatin *n*.
hematocele/*n*: Hämatozele *f*.
hematocolpos/*n*: Hämatokolpos *m*.
hematocrit/*n*: Hämatokrit *m*, HK.
hematocyte/*n*: Hämozyt *m*, Blutzelle *f*.
hematogenous abscess: hämatogener Abszess *m*.
hematogenous osteitis: hämatogene Ostitis *f*.
hematogenous pyelonephritis: hämatogene Pyelonephritis *f*.
hematogenous tuberculosis: hämatogene Tuberkulose *f*.
hematology/*n*: Hämatologie *f*.
hematolysis/*n*: Hämolyse *f*.
hematoma/*n*: a swelling caused by the localized accumulation of blood in a tissue or a space. It is usually composed of clotted blood in different stages of resorption. Most common causes include direct violence, for example a black eye, and internal hemorrhage. Hämatom *n*, Bluterguss *m*.
hematometra/*n*: Hämatometra *f*.
hematopoietic system: hämatopoetisches System *n*.

hematoporphyrin/*n*: Hämatoporphyrin *n*.
hematosalpinx/*n*: Hämatosalpinx *f*.
hematothorax/*n*: Hämothorax *m*.
hematotoxin/*n*: Hämatotoxin *n*.
hematuria/*n*: the presence of red blood cells in the urine. Forms include gross hematuria with visible reddening of urine, and microscopic hematuria only detected by microscopic or chemical examination. Causes include infections of the urinary tract or the kidneys, tumors, or lesions caused by urinary calculus. Hämaturie *f*.
heme/*n*: Häm *n*.
hemeralopia/*n*: Hemeralopie *f*, Tagblindheit *f*.
heme synthesis: Hämsynthese *f*.
hemiagnosia/*n*: Hemiagnosie *f*.
hemianesthesia/*n*: Hemianästhesie *f*.
hemianopia/*n*: Hemianopsie *f*.
hemianopic scotoma: Halbseitenskotom *n*.
hemianopsia/*n*: Hemianopsie *f*.
hemiatrophy/*n*: Hemiatrophie *f*.
hemiballismus/*n*: Hemiballismus *m*.
hemicolectomy/*n*: Hemikolektomie *f*.
hemicrania/*n*: Hemikranie *f*.
hemilateral chorea: Hemichorea *f*.
hemiparaplegic syndrome: a neurologic condition resulting from transverse lesion of the spinal cord due to trauma, tumor, or demyelination which is characterized by spastic paralysis, loss of position sense on the side of the lesion and loss of pain and temperature sense on the opposite side. Brown-Séquard-Syndrom *n*.
hemiparesis/*n*: Hemiparese *f*.
hemiparkinsonism/*n*: Hemiparkinsonismus *m*.
hemiplegia/*n*: partial or complete paralysis of one side of the body, usually due to a lesion to the opposite side of the brain. Causes include a cerebral blood clot or hemorrhage in a blood vessel in the brain. Hemiplegie *f*, Halbseitenlähmung *f*.
hemiplegic gait: hemiplegischer Gang *m*.
hemisphere/*n*: Hemisphäre *f*.
hemizygous/*adj*: hemizygot.
hemizygous gene: hemizygotes Gen *n*.
hemoblastic leukemia: Stammzellenleukämie *f*.
hemochromatosis/*n*: a chronic, progressive disorder which is associated with iron overload and iron deposits in many organs. Forms include autosomal recessive inherited idiopathic hemochromatosis, and acquired hemochromatosis resulting from external iron overload. Hämochromatose *f*.
hemoconcentration/*n*: Hämokonzentration *f*.
hemocyte/*n*: Hämozyt *m*, Blutzelle *f*.
hemocytometer/*n*: Hämozytometer *n*, Zählkammer *f*.
hemodialysis/*n*: Hämodialyse *f*.
hemoglobin/*n*: Hämoglobin *n*, Hb.
hemoglobinopathy/*n*: Hämoglobinopathie *f*.
hemoglobinuria/*n*: presence of hemoglobin in the urine. Causes include hemolytic anemia, incompatible blood transfusions, autoimmune disease, allergic reactions to drugs or nutrients, or infections. Hämoglobinurie *f*.
hemoglobinuric fever: Schwarzwasserfieber *n*.
hemolysin/*n*: Hämolysin *n*.
hemolysis/*n*: Hämolyse *f*.
hemolytic/*adj*: hämolytisch.
hemolytic anemia: hämolytische Anämie *f*.
hemolytic crisis: hämolytische Krise *f*.
hemopericardium/*n*: Hämoperikard *n*.
hemophilia/*n*: X-linked, hereditary bleeding disorders which are characterized by a defect in blood coagulation, due to a lack of certain coagulation factors. Major forms include hemophilia A, or classical hemophilia with a deficiency of factor VIII, and hemophilia B or Christmas disease with a deficiency of factor IX. Hämophilie *f*, Bluterkrankheit *f*.

hemophiliac/*n*: Hämophiler *m*, Bluter *m*.
hemophilic/*adj*: hämophil.
hemophilic arthropathy: hämophile Arthropathie *f*, Blutergelenk *n*.
hemopoiesis/*n*: Hämatopoese *f*, Blutbildung *f*.
hemopoietic cell: hämatopoetische Zelle *f*.
hemoptysis/*n*: Hämoptyse *f*, Bluthusten *m*.
hemorrhage/*n*: escape of blood from a damaged blood vessel, resulting in external or internal bleeding. Severe hemorrhage may result in decrease of blood pressure and shock, and may provoke a life-threatening condition. Hämorrhagie *f*, Blutung *f*.
hemorrhagic anemia: a decrease in the concentration of erythrocytes resulting from blood loss. Acute hemorrhagic anemia is characterized by normocytic and normochromic erythrocytes. Chronic hemorrhagic anemia with continued blood loss results in iron deficiency anemia and microcytic and hypochromic erythrocytes. Blutungsanämie *f*.
hemorrhagic ascites: hämorrhagischer Aszites *m*, Hämaskos *m*.
hemorrhagic bronchitis: Bronchospirochätose *f*, Castellani-Krankheit *f*.
hemorrhagic cyst: hämorrhagische Zyste *f*.
hemorrhagic fever: hämorrhagisches Fieber *n*.
hemorrhagic glomerulonephritis: hämorrhagische Glomerulonephritis *f*.
hemorrhagic pericarditis: hämorrhagische Perikarditis *f*.
hemorrhagic rickets: hämorrhagische Rachitis *f*, Moeller-Barlow-Krankheit *f*.
hemorrhagic shock: hämorrhagischer Schock *m*.
hemorrhagic smallpox: hämorrhagische Pocken *f*.
hemorrhagic stroke: hämorrhagischer Insult *m*.
hemorrhoid/*n*: enlargement of veins of the hemorrhoidal plexus. Symptoms include pain, blood on top of the feces, and defecation disorder. Hämorrhoide *f*.
hemorrhoidal/*adj*: hämorrhoidal.
hemorrhoidal node: Hämorrhoidalknoten *m*.
hemorrhoidectomy/*n*: Hämorrhoidektomie *f*.
hemosalpinx/*n*: Hämatosalpinx *f*.
hemostasis/*n*: Hämostase *f*.
hemostatic/*n*, *adj*: 1. Hämostatikum *n*, Hämostyptikum *n*; 2. hämostatisch, blutstillend.
hemostatic clamp: Gefäßklemme *f*.
hemothorax/*n*: Hämatothorax *m*.
hepar/*n*: Leber *f*.
heparin/*n*: Heparin *n*.
hepatectomy/*n*: Hepatektomie *f*, Leberresektion *f*.
hepatic/*adj*: hepatisch.
hepatic abscess: abscess in the liver, typically multiple hepatic abscesses. Causes include infections, for example ascending infections of the biliary tract, septicemia, or amebiasis. Leberabszess *m*.
hepatic amebiasis: Amöbenhepatitis *f*.
hepatic bile: Lebergalle *f*.
hepatic cell: Leberzelle *f*.
hepatic cirrhosis: a condition of the liver which is characterized by a hardening resulting from faulty regeneration and nodular proliferation of hepatocytes. Causes include chronic infection, for example chronic hepatitis B or hepatitis C, chronic intoxication or alcohol intake, biliary tract obstructions, or metabolic disorders. Symptoms result from an impairment or loss of liver functions and may include liver failure. Leberzirrhose *f*.
hepatic coma: hepatisches Koma *n*.
hepatic cyst: cyst of the liver. Forms include congenital cysts, or acquired cysts, resulting for example from echinococcus infection. Leberzyste *f*.
hepatic dullness: Leberdämpfung *f*.
hepatic encephalopathy: hepatische Enzephalopathie *f*.

H

hepatic failure: Leberversagen *n*.
hepatic fibrosis: a condition of the liver which is characterized by replacement of normal hepatocytes by collagen, interstitial cells, and fibrous tissue. Causes include chronic infection, for example chronic hepatitis B, or hepatitis C, chronic intoxication or alcohol intake, biliary tract obstructions, or metabolic disorders. Symptoms depend on the stage of fibrosis, which may eventually result in liver cirrhosis. Leberfibrose *f*.
hepatic insufficiency: Leberinsuffizienz *f*.
hepatic lobe: Leberlappen *m*.
hepaticocholangiojejunostomy/*n*: Hepatikocholangiojejunostomie *f*.
hepatic porphyria: hepatische Porphyrie *f*.
hepatic portal: Leberpforte *f*.
hepatic pulse: Leberpuls *m*.
hepatic sarcoidosis: Lebersarkoidose *f*.
hepatic segment: Lebersegment *n*.
hepatic vein occlusion: obstruction of the hepatic veins, usually due to thrombosis, phlebitis, or hypercoagulable states. Symptoms include abdominal pain and eventually signs of an acute abdomen, hepatomegaly, and ascites. Lebervenenverschluss *m*, Budd-Chiari-Syndrom *n*.
hepatitis/*n*: acute or chronic inflammation of the liver, usually due to infections, chemical or physical damage, or intoxications. Major forms of infectious hepatitis include viral hepatitis (hepatitis A, B or C). Symptoms include loss of appetite, liver enlargement, nausea, and eventually jaundice; in chronic hepatitis, progressive liver fibrosis and cirrhosis with consecutive liver failure may develop. Hepatitis *f*, Leberentzündung *f*.
hepatization/*n*: Hepatisation *f*.
hepatobiliary/*adj*: hepatobiliär.
hepatocellular adenoma: Leberzelladenom *n*.
hepatocellular carcinoma: a malignant neoplasm originating in liver cells. Main causes include liver cirrhosis resulting from chronic hepatitis B or chronic hepatitis C. hepatozelluläres Karzinom *n*, Leberzellkarzinom *n*.
hepatojugular reflux: hepatojugulärer Reflux *m*.
hepatolenticular/*adj*: hepatolentikulär.
hepatolenticular degeneration: autosomal recessive inherited disorder in copper metabolism. Symptoms include excessive deposition of copper in the liver and other organs, discoloration of the limbus of the cornea, and movement disorders and tremor due to degenerative changes in the basal ganglia of the brain. hepatolentikuläre Degeneration *f*, Wilson-Krankheit *f*.
hepatology/*n*: Hepatologie *f*.
hepatoma/*n*: Hepatom *n*.
hepatomegaly/*n*: Hepatomegalie *f*, Leververgrößerung *f*.
hepatorenal syndrome: rapidly progressive renal failure which occurs in the context of severe liver diseases, for example hepatic cirrhosis. Symptoms include liver failure, edema, arterial hypotonia, hyponatremia. hepatorenales Syndrom *n*.
hepatosplenomegaly/*n*: Hepatosplenomegalie *f*.
hepatotoxic agent: Lebergift *n*.
hepatotoxicity/*n*: Hepatotoxizität *f*.
heptanoic acid: Önanthensäure *f*.
herb/*n*: Kraut *n*, Pflanze *f*.
hereditary/*adj*: hereditär, erblich.
hereditary cerebellar ataxia: Heredoataxia cerebellaris *f*, Marie-Krankheit *f*.
hereditary disease: hereditäre Erkrankung *f*.
hereditary edema: an autosomal dominant disorder which is characterized by episodic attacks of edema of the lips and eyelids or sometimes other areas of the body, caused by a deficiency of C1 inhibitor. hereditäres Angioödem *n*.
hereditary epilepsy: familiäre Epilepsie *f*.

hereditary hemorrhagic telangiectasia: hereditäre Teleangiektasie *f*, Osler-Rendu-Weber-Syndrom *n*, Rendu-Fiessinger-Syndrom *n*.
hereditary hyperbilirubinemia: hereditäre Hyperbilirubinämie *f*, Gilbert-Meulengracht-Syndrom *n*.
hereditary lymphedema: hereditäres Lymphödem *n*, Nonne-Milroy-Syndrom *n*.
hereditary optic atrophy: Leber-Optikusatrophie *f*.
hereditary sensory neuropathy: hereditäre sensible Neuropathie *f*, HSN.
hereditary spinal sclerosis: spinozerebelläre Heredoataxie *f*, Friedreich-Ataxie *f*.
heredodegenerative deafness: heredodegenerative Taubheit *f*.
heredomacular degeneration: tapetoretinale Degeneration *f*, Makuladegeneration *f*.
hermaphroditism/*n*: Hermaphroditismus *m*.
hermetic/*adj*: hermetisch.
hernia/*n*: abnormal opening of a structure or rupture of a muscular wall which allows an internal organ or parts of it to bulge out. Hernie *f*, Bruch *m*.
hernial truss: Bruchband *n*
herniated/*adj*: eingeklemmt.
herniated intervertebral disk: Bandscheibenprotrusion *f*.
hernioplasty/*n*: Hernioplastik *f*.
herniorrhaphy/*n*: Herniorrhaphie *f*.
herniotomy/*n*: Herniotomie *f*.
heroin/*n*: Heroin *n*.
herpes simplex: a condition resulting from infection with herpesvirus types 1 and 2. Symptoms include clusters of small blisters on the skin or mucosa, usually around the lips or in the genital area. Herpes simplex *m*.
herpetic/*adj*: herpetisch.
herpetic fever: Herpes-Infektion *f*.
herpetic keratitis: inflammation of the cornea resulting from infection with herpesvirus. Symptoms include an epithelial infection with characteristic dendritic punctate lesions. Herpes-Keratitis *f*.
herpetic pharyngitis: Pharyngitis herpetica *f*.
herpetic whitlow: an infectious disease of the nail fold, resulting from herpes simplex infection. Symptoms include swelling, formation of a very painful abscess, and inflammation of lymphatic vessels. Herpes-simplex-Paronychie *f*.
hetacillin/*n*: Hetacillin *n*.
heterochromic cataract: Heterochromiestar *m*.
heterochromic cyclitis: heterochrome Zyklitis *f*, Fuchs-Heterochromie *f*.
heterochromosome/*n*: Heterochromosom *n*.
heterocyclic amino acid: heterozyklische Aminosäure *f*.
heterogenous/*adj*: heterogen.
heterograft/*n*: Heterotransplantat *n*, Xenotransplantat *n*.
heterologous/*adj*: heterolog.
heterologous gene: Fremdgen *n*.
heterologous insemination: heterologe Insemination *f*.
heteronymous hemianopia: heteronyme Hemianopsie *f*.
heterophilic antigen: heterophiles Antigen *n*.
heterophoria/*n*: Heterophorie *f*.
heteroplasia/*n*: Heteroplasie *f*.
heteroplastic graft: Heterotransplantat *n*.
heterosexuality/*n*: Heterosexualität *f*.
heterosomal aberration: Geschlechtschromosomenaberration *f*.
heterotopia/*n*: Heterotopie *f*, Ektopie *f*.
heterotopic bone: heterotoper Knochen *m*, heterotope Ossifikation *f*.
heterotopic glioma: heterotopes Gliom *n*.
heterotopic graft: heterotopes Transplantat *n*.
heterotropia/*n*: Heterotropie *f*, Strabismus *m*.
heterotypic antibody: heterotypischer Antikörper *m*.

H

heterozygous/*adj*: heterozygot.

heterozygous thalassemia: Thalassaemia minor *f*.

hexachlorethane/*n*: Hexachlorethan *n*.

hexachlorophene/*n*: Hexachlorophen *n*.

hexacyanoferrate/*n*: Hexacyanoferrat *n*.

hexamethonium bromide: Hexamethoniumbromid *n*.

hexane/*n*: Hexan *n*.

hexcarbacholine bromide: Hexcarbacholinbromid *n*.

hexobarbital/*n*: Hexobarbital *n*.

hexobendine/*n*: Hexobendin *n*.

hexonic acid: Hexonsäure *f*.

hexoprenaline/*n*: Hexoprenalin *n*.

Hgb <*abbr*> **hemoglobin**/*n*: Hämoglobin *n*, Hb.

hGH <*abbr*> **human growth hormone**: menschliches Wachstumshormon *n*, Somatotropin *n*, STH.

hiatal hernia: protrusion, usually of parts of the stomac and the lower esophagus, through the diaphragmatic hiatus. Symptoms may include hiccups, esophageal reflux, dyspnea, substernal pain, and vomiting. Hiatushernie *f*.

hiatus/*n*: Hiatus *m*, Lücke *f*.

hiccup/*n*: Schluckauf *m*, Singultus *m*.

hidradenitis/*n*: Hidradenitis *f*, Schweißdrüsenentzündung *f*.

hidrosis/*n*: Schweißsekretion *f*.

hidrotic ectodermal dysplasia: hidrotische Ektodermaldysplasie *f*, Clouston-Syndrom *n*.

high-altitude pulmonary edema: Höhenlungenödem *n*.

high blood pressure: Bluthochdruck *m*, Hypertonus *m*.

high-caloric/*adj*: kalorienreich, hochkalorisch.

high-density lipoprotein: High-Density-Lipoprotein *n*, Lipoprotein hoher Dichte *n*.

high dose: hohe Dosis *f*.

higher nervous activity: zentralnervöse Aktivität *f*.

high-frequency amplifier: Hochfrequenzverstärker *m*.

high-jumpers' strain: Rotatorenzerrung *f*.

high pelvic position: Trendelenburg-Lagerung *f*.

high-protein diet: eiweißreiche Ernährung *f*.

high-risk/*adj*: risikoreich.

high-risk delivery: Risikogeburt *f*.

high temperature: hohes Fieber *n*.

high-voltage therapy: Hochvolttherapie *f*.

hilar/*adj*: hilär.

hilar adenopathy: Hiluslymphknotenvergrößerung *f*.

hilum-cell tumor: Hiluszelltumor *m*.

hindbrain/*n*: Rhombencephalon *n*.

hinge area: Hinge-Region *f*, flexible Region *f*.

hinged flap: Brückenlappen *m*, Visierlappenplastik *f*.

hip/*n*: Hüfte *f*.

hip bone: Hüftbein *n*.

hip dislocation: Hüftluxation *f*.

hip joint: Hüftgelenk *n*.

hippocratic/*adj*: hippokratisch.

hippocratic face: Facies hippocratica *f*.

hippocratic nail: hippokratischer Nagel *m*, Uhrglasnagel *m*.

hippocratic succussion: Succussio Hippocratis *f*.

hippotherapy/*n*: Hippotherapie *f*, Reittherapie *f*.

hip prosthesis: Hüftgelenkprothese *f*.

hippuric acid: Hippursäure *f*.

hirsutism/*n*: a male hair distribution pattern in women. Forms include idiopathic hirsutism of unknown origin, and acquired hirsutism, usually resulting from increased androgen levels due to underlying diseases of the ovary or adrenal cortex, or decreased estrogen levels. Hirsutismus *m*.

His bundle electrogram: His-Bündel-Elektrokardiogramm *n*.

histamine/*n*: Histamin *n*.

histamine receptor blocker: Histaminrezeptorenblocker *m*.

histidine/*n*: Histidin *n*.

histiocyte/*n*: Histiozyt *m*, Adventitiazelle *f*.

histiocytic lymphoma: histiozytäres Lymphom *n*.
histiocytic medullary reticulosis: medulläre Histiozytose *f*, Robb-Smith-Krankheit *f*.
histiocytic sarcoma: histiozytäres Lymphom *n*.
histiocytoma/*n*: Histiozytom *n*.
histochemistry/*n*: Histochemie *f*.
histocompatibility/*n*: Histokompatibilität *f*.
histogenesis/*n*: Histogenese *f*.
histoincompatibility/*n*: Histoinkompatibilität *f*.
histologic chemistry: Histochemie *f*.
histology/*n*: Histologie *f*.
histoplasmosis/*n*: Histoplasmose *f*.
history taking: Anamneseaufnahme *f*.
HIV <*abbr*> **human immunodeficiency virus**: humanes Immunodefizienz-Virus *n*, HIV.
hives/*n*: Urtikaria *f*.
HIV infection: chronic infectious disease due to infection with Human Immunodeficiency Virus. After an initial period with unspecific signs, symptoms may develop after several months or years and result in increasing immunodeficiency, due to viral infection of immune cells. Without adequate treatment, the Acquired Immune Deficiency Syndrome or AIDS develops. HIV-Infektion *f*.
HLA <*abbr*> **human leukocyte antigene**: humanes Leukozytenantigen *n*, HLA.
hoarseness/*n*: Heiserkeit *f*.
holandric gene: holandrisches Gen *n*.
holistic medicine: ganzheitliche Medizin *f*.
hollow/*n, adj*: 1. Mulde *f*, Vertiefung *f*; 2. hohl.
hollow-back/*n*: Hohlkreuz *n*, Lordose *f*.
hollow cheek: eingefallene Wange *f*.
hollow foot: Hohlfuß *m*.
hollow space: Hohlraum *m*.
holocrine gland: holokrine Drüse *f*.
holodiastolic murmur: holodiastolisches Geräusch *n*.
holosystolic murmur: holosystolisches Geräusch *n*.
homatropine/*n*: Homatropin *n*.
home/*n*: Heim *n*, Pflegeheim *n*.
home care: Hauspflege *f*.
home childbirth: Hausgeburt *f*.
home dialysis: Heimdialyse *f*.
home inmate/*n*: Heimbewohner *m*.
homeopathy/*n*: Homöopathie *f*.
homeostasis/*n*: Homöostase *f*.
homeothermic/*adj*: warmblütig.
home test: Heimtest *m*.
homicide/*n*: Mord *m*.
homogenous/*adj*: homogen.
homogentisic acid: Homogentisinsäure *f*.
homograft/*n*: Allotransplantat *n*.
homolateral/*adj*: homolateral, ipsilateral.
homologous antigen: Alloantigen *n*.
homologous insemination: homologe Insemination *f*.
homonymous hemianopia: homonyme Hemianopsie *f*.
homoplastic graft: Allotransplantat *n*.
homosexuality/*n*: Homosexualität *f*.
homosomal aberration: strukturelle Chromosomenaberration *f*.
homovanillic acid: Homovanillinsäure *f*.
homozygous/*adj*: homozygot.
homozygous thalassemia: Thalassaemia major *f*.
honeycomb lung: Wabenlunge *f*.
hook/*n*: Haken *m*.
hookworm/*n*: Hakenwurm *m*, Ankylostoma *n*.
hordeolum/*n*: infection of the zeisian gland or the meibomian gland of the eyelid caused by bacteria, usually Staphylococcus or Streptococcus. Hordeolum *n*, Gerstenkorn *n*.
horizontal heart: Horizontaltyp *m*.
horizontal maxillary fracture: Le-Fort-I-Unterkieferfraktur *f*.
horizontal plane: Horizontalebene *f*.
horizontal position: Horizontallage *f*.
horizontal transmission: horizontale Übertragung *f*.
horizontal vertigo: Horizontalschwindel *m*.
hormonal/*adj*: hormonal.

H

hormonal contraception: hormonelle Kontrazeption *f*.
hormone/*n*: Hormon *n*.
hormone-dependent: hormonabhängig.
hormone production: Hormonbildung *f*.
hormone receptor: Hormonrezeptor *m*.
hormone therapy: Hormontherapie *f*.
horn/*n*: Horn *n*.
horny scale: Hornhautschuppe *f*.
horseshoe kidney: Hufeisenniere *f*.
horseshoe placenta: Hufeisenplazenta *f*.
hose/*n*: Schlauch *m*.
hospice/*n*: Hospiz *n*.
hospital/*n*: Krankenhaus *n*, Spital *n*.
hospital-acquired/*adj*: nosokomial.
hospital administration: Krankenhausverwaltung *f*.
hospital allowance: Pflegesatz *m*.
hospital infection: Hospitalismus *m*, nosokomiale Infektion *f*.
hospitalization/*n*: Krankenhauseinweisung *f*.
hospital pharmacy: Krankenhausapotheke *f*.
hospital stay: Krankenhausaufenthalt *m*.
host/*n*: Wirt *m*.
hot abscess: heißer Abszess *m*.
hot air: Heißluft *f*.
hot biopsy: heiße Biopsie *f*.
hot compress: heißer Umschlag *m*.
hot gangrene: entzündliche Gangrän *f*.
hotline/*n*: Telephonberatung *f*.
hot stage: Fieberstadium *n*.
hourglass stomach: Uhrglasmagen *m*, Sanduhrmagen *m*.
housewife's neurosis: Putzzwang *m*.
Huhner's test: Huhner-Sims-Test *m*.
human/*n, adj*: 1. Mensch *m*; 2. menschlich.
human albumin: Humanalbumin *n*.
human chorionic gonadotropin: humanes Choriongonadotropin *n*, HCG.
human flea: Menschenfloh *m*, Pulex irritans *m*.
human genetics: Humangenetik *f*.
human insulin: Humaninsulin *n*.
human milk: Muttermilch *f*, Frauenmilch *f*.
humerus/*n*: Oberarm *m*.
humic acid: Huminsäure *f*.
humid/*adj*: feucht.
humidifier/*n*: Raumluftbefeuchter *m*.
humidity/*n*: Feuchtigkeit *f*.
humming-top murmur: venöses Schwirren *n*.
humoral/*adj*: humoral.
humoral allergy: humorale Allergie *f*.
humoral immunity: humorale Immunität *f*.
humoralism/*n*: Humoralpathologie *f*.
humoral transmission: humorale Übertragung *f*.
humpback/*n*: Rundrücken *m*, Kyphose *f*.
hunchback/*n*: Rundrücken *m*, Kyphose *f*.
hunger/*n*: Hunger *m*.
hunger pain: Nüchternschmerz *m*.
hyalin/*n*: Hyalin *n*.
hyaline/*adj*: hyalinartig.
hyaline body: hyalines Körperchen *n*.
hyaline cartilage: hyaliner Knorpel *m*.
hyaline cast: hyaliner Zylinder *m*.
hyaline degeneration: hyaline Degeneration *f*.
hyaline substance: hyaline Substanz *f*.
hyaline thrombus: hyaliner Thrombus *m*.
hyaloid/*n, adj*: 1. Hyalin *n*; 2. hyalin, glasartig.
hyaluronic acid: Hyaluronsäure *f*.
hybrid cell: Hybridzelle *f*.
hydantoic acid: Hydantoinsäure *f*.
hydantoin/*n*: Hydantoin *n*.
hydatid cyst: Hydatidzyste *f*, Echinokokkuszyste *f*.
hydatidiform/*adj*: hydatidiform.
hydatid thrill: Hydatidenschwirren *n*.
hydralazine/*n*: Hydralazin *n*.
hydramnios/*n*: Hydramnion *n*.
hydrastinine/*n*: Hydrastinin *n*.
hydration/*n*: Hydratation *f*.
hydrobromic acid: Bromwasserstoff-

säure *f*.
hydrocarbon/*n*: Kohlenwasserstoff *m*.
hydrocele/*n*: an accumulation of serous fluid in a body cavity, for example testicular hydrocele between the visceral and the parietal layers of the tunica vaginalis in the scrotum. Hydrozele *f*.
hydrocephalus/*n*: enlargement of the head, usually due to impairment of the drainage of cerebrospinal fluid and an abnormally large volume of cerebrospinal fluid within the brain ventricles. Hydrozephalus *m*, Wasserkopf *m*.
hydrochloric acid: Salzsäure *f*.
hydrochloride/*n*: Hydrochlorid *n*.
hydrochlorothiazide/*n*: Hydrochlorothiazid *n*.
hydrocortisone/*n*: Hydrocortison *n*.
hydrocortisone acetate: Hydrocortisonacetat *n*.
hydrocyanic acid: Blausäure *f*, Zyanwasserstoffsäure *f*.
hydroelectric bath: hydroelektrisches Vollbad *n*, Stanger-Bad *n*.
hydroflumethiazide/*n*: Hydroflumethiazid *n*.
hydrogen/*n*: Wasserstoff *m*, H.
hydrogen peroxide: Wasserstoffperoxid *n*.
hydrolysis/*n*: Hydrolyse *f*.
hydrolytic enzyme: hydrolytisches Enzym *n*.
hydrometer/*n*: Aräometer *n*.
hydrometra/*n*: Hydrometra *f*.
hydronephrosis/*n*: Hydronephrose *f*, Wassersackniere *f*.
hydropenia/*n*: Wassermangel *m*, Exsikkose *f*.
hydropericardium/*n*: Hydroperikard *n*.
hydroperitoneum/*n*: Aszites *m*.
hydrophilic ointment: Unguentum hydrophilicum *n*.
hydrophobia/*n*: Hydrophobie *f*, Wasserscheu *f*.
hydropic degeneration: hydropische Degeneration *f*.
hydrops/*n*: Hydrops *m*.
hydrosalpinx/*n*: Hydrosalpinx *f*.
hydrostatic reduction: Einlaufreposition *f*, Kontrastmitteldesinvagination *f*.
hydrotherapy/*n*: Hydrotherapie *f*.
hydrothorax/*n*: Hydrothorax *m*.
hydroxyacetic acid: Hydroxyessigsäure *f*.
hydroxy acid: Hydroxysäure *f*.
hydroxybutyric acid: Hydroxybuttersäure *f*.
hydroxycarbamide/*n*: Hydroxycarbamid *n*.
hydroxychloroquine/*n*: Hydroxychloroquin *n*.
hydroxycolecalciferol/*n*: Hydroxycolecalciferol *n*.
17-hydroxycorticosteroid/*n*: 17-Hydroxykortikosteroid *n*.
17-hydroxycorticosterone/*n*: 17-Hydroxykortikosteron *n*.
hydroxydione/*n*: Hydroxydion *n*.
hydroxyglutamic acid: Hydroxyglutaminsäure *f*.
5-hydroxyindoleacetic acid: 5-Hydroxyindolessigsäure *f*.
hydroxyprogesterone/*n*: Hydroxyprogesteron *n*.
hydroxystilbamidine/*n*: Hydroxystilbamidin *n*.
hydroxytetracycline/*n*: Hydroxytetracyclin *n*, Oxytetracyclin *n*.
5-hydroxytryptamine/*n*: 5-Hydroxytryptamin *n*, Serotonin *n*.
hydroxyurea/*n*: Hydroxyharnstoff *m*.
hydroxyzine/*n*: Hydroxyzin *n*.
hygiene/*n*: Hygiene *f*.
hygroma/*n*: Hygrom *n*.
hygrometer/*n*: Hygrometer *n*.
hygromycin/*n*: Hygromycin *n*.
hygroscopic/*adj*: hygroskopisch.
hymen/*n*: Hymen *m*.
hymenal atresia: atresia and lack of an opening in the hymenal membrane. Symptoms include retention of menstrual blood in the vagina, or in the uterus. Hymenalatresie *f*.
hymenal membrane: Hymen *m*.
hymenoptera/*n*: Hymenoptera *f*.
hymenotomy/*n*: Hymeninzision *f*.
hyoscine/*n*: Hyoscin *n*.
hyoscyamine/*n*: Hyoscyamin *n*, L-Atropin *n*.

hypalgesia/*n*: Hypalgesie *f*.
hyperacidity/*n*: Hyperazidität *f*, Übersäuerung *f*.
hyperalgesia/*n*: Hyperalgesie *f*.
hyperbaric/*adj*: hyperbar.
hyperbaric chamber: Überdruckkammer *f*.
hyperbaric oxygenation: hyperbare Oxygenierung *f*, Sauerstoffüberdrucktherapie *f*.
hyperbaric pressure: Überdruck *m*.
hyperbilirubinemia/*n*: an increased concentration of bilirubin in the blood, resulting for example from increased hemolysis or impaired liver capacity to excrete bilirubin. Symptoms include jaundice and pruritus. Hyperbilirubinämie *f*.
hyperbolic glasses: Hyperbolgläser.
hypercalcemia/*n*: an increased concentration of calcium in the blood, caused for example by pararthyroidism, malignant tumors, endocrine disorders, or as an adverse effect of drugs. Symptoms include formation or renal calculus, loss of appetite, nausea, vomiting, vertigo, cardiac arrhythmia, and mental signs. Hyperkalzämie *f*.
hypercalcemic sarcoidosis: hyperkalzämische Sarkoidose *f*.
hypercapnia/*n*: Hyperkapnie *f*.
hyperchloremic acidosis: hyperchlorämische Azidose *f*.
hyperchlorhydria/*n*: Hyperchlorhydrie *f*.
hypercholesterolemia/*n*: an increased concentration of cholesterol in the blood. Causes include genetic and/or familial factors, and dietary habits. Hypercholesterinämie *f*.
hyperchromatopsia/*n*: Hyperchromatopsie *f*.
hyperchromia/*n*: Hyperchromasie *f*.
hyperchromic anemia: hyperchrome Anämie *f*.
hyperelastic/*adj*: hyperelastisch.
hyperemia/*n*: Hyperämie *f*.
hypereosinophilic syndrome: any condition which is characterized by an excessice amount of eosinophils in the blood, for example eosinophilic lung or Löffler's endocarditis. Hypereosinophiliesyndrom *n*.
hyperesthesia/*n*: Hyperästhesie *f*.
hyperesthetic zone: hyperästhetische Zone *f*.
hyperexcitability/*n*: Übererregbarkeit *f*.
hyperextension/*n*: Hyperextension *f*.
hyperflexion/*n*: Hyperflexion *f*.
hyperglycemia/*n*: Hyperglykämie *f*.
hypergonadism/*n*: Hypergonadismus *m*.
hypergonadotropic hypogonadism: hypergonadotroper Hypogonadismus *m*.
hyperhidrosis/*n*: a condition which is characterized by increased sweating, affecting the whole body or only parts of it. Forms include physiological hyperhidrosis for example in thermoregulation, or secondary hyperhidrosis usually due to endocrine disorders or neurologic diseases, for example lesions of the sympathetic nervous system. Hyperhidrose *f*.
hypericin/*n*: Hypericin *n*.
hyperimmune serum: Hyperimmunserum *n*.
hyperimmunization/*n*: Hyperimmunisierung *f*.
hyperkalemia/*n*: an increased concentration of potassium in the blood. Causes include metabolic disorders like acidosis, blood transfusion, renal failure, endocrine disorders, multiple trauma or burns, and hemolysis. Hyperkaliämie *f*.
hyperkalemic periodic paralysis: hyperkaliämische periodische Lähmung *f*, Gamstorp-Syndrom *n*.
hyperkeratosis/*n*: Hyperkeratose *f*, Hyperkeratosis *f*.
hyperkeratotic ulcer: hyperkeratotisches Ulkus *n*.
hyperkinesis/*n*: Hyperkinese *f*.
hyperkinetic syndrome: hyperkinetisches Syndrom *n*.
hyperlipemia/*n*: Hyperlipidämie *f*.
hyperlipoproteinemia/*n*: Hyperlipoproteinämie *f*.
hypermetropia/*n*: Hypermetropie *f*, Hyperopie *f*, Übersichtigkeit *f*.

hypermnesia/*n*: Hypermnesie *f*.
hypermobility/*n*: gesteigerte Beweglichkeit *f*.
hypermotility/*n*: Hypermotilität *f*.
hypermyotonia/*n*: Muskelhypertonie *f*.
hypernatremia/*n*: an increased concentration of sodium in the blood. Causes include dehydration, endocrine disorders, sodium-containing infusion therapy, or increased water loss. Hypernatriämie *f*.
hypernatremia syndrome: a condition which is characterized by hypertonic hyperhydration and interstitial edema, usually occurring in association with disorders of the central nervous system. Natriumspeichersyndrom *n*.
hypernephroid carcinoma: hypernephroides Karzinom *n*.
hypernephroma/*n*: Hypernephrom *n*.
hyperonychia/*n*: Hyperonychie *f*.
hyperopia/*n*: a condition in which far vision is very good, but near or close objects appear blurred. Hyperopie *f*, Hypermetropie *f*, Übersichtigkeit *f*.
hyperopic astigmatism: hyperopischer Astigmatismus *m*.
hyperosmolar/*adj*: hyperosmolar.
hyperosmolar coma: hyperosmolares Koma *n*.
hyperostosis/*n*: Hyperostose *f*.
hyperostotic spondylosis: Spondylosis hyperostotica *f*.
hyperparathyroidism/*n*: excessive secretion of parathyroid hormone which may be caused by hyperplasia or adenoma of the parathyroid glands, or eventually a hormone-secreting cancer of other organs. Symptoms include hypercalcemia, hypophosphatemia, loss of calcium from bones, formation of kidney stones, vomiting, ileus, and somnolence. Hyperparathyreoidismus *m*.
hyperphagia/*n*: Bulimie *f*.
hyperphoria/*n*: Hyperphorie *f*.
hyperpigmentation/*n*: Hyperpigmentierung *f*.
hyperpituitarism/*n*: Hyperpituitarismus *m*.
hyperplasia/*n*: Hyperplasie *f*.
hyperpotassemia/*n*: an increased concentration of potassium in the blood. Causes include for example metabolic disorders like acidosis, blood transfusion, renal failure, endocrine disorders, multiple trauma or burns, and hemolysis. Hyperkaliämie *f*.
hyperpyrexia/*n*: Hyperpyrexie *f*.
hyperreactive/*adj*: hyperreaktiv.
hypersecretion/*n*: Hypersekretion *f*, verstärkte Sekretion *f*.
hypersensitive/*adj*: überempfindlich.
hypersensitivity/*n*: increased sensitivity of the body against a foreign substance. These substances or allergens can include nutrients like milk or fish proteins, environmental agents such as pollen, chemical substances, drugs, or microorganisms. Manifestations include a variety of immune reactions of the immediate type like urticaria, catarrhal inflammation, or asthma. Hypersensibilität *f*, Überempfindlichkeit *f*.
hypersplenism/*n*: abnormal increase of spleen functions, resulting in increased destruction of aged blood cells. Forms include primary hypersplenism or Banti's disease, and secondary forms, usually due to underlying diseases with spleen involvement. Hypersplenismus *m*.
hypertension/*n*: high blood pressure. Forms include primary hypertension of unknown origin which is apparently not related to any other disease, and secondary hypertension caused by an underlying disease, for example renal artery obstruction, or adrenal tumors. Hypertension *f*, Hypertonie *f*, Bluthochdruck *m*.
hypertensive crisis: hypertensive Krise *f*.
hypertensive heart: Bluthochdruckherz *n*.
hypertensive retinitis: Retinopathia hypertonica *f*.
hyperthermia/*n*: Hyperthermie *f*.
hyperthrombinemia/*n*: Hyperthrombinämie *f*.

H

hyperthymism/*n*: Hyperthymie *f*.

hyperthyroidism/*n*: excessive secretion of thyroid hormones, usually due to hyperfunction of the thyroid gland. Symptoms include weight loss, increased appetite, diarrhea, intolerance to heat, hyperhidrosis, hair loss, fatigue, tachycardia, tremor, and dysmenorrhea. Hyperthyreoidismus *m*, Hyperthyreose *f*.

hyperthyroid ophthalmoplegia: endokriner Exophthalmus *m*.

hypertonia/*n*: Hypertonie *f*, Hypertension *f*, Bluthochdruck *m*.

hypertonic bladder: hypertone Blase *f*.

hypertonic hydrocephalus: hypertensiver Hydrozephalus *m*.

hypertonic uterine dysfunction: hypertone Wehendystokie *f*.

hypertrichosis/*n*: Hypertrichose *f*.

hypertriglyceridemia/*n*: an increased concentration of triglycerides in the blood. Causes include genetic and familial factors, side effects of drugs, and dietary habits. Hypertriglyzeridämie *f*.

hypertrophic/*adj*: hypertroph.

hypertrophic arthritis: hypertrophe Arthritis *f*.

hypertrophic cardiomyopathy: hypertrophe Kardiomyopathie *f*.

hypertrophic conjunctivitis: proliferative Konjunktivitis *f*.

hypertrophic emphysema: Fassthoraxemphysem *n*.

hypertrophic gastritis: Riesenfaltengastritis *f*, Ménétrier-Krankheit *f*.

hypertrophic pharyngitis: hypertrophe Pharyngitis *f*.

hypertrophic pulmonary osteoarthropathy: hypertrophe pulmonale Osteoarthropathie *f*, Marie-Bamberger-Krankheit *f*.

hypertrophic spondylitis: hypertrophe Spondylitis *f*.

hypertrophy/*n*: Hypertrophie *f*.

hyperventilation/*n*: overbreathing with increased breathing rate with excessive alveolar ventilation. Causes include mental factors such as anxiety or fear, or it occurs spontaneously. Overventilation may result in progressive hypocapnia, palpitations, dizziness, paresthesia, and tetany. Hyperventilation *f*.

hypervolemia/*n*: Hypervolämie *f*.

hypesthesia/*n*: Hypästhesie *f*.

hypnagogic hallucination: hypnagoge Halluzination *f*.

hypnopompic hallucination: hypnopompe Halluzination *f*.

hypnosis/*n*: Hypnose *f*.

hypnotherapy/*n*: Hypnotherapie *f*, Schlaftherapie *f*.

hypnotic/*n, adj*: 1. Hypnotikum *n*; 2. hypnotisch.

hypoalbuminemia/*n*: Hypalbuminämie *f*.

hypobromous acid: unterbromige Säure *f*.

hypocalcemia/*n*: less than normal concentration of calcium in the blood. Causes include hypoparathyreoidism, vitamin D deficiency, steatorrhea, pancreatitis, or renal disease associated with retention of phosphate. Hypokalzämie *f*.

hypochloremia/*n*: Hypochlorämie *f*.

hypochloremic azotemia: hypochlorämische Azotämie *f*.

hypochlorhydria/*n*: Hypochlorhydrie *f*.

hypochlorous acid: unterchlorige Säure *f*.

hypocholesterinemic agent: Cholesterinsenker *m*.

hypochondriasis/*n*: Hypochondrie *f*.

hypochromia/*n*: Hypochromasie *f*.

hypochromic/*adj*: hypochrom.

hypochromic anemia: hypochrome Anämie *f*.

hypoderm/*n*: Hypodermis *f*, Subkutis *f*.

hypodermic/*adj*: subkutan.

hypodermic injection: subkutane Injektion *f*.

hypoesthesia/*n*: Hypästhesie *f*.

hypoferric anemia: Eisenmangelanämie *f*.

hypofibrinogenemia/*n*: Hypofibrinogenämie *f*.

hypogammaglobulinemia/*n*: Hypogammaglobulinämie *f*.

hypogastric/*adj*: hypogastrisch.
hypoglossal/*adj*: hypoglossisch.
hypoglossal paralysis: Hypoglossuslähmung *f*.
hypoglycemia/*n*: less than normal concentration of glucose in the blood. Causes include increased concentrations of insulin, for example in pancreatic diseases, liver diseases, endocrine disorders, or malnutrition. Hypoglykämie *f*.
hypoglycemic coma: hypoglykämisches Koma *n*.
hypoglycemic shock: hypoglykämischer Schock *m*.
hypogonadism/*n*: less than normal secretion of sexual hormones by the gonads, caused by disorders of the hypothalamus, the hypophysis, or the testis. Symptoms depend on the extent of hormone deficiency and age of the affected person. Hypogonadismus *m*.
hypogonadotropic hypogonadism: hypogonadotroper Hypogonadismus *m*.
hypoinsulinism/*n*: Hypoinsulinismus *m*.
hypokalemia/*n*: less than normal concentrations of potassium in the blood. Causes include inadequate potassium intake, diarrhea, vomiting, renal diseases, and endocrine disorders or medical treatment. Hypokaliämie *f*.
hypokalemic alkalosis: hypokaliämische Alkalose *f*.
hypomania/*n*: Hypomanie *f*.
hypometria/*n*: Hypometrie *f*.
hyponatremia/*n*: less than normal concentration of sodium in the blood. Causes include dehydration, inadequate sodium intake, endocrine disorders, salt-losing nephropathy, vomiting, diarrhea, renal failure, or cardiac insufficiency. Hyponatriämie *f*.
hypo-osmolar syndrome: a condition which is characterized by hypo-osmolarity of extracellular fluids, for example due to inappropriate secretion of antidiuretic hormone. Symptoms include weakness, confusion, irritability, and convulsions. Hypoosmolaritätssyndrom *n*.
hypoparathyroidism/*n*: less than normal secretion of parathyroid hormone which may be caused by hypoplasia, atrophy or surgical removal of the parathyroid glands. Symptoms include hypocalcemia, hyperphosphatemia, hypercalciuria, tetany, and mental signs. Hypoparathyreoidismus *m*.
hypopharyngeal diverticulum: Pharyngozele *f*, Zenker-Divertikel *n*.
hypophoria/*n*: Hypophorie *f*.
hypophosphatasia/*n*: Hypophosphatasie *f*, Rathbun-Syndrom *n*.
hypophosphatemia/*n*: Hypophosphatämie *f*.
hypophosphorous acid: unterphosphorige Säure *f*.
hypophysectomy/*n*: Hypophysektomie *f*.
hypophysial/*adj*: hypophysär.
hypophysial syndrome: a syndrome which is characterized by obesity, sexual retardation, small growth, visual disorders, and endocrine disturbances, resulting from lesions in the hypothalamus. Fröhlich-Krankheit *f*, Dystrophia adiposogenitalis *f*.
hypophysial tumor: Hypophysentumor *m*.
hypophysial hormone: Hypophysenhormon *n*.
hypophysis/*n*: Hypophyse *f*, Hirnanhangdrüse *f*.
hypopituitarism/*n*: less than normal secretion of anterior pituitary hormones which may be caused by infarction or necrosis of the pituitary gland, tumors, or surgical hypophysectomy. Symptoms include growth retardation, and gonadal, thyroidal, and adrenocortical deficiency. Hypopituitarismus *m*.
hypopituitary gigantism: hypophysärer Riesenwuchs *m*.
hypoplasia/*n*: Hypoplasie *f*, Unterentwicklung *f*.
hypoplastic anemia: hypoplastische Anämie *f*.

H

hypoplastic heart: hypoplastisches Herz *n*.
hypoproteinemia/*n*: Hypoproteinämie *f*.
hypoprothrombinemia/*n*: Hypoprothrombinämie *f*.
hypopyon/*n*: Hypopyon *n*.
hyposecretion/*n*: Hyposekretion *f*.
hyposensitivity/*n*: Hyposensitivität *f*.
hyposmia/*n*: Hyposmie *f*.
hypospadias/*n*: Hypospadie *f*.
hypostasis/*n*: Hypostase *f*.
hypostatic albuminuria: hypostatische Albuminurie *f*.
hyposthenia/*n*: Hyposthenie *f*, Schwäche *f*.
hypotension/*n*: abnormal low tension or pressure, for example reduced muscle tension or low blood pressure. Hypotension *f*, Hypotonie *f*.
hypothalamic/*adj*: hypothalamisch.
hypothalamic amenorrhea: hypothalamische Amenorrhö *f*.
hypothalamic center: Hypothalamuskern *m*.
hypothalamic gigantism: hypothalamischer Riesenwuchs *m*.
hypothalamic hormone: Hypothalamushormon *n*.
hypothalamic pituitary cachexia: hypothalamisch-hypophysäre Kachexie *f*.
hypothalamic releasing hormone: hypothalamisches Releasing-Hormon *n*.
hypothermia/*n*: a body temperature below the normal value of 37° degrees Celsius. Accidental hypothermia is caused by exposure to a cold environment and characterized by a dangerous fall in body temperature, while induced hypothermia is produced intentionally, for example for therapeutic purposes. Hypothermie *f*.
hypothermic coma: Unterkühlungskoma *n*.
hypothesis/*n*: Hypothese *f*.
hypothyroidism/*n*: less than normal secretion of thyroid hormones, usually due to hypofunction or failure of the thyroid gland, for example in autoimmune disorders. Symptoms include lethargy, pallor, dysmenorrhea, and in advanced stages myxedema and coma. Hypothyreoidismus *m*, Hypothyreose *f*.
hypotonia/*n*: abnormally low strength of tension, for example a reduction in muscle tone. Hypotonie *f*, Hypotension *f*.
hypotonic/*adj*: hypoton.
hypotonic cerebral palsy: Foerster-Lähmung *f*, Atonie-Astasie-Syndrom *n*.
hypoventilation/*n*: Hypoventilation *f*.
hypovitaminosis/*n*: lack of one or more essential vitamins, due to malnutrition, increased need of vitamins, or malabsorption, and resulting in severe, sometimes life-threatening conditions. Hypovitaminose *f*, Vitaminmangel *m*.
hypovolemic shock: hypovolämischer Schock *m*.
hypoxia/*n*: Hypoxie *f*, Sauerstoffmangel *m*.
hypoxic hypoxia: hypoxische Hypoxie *f*.
hystera/*n*: Uterus *m*, Gebärmutter *f*.
hysterectomy/*n*: Hysterektomie *f*.
hysteria/*n*: a psychological state resulting from failure to face reality or certain aspects of it, and leading to conversion symptoms, such as paralysis, anesthesia, vomiting, fugue, or other dissociation manifestations. Without detectable organic basis. Hysterie *f*.
hysteric/*adj*: hysterisch.
hysterical amnesia: hysterische Amnesie *f*, psychogene Amnesie *f*.
hysterical attack: psychogener Anfall.
hysterical blindness: hysterische Blindheit *f*.
hysterical convulsion: hysterischer Krampfanfall *m*.
hysterical paralysis: hysterische Lähmung *f*.
hysterical pregnancy: eingebildete Schwangerschaft *f*.
hysterical psychosis: hysterische Psychose *f*.

hysteropathy/*n*: Metropathie *f*.
hysteropexy/*n*: Hysteropexie *f*.
hysteroplasty/*n*: Uterusplastik *f*.
hysterosalpingectomy/*n*: Hysterosalpingektomie *f*.
hysterosalpingography/*n*: Hysterosalpingographie *f*.
hysterotomy/*n*: Hysterotomie *f*.

I

I <*abbr*> **1. iodine; 2. isoleucine; 3. inosine**: 1. Jod *n*, I; 2. Isoleucin *n*; 3. Inosin *n*.
iatrogenic/*adj*: iatrogen.
ibafloxacin/*n*: Ibafloxacin *n*.
ibandronate/*n*: Ibandronsäure *f*.
ibogaine/*n*: Ibogain *n*.
ibufenac/*n*: Ibufenac *n*.
ibuprofen/*n*: Ibuprofen *n*.
ICD <*abbr*> **1. International Classification of Diseases; 2. intrauterine contraceptive device; 3. ischemic coronary disease**: 1. Internationale Klassifikation der Krankheiten *f*, ICD; 2. Intrauterinpessar *n*; 3. ischämische koronare Herzkrankheit *f*.
ice/*n, vb*: 1. Eis *n*; 2. vereisen.
iced spleen: Zuckergussmilz *f*.
ichthyosiform erythroderma: an autosomal recessive disorder which is characterized by generalized congenital ichthyosis, a spastic paraparesis, and oligophrenia. ichthyosiforme Erythrodermie *f*.
ichthyosis/*n*: a skin disorder which is characterized by disorders of keratinization with dry and scaly skin, for example ichthyosis congenita with hyperkeratotic lesions present at birth. Ichthyose *f*, Schuppenkrankheit *f*.
icing liver: Zuckergussleber *f*.
icosahedron/*n*: Ikosaeder *m*.
icteric/*adj*: ikterisch.
icterohemorrhagic fever: an infectious disease caused by the bacterium Leptospira interrogans. Symptoms include high fever, chills, muscle and joint pain, enlargement of the liver, and icterus. ikterische Leptospirose *f*, Weil-Krankheit *f*, Leptospirosis icterohaemorrhagica *f*.
icterus/*n*: increase of bile pigment in the blood causing yellow tinge to conjunctiva, skin, and membranes. Causes include diseases of the liver, gallbladder, bile system or blood disorders, for example hemolysis. Ikterus *m*, Gelbsucht *f*.
ICU <*abbr*> **intensive care unit**: Intensivstation *f*.
idarubicin/*n*: Idarubicin *n*.
idea/*n*: Idee *f*, Vorstellung *f*.
ideal weight: Idealgewicht *n*, Sollgewicht *n*.
identical/*adj*: identisch.
identification/*n*: Identifizierung *f*, Kennzeichnung *f*.
identity disorder: Identitätsstörung *f*.
ideokinetic apraxia: ideokinetische Apraxie *f*.
ideokinetics/*n*: Ideokinese *f*.
ideomotor apraxia: ideomotorische Apraxie *f*.
ideomotor center: ideomotorisches Zentrum *n*.
idiocy/*n*: Idiotie *f*.
idiopathic/*adj*: idiopathisch.
idiopathic aldosteronism: idiopathischer Aldosteronismus *m*, Mach-Syndrom *n*.
idiopathic facial paralysis: idiopathische Fazialislähmung *f*, Bell-Lähmung *f*.
idiopathic fracture: bone fracture resulting from normal movement and not due to trauma or excessive stress. Underlying causes include changes in bone structure or bone diseases, for example osteomalacia or osteoporosis. Spontanfraktur *f*.
idiopathic hypertension: essentieller Hochdruck *m*.

idiopathic multiple pigmented hemorrhagic sarcoma: a neoplasm characterized by vascular proliferation and the development of bluish-red nodules, usually on the skin of the lower extremities, but also on the mucous membranes for example in the mouth or in the lung. Kaposi sarcoma or multiple idiopathic hemorrhagic sarcoma occurs predominantly in elder men, it is endemically in parts of Central Africa. Disseminated forms occur in immunocompromised persons, for example persons with AIDS, and are associated with infection by human herpesvirus 8. Sarcoma idiopathicum multiplex haemorrhagicum *n*, Kaposi-Sarkom *n*.
idiopathic renal acidosis: idiopathische renale Azidose *f*, Lightwood-Albright-Syndrom *n*.
idiopathic respiratory distress of newborn: a syndrome occurring mainly in premature infants, which is characterized by difficulties in breathing, progressive cyanosis, and hyaline membranes on the lining of alveoli. akutes Atemnotsyndrom des Neugeborenen *n*.
idiopathic steatorrhea: a malabsorption syndrome caused by sensitivity to gluten-containing food. It is characterized by the presence of an excessive fat amount in the feces, and large, bulky stools. idiopathische Steatorrhö *f*, Zöliakie *f*, Heubner-Herter-Krankheit *f*.
idiosyncrasy/*n*: Idiosynkrasie *f*.
idioventricular rhythm: Kammereigenrhythmus *m*.
idoxuridine/*n*: Idoxuridin *n*.
iduronic acid: Iduronsäure *f*.
ifosfamide/*n*: Ifosfamid *n*.
ileitis/*n*: inflammation of the lower small intestine. Causes include infections or inflammatory disorders, for example Crohn's disease or regional enteritis. Symptoms include abdominal pain, diarrhea, weight loss and fever, and eventually the formation of intestinal fistula. Ileitis *f*.
ileocecal/*adj*: ileozäkal.
ileocecal insufficiency: Ileozäkalklappeninsuffizienz *f*.
ileocecal valve: Ileozäkalklappe *f*, Bauhin-Klappe *f*.
ileocolitis/*n*: Ileokolitis *f*.
ileocolostomy/*n*: Ileokolostomie *f*.
ileocolotomy/*n*: Ileokolotomie *f*.
ileopexy/*n*: Ileopexie *f*.
ileoproctostomy/*n*: Ileoproktostomie *f*.
ileostomy/*n*: Ileostomie *f*.
ileostomy bag: Stomabeutel *m*.
ileum/*n*: Ileum *n*.
ileus/*n*: stop of transport of intestinal contents due to diminished or absent bowel motility or to obstruction of the intestinal lumen. Symptoms include abdominal pain, vomiting, meteorism, and absence of defacation. Ileus *m*, Darmverschluss *m*.
iliac/*adj*: iliakal.
iliac bone: Ilium *n*, Os ilium *n*.
iliac region: Leistenregion *f*.
iliococcygeal/*adj*: iliokokzygeal.
iliofemoral ligament: Ligamentum iliofemorale *n*, Bertin-Band *n*.
iliofemoral thrombosis: Becken-Bein-Venenthrombose *f*.
ilium/*n*: Ilium *n*, Os ilium *n*.
ill/*adj*: krank.
illegal abortion: krimineller Abort *m*.
illicit drug: illegale Droge *f*.
illiteracy/*n*: Analphabetismus *m*.
illness/*n*: Krankheit *f*.
illness behavior: Krankheitsverhalten *n*.
illumination/*n*: Illumination *f*, Beleuchtung *f*.
illusion/*n*: Illusion *f*.
iloprost/*n*: Iloprost *n*.
IM <*abbr*> **intramuscular**/*adj*: intramuskulär, i.m.
image/*n*: Bild *n*.
image intensification: Bildverstärkung *f*.
imagery/*n*: Vorstellung *f*.
imaging/*n*: Bildgebung *f*, bildgebendes Verfahren *n*.
imatinib/*n*: Imatinib *n*.
imbalance/*n*: Ungleichgewicht *n*, Unausgeglichenheit *f*.

imbecility/*n*: Imbezillität *f*.
imbricated bandage: Dachziegelverband *m*.
imiclopazine/*n*: Imiclopazin *n*.
imidapril/*n*: Imidapril *n*.
imidazole/*n*: Imidazol *n*.
imiglucerase/*n*: Imiglucerase *n*.
imipenem/*n*: Imipenem *n*.
imipramine/*n*: Imipramin *n*.
imiquimod/*n*: Imiquimod *n*.
immature/*adj*: immatur, unreif.
immature birth: Frühgeburt *f*.
immature cataract: unreife Katarakt *f*.
immature delivery: Frühgeburt *f*.
immature infant: Frühgeborenes *n*, Frühchen *n*.
immediate/*adj*: unmittelbar, sofort.
immediate allergy: allergische Reaktion vom Soforttyp *f*.
immediate auscultation/*n*: direkte Auskultation *f*.
immediate complication: Primärkomplikation *f*.
immediate effect: Sofortwirkung *f*.
immediate reaction: Sofortreaktion *f*.
immobility/*n*: Unbeweglichkeit *f*.
immobilization/*n*: Immobilisierung *f*.
immovable bandage: Fixierverband *m*.
immune/*adj*: immun.
immune adherence: Immunadhärenz *f*.
immune-associated/*adj*: immunassoziiert.
immune body: Immunkörper *m*.
immune complex: Immunkomplex *m*.
immune-complex disease: any disorder which is caused by circulating immune complexes, manifesting for example as glomerulonephritis, lupus, rheumatoid arthritis, endocarditis or myocarditis. Immunkomplexkrankheit *f*.
immune globulin: Immunglobulin *n*.
immune hemolysin: Immunhämolysin *n*.
immune reaction: Immunantwort *f*.
immune response: Immunreaktion *f*.
immune serum: Immunserum *n*, Antiserum *n*.
immune-stimulating complex: immunstimulierender Komplex *m*.
immune system: Immunsystem *n*.
immunify/*vb*: immunisieren.
immunity/*n*: Immunität *f*.
immunization/*n*: Immunisierung *f*.
immunoassay/*n*: Immunoassay *m*.
immunochemistry/*n*: Immunchemie *f*.
immunodeficiency/*n*: any disorder which is characterized by an impairment or loss of the normal function of the immune system. Forms include congenital immunodeficiency, for example agammaglobulinemia, or acquired immunodeficiency, for example AIDS as a consequence of HIV infection, or iatrogenic immunodeficiency resulting from therapeutic immunosuppression. Immundefekt *m*, Immundefizienz *f*.
immunodeficiency syndrome: any condition which is characterized by impairment of functions of the immune system. Congenital forms include severe defects of B- and T-lymphocyte development, for example Swiss type agammaglobulinemia, certain hematopoietic stem cell defects, and thymic aplasia. Acquired forms include for example AIDS as a consequence of HIV infection, or may result from other systemic diseases like leukemia or lymphogranulomatosis. Immundefektsyndrom *n*, Immunmangelsyndrom *n*.
immunodiffusion test: Immundiffusionstest *m*.
immunoelectrophoresis/*n*: Immunelektrophorese *f*.
immunofluorescence/*n*: Immunfluoreszenz *f*.
immunogenetics/*n*: Immungenetik *f*.
immunoglobulin/*n*: Immunglobulin *n*.
immunologically competent cell: immunkompetente Zelle *f*, Immunozyt *m*.
immunologic amnesia: Verlust der Immunantwort *m*.
immunologic deficiency: Immundefekt *m*, Immundefizienz *f*.

immunologic depression: Immunsuppression *f*.
immunologic rejection: Abstoßungsreaktion *f*.
immunology/*n*: Immunologie *f*.
immunomodulator/*n*: Immunmodulator *m*.
immunostimulant/*n*: Immunstimulans *n*, immunstimulierende Substanz *f*.
immunosuppressant/*n*: Immunsuppressivum *n*, immunsupprimierende Substanz *f*.
immunosuppressive/*adj*: immunsuppressiv.
immunosuppressive therapy: immunsuppressive Therapie *f*, Immunsuppression *f*.
imolamine/*n*: Imolamin *n*.
impacted/*adj*: impaktiert, eingekeilt.
impacted cerumen: Zeruminalpfropf *m*.
impacted feces: Koprolith *m*, Kotstein *m*.
impacted fracture: eingekeilter Bruch *m*.
impair/*vb*: beeinträchtigen, schädigen.
impaired development: Entwicklungsstörung *f*.
impaired function: Funktionseinschränkung *f*, Unterfunktion *f*.
impairment/*n*: Beeinträchtigung *f*.
impalpable/*adj*: nicht palpabel.
impatent/*adj*: verstopft, verschlossen.
impedance/*n*: Impedanz *f*.
impediment/*n*: Funktionsstörung *f*.
imperforate/*adj*: nicht perforiert, ohne Öffnung.
imperforate anus: Analatresie *f*.
imperforate hymen: atresia and lack of an opening in the hymenal membrane. Symptoms include retention of menstrual blood in the vagina, or in the uterus. Hymenalatresie *f*.
impermeability/*n*: Impermeabilität *f*.
impervious/*adj*: undurchdringlich.
implant/*n, vb*: 1. Implantat *n*; 2. implantieren.
implantation/*n*: Implantation *f*, Nidation *f*.
implanted pacemaker: implantierter Herzschrittmacher *m*.
implanted suture: versenkte Naht *f*.
impotence/*n*: Impotenz *f*, Zeugungsunfähigkeit *f*.
impregnation/*n*: Imprägnation *f*, Befruchtung *f*.
impression/*n*: Impression *f*, Abdruck *m*, Eindruck *m*.
improvement/*n*: Besserung *f*.
impulse/*n*: Impuls *m*, Antrieb *m*, Reiz *m*.
impulse-conducting fiber: Purkinje-Faser *f*.
impulsive action: Triebhandlung *f*.
impulsive behavior: impulsives Verhalten *n*.
inactivate/*vb*: inaktivieren.
inactivated serum: inaktiviertes Serum *n*.
inactivated vaccine: inaktivierter Impfstoff *m*.
inactive gastritis: inaktive Gastritis *f*.
inactive ingredient: Hilfsstoff *m*.
inactivity atrophy: Inaktivitätsatrophie *f*.
inanition/*n*: Inanition *f*.
inarticulate/*adj*: unartikuliert.
inborn/*adj*: angeboren, hereditär.
inborn behavior: Instinktverhalten *n*.
inborn reflex: angeborener Reflex *m*.
inbreeding/*n*: Inzucht *f*.
incapsulation/*n*: Einkapselung *f*.
incarcerated hernia: inkarzerierte Hernie *f*.
incarceration/*n*: Inkarzerierung *f*.
incest/*n*: Inzest *m*.
incest tabu: Inzesttabu *n*.
incidence/*n*: Inzidenz *f*.
incidental cancer: inzidentes Karzinom *n*.
incidental finding: Zufallsbefund *m*.
incidental parasite: Zufallsparasit *m*.
incidental rupture: Spontanruptur *f*.
incipient/*adj*: beginnend, initial.
incision/*n*: Inzision *f*, Schnitt *m*, Eröffnung *f*.
incisional biopsy: Probeexzision *f*.
incisional hernia: Narbenhernie *f*.
incisor/*n*: Schneidezahn *m*.
incisure/*n*: Inzisur *f*, Einschnitt *m*, Einkerbung *f*.

I

inclination/*n*: Inklination *f*, Neigung *f*.
inclusion/*n*: Einschluss *m*, Einlagerung *f*.
inclusion body: Einschlusskörperchen *n*.
incoherence/*n*: Inkohärenz *f*, Zerfahrenheit *f*.
incompatibility/*n*: Inkompatibilität *f*, Unverträglichkeit *f*.
incompatible/*adj*: inkompatibel.
incompetence/*n*: Unfähigkeit *f*, Insuffizienz *f*.
incomplete/*adj*: unvollständig.
incomplete abortion: inkompletter Abort *m*.
incomplete amnesia: partielle Amnesie *f*.
incomplete antibody: inkompletter Antikörper *m*.
incomplete antigen: Hapten *n*.
incomplete bundle branch block: inkompletter Schenkelblock *m*.
incomplete dislocation: Subluxation *f*.
incomplete fistula: inkomplette Fistel *f*.
incomplete fracture: inkomplette Fraktur *f*.
incomplete hernia: unvollständiger Bruch *m*.
incomplete left bundle branch block: Linksverspätung *f*.
incontinence/*n*: Inkontinenz *f*.
incoordination/*n*: Inkoordination *f*, Ataxie *f*.
increase/*n, vb*: 1. Zunahme *f*, Anstieg *m*; 2. zunehmen, wachsen.
increased fremitus: verstärkter Fremitus *m*.
increased respiration: Hyperventilation *f*.
increased secretion: gesteigerte Sekretion *f*, Hypersekretion *f*.
increment/*n*: Inkrement *n*, Zuwachs *m*.
incrustation/*n*: Inkrustation *f*, Krustenbildung *f*.
incubation/*n*: Inkubation *f*.
incubation period: Inkubationszeit *f*.
incubator/*n*: Inkubator *m*, Brutkasten *m*.
incurable/*adj*: inkurabel, unheilbar.
incus/*n*: Amboss *m*.
indapamide/*n*: Indapamid *n*.
indemnity/*n*: Entschädigung *f*, Schadenersatz *m*.
independent variable: unabhängige Variable *f*.
index/*n*: Index *m*, Verhältnis *n*.
index case: Indexpatient *m*.
Indian flap: Stirnlappen *m*.
Indian rhinoplasty: indische Rhinoplastik *f*.
indication/*n*: Indikation *f*, Anzeige *f*.
indicator/*n*: Indikator *m*.
indifferent cell: undifferenzierte Zelle *f*.
indifferent tissue: undifferenziertes Gewebe *n*.
indigenous practitioner: Medizinmann *m*.
indigestible/*adj*: unverdaulich, schwer verdaulich.
indinavir/*n*: Indinavir *n*.
indirect ballottement: indirektes Ballottement *n*.
indirect bilirubin: indirektes Bilirubin *n*.
indirect fracture: indirekte Fraktur *f*.
indirect nuclear division: indirekte Kernteilung *f*, Mitose *f*.
indirect percussion: indirekte Perkussion *f*.
indirect pupillary reaction: indirekte Pupillenreaktion *f*.
individual/*n, adj*: 1. Individuum *n*; 2. individuell.
indocyanine green: Indozyaningrün *n*.
indolacetic acid: Indolessigsäure *f*.
indolent/*adj*: indolent.
indomethacin/*n*: Indometacin *n*.
indoramin/*n*: Indoramin *n*.
indoxyl/*n*: Indoxyl *n*.
induce/*vb*: induzieren, einleiten.
induced abortion: induzierter Abort *m*.
induced delivery: induzierte Geburt *f*.
induced fever: künstliches Fieber *n*.
induced hypothermia: künstliche Hypothermie *f*, kontrollierte Hypothermie *f*.

induced immunity: induzierte Immunität *f*.
induced labor: eingeleitete Wehen.
induced psychosis: a delusion, false belief or psychotic disorder which is induced from an index patient to one or more closely related, formerly inconspicuous persons who simultaneously develop similar symptoms. induzierte Psychose *f*, Folie à deux *f*.
inducer/*n*: Induktor *m*.
inducible enzyme: induzierbares Enzym *n*.
inducing agent: Induktor *m*.
induction/*n*: Induktion *f*, Einleitung *f*.
inductive phase: Induktionsphase *f*.
induration/*n*: Induration *f*, Verhärtung *f*.
industrial/*adj*: Arbeits-, Berufs-.
industrial dermatosis: Berufsdermatose *f*.
indwelling cannula: Verweilkanüle *f*.
indwelling catheter: Verweilkatheter *m*, Dauerkatheter *m*.
inebriant/*n*: Rauschmittel *n*.
inebriation/*n*: Trunkenheit *f*, Rausch *m*.
ineffectivity/*n*: Unwirksamkeit *f*.
inert/*adj*: inert, inaktiv.
inert complex: inerter Komplex *m*.
inertia/*n*: Inertie *f*, Trägheit *f*.
infancy/*n*: Säuglingsalter *n*, Kleinkindalter *n*
infant/*n*: Kind *n*.
infant formula: Milchfertignahrung *f*.
infantile/*adj*: infantil.
infantile amaurotic familial disease: a condition which is characterized by an abnormal accumulation of gangliosides, due to an autosomal recessive defect in the enzyme hexosaminidase. Symptoms include an early onset in the first year of life with psychomotor retardation, paralysis, seizures, and progressive vision loss. infantile amaurotische Idiotie *f*, Tay-Sachs-Syndrom *n*.
infantile cataract: infantile Katarakt *f*.
infantile celiac disease: a malabsorption syndrome caused by sensitivity to gluten-containing food. It is characterized by the presence of an excessive fat amount in the feces, and large, bulky stools. idiopathische Steatorrhö *f*, Zöliakie *f*, Heubner-Herter-Krankheit *f*.
infantile cerebral palsy: zerebrale Kinderlähmung *f*, Little-Krankheit *f*.
infantile dementia: infantile Demenz *f*, Heller-Syndrom *n*.
infantile gastroenteritis: Sommerdiarrhö *f*, epidemische Diarrhö *f*, Cholera infantum *f*.
infantile hypotonia: Floppy-Infant-Syndrom *n*.
infantile lobar emphysema: kongenitales lobäres Emphysem *n*.
infantile myoclonic encephalopathy: Encephalopathia myoclonica infantilis *f*, Kinsbourne-Syndrom *n*.
infantile paralysis: an infectious disease caused by poliovirus, affecting the cells of the central nervous system and especially cells of the anterior column of the spinal cord. Main symptom is a muscular paralysis, sometimes including paralysis of respiratory muscles. Kinderlähmung *f*, Poliomyelitis anterior acuta *f*, Heine-Medin-Krankheit *f*.
infantile progressive bulbar palsy: familiäre infantile progressive Bulbärparalyse *f*, Fazio-Londe-Syndrom *n*.
infantile renal tubular acidosis: infantile tubuläre Azidose *f*.
infantile scurvy: infantiler Skorbut *m*, Möller-Barlow-Krankheit *f*.
infantile spongy degeneration: frühinfantile diffuse spongiöse Dystrophie *f*, Canavan-Krankheit *f*.
infantile uterus: Uterus infantilis *m*.
infantilism/*n*: Infantilismus *m*.
infarct/*n*: Infarkt *m*.
infarcted kidney: Niereninfarkt *m*.
infarction/*n*: Infarzierung *f*, Infarkt *m*.
infect/*vb*: infizieren, anstecken.
infected abortion: komplizierter Abort *m*, putrider Abort *m*.

infected thrombus: septischer Thrombus *m*.
infection/*n*: Infektion *f*.
infection control: Infektionsbekämpfung *f*.
infectiosity/*n*: Infektiosität *f*.
infectious/*adj*: infektiös.
infectious agent: Erreger *m*.
infectious angioma: Angioma serpiginosum *n*.
infectious arthritis: inflammation of one or several joints, due to infection with bacteria, viruses, or other pathogenic microorganisms. Most frequent bacterial infections include Staphylococcus infections, usually after injury. Other forms include tuberculous arthritis, yersiniosis, or rheumatic fever. infektiöse Arthritis *f*.
infectious disease: Infektionskrankheit *f*.
infectious endocarditis: infektiöse Endokarditis *f*.
infectious gastroenteritis: inflammation of the stomach and intestine, resulting from infection with a virus, bacterium, or other pathogenic microorganism. Symptoms include nausea and vomiting, diarrhea, and abdominal discomfort. infektiöse Gastroenteritis *f*, Magen-Darm-Katarrh *m*.
infectious hepatitis: infektiöse Hepatitis *f*.
infectious mononucleosis: an infectious disease caused by Epstein-Barr virus. Mononucleosis or glandular fever is characterized by an increase in number of monocytes, enlargement of lymph nodes, mild elevation of body temperature, enlargement of the spleen, sore throat, and sometimes skin eruption. infektiöse Mononukleose *f*, Pfeiffer-Drüsenfieber *n*.
infectious nucleic acid: infektiöse Nukleinsäure *f*.
infective asthma: infektallergisches Asthma *n*.
infective chorea: Sydenham-Chorea *f*, Chorea minor *f*.
infective dose: infektiöse Dosis *f*, Infektionsdosis *f*.
infective embolism: septische Embolie *f*.
inferior/*adj*: unterer, inferior.
inferior alternate paralysis: Hemiplegia alternans inferior *f*, Millard-Gubler-Syndrom *n*.
inferior pontine syndrome: a neurologic condition due to lesions of the nucleus of the abducent nerve and the pyramidal tract which is characterized by ipsilateral paresis of the abducent nerve and contralateral hemiparesis. unteres Brückensyndrom *n*, Raymond-Syndrom *n*.
inferior vena cava syndrome: Vena-cava-inferior-Syndrom *n*.
infertility/*n*: inability to conceive and become pregnant. Causes include genetic disorders, endocrine disturbances, ovarian dysfunction, tubal obstruction, vaginal dysplasia, and emotional factors. Infertilität *f*.
infestation/*n*: Infestation *f*, Parasitenbefall *m*.
infiltrating growth: infiltrierendes Wachstum *n*.
infiltrating tumor: infiltrierender Tumor *m*.
infiltration/*n*: Infiltration *f*.
infiltration anesthesia: Infiltrationsanästhesie *f*.
infiltrative ophthalmopathy: endokriner Exophthalmus *m*.
infirmary/*n*: Pflegestation *f*, Krankenrevier *n*.
infirmity/*n*: Infirmität *f*, Schwäche *f*, Hinfälligkeit *f*.
inflammation/*n*: Inflammation *f*, Entzündung *f*.
inflammatory bowel disease: entzündliche Darmerkrankung *f*.
inflammatory cell: Entzündungszelle *f*.
inflammatory process: Entzündungsvorgang *m*.
inflammatory reaction: Entzündungsreaktion *f*.
inflammatory rheumatism: generalized disease affecting joints, skin, the heart, and sometimes the central

nervous system, due to an allergic reaction to toxins of the bacterium Streptococcus. rheumatisches Fieber *n*.

inflammatory softening: entzündliche Einschmelzung *f*.

inflammatory symptom: Entzündungszeichen *n*.

inflate/*vb*: aufblähen, insufflieren.

inflexion/*n*: Einwärtsbiegung *f*.

infliximab/*n*: Infliximab *n*.

inflow/*n*: Einfluss *m*, Zufluss *m*.

influenza/*n*: an infectious disease caused by influenza virus. Symptoms include fever, chills, headache, inflammation of the nose, larynx and bronchi, muscular pains, aches in the back and limbs, and gastrointestinal disorders. Influenza *f*, Grippe *f*.

influenzal encephalitis: Grippeenzephalitis *f*.

infolding suture: invertierende Naht *f*.

infranuclear paralysis: infranukleäre Lähmung *f*.

infraorbital neuralgia: Infraorbitalneuralgie *f*.

infrared light: Infrarotlicht *n*.

infrared thermography: Infrarotthermographie *f*.

infrasound/*n*: Infraschall *m*.

infundibular/*adj*: infundibulär, trichterförmig.

infundibular pulmonary stenosis: infundibuläre Pulmonalstenose *f*.

infusion/*n*: Infusion *f*, Aufguss *m*.

infusion pump: Infusionspumpe *f*.

ingestion/*n*: Ingestion *f*, Aufnahme *f*.

ingredient/*n*: Ingredienz *f*, Bestandteil *m*.

ingrown/*adj*: eingewachsen.

ingrown nail: eingewachsener Nagel *m*.

inguinal/*adj*: inguinal.

inguinal canal: Leistenkanal *m*.

inguinal hernia: protrusion of abdominal tissue or organs into the inguinal canal. Forms include direct inguinal hernia which originates between the inferior epigastric artery and the rectus muscle, and indirect inguinal hernia in which the internal opening is the deep inguinal ring. Leistenhernie *f*.

inguinal ligament: Leistenband *n*.

inguinal lymph node: Leistenlymphknoten *m*.

inguinal region: Leistenregion *f*.

inguinal ring: Leistenring *m*.

inguinal testis: Leistenhoden *m*.

inhalation/*n*: Inhalation *f*.

inhalation pneumonia: Inhalationspneumonie *f*, Aspirationspneumonie *f*.

inherent/*adj*: inhärent.

inheritance/*n*: Vererbung *f*.

inhibiting mechanism: Hemmmechanismus *m*.

inhibition/*n*: Inhibition *f*, Hemmung *f*.

inhibitory concentration: Hemmkonzentration *f*.

inhibitory effect: Hemmwirkung *f*.

inhibitory fiber: inhibitorisches Axon *n*.

inhibitory hormone: inhibitorisch wirkendes Hormon *n*.

initial/*adj*: initial.

initial focus: Ausgangsherd *m*.

initial manifestation: Erstmanifestation *f*.

initial vaccination: Erstimpfung *f*.

initial weight: Ausgangsgewicht *n*, Geburtsgewicht *n*.

inject/*vb*: injizieren.

injection/*n*: Injektion *f*.

injection site: Injektionsort *m*.

injure/*vb*: schädigen, verletzen.

injury/*n*: Verletzung *f*, Schädigung *f*, Trauma *n*.

inlay/*n*: Auflage *f*, Einlage *f*, Zahnfüllung *f*.

inmate/*n*: Insasse *m*.

innate/*adj*: angeboren, kongenital.

inner/*adj*: innerer.

inner ear: Innenohr *n*.

innervation/*n*: Innervation *f*.

innocent/*adj*: harmlos, benigne.

innocent murmur: funktionelles Geräusch *n*.

innominate/*adj*: namenlos.

innoxious/*adj*: unschädlich, harmlos.

inoculating loop: Impföse *f*.

inoculation/*n*: Inokulation *f*.
inorganic/*adj*: anorganisch.
inorganic acid: anorganische Säure *f*.
inorganic chemistry: anorganische Chemie *f*.
inosine monophosphate: Inosinmonophosphat *n*, Inosinsäure *f*.
inosinic acid: Inosinsäure *f*, Inosinmonophosphat *n*.
inositol/*n*: Inositol *n*, Inosit *n*.
inpatient/*n*: stationärer Patient *m*.
input/*n*: Eingabe *f*.
insane/*n, adj*: 1. Geisteskranker *m*; 2. geisteskrank.
insanity/*n*: Geisteskrankheit *f*, Psychose *f*.
insect/*n*: Insekt *n*.
insect bite: sting by an insect, which can result in the injection of an allergen or a toxic substance into the body, or may be associated with transmission of diseases, for example malaria through bites by certain types of mosquitoes, tick-borne fever, or tularemia through flies. Insektenstich *m*.
insemination/*n*: Insemination *f*, Befruchtung *f*.
insensible/*adj*: unempfindlich, unmerklich.
insensible perspiration: Perspiratio insensibilis *f*.
insensitivity/*n*: Insensibilität *f*, Unempfindlichkeit *f*.
insertion/*n*: Insertion *f*, Eingliederung *f*.
inside diameter: innerer Durchmesser *m*.
insight/*n*: Einsicht *f*.
insoluble/*adj*: insolubel, unlöslich.
insomnia/*n*: the inability to initiate or to maintain sleep. Causes include external sources such as noise, uncomfortable environmental temperature, or an unfamiliar bed, overstimulation from drugs, coffee or tea. Internal causes include for example emotional upset, pain, or systemic diseases. Insomnie *f*, Schlaflosigkeit *f*.
inspection/*n*: Inspektion *f*, Untersuchung *f*.
inspiration/*n*: Inspiration *f*, Atemzug *m*.
inspiratory/*adj*: inspiratorisch.
inspiratory capacity: Inspirationskapazität *f*.
inspiratory dyspnea: inspiratorische Dyspnoe *f*.
inspiratory pressure: inspiratorischer Druck *m*.
inspiratory stridor: inspiratorischer Stridor *m*.
inspissated/*adj*: eingedickt.
instability/*n*: Instabilität *f*.
instantaneous death: sofortiger Tod *m*.
instillation/*n*: Instillation *f*.
instinct/*n*: Instinkt *m*, Trieb *m*.
instinctive behavior: Instinktverhalten *n*.
instruction/*n*: Anweisung *f*, Anleitung *f*.
instrument/*n*: Instrument *n*, Gerät *n*.
insufficiency/*n*: Insuffizienz *f*.
insular scotoma: isoliertes Skotom *n*.
insulation/*n*: Isolierung *f*, Isolation *f*.
insulin/*n*: Insulin *n*.
insulin allergy: Insulinallergie *f*.
insulin aspart/*n*: Insulinaspart *n*.
insulin detemir/*n*: Insulindetemir *n*.
insulin glargine/*n*: Insulinglargin *n*.
insulin glulisine/*n*: Insulinglulisin *n*.
insulin-induced hypoglycemia: insulinbedingte Hypoglykämie *f*.
insulin-like activity: insulinartige Wirkung *f*.
insulin-like growth factor: insulinartiger Wachstumsfaktor *m*.
insulin lispro/*n*: Insulinlispro *n*.
insulinoma/*n*: neoplasm of the beta cells of the pancreas which is characterized by an excessive secretion of insulin. Symptoms include hyperinsulinemia with severe hypoglycemia. Insulinom *n*.
insulin pump: Insulinpumpe *f*.
insulin receptor: Insulinrezeptor *m*.
insulin resistance: Insulinresistenz *f*.
insulin secretion: Insulinausschüttung *f*.
insulin unit: Insulineinheit *f*.
insulin zinc suspension: Insulin-Zink-Suspension *f*.

insulitis/*n*: Insulitis *f*.
insurance/*n*: Versicherung *f*.
intact/*adj*: intakt, ungestört.
intake/*n*: Aufnahme *f*.
integral dose: Integraldosis *f*, Gesamtdosis *f*.
integrase inhibitor/*n*: Integraseinhibitor *m*.
integument/*n*: Integument *n*.
intellect/*n*: Intellekt *m*.
intelligence quotient: Intelligenzquotient *m*.
intelligence test: Intelligenztest *m*.
intense/*adj*: stark, intensiv.
intensify/*vb*: verstärken.
intensive care: Intensivpflege *f*.
intentional reaction: Willkürreaktion *f*.
intention tremor: Intentionstremor *m*.
interaction/*n*: Interaktion *f*, Wechselwirkung *f*.
interarticular/*adj*: interartikulär.
interatrial septal defect: Vorhofseptumdefekt *m*.
intercalated flap: Zwischenlappen *m*.
intercalated nucleus: Schaltkern *m*.
intercellular/*adj*: interzellulär.
intercellular lymph: Interstitialflüssigkeit *f*.
intercellular space: Interzellularraum *m*.
intercostal/*adj*: interkostal.
intercostal anesthesia: Interkostalanästhesie *f*.
intercostal block: Interkostalblock *m*
intercostal neuralgia: nerve pain located in one or several intercostal spaces. Causes include herpes zoster, diseases of the spinal cord or the vertebral column, or aortic isthmus stenosis. Interkostalneuralgie *f*.
intercostal space: Interkostalraum *m*.
intercourse/*n*: Geschlechtsverkehr *m*, Koitus *m*.
intercristal diameter: Beckenkammlinie *f*.
intercurrent/*adj*: interkurrent.
interdental space: Interdentalraum *m*.
interferon/*n*: Interferon *n*.
intergluteal cleft: Crena ani *f*, Afterfurche *f*.
interlamellar space: Lamellenzwischenraum *m*.
intermaxillary bone: Zwischenkieferknochen *m*, Goethe-Knochen *m*.
intermaxillary fixation: Kieferfixation *f*.
intermediary carcinoma: Intermediärzellkarzinom *n*.
intermediate/*n, adj*: 1. Intermediat *n*, Zwischenprodukt *n*; 2. intermediär.
intermediate-acting insulin: Intermediärinsulin *n*.
intermediate heart: elektrische Mittellage *f*.
intermediate lamella: Schaltlamelle *f*.
intermediate state: Intermediärstadium *n*.
intermenstrual flow: Zwischenblutung *f*.
intermenstrual pain: Mittelschmerz *m*.
intermesenteric anastomosis: Riolan-Anastomose *f*.
intermittent/*adj*: intermittierend.
intermittent carrier: intermittierender Ausscheider *m*.
intermittent claudication: a condition characterized by pain in the legs and intermittent lameness after brief exercise, usually due to partial or complete obstruction of the femoral artery by arteriosclerotic lesions. Claudicatio intermittens *f*.
intermittent explosive disorder: intermittierende explosive Störung *f*.
intermittent fever: intermittierendes Fieber *n*.
intermittent hemoglobinuria: recurrent presence of free hemoglobin in the urine, a characteristic sign for example of paroxysmal nocturnal hemoglobinuria or paroxysmal cold hemoglobinuria. intermittierende Hämoglobinurie *f*, Dressler-Harley-Krankheit *f*.
intermittent proteinuria: intermittierende Proteinurie *f*.
intermittent pulse: Pulsus intermittens *m*.
internal/*adj*: innerlich, innere.

I

internal acoustic canal: innerer Gehörgang *m*.
internal ballottement: direktes Ballottement *n*.
internal bleeding: innere Blutung *f*.
internal conjugate: innerer Beckendurchmesser *m*.
internal ear: Innenohr *n*.
internal fistula: innere Fistel *f*.
internal fixation: interne Fixierung *f*.
internal hemorrhage: innere Blutung *f*.
internal hernia: direkte Leistenhernie *f*, innerer Bruch *m*.
internal medicine: innere Medizin *f*.
internal ophthalmoplegia: Ophthalmoplegia interna *f*.
internal pelvimetry: innere Beckenmessung *f*.
internal rotation: Innenrotation *f*.
internal sensation: Viszerosensibilität *f*.
internal strabismus: Einwärtsschielen *n*, Konvergenzschielen *n*, Esotropie *f*.
internal version: innere Wendung *f*.
international nonproprietary name: internationaler Freiname *m*.
internuclear ophthalmoplegia: internukleäre Ophthalmoplegie *f*.
internuclear paralysis: internukleäre Ophthalmoplegie *f*.
interoceptive sensibility: Viszerosensibilität *f*.
interorbital distance: Augenabstand *m*.
interosseous/*adj*: interossär.
interpelvicoabdominal amputation: Hemipelvektomie *f*, Jaboulay-Amputation *f*.
interphase/*n*: Interphase *f*.
interpleural space: Mediastinum *n*.
interrupted respiration: intermittierende Atmung *f*.
interrupted suture: diskontinuierliche Naht *f*.
interscapulothoracic amputation: interskapulothorakale Amputation *f*.
interspace/*n*: Zwischenraum *m*.
interspinal line: Interspinallinie *f*.
interstitial/*adj*: interstitiell.
interstitial cystitis: interstitielle Zystitis *f*.
interstitial fluid: interstitielle Flüssigkeit *f*.
interstitial nephritis: interstitielle Nephritis *f*.
interstitial radiotherapy: interstitielle Bestrahlung *f*.
interstitial space: Interstitialraum *m*.
intertrigo/*n*: an acute skin disorder with irritation and inflammation, erythema or eczema which affects skin folds or skin surface beneath a pendulous breast, mainly in persons showing obesity. Intertrigo *f*.
intertrochanteric/*adj*: intertrochantär.
intertrochanteric fracture: intertrochantäre Fraktur *f*.
interval/*n*: Intervall *n*.
intervention/*n*: Intervention *f*.
interventional radiology: interventionelle Radiologie *f*.
interventricular/*adj*: interventrikulär.
interventricular septum: Kammerscheidewand *f*.
intervertebral/*adj*: intervertebral.
intervertebral disk: Bandscheibe *f*, Discus intervertebralis *m*.
interview/*n*: Interview *n*, Befragung *f*.
interzonal fiber: Spindelfaser *f*.
intestinal/*adj*: intestinal.
intestinal amebiasis: Amöbenruhr *f*.
intestinal anastomosis: Darmanastomose *f*.
intestinal anthrax: Darmmilzbrand *m*.
intestinal atresia: Darmatresie *f*.
intestinal fistula: Darmfistel *f*.
intestinal flu: Darmgrippe *f*.
intestinal hemorrhage: Darmblutung *f*.
intestinal hormone: Enterohormon *n*.
intestinal infection: Darminfektion *f*, Enteritis *f*.
intestinal lipodystrophy: intestinale Lipodystrophie *f*, Whipple-Krankheit *f*.
intestinal loop: Darmschlinge *f*.

intestinal motility: Darmmotilität *f*.
intestinal perforation: Darmperforation *f*.
intestinal peristalsis: Darmperistaltik *f*, Darmbewegung *f*.
intestinal polyp: Darmpolyp *m*.
intestinal reabsorption: intestinale Rückresorption *f*.
intestinal telangiectasia: intestinale Teleangiektasie *f*.
intestinal tract: Magen-Darm-Kanal *m*.
intestinal villus: Darmzotte *f*.
intestine/*n*: Darm *m*, Intestinum *n*.
intolerance/*n*: Intoleranz *f*, Unverträglichkeit *f*.
intoxication/*n*: uptake of poisonous substances or gas into the body by ingestion, absorption or inhalation and the following action of this substance upon the organism. The term is also used to describe the condition of drunkenness. Intoxikation *f*, Vergiftung *f*.
intra-abdominal/*adj*: intraabdominell.
intra-articular/*adj*: intraartikulär.
intra-articular fracture: intraartikuläre Fraktur *f*.
intra-atrial conduction: intraatriale Reizleitung *f*.
intra-atrial septum: Vorhofseptum *n*.
intracanalicular papilloma: intrakanalikuläres Papillom *n*.
intracavitary radiotherapy: intrakavitäre Strahlentherapie *f*.
intracellular/*adj*: intrazellulär.
intracellular compartment: Intrazellularraum *n*.
intracellular fluid: Intrazellularflüssigkeit *f*.
intracerebral/*adj*: intrazerebral.
intracerebral abscess: Hirnabszess *m*.
intracerebral hematoma: zerebrales Hämatom *n*.
intracerebral hemorrhage: intrazerebrale Blutung *f*.
intracerebral mass: intrakranielle Raumforderung *f*.
intracordial electrocardiography: intrakardiale Elektrokardiographie *f*.
intracranial/*adj*: intrakraniell.
intracranial abscess: intrakranieller Abszess *m*.
intracranial calcification: intrakranielle Kalkablagerung *f*.
intracranial cyst: intrakranielle Zyste *f*.
intracranial hemorrhage: intrakranielle Blutung *f*.
intracranial pressure: intrakranieller Druck *m*.
intractable/*adj*: unbehandelbar.
intradermal/*adj*: intradermal.
intradermal suture: Subkutannaht *f*.
intradermal test: Intrakutantest *m*.
intradermal tuberculin skin testing: intrakutane Tuberkulinprobe *f*, Mendel-Mantoux-Test *m*.
intraductal papilloma: intraduktales Papillom *n*.
intradural/*adj*: intradural.
intrafusal fiber: intrafusale Muskelfaser *f*.
intragastric/*adj*: intragastral.
intrahepatic/*adj*: intrahepatisch.
intramedullary/*adj*: intramedullär.
intramedullary nailing: Marknagelung *f*.
intramembraneous ossification: desmale Ossifikation *f*.
intramural hematoma: Wandhämatom *n*.
intramuscular/*adj*: intramuskulär, i.m.
intranasal/*adj*: intranasal, endonasal.
intranasal administration: intranasale Applikation *f*.
intranasal antrotomy: transnasale Antrotomie *f*.
intraocular/*adj*: intraokular.
intraocular pressure: Augeninnendruck *m*.
intraosseous fixation: intraossäre Fixation *f*.
intraosseous hemangioma: Knochenhämangiom *n*.
intraperiosteal fracture: subperiostale Fraktur *f*.
intraperitoneal pregnancy: Bauchhöhlenschwangerschaft *f*.
intraspinal: intraspinal.
intraspinal abscess: Spinalkanalabszess *m*.

intraspinal pressure: Liquordruck *m*.
intrathecal/*adj*: intrathekal.
intrathoracic/*adj*: intrathorakal.
intrathoracic goiter: retrosternale Struma *f*.
intrathoracic pressure: intrathorakaler Druck *m*.
intrathoracic thyroid: retrosternale Struma *f*.
intrauterine/*adj*: intrauterin.
intrauterine amputation: Amnionschnürfurche *f*.
intrauterine contraceptive: Intrauterinpessar *m*.
intrauterine death: intrauteriner Fruchttod *m*.
intrauterine device: Intrauterinpessar *n*.
intrauterine fracture: Intrauterinfraktur *f*.
intrauterine pregnancy: Intrauteringravidität *f*.
intravaginal/*adj*: intravaginal.
intravaginal administration: intravaginale Applikation *f*.
intravascular coagulation: intravaskuläre Gerinnung *f*.
intravenous/*adj*: intravenös, i.v.
intravenous administration: intravenöse Anwendung *f*.
intravenous cholangiography: intravenöse Cholangiographie *f*.
intravenous feeding: intravenöse Ernährung *f*.
intravenous renal angiography: Nierenangiographie *f*, Renovasographie *f*.
intravenous urography: Infusionsurographie *f*.
intraventricular block: intraventrikulärer Block *m*.
intraventricular conduction: Kammerleitung *f*.
intraventricular hemorrhage: Ventrikelblutung *f*.
intraventricular pressure: Kammerdruck *m*.
intrinsic/*adj*: intrinsisch.
intrinsic allergy: Atopie *f*.
intrinsic asthma: intrinsisches Asthma *n*, endogenes Asthma *n*.
intrinsic factor: intrinsischer Faktor *m*, Castle-Faktor *m*.
introspection/*n*: Introspektion *f*, Selbstbeobachtung *f*.
introvert/*vb, adj*: 1. introvertieren, einwärtswenden; 2. introvertiert.
intubation/*n*: Intubation *f*.
intumescence/*n*: Intumeszenz *f*.
intumescent cataract: Quellungskatarakt *f*.
intussusception/*n*: a condition in which a segment of the intestine is fold in on itself, cutting off the passageway, for example invagination of the ileum into the colon. Intussuszeption *f*, Invagination *f*.
inulin/*n*: Inulin *n*.
inunction/*n*: Inunktion *f*, Einreibung *f*.
invagination/*n*: Invagination *f*.
invalidism/*n*: Invalidität *f*.
invariance/*n*: Invarianz *f*.
invasion/*n*: Invasion *f*, Eindringen *n*.
invasive/*adj*: invasiv.
invasive growth: invasives Wachstum *n*.
invasive method: invasive Methode *f*.
inverse/*adj*: invers, umgekehrt.
inverse astigmatism: irregulärer Astigmatismus *m*.
inverse function: Umkehrfunktion *f*.
inversion/*n*: Inversion *f*, Wendung *f*.
inverted testis: invertierter Hoden *m*.
investigate/*vb*: untersuchen, erforschen.
investigation/*n*: Untersuchung *f*, Erforschung *f*.
investigator/*n*: Forscher *m*, Untersucher *m*.
investment/*n*: Bedeckung *f*, Umkleidung *f*.
involuntary movement: unwillkürliche Bewegung *f*.
involution/*n*: Involution *f*.
involutional depression: Involutionsdepression *f*, senile Depression *f*.
involutional paranoia: Involutionsparanoia *f*.
involutional psychosis: Involutionsmelancholie *f*.
involvement/*n*: Beteiligung *f*, Mitbeteiligung *f*.
iobenzamic acid: Iobenzaminsäure *f*.

iocetamic acid: Iocetaminsäure *f*.
iodic acid: Jodsäure *f*.
iodide/*n*: Jodid *n*.
iodine/*n*: Iod *n*, I, Jod *n*.
iodine deficiency: Jodmangel *m*.
iodine ointment: Jodsalbe *f*.
iodipamic acid: Iodipamid *n*.
iodism/*n*: Jodismus *m*, Jodvergiftung *f*.
iodized oil: Jodöl *n*.
iodized salt: jodiertes Salz *n*, Jodsalz *n*.
iodogorgoric acid: Dijodthyrosin *n*.
iodopsin/*n*: Jodopsin *n*.
iodoxybenzoic acid: Jodbenzoesäure *f*.
ion/*n*: Ion *n*.
ion channel: Ionenkanal *m*.
ion-exchange resin: Austauscherharz *n*.
ionization/*n*: Ionisation *f*, Ionisierung *f*.
ionizing/*adj*: ionisierend.
ionizing radiation: ionisierende Strahlung *f*.
iopamidol/*n*: Iopamidol *n*.
iopanic acid: Iopansäure *f*.
iopromide/*n*: Iopromid *n*.
iosarcol/*n*: Iosarcol *n*.
iotalamic acid: Iotalaminsäure *f*.
iothalamate/*n*: Iothalamat *n*.
iothiouracil/*n*: Iothiouracil *n*.
iotrol/*n*: Iotrol *n*.
iotrolan/*n*: Iotrolan *n*.
ioxaglic acid: Ioxaglinsäure *f*.
ioxitalamic acid: Ioxitalaminsäure *f*.
ipecac/*n*: Ipecacuanha *f*, Brechwurz *f*.
ipratropium bromide: Ipratropiumbromid *n*.
iprazochrome/*n*: Iprazochrom *n*.
iproclozide/*n*: Iproclozid *n*.
ipronidazole/*n*: Ipronidazol *n*.
ipsilateral/*adj*: ipsilateral.
irbesartan/*n*: Irbesartan *n*.
iridectomy/*n*: Iridektomie *f*.
iridocorneal angle: Iridokornealwinkel *m*, Kammerwinkel *m*.
iridocyclitis/*n*: Iridozyklitis *f*.
iridopathy/*n*: Iriserkrankung *f*.
iridoplegia/*n*: Iridoplegie *f*.
iridotomy/*n*: Iridotomie *f*.
irinotecan/*n*: Irinotecan *n*.
iris/*n*: Iris *f*, Regenbogenhaut *f*.
iron/*n, adj*: 1. Eisen *n*, Fe; 2. eisern.
iron-binding capacity: Eisenbindungskapazität *f*.
iron compound: Eisenverbindung *f*.
iron-deficiency anemia: Eisenmangelanämie *f*.
iron-hard tumor: eisenharte Struma *f*, Riedel-Struma *f*.
iron lung: eiserne Lunge *f*.
irradiation/*n*: Irradiation *f*, Bestrahlung *f*.
irradiation cataract: Strahlenkatarakt *f*.
irradiation field: Bestrahlungsfeld *n*.
irreducible/*adj*: nicht reduzierbar.
irregular/*adj*: irregulär, unregelmäßig.
irregular pulse: unregelmäßiger Puls *m*.
irresponsible/*adj*: unzurechnungsfähig.
irreversible coma: irreversibles Koma *n*.
irrigation/*n*: Irrigation *f*, Spülung *f*
irritability/*n*: Irritabilität *f*, Reizbarkeit *f*.
irritable/*adj*: irritabel, reizbar.
irritable bladder: Reizblase *f*.
irritable colon: irritables Kolon *n*, Reizkolon *n*.
irritable heart: neurozirkulatorische Asthenie *f*.
irritable joint: Reizgelenk *n*.
irritant/*n*: Irritans *n*, Reizstoff *m*.
irritant poison: Reizgift *n*.
irritating substance: Reizstoff *m*, Irritans *n*.
irritation/*n*: Irritation *f*, Reizung *f*.
ischemia/*n*: a local, temporary or continued decreased blood supply in a body area or an organ. Causes include constriction or obstruction in the blood vessel supplying that part of the body. Reductions of blood flow may also result from unfavorable body positions. Ischämie *f*.
ischemic/*adj*: ischämisch.
ischemic colitis: ischämische Kolitis *f*.
ischemic gangrene: ischämische Gangrän *f*.
ischemic heart disease: ischämische Herzkrankheit *f*.

ischemic paralysis: ischämische Lähmung *f*.
ischiatic bone: Os ischii *n*, Sitzbein *n*.
isethionic acid: Isethionsäure *f*.
island disease: Scrub-Typhus *m*, Tsutsugamushi-Krankheit *f*.
island of Reil: Reil-Insel *f*, Insula Reilii *f*.
islet/*n*: Insel *f*.
islets of Langerhans: Langerhans-Inseln.
isoallele/*n*: Isoallel *n*.
isoaminile/*n*: Isoaminil *n*.
isoantibody/*n*: Isoantikörper *m*, Alloantikörper *m*.
isoantigen/*n*: Isoantigen *n*, Alloantigen *n*.
isocarboxazid/*n*: Isocarboxazid *n*.
isocitric acid: Isozitronensäure *f*.
isoconazole/*n*: Isoconazol *n*.
isocoria/*n*: Isokorie *f*.
isocortex/*n*: Isocortex *m*, Neokortex *m*.
isoetarine/*n*: Isoetarin *n*.
isoflurane/*n*: Isofluran *n*.
isogeneic/*adj*: isogen, syngen.
isolated explosive disorder: isolierte explosive Störung *f*.
isolateral/*adj*: isolateral, ipsilateral.
isolation/*n*: Isolation *f*, Isolierung *f*.
isolation unit: Isolierstation *f*.
isolysergic acid: Isolysergsäure *f*.
isomer/*n*: Isomer *n*.
isometric/*adj*: isometrisch.
isomorphic/*adj*: isomorph.
isomorphous provocative reaction: isomorpher Reizeffekt *m*, Köbner-Phänomen *n*.
isoniazid/*n*: Isoniazid *n*, Isonikotinsäurehydrazid *n*.
isonicotinic acid: Isonikotinsäure *f*.
isonicotinoylhydrazine/*n*: Isonikotinsäurehydrazid *n*, Isoniazid *n*.
isoperistaltic anastomosis: isoperistaltische Anastomose *f*.
isophane insulin: Isophaninsulin *n*.
isoprenaline/*n*: Isoprenalin *n*, Isoproterenol *n*.
isopropamide iodide: Isopropamidiodid *n*.
isopropanol/*n*: Isopropanol *n*.
isopyknic/*adj*: isopyknisch.
isoriboflavin/*n*: Isoriboflavin *n*.
isosorbide/*n*: Isosorbid *n*.
isotonic saline solution: isotone Kochsalzlösung *f*.
isotope/*n*: Isotop *n*.
isotretinoin/*n*: Isotretinoin *n*.
isovaleric acid: Isovaleriansäure *f*.
isradipine/*n*: Isradipin *n*.
isthmus/*n*: Isthmus *m*, Enge *f*.
Italian flap: italienischer Lappen *m*.
Italian rhinoplasty: italienische Rhinoplastik *f*.
itch/*n, vb*: 1. Jucken *n*, Flechte *f*, Kratzen *n*; 2. jucken, kratzen.
itching/*n, adj*: 1. pruritus, caused by chemical or mechanical skin irritation, or due to emotional causes. General or circumscribed itching can occur as a sign of other diseases, infections, metabolic disorders, allergic reactions, or intoxications. Juckreiz *m*, Pruritus *m*; 2. juckend.
itch mite: Krätzmilbe *f*, Sarcoptes scabiei *f*.
itchy swelling: Quaddel *f*.
iteration/*n*: Iteration *f*.
itraconazole/*n*: Itraconazol *n*.
IUD <*abbr*> **intrauterine device**: Intrauterinpessar *n*.
IV <*abbr*> **intravenous**: intravenös, i.v.
ivermectin/*n*: Ivermectin *n*.
IVF <*abbr*> **in vitro fertilization**: In-vitro-Fertilisation *f*, IVF.
ivory osteoma: Elfenbeintumor *m*.
ixodiasis/*n*: Ixodiasis *f*, Zeckenlähmung *f*.
ixone/*n*: Ixon *n*.

J

J <*abbr*> **joule**: Joule *n*.
jab/*n, vb*: 1. Einspritzung *f*, Spritze *f*; 2. stechen.
jacket/*n, vb*: 1. Umhüllung *f*, Ummantelung *f*; 2. ummanteln, umhüllen.
jacket cancer: Cancer en cuirasse *m*, Panzerkrebs *m*.
jackknife seizures: Nickkrampf *m*, Blitz-Nick-Salaam-Krämpfe.
jacksonian epilepsy: a form of epilepsy which is characterized by focal seizure. The seizure usually begins in the fingers or toes of one hand or foot, and as more nerve cells become affected, the trembling spreads. Jackson-Epilepsie *f*.
jalap/*n*: Jalapenwurzel *f*, Purgierwinde *f*.
Japanese B encephalitis: japanische B-Enzephalitis *f*.
Japanese dysentery: Dysenterie *f*, Bakterienruhr *f*, Shigellose *f*.
jargon aphasia: Jargon Aphasie *f*.
jasmine root: Jasminwurzel *f*.
jaundice/*n*: increase of bile pigment in the blood causing yellow tinge to conjunctiva, skin, and membranes. Causes include diseases of the liver, gallbladder, bile system or blood, for example hemolysis. Gelbsucht *f*, Ikterus *m*.
jaundice of the newborn: jaundice of the neonate due to a transitory inability to excrete bilirubin. In particular, premature infants are affected. In severe cases, nuclear jaundice or kernicterus may occur. Neugeborenenikterus *m*, Icterus neonatorum *m*.
jaw/*n*: Kiefer *m*.
jaw angle: Kieferwinkel *m*.
jawbone: Kieferknochen *m*.
jaw reflex: Unterkieferreflex *m*, Masseterreflex *m*.
jealous delusion: Eifersuchtswahn *m*.
jejunal/*adj*: jejunal.
jejunectomy/*n*: Jejunumresektion *n*.
jejunocolic fistula: jejunokolische Fistel *f*.
jejunoileal fistula: abnormal passage between the jejunum and the ileum, occurring for example as a consequence of chronic inflammation like in regional enteritis. jejunoileale Fistel *f*.
jejunostomy/*n*: Jejunostomie *f*.
jejunum/*n*: Jejunum *n*, Leerdarm *m*.
jellyfish poison: Quallengift *n*.
jellylike/*adj*: gallertartig, gelartig.
jennerian vaccination: Jenner-Pockenimpfung *f*.
jerk/*n, vb*: 1. Muskelzuckung *f*, Krampf *m*; 2. zucken.
jerk thumb: Schnappdaumen *m*.
jerky nystagmus: Rucknystagmus *m*.
jerky pulse: hüpfender Puls *m*.
jet injector: Jetinjektor *m*, Impfpistole *f*.
jet lag: Jetlag *m*, zirkadiane Dysrhythmie *f*.
Job syndrome: an autosomal dominant condition which is characterized by increased concentrations of IgE and eosinophilia. Symptoms include dermatitis, recurrent staphylococcal infections of the skin and the respiratory tract, and mucocutaneous candidiasis. Hiob-Syndrom *n*, Hyper-IgE-Syndrom *n*.
jogging/*n*: Jogging *n*, Dauerlauf *m*.
join/*vb*: vereinigen, verbinden.
joint/*n, adj, vb*: 1. Verbindung *f*, Gelenk *n*; 2. gemeinschaftlich; 3. verbinden.

joint capsule: Gelenkkapsel *f*.
joint mouse: Gelenkmaus *f*, Enarthron *n*.
joint pain: Gelenkschmerz *m*.
joint space: Gelenkraum *m*.
josamycin/*n*: Josamycin *n*.
jugular/*adj*: jugular.
jugular compression: Jugularisdruckversuch *m*.
jugular pulse: Jugularispuls *m*.
jugular venous pressure: Jugularisdruck *m*.
juice/*n*: Flüssigkeit *f*, Saft *m*.
jujube/*n*: Brustbeere *f*.
jumbled speech: Jargonaphasie *f*.
jumping chorea: a condition which is characterized by extreme excitement and rapid, jerky, dyskinetic movements like in dancing, due to rheumatic fever. Choreomanie *f*, Chorea major *f*.
jumping gene: springendes Gen *n*.
jumping sickness: Choreomanie *f*, Chorea major *f*.
jumping thrombosis: Thrombosis migrans *f*.
jumps/*n*: choreatiforme Bewegungen.
junction/*n*: Verbindung *f*, Knotenpunkt *m*.
junctional tachycardia: abnormal heart rate with rapid beating of the heart and more than 75 beats per minute which originates in the atrioventricular node and/or the bundle of His. AV-Knotentachykardie *f*.
juniper oil: Wacholderöl *n*.
just noticeable: eben merklich.
juvenile/*n, adj*: 1. Jugendlicher *m*; 2. juvenil, jugendlich.
juvenile amaurotic idiocy: juvenile amaurotische Idiotie *f*, Stock-Spielmeyer-Vogt-Krankheit *f*.
juvenile chorea: Sydenham-Chorea *f*, Chorea minor *f*.
juvenile diabetes: diabetes mellitus type I with a sudden onset in youth around the age of twelve and in which basal insulin secretion is suddenly reduced or ceasing, possibly due to an autoimmune reaction. juveniler Diabetes *m*.
juvenile distal atrophic paralysis: Charcot-Marie-Tooth-Krankheit *f*.
juvenile gangliosidosis: a condition which is characterized by an abnormal accumulation of gangliosides, due to an autosomal recessive defect in the enzyme hexosaminidase. Symptoms include an early onset in the first year of life with psychomotor retardation, paralysis, seizures, and progressive vision loss. juvenile Gangliosidose *f*, Tay-Sachs-Syndrom *n*.
juvenile histiocytoma: juveniles Xanthogranulom *n*.
juvenile kyphosis: kyphosis of the spine resulting from an ossification disorder and osteochondrosis of unknown origin. Most frequently, the thoracic part of the spine is affected. juvenile Kyphose *f*, Adoleszentenkyphose *f*, Scheuermann-Krankheit *f*.
juvenile macular degeneration: juvenile Makuladegeneration *f*, Stargardt-Syndrom *n*.
juvenile parkinsonism: juvenile Paralysis agitans *f*.
juvenile plane wart: Verruca plana juvenilis *f*.
juvenile psychosis: juvenile Psychose *f*.
juvenile rheumatoid arthritis: rheumatoid arthritis in children and young adolescents. Symptoms include swelling, pain, impaired function, followed by destructions of chondral and osseous substance with impaired growth and development. It is frequently associated with systemic features like rash, anemia, or generalized lymphadenopathy. juvenile rheumatoide Arthritis *f*.
juxta-articular/*adj*: juxtaartikulär.
juxtacortical/*adj*: juxtakortikal.
juxtaglomerular/*adj*: juxtaglomerulär.
juxtaglomerular apparatus: juxtaglomerulärer Apparat *m*.
juxtamedullary/*adj*: juxtamedullär.
juxtaposition/*n*: Juxtaposition *f*, Apposition *f*.
juxtapyloric/*adj*: juxtapylorisch.

K

K <*abbr*> **Kelvin**: Kelvin *n*.

k <*abbr*> **kilo-**: Kilo-.

kala-azar/*n*: an infectious disease caused by the protozoon Leishmania donovani which occurs in tropical regions. Symptoms include fever, chills, anemia, dropsy, and enlargement of liver and spleen. Kala-Azar *f*, viszerale Leishmaniase *f*.

kalium/*n*: Kalium *n*, K.

kallidin/*n*: Kallidin *n*.

kanamycin/*n*: Kanamycin *n*.

Kaposi sarcoma: a neoplasm characterized by vascular proliferation and the development of bluish-red nodules, usually on the skin of the lower extremities, but also on the mucous membranes for example in the mouth or in the lung. Kaposi sarcoma or multiple idiopathic hemorrhagic sarcoma occurs predominantly in elder men, it is endemically in parts of Central Africa. Disseminated forms occur in immunocompromised persons, for example persons with AIDS, and are associated with infection by human herpesvirus 8. Kaposi-Sarkom *n*, Sarcoma idiopathicum multiplex haemorrhagicum *n*.

Karnofsky activity index: Karnofsky-Aktivitätsindex *m*.

karyoblast/*n*: Karyoblast *m*.

karyocyte/*n*: Karyozyt *m*.

karyokinesis/*n*: Karyokinese *f*.

karyon/*n*: Karyon *n*, Zellkern *m*, Nukleus *m*.

karyotype/*n, vb*: 1. Karyotyp *m*; 2. karyotypisieren.

kation/*n*: Kation *n*.

kava/*n*: Kawa *f*.

kawain/*n*: Kavain *n*.

kebuzone/*n*: Kebuzon *n*.

keeled breast: Kielbrust *f*, Pectus carinatum *n*.

keeled chest: Kielbrust *f*, Pectus carinatum *n*.

keel-shaped/*adj*: kielförmig.

keloid/*n*: hardening of a skin area with hypertrophy of connective tissue and collagen, usually resulting from scar formation, burns, or other injury. Keloid *n*.

keloidal/*adj*: keloidal, keloidartig.

kerasin thesaurismosis: Kerasinspeicherkrankheit *f*, Gaucher-Krankheit *f*.

keratectasia/*n*: Keratektasie *f*.

keratectomy/*n*: Keratektomie *f*.

keratic/*adj*: keratisch.

keratin/*n*: Keratin *n*.

keratinization/*n*: Keratinisation *f*, Verhornung *f*.

keratitis/*n*: inflammation of the cornea resulting for example from infection, exposure to physical factors, or generalized diseases. Symptoms include drying changes, minimal superficial punctate lesions, and epithelial opacities, sometimes associated with corneal ulcer and formation of new blood vessels. Keratitis *f*, Hornhautentzündung *f*.

keratohyaline granule: keratohyalines Granulum *n*.

keratolytic/*n, adj*: 1. Keratolytikum *n*; 2. keratolytisch.

keratoma/*n*: Keratom *n*.

keratomalacia/*n*: Keratomalazie *f*.

keratome/*n*: Keratom *n*.

keratometer/*n*: Keratometer *n*, Astigmometer *n*.

keratopathy/*n*: Keratopathie *f*, Hornhauterkrankung *f*.

keratoplasty/*n*: Keratoplastik *f*.
keratoscopy/*n*: Keratoskopie *f*.
keratosis/*n*: Keratose *f*.
kernicterus/*n*: an icterus of the cerebral, cerebellar, and bulbar nuclei, characterized by severe neurologic symptoms. Nuclear jaundice or kernicterus is caused by high levels of bilirubin in the blood of neonates, for example in hemolytic disease of newborn. Kernikterus *m*.
ketamine/*n*: Ketamin *n*.
ketoacid/*n*: Ketonsäure *f*.
ketoconazole/*n*: Ketoconazol *n*.
ketogenic/*adj*: ketogen, ketoplastisch.
ketogenic amino acid: ketoplastische Aminosäure *f*.
ketogenic substance: Ketonkörperlieferant *m*.
ketoglutaric acid: Ketoglutarsäure *f*.
ketone body: Ketonkörper *m*.
ketonemia/*n*: Ketonämie *f*.
ketonuria/*n*: Ketonurie *f*.
ketoprofen/*n*: Ketoprofen *n*.
ketorolac/*n*: Ketorolac *n*.
ketosis/*n*: Ketose *f*.
ketosteroid/*n*: Ketosteroid *n*.
ketotifen/*n*: Ketotifen *n*.
key enzyme: Schlüsselenzym *n*.
key stimulus: Schlüsselreiz *m*.
kidney/*n*: Niere *f*.
kidney abscess: abscess of the renal cortex, usually resulting from pyelonephritis, glomerulitis, or kidney infarction. Symptoms include malaise, fever, chills, and costovertebral angle tenderness. Nierenrindenabszess *m*.
kidney disease: Nierenerkrankung *f*.
kidney failure: Nierenversagen *n*, Niereninsuffizienz *f*.
kidney injury: Nierenverletzung *f*.
kidney stone: hard concretions which can be found in the renal pelvis, and which are typically formed by substances which are excreted by the kidneys, for example calcium, oxalate, urate, uric acid, or phosphates. Symptoms depend on the size of the calculus and may include acute pain, renal colic, dysuria, and eventually hematuria or ureteral obstruction. Nierenstein *m*.
kill/*vb*: töten.
killer cell: Killerzelle *f*.
kinase/*n*: Kinase *f*.
kineplasty/*n*: Kineplastik *f*.
kinesis/*n*: Kinese *f*, Kinetose *f*.
kinesitherapy/*n*: Kinesiotherapie *f*.
kinesthesia/*n*: Kinästhesie *f*.
kinesthetic hallucination: Bewegungshalluzination *f*.
kinesthetic sensibility: Kinästhesie *f*.
kinetic apraxia: kinetische Apraxie *f*.
kinetics/*n*: Kinetik *f*.
kinking/*n*: Kinking *n*, Knickung *f*.
kinky-hair syndrome: an X-linked, recessive condition with a disorder of copper metabolism which is characterized by severe growth retardation, white and kinky hair, cerebral seizures, and degenerative alterations of the central nervous system. Kinky-Hair-Syndrom *n*, Menkes-Syndrom *n*.
kissing bug: Raubwanze *f*, Reduviida *f*.
kissing disease: an infectious disease caused by Epstein-Barr virus. Mononucleosis or glandular fever is characterized by an increase in number of monocytes, enlargement of lymph nodes, mild elevation of body temperature, enlargement of the spleen, sore throat, and sometimes skin eruption. infektiöse Mononukleose *f*, Pfeiffer-Drüsenfieber *n*.
kissing spine: kissing spine, Baastrup-Phänomen *n*.
kissing ulcer: kissing ulcer, Abklatschgeschwür *n*.
kiss of life: Mund-zu-Mund-Beatmung *f*.
kitasamycin/*n*: Kitasamycin *n*.
Klebsiella pneumonia: Klebsiellenpneumonie *f*.
knapsack paralysis: Rucksacklähmung *f*, Tornisterlähmung *f*.
knee/*n*: Knie *n*.
kneecap/*n*: Kniescheibe *f*, Patella *f*.
knee-elbow position: Knie-Ellbogen-Lage *f*.
knee jerk: Patellarsehnenreflex *m*, Quadrizepssehnenreflex *m*, QSR.

knee joint: Kniegelenk *n*.

knee presentation: in obstetrics, the position of the fetus in which the knee is presented and appears first in the uterine cervix. Knielage *f*.

Kneipp cure: Kneipp-Kur *f*.

knife/*n*: Messer *n*.

knob/*n*: Buckel *m*, Auswuchs *m*.

knot/*n, vb*: 1. Knoten *m*; 2. knoten.

knuckle/*n*: Knöchel *m*, Fingerknöchel *m*, Fingergelenk *n*.

koilonychia/*n*: Koilonychie *f*, Hohlnägel.

konimetry/*n*: Koniometrie *f*.

Koplik spots: Koplik-Flecken.

Korotkoff sounds: Korotkow-Geräusche.

kraurosis/*n*: Kraurosis *f*.

Krebs cycle: Krebs-Zyklus *m*, Zitratzyklus *m*.

kreosot/*n*: Kreosot *n*.

Kufs' disease: Kufs-Hallervorden-Krankheit *f*, adulte Zeroidlipofuszinose *f*.

kuru/*n*: Kuru *n*.

kwashiorkor/*n*: a syndrome in children and young adolescents which is characterized by malnutrition, specifically a lack of proteins and amino acids, and may result in growth retardation, dyschromia of the skin, edema, and mental apathy. Kwashiorkor *m*.

kyasanur forest disease: Kyasanur-Wald-Krankheit *f*.

kyphoscoliosis/*n*: Kyphoskoliose *f*.

kyphosis/*n*: a condition in which the vertebral column is abnormally curved in the thoracic area. Forms include congenital malformations of vertebra, generalized bone diseases, acquired forms following rickets, ankylosing spondylitis, or tuberculosis. Kyphose *f*.

kyphotic/*adj*: kyphotisch.

kyphotic pelvis: kyphotisches Becken *n*.

L

L <*abbr*> **1. left; 2. levorotatory; 3. liter**: 1. links; 2. linksdrehend; 3. Liter *m*.
label/*n, vb*: 1. Etikett *n*, Markierung *f*; 2. kennzeichnen.
labetalol/*n*: Labetalol *n*.
labial/*adj*: labial.
labial bar: Labialbügel *m*.
labial reflex: Nasolabialreflex *m*.
labial ulcer: Lippengeschwür *n*.
labile/*adj*: labil.
labile hypertension: labiler Hochdruck *m*.
lability of mood: Stimmungslabilität *f*.
labiomental/*adj*: mentolabial.
labioplasty/*n*: Lippenplastik *f*, Cheiloplastik *f*.
labor/*n*: Arbeit *f*, Wehen.
laboratory/*n*: Labor *n*.
laboratory findings: Laborbefunde.
laboratory medicine: Labormedizin *f*.
laboratory test: Laboruntersuchung *f*.
labor onset: Wehenbeginn *m*.
labyrinth/*n*: Labyrinth *n*.
labyrinthine ataxia: vestibuläre Ataxie *f*.
labyrinthine fluid: Perilymphe *f*.
labyrinthine hearing loss: Innenohrschwerhörigkeit *f*.
labyrinthine nystagmus: Labyrinthnystagmus *m*.
labyrinthine righting reflex: Labyrinthstellreflex *m*.
labyrinthine test: Labyrinthfunktionsprüfung *f*.
labyrinthine vertigo: Labyrinthschwindel *m*.
labyrinthitis/*n*: inflammation of the inner ear, usually resulting from otitis media, meningitis, or other infections of the ear. Symptoms include vertigo, nausea, hearing loss, and nystagmus. Labyrinthitis *f*.
lacerate/*vb*: einreißen.
lacerated wound: Risswunde *f*.
laceration/*n*: a wound that is torn, rather than cut, and is characterized by ragged, irregular edges, and mashed tissue underneath. Lazeration *f*, Einriss *m*.
lacidipine/*n*: Lacidipin *n*.
lack/*n, vb*: 1. Fehlen *n*, Mangel *m*; 2. fehlen.
lack of criminal responsibility: Unzurechnungsfähigkeit *f*.
lacrimal/*adj*: Tränen-.
lacrimal bone: Tränenbein *n*, Os lacrimale *n*.
lacrimal calculus: Dakryolith *m*.
lacrimal canal: Tränengang *m*.
lacrimal fistula: Tränengangsfistel *f*.
lacrimal gland: Tränendrüse *f*.
lacrimal probe: Tränengangsonde *f*.
lacrimal sac: Tränensack *m*.
lacrimation/*n*: Tränenbildung *f*.
lactalbumin/*n*: Laktalbumin *n*.
lactamase/*n*: Laktamase *f*.
lactase/*n*: Laktase *f*.
lactase deficiency: Laktasemangel *m*.
lactate dehydrogenase: Laktatdehydrogenase *f*, LDH.
lactation/*n*: Laktation *f*, Milchsekretion *f*.
lactation amenorrhea: Laktationsamenorrhö *f*.
lactation hormone: Prolaktin *n*.
lactation period: Stillperiode *f*.
lacteal/*adj*: milchig, chylös.
lacteal cyst: Milchzyste *f*.
lacteal fistula: Milchgangsfistel *f*.
lactic acid: Milchsäure *f*.
lactic acidosis: Laktatazidose *f*.

lactiferous/*adj*: laktifer, milchführend.
lactifuge/*n*: Laktifugum *n*.
lactogenic/*adj*: laktogen.
lactose/*n*: Laktose *f*.
lactose intolerance: Laktoseintoleranz *f*.
lacunar/*adj*: lakunär.
lacunar amnesia: lakunäre Amnesie *f*, partielle Amnesie *f*.
lacunar infarction: infarction of the brain which is characterized by multiple small lesions or gaps. Causes include arteriosclerotic changes of blood vessels, resulting in degeneration of brain tissue and encephalomalacia. lakunärer Infarkt *m*.
lacunar state: Status lacunaris *m*.
ladder splint: Drahtleiterschiene *f*, Cramer-Schiene *f*.
lag/*n*: Verzögerung *f*, Latenz w.
laky blood: hämolytisches Blut *n*.
lambdoid/*adj*: lambdaförmig.
lamella/*n*: Lamelle *f*.
lamellar bone: Lamellenknochen *m*.
lamellar cataract: Schichtstar *m*.
lamellar ichthyosis: ichthyosiforme Erythrodermie *f*, Sjögren-Larsson-Syndrom *n*.
lameness/*n*: Lahmheit *f*.
lamina/*n*: Lamina *f*.
laminary/*adj*: laminär
laminated clot: Schichtthrombus *m*.
laminectomy/*n*: Laminektomie *f*.
lamivudine/*n*: Lamivudin *n*.
lamotrigine/*n*: Lamotrigin *n*.
lancet/*n*. Lanzette *f*.
lancinating/*adj*: lanzinierend.
lancinating pain: tearing or sharply cutting pain, occurring for example in tabes dorsalis. lanzinierender Schmerz *m*.
landmark/*n*: Orientierungspunkt *m*.
language/*n*: Sprache *f*.
language development disorder: Sprachentwicklungsstörung *f*.
lanolin/*n*: Lanolin *n*.
lanreotide/*n*: Lanreotid *n*.
lansoprazole/*n*: Lansoprazol *n*.
laparogastrotomy/*n*: Laparogastrotomie *f*.
laparoscopy/*n*: Laparoskopie *f*.
laparotomy/*n*: Laparotomie *f*.
lapse/*n*: Lapsus *m*.
lardaceous liver: Speckleber *f*, Amyloidleber *f*.
lardaceous spleen: Speckmilz *f*, Schinkenmilz *f*.
large/*adj*: groß, weit.
large-bore/*adj*: weitlumig.
large-for-date baby: Riesenkind *n*.
large pelvis: großes Becken *n*.
laronidase/*n*: Laronidase *f*.
larval conjunctivitis: Larvenkonjunktivitis *f*, Myiasis *f*.
larval cyst: Larvenzyste *f*.
larvate depression: larvierte Depression *f*.
laryngeal/*adj*: laryngeal.
laryngeal cancer: malignant neoplasm of the larynx, usually a squamous cell carcinoma localized for example in the vocal cords, between vocal and vestibular folds, or in the hypopharynx. Larynxkarzinom *n*.
laryngeal crisis: Laryngospasmus *m*, Stimmritzenkrampf *m*.
laryngeal cyst: Larynxzyste *f*.
laryngeal diphtheria: Kehlkopfdiphtherie *f*.
laryngeal diverticulum: Kehlkopfdivertikel *n*.
laryngeal granuloma: small fibroma or retention cysts occurring on the vocal cord, resulting from excessive vocal strain. Sängerknötchen *n*.
laryngeal mirror: Kehlkopfspiegel *m*.
laryngeal obstruction: Larynxstenose *f*.
laryngeal paralysis: Kehlkopflähmung *f*.
laryngeal reflex: Kehlkopfreflex *m*, Hustenreflex *m*.
laryngeal stridor: Stridor laryngealis *m*.
laryngeal tuberculosis: Kehlkopftuberkulose *f*.
laryngeal vertigo: Kehlkopfschwindel *m*.
laryngectomy/*n*: Laryngektomie *f*.
laryngismus/*n*: Laryngismus *m*.
laryngitis/*n*: inflammation of the larynx, usually due to infections of the upper respiratory tract. Symp-

toms include dryness and soreness of the throat, hoarseness, cough, dysphagia, and eventually fever. Laryngitis *f*.

laryngology/*n*: Laryngologie *f*.

laryngoscopy/*n*: Laryngoskopie *f*, Kehlkopfspiegelung *f*.

laryngospasm/*n*: Laryngospasmus *m*, Stimmritzenkrampf *m*.

laryngostenosis/*n*: Larynxstenose *f*, Kehlkopfstenose *f*.

laryngotomy/*n*: Laryngotomie *f*.

laryngotracheobronchitis/*n*: Laryngotracheobronchitis *f*.

larynx/*n*: Larynx *m*, Kehlkopf *m*.

laser <*abbr*> **light amplification by stimulated emission of radiation**: Laser *m*.

laser coagulation/*n*: Laserkoagulation *f*.

laser therapy/*n*: Laserbehandlung *f*.

lasting effect: anhaltende Wirkung *f*.

latamoxef/*n*: Latamoxef *n*.

latanoprost/*n*: Latanoprost *n*.

late/*adj*: spät.

late abortion: Spätabort *m*.

late distal hereditary myopathy: Myopathia distalis hereditaria *f*, Welander-Myopathie *f*.

late epilepsy: Spätepilepsie *f*.

late juvenile cerebromacular degeneration: adulte Zeroidlipofuszinose *f*, Kufs-Krankheit *f*.

latency period/*n*: Latenzperiode *f*.

latent cancer: latentes Karzinom *n*.

latent diabetes: impaired glucose tolerance with blood glucose values of an oral glucose tolerance test that are elevated but not high enough to be diagnostic of diabetes mellitus. Latent autoimmune diabetes in adults is a diabetes mellitus type I which is characterized by a late onset of clinical signs of insulin deficiency and mimicks type II diabetes. latenter Diabetes *m*.

latent epilepsy: Epilepsia nonconvulsiva *f*.

latent jaundice: Subikterus *m*.

latent period: Latenzphase *f*.

latent stimulus: unterschwelliger Reiz *m*.

late-onset cerebral sphingolipidosis: adulte Zeroidlipofuszinose *f*, Kufs-Krankheit *f*.

late-onset depression: senile Depression *f*.

late-onset diabetes: Erwachsenendiabetes *m*, Altersdiabetes *m*.

lateral/*adj*: lateral.

lateral column: Seitenstrang *m*.

lateral curvature: Skoliose *f*.

laterality/*n*: Lateralität *f*, Seitenbetonung *f*.

lateral incision: seitliche Inzision *f*.

lateral medullary syndrome: a neurologic condition due to lesions in the lateral medulla oblongata, usually resulting from occlusion of a vertebral artery. Symptoms include ipsilateral loss of temperature and pain sensations of the face and contralateral loss of temperature and pain sensations of the extremities and trunk, ipsilateral ataxia, and Horner's syndrome. laterales Medulla-oblongata-Syndrom *n*, Wallenberg-Syndrom *n*.

lateral position: Seitenlage *f*.

lateral thrombus: wandständiger Thrombus *m*.

lateral tract: Seitenstrang *m*.

lateral ventricle: Seitenventrikel *m*.

late reaction: Reaktion vom verzögerten Typ *f*.

late schizophrenia: Spätschizophrenie *f*.

late syphilis: Spätsyphilis *f*.

late systolic murmur: spätsystolisches Geräusch *n*.

latex agglutination test: Latexagglutinationstest *m*.

lattice/*n*: Gefüge *n*, Gitter *n*.

laughing gas: Lachgas *n*.

lauric acid: Laurinsäure *f*.

lavage/*n, vb*: 1. Spülung *f*, Lavage *f*; 2. spülen.

law/*n*: Gesetz *n*, Prinzip *n*.

laws of refraction: Brechungsgesetze.

laxative/*n, adj*: 1. Laxans *n*, Abführmittel *n*; 2. laxierend.

laxity/*n*: Laxheit *f*.

layer/*n*: Schicht *f*, Lage *f*.

layered/*adj*: geschichtet.
layered suture: Etagennaht *f*.
L-carnitine/*n*: L-Carnitin *n*.
LDL <*abbr*> **low-density lipoprotein**: Low-Density-Lipoprotein *n*, Lipoprotein niedriger Dichte *n*, LDL.
lead/*n, vb*: 1. Blei *n*, Pb, Ableitung *f*; 2. führen, leiten.
lead acetate: Bleiacetat *n*.
lead anemia: Bleianämie *f*.
lead iodide: Bleijodid *n*.
lead-pipe colon: starres Kolon *n*.
lead poisoning: plumbism resulting from absorption or ingestion of lead or lead salt. Symptoms include normochromic anemia, central nervous symptoms like encephalopathy, joint pain, gastrointestinal symptoms and atrophy of the kidneys. Bleivergiftung *f*.
leads: Ableitungen *f*.
leaflet/*n*: Klappensegel *n*, Broschüre *f*.
leak/*n, vb*: 1. Leck *n*; 2. lecken.
leakage/*n*: Leckage *f*.
lean/*adj*: mager.
learning difficulty: Lernschwierigkeit *f*.
lecithin/*n*: Lezithin *n*.
leech/*n, vb*: 1. Blutegel *m*; 2. behandeln, schröpfen.
leflunomid/*n*: Leflunomid *n*.
left atrioventricular valve: Mitralklappe *f*.
left bundle branch block: Linksschenkelblock *m*.
left-handed/*adj*: linkshändig.
left heart: linkes Herz *n*.
left heart bypass: Linksbypass *m*.
left heart failure: Linksherzversagen *n*.
left-to-right shunt: Links-Rechts-Shunt *m*.
left ventricular: linksventrikulär.
left ventricular hypertrophy: Linksherzhypertrophie *f*.
leg/*n*: Bein *n*.
legal abortion: legale Abtreibung *f*.
legal age: Volljährigkeit *f*.
legal medicine: Gerichtsmedizin *f*.
legionnaires' disease: Legionärskrankheit *f*, Legionellose *f*.
leg plaster: Beingips *m*.
leg splint: Beinschiene *f*.
leishmaniasis/*n*: infection with the flagellate protozoa Leishmania. Forms include cutaneous, mucocutaneous, and visceral types, for example kala-azar. Leishmaniase *f*.
length/*n*: Länge *f*.
length-breadth index: Längen-Breiten-Index *m*.
lengthening/*n*: Verlängerung *f*.
length-height index: Längen-Höhen-Index *m*.
length of stay: Krankenhausaufenthaltsdauer *f*.
lenograstim/*n*: Lenograstim *n*.
lens/*n*: Linse *f*.
lens star: Linsenstar *m*.
lenticular/*adj*: linsenförmig, lentikulär.
lenticular astigmatism: Linsenastigmatismus *m*.
lenticular degeneration: Linsendegeneration *f*, Wilson-Krankheit *f*, hepatolentikuläre Degeneration *f*.
lenticular loop: Linsenkernschlinge *f*.
lentiform nucleus: Linsenkern *m*.
lentigo/*n*: Lentigo *f*.
leonine face: Löwengesicht *n*.
leontiasis/*n*: Leontiasis *f*.
lepirudin/*n*: Lepirudin *n*.
leproma/*n*: Leprom *n*.
leprostatic/*n, adj*: 1. Leprostatikum *n*; 2. leprostatisch.
leprosy/*n*: a chronic infectious disease caused by the microorganism Mycobacterium leprae. Forms include nodular leprosy with masses of nodules that cause distortions in other tissues, and neural leprosy in which nerves are affected, resulting in numbness and loss of sensitivity in these areas. Lepra *f*.
leprotic fever: Leprafieber *n*.
leprous nodule: Lepraknoten *m*.
leptomeningitis/*n*: Leptomeningitis *f*.
leptospirosis/*n*: Leptospirose *f*.
lercanidipine/*n*: Lercanidipin *n*.
lesbian/*n, adj*: 1. Lesbe *f*; 2. lesbisch.
lesion/*n*: Läsion *f*, Schädigung *f*.
lesser/*adj*: kleiner, geringer.

lesser circulation: kleiner Kreislauf *m*, Lungenkreislauf *m*.
lesser pelvis: kleines Becken *n*.
lethal/*adj*: letal.
lethal dose: letale Dosis *f*, LD.
lethal factor: Letalfaktor *m*.
lethal gene: Letalgen *n*.
lethality/*n*: Letalität *f*.
lethargic/*adj*: lethargisch.
lethargic encephalitis: Encephalitis lethargica *f*.
lethargy/*n*: Lethargie *f*.
letrozole/*n*: Letrozol *n*.
leucine/*n*: Leucin *n*.
leucinosis/*n*: Leuzinose *f*, Ahornsirupkrankheit *f*.
leukemia/*n*: a malignant disease of the bone marrow, characterized by proliferation and development of leukocytes and/or their precursor cells. Forms include acute or chronic leukemia, according to the degree of cell differentiation, and myelogenous or lymphocytic leukemia according to the predominant type of cell involved. Leukämie *f*.
leukemic pericarditis: leukämische Perikarditis *f*.
leukin/*n*: Leukin *n*.
leukocyte/*n*: Leukozyt *m*.
leukocyte count: Leukozytenzählung *f*, Leukozytenzahl *f*.
leukocytopenia/*n*: Leukozytopenie *f*.
leukocytosis/*n*: Leukozytose *f*.
leukodermia/*n*: a condition which is characterized by the loss of skin pigment in certain areas of the body and consecutive formation of patches of very white skin. Leukoderm *n*.
leukodystrophy/*n*: Leukodystrophie *f*.
leukoencephalitis/*n*: Leukoenzephalitis *f*.
leukonychia/*n*: Leukonychie *f*.
leukopathy/*n*: Leukopathie *f*.
leukopenia/*n*: Leukopenie *f*.
leukoplakia/*n*: white, thickened patches which appear on the skin or mucous membranes following chronic irritation or inflammation. Leukoplakia showing verrucous lesions and associated with hyperkeratosis may be an early sign of malignant neoplasm. Leukoplakie *f*.
leukoplasia/*n*: Leukoplakie *f*.
leukopoiesis/*n*: Leukopoese *f*.
leukorrhea/*n*: Leukorrhö *f*.
leukotomy/*n*: Leukotomie *f*.
leuprorelin/*n*: Leuprorelin *n*.
levallorphan/*n*: Levallorphan *n*.
levamisole/*n*: Levamisol *n*.
levarterenol/*n*: Levarterenol *n*, Noradrenalin *n*.
levator/*n*: Levator *m*, Musculus levator *m*.
levator sign: Levatorzeichen *n*, Cestan-Zeichen *n*.
level/*n*: 1. Niveau *n*, Grad *m*, Spiegel *m*.
lever/*n*: Heber *m*, Löffel *m*.
levetiracetam/*n*: Levetiracetam *n*.
levobunolol/*n*: Levobunolol *n*.
levobupivacaine/*n*: Levobupivacain *n*.
levocetirizine/*n*: Levocetirizin *n*.
levodopa/*n*: Levodopa *n*, L-Dopa *n*.
levodropropizine/*n*: Levodropropizin *n*.
levofloxacin/*n*: Levofloxacin *n*.
levonorgestrel/*n*: Levonorgestrel *n*.
levophilia/*n*: excessive fondness or attraction to objects on the left side of the body, frequently associated with dextrophobia. Levophilie *f*.
levotartaric acid: Linksweinsäure *f*.
levulose/*n*: Lävulose *f*, Fruktose *f*.
LHRH <*abbr*> **luteinizing hormone-releasing hormone**: Luteinisierungshormon freisetzendes Hormon *n*, LHRH.
liability/*n*: Verantwortung *f*, Haftung *f*.
liberate/*vb*: freisetzen, entbinden.
libidinal fixation: libidinöse Bindung *f*.
libido/*n*: Libido *f*.
libido disorder: Libidostörung *f*.
lichen/*n*: acute or chronic skin disorders which are characterized by small, scaly nodules or papules that are usually set very close together. Most frequently occurring forms include lichen planus, lichen sclero-

sus, and lichen simplex chronicus. Lichen *m*, Flechte *f*.
lichenoid amyloidosis: Lichen amyloidosus *m*.
lichenoid dermatosis: lichenartige Dermatose *f*.
lichenoid eczema: lichenförmiges Ekzem *n*.
licorice/*n*: Lakritze *f*.
lid/*n*: Augenlid *n*.
lid drop: Ptosis *f*.
lidocaine/*n*: Lidocain *n*.
lidoflazine/*n*: Lidoflazin *n*.
lid paralysis: Lidlähmung *f*.
L-iduronic acid: L-Iduronsäure *f*.
lienal/*adj*: lienal.
life/*n*: Leben *n*.
life cycle: Lebenszyklus *m*.
life expectancy: Lebenserwartung *f*.
life insurance: Lebensversicherung *f*.
lifeless/*adj*: leblos.
life-saving/*adj*: lebensrettend.
life span/*n*: Lebensspanne *f*, Lebensdauer *f*.
lifestyle/*n*: Lebensweise *f*.
life table: Sterbetafel *f*.
life-threatening/*adj*: lebensbedrohlich.
lifetime: Lebenszeit *f*, Lebensdauer *f*.
lifting/*n*: Lifting *n*, Heben *n*.
ligament/*n*: Ligament *n*, Band *n*.
ligation/*n*: Ligation *f*.
ligature/*n, vb*: 1. Ligatur *f*, Unterbindung *f*; 2. abbinden, unterbinden.
light/*n, adj, vb*: 1. Licht *n*; 2. hell, leicht; 3. beleuchten.
light adaptation: Helladaptation *f*.
light-chain disease: Leichte-Ketten-Krankheit *f*.
light diet: leichte Kost *f*.
light exposure: Lichtexposition *f*.
light-sensitive/*adj*: lichtempfindlich.
ligneous struma: eisenharte Struma Riedel *f*.
lignoceric acid: Lignocerinsäure *f*.
likelihood/*n*: Wahrscheinlichkeit *f*.
lilliputian hallucination: Liliput-Halluzination *f*, Mikropsie *f*.
limb/*n*: Extremität *f*.
limb-girdle muscular dystrophy: Beckengürtelmuskeldystrophie *f*.
limbic/*adj*: limbisch
limbic cortex: limbischer Kortex *m*.
limbic system: limbisches System *n*.
lime/*n, vb*: 1. Kalziumoxid *n*, Limone *f*; 2. kalken.
liminal stimulus: Schwellenreiz *m*.
limit/*n, vb*: 1. Grenze *f*; 2. begrenzen, eingrenzen.
limp/*n, vb, adj*: 1. Hinken *n*; 2. hinken; 3. schlaff, weich.
lincomycin/*n*: Lincomycin *n*.
lincture/*n*: Latwerge *f*, Electuarium *n*.
lindane/*n*: Lindan *n*.
line/*n*: Linie *f*, Kurve *f*.
lineage/*n*: Abstammung *f*.
linear fracture: Längsbruch *m*.
linear osteotomy: gerade Osteotomie *f*.
linear stricture: Längsstriktur *f*.
linen/*n*: Leinen *n*.
linezolid/*n*: Linezolid *n*.
lingering illness: schleichende Krankheit *f*.
lingual goiter: Zungengrundstruma *f*.
lingual tonsil: Zungentonsille *f*.
lingular/*adj*: Zungen-.
liniment/*n*: Liniment *n*.
lining cell: Randsaumzelle *f*.
linitis plastica: Linitis plastica *f*.
link/*n, vb*: 1. Zusammenhang *m*, Verbindung *f*; 2. verbinden.
linkage/*n*: Verbindung *f*, Kopplung *f*.
linoleic acid: Linolsäure *f*.
linolenic acid: Linolensäure *f*.
linseed/*n*: Leinsamen *m*.
lint/*n*: Verbandmull *f*.
lip/*n*: Lippe *f*.
lipase/*n*: Lipase *f*.
lip cleft: congenital failure of union of mesoderm, resulting in a developmental defect and fissure of the upper lip. It can be unilateral, bilateral, or median, and may be associated with defects of the maxilla and palate. Lippenspalte *f*.
lipectomy/*n*: Fettgewebsresektion *f*.
lipemia/*n*: Lipämie *f*.
lipid-lowering/*adj*: lipidsenkend.
lipid membrane: Lipidmembran *f*.
lipid metabolism: Lipidstoffwechsel *m*, Fettstoffwechsel *m*.
lipid storage disease: Lipidspeicherkrankheit *f*.

L

lipoatrophic diabetes: lipoatrophischer Diabetes *m*.
lipoatrophy/*n*: Lipoatrophie *f*.
lipochondrodystrophy/*n*: Lipochondrodystrophie *f*, Pfaundler-Hurler-Syndrom *n*.
lipocyte/*n*: Lipozyt *m*, Fettzelle *f*.
lipodystrophy/*n*: Lipodystrophie *f*.
lipoic acid: Liponsäure *f*.
lipoid/*n, adj*: 1. Lipoid *n*; 2. fettähnlich.
lipoid histiocytoma: Fibroxanthom *n*.
lipoid nephrosis: Lipoidnephrose *f*.
lipoidosis/*n*: Lipoidose *f*.
lipolysis/*n*: Lipolyse *f*.
lipoma/*n*: neoplasm originating from fat cells or adipose tissue, usually benign, and characterized by a soft capsule. It generally occurs in the subcutaneous tissue of the trunk, nucha, or forearms. Lipom *n*.
lipomatosis/*n*: Lipomatose *f*.
lipoprotein/*n*: Lipoprotein *n*.
lipotropic/*adj*: lipotrop.
liquid/*n, adj*: 1. Flüssigkeit *f*; 2. flüssig.
liquid extract: Flüssigextrakt *m*.
liquor/*n*: Liquor *m*, Flüssigkeit *f*.
liquorrhea/*n*: Liquorrhö *f*.
lisinopril/*n*: Lisinopril *n*.
lisping/*n, adj*: 1. speech defect with incorrect pronunciation of the s sound and substitution of s sounds, for example th for s. Lispeln *n*, Sigmatismus *m*; 2. lispelnd.
listeriosis/*n*: Listeriose *f*.
listlessness/*n*: Teilnahmslosigkeit *f*.
lisuride/*n*: Lisurid *n*.
literal agraphia: vollständige Agraphie *f*.
lithagogue/*n*: Lithagogum *n*.
lithiasis/*n*: formation of stones, concretion, or calculi in the body, for example kidney stones in nephrolithiasis. Lithiasis *f*, Steinleiden *n*.
lithium/*n*: Lithium *n*, Li.
lithium salt: Lithiumsalz *n*.
lithocholic acid: Lithocholsäure *f*.
litholapaxy/*n*: Litholapaxie *f*.
litholysis/*n*: Litholyse *f*.
lithotomy/*n*: Lithotomie *f*, Steinschnitt *m*.
lithotomy position: Lithotomieposition *f*, Steinschnittlage *f*.
lithotripsy/*n*: Lithotripsie *f*.
litmus/*n*: Lackmus *m*.
litter/*n*: Krankentrage *f*, Trage *f*.
little toe: kleine Zehe *f*.
little-toe reflex: Puusepp-Reflex *m*.
live/*vb, adj*: 1. leben; 2. lebendig.
live birth: Lebendgeburt *f*.
liveborn/*adj*: lebendgeboren.
liveborn infant: Lebendgeborenes *n*.
liver/*n*: Leber *f*.
liver capsule: Leberkapsel *f*.
liver carcinoma: a malignant neoplasm of the liver, usually a hepatic cellular carcinoma developing in a cirrhotic liver. Most frequent causes of precancerous liver cirrhosis include chronic infections with hepatitis B or C virus, or toxic factors like alcohol. Leberkarzinom *n*.
liver cirrhosis/*n*: loss of normal structure of hepatic tissue with replacement of liver cells by connective tissue, resulting in reduced size of the liver. Most frequent causes of precancerous liver cirrhosis include chronic infections with hepatitis B or C virus, or toxic factors like alcohol. Leberzirrhose *f*.
liver disorder: Lebererkrankung *f*.
liver enzyme: Leberenzym *n*.
liver failure: acute or chronic insufficiency of liver functions, usually due to infections like viral hepatitis or intoxications like mushroom poisoning. Symptoms include elevated liver function tests, increase in bilirubin, blood coagulation disorders, endocrine dysfunction, and neuropsychiatric signs. Leberversagen *n*.
liver function test: Leberfunktionsprobe *f*.
liver transplantation: Lebertransplantation *f*.
live vaccine: Lebendimpfstoff *m*.
livid/*adj*: livid.
living/*adj*: lebend.
load/*n, vb*: 1. Belastung *f*, Ladung *f*; 2. belasten, laden.
lobar/*adj*: lobär.
lobar atelectasis: Lappenatelektase *f*.

lobar pneumonia: Lobärpneumonie *f*.
lobar sclerosis: Lobärsklerose *f*, Pick-Krankheit *f*.
lobe/*n*: Lappen *m*.
lobectomy/*n*: Lobektomie *f*.
lobed placenta: gelappte Plazenta *f*.
lobeline/*n*: Lobelin *n*.
Lobo's disease: Lobo-Krankheit *f*, Blastomycosis queloidana *f*.
lobotomy/*n*: Lobotomie *f*.
lobucavir/*n*: Lobucavir *n*.
lobular aplasia: Lappenaplasie *f*.
lobule/*n*: Läppchen *n*.
local/*adj*: lokal, örtlich.
local anaphylaxis: lokale anaphylaktische Reaktion *f*.
local anesthesia: Lokalanästhesie *f*.
local anesthetic: Lokalanästhetikum *n*.
local convulsion: fokaler Anfall *m*.
local effect: lokale Wirkung *f*.
local flap: Nahplastik *f*.
local immunity: Gewebsimmunität *f*.
local infection: Lokalinfektion *f*.
local irradiation: lokale Strahlentherapie *f*.
localized/*adj*: lokalisiert.
localized amnesia: umschriebene Amnesie *f*.
localized epilepsy: Jackson-Epilepsie *f*.
localized pain: umschriebener Schmerz *m*.
local reaction: Lokalreaktion *f*, Herdreaktion *f*.
local sign: Lokalzeichen *n*, lokales Symptom *n*.
location/*n*: Sitz *m*, Ort *m*.
lochia/*n*: Lochien, Wochenfluss *m*.
locked-in syndrome: a neurologic condition, usually due to a vascular lesion in the pons. Symptoms include quadriplegia and inability to speak with intact consciousness and the ability of voluntary vertical eye movements and blinking. Locked-in-Syndrom *n*.
locked occlusion: Bisssperre *f*.
locking/*n*: Verhakung *f*, Blockade *f*.
lockjaw/*n*: Kieferklemme *f*, Trismus *m*.
locomotor/*adj*: lokomotorisch.
locomotor apparatus: Bewegungsapparat *m*.
locomotor ataxia: lokomotorische Ataxie *f*.
locus/*n*: Ort *m*, Stelle *f*.
lofepramine/*n*: Lofepramin *n*.
logopedics: Logopädie *f*.
logorrhea/*n*: Logorrhö *f*.
logotherapy/*n*: Logotherapie *f*.
loin/*n*: Lende *f*.
lomefloxacin/*n*: Lomefloxacin *n*.
lomustine/*n*: Lomustin *n*.
lonazolac/*n*: Lonazolac *n*.
long-acting/*adj*: lang wirkend.
long-acting insulin: Depotinsulin *n*.
long bone: langer Knochen *m*, Röhrenknochen *m*.
longevity/*n*: Langlebigkeit *f*.
longitudinal/*adj*: länglich, longitudinal.
longitudinal crease: Longitudinalfurche *f*.
longitudinal fracture: Längsbruch *m*.
longitudinal presentation: in obstetrics, a position of the fetus which is in parallel to the long axis of the mother and in which the buttocks or feet appear first in the uterine cervix. Längslage *f*, Geradlage *f*.
long QT syndrome: any condition which is characterized by a prolongation of the Q-T interval in the electrocardiogram. Forms include acquired long QT syndrome, usually due to metabolic or cardiac disorders, due to drug or substance use, and congenital forms like Jervell and Lange-Nielsen syndrome or Romano-Ward syndrome. QT-Verlängerung *f*, familiäres QT-Syndrom *n*.
longsightedness: Weitsichtigkeit *f*, Hyperopie *f*.
long-term care: Langzeitbetreuung *f*.
long-term memory: Langzeitgedächtnis *n*.
look/*n*, *vb*: 1. Blick *m*; 2. sehen.
loop/*n*: Schlinge *f*, Schleife *f*.
loop diuretic: Schleifendiuretikum *n*.
loose/*adj*: locker, frei.
loose joint: Wackelgelenk *n*.
looseness/*n*: Schlaffheit *f*, Lockerung *f*.

loose shoulder: lose Schulter *f*.
loose skin: Cutis laxa *f*, Dermatochalasis *f*.
loperamide/*n*: Loperamid *n*.
lopinavir/*n*: Lopinavir *n*.
loracarbef/*n*: Loracarbef *n*.
lorazepam/*n*: Lorazepam *n*.
lorcainide/*n*: Lorcainid *n*.
lordosis/*n*: an abnormal curvature of the thoracic spine with the convexity toward the front; the cervical and the lumbar spine show a physiological lordosis. Lordose *f*.
lordotic pelvis: Lordosebecken *n*.
lordotic proteinuria: lordotische Proteinurie *f*.
lormetazepam/*n*: Lormetazepam *n*.
lornoxicam/*n*: Lornoxicam *n*.
losartan/*n*: Losartan *n*.
loss/*n*: Verlust *m*.
loss of appetite: Appetitverlust *m*.
loss of conciousness: Bewusstseinsverlust *m*.
loss of memory: Gedächtnisverlust *m*, Amnesie *f*.
loss of vision: Sehverlust *m*.
lot/*n*: Charge *f*.
loteprednol/*n*: Loteprednol *n*.
lotion/*n*: Lösung *f*, Lotion *f*.
loudness/*n*: Lautstärke *f*, Lautheit *f*.
louse/*n*: Laus *f*.
louse-borne relapsing fever: Läuserückfallfieber *n*.
lovastatin/*n*: Lovastatin *n*.
loviride/*n*: Lovirid *n*.
low/*adj*: niedrig.
low-back pain: Kreuzschmerz *m*.
low blood pressure: niedriger Blutdruck *m*, Hypotonus *m*.
low-caloric: kalorienarm.
low-density lipoprotein: Low-Density-Lipoprotein *n*, Lipoprotein niedriger Dichte *n*.
low-dose: niedrig dosiert.
lower abdomen: Unterbauch *m*.
lower arm: Unterarm *m*.
lower extremity: untere Extremität *f*.
lower leg: Unterschenkel *m*.
lower lip: Unterlippe *f*.
lower lobe: Unterlappen *m*.
lower respiratory tract: untere Atemwege.
lower threshold: untere Reizschwelle *f*.
low-fat/*adj*: fettarm.
low-fat milk: Magermilch *f*.
low-grade/*adj*: geringgradig.
low output: niedriges Herzauswurfvolumen *n*.
low-protein diet: eiweißarme Ernährung *f*.
low-purine diet: purinarme Kost *f*.
low-tension pulse: weicher Puls *m*, Pulsus mollis *m*.
lubricant/*n*: Lubrikans *n*, Gleitmittel *n*.
lubrication/*n*: Gleitfähigkeit *f*.
lucid/*adj*: glänzend, klar.
lückenschädel/*n*: Lückenschädel *m*.
lues/*n*: Lues *f*, Syphilis *f*.
luetic curve: Lueskurve *f*.
lukewarm/*adj*: lauwarm.
lumbago/*n*: backache in the loin region, most frequently in the lower lumbar region. Symptoms include acute pain, paresthesia, muscular tenderness, and impairment of functions and movements. Lumbago *f*, Kreuzschmerz *m*.
lumbar/*adj*: lumbal.
lumbar canal: Lumbalkanal *m*.
lumbar hernia: Lendenbruch *m*.
lumbar puncture: Lumbalpunktion *f*.
lumbar region: Lende *f*.
lumbar spine: Lendenwirbelsäule *f*.
lumbar triangle: Lendendreieck *n*.
lumbar vertebra: Lumbalwirbel *m*, LW.
lumen/*n*: Lumen *n*, Gefäßlumen *n*.
lump/*n, vb*: 1. Klumpen *m*, Schwellung *f*; 2. Klumpen bilden.
lumpy jaw: Kieferaktinomykose *f*.
lunacy/*n*: Wahnsinn *m*.
lunate/*adj*: mondförmig, lunatus.
lunate bone: Mondbein *n*, Os lunatum *n*.
lunatic/*n, adj*: 1. Wahnsinniger; 2. geisteskrank, wahnsinnig.
lung/*n*: Lunge *f*.
lung abscess: formation of isolated or multiple abscesses in the lung, usually resulting from pneumonia, aspiration of foreign bodies, thoracic injury, bronchiectasis, or lung tu-

mors. Symptoms include intermittent fever, chills, leukocytosis, painful dyspnea, and sputum stained with blood. Lungenabszess *m*.

lung biopsy: Lungenbiopsie *f*.

lung capacity: Lungenkapazität *f*.

lung disease: Lungenerkrankung *f*.

lung function test: Lungenfunktionsprobe *f*.

lung nodule: Lungenrundherd *m*.

lung sounds: Atemgeräusche.

lung transplantation: Lungentransplantation *f*.

lung volume: Lungenvolumen *n*.

lupoid hepatitis: lupoide Hepatitis *f*.

luteal cell: Lutealzelle *f*.

luteal phase: Lutealphase *f*.

luteinizing/*adj*: luteinisierend.

luteinizing hormone: luteinisierendes Hormon *n*, LH.

luteinizing hormone-releasing hormone agonist: LHRH-Agonist *m*.

luteotropic/*adj*: luteotrop.

lutropin alfa: Lutropin alfa *n*.

luxation/*n*: dislocation of the bones in a joint, usually resulting from force applied at or near the joints, from sudden muscular contractions, from twisting strains on joint ligaments, or when force is transferred to a joint. The joints most frequently dislocated are those of the shoulder, hip, finger, and jaw. Luxation *f*, Dislokation *f*.

luxuriant/*adj*: luxurierend, wuchernd.

luxury gene: Luxusgen *n*.

lymph/*n*: Lymphe *f*.

lymphadenitis/*n*: acute or chronic inflammation of a lymph node, usually due to local, regional, or generalized infection and resulting in swelling and sometimes purulent pseudotumors. Lymphadenitis *f*.

lymphadenoid goiter: Hashimoto-Thyreoiditis *f*.

lymphadenopathy/*n*: Lymphadenopathie *f*.

lymphangiectasia/*n*: Lymphangiektasie *f*.

lymphangiectomy/*n*: Lymphangiektomie *f*.

lymphangioendothelial sarcoma: Lymphangiosarkom *n*.

lymphangitis/*n*: Lymphangitis *f*.

lymphatic/*adj*: lymphatisch.

lymphatic cyst: Lymphozele *f*.

lymphatic drainage: Lymphdrainage *f*.

lymphatic dropsy: Lymphödem *n*.

lymphatic edema: Lymphödem *n*.

lymphatic fistula: Lymphfistel *f*.

lymphatic leukemia: lymphatische Leukämie *f*.

lymphatic node: Lymphknoten *m*.

lymphatic sinus: Lymphknotensinus *m*.

lymphatic system: Lymphsystem *n*.

lymphatic telangiectasia: Lymphangiektasie *f*.

lymphatic vessel: Lymphgefäß *n*.

lymphedema/*n*: Lymphödem *n*.

lymph node: Lymphknoten *m*.

lymph node enlargement: Lymphknotenvergrößerung *f*.

lymphoblast/*n*: Lymphoblast *m*.

lymphoblastic erythroderma: Séza-ry-Syndrom *n*.

lymphoblastic leukemia: Lymphoblastenleukämie *f*.

lymphoblastic lymphoma: lymphoblastisches Lymphom *n*.

lymphoblastoma/*n*: Lymphoblastom *n*.

lymphocyte/*n*: Lymphozyt *m*.

lymphocytic gastritis: lymphozytäre Gastritis *f*.

lymphocytic lymphoma: lymphozytisches Lymphom *n*.

lymphocytoma/*n*: Lymphozytom *n*.

lymphocytopenia/*n*: Lymphozytopenie *f*.

lymphoepithelial carcinoma: a malignant neoplasm of the nasopharynx or the oropharynx which is characterized by the presence of large numbers of lymphoid cells. Symptoms include rapid growth, and early metastases. Lymphoepitheliom *n*.

lymphogram/*n*: Lymphogramm *n*.

lymphogranuloma/*n*: granulomatous changes in the lymphatic tissue, especially in lymph nodes. The term is sometimes used to refer to malignant lymphogranulomatosis or Hodgkin's disease. Lymphogranulom *n*.

lymphography/*n*: Lymphographie *f*.

lymphoid/*adj*: lymphoid, lymphatisch.

lymphoid follicle: Lymphfollikel *m*.

lymphoid interstitial pneumonia: lymphoide interstitielle Pneumonie *f*, LIP.

lymphoma/*n*: any neoplasm of the lymphoid tissue or arising from the lymphoid components of the immune system. Forms include circumscribed or generalized tumors, sometimes with diffuse patterns of infiltration, and are distinguished by histological criteria. Lymphom *n*.

lymphoproliferative disease: lymphoproliferative Erkrankung *f*.

lymphosarcoma/*n*: Lymphosarkom *n*.

lypressin/*n*: Lypressin *n*, 8-Lysinvasopressin *n*.

lysergic acid: Lysergsäure *f*.

lysin/*n*: Lysin *n*, Lys.

lysine vasopressin: 8-Lysinvasopressin *n*, Lypressin *n*.

lysis/*n*: Lyse *f*, Auflösung *f*, Zerfall *m*.

lysis area: Lysehof *m*.

lysoform/*n*: Lysoform *n*.

lysogeny/*n*: Lysogenie *f*.

lysosomal/*adj*: lysosomal.

lysozyme/*n*: Lysozym *n*.

lyssa/*n*: an infectious disease caused by the neurotropic rabies virus transmitted to humans by the bite of infected animals like fox, dog. It affects the central nervous system, resulting in a furious or paralytic form, both frequently fatal. Typical symptoms include paresthesia, pain at inoculation site, agitation, delirium, convulsions, and paralysis. Lyssa *f*, Tollwut *f*.

lytic/*adj*: lytisch, lösend.

lyxosamine/*n*: Lyxosamin *n*.

M

M <*abbr*> **1. male; 2. methionine; 3. myopia**: 1. männlich; 2. Methionin *n*; 3. Myopie *f*.
macaque/*n*: Makakenaffe *m*.
maceration/*n*: Mazeration *f*.
machinelike murmur: Maschinengeräusch *n*.
macies/*n*: Gewichtsverlust *m*.
macrobiotic diet: makrobiotische Ernährung *f*.
macrobiotics/*n*: Makrobiotik *f*.
macrocephaly/*n*: Makrozephalie *f*.
macrocheilia/*n*: Makrocheilie *f*.
macrocyte/*n*: Makrozyt *m*.
macrocytic/*adj*: makrozytär.
macrocytic anemia: makrozytäre Anämie *f*.
macrocytosis/*n*: presence of macrocytes in the blood, occurring for example in macrocytic hemolytic anemia, pernicious anemia, vitamin B_{12} deficiency, or hepatic diseases. Makrozytose *f*.
macrodactyly/*n*: Makrodaktylie *f*.
macroglobulinemia/*n*: Makroglobulinämie *f*.
macroglossia/*n*: Makroglossie *f*.
macrogol/*n*: Macrogol *n*.
macrolide antibiotic: Makrolidantibiotikum *n*.
macromastia/*n*: Makromastie *f*, Brustvergrößerung *f*.
macromelia/*n*: Makromelie *f*.
macromolecule/*n*: Makromolekül *n*.
macrophage/*n*: Makrophage *m*.
macroscopic/*adj*: makroskopisch.
macroscopic anatomy: makroskopische Anatomie *f*.
macrostomia/*n*: Makrostomie *f*.
macula/*n*: Makula *f*.
macular degeneration: degenerative disease of the macula of the eye. Forms include familial juvenile macular degeneration, and several forms which occur with old age. Makuladegeneration *f*.
macular edema: Makulaödem *n*.
macular retinopathy: Makulaerkrankung *f*.
macular sparing: Makulaaussparung *f*.
macular syphilid: fleckiges Syphilid *n*.
macule/*n*: Fleck *m*.
maculopapular/*adj*: makulopapulös.
maculopapular rash: makulopapulöser Ausschlag *m*.
mad/*adj*: toll, geisteskrank.
mad cow disease: an infectious disease of cattle, caused by prions. Symptoms include encephalopathy with destruction of brain tissue. Bovine spongiform encephalopathy may be transmitted to humans by ingestion of prion-containing meat and is associated with a neurologic disease similar to Creutzfeldt-Jakob's disease. Rinderwahnsinn *m*, bovine spongiforme Enzephalopathie *f*, BSE.
madness/*n*: Geisteskrankheit *f*, Wahnsinn *m*.
mafenide/*n*: Mafenid *n*.
magnesium: Magnesium *n*, Mg.
magnet/*n*: Magnet *m*.
magnetic field: Magnetfeld *n*.
magnetism/*n*: Magnetismus *m*.
magnification/*n*: Vergrößerung *f*.
maidenhood/*n*: Jungfräulichkeit *f*.
main bronchus: Hauptbronchus *m*.
main bundle: Hauptbündel *n*.
main cell: Hauptzelle *f*.
main symptom: Hauptsymptom *n*.
maintain/*vb*: aufrechterhalten.
maintenance/*n*: Erhaltung *f*, Erhaltungstherapie *f*.

maintenance dose: Erhaltungsdosis *f*.
major/*adj*: größer, Haupt-.
major affective disorder: typische affektive Störung *f*.
major disability: Schwerbehinderung *f*.
major duodenal papilla: Papilla duodenalis major *f*, Vater-Papille *f*.
major epilepsy: Epilepsia major *f*, Grand mal *n*.
major gene: Hauptgen *n*.
major surgery: großer Eingriff *m*.
major tranquilizer: Major Tranquilizer *m*, Neuroleptikum *n*.
malabsorption syndrome: an inability to absorb and digest food or nutrients adequately, especially fat, vitamins, and carbohydrates. Causes include congenital conditions like metabolic disorders or enzyme deficiency, or alterations of the intestinal wall, for example resulting from inflammation. Malabsorptionssyndrom *n*.
malacia/*n*: Malazie *f*.
maladaptation/*n*: Maladaptation *f*.
maladjustment/*n*: schlechte Anpassung *f*, Fehlanpassung *f*.
malaise/*n*: Unpässlichkeit *f*, Unwohlsein *n*.
malalignment/*n*: Frakturfehlstellung *f*.
malar/*adj*: malar.
malaria/*n*: acute or chronic infectious disease caused by the presence of the parasitic organism Plasmodium falciparum which is transmitted by a female Anopheles mosquito in red blood cells. Symptoms characteristically occur 10 to 14 days after being bitten and include a cycle of fever and chills, headache and nausea. Different varieties of malaria have different cycles. Malaria *f*.
malaria control: Malariabekämpfung *f*.
malarial fever: Malariafieber *n*, Wechselfieber *n*.
malarial hemoglobinuria: Schwarzwasserfieber *n*.
maldigestion/*n*: Maldigestion *f*.
male/*n, adj*: 1. Mann *m*; 2. männlich.
male/female ratio: Geschlechtsverhältnis *n*.
maleic acid: Maleinsäure *f*.
male pattern alopecia: Calvities *f*, Alopezie *f*.
malformation/*n*: Malformation *f*, Fehlbildung *f*.
malformation syndrome: any condition which is characterized by congenital abnormalities, usually due to chromosomal aberrations, mutations, or exogenous or idiopathic disturbances of intrauterine development. Fehlbildungssyndrom *n*.
malformed nail: Nagelfehlbildung *f*.
malic acid: Äpfelsäure *f*.
malignancy/*n*: Malignität *f*.
malignant/*adj*: maligne.
malignant anemia: perniziöse Anämie *f*.
malignant carbuncle: Hautmilzbrand *m*.
malignant fibrous histiocytoma: malignes fibröses Histiozytom *n*, Fibrohistiozytom *n*.
malignant granuloma: malignes Mittelliniengranulom *n*.
malignant histiocytic lymphoma: malignes histiozytäres Lymphom *n*, Retikulumzellsarkom *n*.
malignant hypertension: a severe form of high blood pressure that runs a rapid course and shows continuous diastolic blood pressure above 120 mm. Hg. It causes damage to the walls of the arteries especially in the kidney, and the eye. maligner Hypertonus *m*.
malignant lentigo: Dubreuilh-Hutchinson-Krankheit *f*.
malignant melanoma: a malignant neoplasm originating from melanoblasts. Most frequently localized in the skin or the choroidea of the eye, malignant melanomas may also occur in the gastrointestinal tract, the adrenal glands, or the peritoneum. malignes Melanom *n*.
malignant peripheral glioma: Neurofibrosarkom *n*.
malignant purpura: Waterhouse-Friderichsen-Syndrom *n*.

malignant tertian malaria: Falciparum-Malaria *f*.
malignant tumor: maligner Tumor *m*, Malignom *n*.
malingerer/*n*: Simulant *m*.
malleolus/*n*: Malleolus *m*, Knöchel *m*.
mallet finger: Hammerfinger *m*.
malleus/*n*: Hammer *m*.
malnutrition/*n*: failure to meet nutritional requirements, resulting either from the consumption of an insufficient quantity of food or of one or more essential nutrients, imbalanced diet, or caused by malabsorption and/or faulty utilization of nutrients. Malnutrition *f*, Mangelernährung *f*.
malocclusion/*n*: Malokklusion *f*.
malonic acid: Malonsäure *f*.
malposition/*n*: Fehlstellung *f*.
malpresentation/*n*: an abnormal position of the fetus during labor; usually, the term is used to refer to all presentations other than vertex presentation. anomale Kindslage *f*.
malt/*n*: Malz *n*.
Malta fever: Maltafieber *n*, Brucellose *f*.
maltase/*n*: Maltase *f*.
maltose/*n*: Maltose *f*.
maltreatment/*n*: Misshandlung *f*.
malunion/*n*: a condition in which a broken bone has healed improperly and the broken edges of the bones are not evenly matched together. Frakturheilung in Fehlstellung *f*.
mamilla/*n*: Mamille *f*.
mamillary/*adj*: Mamillen-.
mamillary line: Mamillarlinie *f*.
mamma/*n*: Brust *f*, Mamma *f*.
mammaplasty/*n*: Mammaplastik *f*.
mammary/*adj*: mammär.
mammary abscess: Mammaabszess *m*.
mammary cycle: zyklusabhängige Brustveränderungen.
mammary gland: Glandula mammaria *f*, Brustdrüse *f*.
mammary hypertrophy: Mammahypertrophie *f*.
mammectomy/*n*: Mastektomie *f*.
mammography/*n*: Mammographie *f*.
man/*n*: Mann *m*, Mensch *m*.
management/*n*: Versorgung *f*, Behandlung *f*.
mandatory/*adj*: obligatorisch.
mandatory vaccination: Pflichtimpfung *f*, Impfzwang *m*.
mandelic acid: Mandelsäure *f*.
mandible/*n*: Unterkiefer *m*.
mandibular joint: Kiefergelenk *n*.
mandibular resection: Mandibularesektion *f*.
mandibulo-oculofacial syndrome: a condition which is characterized by dysplasia of the facial bones, congenital cataract, microphthalmos, short stature, dental and nasal deformities, and mental retardation. Hallermann-Streiff-Syndrom *n*.
maneuver/*n*: Handgriff *m*, Manöver *n*.
mangafodipir/*n*: Mangafodipir *n*.
manganese poisoning: Manganvergiftung *f*.
mange mite: Räudemilbe *f*, Krätzmilbe *f*.
mania/*n*: psychiatric disorder characterized by extreme excitement, overproduction of ideas or incoherence in thought, and incessant talking, accompanied by abundant movements and agitation. Manie *f*, Tobsucht *f*.
manic-depressive/*adj*: manisch-depressiv.
manic-depressive psychosis: psychiatric disorder of unknown cause which is characterized by alternating periods of mania-like excitement and depression. manisch-depressive Psychose *f*, bipolare affektive Psychose *f*.
manic psychosis: manische Psychose *f*, Manie *f*.
manifestation/*n*: Manifestation *f*, Erscheinungsform *f*.
manipulation/*n*: Manipulation *f*.
mannerism/*n*: Maniriertheit *f*.
mannitol hexanitrate: Mannitolhexanitrat *n*.
mannomustine/*n*: Mannomustin *n*.
manoeuvre/*n*: Handgriff *m*, Manöver *n*.

manometer/*n*: Manometer *n*.
mantle/*n*: Mantel *m*, Außenhülle *f*.
manual/*n, adj*: 1. Anleitung *f*; 2. manuell.
manual rotation: manuelle Rotation *f*.
manubrium/*n*: Handhabe *f*, Manubrium *n*.
manus/*n*: Hand *f*.
MAO inhibitor: MAO-Hemmer *m*, Monoaminoxidasehemmer *m*.
map/*n, vb*: 1. Karte *f*; 2. kartieren.
maple syrup urine disease: a congenital defect in the metabolism of the amino acids valine, leucine, and isoleucine. This causes a maple syrup odor of urine, seizures, mental retardation, and without dietary treatment early death. Ahornsirupkrankheit *f*.
maplike skull: Landkartenschädel *m*.
mapping/*n*: Mapping *n*, Kartierung *f*.
maprotiline/*n*: Maprotilin *n*.
marasmus/*n*: Marasmus *m*.
marble bone disease: Marmorknochenkrankheit *f*, Albers-Schönberg-Krankheit *f*.
march albuminuria: Marschalbuminurie *f*.
margin/*n*: Rand *m*, Kante *f*.
marginal atelectasis: Randatelektase *f*.
marginal blepharitis: Lidrandentzündung *f*.
marginal keratitis: Randkeratitis *f*.
marginal placenta: Placenta marginata *f*.
marginal psychosis: Randpsychose *f*.
marginal sinus: Marginalsinus *m*, Randsinus *m*.
marginal ulcer: Randulkus *n*.
marginal zone: Randzone *f*.
marijuana/*n*: Marihuana *n*, Haschisch *n*.
marital/*adj*: ehelich.
mark/*n, vb*: 1. Zeichen *n*, Stigma *n*; 2. markieren.
marked/*adj*: ausgeprägt, deutlich.
marker/*n*: Marker *m*, Markersubstanz *f*.
marker protein: Markierungsprotein *n*.
marrow/*n*: Mark *n*, Knochenmark *n*.
marsupialization/*n*: Marsupialisation *f*.
mash/*n, vb*: 1. Brei *m*, Mus *n*; 2. zerquetschen.
mashed food: Breikost *n*.
mask/*n, vb*: 1. Maske *f*; 2. maskieren.
masked fat: gebundenes Fett *n*.
masking audiogram: Lärmaudiogramm *n*.
masklike face: Maskengesicht *n*.
masochism/*n*: Masochismus *m*.
mass/*n*: Masse *f*.
massage/*n*: Massage *f*.
mass examination: Reihenuntersuchung *f*.
massive hemorrhage: Massenblutung *f*.
massive vitreous retraction: Glaskörperretraktion *f*, Stilling-Türk-Duane-Syndrom *n*.
mass psychology: Massenpsychologie *f*.
mast cell: Mastzelle *f*, Mastozyt *m*.
mastectomy/*n*: Mastektomie *f*.
mastery/*n*: Beherrschung *f*.
mastication/*n*: Mastikation *f*, Kaubewegung *f*.
masticatory force: Kaukraft *f*.
masticatory paralysis: Kaumuskellähmung *f*.
masticatory spasm: Trismus *m*.
mastitis/*n*: inflammation of the mammary glands, occurring for example as puerperal mastitis during the childbed period, usually caused by the bacterium Staphylococcus. Symptoms include severe pain, lymphangitis, lymphadenitis, and eventually formation of an abscess. Mastitis *f*.
mastocytoma/*n*: Mastozytom *n*.
mastodynia/*n*: pain or painful tension in the breast, usually occurring during the premenstrual phase, or in association with gynecomastia. Mastodynie *f*, Cooper-Syndrom *n*.
mastoidal/*adj*: warzenförmig, mastoideus.
mastoidectomy/*n*: Mastoidektomie *f*.
mastoiditis/*n*: serous or purulent inflammation of the mucous membrane of the pneumatic cells of the mas-

toid, usually resulting from an inflammation or infection of the middle ear. Symptoms include swelling, pain in the ear, retraction of the posterior wall of the auditory duct, and conduction deafness. Mastoiditis *f*.
mastoid operation: Mastoidektomie *f*.
mastopathy/*n*: any disorder of the mammary gland. The term is also used to describe dysplastic alterations of mammary gland tissue. Symptoms include multiple, palpable cysts and nodules. Mastopathie *f*.
masturbation/*n*: Masturbation *f*.
matched blood: Kreuzblut *n*.
matching/*n, adj*: 1. Matching *n*, Abgleichung *f*, Zuordnung *f*; 2. passend.
material/*n, adj*: 1. Material *n*, Substanz *f*; 2. materiell.
maternal/*adj*: maternal, mütterlich.
maternal mortality: Müttersterblichkeit *f*.
maternal placenta: mütterliche Plazenta *f*.
maternity/*n*: Maternität *f*, Mutterschaft *f*.
maternity protection: Mutterschutz *m*.
maternofetal transmission: maternofetale Transmission *f*, Mutter-Kind-Übertragung *f*.
mating behavior: Paarungsverhalten *n*.
matrix/*n*: Matrix *f*.
matter/*n*: Masse *f*, Substanz *f*.
mattress/*n*: Matratze *f*.
maturation/*n*: Maturation *f*, Reifung *f*.
mature/*vb, adj*: 1. reifen; 2. reif.
mature bacteriophage: reifer Phage *m*.
mature cataract: reife Katarakt *f*.
mature infant: reifes Neugeborenes *n*.
maturity-onset diabetes: Erwachsenendiabetes *m*, Altersdiabetes *m*.
maturity signs: Reifezeichen.
maxillary/*adj*: maxillär.
maxillary osteoma: Oberkieferosteom *n*.
maxillary resection: Maxillaresektion *f*.
maxillary sinus: Kieferhöhle *f*.
maxillary sinusitis: Sinusitis maxillaris *f*, Kieferhöhlenentzündung *f*.
maxillomandibular fixation: Kieferfixation *f*.
maximal/*adj*: maximal.
maximal respiratory capacity: Atemgrenzwert *m*.
maximal stimulus: maximaler Stimulus *m*.
maximal tubular excretory capacity: maximale tubuläre Ausscheidungskapazität *f*.
maximum allowable concentration: maximale Arbeitsplatzkonzentration *f*, MAK.
maximum amount: Höchstmenge *f*.
maze/*n*: Labyrinth *n*.
mazipredone/*n*: Mazipredon *n*.
meal/*n*: Mahlzeit *f*, Essen *n*.
meals on wheels: Essen auf Rädern *n*, fahrbarer Mittagstisch *m*.
mean/*n, adj, vb*: 1. Mittelwert *m*, Mittel *n*; 2. durchschnittlich; 3. mitteln.
mean age: Durchschnittsalter *n*.
mean corpuscular hemoglobin: mittlerer absoluter Hämoglobingehalt *m*, Färbekoeffizient *m*.
mean corpuscular volume: mittleres Zellvolumen *n*.
mean deviation: mittlere Abweichung *f*.
meaning/*n*: Bedeutung *f*.
mean value: Mittelwert *m*.
measles/*n*: an infectious disease caused by the Morbillivirus. Symptoms include fever, a rash of pink spots first appearing in the face and spreading to the entire body and the extremities, redness of the eyes, and mild bronchitis. As complications, pneumonia, middle-ear infection, and encephalitis may occur. Masern *f*.
measure/*n, vb*: 1. Maß *n*, Maßnahme *f*; 2. messen.
measuring tape: Bandmaß *n*.
meat/*n*: Fleisch *n*.
meatal stenosis: Meatusstenose *f*.

meatus/*n*: Gang *m*.
mebendazole/*n*: Mebendazol *n*.
mebeverine/*n*: Mebeverin *n*.
mecamylamine/*n*: Mecamylamin *n*.
mechanical ascites: Stauungsaszites *m*.
mechanical cystitis: mechanische Blasenentzündung *f*.
mechanical ileus: mechanischer Ileus *m*.
mechanical jaundice: Verschlussikterus *m*.
mechanism/*n*: Mechanismus *m*.
meclocycline/*n*: Meclocyclin *n*.
meclofenamic acid: Meclofenaminsäure *f*.
meclofenoxate/*n*: Meclofenoxat *n*.
mecloxamine/*n*: Mecloxamin *n*.
meclozine/*n*: Meclozin *n*.
meconic acid: Mekonsäure *f*.
meconium/*n*: Mekonium *n*, Kindspech *n*.
medazepam/*n*: Medazepam *n*.
medial/*adj*: medial.
medial arteriosclerosis: Mediasklerose *f*, Mönckeberg-Sklerose *f*.
medial ligament: Innenband *n*.
median/*n, adj*: 1. Median *m*, Medianlinie *f*; 2. median.
median effective dose: mittlere effektive Dosis *f*.
median incision: Medianschnitt *m*.
median medullary syndrome: a neurologic condition resulting from lesions of the medulla oblongata which is characterized by lesions of the nucleus of the hypoglossal nerve with speech impairment, and contralateral hemiplegia. paramedianes Oblongatasyndrom *n*, Jackson-Syndrom *n*.
median paralysis: Medianuslähmung *f*.
median plane: Medianebene *f*.
median sagittal plane: Mediansagittalebene *f*.
mediastinal/*adj*: mediastinal.
mediastinal cyst: a fluid-containing sac in the mediastinum. Pericardial cysts contain a clear fluid and can almost always be found immediately adjacent to the pericardium in the anterior mediastinum. Mediastinalzyste *f*.
mediastinal displacement: Mediastinalverdrängung *f*.
mediastinal emphysema: Mediastinalemphysem *n*.
mediastinal flutter: Mediastinalflattern *n*.
mediastinobronchial fistula: Bronchomediastinalfistel *f*.
mediastinum/*n*: Mediastinum *n*.
mediate/*n, vb, adj*: 1. Mediator *m*, Überträgerstoff *m*; 2. vermitteln; 3. mittelbar.
mediate auscultation/*n*: indirekte Auskultation *f*.
mediate percussion: indirekte Perkussion *f*, Plessimeterperkussion *f*.
medical/*adj*: medizinisch, ärztlich.
medical care: medizinische Versorgung *f*.
medical device: medizintechnisches Gerät *n*.
medical education: ärztliche Fortbildung *f*.
medical ethics: medizinische Ethik *f*, Medizinethik *f*.
medical file: medizinisches Dossier *n*.
medical history: Krankengeschichte *f*, Anamnese *f*.
medical informatics: Medizininformatik *f*.
medical malpractice: ärztlicher Kunstfehler *m*.
medical personnel: medizinisches Personal *n*.
medical practitioner: praktischer Arzt *m*.
medical record: Krankenbericht *m*.
medical report: Arztbericht *m*, Arztbrief *m*.
medical sociology: Medizinsoziologie *f*.
medical staff: medizinisches Personal *n*.
medical student: Medizinstudent *m*.
medical therapy: medizinische Behandlung *f*.
medical treatment: ärztliche Behandlung *f*, konservative Therapie *f*.
medicated syrup: Medizinalsirup *m*.
medication/*n*: Medikation *f*.

medicinal/*adj*: medizinisch, medizinal.
medicinal agent: Medikament *n*.
medicinal herb: Medizinalpflanze *f*.
medicinal product: Fertigarzneimittel *n*.
medicinal rash: Arzneimittelexanthem *n*.
medicine/*n*: Medizin *f*, Heilkunde *f*, Arznei *f*.
medicine ball/*n*: Medizinball *m*.
medicolegal/*adj*: forensisch, gerichtsmedizinisch.
medicolegal autopsy: gerichtliche Autopsie *f*.
medicolegal necropsy: gerichtliche Leichenschau *f*.
mediocarpal joint: Karpalgelenk *n*.
mediotarsal amputation: Chopart-Operation *f*.
Mediterranean anemia: Thalassaemia major *f*, Cooley-Anämie *f*.
Mediterranean disease: Mittelmeerkrankheit *f*, β-Thalassämie *f*.
Mediterranean fever: Boutonneuse-Fieber *n*, Mittelmeerfieber *n*, Brucellose *f*.
medium/*n, adj*: 1. Medium *n*, Kulturmedium *n*; 2. mittlere, Mittel-, Durchschnitts-.
medrogestone/*n*: Medrogeston *n*.
medroxyprogesterone/*n*: Medroxyprogesteron *n*.
medrysone/*n*: Medryson *n*.
medulla/*n*: Mark *n*, Medulla *f*.
medullary/*adj*: medullär.
medullary carcinoma: Markschwammkarzinom *n*.
medullary layer: Marklager *n*.
medullary segment: Markscheidensegment *n*.
medullary sheath: Myelinscheide *f*.
medullary space: Markraum *m*.
medullary sponge kidney: Markschwammniere *f*.
medullated/*adj*: markhaltig.
medullated fiber: markhaltige Faser *f*.
medullated nerve: myelinisierter Nerv *m*.
medulloblastoma/*n*: Medulloblastom *n*.
mefenamic acid: Mefenaminsäure *f*.
mefloquine/*n*: Mefloquin *n*.
mefruside/*n*: Mefrusid *n*.
megacephaly/*n*: Megazephalus *m*, Makrozephalie *f*.
megacolon/*n*: abnormal enlargement and dilatation of the colonic parts of the intestine, affecting a colonic segment or the entire colon. Forms include congenital megacolon with abscence of myenteric ganglion cells in the large bowel, and acquired megacolon resulting from chronic constipation. Symptoms include constipation, loss of peristalsis, and swelling of the abdomen. Megakolon *n*.
megakaryoblast/*n*: Megakaryoblast *m*.
megakaryocyte/*n*: Megakaryozyt *m*.
megakaryocytic leukemia: Megakaryozytenleukämie *f*.
megaloblast/*n*: Megaloblast *m*.
megaloblastic anemia: Megaloblastenanämie *f*.
megalocyte/*n*: Megalozyt *m*.
megalomania/*n*: Megalomanie *f*, Größenwahn *m*.
megestrol/*n*: Megestrol *n*.
meibomian cyst: Meibom-Zyste *f*.
meibomian glands: Meibom-Drüsen.
meiosis/*n*: Meiose *f*.
melagatran/*n*: Melagatran *n*.
melancholia/*n*: Melancholie *f*, endogene Depression *f*.
melancholic stupor: depressiver Stupor *m*.
melanin/*n*: Melanin *n*.
melanoma/*n*: any tumor arising from melanoblasts, most frequently located in the skin and the eye. Forms include benign melanomas like nevus, or malignant tumors like melanoblastoma or malignant melanoma. Melanom *n*.
melanosis/*n*: Melanose *f*, Melasma *n*.
melanotic/*adj*: melanotisch.
melanotic sarcoma: Melanosarkom *n*.
melanuric fever: Schwarzwasserfieber *n*.
melissa/*n*: Melisse *f*.
melitracen/*n*: Melitracen *n*.
meloxicam/*n*: Meloxicam *n*.

M

melperone/*n*: Melperon *n*.
melphalan/*n*: Melphalan *n*.
melting/*n*: Schmelzen *n*, Einschmelzen *n*, Verschmelzung *f*.
memantine/*n*: Memantin *n*.
member/*n*: Glied *n*, Gliedmaße *f*.
membrane/*n*: Membran *f*, Häutchen *n*.
membrane potential: Membranpotential *n*.
membranoproliferative glomerulonephritis: membranoproliferative Glomerulonephritis *f*.
membranous conjunctivitis: membranöse Konjunktivitis *f*.
membranous endometritis: membranöse Endometritis *f*.
memory/*n*: Gedächtnis *n*, Speicher *m*.
memory loss: Erinnerungslücke *f*, Amnesie *f*.
menarche/*n*: Menarche *f*.
mendelian theory: Mendel-Vererbungstheorie *f*.
meningeal/*adj*: meningeal.
meningeal granules: Pacchioni-Granulationen.
meningeal headache: meningitischer Kopfschmerz *m*.
meningeal hemorrhage: Subarachnoidalblutung *f*.
meningeal space: Subarachnoidalraum *m*.
meningeal tuberculosis: tuberkulöse Meningitis *f*.
meningioma/*n*: tumor arising from the membranes covering the brain, the meninges. Most meningiomas are related to the dura mater, and characteristically show rather slow growth. Rapidly growing, malignant forms with invasive growth or metastatic spread may occur. Meningiom *n*.
meningism/*n*: Meningismus *m*.
meningitic/*adj*: meningitisch.
meningitis/*n*: inflammation of the membranes covering the brain and spinal cord, caused by bacteria like Meningococcus, by viruses, or other pathogenic microorganisms. Symptoms include fever, neurologic and psychological signs like headache, paralysis, disorientation, or unconsciousness. Meningitis *f*.
meningocele/*n*: Meningozele *f*.
meningococcal infection: Meningokokkeninfektion *f*.
meningococcal meningitis: Meningokokkenmeningitis *f*.
meningococcemia/*n*: Meningokokkensepsis *f*.
meningoencephalitis/*n*: Meningoenzephalitis *f*.
meningoencephalocele/*n*: Meningoenzephalozele *f*.
meniscal/*adj*: Meniskus-.
meniscectomy/*n*: Meniskusentfernung *f*.
meniscus injury: Meniskusverletzung *f*.
menopausal flush: menopausale Hitzewallung *f*.
menopause/*n*: Menopause *f*.
menorrhagia/*n*: excessive, prolonged bleeding during the monthly period. Menorrhagie *f*.
menstrual age: Schwangerschaftsdauer post menstruationem *f*.
menstrual bleeding: Menstruation *f*.
menstrual colic: Dysmenorrhö *f*.
menstrual cycle: Menstruationszyklus *m*.
menstrual edema: prämenstruelles Ödem *n*.
menstrual pain: Menstruationsschmerz *m*.
menstrual period: Menstruation *f*, Periode *f*.
menstrual psychosis: Menstruationspsychose *f*.
menstruation/*n*: Menstruation *f*, Periode *f*.
mental/*adj*: mental, Kinn-.
mental acuity: Geistesschärfe *f*.
mental age: Intelligenzalter *n*.
mental capacity: geistige Fähigkeit *f*.
mental change: psychische Veränderung *f*.
mental deficiency: geistige Retardierung *f*, Oligophrenie *f*.
mental deterioration: geistiger Abbau *m*.
mental development: geistige Entwicklung *f*.

mental disorder: psychische Störung *f*.
mental handicap: geistige Behinderung *f*.
mental health: geistige Gesundheit *f*.
mental illness: Geisteskrankheit *f*.
mental image: Vorstellungsbild *n*.
mentally handicapped: geistig behindert.
mental region: Kinnregion *f*.
mental retardation: a mental condition which is characterized by inadequate development of intelligence and significant impairment of the ability to learn and to develop socially. Causes include for example intrauterine infections, malnutrition, neurologic disorders, genetic syndromes, metabolic diseases; in approximately seventy-five to eighty percent of cases the cause is unknown. geistige Behinderung *f*.
mental stress: psychische Belastung *f*.
menthol/*n*: Menthol *n*.
mepacrine/*n*: Mepacrin *n*.
mephenesin/*n*: Mephenesin *n*.
mephentermine/*n*: Mephentermin *n*.
mepindolol/*n*: Mepindolol *n*.
meproscillarin/*n*: Meproscillarin *n*.
meptazinol/*n*: Meptazinol *n*.
mercaptamine/*n*: Mercaptamin *n*.
mercaptopurine/*n*: Mercaptopurin *n*.
mercapturic acid: Merkaptursäure *f*.
mercurial ointment: Präzipitatsalbe *f*, Unguentum Hydrargyri *n*.
mercurial stomatitis: Quecksilberstomatitis *f*.
mercy killing: Gnadentod *m*, Euthanasie *f*.
meridian/*n*: Meridian *m*.
merocrine gland: merokrine Drüse *f*.
mesalazine/*n*: Mesalazin *n*.
mesangial cell: Mesangiumzelle *f*.
mesangial nephropathy: mesangiale Glomerulonephritis *f*.
mesangiocapillary glomerulonephritis: mesangiokapilläre Glomerulonephritis *f*.
mesarteritis/*n*: Mesarteriitis *f*.
mesencephalic paralysis: Mittelhirnsyndrom *n*.
mesencephalon/*n*: Mesencephalon *n*.
mesenchymal cell: Mesenchymzelle *f*.
mesenchyme/*n*: Mesenchym *n*.
mesenteric/*adj*: mesenterial.
mesenteric cyst: Mesenterialzyste *f*.
mesenteric infarct: infarction of the mesentery and the intestine, usually resulting from acute occlusion of the mesenterial artery. Symptoms include abdominal pain, bloody diarrhea, shock, loss of peristalsis, and necrosis of the intestine. Mesenterialinfarkt *m*.
mesenteric ischemia: mesenteriale Ischämie *f*, Dunbar-Syndrom *n*.
mesenteric thrombosis: Mesenterialarterienthrombose *f*.
mesentery/*n*: Mesenterium *n*.
mesial occlusion: Mesialbiss *m*.
mesitylenic acid: Mesitylensäure *f*.
mesmerism/*n*: Mesmerismus *m*.
mesna/*n*: Mesna *n*.
mesoappendix/*n*: Mesoappendix *f*.
mesoblastic sensibility: Muskelsensibilität *f*.
mesocaval shunt: mesenterikokavaler Shunt *m*.
mesocolon/*n*: Mesokolon *n*.
mesoderm/*n*: Mesoderm *n*.
mesonasal/*adj*: nasomedial.
mesonephroma/*n*: Mesonephrom *n*.
mesosalpinx/*n*: Mesosalpinx *m*.
mesothelioma/*n*: Mesotheliom *n*.
mesothelium/*n*: Mesothel *n*.
messenger ribonucleic acid: Boten-RNS *f*, Messenger-Ribonukleinsäure *f*, mRNA.
messianic delusion: messianischer Wahn *m*.
mesterolone/*n*: Mesterolon *n*.
mestranol/*n*: Mestranol *n*.
mesulfen/*n*: Mesulfen *n*.
mesuximide/*n*: Mesuximid *n*.
metabolic/*adj*: metabolisch.
metabolic acidosis: metabolische Azidose *f*.
metabolic alkalosis: metabolische Alkalose *f*.
metabolic antagonist: Antimetabolit *m*.
metabolic balance: metabolisches Gleichgewicht *n*.

metabolic coma: Stoffwechselkoma *n*.
metabolic disease: Stoffwechselkrankheit *f*.
metabolic disorder: metabolische Störung *f*, Stoffwechselstörung *f*.
metabolic encephalopathy: metabolische Enzephalopathie *f*.
metabolic equilibrium: Stoffwechselgleichgewicht *n*.
metachromatic granule: Babes-Ernst-Polkörperchen *n*.
metabolic pathway: Stoffwechselweg *m*.
metabolic psychosis: Stoffwechselpsychose *f*.
metabolism/*n*: Metabolismus *m*, Stoffwechsel *m*.
metabolite/*n*: Metabolit *m*.
metacarpal/*adj*: metakarpal.
metacarpophalangeal/*adj*: metakarpophalangeal.
metacarpus/*n*: Mittelhand *f*.
metachromatic leukodystrophy: metachromatische Leukodystrophie *f*, familiäre juvenile diffuse Sklerose *f*, Scholz-Bielschowsky-Henneberg-Sklerose *f*.
metal/*n*: Metall *n*.
metal chelate complex: Metallchelatkomplex *m*.
metallic rale: metallisches Rasselgeräusch *n*.
metamfepramone/*n*: Metamfepramon *n*.
metamizole/*n*: Metamizol *n*.
metamorphosis/*n*: Metamorphose *f*.
metanephros/*n*: Metanephros *m*, Nachniere *f*.
metaphase/*n*: Metaphase *f*.
metaphosphoric acid: Metaphosphorsäure *f*.
metaphyseal dysplasia: metaphysäre Dysplasie *f*, Pyle-Krankheit *f*.
metaphysis/*n*: Metaphyse *f*.
metaplasia/*n*: Metaplasie *f*.
metapneumonic empyema: metapneumonisches Empyem *n*.
metapneumonic pleurisy: metapneumonische Pleuritis *f*.
metaraminol/*n*: Metaraminol *n*.
metastasis/*n*: Metastase *f*.
metastasizing septicemia: septische Metastasierung *f*.
metastatic abscess: metastatischer Abszess *m*.
metatarsal/*adj*: metatarsal.
metencephalic/*adj*: metenzephal.
metenolone/*n*: Metenolon *n*.
meteorism/*n*: Meteorismus *m*.
meter/*n*: Meter *m*.
methacholine chloride: Methacholinchlorid *n*.
methadone/*n*: Methadon *n*.
methadone maintenance: medical treatment with methadone which is prescribed as a substitute for heroin or other morphines in drug users. Methadone maintenance programs contribute to a stabilization of the social situation of drug users, and to a reduction of infections which are transmitted via injecting drug use, for example HIV infection. Methadonsubstitution *f*.
methandriol/*n*: Methandriol *n*.
methanol/*n*: Methanol *n*.
methanthelinium bromide: Methantheliniumbromid *n*.
methazolamide/*n*: Methazolamid *n*.
methemoglobin: Methämoglobin *n*, Met-Hb, Hämiglobin *n*.
methemoglobinemia/*n*: Methämoglobinämie *f*.
methicillin/*n*: Methicillin *n*.
methimazole/*n*: Methimazol *n*, Thiamazol *n*.
methionine/*n*: Methionin *n*.
methocarbomal/*n*: Methocarbomal *n*.
method/*n*: Methode *f*, Verfahren *n*.
methotrexate/*n*: Methotrexat *n*.
methoxamine hydrochloride: Methoxaminhydrochlorid *n*.
methoxsalen/*n*: Methoxypsoralen *n*.
methoxyflurane/*n*: Methoxyfluran *n*.
methyl alcohol: Methylalkohol *m*, Methanol *n*.
methyldigoxin/*n*: Methyldigoxin *n*, Medigoxin *n*.
methyldopa/*n*: Methyldopa *n*.
methylergometrine/*n*: Methylergometrin *n*.
methylhydantoic acid: Methylhydantoinsäure *f*.

methylmalonic acid: Methylmalonsäure *f*.
methylmalonic aciduria: Methylmalonazidurie *f*.
methyl orange: Methylorange *n*.
methylpentynol/*n*: Methylpentynol *n*.
methyl-phenyl-tetrahydropyridine/*n*: Methyl-phenyl-tetrahydropyridin *n*, MPTP.
methylprednisolone/*n*: Methylprednisolon *n*.
methylsulfonal/*n*: Methylsulfonal *n*.
methyltestosterone/*n*: Methyltestosteron *n*.
methysergide/*n*: Methysergid *n*.
meticillin/*n*: Meticillin *n*.
metildigoxin/*n*: Metildigoxin *n*, Methyldigoxin *n*.
metipranolol/*n*: Metipranolol *n*.
metoclopramide/*n*: Metoclopramid *n*.
metolazone/*n*: Metolazon *n*.
metoprolol/*n*: Metoprolol *n*.
metric/*adj*: metrisch.
metritis/*n*: inflammation of the uterus. Forms include myometritis with affection of uterine muscles, and endometritis with affection of the mucous membranes of the uterus. Metritis *f*, Myometritis *f*.
metronidazole/*n*: Metronidazol *n*.
metrorrhagia/*n*: bleeding originating from the uterus which is unrelated to monthly bleeding during the menstrual period. Metrorrhagie *f*.
metrosalpingography/*n*: Hysterosalpingographie *f*.
metyrapone/*n*: Metyrapon *n*.
Mexican spotted fever: Rocky-Mountain-Fleckfieber *n*.
mexiletine/*n*: Mexiletin *n*.
mezlocillin/*n*: Mezlocillin *n*.
mianserin/*n*: Mianserin *n*.
miconazole/*n*: Miconazol *n*.
microangiopathy/*n*: stenosis and/or obliteration of small blood vessels and capillaries. Forms include for example diabetic microangiopathy of the retina and the kidney in diabetes mellitus, and thrombotic microangiopathy, as in Moschcowitz' syndrome. Mikroangiopathie *f*.
microbe/*n*: Mikrobe *f*, Mikroorganismus *m*.
microbial/*adj*: mikrobiell.
microbicide/*n, adj*: 1. Mikrobizid *n*; 2. mikrobizid.
microbiology/*n*: Mikrobiologie *f*.
microcephaly/*n*: Mikrozephalie *f*.
microcytosis/*n*: Mikrozytose *f*.
microglia/*n*: Mikroglia *f*.
microglial cell: Mikrogliazelle *f*, Hortega-Zelle *f*.
micrognathia/*n*: Mikrognathie *f*.
micromelia/*n*: Mikromelie *f*.
micrometry/*n*: Mikrometrie *f*.
microorganism/*n*: Mikroorganismus *m*.
micropathology/*n*: Histopathologie *f*.
microphthalmos/*n*: Mikrophthalmus *m*.
microptic hallucination: Mikropsie *f*.
microscope/*n*: Mikroskop *n*.
microscopic/*adj*: mikroskopisch.
microscopic anatomy: mikroskopische Anatomie *f*.
microscopy/*n*: Mikroskopie *f*.
microsome/*n*: Mikrosom *n*.
microsurgery/*n*: Mikrochirurgie *f*.
microtome/*n*: Mikrotom *n*.
micturition/*n*: Miktion *f*.
micturition frequency: Miktionshäufigkeit *f*.
midbrain/*n*: Mittelhirn *n*.
midcycle bleeding: Mittelblutung *f*, Ovulationsblutung *f*.
mid-diastolic murmur: mesodiastolisches Geräusch *n*.
middle ear: Mittelohr *n*.
middle-ear effusion: Seromukotympanon *n*.
middle finger: Mittelfinger *m*.
middle lobe: Mittellappen *m*.
midget/*n*: proportionierter Zwerg *m*.
midline/*n*: Mittellinie *f*, Medianebene *f*.
midline granuloma: Mittelliniengranulom *n*.
midodrine/*n*: Midodrin *n*.
midpain/*n*: Mittelschmerz *m*.
midriff/*n*: Diaphragma *n*.
midstream urine: Mittelstrahlurin *m*.
midwife/*n*: Hebamme *f*, Entbindungspfleger *m*.

M

midwifery/*n*: Geburtshilfe *f*.
mifepristone/*n*: Mifepriston *n*.
miglitol/*n*: Miglitol *n*.
miglustat/*n*: Miglustat *n*.
migraine/*n*: severe, periodic headache, usually one-sided and accompanied by nausea, vomiting, and vision disturbances. Symptoms occur intermittently and can be triggered in some cases by certain stimuli. The exact cause of the disorder is unknown. Migräne *f*.
migrainous neuralgia: Histaminkopfschmerz *m*, Horton-Syndrom *n*.
migrating abscess: Senkungsabszess *m*.
migrating phlebitis: Phlebitis migrans *f*.
migrating thrombosis: Thrombosis migrans *f*.
migratory thrombophlebitis: Thrombophlebitis migrans *f*.
mild/*adj*: mild, leicht.
mild dysentery: leichte Dysenterie *f*.
mild smallpox: Alastrim *n*, Variola minor *f*.
miliary/*adj*: miliar.
miliary abscess: Miliarabszess *m*.
miliary tuberculosis: Miliartuberkulose *f*.
military hospital: Militärhospital *n*, Lazarett *n*.
military medicine: Wehrmedizin *f*.
milk/*n*: Milch *f*.
milk crust: Milchschorf *m*.
milk duct: Milchgang *m*.
milk retention: Milchretention *f*, Milchverhaltung *f*.
milk teeth: Milchgebiss *n*, Milchzähne.
milk thistle: Mariendistel *f*.
milky/*adj*: milchig.
milky ascites: chylöser Aszites *m*.
milky cataract: Milchstar *m*.
milky urine: trüber Urin *m*.
milrinone/*n*: Milrinon *n*.
Milroy's disease: Nonne-Milroy-Krankheit *f*, hereditäres Lymphödem *n*.
miltefosine/*n*: Miltefosin *n*.
milzbrand/*n*: Milzbrand *m*, Anthrax *m*.
mimetic/*n, adj*: 1. Mimetikum *n*; 2. mimetisch, nachahmend.
mimetic behavior: Nachahmungsverhalten *n*.
mimic convulsion: Tic *m*, mimische Zuckung *f*.
mimicry/*n*: Mimikry *f*.
mind/*n*: Geist *m*, Psyche *f*.
mineral/*n, adj*: 1. Mineral *n*; 2. mineralisch.
mineral water: Mineralwasser *n*.
miners' asthma/*n*: Bergmannsasthma *n*, Anthrakose *f*.
minimal/*adj*: minimal.
minimal brain dysfunction: minimale zerebrale Dysfunktion *f*.
minimal care: Grundversorgung *f*.
minimal invasive surgery: minimalinvasive Chirurgie *f*, MIC.
minimum daily requirement: täglicher Mindestbedarf *m*.
minimum dose/*n*: Minimaldosis *f*.
minipill/*n*: Minipille *f*.
minocycline/*n*: Minocyclin *n*.
minor/*adj*: geringer, kleiner.
minor antigen: Kryptantigen *n*.
minor duodenal papilla: Papilla duodenalis minor *f*.
minor epilepsy: Epilepsia minor *f*, Petit mal.
minor surgery: kleiner Eingriff *m*, kleine Chirurgie *f*.
minor tranquilizer: Minor Tranquilizer *m*, Anxiolytikum *n*.
minoxidil/*n*: Minoxidil *n*.
minus lens: Minuslinse *f*.
minute motor activity: Feinmotorik *f*.
minute volume/*n*: Minutenvolumen *n*.
miosis/*n*: Miosis *f*.
mirror/*n*: Spiegel *m*.
mirtazapine/*n*: Mirtazapin *n*.
miscarriage/*n*: loss of an embryo or a fetus before the age of viability. Causes include endocrine or nutritional disorders, immunological reactions, infections, or generalized disease of the mother. Spontanabort *m*.
misdiagnose/*vb*: fehldiagnostizieren.
misinterpretation/*n*: Fehldeutung *f*.
mismatching/*n*: Fehlpaarung *f*.

misoprostol/*n*: Misoprostol *n*.
missed abortion: Missed Abortion, verhaltener Abort *f*.
missing/*adj*: fehlend.
mistletoe/*n*: Mistel *f*.
mite/*n*: Milbe *f*.
mite fever: Fleckfieber *n*.
mithramycin/*n*: Mithramycin *n*.
mitochondrion/*n*: Mitochondrion *n*, Mitochondrium *n*.
mitogenic factor: mitogener Faktor *m*.
mitoguazone/*n*: Mitoguazon *n*.
mitomycin/*n*: Mitomycin *n*.
mitosis/*n*: Mitose *f*.
mitotane/*n*: Mitotan *n*.
mitotic poison: Mitosegift *n*, Spindelgift *n*.
mitoxantrone/*n*: Mitoxantron *n*.
mitral/*adj*: mitral.
mitral click: Mitralöffnungston *m*.
mitral insufficiency: Mitralklappeninsuffizienz *f*.
mitral murmur: Mitralklappengeräusch *n*.
mitral regurgitation: Mitralklappeninsuffizienz *f*.
mitral stenosis: Mitralklappenstenose *f*.
mitral valve: Mitralklappe *f*.
mitral valve prolapse: Mitralklappenprolaps *m*.
mivacurium chloride: Mivacuriumchlorid *n*.
mixed/*adj*: gemischt.
mixed gland: gemischte Drüse *f*.
mixed glioma: gemischtes Gliom *n*.
mixed nerve: gemischter Nerv *m*.
mixed psychosis: Mischpsychose *f*.
mixed thrombus: gemischter Thrombus *m*.
mixed tumor: Mischtumor *m*.
mixed vaccine: Kombinationsimpfstoff *m*.
mixture/*n*: Mixtur *f*, Gemisch *n*.
mizolastine/*n*: Mizolastin *n*.
mnestic/*adj*: mnestisch.
mobile/*adj*: beweglich, fahrbar.
mobile gallbladder: flottierende Gallenblase *f*, wandernde Gallenblase *f*.
mobile scoliosis: korrigierbare Skoliose *f*.
mobility/*n*: Mobilität *f*, Beweglichkeit *f*.
mobilization/*n*: Mobilisation *f*.
moclobemide/*n*: Moclobemid *n*.
mode of action: Wirkmechanismus *m*.
moderate/*adj*: moderat, mäßig.
modified milk: adaptierte Milch *f*.
modified smallpox: Variolois *f*, Variola mitigata *f*.
modify/*vb*: modifizieren, abändern.
modifying gene: Modifikatorgen *n*.
moexipril/*n*: Moexipril *n*.
mofebutazone/*n*: Mofebutazon *n*.
mogigraphia/*n*: Mogigraphie *f*, Schreibkrampf *m*.
moist/*adj*: feucht.
moisten/*vb*: befeuchten.
moist gangrene: feuchte Gangrän *f*.
moist papule: nässende Papel *f*.
moist rale: feuchtes Rasselgeräusch *n*.
moisturizing cream: Feuchtigkeitscreme *f*.
molality/*n*: Molalität *f*.
molar/*n, adj*: 1. Molar *m*, Backenzahn *m*; 2. molar.
molarity/*n*: Molarität *f*.
molar pregnancy: Molenschwangerschaft *f*.
molasses/*n*: Melasse *f*.
mold mycosis: Schimmelpilzmykose *f*.
mole/*n*: Mole *f*, Muttermal *n*.
molecular/*adj*: molekular.
molecular biology: Molekularbiologie *f*.
molecular genetics: Molekulargenetik *f*.
molecular pathology: Molekularpathologie *f*.
molecule/*n*: Molekül *n*.
molgramostim/*n*: Molgramostim *n*.
molsidomine/*n*: Molsidomin *n*.
molybdenic acid: Molybdänsäure *f*.
mometasone furoate: Mometasonfuroat *n*.
monaural/*adj*: monaural.
Mondonesi's reflex: Mondonesi-Reflex *m*, bulbomimischer Reflex *m*.
mongolian spot: Mongolenfleck *m*.
monilial/*adj*: monilial.

monilial vaginitis: inflammation of the vagina, caused by infection with the Candida fungus Monilia. Symptoms include vulvovaginitis, pruritus, and discharge. Candida-Vaginitis *f*, Soorkolpitis *f*.
monitor/*n, vb*: 1. Monitor *m*; 2. überwachen.
monitoring/*n*: Monitoring *n*, Überwachung *f*.
monoamine oxidase inhibitor: Monoaminoxidasehemmer *m*, MAO-Hemmer *m*.
monobasic acid: monobasische Säure *f*.
monobenzone/*n*: Monobenzon *n*.
monoblast/*n*: Monoblast *m*.
monocentric/*adj*: monozentrisch.
monochloracetic acid: Chloressigsäure *f*.
monoclonal/*adj*: monoklonal.
monoclonal antibody: monoklonaler Antikörper *m*.
monocular strabismus: Monokularschielen *n*.
monocyte/*n*: Monozyt *m*.
monocytic leukemia: Monozytenleukämie *f*.
monocytoid cell: monozytäre Zelle *f*.
monogamy/*n*: Monogamie *f*.
monomania/*n*: Monomanie *f*.
mononeuritis/*n*: Mononeuritis *f*.
mononuclear/*adj*: mononukleär, einkernig.
mononucleosis/*n*: an infectious disease caused by Epstein-Barr virus. Mononucleosis or glandular fever is characterized by an increase in number of monocytes, enlargement of lymph nodes, mild elevation of body temperature, enlargement of the spleen, sore throat, and sometimes skin eruption. Mononukleose *f*, Pfeiffer-Drüsenfieber *n*.
monophasic cycle: monophasischer Zyklus *m*, anovulatorischer Zyklus *m*.
monoplegia/*n*: Monoplegie *f*.
monoploid/*adj*: monoploid, haploid.
monopolar/*adj*: unipolar.
monorchidism/*n*: Monorchidie *f*.
monosaccharide/*n*: Monosaccharid *n*.
monosome/*n*: Monosom *n*.
monotherapy/*n*: Monotherapie *f*.
monovalent serum: monovalentes Antiserum *n*.
monstrocellular sarcoma: Monstrezellensarkom *n*.
montelukast/*n*: Montelukast *n*.
mood/*n*: Stimmung *f*, Laune *f*.
mood-congruent psychotic features: stimmungskongruente psychotische Merkmale.
mood disorder: affektive Störung *f*.
moody/*adj*: launisch, schwermütig.
moon/*n*: Mond *m*, Nagelweiß *n*.
moperone/*n*: Moperon *n*.
mopidamol/*n*: Mopidamol *n*.
morazone/*n*: Morazon *n*.
morbid/*adj*: morbid.
morbidity/*n*: Morbidität *f*.
morbilliform/*adj*: morbilliform.
morbilliform eruption: a rash which resembles in pink color, localization, and distribution pattern the Koplik spots which occur in measles. morbilliformer Ausschlag *m*.
morbus/*n*: Morbus *m*, Krankheit *f*.
morgagnian cataract: Morgagni-Katarakt *f*.
morgagnian cyst: Morgagni-Zyste *f*.
morgue/*n*: Leichenhalle *f*.
moribund/*adj*: moribund.
morning-after pill: Postkoitalpille *f*.
morning epilepsy: Aufwachepilepsie *f*.
morning sickness: nausea and vomiting occurring during the first weeks of pregnancy, especially the early morning vomiting. Schwangerschaftserbrechen *n*, Hyperemesis gravidarum *f*.
moroxydine/*n*: Moroxydin *n*.
morphine/*n*: Morphin *n*.
morphine derivative: Morphinderivat *n*.
morphinism/*n*: Morphinismus *m*.
morphium/*n*: Morphium *n*.
morphogenetic field: morphogenetisches Feld *n*.
morphological sex: morphologisches Geschlecht *n*.
morphology/*n*: Morphologie *f*.
mortal/*adj*: sterblich, letal.

mortality/*n*: Mortalität *f*, Sterblichkeit *f*.
mortality risk: Mortalitätsrisiko *n*.
morula/*n*: Morula *f*.
mosaic/*n*: Mosaik *n*.
mosquito/*n*: Moskito *m*, Stechmücke *f*.
mossy/*adj*: moosartig.
mother/*n*: Mutter *f*.
motherhood/*n*: Mutterschaft *f*.
motility/*n*: Motilität *f*, Beweglichkeit *f*.
motion/*n*: Bewegung *f*.
motion sickness: a condition which is characterized by the feeling of nausea and sometimes vomiting and which is caused by motion. Causes include physical factors like diseases of the inner ear, and psychological factors like fear. Kinetose *f*.
motor activity: Motorik *f*.
motor agraphia: motorische Agraphie *f*.
motor aphasia: motorische Aphasie *f*, Broca-Aphasie *f*.
motor area: motorische Rinde *f*.
motor cell: Motoneuron *n*.
motor cortex: motorischer Kortex *m*.
motor discharge: motorische Entladung *f*.
motor endplate: motorische Endplatte *f*.
motor fiber: motorische Nervenfaser *f*.
motor image: Bewegungsbild *n*.
motor neuron: motorisches Neuron *n*, Motoneuron *n*.
motor paralysis: motorische Lähmung *f*.
motor plate: motorische Endplatte *f*.
motor test: motorischer Test *m*.
motor tic: motorischer Tic *m*.
mottled/*adj*: gesprenkelt.
mottled rash: gesprenkelter Ausschlag *m*.
mountain sickness: Höhenkrankheit *f*.
mountain tick fever: Gebirgszeckenfieber *n*, Colorado-Zeckenfieber *n*.
mouth/*n*: Mund *m*.
mouth-to-mouth resuscitation: Mund-zu-Mund-Beatmung *f*.
mouth-to-nose respiration: Mund-zu-Nase-Beatmung *f*.
mouthwash/*n*: Mundspülung *f*.
movement/*n*: Bewegung *f*.
moxaverine/*n*: Moxaverin *n*.
moxibustion/*n*: Moxibustion *f*.
moxidectin/*n*: Moxidectin *n*.
moxifloxacin/*n*: Moxifloxacin *n*.
moxonidin/*n*: Moxonidin *n*.
MS <*abbr*> **multiple sclerosis**: multiple Sklerose *f*, MS.
mucilage/*n*: Muzilago *f*.
mucin/*n*: Muzin *n*.
mucinous adenocarcinoma: schleimbildendes Adenokarzinom *n*.
mucinous adenoma: muzinöses Adenom *n*.
mucinous degeneration: muköse Degeneration *f*.
mucocele/*n*: Mukozele *f*.
mucocellular carcinoma: Siegelringzellkarzinom *n*.
mucoepidermoid carcinoma: schleimbildendes Adenokarzinom *n*.
mucoid/*n, adj*: 1. Mukoid *n*; 2. mukoid.
mucoid carcinoma: Gallertkarzinom *n*.
mucoid degeneration: mukoide Degeneration *f*.
mucoitin-sulfuric acid: Mukoitinschwefelsäure *f*.
mucolytic/*adj*: mukolytisch.
mucolytic agent: Mukolytikum *n*, Expectorans *n*.
mucomembranous enteritis: mukomembranöse Kolitis *f*, Syndrom des irritablen Kolons *n*.
mucoperiosteal flap: mukoperiostaler Lappen *m*.
mucopurulent/*adj*: mukopurulent, schleimig-eitrig.
mucosa/*n*: Mukosa *f*, Schleimhaut *f*.
mucosal immunity: Schleimhautimmunität *f*.
mucous/*adj*: mukös, schleimig.
mucous cell: schleimsezernierende Zelle *f*.
mucous colitis: mukomembranöse Kolitis *f*, Syndrom des irritablen Darms.

M

mucous cyst: Schleimzyste *f*.
mucous diarrhea: schleimige Diarrhö *f*.
mucous gland: muköse Drüse *f*, Schleimdrüse *f*.
mucous membrane: Schleimhaut *f*.
mucous plaque: Plaque muqueuse *f*.
mucous plug: Schleimpfropf *m*.
mucous thread: Schleimfaden *m*.
mucoviscidosis/*n*: an autosomal recessive condition that affects the exocrine, or externally secreting, glands. Major symptoms include maldigestion due to decreased pancreatic exocrine function, and chronic bronchopneumonia due to decreased mucociliary transport. Mukoviszidose *f*, zystische Fibrose *f*.
mucus/*n*: Mukus *m*, Schleim *f*.
mudpack/*n*: Moorpackung *f*.
multicentric cancer: multizentrisches Karzinom *n*.
multiclonal/*adj*: polyklonal.
multifactorial disorder: multifaktorielle Störung *f*.
multifocal chronic atrophic gastritis: multifokale chronische atrophische Gastritis *f*.
multilobate placenta: Placenta multipartita *f*.
multilocular/*adj*: mehrkammerig.
multilocular cyst: mehrkammerige Zyste *f*.
multiple/*adj*: mehrfach, multipel.
multiple birth: Mehrfachgeburt *f*.
multiple endocrine adenoma: an autosomal dominant inherited syndrome which is characterized by the presence of benign or malignant neoplasms of more than one endocrine gland and neurocutaneous alterations. multiple endokrine Neoplasie *f*, MEN.
multiple fracture: Mehrfachbruch *m*.
multiple hamartoma syndrome: an autosomal dominant condition which is characterized by the presence of hamartomatous polyps in the intestine, associated with pigmented lesions on the skin, on the lips, and on buccal mucosa. Peutz-Jeghers-Syndrom *n*.
multiple myeloma: multiples Myelom *n*.
multiple neuritis: Polyneuritis *f*, Polyneuropathie *f*.
multiple personality: multiple Persönlichkeit *f*.
multiple pregnancy: Mehrlingsschwangerschaft *f*.
multiple-puncture test: Tine-Test *m*.
multiple sclerosis: a chronic, progressive disease of the central nervous system of unknown cause. The condition is characterized by multiple scarlike, demyelinating lesions and inflammatory changes on the brain and spinal cord. Symptoms depend on the localization of lesions and may include vision disorders, weakness, paralysis, and tremor. multiple Sklerose *f*, MS.
multiple-system illness: Multisystemerkrankung *f*.
multiple trauma: simultaneous traumatic lesions in one or more regions of the body or organs of which one injury or the summation of the lesions have life-threatening character. Polytrauma *n*.
multipolar cell: multipolares Neuron *n*.
multivesicular body: multivesikuläre Vakuole *f*.
mumbling/*adj*: mussitierend, murmelnd.
mumps/*n*: an infectious disease caused by a paramyxovirus. Symptoms include a characteristic swelling of the parotid glands, pain under the ears or under the chin, and fever. As complication, infections of the pancreas or, predominantly in adults, of the testis may occur. Mumps *m*, Parotitis epidemica *f*.
mupirocin/*n*: Mupirocin *n*.
mural aneurysm: Wandaneurysma *n*.
mural cell: Wandzelle *f*.
mural endocarditis: parietale Endokarditis *f*.
mural salpingitis: entzündliche Tubenverdickung *f*.
mural thrombus: Wandthrombus *m*.
muramic acid: Muraminsäure *f*.

murine/*adj*: murin.
murine plague: Yersiniose *f*.
murine typhus: murines Fleckfieber *n*, Flohfleckfieber *n*.
murmur/*n, vb*: 1. Geräusch *n*; 2. rauschen.
muscarinic agent: muskarinartige Substanz *f*.
muscarinic effect: muskarinartige Wirkung *f*.
muscarinic receptor: muskarinartiger Rezeptor *m*.
muscle/*n*: Muskel *m*.
muscle action potential: Muskelaktionspotential *n*.
muscle cramp: painful, spasmodic contraction of one or more muscles, resulting for example from ischemia, overfatigue, electrolyte imbalance, sometimes also occurring spontaneously or following voluntary movements. Muskelkrampf *m*.
muscle insertion: Muskelansatz *m*.
muscle tone: Muskeltonus *m*.
muscle weakness: Muskelschwache *f*.
muscular/*adj*: muskulär, muskulös.
muscular atrophy: Muskelatrophie *f*.
muscular degeneration: Muskeldegeneration *f*.
muscular dystrophy: degenerative myopathy which is characterized by progressive weakness and atrophy of muscles, resulting from enzyme deficiency. Typically, the nervous system is not involved. Symptoms may include myopathic or waddling gait, and pseudohypertrophy with increase of muscle tissue but without true hypertrophy. Muskeldystrophie *f*.
muscular fatigue: Muskelermüdung *f*.
muscular murmur: Muskelton *m*.
muscular pain: Muskelschmerz *m*.
muscular power: Muskelkraft *f*.
muscular proprioceptive reflex: Muskeleigenreflex *m*, MER.
muscular rheumatism: Weichteilrheumatismus *f*.
muscular rigidity: Muskelsteife *f*.
muscular scoliosis: myopathische Skoliose *f*.
muscular sensibility: Muskelsinn *m*.
muscular tension: Muskelspannung *f*.
muscular tissue: Muskelgewebe *n*.
musculoskeletal system: muskuloskelettales System *n*.
mushroom poisoning: intoxication caused by mushrooms or mushroom toxins. Symptoms depend on the type and the quantity of ingested mushrooms and range from vomiting to liver failure and exitus. Signs may occur immediately after the consumption, or with considerable delay of several days. Pilzvergiftung *f*.
musical murmur: musikalisches Geräusch *n*.
music therapy: Musiktherapie *f*.
mustard poultice: Senfwickel *m*.
mutagen/*n, adj*: 1. Mutagen *n*; 2. mutagen.
mutant/*n*: Mutante *f*.
mutation/*n*: Mutation *f*.
mute/*n, adj*: 1. Stummer *m*; 2. stumm.
mutilate/*vb*: mutilieren, verstümmeln.
mutism/*n*: Mutismus *m*.
myalgia/*n*: circumscribed or generalized muscle pain, occurring for example as a sign of inflammation, injury, or infectious diseases like trichinosis or chronic viral infections. Myalgie *f*.
myasthenia/*n*: muscle weakness. Myasthenia gravis or Erb-Goldflam disease is a neurologic disorder which is considered to be caused by an autoimmune reaction against muscular receptors of acetylcholine. It is characterized by severe muscle weakness following movements or exercise, affecting all voluntary muscles, including eye muscles and respiratory muscles. Myasthenie *f*, Muskelschwäche *f*.
myasthenic crisis: myasthenische Krise *f*.
myasthenic reaction: myasthenische Reaktion *f*.
myasthenic syndrome: a condition which is characterized by muscular weakness, exhaustion, and absent

M

tendon reflexes, usually as paraneoplastic syndrome associated with lung cancer. Lambert-Eaton-Syndrom *n*.

mycete/*n*: Myzet *m*, Pilz *m*.

mycetoma/*n*: Myzetom *n*, Madurabeule *f*.

mycolic acid: Mycolsäure *f*.

mycoplasma/*n*: Mykoplasma *n*.

mycoplasmal pneumonia: Mykoplasmenpneumonie *f*, atypische Pneumonie *f*.

mycosis/*n*: any infection caused by fungi, for example candidiasis. However, mycosis fungoides is a chronic or rapidly progressive form of cutaneous T-cell lymphoma, formerly thought to be of fungal origin. Mykose *f*.

mycotic stomatitis: a fungal infection of the mouth, typically caused by Candida albicans. Symptoms include small white stipples on the mucosa, and eventually painful swallowing. Pilzstomatitis *f*, Soor *m*.

mycotoxin/*n*: Mykotoxin *n*.

mydriasis/*n*: Mydriasis *f*.

myelin/*n*: Myelin *n*.

myelinated/*adj*: myelinisiert, markhaltig.

myelinated fiber: markhaltige Faser *f*.

myelinogenetic field: Flechsig-Zone *f*.

myelitis/*n*: Myelitis *f*.

myelocele/*n*: Myelozele *f*

myelocyte/*n*: Myelozyt *m*.

myeloencephalitis/*n*: Enzephalomyelitis *f*.

myelography/*n*: Myelographie *f*.

myeloid/*adj*: myeloid, myeloisch.

myeloid cell: myeloische Zelle *f*.

myeloid sarcoma: Myelosarkom *n*.

myeloma/*n*: a malignant neoplasma originating from the bone marrow. In Kahler's disease, multiple hematosarcomas are present within the bones or other tissues. Symptoms include spontaneous fracture of bones, and the production of Bence-Jones protein. Myelom *n*, Plasmozytom *n*, Leichte-Ketten-Krankheit *f*.

myelomatosis/*n*: multiples Myelom *n*.

myelomeningocele/*n*: Meningomyelozele *f*.

myelomonocytic leukemia: myelomonozytäre Leukämie *f*.

myelopathic atrophy: progressive Muskeldystrophie *f*.

myelopathy/*n*: 1. any disease or functional disturbance of the spinal cord, for example myelitis or multiple sclerosis affecting the spinal cord. Myelopathie *f*. 2. any disorder of the bone marrow, for example myeloproliferative disorders. Myelopathie *f*.

myeloproliferative syndrome: any disorder which is characterized by proliferation of cells derived from the bone marrow such as erythrocytes, granulocytes, and platelet precursor cells. Forms include for example true polycythemia, essential thrombocythemia, chronic myelocytic leukemia, erythroleukemia, and preleukemic syndromes. myeloproliferatives Syndrom *n*.

myelosclerosis/*n*: Myelosklerose *f*, Osteomyelofibrose *f*.

myelosis/*n*: Myelose *f*.

myoblastoma/*n*: Myoblastenmyom *n*, Abrikossof-Tumor *m*.

myocardial/*adj*: myokardial.

myocardial failure: Herzinsuffizienz *f*.

myocardial infarction: damaging and necrosis of a part of the heart muscle, resulting from insufficient blood supply, usually caused by occlusion of coronary arteries in coronary artery disease. Symptoms include sudden severe pain in the chest, often radiating to the left arm. Myocardial infarction is among the most common causes of sudden death. Myokardinfarkt *m*, Herzinfarkt *m*.

myocardial insufficiency: inability of the heart to a sufficient output of blood at an adequate rate to the body, or an abnormality in diastolic function with venous engorgement, hepatic enlargement, and subcutaneous edema. Causes include for example degenerative or inflammatory changes of the myocardium, coronary artery disease, and myocardial infarction. Herzinsuffizienz *f*.

myocardial reserve: Reservekraft des Herzens.

myocardial sarcoidosis: Myokardsarkoidose *f*.

myocarditis/*n*: acute or chronic inflammation of the heart muscle, usually due to infection, systemic inflammatory disorders, metabolic disorders, or toxic substances. Myokarditis *f*, Herzmuskelentzündung *f*.

myocardium/*n*: Myokard *n*.

myoclonic attack: Myoklonus *m*.

myoclonic contraction: Myoklonus *m*.

myoclonic epilepsy: myoklonischer Anfall *m*, myoklonische Epilepsie *f*.

myoclonus/*n*: repeated, rapid and involuntary contraction spasms of short duration in a muscle or a muscle group. Myoclonus may occur as a sign in various neurologic disorders, for example certain forms of epilepsy. Myoklonus *m*.

myocutaneous flap: Hautmuskellappen *m*.

myofiber/*n*: Muskelfaser *f*.

myofibril/*n*: Myofibrille *f*.

myogenic/*adj*: myogen.

myogenic cell: Myoblast *m*.

myogenic paralysis: myogene Lähmung *f*.

myoglobin/*n*: Myoglobin *n*.

myoglobinuria/*n*: Myoglobinurie *f*.

myoma/*n*: benign neoplasm formed by muscular tissue. Forms include leiomyoma of smooth muscles, for example in the uterus, and rhabdomyoma of the striated muscles, for example in skeletal muscle. Myom *n*.

myomalacia/*n*: Myomalazie *f*.

myomectomy/*n*: Myomektomie *f*.

myometrium/*n*: Myometrium *n*.

myopathic face: Facies myopathica *f*, Sphinxgesicht *n*.

myopathic gait: myopathische Gangstörung *f*.

myopathic potential: myopathisches Muskelaktionspotential *n*.

myopathy/*n*: any disease of the muscles. Forms include muscular dystrophies, idiopathic myopathies, or any muscle disease resulting from metabolic, neurologic, or endocrine disorders. Myopathie *f*, Muskelerkrankung *f*.

myopia/*n*: ophthalmologic disorder in which distant objects produce blurred images, usually resulting from an abnormally long front-to-back diameter of the eye. Myopie *f*, Kurzsichtigkeit *f*.

myopic astigmatism: myoper Astigmatismus *m*.

myoplasty/*n*: Myoplastik *f*, Muskelplastik *f*.

myosarcoma/*n*: Myosarkom *n*.

myosin/*n*: Myosin *n*.

myositis/*n*: acute or chronic inflammation of one or more muscles, caused by bacteria like Staphylococcus, Streptococcus, or associated with skin disease like dermatomyositis. Myositis *f*, Muskelentzündung *f*.

myostatic/*adj*: myostatisch.

myostatic sensibility: Muskelpropriozeptivität *f*.

myotomy/*n*: Myotomie *f*.

myotonia/*n*: Myotonie *f*.

myotonic atrophy: Dystrophia myotonica *f*, Curschmann-Batten-Steinert-Syndrom *n*.

myotonic discharge: myotonische Entladung *f*.

myotonic dystrophy: Dystrophia myotonica *f*, Curschmann-Batten-Steinert-Syndrom *n*.

myotonic myopathy: myotonische Myopathie *f*, Curschmann-Batten-Steinert-Syndrom *n*.

myotonic pupil: Pupillotonie *f*.

myotony/*n*: Myotonie *f*.

myringa/*n*: Trommelfell *n*.

myringitis/*n*: inflammation of the eardrum, sometimes associated with the appearence of serous or hemorrhagic blebs on the membrana tympani. Myringitis *f*, Trommelfellentzündung *f*.

M

myringoplasty/*n*: Myringoplastik *f*.
myringotomy/*n*: Myringotomie *f*, Parazentese *f*.
myristic acid: Myristinsäure *f*.
myxedema/*n*: a condition which is characterized by coarse hair, dry, thickened skin, and goiter, resulting from a congenital or acquired deficiency or complete lack of thyroid hormone. Myxödem *n*.
myxedematous dementia: Kretinismus *m*.
myxedematous goiter: myxödematöse Struma *f*.
myxoid fibroma: Fibromyxom *n*.
myxoma/*n*: a tumor originating from undifferentiated cells of connective tissue, or embryonic cells. Forms include odontogenic myxoma of the jaw, and atrial myxoma of the heart. Myxom *n*.
myxomatous degeneration: mukoide Degeneration *f*.
myxosarcoma/*n*: Myxosarkom *n*.

N

N <*abbr*> **1. newton; 2. nitrogen**: 1. Newton, N; 2. Stickstoff *m*.
Naboth's follicles: Naboth-Eier.
nabumetone/*n*: Nabumeton *n*.
NAD <*abbr*> **1. nicotinamide adenine dinucleotide; 2. nothing abnormal detected**: 1. Nicotinamid-Adenin-Dinucleotid *n*, NAD; 2. ohne pathologischen Befund, o.B.
NADH <*abbr*> **reduced NAD**: reduziertes Nicotinamid-Adenin-Dinucleotid *n*, NADH.
nadifloxacin/*n*: Nadifloxacin *n*.
nadolol/*n*: Nadolol *n*.
NADP <*abbr*> **nicotinamide adenine dinucleotide phosphate**: Nicotinamid-Adenin-Dinucleotid-Phosphat *n*, NADP.
nafarelin acetate: Nafarelinacetat *n*.
nafcillin/*n*: Nafcillin *n*.
nafoxidine/*n*: Nafoxidin *n*.
naftalofos/*n*: Naftalofos *n*.
naftidrofuryl/*n*: Naftidrofuryl *n*.
nagging pain: nagender, bohrender Schmerz *m*.
nail/*n, vb*: 1. Nagel *m*; 2. nageln.
nail bed: Nagelbett *n*.
nail biting: Nägelkauen *n*, Onychophagie *f*.
nail file: Nagelfeile *f*.
nailing/*n*: Nageln *n*, Osteosynthese *f*.
nail plate: Nagelplatte *f*.
nail pulse: visible capillary pulsation under the nail bed. Nagelpuls *m*.
naked/*adj*: nackt.
nalbuphine/*n*: Nalbuphin *n*.
nalidixic acid: Nalidixinsäure *f*.
nalorphine/*n*: Nalorphin *n*, N-Allylnormorphin *n*.
naloxone/*n*: Naloxon *n*.
naltrexone/*n*: Naltrexon *n*.
name/*n*: Name *m*, Bezeichnung *f*.
nanism/*n*: Nanismus *m*, Zwergwuchs *m*.
nanous/*adj*: zwergwüchsig.
nape/*n*: Nacken *m*, Genick *n*.
naphazoline/*n*: Naphazolin *n*.
naphthalene/*n*: Naphthalin *n*.
naphthol/*n*: Naphthol *n*.
naphtholsulfonic acid: Naphtholsulfonsäure *f*.
naphthoquinone/*n*: Naphthochinon *n*.
naphthylaminosulfonic acid: Naphthylaminosulfonsäure *f*.
napkin/*n*: Windel *f*.
naproxen/*n*: Naproxen *n*.
naratriptan/*n*: Naratriptan *n*.
narcissism/*n*: Narzissmus *m*.
narcoanalysis/*n*: Narkoanalyse *f*.
narcolepsy/*n*: a condition which is characterized by periodic, short episodes of sleep any time during the day or the night, sometimes associated with diseases like epilepsy, or a brain tumor. Narkolepsie *f*, Gélineau-Syndrom *n*.
narcoleptic/*adj*: narkoleptisch.
narcosis/*n*: Narkose *f*, Betäubung *f*.
narcotic/*n, adj*: 1. Opiat *n*, Betäubungsmittel *n*, BtM; 2. narkotisch, betäubend.
narcotic receptor: Endorphinrezeptor *m*.
narcotine/*n*: Narcotin *n*, Noscapin *n*.
narrow/*vb, adj*: 1. verengen; 2. eng, schmal.
narrowing/*n*: Verengung *f*, Stenose *f*.
narrow-spectrum antibiotic: Schmalspektrum-Antibiotikum *n*.
nasal/*adj*: nasal.
nasal allergy: allergische Rhinitis *f*.
nasal calculus: Nasenstein *m*, Rhinolith *m*.

nasal cavity: Nasenhöhle *f.*
nasal drop: Nasentropfen.
nasal feeding: Nasensondenernährung *f.*
nasal fold: Nasenfalte *f.*
nasal fracture: breaking of the nasal septum, usually associated with fracture of nasal bone, and resulting in deformity of the nose, nosebleed, and impaired nasal respiration. Nasenscheidewandbruch *m.*
nasal furuncle: furuncle of the nose, characteristically originating from folliculitis or inflammation of sebaceous glands, and associated with the risk of ascending thrombophlebitis affecting the cavernous sinus. Nasenfurunkel *m.*
nasal hemianopia: nasale Hemianopsie *f.*
nasal hemorrhage: Nasenbluten *n*, Epistaxis *f.*
nasal polyp: excessive outgrowths from the mucous membranes of the nose, as pedunculated or sessile polyp. Symptoms include disturbances of nasal respiration, anosmia, hypersecretion, and headache. Nasenpolyp *m.*
nasal respiration: Nasenatmung *f.*
nasal septum: Nasenscheidewand *f.*
nasal sinus: Nasennebenhöhle *f.*
nasal speculum: Nasenspekulum *n.*
nasal vestibule: Nasenvorhof *m*, Vestibulum nasi *n.*
nasitis/*n*: Nasenentzündung *f*, Rhinitis *f.*
nasociliary/*adj*: nasoziliar.
nasogastric/*adj*: nasogastrisch.
nasolacrimal/*adj*: nasolakrimal.
nasopharyngeal/*adj*: nasopharyngeal.
nasopharyngeal carcinoma: malignant neoplasm in the nasopharyngeal region. Symptoms include rhinorrhea, nosebleed, and pain. Nasopharynxkarzinom *n.*
nasopharyngeal speculum: Nasopharyngealspekulum *n.*
nasopharyngoscopy/*n*: Nasopharyngoskopie *f*, Rhinopharyngoskopie *f.*
nasopharynx/*n*: Nasopharynx *m*, Nasenrachenraum *m.*
nasotracheal tube: Nasotrachealtubus *m.*
natality/*n*: Natalität *f*, Geburtenziffer *f.*
natality statistics: Geburtenstatistik *f.*
natalizumab/*n*: Natalizumab *n.*
natamycin/*n*: Natamycin *n.*
nateglinide/*n*: Nateglinid *n.*
native protein: Nativeiweiß *n.*
natremia/*n*: Natriämie *f.*
natural/*adj*: natürlich, nativ.
natural abortion: Spontanabort *m*, Fehlgeburt *f.*
natural contraception: natürliche Kontrazeption *f.*
natural frequency: Eigenfrequenz *f.*
natural history: Naturgeschichte *f*, natürlicher Verlauf *m.*
natural immunity: natürliche Immunität *f.*
nature/*n*: Natur *f*, Wesen *n.*
nausea/*n*: stomach discomfort with the feeling of a need to vomit, accompanied by contractions of pharyngeal, esophageal, and gastric musculature. Nausea *f*, Übelkeit *f*, Brechreiz *m.*
navel/*n*: Nabel *m.*
navicular/*adj*: navikulär, kahnförmig.
navicular abdomen: Kahnbauch *m.*
near/*adj*: nahe, benachbart.
near field: Nahfeld *n.*
near point: Nahpunkt *m.*
nearsightedness/*n*: an ophthalmologic disorder in which distant objects produce blurred images, usually resulting from an abnormally long front-to-back diameter of the eye. Kurzsichtigkeit *f*, Myopie *f.*
nebivolol/*n*: Nebivolol *n.*
nebramycin/*n*: Nebramycin *n.*
nebula/*n*: Nebelfleck *m.*
nebulizer/*n*: Vernebler *m.*
neck/*n*: Hals *m*, Nacken *m*, Zervix *f.*
neck of the femur: Oberschenkelhals *m.*
neck of the tooth: Zahnhals *m.*
neck phenomenon: Nackenzeichen *n*, Lhermitte-Zeichen *n.*
necrobiosis/*n*: Nekrobiose *f.*
necrogenic wart: Leichentuberkel *n.*

necropsy/*n*: Autopsie *f*, Leichenschau *f*.

necrose/*vb*: nekrotisieren.

necrosis/*n*: morphological changes resulting in death of a part of the body, an organ, or cells due to the absence of blood supply and enzymatic degradation. Nekrose *f*.

necrotic/*adj*: nekrotisch.

necrotizing angiitis: nekrotisierende Angiitis *f*.

necrotizing arteritis: nekrotisierende Arteriitis *f*, Panarteriitis nodosa *f*.

necrotizing enterocolitis: nekrotisierende Enterokolitis *f*.

necrotizing hemorrhagic encephalopathy: nekrotisierende hämorrhagische Enzephalopathie *f*, Wernicke-Enzephalopathie *f*.

necrotizing otitis: nekrotisierende Otitis media *f*.

necrotizing ulcerative gingivitis: nekrotisierende ulzerierende Gingivitis *f*.

nedocromil/*n*: Nedocromil *n*.

need/*n, vb*: 1. Bedürfnis *n*, Bedarf *m*; 2. benötigen, brauchen.

need for care: Pflegebedürftigkeit *f*.

needle/*n*: Nadel *f*.

needle aspiration biopsy: Nadelaspirationsbiopsie *f*.

needle holder: Nadelhalter *m*.

needlestick injury: Nadelstichverletzung *f*.

nefazodone/*n*: Nefazodon *n*.

nefopam/*n*: Nefopam *n*.

negation/*n*: Negation *f*, Verneinung *f*.

negative/*adj*: negativ.

negative end-expiratory pressure: negativer endexspiratorischer Beatmungsdruck *m*.

negative feedback: negative Rückkopplung *f*, Gegenkopplung *f*.

negative pressure: negativer Druck *m*, Unterdruck *m*.

negativism/*n*: Negativismus *m*.

negligence/*n*: Nachlässigkeit *f*, Fahrlässigkeit *f*.

nelfinavir/*n*: Nelfinavir *n*.

nematode/*n*: Nematode *f*, Fadenwurm *m*.

neodymium/*n*: Neodym *n*, Nd.

neoformation/*n*: Neubildung *f*.

neomycin/*n*: Neomycin *n*.

neonatal/*adj*: neonatal.

neonatal hepatitis: Neugeborenenhepatitis *f*.

neonatal hyperbilirubinemia: Neugeborenenhyperbilirubinämie *f*.

neonatal jaundice: icterus of the neonate, resulting from inability of the newborn to eliminate bilirubin. Severe forms may result in nuclear jaundice or kernicterus. Neugeborenenikterus *m*.

neonatal mortality: Neugeborenensterblichkeit *f*.

neonatal period: Neugeborenenperiode *f*.

neonatal screening: Neugeborenen-Screening *n*.

neonate/*n*: Neugeborenes *n*.

neonatology/*n*: Neonatologie *f*.

neoplasia/*n*: Neoplasie *f*.

neoplasm/*n*: abnormal, benign or malignant growth with formation of new cells or tissue, eventually with uncontrolled and progressive growth. Malignant neoplasms are characterized by a high degree of anaplasia and show invasive growth or metastatic spread. Neoplasma *n*.

neostigmine/*n*: Neostigmin *n*.

neovascular/*adj*: neovaskulär.

nephrectomy/*n*: Nephrektomie *f*.

nephritic/*adj*: nephritisch.

nephritic edema: nephrotisches Ödem *n*.

nephritis/*n*: acute or chronic, focal or diffuse inflammation of the kidneys, usually caused by bacteria. Glomeruli, tubules, and interstitial renal tissue may be involved. Nephritis *f*, Nierenentzündung *f*.

nephroblastoma/*n*: Nephroblastom *n*, Wilms-Tumor *m*.

nephrocalcinosis/*n*: Nephrokalzinose *f*.

nephrocapsulectomy/*n*: Nierendekapsulation *f*.

nephrogenous polycythemia: nephrogene Polyzythämie *f*, Forssel-Syndrom *n*.

nephrohydrosis/*n*: Hydronephrose *f*.

nephrolithiasis/*n*: formation of kidney stones or renal calculus, typically consisting of substances which are excreted by the kidneys, for example calcium, oxalate, urate, uric acid, or phosphates. Symptoms include acute pain, renal colic, dysuria, and eventually hematuria. Nephrolithiasis *f*.
nephrolithotomy/*n*: Nephrolithotomie *f*.
nephroma/*n*: a renal tumor of the outer portion of the kidney. Nephrom *n*, Nierentumor *m*.
nephron/*n*: Nephron *n*.
nephronic loop: Henle-Schleife *f*.
nephropathy/*n*: Nephropathie *f*, Nierenerkrankung *f*.
nephropexy/*n*: Nephropexie *f*.
nephroptosis/*n*: Nephroptose *f*, Wanderniere *f*.
nephropyelitic/*adj*: pyelonephritisch.
nephrosclerosis/*n*: Nierensklerose *f*.
nephrosis/*n*: Nephrose *f*, nephrotisches Syndrom *n*.
nephrostomy/*n*: Nephrostomie *f*.
nephrotic/*adj*: nephrotisch.
nephrotic syndrome: a condition that results from chronic kidney disorders such as diabetic glomerulosclerosis or renal amyloidosis and which is characterized by persistent marked proteinuria, which results in hypoalbuminemia, edema, and hypercholesterolemia. nephrotisches Syndrom *n*.
nephrotomography/*n*: Nephrotomographie *f*.
nephrotomy/*n*: Nephrotomie *f*.
nephrotoxicity/*n*: Nephrotoxizität *f*.
nephroureterectomy/*n*: Nephroureterektomie *f*.
nerve/*n*: Nerv *m*, Nervus *m*, N.
nerve action potential: Nervenaktionspotential *n*, NAP.
nerve block anesthesia: Leitungsanästhesie *f*.
nerve canal: Nervenkanal *m*.
nerve compression syndrome: any neuropathy in which a peripheral nerve is injured by compression through surrounding tissue, for example carpal tunnel syndrome, Morton's neuralgia, or tarsal tunnel syndrome. Nervenkompressionssyndrom *n*.
nerve conduction: Nervenleitung *f*.
nerve ending: Nervenendigung *f*.
nerve hillock: Axonhügel *m*.
nerve root irritation: irritation of a nerve root, especially of the root of a spinal nerve. Symptoms include pain and paresthesia and/or motor deficiencies in the innervation area. Wurzelirritationssyndrom *n*.
nerve tract: Nervenbahn *f*, Leitungsbahn *f*.
nervonic acid: Nervonsäure *f*.
nervous/*adj*: nervös, Nerven-.
nervous asthma: psychogenes Asthma *n*, nervöses Asthma *n*.
nervous bladder: Reizblase *f*.
nervous breakdown: Nervenzusammenbruch *m*.
nervous conduction: Nervenleitung *f*.
nervous function: Nervenfunktion *f*.
nervous impulse: Nervenimpuls *m*.
nervous system: Nervensystem *n*.
net/*n, adj*: 1. Netz *n*; 2. netto.
netilmycin/*n*: Netilmycin *n*.
nettle/*n*: Urtica *f*, Brennnessel *f*.
nettle rash: Nesselsucht *f*.
network/*n*: Netz *n*, Geflecht *n*, Netzwerk *n*.
neural/*adj*: neural.
neural canal: Neuralrinne *f*.
neural discharge: Neuronenentladung *f*.
neuralgia/*n*: a painful disorder of one or more nerves, usually characterized by sharp, fitful pains in the innervation area of the affected nerve. Causes include infections, metabolic or endocrine disorders, intoxication, injury, or nerve compression. Neuralgie *f*.
neuralgic amyotrophy: neuralgische Schulteramyotrophie *f*.
neuralgic headache: neuralgischer Kopfschmerz *m*.
neuralgic pain: Nervenschmerz *m*.
neural pattern: Innervationsmuster *n*.

N

neural therapy: Neuraltherapie *f*.
neural tube: Neuralrohr *n*.
neural-tube defect: a developmental disorder characterized by the failure of closure of the neural tube during the fourth week of the embryonal period, resulting in conditions such as cleft spine or spina bifida, or myelomeningocele. Neuralrohrdefekt *m*.
neuraminic acid: Neuraminsäure *f*.
neuraminidase/*n*: Neuraminidase *f*.
neurapraxia/*n*: Neurapraxie *f*.
neurasthenia/*n*: Neurasthenie *f*.
neurectomy/*n*: Neurektomie *f*.
neurilemma/*n*: Neurilemm *n*, Schwann-Scheide *f*.
neurinoma/*n*: Neurinom *n*.
neuritic/*adj*: neuritisch.
neuritis/*n*: inflammation of one or more nerves, usually causing a constant, burning pain. The skin is often reddened along the course of the affected nerve. Neuritis may be localized to one nerve or may involve several nerves. Causes include infections, injury, intoxication, or chilling. Neuritis *f*, Nervenentzündung *f*.
neuroblast/*n*: Neuroblast *m*.
neuroblastoma/*n*: a highly malignant tumor of the nervous system which is composed of immature nerve cells. Neuroblastoma typically occurs in children below the age of six, and originates in the adrenal medulla or ganglionic cells of the sympathetic nervous system. Neuroblastom *n*.
neurocirculatory asthenia: neurozirkulatorische Asthenie *f*, DaCosta-Syndrom *n*, Soldatenherz *n*.
neurodegenerative disorder: neurodegenerative Erkrankung.
neurodermatitis/*n*: Neurodermitis *f*, atopisches Ekzem *n*.
neuroepithelial tumor: Neuroepitheliom *n*.
neuroepithelium/*n*: Neuroepithel *n*.
neurofibroma/*n*: Neurofibrom *n*.
neurofibromatosis/*n*: Neurofibromatose *f*, Recklinghausen-Krankheit *f*.
neurogenic arthropathy: neurogene Arthropathie *f*, Charcot-Gelenk *n*.
neurogenic atrophy: neurogene Muskelatrophie *f*.
neurogenic bladder: neurogene Blase *f*.
neurogenic diabetes: neurogener Diabetes *m*.
neurogenic fever: zentrales Fieber *n*.
neurogenic hypertension: neurogener Hochdruck *m*, Entzügelungshochdruck *m*.
neurogenic paralysis: neurogene Lähmung *f*.
neurogenic shock: neurogener Schock *m*.
neuroglia/*n*: Neuroglia *f*.
neuroglioma/*n*: Neurogliom *n*.
neurohormone/*n*: Neurohormon *n*, Neurotransmitter *m*.
neuroleptic/*n*: Neuroleptikum *n*.
neuroleptic malignant syndrome: a neurologic condition which may result from the administration of certain neuroleptic drugs and which is characterized by an increase of body temperature and extrapyramidal symptoms like rigidity, involuntary movements, and facial dyskinesia. malignes Neuroleptikasyndrom *n*.
neurolinguistics/*n*: Neurolinguistik *f*.
neurolipid/*n*: Neurolipid *n*, Sphingolipid *n*.
neurologic deficit: neurologisches Defizit *n*.
neurologic examination: neurologische Untersuchung *f*.
neurologic symptom: neurologisches Symptom *n*.
neurology/*n*: Neurologie *f*.
neurolysis/*n*: Neurolyse *f*.
neuroma/*n*: a tumor originating from a nerve or composed of neural tissue. Forms include congenital neuroma, and neuroma developing in later life, for example following nerve injury, or resulting from hyperplasia of nerve fibers. Neurom *n*.
neuromuscular/*adj*: neuromuskulär.
neuromuscular block: neuromuskulärer Block *m*.

neuromuscular junction: motorische Endplatte *f*.
neuron/*n*: Neuron *n*, Nervenzelle *f*.
neuro-otology/*n*: Otoneurologie *f*.
neuroparalytic/*adj*: neuroparalytisch.
neuroparalytic keratitis: Keratitis neuroparalytica *f*.
neuropathic/*adj*: neuropathisch.
neuropathology/*n*: Neuropathologie *f*.
neuropathy/*n*: any disease of the peripheral or central nervous system. Historically, this term also referred to emotional disorders such as neurasthenia or neurosis. Neuropathie *f*.
neuroplasty/*n*: Nervenplastik *f*.
neuropsychiatry/*n*: Neuropsychiatrie *f*.
neuropsychology/*n*: Neuropsychologie *f*.
neurorrhaphy/*n*: Neurorrhaphie *f*, Nervennaht *f*.
neurosecretory cell: neurosekretorische Zelle *f*.
neurosensory cell: neurosensorische Zelle *f*.
neurosis/*n*: Neurose *f*.
neurosurgery/*n*: Neurochirurgie *f*.
neurosyphilis/*n*: syphilis which affects the central nervous system, usually occurring many months to years after primary infection. Forms include tabes dorsalis, and generalized paresis. Neurosyphilis *f*.
neurotendinous organ: Sehnenorgan *n*.
neurotic/*n, adj*: 1. Neurotiker; 2. neurotisch, Nerven-.
neurotic disorder: Neurose *f*.
neurotmesis/*n*: Neurotmesis *f*.
neurotomy/*n*: Neurotomie *f*.
neurotransmitter/*n*: Neurotransmitter *m*.
neurotrauma/*n*: Nervenverletzung *f*, traumatische Nervenläsion *f*.
neurovisceral lipoidosis: neuroviszerale Lipoidose *f*, Gangliosidose G_{M1} *f*.
neutral/*adj*: neutral.
neutral fat: Neutralfett *n*.
neutralize/*vb*: neutralisieren.
neutralizing antibody: neutralisierender Antikörper *m*.
neutrocclusion/*n*: Neutralbiss *m*.
neutropenia/*n*: Neutropenie *f*, Neutrozytopenie *f*.
neutrophil granules: neutrophile Granula.
neutrophil granulocyte: neutrophiler Granulozyt *m*, Neutrophiler *m*.
neutrophilic/*adj*: neutrophil.
nevirapine/*n*: Nevirapin *n*.
nevoid amentia: Sturge-Weber-Krabbe-Syndrom *n*.
nevus/*n*: a congenital malformation with benign growths on the skin. Forms include pigmented nevus with a characteristic brown color and patches in form of a lentil, and vascular nevus or angioma, consisting of proliferation of blood vessels. Flat, dark moles without hairs which are located in areas that receive constant friction have a tendency to become malignant. Nävus *m*, Muttermal *n*.
nevus-cell nevus: Nävuszellnävus *m*.
newborn/*n, adj*: 1. Neugeborenes *n*; 2. neugeboren.
newborn jaundice: icterus of the neonate, resulting from inability of the newborn to eliminate bilirubin. Severe forms may result in nuclear jaundice or kernicterus. Neugeborenenikterus *m*.
new brain: Neenzephalon *n*.
next-to-end: endständig.
niacin/*n*: Niacin *n*, Nicotinsäure *f*.
niacinamide/*n*: Niacinamid *n*, Nicotinamid *n*.
nicardipine/*n*: Nicardipin *n*.
nicergoline/*n*: Nicergolin *n*.
niche/*n*: Nische *f*, Höhle *f*.
nick/*n, vb*: 1. Schnitt *m*, Kerbe *f*; 2. anschneiden.
niclofolan/*n*: Niclofolan *n*.
nicofuranose/*n*: Nicofuranose *f*.
nicotine/*n*: Nikotin *n*, Nicotin *n*.
nicotine effect: nikotinartige Wirkung *f*.
nicotinic acid: Nicotinsäure *f*.
nicotinic action: nikotinartige Wirkung *f*.

N

nicotinic receptor: nikotinartiger Rezeptor *m*.
nictitating spasm: Spasmus nictitans *m*, Blinzelkrampf *m*, Blepharospasmus *m*.
nictation/*n*: Niktation *f*, Blinzeln *n*.
nidation/*n*: Nidation *f*, Einnistung *f*.
nifedipine/*n*: Nifedipin *n*.
nifenalol/*n*: Nifenalol *n*.
nifenazone/*n*: Nifenazon *n*.
niflumid acid: Nifluminsäure *f*.
nifuratel/*n*: Nifuratel *n*.
nifuroxazide/*n*: Nifuroxazid *n*.
nifurprazin/*n*: Nifurprazin *n*.
night/*n*: Nacht *f*.
night blindness: the inability to see at night or in a low-light environment, resulting from a deficiency of rhodopsin and consecutive malfunctioning of the rods in the retina. Nachtblindheit *f*, Nyktalopie *f*.
night clinic: Nachtklinik *f*.
nightmare/*n*: Alptraum *m*.
night sweat: Nachtschweiß *m*.
night terrors: Pavor nocturnus *m*, Nachtangst *f*.
night walking: walking around during a dreamy state or sleep. Actions and movements during this period are not remembered by the somnambulist. Sleep-wake schedule disorders and postencephalitic lesions are discussed as possibly underlying causes. Schlafwandeln *n*, Somnambulismus *m*.
night watch: Nachtwache *f*.
nilutamide/*n*: Nilutamid *n*.
nilvadipine/*n*: Nilvadipin *n*.
nimodipine/*n*: Nimodipin *n*.
nimorazole/*n*: Nimorazol *n*.
nimustine/*n*: Nimustin *n*.
nipple/*n*: Mamille *f*, Brustwarze *f*, Sauger *m*.
nipple shield: Brustwarzenhütchen *n*.
niridazole/*n*: Niridazol *n*.
nisbuterol/*n*: Nisbuterol *n*.
nisoldipine/*n*: Nisoldipin *n*.
nit/*n*: Nisse *f*.
nitisinone/*n*: Nitisinon *n*.
nitrate/*n*: Nitrat *n*.
nitrefazole/*n*: Nitrefazol *n*.
nitrendipine/*n*: Nitrendipin *n*.
nitric acid: Salpetersäure *f*.
nitric oxide: Stickstoffmonoxid *n*.
nitrofural/*n*: Nitrofural *n*, Nitrofurazon *n*.
nitrofuran/*n*: Nitrofuran *n*.
nitrofurantoin/*n*: Nitrofurantoin *n*.
nitrofurazone/*n*: Nitrofurazon *n*, Nitrofural *n*.
nitrogen/*n*: Stickstoff *m*.
nitroglycerin/*n*: Nitroglycerin *n*.
nitroglycerol/*n*: Nitroglycerin *n*.
nitroprusside/*n*: Nitroprussid *n*.
nitrous acid: salpetrige Säure *f*.
nitrous oxide: Lachgas *n*, Stickoxidul *n*.
nitroxinile/*n*: Nitroxinil *n*.
nitroxoline/*n*: Nitroxolin *n*.
nizatidine/*n*: Nizatidin *n*.
nociception/*n*: Nozizeption *f*, Schmerzwahrnehmung *f*.
nociceptive reflex: Schmerzreflex *m*.
nocturia/*n*: increase in the frequency of urination at night, usually occurring as a symptom in benign prostatic hyperplasia, renal failure, or cardiac insufficiency. Nykturie *f*, nächtliches Wasserlassen *n*.
nocturnal/*adj*: nächtlich.
nocturnal epilepsy: Schlafepilepsie *f*, Epilepsia nocturna *f*.
nocturnal hemoglobinuria: Marchiafava Anämie *f*, paroxysmale nächtliche Hämoglobinurie *f*.
nocturnal penile tumescence: nächtliche Spontanerektion *f*.
nodal arrhythmia: AV-Knoten-Arrhythmie *f*.
nodal escape: Knotenersatzrhythmus *m*.
nodal rhythm: Knotenrhythmus *m*, AV-Rhythmus *m*.
nodal tachycardia: AV-Knoten-Tachykardie *f*.
nodding spasm: Nickkrampf *m*, Blitz-Nick-Salaam-Krämpfe.
node/*n*: Knoten *m*.
nodose rheumatism: Rheumatismus nodosus *m*.
nodular amyloidosis: noduläre Amyloidose *f*.
nodular circumscribed lipomatosis: Madelung-Fetthals *m*.

nodular elastosis of the skin: noduläre Elastose der Haut.
nodular goiter: Struma nodularis *f*, Knotenstruma *f*.
nodular liver cirrhosis: noduläre Leberzirrhose *f*.
nodular lymphoid hyperplasia: noduläre Lymphknotenhyperplasie *f*.
nodule/*n*: Knötchen *n*.
noise/*n*: Geräusch *n*, Lärm *m*.
noise apparatus: Bárány-Lärmtrommel *f*.
noise-induced hearing loss: Lärmschwerhörigkeit *f*.
noise pollution: Lärmbelastung *f*.
noma/*n*: an ulceromembranous gangrene of the mouth found predominantly in children with cachexia, malnutrition, or wasting infectious diseases. Noma *f*, Wasserkrebs *m*.
nomifensine/*n*: Nomifensin *n*.
nonarticular rheumatism: extraartikulärer Rheumatismus *m*.
noncommunicating hydrocephalus: nicht kommunizierender Hydrozephalus *m*, Hydrocephalus occlusus *m*.
noncompetitive inhibition: nichtkompetitive Hemmung *f*.
noncompliance with medical treatment: Nichtbefolgen der ärztlichen Behandlungsmaßnahmen, Noncompliance *f*.
nondominant hemisphere: inferiore Hemisphäre *f*.
noneffective/*adj*: unwirksam.
nonesterified fatty acid: unveresterte Fettsäure *f*.
nongonococcal urethritis: nichtgonorrhoische Urethritis *f*.
non-Hodgkin lymphoma: Non-Hodgkin-Lymphom *n*.
noninflammatory arthritis: any degenerative disease of a joint, usually affecting the joint cartilage. Symptoms include pain, aches, and impairment of function. Arthrose *f*.
noninvasive/*adj*: nichtinvasiv.
noninvasive growth: nichtinvasives Wachstum *n*.
non-ionizing radiation: nichtionisierende Strahlung *f*.
nonmedullated fiber: marklose Faser *f*.
nonobstructive hypertrophic cardiomyopathy: nichtobstruktive Kardiomyopathie *f*.
nonossifying fibroma: nichtossifizierendes Fibrom *n*.
nonoxynol-9/*n*: Nonoxinol 9 *n*.
nonpitting edema: wegdrückbares Ödem *n*.
nonproductive cough: unproduktiver Husten *m*.
nonrenal azotemia: extrarenale Azotämie *f*, Produktionsazotämie *f*.
nonrespiratory alkalosis: metabolische Alkalose *f*.
nonsense syndrome: a dissociative disorder which is characterized by psychological symptoms such as the inability to do anything correctly. Ganser-Syndrom *n*, Scheinblödsinn *m*.
nonsexual generation: ungeschlechtliche Fortpflanzung *f*.
nonspecific stimulation: unspezifischer Reiz *m*.
nonspecific therapy: unspezifische Therapie *f*.
nonspecific urethritis: unspezifische Urethritis *f*.
nonsteroidal anti-inflammatory agents: nichtsteroidale Antiphlogistika.
non-ulcer dyspepsia: nichtulzeröse Dyspepsie *f*.
norepinephrine/*n*: Norepinephrin *n*, Noradrenalin *n*.
norethisterone/*n*: Norethisteron *n*.
norfenefrine/*n*: Norfenefrin *n*.
norfloxacin/*n*: Norfloxacin *n*.
norfluoxetine/*n*: Norfluoxetin *n*.
norgesterone/*n*: Norgesteron *n*.
norgestrel/*n*: Norgestrel *n*.
norlevorphanol/*n*: Norlevorphanol *n*.
norm/*n*: Norm *f*, Standard *m*.
normal/*n, adj*: 1. Normalperson *f*; 2. normal.
normal aciditiy: Normazidität *f*.
normal breathing: Normalatmung *f*.
normalization/*n*: Normalisierung *f*.
normal-pressure hydrocephalus: normotensiver Hydrozephalus *m*.

normal range: Referenzbereich *m*, Normalbereich *m*.
normal rhythm: Normorhythmie *f*.
normal temperature: normale Temperatur *f*.
normal value: Normalwert *m*.
normal vision: Normalsichtigkeit *f*, Emmetropie *f*.
normoblast/*n*: Normoblast *m*.
normochromic anemia: normochrome Anämie *f*.
normocyte/*n*: Normozyt *m*.
normocytic anemia: normozytäre Anämie *f*.
normokalemic periodic paralysis: normokaliämische periodische Lähmung *f*.
nortestosterone/*n*: Nortestosteron *n*.
North American blastomycosis: nordamerikanische Blastomykose *f*, Gilchrist-Krankheit *f*.
nortriptyline/*n*: Nortriptylin *n*.
Norwegian scabies: Scabies norvegica *f*, Boeck-Skabies *f*.
noscapine/*n*: Noscapin *n*, Narcotin *n*.
nose/*n*: Nase *f*.
nosebleed/*n*: hemorrhage from the nasal mucosa, mostly in the nasal septum. Causes include injury, arterial hypertension, blood coagulation disorders, leukemia, or acute infections; in many cases epistaxis occurs without evident cause as idiopathic nosebleed. Nasenbluten *n*, Epistaxis *f*.
nose drops: Nasentropfen.
nosocomial/*adj*: nosokomial.
nosocomial infection: nosokomiale Infektion *f*, Krankenhausinfektion *f*.
nosology/*n*: Nosologie *f*, Krankheitslehre *f*.
nosophobia/*n*: Nosophobie *f*.
nostril/*n*: Nasenloch *n*.
notch/*n*: Kerbe *f*, Einschnitt *m*, Incisura *f*.
noticeable/*adj*: wahrnehmbar, merklich.
notifiable disease: meldepflichtige Krankheit *f*.
notification/*n*: Meldung *f*, Anzeige *f*.
novobiocin/*n*: Novobiocin *n*.
noxious/*adj*: schädlich.
noxious agent: Noxe *f*.
noxiptiline/*n*: Noxiptilin *n*.
nozzle loop reactor: Umlaufdüsenreaktor *m*.
NSAIA <*abbr*> **non-steroidal anti-inflammatory agents**: nichtsteroidale Antiphlogistika.
nuchal region: Nackenregion *f*.
nuchal rigidity: Nackensteife *f*.
nuclear/*adj*: nukleär.
nuclear aplasia: Kernaplasie *f*, Moebius-Syndrom *n*.
nuclear bag: Kernhülle *f*.
nuclear cataract: Kernstar *m*.
nuclear division: Kernteilung *f*.
nuclear dysplasia: Kerndysplasie *f*.
nuclear fusion: Kernfusion *f*.
nuclear jaundice: an icterus of the cerebral, cerebellar, and bulbar nuclei, characterized by severe neurologic symptoms. Nuclear jaundice or kernicterus is caused by high levels of bilirubin in the blood of neonates, for example in hemolytic disease of newborn. Kernikterus *m*.
nuclear magnetic resonance: Kernspinresonanz *f*, NMR.
nuclear medicine: Nuklearmedizin *f*.
nuclear ophthalmoplegia: Kernlähmung *f*, Graefe-Moebius-Syndrom *n*.
nuclear particle: Kernrest *m*, Howell-Jolly-Körperchen *n*.
nuclear radiology: Nuklearmedizin *f*.
nuclear resonance: Kernresonanz *f*.
nuclear segmentation: Kernsegmentierung *f*.
nuclear zone: Kernzone *f*.
nucleated cell: kernhaltige Zelle *f*.
nucleic acid: Nukleinsäure *f*.
nucleocapsid/*n*: Nukleokapsid *n*.
nucleolus/*n*: Nukleolus *m*, Kernkörperchen *n*.
nucleoprotein/*n*: Nukleoprotein *n*.
nucleoside/*n*: Nukleosid *n*.
nucleoside analogue: Nukleosidanalogon *n*.
nucleotide/*n*: Nukleotid *n*.
nucleotide analogue: Nukleotidanalogon *n*.
nucleus/*n*: Kern *m*.
nuclide/*n*: Nuklid *n*.

N

nude/*adj*: nackt.
null hypothesis: Nullhypothese *f*.
numb/*adj*: taub, gefühllos.
number/*n*: Zahl *f*, Anzahl *f*, Nummer *f*.
numbness/*n*: a condition in which an area of the body surface is insensitive when touched or otherwise stimulated. Numbness can be caused for example by various diseases, mulfunctioning of body parts, or nerve disorders, or can be artificially induced to relieve existing pain or to prevent pain by anesthesia. Taubheitsgefühl *n*, Gefühllosigkeit *f*.
numeric/*adj*: numerisch.
numerous/*adj*: zahlreich.
nummular eczema: nummuläres Ekzem *n*.
nummulation/*n*: Geldrollenbildung *f*.
nurse/*n, vb*: 1. Krankenschwester *f*; 2. pflegen, verpflegen.
nurses' aide: Krankenpflegehelfer *m*, Krankenpflegehelferin *f*.
nursing/*n*: Krankenpflege *f*, Pflege *f*, Säugen *n*.
nursing care: Pflege *f*, Krankenpflege *f*.
nursing home: Pflegeheim *n*.
nursing profession: Pflegeberuf *m*.
nursing staff: Pflegepersonal *n*.
nurture/*n, vb*: 1. Ernährung *f*, Pflege *f*, Erziehung *f*; 2. ernähren, pflegen.
nutation/*n*: Nickbewegung *f*, Kopfwackeln *n*.
nutrient/*n, adj*: 1. Nährstoff *m*, Nahrungsstoff *m*; 2. nährend.
nutrient culture medium: Nährboden *m*.
nutriment/*n*: Nahrung *f*, Nahrungsmittel *n*.
nutrition/*n*: Ernährung *f*, Alimentation *f*.
nutritional/*adj*: alimentär.
nutritional availability: Nährwert *m*.
nutritional component: Nährstoffbestandteil *m*.
nutritional deficiency: ernährungsbedingter Mangel *m*.
nutritional dropsy: a condition which is characterized by the presence of generalized edema or dropsy, resulting from protein deficiency in chronically malnourished persons. Hungerödem *n*.
nutritional status: Ernährungszustand *m*.
nutritional value: Nährwert *m*.
nutritionist/*n*: Ernährungswissenschaftler *m*.
nyctalopia/*n*: the inability to see at night or in a low-light environment, resulting from a deficiency of rhodopsin and consecutive malfunctioning of the rods in the retina. Nyktalopie *f*, Nachtblindheit *f*.
nymphomania/*n*: Nymphomanie *f*, Mannstollheit *f*.
nystagmography/*n*: Nystagmographie *f*.
nystagmus/*n*: Nystagmus *m*.
nystagmus goggles: Nystagmusbrille *f*.
nystatin/*n*: Nystatin *n*.

O

O <*abbr*> **oxygen**/*n*: Sauerstoff *m*, O.
oat cell carcinoma: Oat-cell-Karzinom *n*, kleinzelliges Bronchialkarzinom *n*.
obese/*adj*: adipös, übergewichtig.
obesity/*n*: a condition which is characterized by an excess of fat tissue in relation to other body components, and an increase of twentyfive percent or more over normal weight. Obesity or adiposity is typically resulting from a persistent caloric intake that exceeds the energy needs of the body. Causative factors may include constitutional and/or metabolic or endocrine factors, but frequently emotional, cultural, or dietary influences, and lack of physical exercise are the main causes. Obesität *f*, Fettsucht *f*, Übergewicht *n*.
OB-GYN <*abbr*> **obstetrics-gynecology**: Gynäkologie und Geburtshilfe.
object/*n*: Objekt *n*.
object attachment: Objektbindung *f*.
objective/*n, adj*: 1. Ziel *n*, Objektiv *n*; 2. objektiv.
objective symptom: objektives Symptom *n*.
objective vertigo: Drehschwindel *m*.
obligate anaerobe: obligater Anaerobier *m*.
obligate parasite: obligater Parasit *m*.
obligation to treatment: Behandlungspflicht *f*.
oblique/*adj*: schräg, schief.
oblique bandage: Schrägverband *m*.
oblique contracted pelvis: schräg verengtes Becken *n*.
oblique fracture: Querbruch *m*.
oblique presentation: in obstetrics, the position of the fetus when its long body axis crosses the long axis of the maternal body. Usually, the shoulder or an arm presents first. Schräglage *f*.
obliterating endarteritis: Endarteriitis obliterans *f*.
obliteration/*n*: Obliteration *f*.
obsession/*n*: Obsession *f*, Zwangsvorstellung *f*.
obsessional washing: Waschzwang *m*.
obsessive compulsive disorder: Zwangssyndrom *n*.
obsolete/*adj*: obsolet.
obstetric/*adj*: geburtshilflich.
obstetrical conjugate: Conjugata vera obstetrica *f*.
obstetrical forceps: Geburtszange *f*.
obstetrical paralysis: Geburtslähmung *f*.
obstetric complication: Geburtskomplikation *f*.
obstetrician/*n*: Geburtshelfer *m*.
obstetric lever: Geburtslöffel *m*.
obstetrics: Obstetrik *f*, Geburtshilfe *f*.
obstipation/*n*: Obstipation *f*.
obstruction/*n*: Obstruktion *f*, Hindernis *n*.
obstructive anuria: Harnsperre *f*.
obstructive atelectasis: Obstruktionsatelektase *f*.
obstructive emphysema: obstruktives Emphysem *n*.
obstructive hypertrophic cardiomyopathy: obstruktive hypertrophe Kardiomyopathie *f*.
obstructive jaundice: Obstruktionsikterus *m*, Verschlussikterus *m*.
obstructive pneumonia: Obstruktionspneumonie *f*.
obturator/*n*: Obturator *m*, Musculus obturatorius *m*.
obtuse/*adj*: stumpf.

occipital/*adj*: okzipital.
occipital point: Okzipitalpunkt *m*.
occiput presentation: in obstetrics, the position of the fetus where the posterior part of the head presents first and appears first in the uterine cervix. Hinterhauptslage *f*.
occlusal/*adj*: okklusal.
occlusal force: Okklusionskraft *f*.
occlusal pattern: Gebissschema *n*.
occlusion/*n*: Okklusion *f*, Verschluss *m*, Schlussbiss *m*.
occlusive/*adj*: okklusiv.
occlusive bandage: Okklusivverband *m*.
occlusive disease: a condition which is characterized by an occlusion of peripheral blood vessels, resulting in reduced blood supply. Causes include arteriosclerosis, diabetic angiopathy, and inflammatory diseases. Symptoms include alterations of the arterial pulse, decreased skin temperature, trophic disturbances, dysesthesia, and pain. Verschlusskrankheit *f*.
occlusive dressing: Okklusivverband *m*.
occlusive ileus: Okklusionsileus *m*, Verschlussileus *m*.
occlusive thrombus: Verschlussthrombus *m*.
occult/*adj*: okkult.
occult bleeding: okkulte Blutung *f*.
occult blood: okkultes Blut *n*.
occult carcinoma: okkultes Karzinom *n*.
occult fracture: okkulte Fraktur *f*.
occult hydrocephalus: asymptomatischer Hydrozephalus *m*.
occult immunization: stille Feiung *f*.
occupancy/*n*: Okkupanz *f*, Belegung *f*.
occupation/*n*: Beruf *m*.
occupational/*adj*: beruflich.
occupational accident: Arbeitsunfall *m*.
occupational cataract: berufsbedingte Katarakt *f*.
occupational dermatosis: Berufsdermatose *f*.
occupational disease: Berufskrankheit *f*, BK.
occupational eczema: Berufsdermatose *f*.
occupational exposure: berufliche Exposition *f*.
occupational injury: Arbeitsunfall *m*.
occupational medicine: Arbeitsmedizin *f*.
occupational therapy: Arbeitstherapie *f*, Beschäftigungstherapie *f*.
occurrence/*n*: Vorkommen *n*, Auftreten *n*.
octadecanoic acid: Octadecansäure *f*, Stearinsäure *f*.
octreotide/*n*: Octreotid *n*.
ocular/*n, adj*: 1. Okular *n*; 2. okulär.
ocular hypertension: Augeninnendruckerhöhung *f*.
ocular muscular dystrophy: Augenmuskeldystrophie *f*.
ocular nystagmus: okulärer Nystagmus *m*.
ocular palsy: Augenmuskellähmung *f*.
oculist/*n*: Augenarzt *m*.
oculoauriculovertebral syndrome: a dysplastic syndrome which is characterized by facial hypoplasia, anomalies of the ear with conductive deafness, skin appendages, and vertebral hypoplasia. okuloaurikuläres Syndrom *n*, Goldenhar-Syndrom *n*.
oculocardiac reflex: okulokardialer Reflex *m*, Bulbusreflex *m*.
oculocephalic reflex: okulozephaler Reflex *m*, Puppenaugenphänomen *n*.
oculocerebrorenal syndrome: an X-linked recessive syndrome which is characterized by metabolic disorders and hyperaminoaciduria, congenital cataract, glaucoma, craniofacial anomalies, hypotonia, and mental retardation. okulozerebrorenales Syndrom *n*, Lowe-Syndrom *n*.
oculocutaneous syndrome: a syndrome of unknown origin that occurs mainly at the age of 30 to 50 years and which is characterized by cranial nerve palsy, nuchal rigidity, iridocyclitis, uveitis, and discoloration of the skin, vitiligo, and alopecia. Vogt-Koyanagi-Syndrom *n*.

oculo-dentodigital dysplasia: an autosomal dominant syndrome which is characterized by facial dysplasia with hypertelorism, thin nose, microphthalmia, and skeletal dysplasia. okulodentodigitales Syndrom *n*, ODD-Syndrom *n*.
oculoglandular syndrome: a syndrome which is characterized by unilateral granulomatous conjunctivitis and swelling of submandibular and preauricular lymph nodes. Causes include various infectious diseases, for example lymphogranuloma venereum, syphilis, tularemia, tuberculosis, cat-scratch disease, and sporotrichosis. okuloglanduläres Syndrom *n*, Parinaud-Konjunktivitis *f*.
oculogyric crisis: okulogyre Krise *f*, Blickkrampf *m*.
oculogyric spasm: okulogyre Lähmung *f*.
oculomotor/*adj*: okulomotorisch.
oculomotor apraxia: okulomotorische Apraxie, Cogan-Syndrom *n*.
oculomotor hemiplegia: Hemiplegia alternans oculomotoria *f*, Weber-Syndrom *n*.
oculovestibuloauditory syndrome: a syndrome of unknown origin which is characterized by parenchymatous keratitis, conductive hearing loss, vertigo and tinnitus. Cogan-Syndrom *n*.
ocytocin/*n*: Oxytocin *n*.
odd/*adj*: ungerade.
odontalgia/*n*: Odontalgie *f*, Zahnschmerz *m*.
odontoameloblastoma/*n*: Odontoameloblastom *n*.
odontogenic fibroma: odontogenes Fibrom *n*.
odontology/*n*: Odontologie *f*, Zahnheilkunde *f*.
odontoma/*n*: a benign neoplasm of odontogenic origin which develops from the same tissue from which teeth are formed. Odontom *n*.
odor/*n*: Odor *m*, Geruch *m*.
odorless/*adj*: geruchslos, geruchsfrei.
oenanthylic acid: Önanthensäure *f*.
office/*n*: Praxis *f*, Büro *n*.
officinal/*n, adj*: 1. offizinelles Arzneimittel *n*; 2. offizinell.
off-position/*n*: Nullstellung *f*, Aus-Stellung *f*.
ofloxacin/*n*: Ofloxacin *n*.
Ogino-Knaus method: Knaus-Ogino-Methode *f*, Kalendermethode *f*.
oil/*n*: Öl *n*.
oil-aspiration pneumonia: Ölpneumonie *f*, Pneumolipidose *f*.
oil immersion: Ölimmersion *f*.
ointment/*n*: Salbe *f*, Unguentum *n*.
olanzapine/*n*: Olanzapin *n*.
old/*adj*: alt.
old age: hohes Alter *n*, Senium *n*.
old brain: Urhirn *n*, Palaeoencephalon *n*.
old sight: Alterssichtigkeit *f*, Presbyopie *f*.
old tuberculin: Alttuberkulin *n*.
oleandomycin/*n*: Oleandomycin *n*.
olecranon/*n*: Olekranon *n*.
olefinic acid: Olefinsäure *f*.
oleic acid: Ölsäure *f*.
olfactive hallucination: Geruchshalluzination *f*.
olfactometry/*n*: Olfaktometrie *f*.
olfactory/*adj*: olfaktorisch.
olfactory area: Riechzentrum *n*.
olfactory bundle: Riechbahn *f*, Tractus olfactorius *m*.
olfactory cell: Riechzelle *f*.
olfactory center: Riechzentrum *n*.
olfactory cortex: olfaktorischer Kortex *m*.
olfactory fiber: Riechnerv *m*, Nervus olfactorius *m*.
olfactory genital dysplasia: olfaktogenitales Syndrom *n*, Kallmann-Syndrom *n*.
olfactory nerve: Riechnerv *m*, Nervus olfactorius *m*.
olfactory neuroepithelium: Riechepithel *n*.
olfactory threshold: Geruchsschwelle *f*.
oligemic shock: hypovolämischer Schock *m*.
oligodendroglial cell: Oligodendroglia *f*.
oligodendroglioma/*n*: Oligodendrogliom *n*.

O

oligomenorrhea/*n*: disturbances of the menstruation with abnormally prolonged intervals of menstrual flow, usually caused by ovarian failure. Oligomenorrhö *f*.
oligospermia/*n*: Oligospermie *f*.
oligotrichy/*n*: Oligotrichie *f*.
oliguria/*n*: decreased amount of urine production with less than 500 ml of urine over a period of 24 hours. Causes include fluid loss, renal failure, or obstruction of the urinary tract. Oligurie *f*.
olivopontocerebellar atrophy: olivopontozerebelläre Atrophie *f*, Déjerine-Thomas-Syndrom *n*.
olmesartan/*n*: Olmesartan *n*.
olopatadine/*n*: Olopatadin *n*.
olsalazine/*n*: Olsalazin *n*.
omalizumab/*n*: Omalizumab *n*.
omental cyst: Omentumzyste *f*.
omentitis/*n*: Omentitis *f*.
omentopexy/*n*: Omentopexie *f*.
omentum/*n*: Omentum *n*, Netz *n*.
omeprazole/*n*: Omeprazol *n*.
omphalic/*adj*: umbilikal.
omphalitis/*n*: inflammation of the umbilicus. Omphalitis *f*, Nabelentzündung *f*.
omphalocele/*n*: Omphalozele *f*, Nabelschnurbruch *m*.
on call: Rufbereitschaft *f*.
once a day: einmal täglich.
oncocytic adenoma: onkozytäres Adenom *n*, Hürthle-Zelladenom *n*.
oncocytic carcinoma: a malignant neoplasm which is composed by oncocytes. It is most frequently found in the thyroid and parathyroid gland, in the pituitary gland, and in salivary glands. Onkozytom *n*.
oncofetal antigen: onkofetales Antigen *n*.
oncogenic virus: onkogenes Virus *n*.
oncology/*n*: Onkologie *f*.
ondansetron/*n*: Ondansetron *n*.
on-demand: On-Demand, auf Verlangen.
one-sided/*adj*: einseitig.
one-sided chorea: Hemichorea *f*.
onion scale lesion: zwiebelschalenartige Läsion *f*.
on-off: On-off-, intermittierend.
onset/*n*: Beginn *m*, Ausbruch *m*.
ontogenesis/*n*: Ontogenese *f*.
onychia/*n*: Onychie *f*.
onychodystrophy/*n*: Onychodystrophie *f*.
onychogryposis/*n*: Onychogrypose *f*.
onychomycosis/*n*: a mycosis or tinea involving the nails of finger and/or toes. Symptoms include dyschromasia of nails, hyperkeratosis beneath the nail plate, and separation of the nail plate from the nail bed. Onychomykose *f*, Nagelmykose *f*.
oocyst/*n*: Oozyste *f*.
oocyte/*n*: Oozyt *m*, Ovozyt *m*.
oogenesis/*n*: Oogenese *f*.
oophorectomy/*n*: Oophorektomie *f*.
oophoritis/*n*: inflammation of an ovary, usually following salpingitis. The formation of an ovarian abscess may occasionally occur. Oophoritis *f*.
oophoron/*n*: Oophoron *n*, Ovar *n*.
oophorosalpingectomy/*n*: Oophorosalpingektomie *f*.
ootomy/*n*: Ootomie *f*.
ooze/*vb*: sickern, durchsickern.
oozing hemorrhage: Sickerblutung *f*.
opacity/*n*: Opazität *f*, Undurchsichtigkeit *f*.
opaque/*adj*: opak, undurchsichtig.
opaque catheter: schattengebender Katheter *m*.
opaque meal: Kontrastmittelbreimahlzeit *f*.
open-angle glaucoma: Weitwinkelglaukom *n*.
open biopsy: offene Biopsie *f*.
open dislocation: offene Luxation *f*.
open fracture: offener Bruch *m*.
opening/*n*: Öffnung *f*, Orifizium *n*.
open operation: offener Eingriff *m*.
open pneumothorax: offener Pneumothorax *m*.
open reduction: offene Reposition *f*.
open tenotomy: offene Tenotomie *f*.
open tuberculosis: offene Tuberkulose *f*.
operating room: Operationssaal *m*, OP.
operation/*n*: Operation *f*, Bedienung *f*.

operative ankylosis: Arthrodese *f*.
operative cholangiography: intraoperative Cholangiographie *f*.
operative delivery: Schnittentbindung *f*.
ophthalmia/*n*: any inflammation or irritation of the eye, the conjunctiva, or deeper structures of the eye, for example as gonorrheal ophthalmia or gonoblennorhea caused by Gonococcus. Ophthalmie *f*.
ophthalmic/*adj*: Augen-.
ophthalmic ointment: Augensalbe *f*.
ophthalmography/*n*: Ophthalmographie *f*.
ophthalmology/*n*: Ophthalmologie *f*, Augenheilkunde *f*.
ophthalmoneuritis/*n*: Sehnervenentzündung *f*, Neuritis nervi optici *f*.
ophthalmopathy/*n*: Ophthalmopathie *f*, Augenerkrankung *f*.
ophthalmoplegia/*n*: paralysis of the eye muscles. Forms include for example external ophthalmoplegia with paralysis of the external ocular muscles, and internal ophthalmoplegia with paralysis of the iris and ciliary apparatus. Ophthalmoplegie *f*, Augenmuskellähmung *f*.
ophthalmoplegic migraine: Migraine ophthalmoplégique *f*.
ophthalmoscopy/*n*: Ophthalmoskopie *f*, Augenspiegelung *f*.
opiate/*n*: Opiat *n*.
opiate dependence: Opiatabhängigkeit *f*.
opiate-like: opiatartig.
opioid/*n*: Opioid *n*.
opipranol/*n*: Opipranol *n*.
opisthorchiasis/*n*: Opisthorchiasis *f*.
opisthotonos/*n*: hyperextension of the body with arched-back position while head and heels remain in contact with the ground. Causes include cerebellar neoplasms, intoxications, and mental conditions. Opisthotonus *m*.
opium/*n*: Opium *n*.
opium tincture: Opiumtinktur *f*.
opponent/*n*: Musculus opponens *m*.
opportunistic/*adj*: opportunistisch.
opportunistic infection: opportunistische Infektion *f*.
OPSI syndrome <*abbr*> **overwhelming postsplenectomy infection syndrome**: a fulminant progressive septicemia with Streptococcus pneumoniae or Haemophilus influenzae, usually occurring after splenectomy. OPSI-Syndrom *n*.
opsonin/*n*: Opsonin *n*.
opsonizing antibody: opsonierender Antikörper *m*.
optic/*adj*: optisch.
optic agraphia: optische Agraphie *f*.
optical activity: optische Aktivität *f*.
optical center: Sehzentrum *n*.
optical illusion: optische Täuschung *f*.
optic atrophy: Optikusatrophie *f*, Sehnervenatrophie *f*.
optic chiasm: Chiasma opticum *n*, Sehnervenkreuzung *f*.
optic disk: Sehnervenpapille *f*.
optic fissure: Augenbecherspalte *f*.
optic glioma: Optikusgliom *n*.
optician/*n*: Optiker *m*.
optic neuritis: Sehnervenentzündung *f*, Neuritis nervi optici *f*.
optic papilla: Sehnervenpapille *f*.
optics/*n*: Optik *f*.
optimal dose: Optimaldosis *f*.
optimum/*n, adj*: 1. Optimum *n*; 2. optimal.
option/*n*: Option *f*, Auswahl *f*.
optokinetic nystagmus: optokinetischer Nystagmus *m*.
optometry/*n*: Optometrie *f*.
oral/*adj*: oral.
oral administration: orale Applikation *f*.
oral candidiasis: fungal infection of the mouth, typically caused by Candida albicans. Symptoms include small white stipples on the mucosa, and eventually painful swallowing. Mundsoor *m*.
oral cavity: Mundhöhle *f*.
oral contraceptive: orales Kontrazeptivum *n*.
oral hygiene: Mundhygiene *f*, Mundpflege *f*.
oral therapy: orale Therapie *f*.
oral vaccination: Schluckimpfung *f*.

orazamide/*n*: Orazamid *n*.
orbicular/*adj*: kreisrund, orbicularis.
orbiculopupillary reflex: Orbikularisphänomen *n*, Westphal-Pilcz-Zeichen *n*.
orbit/*n*: Augenhöhle *f*.
orbital/*adj*: orbital.
orchidectomy/*n*: Orchidektomie *f*.
orchidoepididymitis/*n*: Orchiepididymitis *f*.
orchidopexy/*n*: Orchidopexie *f*.
orchiectomy/*n*: Orchiektomie *f*.
orchis/*n*: Hoden *m*.
orchitis/*n*: inflammation of the testicle, usually in association with an infectious disease like gonorrhea, tuberculosis, or epidemic parotitis. Symptoms include swelling, fever, and pain. Orchitis *f*, Hodenentzündung *f*.
orciprenaline/*n*: Orciprenalin *n*.
order/*n*: Ordnung *f*, Reihenfolge *f*.
orexia/*n*: Orexie *f*, Heißhunger *m*.
organ/*n*: Organ *n*.
organ donation: Organspende *f*.
organ dose: Organdosis *f*.
organ failure: Organversagen *n*.
organic/*adj*: organisch.
organic acid: organische Säure *f*.
organic chemistry: organische Chemie *f*.
organic disease: organische Erkrankung *f*.
organic disorder: organische Störung *f*.
organic mental disorder: any psychological disorder that is caused by metabolic, endocrine or structural abnormalities in the body. organisch bedingte psychische Störung *f*.
organic psychosis: organische Psychose *f*, hirnorganisches Psychosyndrom *n*.
organic therapy: Frischzellentherapie *f*.
organism/*n*: Organismus *m*, Mikroorganismus *m*.
organized thrombus: organisierter Thrombus *m*.
organ recipient: Organempfänger *m*.
organ-specific/*adj*: organspezifisch.
orgasm/*n*: Orgasmus *m*.
orgasmic dysfunction: Orgasmusstörung *f*.
orgotein/*n*: Orgotein *n*.
oriental bedbug: Cimex hemipterus *m*.
oriental boil: Orientbeule *f*.
oriental hemoptysis: Paragonimiasis *f*.
oriental schistosomiasis: Schistosomiasis japonica *f*.
oriental sore: Orientbeule *f*.
orientation/*n*: Orientierung *f*, Ausrichtung *f*.
orienting response: Orientierungsreaktion *f*.
orifice/*n*: Körperöffnung *f*, Orifizium *n*.
origin/*n*: Ursprung *m*, Ursache *f*, Entstehung *f*.
orlistat/*n*: Orlistat *n*.
ornidazole/*n*: Ornidazol *n*.
ornithosis/*n*: Ornithose *f*.
orofacial/*adj*: orofazial.
orofaciodigital syndrome: any syndrome which is characterized by congenital abnormalities of the face, mouth, and digits. Forms include type I or Papillon-Léage and Psaume syndrome, type II or Mohr syndrome, and types III-VIII with deformations of the bones, the genitalia, and the central nervous system. orofaziodigitales Syndrom *n*, OFD-Syndrom *n*.
oropharyngeal/*adj*: oropharyngeal.
oropharynx/*n*: Oropharynx *m*.
orotic acid: Orotsäure *f*.
orotic aciduria: Orotazidurie *f*.
orphan/*n*: Waise *m*.
orphenadrine/*n*: Orphenadrin *n*.
orthodontics: Orthodontie *f*, Kieferorthopädie *f*.
orthomolecular/*adj*: orthomolekular.
orthopedic bed: Streckbett *n*.
orthopedics/*n*: Orthopädie *f*.
orthopedic shoe: orthopädischer Schuh *m*.
orthophosphoric acid: Orthophosphorsäure *f*.
orthopic transplantation: orthotope Transplantation *f*.
orthoptics/*n*: Orthoptik *f*.

orthoscopy/*n*: Orthoskopie *f*.
orthosis/*n*: Orthese *f*.
orthostatic/*adj*: orthostatisch.
orthostatic hypotension: orthostatische Hypotonie *f*.
orthostatic proteinuria: lordotische Proteinurie *f*.
orthostatic syncope: orthostatische Synkope *f*.
orthostatic tachycardia: orthostatische Tachykardie *f*.
orthotic/*adj*: orthetisch.
orthotopic graft: orthotopes Transplantat *n*.
os/*n*: Mund *m*, Knochen *m*.
oscillation/*n*: Oszillation *f*, Schwingung *f*.
oseltamivir/*n*: Oseltamivir *n*.
Osgood-Schlatter disease: Osgood-Schlatter-Syndrom *n*, aseptische Tibiakopfnekrose *f*.
osmic acid: Osmiumsäure *f*.
osmolality/*n*: Osmolalität *f*.
osmolarity/*n*: Osmolarität *f*.
osmole/*n*: Osmol *n*.
osmometry/*n*: Osmometrie *f*.
osmotic/*adj*: osmotisch.
osmotic diuresis: osmotische Diurese *f*.
osmotic diuretic: Osmodiuretikum *n*.
osmotic nephrosis: osmotische Nephrose *f*.
osseous/*adj*: knöchern.
osseous cell: Osteozyt *m*.
osseous junction: knöcherne Verbindung *f*, Gelenk *n*.
osseous lamella: Knochenlamelle *f*
ossicle/*n*: Knöchelchen *n*.
ossification/*n*: Ossifikation *f*, Knochenentwicklung *f*.
ossification center: Knochenkern *m*.
ossifying fibroma: Fibroosteom *n*, Osteofibrom *n*.
ostalgia/*n*: Knochenschmerz *m*.
ostectomy/*n*: Ostektomie *f*, Knochenresektion *f*.
osteitis/*n*: bone inflammation, originating in or involving the haversian spaces. Symptoms include enlargement of the bone, tenderness, and pain. Osteitis *f*, Ostitis *f*.
osteoarthritis/*n*: Osteoarthritis *f*.
osteoarthropathy/*n*: Osteoarthropathie *f*.
osteoarthrosis/*n*: a noninflammatory degenerative joint disease, characterized by a degeneration of joint cartilage which becomes soft and wears unevenly. As causative factors, chronic irritation of the joints, and normal wear and tear are discussed. Symptoms include pain, aches, and stiffness, enlargement of the fingers at the last joint, but seldom serious bone deformity. Osteoarthrose *f*.
osteoblast/*n*: Osteoblast *m*.
osteoblastic cancer: osteoblastischer Tumor *m*.
osteoblastoma/*n*: Osteoblastom *n*.
osteochondral/*adj*: osteochondral.
osteochondritis/*n*: inflammation of bone and cartilage which may eventually result in the splitting of pieces of cartilage into the joint, or destruction and necrosis in the cartilage. Osteochondritis *f*.
osteochondrodysplasia/*n*: Osteochondrodysplasie *f*.
osteochondroma/*n*: Osteochondrom *n*.
osteoclast/*n*: Osteoklast *m*.
osteocystoma/*n*: Knochenzyste *f*.
osteocyte/*n*: Osteozyt *m*.
osteodystrophy/*n*: dystrophy of bones resulting in defective bone formation, resulting for example from disorders of the phosphorus and calcium metabolism. Symptoms include bone pain, spontaneous fractures, and formation of bone cysts. Osteodystrophie *f*.
osteofibroma/*n*: Osteofibrom *n*.
osteogenesis/*n*: Osteogenese *f*, Knochenentwicklung *f*.
osteogenic cell: Osteoblast *m*.
osteogenic sarcoma: Osteosarkom *n*.
osteogenous/*adj*: osteogen.
osteoid osteoma: osteoides Osteom *n*, Osteoidosteom *n*.
osteolysis/*n*: Osteolyse *f*.
osteolytic cancer: osteolytischer Tumor *m*.
osteoma/*n*: Osteom *n*.
osteomalacia/*n*: softening of the bones, due to a mineralization disorder

caused by malnutrition, metabolic disorders, or increased elimination of essential minerals. Symptoms include painful bone deformity. Osteomalazie *f*.

osteomyelitis/*n*: acute or chronic inflammatory disease of bones originating in or involving the bone marrow, usually caused by bacterial infection with Streptococcus or Staphylococcus, for example following open fracture. Symptoms include sudden pain in the bone, and fever. Osteomyelitis *f*.

osteomyelofibrotic syndrome: presence of fibrous tissue in the bone marrow, usually due to chemical or physical damage such as irradiation or associated with Hodgkin's disease or a myeloproliferative disorder like polycythemia vera. Osteomyelofibrose *f*.

osteopathic scoliosis: osteopathische Skoliose *f*.

osteopathy/*n*: Osteopathie *f*.

osteopetrosis/*n*: Osteopetrose *f*, Marmorknochenkrankheit *f*.

osteophony/*n*: Knochenschallleitung *f*.

osteophyte/*n*: Osteophyt *m*.

osteoplast/*n*: Osteoplast *m*, Osteoblast *m*.

osteoporosis/*n*: a gradual decrease in the amount and strength of bone tissue, typically occurring with old age, but also after trauma or long periods of immobilization, and in association with endocrine disorders. Bones usually affected first in osteoporosis are the vertebrae and the pelvis. Osteoporosis results in thinning of the vertebrae, which are then compressed by the body weight and eventually may break and collapse. Symptoms include back pain, and spontaneous fractures of bones. Osteoporose *f*.

osteoporosis with renal diabetes: renale Osteodystrophie *f*.

osteosarcoma/*n*: Osteosarkom *n*, Knochensarkom *n*.

osteosclerosis/*n*: Osteosklerose *f*.

osteosclerotic anemia: osteosklerotische Anämie *f*.

osteotome/*n*: Osteotom *n*.

osteotomy/*n*: Osteotomie *f*.

ostium/*n*: Öffnung *f*, Mündung *f*.

otalgia/*n*: pain localized, but not necessarily originating in the ear. Earache originating in the ear may be caused by otitis or injury, reflex pain in the ear can be due to dental disease, diseases of the nasopharynx, or neurologic disorders affecting cranial nerves. Otalgie *f*, Ohrenschmerz *m*.

OTC drug <*abbr*> **over the counter drug**: frei verkäufliches Medikament *n*.

otic cerebral abscess: otogener Hirnabszess *m*.

otic fluid: Endolymphe *f*.

otitic encephalitis: otogene Enzephalitis *f*.

otitis/*n*: inflammation of the ear. Forms include external otitis with inflammation of the outer ear duct, otitis media with an infection of the middle ear, usually caused by the spread of bacterial infection from the throat, and labyrinthitis with inflammation of the inner ear. Otitis *f*, Ohrenentzündung *f*.

otodynia/*n*: Otalgie *f*, Ohrenschmerz *m*.

otolith/*n*: Otolith *m*.

otology/*n*: Otologie *f*, Ohrenheilkunde *f*.

otomycosis/*n*: Otomykose *f*.

otopalatodigital syndrome: an X-linked syndrom which mainly affects male infants. Type I is characterized by short stature, mental retardation, conductive hearing loss, and facial dysplasia. Type II is characterized by microcephaly, microstomy, cleft palate, hypoplasia of the thumbs, and curved lower extremities. otopalatodigitales Syndrom *n*, OPD-Syndrom *n*.

otoplasty/*n*: Otoplastik *f*.

otorhinolaryngology/*n*: Otorhinolaryngologie *f*, Hals-Nasen-Ohren-Heilkunde *f*, HNO.

otosclerosis/*n*: hearing loss with conductive deafness caused by hardening of the tissues and bones in the inner ear. Otosklerose *f*.
otoscopy/*n*: Otoskopie *f*, Ohrenspiegelung *f*.
ototoxicity/*n*: Ototoxizität *f*.
ouch-ouch disease: Itai-Itai-Krankheit *f*.
outbreak/*n*: Ausbruch *m*.
outcome/*n*: Ergebnis *n*.
outdated/*adj*: überholt.
outer ear: äußeres Ohr *n*.
outer membrane: Außenmembran *f*.
outer nuclear membrane: äußere Kernhülle *f*.
outflow/*n*: Ausfluss *m*.
outgrowth/*n*: Auswuchs *m*.
outlay/*n*: Onlay-Span *m*.
outlet/*n*: Ausgang *m*, Öffnung *f*.
outlook/*n*: Prognose *f*.
outpatient/*n*: ambulanter Patient.
outpatient clinic: Poliklinik *f*.
outpatient service: ambulante Versorgung *f*.
outside/*adj*: außen, außerhalb.
oval/*adj*: eiförmig, oval.
ovarian/*adj*: ovarial.
ovarian amenorrhea: ovarielle Amenorrhö *f*.
ovarian cancer: malignant neoplasm of the ovary originating in the superficial epithelial layers of the ovary. Initial tumor stages frequently cause no signs. Symptoms of more advanced tumor stages include ascites and palpable mass. Ovarialkarzinom *n*.
ovarian colic: kolikartiger Ovarschmerz *m*.
ovarian cycle: ovarieller Zyklus *m*.
ovarian cyst: retention cyst of the ovary, formed by enlargement of an ovarian follicle or developed from a corpus luteum. Cystic masses also occur in cystadenoma of the ovary, or ovarian endometriosis, and polycystic ovary syndrome. Ovarialzyste *f*.
ovarian follicle: Eifollikel *m*.
ovarian pregnancy: Ovarialgravidität *f*.
ovarian seminoma: Dysgerminom *n*.
ovarian steroid: ovarielles Steroid *n*.
ovarian tumor: Ovarialtumor *m*.
ovariectomy/*n*: Ovariektomie *f*.
ovariotomy/*n*: Ovariotomie *f*.
ovary/*n*: Ovar *n*, Eierstock *m*.
ovary abscess: Ovarialabszess *m*.
ovary torsion: Ovarialtorsion *f*.
overactive/*adj*: hyperaktiv.
overaging/*n*: Überalterung *f*.
overanxious disorder: Angstsyndrom mit Überängstlichkeit.
overbite/*n*: Überbiss *m*.
overcharged idea: überwertige Idee *f*.
overcompensation/*n*: Überkompensation *f*.
overdetermination/*n*: Multidetermination *f*.
overdosage/*n*: Überdosierung *f*.
overdose/*n*: Überdosis *f*.
overeating/*n*: Hyperphagie *f*.
overexposure/*n*: Überbelichtung *f*.
overflow/*n, vb*: 1. Überlauf *m*; 2. überlaufen.
overflow incontinence: Überlaufinkontinenz *f*.
overgrowth/*n*: vermehrtes Wachstum *n*.
overlap/*n, vb*: 1. Überlappung *f*; 2. überlappen.
overlay/*n, vb*: 1. Überzug *m*, 2. überschichten, überlagern.
overload/*n*: Überlastung *f*, Überladung *f*.
overpressure/*n*: Überdruck *m*.
overriding aorta: reitende Aorta *f*.
overriding head: reitender Kopf *m*.
overshoot/*n*: Überschwingung *f*.
overstimulation/*n*: Reizüberflutung *f*.
overstrain/*n, vb*: 1. Überlastung *f*, Überanstrengung *f*; 2. überlasten.
oversuppression syndrome: Oversuppression-Syndrom *n*.
overt/*adj*: manifest, explizit.
overt diabetes: manifester Diabetes *m*.
over the counter: frei verkäuflich.
overweight/*n*: a condition which is characterized by an increase in weight ten percent or more over normal weight. Overweight is typically

resulting from a persistent caloric intake that exceeds the energy needs of the body. Causative factors may include constitutional and/or metabolic or endocrine factors, but frequently emotional, cultural, or dietary influences, and lack of physical exercise are the main causes. Übergewicht *n*.
oviduct/*n*: Eileiter *m*, Tuba uterina *f*.
oviform/*adj*: eiförmig.
ovulation/*n*: Ovulation *f*.
ovulation induction: Ovulationsinduktion *f*.
ovulation inhibitor: Ovulationshemmer *m*.
ovulation method: Ovulationsmethode *f*.
ovulation timing: Eisprungbestimmung *f*.
ovule/*n*: Ei *n*.
ovum/*n*: Ei *n*.
owl's eye cell: Eulenaugenzelle *f*.
oxabolone/*n*: Oxabolon *n*.
oxaceprol/*n*: Oxaceprol *n*.
oxacillin/*n*: Oxacillin *n*.
oxalate calculus: Oxalatstein *m*.
oxalated blood: Oxalatblut *n*.
oxalic acid: Oxalsäure *f*.
oxaliplatin/*n*: Oxaliplatin *n*.
oxaloacetic acid: Oxalessigsäure *f*.
oxalosuccinic acid: Oxalbernsteinsäure *f*.
oxaluria/*n*: Oxalurie *f*.
oxaluric acid: Oxalursäure *f*.
oxamic acid: Oxaminsäure *f*.
oxamycin/*n*: Oxamycin *n*.
oxanamide/*n*: Oxanamid *n*.
oxandrolone/*n*: Oxandrolon *n*.
oxaprozin/*n*: Oxaprozin *n*.
oxatomide/*n*: Oxatomid *n*.
oxazepam/*n*: Oxazepam *n*.
oxazolam/*n*: Oxazolam *n*.
oxcarbazepine/*n*: Oxcarbazepin *n*.
oxetacaine/*n*: Oxetacain *n*.
oxiconazole/*n*: Oxiconazol *n*.
oxidant/*n*: Oxidant *m*, Oxidationsmittel *n*.
oxidation/*n*: Oxidation *f*.
oxidation-reduction reaction: Redoxreaktion *f*.
oxide/*n*: Oxid *n*.
oxidized hemoglobin: oxygeniertes Hämoglobin *n*, Oxyhämoglobin *n*.
oximetry/*n*: Oxymetrie *f*, Sauerstoffmessung *f*.
oxitriptan/*n*: Oxitriptan *n*.
oxitropium bromide: Oxitropiumbromid *n*.
oxoline/*n*: Oxolin *n*.
oxolinic acid: Oxolinsäure *f*.
oxprenolol/*n*: Oxprenolol *n*.
oxybutynin/*n*: Oxybutynin *n*.
oxybutyric acid: Hydroxybuttersäure *f*.
oxycephaly/*n*: Spitzschädel *m*, Akrozephalie *f*.
oxyclozanide/*n*: Oxyclozanid *n*.
oxygen/*n*: Sauerstoff *m*.
oxygenation/*n*: Oxygenation *f*, Sauerstoffzufuhr *f*.
oxygen capacity: Sauerstoffkapazität *f*.
oxygen deficiency: Sauerstoffmangel *m*.
oxygen mask: Sauerstoffmaske *f*.
oxygen tent: Sauerstoffzelt *n*.
oxygen therapy: Sauerstoffbehandlung *f*.
oxygen uptake: Sauerstoffaufnahme *f*.
oxygen utilization: Sauerstoffutilisation *f*.
oxygen want: Sauerstoffbedarf *m*.
oxyhemoglobin/*n*: oxygeniertes Hämoglobin *n*, Oxyhämoglobin *n*.
oxymesterone/*n*: Oxymesteron *n*.
oxymetholone/*n*: Oxymetholon *n*.
oxynaphthoic acid: Oxynaphthoesäure *f*.
oxynervonic acid: Oxynervonsäure *f*.
oxyntic/*adj*: säureproduzierend.
oxypertine/*n*: Oxypertin *n*.
oxyphenbutazone/*n*: Oxyphenbutazon *n*.
oxyphencyclimine/*n*: Oxyphencyclimin *n*.
oxyphenisatin/*n*: Oxyphenisatin *n*.
oxyphenylacetic acid: Hydroxyphenylessigsäure *f*.
oxyphilic adenoma: oxyphiles Adenom *n*, Hürthle-Zelladenom *n*.
oxyphilic carcinoma: a malignant neoplasm which is composed by on-

cocytes. It is most frequently found in the thyroid and parathyroid gland, in the pituitary gland, and in salivary glands. Onkozytom *n*, Hürthle-Zellkarzinom *m*.

oxytetracycline/*n*: Oxytetracyclin *n*, Hydroxytetracyclin *n*.

oxytocic/*n, adj*: 1. Oxytocicum *n*, Wehenmittel *n*; 2. wehenauslösend.

oxytocin/*n*: Oxytocin *n*.

oxyuriasis/*n*: infection of the intestine with oxyurid. Symptoms include pruritus of the anus, diarrhea, nausea, and vomiting. Oxyuriasis *f*, Enterobiasis *f*.

ozena/*n*: chronic-atrophic inflammation of the lining of the nose, frequently associated with Klebsiella ozaenae. Symptoms include the production of a mucopurulent, foul-smelling discharge. Ozäna *f*, atrophische Rhinitis *f*.

ozone/*n*: Ozon *n*.

ozone sickness: Ozonkrankheit *f*.

P

P <*abbr*> **1. phosphorus; 2. plasma**: 1. Phosphor *m*, P; 2. Plasma *n*.
pace/*n, vb*: 1. Schritt *m*, Tempo *n*; 2. schreiten, Tempo bestimmen.
pacemaker/*n*: Schrittmacher *m*.
pacemaker registration card: Herzschrittmacher-Pass *m*.
pachydermia/*n*: thickening of the skin resulting from hyperplasia of all skin layers. Forms include congenital pachydermia, and pachydermia associated with inflammatory diseases like elephantiasis or myxedema. Pachydermie *f*.
pachymeningitis/*n*: Pachymeningitis *f*.
pacifier/*n*: Schnuller *m*, Beruhigungsmittel *n*.
pacing/*n*: Stimulation *f*, Frequenzstimulierung *f*.
package/*n*: Packung *f*.
package insert: Packungsbeilage *f*, Beipackzettel *m*.
packed-cell volume: Hämatokrit *m*, Hk.
paclitaxel/*n*: Paclitaxel *n*.
PACS <*abbr*> **Picture Archiving and Communication System**: Bild-Archiv-Kommunikations-System *n*.
pad/*n*: Kompresse *f*, Polster *n*.
pagetoid osteitis: Paget-Krankheit *f*, Ostitis deformans *f*.
pain/*n*: Schmerz *m*.
pain assessment card: Schmerzbeurteilungsbogen *m*.
pain conduction: Schmerzleitung *f*.
pain disorder: any condition which is characterized by acute, chronic, or intermittent pain. Schmerzsyndrom *n*.
pain ending: Nozizeptor *m*, Schmerzrezeptor *m*.
painful menstruation: menstruation which is associated with colic-like pain not related to the intensity of the bleeding. Causes include organic diseases, for example of the uterus, and mental factors; idiopathic dysmenorrhea occurs without detectable cause. Dysmenorrhö *f*.
painful ophthalmoplegia: Tolosa-Hunt-Syndrom *n*, Orbitaspaltsyndrom *n*.
painful swallowing: Schluckschmerz *m*.
painkiller/*n*: Schmerzmittel *n*, Analgetikum *n*.
painless/*adj*: schmerzlos, indolent.
pain management: Schmerzbehandlung *f*.
pain reflex: Schmerzreflex *m*.
pains: Wehen *f*.
paint/*n, vb*: 1. Tinktur *f*; 2. einpinseln.
pairing/*n*: Paarung *f*.
palatal paralysis: Gaumenmuskellähmung *f*.
palate/*n*: Gaumen *m*.
palate retractor: Gaumenhaken *m*.
palatine cleft: Gaumenspalte *f*.
palatine tonsil: Gaumenmandel *f*.
palatoplasty/*n*: Palatoplastik *f*, Gaumenplastik *f*.
palatoplegia/*n*: Gaumensegellähmung *f*.
pale thrombus: weißer Thrombus *m*.
palindromic rheumatism: palindromischer Rheumatismus *m*.
pallesthetic sensibility: Pallästhesie *f*, Vibrationsempfinden *n*.
palliation/*n*: Linderung *f*.
palliative/*n, adj*: 1. Palliativum *n*; 2. palliativ.
palliative care: Palliativpflege *f*, Palliativversorgung *f*.

palliative surgery: Palliativoperation *f*.
palliative treatment: Palliativbehandlung *f*.
pallid/*adj*: bleich, blass.
pallidal syndrome: any neurologic disorder resulting from lesions in the globus pallidus. Symptoms include impairment of movement, rigidity, tremor, a tendency to fall, a monotonous voice, and micrographia. Pallidumsyndrom *n*.
pallor/*n*: Blässe *f*.
palm/*n*: Hohlhand *f*.
palmar/*adj*: palmar.
palmar contraction: progredient, often bilateral contracture of one or several fingers, resulting from a retraction of the palmar aponeurosis. Dupuytren-Palmarkontraktur *f*.
palmar crease: Handfurche *f*.
palmar erythema: Palmarerythem *n*.
palmar phlegmon: Hohlhandphlegmone *f*.
palmar reflex: Palmarreflex *m*
palmitic acid: Palmitinsäure *f*.
palmitoleic acid: Palmitoleinsäure *f*.
palonosetron/*n*: Palonosetron *n*.
palpation/*n*: Palpation *f*.
palpebra/*n*: Augenlid *n*.
palpebral fissure: Lidspalte *f*.
palpebronasal fold: Lidfalte *f*, Epikanthus *m*.
palpitation/*n*: Palpitation *f*, Herzklopfen *n*.
palsy/*n*: impairment or complete loss of motor function, and paralysis due to muscular or neural lesions. Lähmung *f*, Paralyse *f*.
paludism/*n*: Paludismus *m*, Malaria *f*.
pamidronate/*n*: Pamidronsäure *f*.
pampiniform body: Epoophoron *n*.
panacinar emphysema: panazinäres Lungenemphysem *n*.
panarteritis/*n*: Panarteriitis *f*.
panarthritis/*n*: Panarthritis *f*.
pancarditis/*n*: Pankarditis *f*.
pancreas/*n*: Pankreas *n*, Bauchspeicheldrüse *f*.
pancreatectomy/*n*: Pankreatektomie *f*.
pancreatic/*adj*: pankreatisch.
pancreatic abscess: Pankreasabszess *m*.
pancreatic amylase: Pankreasamylase *f*.
pancreatic calcification: Pankreaskalzifizierung *f*.
pancreatic cancer: malignant neoplasm of the pancreas, usually an adenocarcinoma. Initial tumor stages frequently cause no signs; symptoms of more advanced tumor stages include pain in the epigastric region and/or in the right dorsolumbar area, loss of appetite, weight loss, vomiting, gastrointestinal signs, and eventually jaundice. Pankreaskarzinom *n*.
pancreatic colic: Pankreaskolik *f*.
pancreatic insufficiency: Pankreasinsuffizienz *f*.
pancreatic islet: Langerhans-Insel *f*.
pancreatic lipase: Pankreaslipase *f*.
pancreatic transplantation: Pankreastransplantation *f*.
pancreaticoduodenostomy/*n*: Pankreatoduodenostomie *f*.
pancreatin/*n*: Pankreatin *n*.
pancreatitis/*n*: acute or chronic inflammation of the pancreas as a consequence of biliary disorders, alcohol consumption, or from trauma. Pankreatitis *f*.
pancreozymin/*n*: Pankreozymin *n*.
pancuronium bromide: Pancuroniumbromid *n*.
pandemic/*n, adj*: 1. in epidemiology, the occurrence of a disease, especially an infectious disease, all over the world or a continent. Pandemie *f*; 2. pandemisch.
panel/*n*: Arztregister *n*, Panel *n*.
panencephalitis/*n*: Panenzephalitis *f*.
pang/*n*: plötzlicher, stechender Schmerz *m*.
panhypopituitarism/*n*: Panhypopituitarismus *m*.
panic/*n, adj, vb*: 1. Panik *f*; 2. panisch; 3. erschrecken, in Panik geraten.
panic attack: Panikattacke *f*.
panic disorder: Paniksyndrom *n*.
panmural cystitis: transmurale Blasenentzündung *f*.

P

panmyelophthisis/*n*: Panmyelophthise *f*.
panniculitis/*n*: Pannikulitis *f*.
panophthalmitis/*n*: Panophthalmitis *f*.
pansystolic murmur: holosystolisches Geräusch *n*.
pantoprazole/*n*: Pantoprazol *n*.
pantothenic acid: Pantothensäure *f*.
Papanicolaou smear: Papanicolaou-Abstrich *m*.
papaverine/*n*: Papaverin *n*.
papilla/*n*: Papille *f*, Sehnervenpapille *f*.
papillary adenocarcinoma: papilläres Adenokarzinom *n*.
papillary carcinoma: a malignant neoplasm which is characterized microscopically by its papillary structures. It is most frequently found in the urinary bladder, in the ovaries, and in the thyroid gland. Papillenkarzinom *n*.
papillary stasis: Stauungspapille *f*.
papilledema/*n*: edematous swelling of the optic nerve at the site where the nerve enters the eye. Papillenödem *n*.
papillitis/*n*: Papillitis *f*.
papilloma/*n*: Papillom *n*.
papillomacular bundle: papillomakuläres Bündel *n*, Makulabündel *n*.
papillosphincterotomy/*n*: Papillosphinkterotomie *f*.
papular/*adj*: papulös.
papule/*n*: Papel *f*.
papuloerosive erythema: papuloerosive Windeldermatitis *f*.
para-albumin/*n*: Paralbumin *n*.
para-aminobenzoic acid: Para-Aminobenzoesäure *f*, PABA.
para-aminohippuric acid: Para-Aminohippursäure *f*.
para-aminosalicylic acid: Para-Aminosalicylsäure *f*, PAS.
paracentesis/*n*: Parazentese *f*.
paracentral scotoma: parazentrales Skotom *n*.
paracentric inversion: parazentrische Chromosomeninversion *f*.
paracetamol/*n*: Paracetamol *n*.
paracrine effect: parakriner Effekt *m*.
paracusia/*n*: Parakusis *f*.
paradoxical/*adj*: paradox.
paradoxical diaphragmatic contraction: paradoxe Zwerchfellbewegung *f*.
paradoxical embolism: paradoxe Embolie *f*.
paradoxical incontinence: Überlaufinkontinenz *f*.
paradoxical pulse: Pulsus paradoxus *m*.
paradoxical pupillary reaction: paradoxe Pupillenreaktion *f*.
paradoxical respiration: paradoxe Atmung *f*.
paraffin cancer: Paraffinkrebs *m*.
paraflutizide/*n*: Paraflutizid *n*.
parahepatitis/*n*: Perihepatitis *f*.
parainfluenza/*n*: Parainfluenza *f*.
paraldehyde/*n*: Paraldehyd *m*.
paralysis/*n*: impairment or complete loss of the power of movement in one or more parts of the body. Paralyse *f*, Lähmung *f*.
paralytic/*n, adj*: 1. Paralytiker *m*; 2. paralytisch.
paralytic dementia: Dementia paralytica *f*, progressive Paralyse *f*.
paralytic ileus: paralytischer Ileus *m*.
paralytic incontinence: Sphinkterinkontinenz *f*.
paralytic rabies: paralytische Tollwut *f*.
paralytic strabismus: Lähmungsschielen *n*.
paralytic vertigo: paralytischer Schwindel *m*.
paramalta fever: brucelloseartiges Fieber *n*.
paramedian/*adj*: paramedian.
paramedian incision: Paramedianschnitt *m*.
paramedical/*n, adj*: 1. Angehöriger eines medizinischen Assistenzberufs; 2. paramedizinisch.
paramethadione/*n*: Paramethadion *n*.
paramethasone/*n*: Paramethason *n*.
paramethasone acetate: Paramethasonacetat *n*.
parametritis/*n*: inflammation of the parametrium, the tissue which sur-

rounds and supports the uterus, mostly caused by bacteria like Streptococcus or Staphylococcus. Symptoms include fever, and pain in the lower abdomen. Parametritis *f*.
parametrium/*n*: Parametrium *n*.
paramnesia/*n*: Paramnesie *f*.
paramyxovirus/*n*: Paramyxovirus *n*.
paranasal sinus: Nasennebenhöhle *f*.
paraneoplastic/*adj*: paraneoplastisch.
paraneoplastic cerebellar atrophy: paraneoplastische Kleinhirnatrophie *f*.
paraneoplastic polyneuropathy: paraneoplastische Polyneuropathie *f*.
paranephric abscess: epinephritischer Abszess *m*.
paranoia/*n*: a chronic psychosis. Symptoms include fears, suspicion, and well-organized imaginery thoughts. Paranoia *f*, systematisierter Wahn *m*.
paranoid/*adj*: paranoid.
paranoid disorder: paranoide Störung *f*.
paranoid psychosis: Paranoia *f*, systematisierter Wahn *m*.
paranoid schizophrenia: paranoide Schizophrenie *f*.
paraoxon/*n*: Paraoxon *n*.
paraparetic gait: paretischer Gang *m*.
parapharyngeal abscess: parapharyngealer Abszess *m*.
paraphimosis/*n*: Paraphimose *f*.
paraplegia/*n*: complete loss of motor function in the legs and lower part of the body, typically associated with dysesthesia, as a result of a disease or injury to the spinal cord. Paraplegie *f*.
para-position/*n*: Parastellung *f*.
pararectal/*adj*: pararektal.
pararectal incision: Pararektalschnitt *m*.
parasagittal plane: Paramedianebene *f*.
parasinoidal space: parasinoidaler Raum *m*.
parasite/*n*: Parasit *m*.
parasitic hemoptysis: Paragonimiasis *f*.
parasiticide/*n*: Parasitizid *n*.
parasomnia/*n*: sleep disorder, resulting from brain disease, or reduced state of consciousness with episodes of somnolence. Parasomnie *f*, Schlafstörung *f*.
parasympathic/*adj*: parasympathisch.
parasystole/*n*: Parasystole *f*.
parasystolic rhythm: Parasystolie *f*.
parathion/*n*: Parathion *n*.
parathormone/*n*: Parathormon *n*, Parathyrin *n*.
parathyroid/*n, adj*: 1. Parathyreoidea *f*, Nebenschilddrüse *f*; 2. parathyreoidal.
parathyroid adenoma: Nebenschilddrüsenadenom *n*.
parathyroid hormone: Parathormon *n*, Parathyrin *n*.
parathyroid insufficiency: Nebenschilddrüseninsuffizienz *f*, Hypoparathyreoidismus *m*.
parathyroid osteodystrophy: hyperparathyreoide Osteodystrophie *f*.
paratyphoid/*n*: Paratyphus *m*.
paraurethral gland: Paraurethraldrüse *f*.
paravaginal incision: Paravaginalschnitt *m*.
paravertebral block: Paravertebralanästhesie *f*.
paravesical/*adj*: paravesikal.
parchment skin: Pergamenthaut *f*.
parecoxib/*n*: Parecoxib *n*.
parenchyma/*n*: Parenchym *n*.
parenchymal/*adj*: parenchymatös.
parenchymatous degeneration: parenchymatöse Degeneration *f*.
parenchymatous goiter: Kolloidstruma *f*.
parenchymatous hemorrhage: Gewebsblutung *f*.
parent/*n*: Elternteil *n*.
parental/*adj*: elterlich.
parental generation: Elterngeneration *f*.
parenteral/*adj*: parenteral.
parenteral nutrition: parenterale Ernährung *f*.
parenteric fever: Paratyphus *m*.
parents/*n*: Eltern.
paresis/*n*: impairment of the power of movement in one or more parts

of the body; slight or incomplete paralysis. Parese *f*.

paresthesia/*n*: any disturbance in the perception of stimuli, a disorder of sense. Usually used to refer to disturbances in touch sensation, such as formication, burning. Parästhesie *f*, Missempfindung *f*.

pargyline/*n*: Pargylin *n*.

paricalcitol/*n*: Paricalcitol *n*.

parietal/*adj*: parietal.

parietal bone: Scheitelbein *n*.

parietal cell: Parietalzelle *f*.

parity/*n*: Gebärfähigkeit *f*.

parkinsonism/*n*: chronic progressive disorder of the central nervous system of unknown origin, associated with a dopamine deficiency. Symptoms include bi- or unilateral tremor, rigidity of the muscles, slowness of movement, and akinesia. Parkinsonismus *m*, Parkinson-Syndrom *n*.

parodontitis/*n*: inflammation of the parodontium, resulting for example from infections or exposure to toxic substances. Parodontitis *f*.

paromomycin/*n*: Paromomycin *n*.

paronychia/*n*: an infectious disease of the nail fold, mostly due to bacterial infection with Staphylococcus or Streptococcus, or resulting from herpes simplex infection. Symptoms include swelling, formation of a very painful abscess, and inflammation of lymphatic vessels. Paronychie *f*, Nagelgeschwür *n*, Umlauf *m*.

paroophoritis/*n*: Paroophoritis *f*.

parosmia/*n*: Parosmie *f*, Riechstörung *f*.

parosteal sarcoma: periostales Sarkom *n*.

parotid/*n*: Parotis *f*, Ohrspeicheldrüse *f*.

parotidectomy/*n*: Parotidektomie *f*.

parotitis/*n*: inflammation of the parotid gland, usually occurring as epidemic parotitis following viral infection, or in association with other infectious diseases like typhoid fever, scarlet fever, or bacterial infection. Parotitis *f*.

paroxetin/*n*: Paroxetin *n*.

paroxysm/*n*: Paroxysmus *m*, Anfall *m*.

paroxysmal cold hemoglobinuria: paroxysmale Kältehämoglobinurie *f*, Donath-Landsteiner-Syndrom *n*.

paroxysmal cough: Hustenparoxysmus *m*.

paroxysmal lacrimation: Phänomen der paroxysmalen Tränen *n*, Krokodilstränenphänomen *n*.

paroxysmal nocturnal hemoglobinuria: chronic hemolytic anemia with nocturnal excretion of hemoglobin in the urine. Symptoms include episodes of jaundice and mild splenomegaly. paroxysmale nächtliche Hämoglobinurie *f*, Marchiafava-Anämie *f*.

paroxysmal sleep: Schlafanfall *m*.

paroxysmal supraventricular arrhythmia: paroxysmale supraventrikuläre Arrhythmie *f*.

paroxysmal supraventricular tachycardia: paroxysmale supraventrikuläre Tachykardie *f*.

parrot fever: Papageienkrankheit *f*, Psittakose *f*.

parry fracture: Monteggia-Fraktur *f*.

part/*n*: Teil *m*.

parthenogenesis/*n*: Parthenogenese *f*.

partial abortion: inkompletter Abort *m*.

partial agonist: partieller Agonist *m*.

partial amputation: Teilamputation *f*.

partial antagonist: partieller Antagonist *m*.

partial antigen: Hapten *n*.

partial block: Partialblock *m*, AV-Block II. Grades *m*.

partial cystectomy: Blasenteilresektion *f*.

partial epilepsy: Herdepilepsie *f*.

partial fracture: unvollständiger Bruch *m*.

partial hearing loss: partieller Hörverlust *m*.

partial recovery: Defektheilung *f*.

partial thromboplastin time: partielle Thromboplastinzeit *f*, PTZ.

partial volume: Partialvolumen *n*.

particle/*n*: Partikel *n*, Teilchen *n*.

partition/*n*: Teilung *f*, Unterteilung *f*.

partner therapy: Partnertherapie *f*.
parturient canal: Geburtskanal *m*.
parturition/*n*: Geburt *f*, Partus *m*.
parumbilical/*adj*: paraumbilikal.
passage/*n*: Passage *f*.
passive/*adj*: passiv.
passive congestion: venöse Stauung *f*.
passive cutaneous anaphylaxis: passive kutane Anaphylaxie *f*.
passive immunity: passive Immunität *f*.
passive protection: passive Immunisierung *f*.
passive tremor: Ruhetremor *m*.
paste/*n*: Paste *f*, Salbe *f*.
pasteurization/*n*: Pasteurisation *f*.
pastil/*n*: Pastille *f*.
pasty/*adj*: pastös.
patch/*n*: Fleck *m*, Flicken *m*, Lappen *m*, Patch *n*.
patch test: Patchtest *m*, Läppchentest *m*.
patchy alopecia: Pseudopelade *f*.
patchy lesion: fleckförmige Läsion *f*.
patella/*n*: Kniescheibe *f*.
patellar fracture: breaking of the patella, resulting from direct trauma or muscle tear. Symptoms include local pain, knee joint effusion, and impaired ability to stretch the lower leg. Patellafraktur *f*.
patellar tendon reflex: Patellarsehnenreflex *m*, Quadrizepssehnenreflex *m*, QSR.
patellectomy/*n*: Patellaentfernung *f*.
patency/*n*: Durchgängigkeit *f*.
patent/*n, adj*: 1. Patent *n*; 2. offen.
patent medicine: Markenpräparat *n*.
paternity test: Vaterschaftstest *m*.
pathoanatomy/*n*: pathologische Anatomie *f*.
pathogen/*n*: pathogener Mikroorganismus *m*.
pathogenesis/*n*: Pathogenese *f*.
pathogenic/*adj*: pathogen.
pathogenetic mechanism: pathogenetischer Mechanismus *m*, Pathomechanismus *m*.
pathognomonic/*adj*: pathognomonisch.
pathognomonic sign: pathognomonisches Zeichen *n*.
pathologic/*adj*: pathologisch.
pathologic atrophy: pathologische Atrophie *f*.
pathologic change: krankhafte Veränderung *f*.
pathologic fracture: bone fracture resulting from normal movement and not due to trauma or excessive stress. Underlying causes include changes in bone structure or bone diseases, for example osteomalacia or osteoporosis. Spontanfraktur *f*, pathologische Fraktur *f*.
pathologic histology: Histopathologie *f*.
pathologic intoxication: pathologischer Rausch *m*.
pathologic ossification: pathologische Ossifikation *f*.
pathology/*n*: Pathologie *f*.
pathophysiology/*n*: Pathophysiologie *f*.
pathway/*n*: Weg *m*, Bahn *f*.
patient/*n*: Patient *m*.
patient advocacy: Patientenanwalt *m*.
patient dose: Patientendosis *f*.
patient lift: Patientenheber *m*.
patient's history: Krankengeschichte *f*, Anamnese *f*.
pattern/*n*: Muster *n*, Schema *n*.
patulous/*adj*: ausgedehnt, erweitert.
PCR <*abbr*> **polymerase chain reaction**: Polymerasekettenreaktion *f*, PCR.
peak/*n*: Spitze *f*, Höhepunkt *m*, Zacke *f*.
pearly body: Hornperle *f*, Epithelperle *f*.
pectin/*n*: Pektin *n*.
pectoral girdle: Schultergürtel *m*.
pedal/*adj*: Fuß-.
pedal spasm: Fußkrampf *m*.
pediatric/*adj*: pädiatrisch.
pediatrics/*n*: Pädiatrie *f*, Kinderheilkunde *f*.
pedicle flap: Stiellappen *m*.
pediculicide/*n*: Pedikulizid *n*, Läusemittel *n*.
pediculosis/*n*: infestation with lice, typically affecting the scalp or hairy parts of the body, transmitted by direct person-to-person contact, clo-

thing, or bedding. Symptoms include inflammation of the skin, itching, and visible white eggs on the hair. Pedikulose *f*, Läusebefall *m*.

peduncle/*n*: Stiel *m*.

pedunculated cyst: gestielte Zyste *f*.

pedunculated polyp: gestielter Polyp *m*.

peeling/*n*: Schälen *n*, Abschälen *n*.

PEEP <*abbr*> **positive end-expiratory pressure**: PEEP, positiver endexspiratorischer Beatmungsdruck *m*.

pefloxacin/*n*: Pefloxacin *n*.

peg/*n*: Nagel *m*, Dübel *m*, Zapfen *m*.

pegaspargase/*n*: Pegaspargase *n*.

pegfilgrastim/*n*: Pegfilgrastim *n*.

peginterferon/*n*: Peginterferon *n*, pegyliertes Interferon *n*.

pegvisomant/*n*: Pegvisomant *n*.

pegylated interferon: pegyliertes Interferon *n*, Peginterferon *n*.

pellagra/*n*: disease caused by the lack of niacin or the inability to utilize niacin. Symptoms include dermatitis, inflammation of mucous membranes, diarrhea, and mental disturbances. Pellagra *n*.

pellet/*n*: Pellet *n*, Kügelchen *n*.

pellicle/*n*: dünne Membran *f*, Häutchen *n*.

pellucidal cyst: Septum-pellucidum-Zyste *f*.

pelvic/*adj*: pelvin.

pelvic aperture: Beckenapertur *f*.

pelvic axis: Beckenachse *f*.

pelvic floor: Beckenboden *m*.

pelvic girdle: Beckengürtel *m*.

pelvic inclination: Beckenneigung *f*.

pelvic index: Beckenindex *m*.

pelvic inflammatory disease: any pelvic inflammation involving the adnexa uteri and the upper female genital tract. Adnexitis *f*.

pelvic inlet: Beckeneingang *m*.

pelvic kidney: Beckenniere *f*.

pelvic osteotomy: Beckenosteotomie *f*.

pelvic outlet: Beckenausgang *m*.

pelvic plane: Beckenebene *f*.

pelvic presentation: in obstetrics, the position of the fetus in which the buttocks or feet are presented and appear first in the uterine cervix. Beckenendlage *f*.

pelvic vein thrombosis: Beckenvenenthrombose *f*.

pelvimetry/*n*: Pelvimetrie *f*, Beckenmessung *f*.

pelviography/*n*: Pelvigraphie *f*.

pelvirectal abscess: pelvirektaler Abszess *m*.

pelvis/*n*: Becken *n*.

pemphigoid/*n*: a group of subepidermal blistering skin diseases which can be distinguished from those of the pemphigus group. Pemphigoid *n*.

pemphigus/*n*: a group of skin disorders of unknown origin which are characterized by intraepidermal blistering. Pemphigus *m*.

penbutolol/*n*: Penbutolol *n*.

penciclovir/*n*: Penciclovir *n*.

pendular/*adj*: pendelnd.

pendular movement: Pendelbewegung *f*.

penectomy/*n*: Penektomie *f*, Penisamputation *f*.

penetrating ulcer: penetrierendes Ulkus *n*.

penetration/*n*: Penetration *f*, Eindringen *n*.

penfluridol/*n*: Penfluridol *n*.

penflutizide/*n*: Penflutizid *n*.

penicillamine/*n*: Penicillamin *n*.

penicillanic acid: Penicillansäure *f*.

penicillenic acid: Penicillensäure *f*.

penicillic acid: Penicillinsäure *f*.

penicillin/*n*: Penicillin *n*.

penicillinase/*n*: Penicillinase *f*.

penicilloic acid: Penicilloinsäure *f*.

penile/*adj*: penil.

penile deviation: Penisdeviation *f*.

penile induration/*n*: Induratio penis plastica *f*, Peyronie-Krankheit *f*.

penile reflex: Bulbocavernosusreflex *m*.

penile root: Penisschaft *m*.

penis envy: Penisneid *m*.

pension neurosis: Rentenneurose *f*.

pentaerythrityl tetranitrate: Pentaerithrityltetranitrat *n*.

pentafuside/*n*: Pentafusid *n*.

pentagastrin/*n*: Pentagastrin *n*.

pentamethonium/*n*: Pentamethonium *n*.
pentamidine/*n*: Pentamidin *n*.
pentetreotide/*n*: Pentetreotid *n*.
pentobarbital/*n*: Pentobarbital *n*.
pentosan/*n*: Pentosan *n*.
pentose/*n*: Pentose *f*.
pentosuria/*n*: Pentosurie *f*.
pentoxifylline/*n*: Pentoxifyllin *n*.
pepsin/*n*: Pepsin *n*.
peptic/*adj*: peptisch.
peptic esophagitis: peptische Ösophagitis *f*.
peptic ulcer: an erosive sore in the wall of the stomach or the small intestine which erodes through the inner mucous membrane lining and into the deeper muscular wall. peptisches Ulkus *n*.
peptide/*n*: Peptid *n*.
peracetic acid: Peressigsäure *f*.
percentile/*n*: Perzentil *n*.
perception/*n*: Perzeption *f*, Wahrnehmung *f*.
perceptive deafness: sensorineurale Taubheit *f*.
perceptual field: Wahrnehmungsfeld *n*.
perceptual illusion: Wahrnehmungstäuschung *f*.
perchloric acid: Perchlorsäure *f*.
percussion/*n*: Perkussion *f*.
percussion sound: Klopfschall *m*.
percutaneous/*adj*: perkutan.
percutaneous transhepatic cholangiography: perkutane transhepatische Cholangiographie *f*.
percutaneous transluminal angioplasty: perkutane transluminale Angioplastie *f*.
perforating appendicitis: perforierende Appendizitis *f*.
perforating peritonitis: perforierende Peritonitis *f*.
perforating ulcer: Ulcus perforans *n*, Ulkusperforation *f*.
perforation/*n*: Perforation *f*.
perform/*vb*: durchführen.
performance/*n*: Leistung *f*.
perfusion/*n*: Perfusion *f*, Durchblutung *f*.
pergolide/*n*: Pergolid *n*.
perhexiline/*n*: Perhexilin *n*.
perianal reflex: Analreflex *m*.
periangioma/*n*: Hämangioperizytom *n*.
periaortic/*adj*: paraaortal.
periarteritis/*n*: Periarteriitis *f*.
periarthritis/*n*: Periarthritis *f*.
periarticular calcification: periartikuläre Kalkeinlagerung *f*.
pericapillary cell: Adventitiazelle *f*, Perizyt *m*.
pericardial/*adj*: perikardial.
pericardial calcification: Perikardverkalkung *f*.
pericardial effusion: Perikarderguss *m*.
pericardial fluid: Herzbeutelflüssigkeit *f*.
pericardial friction: Perikardreiben *n*.
pericardial murmur: Perikardreiben *n*.
pericardial rub: Perikardreiben *n*.
pericarditis/*n*: inflammation of the sac which surrounds the heart, resulting from direct or indirect traumatic injury, or in association with other diseases like infections or hypersensitivity reaction. Symptoms include local pain, fever, tachycardia, effusion, and tamponade. Perikarditis *f*, Herzbeutelentzündung *f*.
pericardium/*n*: Perikard *n*, Herzbeutel *m*.
pericentric inversion: perizentrische Chromosomeninversion *f*.
perichondral ossification: perichondrale Ossifikation *f*.
perichondritis/*n*: inflammation of the perichondrium, eventually resulting in abscess formation and destruction of perichondrial tissue. Perichondritis *f*.
perichondrium/*n*: Perichondrium *n*.
pericolitis/*n*: Perikolitis *f*.
pericorneal/*adj*: perikorneal.
peridural/*adj*: peridural.
peridural anesthesia: Periduralanästhesie *f*.
perilymph/*n*: Perilymphe *f*.
perimeter/*n*: Perimeter *n*.
perinatal/*adj*: perinatal.

perinatal mortality: Perinatalsterblichkeit *f*.
perinatal period: Perinatalzeit *f*.
perinatology/*n*: Perinatologie *f*.
perineal/*adj*: perineal.
perineal laceration: Dammriss *m*.
perineal prostatectomy: perineale Prostatektomie *f*.
perineal section: externe Urethrotomie *f*.
perineorrhaphy/*n*: Perineorrhaphie *f*.
perinephric/*adj*: perinephritisch, perirenal.
perinephric abscess: perinephritischer Abszess *m*.
perinephric hematoma: perirenales Hämatom *n*.
perineum/*n*: Perineum *n*, Damm *m*.
perineurial cell: Perineuriumzelle *f*.
perineurium/*n*: Perineurium *n*.
period/*n*: Periode *f*, Phase *f*, Zeitraum *m*.
periodic/*adj*: periodisch.
periodic acid: Perjodsäure *f*.
periodic breathing: periodische Atmung *f*, Cheyne-Stokes-Atmung *f*.
periodic drinking bout: periodischer Alkoholismus *m*, Dipsomanie *f*.
periodic fever: periodisches Fieber *n*.
periodic paralysis: periodische Lähmung *f*, Adynamia episodica hereditaria *f*.
periodic psychosis: periodische Psychose *f*, manisch-depressive Psychose *f*.
periodic respiration: periodische Atmung *f*.
period of filling: Füllungszeit *f*.
period of life: Lebensabschnitt *m*.
periodontal/*adj*: alveolär, parodontal.
periorbital/*adj*: periorbital.
periorchitis/*n*: Periorchitis *f*.
periosteal/*adj*: periostal.
periosteal reflex: Sehnenreflex *m*.
periosteal retractor: Periosthaken *m*.
periosteal tissue: Periost *n*.
periosteoplastic amputation: subperiostale Amputation *f*.
periostitis/*n*: acute or chronic inflammation of the membrane surrounding a bone, the periosteum, usually resulting from trauma, local or generalized infection. Periostitis *f*.
peripheral/*adj*: peripher.
peripheral arterial occlusive disease: occlusion of a peripheral artery, most frequently located in the lower extremities, and usually resulting from arteriosclerosis or associated with diabetic angiopathy, arteritis, or embolism. Symptoms include alterations of the arterial pulse, decreased skin temperature, trophic disturbances, dysesthesia, and pain. periphere arterielle Verschlusskrankheit *f*.
peripheral blood: peripheres Blut *n*.
peripheral circulatory failure: peripheres Kreislaufversagen *n*.
peripheral cyanosis: periphere Zyanose *f*.
peripheral glioma: Neurilemmom *n*.
peripheral neuropathy: periphere Neuropathie *f*.
peripheral resistance: peripherer Widerstand *m*.
periportal cirrhosis: periportale Zirrhose *f*.
periportal liver cirrhosis: periportale Zirrhose *f*.
periproctic abscess: periproktitischer Abszess *m*, abszedierende Periproktitis *f*.
periproctitis/*n*: Periproktitis *f*.
perirectal abscess: pararektaler Abszess *m*.
perirectal fistula: Analfistel *f*.
peristalsis/*n*: Peristaltik *f*.
peristaltic movement: Peristaltik *f*.
peristaltic sound: Darmgeräusch *n*.
peritomy/*n*: Peritomie *f*, Periektomie *f*.
peritoneal/*adj*: peritoneal.
peritoneal carcinomatosis: dissemination of malignant tumor cells in the peritoneum. Peritonealkarzinose *f*.
peritoneal dialysis: Peritonealdialyse *f*.
peritoneal dropsy: Aszites *m*.
peritoneal lavage: Peritoneallavage *f*, Abdominallavage *f*.
peritoneal space: Peritonealhöhle *f*.

peritoneum/*n*: Peritoneum *n*, Bauchfell *n*.
peritonitis/*n*: inflammation of the lining tissue of the abdominal cavity, usually caused by microorganisms that infect the peritoneum following trauma or unsterile surgery. Forms include circumscribed or generalized, acute or chronic peritonitis. Symptoms include intense pain and tenderness. Peritonitis *f*.
peritonsillar/*adj*: peritonsillär.
peritonsillar abscess: inflammation of the peritonsillar connective tissue, usually following chronic tonsillitis. Symptoms include formation of phlegmon and abscess, cervical pain, and painful swallowing. Peritonsillarabszess *m*, Retrotonsillarabszess *m*.
periungual fibroma: periunguales Fibrom *n*, Koenen-Tumor *m*.
periurethritis/*n*: Periurethritis *f*.
perivascular cell: Adventitiazelle *f*, Perizyt *m*.
perivascular glial cell: Mikrogliazelle *f*, Hortega-Zelle *f*.
perivascular sheath: Gefäßscheide *f*.
perivascular space: Perivaskulärraum *m*, Virchow-Robin-Raum *m*.
permanent callus: bleibender Kallus *m*.
permanent dentition: permanentes Gebiss *n*.
permanent stricture: Dauerstriktur *f*.
permanganic acid: Permangansäure *f*.
permeability/*n*: Permeabilität *f*.
permethrin/*n*: Permethrin *n*.
permissiveness/*n*: Permissivität *f*.
pernicious/*adj*: perniziös.
pernicious anemia: perniziöse Anämie *f*, Hunter-Addison-Anämie *f*.
perniosis/*n*: Perniose *f*, Kälteschaden *m*.
peroneal/*adj*: peroneal, fibular.
peroneal-nerve phenomenon: Fibularisphänomen *n*, Lust-Phänomen *n*.
peroneal paralysis: paralysis of the peroneal nerve. Symptoms include partial or complete loss of certain muscles of the foot and the toes, resulting in a characteristic steppage gait. Fibularislähmung *f*, Peroneuslähmung *f*.
peroxyacetic acid: Peressigsäure *f*.
perphenazine/*n*: Perphenazin *n*.
persecutory delusion: Verfolgungswahn *m*.
perseveration/*n*: Perseveration *f*.
persist/*vb*: persistieren, andauern.
persistent idea: Zwangsidee *f*.
persistent proteinuria: persistierende Proteinurie *f*.
persistent vomiting: unstillbares Erbrechen *n*.
person/*n*: Person *f*.
personal hygiene: Körperhygiene *f*, Körperpflege *f*.
personality/*n*: Persönlichkeit *f*, Charakter *m*.
personnel/*n*: Personal *n*.
perspiration/*n*: Perspiration *f*, Schwitzen *n*.
persulfuric acid: Perschwefelsäure *f*.
pertussis/*n*: an infectious disease caused by the bacterium Bordetella pertussis, characterized by epidsodes of paroxysmal coughing punctuated by whooping noises between episodes during periods of inspiration. Keuchhusten *m*, Pertussis *f*.
peruvian wart: Peru-Warze *f*, Verruga peruana *f*.
pes/*n*: Fuß *m*.
pessary/*n*: Pessar *n*.
pest/*n*: Plage *f*, Pest *f*.
petechial/*adj*: petechial.
petechial hemorrhage: petechiale Blutung *f*.
petechial rash: petechiale Hautblutung *f*.
petrifaction/*n*: Petrifikation *f*, Versteinerung *f*.
pétrissage/*n*: Pétrissage *f*, Knetmassage *f*.
petrous/*adj*: steinartig, Felsenbein-.
PET scanning: Positronenemissionstomographie *f*, PET.
phage/*n*: Phage *m*.
phagedenic ulcer: phagedänisches Ulkus *n*.
phage-typing: Phagentypisierung *f*.
phagocyte/*n*: Phagozyt *m*.

phagocytosis/*n*: Phagozytose *f*.
phalangitis/*n*: Phalanxentzündung *f*.
phallic/*adj*: phallisch.
phantasy/*n*: Phantasie *f*.
phantom limb: Phantomglied *n*.
phantom limb pain: Phantomschmerz *m*.
pharmaceutical/*n, adj*: 1. Pharmakon *n*, Arzneimittel *n*; 2. pharmazeutisch.
pharmaceutical agent: Arzneimittel *n*, Medikament *n*.
pharmaceutical aid: Arzneimittelhilfsstoff *m*.
pharmaceutical chemistry: pharmazeutische Chemie *f*.
pharmaceutics/*n*: Pharmazie *f*.
pharmacoepidemiology/*n*: Pharmakoepidemiologie *f*.
pharmacogenetics/*n*: Pharmakogenetik *f*.
pharmacognosy/*n*: Pharmakognosie *f*.
pharmacokinetics/*n*: Pharmakokinetik *f*.
pharmacologic/*adj*: pharmakologisch.
pharmacological castration: medikamentöse Kastration *f*.
pharmacologist/*n*: Pharmakologe *m*.
pharmacology/*n*: Pharmakologie *f*.
pharmacopoeia/*n*: Pharmakopoe *f*, Arzneibuch *n*.
pharmacotherapy/*n*: Pharmakotherapie *f*, medikamentöse Behandlung *f*.
pharmacovigilance/*n*: Pharmakovigilanz *f*.
pharmacy/*n*: Apotheke *f*, Pharmazie *f*, Arzneimittelherstellung *f*.
pharyngeal/*adj*: pharyngeal.
pharyngeal arch: Kiemenbogen *m*.
pharyngeal cleft: Kehlkopfspalte *f*.
pharyngeal diphtheria: diphtherische Angina *f*.
pharyngeal diverticulum: Pharynxdivertikel *n*.
pharyngeal paralysis: Pharynxlähmung *f*.
pharyngeal pouch: Kiementasche *f*.
pharyngeal reflex: Rachenreflex *m*, Würgreflex *m*.
pharyngeal space: Rachenraum *m*.
pharyngeal tube: Rachentubus *m*.
pharyngectomy/*n*: Pharyngektomie *f*.
pharyngism/*n*: Pharyngismus *m*.
pharyngitis/*n*: inflammation of the pharynx, in its acute form usually associated with acute infections of the upper respiratory tract, as chronic pharyngitis for example associated with exposure to dust and smoke. Pharyngitis *f*, Rachenentzündung *f*.
pharyngoconjunctival fever: Pharyngokonjunktivalfieber *n*.
pharyngoesophageal diverticulum: Pharyngozele *f*, Zenker-Divertikel *n*.
pharyngolaryngectomy/*n*: Pharyngolaryngektomie *f*.
pharyngoplasty/*n*: Pharyngoplastik *f*.
pharyngoscopy/*n*: Pharyngoskopie *f*.
pharyngotomy/*n*: Pharyngotomie *f*.
phase/*n*: Phase *f*, Periode *f*.
phase-contrast microscope: Phasenkontrastmikroskop *n*.
phasic arrhythmia: respiratorische Arrhythmie *f*.
phenacemide/*n*: Phenacemid *n*.
phenacetin/*n*: Phenacetin *n*.
phenamacide/*n*: Phenamacid *n*.
phenelzine/*n*: Phenelzin *n*.
phenethicillin/*n*: Phenethicillin *n*.
phenethicillin potassium: Phenethicillin-Kalium *n*.
phenic acid: Karbolsäure *f*, Phenol *n*.
phenindione/*n*: Phenylindandion *n*.
pheniprazine/*n*: Pheniprazin *n*.
phenol red: Phenolrot *n*.
phenomenon/*n*: Phänomen *n*, Zeichen *n*.
phenothiazine/*n*: Phenothiazin *n*.
phenotype/*n*: Phänotyp *m*.
phenotypic resistance: phänotypische Resistenz *f*.
phenoxybenzamine/*n*: Phenoxybenzamin *n*.
phenoxymethylpenicillin/*n*: Phenoxymethylpenicillin *n*, Penicillin V *n*.
phenprobamate/*n*: Phenprobamat *n*.
phenprocoumon/*n*: Phenprocoumon *n*.
phensuximide/*n*: Phensuximid *n*.

phentolamine/*n*: Phentolamin *n*.
phenyl/*n*: Phenyl *n*.
phenylacetic acid: Phenylessigsäure *f*.
phenylalanine/*n*: Phenylalanin *n*, Phe.
phenylbutazone/*n*: Phenylbutazon *n*.
phenylephrine/*n*: Phenylephrin *n*.
phenylethylbarbituric acid: Phenyläthylbarbitursäure *f*, Phenobarbital *n*.
phenylketonuria/*n*: hereditary disorder of phenylalanine metabolism caused by an enzyme deficiency, and without dietary phenylalanine restriction resulting in mental retardation and neurologic signs like seizures. Phenylketonurie *f*, Fölling-Krankheit *f*.
phenylmercuric borate: Phenylmercuriborat *n*.
phenylpropanolamine/*n*: Phenylpropanolamin *n*.
phenylpyruvic acid: Phenylbrenztraubensäure *f*.
phenylpyruvic amentia: Phenylketonuriedemenz *f*.
phenyltoloxamine/*n*: Phenyltoloxamin *n*.
phenytoin/*n*: Phenytoin *n*, Diphenylhydantoin *n*.
pheochrome cell: phäochrome Zelle *f*.
phlebectomy/*n*: Phlebektomie *f*.
phlebitis/*n*: inflammation of a vein, most frequently located in the leg, and usually associated with the formation of a blood clot and phlebothrombosis. Phlebitis *f*, Venenentzündung *f*.
phlebothrombosis/*n*: formation of a blood clot in a vein, not due to inflammation of the wall of the vein. Phlebothrombose *f*.
phlebotomus fever: Phlebotomusfieber *n*, Pappataci-Fieber *n*.
phlegmasia/*n*: Phlegmasie *f*.
phlegmon/*n*: diffuse, purulent infiltration of subcutaneous layers of the skin or connective tissue, typically caused by bacteria like Staphylococcus or Streptococcus. Phlegmone *f*.
phlegmonous adenitis: Drüsenphlegmone *f*.
phlegmonous enteritis: phlegmonöse Enteritis *f*.
phlegmonous gastritis: phlegmonöse Gastritis *f*.
phlyctena/*n*: Phlyktäne *f*, Bläschen *n*.
phlyctenular/*adj*: phlyktänulär.
phlyctenular eczema: phlyktänuläres Ekzem *n*.
phobia/*n*: extreme fear of a situation, an object, or a localization which is not based on a rational cause, for example fear of objects on the right side of the body in dextrophobia. Phobie *f*.
phobic disorder: phobische Störung *f*.
phocomelia/*n*: Phokomelie *f*.
phonation/*n*: Phonation *f*.
phoniatrics/*n*: Phoniatrie *f*.
phonocardiogram/*n*: Phonokardiogramm *n*.
phosphatase/*n*: Phosphatase *f*.
phosphate/*n*: Phosphat *n*.
phosphaturia/*n*: Phosphaturie *f*.
phosphoglyceric acid: Phosphoglycerinsäure *f*.
phospholipid/*n*: Phospholipid *n*.
phosphomolybdic acid: Phosphomolybdänsäure *f*.
phosphonecrosis/*n*: Phosphornekrose *f*.
phosphorus/*n*: Phosphor *m*, P.
phosphoric acid: Phosphorsäure *f*.
phosphorous acid: phosphorige Säure *f*.
phosphorylation/*n*: Phosphorylierung *f*.
phosphotungstic acid: Phosphorwolframsäure *f*.
photic stimulation: Photostimulation *f*.
photoallergy/*n*: Lichtallergie *f*.
photochemistry/*n*: Photochemie *f*.
photoelectric/*adj*: photoelektrisch.
photography/*n*: Photographie *f*.
photophobia/*n*: Photophobie *f*, Lichtscheu *f*.
photopic adaptation: Helladaptation *f*.
photopic vision: photopisches Sehen *n*, Tagessehen *n*.

photoreceptor/*n*: Photorezeptor *m*.
photosensitive epilepsy: photogene Epilepsie *f*.
photosensitive porphyria: photosensitive Porphyrie *f*.
photosensitization/*n*: Photosensibilisierung *f*.
phrenicectomy/*n*: Phrenikusresektion *f*.
phrenic paralysis: Phrenikuslähmung *f*.
phrenoplegia/*n*: Zwerchfelllähmung *f*.
phrenosin/*n*: Phrenosin *n*, Cerebron *n*.
phrygian cap: phrygische Mütze *f*.
phthalic acid: Phthalsäure *f*.
phycomycotic infection: Mukormykose *f*.
phylogeny/*n*: Phylogenie *f*, Phylogenese *f*.
physiatrics/*n*: Physiatrik *f*, physikalische Therapie *f*.
physical/*adj*: physisch, körperlich, physikalisch.
physical disability: Körperbehinderung *f*, körperliche Behinderung *f*.
physical disorder: körperliche Störung *f*.
physical effort: körperliche Anstrengung *f*.
physical examination: körperliche Untersuchung *f*.
physical finding: körperlicher Untersuchungsbefund *m*.
physical handicap: Körperbehinderung *f*, körperliche Behinderung *f*.
physical sign: körperliches Symptom *n*.
physical stress: körperliche Belastung *f*.
physical therapy: physikalische Therapie *f*.
physical training: körperliche Übung *f*.
physician/*n*: Arzt *m*.
physician assistant: Arzthelferin *f*, Arzthelfer *m*.
physician-patient relation: Arzt-Patient-Beziehung *f*.
physicist/*n*: Physiker *m*.
physiologic/*adj*: physiologisch.
physiologic age: physiologisches Alter *n*.
physiologic albuminuria: physiologische Albuminurie *f*.
physiologic amenorrhea: physiologische Amenorrhö *f*.
physiologic atrophy: physiologische Atrophie *f*.
physiologic availability: physiologische Verfügbarkeit *f*.
physiologic jaundice: physiologischer Ikterus *m*.
physiologic ossification: Knochenbildung *f*, Osteogenese *f*.
physiologic proteinuria: physiologische Proteinurie *f*.
physiology/*n*: Physiologie *f*.
physiotherapy/*n*: Physiotherapie *f*.
physique/*n*: Physis *f*, Körperbau *m*.
physostigmine/*n*: Physostigmin *n*.
phytic acid: Phytinsäure *f*.
phytol/*n*: Phytol *n*.
pia-arachnoid space: Subarachnoidalraum *m*.
pickwickian syndrome: a condition characterized by excessive obesity, hypoventilation, somnolence, and an increase in red blood cells. Pickwick-Syndrom *n*.
picric acid: Pikrinsäure *f*, Trinitrophenol *n*.
picric itch: Pikrinsäuredermatitis *f*.
picrotoxin/*n*: Pikrotoxin *n*.
picture/*n*: Bild *n*.
piezogenic pedal papule: piezogene Fußpapel *f*.
pigeon chest: Hühnerbrust *f*, Pectus carinatum *n*.
pigment/*n*: Pigment *n*.
pigmental spot: Pigmentfleck *m*.
pigmentary change: Pigmentanomalie *f*.
pigmentary dermatosis: Pigmentdermatose *f*.
pigmentary retinopathy: Retinitis pigmentosa *f*.
pigmentation/*n*: Pigmentierung *f*.
pigmentation disorder: Pigmentanomalie *f*.
pigment border: Pigmentsaum *m*.
pigmented liver: Pigmentleber *f*.
pilar/*adj*: haarig, pilar.

pilar cone: Haarkegel *m*.
pilar cyst: Talgdrüse *f*.
piles: enlargement of veins of the hemorrhoidal plexus. Symptoms include pain, blood on top of the feces, and defecation disorder. Hämorrhoiden.
pill/*n*: Pille *f*.
pillow/*n*: Kissen *n*.
pill-rolling tremor: Pillendrehertremor *m*.
pillular mass: Pillenmasse *f*.
pilocarpine/*n*: Pilocarpin *n*.
piloerection/*n*: Piloarrektion *f*.
pilonidal sinus: a cystic cavity or channel, usually occurring in the coccygeal region, which contains hair. Pilonidalsinus *m*.
piloting trocar: Führungstrokar *m*.
pilot study: Pilotstudie *f*, Vorversuch *m*.
pimecrolimus/*n*: Pimecrolimus *n*.
pimozide/*n*: Pimozid *n*.
pimple/*n*: Pustel *f*, Papel *f*, Pickel *m*.
pin/*n*: Stift *m*, Nadel *f*.
pindolol/*n*: Pindolol *n*.
pineal/*adj*: Pineal-, pinealis.
pineal body: Zirbeldrüse *f*.
pineal gland: Pinealdrüse *f*, Zirbeldrüse *f*.
pinealoma/*n*: Pinealom *n*.
pineal organ: Pinealdrüse *f*, Zirbeldrüse *f*.
ping-pong fracture: Schädelimpressionsfraktur *f*.
pinguecula/*n*: Pinguecula *f*.
pink disease: Rosakrankheit *f*, Akrodynie *f*, Feer-Krankheit *f*.
pinkeye/*n*: akute Konjunktivitis *f*, rotes Auge *n*.
pinning/*n*: Nagelung *f*.
pinocytosis/*n*: Pinozytose *f*.
pinworm/*n*: Fadenwurm *m*, Nematode *f*.
pioglitazone/*n*: Pioglitazon *n*.
pipamperone/*n*: Pipamperon *n*.
pipazethate/*n*: Pipazetat *n*.
pipemedic acid: Pipemidsäure *f*.
pipenzolate bromide: Pipenzolatbromid *n*.
piperacillin/*n*: Piperacillin *n*.
piperazine/*n*: Piperazin *n*.
piperazine hexahydrate: Piperazinhexahydrat *n*.
piperidine/*n*: Piperidin *n*.
piperidolate/*n*: Piperidolat *n*.
piperidyl/*n*: Piperidyl *n*.
piperocaine/*n*: Piperocain *n*.
piperonyl butoxide: Piperonylbutoxid *n*.
pipet/*vb*: pipettieren.
pipoxolan/*n*: Pipoxolan *n*.
piracetam/*n*: Piracetam *n*.
pirbuterol/*n*: Pirbuterol *n*.
pirenzepine/*n*: Pirenzepin *n*.
piretanide/*n*: Piretanid *n*.
piribedil/*n*: Piribedil *n*.
piridoxilate/*n*: Piridoxilat *n*.
piritramide/*n*: Piritramid *n*.
piroplasmosis/*n*: Piroplasmose *f*, Babesiose *f*.
piroxicam/*n*: Piroxicam *n*.
pirprofen/*n*: Pirprofen *n*.
pisiform bone: Erbsenbein *n*.
pistol-shot sound: Pistolenschussphänomen *n*, Duroziez-Geräusch *n*.
pit/*n*: Grube *f*, Delle *f*.
pitted nail: Grübchennagel *m*, Tüpfelnagel *m*.
pitting edema: dellenbildendes Ödem *n*.
pituitary/*n, adj*: 1. Hypophyse *f*, Hypophysenextrakt *m*, 2. pituitär, hypophysär.
pituitary adenoma: a benign neoplasm of the anterior pituitary gland. Histologically distinguished are basophil, chromophobe, and eosinophil adenomas. Symptoms include endocrine disturbances, and signs of intracranial mass. Hypophysenadenom *n*.
pituitary amenorrhea: hypophysäre Amenorrhö *f*.
pituitary apoplexy: Hypophysenvorderlappeninfarkt *m*.
pituitary dysfunction: Pituitarismus.
pituitary gigantism: hypophysärer Riesenwuchs *m*.
pituitary gland: Hirnanhangdrüse *f*.
pituitary gonadotropin: hypophysäres Gonadotropin *n*.
pituitary hormone: Hypophysenhormon *n*.

pituitary infarction: infarction of the pituitary gland. Symptoms include signs of hypopituitarism and pituitary insufficiency. Hypophyseninfarkt *m*.

pituitary insufficiency: partial or complete loss of function of the pituitary gland, typically resulting from necrosis, tumor, or inflammation of the pituitary gland. Symptoms are due to the diminuition of endocrine function and include regression of secondary sex characteristics, hair loss, hypogonadism, hypoglycemia, fatigue, and lethargy. Hypophyseninsuffizienz *f*.

pityriasis/*n*: disease of the skin in which the main symptom is a scaly skin. Pityriasis *f*, Kleienflechte *f*.

pivampicillin/*n*: Pivampicillin *n*.

pizotifen/*n*: Pizotifen *n*.

placebo/*n*: Placebo *n*.

placebo effect: Placeboeffekt *m*.

placement/*n*: Platzierung *f*.

placenta/*n*: Plazenta *f*, Mutterkuchen *m*.

placental/*adj*: plazentar.

placental barrier: Plazentaschranke *f*.

placental bed: Deziduaplatte *f*.

placental hormone: Plazentahormon *n*.

placental insufficiency: impairment of the placenta function, occurring for example as a consequence of malnutrition, intoxication or vascular insufficency, and resulting in dystrophia and growth retardation of the fetus, and an increased risk of intrauterine death. Plazentainsuffizienz *f*.

placental presentation: in obstetrics, a placenta which develops in the lower segment of the uterus and may even cover the entire cervical canal, associated with the risk of premature separation and hemorrhage. Placenta praevia *f*.

placental transfer: diaplazentare Übertragung *f*.

placental transfusion syndrome: in twin pregnancy, the flow of fetal blood from one fetus to the other via an arteriovenous or arterial anastomosis, resulting in the birth of one anemic and one plethoric twin. Syndrom der fetofetalen Bluttransfusion *n*, fetofetale Transfusion *f*.

placental transmission: diaplazentare Übertragung *f*.

placing reflex: Stellreaktion *f*.

placode/*n*: Plakode *f*.

plagiocephaly/*n*: Plagiozephalie *f*.

plague/*n*: an infectious disease caused by the bacterium Yersinia pestis and transmitted by fleas of rats. Forms include bubonic plague which causes swelling of the lymph nodes and is associated with hemorrhage, necrotic purpura and gangrene, and pneumonic or pulmonic plague which affects the lungs. Pest *f*, Seuche *f*.

plane/*n*: Ebene *f*, Körperebene *f*.

plane articulation: ebenes Gelenk *n*.

plane bone: planer Knochen *m*.

plane wart: Verruca plana *f*.

planning/*n*: Planung *f*.

plant agglutinin: pflanzliches Agglutinin *n*, Phytagglutinin *n*.

plantar/*adj*: plantar.

plantar wart: painful wart occurring on the bottom of the foot. Verruca plantaris *f*.

plaque/*n*: Plaque *f*, Fleck *m*.

plasma/*n*: Plasma *n*, Blutplasma *n*.

plasma cell: Plasmazelle *f*.

plasma coagulation factor: plasmatischer Gerinnungsfaktor *m*.

plasmacytosis/*n*: Plasmozytose *f*.

plasma exchange: Plasmaaustausch *m*.

plasma membrane: Plasmamembran *f*.

plasmapheresis/*n*: Plasmapherese *f*.

plasma thromboplastin antecedent: Faktor XI *m*.

plasmatic/*adj*: plasmatisch.

plasmid/*n*: Plasmid *n*.

plaster/*n*: Pflaster *n*, Gipsverband *m*.

plaster body cast: Gipslonguette *f*.

plaster impression: Abdruckgips *m*.

plastic/*n, adj*: 1. Plastik *n*; 2. plastisch.

plastic surgery: plastische Chirurgie *f*.

plate/*n*: Platte *f*.
platelet/*n*: Plättchen *n*, Thrombozyt *m*.
platelet aggregation: Thrombozytenaggregation *f*.
platelet count: Thrombozytenzählung *f*, Thrombozytenzahl *f*.
platelike atelectasis: Plattenatelektase *f*, Fleischner-Atelektase *f*.
platyhelminth/*n*: Plathelminthe *f*, Plattwurm *m*.
play therapy: Spieltherapie *f*.
pleasure principle: Lustprinzip *n*.
pledget/*n*: Tupfer *m*.
plegia/*n*: Plegie *f*.
pleomorphic adenoma: pleomorphes Adenom *n*.
pleomorphism/*n*: Pleomorphismus *m*, Polymorphie *f*.
plessimetric percussion: Plessimeterperkussion *f*.
plethora/*n*: Plethora *f*, Volumenüberfüllung *f*.
plethysmography/*n*: Plethysmographie *f*.
pleura/*n*: Pleura *f*, Rippenfell *n*.
pleural/*adj*: pleural.
pleural drainage: Pleuradrainage *f*.
pleural effusion: the presence of fluid in the pleural space as exudate or transudate, typically occurring in association with bronchial carcinoma, or carcinomatous pleurisy. Pleuraerguss *m*.
pleural empyema: the presence of pus in the pleural space, resulting for example from lung infarction, perforating thoracic injury, or hematogenous spread of microorganisms. Pleuraempyem *n*.
pleural fibrosis: Pleurafibrose *f*.
pleural friction: Pleurareiben *n*.
pleural lavage: Pleuraspülung *f*.
pleural mesothelioma: Pleuramesotheliom *n*.
pleural pressure: Pleuradruck *m*.
pleural rub: Pleurareiben *n*.
pleural sac: Pleurahöhle *f*.
pleural space: Pleurahöhle *f*.
pleurisy/*n*: inflammation of the pleura, most commonly caused by viral or bacterial infection. Forms include dry pleurisy in which the protective fluid between the two pleura layers is partially replaced by fibrin, and serofibrinous pleurisy, or pleurisy with effusion, which is caused by an excess accumulation of fluid between the two pleura layers. Pleuritis *f*, Pleurareizung *f*.
pleurobronchial fistula: Bronchopleuralfistel *f*.
pleuropericardial rub: Pleuroperikardialreiben *n*.
plexiform neuroma: rankenförmiges Neurom *n*, Verneuil-Neurom *n*.
plexopathy/*n*: Plexusschädigung *f*.
plexus/*n*: Geflecht *n*, Plexus *m*.
plica/*n*: Falte *f*, Plica *f*.
pliers/*n*: Zange *f*.
plug/*n, vb*: 1. Pfropf *m*, Stecker *m*; 2. ausstopfen, tamponieren.
plumbism/*n*: lead poisoning resulting from absorption or ingestion of lead or lead salt. Symptoms include normochromic anemia, central nervous symptoms like encephalopathy, joint pain, gastrointestinal symptoms and atrophy of the kidneys. Bleivergiftung *f*.
plural pregnancy: Mehrfachschwangerschaft *f*.
pluriglandular adenomatosis: an autosomal dominant inherited syndrome which is characterized by the presence of benign or malignant neoplasms of more than one endocrine gland and neurocutaneous alterations. pluriglanduläre Adenomatose *f*, multiple endokrine Neoplasie *f*, MEN.
pluripotent state: pluripotentes Stadium *n*.
pluripotent stem cell: pluripotente Stammzelle *f*.
pneumatic/*adj*: pneumatisch.
pneumatocele/*n*: Pneumatozele *f*, Pneumozele *f*.
pneumatogram/*n*: Spirogramm *n*.
pneumaturia/*n*: Pneumaturie *f*.
pneumococcal meningitis: Pneumokokkenmeningitis *f*.
pneumococcal nephritis: Pneumokokkennephritis *f*.

pneumococcal pneumonia: Pneumokokkenpneumonie *f*.
pneumoconiosis/*n*: Pneumokoniose *f*, Staublungenkrankheit *f*.
Pneumocystis jirovecii pneumonia: Pneumocystis-jirovecii-Pneumonie *f*.
pneumography/*n*: Pneumographie *f*, Pneumoradiographie *f*.
pneumonectomy/*n*: Pneumonektomie *f*.
pneumonia/*n*: infection of the lungs which can be caused by different kinds of microorganisms, by physical factors or chemical substances. Symptoms include high fever, chills, coughing, and difficult, rapid breathing. Pneumonie *f*, Lungenentzündung *f*.
pneumonitis/*n*: Pneumonitis *f*.
pneumoperitonitis/*n*: Pneumoperitonitis *f*.
pneumothorax/*n*: abnormal entrance of air into the lung sac which may result from trauma or a pathological process or may occur spontaneously, causing an imbalance of pressures and difficult respiration. Pneumothorax *m*.
pock/*n*: Pustel *f*, Blatter *f*.
pocket/*n, vb*: 1. Tasche *f*, Hohlraum *m*.
podology/*n*: Fußpflege *f*.
podophyllin/*n*: Podophyllin *n*.
podophyllotoxin/*n*: Podophyllotoxin *n*.
poikilocytosis/*n*: Poikilozytose *f*.
point/*n, vb*: 1. Punkt *m*, Spitze *f*; 2. hinweisen, zeigen, punktieren.
pointed wart: Kondylom *n*, Feigwarze *f*.
point mutation: Punktmutation *f*.
poison/*n, vb*: 1. Gift *n*; 2. vergiften.
pokeweed mitogen: Kermesbeerenmitogen *n*.
polar/*adj*: polar.
polar body: Polkörperchen *n*.
polarity/*n*: Polarität *f*.
polar presentation: in obstetrics, a position of the fetus which is in parallel to the long axis of the mother and in which the buttocks or feet appear first in the uterine cervix. Längslage *f*, Geradlage *f*.
polar zone: Polzone *f*.
pole/*n*: Pol *m*, Eipol *m*.
polioencephalitis/*n*: Polioenzephalitis *f*.
poliomyelitis/*n*: an infectious disease caused by poliovirus, affecting the cells of the central nervous system and especially cells of the anterior column of the spinal cord. Main symptom is a muscular paralysis, sometimes including paralysis of respiratory muscles. Poliomyelitis *f*, Kinderlähmung *f*.
poliomyelitis vaccine: Polioimpfstoff *m*.
pollakisuria/*n*: Pollakisurie *f*.
pollution/*n*: Pollution *f*, Verunreinigung *f*.
polyadenopathy/*n*: Polyadenopathie *f*.
polyarteritis/*n*: Polyarteriitis *f*.
polyarthritis/*n*: simultaneous inflammation of several joints, occurring for example in rheumatic fever. Polyarthritis *f*.
polychondritis/*n*: Polychondritis *f*.
polyclonal antibody: polyklonaler Antikörper *m*.
polycystic/*adj*: polyzystisch.
polycystic kidney: Zystenniere *f*.
polycystic ovary syndrome: a syndrome which is characterized by the presence of polycystic ovaries. Symptoms include oligomenorrhea or amenorrhea, anovulation, and a male pattern of hair distribution. A PCO syndrome may occur as side effect of certain drugs. polyzystisches Ovarialsyndrom *n*, Stein-Leventhal-Syndrom *n*.
polycystic renal disease: polyzystische Nephropathie *f*.
polycythemia/*n*: condition which is characterized by an absolute or relative excess of red blood cells, resulting for example from myeloproliferative disorders like Vaquez-Osler disease. Polyzythämie *f*.
polydactyly/*n*: Polydaktylie *f*.
polydipsia/*n*: continued excessive fluid intake, as a consequence of or-

ganic disorders such as dehydration in diabetes, a reaction to medication or ingestion of a substance, or from an emotional cause. Polydipsie *f*.

polygamy/*n*: Polygamie *f*.

polyglandular adenomatosis: an autosomal dominant inherited syndrome which is characterized by the presence of benign or malignant neoplasms of more than one endocrine gland and neurocutaneous alterations. multiple endokrine Neoplasie *f*, MEN.

polyhedral cell: polyedrische Zelle *f*.

polymenorrhea/*n*: Polymenorrhö *f*.

polymerase chain reaction: Polymerasekettenreaktion *f*, PCR.

polymorphism/*n*: Polymorphie *f*, Polymorphismus *m*.

polymorphonuclear granulocyte: Polymorphkerniger *m*.

polymorphonuclear leukocyte: Polymorphkerniger *m*.

polymorphous chorea: Gilles-de-la-Tourette-Syndrom *n*.

polymyopathy/*n*: Polymyopathie *f*.

polymyositis/*n*: Polymyositis *f*.

polymyxin/*n*: Polymyxin *n*.

polyneuritic psychosis: Wernicke-Korsakoff-Psychose *f*.

polyneuritis/*n*: simultaneous inflammation of several nerves. In cranial polyneuritis or mononeuritis multiplex several cranial nerves are involved; acute idiopathic polyneuritis or Guillain-Barré syndrome is characterized by rapidly ascending motor neuron paralysis. Polyneuritis *f*.

polyneuropathy/*n*: pathological change and functional disturbances of several peripheral nerves at the same time. Causes include chronic alcohol consumption, or intoxication with drugs or chemical substances, for example arsenic. Polyneuropathie *f*.

polyopia/*n*: Polyopie *f*.

polyostotic fibrous dysplasia: polyostotische Fibrodysplasie *f*, Jaffé-Lichtenstein-Syndrom *n*.

polyp/*n*: excessive outgrowths from the mucous membranes of the nose, or internal organs like intestines or bladder. Polyp *m*.

polypoid carcinoma: polypoides Karzinom *n*.

polypoid hyperplasia: polypoide Hyperplasie *f*.

polyposis/*n*: Polypose *f*.

polysaccharide/*n*: Polysaccharid *n*.

polysomaty/*n*: Polysomatie *f*.

polythiazide/*n*: Polythiazid *n*.

polyunsaturated/*adj*: mehrfach ungesättigt.

polyunsaturated fatty acid: mehrfach ungesättigte Fettsäure *f*.

polyuria/*n*: excessive urination, occurring as a symptom of metabolic disorders like diabetes insipidus or diabetes mellitus, or compensatory after a period of anuria. Polyurie *f*.

polyvalent vaccine: polyvalenter Impfstoff *m*.

pompholyx/*n*: Pompholyx *f*.

pontine/*adj*: pontin.

pontine sleep: REM-Schlaf *m*, desynchronisierter Schlaf *m*, paradoxer Schlaf *m*.

pontine syndrome: a neurologic syndrome resulting from lesions of the pontine region which is characterized by hemiataxia, adiadochokinesis, Horner syndrome, and dissociated sensitivity disorders. Brückensyndrom *n*.

pool/*n*: Pool *m*, Ansammlung *f*, Reservoir *n*.

pooled plasma: Mischplasma *n*.

poor prognosis: schlechte Prognose *f*.

poor response: schlechtes Ansprechen *n*.

popliteal/*adj*: popliteal.

popliteal bursitis: Poplitealzyste *f*, Baker-Zyste *f*.

popliteal fossa: Kniekehle *f*.

population/*n*: Population *f*, Bevölkerung *f*, Kollektiv *n*.

population distribution: Bevölkerungsverteilung *f*.

population pyramid: Bevölkerungspyramide *f*.

population study: Bevölkerungsstudie *f*.

porcine insulin: Schweineinsulin *n*.

P

pore/*n*: Öffnung *f*, Pore *f*.
porencephalic cyst: Porenzephalie *f*.
porencephaly/*n*: Porenzephalie *f*.
porfimer/*n*: Porfimer *n*.
porphobilinogen/*n*: Porphobilinogen *n*.
porphyria/*n*: Porphyrie *f*.
porphyric neuropathy: porphyrische Neuropathie *f*.
porphyrin/*n*: Porphyrin *n*.
porphyrinogen/*n*: Porphyrinogen *n*.
portal/*n, adj*: 1. Eingang *m*, Pforte *f*; 2. portal.
portal block: Pfortaderblock *m*.
portal circulation: Portalkreislauf *m*.
portal cirrhosis: Laennec-Leberzirrhose *f*.
portal hypertension: increased pressure in the area of the portal vein, caused by intra- or extrahepatic disorders like liver cirrhosis, thrombosis, or liver fibrosis. Symptoms include splenomegaly, ascites, and varicosis of esophageal and gastric veins. portale Hypertension *f*.
portal system: Pfortadergebiet *n*.
portal venography: Portographie *f*.
portal venous pressure: Portalvenendruck *m*.
portion/*n*: Teil *m*, Anteil *m*.
portocaval anastomosis: portokavale Anastomose *f*.
portocaval encephalopathy: hepatische Enzephalopathie *f*.
portacaval shunt: portokavaler Shunt *m*.
posaconazol/*n*: Posaconazol *n*.
position/*n*: Position *f*, Lage *f*.
positional failure: Haltungsschaden *m*.
positional nystagmus: Stellungsnystagmus *m*, Lagenystagmus *m*.
positional vertigo: Lageschwindel *m*.
positive/*adj*: positiv.
positive cardiac inotropic agent: positiv inotrop wirkende Substanz *f*.
positive end-expiratory pressure: positiver endexspiratorischer Beatmungsdruck *m*, PEEP.
positive feedback: positive Rückkopplung *f*.
positive pressure: Überdruck *m*.
positron emission tomography: Positronenemissionstomographie *f*.
posology/*n*: Posologie *f*.
postabortal/*adj*: postabortiv.
postabortal sepsis: Abortsepsis *f*.
postauricular incision: retroaurikuläre Inzision *f*.
postbranchial body: Ultimobranchialkörper *m*.
postcardiotomy syndrome: a condition occurring after cardiac surgery or myocardial infarction which is characterized by fever, pleurisy, and pericarditis. Postkardiotomiesyndrom *n*, Dressler-Syndrom *n*.
postcoital contraception: postkoitale Kontrazeption *f*.
postconceptional gestational period: Schwangerschaftsdauer post conceptionem *f*.
postconcussional syndrome: physical and mental symptoms that may occur after concussion of the brain, for example amnesia, headache, dizziness, irritability, insomnia, anxiety, and impairment of memory and concentration. postkommotionelles Syndrom *n*.
postencephalitic parkinsonism: postenzephalitisches Parkinson-Syndrom *n*.
postepileptic paralysis: postiktale Lähmung *f*, Todd-Paralyse *f*.
posterior/*adj*: hinterer, posterior.
posterior asynclitism: Hinterscheitelbeineinstellung *f*.
posterior horn cell: Hinterhornzelle *f*.
posterior lobe: Hinterlappen *m*.
posterior rhizotomy: hintere Rhizotomie *f*, Foerster-Operation *f*.
posterior root: Hinterwurzel *f*.
postexposure/*adj*: postexpositionell.
postgastrectomy syndrome: a syndrome characterized by gastrointestinal and cardiovascular signs and symptoms like diarrhea, nausea, weakness, sweating, palpitation, headache etc. following food intake in persons who had gastrectomy. Postgastrektomiesyndrom *n*, Dumpingsyndrom *n*.

posthemorrhagic anemia: Blutungsanämie *f*.
postherpetic neuralgia: postherpetische Neuralgie *f*.
postictal/*adj*: postiktal.
postictal sleep: postepileptische Schlafphase *f*.
postinfectious arthritis: postinfektiöse Arthritis *f*, Begleitarthritis *f*.
postinfectious encephalitis: postinfektiöse Enzephalitis *f*.
postmature infant: übertragenes Kind *n*.
postmaturity/*n*: Überreife *f*.
postmenopausal osteoporosis: Involutionsosteoporose *f*.
postmortal/*adj*: post mortem.
postnasal space: Nasenrachenraum *m*.
postnatal development: nachgeburtliche Entwicklung *f*, Reifung *f*.
postnatal mortality: Säuglingssterblichkeit *f*.
postneonatal period: Säuglingsalter *n*.
postoperative irradiation: Nachbestrahlung *f*.
postpartal pituitary necrosis: Hypophysennekrose *f*, Sheehan-Syndrom *n*.
post partum amenorrhea: postpartale Amenorrhö *m*.
post partum period: Nachgeburtsperiode *f*.
postprandial/*adj*: postprandial.
postradiation fibrosis: Strahlenfibrose *f*.
postrenal anuria: postrenale Anurie *f*.
postspinal headache: postpunktioneller Kopfschmerz *m*.
poststreptococcal glomerulonephritis: Poststreptokokkennephritis *f*.
postsurgical infection: postoperative Infektion *f*.
postsynaptic inhibition: postsynaptische Hemmung *f*.
post-term birth: Spätgeburt *f*.
post-transfusion hepatitis: Transfusionshepatitis *f*.
post-traumatic amnesia: posttraumatische Amnesie *f*.
post-traumatic cervical syndrome: a syndrome occurring after indirect trauma to the neck, for example a whiplash injury, which is characterized by pain, muscle spasm, headache, paresthesia, and vision disturbances. posttraumatisches Halswirbelsäulensyndrom *n*.
post-traumatic epilepsy: posttraumatische Epilepsie *f*.
post-traumatic osteoporosis: Sudeck-Syndrom *n*.
post-traumatic stress disorder: posttraumatisches Belastungssyndrom *n*.
postural/*adj*: Lage-, Stellungs-.
postural change: Lagewechsel *m*.
postural drainage: Lagedrainage *f*.
postural fixation: Lagefixation *f*.
postural ischemia: lagebedingte Ischämie *f*.
postural nystagmus: Stellungsnystagmus *m*, Lagenystagmus *m*.
postural reflex: Stellreflex *m*, Lagereflex *m*.
postural vertigo: Lageschwindel *m*.
posture/*n*: Körperhaltung *f*, Körperstellung *f*.
postvaccinal/*adj*: postvakzinal.
postvaccinal encephalitis: postvakzinale Enzephalitis *f*, Impfenzephalitis *f*.
potassium/*n*: Kalium *n*, K.
potassium bromide: Kaliumbromid *n*.
potassium dichromate: Kaliumdichromat *n*.
potassium-losing nephritis: Kaliumverlustnephritis *f*.
potassium permanganate: Kaliumpermanganat *n*.
potato nose: Kartoffelnase *f*, Rhinophym *n*.
potency/*n*: Potenz *f*, Wirkpotential *n*.
potent/*adj*: potent.
potential/*n*: Potential *n*.
potential years of life lost: potentielle Lebensverkürzung *f*.
pouch/*n*: Sack *m*, Tasche *f*.
poultice/*n*: Umschlag *m*.
povidone iodine: Povidon-Iod *n*, PVP-Jodlösung *f*.

powder/*n, vb*: 1. Puder *m*, Pulver *n*; 2. pudern, pulverisieren.
powdered extract: Trockenextrakt *m*.
power/*n*: Stärke *f*, Macht *f*, Energie *f*.
pox/*n*: blisters and scars on the skin as a symptom of certain diseases, for example chickenpox, smallpox. Pocken *f*, Blattern *f*.
practice/*n, vb*: 1. Praxis *f*, Gewohnheit *f*, Verfahren *n*; 2. praktizieren, ausüben.
practitioner/*n*: praktischer Arzt *m*, Praktiker *m*.
practolol/*n*: Practolol *n*.
prajmalium bitartrate: Prajmaliumbitartrat *n*.
pralidoxime/*n*: Pralidoxim *n*.
pramipexol/*n*: Pramipexol *n*.
pramiverine/*n*: Pramiverin *n*.
prasterone/*n*: Prasteron *n*.
pravastatin/*n*: Pravastatin *n*.
praziquantel/*n*: Praziquantel *n*.
prazosin/*n*: Prazosin *n*.
preanesthesia/*n*: Pränarkose *f*.
preauricular cyst: präaurikuläre Zyste *f*.
preauricular fistula: Präaurikularsinus *m*.
precancer/*n*: Präkanzerose *f*.
precancerous dermatosis: präkanzeröse Dermatose *f*, Bowen-Krankheit *f*.
precentral motor cortex: präzentraler motorischer Kortex *m*.
precipitate labor: Sturzgeburt *f*.
precipitation/*n*: Präzipitation *f*.
precipitation test: Präzipitationsreaktion *f*.
precipitin/*n*: Präzipitin *n*.
precocious puberty: Pubertas praecox *f*.
precocity/*n*: Frühreife *f*.
precollagenous fiber: präkollagene Faser *f*.
precordial/*adj*: präkordial.
precordial leads: präkordiale Ableitungen, Brustwandableitungen, Wilson-Ableitungen.
precordial pain: Präkordialschmerz *m*.
precursory symptom: Prodromalzeichen *n*.
predictor/*n*: Prädiktor *m*.
prednicarbate/*n*: Prednicarbat *n*.
prednimustine/*n*: Prednimustin *n*.
prednisolone/*n*: Prednisolon *n*.
prednisolone acetate: Prednisolonacetat *n*.
prednisolone sodium phosphate: Prednisolon-Natriumphosphat *n*.
prednisone/*n*: Prednison *n*.
prednylidene/*n*: Prednyliden *n*.
preeclampsia/*n*: Präeklampsie *f*.
preeclamptic toxemia: präeklamptische Toxämie *f*.
preexisting condition: vorbestehende Erkrankung *f*.
prefrontal/*adj*: präfrontal.
pregabalin/*n*: Pregabalin *n*.
pregnancy/*n*: Schwangerschaft *f*, Gravidität *f*.
pregnancy complication: Schwangerschaftskomplikation *f*.
pregnancy test: Schwangerschaftstest *m*.
pregnanediol/*n*: Pregnandiol *n*.
pregnant/*adj*: schwanger.
prehension arm: Greifarm *m*.
preinfarction angina: Präinfarktsyndrom *n*.
preinvasive carcinoma: präinvasives Karzinom *n*.
prejudice/*n*: Vorurteil *n*.
premature/*adj*: prämatur, vorzeitig.
premature beat: Extrasystole *f*.
premature birth: according to criteria of the World Health Organization (WHO), birth of an immature infant occurring before pregnancy week 37 or day 259 after the last menstruational period. Frühgeburt *f*.
premature ejaculation: expulsion of semen before or in the very beginning of sexual intercourse. vorzeitige Ejakulation *f*, Ejaculatio praecox *f*.
premature infant: Frühgeborenes *n*.
premature rupture of membranes: vorzeitiger Blasensprung *m*.
premature systole: vorzeitig einfallende Extrasystole *f*.
prematurity/*n*: Unreife *f*.
premenopausal/*adj*: prämenopausal.
premenstrual/*adj*: prämenstruell.

premenstrual headache: prämenstrueller Kopfschmerz *m*.
premenstrual phase: Prämenstruationsphase *f*.
premenstrual swelling: prämenstruelle Schwellung *f*.
premenstrual syndrome: recurrent syndrome occurring before menstruation, attributed to endocrine or neurovegetative dysfunction. Symptoms include mastodynia, dysmenorrhea, headache, psychological signs, edema, and gastrointestinal signs. prämenstruelles Syndrom *n*.
premolar/*n*: Prämolar *m*.
premotor cortex: prämotorischer Kortex *m*.
prenatal/*adj*: pränatal.
prenatal care: Schwangerenbetreuung *f*.
prenatal development: Embryonalentwicklung *f*.
prenatal diagnosis: pränatale Diagnose *f*.
prenatal period: Pränatalzeit *f*, Pränatalperiode *f*.
prenatal screening: pränatales Screening *n*.
prenatal syphilis: angeborene Syphilis *f*.
prenylamine/*n*: Prenylamin *n*.
preoperative preparation: Operationsvorbereitung *f*
preoperative radiotherapy: präoperative Strahlentherapie *f*.
preparation/*n*: Präparation *f*, Vorbereitung *f*.
prepuberty/*n*: Präpubertät *f*.
prepuce/*n*: Vorhaut *f*, Präputium *n*.
preputial concretion: Vorhautkonkrement *n*, Smegmolith *m*.
prerenal anuria: prärenale Anurie *f*.
prerenal azotemia: extrarenale Azotämie *f*, Produktionsazotämie *f*.
prerenal failure: prärenales Nierenversagen *n*.
prerequisite/*n, adj*: 1. Voraussetzung *f*; 2. notwendig.
presbyacusis/*n*: Presbyakusis *f*, Altersschwerhörigkeit *f*.
presbyophrenia/*n*: Presbyophrenie *f*, senile Demenz *f*.
presbyopia/*n*: loss of elasticity in eyes which occurs in old age and which results in accomodation disturbances and hyperopia. Presbyopie *f*, Alterssichtigkeit *f*.
prescribe/*vb*: verschreiben, verordnen.
prescription/*n*: Verordnung *f*, Rezept *n*.
prescription drug: verschreibungspflichtiges Medikament *n*.
prescription fee: Rezeptgebühr *f*.
presence/*n*: Vorliegen *n*.
presenile dementia: präsenile Demenz *f*.
presenile psychosis: präsenile Psychose *f*.
presentation/*n*: Kindseinstellung *f*, Kindslage.
presentation of the cord: in obstetrics, a prolapse of the umbilical cord into the vagina before delivery. Nabelschnurvorfall *m*.
present condition: Status praesens *m*.
presenting symptom: subjektives Hauptsymptom *n*.
pressure/*n*: Druck *m*, Wucht *f*.
pressure dressing: Druckverband *m*.
pressure necrosis: Drucknekrose *f*.
pressure sore: lesion over prominent areas on the body of a bedridden person, caused by prolonged pressure. Initial symptoms include reddening of the skin, and formation of blisters, leading to necrotic alterations, and lesions involving lower layers of the tissue, muscle, and sometimes skeletal bones. Druckgeschwür *n*, Dekubitus *m*.
presynaptic inhibition: präsynaptische Hemmung *f*.
presystolic/*adj*: präsystolisch.
presystolic murmur: Präsystolikum *n*.
preterm infant: Frühgeborenes *n*.
pretibial fever: prätibiales Fieber *n*, Fort-Bragg-Fieber *n*.
prevalence/*n*: Prävalenz *f*.
prevent/*vb*: vorbeugen, verhindern.
prevention/*n*: Prävention *f*, Vorbeugung *f*.
preventive/*adj*: präventiv.

priapism/*n*: continued, painful erection of the penis without sexual stimulus, eventually associated with cystitis or urethritis, or occurring as a sign of certain diseases of the spinal cord. Priapismus *m*.
prickle/*n*: Korn *n*, Körnchen *n*.
prickle cell: Plattenepithelzelle *f*.
pridinol/*n*: Pridinol *n*.
primaquine/*n*: Primaquin *n*.
primary/*adj*: primär.
primary adrenocortical insufficiency: Addison-Krankheit *f*, Nebennierenrindeninsuffizienz *f*.
primary alcohol: primärer Alkohol *m*.
primary aldosteronism: primärer Aldosteronismus *m*, Conn-Syndrom *n*.
primary amenorrhea: primäre Amenorrhö *f*.
primary amine: primäres Amin *n*.
primary amyloidosis: primäre Amyloidose *f*.
primary biliary cirrhosis: primäre biliäre Zirrhose *f*.
primary bone: embryonale Knochenanlage *f*.
primary cancer: Primärtumor *m*.
primary care: Grundversorgung *f*.
primary degenerative dementia: primär degenerative Demenz *f*.
primary dentition: erste Dentition *f*, Milchgebiss *n*.
primary filtration: Vorfilterung *f*.
primary follicle: Primärfollikel *m*.
primary glaucoma: primäres Glaukom *n*.
primary infection: Primärinfektion *f*.
primary lateral sclerosis: primäre Lateralsklerose *f*, Erb-Sklerose *f*.
primary lesion: Primäraffekt *m*.
primary polycythemia: Polycythaemia vera *f*, Vaquez-Osler-Krankheit *f*.
primary prevention: Primärprävention *f*.
primary progressive amyotrophy: degenerative myopathy which is characterized by progressive weakness and atrophy of muscles, resulting from enzyme deficiency. Typically, the nervous system is not involved. Symptoms may include myopathic or waddling gait, and pseudohypertrophy with increase of muscle tissue but without true hypertrophy. Muskeldystrophie *f*.
primary sclerosing cholangitis: primär sklerosierende Cholangitis *f*.
primary sore: harter Schanker *m*, Primäraffekt *m*.
primary spastic paraplegia: primäre Lateralsklerose *f*.
primary sterility: primäre Sterilität *f*.
primary suture: Primärverschluss *m*.
primary syphilis: primäre Syphilis *f*.
primary tumor: Primärtumor *m*.
primary urine: Primärharn *m*.
primate/*n*: Primat *m*.
primidone/*n*: Primidon *n*.
primiparous/*adj*: primipar.
primitive bone: Primitivknochen *m*.
primitive brain: Archenzephalon *n*.
primitive gut: Archenteron *n*, Urdarm *m*.
primitive organ: Urorgan *n*.
primitive perineal body: Primitivknoten *m*.
primitive reflex: primitiver Reflex *m*, frühkindlicher Reflex *m*.
primordial germ cell: Urkeimzelle *f*.
primordial gigantism: primordialer Riesenwuchs *m*.
primordial ovarian follicle: Primordialfollikel *m*.
principle/*n*: Prinzip *n*.
prion/*n*: Prion *n*.
prismatic spectacles: Prismenbrille *f*.
prison hospital: Gefängniskrankenhaus *n*.
privacy/*n*: Privatsphäre *f*.
probability/*n*: Wahrscheinlichkeit *f*.
proband/*n*: Proband *m*, Versuchsperson *f*.
probe/*n, vb*: 1. Sonde *f*; 2. sondieren.
probenecid/*n*: Probenecid *n*.
probing/*n*: Sondierung *f*.
problem/*n*: Problem *n*.
probucol/*n*: Probucol *n*.
procainamide/*n*: Procainamid *n*.
procaine/*n*: Procain *n*.
procaine penicillin G: Procainpenicillin G *n*.
procarbazine/*n*: Procarbazin *n*.
procaterol/*n*: Procaterol *n*.

procedure/*n*: Verfahren *n*, Vorgehen *n*, Behandlungsmethode *f*.
process/*n*: Prozess *m*, Verfahren *n*, Fortsatz *m*.
procidentia/*n*: Prolaps *m*.
procoagulant/*n*: Gerinnungsfaktorvorstufe *f*.
procreative capacity: Zeugungsfähigkeit *f*.
proctalgia/*n*: Proktalgie *f*.
proctectomy/*n*: Proktektomie *f*.
proctitis/*n*: inflammation of the rectum and/or anus, caused by pathogenic microorganisms, or physical damage, for example resulting from radiation therapy of the cervix. Proktitis *f*.
proctocele/*n*: Proktozele *f*, Rektozele *f*.
proctoscopy/*n*: Proktoskopie *f*.
procyclidine/*n*: Procyclidin *n*.
prodromal/*adj*: prodromal.
prodromal stage: Prodromalstadium *n*.
prodrug/*n*: Pro-Drug *n*, Arzneimittelvorstufe *f*.
product/*n*: Produkt *n*, Ergebnis *n*.
productive cough: produktiver Husten *m*.
professional ethics: Deontologie *f*.
professional spasm: Beschäftigungskrampf *m*.
profuse rash: profuser Ausschlag *m*.
progeny/*n*: Nachkommenschaft *f*.
progeria/*n*: a condition which is characterized by premature aging, possibly caused by a genetic disorder, with death occurring around the age of ten years due to arteriosclerosis. Progerie *f*, Hutchinson-Gilford-Syndrom *n*.
progestational phase: Lutealphase *f*.
progesterone/*n*: Progesteron *n*.
progestin/*n*: Progestin *n*.
proglumetacin/*n*: Proglumetacin *n*.
proglumide/*n*: Proglumid *n*.
prognathism/*n*: Prognathie *f*.
prognosis/*n*: Prognose *f*, Vorhersage *f*.
prognostic/*n, adj*: 1. prognostisches Zeichen *n*; 2. prognostisch.
progranulocytic leukemia: Promyelozytenleukämie *f*.
progress/*n, vb*: 1. Fortschritt *m*, Progredienz *f*; 2. voranschreiten, fortschreiten.
progressive/*adj*: progressiv, progredient.
progressive bacterial synergistic gangrene: progrediente Gangrän *f*.
progressive bulbar paralysis: progressive Bulbärparalyse *f*.
progressive cerebellar tremor: Dyssynergia cerebellaris myoclonica *f*.
progressive diaphyseal dysplasia: Camurati-Engelmann-Syndrom *n*, Osteopathia hyperostotica multiplex infantilis *f*.
progressive facial atrophy: Hemiatrophia facialis progressiva *f*, Romberg-Syndrom *n*.
progressive lingual hemiatrophy: progressive Zungenatrophie *f*, Melkersson-Rosenthal-Syndrom *n*.
progressive lipodystrophy: Lipodystrophia progressiva *f*, Simons-Syndrom *n*.
progressive muscular dystrophy: degenerative myopathy which is characterized by progressive weakness and atrophy of muscles, resulting from enzyme deficiency. Typically, the nervous system is not involved. Symptoms may include myopathic or waddling gait, and pseudohypertrophy with increase of muscle tissue without true hypertrophy. progressive Muskeldystrophie *f*.
progressive myoclonic epilepsy: progressive Myoklonus-Epilepsie *f*, Lafora-Epilepsie *f*.
progressive nuclear amyotrophy: progressive nukleäre Muskelatrophie *f*.
progressive ophthalmoplegia: obere Bulbärparalyse *f*, Graefe-Syndrom *n*.
progressive pigmented purpuric dermatosis: progressive Pigmentdermatose *f*, Schamberg-Dermatose *f*.
progressive scleroderma: progressives Skleroderm *n*.
progressive spinal muscular dystrophy: spinale progressive Muskelatrophie *f*, Aran-Duchenne-Syndrom *n*.

P

progressive subcortical encephalopathy: subkortikale arteriosklerotische Enzephalopathie *f*, Binswanger-Enzephalopathie *f*.
progressive supranuclear palsy: progressive supranukleäre Lähmung *f*, Steele-Richardson-Olszewski-Syndrom *n*.
progressive traumatic encephalopathy: Boxerenzephalopathie *f*.
proguanil hydrochloride: Proguanil *n*.
projection/*n*: Projektion *f*, Verlagerung *f*.
prolactin/*n*: Prolaktin *n*.
prolactinoma/*n*: Prolaktinom *n*.
prolactin-secreting pituitary adenoma: Prolaktinom *n*.
prolapse/*n, vb*: 1. Prolaps *m*, Vorfall *m*; 2. vorfallen, prolabieren.
prolapsed arm: Armvorfall *m*.
prolapse of intervertebral disk: dislocation and protrusion of the nucleus pulposus or anulus fibrosus of the intervertebral disk. Symptoms depend on the location and may include pain, abnormal reflex responses, and paresis. Bandscheibenvorfall *m*.
proliferation/*n*: Proliferation *f*.
proliferative fibrosis: proliferative Fibrose *f*.
proliferative stage: Proliferationsphase *f*.
prolintane/*n*: Prolintan *n*.
prolonged fever: anhaltendes Fieber *n*.
prolonged pregnancy: Übertragung *f*.
prolonged rupture of membranes: verspäteter Blasensprung *m*.
prominent ear: abstehendes Ohr *n*.
promiscuity/*n*: Promiskuität *f*.
promonocyte/*n*: Promonozyt *m*.
promontory/*n*: Promontorium.
promyelocytic leukemia: Promyelozytenleukämie *f*.
pronation-supination test: Pronations-Supinations-Versuch *m*.
prone/*adj*: in Bauchlage, geneigt.
proof/*n*: Beweis *m*, Nachweis *m*.
propafenone/*n*: Propafenon *n*.
propamidine/*n*: Propamidin *n*.
propanidid/*n*: Propanidid *n*.
propanol/*n*: Propanol *n*, Propylalkohol *m*.
propantheline bromide: Propanthelinbromid *n*.
propellant/*n*: Treibmittel *n*.
properdin/*n*: Properdin *n*.
prophylactic treatment: prophylaktische Behandlung *f*.
prophylaxis/*n*: Prophylaxe *f*, Krankheitsverhütung *f*.
propicillin/*n*: Propicillin *n*.
propionic acid: Propionsäure *f*.
propionic acidemia: Propionazidämie *f*.
propionyl/*n*: Propionyl *n*.
propionylsalicylic acid: Propionylsalicylsäure *f*.
propiverine/*n*: Propiverin *n*.
propofol/*n*: Propofol *n*.
propolis/*n*: Propolis *n*, Bienenharz *n*.
propoxycaine/*n*: Propoxycain *n*.
propranolol/*n*: Propranolol *n*.
proprioception/*n*: Propriozeption *f*.
proprioceptive reflex: propriozeptiver Reflex *m*.
proprioceptive sensation: Propriozeptivität *f*.
proprioceptor/*n*: Propriorezeptor *m*.
propulsion/*n*: Propulsion *f*, Antepulsion *f*.
propyl alcohol: Propylalkohol *m*, Propanol *n*.
propylhexedrine/*n*: Propylhexedrin *n*.
proquazone/*n*: Proquazon *n*.
prospective study: prospektive Studie *f*.
prostacyclin/*n*: Prostazyklin *n*.
prostaglandin: Prostaglandin *n*.
prostanoid/*n*: Prostanoid *n*.
prostate/*n*: Prostata *f*, Vorsteherdrüse *f*.
prostatectomy/*n*: Prostatektomie *f*.
prostatic adenoma: Prostataadenom *n*.
prostatic cancer: malignant neoplasm of the prostate, most frequently an adenocarcinoma located in the posterior prostate region. Initial tumor stages frequently cause no signs; symptoms of more advanced tumor stages include urination

disorders, hematuria, and bone pain following metastatic spread of tumor cells. Prostatakarzinom *n*.
prostatic concretion: Prostatakonkrement *n*.
prostatic resection: Prostataresektion *f*.
prostatitis/*n*: inflammation of the prostate, usually caused by bacterial infection. Symptoms include pain in the inguinal and perineal region, pollakiuria, and painful urination. Prostatitis *f*.
prosthesis/*n*: Prothese *f*.
prosthetic vascular graft: Gefäßprothesenimplantat *n*.
prostitution/*n*: Prostitution *f*.
prostration/*n*: Prostration *f*, hochgradige Erschöpfung *f*.
protamine/*n*: Protamin *n*.
protamine insulin: Protamin-Insulin *n*.
protease inhibitor: Proteaseinhibitor *m*.
protection/*n*: Schutz *m*, Schutzvorrichtung *f*.
protective antibody: protektiver Antikörper *m*.
protective bandage: Schutzverband *m*.
protective barrier: Schutzschranke *f*.
protective effect: Schutzwirkung *f*.
protective function: Schutzfunktion *f*.
protective immunization: Schutzimpfung *f*.
protective mechanism: Schutzmechanismus *m*.
protective ointment: Schutzsalbe *f*.
protective reflex: Schutzreflex *m*.
protective response: Schutzreaktion *f*.
protective spectacles: Schutzbrille *f*.
protective vaccination: Schutzimpfung *f*.
protein/*n*: Protein *n*, Eiweiß *n*.
protein binding capacity: Proteinbindungskapazität *f*.
protein deficiency: Eiweißmangel *m*.
protein-losing enteropathy: Eiweißverlustsyndrom *n*, exsudative Enteropathie *f*.
protein-modified fasting: proteinmodifiziertes Fasten *n*.
protein test: Eiweißprobe *f*.
proteinuria/*n*: presence of excessive amounts of protein in the urine. Proteinuria may be a sign of kidney disease, systemic disorders, or protein-secreting tumors, for example multiple myeloma. Proteinurie *f*.
proteolysis/*n*: Proteolyse *f*.
proteolytic enzyme: proteolytisches Enzym *n*.
prothipendyl/*n*: Prothipendyl *n*.
prothrombin/*n*: Prothrombin *n*, Faktor II *m*.
prothromboplastin time: Prothromboplastinzeit *f*.
protionamide/*n*: Protionamid *n*.
protirelin/*n*: Protirelin *n*.
protocatechuic acid: Protokatechusäure *f*.
proton pump inhibitor: Protonenpumpenhemmer *m*.
protopathic sensation: protopathische Sensibilität *f*.
protoplasm/*n*: Protoplasma *n*.
prototype/*n*: Prototyp *m*.
protozoan/*n*: Protozoon *n*.
protracted/*adj*: protrahiert.
protracted irradiation: protrahierte Bestrahlung *f*.
protruded disk: Bandscheibenprotrusion *f*.
protuberance/*n*: Protuberanz *f*.
proud flesh: Granulationsgewebe *n*, Wucherung *f*.
proviral/*adj*: proviral.
provisional amputation: provisorische Amputation *f*.
provisional callus: temporärer Kallus *m*.
provitamin/*n*: Provitamin *n*.
proximal/*adj*: proximal.
prune-belly syndrome: a rare congenital malformation syndrome which is characterized by hypoplasia or aplasia of abdominal musculature, abnormalities of the kidneys and the urinary tract, and absence or nondescent of the testes. Prune-Belly-Syndrom *n*, Bauchdeckenaplasie *f*.

pruritus/*n*: itching, caused by chemical or mechanical skin irritation, or due to emotional causes. General or circumscribed pruritus can occur as a sign of other diseases, infections, metabolic disorders, allergic reactions, or intoxications. Pruritus *m*, Hautjucken *n*.

pseudarthrosis/*n*: Pseudarthrose *f*, Falschgelenkbildung *f*.

pseudobulbar/*adj*: pseudobulbär.

pseudobulbar paralysis: Pseudobulbärparalyse *f*.

pseudocyst/*n*: Pseudozyste *f*.

pseudofollicular salpingitis: pseudofollikuläre Salpingitis *f*.

pseudohypertrophic muscular dystrophy: pseudohypertrophe Muskeldystrophie *f*.

pseudomembranous bronchitis: Bronchitis pseudomembranacea *f*.

pseudomembranous colitis: pseudomembranöse Kolitis *f*.

pseudomembranous conjunctivitis: Conjunctivitis pseudomembranosa *f*.

pseudomembranous croup: diphtherischer Krupp *m*.

pseudomembranous enterocolitis: pseudomembranöse Kolitis *f*.

pseudomonad/*n*: Pseudomonade *f*.

pseudomyasthenia/*n*: Pseudomyasthenie *f*, Lambert-Eaton-Syndrom *n*.

pseudoparalysis/*n*: Pseudoparalyse *f*.

pseudopod/*n*: Pseudopodium *n*.

psittacosis/*n*: Psittakose *f*, Papageienkrankheit *f*.

psoas sign: Psoaszeichen *n*.

psoriasis/*n*: chronic skin disorder of unknown origin which is characterized by development of red scaly patches, located predominantly in the elbow and/or popliteal cavity. Psoriasis *f*.

psychasthenia/*n*: Psychasthenie *f*.

psyche/*n*: Psyche *f*, Seele *f*.

psychiatry/*n*: Psychiatrie *f*.

psychic/*adj*: psychisch.

psychic blindness: Seelenblindheit *f*, optische Agnosie *f*.

psychic tension: psychische Anspannung *f*.

psychic trauma: psychisches Trauma *n*.

psychoanalysis/*n*: Psychoanalyse *f*.

psychobiology/*n*: Psychobiologie *f*.

psychogenic/*adj*: psychogen, seelisch bedingt.

psychogenic amenorrhea: psychogene Amenorrhö *f*.

psychogenic amnesia: psychogene Amnesie *f*, hysterische Amnesie *f*.

psychological/*adj*: psychologisch.

psychology/*n*: Psychologie *f*.

psychometric test: psychometrischer Test *m*.

psychomotor/*adj*: psychomotorisch.

psychomotor attack: Dämmerattacke *f*.

psychomotor development: psychomotorische Entwicklung *f*.

psychomotor epilepsy: psychomotorischer Anfall *m*, Temporallappenepilepsie *f*.

psychomotor hallucination: psychomotorische Halluzination *f*.

psychomotor retardation: psychomotorischer Entwicklungsrückstand *m*.

psychomotor seizure: psychomotorischer Anfall *m*.

psychomotor test: psychomotorischer Test *m*.

psychoneuroimmunology/*n*: Psychoneuroimmunologie *f*.

psychoneurosis/*n*: Psychoneurose *f*, Neurose *f*.

psychooncology/*n*: Psychoonkologie *f*.

psychopath/*n*: Psychopath *m*.

psychopathology/*n*: Psychopathologie *f*.

psychophysical law: psychophysisches Gesetz *n*.

psychosexual/*adj*: psychosexuell.

psychosis/*n*: a mental disorder which is characterized by severe impairment of the personality and is associated with perception disorders, delusions, hallucinations, and incomprehensive judgment of which the affected person is not aware. Psychose *f*.

psychosis of pregnancy: Schwangerschaftspsychose *f*.

psychosomatic/*adj*: psychosomatisch.
psychosomatic disease: psychosomatische Erkrankung *f*.
psychosomatic disorder: psychosomatische Störung *f*.
psychotherapy/*n*: Psychotherapie *f*.
psychotic/*adj*: psychotisch.
psychotic features: psychotische Merkmale.
pteroic acid: Pteroinsäure *f*.
pteroylglutamic acid: Pteroylglutaminsäure *f*.
pterygium/*n*: Pterygium *n*, Flügelfell *n*.
ptosis/*n*: Ptose *f*, Senkung *f*.
ptyalism/*n*: Ptyalismus *m*, Sialorrhö *f*.
ptyalography/*n*: Sialographie *f*.
ptyalolithiasis/*n*: Sialolithiasis *f*.
pubertal epilepsy: Pubertätsepilepsie *f*.
puberty/*n*: Pubertät *f*.
pubescence/*n*: Pubertätsphase *f*.
pubescent uterus: Uterus infantilis *m*.
pubic bone: Schambein *n*, Os pubis *n*.
pubic louse: Schamlaus *f*, Filzlaus *f*.
publication/*n*: Veröffentlichung *f*.
public health: Gesundheitswesen *n*.
pudding face: Vollmondgesicht *n*.
pudendal anesthesia: Pudendusanästhesie *f*.
pudendal neuralgia: Pudendusneuralgie *f*.
puerile/*adj*: pueril, kindlisch.
puerperal/*adj*: puerperal.
puerperal convulsion: Wochenbettkrampf *m*.
puerperal depression: Wochenbettdepression *f*.
puerperal endometritis: Endometritis puerperalis *f*, Wochenbettendometritis *f*.
puerperal fever: Puerperalfieber *n*, Wochenbettfieber *n*.
puerperal period: Wochenbett *n*.
puerperal psychosis: Wochenbettpsychose *f*.
puerperal sepsis: an infectious disease following birth or abortion, typically caused by the bacteria Streptococcus or Staphylococcus. Childbed fever can affect the entire birth channel, the uterine cavity, and may eventually result in septic shock. Puerperalfieber *n*, Wochenbettfieber *n*, Kindbettfieber *n*.
puerperal thrombosis: Wochenbettthrombose *f*.
puerperium/*n*: Puerperalperiode *f*, Kindbett *n*, Wochenbett *n*.
puff/*n*: Stoß *m*, blasendes Geräusch *n*, Puff *m*.
puffed/*adj*: aufgedunsen.
pugilistic attitude: Fechterstellung *f*.
pulmonary/*adj*: pulmonal.
pulmonary abscess: formation of one or more abscesses in the lung, mostly caused by aerobic bacteria and occurring after pneumonia, aspiration of a foreign body, perforating thoracic injury, or lung tumors. Symptoms include intermittent fever, chills, and painful breathing. Lungenabszess *m*.
pulmonary anthrax: Lungenmilzbrand *m*.
pulmonary aspergillosis: Lungenaspergillose *f*.
pulmonary biopsy: Lungenbiopsie *f*.
pulmonary circulation: Lungenkreislauf *m*, kleiner Kreislauf *m*.
pulmonary compliance: Lungencompliance *f*.
pulmonary congestion: Stauungslunge *f*, Lungenstauung *f*.
pulmonary cyanosis: pulmonale Zyanose *f*.
pulmonary cyst: Lungenzyste *f*.
pulmonary diffusing capacity: pulmonale Diffusionskapazität *f*.
pulmonary disease: Lungenerkrankung *f*.
pulmonary edema: abnormal accumulation of fluid in the lung tissue, mostly a transudate due to changes in capillary permeability. Underlying disorders include cardiovascular diseases like heart insufficiency, hypertension, myocardial infarction, renal failure, certain infectious diseases, and intoxication. Symptoms include dyspnea, in some cases foamy expectoration, and cyanosis. Lungenödem *n*.

pulmonary embolectomy: pulmonale Embolektomie *f*, Trendelenburg-Operation *f*.

pulmonary embolism: sudden blocking of the pulmonary artery or its branches by a blood clot, fat drops, air, or foreign body. Site of origin of blood clots resulting in pulmonary embolism is frequently a thrombosis of veins in the lower extremity, followed by blood clots originating in the right heart. Symptoms depend on the localization and the size of the affected area and may include acute cor pulmonale, thoracic pain, cardiovascular failure, and dyspnea. Lungenembolie *f*.

pulmonary emphysema: pathological accumulation of air in the pulmonary tissue, resulting in dilatation or destruction of pulmonary alveoli and distention of the thorax. Lungenemphysem *n*.

pulmonary fibrosis: formation of fibrous tissue in the lung which replaces the pulmonary alveolar walls. Symptoms include dyspnea, coughing, eventually fever, and weight loss. The chronic or idiopathic pulmonary fibrosis can be associated with diseases like sarcoidosis, hemosiderosis, sclerodermia, rheumatoid arthritis, or irradiation; acute and rapidly fatal forms occur in Hamman-Rich syndrome or Goodpasture syndrome. Lungenfibrose *f*.

pulmonary function test: Lungenfunktionsprobe *f*.

pulmonary gangrene: Lungengangrän *f*.

pulmonary heart disease: acute or chronic overload of the right ventricle of the heart, due to diseases which affect the structure of the lungs, or pulmonary embolism. Symptoms include an increase in size or a dilatation of the right ventricle. Cor pulmonale *n*.

pulmonary hemorrhage: Lungenblutung *f*.

pulmonary hypertension: pulmonale Hypertension *f*.

pulmonary infarction: Lungeninfarkt *m*.

pulmonary insufficiency: 1. decreased respiratory function, occurring as a ventilation disorder, or disturbance in pulmonary blood circulation. Forms include obstructive pulmonary disease with bronchial stenosis, and restrictive pulmonary disease with impaired lung compliance. pulmonale Insuffizienz *f*, respiratorische Insuffizienz *f*. 2. insufficent closure of the pulmonic semilunar valve of the heart, resulting in backflow of blood from the pulmonary artery into the right ventricle. Pulmonalklappeninsuffizienz *f*.

pulmonary perfusion: Lungendurchblutung *f*, Lungenperfusion *f*.

pulmonary plague: Lungenpest *f*.

pulmonary pressure: Pulmonalisdruck *m*.

pulmonary-renal syndrome: a condition resulting from formation of autoantibodies against the basement membranes of the renal glomeruli and pulmonary alveoli. Symptoms include life-threatening pulmonary hemorrhage, dyspnea, proteinuria, renal failure, anemia, and arterial hypertension. renopulmonales Syndrom *n*, Goodpasture-Syndrom *n*.

pulmonary resection: Lungenresektion *f*.

pulmonary sarcoidosis: Lungensarkoidose *f*.

pulmonary schistosomiasis: Lungenbilharziose *f*, Schistosomiasis pulmonalis *f*.

pulmonary sequestration: Lungensequester *m*.

pulmonary shunt: pulmonaler Shunt *m*.

pulmonary stenosis: Pulmonalstenose *f*.

pulmonary surfactant: Surfactantfaktor *m*, Antiatelektasefaktor *m*, AAF.

pulmonary tuberculosis: Lungentuberkulose *f*.

pulmonary valve: Pulmonalklappe *f*.

pulmonectomy/*n*: Pneumektomie *f*.

pulmonic murmur: Pulmonalgeräusch *n*.
pulmonic second sound: zweiter Herzton *m*, Pulmonaliston *m*.
pulmonology/*n*: Pulmologie *f*.
pulp/*n*: Pulpa *f*, Fleisch *n*.
pulpitis/*n*: Pulpitis *f*.
pulsate/*vb*: pulsieren.
pulsation/*n*: Pulsation *f*.
pulse/*n, vb*: 1. Puls *m*, P, Impuls *m*; 2. pulsieren, klopfen.
pulsed laser: gepulster Laser *m*.
pulse height: Pulshöhe *f*.
pulseless disease: Aortenbogensyndrom *n*, Takayasu-Krankheit *f*.
pulse rate: Pulsfrequenz *f*.
pump/*n, vb*: 1. Pumpe *f*; 2. pumpen.
punch biopsy: Stanzbiopsie *f*.
punctate/*n, adj*: 1. Punktat *n*; 2. punktiert, punktförmig.
punctate basophilia: basophile Tüpfelung *f*.
punctate bleeding: Kapillarblutung *f*.
punctate hemorrhage: punktförmige Hämorrhagie *f*.
punctate retinitis: Retinitis punctata *f*.
puncture/*n, vb*: 1. Punktur *f*, Einstich *m*; 2. punktieren.
pupil/*n*: Pupille *f*.
pupil dilatation: Pupillenerweiterung *f*, Mydriasis *f*.
pupillary athetosis: Athetosis pupillaris *f*, Hippus *m*.
pupillary reflex: Pupillenreflex *m*, Lichtreflex *m*.
pure/*adj*: rein, sauber.
pure agraphia: isolierte Agraphie *f*.
pure oxygen: reiner Sauerstoff *m*.
purgation/*n*: Abführen *n*.
purified tuberculin: Calmette-Tuberkulin *n*.
purpura/*n*: Purpura *f*.
purpuric acid: Purpursäure *f*.
purr/*vb*: schnurren, summen.
purulent/*adj*: purulent, eitrig.
purulent pericarditis: eitrige Perikarditis *f*.
purulent sputum: eitriges Sputum *n*.
pus/*n*: Eiter *m*.
pustular eczema: pustulöses Ekzem *n*.
pustular psoriasis: Psoriasis pustulosa *f*.
pustular rash: pustulöser Ausschlag *m*.
pustular syphilid: pustulöses Syphilid *n*.
pustule/*n*: Pustel *f*.
putrefaction/*n*: Putrefaktion *f*, Verwesung *f*.
pyelitis/*n*: Pyelitis *f*.
pyelography/*n*: Pyelographie *f*.
pyelolithotomy/*n*: Pyelolithotomie *f*.
pyelonephritis/*n*: inflammation of the pelvis of the kidney, frequently involving tubules, glomeruli, and blood vessels, usually caused by bacterial infection. Acute pyelonephritis is characterized by fever, chills, and pain in the dorsolumbar region. Chronic pyelonephritis is characterized by headache, thirst, polyuria, arterial hypertonia, slightly elevated body temperature, and tenderness in the dorsolumbar area. Pyelonephritis *f*.
pyelorenal reflux: pyelorenaler Reflux *m*.
pyelotubular backflow: pyelotubulärer Rückstau *m*.
pyemia/*n*: Pyämie *f*.
pyemic abscess: septischer Abszess *m*.
pyknic/*adj*: pyknisch.
pyknocytosis/*n*: Pyknozytose *f*.
pyknosis/*n*: Pyknose *f*.
pyknotic cell: pyknotische Zelle *f*.
pyloric/*adj*: pylorisch.
pyloric insufficiency: Pylorusinsuffizienz *f*.
pyloric stenosis: pathologic decrease in the diameter of the distal aperture of the stomach, the pylorus. It may be congenital as in hypertrophic pyloric stenosis or acquired due to an ulceration or carcinoma. Pylorusstenose *f*.
pylorogastrectomy/*n*: Pylorogastrektomie *f*.
pyloroplasty/*n*: Pyloroplastik *f*.
pylorus/*n*: Magenpförtner *m*, Pylorus *m*.
pyoderma/*n*: Pyodermie *f*.

pyogenic/*adj*: eiterbildend, pyogen.
pyometra/*n*: Pyometra *f*.
pyometritis/*n*: Pyometritis *f*.
pyonephrosis/*n*: Pyonephrose *f*, Eitersackniere *f*.
pyorrhea/*n*: Pyorrhö *f*, eitriger Ausfluss *m*.
pyorrhea pocket: Eiterhöhle *f*.
pyosalpinx/*n*: Pyosalpinx *f*.
pyramid/*n*: Pyramide *f*.
pyramidal/*adj*: pyramidal.
pyramidal cell: Pyramidenzelle *f*.
pyramidal fracture: Pyramidenfraktur *f*, LeFort-II-Fraktur *f*.
pyramidal neuron: Pyramidenbahnzelle *f*.
pyramidal tract: Pyramidenbahn *f*.
pyrantel/*n*: Pyrantel *n*.
pyrazinamide/*n*: Pyrazinamid *n*.
pyrexia/*n*: Pyrexie *f*, Fieber *n*.
pyrexial headache: Fieberkopfschmerz *m*.
pyridine/*n*: Pyridin *n*.
pyridostigmine bromide: Pyridostigminbromid *n*.
pyridoxic acid: Pyridoxinsäure *f*.
pyridoxine/*n*: Pyridoxin *n*.
pyrimethamine/*n*: Pyrimethamin *n*.
pyrimidine/*n*: Pyrimidin *n*.
pyrithione zinc: Pyrithion-Zink *n*.
pyrogen/*n*: Pyrogen *n*.
pyroglutamic acid: Pyroglutaminsäure *f*, 5-Oxoprolin *n*.
pyrophosphoric acid: Pyrophosphorsäure *f*.
pyrosis/*n*: burning pain in the stomach and gullet, associated with acid taste in the mouth, often associated with gastroesophageal reflux or dyspepsia. Pyrosis *f*, Sodbrennen *n*.
pyrrole/*n*: Pyrrol *n*, Imidol *n*.
pyrrolidine/*n*: Pyrrolidin *n*.
pyruvic acid: Brenztraubensäure *f*.
pyuria/*n*: Pyurie *f*.

Q

Q-fever: an infectious disease caused by the bacterium Coxiella burneti. Flue-like symptoms, including fever, chills, headache, mayalgia, and malaise. Q-Fieber *s*.
qhat/*n*: Kat *s*.
QOL <*abbr*> **quality of life**: Lebensqualität *w*.
QT syndrome: any condition which is characterized by a prolongation of the Q-T interval in the elctrocardiogram. Forms include acquired long QT syndrome, usually due to metabolic or cardiac disorders, due to drug or substance use, and congenital forms like Jervell and Lange-Nielsen syndrome or Romano-Ward syndrome. QT-Syndrom *s*.
quack/*n*: Quacksalber *m*.
quackery/*n*: Quacksalberei *w*.
quadrantic hemianopia: Quadrantenhemianopsie *w*.
quadrant resection: Quadrantenresektion *w*.
quadrate/*adj*: quadratisch.
quadriceps reflex: Quadrizepssehnenreflex *m*, Patellarsehnenreflex *m*.
quadriplegia/*n*: Tetraplegie *w*.
qualitative/*adj*: qualitativ.
quality/*n*: Qualität *w*.
quality factor: Qualitätsfaktor *m*.
quality of life: Lebensqualität *w*.
quantity/*n*: Quantität *w*, Menge *w*.
quantum/*n*: Quantum *s*, Menge *w*.
quarantine/*n, vb*: 1. Quarantäne *w*; 2. unter Quarantäne stellen, isolieren.
quarantine period: Quarantänezeit *w*.
quartan fever: Viertagefieber *s*, Quartana *w*, Malaria quartana *w*.
quartan malaria: Quartana *w*, Malaria quartana *w*.
quartile deviation: Quartilabweichung *w*.
quartz lamp: Quarzlampe *w*.
quaternary/*adj*: quartär.
quaternary amine: quartäres Amin *s*.
queasiness/*n*: Übelkeit *w*, Unwohlsein *s*.
querulant/*n*: Querulant *m*.
questionnaire/*n*: Fragebogen *m*.
quetiapine/*n*: Quetiapin *s*.
quick/*adj*: schnell.
quick pulse: schneller Puls *m*.
quicksilver/*n*: Quecksilber *s*, Hydrargyrum *s*, Hg.
quiescent/*adj*: ruhend, inaktiv.
quiet/*adj*: ruhig, still.
quillaic acid: Quillajasäure *w*.
quilled suture: Zapfennaht *w*.
quilted suture: Matratzennaht *w*.
quina/*n*: Chinarinde *w*, Cinchona *w*.
quinacrine/*n*: Mepacrin *s*.
quinagolide/*n*: Quinagolid *s*.
quinaldinic acid: Chinaldinsäure *w*.
quinapril/*n*: Quinapril *s*.
quinaprilat/*n*: Quinaprilat *s*.
quinethazone/*n*: Quinethazone *s*.
quinic acid: Chinasäure *w*.
quinidine/*n*: Chinidin *s*.
quinine/*n*: Chinin *s*.
quininism/*n*: intoxication with quinine. Symptoms include headache, buzzing, vomiting, scotoma, delirium, and eventually irreversible blindness and inner ear defect. Chininvergiftung *w*.
quinol/*n*: Chinol *s*.
quinoline/*n*: Chinolin *s*.
quinolinic acid: Chinolinsäure *w*.
quinolinol/*n*: Chinolinol *s*.
quinolone/*n*: Chinolon *s*.
quinone/*n*: Chinon *s*.
quinosol/*n*: Chinosol *s*.

quinsy/*n*: peritonsillar inflammation with abscess formation, usually occurring as a consequence of chronic tonsillitis. Symptoms include pain in the cervical region and palate, edematous swelling, and lymphadenitis. Peritonsillarabszess *m*.
quintan fever: Fünftagefieber *s*, Wolhynisches Fieber *s*.
quintiofos/*n*: Quintiofos *s*.
quintuple/*n*: Fünfling *m*.
quinupristine/*n*: Quinupristin *s*.
quiver/*n, adj*: 1. Zittern *s*, Zuckung *w*; 2. zittern, zucken.
quota/*n*: Quote *w*.
quota sample: Stichprobe *w*.
quotidian/*adj*: täglich.
quotidian malaria: Quotidiana *w*.
quotient/*n*: Quotient *m*.
Q wave: Q-Zacke *w*.
Q-wave infarction: Q-Wave-Infarkt *m*.

R

r <*abbr*> **recombinant/*adj***: rekombinant, r.

R <*abbr*> **1. roentgen; 2. respiratory exchange ratio**: 1. Röntgen *n*; 2. Gasaustauschquotient *m*.

rabbit fever: an infectious disease caused by the bacterium Francisella tularensis and transmitted from small rodents like rabbits to humans by insects. Symptoms include fever, ulcerative, papular lesions, and lymphadenitis. Hasenfieber *n*, Tularämie *f*.

rabeprazole/*n*: Rabeprazol *n*.

rabies/*n*: an infectious disease caused by the neurotropic rabies virus transmitted to humans by the bite of infected animals like fox or dogs. It affects the central nervous system, resulting in a furious or paralytic form, both frequently fatal. Typical symptoms include paresthesia, pain at inoculation site, agitation, delirium, convulsions, and paralysis. Rabies *f*, Tollwut *f*.

rabies vaccine: Tollwutvakzine *f*.

race/*n*: Rasse *f*.

racecadotril/*n*: Racecadotril *n*.

racefemine/*n*: Racefemin *n*.

racemose aneurysm: rankenförmiges Aneurysma *n*.

racemose hemangioma: Rankenhämangiom *n*.

rachial/*adj*: spinal.

rachitic bead: rachitischer Rosenkranz *m*.

rachitic chest: rachitischer Thorax *m*.

rachitic pelvis: rachitisches Becken *n*.

radial/*adj*: radial.

radial aplasia: Radiusaplasie *f*.

radial head: Radiusköpfchen *n*.

radial incision: Kreisbogenschnitt *m*.

radial palsy: Radialislähmung *f*.

radial paralysis: Radialislähmung *f*.

radial pulse: Radialispuls *m*.

radiant/*adj*: strahlend.

radiant energy: Strahlungsenergie *f*.

radiation/*n*: Strahlung *f*.

radiation biology: Strahlenbiologie *f*.

radiation castration: Strahlenkastration *f*, Kastrationsbestrahlung *f*.

radiation exposure: Strahlenexposition *f*.

radiation fibrosis: Strahlenfibrose *f*.

radiation-induced chromosomal aberration: strahleninduzierte Chromosomenaberration *f*.

radiation protection: Strahlenschutz *m*.

radiation therapy: Strahlentherapie *f*.

radical/*n, adj*: 1. Radikal *n*; 2. radikal.

radical excision: Radikalentfernung *f*.

radical mastectomy: radikale Mastektomie *f*, Halsted-Operation *f*.

radical maxillary antrotomy: Kieferhöhlenradikaloperation *f*, Caldwell-Luc-Operation *f*.

radical scavenger: Radikalfänger *m*.

radical surgery: Radikaloperation *f*.

radicotomy/*n*: Radikotomie *f*, Radikulotomie *f*.

radicular neuralgia: Wurzelneuralgie *f*.

radicular pain: radikulärer Schmerz *m*.

radicular syndrome: any condition resulting from lesions to the spinal nerve roots, for example caused by compression of a protruded disk. Symptoms may include motor or sensory impairments such as paralysis, hypesthesia, or paresthesia. Wurzelsyndrom *n*.

radiculitis/*n*: inflammation of a nerve root, especially of the root of a spinal nerve. Symptoms include pain and dysesthesia and/or motor deficiencies in the innervation area. Radikulitis *f*.

radiculoneuritic syndrome: a neurologic disorder of unknown etiology, possibly due to an autoimmune disorder following viral or bacteria infection. Symptoms include polyneuritis, ascending motor neuron paralysis and muscular weakness, initial paralysis of the legs, ascending to the arms and trunk. Radikuloneuritis *f*, Guillain-Barré-Syndrom *n*.

radioactive/*adj*: radioaktiv.

radioactive constant: Zerfallskonstante *f*.

radioactive nuclide: Radionuklid *n*.

radioactivity/*n*: Radioaktivität *f*.

radioallergosorbent test: Radioallergosorbenttest *m*, RAST.

radioautography/*n*: Autoradiographie *f*.

radiobiology/*n*: Radiobiologie *f*, Strahlenbiologie *f*.

radiocarpal joint: Radiokarpalgelenk *n*, Articulatio radiocarpalis *f*.

radioelement/*n*: radioaktives Element *n*.

radioepithelioma/*n*: Strahlenkarzinom *n*.

radiographic examination: Röntgenuntersuchung *f*.

radiographic field: Aufnahmefeld *n*.

radiographic picture: Röntgenbild *n*.

radiographic technique: Aufnahmetechnik *f*.

radiography/*n*: Röntgenaufnahme *f*.

radioimmunoassay/*n*: Radioimmunoassay *m*.

radioimmunoprecipitation assay/*n*: Radioimmunpräzipitationstest *m*.

radiologic/*adj*: radiologisch.

radiologic castration: Strahlenkastration *f*, Kastrationsbestrahlung *f*.

radiologic protection: Strahlenschutz *m*.

radiologic technician: Röntgenassistent *m*.

radiology/*n*: Radiologie *f*.

radionuclide/*n*: Radionuklid *n*.

radiopaque medium: Kontrastmittel *n*.

radiosensitivity/*n*: Strahlenempfindlichkeit *f*.

radiotherapy/*n*: Röntgentherapie *f*, Strahlentherapie *f*.

radius fracture: Radiusfraktur *f*.

rage reaction: Wutreaktion *f*.

railroad sickness: Kinetose *f*.

rainbow syndrome: a vision disorder which is characterized by a rainbow-colored ring seen around lights surrounding a body or image. Halo *m*.

raised temperature: erhöhte Temperatur *f*.

rale/*n, vb*: 1. Rasselgeräusch *n*; 2. rasseln.

raloxifene/*n*: Raloxifen *n*.

ramification/*n*: Verzweigung *f*, Verästelung *f*.

ramipril/*n*: Ramipril *n*.

random/*n, adj*: 1. Zufall; 2. zufällig.

random error: zufälliger Fehler *m*.

randomization/*n*: Randomisierung *f*.

randomized controlled trial: randomisierte kontrollierte Studie *f*.

random selection: Zufallsstichprobe *f*, zufällige Auswahl *f*.

range/*n*: Bereich *m*, Variationsbreite *f*.

ranibizumab/*n*: Ranibizumab *n*.

ranitidine/*n*: Ranitidin *n*.

ranula/*n*: swelling under the tongue due to the obstruction of the excretory ducts of a salivary gland. Ranula *f*, Froschgeschwulst *f*.

rape/*n, vb*: 1. Vergewaltigung *f*; 2. vergewaltigen.

rapid/*adj*: schnell.

rapid diagnosis: Schnelldiagnose *f*.

rapid eye movement: schnelle Augenbewegung *f*.

rapidly increasing pulse: Kletterpuls *m*.

rapid onset: plötzlicher Ausbruch *m*, akuter Beginn *m*.

rapid test: Schnelltest *m*.

rare/*adj*: selten.

rarefying osteitis: Osteoporose *f*.

rasagiline/*n*: Rasagilin *n*.

rasburicase/*n*: Rasburicase *f*.

rash/*n*: Ausschlag *m*, Exanthem *n*.
rat-bite fever: an infectious disease caused by the bacterium Spirillum minus, transmitted to humans by the bite of an infected rodent. Symptoms include a painful lesion at the inoculation site, lymphadenitis, recurrent fever, muscle and joint pain. Rattenbissfieber *n*.
rate/*n*: Rate *f*, Anteil *m*, Verhältnis *n*.
rating/*n*: Bewertung *f*, Einschätzung *f*.
ratio/*n*: Verhältnis *n*, Relation *f*.
rationalization/*n*: Rationalisierung *f*.
rattle/*n, vb*: 1. Rasseln *n*, Röcheln *n*; 2. rasseln, röcheln.
raucous/*adj*: rau, heiser.
rauwolfia alkaloid: Rauwolfia-Alkaloid *n*.
rave/*vb*: phantasieren, delirieren.
raw/*adj*: roh.
ray/*n*: Strahl *m*.
reabsorption/*n*: Rückresorption *f*, Rückabsorption *f*.
reactant/*n*: Reagenz *n*, Reaktionspartner *m*.
reaction/*n*: Reaktion *f*.
reactive/*adj*: reaktiv.
reactive depression: depression or severe lowering of mood tone as a reaction to an external event or situation, for example loss of a closely related person. reaktive Depression *f*.
reactive psychosis: reaktive Psychose *f*.
reactivity/*n*: Reaktivität *f*, Reaktionsfähigkeit *f*.
read error: Ablesefehler *m*.
readiness/*n*: Bereitschaft *f*.
reading/*n*: Lesen *n*, Ablesen *n*.
reading spectacles: Lesebrille *f*.
readmission/*n*: Wiederaufnahme *f*.
reagent/*n*: Reagenz *n*.
real anxiety: Realangst *f*.
reality orientation: Realitätsbezug *m*.
real-time/*n*: Real-Time *f*, Echtzeit *f*.
reanimation/*n*: Reanimation *f*.
reappearance/*n*: Wiederauftreten *n*.
reason/*n*: Verstand *m*, Ursache *f*.
rebound/*n*: Rebound *m*, Rückstoß *m*.
reboxetine/*n*: Reboxetin *n*.
rebreathing bag: Rückatmungsbeutel *m*.
recall/*vb*: erinnern.
recent/*adj*: rezent, kürzlich.
recent memory: Merkfähigkeit *f*, Kurzzeitgedächtnis *n*.
receptive/*adj*: rezeptiv.
receptive aphasia: sensorische Aphasie *f*.
receptor/*n*: Rezeptor *m*, Empfänger *m*.
recess/*n*: Ausbuchtung *f*, Nische *f*, Aussparung *f*.
recessive/*adj*: rezessiv.
recessive gene: rezessives Gen *n*.
reciprocal/*adj*: reziprok.
reciprocal action: Wechselwirkung *f*.
reciprocal beat: reziproke Erregung *f*.
reciprocal effect: Wechselwirkung *f*.
reciprocal gene: reziprokes Gen *n*.
reciprocal rhythm: reziproker Rhythmus *m*.
reclination/*n*: Reklination *f*.
recognition/*n*: Erkennung *f*, Bewusstsein *n*.
recombinant/*n, adj*: 1. Rekombinante *f*; 2. rekombinant, r.
recombination/*n*: Rekombination *f*.
recommanded daily allowance: empfohlene tägliche Menge *f*.
reconstructive/*adj*: rekonstruktiv.
reconstructive operation: Wiederherstellungschirurgie *f*.
reconstructive rhinoplasty: rekonstruktive Rhinoplastik *f*.
reconstructive surgery: Wiederherstellungschirurgie *f*.
record/*n, vb*: 1. Bericht *m*, Aufzeichnung *f*; 2. registrieren, aufzeichnen.
recorder/*n*: Aufzeichnungsgerät *n*.
recording/*n*: Aufzeichnung *f*.
recovery/*n*: Erholung *f*, Rekonvaleszenz *f*.
recovery phase: Erholungsphase *f*.
recovery room: Aufwachstation *f*, Wachstation *f*.
recreation/*n*: Erholung *f*.
recrudescence/*n*: Rekrudeszenz *f*, Wiederauftreten *n*.
recrudescent typhus: recurrence of a typhus fever caused by reactivation of Rickettsia prowazekii, eventually

occurring several years after primary infection. Brill-Zinsser-Krankheit *f*.

recruitment/*n*: Rekrutierung *f*, Lautstärkeausgleich *m*.

rectal/*adj*: rektal.

rectal administration: rektale Applikation *f*.

rectal carcinoma: malignant neoplasm of the rectum or the lower bowel. Symptoms include bloody stools, weight loss, pain, and constipation alternating with diarrhea. Rektumkarzinom *n*.

rectal examination: rektale Untersuchung *f*.

rectal fistula: Rektalfistel *f*.

rectal incontinence: Stuhlinkontinenz *f*.

rectal prolapse: Rektumprolaps *m*.

rectal retractor: Rektumspreizer *m*.

rectal speculum: Rektalspekulum *n*.

rectal stricture: Rektumstriktur *f*.

rectal swab: Rektumabstrich *m*.

rectal temperature: Rektaltemperatur *f*.

rectoanal/*adj*: anorektal.

rectocele/*n*: Rektozele *f*.

rectoscopy/*n*: Rektoskopie *f*.

rectosigmoid anastomosis: Rektum-Sigmoid-Anastomose *f*.

rectosigmoidoscopy/*n*: Rektosigmoideoskopie *f*.

rectostomy/*n*: Proktostomie *f*.

rectouterine pouch: Douglas-Raum *m*.

rectovaginal fistula: Rektovaginalfistel *f*.

rectovesical/*adj*: rektovesikal.

rectovesical fistula: abnormal communication between the rectum and the urinary bladder, often due to invasive growth of a malignant tumor, or resulting from physical damage. Symptoms include severe inflammation of the urinary bladder with signs of cystitis, and the presence of feces in the urine. Rektovesikalfistel *f*.

rectus sheath: Rektusscheide *f*.

recumbent/*adj*: liegend, rekliniert.

recuperation/*n*: Erholung *f*, Rekonvaleszenz *f*.

recur/*vb*: rezidivieren.

recurrence/*n*: Wiederauftreten *n*, Rezidiv *n*.

recurrent encephalopathy: palindromische Enzephalopathie *f*.

recurrent fever: an infectious disease caused by the bacteria Spirochaeta and transmitted by lice. Characteristically, several periods of high fever alternate with periods of normal body temperature. Rückfallfieber *n*.

recurrent inhibition: rekurrente Hemmung *f*, Renshaw-Hemmung *f*.

recurrent major depression: rezidivierende typische Depression *f*.

red/*adj*: rot.

red blindness: Rotblindheit *f*.

red blood cell: rotes Blutkörperchen *n*, Erythrozyt *m*.

red bug: Trombiculamilbe *f*, Laufmilbe *f*.

red cell: rotes Blutkörperchen *n*, Erythrozyt *m*.

red cell count: Erythrozytenzahl *f*, Erythrozytenzählung *f*.

red-green blindness: Rotgrünblindheit *f*, Deuteranopie *f*.

red marrow: rotes Knochenmark *n*.

redness/*n*: Rötung *f*, Rubor *m*.

red neuralgia: Erythromelalgie *f*.

redressement/*n*: Verbandswechsel *m*, Fraktureinrichtung *f*.

red thrombus: roter Thrombus *m*.

reduced hemoglobin: reduziertes Hämoglobin *n*.

reduced respiration: Hypoventilation *f*.

reducible hernia: reponierbare Hernie *f*.

reduction/*n*: Abnahme *f*, Reduktion *f*, Reposition *f*.

reductional division: Reduktionsteilung *f*, Meiose *f*.

reduction diet: Reduktionsdiät *f*.

reduction en bloc: Blockresektion *f*.

reeling gait: schwankender Gang *m*.

reentrant pathway: Reentryleitungsweg *m*.

reentrant tachycardia: Reentrytachykardie *f*.

reentry mechanism: Reentrymecha-

nismus *m*.
refer/*vb*: beziehen, hinweisen, überweisen.
reference/*n*: Bezugnahme *f*, Hinweis *m*, Literaturangabe *f*.
reference group: Bezugsgruppe *f*.
reference range: Referenzbereich *m*.
referral/*n*: Überweisung *f*.
referred otalgia: reflektorische Otalgie *f*.
referred pain: pain felt in a part of the body other than in its place of origin. fortgeleiteter Schmerz *m*.
reflection/*n*: Reflexion *f*, Spiegelung *f*.
reflex/*n*: Reflex *m*.
reflex automatism: Reflexautomatie *f*.
reflex therapy: Reflextherapie *f*.
reflux/*n*: Reflux *m*.
refraction/*n*: Refraktion *f*, Brechung *f*.
refractive ametropia: Refraktionsanomalie *f*.
refractive error: Brechungsfehler *m*, Refraktionsanomalie *f*.
refractive index: Brechungsindex *m*.
refractive power: Brechkraft *f*.
refractory/*adj*: refraktär, obstinat.
refractory period: Refraktärperiode *f*.
refractory phase: Refraktärperiode *f*.
refractory rickets: Vitamin-D-resistente Rachitis *f*.
refrigeration/*n*: Kühlung *f*.
refusal/*n*: Ablehnung *f*, Weigerung *f*.
regard/*n, vb*: 1. Aufmerksamkeit *f*; 2. betrachten.
regeneration/*n*: Regeneration *f*.
regenerative process: Regenerationsvorgang *m*.
regimen/*n*: Regime *n*, Therapieplan *m*, Diätverordnung *f*.
region/*n*: Region *f*, Bereich *m*, Areal *n*.
regional/*adj*: regional.
regional anesthesia: Lokalanästhesie *f*.
regional block: Lokalanästhesie *f*.
regional colitis: Colitis regionalis *f*, Crohn-Krankheit *f*.
regional enteritis: chronic inflammatory disease of the gastrointestinal tract of unknown cause, mostly affecting the terminal ileum, and the colon. Symptoms include abdominal pain, diarrhea, weight loss and fever, and formation of intestinal fistula. Enteritis regionalis *f*, Crohn-Krankheit *f*.
regional ileitis: Enteritis regionalis *f*, Crohn-Krankheit *f*.
regional perfusion: Regionalperfusion *f*.
region of accommodation: Akkommodationsbereich *m*.
register/*n, vb*: 1. Register *n*, Verzeichnis *n*; 2. registrieren.
registered nurse: examinierte Krankenschwester *f*.
regression/*n*: Regression *f*, Rückbildung *f*.
regression analysis: Regressionsanalyse *f*.
regular insulin: Normalinsulin *n*, Altinsulin *n*.
regular rhythm: regelmäßiger Rhythmus *m*.
regulation/*n*: Regelung *f*, Steuerung *f*, Vorschrift *f*.
regurgitant murmur: Regurgitationsgeräusch *n*.
regurgitation/*n*: Regurgitation *f*.
rehabilitation/*n*: Rehabilitation *f*
reinfarction/*n*: Reinfarkt *m*.
reinfection/*n*: Reinfektion *f*.
reinforcement/*n*: Verstärkung *f*.
rejection/*n*: Abstoßung *f*, Ablehnung *f*, Zurückweisung *f*.
relapse/*n, vb*: 1. Rezidiv *n*, Rückfall *m*; 2. rezidivieren.
relapse rate: Rezidivrate *f*.
relapsing febrile non-suppurative panniculitis: Panniculitis nodularis non suppurativa febrilis et recidivans *f*, Pfeifer-Weber-Christian-Syndrom *n*.
relapsing fever: an infectious disease caused by the bacteria Spirochaeta and transmitted by lice. Characteristically, several periods of high fever alternate with periods of normal body temperature. Rückfallfieber *n*.
relapsing malaria: rekurrierende Malaria *f*.

R

relapsing ophthalmoplegia: Migraine ophtalmoplégique *f*.
relapsing polyneuropathy: rezidivierende Polyneuropathie *f*.
related/*adj*: verwandt.
relation/*n*: Relation *f*, Verhältnis *n*.
relationship/*n*: Verwandtschaft *f*, Beziehung *f*.
relative/*n, adj*: 1. Verwandter *m*; 2. relativ.
relative aperture: Öffnungsverhältnis *n*.
relative density: spezifische Dichte *f*.
relative hemianopia: relative Hemianopsie *f*.
relative refractory period: relative Refraktärperiode *f*.
relaxant/*n, adj*: 1. Relaxans *n*; 2. relaxierend.
relaxation/*n*: Relaxation *f*, Entspannung *f*.
relaxation incision: Entlastungsschnitt *m*.
relaxin/*n*: Relaxin *n*.
relay cell: Relaiszelle *f*.
release/*n, vb*: 1. Freisetzung *f*, Entlassung *f*; 2. freisetzen.
releasing/*adj*: freisetzend.
releasing factor: Releasing-Faktor *m*.
releasing hormone: Releasing-Hormon *n*.
relevance/*n*: Relevanz *f*.
reliability/*n*: Reliabilität *f*, Zuverlässigkeit *f*.
relief/*n*: Entlastung *f*, Erleichterung *f*, Milderung *f*.
relieve/*vb*: erleichtern, mildern, entlasten.
relieving incision: Entlastungsschnitt *m*.
relieving posture: Schonhaltung *f*.
remain/*vb*: verbleiben.
remainder/*n*: Rückstand *m*.
remedy/*n*: Remedium *n*, Heilmittel *n*, Medikament *n*.
remembrance/*n*: Erinnerung *f*.
remission/*n*: Remission *f*.
remittent/*adj*: remittierend.
remnant/*n*: Überrest *m*.
remote/*adj*: distal, entfernt.
removal/*n*: Entfernung *f*, Beseitigung *f*.
renal/*adj*: renal, Nieren-.
renal abscess: abscess of the renal cortex, usually resulting from pyelonephritis, glomerulitis, or kidney infarction. Symptoms include malaise, fever, chills, and costovertebral angle tenderness. Nierenrindenabszess *m*.
renal adenocarcinoma: Nierenzellkarzinom *n*.
renal albuminuria: renale Albuminurie *f*.
renal amino acid diabetes: Aminosäurediabetes *m*, Fanconi-Abderhalden-Syndrom *n*.
renal amyloidosis: Nierenamyloidose *f*.
renal anuria: renale Anurie *f*.
renal arteriography: Nierenarteriographie *f*.
renal blood flow: Nierendurchblutung *f*.
renal calculus: hard concretions which can be found in the renal pelvis, and which are typically formed by substances which are excreted by the kidneys, for example calcium, oxalate, urate, uric acid, or phosphates. Symptoms depend on the size of the calculus and may include acute pain, renal colic, dysuria, and eventually hematuria or ureteral obstruction. Nierenstein *m*.
renal carbuncle: Nierenkarbunkel *m*, Nierenabszess *m*.
renal cast: Harnzylinder *m*.
renal cell carcinoma: malignant neoplasm of the kidney, predominantly occurring in male persons aged over fifty. Symptoms include initially painless hematuria, dorsolumbar pain, and a palpable tumor in the kidney region. Nierenzellkarzinom *n*.
renal clearance: Nierenclearance *f*.
renal colic: Nierenkolik *f*.
renal congestion: Nierenstauung *f*.
renal cortical adenoma: Nierenrindenadenom *n*.
renal cyst: solitary or multiple cysts in the kidney tissue, occurring as congenital polycystic kidney, or as

a consequence of other kidney disorders as for example pyelonephritis or renal tuberculosis. Nierenzyste *f*.
renal diabetes: renaler Diabetes *m*.
renal dysplasia: Nierendysplasie *f*.
renal ectopia: Nierendystopie *f*.
renal embolism: Nierenembolie *f*.
renal failure: inability of the kidney to filtrate and excrete metabolites and to retain electrolytes, resulting in uremia. Symptoms of acute renal failure include initially reduced urination or anuria, followed by polyuria, and a disordered water and electrolyte balance. Chronic renal failure is characterized by nocturnal urination, and cardiovascular, gastrointestinal, and neurologic signs. Nierenversagen *n*.
renal fibrosis: Nierenfibrose *f*.
renal fistula: Nierenfistel *f*.
renal function: Nierentätigkeit *f*.
renal fusion: Fusionsniere *f*, Verschmelzungsniere *f*.
renal hemorrhage: Nierenblutung *f*, Nephrorrhagie *f*.
renal hypertension: renaler Hochdruck *f*.
renal infarction: infarct of the kidney, typically due to cardiovascular diseases, endocarditis, or arteriosclerosis. Symptoms include abdominal pain, hematuria, oliguria or anuria. Niereninfarkt *m*.
renal insufficiency: decreased renal function with insufficiency of the kidney to filtrate and excrete metabolites and to retain electrolytes. Symptoms include a disordered water and electrolyte balance. Niereninsuffizienz *f*.
renal lipoidosis: Lipoidnephrose *f*, Fettniere *f*.
renal osteodystrophy: trophic disorder of bones resulting from chronic kidney disease with impaired renal function, and disorders of the phosphorus and calcium metabolism. The disease may lead to defective bone formation, osteomalacia, and osteoporosis. renale Osteodystrophie *f*, Rachitis renalis *f*.
renal pelvic obstruction: Nierenbeckenverlegung *f*.
renal pelvis: Nierenbecken *n*.
renal rickets: Rachitis renalis *f*, renale Osteodystrophie *f*.
renal sclerosis: Nephrosklerose *f*.
renal threshold: Nierenschwelle *f*.
renal transplantation: Nierentransplantation *f*.
renal tuberculosis: Nierentuberkulose *f*, Nephrophthisis *f*.
renal tubular acidosis: renale tubuläre Azidose *f*.
renin/*n*: Renin *n*.
renovascular hypertension: renovaskulärer Hochdruck *m*.
repaglinide/*n*: Repaglinid *n*.
repair/*n, vb*: 1. Reparatur *f*, Instandsetzung *f*; 2. reparieren.
repair mechanism: Reparaturmechanismus *m*.
repeat/*n, vb*: 1. Wiederholung *f*; 2. wiederholen.
repeated vaccination: Wiederholungsimpfung *f*.
repellent/*n, adj*: 1. Repellent *n*; 2. abstoßend.
repetition compulsion: Wiederholungszwang *m*.
replacement/*n*: Austausch *m*, Ersatz *m*.
replication/*n*: Replikation *f*, Wiederholung *f*.
report/*n, vb*: 1. Bericht *m*; 2. berichten, melden.
reporting/*n*: Dokumentation *f*, Bericht *m*.
repository injection: Depotinjektion *f*.
repository penicillin: Depotpenicillin *n*.
repression/*n*: Repression *f*, Unterdrückung *f*, Hemmung *f*.
reproduction/*n*: Reproduktion *f*, Fortpflanzung *f*.
reproductive age: fortpflanzungsfähiges Alter *n*.
reproductive biology: Reproduktionsbiologie *f*.
reproductive cell: Keimzelle *f*.
reproductive period: Fortpflanzungsperiode *f*.

reproterol/*n*: Reproterol *n*.
requirement/*n*: Erfordernis *n*, Bedarf *m*.
rescue/*n, vb*: 1. Rettung *f*; 2. retten, bergen.
research/*n, vb*: 1. Forschung *f*; 2. erforschen.
resection/*n*: Resektion *f*.
resectoscope/*n*: Resektoskop *n*.
resemblance/*n*: Ähnlichkeit *f*.
reserpine/*n*: Reserpin *n*.
reserve/*n*: Reserve *f*, Vorrat *m*.
reset/*vb*: zurücksetzen, reponieren.
residual/*adj*: residual.
residual body: Residualkörperchen *n*.
residual cyst: Residualzyste *f*.
residual delusion: Residualwahn *m*.
residual schizophrenia: Residualschizophrenie *f*.
residual urine: Restharn *m*.
residual volume: Residualvolumen *n*.
residue/*n*: Residuum *n*, Rückstand *m*.
resin/*n*: Harz *m*.
resistance/*n*: Resistenz *f*.
resistant/*adj*: resistent, widerstandsfähig.
resistant maculopapular scaly erythroderma: Parapsoriasis en plaque *f*.
resocortol/*n*: Resocortol *n*.
resolution/*n*: Auflösung *f*.
resolvent/*n*: Resolvens *n*, Lösungsmittel *n*.
resonance/*n*: Resonanz *f*, Schall *m*.
resonant frequency: Resonanzfrequenz *f*.
resorption/*n*: Resorption *f*.
respiration/*n*: Respiration *f*, Atmung *f*.
respiration rate: Atemfrequenz *f*.
respirator/*n*: Respirator *m*, Beatmungsgerät *n*.
respiratory/*adj*: respiratorisch.
respiratory acidosis: respiratorische Azidose *f*.
respiratory air: Atemluft *f*.
respiratory alkalosis: respiratorische Alkalose *f*.
respiratory arrhythmia: respiratorische Arrhythmie *f*.
respiratory capacity: Atemgrenzwert *m*.
respiratory center: Atemzentrum *n*.
respiratory chain: Atmungskette *f*.
respiratory depression: Atemdepression *f*.
respiratory disease: Atemwegserkrankung *f*.
respiratory distress: Atemnot *f*.
respiratory failure: decreased respiratory function, occurring as a ventilation disorder, or disturbance in pulmonary blood circulation. Forms include obstructive pulmonary disease with bronchial stenosis, and restrictive pulmonary disease with impaired lung compliance. respiratorische Insuffizienz *f*.
respiratory frequency: Atemfrequenz *f*.
respiratory infection: Atemwegsinfektion *f*.
respiratory minute volume: Atemminutenvolumen *n*.
respiratory obstruction: Atembehinderung *f*.
respiratory organ: Atemorgan *n*.
respiratory rate: Atemfrequenz *f*.
respiratory reserve: Atemreserve *f*, Reservevolumen *n*.
respiratory sound: Atemgeräusch *n*.
respiratory system: Atemtrakt *m*.
respiratory tract: Respirationstrakt *m*, Atemwege.
respiratory tract infection: Atemwegsinfektion *f*.
respiratory volume: Atemvolumen *n*.
respirometry/*n*: Spirometrie *f*.
response/*n*: Antwort *f*, Reaktion *f*.
responsiveness/*n*: Anregbarkeit *f*, Reaktionsfähigkeit *f*.
rest/*n, vb*: 1. Ruhe *f*, Erholung *f*, Rest *m*, Auflage *f*; 2. ruhen, liegen.
resting/*adj*: ruhend.
resting cell: Ruhezelle *f*.
resting state: Ruhephase *f*.
resting tremor: Ruhetremor *m*.
restless/*adj*: ruhelos.
restless legs: Restless Legs, Wittmaack-Ekbom-Syndrom *n*.
restlessness/*n*: Unruhe *f*.
rest pain: Ruheschmerz *m*.
rest position: Ruhestellung *f*.
restriction/*n*: Restriktion *f*.
result/*n, vb*: 1. Resultat *n*, Ergebnis *n*,

Produkt *n*; 2. resultieren.
resurrection bone: Sakralbein *n*, Kreuzbein *n*, Os sacrum *n*.
resuscitation/*n*: Reanimation *f*, Wiederbelebung *f*.
resuscitation time: Wiederbelebungszeit *f*.
retain/*vb*: zurückhalten.
retained lochia: Lochienstauung *f*.
retained placenta: Plazentaretention *f*.
retained testis: Kryptorchismus *m*.
retardation/*n*: Retardierung *f*, Verzögerung *f*.
retching/*n*: Würgen *n*, Erbrechen *n*.
retention/*n*: Retention *f*, Zurückhalten *n*.
reteplase/*n*: Reteplase *f*.
reticular/*adj*: retikulär.
reticular fiber: Gitterfaser *f*, Retikulinfaser *f*.
reticular tissue: retikuläres Bindegewebe *n*.
reticulate body: Retikulärzelle *f*.
reticulin/*n*: Retikulin *n*.
reticulocyte/*n*: Retikulozyt *m*.
reticulocytosis/*n*: Retikulozytose *f*.
reticuloendothelial/*adj*: retikuloendothelial.
reticulosis/*n*: Retikulose *f*.
reticulum cell sarcoma: Retikulumzellsarkom *n*.
retina/*n*: Retina *f*, Netzhaut *f*.
retinal/*n, adj*: 1. Retinal *n*; 2. retinal.
retinal adaptation: Netzhautadaptation *f*.
retinal area: Netzhautbezirk *m*.
retinal astigmatism: Netzhautastigmatismus *m*.
retinal cone: Netzhautzapfen *m*.
retinal correspondence: Netzhautkorrespondenz *f*.
retinal detachment: partial or complete detachment of the retina, resulting from retinal lesions, or caused by accumulation of subretinal fluid. Symptoms include photopsia and scotoma. Netzhautablösung *f*.
retinal disease: Retinopathie *f*.
retinal dysplasia: Netzhautdysplasie.
retinal embolism: Netzhautembolie *f*.
retinal hemorrhage: Netzhautblutung *f*.
retinal image: Netzhautbild *n*.
retinal perception: Netzhautwahrnehmung *f*.
retinal pigment: Netzhautpigment *n*.
retinal rupture: Netzhautruptur *f*.
retinal tear: rupture of the retina, occurring typically as a consequence of vascular diseases and caused by concussion of the head or sudden eye movements. Netzhauteinriss *m*.
retinitis/*n*: inflammation of the retina, typically caused by viral infection, for example herpesvirus. Frequently associated with immune deficiency, other parts of the eye may also be affected. Retinitis *f*, Netzhautentzündung *f*.
retinoblastoma/*n*: Retinoblastom *n*.
retinoic acid: Retinsäure *f*.
retinol/*n*: Retinol *n*.
retinopathy/*n*: Retinopathie *f*.
retirement/*n*: Ruhestand *m*.
retort/*n*: Retorte *f*.
retracted nipple: retrahierte Mamille *f*.
retraction/*n*: Retraktion *f*.
retraction syndrome: an ophthalmologic syndrome which is characterized by congenital aplasia of the abducent nerve. Symptoms include impairment of ocular abduction and retraction of the eye on attempted adduction. Retraktionssyndrom *n*, Stilling-Türk-Duane-Syndrom *n*.
retractor/*n*: Spreizhaken *m*.
retrad/*adj*: rückwärts.
retroactive/*adj*: retroaktiv, rückwirkend.
retroactive amnesia: retrograde Amnesie *f*.
retrobulbar/*adj*: retrobulbär.
retrobulbar neuritis: Retrobulbärneuritis *f*.
retrobulbar space: Retrobulbärraum *m*.
retrocardiac space: Retrokardialraum *m*, Holzknecht-Raum *m*.
retrocochlear/*adj*: retrokochlear.
retroflexed/*adj*: retroflektiert.
retrograde/*adj*: retrograd.

R

retrograde amnesia: retrograde Amnesie *f*.
retrograde block: retrograder Block *m*.
retrograde cholangiography: retrograde Cholangiographie *f*.
retrograde degeneration: retrograde Degeneration *f*.
retromammary abscess: retromammärer Abszess *m*.
retroperitoneal/*adj*: retroperitoneal.
retroperitoneal fibrosis: idiopathische retroperitoneale Fibrose *f*, Ormond-Syndrom *n*.
retroperitoneal hematoma: Retroperitonealhämatom *n*.
retroperitoneal hernia: Cooper-Hernie *f*, Treitz-Hernie *f*, enzystierte Leistenhernie *f*.
retroperitoneal space: Retroperitonealraum *m*.
retropharyngeal/*adj*: retropharyngeal.
retropharyngeal abscess: Retropharyngealabszess *m*.
retroplacental hematoma: retroplazentares Hämatom *n*.
retropubic prostatectomy: retropubische Prostatektomie *f*.
retrospective/*adj*: retrospektiv.
retrosternal goiter: retrosternale Struma *f*.
retrosternal pain: Retrosternalschmerz *m*.
retrosternal space: Retrosternalraum *m*.
retrotonsillar abscess: Retrotonsillarabszess *m*, Peritonsillarabszess *m*.
re-uptake/*n*: Re-uptake, Wiederaufnahme *f*.
revaccination/*n*: Wiederholungsimpfung *f*.
reversal/*n*: Umkehr *f*.
reverse/*vb, adj*: 1. umkehren; 2. umgekehrt.
reverse transcriptase inhibitor: Reverse-Transkriptase-Inhibitor *m*.
reversible ischemic neurologic deficit: reversibles ischämisches neurologisches Defizit *n*, RIND.
review/*n, vb*: 1. Überblick *m*, Überprüfung *f*; 2. überprüfen.
revitalization/*n*: Revitalisierung *f*.
revolutions per minute: Umdrehungen pro Minute, Drehzahl *f*.
rhabdomyolysis/*n*: Rhabdomyolyse *f*.
Rh blood groop: Rh-Blutgruppe *f*.
rhesus incompatibility: Rhesusinkompatibilität *f*.
rheumatic/*adj*: rheumatisch.
rheumatic chorea: Chorea rheumatica *f*, Sydenham-Chorea *f*.
rheumatic endocarditis: rheumatische Endokarditis *f*.
rheumatic fever: generalized disease affecting joints, skin, the heart, and sometimes the central nervous system, due to an allergic reaction to toxins of the bacterium Streptococcus. rheumatisches Fieber *n*, Febris rheumatica *f*.
rheumatic heart disease: rheumatische Herzkrankheit *f*.
rheumatic nodule: Rheumaknötchen *n*.
rheumatism/*n*: any condition which is characterized by pain, swelling and deformity of joints and muscles, and is associated with functional impairment. Rheuma *n*, Rheumatismus *m*.
rheumatoid/*adj*: rheumatoid.
rheumatoid arthritis: chronic systemic disease affecting the connective tissue, predominantly of the joints, of unknown origin. Symptoms include swelling, pain, impaired function, followed by destructions of chondral and osseous substance, deformity and abnormal position like ulnar drift. rheumatoide Arthritis *f*, chronische Polyarthritis *f*.
rheumatoid factor: Rheumafaktor *m*.
rheumatoid polyarthritis: rheumatoide Polyarthritis *f*.
rheumatology/*n*: Rheumatologie *f*.
rhGH <*abbr*> **recombinant human growth hormone**: rekombinantes menschliches Wachstumshormon *n*.
Rh incompatibility: Rhesusinkompatibilität *f*.
rhinitis/*n*: inflammation of the lining of the nose. Symptoms include nasal

pruritus, sneezing, hypersecretion, and swelling of the nasal mucosa with nose obstruction. Rhinitis *f*, Nasenschleimhautentzündung *f*.
rhinopharyngitis/*n*: Rhinopharyngitis *f*.
rhinoplasty/*n*: Rhinoplastik *f*, plastische Nasenoperation *f*.
rhinorrhea/*n*: Rhinorrhö *f*.
rhinoscopy/*n*: Rhinoskopie *f*, Nasenspiegelung *f*.
rhizotomy/*n*: Rhizotomie *f*, Radikulotomie *f*.
rhodanic acid: Rhodanin *n*.
Rhodesian trypanosomiasis: afrikanische Trypanosomiasis *f*.
rhodopsin/*n*: Rhodopsin *n*, Sehpurpur *n*.
rhombencephalon/*n*: Rhombencephalon *n*, Rautenhirn *n*.
rhonchus/*n*: Rhonchus *m*, Rasselgeräusch *n*.
rhythm/*n*: Rhythmus *m*.
rib/*n*: Rippe *f*, Costa *f*.
ribavirin/*n*: Ribavirin *n*.
ribbon/*n*: Band *n*, Streifen *m*.
ribbon-like keratitis: Bandkeratitis *f*.
rib cage: Brustkorb *m*.
rib-cutting forceps: Rippenzange *f*.
riboflavin/*n*: Riboflavin *n*, Vitamin B_2 *n*.
ribonuclease/*n*: Ribonuklease *f*, RNase *f*.
ribonucleic acid: Ribonukleinsäure *f*, RNS.
ribosomal/*adj*: ribosomal.
ribosomal ribonucleic acid: ribosomale Ribonukleinsäure *f*.
ribosome/*n*: Ribosom *n*.
ribostamycin/*n*: Ribostamycin *n*.
ricinoleic acid: Rizinolsäure *f*.
ricinus oil: Rizinusöl *n*.
rickets/*n*: a disease caused by the lack of vitamin D or the inability to utilize vitamin D. Symptoms in small children include disturbances in bone metabolism resulting in malformation of bones. Rachitis *f*.
rickettsia/*n*: Rickettsie *f*.
rider's bone: Reiterknochen *m*.
ridge/*n*: Kamm *m*, Knochenleiste *f*.
rifabutin/*n*: Rifabutin *n*.
rifampicin/*n*: Rifampicin *n*.
rifamycin/*n*: Rifamycin *n*.
right atrioventricular valve: Trikuspidalklappe *f*.
right bundle branch block: Rechtsschenkelblock *m*.
right-handed/*adj*: rechtshändig.
right heart: rechtes Herz *n*.
right heart failure: Rechtsherzversagen *n*, Rechtsherzinsuffizienz *f*.
right occipitotransverse position: rechte hintere Querlage *f*.
right-sided angiography: Dextrokardiographie *f*.
right-to-left shunt: Rechts-Links-Shunt *m*.
right to treatment: Recht auf Behandlung *f*.
right ventricular hypertrophy: Rechtsherzhypertrophie *f*.
rigidity/*n*: Rigidität *f*, Rigor *m*.
rigid spine: Wirbelsäulenversteifung *f*.
rigor/*n*: Rigor *m*, Rigidität *f*.
riluzole/*n*: Riluzol *n*.
rimantadine/*n*: Rimantadin *n*.
rimexolone/*n*: Rimexolon *n*.
rimonabant/*n*: Rimonabant *n*.
ring/*n*: Ring *m*.
ring finger: Ringfinger *m*.
ring scotoma: Ringskotom *n*.
ringworm/*n*: chronic infectious disease of the skin, typically caused by the fungus Trichophyton. Symptoms include ring-shaped lesions. Tinea *f*.
rinsing fluid: Spülflüssigkeit *f*.
ripe cataract: reifer Star *m*, Cataracta maturata *f*.
ripening/*n*: Reifung *f*.
risedronate/*n*: Risedronsäure *f*.
risk/*n, vb*: 1. Risiko *n*; 2. riskieren.
risk assessment: Risikobewertung *f*.
risk behavior: Risikoverhalten *n*.
risk factor: Risikofaktor *m*.
risk group: Risikogruppe *f*.
risk-taking behavior: Risikoverhalten *n*.
risperidone/*n*: Risperidon *n*.
ritodrine/*n*: Ritodrin *n*.
ritonavir: Ritonavir *n*.
rituximab/*n*: Rituximab *n*.

rivastigmine/*n*: Rivastigmin *n*.
rizatriptan/*n*: Rizatriptan *n*.
RNA <*abbr*> **ribonucleic acid**: Ribonukleinsäure *f*, RNS.
road accident: Verkehrsunfall *m*.
rocking bed: Schaukelbett *n*.
Rocky Mountain spotted fever: Rocky-Mountain-Fieber *n*, Felsengebirgsfieber *n*.
rocuronium bromide: Rocuroniumbromid *n*.
rod/*n*: Stab *m*, Stäbchen *n*.
rodent/*n*: Nagetier *n*.
roentgen/*n*: Röntgen *n*.
roentgenographic finding: Röntgenbefund *m*.
roentgenography/*n*: Röntgenaufnahme *f*.
roentgenology/*n*: Radiologie *f*.
rolitetracycline/*n*: Rolitetracyclin *n*.
roof of skull: Schädeldach *n*, Kalotte *f*.
room/*n*: Raum *m*, Zimmer *n*.
room disinfection: Raumdesinfektion *f*.
root/*n*: Wurzel *f*, Radix *f*.
root resection: Wurzelresektion *f*.
root stimulation: Nervenwurzelstimulation *f*.
rope flap: Rundstiellappen *m*.
ropinirole/*n*: Ropinirol *n*.
ropivacaine/*n*: Ropivacain *n*:
rosacea/*n*: a skin disease with permanent skin changes, usually of the face, with redness over the nose and cheeks. Rosazea *f*, Acne rosacea *f*.
rose spot: Typhusroseola *f*.
rosewood oil: Rosenholzöl *n*.
rosiglitazone/*n*: Rosiglitazon *n*.
rosoxacin/*n*: Rosoxacin *n*.
rotating irradiation: Rotationsbestrahlung *f*.
rotation/*n*: Rotation *f*, Umdrehung *f*, Wendung *f*.
rotation flap: Rotationslappen *m*, Schwenklappen *m*.
rotator cuff: Rotatorenmanschette *f*.
rotatory nystagmus: Rotationsnystagmus *m*, Drehnystagmus *m*.
rotatory spasm: Drehkrampf *m*.
rotatory tic: Spasmus rotatorius *m*.
rotatory vertigo: Drehschwindel *m*.
rough/*adj*: roh, rau.
roughness/*n*: Rauheit *f*.
rouleau formation: Rouleaubildung *f*, Geldrollenbildung *f*.
round/*adj*: rund.
round back: Rundrücken *m*.
round lesion: Rundschatten *m*, Rundherd *m*.
round pelvis: rundes Becken *n*.
route/*n*: Route *f*, Weg *m*, Zugangsweg *m*.
route of infection: Infektionsweg *m*.
routine/*n*: Routine *f*.
routine examination: Routineuntersuchung *f*.
routinely/*adj*: routinemäßig.
roxithromycin/*n*: Roxithromycin *n*.
rub/*n, vb*: 1. Reibegeräusch *n*, Reiben *n*; 2. reiben, einreiben.
rubber/*n*: Gummi *n*.
rubber bandage: elastische Binde *f*.
rubber glove: Gummihandschuh *m*.
rubefacient/*n, adj*: 1. Rubefaziens *n*; 2. rötend.
rubella/*n*: an acute infection which is caused by rubella virus. Symptoms include high fever, and a characteristic skin rash with exanthema and pink patches. Congenital rubella can be a fatal disease and is frequently associated with a wide range of severe congenital malformations, for example of the central nervous system. Rubella *f*, Röteln *f*.
rubella embryopathy: Rötelnembryopathie *f*, Gregg-Syndrom *n*.
rudimentary bone: Rudimentärknochen *m*.
rugby knee: aseptische Tibianekrose *f*, Osgood-Schlatter-Syndrom *n*.
rugine/*n*: Raspatorium *n*.
rule/*n*: Norm *f*, Gesetz *n*, Prinzip *n*.
rule out/*vb*: ausschließen.
rumination/*n*: Rumination *f*, Wiederkäuen *n*.
runaround/*n*: an infectious disease of the nail fold, mostly due to bacterial infection with Staphylococcus or Streptococcus, or resulting from herpes simplex infection. Symptoms include swelling, formation of a very

painful abscess, and inflammation of lymphatic vessels. Umlauf *m*, Panaritium *n*.
running/*adj*: fortlaufend.
runt disease: Runt-Krankheit *f*, Zwergenkrankheit *f*.
rupia/*n*: Rupia *f*.
rupture/*n, vb*: 1. Ruptur *f*, Riss *m*; 2. rupturieren, reißen.
rupture of membranes: Blasensprung *m*.
rusty sputum: rostbraunes Sputum *n*.

S

S <*abbr*> **1. siemens; 2. sulfur; 3. serum**: 1. Siemens *n*; 2. Schwefel *m*, S; 3. Serum *n*.
saber-shaped tibia: outward curved tibia, eventually associated with a slight anteflexion, usually due to inflammation of the periosteum in congenital syphilis. Säbelscheidentibia *f*.
sac/*n*: Sack *m*, Tasche *f*.
saccade/*n*: Sakkade *f*.
saccadic movement: ruckartige Bewegung *f*.
saccharic acid: Zuckersäure *f*.
saccharide/*n*: Saccharid *n*.
saccharin/*n*: Saccharin *n*.
sacciform kidney: Sackniere *f*.
saccular aneurysm: sackförmiges Aneurysma *n*.
saccular bronchiectasis: sackförmige Bronchiektasie *f*.
sacculated bladder: Divertikelblase *f*.
sacculated uterus: Uteruswandaussackung *f*.
sacculation/*n*: Sakkulation *f*, Sackbildung *f*.
sacral/*adj*: sakral.
sacral anesthesia: Sakralanästhesie *f*.
sacral bone: Sakralbein *n*, Os sacrum *n*.
sacral canal: Sakralkanal *m*.
sacral cyst: Steißbeinzyste *f*.
sacralization/*n*: Sakralisation *f*.
sacral scoliosis: Beckenskoliose *f*.
sacral vertebra: Sakralwirbel *m*.
sacrococcygeal fistula: Steißbeinfistel *f*.
sacroiliac articulation: Sakroiliakalgelenk *n*.
sacrum/*n*: Sakrum *n*, Os sacrum *n*.
saddle-block anesthesia: Sattelblockanästhesie *f*.
saddle joint: Sattelgelenk *n*.
saddle nose: Sattelnase *f*.
sadism/*n*: Sadismus *m*.
sadness/*n*: Traurigkeit *f*.
sadomasochism/*n*: Sadomasochismus *m*.
safety profile: Sicherheitsprofil *n*.
sagittal/*adj*: sagittal.
sagittal plane: Sagittalebene *f*.
Saint Anthony's fire: Sankt-Antons-Feuer *n*, Ergotismus *m*.
Saint John's wort: Johanniskraut *n*.
Saint Vitus' dance: Veitstanz *m*, Chorea *f*.
salbutamol/*n*: Salbutamol *n*.
salicylate/*n*: Salicylat *n*.
salicylic acid: Salicylsäure *f*.
salicylsalicylic acid: Disalicylsäure *f*.
salicylsulfonic acid: Sulfosalicylsäure *f*.
salicyluric acid: Salicylursäure *f*.
saline/*adj*: salzig, salzhaltig.
saline solution: Salzlösung *f*.
saliva/*n*: Speichel *m*.
salivary/*adj*: Speichel-, Sialo-.
salivary calculus: Speichelstein *m*, Sialolith *m*.
salivary fistula: Speicheldrüsenfistel *f*.
salivary gland: Speicheldrüse *f*.
salivary secretion: Speichelsekretion *f*.
salivary stone: Speicheldrüsenstein *m*.
salivary tumor: benign or malignant neoplasm of a salivary gland, usually in the parotid gland. Symptoms may include swelling, pain, and salivary duct obstruction. Speicheldrüsentumor *m*.
salivation/*n*: Salivation *f*, Speichelfluss *m*.

salmeterol/*n*: Salmeterol *n*.

salpingectomy/*n*: Salpingektomie *f*.

salpingitis/*n*: 1. inflammation of the fallopian tube, the tuba uterina. Salpingitis *f*, Eileiterentzündung *f*. 2. inflammation of the eustachian tube, the tuba auditiva. Salpingitis *f*, Syringitis *f*.

salpingography/*n*: Salpingographie *f*.

salpingostomy/*n*: Salpingostomie *f*.

salpinx/*n*: Salpinx *f*, Tube *f*.

salt/*n, vb*: 1. Salz *n*; 2. salzen.

saltatory conduction: saltatorische Erregungsleitung *f*.

saltatory mutation: Sprungmutation *f*.

saltatory spasm: Nickkrampf *m*, Blitz-Nick-Salaam-Krämpfe.

salt-depletion syndrome: a condition which is characterized by dehydration, weakness, muscle cramps, hypovolemia, orthostatic hypotension, and shock due to excessive loss of salt by vomiting, diarrhea, or kidney disease. Salzverlustsyndrom *n*, Thorn-Syndrom *n*.

salt-losing nephritis: Salzverlustnephritis *f*.

saluretic/*n, adj*: 1. Saluretikum *n*; 2. saluretisch.

salutary/*adj*: heilsam.

salvage/*n, vb*: 1. Rettung *f*; 2. bergen, retten.

salvarsan/*n*: Salvarsan *n*.

salverine/*n*: Salverin *n*.

samarium/*n*: Samarium *n*, Sm.

sample/*n*: Probe *f*, Stichprobe *f*.

sample storage: Probenaufbewahrung *f*.

sampling/*n*: Probenentnahme *f*, Stichprobenerhebung *f*.

sanatorium/*n*: Sanatorium *n*.

sand/*n*: Sand *m*.

sandfly fever: Sandfliegenfieber *n*, Phlebotomusfieber *n*, Pappataci-Fieber *n*.

sane/*adj*: gesund.

sanitary/*adj*: sanitär, hygienisch.

sanitary napkin: Hygienebinde *f*.

sanitary regimen: Regimen sanitatis *n*, Hygienemaßnahme *f*.

sanitation/*n*: Sanitation *f*.

sanity/*n*: Gesundheit *f*, normaler Geisteszustand *m*.

saphenectomy/*n*: Saphenaresektion *f*.

saponification/*n*: Saponifikation *f*.

saponin/*n*: Saponin *n*.

saprophyte/*n*: Saprophyt *m*.

sapropterin/*n*: Sapropterin *n*.

saquinavir/*n*: Saquinavir *n*.

saralasin/*n*: Saralasin *n*.

sarcoid/*n, adj*: 1. Sarkoid *n*; 2. sarkoidartig.

sarcoidosis/*n*: a chronic, systemic inflammatory disease of unknown origin which can affect any organ; mainly the lung, the skin, and joints are involved. Characterized by the presence of granulomatous, noncaseating cells. Sarkoidose *f*, Besnier-Boeck-Schaumann-Krankheit *f*.

sarcolactic acid: Muskelmilchsäure *f*.

sarcolemma/*n*: Sarkolemm *n*.

sarcoma/*n*: Sarkom *n*.

sarcoptic itch: Krätzmilbenkrankheit *f*, Skabies *f*

sardonic laugh: Risus sardonicus *m*.

SARS <*abbr*> **severe acute respiratory syndrome**: an infectious disease caused by a Coronavirus. Initial symptoms include fever and dyspnea, and may, without treatment, result in acute respiratory failure. SARS was first described in China in 2003. SARS, schweres akutes Atemwegssyndrom *n*.

satellite/*n*: Satellit *m*.

satiation point: Sättigungspunkt *m*.

satiety/*n*: Sattheit *f*, Sättigungsgefühl *n*.

satisfaction/*n*: Befriedigung *f*, Sättigung *f*.

saturated fatty acid: gesättigte Fettsäure *f*.

saturation/*n*: Sättigung *f*.

saturnism/*n*: Saturnismus *m*, Bleivergiftung *f*.

saw/*n*: Säge *f*.

saw palmetto: Sägezahnpalme *f*.

scab/*n, vb*: 1. Kruste *f*, Schorf *m*, Aussatz *m*; 2. verkrusten.

scabies/*n*: an infectious disease of the skin, caused by the itch mite. Symptoms include pruritus and charac-

teristic lesions in form of fine tunnel-shaped burrows. Skabies *f*, Krätze *f*.
scald/*n*: Verbrühung *f*.
scale/*n, vb*: 1. Skala *f*, Schuppe *f*, Zahnstein *m*; 2. abschälen, abschilfern.
scalp/*n*: Skalp *m*.
scalpel/*n*: Skalpell *n*.
scan/*n, vb*: 1. Scan *m*; 2. scannen, abtasten.
scanner/*n*: Scanner *m*.
scanning speech: skandierende Sprache *f*.
scaphocephaly/*n*: Skaphokephalie *f*.
scaphoid abdomen: Kahnbauch *m*.
scaphoid fracture: fracture of the scaphoid bone of the hand, eventually associated with bone dislocation. Skaphoidfraktur *f*, Kahnbeinbruch *m*.
scaphoid scapula: Skapulakonkavität *f*.
scaphoid thorax: Kahnthorax *m*.
scapula/*n*: Skapula *f*, Schulterblatt *n*.
scapular line: Interskapularlinie *f*.
scar/*n, vb*: 1. Narbe *f*; 2. vernarben.
scar contracture: Narbenkontraktur *f*.
scarf/*n*: Dreiecktuch *n*.
scarification/*n*: Skarifikation *f*.
scarlatinal nephritis: Scharlachnephritis *f*.
scarlet fever: an infectious disease caused by hemolytic staphylococci. Symptoms include fever, a characteristic erythematous rash of the trunk and the palm, pharyngitis, tonsillitis, and strawberry tongue. Scharlach *m*.
scarlet fever rash: Scharlachausschlag *m*, Scharlachexanthem *n*.
scarred uterus: narbiger Uterus *m*.
scarring/*n*: Vernarbung *f*.
scatter/*n, vb*: 1. Streuung *f*; 2. streuen.
scattered radiation: Streustrahlung *f*.
scavenger cell: Fresszelle *f*, Abräumzelle *f*.
schistocyte/*n*: Schistozyt *m*.
schistosomiasis/*n*: infection with Schistosoma which are transmitted by fresh-water snails. Chronic schistosomiasis mostly affects the skin, the intestinal tract, the urogenital tract, and the liver and may lead to portal hypertension and bladder carcinoma. Schistosomiasis *f*, Bilharziose *f*.
schistosomal dysentery: Schistosomen-Dysenterie *f*.
schizoaffective disorder: schizoaffektive Störung *f*.
schizoid personality: schizoider Charaktertyp *m*.
schizophrenia/*n*: psychiatric disorder of unknown origin. Symptoms include a variety of manifestations in which affected persons show disturbances in form and content of thought, mood, and self-perception resulting in misinterpretation or loss of contact to reality. Schizophrenie *f*.
schizophreniform disorder: schizophreniforme Störung *f*.
schizothymic personality: schizoider Charaktertyp *m*.
school age: Schulalter *n*.
school health care: schulärztlicher Dienst *m*.
sciatic dislocation: Ischiassyndrom *n*.
sciatica/*n*: pain syndrome, usually caused by protrusion of a lumbar intervertebral disk. Characteristical symptoms include radiating pain from the spine into the buttocks and the leg. Ischiassyndrom *n*, Hexenschuss *m*.
sciatic nerve: Nervus ischiadicus *m*, Ischiadikus *m*.
sciatic neuralgia: Ischialgie *f*.
sciatic spine: Sitzbeinstachel *m*, Spina ischiadica *f*.
science/*n*: Wissenschaft *f*.
scintigraphy/*n*: Szintigraphie *f*.
scintillating scotoma: Flimmerskotom *n*, Teichopsie *f*.
scintillation/*n*: Szintillation *f*.
scirrhous/*adj*: szirrhös.
scirrhous adenocarcinoma: Gallertkarzinom *n*.
scirrhous carcinoma: szirrhöses Karzinom *n*.
scirrhus/*n*: Szirrhus *m*.
scissor gait: Scherengang *m*.

scissors/*n*: Schere *f*.
sclera/*n*: Sklera *f*.
scleredema/*n*: Sklerödem *n*.
scleritis/*n*: inflammatory disease of the outer coat of the eye, the sclera. Skleritis *f*.
sclerodactyly/*n*: Sklerodaktylie *f*.
scleroderma/*n*: a chronic disorder of the skin and connective tissue of unknown origin. Symptoms include characteristically thickened, hard and white patches of skin. Sklerodermie *f*, Skleroderm *n*.
scleroma of the nose: Rhinosklerom *n*.
sclerosing angioma: sklerosierendes Angiom *n*, Histiozytom *n*.
sclerosing injection: Sklerosierung *f*.
sclerosing osteitis: sklerosierende Ostitis *f*, Knochensklerosierung *f*.
sclerosis/*n*: a hardening or induration of an organ or a tissue, resulting for example from inflammation and excessive formation of connective tissue. Sklerose *f*.
sclerotic/*adj*: sklerotisch.
sclerotic acid: Sklerotinsäure *f*.
sclerotomy/*n*: Sklerotomie *f*.
scolex/*n*: Skolex *m*.
scoliosis/*n*: lateral curvature of the spine to one side or the other. Skoliose *f*.
scoliotic pelvis: Skoliosebecken *n*.
scoop/*n*: Löffel *m*.
scopolamine/*n*: Scopolamin *n*.
scopophilia/*n*: Skopophilie *f*, Voyeurismus *m*.
scorbutic position: Hampelmannphänomen *n*.
scorbutic stomatitis: Stomatitis scorbutica *f*.
score/*n, vb*: 1. Score *m*, Bewertungsziffer *f*; 2. scoren, bewerten.
scotoma/*n*: an area of partial or complete blindness within the normal visual field. Causes include glaucoma, retrobulbar neuritis, migraine, or retinitis pigmentosa. Skotom *n*, Gesichtsfeldausfall *m*.
scotopic adaptation: Dunkeladaptation *f*.
scotopic vision: skotopisches Sehen *n*, Dämmerungssehen *n*.
scout film: Nativaufnahme *f*, Übersichtsaufnahme *f*.
scrape/*n, vb*: 1. Kratzen *n*; 2. schaben, kratzen.
scraper/*n*: Schaber *m*.
scratch/*n, vb*: 1. Kratzen *n*, Schramme *f*; 2. kratzen, ritzen.
scratch test: Scratch-Test *m*, Skarifikationstest *m*.
scream/*n, vb*: 1. Geschrei *n*; 2. kreischen.
screen/*n*: Schirm *m*.
screening/*n*: Screening *n*, Reihenuntersuchung *f*.
screening test: Screeningtest *m*, Reihentest *m*.
scrotal/*adj*: skrotal.
scrotal hernia: Skrotalhernie *f*.
scrotal hydrocele: accumulation of serous fluid in the scrotum following local inflammation or trauma. Skrotumhydrozele *f*.
scrotal reflex: Skrotalreflex *m*.
scrub disinfection: Scheuerdesinfektion *f*.
scrub typhus: Scrub-Typhus *m*, Tsutsugamushi-Krankheit *f*.
scurf/*n*: Kopfschuppen.
scurvy/*n*: a disease caused by the lack of vitamin C or the inability to utilize vitamin C or ascorbic acid which is an essential cofactor in intracellular redox reactions. Initial symptoms of vitamin C deficiency include fatigue, irritability, joint and limb pain, and proneness to infections; in later stages generalized hemorrhage, scorbutic stomatitis, gingivitis, and tooth loss may occur. Skorbut *m*.
scutulum/*n*: Skutulum *n*.
scybala: Skybala, Kotballen.
seagull murmur: Seagull-Geräusch *n*, Seemöwengeräusch *n*.
seal/*n, vb*: 1. Siegel *n*, Verschluss *m*; 2. verschließen, abdichten.
seal-fin deformity: Flossenhand *f*, Ulnardeviation *f*.
seam/*n*: Naht *f*, Verschmelzungslinie *f*.
seasickness/*n*: Seekrankheit *f*.
seaside resort: Seebad *n*.

season/*n*: Jahreszeit *f*, Saison *f*.
seasonal nasal allergy: allergic rhinitis caused by specific airborne allergens like pollen. Typical symptoms include acute inflammatory reaction of the nasal mucosa and conjunctivitis. Heuschnupfen *m*.
seat-belt syndrome: Seat-Belt-Syndrom *n*, Sicherheitsgurtsyndrom *n*.
seaweed/*n*: Seetang *m*, Alge *f*, Seegras *n*.
sebaceous/*adj*: talgig.
sebaceous adenoma: Adenoma sebaceum *n*, Nävus Pringle *m*.
sebaceous carcinoma: a rare, malignant tumor of a sebaceous gland, showing eventually lipid secretion. Talgdrüsenkarzinom *n*.
sebaceous cyst: Talgzyste *f*.
sebaceous gland: Talgdrüse *f*.
seborrhea/*n*: Seborrhö *f*.
seborrheic blepharitis: squamöse seborrhoische Blepharitis *f*.
seborrheic dermatitis: chronic skin disorder characterized by the presence of erythrema and sebaceous patches, predominantly located at the head and the trunk. seborrhoische Dermatitis *f*.
secnidazole/*n*: Secnidazol *n*.
secondary alcohol: sekundärer Alkohol *m*.
secondary aldosteronism: sekundärer Aldosteronismus *m*.
secondary amenorrhea: sekundäre Amenorrhö *f*.
secondary amine: sekundäres Amin *n*.
secondary amyloidosis: sekundäre Amyloidose *f*.
secondary bone: Sekundärknochen *m*.
secondary cataract: Nachstar *m*.
secondary cyst: Tochterzyste *f*.
secondary dentition: zweite Dentition *f*, permanentes Gebiß *n*.
secondary follicle: Sekundärfollikel *m*.
secondary fracture: bone fracture resulting from normal movement and not due to trauma or excessive stress. Underlying causes include changes in bone structure or bone diseases, for example osteomalacia or osteoporosis. Spontanfraktur *f*, pathologische Fraktur *f*.
secondary glaucoma: sekundäres Glaukom *n*.
secondary hemorrhage: Nachblutung *f*.
secondary hypertension: symptomatische Hypertonie *f*.
secondary otalgia: Irritationsotalgie *f*.
secondary prevention: Sekundärprävention *f*.
secondary sclerosing cholangitis: sekundär sklerosierende Cholangitis *f*.
secondary sickness: Folgekrankheit *f*.
secondary suture: Sekundärnaht *f*.
secondary syphilis: sekundäre Syphilis *f*.
secondary tumor: Zweittumor *m*, Sekundärtumor *m*.
second-degree atrioventricular block: AV-Block II. Grades *m*.
second indication: zusätzliche Indikation *f*.
second-look procedure: Second-Look-Operation *f*.
second order symptom: Symptom zweiten Ranges *n*.
second sound: zweiter Herzton *m*.
second systolic phase: Austreibungsphase *f*.
secretin/*n*: Sekretin *n*.
secretion/*n*: Sekretion *f*, Absonderung *f*.
secretory cyst: Retentionszyste *f*.
secretory granule: sekretorische Vakuole *f*.
secretory phase: Sekretionsphase *f*, Lutealphase *f*.
section/*n, vb*: 1. Sektion *f*, Schnitt *m*, Sectio *f*; 2. schneiden.
security/*n*: Sicherheit *f*.
sedative/*n, adj*: 1. Sedativum *n*; 2. sedierend.
sediment/*n*: Sediment *n*.
sedimentation rate: Sedimentationsrate *f*.
sedimentation reaction: Blutkörperchensenkungsreaktion *f*, BSG.
seed/*n*: 1. Samenkorn *n*, Seed *n*, Ra-

dioisotopenpräparat *n*.
segment/*n*: Segment *n*, Abschnitt *m*.
segmental/*adj*: segmental.
segmental anesthesia: segmentale Anästhesie *f*.
segmental atelectasis: Segmentatelektase *f*.
segmental block: segmentale Anästhesie *f*.
segmental bronchus: Segmentbronchus *m*.
segmentation/*n*: Segmentierung *f*.
segmented cell: segmentierter Neutrophiler *m*.
segmentum/*n*: Segment *n*, Abschnitt *m*.
segregation/*n*: Segregation *f*, Aufspaltung *f*.
seizure/*n*: Anfall *m*, Krampf *m*.
selamectin/*n*: Selamectin *n*.
selection/*n*: Selektion *f*, Auswahl *f*.
selective culture medium: Selektivnährboden *m*.
selegiline/*n*: Selegilin *n*.
selenium/*n*: Selen *n*, Se.
self/*n, adj*: 1. Selbst *n*, Ego *n*; 2. Selbst-, Auto-.
self antigen: Autoantigen *n*.
self-control/*n*: Selbstkontrolle *f*.
self-esteem/*n*: Selbsteinschätzung *f*.
self-glucose monitoring: Blutzuckerselbstkontrolle *f*.
self-help group: Selbsthilfegruppe *f*.
self-hypnosis: Autohypnose *f*.
self-induced reflex: Eigenreflex *m*.
self-medication/*n*: Selbstmedikation *f*.
self-rating/*n*: Selbstbewertung *f*.
self-retaining catheter: selbsthaltender Katheter *m*.
self-treatment: Eigenbehandlung *f*.
semantic alexia: semantische Alexie *f*.
semantic aphasia: semantische Aphasie *f*.
semen/*n*: Samen *m*, Samenflüssigkeit *f*.
semen analysis: Spermauntersuchung *f*.
semiconductor/*n*: Halbleiter *m*.
semilunar/*adj*: halbmondförmig.
semilunar body: Gianuzzi-Halbmond *m*.
semilunar valve: Semilunarklappe *f*.
seminal/*adj*: Samen-.
seminal carcinoma: a malignant neoplasm of the testis composed by germ cells. Symptoms include initially painless swelling and tumescence of the testis, dysuria, and eventually gynecomastia as a result of endocrine dysfunction. Seminom *n*.
seminal cyst: Samenzyste *f*.
seminal vesicle: Samenblase *f*.
seminal vesiculitis: inflammation of the seminal vesicle, usually caused by bacteria, for example Gonococcus. Typical symptoms include fever, pain, and painful urination. Spermatozystitis *f*, Samenblasenentzündung *f*.
seminiferous/*adj*: samenführend, seminifer.
seminoma/*n*: Seminom *n*.
semipermeable membrane: semipermeable Membran *f*.
semiprone position: Sims-Lage *f*.
semisynthetic steroid: semisynthetisches Steroid *n*.
semivertical heart: Indifferenztyp *m*.
senescence/*n*: Seneszenz *f*, Altern *n*.
senile/*adj*: senil.
senile alopecia: Altersalopezie *f*.
senile cataract: Altersstar *m*, Cataracta senilis *f*.
senile deafness: progressive hearing loss as a result of changes in the inner ear occurring with age. Altersschwerhörigkeit *f*, Presbyakusis *f*.
senile dementia: senile Demenz *f*.
senile depression: senile Depression *f*.
senile disciform degeneration: senile Makularetinitis *f*.
senile emphysema: Altersemphysem *n*.
senile gangrene: senile Gangrän *f*, arteriosklerotische Gangrän *f*.
senile keratosis: Keratosis senilis *f*.
senile plaque: senile Plaque *f*, Altersplaque *f*.
senile psychosis: Alterspsychose *f*.
senile wart: yellow to black, circumscribed seborrheic patch in form of

a wart, occurring with old age. Alterswarze *f*.
senility/*n*: Senilität *f*.
senium/*n*: Senium *n*, hohes Alter *n*.
sensation/*n*: Sensation *f*, Sinnesempfindung *f*.
sense/*n, vb*: 1. Sinn *m*; 2. empfinden.
sensible perspiration: Perspiratio sensibilis *f*, Transpiration *f*.
sensibility/*n*: Sensibilität *f*, Sinneswahrnehmung *f*.
sensibilization/*n*: Sensibilisierung *f*.
sensible/*adj*: fühlbar.
sensitive/*adj*: sensibel, sensitiv, empfindlich.
sensitivity/*n*: Sensitivität *f*.
sensitization/*n*: Sensibilisierung *f*.
sensitized/*adj*: sensibilisiert.
sensor/*n*: Sinnesorgan *n*, Sensor *m*.
sensorial/*adj*: sensorisch.
sensorimotor cortex: sensomotorische Rinde *f*.
sensorineural hearing loss: complete loss of hearing resulting from a defect in the inner ear, the acoustic nerve, or auditory areas of the brain. zentrale Taubheit *f*.
sensory/*adj*: sensorisch.
sensory abnormality: Sensibilitätsstörung *f*.
sensory aphasia: aphasia with difficulties in comprehending spoken or even written language, resulting from lesions in the auditory and visual cortical centers. sensorische Aphasie *f*, Wernicke-Aphasie *f*.
sensory area: sensorische Rinde *f*.
sensory ataxia: sensorische Ataxie *f*.
sensory cell: Sinneszelle *f*.
sensory center: Sinneszentrum *n*.
sensory cortex: sensorisches Rindenareal *n*.
sensory disorder: any change in the perception of sensory stimuli. Underlying causes include dysfunctions or pathological changes of peripheral nerves or cerebral lesions. Sensibilitätsstörung *f*.
sensory dissociation: dissoziierte Sensibilitätsstörung *f*.
sensory fiber: sensorische Faser *f*.
sensory hair: Sinneshaar *n*.
sensory hallucination: Empfindungshalluzination *f*.
sensory illusion: Pseudoästhesie *f*.
sensory loss: Sensibilitätsverlust *m*.
sensory neuron: sensorisches Neuron *n*.
sensory paralysis: Pseudoparalyse *f*.
sensory perception: Sinneswahrnehmung *f*.
sensory threshold: Empfindungsschwelle *f*.
separation bleeding: Lösungsblutung *f*.
sepsis/*n*: systemic disease caused by pathogenic microorganisms, for example bacteria, fungi, and/or their toxins. Symptoms may include intermittent fever, splenomegaly, tachycardia, and hematologic alterations. Sepsis *f*.
septal defect: 1. defect of the nasal septum as a result of injury, infectious rhinitis, or intranasal drug application. Septumdefekt *m*, Nasenscheidewanddefekt *m*. 2. defect of the atrioventricular septum of the heart, for example atrial septal defect, ventricular septal defect. Septumdefekt *m*.
septal deviation: deformity of the nasal septum with abnormal anatomical position, usually resulting from injury. Symptoms can include nasal airway obstruction and impaired sense of smell. Septumdeviation *f*, Nasenscheidewanddeviation *f*.
septal perforation: Septumperforation *f*.
septate/*adj*: septiert.
septate gallbladder: septierte Gallenblase *f*.
septate hymen: Hymen septus *m*.
septate vagina: septierte Vagina *f*, Vagina septata *f*.
septic/*adj*: septisch.
septic abortion: septischer Abort *m*.
septicemia/*n*: Septikämie *f*, Sepsis *f*.
septic fever: septische Temperaturen.
septic granuloma: septisches Granulom *n*.
septic pericarditis: septische Perikarditis *f*.

septic peritonitis: septische Peritonitis *f*.
septic shock: septischer Schock *m*.
septic sore throat: Streptokokkenangina *f*.
septic thrombus: infizierter Thrombus *m*.
septum/*n*: Septum *n*, Scheidewand *f*.
sequel/*n*: Folge *f*.
sequence/*n*: Sequenz *f*, Folge *f*.
sequencing/*n*: Sequenzierung *f*.
sequential/*adj*: sequentiell.
sequential oral pill: Mehrphasenpille *f*.
sequential pacing: sequentielle Stimulation *f*.
sequestration/*n*: Sequestration *f*, Sequesterbildung *f*.
serial/*adj*: seriell.
series/*n*: Serie *f*, Reihe *f*.
serial epilepsy: Anfallsserie *f*.
serial fracture: Serienfraktur *f*.
seriously ill: schwer krank.
seriously injured: schwer verletzt.
seroalbuminous/*adj*: seroalbuminös.
serofibrinous pericarditis: Pericarditis serofibrinosa *f*.
serofibrinous pleurisy: serofibrinöse Pleuritis *f*.
serologic/*adj*: serologisch.
serologic diagnosis: serologische Diagnose *f*.
seroma/*n*: Serom *n*.
serositis/*n*: Serositis *f*.
serothorax/*n*: seröser Pleuraerguss *m*.
serotonin/*n*: Serotonin *n*.
serous/*adj*: serös.
serous cell: seröse Zelle *f*.
serous cyst: seröse Zyste *f*.
serous fluid: seröse Flüssigkeit *f*.
serous gland: seröse Drüse.
serous otitis: inflammation of the middle ear, sometimes resulting from obstruction of the eustachian tube. Symptoms may include the accumulation of a serous fluid and conduction hearing loss. seröse Otitis *f*.
serous peritonitis: seröse Peritonitis *f*.
serous pleurisy: seröse Pleuritis *f*.
serous sac: seröse Höhle *f*.
serous synovitis: seröse Synovitis *f*.
serpent worm: Medinawurm *m*, Dracunculus medinensis *m*.
serpiginous/*adj*: serpiginös, kriechend.
serpiginous ulcer: a suppurative ulcer of the cornea of the eye, due usually to bacterial infection with Pneumococcus or to fungal infection. Ulcus serpens *n*, serpiginöses Hornhautgeschwür *n*.
serrapeptase/*n*: Serrapeptase *f*.
serration/*n*: Zähnung *f*, Zahnung *f*.
sertindole/*n*: Sertindol *n*.
sertraline/*n*: Sertralin *n*.
serum/*n*: Serum *n*.
serum level: Serumspiegel *m*.
serum mark: Serumnarbe *f*.
serum therapy: Serumtherapie *f*.
sesamoid bone: Sesambein *n*.
sessile/*adj*: sessil, breitbasig.
sessile polyp: breitbasig aufsitzender Polyp *m*.
setup/*n*: Aufstellung *f*.
sevelamer/*n*: Sevelamer *n*.
seven-day fever: Siebentagefieber *n*, Nanukayami *n*.
severe/*adj*: schwer, heftig.
severe acute respiratory syndrome: an infectious disease caused by a Coronavirus. Initial symptoms include fever and dyspnea, and may, without treatment, result in acute respiratory failure. SARS was first described in China in 2003. SARS, schweres akutes Atemwegssyndrom *n*.
severe combined immunodeficiency: immunologic disorder with a severe defect of B- and T-lymphocyte development, for example Swiss type of agammaglobulinemia, certain hematopoietic stem cell defects, and thymic aplasia. schwerer kombinierter Immundefekt *m*.
severe disability: Schwerbehinderung *f*.
severely ill: schwer krank.
sevoflurane/*n*: Sevofluran *n*.
sew/*vb*: nähen.
sewer/*n*: Heftmaschine *f*, Nahtapparat *m*.

S

sex/*n*: Geschlecht *n*, Sexualität *f*.
sex chromatin: Geschlechtschromatin *n*, Barr-Körperchen *n*.
sex drive: Geschlechtstrieb *m*, Libido sexualis *f*.
sex education: Sexualaufklärung *f*.
sex-hormone binding globulin: Sexualhormon-bindendes Globulin *n*, SHBG.
sex-linked gene: geschlechtsgebundenes Gen *n*.
sex offense: Sexualdelikt *n*.
sexology/*n*: Sexologie *f*, Sexualwissenschaft *f*.
sex ratio: Geschlechtsverteilung *f*.
sex-specific/*adj*: geschlechtsspezifisch.
sexual/*adj*: sexuell.
sexual anesthesia: Frigidität *f*.
sexual behavior: Sexualverhalten *n*.
sexual contact: Sexualkontakt *m*.
sexual cycle: Geschlechtszyklus *m*.
sexual dysfunction: any disorder characterized by impairment or disturbance of sexual response, including sexual arousal disorders, or erectile dysfunction. sexuelle Funktionsstörung *f*.
sexual generation: geschlechtliche Fortpflanzung *f*.
sexuality/*n*: Sexualität *f*.
sexually transmitted disease: any infectious disease that is transmitted from person to person predominantly or exclusively through sexual contacts. Sexually transmitted or venereal diseases include for example syphilis, gonorrhea, soft chancre, HIV infection, chlamydial infection, and Mycoplasma infection. sexuell übertragbare Krankheit *f*, Geschlechtskrankheit *f*.
sexual offender: Sexualstraftäter *m*.
sexual reproduction: geschlechtliche Fortpflanzung *f*.
sexual transmission: sexuelle Übertragung *f*.
shadow/*n*: Schatten *m*, Verschattung *f*.
shadow corpuscle: Erythrozytenschatten *m*.
shaft/*n*: Schaft *m*, Knochenschaft *m*.
shake/*vb*: schütteln.
shaking/*n, adj*: 1. Schütteln *n*, Tremor *m*; 2. schüttelnd.
shaking ague: Schüttelfrost *m*.
shaking mixture: Schüttelmixtur *f*.
shaking palsy: Schüttellähmung *f*, Paralysis agitans *f*.
shallow breathing: flache Atmung *f*.
sham/*n, vb*: 1. Schein *m*, Betrug *m*; 2. vortäuschen, sich krank stellen, simulieren.
shape/*n, vb*: 1. Form *f*; 2. formen.
shared delusion: a false belief or psychotic disorder which is induced from an index patient to one or more closely related, formerly inconspicuous persons who simultaneously develop similar symptoms. induzierte Psychose *f*, Folie à deux *f*.
sharp/*adj*: scharf.
sharp wave: spitze Welle *f*.
shatter/*vb*: zertrümmern.
shear fracture: Scherfraktur *f*.
shearing force: Scherkraft *f*.
sheath/*n*: Scheide *f*, Hülle *f*.
shedding/*n*: Shedding *n*, Abschilferung *f*.
sheep cell agglutination: Schafzellagglutination *f*.
sheet/*n*: Blatt *n*, Laken *n*.
shelf/*n*: Bord *n*, Sockel *m*.
shelf life: Haltbarkeit *f*, Lagerdauer *f*.
shell/*n*: Schale *f*, Rinde *f*.
shellfish poisoning: Muschelvergiftung *f*.
shield/*n, vb*: 1. Schild *m*, Schirm *m*; 2. abschirmen.
shift/*n, vb*: 1. Verschiebung *f*; 2. verschieben.
shifting pacemaker: wandernder Schrittmacher *m*.
Shiga's dysentery: Shigellose *f*, Dysenterie *f*, Bakterienruhr *f*.
shin/*n*: Schienbein *n*.
shinbone fracture/*n*: fracture of the tibia. Forms include tibial plateau fracture, malleolar fracture with tibia involvement, or simultaneous fracture of tibia and fibula. Tibiafraktur *f*.
shingles/*n*: an infectious disease of the skin, caused by reactivation of varicella-zoster virus. Predominant-

ly located in the thoracic region, symptoms include a papular exanthema, typically in the area of innervation of a sensory ganglion, and painful sensations. As complications, herpetic encephalitis, involvement of the eye, or general dissemination can occur. Zoster *m*, Gürtelrose *f*, Herpes zoster *m*.

shipyard conjunctivitis/*n*: epidemische Keratokonjunktivitis *f*.

shirt-stud abscess: Knopflochabszess *m*.

shiver/*vb*: zittern.

shivers/*n*: Schüttelfrost *m*.

shock/*n*: a life-threatening medical condition resulting from decreased effective circulating blood volume and profound metabolic disturbances. Symptoms include hypotension, tachycardia, respiratory insufficiency, and anuria. Schock *m*.

shoe/*n*: Schuh *m*.

shooting pain: einschießender Schmerz *m*.

short/*adj*: kurz.

shortage/*n*: Mangel *m*, Knappheit *f*.

short bone: kurzer Knochen *m*.

short cone: kurzer Tubus *m*.

shortening/*n, adj*: 1. Verkürzung *f*; 2. verkürzend.

shortness of breath: Kurzatmigkeit *f*, Dyspnoe *f*.

shortsightedness/*n*: Kurzsichtigkeit *f*, Myopie *f*.

short-term/*adj*: kurzfristig.

short-term memory: Kurzzeitgedächtnis *n*.

short wave diathermy: Kurzwellendiathermie *f*.

shot/*n*: Schuss *m*, Injektion *f*.

shotty breast: zystische Mastopathie *f*.

shoulder/*n*: Schulter *f*.

shoulder blade/*n*: Schulterblatt *n*, Scapula *f*.

shoulder presentation/*n*: in obstetrics, the position of the fetus in which the shoulder appears first in the uterine cervix. Schultervorfall *m*, Schulterlage *f*.

shower/*n*: Dusche *f*, Brausebad *n*.

shrinkage/*n*: Schrumpfen *n*, Schwund *m*.

shuffle/*vb*: schlurfen.

shunt/*n*: Shunt *m*, Nebenschluss *m*.

shunt cyanosis: Shuntzyanose *f*.

SI <*abbr*> **Système International d'Unités**: Système International d'Unités, SI-System *n*.

sialadenitis/*n*: Sialadenitis *f*.

sialic acid: Sialinsäure *f*.

sialogogue/*n*: Sialagogum *n*.

sialolithiasis/*n*: a disease characterized by the presence of one or more stones or concrements in the ducts of salivary glands, most frequently in the submaxillary gland. Sialolithiasis *f*.

sibilant rale: giemendes Rasselgeräusch *n*.

siblings/*n*: Geschwister.

sibutramine/*n*: Sibutramin *n*.

sick/*n, adj*: 1. Kranker *m*; 2. krank, leidend.

sick bay/*n*: Krankenrevier *n*.

sick leave/*n*: Krankschreibung *f*.

sickle cell: Sichelzelle *f*, Drepanozyt *m*.

sickle-cell anemia: hereditary blood disorder characterized by an intermittent lysis of red blood cells due to the presence of abnormal hemoglobin. Symptoms may include attacks of joint pain, intermittent abdominal pain, and skin ulcerations at the lower limbs. Sichelzellenanämie *f*.

sickle hemoglobin: Sichelzellenhämoglobin *n*, HbS.

sickly/*adj*: schwächlich, krankhaft.

sickness/*n*: Erkrankung *f*, Krankheit *f*.

sickness concept: Krankheitskonzept *n*.

sick sinus syndrome: a condition which is characterized by an abnormality of sinoatrial node function, usually due to coronary arteriosclerosis, myocarditis, or alterations of the cardial muscles. Symptoms include bradycardia and sinus arrest or block. Sick-Sinus-Syndrom *n*, Sinusknotensyndrom *n*.

side/*n*: Seite *f*.

sidechain: Seitenkette *f*.
side effect: Nebenwirkung *f*, unerwünschte Wirkung *f*.
sideroachrestic anemia: sideroachrestische Anämie *f*, chronisch-refraktäre Anämie *f*.
sideroblastic anemia: Sideroblastenanämie *f*, sideroachrestische Anämie *f*.
siderocytosis/*n*: Siderozytose *f*.
sideropenic anemia: blood disorder characterized by a decrease of red blood cells due to iron deficiency. Eisenmangelanämie *f*.
sideropenic syndrome: a condition usually due to severe and chronic iron deficiency. Symptoms include painful swallowing, atrophy of mucous membranes of the mouth, throat, and esophagus, and iron deficiency anemia. Plummer-Vinson-Syndrom *n*.
siderosis/*n*: Siderose *f*, Eisenablagerung *f*.
siderotic splenomegaly: Gandy-Gamna-Milz *f*.
side-to-side shunt: Seit-zu-Seit-Anastomose *f*.
SIDS <*abbr*> **sudden infant death syndrome**: sudden death of an infant during the first year of life, characteristically during sleep, without detectable organic cause. The exact etiology is unknown, factors such as environmental temperature, abdominal position during sleep, and pre- or postnatal exposure to tobacco smoke are discussed. plötzlicher Kindstod *m*.
sigh respiration: Seufzeratmung *f*.
sight/*n*: Sicht *f*, Sehvermögen *n*.
sight test: Sehtest *m*.
sigmoid/*n*: Sigmoid *n*.
sigmoid bladder: Sigmablase *f*.
sigmoid carcinoma: a malignant neoplasm of the sigmoid colon. Symptoms include bloody stools, weight loss, pain, and constipation alternating with diarrhea. Sigmakarzinom *n*.
sigmoid diverticulum: Sigmadivertikel *n*.
sigmoidoscopy/*n*: Sigmoidoskopie *f*.
sigmoidostomy/*n*: Sigmoidostomie *f*.
sign/*n*: Zeichen *n*, Symptom *n*.
signal/*n*: Signal *n*, Anzeichen *n*.
signature/*n*: Signatur *f*.
sign blindness: visuelle Asymbolie *f*.
significance/*n*: Bedeutung *f*, Signifikanz *f*.
sign language: Zeichensprache *f*.
sildenafil/*n*: Sildenafil *n*.
silence/*n*: Stille *f*, Ruhe *f*.
silent area: stummes Areal *n*.
silent gap: auskultatorische Lücke *f*.
silent gene: stilles Gen *n*.
silent kidney: stumme Niere *f*.
silent mastoiditis: okkulte Mastoiditis *f*.
silent myocardial infarction: stummer Myokardinfarkt *m*.
silent period: silent period, stummes Intervall *n*, Pause *f*.
silibinin/*n*: Silibinin *n*.
silicic acid: Kieselsäure *f*.
silicon breast implant: Silikonbrustimplantat *n*.
silicosis/*n*: chronic lung disease resulting from inhalation of stone dust containing silicon dioxide. A late onset occurring years after dust exposure is possible. Symptoms include fatigue, dyspnea, and cyanosis. Silikose *f*.
silver nitrate: Silbernitrat *n*, Argentum nitricum *n*.
simian crease: Affenfurche *f*, Vierfingerfurche *f*.
simian virus: Simianvirus *n*.
similar/*adj*: ähnlich.
simple/*adj*: unkompliziert, einfach.
simple dislocation: einfache Luxation *f*.
simple ointment: weiße Salbe *f*.
simple schizophrenia: Schizophrenia simplex *f*.
simple synovitis: unkomplizierte Synovitis *f*.
simple urethritis: unspezifische Urethritis.
simulation/*n*: Simulation *f*.
simulator/*n*: Simulator *m*.
simvastatin/*n*: Simvastatin *n*.
sincalide/*n*: Sincalid *n*.
sinew/*n*: Sehne *f*.

singers' nodules: small fibroma or retention cysts occurring on the vocal cord, resulting from excessive vocal strain. Sängerknötchen *n*.
single/*adj*: einfach, einmalig, alleinstehend.
single-agent therapy: Monotherapie *f*.
single-copy gene: Einzelkopie-Gen *n*.
single cyst: Solitärzyste *f*.
single dose: Einzeldosis *f*.
single episode major depression: typische depressive Episode *f*.
single photon emission computed tomography: Single-Photon-Emissions-Computertomographie *f*, SPECT.
single-stranded: einstrangig.
single-stranded DNA: einstrangige DNA *f*.
single-use: Einweg-.
sinistrocardia/*n*: Sinistrokardie *f*, Lävokardie *f*.
sinoatrial block: sinuatrialer Block *m*, SA-Block *m*.
sinoatrial node: Sinusknoten *m*, Keith-Flack-Knoten *m*.
sinus/*n*: Sinus *m*, Bucht *f*, Nebenhöhle *f*.
sinus arrhythmia: irregular rhythm in heart rate resulting from a variation of impulses from the sinoatrial node. Sinusarrhythmie *f*.
sinusitis/*n*: acute or chronic inflammation of a paranasal sinus, for example inflammation of the ethmoidal, frontal, maxillary, or sphenoidal sinuses. Sinusitis *f*.
sinus node: Sinusknoten *m*, Keith-Flack-Knoten *m*.
sinusoid/*n, adj*: 1. Sinusoid *n*; 2. sinusförmig.
sinusoidal rhythm: sinusartiger Rhythmus *m*.
siomycin/*n*: Siomycin *n*.
sirolimus/*n*: Sirolimus *m*.
sisomicin/*n*: Sisomicin *n*.
sitosterol/*n*: Sitosterin *n*.
situation/*n*: Situation *f*, Lage *f*.
situational/*adj*: situativ.
situational psychosis: reaktive Psychose *f*.
situation therapy: Milieutherapie *f*.
size/*n*: Größe *f*.
skeletal age: Knochenalter *n*.
skeletal dysplasia: Osteochondrodysplasie *f*.
skeletal muscle: Skelettmuskel *m*.
skeletal tuberculosis: Knochentuberkulose *f*.
skeleton/*n*: Skelett *n*.
skeleton deformity: Skelettdeformität *f*.
skew deviation: inward and downward rotation of the eyeball, occurring for example as a symptom of certain brain stem lesions. Skew deviation, Hertwig-Magendie-Syndrom *n*.
skill/*n*: Fähigkeit *f*, Geschicklichkeit *f*.
skimmed milk: Magermilch *f*.
skin/*n*: Haut *f*.
skin biopsy: Hautbiopsie *f*.
skinfold/*n*: Hautfalte *f*.
skin lesion: Hautläsion *f*.
skin rash: dermal lesion with eruption, exanthema, or efflorescence of the skin. Hautausschlag *m*.
skin test: Hauttest *m*, Hautprobe *f*.
skin test dose: Hauttestdosis *f*.
skip lesion: Skip Lesion *f*.
skull/*n*: Schädel *m*.
skull base: Schädelbasis *f*.
skull fracture: fracture of the bony structure of the head, affecting the cranial bones or the bones of the face. Schädelfraktur *f*.
sleep/*n, vb*. 1. Schlaf *m*; 2. schlafen.
sleep-apnea syndrome: a momentary cessation of breathing during sleep due to a disorder in respiratory regulation. The most common form is an obstructive sleep apnea resulting from obstructions of extrathoracic airways. Schlafapnoesyndrom *n*.
sleeping sickness: any disease characterized by apathy, lethargy and increased sleeping periods, for example lethargic encephalitis or African trypanosomiasis. Schlafkrankheit *f*.
sleeplessness/*n*: Schlaflosigkeit *f*, Insomnie *f*.
sleep therapy: Schlafbehandlung *f*, Schlaftherapie *f*.

sleepwalking/*n*: walking around during a dreamy state or sleep. Actions and movements during this period are not remembered by the somnambulist. Sleep-wake schedule disorders and postencephalitic lesions are discussed as possibly underlying causes. Schlafwandeln *n*, Somnambulismus *m*.
sleeve/*n*: Schutzhülle *f*, Ärmel *m*.
slice/*n*: Scheibe *f*, Schicht *f*.
slide/*n, vb*: 1. Gleiten *n*, Objektträger *m*, Dia *n*; 2. gleiten, rutschen.
sliding flap: Verschiebelappen *m*.
sliding hernia: Gleitbruch *m*.
slight/*adj*: schwach.
slight temperature: leichtes Fieber *n*.
slim/*adj*: schlank, schwach.
slime mold: Schleimpilz *m*, Myxomyzet *m*.
sling/*n*: Schlinge *f*, Armschlinge *f*.
slip/*vb*: ausgleiten, ausrutschen.
slipped disk: Bandscheibenvorfall *m*.
slipped shoulder: dislocation of the shoulder joint. Forms include posttraumatic and constitutional shoulder dislocation. Schultergelenkluxation *f*.
slit lamp: Spaltlampe *f*.
slope/*n*: Neigung *f*, Abhang *m*.
slow/*adj*: langsam.
slow distal hereditary myopathy: Myopathia distalis hereditaria *f*, Welander-Myopathie *f*.
slow infection: schleichende Infektion *f*, Slow-Infection *f*.
slow wave: langsame Welle *f*.
sludge/*n*: Schlamm *m*, Rückstand *m*.
sludged blood: Sludge-Phänomen *n*, Geldrollenbildung *f*, Erythrozytenaggregation *f*.
sluggish/*adj*: träge.
slurred speech: verwaschene Sprache.
slurry/*n*: Aufschlämmung *f*.
small/*adj*: klein.
small-cell carcinoma: kleinzelliges Karzinom *n*.
small pelvis: kleines Becken *n*.
smallpox/*n*: highly infectious disease caused by variola virus, an orthopoxvirus. Symptoms include high fever, pain, vomiting, and an eruption of red spots which transform into blisters, filled with pus. Pocken *f*, Variola *f*.
smallpox vaccine: Pockenvakzine *f*.
small weak pulse: Pulsus parvus *m*.
smear/*n, vb*: 1. Abstrich *m*; 2. schmieren, ausstreichen.
smear test: Papanicolaou-Test *m*.
smegma/*n*: Smegma *n*.
smell/*n, vb*: 1. Geruch *m*; 2. riechen.
smoking/*n*: Rauchen *n*.
smooth/*adj*: glatt.
smooth diet: Schonkost *f*.
smooth muscle: glatter Muskel *m*.
snake venom: Schlangengift *n*.
snapping/*adj*: schnappend, schnellend.
snapping finger: schnellender Finger *m*.
snapping tendon: schnappende Sehne *f*.
sneeze/*n, vb*: 1. Niesen *n*; 2. niesen.
sniffing/*n*: Schnüffeln *n*.
snooze/*vb*: dösen.
snore/*n, vb*: 1. noise when breathing during sleep, caused by vibration of the uvula and the soft palate or by nose or throat obstruction. Schnarchen *n*; 2. schnarchen.
snoring rale: schnarchendes Geräusch *n*.
snow blindness: Schneeblindheit *f*.
soap/*n*: Seife *f*.
sober/*adj*: nüchtern.
social/*adj*: sozial.
social agnosia: soziale Agnosie *f*.
social insurance: Sozialversicherung *f*.
social psychiatry: Sozialpsychiatrie *f*.
social system: soziales System *n*.
sociology/*n*: Soziologie *f*.
sociomedical/*adj*: sozialmedizinisch.
socket/*n*: Gelenkpfanne *f*, Sockel *m*, Fassung *f*.
socket joint: Kugelgelenk *n*.
sodium/*n*: Natrium *n*, Na.
sodium aurothiomalate: Natriumaurothiomalat *n*.
sodium channel: Natriumkanal *m*.
sodium chloride: Natriumchlorid *n*, Kochsalz *n*.
sodium chloride solution: Kochsalzlösung *f*.

sodium nitrate: Natriumnitrat *n*, Salpeter *m*.
sodium nitrite: Natriumnitrit *n*.
sodium nitroprusside: Natriumnitroprussid *n*, Nitroprussidnatrium *n*.
sodium-restricted diet: kochsalzarme Diät *f*.
soft/*adj*: weich.
soft-bodied tick: Lederzecke *f*, Argasida *f*.
soft catheter: flexibler Katheter *m*.
soft chancre: sexually transmitted infection due to Haemophilus ducreyi, characterized by one or more painful ulcerative lesions most commonly located at the external genitalia. weicher Schanker *m*, Ulcus molle *n*.
softening/*n*: Erweichung *f*, Malazie *f*.
soft fibroma: Fibroma molle *n*, Fibrolipom *n*.
soft papilloma: Papilloma molle *n*.
soft pulse: weicher Puls *m*.
soft sore: weicher Schanker *m*, Ulcus molle *n*.
soft tissue: Bindegewebe *n*.
soft-tissue sarcoma: Weichteilsarkom *n*.
soft-tissue tumor: benign or malignant neoplasm of the non-osseous tissues. Weichteiltumor *m*.
soil bacterium: Bodenbakterium *n*.
solar/*adj*: solar.
solar blindness: UV-Blindheit *f*.
solar dermatitis: skin disorder following longterm exposure to sunlight with multiple horny or verrucous tumors. aktinische Keratose *f*.
solar fever: Sonnenstich *m*.
solar ophthalmia: Blendungskonjunktivitis *f*.
solar plexus: Solarplexus *m*, Plexus coeliacus *m*.
solar radiation: Sonnenstrahlung *f*.
solar treatment: Heliotherapie *f*.
solar urticaria: Lichturtikaria *f*.
soldier's heart: Soldatenherz *n*, neurozirkulatorische Asthenie *f*, DaCosta-Syndrom *n*.
sole/*n*: Fußsohle *f*.
solifenacin/*n*: Solifenacin *n*.
solid/*n, adj*: 1. feste Substanz *f*; 2. solide, fest.
solid bone: Kompakta *f*, Substantia compacta *f*.
solid extract: fester Extrakt *m*.
solitary/*adj*: solitär.
solitary cyst: Solitärzyste *f*.
solitary follicle: Solitärfollikel *m*.
soluble antigen: S-Antigen *n*.
soluble complex: löslicher Komplex *m*.
soluble insulin: Normalinsulin *n*, Altinsulin *n*.
solution/*n*: Lösung *f*.
solvent/*n, adj*: 1. Solvens *n*, Lösungsmittel *n*; 2. lösend.
somatic/*adj*: somatisch, körperlich.
somatic cell: Körperzelle *f*.
somatic conversion: Konversionshysterie *f*.
somatic pain: somatischer Schmerz *m*.
somatic sex: Körpergeschlecht *n*.
somatization disorder: Somatisierungsstörung *f*, Somatisierungssyndrom *n*.
somatoform disorder: somatoforme Störung *f*.
somatology/*n*: Somatologie *f*, Körperlehre *f*.
somatorelin/*n*: Somatorelin *n*.
somatosensory cortex: somatosensibler Kortex *m*.
somatosensory evoked potential: somatosensibel evoziertes Potential *n*, SEP.
somatostatin/*n*: Somatostatin *n*.
somnambulism/*n*: walking around during a dreamy state or sleep. Actions and movements during this period are not remembered by the somnambulist. Sleep-wake schedule disorders and postencephalitic lesions are discussed as possibly underlying causes. Somnambulismus *m*, Schlafwandeln *n*.
somnolence/*n*: Somnolenz *f*.
sonography/*n*: Sonographie *f*, Ultraschallsonographie *f*.
soot/*n*: Ruß *m*.
soot cancer: Schornsteinfegerkrebs *m*.
soporific/*n, adj*: 1. Schlafmittel *n*; 2. einschläfernd.

sorbic acid: Sorbinsäure *f*.
sorbitol/*n*: Sorbitol *n*, Sorbit *n*.
sore/*n, adj*: 1. Geschwür *n*, Ulkus *n*; 2. schmerzhaft.
sore throat: Angina *f*, Halsentzündung *f*.
sorrow/*n*: Kummer *m*, Sorge *f*.
sotalol/*n*: Sotalol *n*.
soul/*n*: Seele *f*, Psyche *f*.
sound/*n, vb*: 1. Geräusch *n*, Schall *m*, Sonde *f*; 2. klingen, sondieren.
source/*n*: Quelle *f*, Ursprung *m*.
South American blastomycosis: südamerikanische Blastomykose *f*, Almeida-Krankheit *f*, Parakokzidioidomykose *f*.
South American trypanosomiasis: südamerikanische Trypanosomiasis *f*, Chagas-Krankheit *f*.
space/*n*: Raum *m*.
space orientation: Raumorientierung *f*.
spade finger: Pratzenhände.
span/*n*: Spanne *f*, Zeitintervall *n*.
sparfloxacin/*n*: Sparfloxacin *n*.
sparing/*n*: Aussparung *f*.
sparteine/*n*: Spartein *n*.
spasm/*n*: Spasmus *m*, Zuckung *f*.
spasmodic/*adj*: spasmodisch, krampfartig.
spasmodic asthma: Asthma bronchiale *n*, Bronchialasthma *n*.
spasmodic laughter: Lachkrampf *m*.
spasmodic pain: krampfartiger Schmerz *m*.
spasmolytic/*adj*: spasmolytisch.
spastic/*n, adj*: 1. Spastiker *m*; 2. spastisch, krampfhaft.
spastic bulbar paralysis: Pseudobulbärparalyse *f*.
spastic colon: chronic dysfunction of the lower gastrointestinal tract without detectable pathological alterations. Symptoms include flatulence, intermittent diarrhea, intermittent constipation, and abdominal pain. irritables Kolon *n*, Reizkolon *n*.
spastic diplegia: spastische Diplegie *f*, Little-Krankheit *f*.
spastic gait: spastischer Gang *m*.
spastic hemiplegia: spastische Hemiplegie *f*.
spasticity/*n*: sustained increased muscle tension. Spastizität *f*, Spastik *f*.
spastic paralysis: spastische Lähmung *f*.
spastic paraplegia: spastische Paraplegie *f*.
spatial/*adj*: räumlich.
spatula/*n*: Spatel *m*.
speaking aid: Sprechhilfe *f*.
speaking tube: Sprechkanüle *f*.
speaking voice: Sprechstimme *f*.
species/*n*: Spezies *f*, Art *f*.
species-specific/*adj*: artspezifisch.
specific/*n, adj*: 1. Spezifikum *n*; 2. spezifisch.
specific granule: spezifisches Granulom *n*.
specific parasite: wirtspezifischer Parasit *m*.
specific urethritis: gonorrhoische Urethritis.
specimen/*n*: Probe *f*, Untersuchungsmaterial *n*, Muster *n*.
spectacles/*n*: Brille *f*.
spectinomycin/*n*: Spectinomycin *n*.
spectrometry/*n*: Spektrometrie *f*.
spectrophotometry/*n*: Spektrophotometrie *f*.
spectroscopic test: spektroskopische Untersuchung *f*.
spectroscopy/*n*: Spektroskopie *f*.
spectrum/*n*: Spektrum *n*.
speculum/*n*: Spekulum *n*, Spiegel *m*.
speech audiogram: Sprachaudiogramm *n*.
speech center: Sprachzentrum *n*.
speech reception threshold: Sprachwahrnehmungsschwelle *f*.
speech therapy: Sprachtherapie *f*.
speed/*n*: Geschwindigkeit *f*, Speed *n*, Amphetamin *n*.
sperm/*n*: Spermie *f*, Sperma *n*.
spermatic/*adj*: spermatisch.
spermatic cord: Samenstrang *m*.
spermatic hydrocele: Spermatozele *f*.
spermaticide/*n*: Spermizid *n*.
spermatid/*n*: Spermatide *f*.
spermatocele/*n*: cystic enlargement of the epididymis or the testis, due to accumulation of spermatozoa. Spermatozele *f*.

spermatocyte/*n*: Spermatozyt *m*.
spermatogenesis/*n*: Spermatogenese *f*.
spermatozoon/*n*: Spermatozoon *n*.
sperm cell: Spermie *f*, Spermatoblast *m*.
spermicidal agent: Spermizid *n*.
spermicide/*n*: Spermizid *n*.
sperm motility: Spermienmotilität *f*.
sperm transport: Spermientransport *m*.
sphenoid/*n, adj*: 1. Keilbein *n*, Os sphenoidale *n*; 2. keilförmig, sphenoidal.
sphenoidal sinusitis: Sinusitis sphenoidalis *f*, Sphenoiditis *f*.
sphenoidal wing: Keilbeinflügel *m*.
spheric aberration: sphärische Aberration *f*.
spherocyte/*n*: Sphärozyt *m*, Kugelzelle *f*.
spherocytic anemia: Sphärozytose *f*.
spherocytosis/*n*: Sphärozytose *f*.
spheroidal articulation: Sphäroidgelenk *n*.
sphincter/*n*: Sphinkter *m*, Schließmuskel *m*.
sphincterotomy/*n*: Sphinkterotomie *f*.
sphincter weakness: Sphinkterschwäche *f*.
sphingolipidosis/*n*: Sphingolipidose *f*.
sphygmography/*n*: Sphygmographie *f*.
sphygmomanometry/*n*: Sphygmomanometrie *f*, Blutdruckmessung *f*.
spica bandage: Kornährenverband *m*, Bindenverband *m*.
spicular/*adj*: spornförmig.
spicule/*n*: Spitze *f*.
spider-burst: Besenreiservarizen.
spider nevus: Spider-Nävus *m*, Naevus araneus *m*.
spike/*n*: Spitze *f*, Zacke *f*, Spike *m*.
spike potential: Spike *m*, Spitzenpotential *n*.
spina/*n*: Stachel *m*, Rückgrat *n*.
spinach stool: Spinatstuhl *m*.
spinal/*adj*: spinal.
spinal anesthesia: Spinalanästhesie *f*, Lumbalanästhesie *f*.
spinal angioma: spinales Angiom *n*.
spinal apoplexy: spinale Apoplexie *f*.
spinal ataxia: spinale Ataxie *f*.
spinal block: Spinalanästhesie *f*.
spinal canal: Spinalkanal *m*.
spinal cell: Rückenmarkzelle *f*.
spinal center: Rückenmarkzentrum *n*.
spinal column: Wirbelsäule *f*.
spinal compression: Rückenmarkkompression *f*.
spinal cord: Rückenmark *n*.
spinal cord lesion: Rückenmarkschädigung *f*.
spinal fusion: Wirbelverschmelzung *f*.
spinal ganglion: Spinalganglion *n*.
spinal hemorrhage: Rückenmarkblutung *f*.
spinal marrow: Rückenmark *n*.
spinal muscular atrophy: spinale Muskeldystrophie *f*.
spinal nerve: Spinalnerv *m*.
spinal puncture: Spinalpunktion *f*, Lumbalpunktion *f*.
spinal reflex: spinaler Reflex *m*, Rückenmarkreflex *m*.
spinal root: Rückenmarkwurzel *f*.
spinal segment: Rückenmarksegment *n*.
spinal shock: spinaler Schock *m*.
spinal stenosis: Spinalkanalstenose *f*.
spinal tap: Lumbalpunktion *f*.
spindle/*n*: Spindel *f*.
spindle cell carcinoma: Spindelzellkarzinom *n*.
spindle poison: Spindelgift *n*, Mitosegift *n*.
spine/*n*: Rückgrat *n*, Stachel *m*.
spine sign: Kniekussphänomen *n*.
spinocerebellar ataxia: spinozerebelläre Ataxie *f*, Friedreich-Ataxie *f*.
spinous/*adj*: dornförmig.
spinous plane: Spina-iliaca-Ebene *f*.
spiral fracture: Spiralfraktur *f*.
spiral organ: Organum spirale *n*, Corti-Organ *n*.
spiral-tip catheter: Spiralkatheter *m*.
spiramycin/*n*: Spiramycin *n*.
spirapril/*n*: Spirapril *n*.
spirillary fever: Spirillum-minus-Krankheit *f*, Sodoku *n*.

spirit/*n*: Spiritus *m*, Geist *m*, Seele *f*.
spirochetal infection: Spirochätose *f*.
spirography/*n*: Spirographie *f*.
spirometry/*n*: Spirometrie *f*.
spironolactone/*n*: Spironolacton *n*.
spit/*n, vb*: 1. Speichel *m*; 2. spucken.
splanchnic/*adj*: viszeral.
splanchnic block: Splanchnikusblockade *f*.
splanchnicectomy/*n*: Splanchnikektomie *f*.
splanchnic nerve: Splanchnikus *m*, Nervus splanchnicus *m*.
splanchnic wall: Viszeropleura *f*, viszerales Mesoderm *n*.
splashing sound: Plätschergeräusch *n*, Clapotement *n*.
splayfoot/*n*: Spreizfuß *m*.
spleen/*n*: Milz *f*.
splenectomy/*n*: Splenektomie *f*, Milzexstirpation *f*.
splenic/*adj*: Milz-, lienal.
splenic fever: Anthrax *m*, Milzbrand *m*.
splenic rupture: tearing apart of the spleen resulting from traumatic injury. Clinical signs include hypotension and shock due to severe hemorrhage. Milzruptur *f*.
splenography/*n*: Splenographie *f*.
splenohepatomegaly/*n*: enlargement of the spleen and the liver, resulting for example from infections or metabolic disorders. Hepatosplenomegalie *f*.
splenomegaly/*n*: Splenomegalie *f*, Milzvergrößerung *f*.
splenoportal venography: Splenoportographie *f*.
splenorenal shunt: splenorenaler Shunt *m*.
splicing/*n*: Spleißen *n*, Splicing *n*.
splint/*n, vb*: 1. Schiene *f*; 2. schienen.
splinter/*n, vb*: 1. Splitter *m*; 2. splittern, zersplittern.
splintered fracture: Splitterfraktur *f*.
split-brain state: Split-Brain-Syndrom *n*.
split foot: Spaltfuß *m*.
split hand: Spalthand *f*.
split personality: gespaltene Persönlichkeit *f*.
split sound: gespaltener Herzton *m*.
splitting-off: Abspaltung *f*.
splitting of heart sounds: Spaltung der Herztöne.
spoke bone: Speiche *f*, Radius *m*.
spondylarthrosis/*n*: Spondylarthrose *f*.
spondylitis/*n*: inflammation of the vertebrae of the spinal column, frequently affecting adjoint intervertebral disks. Most commonly due to bacterial infections, it also occurs in noninfectious systemic diseases such as Bekhterev's arthritis. Spondylitis *f*.
spondylolisthetic pelvis: Spondylolisthesisbecken *n*, Rokitansky-Becken *n*.
spondylolysis/*n*: Spondylolyse *f*.
spondylosis/*n*: Spondylose *f*.
sponge/*n*: Schwamm *m*.
sponge kidney: Schwammniere *f*.
spongioblast/*n*: Spongioblast *m*.
spongiform encephalopathy: spongiforme Enzephalopathie *f*.
spongiform leukodystrophy: autosomal recessive degeneration of the central nervous system with early onset. Symptoms include psychomotor retardation, muscle hypertonia and/or hypotonia, vision loss, and cerebral seizures. spongiforme Leukodystrophie *f*, Canavan-Krankheit *f*.
spongiose/*adj*: spongiös.
spongiositis/*n*: Corpus-spongiosum-Entzündung *f*.
spongy bone: Spongiosa *f*, Substantia spongiosa *f*.
sponsor/*n*: Sponsor *m*, Schirmherr *m*.
spontaneous/*adj*: spontan.
spontaneous abortion: Spontanabort *m*.
spontaneous breathing: Spontanatmung *f*.
spontaneous delivery: Spontangeburt *f*.
spontaneous epilepsy: Spontanepilepsie *f*.
spontaneous evolution: Selbstentwicklung *f*.
spontaneous fracture: bone fracture resulting from normal movement

and not due to trauma or excessive stress. Underlying causes include changes in bone structure or bone diseases, for example osteomalacia or osteoporosis. Spontanfraktur *f*, pathologische Fraktur *f*.
spontaneous healing: Spontanheilung *f*.
spontaneous hemorrhage: Spontanblutung *f*.
spontaneous inversion: Spontanwendung *f*.
spontaneous labor: Spontangeburt *f*.
spontaneous luxation: Spontanluxation *f*.
spontaneous movement: Spontanbewegung *f*.
spontaneous pneumothorax: Spontanpneumothorax *m*.
spontaneous recovery: Spontanheilung *f*.
spontaneous regression: Spontanrückbildung *f*.
spontaneous remission: Spontanremission *f*.
spontaneous respiration: Spontanatmung *f*.
spontaneous rupture: spontaner Blasensprung *m*.
spontaneous version: spontane Wendung *f*.
spoon/*n*: Löffel *m*.
spoonful/*adj*: löffelvoll.
spoon nail: Löffelnagel *m*, Koilonychie *f*.
sporadic/*adj*: sporadisch.
spore/*n*: Spore *f*.
sporotrichosis/*n*: Sporotrichose *f*.
sport/*n*: Sport *m*.
sports medicine: Sportmedizin *f*.
sporulation/*n*: Sporenbildung *f*.
spot/*n, vb*: 1. Fleck *m*, Tüpfelung *f*; 2. sprenkeln, tüpfeln.
spotted/*adj*: gefleckt.
spotted fever: Fleckfieber *n*.
spotting/*n*: Spotting *n*, Schmierblutung *f*.
sprain fracture: Distorsionsfraktur *f*.
spray/*n, vb*: 1. Spray *n*, Zerstäuber *m*; 2. sprayen, sprühen.
spread/*n, vb*: 1. Ausbreitung *f*; 2. ausbreiten.
spread foot: Spreizfuß *m*.
spreading/*n, adj*: 1. Ausbreitung *f*, Verbreitung *f*; 2. spreitend.
spreading factor: Spreading-Faktor *m*.
spreading pigmented actinic keratosis: spreitende pigmentierte aktinische Keratose *f*.
spring catarrh: Frühjahrskonjunktivitis *f*.
spring-summer encephalitis: tick-borne infectious disease of the central nervous system, including the brain. Different forms like Central European encephalitis, Russian encephalitis, and others exist. Symptoms include a prodromal period with flulike signs, followed by meningitis, encephalitis and flaccid paralysis. Frühsommerenzephalitis *f*.
sprout/*n, vb*: 1. Spross *m*, Ableger *m*; 2. keimen, sprießen.
spur/*n*: Sporn *m*, Knochenzacke *f*.
spur cell: Akanthozyt *m*.
spurious/*adj*: falsch, unecht.
spurious parasite: Pseudoparasit *m*.
spurious polycythemia: relative Polyzythämie *f*.
spurious pregnancy: Pseudoschwangerschaft *f*.
sputum/*n*: Sputum *n*, Auswurf *m*.
squama/*n*: Schuppe *f*, Hautschuppe *f*.
squamous/*adj*: squamös, schuppenförmig.
squamous cell: Schuppenzelle *f*.
squamous cell carcinoma: malignant neoplasm developing from squamous epithelium, most frequently occurring in the skin and mucosa. Symptoms depend on the localization. Squamous cell carcinomas of the skin may initially present as hyperkeratotic lesions, showing rapid growth. Plattenepithelkarzinom *n*.
squamous metaplasia: Plattenepithelmetaplasie *f*.
square/*n, adj*: 1. Quadrat *n*; 2. quadratisch.
squash/*n, vb*: 1. Brei *m*; 2. quetschen, zerdrücken.
squatting/*n*: Squatting *n*, Hockerstellung *f*.

squeeze/*vb*: zusammendrücken, quetschen, pressen, einzwängen.
squill glycoside: Scilla-Glykosid *n*.
squint/*n, vb*: 1. eye disorder with deviation of the visual axis, resulting in loss of convergence and the perception of two images of a single object. Schielen *n*, Strabismus *m*; 2. schielen.
squint angle: Schielwinkel *m*.
squint deviation: Schielwinkel *m*.
stab/*n, vb*: 1. Stich *m*; 2. stechen.
stabbing/*adj*: stechend.
stability/*n*: Stabilität *f*, Festigkeit *f*.
stable/*adj*: stabil, beständig.
stable complex: beständiger Komplex *m*.
stab wound: any wound resulting from injury of a cutting instrument, typically a knife. Complications include injuries of blood vessels or internal organs, wound infection, or presence foreign bodies. Stichwunde *f*.
staff/*n*: Personal *n*, Stab *m*.
staff of Aesculapius: Äskulapstab *m*.
stage/*n, vb*: 1. Stadium *n*, Plattform *f*; 2. in Stadien einteilen.
stagger/*vb*: wanken, taumeln.
staggering gait: schwankender Gang *m*, ataktischer Gang *m*.
staging/*n*: Staging *n*, Stadieneinteilung *f*.
stain/*n, vb*: 1. Färbung *f*, Farbstoff *m*, Fleck *m*; 2. färben.
stainability/*n*: Anfärbbarkeit *f*.
staining/*n*: Färben *n*, Färbung *f*.
stainless/*adj*: rostfrei.
staircase phenomenon: Treppenphänomen *n*.
stalk/*n*: Stängel *m*, Stiel *m*.
stammer/*vb*: stottern, stammeln.
stamping gait: stampfender Gang *m*.
stance/*n*: Haltung *f*.
standard/*n*: Standard *m*, Maß *n*, Norm *f*.
standard error: mittlerer Fehler *m*.
standardization/*n*: Standardisierung *f*, Vereinheitlichung *f*
standardized opium: eingestelltes Opium *n*.
standard leads: Standardableitungen.
standard test: Standardtest *m*.
stand-by pacemaker: Stand-by-Schrittmacher *m*.
standing position: Stand *m*.
standstill/*n*: Stillstand *m*.
stannic acid: Zinnsäure *f*.
stanozolol/*n*: Stanozolol *n*.
stapedectomy/*n*: Stapedektomie *f*.
stapedial tenotomy: Stapediotenotomie *f*.
stapedius/*n*: Stapedius *m*, Musculus stapedius *m*.
stapes/*n*: Steigbügel *m*.
staphylococcal infection: bacterial infection due to Staphylococcus, frequently causing purulent infections like furuncles, bone inflammation, whitlow and other. Staphylococcal toxins may cause food poisoning and toxic shock syndrome. Staphylokokkeninfektion *f*.
staphylococcal pneumonia: Staphylokokkenpneumonie *f*.
staphylococcus/*n*: Staphylococcus *m*, Staphylokokkus *m*.
staphyloma/*n*: Staphylom *n*.
staphylorrhaphy/*n*: Staphylorrhaphie *f*.
stapler/*n*: Klammernahtgerät *n*.
star/*n*: Stern *m*.
starch/*n*: Stärke *f*.
starch test: Stärkeprobe *f*.
start/*n, vb*: 1. Anfang *m*; 2. anfangen, beginnen.
startle myoclonus: Schreckmyoklonus *m*.
startle response: Schreckreaktion *f*.
starvation/*n*: Verhungern *n*, Hungertod *m*.
starve/*vb*: hungern.
stasis/*n*: Stauung *f*, Stase *f*.
state/*n*: Status *m*, Zustand *m*.
static/*n, adj*: 1. Bakteriostatikum *n*; 2. statisch.
static convulsion: Nickkrampf *m*, Blitz-Nick-Salaam-Krämpfe.
static gangrene: venöse Gangrän *f*.
static imaging: Standbildverfahren *n*.
static reflex: Stellreflex *m*, Lagereflex *m*.
static sense: Gleichgewichtssinn *m*.
statin/*n*: Statin *n*.

stationary/*adj*: stationär, stillstehend, gleichbleibend.
station test: Romberg-Versuch *m*.
statistical/*adj*: statistisch.
statistics/*n*: Statistik *f*.
stature/*n*: Statur *f*.
status/*n*: Status *m*, Zustand *m*.
stavudine/*n*: Stavudin *n*.
stay/*n, vb*: 1. Aufenthalt *m*; 2. bleiben.
STD <*abbr*> **sexually transmitted disease**: any infectious disease that is transmitted from person to person predominantly or exclusively through sexual contacts. Sexually transmitted or venereal diseases include for example syphilis, gonorrhea, soft chancre, HIV infection, chlamydial infection, and Mycoplasma infection. sexuell übertragbare Krankheit *f*, Geschlechtskrankheit *f*.
steady/*adj*: gleichbleibend, beständig.
steady period: Eröffnungsperiode *f*.
steady state: Steady State *m*, Fließgleichgewicht *n*.
steal/*n, vb*: 1. Steal-Effekt *m*, Anzapfsyndrom *n*; 2. stehlen.
stearic acid: Stearinsäure *f*.
steatoma/*n*: Steatom *n*.
steatorrhea/*n*: presence of an excessive fat amount in the feces, due to maldigestion of fat, for example resulting from exocrine pancreatic disease. Steatorrhö *f*, Fettstuhl *m*.
steatosis/*n*: Steatose *f*, Steatosis *f*, Verfettung *f*.
stellate/*adj*: sternförmig.
stellate angioma: Spider Nävus *m*, Naevus araneus *m*.
stellate cell: Sternzelle *f*.
stem/*n*: Stamm *m*, Hauptachse *f*.
stem cell: Stammzelle *f*.
stenosis/*n*: pathologic decrease in the diameter of a blood vessel, an organ duct, an opening, or an orifice. Stenose *f*, Verengung *f*.
stenotic/*adj*: stenotisch.
stenotic murmur: Stenosegeräusch *n*.
stenotic respiration: Stenoseatmung *f*.
stenoxenous parasite: stenoxener Parasit *m*.
stent/*n*: Stent *m*, Stentabdruck *m*.
step/*n, vb*: 1. Schritt *m*; 2. schreiten, gehen.
stepping/*n*: Schreitphänomen *n*.
stercobilin/*n*: Sterkobilin *n*.
stercolith/*n*: Sterkolith *m*, Kotstein *m*.
stercoral abscess: Sterkoralabszess *m*.
stercoral colic: Sterkoralkolik *f*.
stercoral fistula: Kotfistel *f*.
stereoanesthesia/*n*: Stereoanästhesie *f*.
stereognosis/*n*: Stereognosie *f*.
sterognostic sense: stereognostischer Tastsinn *m*.
stereotaxic/*adj*: stereotaktisch.
sterile/*adj*: steril.
sterile abscess: steriler Abszess *m*.
sterility/*n*: Sterilität *f*, Zeugungsunfähigkeit *f*, Keimfreiheit *f*.
sterilization/*n*: Sterilisation *f*.
sterilizer/*n*: Sterilisator *m*.
sternal/*adj*: sternal.
sternal biopsy: Sternalpunktion *f*.
sternal pain: Sternumschmerz *m*.
sternal puncture: Sternalpunktion *f*.
steroid/*n*: Steroid *n*.
steroid acne: Steroidakne *f*.
steroidal anti-inflammatory agent: steroidales antiinflammatorisches Antirheumatikum *n*.
sterol/*n*: Sterol *n*, Sterin *n*
stertorous respiration: röchelndes Atmen *n*.
stethoscope/*n*: Stethoskop *n*.
sticking plaster: Heftpflaster *n*.
sticky/*adj*: klebrig, zäh.
stiff/*adj*: steif.
stiffening/*n*: Versteifung *f*.
stiff neck: Nackensteife *f*.
stiff spine: rigidity of the spinal column resulting from ossification of the spinal joints, for example due to ankylosing spondylitis. Wirbelsäulenversteifung *f*, Bambusstabwirbelsäule *f*.
stigma/*n*: Stigma *n*, Markierung *f*.
stigmatization/*n*: Stigmatisierung *f*.
stilbamidine/*n*: Stilbamidin *n*.
stillbirth/*n*: Totgeburt *f*.
stillborn/*adj*: totgeboren.
stimulant/*n, adj*: 1. Stimulans *n*, Stimulator *m*; 2. stimulierend.

stimulate/*vb*: stimulieren.
stimulation/*n*: Stimulation *f*.
stimulus/*n*: Stimulus *m*, Reiz *m*.
stimulus generalization: Reizgeneralisierung *f*.
sting/*n*: Stich *m*.
stipple cell: Tüpfelzelle *f*.
stippled/*adj*: getüpfelt.
stippled epiphysis: Stippchenepiphyse *f*.
stirrup/*n*: Extensionsbügel *m*, Steigbügel *m*.
stitch/*n, vb*: 1. Stich *m*, Naht *f*, Stechen *n*; 2. nähen, stechen.
stomach/*n*: Magen *m*.
stomach pump: Magenpumpe *f*.
stomach ulcer: Magenulkus *n*.
stomatitis/*n*: inflammation of the mouth and the oral mucosa, occurring from bacterial, viral or fungal infection or as concomitant sign in other conditions, like metabolic diseases or intoxications. Stomatitis *f*.
stomatology/*n*: Stomatologie *f*.
stone/*n*: Stein *m*.
stool/*n*: Stuhl *m*, Kot *m*.
storage/*n*: Aufbewahrung *f*, Einlagerung *f*, Speicherung *f*.
storage disease: Speicherkrankheit *f*, Thesaurismose *f*.
stored blood: Blutkonserve *f*.
stove-in chest: instabiler Thorax *m*.
strabismus/*n*: eye disorder with deviation of the visual axis, resulting in loss of convergence and the perception of two images of a single object. Strabismus *m*, Schielen *n*.
strabismic amblyopia: Schielamblyopie *f*.
strabismus operation: Schieloperation *f*.
straight/*adj*: gerade.
strain/*n, vb*: 1. Abstammung *f*, Stamm *m*, Überanstrengung *f*, Zerrung *f*; 2. überanstrengen, belasten.
strait/*n*: Enge *f*.
straitjacket/*n*: Zwangsjacke *f*.
strand/*n*: Strang *m*.
strangulated hernia: strangulierte Hernie *f*.
strangulation/*n*: Strangulierung *f*, Abschnürung *f*.
strap/*n*: Gurt *m*, Riemen *m*.
stratification/*n*: Stratifikation *f*.
stratified thrombus: Schichtthrombus *m*, gemischter Thrombus *m*.
strawberry gallbladder: Erdbeergallenblase *f*, Stippchengallenblase *f*.
strawberry tongue: red tongue with white stipples, occurring as a characteristic sign during the early stage of scarlet fever. Erdbeerzunge *f*.
streak/*n*: Streifen *m*, Stria.
stream/*n, vb*: 1. Fluss *m*, Strom *m*; 2. fließen, strömen.
strength/*n*: Kraft *f*, Stärke *f*.
strengthen/*vb*: kräftigen, stärken.
strengthening agent: Stärkungsmittel *n*, Roborans *n*.
streptobacillary fever: Erythema arthriticum epidemicum *n*, Haverhill-Fieber *n*.
streptococcal carditis: Streptokokkenkarditis *f*.
streptococcal infection: Streptokokkeninfektion *f*.
streptokinase/*n*: Streptokinase *f*.
streptolysin/*n*: Streptolysin *n*.
streptomycin/*n*: Streptomycin *n*.
streptomycin sulfate: Streptomycinsulfat *n*.
stress/*n, vb*: 1. Stress *m*, Belastung *f*; 2. belasten.
stress fracture: fracture of the bone due to unusual strain on or repeated trauma of a bone, mostly located in the lower limbs. Belastungsfraktur *f*, Deutschländer-Fraktur *f*.
stress-induced amenorrhea: stressbedingte Amenorrhö *f*.
stretch/*n, vb*: 1. Strecken *n*, Anspannung *f*; 2. anspannen, strecken.
stretcher/*n*: Krankentrage *f*, Trage *f*.
stretch reflex: Dehnungsreflex *m*.
striate/*adj*: gestreift.
striated muscle: quergestreifter Muskel *m*.
stricture/*n*: Striktur *f*.
stridor/*n*: Stridor *m*.
string/*n*: Band *n*, Bindfaden *m*.
strip/*n, vb*: 1. Streifen *m*; 2. abstreifen, abziehen.
stripper's asthma: Byssinose *f*.
stripping/*n*: Abziehen *n*, Abstreifen

n, Stripping *n*.

stroke/*n*: any sudden and severe attack. The term is frequently used to describe cerebral stroke or apoplexy, a condition characterized by sudden onset and a variety of symptoms due to acute brain hemorrhage or infarction. Anfall *m*, Schlaganfall *m*, Apoplexie *f*.

stroma cell: Stromazelle *f*.

strong/*adj*: stark, kräftig.

strong pulse: kräftiger Puls *m*.

strophanthidin/*n*: Strophanthidin *n*.

strophanthin/*n*: Strophanthin *n*.

structural gene: Strukturgen *n*.

structural scoliosis: unkorrigierbare Skoliose *f*.

structure/*n*: Struktur *f*, Architektonik *f*.

struggle/*n, vb*: 1. Kampf *m*; 2. kämpfen.

struma/*n*: diffuse or nodular enlargement of the thyroid gland, due for example to iodide deficiency, enzymatic or metabolic disorders of the thyroid gland. Struma *f*, Kropf *m*.

strychnine/*n*: Strychnin *n*.

student nurse: Schwesternschülerin *f*.

student of medicine: Medizinstudent *m*.

study/*n, vb*: 1. Untersuchung *f*, Studie *f*; 2. studieren, untersuchen.

study design: Studiendesign *n*.

stump/*n*: Stumpf *m*, Organstumpf *m*.

stump foot: Klumpfuß *m*.

stun/*vb*: betäuben.

stupidity/*n*: Stupidität *f*.

stupor/*n*: a psychiatric disorder with a state of decreased feeling and reduced responsiveness. The term is also used to describe conditions with loss of physical and/or mental activity. Benommenheit *f*, Stupor *m*.

stuttering/*n*: Stottern *n*.

sty/*n*: infection of the zeisian gland or the meibomian gland of the eyelid caused by bacteria, usually Staphylococcus or Streptococcus. Gerstenkorn *n*, Hordeolum *n*.

stylet/*n*: Stilett *n*, Sonde *f*, Mandrin *m*.

styloidectomy/*n*: Styloidektomie *f*.

styptic/*n, adj*: 1. Styptikum *n*, blutstillendes Mittel *n*; 2. blutstillend.

subacute/*adj*: subakut.

subacute bacterial endocarditis: infectious endocarditis with a prolonged clinical course, usually due to infection with the bacterium Streptococcus or fungi. Subakute Endokarditis *f*, Endocarditis lenta *f*.

subacute necrotic myelitis: subakute nekrotisierende Myelitis *f*, Foix-Alajouanine-Krankheit *f*.

subacute necrotizing encephalopathy: subakute nekrotisierende Enzephalomyelopathie *f*, Leigh-Enzephalomyelopathie *f*.

subacute nodular migratory panniculitis: subakute noduläre Pannikulitis *f*.

subacute rheumatism: chronischer Rheumatismus *m*.

subacute sclerosing panencephalitis: inflammation of the brain, usually due to infection with measles virus and typically affecting children and adolescents. Characteristic symptoms include cerebral dysfunction developing over weeks to months. subakute sklerosierende Panenzephalitis *f*, Einschlusskörperchenenzephalitis Dawson *f*.

subarachnoid hemorrhage: intracranial bleeding into the subarachnoid space, usually resulting from angioma or rupture of an aneurysm of a cerebral artery. Clinical signs may range from mild headache to unconsciousness with coma and decerebration rigidity. Subarachnoidalblutung *f*.

subarachnoiditis/*n*: Leptomeningitis *f*.

subarachnoid space: Subarachnoidalraum *m*.

subatmospheric pressure: Unterdruck *m*.

subcapsular cataract: Cataracta subcapsularis *f*.

subchorionic hematoma: Blutmole *f*, Breus-Mole *f*.

subclavian/*adj*: Subklavia-.

subclavian steal: decreased blood flow in the vertebral artery due to a stenosis or occlusion of the subclavian artery and a reversal of blood flow. Symptoms may include vertigo, dizziness, visual and auditory disturbances. Subclavian-Steal-Syndrom *n*, Anzapfsyndrom der Arteria subclavia *n*.
subclavicular murmur: Subklavikulargeräusch *n*.
subclinical/*adj*: subklinisch.
subclinical diabetes: latenter Diabetes *m*.
subclinical scurvy: asymptomatischer Skorbut *m*.
subconjunctival hemorrhage: Konjunktiveneinblutung *f*.
subcorneal pustular dermatosis: subkorneale bullöse Dermatose *f*.
subcortical aphasia: subkortikale Aphasie *f*, Leitungsaphasie *f*.
subcostal incision: Rippenbogenrandschnitt *m*.
subcrepitant/*adj*: leise knisternd.
subcutaneous emphysema: subkutanes Emphysem *n*.
subdiaphragmatic abscess: subphrenischer Abszess *m*.
subdural/*adj*: subdural.
subdural abscess: Subduralabszess *m*.
subdural bleeding: Subduralblutung *f*.
subdural cavity: Subduralraum *m*.
subdural hematoma: accumulation of blood in the subdural space, usually due to a traumatic injury of the brain and cerebral blood vessels. Symptoms may include unconsciousness, focal neurologic signs, and pupillomotor disorders. Subduralhämatom *n*.
subdural hemorrhage: Subduralblutung *f*.
subdural space: Subduralraum *m*.
suberosis/*n*: Suberose *f*, Korkstaublunge *f*.
subicteric/*adj*: subikterisch.
subjacent/*adj*: tiefer liegend.
subject/*n*: Subjekt *n*, Person *f*, Proband *m*.
subjective/*adj*: subjektiv.
subjective sensation: subjektive Wahrnehmung *f*.
subjective sign: subjektives Symptom *n*.
subjective symptom: subjektives Symptom *n*.
sublethal gene: subletales Allel *n*.
subliminal/*adj*: unterschwellig.
subliminal perception: unterschwellige Wahrnehmung *f*.
sublingual/*adj*: sublingual.
sublingual administration: sublinguale Anwendung *f*.
sublingual cyst: Ranula *f*, Froschgeschwulst *n*.
sublingual gland: Unterzungendrüse *f*, Glandula sublingualis *f*.
sublingual papilla: Caruncula sublingualis *f*.
sublingual tablet: Sublingualtablette *f*.
submaxillary/*adj*: submaxillar.
submeningeal/*adj*: submeningeal.
submental fistula: Unterkieferfistel *f*.
submucosal/*adj*: submukös.
submucous plexus: submuköser Plexus *m*, Meissner-Plexus *m*.
suboccipital puncture: Subokzipitalpunktion *f*.
suboptimal/*adj*: suboptimal.
subperiosteal amputation: subperiostale Amputation *f*.
subperiosteal fracture: subperiostale Fraktur *f*.
subphrenic abscess: subphrenischer Abszess *m*.
subpleural collapse: Mantelatelektase *f*.
subscription/*n*: Subscriptio *f*, Zubereitungsanweisung *f*.
subscurvy state: asymptomatischer Skorbut *m*.
subsidiarity/*n*: Subsidiarität *f*.
subsistence diet: Nahrungsbedarf *m*, lebensnotwendige Nahrungsmenge *f*.
substance/*n*: Substanz *f*, Stoff *m*.
substance abuse: excessive use of any chemical or biological substance (for example prescription drugs, illegal drugs, weed) with continuous or pe-

riodical compulsion to take the substance. Stoffabhängigkeit *f*.
substance-induced psychosis: substanzbedingte Psychose *f*.
substernal goiter: Retrosternalstruma *f*.
substitute/*n, vb*: 1. Ersatz *m*, Substitution *f*; 2. substituieren, ersetzen.
substrate/*n*: Substrat *n*.
subtemporal decompression: subtemporale Dekompression *f*, Cushing-Operation *f*.
subthreshold/*adj*: unterschwellig.
subthreshold stimulus: unterschwelliger Reiz *m*.
subtle sign: dezentes Anzeichen *n*.
subtotal/*adj*: subtotal.
subtotal gastrectomy: subtotale Gastrektomie *f*.
subtraction angiography: Subtraktionsangiographie *f*.
subtrochanteric fracture: subtrochantäre Fraktur *f*.
subtrochanteric osteotomy: subtrochantäre Osteotomie *f*.
subungual hematoma: Nagelhämatom *n*.
subunit/*n*: Untereinheit *f*, Subunit *f*.
subvital factor: Subvitalfaktor *m*.
sub-whole: Teilganzes *n*.
succenturiate placenta: Placenta succenturiata *f*, Nebenplazenta *f*.
success/*n*: Erfolg *m*.
succinic acid: Bernsteinsäure *f*.
succubus/*n*: Succubus *m*.
succulence/*n*: Sukkulenz *f*.
succulent hand: geschwollene Hand *f*.
succussion/*n*: Erschütterung *f*.
suck/*vb*: lutschen, saugen.
sucking cushion: Saugpolster *n*.
sucking reflex: Saugreflex *m*.
suckling/*n*: Brustkind *n*, Säugling *m*.
suck reflex: Saugreflex *m*.
sucralfate/*n*: Sucralfat *n*.
suction curettage: Saugkürettage *f*.
suction drainage: Saugdrainage *f*.
sudanophilic diffuse sclerosis: diffuse sudanophile Hirnsklerose *f*.
sudden/*adj*: plötzlich.
sudden cardiac death: unexpected death following sudden cardiac arrest, mostly resulting from asystolia or ventricular arrhythmia due to coronary heart disease or myocardial infarction. plötzlicher Herztod *m*.
sudden deafness: sudden hearing loss due to an ischemia of the inner ear. Hörsturz *m*.
sudden infant death: sudden death of an infant during the first year of life, characteristically during sleep, without detectable organic cause. The exact etiology is unknown, factors such as environmental temperature, abdominal position during sleep, and pre- or postnatal exposure to tobacco smoke are discussed. plötzlicher Kindstod *m*.
sudoriparous abscess: Schweißdrüsenabszess *m*.
suffer/*vb*: erleiden, leiden.
sufficiency/*n*: Suffizienz *f*.
sufficient/*adj*: suffizient, ausreichend.
suffocate/*vb*: ersticken.
suffocative bronchitis: Bronchopneumonie *f*.
sugar/*n*: Zucker *m*.
sugar-coated: mit Zucker überzogen.
sugar-coated tablet: Dragée *n*.
sugar substitute: Zuckeraustauschstoff *m*.
suggestibility/*n*: Suggestibilität *f*.
suggestion therapy: Suggestionstherapie *f*.
suicidal state: suizidales Syndrom *n*.
suicide/*n*: any action of taking one's own life which may for example be related to psychiatric disorders, for example endogenous depression, or critical life situations. Suizid *m*, Selbsttötung *f*.
sulbactam/*n*: Sulbactam *n*.
sulcus/*n*: Rinne *f*, Furche *f*.
sulfacarbamide/*n*: Sulfacarbamid *n*.
sulfaguanidine/*n*: Sulfaguanidin *n*.
sulfamoxole/*n*: Sulfamoxol *n*.
sulfan blue: Sulfanblau *n*.
sulfanilamide/*n*: Sulfanilamid *n*.
sulfanilic acid: Sulfanilsäure *f*.
sulfasalazine/*n*: Sulfasalazin *n*.
sulfatide/*n*: Sulfatid *n*.
sulfide/*n*: Sulfid *n*.

sulfinic acid: Sulfinsäure *f*.
sulfinpyrazone/*n*: Sulfinpyrazon *n*.
sulfocyanic acid: Schwefelzyanwasserstoffsäure *f*.
sulfonamide/*n*: Sulfonamid *n*.
sulfonic acid: Sulfonsäure *f*.
sulfosalicylic acid: Sulfosalizylsäure *f*.
sulfur/*n, vb*: 1. Schwefel *m*, S; 2. schwefeln, ausschwefeln.
sulfuric acid: Schwefelsäure *f*.
sulfurous acid: schweflige Säure *f*.
sulindac/*n*: Sulindac *n*.
suloctidil/*n*: Suloctidil *n*.
sulpiride/*n*: Sulpirid *n*.
sulprostone/*n*: Sulproston *n*.
sultamicillin/*n*: Sultamicillin *n*.
sultiame/*n*: Sultiam *n*.
sumatriptan/*n*: Sumatriptan *n*.
summation effect: Summationseffekt *m*.
summer encephalitis: Sommerenzephalitis *f*, Encephalitis japonica *f*.
sunburn/*n*: inflammatory reaction of the skin to exposure to sunrays. Typical symptoms include erythema, and eventually blisters. Sonnenbrand *m*.
sunken nipple: Hohlwarze *f*.
sun protection: Sonnenschutz *m*.
sunset phenomenon: Sonnenuntergangsphänomen *n*.
sunspot/*n*: Sonnenfleck *m*, Sommersprosse *f*.
superacute/*adj*: perakut.
superalimentation/*n*: Hyperalimentation *f*.
superciliary/*adj*: Augenbrauen-.
superfecundation/*n*: Superfekundation *f*.
superfemale/*n*: Superfemale *f*, Triple-X-Syndrom *n*, XXX-Frau *f*.
superficial bleeding: oberflächliche Blutung *f*.
superficial reflex: oberflächlicher Hautreflex *m*.
superior/*adj*: oberer.
superior caval syndrome: Vena-cava-superior-Syndrom *n*.
superior hemorrhagic polioencephalitis: Pseudoencephalitis haemorrhagica superior *f*, Wernicke-Enzephalopathie *f*.
superiority/*n*: Überlegenheit *f*.
superior vena cava syndrome: a condition which is characterized by venous dilatation, cyanosis, and edema of the upper parts of the body due to compression and obstruction of the superior vena cava, for example due to intrathoracic tumors, aortic aneurysm, or lymph node metastases. Vena-cava-superior-Syndrom *n*.
supernumerary bone: akzessorischer Knochen *m*.
supernumerary mamma: mammary gland present in excess to the normal number of two, usually found along the embryonic milk line. akzessorische Mamma *f*.
supination/*n*: Supination *f*, Rückenlagerung *f*.
supine position: Rückenlage *f*.
supplementary/*adj*: ergänzend.
supplementary food: Beikost *f*.
supply/*n, vb*: 1. Zufuhr *f*, Versorgung *f*; 2. versorgen, beliefern.
support/*n, vb*: 1. Unterstützung *f*, Abstützung *f*; 2. unterstützen, stützen.
supporting tissue: Stützgewebe *n*.
suppository/*n*: Suppositorium *n*, Zäpfchen *n*.
suppress/*vb*: supprimieren, unterdrücken.
suppressed breathing: Schonatmung *f*.
suppression/*n*: Unterdrückung *f*, Verdrängung *f*.
suppurating ulcer: Eitergeschwür *n*.
suppuration/*n*: Eiterung *f*.
suppurative arthritis: eitrige Arthritis *f*.
suppurative pyelitis: Nierenbeckenabszess *m*.
supraclavicular fossa: Supraklavikulargrube *f*.
supracondylar amputation: suprakondyläre Amputation *f*.
supracondylar fracture: suprakondyläre Fraktur *f*.
suprahepatic abscess: subphrenischer Abszess *m*.
supraliminal stimulus: überschwelliger Reiz *m*.

supranodal tachycardia: heterotope Tachykardie *f*.
supranuclear palsy: supranukleäre Lähmung *f*.
supranuclear paralysis: supranukleäre Lähmung *f*.
supraorbital/*adj*: supraorbital.
supraorbital arch: Orbitarand *m*, Margo supraorbitalis *m*.
suprapontine/*adj*: suprapontin.
suprapubic cystotomy: suprapubische Zystotomie *f*.
suprapubic prostatectomy: suprapubische Prostataenukleation *f*.
suprapubic puncture: suprapubische Blasenpunktion *f*.
suprapubic space: suprapubisches Dreieck *n*.
supraventricular tachycardia: supraventrikuläre Tachykardie *f*.
sural/*adj*: Waden-.
suramin/*n*: Suramin *n*.
suramin sodium: Suraminnatrium *n*.
surdocardiac syndrome: autosomal recessive disorder with sensorineural deafness, ventricular tachycardia and/or ventricular fibrillation. surdokardiales Syndrom *n*, kardioauditives Syndrom *n*, Jervell-Lange-Nielsen-Syndrom *n*.
surface/*n*: Oberfläche *f*.
surface-active: oberflächenaktiv.
surface anesthesia: Oberflächenanästhesie *f*, Schleimhautanästhesie *f*.
surface antigen: Oberflächenantigen *n*.
surfactant/*n*: Surfactant *n*, Oberflächenfaktor *m*.
surgeon's knot: chirurgischer Knoten *m*.
surgery/*n*: Chirurgie *f*, Operation *f*, Operationsraum *m*.
surgical/*adj*: chirurgisch, operativ.
surgical abdomen: condition with rapid onset of abdominal pain, vomiting, meteorism, and muscular defense, requiring emergency diagnostics. An acute abdomen typically indicates a disease requiring surgical intervention. akutes Abdomen *n*.
surgical castration: operative Kastration *f*.
surgical division: operative Spaltung *f*.
surgical exposure: chirurgische Freilegung *f*.
surgical glove: OP-Handschuh *m*.
surgical gut: Catgut *n*.
surgical hook: Wundhaken *m*.
surgical knife: Skalpell *n*.
surgical microscope: Operationsmikroskop *n*.
surgical procedure: Operationsverfahren *n*.
surgical saw: Operationssäge *f*.
surgical shunt: operativer Shunt *m*.
surgical team: Operationsteam *n*.
surgical wound: Operationswunde *f*.
surplus/*n*: Überschuss *m*.
surrogate marker: Surrogatmarker *m*.
survival/*n*: Überleben *n*.
survival time: Überlebenszeit *f*, Überlebensdauer *f*.
survive/*vb*: überleben.
susceptibility/*n*: Empfindlichkeit *f*, Empfänglichkeit *f*.
susceptible/*adj*: empfänglich, empfindlich.
suspension/*n*: Suspension *f*, Aufschwemmung *f*, Aufhängung *f*.
suspensory mechanism: Stützmechanismus *m*.
sustentacular cell: Stützzelle *f*.
sustentacular fiber: Stützfaser *f*.
sustentacular tissue: Stützgewebe *n*.
sutural cataract: Nahtstar *m*.
suture/*n, vb*: 1. Naht *f*, Nahtmaterial *n*; 2. nähen.
suxamethonium/*n*: Suxamethonium *n*.
suxamethonium chloride: Suxamethoniumchlorid *n*.
suxibuzone/*n*: Suxibuzon *n*.
swab/*n, vb*: 1. Abstrich *m*, Tupfer *m*; 2. betupfen, abtupfen.
swallowing/*n*: Schlucken *n*.
swallowing reflex: Schluckreflex *m*.
sweat/*n, vb*: 1. Schweiß *m*; 2. schwitzen.
sweat gland: Schweißdrüse *f*, Duftdrüse *f*.
Swedish porphyria: akute intermittierende Porphyrie *f*.

sweetener/*n*: Süßstoff *m*.
swell/*vb*: schwellen.
swelling/*n*: Schwellung *f*, Quellung *f*, Geschwulst *f*.
swimmers' ear: Schwimmbadotitis *f*.
swineherds' disease: Schweinehüterkrankheit *f*, Leptospirose *f*, Weil-Krankheit *f*.
swing/*n, vb*: 1. Schwingung *f*, Schwung *m*; 2. schwingen, pendeln.
swing-through gait: Pendelgang *m*.
switch/*n, vb*: 1. Schalter *m*, Übergang *m*, Wechsel *m*; 2. schalten, umstellen.
swollen/*adj*: geschwollen, aufgetrieben.
sycosis/*n*: Sykose *f*.
sylvan yellow fever: Dschungelgelbfieber *n*.
symbiosis/*n*: Symbiose *f*.
symbiotic psychosis: symbiotische Psychose *f*.
symbolic agnosia: Asymbolie *f*.
symmetry/*n*: Symmetrie *f*.
sympathectomy/*n*: Sympathektomie *f*.
sympathetic/*adj*: sympathisch.
sympathetic block: Sympathikusausschaltung *f*.
sympathetic blocking agent: Sympatholytikum *n*.
sympathetic chain: Truncus sympathicus *m*, Grenzstrang *m*.
sympathetic nervous system: sympathisches Nervensystem *n*.
sympathetic ophthalmia: sympathische Ophthalmie *f*.
sympathicus/*n, adj*: 1. Sympathikus *m*, Nervus sympathicus *m*; 2. sympathisch.
symphysiectomy/*n*: Symphysenresektion *f*.
symphysis/*n*: Symphyse *f*.
symptom/*n*: Symptom *n*, Krankheitszeichen *n*.
symptomatic/*adj*: symptomatisch.
symptomatic alopecia: Alopecia symptomatica *f*.
symptomatic epilepsy: symptomatische Epilepsie *f*.
symptomatic headache: symptomatischer Kopfschmerz *m*.
symptomatic treatment: symptomatische Behandlung *f*.
symptom-free: symptomfrei, asymptomatisch.
symptoms and signs: Symptomatik *f*.
symptothermal method: Symptothermalmethode *f*.
synapse/*n*: Synapse *f*.
synaptic button: Endplatte *f*.
synaptic conduction: synaptische Überleitung *f*.
synaptic receptor: synaptischer Rezeptor *m*.
synarthrosis/*n*: Synarthrose *f*.
synchondrosis/*n*: Synchondrose *f*.
synchronism/*n*: Synchronismus *f*, Synchronie *f*.
synchronization/*n*: Synchronisation *f*.
synchronized sleep: synchronisierter Schlaf *m*, Non-REM-Schlaf *m*.
synchronous pacemaker: synchroner Schrittmacher *m*.
synclitism/*n*: Synklitismus *m*.
syncope/*n*: Synkope *f*.
syncytia formation: Synzytienbildung *f*.
syncytial cell: Synzytiumzelle *f*.
syndrome/*n*: Syndrom *n*, Symptomenkomplex *m*.
syndrome of inappropriate ADH secretion: a chronic condition which is characterized by an excessive secretion of antidiuretic hormone or AHD-like peptids, resulting in hyperhydration, decreased osmotic pressure of plasma and extracellular fluids, renal excretion of sodium, and hyponatremia. Syndrom der inappropriaten ADH-Sekretion *f*, Schwartz-Bartter-Syndrom *n*.
synechia/*n*: an abnormal union of two parts, for example synechia vulvae with a congenital fusion of the margins of the labia minora, or anterior synechia of the eye with adhesions between the iris and the cornea. Synechie *f*.
synergistic action: synergistische Wirkung *f*.
synergy/*n*: Synergie *f*, Synergismus *m*.

syngeneic graft: syngenes Transplantat *n*, Isograft *n*.
synophthalmia/*n*: Synophthalmie *f*.
synostosis/*n*: Synostose *f*.
synovectomy/*n*: Synovektomie *f*.
synovial/*adj*: synovial.
synovial cyst: Synovialzyste *f*.
synovial fluid: Synovia *f*.
synovial hernia: Hernia synovialis *f*.
synovial sac: Synovialtasche *f*.
synovial villus: Synovialzotte *f*.
synovitis/*n*: inflammation of the lining of a joint, typically due to an arthritis. Symptoms may include accumulation of fluid in the joint, and desctruction of chondreous or osseous tissue. Synovitis *f*.
synthesis/*n*: Synthese *f*.
synthetic/*n, adj*: 1. Kunststoff *m*; 2. synthetisch.
synzyme/*n*: Synzym *n*.
syphilid/*n*: Syphilid *n*.
syphilis/*n*: sexually transmitted infection with the bacterium Treponema pallidum. Primary syphilis is characterized by soft chancre, secondary syphilis by widespread mucocutaneous lesions (syphilids) and generalized swelling of lymph nodes; tertiary or late syphilis occurs after months or several years and is characterized by organ lesions, inflammation of blood vessels, and involvement of the central nervous system. Syphilis *f*, Lues *f*.
syphilitic hyperplastic pachymeningitis: Pachymeningitis cervicalis hypertrophica *f*.
syphilitic osteochondritis: Osteochondritis syphilitica *f*.
syphilitic rash: syphilitisches Exanthem *n*.
syphilitic ulcer: Ulcus durum *n*, harter Schanker *m*.
syringe/*n*: Spritze *f*.
syringomyelia/*n*: Syringomyelie *f*.
syringotomy/*n*: Syringotomie *f*, Fistelspaltung *f*.
syrosingopine/*n*: Syrosingopin *n*.
syrup/*n*: Sirup *m*.
system/*n*: System *n*.
systematic error: systematischer Fehler *m*.
systematics/*n*: Systematik *f*.
systematic vertigo: Drehschwindel *m*.
systematized delusion: systematisierter Wahn *m*, Wahnsystem *n*.
systemic/*adj*: systemisch, generell.
systemic acne: Acne fulminans *f*.
systemic anaphylaxis: generalisierte anaphylaktische Reaktion *f*.
systemic blastomycosis: systemische Blastomykose *f*.
systemic circulation: Körperkreislauf *m*, großer Kreislauf *m*.
systemic disease: Systemerkrankung *f*, Allgemeinkrankheit *f*.
systemic mycosis: generalized fungal infection, usually occurring in persons with compromised immune system, for example severe immunodeficiency or suppression of immune functions. Systemmykose *f*.
systemic reaction: Allgemeinreaktion *f*.
systole/*n*: Systole *f*.
systolic/*adj*: systolisch.
systolic click: systolischer Click *m*.
systolic hypertension: systolischer Hochdruck *m*.
systolic murmur: systolisches Geräusch *n*, Systolikum *n*.
systolic pressure: systolischer Blutdruck *m*.
systolic retraction: systolische Einziehung *f*.
syzygiology/*n*: Syzygiologie *f*.

T

T <*abbr*> **1. temperature; 2. threonine**: 1. Temperatur *f*; 2. Threonin *n*, Thr.
tabby cat heart: Tigerherz *n*.
tabes/*n*: 1. gradual deterioration or wasting as a consequence of chronic illness. Tabes *f*, Auszehrung *f*; 2. tabes dorsalis, a neurologic disorder typically occurring several years after the infection with syphilis and characterized by degenerative lesions of the posterior roots and the posterior columns of the spinal cord. Symptoms include disorders of vibratory sense, dyscoordinated movements, ataxia, paroxysmal, lancinating pain at various locations, and trophic disorders of the joints. Tabes dorsalis *f*.
tabetic/*adj*: tabisch.
tabetic arthropathy: tabische Arthropathie *f*.
tabetic crisis: tabische Krise *f*.
tabetic dissociation: tabische Dissoziation *f*.
tabetic gait: tabischer Gang *m*.
tabetic neurosyphilis: Tabes dorsalis *f*.
table/*n*: Tisch *m*, Tabelle *f*.
tablespoon/*n*: Esslöffel *m*.
tablet/*n*: Tablette *f*.
tacalcitol/*n*: Tacalcitol *n*.
tachyarrhythmia/*n*: Tachyarrhythmie *f*.
tachycardia/*n*: abnormal heart rate with rapid beating of the heart and more than 100 beats per minute. Forms are differentiated according to the locus of origin, for example atrial tachycardia, ventricular or supraventricular tachycardia. Tachykardie *f*.
tack/*n, vb*: 1. Heftstich *m*; 2. anheften.
tacrine/*n*: Tacrin *n*.
tacrolimus/*n*: Tacrolimus *m*.
tactile/*adj*: taktil.
tactile agnosia: taktile Agnosie *f*, Stereoagnosie *f*, Tastblindheit *f*.
tactile discrimination: Tastunterscheidung *f*.
tactile field: Tastfeld *n*.
tactile hallucination: haptische Halluzination *f*.
tactile image: Tasteindruck *m*.
tactile papilla: Tastkörperchen *n*.
tactile perception: Tastwahrnehmung *f*.
tactile receptor: Tastrezeptor *m*.
tactile sense: Tastsinn *m*.
tactual illusion: Tasttäuschung *f*.
tadalafil/*n*: Tadalafil *n*.
taenia/*n*: Tänie *f*.
tag/*n, vb*: 1. Markierung *f*, Anhang *m*; 2. markieren.
tail/*n*: Schwanz *m*.
tailor's muscle: Schneidermuskel *m*, Musculus sartorius *m*.
take up/*vb*: aufnehmen.
talinolol/*n*: Talinolol *n*.
talipes/*n*: congenital or acquired foot deformity with abnormal position or form of the foot, resulting from malformations of the tendons, and frequently associated with bone malformations. According to the malformation, different forms are distinguished, for example talipes equinus, talipes valgus, talipes varus. Fußdeformität *f*, Klumpfuß *m*.
talk/*n, vb*: 1. Rede *f*, Sprache *f*; 2. sprechen.
talkative/*adj*: geschwätzig.
talocalcaneonavicular joint: vorderes Sprunggelenk *n*, Articulatio talocalcaneonavicularis *f*.

talocrural joint: oberes Sprunggelenk *n*, Articulatio talocruralis *f*.
talon/*n*: Ferse *f*.
talus/*n*: Sprungbein *n*.
tamoxifen/*n*: Tamoxifen *n*.
tampon/*n*: Tampon *m*.
tamponade/*n, vb*: 1. Tamponade *f*; 2. tamponieren.
tamsulosin/*n*: Tamsulosin *n*.
tank ventilator: eiserne Lunge *f*.
Tanner stages: Tanner-Stadien.
tannic acid: Tanninsäure *f*, Gerbsäure *f*.
tantrum/*n*: Raptus *m*.
tap/*n, vb*: 1. Drainage *f*, Perkussion *f*; 2. perkutieren, drainieren.
tape/*n*: Band *n*, Pflaster *n*.
tapetal cell: Tapetenschichtzelle *f*.
tapetochoroidal dystrophy: Chorioideremie *f*.
tapetoretinal degeneration: tapetoretinale Degeneration *f*.
tapeworm/*n*: Bandwurm *m*, Taenia *f*.
tapir snout sign: Tapirlippenzeichen *n*.
tapping/*n*: Klopfen *n*.
tap water: Leitungswasser *n*.
tar acne: Teerakne *f*.
target/*n*: Ziel *n*.
tarry stool: Teerstuhl *m*.
tarsal/*adj*: tarsal.
tarsal cyst: Meibom-Zyste *f*.
tarsalgia/*n*: Tarsalgie *f*.
tarsal tunnel syndrome: nerve compression syndrome with compression of the posterior tibial nerve through surrounding tissue of the calcaneal canal. Symptoms include local pain, paresthesia in the toes, and impairment of sensorial and motor nerve functions, including hypesthesia and paralysis. Tarsaltunnelsyndrom *n*.
tarsectomy/*n*: Tarsusresektion *f*.
tarsorrhaphy/*n*: Tarsorrhaphie *f*.
tarsus/*n*: Tarsus *m*, Lidplatte *f*.
tartaric acid: Weinsäure *f*.
tartrate/*n*: Tartrat *n*.
tasonermin/*n*: Tasonermin *n*.
taste/*n, vb*: 1. Geschmack *m*; 2. schmecken.
taste blindness: Ageusie *f*.
taste bud: Geschmacksknospe *f*.
tasteless/*adj*: geschmacklos.
taste quality: Geschmacksqualität *f*.
tattoo/*n, vb*: Tätowierung *f*; 2. tätowieren.
taurocholate/*n*: Taurocholat *n*.
taurocholic acid: Taurocholsäure *f*.
taxonomy/*n*: Taxonomie *f*.
tazarotene/*n*: Tazaroten *n*.
tazobactam/*n*: Tazobactam *n*.
TB <*abbr*> **tuberculosis**: Tuberkulose *f*, TB.
teaching hospital: Lehrkrankenhaus *n*.
teaching nurse: Schulschwester *f*.
team/*n*: Team *n*, Gruppe *f*.
team care: Gruppenpflege *f*.
tear/*n, vb*: 1. Riss *m*, Träne *f*; 2. reißen, rupturieren, tränen.
tearing of a ligament: Bänderzerrung *f*.
teaspoon/*n*: Teelöffel *m*.
teat/*n*: Brustwarze *f*, Mamille *f*.
technical/*adj*: technisch.
technician/*n*: Techniker *m*.
technique/*n*: Verfahren *n*, Technik *f*.
tectal/*adj*: Tectum-.
teething/*n*: Zahnen *n*.
tegafur/*n*: Tegafur *n*.
tegaserod/*n*: Tegaserod.
tegmental mesencephalic paralysis: Benedikt-Syndrom *n*, unteres Nucleus-ruber-Syndrom *n*.
tegumental/*adj*: integumental.
teichoic acid: Teichoinsäure *f*.
teicoplanin/*n*: Teicoplanin *n*.
tela/*n*: Gewebe *n*.
telbivudine/*n*: Telbivudin *n*.
telangiectasia/*n*: congenital or acquired dilatation of small blood vessels, typically occurring on multiple locations of the body, including skin and mucosal membranes. Teleangiektasie *f*.
telangiectatic angioma: planes Angiom *n*, Kapillarangiom *n*.
telecobalt therapy: Telekobalttherapie *f*.
telemetry/*n*: Telemetrie *f*.
telepathy/*n*: Telepathie *f*, Gedankenlesen *n*.
telephone hotline: Telefonberatung.

telithromycin/*n*: Telithromycin *n*.
tellurism/*n*: Tellurschädigung *f*.
telmisartan/*n*: Telmisartan *n*.
temazepam/*n*: Temazepam *n*.
temocapril/*n*: Temocapril *n*.
temozolomide/*n*: Temozolomid *n*.
temp <*abbr*> **temperature**/*n*: Temperatur *f*, T.
temper/*n*: Stimmung *f*.
temperament/*n*: Temperament *n*.
temperate/*adj*: temperent.
temperate bacteriophage: temperenter Phage *m*.
temperature/*n*: Temperatur *f*, T.
temperature-dependent/*adj*: temperaturabhängig.
temperature tracer: Temperaturfühler *m*.
template/*n*: Abdruck *m*, Matrize *f*.
temple/*n*: Schläfe *f*.
temporal/*adj*: temporal.
temporal arteritis: Arteriitis temporalis *f*, Riesenzellarteriitis *f*, Horton-Arteriitis *f*.
temporal epilepsy: Temporallappenepilepsie *f*.
temporal hemianopia: temporale Hemianopsie *f*.
temporal lobe: Temporallappen *m*, Schläfenlappen *m*.
temporal pallor: temporale Papillenabblassung *f*.
temporary pacing: temporärer Schrittmacher *m*.
temporomandibular/*adj*: temporomandibulär.
temporomandibular syndrome: a syndrome which is characterized by facial pain and pain in the mandibular joint, due to degenerative alterations of the mandibula, as caused in some cases of occlusal disharmony. Temporomandibularsyndrom *n*, Costen-Syndrom *n*.
tender/*adj*: empfindlich, weich.
tenderness/*n*: Empfindlichkeit *f*, Berührungsschmerzhaftigkeit *f*.
tendinitis/*n*: inflammation of a tendon, frequently associated with systemic inflammatory or rheumatic disease, for example Reiter's syndrome. Tendinitis *f*.
tendinous synovitis: Tendovaginitis *f*, Sehnenscheidenentzündung *f*.
tendinous xanthoma: tendinöses Xanthom *n*, Sehnenxanthom *n*.
tendon/*n*: Sehne *f*.
tendon reflex: Sehnenreflex *m*.
tendon sheath: Sehnenscheide *f*.
tendoplasty/*n*: Tendoplastik *f*, Sehnenplastik *f*.
tendovaginitis/*n*: Tendovaginitis *f*, Sehnenscheidenentzündung *f*.
tenecteplase/*n*: Tenecteplase *f*.
tenesmus/*n*: Tenesmus *m*.
teniposide/*n*: Teniposid *n*.
tennis elbow: a condition which is characterized by pain in the arm and inflammatory reaction of the epicondylus and the tendons, caused by excessive strain, particularly occurring when twisting inward. Tennisellenbogen *m*, Epikondylitis *f*.
tenofovir disoproxil/*n*: Tenofovirdisoproxil *n*.
tenoplasty/*n*: Tendoplastik *f*.
tenorrhaphy/*n*: Tenorrhaphie *f*.
tenositis/*n*: Tendinitis *f*.
tenosynovitis/*n*: acute or chronic inflammation of a tendon and its sheath. Symptoms include pain, and impaired function. Tenosynovitis *f*, Tendovaginitis *f*, Sehnenscheidenentzündung *f*.
tenotomy/*n*: Tenotomie *f*.
tense/*adj*: straff, angespannt.
tension/*n*: Spannung *f*, Dehnung *f*.
tension headache: Spannungskopfschmerz *m*.
tensor/*n*: Tensor *m*, Musculus tensor *m*.
tent/*n*: Zelt *n*.
tentative/*adj*: versuchsweise.
tentative diagnosis: Verdachtsdiagnose *f*.
tentorial hernia: Tentoriumshernie *f*.
tenuous/*adj*: dünn.
tepid/*adj*: lauwarm.
teratism/*n*: Fehlbildung *f*, Malformation *f*.
teratoblastoma/*n*: Teratoblastom *n*.
teratogenic/*adj*: teratogen.
teratoid carcinoma: a malignant neoplasm composed of malignant germ

cells, with the most frequent localization in the testis. Teratokarzinom *n*.
teratoma/*n*: Teratom *n*.
terazosin/*n*: Terazosin *n*.
terbutaline/*n*: Terbutalin *n*.
terconazole/*n*: Terconazol *n*.
terbinafine/*n*: Terbinafin *n*.
terebrant/*adj*: stechend, bohrend.
terfenadine/*n*: Terfenadin *n*.
terizidone/*n*: Terizidon *n*.
terminal/*n, adj*: 1. Endigung *f*; 2. terminal, final.
terminal bar: Schlussleiste *f*.
terminal care: Sterbebegleitung *f*.
terminal hair: Terminalhaar *n*.
terminal ileitis: Ileitis terminalis *f*.
terminal illness: terminale Krankheit *f*.
terminal organ: Endorgan *n*.
termination/*n*: Beendigung *f*.
term infant: termingerechtes Kind *n*.
terminology/*n*: Terminologie *f*.
terminoterminal/*adj*: End-zu-End-.
terminoterminal anastomosis: End-zu-End Anastomose *f*.
territory/*n*: Gebiet *n*.
tertatolol/*n*: Tertatolol *n*.
tertian/*n*: Tertiana *f*.
tertiary/*adj*: tertiär.
tertiary alcohol: tertiärer Alkohol *m*.
tertiary amine: tertiäres Amin *n*
tertiary follicle: Tertiärfollikel *m*, Graaf-Follikel *m*.
tertiary prevention: Tertiärprävention *f*.
tertiary syphilis: tertiäre Syphilis *f*.
tesselated fundus: gesprenkelter Fundus *m*.
test/*n, vb*: 1. Test *m*, Probe *f*; 2. testen, erproben.
testicle/*n*: Hoden *m*.
testicular/*adj*: testikulär.
testicular adenoma: testikuläres Adenom *n*.
testicular cancer: malignant neoplasm of the testicle, most frequently occurring as seminoma, a type of germ cell tumor. Symptoms include initially painless swelling and tumescence of the testis, dysuria, and eventually gynecomastia as a result from endocrine dysfunction. Hodenkrebs *m*.
testicular cord: Samenstrang *m*, Funiculus spermaticus *m*.
testicular ectopia: abnormal position of one or both testicles, most frequently occurring as undescended testis which remains in the inguinal canal. Hodendystopie *f*.
testicular feminization: testikuläre Feminisierung *f*.
testicular steroid: Testosteron *n*.
testicular torsion: abrupt twisting of the testicle, resulting in interruption of testicular blood supply. Symptoms include severe pain, swelling of the testicles, and necrosis of the testis. Hodentorsion *f*.
testicular tumescence: Hodenschwellung *f*.
testimony/*n*: Gutachten *n*.
testis/*n*: Hoden *m*.
test meal: Probemahlzeit *f*.
testolactone/*n*: Testolacton *n*.
testosterone/*n*: Testosteron *n*.
testosterone phenylpropionate: Testosteronphenylpropionat *n*.
test result: Testergebnis *n*.
test solution: Testlösung *f*.
test strip: Teststreifen *m*.
test subject: Versuchsperson *f*.
test tube: Reagenzglas *n*.
test value: Testwert *m*.
tetanic contraction: tetanische Zuckung *f*.
tetanization/*n*: Tetanisierung *f*.
tetanoid/*adj*: tetanusartig.
tetanus/*n*: an infectious disease caused by the bacterium Clostridium tetani which is characterized by painful tonic seizures and spasms of voluntary muscles. Tetanus *m*, Starrkrampf *m*.
tetanus antitoxin: Tetanusantitoxin *n*.
tetanus vaccine: Tetanusimpfstoff *m*.
tetany/*n*: a condition which is characterized by painful muscle spasms with convulsive movements, usually due to calcium deficiency or emotional conditions. Tetanie *f*.
tetrabenazine/*n*: Tetrabenazin *n*.

T

tetraboric acid: Tetraborsäure *f*.
tetracaine/*n*: Tetracain *n*.
tetrachloroethylene/*n*: Tetrachlorethylen *n*.
tetracosanic acid: Tetracosansäure *f*.
tetracycline/*n*: Tetracyclin *n*.
tetradactyly/*n*: Tetradaktylie *f*.
tetrahydrofolic acid: Tetrahydrofolsäure *f*.
tetramelic/*adj*: viergliedrig.
tetraplegia/*n*: Tetraplegie *f*.
tetrofosmin/*n*: Tetrofosmin *n*.
tetroxoprim/*n*: Tetroxoprim *n*.
text blindness: Alexie *f*.
thalamectomy/*n*: Thalamusausschaltung *f*, Thalamotomie *f*.
thalamic/*adj*: thalamisch.
thalamic pain: Thalamusschmerz *m*.
thalamic syndrome: a neurologic syndrome which results from thalamic lesions, usually due to impairment of cerebral blood flow or eventually a brain tumor. Symptoms may include spontaneous, severe pain of the opposite body parts, especially in the face and the hand, hyperkinesis, hypesthesia and hypalgesia and sometimes sensory ataxia. Thalamussyndrom *n*, Déjerine-Roussy-Syndrom *n*.
thalamus/*n*: Thalamus *m*.
thalassemia/*n*: an autosomal recessive, hereditary disorder of hemoglobin synthesis, resulting in hypochromic, hemolytic anemia. Forms include the homozygous thalassemia major or Cooley's anemia, and the heterozygous thalassemia minor. Thalassämie *f*.
thalassotherapy/*n*: Thalassotherapie *f*.
thalidomide/*n*: Thalidomid *n*.
thalidomide syndrome: a congenital malformation syndrome caused by administration of thalidomide to the mother during pregnancy. Symptoms depend on the developmental stage of the embryo or fetus when exposed to the drug and may include hypoplasia or aplasia of the extremities, ear malformations, cranial nerve lesions, and abnormalities of internal organs. Thalidomidembryopathie *f*.
thallium/*n*: Thallium *n*, Tl.
thanatophoric dysplasia: thanatophorischer Minderwuchs *m*.
thaw/*vb*: auftauen, schmelzen.
theca/*n*: Hülle *f*, Kapsel *f*.
theca cell tumor: Thekazelltumor *m*.
thenar/*n*: Daumenballen *m*.
theobromine/*n*: Theobromin *n*.
theophylline/*n*: Theophyllin *n*.
theophylline ethylendiamine: Theophyllin-Ethylendiamin *n*.
theory/*n*: Theorie *f*.
therapeutic/*adj*: therapeutisch.
therapeutic agent: Heilmittel *n*.
therapeutic dose: therapeutische Dosis *f*.
therapeutic fever: therapeutisches Fieber *n*.
therapeutic index: therapeutischer Index *m*, therapeutische Breite *f*.
therapeutic indication: therapeutische Indikation *f*.
therapeutic nihilism: therapeutischer Nihilismus *m*.
therapeutic occupation: Heilberuf *m*.
therapeutic pneumothorax: therapeutischer Pneumothorax *m*.
therapeutic radiology: Strahlentherapie *f*.
therapeutic range: therapeutische Breite *f*.
therapeutic response: therapeutisches Ansprechen *n*.
therapeutic risk: Behandlungsrisiko *n*.
therapeutics/*n*: Therapeutik *f*.
therapeutic vaccine: therapeutischer Impfstoff *m*.
therapy/*n*: Therapie *f*, Behandlung *f*.
thermal balance: Wärmehaushalt *m*.
thermal test: Temperatursinnesprüfung *f*.
thermesthesia/*n*: Thermästhesie *f*.
thermic denaturation: Hitzedenaturierung *f*.
thermodilution technique: Thermodilutionsverfahren *n*.
thermography/*n*: Thermographie *f*.
thermolabile/*adj*: thermolabil.
thermometer/*n*: Thermometer *n*.
thermophilic/*adj*: thermophil.

thermoregulatory center: Thermoregulationszentrum *n*.
thermostable/*adj*: thermostabil.
thermostat/*n*: Thermostat *m*.
thesaurosis/*n*: Thesaurismose *f*, Speicherkrankheit *f*.
thevetin/*n*: Thevetin *n*.
thiamazole/*n*: Thiamazol *n*, Methimazol *n*.
thiambutosine/*n*: Thiambutosin *n*.
thiamine/*n*: Thiamin *n*, Vitamin B_1 *n*.
thiamphenicol/*n*: Thiamphenicol *n*.
thick/*adj*: dick.
thickened skin: Hautverdickung *f*.
thickener/*n*: Verdickungsmittel *n*.
thickening/*n*: Verdickung *f*.
thickness/*n*: Dicke *f*.
thick voice: belegte Stimme *f*.
thigh/*n*: Oberschenkel *m*.
thin/*adj*: dünn, mager.
thinking/*n*: Denken *n*.
thin-layer chromatography: Dünnschichtchromatographie *f*.
thinner/*n*: Verdünner *m*.
thinness/*n*: Dünne *f*, Dünnheit *f*.
β-thio α-aminopropionic acid: Cystein *n*, Zystein *n*.
thiobarbituric acid: Thiobarbitursäure *f*.
thioctic acid: Thioctansäure *f*.
thiocyanic acid: Thiozyansäure *f*.
thiolactic acid: Thiomilchsäure *f*.
thiosulfuric acid: Thioschwefelsäure *f*.
thiotepa/*n*: Thiotepa *n*.
thiouracil/*n*: Thiouracil *n*.
third sound: dritter Herzton *m*.
thirst/*n*: Durst *m*.
thirst center: Durstzentrum *n*.
thoracic/*adj*: thorakal.
thoracic cavity: Brusthöhle *f*.
thoracic outlet: Thoraxapertur *f*.
thoracic-pelvic-phalangeal dystrophy: asphyxierende Thoraxdystrophie *f*, Jeune-Krankheit *f*.
thoracic respiration: Thorakalatmung *f*.
thoracic spine: Brustwirbelsäule *f*.
thoracic surgery: Thoraxchirurgie *f*.
thoracic vertebra: Brustwirbel *m*.
thoracoabdominal/*adj*: thorakoabdominal.
thoracocentesis/*n*: Thorakozentese *f*.
thoracoplasty/*n*: Thorakoplastik *f*.
thoracoscopy/*n*: Thorakoskopie *f*.
thoracotomy/*n*: Thorakotomie *f*.
thorax/*n*: Brustkorb *m*.
thornapple/*n*: Stechapfel *m*.
thought/*n*: Gedanke *m*.
thread/*n*: Faden *m*.
threadworm/*n*: Fadenwurm *m*, Nematode *f*.
thready pulse: fadenförmiger Puls *m*.
threatened abortion: drohender Abort *m*.
three-chambered heart: Cor triloculare *n*.
three-day fever: Dreitagefieber *n*.
three-dimensional/*adj*: dreidimensional.
three-glass test: Dreigläserprobe *f*.
threshold/*n*: Schwelle *f*.
threshold effect: Schwelleneffekt *m*.
threshold erythema dose: Erythemschwellendosis *f*.
threshold stimulus: Schwellenreiz *m*.
thrill/*n, vb*: 1. heart murmur or abnormal blood vessel tremor that can be felt by the examinating physician as a vibration. Schwirren *n*, Schnurren *n*; 2. erschüttern, erschauern.
throat/*n*: Hals *m*, Kehle *f*.
throat swab: Rachenabstrich *m*.
throb/*n, vb*: 1. Pulsschlag *m*, Schlagen *n*; 2. schlagen, pulsieren.
throbbing pain: klopfender Schmerz *m*.
thrombectomy/*n*: Thrombektomie *f*.
thrombelastography/*n*: Thrombelastographie *f*.
thrombin/*n*: Thrombin *n*.
thromboangiitis/*n*: Thrombangitis *f*.
thromboarteritis/*n*: Thrombarteriitis *f*.
thrombocyte/*n*: Thrombozyt *m*.
thrombocyte aggregation: Thrombozytenaggregation *f*.
thrombocythemia/*n*: increase in the number of blood platelets in the peripheral blood, occurring for example in myeloproliferative disorders. Thrombozythämie *f*.
thrombocytopenia/*n*: decrease in the number of blood platelets in the pe-

T

ripheral blood, occurring for example in immunological disorders, infectious diseases, bone marrow disorders, or resulting from mechanical destruction of thrombocytes. Thrombozytopenie *f*.

thrombocytopenic purpura: thrombozytopenische Purpura *f*.

thrombocytosis/*n*: Thrombozytose *f*.

thrombokinase/*n*: Thrombokinase *f*, Prothrombinaktivator *m*.

thrombolytic/*adj*: thrombolytisch.

thrombopenia/*n*: Thrombopenie *f*, Thrombozytopenie *f*.

thrombophlebitic splenomegaly: Milzvenenthrombose *f*, Opitz-Krankheit *f*.

thrombophlebitis/*n*: inflammation of a vein associated with thrombosis, most frequently located in the veins of the lower extremity. Thrombophlebitis *f*.

thromboplastin/*n*: Thromboplastin *n*.

thromboplastin time: Thromboplastinzeit *f*.

thrombosis/*n*: formation or presence of a blood clot within a blood vessel. Locations predominantly affected include the heart valves, coronary arteries, basilar vessels of the brain, the mesenteric artery and arteries of the legs, as well as the pelvic veins and the veins of the leg. Thrombose *f*.

thrombotic gangrene: thrombotische Gangrän *f*.

thrombotic thrombocytopenic purpura: thrombotisch-thrombozytopenische Purpura *f*, Moschcowitz-Krankheit *f*.

thrombus/*n*: Thrombus *m*.

through-and-through suture: transmurale Naht *f*.

throughput/*n*: Durchsatz *m*.

throw up/*vb*: erbrechen.

thrush/*n*: fungal infection of the mouth and throat, typically caused by Candida albicans. Symptoms include small white stipples on the mucosa, and eventually painful swallowing. Soor *m*, Pilzstomatitis *f*.

thumb/*n*: Daumen *m*.

thumb sign: Daumenzeichen *n*, Froment-Zeichen *n*.

thymectomy/*n*: Thymektomie *f*.

thyme oil: Thymianöl *n*.

thymic aplasia: Thymusaplasie *f*.

thymic cyst: Thymuszyste *f*.

thymic hormone: Thymushormon *n*, Thymusfaktor *m*.

thymic-parathyreoid aplasia: DiGeorge-Syndrom *n*.

thymidine/*n*: Thymidin *n*.

thymine/*n*: Thymin *n*, Thy.

thyminic acid: Thyminsäure *f*.

thymocyte/*n*: Thymozyt *m*.

thymol/*n*: Thymol *n*.

thymoma/*n*: Thymom *n*.

thymus/*n*: Thymus *m*.

thymus corpuscle: Hassall-Körperchen *n*.

thymus hyperplasia: Thymushyperplasie *f*.

thyroglobulin/*n*: Thyreoglobulin *n*.

thyroglossal/*adj*: thyreoglossal.

thyroglossal cyst: Thyreoglossuszyste *f*.

thyroid/*n, adj*: 1. Schilddrüse *f*; 2. thyreoidal.

thyroid adenoma: adenoma of the thyroid gland, occurring in several, histologically distinguished forms. Schilddrüsenadenom *n*.

thyroid carcinoma: malignant neoplasm of the thyroid gland, classified into different forms like follicular, papillary, medullary, anaplastic, or otherwise nonspecified carcinoma. Symptoms include a solitary node in the thyroid gland, and eventually referred pain of the mandibular region and the neck. Schilddrüsenkarzinom *n*.

thyroidectomy/*n*: Thyreoidektomie *f*.

thyroid gland: Thyroidea *f*, Schilddrüse *f*.

thyroid hormone: Schilddrüsenhormon *n*.

thyroid insufficiency: Hypothyreose *f*.

thyroiditis/*n*: inflammation of the thyroid gland. Forms include acute, purulent thyreoiditis of infectious origin, autoimmune thyroiditis, and inflammation due to other causes, for example irradiation or systemic diseases like sarcoidosis. Thyreoiditis *f*.

thyrotoxic coma: thyreotoxisches Koma *n*.

thyrotoxic crisis: thyreotoxische Krise *f*.

thyrotoxic ophthalmopathy: endokrine Ophthalmopathie *f*.

thyrotoxicosis/*n*: Thyreotoxikose *f*.

thyrotrophin/*n*: Thyrotrophin *n*.

thyrotropic/*adj*: thyreotrop.

thyrotropic hormone: Thyrotropin *n*.

thyrotropin/*n*: Thyrotropin *n*.

thyroxine/*n*: Thyroxin *n*, T_4.

thyroxine-binding globulin: thyroxinbindendes Globulin *n*, TBG.

TIA <*abbr*> **transient ischemic attack**: transitorische ischämische Attacke *f*, TIA.

tiabendazole/*n*: Tiabendazol *n*.

tiagabine/*n*: Tiagabin *n*.

tiapride/*n*: Tiaprid *n*.

tiaprofenic acid: Tiaprofensäure *f*.

tibia/*n*: Schienbein *n*.

tibiofibular joint: Tibiofibulargelenk *n*.

tibolone/*n*: Tibolon *n*.

tic/*n*: sudden, involuntary or habitual movement due to muscular contraction or twitch, typically of the face muscles. Tic *m*.

ticarcillin/*n*: Ticarcillin *n*.

tic disorder: Ticstörung *f*.

tick/*n*: Zecke *f*.

tick-borne encephalitis: an infectious disease with inflammation of the brain, following tick bites which can transmit the pathogenic viruses. In certain European regions, endemic occurrence of spring-summer encephalitis has been described. Zeckenenzephalitis *f*.

tick-borne relapsing fever: Zeckenrückfallfieber *n*.

tick fever: Zeckenbissfieber *n*.

tickle/*n, vb*: 1. Kitzelgefühl *n*; 2. kitzeln.

tickling cough: Reizhusten *m*.

ticlopidine/*n*: Ticlopidin *n*.

tidal air: Atemluft *f*.

tidal drainage: Überlaufdrainage *f*.

tidal volume: Atemzugvolumen *n*.

tidal wave: Woge *f*.

tide/*n*: Anflutung *f*.

tie/*n, vb*: 1. Verbindung *f*, Nexus *m*; 2. verknüpfen.

tight/*adj*: eng, straff.

tiglic acid: Tiglinsäure *f*.

tigroid fundus: gesprenkelter Fundus *m*.

tigrolysis/*n*: Tigrolyse *f*.

tilt angle: Neigungswinkel *m*.

tiludronic acid: Tiludronsäure *f*.

time/*n*: Zeit *f*.

time course: zeitlicher Verlauf *m*.

timed vital capacity: Sekundenkapazität *f*.

time-release preparation: Retardpräparat *n*.

time span: Zeitspanne *f*.

timid/*adj*: ängstlich, befangen.

timolol/*n*: Timolol *n*.

tincture/*n*: Tinktur *f*.

tinea/*n*: chronic infectious disease of the skin, typically caused by the fungus Trichophyton. Symptoms include ring-shaped lesions, therefore tinea is popularly called ringworm. Tinea *f*.

tingling/*n*: Prickelgefühl *n*, Kitzeln *n*.

tinidazole/*n*: Tinidazol *n*.

tinnitus/*n*: auditory sensation with abnormal noises in the ear for which there exists no external source, typically in the form of buzzing, clicking or a dull sound. Tinnitus *m*.

tinzaparin/*n*: Tinzaparin *n*.

tioconazole/*n*: Tioconazol *n*.

tioguanine/*n*: Tioguanin *n*.

tiopronin/*n*: Tiopronin *n*.

tiotixene/*n*: Tiotixen *n*.

tiotropium bromide: Tiotropiumbromid *n*.

tip/*n*: Spitze *f*.

tip foot: Spitzfuß *m*, Pferdefuß *m*.

tipranavir/*n*: Tipranavir *n*.

tiracizine/*n*: Tiracizin *n*.

tired/*adj*: müde.

tired of life: lebensmüde.

tirofiban/*n*: Tirofiban *n*.

tissue/*n*: Gewebe *n*.

T

tissue bank: Gewebebank *f*.
tissue protein: Gewebeprotein *n*.
tissue space: Interzellularraum *m*, IZR.
tissue transplant: Gewebetransplantat *n*.
titer/*n*: Titer *m*.
titration/*n*: Titration *f*.
tixocortol/*n*: Tixocortol *n*.
tizanidine/*n*: Tizanidin *n*.
tobacco bag suture: Tabakbeutelnaht *f*.
tobacco mosaic virus: Tabakmosaikvirus *n*.
tobramycin/*n*: Tobramycin *n*.
tocainide/*n*: Tocainid *n*.
tocography/*n*: Tokographie *f*.
tocolysis/*n*: Tokolyse *f*.
tocopherol/*n*: Tocopherol *n*, Vitamin E *n*.
toddle/*vb*: watscheln.
toddler/*n*: Kleinkind *n*.
toe/*n*: Zehe *f*.
toilet training: Toilettentraining *n*.
tolazamide/*n*: Tolazamid *n*.
tolbutamide/*n*: Tolbutamid *n*.
tolcapone/*n*: Tolcapon *n*.
tolciclate/*n*: Tolciclat *n*.
tolerable/*adj*: tolerabel.
tolerance/*n*: Toleranz *f*, Verträglichkeit *f*.
tolerance dose: Toleranzdosis *f*.
tolerance range: Toleranzbereich *m*.
tolerance test: Toleranztest *m*, Belastungsprobe *f*.
tolerate/*vb*: tolerieren.
toliprolol/*n*: Toliprolol *n*.
tolmetin/*n*: Tolmetin *n*.
tolterodine/*n*: Tolterodin *n*.
tomography/*n*: Tomographie *f*.
tonal discrimination: Tonhöhenunterscheidung *f*.
tonal fusion: Tonverschmelzung *f*.
tone/*n*: Ton *m*, Tonus *m*.
tongs/*n*: Zange *f*.
tongue/*n*: Zunge *f*.
tongue blade: Zungenspatel *m*.
tongue flap: Zungenlappen *m*.
tongueworm/*n*: Zungenwurm *m*.
tonic-clonic/*adj*: tonisch-klonisch.
tonic-clonic seizure: tonisch-klonischer Anfall *m*.
tonic convulsion: tonischer Krampf *m*.
tonic diplegia: spastische Diplegie *f*.
tonic epilepsy: tonischer Anfall *m*.
tonic muscular contraction: tetanische Muskelkontraktion *f*.
tonic pupil: Pupillotonie *f*.
tonography/*n*: Tonographie *f*.
tonometry/*n*: Tonometrie *f*.
tonsil/*n*: Tonsille *f*, Mandel *f*.
tonsillar ring: lymphatischer Rachenring *m*, Waldeyer-Rachenring *m*.
tonsillectomy/*n*: Tonsillektomie *f*.
tonsillitis/*n*: inflammation of the tonsils, usually caused by bacteria or a virus. Symptoms of acute tonsillitis include fever, shivers, coated tongue, and painful enlargement of cervical lymph nodes. Tonsillitis *f*.
tonsillotomy/*n*: Tonsillotomie *f*, Adenotomie *f*.
tool/*n*: Werkzeug *n*, Instrument *n*.
tooth/*n*: Zahn *m*.
tooth discoloration: Zahnverfärbung *f*.
toothless/*adj*: zahnlos.
toothpick/*n*: Zahnstocher *m*.
top/*n*: Spitze *f*.
tophaceous gout: tophische Gicht *f*.
tophic concretion: Tophus *m*.
topical/*adj*: topisch.
topical administration: lokale Anwendung *f*.
topiramate/*n*: Topiramat *n*.
topographic anatomy: topographische Anatomie *f*.
topographic relationship: topographische Beziehung *f*.
topography/*n*: Topographie *f*.
topothecan/*n*: Topotecan *n*.
torasemide/*n*: Torasemid *n*.
toremifene/*n*: Toremifen *n*.
torpor/*n*: Torpidität *f*, Torpor *m*.
torsion/*n*: Torsion *f*.
torsional deformity: Torsionsdeformität *f*.
torsion forceps: Torsionsklemme *f*.
torsion spasm: Torsionsdystonie *f*.
torso/*n*: Rumpf *m*.
torticollis/*n*: a condition in which the head is turned to one side due to spastic contraction or malformation of

the cervical muscles. Tortikollis *m*, Schiefhals *m*.
tortuous/*adj*: gewunden.
total/*n, adj*: 1. Gesamtheit *f*; 2. gesamt.
total aphasia: Globalaphasie *f*.
total bilirubin: Gesamtbilirubin *n*.
total daily intake: tägliche Gesamtzufuhr *f*.
total filtration: Gesamtfilterung *f*.
total lung capacity: Totalkapazität *f*.
total metabolism: Gesamtumsatz *m*.
total removal: Totalexstirpation *f*.
total shunt: Totalshunt *m*.
total volume: Gesamtmenge *f*.
totipotential cell: omnipotente Zelle *f*.
touch/*n, vb*: 1. Berührung *f*, Tastgefühl *n*; 2. berühren.
touch perception: Tastwahrnehmung *f*.
touch spot: Tastpunkt *m*.
tough/*adj*: zäh.
tourniquet/*n*: Tourniquet *m*, Stauschlauch *m*.
towel clip: Tuchklemme *f*.
toxemia/*n*: Toxämie *f*, Blutvergiftung *f*.
toxic/*adj*: toxisch.
toxic amblyopia: toxische Amblyopie *f*.
toxic anemia: toxische Anämie *f*.
toxic cyanosis: autotoxische Zyanose *f*.
toxic diffuse goiter: diffuse toxische Struma *f*.
toxic encephalopathy: toxische Enzephalopathie *f*.
toxic epidermolysis: Epidermolysis acuta toxica *f*, Lyell-Syndrom *n*.
toxic goiter: toxische Struma *f*.
toxic granule: toxisches Granulom *n*.
toxic hepatitis: toxische Hepatitis *f*.
toxicity/*n*: Toxizität *f*.
toxicology/*n*: Toxikologie *f*.
toxicosis/*n*: Toxikose *f*.
toxicosis of pregnancy: Schwangerschaftstoxikose *f*.
toxic psychosis: Intoxikationspsychose *f*.
toxic shock: toxischer Schock *m*.
toxic shock syndrome: a condition which is characterized by high fever, conjunctivitis, exanthema, desquamation of the skin, shock, gastrointestinal symptoms, and impaired consciousness, most likely to be caused by endotoxins produced by Staphylococcus aureus. Syndrom des toxischen Schocks *n*.
toxic/therapeutic ratio: therapeutische Breite *f*.
toxic thyroid adenoma: toxisches Schilddrüsenadenom *n*.
toxin/*n*: Toxin *n*.
toxoid/*n*: Toxoid *n*.
toxoplasmic cyst: Toxoplasmosezyste *f*.
toxoplasmic encephalitis: Toxoplasmose-Enzephalitis *f*.
toxoplasmosis/*n*: an infectious disease caused by the protozoon Toxoplasma gondii. Toxoplasmosis, transmitted by the mother, can affect the fetus and cause severe lesions of the central nervous system, including hydrocephalus, and the eye. In adolescents and adults, a benign course as well as toxoplasmic encephalitis are possible. In immunocompromised patients, a reactivation of a previous infection may occur. Toxoplasmose *f*.
TPHA test <*abbr*> **treponema pallidum hemagglutination test**: Treponema-pallidum-Hämagglutinationstest *m*, TPHA-Test *m*.
trabecular adenoma: trabekuläres Adenom *n*.
trabecular bone: Spongiosa *f*.
trabecular carcinoma: trabekuläres Karzinom *n*.
trabeculated bladder: Balkenblase *f*.
trabeculation/*n*: Trabekelbildung *f*.
trace/*n, vb*: 1. Spur *f*; 2. aufspüren.
trace element: Spurenelement *n*.
tracer/*n*: Tracer *m*, Markierungssubstanz *f*.
trachea/*n*: Luftröhre *f*.
tracheal stenosis: Trachealstenose *f*.
tracheal tube: Trachealtubus *m*.
tracheitis/*n*: inflammation of the windpipe, usually associated with laryngitis and bronchitis. Tracheitis *f*.
trachelo-: Trachelo-, Zervix-.

trachelorrhaphy/*n*: Zervixnaht *f*.
tracheo-: Tracheo-.
tracheobronchitis/*n*: Tracheobronchitis *f*.
tracheoesophageal fistula: Ösophagotrachealfistel *f*.
tracheostenosis/*n*: Trachealstenose *f*.
tracheostomy/*n*: Tracheostomie *f*.
tracheostomy tube: Trachealkanüle *f*.
tracheotomy/*n*: Tracheotomie *f*.
trachoma/*n*: an infectious disease of the eye, caused by the bacterium Chlamydia trachomatis. Symptoms include swelling of the conjunctiva and hypersecretion, followed by the formation of so-called trachoma inclusion bodies. Conjunctivitis trachomatosa *f*, Trachom *n*.
trachoma inclusion conjunctivitis: Trachomeinschlusskörperchen-Konjunktivitis *f*, TRIC.
trachomatous conjunctivitis: Conjunctivitis trachomatosa *f*, Trachom *n*.
track/*n*: Spur *f*, Bahn *f*.
tract/*n*: Bahn *f*, Trakt *m*.
traction/*n*: Traktion *f*, Extension *f*.
traction apparatus: Streckapparat *m*.
traction bed: Extensionsbett *n*.
traction table: Extensionstisch *m*.
tractotomy/*n*: Traktotomie *f*.
traffic accident: Verkehrsunfall *m*.
tragus pain: Tragusdruckschmerz *m*.
trait/*n*: Eigenschaft *f*, Charakterzug *m*.
tramadol/*n*: Tramadol *n*.
tramazoline/*n*: Tramazolin *n*.
trance/*n*: Trance *f*, Dämmerzustand *m*.
trandolapril/*n*: Trandolapril *n*.
tranexamic acid: Tranexamsäure *f*.
tranquilizer/*n*: Tranquilizer *m*.
transabdominal/*adj*: transabdominal.
transabdominal amniocentesis: transabdominelle Amniozentese *f*.
transactional analysis: Transaktionsanalyse *f*.
transaminase/*n*: Transaminase *f*.
transbronchial biopsy: transbronchiale Lungenbiopsie *f*.
transcervical amniocentesis: transzervikale Amniozentese *f*.
transcervical fracture: intrakapsuläre Oberschenkelhalsfraktur *f*.
trans configuration: trans-Konfiguration *f*.
transcortical aphasia: transkortikale Aphasie *f*, Lichtheim-Aphasie *f*.
transcortical apraxia: transkortikale Apraxie *f*.
transcription/*n*: Transkription *f*.
transcultural psychiatry: interkulturelle Psychiatrie *f*.
transcutaneous electric nerve stimulation: transkutane elektrische Nervenstimulation *f*, TENS.
transcutaneous oximetry: perkutane Sauerstoffmessung *f*, Pulsoxymetrie *f*.
transdermal/*adj*: transdermal.
transfer/*n, vb*: 1. Transfer *m*, Übertragung *f*; 2. übertragen.
transfixion suture: Durchstichnaht *f*.
transformation/*n*: Transformation *f*.
transfusion/*n*: Transfusion *f*.
transfusion-associated hepatitis: Posttransfusionshepatitis *f*, Transfusionshepatitis *f*.
transgenic/*adj*: transgen.
transient cerebral ischemia: transitorische ischämische Attacke *f*, TIA.
transient global amnesia: transitorische Globalamnesie *f*.
transient hypertension: intermittierender Hypertonus *m*.
transient ischemic attack: transitorische ischämische Attacke *f*, TIA.
transient macular edema: passageres Makulaödem *n*, Berlin-Ödem *n*.
transient monocular blindness: einseitige Amaurosis fugax *f*.
transient proteinuria: transitorische Proteinurie *f*.
transitional cell: Übergangsepithelzelle *f*.
transitional cell carcinoma: Urothelkarzinom *n*, Übergangsepithelkarzinom *n*.
transitional phase: Durchgangsstadium *n*, Übergangsphase *f*.
transitional psychosis: Durchgangspsychose *f*.
transitional stage: Übergangsstadium *n*.

transition state: Übergangszustand *m*.
translocation/*n*: Translokation *f*, T.
transluminal arterial dilatation: transluminale Angioplastie *f*.
transmission/*n*: Transmission *f*, Übertragung *f*.
transmission electron microscopy: Transmissionselektronenmikroskopie *f*.
transmit/*vb*: übertragen.
transmitted murmur: fortgeleitetes Geräusch *n*.
transmitter substance: Neurotransmitter *m*.
transmural colitis: transmurale Kolitis *f*.
transmural myocardial infarction: transmuraler Infarkt *m*.
transmural pressure: Wanddruck *m*.
transnasal approach: transnasaler Zugang *m*.
transparency/*n*: Transparenz *f*.
transpiration/*n*: Transpiration *f*.
transplacental/*adj*: transplazentar, diaplazentar.
transplant/*n, vb*: 1. Transplantat *n*; 2. transplantieren.
transplantation/*n*: Transplantation *f*.
transplant bank: Organbank *f*.
transplant recipient: Transplantatempfänger *m*.
transport/*n, vb*: 1. Transport *m*; 2. transportieren.
transportation of patients: Krankentransport *m*.
transposition/*n*: Transposition *f*.
transposition of the arterial trunk: Transposition der großen Gefäße, TGA.
transsexualism/*n*: Transsexualismus *m*.
transsexual surgery: operative Geschlechtsumwandlung *f*.
transthoracic approach: transthorakaler Zugang *m*.
transtrochanteric osteotomy: intertrochantäre Osteotomie *f*.
transudate/*n*: Transsudat *n*.
transurethral prostatectomy: transurethrale Prostataresektion *f*, TURP.
transventricular closed valvulotomy: transventrikuläre Infundibulektomie *f*, Brock-Operation *f*.
transverse/*adj*: transversal.
transverse diameter: Querdurchmesser *m*.
transverse facial fracture: LeFort-III-Fraktur *f*.
transverse fracture: Transversalbruch *m*, Querfraktur *f*.
transverse myelitis: inflammation of the spinal cord, extending from one side to the other, as distinguished from other forms of myelitis which may affect circumscribed structures only. Myelitis transversa *f*, Querschnittmyelitis *f*.
transverse plane: Transversalebene *f*.
transverse presentation: in obstetrics, the position of the fetus when the long axis of its body is situated at a right angle to the long axis of the maternal body. Querlage *f*.
transvestism/*n*: Transvestismus *m*.
tranylcypromine/*n*: Tranylcypromin *n*.
trapezius/*n*: Trapezius *m*, Musculus trapezius *m*.
trapezoid/*n, adj*: 1. Vieleckbein *n*, Os trapezoideum *n*; 2. trapezförmig.
trapped placenta: Plazentaretention *f*.
trauma/*n*: Trauma *n*, Verletzung *f*.
trauma center: traumatologisches Zentrum *n*.
traumatic/*adj*: traumatisch.
traumatic alopecia: mechanische Alopezie *f*.
traumatic amenorrhea: traumatische Amenorrhö *f*, Asherman-Fritsch-Syndrom *n*.
traumatic amnesia: traumatische Amnesie *f*.
traumatic amputation: Amputationstrauma *n*.
traumatic deafness: traumatischer Hörverlust *m*.
traumatic epilepsy: posttraumatische Epilepsie *f*.
traumatic gangrene: traumatische Gangrän *f*.

traumatic headache: posttraumatischer Kopfschmerz *m*.
traumatic parkinsonism: traumatisches Parkinson-Syndrom *n*.
traumatic pneumonia: Kontusionspneumonie *f*.
traumatic pneumothorax: traumatischer Pneumothorax *m*.
traumatic seizure: posttraumatische Epilepsie *f*.
traveller's diarrhea: Reisediarrhö *f*.
travel medicine: Reisemedizin *f*.
travel sickness: Reisekrankheit *f*, Kinetose *f*.
travoprost/*n*: Travoprost *n*.
trazodone/*n*: Trazodon *n*.
treadmill/*n*: Laufband *n*.
treat/*vb*: behandeln.
treatment/*n*: Behandlung *f*, Therapie *f*.
treatment duration: Behandlungsdauer *f*.
treatment option: Behandlungsmöglichkeit *f*.
trematode/*n*: Trematode *f*, Saugwurm *m*.
trembling/*n, adj*: 1. Zittern *n*, Tremor *m*; 2. zitternd.
tremor/*n*: involuntary, sometimes rhythmic shake or quiver. The trembling can be slow or fast, transient or permanent. Tremor *m*, Zittern *n*.
tremulous iris: Irisschlottern *n*, Iridodenesis *f*.
trench/*n*: Grube *f*.
trench fever: Wolhynisches Fieber *n*.
trend/*n*: Trend *m*, Neigung *f*.
treosulfan/*n*: Treosulfan *n*.
trephination/*n*: Trepanation *f*.
trephine biopsy: Trokarbiopsie *f*.
treponema pallidum hemagglutination test: Treponema-pallidum-Hämagglutinationstest *m*, TPHA-Test *m*.
tretamine/*n*: Tretamin *n*.
tretinoin/*n*: Tretinoin *n*, Vitamin-A-Säure *f*.
triage/*n*: Triage *f*.
trial/*n*: Studie *f*, Prüfung *f*.
trial and error method: empirisches Verfahren *n*.
triamcinolone/*n*: Triamcinolon *n*.
triamcinolone acetonide: Triamcinolonacetonid *n*.
triamterene/*n*: Triamteren *n*.
triangle/*n*: Dreieck *n*.
triangular bandage: Dreiecktuch *n*.
triangular pelvis: dreieckiges Becken *n*.
triazolam/*n*: Triazolam *n*.
tribenoside/*n*: Tribenosid *n*.
tribromomethane/*n*: Tribrommethan *n*, Bromoform *n*.
triceps/*n*: Trizeps *m*, Musculus triceps *m*.
trichiasis/*n*: Trichiasis *f*.
trichinosis/*n*: disease caused by the nematode parasite Trichinella spiralis which can be found in raw pork or horse meat. Symptoms include diarrhea, muscle pain, edema of the eyelid, dysphagia, and fever, in severe cases encephalitis can occur. Trichinose *f*.
trichinous/*adj*: trichinös.
trichlormethiazide/*n*: Trichlormethiazid *n*.
trichloroacetic acid: Trichloressigsäure *f*.
trichloroethylene/*n*: Trichloräthylen *n*, Tri.
trichopathy/*n*: Haarerkrankung *f*.
trichophytosis/*n*: Trichophytose *f*.
trichterbrust/*n*: Trichterbrust *f*.
tricuspid insufficiency: Trikuspidalklappeninsuffizienz *f*.
tricuspid murmur: Trikuspidalgeräusch *n*, Trikuspidalton *m*.
tricuspid stenosis: Trikuspidalklappenstenose *f*.
trifluperidol/*n*: Trifluperidol *n*.
trifluridine/*n*: Trifluridin *n*.
trifocal glasses: Trifokalgläser.
trigeminal/*adj*: Trigeminus-.
trigeminal decompression: Trigeminusdekompression *f*.
trigeminal neuralgia: painful disorder in a branch of the trigeminal nerve. Symptoms include an onset typically around the age of 50, and intensely painful attacks. Trigeminusneuralgie *f*.
trigeminal pulse: Trigeminie *f*.

trigeminal rhizotomy: retroganglionäre Neurotomie *f*, Dandy-Operation *f*.
trigger/*n, vb*: 1. Auslöser *m*; 2. auslösen.
trigger point: Triggerpunkt *m*, Reizpunkt *m*.
trigger thumb: schnappender Daumen *m*.
trigone/*n*: Dreieck *n*.
trihexyphenidyl/*n*: Trihexyphenidyl *n*.
trimalleolar fracture: trimalleolärer Knochenbruch *m*.
trimetaphan camsylate: Trimetaphancamsilat *n*.
trimethadione/*n*: Trimethadion *n*.
trimethoprim/*n*: Trimethoprim *n*.
trimetozine/*n*: Trimetozin *n*.
trimipramine/*n*: Trimipramin *n*.
triparanol/*n*: Triparanol *n*.
triple/*adj*: dreifach.
triple anastomosis: Dreifachanastomose *f*.
triple combination: Dreifachkombination *f*.
triplegia/*n*: Triplegie *f*.
triple rhythm: Trigeminie *f*.
triplet pregnancy: Drillingsschwangerschaft *f*.
triple vaccination: Dreifachimpfung *f*.
triple-X syndrome: a chromosomal aberration which is characterized by the presence of a third X chromosome, the karyotype is 48,XXX. Affected females do not show changes in the phenotype and are usually fertile. Triple-X-Syndrom *n*, XXX-Frau *f*.
triploid/*adj*: triploid.
triptan/*n*: Triptan *n*.
trismus/*n*: Trismus *m*, Kieferklemme *f*.
trisomy/*n*: Trisomie *f*.
trisomy syndrome: any syndrome which is characterized by the presence of an extra chromosome, usually one chromosome is present in three copies. Forms include for example trisomy 13 syndrome or trisomy 21 syndrome, the so-called Down syndrome. Trisomiesyndrom *n*.
trivial/*adj*: trivial.
trocar/*n*: Trokar *m*.
trochanter/*n*: Trochanter *m*.
trochlea/*n*: Rolle *f*.
trochlear/*adj*: trochlear.
trochlear paralysis: Trochlearislähmung *f*.
trofosfamide/*n*: Trofosfamid *n*.
tromantadine/*n*: Tromantadin *n*.
trophedema/*n*: Trophödem *n*.
trophic/*adj*: trophisch.
trophic fracture: pathologische Fraktur *f*.
trophic ulcer: trophisches Ulkus *n*.
trophoblast/*n*: Trophoblast *m*.
trophoneurosis/*n*: Trophoneurose *f*.
tropic acid: Tropasäure *f*.
tropical/*adj*: tropisch.
tropical bubo: Bubo *m*, Lymphogranuloma venereum *n*.
tropical disease: Tropenkrankheit *f*.
tropical splenomegaly: tropische Splenomegalie *f*, Kala-Azar *f*, viszerale Leishmaniase *f*.
tropicamide/*n*: Tropicamid *n*.
tropine/*n*: Tropin *n*.
tropisetron/*n*: Tropisetron *n*.
trospium chloride: Trospiumchlorid *n*.
trough/*n*: Rinne *f*.
trovafloxacin/*n*: Trovafloxacin *n*.
true/*adj*: wahr, echt, unverfälscht
true aneurysm: echtes Aneurysma *n*.
true chancre: harter Schanker *m*, Primäraffekt *m*.
true cyst: echte Zyste *f*.
true hermaphroditism: echter Hermaphroditismus *m*.
true pelvis: kleines Becken *n*.
truncal/*adj*: trunkulär.
truncular vagotomy: trunkuläre Vagotomie *f*.
trunk apraxia: Rumpfataxie *f*.
try/*vb*: versuchen, erproben.
trypanosomiasis/*n*: Trypanosomiasis *f*.
trypsin/*n*: Trypsin *n*.
trypsinogen/*n*: Trypsinogen *n*.
tryptophan/*n*: Tryptophan *n*, Trp.
tubal/*adj*: tubar.

tubal abortion: Tubarabort *m*, tubarer Abort *m*.
tubal dropsy: Hydrosalpinx *f*.
tubal ligation: Tubenligatur *f*.
tubal pregnancy: Tubargravidität *f*.
tubal rupture: Eileiterruptur *f*.
tubal transport: Tubentransport *m*.
tube/*n*: Sonde *f*, Röhre *f*, Tube *f*.
tubed flap: Rundstiellappen *m*.
tube feeding: Sondenernährung *f*.
tube patency: Tubendurchgängigkeit *f*.
tubercle/*n*: Tuberkel *n*, Knötchen *n*.
tubercle bacillus: Tuberkelbazillus *m*.
tubercular/*adj*: höckerig, tuberkulös.
tuberculid/*n*: Tuberkulid *n*.
tuberculin/*n*: Tuberkulin *n*.
tuberculin-like reaction: tuberkulinartige Reaktion *f*.
tuberculin reaction: Tuberkulinreaktion *f*.
tuberculoid leprosy: tuberkuloide Lepra *f*.
tuberculosis/*n*: an infectious disease of humans and animals caused by Mycobacterium tuberculosis or Mycobacterium bovis, characterized by the presence of tuberculous, cheesy nodules which may show a variety of morphologic features, and can be limited to one localization or occur in a disseminated form. Mycobacteria can be transmitted via droplet infection and are most frequently inhaled. Tuberculosis most frequently affects the lungs, but also skin, bone, brain, and other organs may be involved. Tuberkulose *f*, TB.
tuberculosis reactivation: Tuberkulosereaktivierung *f*.
tuberculostatic/*n, adj*: 1. Tuberkulostatikum *n*; 2. tuberkulostatisch.
tuberculous/*adj*: tuberkulös.
tuberculous arthritis: tuberkulöse Arthritis *f*.
tuberculous cystitis: Blasentuberkulose *f*.
tuberculous lymphadenitis: Lymphknotentuberkulose *f*.
tuberculous nephritis: Nierentuberkulose *f*.
tuberculous pneumonia: tuberkulöse Pneumonie *f*.
tuberculous spondylitis: Spondylitis tuberculosa *f*, Wirbeltuberkulose *f*.
tuberculum/*n*: Höcker *m*, Knötchen *n*.
tuberosity/*n*: Rauigkeit *f*, Tuberositas *f*.
tuberous/*adj*: tuberös.
tuberous angioma: tuberöses Angiom *n*.
tuberous sclerosis: tuberöse Hirnsklerose *f*, Bourneville-Pringle-Syndrom *n*.
tubocurarine/*n*: Tubocurarin *n*.
tubo-ovarian/*adj*: tuboovarial.
tubo-ovarian abscess: Tuboovarialabszess *m*.
tubo-ovariectomy/*n*: Salpingoophorektomie *f*.
tubular/*adj*: tubulär.
tubular adenoma: tubuläres Adenom *n*.
tubular bone: Röhrenknochen *m*.
tubular cyst: Tubuluszyste *f*.
tubular gland: tubulöse Drüse *f*.
tubular proteinuria: tubuläre Proteinurie *f*.
tubular reabsorption: tubuläre Rückresorption *f*.
tubule/*n*: Röhrchen *n*, Kanal *m*.
tubuloacinar gland: tubuloazinöse Drüse *f*.
tuft fracture: Berstungsbruch *m*.
tuitonal analysis: Lehranalyse *f*.
tularemia/*n*: an infectious disease caused by the bacterium Francisella tularensis and transmitted from small rodents to humans by insects. Symptoms include fever, ulcerative, papular lesions, and lymphadenitis. Tularämie *f*, Hasenfieber *n*.
tularemic pneumonia: tularämische Pneumonie *f*.
tulathromycin/*n*: Tulathromycin *n*.
tulobuterol/*n*: Tulobuterol *n*.
tumescence/*n*: Tumeszenz *f*, Schwellung *f*.
tumor/*n*: any growth or swelling of body tissue. The term is frequently used to designate benign or malignant neoplastic growth with forma-

tion of new cells or tissue. Tumor *m*.
tumor-associated antigen: tumorassoziiertes Antigen *n*.
tumor growth: Tumorwachstum *n*.
tumor-induced anemia: Tumoranämie *f*.
tumorlike lesion: Pseudotumor *m*.
tumor necrosis factor: Tumor-Nekrose-Faktor *m*, TNF.
tumor-specific antigen: Tumorantigen *n*.
tumor staging: Tumorstaging *n*, Tumorstadieneinteilung *f*.
tumor virus: Tumorvirus *n*, Onkovirus *n*.
tumultuous contractions: unkoordinierte Wehen.
tungstic acid: Wolframsäure *f*.
tunic/*n*: Hülle *f*.
tunnel/*n*: Tunnel *m*, Kanal *m*.
turbid urine: trüber Urin *m*.
turbinate/*n, adj*: 1. Nasenmuschel *f*; 2. gewunden.
turbinectomy/*n*: Konchektomie *f*.
turgid/*adj*: geschwollen.
turgor/*n*: Turgor *m*, Schwellung *f*.
turnover/*n*: Turnover *m*, Umsatz *m*.
tussive syncope: Hustensynkope *f*.
tweezers/*n*: Pinzette *f*.
twilight blindness: Dämmerungsamblyopie *f*.
twin birth: Zwillingsgeburt *f*.
twinge/*n*: Zwicken *n*.
twins: Zwillinge
twin transfusion syndrome: in twin pregnancy, the flow of fetal blood from one fetus to the other via an arteriovenous or arterial anastomosis, resulting in the birth of one anemic and one plethoric twin. Syndrom der fetofetalen Bluttransfusion, fetofetale Transfusion *f*.
twisted cord: Nabelschnurumschlingung *f*.
twisting/*n*: Drehung *f*.
twitch/*n, vb*: 1. Zuckung *f*; 2. zucken.
two-glass test: Zweigläserprobe *f*.
two-point discrimination: Zweipunktediskrimination *f*.
two-way catheter: Zweiwegkatheter *m*.
tylosin/*n*: Tylosin *n*.
tympanectomy/*n*: Tympanektomie *f*.
tympanic/*adj*: tympanisch.
tympanic canal: Paukengang *m*.
tympanic membrane: Trommelfell *n*.
tympanic resonance: Tympanie *f*.
tympanitic resonance: tympanitisches Geräusch *n*.
tympanoplasty/*n*: Tympanoplastik *f*.
tympanotomy/*n*: Parazentese *f*.
tympanum/*n*: Trommel *f*, Tympanum *n*, Paukenhöhle *f*.
type/*n, vb*: 1. Typ *m*; 2. typisieren.
typhoid/*n, adj*: 1. Typhoid *n*; 2. typhusähnlich.
typhoid fever: an infectious disease caused by the bacterium Salmonella typhi. Symptoms include fever, intense fatigue, stupor, and diarrhea. Typhus *m*.
typhoid pneumonia: Typhuspneumonie *f*.
typhoid spot: Typhusroseola *f*.
typhus/*n*: arthropod-borne, infectious diseases caused by Rickettsia bacteria. Symptoms and clinical course vary in intensity, depending on the Rickettsia strain. Signs may include initial fever, headache, swelling of the face, conjunctivitis, laryngitis, bronchitis, and dyspnea, followed by the eruption of a macular exanthema. Fleckfieber *n*, Flecktyphus *m*.
typhus fever: Fleckfieber *n*, Flecktyphus *m*.
typical/*adj*: typisch.
typing/*n*: Typisierung *f*.
tyrosine/*n*: Tyrosin *n*, Tyr.

T

U

U <*abbr*> **1. uracil; 2. uranium; 3. uridine**: 1. Uracil *n*; 2. Uran *n*, U; 3. Uridin *n*.
U. <*abbr*> **unit**: Einheit *f*.
ubiquinone/*n*: Ubichinon *n*.
ubiquitous/*adj*: ubiquitär.
ulcer/*n*: sores on the skin or mucosa, and also of internal organs of the body, for example the stomach, resulting from local damage or systemic disease. Ulkus *n*, Geschwür *n*.
ulcerate/*vb*: ulzerieren.
ulceration/*n*: Ulzeration *f*, Geschwürbildung *f*.
ulcerative colitis: chronic inflammatory disease of the colon of unknown origin, resulting in the development of mucosal and submucosal ulcerations. Symptoms include abdominal pain, rectal bleeding, and rectal discharge. Colitis ulcerosa *f*.
ulcerative stomatitis: ulzeröse Stomatitis *f*.
ulcer niche: Ulkusnische *f*.
ulceromembranous gingivitis: nekrotisierende ulzerierende Gingivitis *f*, ulzeromembranöse Gingivitis *f*.
ulceromembranous pharyngitis: ulzeromembranöse Pharyngitis *f*.
ulcer pain: Ulkusschmerz *m*.
ulna/*n*: Ellbogen *m*, Ulna *f*.
ulnar/*adj*: ulnar.
ulnar drift: ulnare Deviation *f*.
ulnar fracture: breaking of the ulnar bone, typically located within the olecranon. Ulnafraktur *f*.
ulnar head: Ulnaköpfchen *n*.
ulnar reflex: Ulnarreflex *m*.
ultimobranchial body: Ultimobranchialkörper *m*.
ultracentrifuge/*n*: Ultrazentrifuge *f*.
ultrafiltration/*n*: Ultrafiltration *f*.
ultrasonic cephalometry: Ultraschall-Schädelumfangsbestimmung *f*.
ultrasonic frequency: Ultraschallfrequenz *f*.
ultrasonographic examination: Ultraschalluntersuchung *f*.
ultrasonography/*n*: Ultraschallsonographie *f*.
ultrasound/*n*: Ultraschall *m*.
ultrastructure/*n*: Ultrastruktur *f*, Feinstruktur *f*.
ultraviolet/*n, adj*: 1. Ultraviolettstrahlung *f*; 2. ultraviolett, UV-.
ultraviolet filter: Ultraviolettfilter *m*.
ultraviolet ophthalmia: Conjunctivitis actinica *f*, aktinische Konjunktivitis *f*.
umbauzonen: Looser-Umbauzonen.
umbilical/*adj*: umbilikal, Nabel-.
umbilical cord: Nabelschnur *f*.
umbilical cyst: Nabelschnurzyste *f*.
umbilical diphtheria: Nabeldiphtherie w.
umbilical fistula: Nabelfistel *f*.
umbilical granuloma: formation of red-blue granulation tissue in the navel area of newborn infants, resulting from a disturbance in epithelialization. Nabelgranulom *n*.
umbilical hemorrhage: Nabelblutung *f*.
umbilical hernia: abdominal hernia with eventual protrusion of intestine into the umbilicus. Nabelbruch *m*, Nabelhernie *f*.
umbilicus/*n*: Nabel *m*, Umbilicus *m*.
umbrella/*n*: Schirm *m*.
unattached anxiety: frei flottierende Angst *f*.
unbalance/*n*: Gleichgewichtsstörung

f, Ungleichgewicht *n*.
unciform/*adj*: hakenförmig.
uncinariasis/*n*: Uncinariasis *f*, Hakenwurmkrankheit *f*.
uncinate seizure: Unzinatusanfall *m*.
unconditioned reflex: unkonditionierter Reflex *m*.
unconsciousness/*n*: state in which a person is unaware of the external environment and, depending on the degree of unconsciousness, shows limited or no reaction to external sensory stimuli. Bewusstlosigkeit *f*.
unconventional therapy: unkonventionelle Therapie *f*.
unction/*n*: Unktion *f*, Einreibemittel *n*.
uncture/*n*: Salbe *f*.
undecylenic acid: Undecylensäure *f*.
under/*adv*: unter, unterhalb.
underexposure/*n*: Unterbelichtung *f*.
underlying disease: Grundkrankheit w.
undermine/*vb*: unterhöhlen.
underreporting/*n*: Untererfassung *f*.
undertable image intensifier: Untertisch-Bildverstärker *m*.
underwater massage: Unterwassermassage *f*.
underweight/*n*: Untergewicht *n*.
undescended testis: Kryptorchismus *m*.
undifferentiated/*adj*: undifferenziert.
undifferentiated carcinoma: undifferenziertes Karzinom *n*.
undifferentiated cell: undifferenzierte Zelle *f*.
undress/*vb*: entkleiden, ausziehen.
undulant fever: fever which is characterized by longer periods of continuously elevated body temperature, alternating with fever-free periods. For example, undulant fever can be a sign of lymphogranulomatosis, or of brucellosis, an infectious disease and zoonosis caused by Brucella organism. undulierendes Fieber *n*.
undulatory/*adj*: wellenförmig.
unequal/*adj*: ungleich.
unequal pulse: ungleicher Puls *m*.
uneven/*adj*: ungerade, uneben.
unfavorable/*adj*: ungünstig.
unfertilized ovum: unbefruchtetes Ei *n*.
unfold/*vb*: entfalten.
unformed/*adj*: ungeformt, formlos.
unguent/*n*: Salbe *f*.
unguinal/*adj*: Nagel-.
unhealthy/*adj*: ungesund, gesundheitsschädigend.
unicameral cyst: einkammerige Zyste *f*.
unicellular/*adj*: einzellig.
unidimensionality/*n*: Eindimensionalität *f*.
unidirected/*adj*: unidirektional.
unidirectional block: unidirektionaler Block *m*.
unifocal/*adj*: unifokal.
uniform/*adj*: uniform, gleichförmig, gleichmäßig.
unilateral/*adj*: unilateral.
unilateral ataxia: Hemiataxie *f*, Halbseitenataxie *f*.
unilateral athetosis: Hemiathetose *f*.
unilateral chorea: Hemichorea *f*.
unilateral paralysis: Hemiplegie *f*, einseitige Lähmung *f*.
unilocular cyst: einkammerige Zyste *f*.
uninterrupted suture: fortlaufende Naht *f*.
union/*n*: Vereinigung *f*, Verbindung *f*.
uniovular twins: eineiige Zwillinge.
unipolar cell: unipolares Neuron *n*.
unipolar leads: unipolare Ableitungen.
unipolar psychosis: unipolare Depression *f*.
unisexual reproduction: eingeschlechtliche Fortpflanzung *f*, Parthenogenese *f*.
unit/*n*: Einheit *f*, Apparatekonfiguration *f*.
univalent vaccine: univalenter Impfstoff *m*.
universal donor: Universalspender *m*.
unknown/*adj*: unbekannt.
unknown primary neoplasm: unbekannter Primärtumor *m*.

unloading/*n*: Entladung *f*.
unmodified/*adj*: unverändert, nativ.
unmyelinated fiber: marklose Faser *f*.
unoprostone/*n*: Unoproston *n*.
unreactive/*adj*: nicht reaktiv, ohne Reaktion.
unreduced dislocation: nicht reponierte Luxation *f*.
unreliable/*adj*: unzuverlässig.
unresectable/*adj*: nicht resezierbar.
unresolved pneumonia: persistierende Pneumonie *f*.
unsaturated/*adj*: ungesättigt.
unsaturated fatty acid: ungesättigte Fettsäure *f*.
unstable/*adj*: instabil, labil.
unstable complex: unbeständiger Komplex *m*.
untreatable/*adj*: unbehandelbar, nicht behandelbar.
unwanted/*adj*: unerwünscht, ungewollt.
unwell/*adj*: unwohl, unpässlich.
unwholesome/*adj*: ungesund, gesundheitsschädigend.
upper arm: Oberarm *m*.
upper extremity: obere Extremität *f*.
upper lip: Oberlippe *f*.
upper lobe: Oberlappen *m*.
upper respiratory tract: obere Atemwege.
upper respiratory tract infection: Infektion der oberen Atemwege.
upper threshold: obere Reizschwelle *f*.
upright/*adj*: aufrecht.
upside-down stomach: upside-down stomach.
uptake/*n, vb*: 1. Aufnahme *f*; 2. aufnehmen.
urachal fistula: Urachusfistel *f*.
urachus/*n*: Urachus *m*, Harngang *m*.
uracil/*n*: Uracil *n*.
uracil mustard: Uracil-Lost *m*.
urapidil/*n*: Urapidil *n*.
urate/*n*: Urat *n*.
urate kidney: Uratnephropathie *f*.
uratic arthritis: Gicht *f*.
uratic conjunctivitis: Uratkonjunktivitis *f*.
urban plague: Rattenpest *f*.
urea/*n*: Urea, Harnstoff *m*.
urea cycle: Harnstoffzyklus *m*, Krebs-Henseleit-Zyklus *m*.
uremia/*n*: presence of substances which are usually excreted with the urine in the blood as a result of acute or chronic renal failure. Symptoms include anuria, vomiting, anorexia, pruritus, and various laboratory abnormalities like hyperkalemia and hyponatremia. Urämie *f*.
uremic acidosis: urämische Azidose *f*.
uremic coma: urämisches Koma *n*.
uremic convulsion: urämischer Krampf *m*.
uremic encephalopathy: urämische Enzephalopathie *f*.
uremic gastritis: urämische Gastritis *f*.
uremic polyneuropathy: urämische Polyneuropathie *f*.
ureter/*n*: Harnleiter *m*, Ureter *m*.
ureteral/*adj*: Harnleiter-, Ureter-.
ureteral calculus: Ureterstein *m*.
ureteral colic: Ureterkolik *f*.
ureteral fistula: Ureterfistel *f*.
ureteral obstruction: Ureterverschluss *m*.
ureteral stenosis: Ureterstenose *f*.
ureteral stone: Ureterstein *m*.
ureterectomy/*n*: Ureterektomie *f*.
ureteritis/*n*: Ureteritis *f*.
ureterocele/*n*: Ureterozele *f*.
ureterography/*n*: Ureterographie *f*.
ureterolith/*n*: a stone or calculus in the ureter. Symptoms may include pain, referring into the lower abdominal area, hematuria, urinary obstruction, and anuria. Ureterstein *m*.
ureterolithotomy/*n*: Ureterolithotomie *f*.
ureterostenosis/*n*: Ureterstenose *f*.
ureterovesical obstruction: ureterovesikale Obstruktion *f*.
urethane/*n*: Urethan *n*.
urethra/*n*: Urethra *f*, Harnröhre *f*.
urethral/*adj*: urethral, Urethra-, Harnröhren-.
urethral discharge: Harnröhrenausfluss *m*.
urethral fever: Urethralfieber *n*.
urethral glands: Urethraldrüsen *f*.

urethral obstruction: Harnröhrenobstruktion *f*.
urethral stricture: decrease in the urethral caliber, as a consequence of hyperplastic inflammation or scar formation due to infection or traumatic lesion. Strictures may result in stenosis of the urethra with urinary obstruction. Harnröhrenstriktur *f*.
urethritis/*n*: inflammation of the urethra. Symptoms include pain, dysuria, and urethral discharge. Chronic urethritis may result in stenosis of the urethra with urinary obstruction. Urethritis *f*.
urethrocystocele/*n*: Urethrozystozele *f*.
urethrography/*n*: Urethrographie *f*.
urethroplasty/*n*: Urethroplastik *f*.
urethroscopy/*n*: Urethroskopie *f*.
urethrostenosis/*n*: Harnröhrenstenose *f*.
urethrotomy/*n*: Urethrotomie *f*.
urethrovaginal/*adj*: urethrovaginal.
urge incontinence: Urge-Inkontinenz *f*, Dranginkontinenz *f*.
uric acid: Harnsäure *f*.
uridylic acid: Uridylsäure *f*.
urinal/*n, adj*: 1. Urinflasche *f*, Harnbehälter *m*; 2. urinal.
urinalysis/*n*: Urinstatus *m*, Urinuntersuchung *f*.
urinary/*adj*: Harn-, Urin-.
urinary abscess: Urinphlegmone *f*.
urinary albumin excretion: Albuminurie *f*.
urinary bladder: Harnblase *f*.
urinary calculus: Harnstein *m*, Harnkonkrement *n*.
urinary cast: Harnzylinder *m*.
urinary concentration: Urinkonzentration *f*.
urinary cyst: Urinzyste *f*.
urinary fistula: Urinfistel *f*.
urinary incontinence: inability to control urination, as urge incontinence, overflow incontinence, stress incontinence, or paralytic incontinence. Harninkontinenz *f*.
urinary nitrogen: Harnstickstoff *m*.
urinary obstruction: Harnabflussbehinderung *f*.
urinary phlegmon: Urinphlegmone *f*.
urinary reflex: Miktionsreflex *m*.
urinary retention: Harnretention *f*, Harnverhaltung *f*.
urinary sediment: Harnsediment *n*.
urinary stone: Urolith *m*, Harnstein *m*.
urinary stress incontinence: Stressinkontinenz *f*.
urinary stuttering: Harnstottern *n*.
urinary tract: Harntrakt *m*.
urinary tract infection: infection of the urinary tract, typically caused by bacteria, which may affect the urethra, the bladder, the ureters, and the kidneys. Initial symptoms include urination disorders like dysuria or pollakiuria. Harnweginfektion *f*.
urination/*n*: Miktion *f*, Wasserlassen *n*.
urine/*n*: Urin *m*, Harn *m*.
uriniferous/*adj*: harnleitend.
urinometry/*n*: Urometrie *f*.
urobenzoic acid: Hippursäure *f*.
urobilin/*n*: Urobilin *n*.
urobilinogen/*n*: Urobilinogen *n*.
urocanic acid: Urokaninsäure *f*.
urocele/*n*: Urozele *f*.
urochrome/*n*: Urochrom *n*.
uroflowmetry/*n*: Uroflowmetrie *f*.
urogenital/*adj*: urogenital.
urogenital system: Urogenitaltrakt *m*.
urogenital tuberculosis: Urogenitaltuberkulose *f*.
urography/*n*: Urographie *f*.
urokinase/*n*: Urokinase *f*.
urolithiasis/*n*: a condition which is characterized by the formation of urinary calculus in the kidney or in the ureter, or by the presence of a stone in the urinary tract. Urolithiasis *f*.
urologic stent: urologischer Stent *m*.
urology/*n*: Urologie *f*.
uronic acid: Uronsäure *f*.
ursodeoxycholic acid: Ursodeoxycholsäure *f*.
urticaria/*n*: skin alteration characterized by papular eruptions, pruritus,

and burning sensations. Urticaria can be a symptom of an allergic reaction, exposure to a physical substance, or idiopathic without detectable cause. Urtikaria *f*, Nesselsucht *f*.
use/*n, vb*: 1. Anwendung *f*, Verwendung *f*; 2. anwenden, benutzen.
user/*n*: Benutzer.
usual/*adj*: üblich, gewöhnlich.
uterine/*adj*: uterin.
uterine amenorrhea: uterine Amenorrhö *f*.
uterine aplasia: Uterusaplasie *f*.
uterine atrophy: Uterusatrophie *f*.
uterine bleeding: Uterusblutung *f*.
uterine cavity: Gebärmutterhöhle *f*.
uterine displacement: Gebärmutterverlagerung *f*.
uterine forceps: Uteruszange *f*.
uterine hemorrhage: Uterusblutung *f*.
uterine insufficiency: Wehenschwäche *f*.
uterine perforation: Uterusperforation *f*.
uterine probe: Uterussonde *f*.
uterine prolapse: abnormal descent of the uterus within the vaginal orifice or below, occurring as a result from muscular weakness of the pelvic floor or traumatic injury. Gebärmuttervorfall *m*.
uterine rupture: Uterusruptur *f*.
uterine sound: Uterussonde *f*.
uterine stimulant: Wehenmittel *n*.
uterine tube: Tuba uterina *f*, Eileiter *m*.
uteropexy/*n*: Hysteropexie *f*.
uteroplacental apoplexy: uteroplazentare Apoplexie *f*, Couvelaire-Syndrom *n*.
uterovesical fistula: Uterovesikalfistel *f*.
uterus/*n*: Uterus *m*, Gebärmutter *f*.
utilization of oxygen: Sauerstoffutilisation *f*.
utricle/*n*: Utriculus *m*.
uvea/*n*: Uvea *f*.
uveitis/*n*: inflammation of the tissue layer of the eye, the uvea, as anterior uveitis involving the iris and ciliary body, as posterior uveitis involving the posterior parts of the eye with choroiditis and chorioretinitis. Uveitis *f*.
uveoparotid fever: Heerfordt-Syndrom *n*.
UV lamp: UV-Lampe *f*.
UV radiation: UV-Strahlung *f*.
uvula/*n*: Zäpfchen *n*.
uvulectomy/*n*: Uvulektomie *f*, Staphylektomie *f*.
uvulotomy/*n*: Staphylotomie *f*.
U wave: U-Welle *f*.
uzarin/*n*: Uzarin *n*.

V

V <*abbr*> **1. vanadium; 2. vision**: 1. Vanadium *n*, V; 2. Sehvermögen *n*.
vacancy/*n*: Vakanz *f*, vakante Bindungsstelle *f*.
vacant/*adj*: leer, nicht besetzt.
vaccinal fever: Impffieber *n*.
vaccinate/*vb*: impfen.
vaccination/*n*: Vakzination *f*, Impfung *f*.
vaccination certificate: Impfnachweis *m*.
vaccine/*n*: Impfstoff *m*, Vakzine *f*.
vaccinia/*n*: Vaccinia *f*, Windpocken *f*.
vacuolar/*adj*: vakuolär.
vacuolar degeneration: vakuoläre Degeneration *f*.
vacuolar myelopathy: vakuoläre Myelopathie *f*.
vacuolated cell: vakuolisierte Zelle *f*.
vacuole/*n*: Vakuole *f*.
vacuum/*n*: Vakuum *n*.
vagabond's disease: Vagabundenhaut *f*, Vagantenhaut *f*.
vagal/*adj*: vagal.
vagal arrhythmia: Vagusarrhythmie *f*.
vagal crisis: Vaguskrise *f*.
vagal escape: vagaler Ersatzrhythmus *m*.
vagal paralysis: Vaguslähmung *f*.
vagal pulse: Vaguspuls *m*.
vagina/*n*: Scheide *f*, Vagina *f*.
vaginal/*adj*: vaginal.
vaginal administration: intravaginale Applikation *f*.
vaginal aplasia: Vaginalaplasie *f*.
vaginal atresia: Vaginalatresie *f*.
vaginal ballottement: direktes Ballottement *n*.
vaginal bleeding: vaginale Blutung *f*, Scheidenblutung *f*.
vaginal candidiasis: Candida-Vaginitis *f*.
vaginal carcinoma: a malignant neoplasm of the vagina. Symptoms include bloody discharge or vaginal bleeding, and enlargement of inguinal lymph nodes. Vaginalkarzinom *n*.
vaginal cyst: Vaginalzyste *f*.
vaginal cytology: Vaginalzytologie *f*, Kolpozytologie *f*.
vaginal delivery: natürliche Entbindung *f*, vaginale Geburt *f*.
vaginal discharge: abnormal, viscid excretion from the vagina, typically resulting from mechanical or chemical irritation of the vaginal mucosa, or as a bodily symptom of psychic origin. Ausfluss *m*, Fluor vaginalis *m*.
vaginal douche: Scheidenspülung *f*.
vaginal fluid: Scheidenflüssigkeit *f*.
vaginal hemorrhage: Scheidenblutung *f*, vaginale Blutung *f*.
vaginal mycosis: Vaginalmykose *f*.
vaginal orifice: Scheideneingang *m*
vaginal pessary: Scheidenpessar *n*.
vaginal prolapse: Scheidenvorfall *m*, Vaginalprolaps *m*.
vaginal smear: Scheidenabstrich *m*.
vaginal spasm: Scheidenkrampf *m*, Vaginismus *m*.
vaginal speculum: Scheidenspekulum *n*.
vaginal stenosis: Vaginalstenose *f*.
vaginal tampon: Scheidentampon *m*.
vaginal vault: Scheidengewölbe *n*.
vaginal wall: Scheidenwand *f*.
vaginal wash: Scheidenspülung *f*.
vaginism/*n*: Vaginismus *m*, Scheidenkrampf *m*.
vaginitis/*n*: inflammation of the vagina, typically resulting from bacterial or fungal infection. Symptoms inclu-

de pain and purulent vaginal discharge. Vaginitis *f*, Kolpitis *f*, Scheidenentzündung *f*.
vaginocele/*n*: Vaginozele *f*, Kolpozele *f*.
vaginography/*n*: Vaginographie *f*.
vaginoplasty/*n*: Vaginaplastik *f*, Scheidenplastik *f*.
vagoaccessory hypoglossal paralysis: paramedianes Oblongatasyndrom *n*, Jackson-Syndrom *n*.
vagolysis/*n*: Vagolyse *f*.
vagotomy/*n*: Vagotomie *f*.
vagovagal/*adj*: vagovagal.
vagovagal reflex: Vagovagalreflex *m*.
vagueness/*n*: Unschärfe *f*, Verschwommenheit *f*.
vagus nerve/*n*: Vagus *m*, Nervus vagus *m*.
valaciclovir/*n*: Valaciclovir *n*.
valdecoxib/*n*: Valdecoxib *n*.
valerianic acid: Valeriansäure *f*.
valerian tincture: Baldriantinktur *f*.
valganciclovir/*n*: Valganciclovir *n*.
valgus position: Valgusstellung *f*.
validation/*n*: Validierung *f*.
valine/*n*: Valin *n*.
valinomycin/*n*: Valinomycin *n*.
valnemulin/*n*: Valnemulin *n*.
valproate/*n*: Valproat *n*.
valproic acid: Valproinsäure *f*.
Valsalva maneuver: Valsalva-Versuch *m*.
valsartan/*n*: Valsartan *n*.
value/*n*: Wert *m*.
valve/*n*: Klappe *f*, Valva *f*.
valve dehiscence: Klappendehiszenz *f*.
valve prolapse: Herzklappenprolaps *m*.
valvula/*n*: kleine Klappe *f*, Valvula *f*.
valvular/*adj*: valvulär.
valvular calcification: Herzklappenverkalkung *f*.
valvular defect: Herzklappenfehler *m*.
valvular insufficiency: dysfunction and improper closure of a heart valve which admits a backflow of blood. Herzklappeninsuffizienz *f*.
valvular pneumothorax: Ventilpneumothorax *m*.
valvular stenosis: Klappenstenose *f*, Ventilstenose *f*.
valvulotomy/*n*: Valvulotomie *f*.
vanadic acid: Vanadinsäure *f*.
vancomycin/*n*: Vancomycin *n*.
vanillic acid: Vanillinsäure *f*.
vanillylmandelic acid: Vanillinmandelsäure *f*.
vanish/*vb*: schwinden.
vanishing lung: progressive Lungendystrophie *f*.
vaporization/*n*: Verdampfung *f*, Vaporisation *f*.
vardenafil/*n*: Vardenafil *n*.
varenicline/*n*: Vareniclin *n*.
variability/*n*: Variabilität *f*.
variable/*n, adj*: 1. Variable *f*; 2. variabel, veränderlich.
variance analysis: Varianzanalyse *f*.
variant/*n*: Variante *f*.
variation/*n*: Variation *f*, Abwandlung *f*, Veränderung *f*.
variceal hemorrhage: Varizenblutung *f*.
varicella: highly contagious infectious disease caused by varicella-zoster virus. Symptoms include vesicular skin lesions with intensive pruritus, and mild constitutional symptoms. In adults, pneumonia and encephalitis can occur as complications. Varizellen, Windpocken.
varicella-zoster virus: Varicella-Zoster-Virus *n*, VZV.
varicocele/*n*: varicose veins of the pampiniform plexus, causing a soft tumefaction in the scrotal region and sometimes pain. Varikozele *f*.
varicose/*adj*: varikös.
varicose bronchiectasis: sackförmige Bronchiektasie *f*.
varicose eczema: Stauungsekzem *n*.
varicose ophthalmia: variköse Ophthalmie *f*.
varicose vein: variköse Vene *f*, Varize *f*.
varicosis/*n*: a condition which is characterized by swollen veins, resulting from improper vein valve function, or secondary to obstruction of major veins and collateral circulation. Varikose *f*.

variegate porphyria: Porphyria variegata *f*.
variety/*n*: Varietät *f*, Verschiedenheit *f*.
variola/*n*: a highly infectious disease caused by variola virus, an orthopoxvirus. Symptoms include high fever, pain, vomiting, and an eruption of red spots which transform into blisters, filled with pus. Variola *f*, Pocken *f*.
variola virus: Variolavirus *n*.
varix/*n*: Varize *f*.
varus position: Varusstellung *f*.
vary/*vb*: variieren, verändern.
vas/*n*: Gefäß *n*.
vascular/*adj*: vaskulär.
vascular band: Gefäßband *n*.
vascular bed: Gefäßbett *n*.
vascular clamp: Gefäßklemme *f*.
vascular dementia: vaskuläre Demenz *f*.
vascular filling: Gefäßfüllung *f*.
vascular headache: vaskulär bedingter Kopfschmerz *m*.
vascular hemophilia: vaskuläre Hämophilie *f*, Angiohämophilie *f*.
vascular hypertension: vaskulärer Hochdruck *m*.
vascularization/*n*: Vaskularisierung *f*.
vascular lesion: Gefäßläsion *f*.
vascular loop: Gefäßschleife *f*.
vascular obliteration: Gefäßverödung *f*.
vascular occlusion: Gefäßverschluss *m*.
vascular plexus: Gefäßgeflecht *n*.
vascular resection: Gefäßresektion *f*.
vascular resistance: Gefäßwiderstand *m*.
vascular sclerosis: Gefäßsklerose *f*.
vascular spasm: Vasospasmus *m*, Angiospasmus *m*.
vascular surgery: Gefäßchirurgie *f*.
vascular system: Kreislaufsystem *n*.
vascular transplantation: Gefäßtransplantation *f*.
vasculitis/*n*: Vaskulitis *f*, Angiitis *f*.
vasectomy/*n*: Vasektomie *f*.
vaseline/*n*: Vaselin *n*.
vasoactive/*adj*: vasoaktiv.
vasoactive amine: vasoaktives Amin *n*.
vasoactive intestinal peptide: vasoaktives intestinales Peptid *n*, VIP.
vasoconstriction/*n*: Vasokonstriktion *f*.
vasodilatation/*n*: Vasodilatation *f*.
vasomotor/*n, adj*: 1. Vasomotor *m*; 2. vasomotorisch.
vasomotor headache: Vasomotorenkopfschmerz *m*.
vasomotor paralysis: Vasomotorenlähmung *f*.
vasomotor rhinitis: Rhinitis vasomotorica *f*.
vasomotor spasm: Vasomotorenspasmus *m*.
vasopressin/*n*: Vasopressin *n*, antidiuretisches Hormon *n*, ADH.
vasopressor/*n*: Vasopressor *m*, vasopressorische Substanz *f*.
vasospasm/*n*: sudden decrease in the caliber of a blood vessel. Vasospasmus *m*, Angiospasmus *m*.
vasotomy/*n*: Vasotomie *f*.
vasotonic/*adj*: vasotonisch.
vasovagal/*adj*: vasovagal.
vasovagal syncope: vasovagale Synkope *f*, Vasovagalsyndrom *n*.
vault/*n*: Gewölbe *n*, Kuppel *f*.
VDRL test <*abbr*> **venereal disease research laboratory test**: VDRL Test *m*.
vector/*n*: Vektor *m*, Träger *m*.
vectorial/*adj*: vektoriell.
vecuronium bromide: Vecuroniumbromid *n*.
vedaprofen/*n*: Vedaprofen *n*.
vegetable oil: Pflanzenöl *n*.
vegetation/*n*: Vegetation *f*.
vegetative/*adj*: vegetativ, ungeschlechtlich.
vegetative dysfunction: vegetative Dysfunktion *f*.
vegetative nervous system: vegetatives Nervensystem *n*.
vegetative reproduction: vegetative Reproduktion *f*.
vegetative stage: vegetatives Stadium *n*.
vehicle/*n*: Vehikel *n*, Träger *m*.
veil/*n*: Schleier *m*, Eihaut *f*.

vein/*n*: Vene *f*, Vena *f*.
vein thrombosis: Venenthrombose *f*.
velocity of nerve conduction: Nervenleitungsgeschwindigkeit *f*.
velopharyngeal insufficiency: Gaumensegelinsuffizienz *f*.
vena cava syndrome: Vena-cava-Syndrom *n*, Kavasyndrom *n*.
venereal/*adj*: venerisch.
venereal arthritis: Reiter-Arthritis *f*.
venereal disease: any infectious disease that is transmitted from person to person predominantly or exclusively through sexual contacts. Sexually transmitted diseases include for example syphilis, gonorrhea, soft chancre, HIV infection, chlamydial infection, and Mycoplasma infection. Geschlechtskrankheit *f*.
venereal granuloma: Granuloma inguinale *n*.
venereal sore: Genitalulkus *n*.
venerology/*n*: Venerologie *f*.
Venezuelan encephalitis: Encephalomyelitis equina *f*, Pferdeenzephalitis *f*, venezolanische Enzephalitis *f*.
venlafaxine/*n*: Venlafaxin *n*.
venoarterial/*adj*: arteriovenös.
venography/*n*: Venographie *f*.
venom/*n*: tierisches Gift *n*.
veno-occlusive disease: venöse Verschlusskrankheit *f*.
venous/*adj*: venös.
venous aneurysm: venöses Aneurysma *n*.
venous angle: Angulus venosus *m*, Venenwinkel *m*.
venous blood: venöses Blut *n*.
venous bypass: Venenbypass *m*.
venous congestion: venöse Stauung *f*.
venous disorder: Venenerkrankung *f*.
venous embolism: venöse Embolie *f*.
venous gangrene: venöse Gangrän *f*.
venous hemorrhage: venöse Blutung *f*.
venous hypertension: venöser Hochdruck *m*.
venous insufficiency: Veneninsuffizienz *f*.
venous pressure: venöser Blutdruck *m*.
venous pulse: Venenpuls *m*.
venous sclerosis: Phlebosklerose *f*.
venous stasis: Venostase *f*.
venous valve: Venenklappe *f*.
ventilation/*n*: Ventilation *f*, Lüftung *f*, Atmung *f*.
ventilator/*n*: Respirator *m*, Beatmungsgerät *n*.
ventilatory frequency: Atemfrequenz *f*.
ventral/*adj*: ventral.
ventral hernia: Bauchwandhernie *f*, Laparozele *f*.
ventral root: Vorderwurzel *f*.
ventricle/*n*: Ventrikel *m*, Kammer *f*.
ventricle filling: Ventrikelfüllung *f*.
ventricular/*adj*: ventrikulär.
ventricular aneurysm: Ventrikelaneurysma *n*, Kammeraneurysma *n*.
ventricular arrhythmia: cardiac arrhythmia originating in the ventricles. ventrikuläre Arrhythmie *f*.
ventricular assist device: Herzkammerschrittmacher *m*.
ventricular automatism: Kammerautomatie *f*.
ventricular beat: Kammerextrasystole *f*.
ventricular bigeminy: Kammerbigeminie *f*.
ventricular block: Kammerblock *m*.
ventricular complex: Kammerkomplex *m*.
ventricular conduction: Kammerleitung *f*.
ventricular escape: Kammerersatzrhythmus *m*.
ventricular fibrillation: Kammerflimmern *n*.
ventricular fluid: Ventrikelflüssigkeit *f*.
ventricular flutter: Kammerflattern *n*.
ventricular hypotension: erniedrigter Ventrikeldruck *m*.
ventricular outflow obstruction: Ventrikelausflussbehinderung *f*.
ventricular pacemaker: Kammerschrittmacher *m*.
ventricular pacing: kammergesteuerte Herzschrittmacherfunktion *f*, Kammerstimulation *f*.
ventricular puncture: Ventrikel-

punktion *f*.
ventricular rate: Kammerfrequenz *f*.
ventricular rhythm: Kammerrhythmus *m*.
ventricular septal defect: Ventrikelseptumdefekt *m*, VSD.
ventricular septal disease: Roger-Syndrom *n*.
ventricular standstill: Kammerasystolie *f*, ventrikulärer Herzstillstand *m*.
ventricular systole: Kammersystole *f*.
ventricular tachycardia: cardiac arrhythmia with abnormally rapid ventricular rhythm, generated in the ventricles. Kammertachykardie *f*.
ventricular volume: Ventrikelvolumen *n*.
ventriculoatrial shunt: ventrikuloatrialer Shunt *m*.
ventriculocisternal anastomosis: Ventrikulozisternostomie *f*.
ventriculography/*n*: Ventrikulographie *f*.
ventriculojugular shunt: ventrikulojugulärer Shunt *m*.
ventriculoperitoneal shunt: ventrikuloperitonealer Shunt *m*.
ventriculopuncture/*n*: Ventrikelpunktion *f*.
venule/*n*: Venole *f*.
verapamil/*n*: Verapamil *n*.
veratrum/*n*: Veratrum *n*, Nieswurz *f*, weißer Germer *m*.
verbal ability: Sprachvermögen *n*.
verbal agraphia: verbale Agraphie *f*.
verbal alexia: verbale Alexie *f*, Wortblindheit *f*.
verification/*n*: Verifikation *f*, Bestätigung *f*.
vermicular colic: Blinddarmkolik *f*.
vermiform/*adj*: wurmförmig.
vermifuge/*n*: Vermifugum *n*, Vermizid *n*, Anthelminthikum *n*.
vermin/*n*: Ungeziefer *n*, Schädling *m*.
vernal conjunctivitis: Conjunctivitis vernalis *f*, Frühjahrskonjunktivitis *f*.
verruca/*n*: a circumscribed growth on the skin, sometimes caused by human papillomavirus. Warze *f*, Verruca *f*.
verrucous carcinoma: verruköses Plattenepithelkarzinom *n*.
verrucous carditis: verruköse Endokarditis *f*.
verrucous eczema: Dermatitis verrucosa *f*, Chromomykose *f*.
verrucous endocarditis: verruköse Endokarditis *f*.
verrucous vegetation: verruköse Vegetation *f*.
version/*n*: Wendung *f*.
versive epilepsy: Versivanfall *m*, Adversivkrämpfe.
vertebra/*n*: Wirbel *m*.
vertebral/*adj*: vertebral.
vertebral angiography: Vertebralarterienangiographie *f*.
vertebral-basilar circulation: vertebrobasiliärer Kreislauf *m*.
vertebral block: Wirbelblock *m*.
vertebral-cervical strain: posttraumatisches Halswirbelsäulensyndrom *n*.
vertebral column: Wirbelsäule *f*.
vertebral dislocation: Wirbelluxation *f*.
vertebral fracture: breaking of a vertebra of the spinal column, resulting from direct trauma, hyperextension, hyperflexion, or torsion of the spinal column. Wirbelfraktur *f*.
vertebral fusion: Wirbelfusion *f*, Blockwirbel *m*.
vertebral insufficiency: Arteria-vertebralis-Insuffizienz *f*.
vertebral process: Wirbelfortsatz *m*.
vertebrobasilar/*adj*: vertebrobasilär.
verteporfin/*n*: Verteporfin *n*.
vertex/*n*: Scheitel *m*.
vertex presentation: in obstetrics, the position of the fetus in which the vertex of the skull appears first in the uterine cervix. Scheitellage *f*.
vertical/*adj*: vertikal.
vertical heart: Steiltyp *m*.
vertical plane: Vertikalebene *f*.
vertical position: senkrechte Lage *f*.
vertical transmission: vertikale Übertragung *f*.
vertigo/*n*: a dizziness and the illusion that one's own body or the environment is whirling, resulting from dis-

eases of the inner ear or the vestibular centers with differing perceptions of vestibular, proprioceptive, and optic sensations. Schwindel *m*, Vertigo *f*.

very-low-density lipoprotein: Lipoprotein sehr niedriger Dichte *n*.

vesica/*n*: Blase *f*, Harnblase *f*.

vesical/*adj*: vesikal.

vesical calculus: Blasenstein *m*.

vesical diverticulum: Blasendivertikel *n*.

vesical ectopia: Blasenektopie *f*.

vesical fistula: Blasenfistel *f*.

vesical outlet: Blasenausgang *m*.

vesical reflex: Blasenreflex *m*.

vesical schistosomiasis: Blasenbilharziose *f*.

vesicant/*n, adj*: 1. Epispastikum *n*, blaseninduzierende Substanz *f*; 2. blasenziehend.

vesicle/*n*: Bläschen *n*, Vesikel *f*.

vesicoabdominal fistula: Vesikoabdominalfistel *f*.

vesicocele/*n*: Vesikozele *f*.

vesicointestinal fistula: vesikointestinale Fistel *f*.

vesicorectal fistula: Rektovesikalfistel *f*.

vesicospinal center: Blasenzentrum *n*.

vesicoureteral reflux: vesikoureteraler Reflux *m*.

vesicovaginal/*adj*: vesikovaginal.

vesicovaginal fistula: Vesikovaginalfistel *f*.

vesicular/*adj*: vesikular, blasenförmig.

vesicular breathing: Vesikuläratmung *f*.

vesicular eruption: bläschenförmiger Ausschlag *m*.

vesicular rale: Vesikuläratmen *n*.

vesicular rash: bläschenförmiger Ausschlag *m*.

vesicular sound: vesikuläres Atemgeräusch *n*.

vesicular stomatitis: inflammation of the mouth and the oral mucosa, occurring from viral infection, for example herpes virus, characterized by the formation of yellowish vesicles that rupture and produce painful ulcers. vesikuläre Stomatitis *f*.

vesiculitis/*n*: Vesikulitis *f*.

vessel/*n*: Gefäß *n*.

vessel wall: Gefäßwand *f*.

vestibular/*adj*: vestibulär.

vestibular nystagmus: Vestibularnystagmus *m*.

vestibular organ: statisches Organ *n*, Vestibularapparat *m*.

vestibular paralysis: Vestibularislähmung *f*.

vestibular vertigo: Vestibularisschwindel *m*.

vestibule/*n*: Vorhof *m*.

vestigial/*adj*: rudimentär.

veterinary medicine: Veterinärmedizin *f*.

viable/*adj*: lebendig, lebensfähig, vermehrungsfähig.

vial/*n*: Phiole *f*, Medizinalfläschchen *n*.

vibration/*n*: Vibration *f*.

vibratory sensibility: Vibrationsempfinden *n*.

vicarious/*adj*: vikariierend.

vicarious hemoptysis: vikariierende Hämoptyse *f*.

vicarious menstruation: vikariierende Menstruation *f*.

vicriviroc/*n*: Vicriviroc *n*.

vidarabine/*n*: Vidarabin *n*.

view/*n, vb*: 1. Sicht *f*, Aufnahme *f*; 2. betrachten, sichten.

vigabatrin/*n*: Vigabatrin *n*.

vigil ambulatory automatism: Automatismus ambulatorius vigilis *m*.

vigilance/*n*: Vigilanz *f*.

vigil coma: Coma vigile *n*, Wachkoma *n*.

villous/*adj*: villös, zottig.

villous adenoma: Zottenadenom *n*.

villous arthritis: villöse Synovitis *f*.

villous atrophy: Zottenatrophie *f*.

villous carcinoma: Zottenkrebs *m*.

villous placenta: Zottenplazenta *f*.

villus/*n*: Zotte *f*, Villus *m*.

viloxazine/*n*: Viloxazin *n*.

vinblastine/*n*: Vinblastin *n*.

vincaine/*n*: Vincain *n*.

vincamine/*n*: Vincamin *n*.

vincristine/*n*: Vincristin *n*.

vindesine/*n*: Vindesin *n*.
vinorelbine/*n*: Vinorelbin *n*.
vinpocetine/*n*: Vinpocetin *n*.
violence/*n*: Gewalt *f*, Gewalteinwirkung *f*.
violent death: gewaltsamer Tod *m*.
viomycin/*n*: Viomycin *n*.
viquidil/*n*: Viquidil *n*.
viral/*adj*: viral.
viral disease: Viruserkrankung *f*.
viral encephalitis: Virusenzephalitis *f*.
viral enteritis: Virusenteritis *f*.
viral hepatitis: acute or chronic inflammation of the liver, due to a viral infection. Major forms of viral hepatitis include hepatitis A, B and C. Symptoms include loss of appetite, liver enlargement, nausea, and eventually jaundice; in chronic hepatitis, progressive liver fibrosis and cirrhosis with consecutive liver failure may develop. Virushepatitis *f*.
viral infection: Virusinfektion *f*.
viral load: Viruslast *f*.
viral particle: Viruspartikel *n*, Virion *n*.
viral strain: Virusstamm *m*.
virginiamycin/*n*: Virginiamycin *n*.
virilization/*n*: Virilisierung *f*, Vermännlichung *f*.
virilizing adenoma: virilisierendes Adenom *n*.
virion/*n*: Virion *n*, Viruspartikel *n*.
virology/*n*: Virologie *f*.
virostatic/*n, adj*: 1. Virostatikum *n*; 2. virostatisch.
virucidal/*adj*: viruzid.
virulence/*n*: Virulenz *f*.
virulent/*adj*: virulent.
virulent bacteriophage: virulenter Phage *m*.
virulent bubo: schankröser Bubo *m*, virulenter Bubo *m*.
virus/*n*: Virus *n*.
visceral/*adj*: viszeral.
visceral arch: Viszeralbogen *m*, Kiemenbogen *m*.
visceral ectopia: Eingeweideekstrophie *f*.
visceral fissure: Kiemenspalte *f*.
visceral inversion: Situs inversus *m*.
visceral leishmaniasis: an infectious disease caused by the protozoon Leishmania donovani which occurs in tropical regions. Symptoms include fever, chills, anemia, dropsy, and enlargement of liver and spleen. viszerale Leishmaniase, Kala-Azar *f*.
visceral pain: Eingeweideschmerz *m*.
visceral sensation: Viszerosensibilität *f*.
visceral wall: Viszeropleura *f*, viszerales Mesoderm *n*.
visceroceptor/*n*: Viszerozeptor *m*.
viscometer/*n*: Viskosimeter *n*.
viscosity/*n*: Viskosität *f*.
viscous/*adj*: viskös.
visible/*adj*: sichtbar.
vision/*n*: Vision *f*, Sehvermögen *n*.
vision disorder: Sehstörung *f*.
vision test: Sehtest *m*.
visit/*n, vb*: 1. Visite *f*, Arztbesuch *m*; 2. besuchen, visitieren.
visiting time: Besuchszeit *f*.
visual/*adj*: visuell, sichtbar.
visual acuity: Sehschärfe *f*.
visual agnosia: optische Agnosie *f*, Seelenblindheit *f*.
visual angle: Sehwinkel *m*, Gesichtswinkel *m*.
visual apraxia: konstruktive Apraxie *f*.
visual area: Sehrinde *f*.
visual cell: Sehzelle *f*.
visual center: Sehzentrum *n*.
visual cone: Netzhautzapfen *m*.
visual cortex: Sehrinde *f*.
visual disorder: Sehstörung *f*.
visual epilepsy: visuelle Epilepsie *f*.
visual evoked potential: visuell evoziertes Potential *n*, VEP.
visual field: Sehfeld *n*, Gesichtsfeld *n*.
visual image: visuelles Bild *n*.
visual loss: Visusverlust *m*.
visual perception: optische Wahrnehmung *f*.
visual pigment: Sehpigment *n*.
visual power: Sehleistung *f*.
visual-spatial agnosia: räumliche Agnosie *f*.
visual yellow: Sehgelb *n*, Xanthopsin *n*.

visus/*n*: Visus *m*, Sehschärfe *f*.
vital/*adj*: vital, lebend, lebenswichtig.
vital capacity: Vitalkapazität *f*, VK.
vital energy: Lebenskraft *f*.
vital function: lebenswichtige Funktion *f*.
vital indication: Vitalindikation *f*.
vitality/*n*: Vitalität *f*.
vital reaction: Vitalreaktion *f*.
vital signs: Lebenszeichen.
vitamin/*n*: Vitamin *n*.
vitamin deficiency: lack of one or more essential vitamins, due to malnutrition, increased need of vitamins, or malabsorption, and resulting in severe, sometimes life-threatening conditions such as scurvy, or rickets. Vitaminmangel *m*, Hypovitaminose *f*.
vitamin D-resistant rickets: Vitamin-D-resistente Rachitis *f*.
vitamin enrichment: Vitaminanreicherung *f*.
vitamin precursor: Provitamin *n*.
vitellin/*n*: Vitellin *n*.
vitelline fistula: Dottersackfistel *f*.
vitelline membrane: Dottersackmembran *f*.
vitreous/*adj*: gläsern, vitreus.
vitreous body: Glaskörper *m*.
vitreous hemorrhage: Glaskörperhämorrhagie *f*.
vitreous traction: Glaskörpertraktion *f*.
vitriol/*n*: Vitriol *n*.
viviparity/*n*: Viviparie *f*.
vivisection/*n*: Vivisektion *f*.
VLDL <*abbr*> **very-low-density lipoprotein**: Lipoprotein sehr niedriger Dichte *n*, VLDL.
vocabulary test: Worttest *m*.
vocal/*adj*: vokal.
vocal cord: Stimmband *n*.
vocal fremitus: Stimmfremitus *m*.
vocal nodule: small fibroma or retention cysts occurring on the vocal cord, resulting from excessive vocal strain. Sängerknötchen *n*.
vocal resonance: Stimmschall *m*.
vocational/*adj*: beruflich.
vocational rehabilitation: berufliche Rehabilitation *f*.
voice/*n*: Stimme *f*.
voice training: Stimmtraining *n*.
void/*n, vb*: 1. Hohlraum *m*, Lücke *f*; 2. leeren.
voiding/*n*: Entleerung *f*.
voiding cystography: Miktionszystographie *f*.
voiding cysturethrogram: Miktionszysturethrogramm *n*.
vol <*abbr*> **volume**/*n*: Volumen *n*.
volar flexion: Volarflexion *f*.
volatile/*adj*: ätherisch, gasförmig, volatil.
volition/*n*: Wollen *n*.
voltage/*n*: Spannung *f*.
volume/*n*: Volumen *n*.
volume replacement: Volumenersatz *m*.
volumetric solution: Standardlösung *f*.
voluntary movement: Willkürbewegung *f*.
volunteer/*n*: Freiwilliger *m*.
volvulus/*n*: twisting of an internal organ, most frequently observed in the bowel, causing obstruction and ileus. Volvulus *m*.
vomeral organ: Jacobson-Organ *n*.
vomit/*n, vb*: 1. Vomitus *m*; 2. erbrechen.
vomiting/*n*: casting-up of the stomach or intestine content through the mouth. Causes include bodily disorders like inflammations of the gastrointestinal tract, central nervous diseases, or metabolic disorders. Vomiting can be of psychic origin, or may be caused by external factors, for example intoxication, drug-induced vomiting. Erbrechen *n*, Emesis *f*.
vomiting of pregnancy: nausea and vomiting occurring during the first weeks of pregnancy, especially the early morning vomiting. Schwangerschaftserbrechen *n*, Hyperemesis gravidarum *f*.
vomiting reflex: Würgreflex *m*.
vomitory/*n*: Brechmittel *n*, Emetikum *n*.
voriconazole/*n*: Voriconazol *n*.
voyeurism/*n*: Voyeurismus *m*.

vulva/*n*: Vulva *f*.
vulva retractor/*n*: Vulvaspreizer *m*.
vulvectomy/*n*: Vulvektomie *f*.
vulvitis/*n*: inflammation of the female external genitalia, usually caused by infection. Frequently associated with physical or chemical lesions of the vulva, or metabolic disorders, for example diabetes mellitus. Vulvitis *f*.
vulvovaginal candidiasis: Candida-Vulvovaginitis *f*.
vulvovaginitis/*n*: acute or chronic inflammation of the vulva and vagina, usually caused by infection with bacteria like Streptococcus, Staphylococcus, Escherichia coli, Gonococcus, or other. Vulvovaginitis *f*.
VZV <*abbr*> **varicella-zoster virus**: Varicella-Zoster-Virus *n*, VZV.

W

W <*abbr*> **1. watt; 2. tungsten**: 1. Watt; 2. Tungsten *n*, Wolfram *n*.
wad/*n, vb*: 1. Bausch *m*; 2. polstern.
wadding/*n*: Watte *f*.
waddle/*vb*: watscheln.
waddling gait: Watschelgang *m*.
waist/*n*: Taille *f*.
waiting period: Wartezeit *f*.
waiting room: Wartezimmer *n*.
wakefulness/*n*: Schlaflosigkeit *f*.
wake-sleep cycle: Wach-Schlaf-Rhythmus *m*.
waking dream: Wachtraum *m*.
waking epilepsy: Aufwachepilepsie *f*.
Waldeyer's tonsillar ring: Waldeyer-Rachenring *m*.
walk/*n, vb*: 1. Gang *m*; 2. gehen.
walker/*n*: Gehstütze *f*.
walking cast: Gehgips *m*.
walking reflex: Schreitreflex *m*.
walking stick: Gehstock *m*.
wall/*n*: Wall *m*, Wand *f*.
walled abscess: abgekapselter Abszess *m*.
wallerian degeneration: Waller-Degeneration *f*.
wall stress: Wandspannung *f*.
wandering/*n, adj*: 1. Wanderung *f*; 2. wandernd.
wandering abscess: Senkungsabszess *m*.
wandering kidney: Wanderniere *f*.
wandering liver: Wanderleber *f*.
ward/*n*: Abteilung *f*, Station *f*.
warfarin/*n*: Warfarin *n*.
war gas: Kampfgas *n*.
warm/*n, adj, vb*: 1. Wärme *f*; 2. warm; 3. erwärmen.
warm agglutinin: Wärmeagglutinin *n*.
warm nodule: heißer Knoten *m*.
war neurosis: Kriegsneurose *f*.
warning/*n*: Warnung *f*.
wart/*n*: a circumscribed growth on the skin, sometimes caused by human papillomavirus. Warze *f*, Verruca *f*.
warty papilloma: warzenförmiges Papillom *n*.
wash/*n, vb*: 1. Spülung *f*, Lotion *f*; 2. waschen, spülen.
wash out/*vb*: auswaschen.
wasp sting: Wespenstich *m*.
wastage/*n*: Verlust *m*.
waste/*n, vb*: 1. Abfall *m*; 2. verschwenden, auszehren.
wasting/*n*: Schwund *m*, Auszehrung *f*.
wasting disease: auszehrende Krankheit *f*.
wasting syndrome: any condition which is characterized by severe wasting, involuntary weight loss of more than ten percent, chronic diarrhea, weakness, and eventually fever. Causes include chronic infection, or intoxications. Auszehrungssyndrom *n*.
watch-glass nail: Uhrglasnagel *m*.
water/*n*: Wasser *n*.
water-clear cell: wasserhelle Zelle *f*.
water cure: Wasserbehandlung *f*, Hydrotherapie *f*.
water for injection: Aqua ad iniectionem *f*.
water loss: Wasserverlust *m*.
watershed infarction: Grenzlinieninfarkt *m*.
water-soluble/*adj*: wasserlöslich.
watery diarrhea: wässrige Diarrhö *f*.
watery stool: wässriger Stuhl *m*.
wave/*n*: Welle *f*.
wavelength/*n*: Wellenlänge *f*.
wax/*n*: Wachs *n*.

waxy cast: Wachsabdruck *m*, Wachszylinder *m*.
waxy degeneration: wachsige Muskeldegeneration *f*.
waxy kidney: Wachsniere *f*, Amyloidniere *f*.
waxy liver: Wachsleber *f*, Amyloidleber *f*.
waxy spleen: Wachsmilz *f*, Schinkenmilz *f*.
way of life: Lebensweise *f*.
weak/*adj*: schwach.
weak foot: Senkfuß *m*.
weakness/*n*: Schwäche *f*, Schwächezustand *m*.
weak pulse: schwacher Puls *m*.
wean/*vb*: abstillen, entwöhnen.
weaning/*n*: Abstillen *n*, Entwöhnung *f*.
weanling/*n*: Flaschenkind *n*.
weariness/*n*: Ermüdung *f*.
weather factor: Witterungseinfluss *m*.
web/*n*: Gewebe *n*, Netz *n*.
webbed fingers: Syndaktylie *f*.
webbed neck: skin fold in the neck region, extending from the mastoid region to the acromion. A congenital condition, with bilateral folds typically occurring in conjunction with genetic syndromes, for example Ullrich Turner syndrome. Pterygium colli *n*.
wedge bone: Keilbein *n*.
wedged hepatic pressure: Portalvenenkatheterdruck *m*.
wedge pressure: Wedge-Druck *m*, Pulmonalarterienverschlussdruck *m*.
weep/*vb*: weinen, nässen.
weeping dermatitis: nässende Dermatitis *f*.
weigh/*vb*: wiegen.
weight/*n*: Gewicht *n*.
weight control: Gewichtskontrolle *f*.
weight gain: Gewichtszunahme *f*.
weight loss: Gewichtsverlust *m*.
weight reduction diet: Reduktionskost *f*.
welfare/*n*: Wohlfahrt *f*, Fürsorge *f*.
welfare organization: Wohlfahrtsverband *m*.
well-balanced/*adj*: ausgeglichen.
wellness/*n*: Wohlbefinden *n*.
wen/*n*: Talgdrüsenzyste *f*.
West African sleeping sickness: Trypanosomiasis gambiensis *f*.
wet/*adj*: feucht, nass.
wet compress: feuchter Umschlag *m*.
wet cough: produktiver Husten *m*.
wet dream: nächtliche Pollution *f*.
wet dropsy: feuchte Beriberi *f*.
wet gangrene: feuchte Gangrän *f*.
wet nurse: Amme *f*.
wet pleurisy: exsudative Pleuritis *f*.
wetting/*n*: Durchnässung *f*, Anfeuchten *n*.
wheal/*n*: Quaddel *f*.
wheelchair/*n*: Rollstuhl *m*.
wheeze/*vb*: keuchen, schnaufen.
wheezing/*n*: Stenoseatmung *f*, Giemen *n*.
whiplash injury: injury of the cervical spine, resulting from flexion and hyperextension of the body, as occurring in car accidents. Peitschenhiebtrauma *n*, Schleudertrauma *n*.
whipworm/*n*: Peitschenwurm *m*, Trichuris trichiura *f*.
whirl/*n, vb*: 1. Wirbel *m*; 2. wirbeln.
whispering resonance: Flüsterschall *m*.
whispering voice: Flüsterstimme *f*.
whisper test: Flüsterprobe *f*.
whistle/*n, vb*: 1. Pfeife *f*; 2. pfeifen.
whistle-tip catheter: Flötenschnabelkatheter *m*.
whistling deformity: Pfeifengesicht *n*.
whistling face-windmill vane hand syndrome: an autosomal dominant malformation syndrome which is characterized by facial dysmorphia, hypertelorism, small mouth, contracture of hand muscles, talipes equinovarus, and growth retardation. kraniokarpotarsale Dystrophie *f*, Freeman-Sheldon-Syndrom *n*.
whistling sound: Pfeifgeräusch *n*.
white atrophy: Atrophie blanche *f*.
white bile: weiße Galle *f*.
white blood cell: weißes Blutkörperchen *n*, Leukozyt *m*.

white blood count: Leukozytenzählung *f*.
white-cap/*n*: Favus *m*, Kopfgrind *m*.
white cell: Leukozyt *m*.
white finger: Digitus mortuus *m*, Reil-Finger *m*.
white head: Favus *m*, Kopfgrind *m*.
white lotion: Lotio alba *f*.
white macule: Weißfleck *m*.
white ointment: weiße Salbe *f*.
white patch: Milchfleck *m*.
white plague: Tuberkulose *f*.
white pneumonia: Pneumonia alba *f*.
white precipitate ointment: weiße Präzipitatsalbe *f*.
white sound: Wärmerauschen *n*.
white substance: weiße Substanz *f*.
white swelling: Tumor albus *m*.
white thrombus: weißer Thrombus *m*, Abscheidungsthrombus *m*.
whitlow/*n*: an infectious disease of the nail fold, mostly due to bacterial infection with Staphylococcus or Streptococcus, or resulting from herpes simplex infection. Symptoms include swelling, formation of a very painful abscess, and inflammation of lymphatic vessels. Nagelgeschwür *n*, Paronychie *f*, Umlauf *m*.
WHO <*abbr*> **World Health Organization**: Weltgesundheitsorganisation *f*.
whole/*n, adj*: 1. Ganze *n*, Ganzheit *f*; 2. voll, ganz.
whole blood: Vollblut *n*.
whole-body computed tomography: Ganzkörpertomographie *f*.
whole-body radiotherapy: Ganzkörperbestrahlung *f*.
whooping/*n*: Keuchen *n*.
whooping cough: an infectious disease caused by the bacterium Bordetella pertussis, characterized by episodes of paroxysmal coughing punctuated by whooping noises between episodes during periods of inspiration. Keuchhusten *m*, Pertussis *f*.
wide/*adj*: weit.
wide-angle glaucoma: Weitwinkelglaukom *n*.
widening/*n*: Verbreiterung *f*.
widespread/*adj*: weitverbreitet.
width/*n*: Weite *f*, Spannbreite *f*.
wild/*adj*: wild.
wild-type/*n*: Wildtyp *m*.
will/*n*: Wille *m*.
willful/*adj*: willkürlich.
willow fracture: Grünholzfraktur *f*, Biegungsbruch *m*.
wind/*n*: Wind *m*, Blähung *f*.
window/*n*: Fenster *n*.
window technique: Fenstertechnik *f*.
windpipe/*n*: Luftröhre *f*.
wing/*n*: Flügel *m*.
winged scapula: Scapula alata *f*.
winking reflex: Blinzelreflex *m*, Orbikularisreaktion *f*.
winking spasm: Blinzelkrampf *m*, Blepharospasmus *m*.
winking tic: Blinzeltic *m*.
wire fixation: Drahtfixation *f*.
wire-like pulse: Drahtpuls *m*.
wire saw: Gigli-Säge *f*.
wiring/*n*: Drahtschienung *f*.
wisdom tooth: Weisheitszahn *m*.
withdrawal/*n*: Entnahme *f*, Entzug *m*.
withdrawal bleeding: Abbruchblutung *f*, Entzugsblutung *f*.
withdrawal symptom: any sign or symptom an alcohol, drug or narcotics addict experiences when the use of the substance is stopped abruptly. Entzugssymptom *n*.
wobble/*vb*: schlottern, wackeln.
wolffian cyst: Wolff-Zyste *f*.
woman/*n*: Frau *f*.
womb/*n*: Gebärmutter *f*.
woodchuck/*n*: Murmeltier *n*.
wooden/*adj*: bretthart, hölzern.
wooden shoe heart: Holzschuhherz *n*.
woody thyroiditis: Riedel-Struma *f*.
woolsorter's disease: Wollarbeiterkrankheit *f*, Weberhusten *m*.
word blindness: Wortblindheit *f*, Alexie *f*.
word deafness: Worttaubheit *f*, auditorische Aphasie *f*.
work/*n, vb*: 1. Arbeit *f*; 2. arbeiten.
work of grief: Trauerarbeit *f*.
work therapy: Arbeitstherapie *f*, Ergotherapie *f*.
World Health Organization: Weltgesundheitsorganisation *f*.

worm/*n*: Wurm *m*.
worm infestation: Wurmbefall *m*.
worsen/*vb*: verschlechtern, verschlimmern.
worsening/*n*: Verschlechterung *m*.
wound/*n, vb*: 1. an injury or break in the normal continuity of structures or tissue, for example a skin wound, or an injury of internal organs. Wunde *f*; 2. verwunden.
wound care: Wundversorgung *f*.
wound clip: Wundklammer *f*.
wound dressing: Wundverband *m*.
wounded/*n, adj*: 1. Verwundeter *m*; 2. verwundet.
woven bone: Primitivknochen *m*.
WPW syndrome <*abbr*> **Wolff-Parkinson-White syndrome**: a cardiac syndrome which is characterized by an abnormally short P-Q interval in the electrocardiogram. Symptoms include arrhythmia, atrial supraventricular tachycardia, and ventricular and/or atrial fibrillation. Wolff-Parkinson-White-Syndrom *n*, WPW-Syndrom *n*.
wrap/*vb*: ummanteln.
wrench/*n, vb*: 1. Verrenkung *f*, Verstauchung *f*; 2. verstauchen, verzerren.
Wright stain: Wright-Färbung *f*.
wrinkle/*n*: Hautfältchen *n*.
wrist/*n*: Handgelenk *n*, Handwurzel *f*.
writer's cramp: Schreibkrampf *m*, Mogigraphie *f*.
writing and reading disability: Schreib-Lese-Schwäche *f*.
wryneck/*n*: a condition in which the head is turned to one side due to spastic contraction or malformation of the cervical muscles. Schiefhals *m*, Tortikollis *m*.

X

X <*abbr*> **xanthosine/*n***: Xanthosin *n*.
xanthic/*adj*: gelblich, Xanthin-.
xanthine/*n*: Xanthin *n*, X.
xanthochromia/*n*: Xanthochromie *f*.
xanthochromic/*adj*: xanthochrom.
xanthocillin/*n*: Xanthocillin *n*.
xanthofibroma/*n*: Xanthofibrom *n*, Histiozytom *n*.
xanthogranulomatous pyelonephritis: xanthogranulomatöse Pyelonephritis *f*.
xanthoma/*n*: Xanthom *n*.
xanthomatosis/*n*: a condition which is characterized by the presence of multiple, disseminated xanthomas of the skin, mucosal membranes, and tendons, occurring as a symptom of hyperlipidemia or as idiopathic disorder with normal levels of cholesterol. Xanthomatose *f*, generalisiertes Xanthom *n*.
xanthomatous polyarthritis: xanthomatöse Polyarthritis *f*.
xanthoproteic acid: Xanthoproteinsäure *f*.
xanthurenic acid: Xanthurensäure *f*.
xanthylic acid: Xanthylsäure *f*.
xantocillin/*n*: Xantocillin *n*.
xantorubin/*n*: Xantorubin *n*.
x-axis: X-Achse *f*, Abszisse *f*.
X chromosome: X-Chromosom *n*.
xenobiotic/*n, adj*: 1. Xenobiotikum *n*; 2. xenobiotisch.
xenogeneic graft: xenogenes Transplantat *n*, Heterotransplantat *n*.
xenograft/*n*: Xenotransplantat *n*, Heterotransplantat *n*.
xenophobia/*n*: Xenophobie *f*, Fremdenfurcht *f*.
xeroderma/*n*: a skin disease characterized by dryness, desquamation, and discoloration of the skin. Xeroderma *n*, Xerodermie *f*.
xerodermic idiocy: Xeroderma pigmentosum *n*, deSanctis-Cacchione-Syndrom *n*.
xerophthalmia/*n*: condition of the eye in which the conjunctival membrane of the eyelid and eyeball is dry and thickened, occurring as a consequence of vitamin A deficiency or due to other ophthalmologic diseases like trachoma. Xerophthalmie *f*.
xeroradiography/*n*: Xeroradiographie *f*.
xerosis/*n*: Xerose *f*.
xerostomia/*n*: abnormal dryness of the mouth, resulting from salivary gland dysfunction, due for example to an atrophy of the salivary glands, vitamin A deficiency, exposure to X-rays, or systemic diseases like Sjögren's syndrome. Xerostomie *f*, Mundtrockenheit *f*.
xibornol/*n*: Xibornol *n*.
ximelagatran/*n*: Ximelagatran *n*.
ximoprofen/*n*: Ximoprofen *n*.
xinomiline/*n*: Xinomilin *n*.
xipamide/*n*: Xipamid *n*.
xiphoid/*n, adj*: 1. Schwertfortsatz *m*; 2. schwertförmig.
xiphoiditis/*n*: Xiphoiditis *f*.
xiphoid process: Schwertfortsatz *m*.
xipranolol/*n*: Xipranolol *n*.
X-linked gene: X-chromosomal gebundenes Gen *n*.
X-linked lymphoproliferative syndrome: X-linked immunodeficiency with undue susceptibility to Epstein-Barr virus, characterized by fulminating infectious mononucleosis, agammaglobulinemia, or bone-

marrow aplasia. X-chromosomal vererbtes lymphoproliferatives Syndrom *n*.

x-radiation/*n*: Röntgenstrahlung *f*.

x-ray/*vb*: röntgen.

x-ray apparatus: Röntgengerät *n*.

x-ray castration: Röntgenkastration *f*.

x-ray film: Röntgenfilm *m*.

x-rays: X-Strahlen, Röntgenstrahlen.

x-ray therapy: Röntgentherapie *f*.

xylamidine/*n*: Xylamidin *n*.

xylazine/*n*: Xylazin *n*.

xylenol/*n*: Xylenol *n*.

xylidine/*n*: Xylidin *n*.

xylidine red: Xylidinrot *n*.

xylocaine/*n*: Xylocain *n*.

xylocoumarol/*n*: Xylokumarol *n*.

xyloflavine/*n*: Xyloflavin *n*.

xylometazoline/*n*: Xylometazolin *n*.

xylose/*n*: Xylose *f*.

xylosuria/*n*: Xylosurie *f*.

xyphoid/*adj*: schwertförmig.

xysma/*n*: Xysma *n*.

xyster/*n*: Xyster *m*, Schaber *m*.

XZ syndrome <*abbr*> **X zero syndrome**: a syndrome which is characterized by a chromosomal mosaic (45,X0). Symptoms include short stature, neck webbing, primary amenorrhea, shield thorax, and distanced mammary papillas. X0-Syndrom *n*, Ullrich-Turner-Syndrom *n*.

X

Y

y <*abbr*> **1. yellow; 2. young**: 1. gelb; 2. jung.
yam/*n*: Yamswurzel *f*.
yawn/*n, vb*: 1. Gähnen *n*; 2. gähnen.
yaws/*n*: a tropical infectious disease caused by Treponema pertenue, characterized by skin lesions similar to syphilitic lesions, and, without treatment, resulting in ulcerative lesions. Frambösie *f*.
y-axis: Y-Achse *f*, Ordinate *f*.
Y chromosome: Y-Chromosom *n*.
year/*n*: Jahr *n*.
year of birth: Geburtsjahr *n*.
yeast/*n, vb*: 1. Hefe *f*; 2. gären.
yeast infection: Hefepilzinfektion *f*.
yeastlike fungus: Hefepilz *m*.
yeast plasmid: Hefeplasmid *n*.
yellow/*n, adj*: 1. Gelb *n*; 2. gelb.
yellow body: Gelbkörper *m*.
yellow fat: gelbes Fett *n*.
yellow fever: Gelbfieber *n*.
yellow fiber: elastische Faser *f*.
yellowish/*adj*: gelblich.
yellow spot: gelber Fleck *m*, Macula lutea *f*.
yellow vision: Xanthopsie *f*, Gelbsehen *n*.
yersinia/*n*: Yersinia *f*.
yersinia infection: Yersiniose *f*.
yersinial arthritis: Yersinia-Arthritis *f*.
yersiniosis/*n*: an infectious disease caused by strains of the bacterium Yersinia. Symptoms include gastroenteritis, mesenteric lymphadenitis, erythema nodosum, and polyarthritis. Yersiniose *f*.
yew berry: Eibe *f*.
yield increase: Ausbeuteerhöhung *f*.
Y ligament: Ligamentum iliofemorale *n*, Bertin-Band *n*.
Y-linked gene: Y-chromosomal gebundenes Gen *n*.
yogurt/*n*: Yoghurt *m*.
yohimbic acid: Yohimbinsäure *f*.
yohimbine/*n*: Yohimbin *n*.
yoke bone: Jochbein *n*, Os zygomaticum *n*.
yolk/*n*: Dotter *m*, Eigelb *n*.
yolk sac: Dottersack *m*.
young/*adj*: jung.
youth/*n*: Jugend *f*.
Y-plasty/*n*: Y-Plastik *f*.
yr <*abbr*> **year**/*n*: Jahr *n*.
y-shaped/*adj*: Y-förmig.

Z

Z <*abbr*> **1. atomic number; 2. proton number**: 1. Ordnungszahl *f*, OZ; 2. Protonenzahl *f*.
zalcitabine/*n*: Zalcitabin *n*.
zaleplon/*n*: Zaleplon *n*.
zanamivir/*n*: Zanamivir *n*.
zapizolam/*n*: Zapizolam *n*.
z band/*n*: Z-Streifen *m*.
z chart: Z-Diagramm *n*.
z disk/*n*: Z-Streifen *m*.
zein agar: Zeinagar *m*.
zeisian stye: infection of the zeisian gland of the eyelid caused by bacteria, usually Staphylococcus or Streptococcus. Gerstenkorn *n*, Hordeolum externum *n*.
zepastine/*n*: Zepastin *n*.
zeranol/*n*: Zeranol *n*.
zero/*n*: Null *f*, Nullpunkt *m*.
zero order kinetics: Kinetik nullter Ordnung *f*.
zetidoline/*n*: Zetidolin *n*.
Z-flap/*n*: Z-Lappen *m*.
ziconotide/*n*: Ziconotid *n*.
zidovudine/*n*: Zidovudin *n*.
zimelidine/*n*: Zimelidin *n*.
zinc/*n*: Zink *n*, Zn.
zinc ointment: Zinksalbe *f*.
zinc oxide: Zinkoxid *n*.
zinstatin/*n*: Zinstatin *n*.
zinterol/*n*: Zinterol *n*.
zinviroxime/*n*: Zinviroxim *n*.
zipeprol/*n*: Zipeprol *n*.
ziprasidone/*n*: Ziprasidon *n*.
z line/*n*: Z-Streifen *m*.
zocainone/*n*: Zocainon *n*.
zofenopril/*n*: Zofenopril *n*.
zoficonazole/*n*: Zoficonazol *n*.
zolamine/*n*: Zolamin *n*.
zolazepam/*n*: Zolazepam *n*.
zoledronic acid: Zoledronsäure *f*.
zolertine/*n*: Zolertin *n*.
zolmitriptan/*n*: Zolmitriptan *n*.
zoloperone/*n*: Zoloperon *n*.
zolpidem/*n*: Zolpidem *n*.
zomepirac/*n*: Zomepirac *n*.
zona/*n*: Gürtel *m*, Bezirk *m*.
zonal/*adj*: zonal.
zonal layer: Stratum zonale *n*.
zone/*n*: Zone *f*.
zone of inhibition: Hemmzone *f*.
zone therapy: Reflexzonentherapie *f*.
zonisamide/*n*: Zonisamid *n*.
zonula/*n*: Zonula *f*, Zone *f*.
zonular cataract: Schichtstar *m*.
zonular scotoma: Zentralskotom *n*.
zooanthroponosis/*n*: Zooanthroponose *f*.
zoology/*n*: Zoologie *f*.
zoom lens: Zoom-Optik *f*.
zoonosis/*n*: infectious disease of animals that can be transmitted to humans and may cause human disease, for example psittacosis, brucellosis, or bovine tuberculosis. Zoonose *f*.
zooparasite/*n*: Zooparasit *m*.
zoophobia/*n*: Tierphobie *f*.
zoospermia/*n*: Zoospermie *f*.
zoospore/*n*: Zoospore *f*.
zoosterol: Zoosterin *n*.
zopiclone/*n*: Zopiclon *n*.
zorubicin/*n*: Zorubicin *n*.
zoster/*n*: an infectious disease of the skin, caused by reactivation of varicella-zoster virus. Predominantly located in the thoracic region, symptoms include a papular exanthema, typically in the area of innervation of a sensory ganglion, and painful sensations. As complications, herpetic encephalitis, involvement of the eye, or dissemination can occur. Zoster *m*, Gürtelrose *f*, Herpes zoster *m*.
zosteriform/*adj*: zosterartig.

zotepine/*n*: Zotepin *n*.
zoxazolamine/*n*: Zoxazolamin *n*.
Z-plasty/*n*: Z-Plastik *f*.
zuclopenthixol/*n*: Zuclopenthixol *n*.
zygomatic/*adj*: zygomatisch.
zygomatic arch: Jochbogen *m*.
zygomatic bone: Jochbein *n*.
zygomaticofrontal/*adj*: zygomatikofrontal.
zygomycetes: Zygomyzeten.
zygote/*n*: Zygote *f*.
zymogen/*n, adj*: 1. Zymogen *n*; 2. zymogen.
zymotic/*adj*: zymotisch.

Deutsch – Englisch

A

A Abk. **1. Adenin** *n*; **2. Akkomodation** *f*; **3. Arterie** *f*: 1. adenine; 2. accommodation; 3. artery, a.
Aaron-Appendizitiszeichen *n*: Aaron sign.
Abacavir *n*: abacavir.
abakteriell: abacterial.
Abarelix *n*: abarelix.
Abbau *m*: degradation, breakdown; **biologischer** ≈ biodegradation; **geistiger** ≈ mental deterioration.
abbaubar: degradable.
abbinden: ligature, bind.
Abbindung *f*: ligature, ligation.
Abbruchblutung *f*: withdrawal bleeding.
Abdomen *n*: abdomen, belly; **akutes** ≈ acute abdomen.
abdominal: abdominal.
Abdominalhoden *m*: abdominal testis.
Abdominalkolik *f*: abdominal colic.
Abdominallavage *f*: peritoneal lavage.
Abdruck *m*: impression, cast, template.
Abdruckgips *m*: impression plaster.
Abduktion *f*: abduction.
Abduzenslähmung *f*: abducens paralysis.
abduzieren: abduce, abduct.
aberrant: aberrant.
Aberration *m*: aberration; **chromatische** ≈ chromatic aberration; **sphärische** ≈ spheric aberration.
Abfluss *m*: drain, outlet.
Abformen *n*: casting, molding.
Abführen *n*: purgation, purging.
Abführmittel *n*: laxative, cathartic.
abgetötet: killed, inactivated.
abhängig: dependent, addicted.
Abhängigkeit *f*: dependency, addiction.
abhören: auscultate.
Abietinsäure *f*: abietic acid.
Abklatschgeschwür *n*: kissing ulcer.
Abklatschtumor *m*: contact cancer.
abklemmen: clamp.
abklingen: die away, fade.
abkratzen: abrade.
Ablagerung *f*: deposit, deposition.
Ablationstherapie *f*: ablative therapy; **hormonelle** ≈ endocrine ablative therapy.
Ablatio retinae *f*: retinal detachment.
Ableitung *f*: lead, derivation, revulsion.
Ableitungen *f*: leads; **bipolare** ≈ bipolar leads; **präkordiale** ≈ precordial leads, Wilson's leads; **unipolare** ≈ unipolar leads.
Ablenkung *f*: deflection, diversion.
Ablesegenauigkeit *f*: accuracy in reading.
Ablösung *f*: detachment, separation.
Abmagerungssyndrom, dienzephales *n*: diencephalic syndrome of infancy, Russell syndrome.
Abnabelung *f*: cutting of the umbilical cord, omphalotomy.
Abnahme *f*: decrease, decline, reduction.
abnorm: abnormal, anomalous.
Abnormalität *f*: abnormality.
ABNull-Blutgruppe *f*: AB0 blood group.
Abort *m*: abortion; **drohender** ≈ threatened abortion; **einzeitiger** ≈ complete abortion; **febriler** ≈ febrile abortion; **habitueller** ≈ habitual abortion; **induzierter** ≈ induced abortion; **inkompletter** ≈ incomplete abortion; **komplizierter** ≈ infected abortion; **putrider** ≈ infected abortion;

septischer ≈ septic abortion; **tubarer** ≈ tubal abortion; **verhaltener** ≈ incomplete abortion; **vollständiger** ≈ complete abortion.
Abortsepsis *f*: postabortal sepsis.
Abrasio *f*: abrasion.
Abrasionsfacetten: wear facets.
Abraumzelle *f*: microglial cell.
Abrikossoff-Tumor *m*: Abrikosov's tumor, granular cell tumor.
Abriss *m*: avulsion.
Absaugen *n*: suction, mechanical aspiration.
Abschälen *n*: stripping, peeling.
Abschälungsfraktur *f*: flake fracture, cleavage fracture.
Abscheidungsthrombus *m*: white thrombus.
Abschilferung *f*: desquamation, exfoliation, shedding.
Abschnitt *m*: segment, stadium.
Abschnürung *f*: strangulation, constriction.
abschürfen: excoriate, abrade.
Abschürfung *f*: excoriation, abrasive.
Abschuppung *f*: desquamation, exfoliation.
Abschwächung *f*: attenuation.
Absence *f*: absence, absent state; **komplexe** ≈ complex partial seizure.
Absinth *m*: absinthe.
Absinthismus *m*: absinthism.
Absonderung *f*: discharge, secretion, isolation.
Absorptionsatelektase *f*: absorption atelectasis.
Abspaltung *f*: splitting-off.
Absprengungsbruch *m*: chip fracture.
Abstammung *f*: origin, filiation.
Abstammungslehre *f*: theory of evolution, Darwin's theory.
Abstillen *n*: weaning, ablactation.
Abstinenzsyndrom *n*: abstinence syndrome, withdrawal syndrome.
abstoßen: reject, repulse.
Abstoßung *f*: rejection, repulsion.
Abstoßungsreaktion *f*: immunologic rejection.
abstreifen: strip.
Abstreifen *n*: stripping.
Abstrich *m*: smear, swab; **zytologischer** ≈ cytologic smear.
Abstützung *f*: support, bracing.
Abszedierung *f*: abscess formation.
Abszess *m*: abscess; **abgekapselter** ≈ walled abscess; **appendizitischer** ≈ appendiceal abscess; **embolischer** ≈ embolic abscess; **epiduraler** ≈ epidural abscess; **extraduraler** ≈ extradural abscess; **gekammerter** ≈ encapsulated abscess; **hämatogener** ≈ hematogenous abscess; **heißer** ≈ hot abscess; **intrakranieller** ≈ intracranial abscess; **kalter** ≈ cold abscess; **metastatischer** ≈ metastatic abscess; **parapharyngealer** ≈ parapharyngeal abscess; **pararektaler** ≈ perirectal abscess; **periapikaler** ≈ periapical abscess; **periproktischer** ≈ periproctic abscess; **retromammärer** ≈ retromammary abscess; **septischer** ≈ pyemic abscess; **steriler** ≈ sterile abscess; **subphrenischer** ≈ subdiaphragmatic abscess.
Abszisse *f*: abscissa, x-axis.
Abteilung *f*: department, ward.
Abtreibung *f*: abortion.
abtupfen: swab, dab.
Abusus *m*: abuse.
Abwehr *f*: defense.
abwehren: defend, repel.
Abwehrhaltung *f*: defensiveness.
Abwehrmechanismus *m*: defense mechanism, host defense.
Abwehrreaktion *f*: defense reaction.
Abwehrreflex *m*: withdrawal reflex.
Abwehrspannung *f*: muscular defense.
abweichen: deviate.
Abweichung *f*: aberrance, deviation.
abziehen: strip.
Abzym *n*: abzyme.
Acamprosat *n*: acamprosate.
Acarbose *n*: acarbose.
Acariasis *f*: acariasis.
Acebutolol *n*: acebutolol.
Acecarbromal *n*: acecarbromal.
Aceclidin *n*: aceclidine.
Aceclofenac *n*: aceclofenac.
Acefyllinpiperazin *n*: acefylline piperazine.
ACE-Hemmer *m*: angiotensin-converting enzyme inhibitor, ACE inhibitor.

Acemetacin *n*: acemetacin.
Acenocoumarol *n*: acenocoumarol.
Acetaldehyd *m*: acetaldehyde.
Acetaminophen *n*: acetaminophen.
Acetanilid *n*: acetanilid.
Acetazolamid *n*: acetazolamide.
Acetessigsäure *f*: acetoacetic acid.
Aceton *n*: acetone.
Acetonämie *f*: acetonemia.
Acetongeruch *m*: acetone breath, fruity breath.
Acetonkörper *m*: acetone body.
Acetonurie *f*: acetonuria.
Acetrizoesäure *f*: acetrizoic acid.
Acetylcholin *n*: acetylcholine.
Acetylcholinesterase *f*: acetylcholinesterase.
Acetyl-CoA *n*: acetyl-CoA, acetylcoenzyme A.
Acetylcystein *n*: acetylcysteine.
Acetylsalicylsäure *f*: acetylsalicylic acid.
Achalasie *f*: achalasia.
Achillessehne *f*: Achilles tendon.
Achillessehnenreflex *m*: Achilles tendon reflex, ankle jerk.
Achillobursitis *f*: achillobursitis.
Achlorhydrie *f*: achlorhydria.
Acholie *f*: acholia.
Achondrogenesis *f*: achondrogenesis.
Achondroplasie *f*: achondroplasia.
Achromasie *f*: achromia.
achromatisch: achromatic.
Achromatopsie *f*: achromatopia.
Achse *f*: axis; **optische** ≈ optic axis, visual line.
Achselhöhle *f*: armpit, axillary space.
Achsellymphknoten *m*: axillary lymph node.
Achselvenenthrombose *f*: effort thrombosis, Paget-von Schroetter syndrome.
Achsenametropie *f*: axial ametropia.
Achsenhyperopie *f*: axial hyperopia.
Achsensymptom *n*: axial symptom.
Achsenzylinder *m*: axis cylinder, axon.
Achternaht *f*: figure-of-eight suture.
Achylia gastrica *f*: achylia gastrica.
Aciclovir *n*: acyclovir.
Acidomycin *n*: acidomycin.
Acitretin *n*: acitretin.
Aclarubicin *n*: aclarubicin.
Acne fulminans *f*: systemic acne, acne fulminans.
Acne rosacea *f*: acne rosacea, rosacea.
Acne vulgaris *f*: common acne, acne vulgaris.
Acriflaviniumchlorid *n*: acriflaviniumchloride.
Acrylamidgelelektrophorese *f*: acrylamide gel electrophoresis.
Actinomycin *n*: actinomycin.
Adaktylie *f*: adactylia.
Adalimumab *n*: adalimumab.
Adamsapfel *m*: Adam's apple.
Adapalen *n*: adapalene.
Adaptation *f*: adaptation.
Adaptation post partum, kindliche: neonatal adaptation.
Adaptionsschiene *f*: coaptation splint.
Addison-Anämie *f*: Addison's anemia, pernicious anemia.
Addison-Bronzehaut *f*: bronzed skin.
Addison-Krankheit *f*: Addison's disease, chronic adrenocortical insufficiency.
Addison-Krise *f*: Addisonian crisis, acute adrenocortical insufficiency.
Adduktion *f*: adduction.
Adduktionsfraktur *f*: adduction fracture.
Adduktorenkanal *m*: adductor canal.
Adefovir *n*: adefovir.
adendritisch: adendritic.
Adenitis *f*: adenitis.
Adenoameloblastom *n*: adenomatoid odontogenic tumor.
Adenoepitheliom *n*: adenoepithelioma.
Adenofibrom *n*: adenofibroma.
Adenohypophyse *f*: adenohypophysis, anterior pituitary.
adenoid: adenoid.
Adenokarzinom *n*: adenocarcinoma; **follikuläres** ≈ follicular adenocarcinoma; **papilläres** ≈ papillary adenocarcinoma; **schleimbildendes** ≈ mucinous adenocarcinoma.
Adenolymphom *n*: adenolymphoma, Whartin's tumor.
Adenom *n*: adenoma; **basophiles** ≈ basophil adenoma; **chromophobes**

≈ chromophobe adenoma; **eosinophiles** ≈ eosinophil adenoma, acidophil adenoma; **follikuläres** ≈ follicular adenoma; **onkozytäres** ≈ oncocytic adenoma; **pleomorphes** ≈ pleomorphic adenoma; **toxisches** ≈ toxic thyroid adenoma; **trabekuläres** ≈ trabecular adenoma; **tubuläres** ≈ tubular adenoma; **virilisierendes** ≈ virilizing adenoma; **zystisches** ≈ cystic adenoma.

Adenoma sebaceum *n*: sebaceous adenoma.

Adenomatose *f*: adenomatosis; **multiple endokrine** ≈ multiple endocrine adenomatosis, MEA, Wermer syndrome.

Adenomyom *n*: adenomyoma.

Adenomyosis *f*: adenomyosis.

Adenopathie *f*: adenopathy.

Adenosarkom *n*: adenosarcoma.

Adenosin *n*: adenosine.

Adenosindiphosphat *n*: adenosine diphosphate.

Adenosinmonophosphat *n*: adenosine monophosphate; **zyklisches** ≈ cyclic adenosine monophosphate.

Adenosinphosphat *n*: adenosine phosphate.

Adenosintriphosphat *n*: adenosine triphosphate.

Adenosintriphosphatase *f*: adenosine triphosphatase.

Adenotomie *f*: adenotomy, tonsillotomy.

Adenovirus-Vektor *m*: adenovirus vector.

Adenylsäure *f*: adenylic acid.

Adenylzyklase *f*: adenyl cyclase.

Ader *f*: blood vessel.

Aderhaut *f*: choroid.

Aderhautentzündung *f*: choroiditis.

Aderhautkolobom *n*: coloboma of the choroid.

Aderhautsklerose *f*: choroidal sclerosis.

Aderhautspalte *f*: choroid fissure.

Aderlass *m*: bloodletting.

Adhärenz *f*: adherence.

Adhäsion *f*: adhesion.

Adhäsionsverband *m*: adhesive adsorbent dressing.

Adhäsivität *f*: adhesiveness.

Adie-Syndrom *n*: Adie's syndrome, pupillotonic pseudotabes.

adipös: adipose, obese.

Adipositas *f*: adiposis, fatness.

Adipozyt *m*: adipocyte, fat cell.

Adiuretin *n*: antidiuretic hormone, ADH.

Adjuvans *n*: adjuvant.

adjuvant: adjuvant.

Adnexektomie *f*: adnexectomy.

Adnexitis *f*: adnexitis, pelvic inflammatory disease.

Adoleszentenkyphose *f*: juvenile kyphosis, Scheuermann's disease.

Adoption *f*: adoption.

Adrenalektomie *f*: adrenalectomy.

Adrenalin *n*: adrenaline, epinephrine.

adrenerg: adrenergic, sympathomimetic.

adrenogenital: adrenogenital.

adrenokortikal: adrenocortical.

Adrenokortikosteroid *n*: adrenocorticosteroid.

adrenokortikotrop: adrenocorticotropic.

Adrenoleukodystrophie *f*: adrenoleukodystrophy, Schilder-Addison complex.

adrenolytisch: adrenolytic.

Adriamycin *n*: adriamycin.

Adstringens *n*: astringent, constringent.

adult: adult.

Adventitiazelle *f*: adventitial cell.

Adversivanfall *m*: adversive attack, adversive seizure.

Adversivbewegung *f*: adversive movement.

Adversivepilepsie *f*: adversive epilepsy.

Adynamia episodica hereditaria *f*: familial hyperkalemic periodic paralysis, Gamstorp's disease.

ängstlich: anxious, timid.

Ängstlichkeit *f*: anxiety.

A-Enzephalitis *f*: encephalitis A, encephalitis lethargica.

Äpfelsäure *f*: malic acid.

Äquationsteilung *f*: equational division.

Äquatorialplatte *f*: equatorial plate.

Äquilibrierung *f*: equilibration.
Äquilibrium *n*: equilibrium.
Äquivalent *n*: equivalent; **epileptisches** ≈ epileptic equivalent; **kalorisches** ≈ calorie equivalent.
Äquivalentdosis *f*: roentgen equivalent man, REM.
Ärmel *m*: sleeve.
aerob: aerobe, aerobic.
Aerobier *m*: aerobe, aerobic bacteria.
Aerodontalgie *f*: aerodontalgia.
Aerophagie *f*: aerophagia, air swallowing.
Aerosol *n*: aerosol.
Aerozele *f*: aerocele.
Ärztin *f*: physician, doctor.
ärztlich: iatric, medical.
Äskulapstab *m*: staff of Aesculapius, caduceus.
Ästivoautumnalfieber *n*: estivoautumnal fever.
Äthanol *n*: ethanol, ethylalcohol.
ätherisch: ethereal, volatile.
Äthernarkose *f*: ether narcosis.
Äthylalkohol *m*: ethyl alcohol, ethanol.
Äthylendiamintetraessigsäure *f*: ethylendiamine tetraacetic acid, EDTA.
Ätiologie *f*: etiology.
ätiologisch: etiologic.
ätiopathologisch: etiopathic.
ätzend: caustic, acrid.
Ätzgastritis *f*: corrosive gastritis.
äußerlich: external.
afebril: afebrile, nonfebrile.
Affekt *m*: affect, emotion; **inadäquater** ≈ dissociated affect.
Affektabfuhr *m*: affective discharge.
affektinduziert: affect-induced.
Affektion *f*: affection.
Affektkrampf, respiratorischer *m*: breath-holding, reflex anoxic crisis.
Affektpsychose *f*: affective psychosis.
Affektstörung *f*: affective disorder.
Affenfurche *f*: simian crease.
afferent: afferent.
Affinitätschromatographie *f*: affinity chromatography.
affizieren: affect.
Afibrinogenämie *f*: afibrinogenemia.
Aflatoxin *n*: aflatoxin.
After *m*: anus; **künstlicher** ≈ artificial anus.
Afterfurche *f*: anal cleft, gluteal cleft.
Afterload: afterload.
Afterloading-Verfahren *n*: afterloading technique.
Agalaktie *f*: agalactia.
Agalsidase *f*: agalsidase.
Agammaglobulinämie *f*: agammaglobulinemia.
aganglionär: aganglionic.
Agar *m*: agar.
Agaricinsäure *f*: agaricic acid.
Agenesie *f*: agenesis.
Agens *n*: agent.
Ageusie *f*: ageusia, taste blindness.
Agglutination *f*: agglutination.
Agglutinin *n*: agglutinin; **pflanzliches** ≈ plant agglutinin.
Aggravation *f*: aggravation.
Aggregat *n*: aggregate.
Aggressin *n*: aggressin.
Aggression *f*: aggression.
Aggressivität *f*: aggressivity.
Agitiertheit *f*: agitation.
Aglepriston *n*: aglepristone.
Agnathie *f*: agnathia.
Agnosie *f*: agnosia; **akustische** ≈ acoustic agnosia; **optische** ≈ visual agnosia; **pragmatische** ≈ apraxic agnosia; **räumliche** ≈ visual-spatial agnosia; **taktile** ≈ tactile agnosia.
Agonie *f*: agony, death struggle.
Agonist *m*: agonist, agonistic muscle.
Agoraphobie *f*: agoraphobia, street phobia.
Agranulozytose *f*: agranulocytosis.
Agraphie *f*: agraphia; **aphasische** ≈ aphasic agraphia; **apraktische** ≈ apraxic agraphia; **isolierte** ≈ pure agraphia; **konstruktive** ≈ constructive agraphia; **verbale** ≈ verbal agraphia; **vollständige** ≈ absolute agraphia.
Ahornsirupkrankheit *f*: maple syrup urine disease, leucinosis.
AIDS *n*: acquired immunodeficiency syndrome, AIDS.
AIDS-definierende Erkrankung *f*: AIDS-defining disease.
Akalkulie *f*: acalculia.
Akanthom *n*: acanthoma.

Akanthose *f*: acanthosis.
Akanthozyt *m*: acanthocyte, spur cell.
Akapnie *f*: acapnia.
Akarizid *n*: acaricide.
Akatalasie *f*: acatalasia, Takahara's disease.
Akathisie *f*: akathisia.
Akinesie *f*: akinesia.
akinetisch: akinetic.
Akklimatisierung *f*: acclimatization.
Akkommodation *f*: accommodation.
Akkommodationsbereich *m*: range of accommodation, range of convergence.
Akkommodationskonvergenz *f*: accommodative convergence.
Akkommodationslähmung *f*: paralysis of accommodation.
Akkommodationsschielen *n*: accommodative strabismus.
Akkretionswachstum *n*: accretionary growth.
Akkumulation *f*: accumulation.
Akme *f*: acme, peak.
Akne *f*: acne, common acne; **androgenetische** ≈ androgenetic acne; **juvenile** ≈ adolescent acne.
Akonit *n*: aconite.
Akonitin *n*: aconitine.
Akonitsäure *f*: aconitic acid.
Akorie *f*: acorea, absence of pupil.
Akrodermatitis *f*: acrodermatitis.
Akrodynie *f*: acrodynia, Feer's disease, pink disease.
Akrokeratose *f*: acrokeratosis.
Akromegalie *f*: acromegaly, Marie syndrome.
Akromelie *f*: acromelia, acromelic dwarfism.
akromioklavikulär: acromioclavicular.
akromioskapular: acromioscapular.
Akronym *n*: acronym.
Akrosomengranulum *n*: acrosomal granule.
Akrosomenkörperchen *n*: acrosomal cone.
Akrozephalie *f*: acrocephaly.
Akrozephalosyndaktylie *f*: acrocephalosyndactyly.
Akrozyanose *f*: acrocyanosis.
Akrylsäure *f*: acrylic acid.
Aktinfilament *n*: actin filament.
aktinisch: actinic.
Aktinodermatitis *f*: actinic dermatitis.
Aktinomykose *f*: actinomycosis.
Aktionspotential *n*: action potential.
Aktivator *m*: activator, activating agent.
Aktivität *f*: activity; **katalytische** ≈ catalytic activity; **pseudomyotonische** ≈ pseudomyotonic discharge; **zentralnervöse** ≈ higher nervous activity.
Aktomyosin *n*: actomyosin.
Aktualneurose *f*: actual neurosis.
Akupressur *f*: acupressure.
Akupunktur *f*: acupuncture.
Akustik *f*: acoustics.
Akustikusneurinom *n*: acoustic neurinoma.
akustisch: acoustic, auditory.
akut: acute.
Akutpflege *f*: acute care.
Akutversorgung *f*: acute care.
Akzeptor *m*: acceptor.
akzessorisch: accessory, supernumerary.
akzidentell: accidental.
Alanin *n*: alanine.
Alastrim *n*: alastrim, variola minor.
Alatrofloxacin *n*: alatrofloxacin.
Albendazol *n*: albendazole.
Albers-Schönberg-Krankheit *f*: Albers-Schönberg disease, osteopetrosis.
Albinismus *m*: albinism.
Albright-Krankheit *f*: Albright's hereditary osteodystrophy, fibrocystic osteitis.
Albumin *n*: albumin.
Albuminurie *f*: albuminuria; **akzidentelle** ≈ accidental albuminuria; **hypostatische** ≈ hypostatic albuminuria; **nächtliche** ≈ nyctalbuminuria; **orthostatische** ≈ orthostatic albuminuria; **physiologische** ≈ physiologic albuminuria.
Alclometason *n*: alclometasone.
Alcuroniumchlorid *n*: alcuronium chloride.
Aldehyd *m*: aldehyde.
Aldesleukin *n*: aldesleukin.

Aldobionsäure *f*: aldobionic acid.
Aldosteron *n*: aldosterone.
Aldosteronismus *m*: aldosteronism; **idiopathischer** ≈ idiopathic aldosteronism; **primärer** ≈ primary aldosteronism, Conn syndrome; **sekundärer** ≈ secondary aldosteronism.
Alemtuzumab *n*: alemtuzumab.
Alendronsäure *f*: alendronic acid.
Alexie *f*: alexia, word blindness; **aphasische** ≈ aphasic alexia; **semantische** ≈ semantic alexia; **verbale** ≈ verbal alexia.
Alfacalcidol *n*: alfacalcidol.
Alfatradiol *n*: alfatradiol.
Alfentanil *n*: alfentanil.
Alfuzosin *n*: alfuzosin.
Alge *f*: seaweed.
Alginsäure *f*: alginic acid.
Algorithmus *m*: algorithm; **therapeutischer** ≈ treatment algorithm.
Alienation *f*: alienation.
alimentär: alimentary, nutritional.
Alimentation *f*: alimentation, nutrition.
Alitretinoin *n*: alitretinoin.
Alizaprid *n*: alizapride.
Alkali *n*: alkali.
Alkalireserve *f*: alkali reserve.
alkalisch: alkaline.
Alkaliurie *f*: alkalinuria.
Alkaloid *n*: alkaloid.
Alkalose *f*: alkalosis; **hypokaliämische** ≈ hypokalemic alkalosis; **kompensierte** ≈ compensated alkalosis; **kongenitale** ≈ congenital gastrointestinal alkalosis; **metabolische** ≈ metabolic alkalosis; **respiratorische** ≈ respiratory alkalosis.
Alkaptonurie *f*: alkaptonuria.
Alkohol *m*: alcohol; **absoluter** ≈ absolute alcohol; **primärer** ≈ primary alcohol; **sekundärer** ≈ secondary alcohol; **tertiärer** ≈ tertiary alcohol.
Alkoholabhängigkeit *f*: alcohol dependence.
Alkoholabusus *m*: alcohol abuse, alcoholism.
Alkoholdehydrogenase *f*: alcohol dehydrogenase.
Alkoholdelir *n*: alcoholic delirium.
Alkoholdemenz *f*: alcoholic dementia, Korsakoff syndrome.
Alkoholentzugsdelir *n*: alcohol withdrawal delirium.
Alkoholenzephalopathie *f*: alcoholic encephalopathy.
Alkoholhepatitis *f*: alcoholic hepatitis.
Alkoholiker *m*: alcoholic.
Alkoholintoxikation *f*: alcoholic intoxication.
alkoholisch: alcoholic.
Alkoholismus *m*: alcoholism, habitual excessive drinking; **periodischer** ≈ periodic drinking bout.
Alkoholkonsum *m*: alcohol consumption.
Alkoholkrankheit *f*: alcoholism.
Alkoholneuropathie *f*: alcoholic polyneuropathy.
Alkoholparanoia *f*: alcoholic paranoia.
Alkoholpsychose *f*: alcoholic psychosis.
Alkylanzien: alkylating agents.
Alkylierung *f*: alkylation.
Allantois *f*: allantois.
Allantoisplazenta *f*: allantoic placenta.
Allel *n*: allele.
Allelie *f*: allelism.
allelomorph: allelomorph.
Allergen *n*: allergen.
Allergenexpositionstest *m*: allergen challenge.
Allergentestung *f*: allergen testing.
Allergie *f*: allergy; **humorale** ≈ humoral allergy; **zelluläre** ≈ cell-mediated allergy.
allergisch: allergic.
Alles-oder-Nichts-Gesetz *n*: all-or-none law.
Allgemeinanästhesie *f*: general anesthesia.
Allgemeinchirurgie *f*: general surgery.
Allgemeinerkrankung *f*: systemic disease.
Allgemeinmedizin *f*: family practice.
Allgemeinmediziner *m*: general practitioner.
Allgemeinnarkose *f*: general anesthesia.

Allgemeinreaktion *f*: general reaction, systemic reaction.
Allgemeinsymptom *n*: constitutional symptom.
Allgemeinzustand *m*: general condition.
Allheilmittel *n*: universal remedy, panacea, cure-all.
Alloantigen *n*: alloantigen, isoantigen.
Alloantikörper *m*: alloantibody, isoantibody.
Allobarbital *n*: allobarbital.
Allochirie *f*: allochiria.
allogen: allogeneic.
Allograft *n*: allograft.
Allokation *f*: allocation.
Allopathie *f*: allopathy.
Allophansäure *f*: allophanic acid.
Alloplastie *f*: alloplasty.
Alloplastik *f*: alloplasty.
Allopurinol *n*: allopurinol.
Allotransplantat *n*: allotransplant, allograft.
Alloxan-Diabetes *m*: alloxan diabetes.
Almeida-Krankheit *f*: Almeida's disease, paracoccidioidomycosis.
Almotriptan *n*: almotriptan.
Aloe *f*: aloe.
Alopecia androgenetica *f*: androgenetic alopecia.
Alopecia symptomatica diffusa *f*: symptomatic alopecia.
Alopezie *f*: alopecia, baldness; **atrophische** ≈ atrophical alopecia; **kongenitale** ≈ congenital alopecia; **mechanische** ≈ traumatic alopecia.
Alpers-Syndrom *n*: Alpers syndrome, diffuse cortical sclerosis.
Alphablocker *m*: alpha blocker.
Alphafetoprotein *n*: alpha-fetoprotein, AFP.
Alphakettenkrankheit *f*: alpha chain disease, Franklin's disease.
Alpharezeptorenblocker *m*: alpha blocker.
Alphastrahl *m*: alpha ray.
Alphawelle *f*: alpha wave.
Alprazolam *n*: alprazolam.
Alprenolol *n*: alprenolol.
Alprostadil *n*: alprostadil.
Alptraum *m*: nightmare.
alt: old.
Altenbetreuung *f*: care for the aged.
Altenpflegerin *f*: geriatric nurse.
Alter *n*: age; **biologisches** ≈ physiologic age; **chronologisches** ≈ chronological age; **fortpflanzungsfähiges** ≈ reproductive age; **funktionelles** ≈ functional age; **gebärfähiges** ≈ childbearing age, reproductive age; **hohes** ≈ old age, senility.
Altern *n*: aging, senescence.
Alternativmedizin *f*: alternative medicine.
alternierend: alternating.
Altersabhängigkeit *f*: age dependency.
Altersalopezie *f*: senile alopecia.
Altersdemenz *f*: senile dementia, Kahlbaum-Wernicke syndrome.
Altersdepression *f*: senile depression.
Altersdiabetes *m*: late-onset diabetes mellitus.
Altersemphysem *n*: aging-lung emphysema.
Altersplaque *f*: senile plaque.
Alterspsychiatrie *f*: geriatric psychiatry.
Alterspsychose *f*: senile psychosis.
Altersschwerhörigkeit *f*: presbyacusis.
Alterssichtigkeit *f*: presbyopia.
Altersstar *m*: senile cataract.
Altersverteilung *f*: age distribution.
Alterswarze *f*: senile wart.
Alterung *f*: aging; **vorzeitige** ≈ premature senility.
Altgedächtnis *n*: remote memory.
Altinsulin *n*: regular insulin.
Altretamin *n*: altretamine.
Alttuberkulin *n*: old tuberculin.
alveolär: alveolar, periodontal.
Alveolarabszess *m*: apical abscess.
Alveolardruck *m*: alveolar pressure.
Alveolardysplasie, kongenitale *f*: congenital alveolar dysplasia.
Alveolarfortsatz *m*: alveolar process, dental process.
Alveolarluft *f*: alveolar air.
Alveolarmakrophage *m*: alveolar macrophage.
Alveolarmembran *f*: respiratory membrane.

Alveolarspalte *f*: alveolar cleft.
Alveolarzellkarzinom *n*: alveolar cell carcinoma.
Alveole *f*: alveolus, air cell.
Alveolitis *f*: alveolitis; **allergische** ≈ allergic alveolitis; **exogene allergische** ≈ extrinsic allergic alveolitis; **fibrosierende** ≈ fibrosing alveolitis.
alveolokapillär: alveolocapillary.
Alzheimer-Demenz *f*: Alzheimer's dementia, Alzheimer's disease.
Amalgam *n*: amalgam.
Amantadin *n*: amantadine.
Amastie *f*: amastia.
Amaurose *f*: amaurosis, blindness.
Amaurosis fugax *f*: amaurosis fugax; **einseitige** ≈ transient monocular blindness.
amaurotisch: amaurotic.
Ambenoniumchlorid *n*: ambenonium chloride.
Ambivalenz *f*: ambivalence.
Amblyopie *f*: amblyopia; **toxische** ≈ toxic amblyopia.
Amboss *m*: incus, anvil.
Ambroxol *n*: ambroxol.
Ambu-Beatmungsbeutel *m*: Ambu resuscitator bag.
Ambucetamid *n*: ambucetamide.
ambulant: ambulatory.
Ambulanz *f*: outpatient clinic.
Ambutoniumbromid *n*: ambutonium bromide.
Amcinonid *n*: amcinonide.
Amebom *n*: ameboma.
Ameisenlaufen *n*: formication, Magnan symptom.
Ameisensäure *f*: formic acid.
Amelie *f*: amelia.
Ameloblast *m*: ameloblast, adamantoblast.
Ameloblastenfibrom *n*: ameloblastic fibroma.
Ameloblastenodontom *n*: ameloblastic odontoma.
Ameloblastom *n*: ameloblastoma.
Ameloblastosarkom *n*: ameloblastosarcoma, ameloblastic sarcoma.
Amenorrhö *f*: amenorrhea; **funktionelle** ≈ functional amenorrhea; **hypophysäre** ≈ pituitary amenorrhea; **hypothalamische** ≈ hypothalamic amenorrhea; **ovarielle** ≈ ovarian amenorrhea; **physiologische** ≈ physiological amenorrhea; **postpartale** ≈ post-partum amenorrhea; **primäre** ≈ primary amenorrhea; **psychogene** ≈ psychogenic amenorrhea; **sekundäre** ≈ secondary amenorrhea; **stressbedingte** ≈ stress-induced amenorrhea; **traumatische** ≈ traumatic amenorrhea, Asherman syndrome; **uterine** ≈ uterine amenorrhea; **zentrale** ≈ central amenorrhea.
Amenorrhö-Galaktorrhö-Syndrom *n*: galactorrhea-amenorrhea syndrome, Albright-Forbes syndrome.
Amentia *f*: amentia.
Ametropie *f*: ametropia.
Ameziniummetilsulfat *n*: amezinium metilsulfate.
Amfepramon *n*: amfepramone.
Amfetaminil *n*: amfetaminil.
Amid *n*: amide.
Amifostin *n*: amifostine.
Amikacin *n*: amikacin.
Amilomer *n*: amilomer.
Amilorid *n*: amiloride.
Amin *n*: amine; **biogenes** ≈ biogenic amine; **primäres** ≈ primary amine; **quartäres** ≈ quaternary amine; **sekundäres** ≈ secondary amine; **tertiäres** ≈ tertiary amine; **vasoaktives** ≈ vasoactive amine.
Aminoazidurie *f*: aminoaciduria.
Aminobenzoat *n*: aminobenzoate.
p-Aminobenzoesäure *f*: p-aminobenzoic acid, PABA.
Aminobuttersäure *f*: aminobutyric acid.
Aminocapronsäure *f*: aminocaproic acid.
Aminoessigsäure *f*: aminoacetic acid, glycine.
Aminoglutethimid *n*: aminoglutethimide.
Aminohippursäure *f*: aminohippuric acid.
Aminohydroxybenzoesäure *f*: aminohydroxybenzoic acid.
α-Amino-ß-hydroxypropionsäure *f*: alpha-aminobetahydroxypropionic acid.

A

α-Aminoisovaleriansäure *f*: 2-aminoisovaleric acid, valine.
δ-Aminolävulinsäure *f*: δ-aminolevulinic acid.
Aminopropionsäure *f*: 2-aminopropionic acid.
Aminopterin *n*: aminopterin.
Aminosäure *f*: amino acid; **aromatische** ≈ aromatic amino acid; **essentielle** ≈ essential amino acid; **ketoplastische** ≈ ketogenic amino acid; **verzweigtkettige** ≈ branched-chain amino acid.
Aminosäurediabetes *m*: amino acid diabetes.
Aminosalizylsäure *f*: aminosalicylic acid.
Amiodaron *n*: amiodarone.
Amiphenazol *n*: amiphenazole.
Amisulprid *n*: amisulpride.
Amitose *f*: amitosis.
Amitriptylin *n*: amitriptyline.
Amitriptylinoxid *n*: amitriptylinoxide.
Amlodipin *n*: amlodipine.
Amme *f*: wet nurse, fosterer.
Ammoniak *n*: ammonia.
Ammoniumchlorid *n*: ammonium chloride.
Ammonshorn *n*: Ammon's formation, cornu Ammonis.
Amnesie *f*: amnesia, memory loss; **anterograde** ≈ anterograde amnesia; **begrenzte** ≈ circumscribed amnesia; **elektive** ≈ affective amnesia; **hysterische** ≈ hysterical amnesia; **lakunäre** ≈ lacunar amnesia; **partielle** ≈ incomplete amnesia; **posttraumatische** ≈ posttraumatic amnesia; **psychogene** ≈ hysterical amnesia; **retrograde** ≈ retrograde amnesia; **transitorische** ≈ transient amnesia; **traumatische** ≈ traumatic amnesia; **umschriebene** ≈ localized amnesia.
Amniographie *f*: amniography.
Amnion *n*: amnion, amniotic sac.
Amnionfalte *f*: amniotic fold.
Amnionflüssigkeit *f*: amniotic fluid.
Amnionhöhle *f*: amniotic cavity.
Amnionschnürfurche *f*: amniotic constriction.
Amnionstrang *m*: amniotic band.
Amnioskopie *f*: amnioscopy.
amniotisch: amniotic.
Amniotomie *f*: amniotomy.
Amniozele *f*: amniocele.
Amniozentese *f*: amniocentesis; **transabdominelle** ≈ transabdominal amniocentesis; **transzervikale** ≈ transcervical amniocentesis.
Amobarbital *n*: amobarbital.
Amodiaquin *n*: amodiaquine.
Amöbe *f*: ameba.
Amöbenbalanitis *f*: amebic balanitis.
Amöbendysenterie *f*: amebic dysentery, amebic diarrhea.
Amöbengranulom *n*: amebic granuloma.
Amöbenhepatitis *f*: amebic hepatitis, hepatic amebiasis.
Amöbenkolitis *f*: amebic colitis.
Amöbenruhr *f*: amebic diarrhea, amebic dysentery.
Amöbenzyste *f*: amebic cyst.
Amöbiasis *f*: amebiasis.
amorph: amorphous.
Amoxicillin *n*: amoxicillin.
Amphetamin *n*: amphetamine.
Amphotericin B *n*: amphotericin B.
amphoterisch: amphoteric.
Ampicillin *n*: ampicillin.
Amprenavir *n*: amprenavir.
Ampulle *f*: ampule, ampulla.
Amputation *f*: amputation, ablation; **aperiostale** ≈ aperiosteal amputation, Bunge's amputation; **interskapulothorakale** ≈ interscapulothoracic amputation; **subperiostale** ≈ subperiosteal amputation; **suprakondyläre** ≈ supracondylar amputation.
Amputationsneurom *n*: amputation neuroma, false neuroma.
Amputationsstumpf *m*: amputation stump.
Amputationstrauma *n*: traumatic amputation.
Amrinon *n*: amrinone.
Amsacrin *n*: amsacrine.
Amylase *f*: amylase.
Amylnitrit *n*: amyl nitrite.
Amyloidablagerung *f*: amyloid deposit.
Amyloidkörperchen *n*: amyloid body.

Amyloidleber *f*: albuminoid liver, amyloid liver.
Amyloidmilz *f*: amyloid spleen.
Amyloidniere *f*: waxy kidney.
Amyloidose *f*: amyloidosis, Virchow's degeneration.
Amyotonia congenita *f*: amyotonia congenita.
Amyotonie *f*: amyotonia.
amyotroph: amyotrophic.
Amyotrophie *f*: amyotrophy, myatrophy.
anabol: anabolic.
Anabolikum *n*: anabolic.
Anabolismus *m*: anabolism.
Anämie *f*: anemia; **achrestische** ≈ achrestic anemia, Wilkinson's anemia; **aplastische** ≈ aplastic anemia; **autoimmunhämolytische** ≈ autoimmune hemolytic disease; **chronische** ≈ chronic anemia; **hämolytische** ≈ hemolytic anemia; **hyperchrome** ≈ hyperchromic anemia; **hypochrome** ≈ hypochromic anemia; **hypoplastische** ≈ hypoplastic anemia; **kongenitale aplastische** ≈ congenital hypoplastic anemia, Diamond-Blackfan syndrome; **kongenitale dyserythropoetische** ≈ congenital dyserythropoietic anemia; **makrozytäre** ≈ macrocytic anemia; **megaloblastäre** ≈ megaloblastic anemia; **normochrome** ≈ normochromic anemia; **normozytäre** ≈ normocytic anemia; **perniziöse** ≈ pernicious anemia, Biermer's anemia; **schwere aplastische** ≈ severe aplastic anemia; **sideroachrestische** ≈ sideroachrestic anemia; **therapierefraktäre sideroachrestische** ≈ acquired sideroachrestic anemia; **toxische** ≈ toxic anemia.
Anämiegeräusch *n*: anemic murmur.
anämisch: anemic.
Anaerobier *m*: anaerobe, anaerobic bacteria; **fakultativer** ≈ facultative anaerobe; **obligater** ≈ obligate anaerobe.
Anästhesie *f*: anesthesia; **segmentale** ≈ segmental anesthesia, segmental block; **spinale** ≈ spinal anesthesia.
Anästhesiologie *f*: anesthesiology.
Anästhetikum *n*: anesthetic.
Anakinra *n*: anakinra.
Anakrotie *f*: anacrotism.
anal: anal.
Analatresie *f*: anal atresia, imperforate anus.
Analbuminämie *f*: analbuminemia.
Analeptikum *n*: analeptic.
Analfissur *f*: anal fissure.
Analfistel *f*: anal fistula.
Analgesie *f*: analgesia; **patientengesteuerte** ≈ on-demand analgesia.
Analgetikanephropathie *f*: analgesic nephropathy.
Analgetikum *n*: analgesic drug, analgetic, painkiller.
analgetisch: analgesic, analgetic.
Analkarzinom *n*: anal carcinoma.
analog: analogous.
Analogstoff *m*: analogue.
Analpapille *f*: anal papilla.
Analphabetismus *m*: illiteracy.
Analprolaps *m*: anal prolapse.
Analreflex *m*: anal reflex, perianal reflex.
Analregion *f*: anal region.
Analyse *f*: analysis.
Anamnese *f*: medical history, patient's history.
anamnestisch: anamnestic.
anankastisch: anancastic.
anaklitisch: anaclitic.
Anaphase *f*: anaphase.
Anaphylaxie *f*: anaphylaxis, anaphylactic reaction; **aktive** ≈ active anaphylaxis; **passive kutane** ≈ passive cutaneous anaphylaxis; **umgekehrte passive kutane** ≈ reverse passive anaphylaxis.
Anaplasie *f*: anaplasia, dedifferentiation.
Anastomose *f*: anastomosis; **antiperistaltische** ≈ antiperistaltic anastomosis; **aortopulmonale** ≈ aorticopulmonary anastomosis; **arteriovenöse** ≈ arteriovenous anastomosis; **gastroduodenale** ≈ Billroth's anastomosis; **isoperistaltische** ≈ isoperistaltic anastomosis; **portokavale** ≈ portocaval anastomosis.
Anastomosenoperation *f*: anastomotic operation.

Anastomosenulkus *n*: anastomotic ulcer.
Anastrozol *n*: anastrozole.
Anatomie *f*: anatomy; **angewandte** ≈ applied anatomy; **beschreibende** ≈ descriptive anatomy; **pathologische** ≈ pathologic anatomy; **topographische** ≈ topographic anatomy.
anatomisch: anatomical.
Anazidität *f*: anacidity.
Ancrod *n*: ancrod.
Ancylostoma *n*: ankylostoma.
Ancylostomiasis *f*: ankylostomiasis.
Androblastom *n*: androblastoma, Sertoli-Leydig cell tumor.
androgen: androgenic.
Androgen *n*: androgen.
android: android.
Andrologie *f*: andrology.
Androstanolon *n*: androstanolone.
Androstendion *n*: androstenedione.
Androstenon *n*: androstenone.
Androsteron *n*: androsterone.
Anenzephalie *f*: anencephaly.
Anergie *f*: anergia, lack of energy.
Anethol *n*: anethole.
Aneuploidie *f*: aneuploidy.
Aneurysma *n*: aneurysm; **arteriovenöses** ≈ arteriovenous aneurysm; **beerenförmiges** ≈ berry aneurysm; **disseziierendes** ≈ dissecting aneurysm; **echtes** ≈ true aneurysm; **falsches** ≈ false aneurysm; **intrakranielles** ≈ intracranial aneurysm; **mykotisches** ≈ mycotic aneurysm, bacterial aneurysm; **rankenförmiges** ≈ cirsoid aneurysm; **sackförmiges** ≈ saccular aneurysm.
Aneurysmaschwirren *n*: aneurysmal thrill.
Aneurysmawandaussackung *f*: aneurysmal sac.
Anfälligkeit *f*: disposition, proneness, susceptibility.
Anfärbbarkeit *f*: stainability.
Anfall *m*: attack, insult, seizure, stroke; **apoplektiformer** ≈ apoplectiform attack; **atonischer** ≈ atonic seizure; **epileptischer** ≈ epileptic attack; **fokaler** ≈ focal attack; **generalisierter** ≈ generalized seizure; **kataplektischer** ≈ cataplectic crisis; **komplexer partieller** ≈ complex absence; **myoklonischer** ≈ myoclonic seizure; **psychogener** ≈ hysterical attack; **psychomotorischer** ≈ psychomotor seizure; **tonischer** ≈ tonic spasm; **tonisch-klonischer** ≈ tonic-clonic seizure; **vasovagaler** ≈ Gowers syndrome.
Anfallsserie *f*: serial epilepsy.
anfeuchten: damp, wet.
Anflutung *f*: tide.
anfrischen: refresh.
angeboren: inborn, innate.
Angewohnheit *f*: habit.
Angiektasie *f*: angiectasia.
angiektatisch: angiectatic.
Angiitis *f*: angiitis, vasculitis; **allergische granulomatöse** ≈ allergic angiitis, Churg-Strauss disease; **granulomatöse** ≈ granulomatous angiitis; **nekrotisierende** ≈ necrotizing angiitis.
Angina *f*: angina; **agranulozytäre** ≈ agranulocytic angina; **diphtherische** ≈ pharyngeal diphtheria, Bretto-neau's disease.
Angina abdominalis *f*: abdominal angina.
Angina pectoris *f*: angina pectoris, cardiac angina; **instabile** ≈ unstable angina; **stabile** ≈ angina of effort; **vasospastische** ≈ Prinzmetal's angina.
Angiogramm *n*: angiogram.
Angiographie *f*: angiography.
Angiohämophilie *f*: angiohemophilia, vascular hemophilia.
Angiokardiographie *f*: angiocardiography.
Angiom *n*: angioma; **arteriovenöses** ≈ arteriovenous angioma; **planes** ≈ telangiectatic angioma; **sklerosierendes** ≈ sclerosing angioma; **spinales** ≈ spinal angioma; **tuberöses** ≈ tuberous angioma.
Angioma serpiginosum *f*: angioma serpiginosum, infectious angioma.
Angiomatose *f*: angiomatosis; **enzephalofaziale** ≈ encephalofacial angiomatosis, Wyatt syndrome; **kongenitale** ≈ congenital dysplastic angiomatosis.

angioneurotisch: angioneurotic.
Angioödem *n*: angioneurotic edema; **hereditäres** ≈ hereditary edema.
Angiopathie *f*: angiopathy; **diabetische** ≈ diabetic angiopathy.
Angioplastie *f*: angioplasty; **perkutane transluminale** ≈ percutaneous transluminal angioplasty, balloon angioplasty; **transluminale** ≈ transluminal arterial dilatation.
Angiosarkom *n*: angiosarcoma.
Angiospasmus *m*: angiospasm, vasospasm.
Angiotensin *n*: angiotensin.
Angiotensinamid *n*: angiotensinamide.
Angiotensin umwandelndes Enzym *n*: angiotensin converting enzyme, ACE.
Angiozyste *f*: angiocyst.
angrenzen: join, abut.
Angst *f*: anxiety; **existentielle** ≈ existential anxiety; **frei flottierende** ≈ unattached anxiety; **pathologische** ≈ pathologic fear.
Angstattacke *f*: anxiety attack.
Angstneurose *f*: anxiety neurosis.
Angstsyndrom *n*: anxiety disorder.
Angularissyndrom *n*: angular gyrus syndrome, Gerstmann syndrome.
Angulus infectiosus *m*: angular stomatitis, angular cheilitis.
Anhänglichkeit *f*: attachment.
Anhang *m*: appendage, appendix, annex, tag.
Anhebung *f*: elevation.
anheften: tack, attach.
Anhidrose *f*: anhidrosis.
Anhidrosis hypotrichotica polydysplastica *f*: anhidrotic ectodermal dysplasia, Christ-Siemens syndrome.
anikterisch: anicteric, nonicteric.
Anilinkrebs *m*: aniline carcinoma.
Anion *n*: anion.
Anionenaustauscher *m*: anion exchanger.
Aniseikonie *f*: aniseikonia.
Anisokorie *f*: anisocoria.
Anisometropie *f*: anisometropia.
Anisozytose *f*: anisocytosis.
Anissäure *f*: anisic acid.
Ankyloblepharon *n*: ankyloblepharon.
Ankyloglosson *n*: ankyloglossia.
Ankylose *f*: ankylosis; **extraartikuläre** ≈ extra-articular ankylosis; **extrakapsuläre** ≈ extracapsular ankylosis; **falsche** ≈ extra-articular ankylosis; **fibröse** ≈ fibrous ankylosis; **knöcherne** ≈ bony ankylosis, true ankylosis.
ankylosierend: ankylosing.
Anlage *f*: assembly, disposition, predisposition.
Anlagerung *f*: accretion, apposition.
Anlegespan *m*: onlay graft.
Anode *f*: anode.
Anodenschlusszuckung *f*: anodal closure contraction.
anogenital: anogenital.
anomal: anomalous.
Anomalie *f*: anomaly.
Anomie *f*: anomia, nominal aphasia.
Anonychie *f*: anonychia.
anonym: anonymous.
Anorchidie *f*: anorchism.
anorektal: anorectal.
Anorexia nervosa *f*: anorexia nervosa.
Anorexie *f*: anorexia.
anorganisch: inorganic, anorganic.
Anorgasmie *f*: anorgasmy.
anormal: abnormal.
Anosmie *f*: anosmia, olfactory anesthesia.
anovulatorisch: anovulatory.
Anoxämie *f*: anoxemia, anoxia.
Anoxie *f*: anoxia, anoxemia.
Anpassung *f*: adaptation, adjustment; **genetische** ≈ genetic adaptation; **phänotypische** ≈ phenotypic adaptation; **schlechte** ≈ maladjustment; **soziale** ≈ social adaptation, social adjustment.
Anpassungshypertrophie *f*: adaptive hypertrophy.
Anpassungsreaktion *f*: adjustment reaction.
Anpassungssyndrom, allgemeines *n*: general adaptation syndrome.
Anpassungsverhalten *n*: adaptive behavior.
Anregbarkeit *f*: excitability.
Anregung *f*: excitation, stimulation.

A

Anreicherung *f*: enrichment.
Ansammlung *f*: agglomeration, pool.
Ansamycin *n*: ansamycin.
Ansatz *m*: appendage, insertion.
Ansaugung *f*: aspiration.
Anschoppung *f*: engorgement, congestion.
Anschwellung *f*: swelling.
Anserin *n*: anserine.
Anspannung *f*: tension, stretch; **psychische** ≈ psychic tension.
Anspannungskopfschmerz *m*: exertional headache.
Anspannungston *m*: tension sound.
Anspannungszeit des Herzens: isometric period of the cardiac cycle.
ansprechen: respond.
Ansprechen *n*: response; **therapeutisches** ≈ therapeutic response.
ansteckend: infectious, communicable, contagious.
Ansteckung *f*: infection, contamination.
Anstieg *m*: increase, rise.
Anstrengung *f*: effort, exertion; **körperliche** ≈ physical effort.
Anstrengungsalbuminurie *f*: exercise albuminuria.
Anstrengungsasthma *n*: exercise-induced asthma.
Antagonismus *m*: antagonism.
Antagonist *m*: antagonistic drug, antagonistic muscle; **partieller** ≈ partial antagonist; **reiner** ≈ full antagonist.
antagonistisch: antagonistic, counteractive.
antazid: antacid.
Antazidum *n*: antacid, acid-inhibiting agent.
Antazolin *n*: antazoline, imidamine.
Antefixation *f*: antefixation.
Anteflexion *f*: anteflexation.
Antepulsion *f*: propulsion.
anterograd: anterograde.
Anteversion *f*: anteversion.
Anthelminthikum *n*: anthelminthic, vermifuge.
Anthrachinon *n*: anthraquinone.
Anthrakose *f*: anthracosis, coal worker's pneumoconiosis.
Anthramycin *n*: anthramycin.
Anthrax *m*: anthrax, splenic fever.
Anthrazyklin *n*: anthracycline.
Anthropologie *f*: anthropology.
Anthropometrie *f*: anthropometry.
antiadrenerg: antiadrenergic, sympathicolytic.
Antiadrenergikum *n*: antiadrenergic.
Antiandrogen *n*: antiandrogen.
Antiantikörper *m*: antiantibody.
Antiarrhythmikum *n*: antiarrhythmic drug.
Antiatelektasefaktor *m*: pulmonary surfactant.
Antibabypille *f*: birth control pill.
Antibasalmembran-Antikörper-Glomerulonephritis *f*: antiglomerular basement membrane antibody glomerulonephritis.
Antibiotikacreme *f*: antibiotic creme.
Antibiotika-Enterokolitis *f*: antibiotic enterocolitis.
Antibiotikaresistenz *f*: antibiotic resistance.
Antibiotikum *n*: antibiotic, antibacterial agent.
antibiotisch: antibiotic.
anticholinerg: anticholinergic.
Antidepressivum *n*: antidepressant drug, antidepressant; **trizyklisches** ≈ tricyclic.
Antidiabetikum *n*: antidiabetic.
antidiabetisch: antidiabetic.
Antidiuretikum *n*: antidiuretic.
antidiuretisch: antidiuretic.
Antidot *n*: antidote, antitoxin.
Antiepileptikum *n*: antiepileptic drug, antiepileptic.
Antigen *n*: antigen; **blutgruppenspezifisches** ≈ group-specific antigen; **carcinoembryonales** ≈ carcinoembryonic antigen, CEA; **heterophiles** ≈ heterophil antigen; **kreuzreagierendes** ≈ cross-reacting antigen; **onkofetales** ≈ oncofetal antigen.
Antigen-Drift *f*: antigen drift, antigenic drift.
antigenpräsentierend: antigen presenting.
Antigen-Shift *m*: antigen shift, antigenic shift.
Antigenvariation *f*: antigenic variation.

Antigenverschiebung *f*: antigen shift, antigenic shift.
Antiglobulin *n*: antiglobulin.
Antiglobulintest *m*: antiglobulin test.
antihelminthisch: anthelminthic.
Antihistaminikum *n*: antihistamine.
Antihumanglobulin *n*: antihuman globulin.
antiinflammatorisch: anti-inflammatory.
Antikoagulans *n*: anticoagulant.
Antikoagulanzientherapie *f*: anticoagulant therapy.
Antikodon *n*: anticodon, nodoc.
Antikörper *m*: antibody; **agglutinierender** ≈ agglutinating antibody; **antimitochondrialer** ≈ antimitochondrial antibody; **antinukleärer** ≈ antinuclear antibody; **heterophiler** ≈ heterophilic antibody; **heterotypischer** ≈ heterotypic antibody; **homozytotroper** ≈ homocytotropic antibody; **inkompletter** ≈ incomplete antibody; **komplementbindender** ≈ complementfixing antibody; **kompletter** ≈ complete antibody; **monoklonaler** ≈ monoclonal antibody; **mütterlicher** ≈ maternal antibody; **oligoklonaler** ≈ oligoclonal antibody; **polyklonaler** ≈ polyclonal antibody; **protektiver** ≈ protective antibody; **zellständiger** ≈ cell-bound antibody; **zytophiler** ≈ cytophilic antibody; **zytotoxischer** ≈ cytotoxic antibody.
Antikörpertiter *m*: antibody titre.
Antikonvulsivum *n*: anticonvulsant.
Antikonzeptivum *n*: contraceptive.
Antilymphozytenserum *n*: antilymphocyte serum.
Antimetabolit *m*: antimetabolite.
antimikrobiell: antimicrobial.
Antimitotikum *n*: antimitotic.
Antimon *n*: antimony.
Antimonsäure *f*: antimonic acid.
Antimykotikum *n*: antimycotic, antifungal.
antinukleär: antinuclear.
Antiöstrogen *n*: antiestrogen.
antiperistaltisch: antiperistaltic.
Antiphlogistikum *n*: antiphlogistic, anti-inflammatory; **nicht-steroidales** ≈ non-steroidal anti-inflammatory agent.
antiphlogistisch: antiphlogistic, anti-inflammatory.
Antipsychotikum *n*: antipsychotic.
antipyretisch: antipyretic, antifebrile, febrifugal.
antirachitisch: antirachitic.
antiretroviral: antiretroviral.
Antirheumatikum *n*: antirheumatic; **antiinflammatorisches steroidales** ≈ steroidal anti-inflammatory agent.
Antisepsis *f*: antisepsis.
antiseptisch: antiseptic.
Antiserum *n*: antiserum, immune serum; **monovalentes** ≈ monovalent antiserum; **polyvalentes** ≈ polyvalent antiserum.
Antispasmodikum *n*: antispasmodic.
Antithrombin *n*: antithrombin.
Antitoxin *n*: antitoxin, antidote.
antiviral: antiviral.
antral: antral.
Antrektomie *f*: antrectomy.
Antriebshemmung *f*: block of impulse.
antriebslos: adynamic.
Antroskopie *f*: antroscopy.
Antrotomie *f*: antrotomy.
Antrum *n*: antrum, mastoid antrum.
Antrumdrainage *f*: antrostomy.
Antrumgastritis *f*: antral gastritis.
Antrumzyste *f*: antral cyst.
Anurie *f*: anuria; **echte** ≈ renal anuria; **postrenale** ≈ postrenal anuria; **prärenale** ≈ prerenal anuria; **renale** ≈ renal anuria.
Anus *m*: anus.
anwenden: apply, use.
Anwendung *f*: administration, application, use; **äußere** ≈ external administration; **intravaginale** ≈ intravaginal administration; **klinische** ≈ clinical application; **orale** ≈ oral administration; **perkutane** ≈ cutaneous administration; **sublinguale** ≈ sublingual administration; **topische** ≈ topical administration.
Anwendungsschema *n*: administration schedule.
Anxiolytikum *n*: anxiolytic, minor tranquilizer.

anxiolytisch: anxiolytic.
Anzahl *f*: number.
Anzapfsyndrom *n*: steal syndrome; **aortoiliakales** ≈ aortoiliac steal syndrome.
Anzapfsyndrom der Arteria subclavia *n*: subclavian steal syndrome, subclavian steal.
Anzeichen *n*: sign, symptom, signal.
anzeigepflichtig: notifiable.
anzüchten: culture.
Aorta *f*: aorta; **doppelte** ≈ double aorta; **reitende** ≈ overriding aorta, dextroposed aorta.
aortal: aortic.
Aortenaneurysma *n*: aortic aneurysm; **abdominales** ≈ abdominal aneurysm; **thorakales** ≈ thoracic aneurysm.
Aortenbifurkationssyndrom *n*: aortoiliac occlusive disease, Leriche syndrome.
Aortenbogen *m*: aortic arch, arch of the aorta; **doppelter** ≈ double aortic arch.
Aortenbogenangiographie *f*: aortic arch angiography.
Aortenbogensyndrom *n*: aortic arch syndrome, Takayasu's arteritis, pulseless disease.
Aortendruck *m*: aortic pressure.
Aortenherz *n*: boat-shaped heart.
Aorteninsuffizienz *f*: aortic insufficiency.
Aortenklappe *f*: aortic valve.
Aortenklappeninsuffizienz *f*: aortic valve insufficiency.
Aortenklappenprolaps *m*: aortic valve prolapse.
Aortenklappenstenose *f*: aortic valve stenosis.
Aortenmurmeln *n*: aortic murmur.
Aortenplastik *f*: aortoplasty.
Aortenpuls, abdomineller *m*: abdominal pulse.
Aortenruptur *f*: aortic rupture.
Aortensklerose *f*: aortic sclerosis.
Aortenstenose *f*: aortic stenosis; **subvalvuläre** ≈ subvalvular aortic stenosis; **supravalvuläre** ≈ supravalvular aortic stenosis; **valvuläre** ≈ aortic valve stenosis; **verkalkende** ≈ calcified aortic stenosis.
Aortenverkalkung *f*: aortic calcification.
Aortenwand *f*: aortic wall.
Aortitis *f*: aortitis.
aortoiliakal: aortoiliac.
aortokoronar: aortocoronary.
aortopulmonal: aortopulmonary.
Apalcillin *n*: apalcillin.
Apathie *f*: apathy.
Aperistaltik *f*: aperistalsis.
Apertur *f*: aperture, opening.
Apgar-Index *m*: Apgar score.
Aphagie *f*: aphagia.
Aphakie *f*: aphakia.
Aphasie *f*: aphasia; **amnestische** ≈ amnesic aphasia; **auditorische** ≈ word deafness; **globale** ≈ global aphasia, total aphasia; **kortikale** ≈ cortical aphasia; **motorische** ≈ motor aphasia, Broca's aphasia; **semantische** ≈ semantic aphasia; **sensorische** ≈ sensory aphasia, Wernicke's aphasia; **subkortikale** ≈ subcortical aphasia; **transkortikale** ≈ transcortical aphasia, Lichtheim's aphasia.
Aphonie *f*: aphonia, tonelessness.
Aphrodisiakum *n*: aphrodisiac.
Aphthe *f*: aphtha, aphthous ulcer.
aphthös: aphthous.
Apikalkörper *m*: apical body.
Apikoektomie *f*: apicectomy.
Aplanat *m*: aplanatic lens.
Aplasie *f*: aplasia.
aplastisch: aplastic.
Aplaviroc *n*: aplaviroc.
Apnoe *f*: apnea.
Apoferritin *n*: apoferritin.
apokrin: apocrine.
Apomorphin *n*: apomorphine.
Aponeurose *f*: aponeurosis.
Apophyse *f*: apophysis.
Apophysenfraktur *f*: apophyseal fracture.
Apophysenlösung *f*: apophyseal fracture.
Apoplexia retinalis *f*: apoplectic retinopathy.
Apoplexie *f*: apoplexy; **lakunäre** ≈ lacunar stroke; **spinale** ≈ spinal apoplexy; **uteroplazentare** ≈ uteroplacental apoplexy, Couvelaire's ute-

rus; **zerebrale** ≈ cerebral apoplexy, cerebral stroke.
Apoptose *f*: apoptosis, programmed cell death.
Apotheke *f*: pharmacy.
Apparat *m*: apparatus, appliance, device, machine; **juxtaglomerulärer** ≈ juxtaglomerular apparatus.
Appendektomie *f*: appendectomy.
Appendix *f*: appendix, appendage.
Appendixphlegmone *f*: appendiceal phlegmon.
Appendizitis *f*: appendicitis; **akute** ≈ acute appendicitis; **perforierende** ≈ perforating appendicitis.
Appendizitiszeichen: appendicitis signs.
Apperzeption *f*: apperception.
Appetit *m*: appetite.
Appetitverlust *m*: loss of appetite.
Appetitzügler *m*: appetite depressant, anorexiant.
Applanatlinse *f*: aplanatic lens.
Applikation *f*: administration.
Applikator *m*: applicator.
Apposition *f*: apposition.
Apprehension *f*: apprehension.
Apraclonidin *n*: apraclonidine.
Apramycin *n*: apramycin.
Apraxie *f*: apraxia; **gliedkinetische** ≈ akinetic apraxia; **ideokinetische** ≈ ideokinetic apraxia; **ideomotorische** ≈ ideomotor apraxia; **kinetische** ≈ kinetic apraxia; **konstruktive** ≈ constructive apraxia; **okulomotorische** ≈ oculomotor apraxia.
Aprepitant *n*: aprepitant.
Aprindin *n*: aprindine.
Aptyalismus *m*: aptyalism, asialia.
Apudom *n*: apudoma.
Aqua ad iniectionem *f*: water for injection.
Aquädukt *m*: aqueduct.
Aquäduktstenose *f*: aqueduct stenosis.
Arabin *n*: arabin.
Arachidonsäure *f*: arachidonic acid.
Arachinsäure *f*: arachic acid.
Arachnodaktylie *f*: arachnodactyly.
Arachnoidea *f*: arachnoid, arachnoid membrane.
Aräometer *n*: areometer, hydrometer.
Aran-Duchenne-Muskeldystrophie *f*: Aran-Duchenne muscular dystrophy.
Arbeitsbelastung *f*: work load.
Arbeitsmedizin *f*: occupational medicine.
Arbeitsphysiologie *f*: work physiology.
Arbeitsplatzkonzentration, maximale *f*: maximum allowable concentration.
Arbeitstherapie *f*: work therapy, ergotherapy.
arbeitsunfähig: disabled, incapable of working.
Arbeitsunfall *m*: occupational accident, occupational injury.
Arborisation *f*: arborization.
Arborisationsblock *m*: arborization block.
Arbovirose *f*: arthropod-borne disease.
Archenteron *n*: archenteron, primitive gut.
Archenzephalon *n*: archencephalon, primitive brain.
Architektonik *f*: architecture, structure.
Areal *n*: area, region.
Arecolin *n*: arecolin.
Areola *f*: areola.
Argasida *f*: argasid.
Argatroban *n*: argatroban.
argentaffin: argentaffin.
Arginin *n*: arginine.
Argininbernsteinsäure *f*: argininosuccinic acid.
Argininbernmsteinsäurekrankheit *f*: argininosuccinicaciduria.
Argininosukzinat *n*: argininosuccinate.
Argininosukzinurie *f*: argininosuccinicaciduria.
Argyrie *f*: argyria.
argyrophil: argyrophil.
Aripiprazol *n*: aripiprazol.
Arm *m*: arm, brachium.
Armlösung *f*: arm extraction.
Armplexus *m*: brachial plexus.
Armplexuslähmung *f*: brachial plexus paralysis; **obere** ≈ upper brachial

plexus paralysis, Erb-Duchenne paralysis; **untere** ≈ lower brachial plexus paralysis, Klumpke's paralysis.
Armschlinge *f*: arm sling.
Armumfang *m*: arm circumference.
Armvorfall *m*: arm presentation, arm prolapse.
Arnold-Chiari-Fehlbildung *f*: Arnold-Chiari deformity.
Aromatasehemmer *m*: aromatase inhibitor.
Arousal-Effekt *m*: arousal effect.
Arrhenoblastom *n*: arrhenoblastoma, Sertoli-Leydig cell tumor.
Arrhythmie *f*: arrhythmia; **paroxysmale supraventrikuläre** ≈ paroxysmal supraventricular arrhythmia; **respiratorische** ≈ respiratory arrhythmia; **ventrikuläre** ≈ ventricular arrhythmia.
arrhythmisch: arrhythmic.
Arsen *n*: arsenic.
Arsenamblyopie: arsenic amblyopia.
Arsenkrebs *m*: arsenic cancer.
Arsenneuropathie *f*: arsenic neuropathy.
Arsenpigmentierung *f*: arsenic pigmentation.
Arsensäure *f*: arsenic acid.
Arsinsäure *f*: arsinic acid.
Arsonsäure *f*: arsonic acid.
Artefakt *n*: artefact, artifact.
artefiziell: artificial, factitious.
Arteria *f*: artery, arteria, a.
Arteria-basilaris-Insuffizienz *f*: basilar insufficiency.
Arteria-carotis-Stenose *f*: carotid stenosis.
Arteria-vertebralis-Insuffizienz *f*: vertebral insufficiency.
Arterie *f*: arteria, artery, a.
arteriell: arterial.
Arteriendruck *m*: arterial blood pressure.
Arteriengeräusch *n*: arterial murmur.
Arterienpuls *m*: arterial pulse.
Arterienrauschen *n*: arterial murmur.
Arterienschwirren *n*: arterial thrill.
Arterienspasmus *m*: arterial spasm.
Arterienthrombose *f*: arterial thrombosis.
Arterienverengung *f*: arterial stenosis.
Arterienverkalkung *f*: arteriosclerosis, arterial calcification.
Arterienverschluss *m*: artery occlusion, arterial obstruction.
Arteriitis *f*: arteritis.
Arteriitis granulomatosa *f*: granulomatous arteritis, giant-cell arteritis, Horton's arteritis.
Arteriitis temporalis *f*: temporal arteritis, giant-cell arteritis, Horton's arteritis.
Arteriographie *f*: arteriography; **selektive** ≈ selective arteriography.
Arteriole *f*: arteriole.
Arteriolosklerose *f*: arteriolosclerosis, arteriolar sclerosis.
Arteriosklerose *f*: arteriosclerosis, arterial sclerosis.
arteriosklerotisch: arteriosclerotic.
Arteriospasmus *m*: arteriospasm.
Arteriotomie *f*: arteriotomy.
arteriovenös: arteriovenous.
Arthralgie *f*: arthralgia.
Arthritis *f*: arthritis; **chronisch entzündliche** ≈ chronic inflammatory arthritis; **eitrige** ≈ suppurative arthritis; **hypertrophe** ≈ hypertrophic arthritis; **infektiöse** ≈ infectious arthritis; **juvenile rheumatoide** ≈ juvenile rheumatoid arthritis; **kristallinduzierte** ≈ crystal arthritis; **postenteritische** ≈ enteropathic reactive arthritis; **postinfektiöse** ≈ postinfectious arthritis; **rheumatoide** ≈ rheumatoid arthritis; **syphilitische** ≈ syphilitic arthritis; **tuberkulöse** ≈ tuberculous arthritis.
arthritisch: arthritic.
Arthritis urica *f*: gouty arthritis.
Arthrodese *f*: arthrodesis, artificial ankylosis.
Arthrographie *f*: arthrography.
Arthrolith *m*: arthrolith, joint calculus.
Arthropathie *f*: arthropathy; **hämophile** ≈ hemophilic arthropathy; **neurogene** ≈ neurogenic arthropathy, Charcot's joint; **psoriatische** ≈ psoriatic arthritis; **tabische** ≈ tabetic osteoarthropathy.

Arthroplastik *f*: arthroplasty.
Arthropode *m*: arthropod.
Arthrose *f*: arthrosis, noninflammatory arthritis.
Arthroskopie *f*: arthroscopy.
Arthrotomie *f*: arthrotomy.
Articain *n*: articaine.
Articulatio *f*: articulation, joint.
artifiziell: artificial, factitious.
artikulär: articular.
Artikulation *f*: articulation.
artspezifisch: species-specific.
arytänoid: arytenoid.
Arytänoidektomie *f*: arytenoidectomy, Kelly's operation.
Arznei *f*: drug, medicine.
Arzneibuch *n*: pharmacopeia, pharmacopoeia.
Arzneiformel *f*: formula.
Arzneimittel *n*: pharmaceutical agent, drug; **frei verkäufliches** ≈ over the counter drug, OTC drug; **offizinelles** ≈ officinal; **verschreibungspflichtiges** ≈ prescription drug.
Arzneimittelexanthem *n*: drug eruption, drug rash.
Arzneimittelinteraktion *f*: drug interaction.
Arzneimittelprüfung *f*: drug evaluation.
Arzneimittelunverträglichkeit *f*: drug intolerance.
Arzneimittelverordnung *f*: drug prescribing.
Arzneimittelvorstufe *f*: prodrug.
Arzneimittelwechselwirkung *f*: drug-drug interaction.
Arzneimittelwirkung *f*: drug action.
Arzneimittelzulassungsbehörde *f*: drug regulatory authority.
Arzt *m*: physician, doctor; **praktischer** ≈ practitioner.
Arztbrief *m*: medical report.
Arzt für Allgemeinmedizin: general practitioner.
Arzthelfer *m*: physician assistant.
Arzt-Patient-Beziehung *f*: physician-patient relation.
Arztwahl, freie *f*: free choice of doctor.
Asbestkrebs *m*: asbestos cancer.
Asbestose *f*: asbestosis.
Ascaridol *n*: ascaridol.
Aschheim-Zondek-Schwangerschaftstest *m*: Aschheim-Zondek pregnancy test.
Aschoff-Tawara-Knoten *m*: node of Aschoff and Tawara, atrioventricular node.
Ascites *m*: ascites, ascitic fluid.
Ascorbinsäure *f*: ascorbic acid, vitamin C.
Asepsis *f*: asepsis.
aseptisch: aseptic.
asexuell: asexual.
Asherman-Fritsch-Syndrom *n*: Asherman syndrome, traumatic amenorrhea.
Asialie *f*: asialia, aptyalism.
Askariasis *f*: ascariasis.
Asomnie *f*: asomnia, insomnia.
Asparaginase *f*: asparaginase.
Asparaginsäure *f*: aspartic acid.
Aspergillom *n*: aspergilloma.
Aspergillose *f*: aspergillosis.
Aspergillsäure *f*: aspergillic acid.
Aspermie *f*: aspermia.
Asphyxie *f*: asphyxia.
Aspiration *f*: aspiration.
Aspirationsbiopsie *f*: aspiration biopsy.
Aspirationsnadel *f*: aspirating needle.
Aspirationspneumonie *f*: aspiration pneumonia, inhalation pneumonia.
Assimilationsbecken *n*: assimilation pelvis.
Astasie-Abasie-Syndrom *n*: astasia-abasia.
Asteatose *f*: asteatosis.
Astemizol *n*: astemizole.
Astereognosie *f*: astereognosis, stereoagnosis.
Asterixis *f*: asterixis, flapping tremor.
Asthenie *f*: asthenia; **neurozirkulatorische** ≈ neurocirculatory asthenia, DaCosta syndrome.
asthenisch: asthenic.
Asthenopie *f*: asthenopia.
Asthma *n*: asthma; **allergisches** ≈ allergic asthma; **endogenes** ≈ intrinsic asthma; **extrinsisches** ≈ extrinsic asthma; **infektallergisches** ≈ infec-

A

tious asthma; **intrinsisches** ≈ intrinsic asthma; **kardiales** ≈ cardiac asthma; **psychogenes** ≈ nervous asthma.
Asthma bronchiale *n*: bronchial asthma.
Asthmahusten *m*: asthmatic cough.
asthmatisch: asthmatic.
Astigmatismus *m*: astigmatism; **gerader** ≈ direct astigmatism; **hyperopischer** ≈ hyperopic astigmatism; **irregulärer** ≈ inverse astigmatism; **myoper** ≈ myopic astigmatism; **regulärer** ≈ direct astigmatism.
Astigmatometer *n*: astigmatometer.
Astroblastom *n*: astroblastoma.
Astroglia *f*: astroglia.
Astronautenkost *f*: astronautic diet.
Astrozyt *m*: astrocyte.
Astrozytom *n*: astrocytoma.
Asymbolie *f*: asymbolia.
Asymmetrie *f*: asymmetry.
asymptomatisch: asymptomatic, symptom-free.
asynchron: asynchronous.
Asynergie *f*: asynergia.
Asynklitismus *m*: asynclitism.
Asystolie *f*: asystolia.
aszendierend: ascending.
Aszites *m*: ascites, ascitic fluid; **chylöser** ≈ chylous ascites; **gallertartiger** ≈ gelatinous ascites; **hämorrhagischer** ≈ hemorrhagic ascites.
Aszitespunktion *f*: abdominal puncture.
ataktisch: atactic, ataxic.
Atavismus *m*: atavism.
Ataxie *f*: ataxia; **alkoholbedingte** ≈ alcoholic ataxia; **hereditäre** ≈ familial ataxia, Sanger-Brown ataxia; **kinetische** ≈ dynamic ataxia; **lokomotorische** ≈ locomotor ataxia; **sensorische** ≈ sensory ataxia; **spinale** ≈ spinal ataxia; **spinozerebelläre** ≈ spinocerebellar ataxia; **vestibuläre** ≈ vestibular ataxia; **zerebelläre** ≈ cerebellar ataxia.
Atazanavir *n*: atazanavir.
Atelektase *f*: atelectasis.
Atelektaseknistern *n*: atelectatic rale.
Atem *m*: breath.
Atembehinderung *f*: respiratory obstruction.
Atembeklemmung *f*: difficulty in breathing.
Atemdepression *f*: respiratory depression.
Atemexkursion *f*: respiratory excursion.
Atemfrequenz *f*: respiratory frequency, respiration rate.
Atemgeräusch *n*: breath sounds, respiratory sound, rale; **amphorisches** ≈ amphoric rale, bottle sound; **schnarchendes** ≈ snoring rale; **vesikuläres** ≈ vesicular sound, vesicular rale.
Atemgrenzwert *m*: maximum breathing capacity, maximal respiratory capacity.
atemlos: breathless.
Atemluft *f*: tidal air, respiratory air.
Atemminutenvolumen *n*: respiratory minute volume.
Atemnot *f*: difficult breathing, respiratory distress.
Atemnotsyndrom *n*: respiratory distress syndrome.
Atemnotsyndrom des Neugeborenen, akutes *n*: idiopathic respiratory distress of newborn.
Atemorgane: respiratory organs.
Atemreserve *f*: respiratory reserve, breathing reserve.
Atemstillstand *m*: cessation of breathing, apnea.
Atemtöne: breath sounds.
Atemtrakt *m*: respiratory system.
Atemübungen: breathing exercises.
Atemwege: respiratory system, respiratory tract; **obere** ≈ upper respiratory tract; **untere** ≈ lower respiratory tract.
Atemwegserkrankung *f*: respiratory tract disease; **chronische** ≈ chronic respiratory disease; **obstruktive** ≈ obstructive disease; **restriktive** ≈ restrictive disease.
Atemwegsinfektion *f*: respiratory tract infection.
Atemwegsobstruktion *f*: airway obstruction.
Atemwegssyndrom, schweres akutes *n*: severe acute respiratory syndrome, SARS.

Atemwegswiderstand *m*: airway resistance.
Atemzentrum *n*: respiratory center; **medulläres** ≈ bulbar respiratory center.
Atemzug *m*: breath, inspiration.
Atemzugvolumen *n*: tidal volume.
Atenolol *n*: atenolol.
Atevirdin *n*: atevirdine.
atherogen: atherogenic.
Atherom *n*: atheroma.
Atherosklerose *f*: atherosclerosis.
atherosklerotisch: atherosclerotic.
Athetose *f*: athetosis, posthemiplegic chorea.
Athétose double *f*: bilateral athetosis, Vogt's disease.
Atlas-Axisgelenk *n*: atlantoaxial joint.
atmen: breathe, respire, inspire.
Atmen *n*: respiration, breathing.
Atmosphärendruck *m*: atmospheric pressure.
Atmung *f*: ventilation, breathing, respiration; **aerobe** ≈ aerobic respiration; **anaerobe** ≈ anaerobic respiration; **autonome** ≈ autonomous breathing; **flache** ≈ shallow breathing; **intermittierende** ≈ interrupted respiration, Biot's breathing; **paradoxe** ≈ paradoxical respiration; **periodische** ≈ periodic breathing, cogwheel respiration; **röchelnde** ≈ stertor.
Atmungskette *f*: respiratory chain.
Atonie *f*: atonia.
Atonie-Astasie-Syndrom *n*: atonic diplegia, Foerster syndrome.
Atopie *f*: atopy, atopic allergy.
atopisch: atopic.
Atorvastatin *n*: atorvastatin.
Atosiban *n*: atosiban.
Atovaquon *n*: atovaquone.
Atracuriumbesilat *n*: atracurium besilate.
atraumatisch: atraumatic.
Atresie *f*: atresia, imperforation.
atrial: atrial.
atrioventrikulär: atrioventricular.
Atrioventrikularblock *m*: atrioventricular block.
Atrioventrikularbündel *n*: atrioventricular bundle.
Atrioventrikularkanal *m*: atrioventricular canal.
Atrioventrikularklappe *f*: atrioventricular valve.
Atrioventrikularknoten *m*: atrioventricular node, His-Tawara node.
Atropa belladonna *f*: belladonna.
Atrophie *f*: atrophy, atrophia; **braune** ≈ brown atrophy; **fettige** ≈ fatty atrophy; **generalisierte** ≈ general atrophy; **kompensatorische** ≈ compensatory atrophy; **olivopontozerebellare** ≈ olivopontocerebellar atrophy, Déjerine-Thomas syndrome.
Atrophie blanche *f*: white atrophy.
atrophisch: atrophic.
Atropin *n*: atropine.
Attacke *f*: attack; **transitorische ischämische** ≈ transient ischemic attack, TIA.
attenuiert: attenuated.
Attenuierung *f*: attenuation.
Attest *n*: certificate.
Attribution *f*: attribution.
Atypie *f*: atypia.
atypisch: atypical, aberrant.
Audiogramm *n*: audiogram.
Audiometrie *f*: audiometry.
Audiometrieschwelle *f*: audiometric threshold.
Auer-Stäbchen *n*: Auer rods.
aufblähen: inflate.
Aufenthaltsdauer *f*: hospitalization length.
Aufflackern *n*: flare, flare-up.
Auffrischungsdosis *f*: recall dose, booster dose.
aufgedunsen: bloated, puffed.
aufgetrieben: inflated, swollen.
Aufguss *m*: infusion.
Aufhängung *f*: suspension.
Aufklärung *f*: education, patient information; **gesundheitliche** ≈ health education, health information.
Auflage *f*: inlay, onlay, rest.
Auflagefläche *f*: contact surface.
Auflagerung *f*: apposition.
Auflichtmikroskopie *f*: bright-field microscopy.
Auflösung *f*: resolution, dissolution, lysis.

Aufmerksamkeit *f*: attention, regard.
Aufmerksamkeits-Hyperaktivitätsstörung *f*: attention deficit disorder.
Aufnahme *f*: patient reception, admission, substance ingestion, uptake; **kutane** ≈ cutaneous absorption, cutaneous uptake; **tolerierbare tägliche** ≈ acceptable daily intake.
Aufnahmefeld *n*: radiographic field.
Aufnahmetechnik *f*: radiographic technique.
Aufschub *m*: delay.
Aufschwemmung *f*: suspension.
Aufspaltung *f*: splitting, decomposition, breakdown, segregation.
aufstoßen: eruct, belch.
Auftreibung *f*: ballooning, distention.
Auftrennung *f*: segregation, dissection; **stumpfe** ≈ blunt dissection.
Auftreten *n*: occurrence, emergence.
Aufwachepilepsie *f*: waking epilepsy, morning epilepsy.
Aufwachstation *f*: recovery room.
Aufwachtemperatur *f*: basal temperature.
Aufwärtsbewegung *f*: upward movement.
Aufwallen *n*: ebullition.
Aufwallung *f*: effervescence.
Augapfel *m*: eyeball.
Auge *n*: eye; **blaues** ≈ black eye; **bloßes** ≈ naked eye; **fixierendes** ≈ fixating eye; **rotes** ≈ pink eye.
Augenabschnitt *m*: eye segment; **vorderer** ≈ anterior eye segment.
Augenabstand *m*: interorbital distance.
Augenbecherspalte *f*: fetal fissure of eye.
Augenbewegung *f*: eye movement; **schnelle** ≈ rapid eye movement, REM.
Augenbläschen *n*: optic vesicle.
Augenbraue *f*: eyebrow.
Augendruckversuch *m*: oculocardiac reflex, Aschner's reflex.
Augenerkrankung *f*: ophthalmopathy, oculopathy.
Augenheilkunde *f*: ophthalmology.
Augenhintergrund *m*: fundus of eye, eyeground.
Augenhöhle *f*: orbita.
Augeninnendruck *m*: intraocular pressure, ophthalmotonus; **erhöhter** ≈ ocular hypertension; **normaler** ≈ normal intraocular tension.
Augeninnendruckmessung *f*: ophthalmotonometry.
Augenkammer *f*: chamber of eye, vitreous chamber; **hintere** ≈ posterior chamber of eye; **vordere** ≈ anterior chamber of eye, aqueous chamber.
Augenlid *n*: eyelid, palpebra.
Augenlinse *f*: lens.
Augenmuskel *m*: muscle of eye, ocular muscle.
Augenmuskellähmung *f*: ophthalmoplegia, ocular palsy; **äußere** ≈ external ophthalmoplegia, Ballett's disease; **innere** ≈ internal ophthalmoplegia; **konjugierte** ≈ conjugate paralysis.
Augenprothese *f*: ocular prosthesis, artificial eye.
Augensalbe *f*: eye ointment, ophthalmic ointment.
Augenspiegel *m*: ophthalmoscope, funduscope.
Augentropfen: eyedrops.
Aura *f*: aura; **akustische** ≈ auditory aura; **epileptische** ≈ epileptic aura; **generalisierte epileptische somatische** ≈ generalized epileptic somatic sensation; **gustatorische** ≈ gustatory aura; **optische** ≈ visual aura; **vertiginöse** ≈ vertiginous aura.
Auranofin *n*: auranofin.
aurikolotemporal: auriculotemporal.
Aurikularanhang *m*: auricular appendage.
aurikulotemporal: auriculotemporal.
Aurothioglukose *f*: aurothioglucose.
ausatmen: expire.
ausbreiten: spread, generalize, disseminate.
Ausbreitung *f*: extension, expansion, spread, spreading.
Ausbruch *m*: onset, outbreak, eruption of disease; **plötzlicher** ≈ rapid onset.
Ausbuchtung *f*: recess.
Ausdehnung *f*: extension, dimension.

Ausdruckstherapie *f*: expressive therapy.
Ausfall *m*: deficit.
Ausfluss *m*: discharge, outflow.
Ausführungsgang *m*: duct.
Ausgang *m*: exit, outlet.
Ausgangsgewicht *n*: initial weight.
Ausgangsherd *m*: initial focus.
ausgedehnt: extended, disseminated.
ausgleiten: slip.
Ausgussstein *m*: staghorn calculus.
Aushöhlung *f*: excavation.
Auskultation *f*: auscultation; **direkte** ≈ direct auscultation, immediate auscultation; **indirekte** ≈ mediate auscultation; **stethoskopische** ≈ stethoscopy.
auskultatorisch: auscultatory.
auskultieren: auscultate.
Auslese *f*: selection.
Auslöschphänomen *n*: extinction sign, Schultz-Charlton reaction.
auslösen: trigger, elicit a response, release.
Ausräumung *f*: dissection.
Ausrenkung *f*: dislocation.
ausrutschen: slip.
Aussatz *m*: leprosy.
Ausschabung *f*: abrasion.
Ausschälungsoperation *f*: stripping.
ausscheiden: excrete, exudate, discharge.
Ausscheider *m*: excreter, secretor.
Ausscheidung *f*: excretion, elimination, secretion; **tubuläre** ≈ renal tubular excretion.
Ausscheidungskapazität *f*: excretory capacity; **maximale tubuläre** ≈ maximal tubular excretory capacity.
Ausscheidungsorgan *n*: excretory organ.
Ausscheidungspyelographie *f*: excretion pyelography, intravenous pyelography.
Ausscheidungsrate *f*: elimination rate.
Ausscheidungsurographie *f*: descending urography.
Ausschlag *m*: exanthem, rash; **bläschenförmiger** ≈ vesicular rash; **gesprenkelter** ≈ mottled rash; **makulopapulöser** ≈ maculopapular rash; **profuser** ≈ profuse rash; **pustulöser** ≈ pustular rash; **scarlatiniformer** ≈ scarlet rash.
Ausschluss *m*: exclusion.
Ausschlussdiagnose *f*: diagnosis by exclusion.
Außenrotation *f*: external rotation, lateral rotation.
Aussparung *f*: recess, sparing.
ausspeien: spit, vomit.
ausströmen: escape, effluve.
Ausstülpung *f*: evagination.
Austausch *m*: exchange, replacement.
Austauscherharz *n*: ion-exchange resin.
Austauschtransfusion *f*: blood exchange transfusion.
austreiben: eject, expel.
Austreibung *f*: expulsion, ejection.
Austreibungsgeräusch *n*: ejection murmur.
Austreibungsperiode *f*: expulsive stage.
Austreibungsphase *f*: ejection phase, systolic phase of contraction.
Austreibungston *m*: ejection click, ejection sound.
Austreibungswehen: expulsive pains.
Austrittsblock *m*: exit block.
Austrocknung *f*: desiccation, exsiccosis.
Auswärtschielen *n*: external strabismus, divergent squint.
Auswahl *f*: selection.
Auswaschphänomen *n*: wash-out phenomenon.
Auswuchs *m*: outgrowth, knob, tuber.
Auswurf *m*: sputum, expectoration; **blutig tingierter** ≈ blood-tinged sputum; **eitriger** ≈ purulent sputum; **grünlicher** ≈ green sputum; **klarer** ≈ colorless sputum.
Auswurfvolumen des Herzens *n*: cardiac ejection volume.
Auszehrung *f*: wasting.
Auszehrungssyndrom *n*: wasting syndrome.
Auszug *m*: extract, tincture.
Autismus *m*: autism; **frühkindlicher** ≈ early infantile autism, Kanner syndrome.
autistisch: autistic.

Autoagglutination *f*: autoagglutination.
Autoantigen *n*: autoantigen.
Autoantikörper *m*: autoantibody, autoimmune antibody.
autogen: autogenous, autogenic.
Autograft *n*: autologous graft.
Autohypnose *f*: self-hypnosis.
autoimmun: autoimmune.
Autoimmunantwort *f*: autoimmune response.
Autoimmunglomerulonephritis *f*: autoimmune glomerulonephritis.
Autoimmunisierung *f*: autoimmunization.
Autoimmunität *f*: autoimmunity.
Autoimmunkrankheit *f*: autoimmune disease.
Autoimmunthyreoiditis *f*: autoimmune thyroiditis.
Autoinfektion *f*: autoinfection.
Autointoxikation *f*: autointoxication.
Autokatalyse *f*: autocatalysis.
Autoklav *m*: autoclave.
Autolyse *f*: autolysis, autodigestion.
Automatismus *m*: automatism, automatic behavior.
Autoplastik *f*: autoplasty, autograft.
Autopsie *f*: autopsy, necropsy; **gerichtliche** ≈ forensic autopsy, medicolegal autopsy.
Autopsiebefund *m*: autopsy findings.
Autoradiographie *f*: autoradiography.
autosomal: autosomal.
Autosuggestion *f*: autosuggestion.
Autotransfusion *f*: autotransfusion.
Autotransplantat *n*: autotransplant.
Autumnalkatarrh *m*: autumnal catarrh.
auxiliär: auxiliary.
avaskulär: avascular.
AV-Block *m*: atrioventricular block.
Avellis-Syndrom *n*: Avellis-Longhi syndrome, ambiguospinothalamic paralysis.
Aversion *f*: aversion, dislike.
Aversivreiz *m*: aversive stimulus.
AV-Fistel *f*: arteriovenous fistula.
aviär: avian.
avirulent: avirulent.
Avitaminose *f*: avitaminosis, vitamin deficiency.
AV-Knoten *m*: atrioventricular node, AV-node, His-Tawara node.
AV-Knoten-Arrhythmie *f*: nodal arrhythmia.
AV-Knoten-Bradykardie *f*: nodal bradycardia.
AV-Knoten-Ersatzrhythmus *m*: atrioventricular escape.
AV-Knoten-Tachykardie *f*: atrioventricular junctional tachycardia, nodal tachycardia.
AV-Rhythmus *m*: atrioventricular rhythm, nodal rhythm.
AV-Überleitung *f*: atrioventricular conduction.
axillär: axillary.
Axillarislähmung *f*: axillary paralysis.
Axillarlinie *f*: axillary line.
Axon *n*: axon, axis cylinder.
Axonhügel *m*: axon hillock, nerve hillock.
Axonotmesis *f*: axonotmesis.
Azamethonium *n*: azamethonium, pentamethazene.
Azamethoniumbromid *n*: azamethonium bromide.
Azapropazon *n*: azapropazone.
Azatadin *n*: azatadine.
Azathioprin *n*: azathioprine.
Azelainsäure *f*: azelaic acid.
Azelastin *n*: azelastine.
azellulär: acellular.
azephal: acephalic.
Azephalie *f*: acephaly.
Azetabulumplastik *f*: acetabuloplasty.
Azidämie *f*: acidemia, acidosis.
Azidamfenicol *n*: azidamfenicol.
Azidität *f*: aciditiy.
Azidocillin *n*: azidocillin.
azidophil: acidophil, oxyphilic.
Azidose *f*: acidosis; **hyperchlorämische** ≈ hyperchloremic acidosis; **idiopathische renale** ≈ idiopathic renal acidosis; **infantile tubuläre** ≈ infantile renal tubular acidosis; **kompensierte** ≈ compensated acidosis; **metabolische** ≈ metabolic acidosis; **renale tubuläre** ≈ renal tubular acidosis, Lightwood-Albright syndrome; **respiratorische** ≈ respir-

atory acidosis; **urämische** ≈ uremic acidosis.
Azidothymidin *n*: azidothymidine.
Azidurie *f*: aciduria.
azinös: aciniform.
Azinuszelle *f*: acinar cell.
Azinuszellkarzinom *n*: acinar cell carcinoma.
Azithromycin *n*: azithromycin.
Azlocillin *n*: azlocillin.
Azoospermie *m*: azoospermia.
Azosemid *n*: azosemide.
Azotämie *f*: azotemia; **chloroprive** ≈ hypochloremic azotemia; **extrarenale** ≈ extrarenal azotemia; **hypochlorämische** ≈ hypochloremic azotemia.
Azoturie *f*: azoturia.
Aztreonam *n*: aztreonam.
Azurgranulum *n*: azurophilic granule.
azurophil: azurophilic.
Azyklovir *n*: acyclovir, aciclovir.

B

B Abk. **Bor** *n*: boron, B.
Baastrup-Zeichen *n*: Baastrup's disease, kissing spine.
Babes-Ernst-Körperchen *n*: Babes-Ernst corpuscles, metachromatic granules.
Babesiasis *f*: babesiosis, piroplasmosis.
Babinski-Zeichen *n*: Babinski sign, pronation sign.
Babyöl *n*: baby oil.
Bacampicillin *n*: bacampicillin.
Bacillin *n*: bacillin.
Bacillus *m*: bacillus.
Bacitracin *n*: bacitracin.
Bacitrin *n*: bacitrin.
Backe *f*: cheek.
Backenschleimhaut *f*: buccal mucosa.
Backenzahn *m*: cheektooth, molar.
Baclofen *n*: baclofen.
Bad *n*: bath.
Badezusatz *m*: bath additive.
Bäfverstedt-Syndrom *n*: Bäfverstedt syndrome, benign lymphocytic reticulosis.
Bändelung *f*: banding.
Bänderzerrung *f*: tearing of a ligament.
Bagassose *f*: bagassosis.
Bahn *f*: path, pathway, tract.
Bahnung *f*: facilitation.
Baker-Zyste *f*: Baker cyst, popliteal bursitis.
Bakteriämie *f*: bacteremia, bacteriemia.
Bakterie *f*: bacterium.
bakteriell: bacterial.
Bakterienembolie *f*: bacterial embolism.
Bakterienfilter *m*: bacterial filter.
Bakterienruhr *f*: bacillary dysentery.
Bakterienstamm *m*: bacterial strain.
Bakterientoxin *n*: bacterial toxin.
Bakterienzylinder *m*: bacterial cast.
Bakteriologie *f*: bacteriology.
bakteriolytisch: bacteriolytic.
Bakteriophage *m*: bacteriophage, phage.
Bakteriostatikum *n*: bacteriostatic.
bakteriostatisch: bacteriostatic.
Bakterium *n*: bacterium; **säurefestes** ≈ acid-fast bacterium.
Bakteriurie *f*: bacteriuria.
bakterizid: bactericidal.
Balanitis *f*: balanitis; **erosive** ≈ erosive balanitis; **gangränöse** ≈ gangrenous balanitis.
Balanoblennorrhö *f*: balanoblennorrhea.
Baldriantinktur *f*: valerian tincture.
Balint-Gruppe *f*: Balint group.
Balkan-Nephritis *f*: Balkan nephropathy, epidemic nephropathy.
Balkenblase *f*: trabeculated bladder.
Balkensyndrom *n*: callosal syndrome.
Ballaststoff *m*: dietary fiber.
Ballonangioplastie *f*: balloon angioplasty.
Ballondilatation *f*: balloon dilatation.
Ballottement *n*: ballottement; **direktes** ≈ internal ballottement, vaginal ballottement; **indirektes** ≈ indirect ballottement.
Balneologie *f*: balneology.
Baló-Sklerose *f*: Baló's disease, concentric sclerosis.
Balsam *m*: balsam, balm.
Bambusstabwirbelsäule *f*: bamboo spine, stiff spine.
Bambuterol *n*: bambuterol.
Band *n*: band, tape, ribbon, ligament, chord.
Bandage *f*: bandage.
Bandenspektrum *n*: band spectrum.

Bandkeratitis *f*: band keratitis, ribbon-like keratitis.
Bandscheibe *f*: intervertebral disk.
Bandscheibenerkrankung *f*: diskopathy.
Bandscheibenprotrusion *f*: intervertebral disk protrusion.
Bandscheibenvorfall *m*: prolapse of intervertebral disk, disk prolapse.
Bandwurm *m*: cestode, tapeworm.
Bang-Krankheit *f*: Bang's disease.
Banti-Krankheit *f*: Banti's disease, congestive splenomegaly.
Bárány-Lärmtrommel *f*: Bárány's drum.
Barbital *n*: barbital, diethylbarbituric acid.
Barbiturat *n*: barbiturate.
Barbitursäure *f*: barbituric acid.
Bariumkontrasteinlauf *m*: barium enema.
Barootitis *f*: barotraumatic otitis.
Barorezeptor *m*: baroreceptor.
Barosinusitis *f*: barosinusitis, barotraumatic sinusitis.
Barré-Lieou-Syndrom *n*: Barré-Lieou syndrome, cervical migraine.
Barr-Körperchen *n*: Barr's body, x chromatin.
Bársony-Teschendorf-Syndrom *n*: Bársony-Teschendorf syndrome, diffuse esophageal spasm.
Bartflechte *f*: barber's itch.
Bartholini-Abszess *m*: bartholinian abscess.
Bartholinitis *f*: bartholinitis.
Basaliom *n*: basalioma.
Basalis *f*: basal layer.
Basalkörperchen *n*: basal body, basal corpuscle.
Basalmembran *f*: basal membrane; **glomeruläre** ≈ glomerulal basement membrane.
Basaltemperatur *f*: basal body temperature.
Basalzelle *f*: basal cell.
Basalzellenschicht *f*: basal layer.
Basalzellkarzinom *n*: basal cell carcinoma.
Basalzellnävussyndrom *n*: basal-cell nevus syndrome, Gorlin syndrome.
Base *f*: base.
Basedow-Krankheit *f*: Basedow's disease, thyrotoxic cachexia.
Basedow-Struma *f*: exophthalmic goiter.
Basenpaarung *f*: base pairing.
Basenüberschuss *m*: base excess.
basilär: basilar.
Basilarisinsuffizienz *f*: basilar insufficiency.
Basilarmembran *f*: basilar membrane.
Basis *f*: basis, base.
basisch: alkaline.
basophil: basophil.
Basophilenleukämie *f*: basophilic leukemia.
Basophiler *m*: basophilic cell, basophilic leukocyte.
Basophilie *f*: basophilia.
Batroxobin *n*: batroxobin.
Bauch *m*: abdomen, belly.
Bauchatmung *f*: abdominal breathing, abdominal respiration.
Bauchchirurgie *f*: abdominal surgery.
Bauchdeckenaplasie *f*: abdominal muscle deficiency syndrome, prune-belly syndrome.
Bauchdeckenfistel *f*: abdominal fistula.
Bauchdeckenreflex *m*: superficial abdominal reflex.
Bauchfell *n*: peritoneum.
Bauchhautreflex *m*: abdominal cutaneous reflex.
Bauchhöhle *f*: abdominal cavity.
Bauchhöhlenpunktion *f*: abdominal puncture.
Bauchhöhlenschwangerschaft *f*: abdominal pregnancy.
Bauchlage *f*: abdominal position.
Bauchmuskel *m*: abdominal muscle.
Bauchmuskelreflex *m*: abdominal reflex.
Bauchpresse *f*: abdominal pressure.
Bauchregion *f*: abdominal region.
Bauchschmerz *m*: abdominal pain, bellyache.
Bauchspeicheldrüse *f*: pancreas.
Bauchtrauma *n*: abdominal trauma.
Bauchwand *f*: abdominal wall.
Bauhin-Klappe *f*: Bauhin's valve, ileocecal valve.

B

Bausch *m*: wad.
bazillär: bacillary.
bazilliform: bacilliform.
Bazillophobie *f*: bacillophobia.
Bazillurie *f*: bacilluria.
Bazillus *m*: bacillus.
Beatmung *f*: ventilation, respiration; **assistierte** ≈ assisted breathing; **künstliche** ≈ artificial respiration.
Beatmungsbeutel *m*: breathing bag.
Beatmungsdruck *m*: ventilator pressure; **negativer endexspiratorischer** ≈ negative end-expiratory pressure; **positiver endexspiratorischer** ≈ positive end-expiratory pressure.
Beatmungsgerät *n*: respirator, ventilator.
Becaplermin *n*: becaplermin.
Becherzelle *f*: beaker cell, goblet cell.
Bechterew-Syndrom *n*: Bekhterev's arthritis, ankylosing spondylitis.
Becken *n*: pelvis; **androides** ≈ funnel-shaped pelvis; **anthropoides** ≈ anthropoid pelvis; **asymmetrisches** ≈ asymmetrical pelvis; **dreieckiges** ≈ triangular pelvis; **enges** ≈ contracted pelvis; **flaches** ≈ flat pelvis; **großes** ≈ greater pelvis, false pelvis; **gynäkoides** ≈ gynecoid pelvis; **kleines** ≈ small pelvis, true pelvis; **knöchernes** ≈ bony pelvis; **kyphotisches** ≈ kyphotic pelvis; **rachitisches** ≈ rachitic pelvis; **schräg verengtes** ≈ oblique contracted pelvis.
Beckenachse *f*: pelvic axis.
Beckenapertur *f*: pelvic aperture.
Beckenausgang *m*: pelvic outlet.
Beckenausgangsdurchmesser *m*: conjugate of the outlet.
Becken-Bein-Venenthrombose *f*: iliofemoral thrombosis.
Beckenboden *m*: pelvic floor.
Beckendurchmesser *m*: conjugate, pelvic diameter; **äußerer** ≈ external conjugate; **innerer** ≈ internal conjugate; **schräger** ≈ diagonal diameter.
Beckenebene *f*: pelvic plane.
Beckeneingang *m*: pelvic inlet.
Beckenendlage *f*: pelvic presentation.
Beckengürtel *m*: pelvic girdle, cingulum pelvicum.
Beckengürtelmuskeldystrophie *f*: limb-girdle muscular dystrophy.
Beckenindex *m*: pelvic index.
Beckenkammlinie *f*: intercristal diameter.
Beckenmessung *f*: pelvimetry.
Beckenneigung *f*: pelvic inclination.
Beckenniere *f*: pelvic kidney.
Beckenobliquität *f*: pelvic obliquity.
Beckenosteotomie *f*: pelvic osteotomy.
Beckenskoliose *f*: sacral scoliosis.
Beckenvenenthrombose *f*: pelvic vein thrombosis.
Beclamid *n*: beclamide.
Beclometason *n*: beclometasone.
Bedarfsschrittmacher *m*: demand pacemaker.
bedingt: conditioned.
Bedingung *f*: condition, circumstance.
Bedside-Methode *f*: bedside method.
Beeinträchtigung *f*: impairment.
Befall *m*: invasion, infestation.
Befehlsautomatismus *m*: command automatism.
Befinden *n*: condition, state.
Befriedigung *f*: satisfaction.
befruchten: fertilize, fecundate.
Befruchtung *f*: insemination, fertilization, fecundation; **extrakorporale** ≈ homologous extrauterine insemination; **künstliche** ≈ artificial insemination.
Befund *m*: finding; **klinischer** ≈ clinical finding; **mikroskopischer** ≈ microscopic picture.
Beginn *m*: start, onset; **akuter** ≈ rapid onset.
Begleitarthritis *f*: reactive arthritis.
Begleiteffekt *m*: associated affect, accompanying effect.
Begleiterkrankung *f*: accompanying illness, associated disease.
Begleitmedikation *f*: adjuvant medication.
Begleitschielen *n*: concomitant strabismus.
Begleitsymptom *n*: accessory symptom, concomitant symptom.
Begrenzung *f*: limitation, boundary.
Begutachtung *f*: expert appraisement.

Behaarung *f*: hairiness.
behandeln: treat.
Behandlung *f*: treatment, therapy; **ambulante** ≈ outpatient care; **medikamentöse** ≈ pharmacotherapy; **medizinische** ≈ medical treatment; **palliative** ≈ palliative treatment; **symptomatische** ≈ symptomatic treatment.
Behandlungsdauer *f*: treatment duration.
Behandlungsmethode *f*: procedure.
Behandlungsmöglichkeit *f*: treatment option.
Behandlungspflicht *f*: obligation to treatment.
Behandlungsrisiko *n*: therapeutic risk.
Behandlungszimmer *n*: consulting room, treatment room.
Behaviorismus *m*: behaviorism, behavioristic psychology.
Behçet-Syndrom *n*: Behçet syndrome, oculobuccogenital syndrome.
behindert: disabled, handicapped.
Behinderter *m*: disabled person, handicapped.
Behinderung *f*: disability, disablement, handicap; **geistige** ≈ mental handicap, mental retardation; **körperliche** ≈ physical disability, physical handicap.
Behinderungsbewältigung *f*: handicap management.
beidhändig: bimanual.
beidohrig: binaural.
Beikost *f*: supplementary food.
Bein *n*: leg.
Beingips *m*: leg plaster.
Beinschiene *f*: leg splint.
Beipackzettel *m*: package insert.
beißen: bite.
Bejel *n*: bejel, nonvenereal syphilis.
Beklemmung *f*: oprression, constriction.
Belag *m*: coat, film, fur.
belasten: stress, strain, load, exert.
belastend: stressful.
Belastung *f*: stress, strain, burden, exertion, load; **körperliche** ≈ physical stress; **linksventrikuläre** ≈ left ventricular strain; **psychische** ≈ mental stress; **rechtsventrikuläre** ≈ right ventricular strain.
Belastungsalbuminurie *f*: exercise albuminuria.
Belastungsangina *f*: exertion angina, angina of effort.
Belastungsbruch *m*: strain fracture.
Belastungsdyspnoe *f*: exertional dyspnea.
Belastungsfraktur *f*: stress fracture.
Belastungsprobe *f*: tolerance test.
Belastungsproteinurie *f*: exercise proteinuria.
Belastungssyndrom, posttraumatisches *n*: post-traumatic stress disorder.
Belastungstest *m*: exercise test, stress test.
Belegung *f*: occupancy.
Belegzelle *f*: parietal cell, acid cell.
Belichtung *f*: exposure.
beliefern: deliver, supply.
Belladonna *f*: belladonna.
Bellhusten *m*: barking cough.
Bell-Lähmung *f*: Bell's palsy, idiopathic facial paralysis.
Bell-Spasmus *m*: facial spasm.
Bemegrid *n*: bemegride.
Bemetizid *n*: bemeticzide.
Benactyzin *n*: benactyzine.
Benazepril *n*: benazepril
Bencyclan *n*: bencyclane.
Bendamustin *n*: bendamustine.
Bendroflumethiazid *n*: bendroflumethiazide.
Benedikt-Syndrom *n*: Benedikt syndrome, inferior red nucleus syndrome.
Benethamin-Penizillin *n*: benethamine penicillin G.
Benfotiamin *n*: benfotiamine.
benigne: benign.
Benommenheit *f*: dizziness, drowsiness, stupor.
Benorteron *n*: benorterone.
Benperidol *n*: benperidol.
Benproperin *n*: benproperine.
Benserazid *n*: benserazide.
Bentiromid *n*: bentiromide.
Benzaldehyd *m*: benzaldehyde.
Benzalkoniumchlorid *n*: benzalkonium chloride.

Benzathin *n*: benzathine.
Benzathin-Benzylpenicillin *n*: benzathine benzylpenicillin.
Benzathin-Penicillin *n*: benzathine penicillin.
Benzatropin *n*: benzatropine, benztropine.
Benzbromaron *n*: benzbromarone.
B-Enzephalitis, japanische *f*: Japanese B encephalitis, Russian autumnal encephalitis.
Benzilonbromid *n*: benzilonium bromide.
Benzocain *n*: benzocaine.
Benzoctamin *n*: benzoctamine.
Benzodepa *n*: benzodepa.
Benzodiazepin *n*: benzodiazepine.
Benzoesäure *f*: benzoic acid.
Benzothiazidinderivat *n*: benzothiadiazide.
Benzoylaminoessigsäure *f*: benzoylaminoacetic acid.
Benzoylglukuronsäure *f*: benzoylglucuronic acid.
Benzydamin *n*: benzydamine.
Benzydiamin *n*: benzydiamine.
Benzylpenicillin *n*: benzylpenicillin.
beobachten: observe.
beraten: counsel, advise, consult.
Beratung *f*: counseling, consultation, guidance.
Bereich *m*: region, range, sector, area.
Bergmannsasthma *n*: miners' asthma.
Beriberi *f*: beriberi; **feuchte** ≈ wet beriberi; **trockene** ≈ dry beriberi.
Berlin-Netzhauttrübung *f*: Berlin's disease.
Bernsteinsäure *f*: succinic acid.
Berstungsbruch *m*: bursting fracture, tuft fracture.
Bertin-Band *n*: Bertin's ligament, iliofemoral ligament.
berühren: touch, contact.
Berührungsschmerzhaftigkeit *f*: tenderness.
Berufsdermatose *f*: occupational dermatosis.
Berufsekzem *n*: occupational eczema.
Berufskrankheit *f*: occupational disease.
Berufsunfähigkeit *f*: disablement.
Berufsunfall *m*: occupational accident.
Beruhigungsmittel *n*: sedative, tranquilizer, pacifier.
Berylliumkrankheit *f*: berylliosis.
Beschäftigungskrampf *m*: occupational cramp, functional spasm.
Beschäftigungstherapie *f*: occupational therapy.
Bescheinigung *f*: certificate.
Beschneidung *f*: circumcision.
Beschwerden: complaints.
Beseitigung *f*: removal.
Besenreiservarizen: spider-burst varices.
Besiedelung *f*: colonization.
Besnier-Boeck-Schaumann-Syndrom *n*: Besnier-Boeck disease, sarcoidosis.
Besserung *f*: improvement.
beständig: stable, steady.
Bestätigung *f*: verification, confirmation.
Bestätigungstest *m*: confirmation test.
Bestandteil *m*: component, compound, ingredient.
Bestrahlung *f*: irradiation, radiation therapy; **intrakavitäre** ≈ intracavitary irradiation; **protrahierte** ≈ protracted irradiation.
Bestrahlungsfeld *n*: irradiation field.
Besuchszeit *f*: visiting hours.
Betablocker *m*: beta-blocker.
betäuben: anesthetize, narcotize.
Betäubung *f*: anesthesia, narcotization.
Betäubungsmittel *n*: analgetic, narcotic.
Betahistin *n*: betahistine.
Betamethason *n*: betamethasone.
Betamethasonacetat *n*: betamethasone acetate.
Betamethasonnatriumphosphat *n*: betamethasone sodium phosphate.
Betarezeptorenblocker *m*: beta blocker, beta-adrenergic antagonist.
Betawelle *f*: beta wave.
Betaxolol *n*: betaxolol.
Betazol *n*: betazole.
Beteiligung *f*: involvement, participation.

Betonung *f*: accentuation; **präsystolische** ≈ presystolic accentuation.
Betreuung *f*: care.
Bettenkapazität *f*: bed capacity.
bettlägerig: bedfast, bedridden.
Bettnässen *n*: bedwetting, enuresis.
Bettpfanne *f*: bedpan.
Bettruhe *f*: bed rest.
Bettwanze *f*: bedbug.
betupfen: swab.
Beugekontraktur *f*: flexion contracture.
Beugereflex *m*: flexor reflex.
Beule *f*: boil, bump, button.
Beulenpest *f*: bubonic plague, black death.
Beurteilung *f*: judgement, assessment.
Beutel *f*: bag, bursa.
Bevölkerung *f*: population.
Bevölkerungsentwicklung *f*: demographic development.
Bevölkerungspyramide *f*: population pyramid.
Bevölkerungsstruktur *f*: demographic structure.
Bevölkerungsstudie *f*: population study.
Bewältigungsverhalten *n*: coping behavior.
beweglich: ambulatory, mobile, movable.
Beweglichkeit *f*: motility, mobility.
Bewegung *f*: movement, motion; **choreatiforme** ≈ choreiform movement; **intentionale** ≈ intention movement; **körperliche** ≈ exercise; **ruckartige** ≈ saccadic movement; **spontane** ≈ spontaneous movement; **unwillkürliche** ≈ involuntary movement; **willkürliche** ≈ voluntary movement, active movement.
Bewegungsapparat *m*: locomotor apparatus.
Bewegungsautomatismus *m*: automatic movement.
Bewegungsbild *n*: motor image.
Bewegungshalluzination *f*: kinesthetic hallucination.
Bewegungsstörung *f*: movement disorder.
Bewegungsunruhe *f*: akathisia.
Bewertung *f*: evaluation, rating.
Bewertungsziffer *f*: score.
bewirken: effect.
bewusst: conscious, aware.
bewusstlos: unconscious.
Bewusstlosigkeit *f*: unconsciousness, blackout.
Bewusstsein *n*: consciousness, awareness; **klares** ≈ full consciousness.
Bewusstseinstrübung *f*: clouding of consciousness.
Bewusstseinsveränderung *f*: altered consciousness.
Bewusstseinsverlust *m*: loss of conciousness.
Bexaroten *n*: bexarotene.
Bezafibrat *n*: bezafibrate.
Beziehung *f*: relation, relationship; **topographische** ≈ topographic relationship.
Beziehungsidee *f*: idea of reference.
Bezirk *f*: site, zone.
Bezoar *m*: bezoar, gastrolith.
Bezugsgruppe *f*: reference group.
Bicalutamid *n*: bicalutamide.
Bichat-Wangenfettpfropf *m*: Bichat's fatty body of the cheek.
Biegung *f*: bend, flexure.
Biegungsbruch *m*: bending fracture.
Bielschowsky-Syndrom *n*: Bielschowsky-Jansky disease, Bielschowsky-Dollinger syndrome, late infantile ceroid lipofuscinosis.
Bienengift *n*: bee venom, apisin.
Bienenstich *m*: bee sting.
Bierherz *n*: beer heart.
bifaszikulär: bifascicular.
Bifokalbrille *f*: bifocal spectacles.
Bifonazol *n*: bifonazole.
Bigeminie *f*: bigeminy, bigeminal rhythm, coupled pulse.
Biguanid *n*: biguanide.
Bikarbonat *n*: bicarbonate.
Bikonkavlinse *f*: biconcave lens.
Bikonvexlinse *f*: biconvex lens.
Bikuspidalklappe *f*: bicuspid valve.
bilateral: bilateral.
Bild *n*: image, picture; **klinisches** ≈ clinical picture, clinical presentation; **stereoskopisches** ≈ stereoscopic image; **virtuelles** ≈ virtual image; **visuelles** ≈ visual image.

Bild-Archiv-Kommunikations-System *n*: Picture Archiving and Communication System, PACS.
Bildauswertung *f*: image interpretation.
Bildebene *f*: image plane.
bilden: form, produce.
Bildgebung *f*: imaging; **dynamische** ≈ dynamic imaging.
Bildkontrast *m*: image contrast.
Bildverstärkung *f*: image amplification.
Bilharzia *f*: bilharzia.
Bilharziose *f*: bilharziosis, schistosomiasis.
biliär: biliary, bilious.
Bilirubin *n*: bilirubin; **direktes** ≈ direct bilirubin; **indirektes** ≈ indirect bilirubin; **konjugiertes** ≈ conjugated bilirubin; **unkonjugiertes** ≈ unconjugated bilirubin.
Bilirubinämie *f*: bilirubinemia.
Bilirubinurie *f*: bilirubinuria.
Biliverdin *n*: biliverdin.
bimanuell: bimanual.
Bimatoprost *n*: bimatoprost.
binär: binary.
binasal: binasal.
binaural: binaural.
Binde *f*: bandage; **elastische** ≈ elastic bandage.
Bindegewebe *n*: connective tissue, soft tissue; **elastisches** ≈ elastic tissue; **interstitielles** ≈ interstitial tissue, stroma; **kollagenes** ≈ collagenous connective tissue; **retikuläres** ≈ reticular connective tissue, reticulothelium.
Bindegewebserkrankung *f*: connective tissue disease.
Bindegewebsfaser *f*: connective-tissue fiber.
Bindegewebstumor *m*: soft tissue tumor, connective tumor.
Bindehaut *f*: conjunctiva.
Bindehautentzündung *f*: conjunctivitis.
Bindenverband *m*: spica bandage.
Bindung *f*: binding, attachment, union.
Bindungskapazität *f*: binding capacity.
Bindungsstelle *f*: binding site.
binokulär: binocular.
Binokularsehen *n*: binocular vision.
Binswanger-Enzephalopathie *f*: Binswanger's encephalitis, progressive subcortical encephalopathy.
Biochemie *f*: biochemistry.
Bioethik *f*: bioethics.
Biogenese *f*: biogenesis.
Biokompatibilität *f*: biocompatibility.
Biologie *f*: biology.
Biomechanik *f*: biomechanics.
Biomedizin *f*: biomedicine.
Biometrie *f*: biometry.
Biophysik *f*: biophysics.
Bioprothese *f*: bioprosthesis.
Biopsie *f*: biopsy; **endoskopische** ≈ endoscopic biopsy; **heiße** ≈ hot biopsy; **offene** ≈ open biopsy.
Biopsiematerial *n*: biopsy material.
Biorhythmus *m*: biorhythm, biologic rhythm.
Biorückkoppelung *f*: biofeedback.
Biosynthese *f*: biosynthesis.
Biotechnologie *f*: biotechnology, biomedical engineering.
Biotin *n*: biotin.
Bioverfügbarkeit *f*: bioavailability.
Biperiden *n*: biperiden.
biphasisch: biphasic, diphasic.
bipolar: bipolar, dipolar.
Bisexualität *f*: bisexuality.
Bisoprolol *n*: bisoprolol.
Biss *m*: bite; **geschlossener** ≈ closed bite; **offener** ≈ open bite.
Bisssperre *f*: locked occlusion.
Bisswunde *f*: bite wound.
Bistouri *n*: bistoury.
bitemporal: bitemporal.
Bithionol *n*: bithionol.
Bivalirudin *n*: bivalirudin.
biventrikulär: biventricular.
Bizepsreflex *m*: biceps reflex.
Blähung *f*: flatulence, wind.
Bläschen *n*: bubble, blister, vesicle, phlyctenula.
Bläschenatmen *n*: vesicular breathing.
Blässe *f*: pallor, whiteness.
blande: bland.
Blase *f*: bladder, vesica, bubble; **auto-**

nome ≈ autonomous bladder, denervated bladder; **hypertone** ≈ hypertonic bladder; **neurogene** ≈ neurogenic bladder.
Blasenausgang *m*: vesical outlet.
Blasenausschlag *m*: bullous eruption.
Blasenbilharziose *f*: bladder schistosomiasis.
Blasendivertikel *n*: bladder diverticulum.
Blasenekstrophie *f*: bladder exstrophy.
Blasenektopie *f*: vesical ectopia.
Blasenentzündung *f*: cystitis; **akute** ≈ acute cystitis; **chronische** ≈ chronic cystitis; **transmurale** ≈ panmural cystitis.
Blasenfistel *f*: bladder fistula.
blasenförmig: vesicular.
Blasengalle *f*: cystic bile.
Blasenhals *m*: bladder-neck.
Blasenhernie *f*: vesicocele, cystocele.
Blaseninkontinenz *f*: urinary incontinence.
Blaseninstillation *f*: bladder instillation.
Blasenkäfer *m*: blister beetle, cantharides.
Blasenkarzinom *n*: bladder cancer.
Blasenkolik *f*: cystic colic.
Blasenpunktion *f*: bladder puncture; **suprapubische** ≈ suprapubic puncture.
Blasenreflex *m*: bladder reflex.
Blasensprengung *f*: amniotomy.
Blasensprung *m*: rupture of membranes; **spontaner** ≈ spontaneous rupture; **verspäteter** ≈ prolonged rupture of membranes; **vorzeitiger** ≈ premature rupture of membranes.
Blasenstein *m*: bladder stone, cystolith.
Blasentee *m*: diuretic tea.
Blasentraining *n*: bladder training.
Blasentuberkulose *f*: tuberculous cystitis.
Blasenzentrum *n*: vesical center, micturition center.
blasenziehend: vesicant, epispastic.
blass: pale, white-faced.
Blastomycin *n*: blastomycin.
Blastomykose *f*: blastomycosis; **europäische** ≈ European blastomycosis, cryptococcosis; **nordamerikanische** ≈ North American blastomycosis, Gilchrist's mycosis; **südamerikanische** ≈ South American blastomycosis, paracoccidioidomycosis.
Blattern *f*: variola, smallpox.
Blaublindheit *f*: blue blindness, tritanopia.
Blaue-Gummiblasen-Nävus-Syndrom *n*: blue rubber bleb nevus.
Blausäure *f*: hydrocyanic acid, hydrogen cyanide.
Bleiacetat *n*: lead acetate.
Bleianämie *f*: lead anemia.
bleich: pale, white-faced.
Bleichmittel *n*: bleacher.
Bleijodid *n*: lead iodide.
Bleivergiftung *f*: lead poisoning, saturnism.
Blende *f*: grid, blind, diaphragm.
Blendeneinstellung *f*: diaphragm position.
Blendungskonjunktivitis *f*: solar ophthalmia.
Blennorrhö *f*: blennorrhea.
Bleomycin *n*: bleomycin.
Blepharitis *f*: blepharitis; **squamöse seborrhoische** ≈ seborrheic blepharitis.
Blepharospasmus *m*: blepharospasm, nictitating spasm, winking spasm.
Blick *m*: look, gaze; **konjugierter** ≈ conjugated gaze.
Blickkrampf *m*: oculogyric crisis.
Blicklähmung *f*: paralysis of gaze.
blind: blind.
Blinddarm *m*: appendix, blindgut, cecum.
Blinddarmentzündung *f*: appendicitis.
Blinddarmkolik *f*: appendicular colic.
Blindheit *f*: blindness; **hysterische** ≈ hysterical blindness, psychanopsia; **völlige** ≈ amaurosis.
Blindpassage *f*: blind passage.
Blindsack *m*: blind pouch, caecus.
Blinzelkrampf *m*: winking spasm, nictitating spasm.
blinzeln: nictitate, wink, blink.
Blinzelreflex *m*: winking reflex, blinking reflex.

Blinzeltic *m*: winking spasm.
Blitz *m*: flash, lightning.
Blitz-Nick-Salaam-Krämpfe: saltatory spasm, saltatory tic.
Blitzstar *m*: electrical cataract.
Block *m*: block; **alveolokapillärer** ≈ alveolar-capillary block; **anterograder** ≈ anterograde block; **atrioventrikulärer** ≈ atrioventricular block; **intraventrikulärer** ≈ intraventricular block; **neuromuskulärer** ≈ neuromuscular block; **retrograder** ≈ retrograde block; **sinuatrialer** ≈ sinoatrial block; **unidirektionaler** ≈ unidirectional block.
Blockade *f*: blockade.
Blockresektion *f*: reduction en bloc.
Blockwirbel *m*: vertebral fusion.
Blotting-Technik *f*: blotting technique.
Blut *n*: blood; **defibriniertes** ≈ defibrinated blood; **geronnenes** ≈ clotted blood; **hämolytisches** ≈ laky blood; **okkultes** ≈ occult blood; **peripheres** ≈ peripheral blood.
Blutarmut *f*: anemia.
Blutausstrich *m*: blood smear.
Blutbank *f*: blood bank.
Blutbild *n*: blood count.
Blutbildung *f*: blood formation, hematopoiesis.
Blutdruck *m*: blood pressure; **diastolischer** ≈ diastolic blood pressure; **hoher** ≈ high blood pressure; **niedriger** ≈ low high blood pressure; **systolischer** ≈ systolic pressure.
Blutdruckmessung *f*: blood pressure measurement.
Blutdrucksenkung *f*: lowering of the blood pressure.
Blutegel *m*: leech, hirudinea, sanguisuga.
Bluter *m*: bleeder, hemophiliac.
Blutergelenk *n*: hemophilic arthropathy.
Bluterguss *m*: hematoma.
Bluterkrankheit *f*: bleeding disorder, hemophilia.
Blutersatz *m*: blood substitution.
Blutfluss *m*: bloodstream.
Blutgasanalyse *f*: blood gas analysis.
Blutgefäß *n*: blood vessel.
Blutgerinnsel *n*: blood clot.
Blutgerinnung *f*: blood coagulation.
Blutglukose *f*: blood glucose.
Blutgruppe *f*: blood group.
Blutgruppenbestimmung *f*: blood grouping.
Blut-Hirn-Schranke *f*: blood-brain barrier.
Bluthochdruck *m*: hypertonus, hypertension.
Bluthochdruckherz *n*: hypertensive heart.
blutig: bloody.
Blutkörperchen *n*: blood corpuscle, blood cell; **rotes** ≈ red blood cell, erythrocyte; **weißes** ≈ white blood cell, leukocyte.
Blutkörperchensenkungsgeschwindigkeit *f*: erythrocyte sedimentation rate.
Blutkörperchenvolumen *n*: corpuscular volume.
Blutkreislauf *m*: blood circulation.
Blutkultur *f*: blood culture, hemoculture.
blutleer: bloodless.
Blutmole *f*: hemorrhagic mole, Breus mole.
Blutplasma *n*: plasma.
Blutprobe *f*: blood sample, blood specimen.
Blutprobenauskreuzung *f*: crossmatching.
Blutschwamm *m*: hemangioma.
Blutspende *f*: blood donation.
blutstillend: hemostyptic.
Blutstillung *f*: arrest of bleeding, hemostasis.
Blutsverwandtschaft *f*: consanguinity.
Bluttransfusion *f*: blood transfusion.
Blutung *f*: bleeding, hemorrhage; **äußere** ≈ external hemorrhage; **arterielle** ≈ arterial hemorrhage; **epidurale** ≈ epidural hemorrhage; **funktionelle** ≈ functional bleeding; **gastrointestinale** ≈ gastrointestinal hemorrhage; **innere** ≈ internal bleeding, internal hemorrhage; **intrakranielle** ≈ intracranial hemorrhage; **intrazerebrale** ≈ intracerebral hemorrhage; **lebensgefährliche** ≈ cri-

tical hemorrhage; **massive** ≈ massive hemorrhage; **oberflächliche** ≈ superficial bleeding; **okkulte** ≈ occult bleeding; **petechiale** ≈ petechial hemorrhage; **subdurale** ≈ subdural hemorrhage; **vaginale** ≈ vaginal bleeding; **zerebrale** ≈ cerebral hemorrhage.
Blutungsanämie *f*: posthemorrhagic anemia.
Blutungszeit *f*: bleeding time.
Bluntersuchung *f*: blood test.
Blutvergiftung *f*: blood poisoning.
Blutverlust *m*: blood loss.
Blutversorgung *f*: blood supply.
Blutvolumen *n*: blood volume.
Blutzelle *f*: blood cell, hemocyte.
Blutzucker *m*: blood sugar, blood glucose.
Blutzuckerselbstkontrolle *f*: self-glucose monitoring.
Bodenbakterium *n*: soil bacterium.
Bodenkrätze *f*: ground itch, uncinerial dermatitis.
Body-Mass-Index *m*: body mass index.
Boeck-Skabies *f*: Norwegian scabies.
Bogaert-Divry-Syndrom *n*: Bogaert-Divry syndrome, diffuse corticomeningeal angiomatosis.
Bogaert-Scherer-Epstein-Syndrom *n*: cerebrotendinous xanthomatosis.
Bogen *m*: arc, arch, bow.
Bohrloch *n*: bur hole.
Bolus *m*: bolus.
Bolusinjektion *f*: bolus injection.
Boosterdosis *f*: booster dose, recall dose.
Bopindolol *n*: bopindolol.
Borborygmus *m*: borborygmus.
Borderline-Persönlichkeitsstörung *f*: borderline personality disorder.
Borke *f*: bark, crust.
Borkenkrätze *f*: Norwegian scabies.
Bornaprin *n*: bornaprine.
Bornholmer Krankheit *f*: Bornholm disease, epidemic benign dry pleurisy.
Borrowing-lending-Phänomen *n*: borrowing-lending hemodynamic phenomenon.
Borsäure *f*: boric acid.
Bortezomib *n*: bortezomib.
Bosentan *n*: bosentan.
Boten-RNS *f*: messenger ribonucleic acid, mRNA.
Botulin *n*: botulin.
Botulinusantitoxin *n*: antibotulinism serum.
Botulinustoxin *n*: botulinum toxin.
Botulismus *m*: botulism.
Bougie *m*: bougie.
Bouillon *f*: broth.
Bourneville-Pringle-Syndrom *n*: Bourneville's phakomatosis, tuberous sclerosis.
Boutonneuse-Fieber *n*: boutonneuse fever, Kenya tick typhus.
Bowen-Darier-Dermatose *f*: Bowen's precancerous dermatosis.
Boxerenzephalopathie *f*: punch-drunk syndrome, progressive traumatic encephalopathy.
brachial: brachial.
Brachialislähmung *f*: brachial palsy, brachial plexus paralysis.
Brachytherapie *f*: brachytherapy, implant radiotherapy.
Brachyzephalie *f*: brachycephaly.
Bradyarrhythmie *f*: bradyarrhythmia.
Bradykardie *f*: bradycardia.
Bradykardie-Tachykardie-Syndrom *n*: bradytachycardia.
Bradykinin *n*: bradykinin.
Branchialbogen *m*: branchial arch.
Brand *m*: gangrene, sphacelus.
Brandblase *f*: burn blister.
Brandverletzung *f*: burn injury.
Braue *f*: eyebrow.
Brausebad *n*: shower.
Braxton-Hicks-Kontraktion *f*: Braxton-Hicks contraction, false uterine contraction.
Braxton-Hicks-Wendung *f*: Braxton-Hicks version, bipolar version.
Brechkraft *f*: refractive power.
Brechmittel *n*: emetic, vomitory.
Brechreiz *m*: nausea, vomiturition.
Brechungsfehler *m*: refractive error.
Brechungsgesetze: laws of refraction.
Brechungshyperopie *f*: curvature hyperopia.
Brechungsindex *m*: refractive index.

Brechungsmyopie *f*: curvature myopia.
Brechwurz *f*: ipecac.
Breikost *f*: mashed food.
Breitband-Antibiotikum *n*: broad-spectrum antibiotic.
Breitband-Neuroleptikum *n*: broad-spectrum neuroleptic.
breitbasig: sessile.
Breite *f*: breadth, wideness; **therapeutische** ≈ therapeutic range.
Brenner-Tumor *m*: Brenner tumor, oophoroma folliculare.
Brennpunkt *m*: focus.
Brennweite *f*: focal distance.
Brennwert *m*: caloric value.
Brenztraubensäure *f*: pyruvic acid.
Brephoplastik *f*: brephoplastic graft.
bretthart: boardlike, wooden.
Bretylium *n*: bretylium.
Breus-Mole *f*: Breus mole, tuberous mole.
Brille *f*: glasses, spectacles.
Brillenhämatom *n*: bilateral periocular hematoma.
Brill-Symmers-Krankheit *f*: Brill-Symmers disease, giant follicular lymphoma.
Brill-Zinsser-Krankheit *f*: Brill-Zinsser disease, benign typhus.
Brimonidin *n*: brimonidine.
Brinzolamid *n*: brinzolamide.
Brittle-Diabetes *m*: brittle diabetes mellitus.
Brivudin *n*: brivudine.
Broca-Aphasie *f*: Broca's aphasia, motor aphasia.
Brock-Operation *f*: Brock's infundibulectomy, transventricular closed valvulotomy.
Bromhidrose *f*: bromhidrosis, bromidrosis.
Bromidvergiftung *f*: bromide poisoning, bromism.
Bromindion *n*: bromindione.
Bromisoval *n*: bromisoval.
Bromocriptin *n*: bromocriptine.
5-Bromodesoxyuridin *n*: 5-bromodeoxyuridine.
Bromoform *n*: tribromomethane.
Bromoprid *n*: bromopride.
Bromperidol *n*: bromperidol.
Brompheniramin *n*: brompheniramine.
Bromuracil *n*: bromouracil.
Bromwasserstoffsäure *f*: hydrobromic acid.
bronchial: bronchial.
Bronchialadenom *n*: bronchial adenoma.
Bronchialallergie *f*: bronchial allergy.
Bronchialasthma *n*: bronchial asthma.
Bronchialatmen *n*: bronchial respiration.
Bronchialfremitus *m*: bronchial fremitus.
Bronchialkarzinom *n*: bronchial carcinoma; **kleinzelliges** ≈ oat cell carcinoma.
Bronchialkatarrh *m*: bronchitis.
Bronchiallavage *f*: bronchial lavage.
Bronchiektasie *f*: bronchiectasis; **sackförmige** ≈ saccular bronchiectasis; **spindelförmige** ≈ fusiform bronchiectasis; **trockene** ≈ dry bronchiectasis; **zylindrische** ≈ cylindric bronchiectasis; **zystische** ≈ cystic bronchiectasis.
Bronchiole *f*: bronchiole.
Bronchiolitis *f*: bronchiolitis.
Bronchitis *f*: bronchitis; **akute** ≈ acute bronchitis; **chronische** ≈ chronic bronchitis; **kruppöse** ≈ croupous bronchitis; **pseudomembranöse** ≈ pseudomembranous bronchitis; **trockene** ≈ dry bronchitis.
bronchoalveolär: bronchoalveolar.
Bronchodilatation *f*: bronchodilatation.
bronchogen: bronchogenic.
Bronchographie *f*: bronchography.
Broncholith *m*: broncholith, bronchial calculus.
Bronchomediastinalfistel *f*: mediastinobronchial fistula.
Bronchopleuralfistel *f*: pleurobronchial fistula.
Bronchopneumonie *f*: bronchopneumonia, lobular pneumonia.
Bronchoskop *n*: bronchoscope.
Bronchoskopie *f*: bronchoscopy.
Bronchospasmus *m*: bronchospasm,

bronchial spasm.
Bronchospirochätose *f*: bronchospirochetosis, Castellani's bronchitis.
Bronchostenose *f*: bronchial stenosis.
Bronchus *m*: bronchial tube, bronchus.
Bronchusfistel *f*: bronchial fistula.
Bronchusverlegung *f*: bronchial obstruction.
Bronzediabetes *m*: bronze diabetes.
Bronzehaut *f*: bronzed skin.
Bronzehautkrankheit *f*: Addison's disease.
Brotizolam *n*: brotizolam.
Brown-Séquard-Syndrom *n*: Brown-Séquard syndrome, hemiparaplegic syndrome.
Brown-Symmers-Krankheit *f*: Brown-Symmers disease, acute infantile encephalopathy.
Brucellose *f*: brucellosis, Bang's disease.
Bruch *m*: fracture, break, hernia; **eingekeilter** ≈ impacted fracture; **innerer** ≈ internal hernia; **komplizierter** ≈ complicated fracture; **offener** ≈ open fracture; **reponierbarer** ≈ reducible hernia; **unvollständiger** ≈ partial fracture.
Bruchband *n*: hernia truss, hernia bandage.
Brucheinklemmung *f*: incarcerated hernia, impaction.
Brucin *n*: brucine.
Brudzinski-Nackenzeichen *n*: Brudzinski sign.
Brückenlappen *m*: bridge flap, hinged flap.
Brückensyndrom *n*: pontine syndrome; **laterales** ≈ lateral pontine syndrome; **oberes** ≈ superior pontine syndrome, Cestan-Raymond syndrome; **paramedianes** ≈ paramedian pontine syndrome; **unteres** ≈ inferior pontine syndrome, Raymond syndrome.
Bruit du pot fêlé: cracked-pot sound.
Brust *f*: chest, breast.
Brustbeere *f*: jujube.
Brustdrüse *f*: mamma, breast.
Brustdrüsenabszess *m*: mammary abscess, intramammary abscess.
Brusternährung *f*: breast-feeding.
Brusthöhle *f*: thoracic cavity.
Brustkorb *m*: thorax, chest.
Brustkrebs *m*: breast cancer.
Brustselbstuntersuchung *f*: breast self-examination.
Brustvergrößerung *f*: breast augmentation, macromastia.
Brustwand *f*: chest wall.
Brustwandableitungen: precordial leads, Wilson's leads.
Brustwarze *f*: breast nipple, thele; **überzählige** ≈ supernumerary nipple.
Brustwarzenkappe *f*: nipple shield.
Brustwirbel *m*: thoracic vertebra.
Brutkasten *m*: incubator.
Bubo *m*: bubo, tropical adenitis; **schankröser** ≈ chancroidal bubo, virulent bubo; **virulenter** ≈ virulent bubo, chancroidal bubo.
Bubonenpest *f*: bubonic plague.
Bucht *f*: bay, sinus.
Buckel *m*: hump, knob, boss.
Buclizin *n*: buclizine.
Buclosamid *n*: buclosamide.
Budd-Chiari-Syndrom *n*: Budd-Chiari disease, hepatic vein occlusion.
Budesonid *n*: budesonide.
Budipin *n*: budipine.
Bündel *n*: bundle, leash; **aberrierendes** ≈ aberrant bundle; **papillomakuläres** ≈ papillomacular bundle.
Bürstensaum *m*: cuticular ridge, cuticular border.
Buflomedil *n*: buflomedil.
bukkal: buccal.
Bulbärapoplexie *f*: bulbar apoplexy.
Bulbärenzephalitis *f*: bulbar encephalitis.
Bulbärparalyse *f*: bulbar paralysis; **familiäre infantile progressive** ≈ infantile progressive bulbar palsy, Fazio-Londe disease; **progrediente** ≈ progressive bulbar palsy, glossolabial paralysis.
Bulbärpoliomyelitis *f*: acute bulbar polioencephalitis.
Bulbocavernosusreflex *m*: penile reflex.
Bulbourethraldrüse *f*: bulbourethral gland, Cowper's gland.
Bulbus *m*: bulbus, bulb.

Bulbusreflex *m*: oculocardiac reflex, Aschner's phenomenon.
Bulimie *f*: bulimia, binging, hyperorexia.
bullös: bullous.
Bumadizon *n*: bumadizone.
Bumetanid *n*: bumetanide.
Bunazosin *n*: bunazosin.
Bunge-Amputation *f*: Bunge's amputation, aperiosteal amputation.
Bunitrolol *n*: bunitrolol.
Buparonolol *n*: bupranolol.
Bupivacain *n*: bupivacaine.
Bupranolol *n*: bupranolol.
Buprenorphin *n*: buprenorphine.
Bupropion *n*: bupropion.
Burkitt-Lymphom *n*: Burkitt's tumor, African lymphoma.
Bursitis *f*: bursitis, bursal synovitis.
Busen *m*: bust, bosom.
Buserelin *n*: buserelin.
Buspiron *n*: buspirone.
Busulfan *n*: busulfan.
Butalamin *n*: butalamine.
Butamirat *n*: butamirate.
Butan *n*: butane.
Butanol *n*: butanol.
Butenafin *n*: butenafine.
Butethal *n*: butethal.
Butinolin *n*: butinoline.
Butizid *n*: butizide.
Buttersäure *f*: butyric acid.
Butylparaben *n*: butylparaben.
Butylradikal *n*: butyl.
Butylscopolamin *n*: butylscopolamine.
Butyrometer *n*: butyrometer.
Butyrophenon *n*: butyrophenone.
Bypass *m*: bypass; **aortokoronarer** ≈ aortocoronary artery bypass; **extraanatomischer** ≈ extra-anatomic bypass; **kardiopulmonaler** ≈ cardiopulmonary bypass.
Bypass-Operation *f*: bypass surgery.
Byssinose *f*: byssinosis, flax-dressers' disease.

C

C Abk. **1. Celsius; 2. Komplement** *n*; **3. Kohlenstoff** *m*: 1. Celsius; 2. complement; 3. carbon.
Cabergolin *n*: cabergoline.
Cactinomycin *n*: cactinomycin.
Cafaminol *n*: cafaminol.
Caissonkrankheit *f*: caisson disease, decompression sickness.
α-Calcidol *n*: alphacalcidol.
Calcifediol *n*: calcifediol.
Calciferol *n*: calciferol.
Calcipotriol *n*: calcipotriol.
Calcitonin *n*: calcitonin.
Calcitriol *n*: calcitriol.
Calcium *n*: calcium, Ca.
Calciumpantothenat *n*: calcium pantothenate.
Caldwell-Luc-Kieferhöhlenradikaloperation *f*: Caldwell-Luc operation, radical maxillary antrostomy.
Callositas *f*: callosity.
Calmette-Tuberkulin *n*: purified tuberculin.
Calvities *f*: common male baldness, male pattern alopecia.
Camazepam *n*: camazepam.
Camurati-Engelmann-Syndrom *n*: Camurati-Engelmann disease, progressive diaphyseal dysplasia.
Canavan-Syndrom *n*: Canavan's diffuse sclerosis, spongiform leukodystrophy.
Cancer en cuirasse *m*: cancer en cuirasse, corset cancer.
Candida *f*: candida.
Candida-Mykose *f*: candidiasis, candidosis.
Candida-Vaginitis *f*: candidal vaginitis, monilial vaginitis.
Candida-Vulvovaginitis *f*: candida vulvovaginitis, vulvovaginal candidiasis.
Candidiasis *f*: candidiasis, candidosis; **orale** ≈ oral candidiasis, thrush.
Candidulin *n*: candidulin.
Cannabis *n*: cannabis, hemp.
Canrenoinsäure *f*: canrenoic acid.
Cantharidinsäure *f*: cantharidic acid.
Capecitabin *n*: capecitabine.
Capreomycin *n*: capreomycin.
Capronsäure *f*: caproic acid.
Caprylsäure *f*: caprylic acid.
Captodiamin *n*: captodiamine.
Captopril *n*: captopril.
Caramiphen *n*: caramiphen.
Carazolol *n*: carazolol.
Carbachol *n*: carbachol, carbamylcholine.
Carbamazepin *n*: carbamazepine.
Carbaminsäure *f*: carbamic acid.
Carbamylphosphat *n*: carbamylphosphate.
Carbenicillin *n*: carbenicillin.
Carbenoxolon *n*: carbenoxolone.
Carbidopa *n*: carbidopa.
Carbimazol *n*: carbimazole.
Carbocistein *n*: carbocisteine.
Carbonsäure *f*: carbonic acid.
Carboxyhämoglobin *n*: carboxyhemoglobin.
Carbromal *n*: carbromal.
Carbuterol *n*: carbuterol.
Carcinoma in situ *n*: intraepithelial carcinoma, intraepidermal carcinoma.
Carisoprodol *n*: carisoprodol, isopropyl meprobamate.
Carmustin *n*: carmustine, bis-chlor nitrosurea.
Carnitin *n*: carnitine.
Carotin *n*: carotene.
Carotis *f*: carotid, carotid artery.
Carprofen *n*: carprofen.
Carteolol *n*: carteolol.

Carter-Krankheit *f*: Carter's mycetoma.
Carvedilol *n*: carvedilol.
Casein *n*: casein.
Casoni-Intrakutantest *m*: Casoni skin test, echinococcus skin test.
Caspofungin *n*: caspofungin.
Castellani-Krankheit *f*: Castellani's bronchitis, bronchospirochetosis.
Castle-Faktor *m*: Castle's factor, intrinsic factor.
Castleman-Tumor *m*: Castleman's disease, giant follicular hyperplasia.
Castoröl *n*: castor oil.
Cataracta electrica *f*: electrical cataract.
Cataracta fluida *f*: fluid cataract.
Cataracta maturata *f*: ripe cataract.
Cataracta senilis *f*: senile cataract.
Cataracta subcapsularis *f*: subcapsular cataract.
Catgut *n*: catgut, surgical gut.
Cava-inferior-Syndrom *n*: inferior caval syndrome.
Cava-superior-Syndrom *n*: superior caval syndrome.
Cefacetril *n*: cefacetril.
Cefaclor *n*: cefaclor.
Cefadroxil *n*: cefadroxil.
Cefalexin *n*: cefalexin, cephalexin.
Cefaloridin *n*: cefaloridine, cephaloridine.
Cefalotin *n*: cefalotin, cephalothin.
Cefamandol *n*: cefamandole.
Cefazedon *n*: cefazedone.
Cefazolin *n*: cefazolin.
Cefmenoxim *n*: cefmenoxime.
Cefoperazon *n*: cefoperazone.
Cefotaxim *n*: cefotaxime.
Cefotetan *n*: cefotetan.
Cefotiam *n*: cefotiam.
Cefoxitin *n*: cefoxitin.
Cefpodoxim *n*: cefpodoxim.
Cefradin *n*: cefradine.
Cefsulodin *n*: cefsulodin.
Ceftazidim *n*: ceftazidime.
Ceftizoxim *n*: ceftizoxime.
Ceftriaxon *n*: ceftriaxone.
Cefuroxim *n*: cefuroxime.
Celecoxib *n*: celecoxib.
Celiprolol *n*: celiprolol.
Cellulose *f*: cellulose.
Celsius-Skala *f*: centigrade scale.
Centrum-Collum-Diaphysenwinkel *m*: collodiaphyseal angle.
Cephalosporin *n*: cephalosporin.
Cerebronsäure *f*: cerebronic acid.
Certoparin *n*: certoparin.
Certoparinnatrium *n*: certoparin sodium.
Ceruletid *n*: ceruletide.
Cervix *f*: cervix, neck.
Cestan-Zeichen *n*: Cestan sign, levator sign.
Cestoda *f*: cestode.
Cetrorelix *n*: cetrorelix.
Cetuximab *n*: cetuximab.
Chagas-Krankheit *f*: Chagas' disease, South American trypanosomiasis.
Charakter *m*: character, person, personality; **abhängiger** ≈ dependent personality; **aggressiver** ≈ aggressive personality; **autoritärer** ≈ authoritarian personality; **genitaler** ≈ genital character; **oraler** ≈ oral character; **schizoider** ≈ schizoid personality; **zyklothymer** ≈ cyclothymic personality.
Charakteristikum *n*: characteristic, feature.
Charaktertyp *m*: personality; **schizoider** ≈ schizothymic personality.
Charakterzug *m*: character trait.
Charcot-Gelenk *n*: Charcot's joint, neurogenic arthropathy.
Charcot-Hand *f*: Charcot's hand.
Charcot-Marie-Tooth-Krankheit *f*: Charcot-Marie-Tooth syndrome, hereditary sensorimotor neuropathy.
Charcot-Zeichen *n*: Charcot sign.
Charge *f*: batch, lot.
Cheilitis *f*: cheilitis.
Cheilitis angularis *f*: angular cheilitis, angular stomatitis.
Cheiloplastik *f*: cheiloplasty, labioplasty.
Chelatbildner *m*: chelating agent.
Chelatkomplex *m*: chelate complex.
Chemie *f*: chemistry; **klinische** ≈ clinical chemistry; **pharmazeutische** ≈ pharmaceutical chemistry.
Chemokinese *f*: chemokinesis.
Chemolitholyse *f*: chemical litholysis.

Chemorezeptor *m*: chemoreceptor, chemical ceptor.
Chemosis *f*: chemosis.
Chemotaxis *f*: chemotaxis.
Chemotherapeutikum *n*: chemotherapeutic agent.
Chemotherapie *f*: chemotherapy.
Chemotropismus *m*: chemotropism.
Chenodeoxycholsäure *f*: chenodeoxycholic acid.
Cheyne-Stokes-Atmung *f*: Cheyne-Stokes breathing, periodic breathing.
Chiasma *n*: chiasm.
Chikungunya-Fieber *n*: chikungunya.
Chimäre *f*: chimera.
Chinaldinsäure *f*: quinaldinic acid.
Chinarinde *f*: cinchona, quinquina.
Chinasäure *f*: quinic acid.
Chinidin *n*: quinidine.
Chinin *n*: quinine.
Chininrausch *m*: quininism.
Chininvergiftung *f*: quinine poisoning, Tommaselli syndrome.
Chinol *n*: quinol.
Chinolin *n*: quinoline.
Chinolinol *n*. quinolinol.
Chinolinsäure *f*: quinolinic acid.
Chinolon *n*: quinolone.
Chinon *n*: quinone.
Chinosol *n*: quinosol.
Chi-Quadrat-Test *m*: chi-squared test.
Chiropraxis *f*: chiropractic, manipulative medicine.
Chirurgie *f*: surgery; **erhaltende** ≈ conservative surgery; **kleine** ≈ minor surgery; **minimal-invasive** ≈ minimal invasive surgery; **plastische** ≈ plastic surgery.
chirurgisch: surgical.
Chlamydieninfektion *f*: chlamydia infection.
Chlamydiensalpingitis *f*: chlamydial salpingitis.
Chloasma *n*: chloasma.
Chlorakne *f*: chlor acne, halogen acne.
Chloralformamid *n*: chloral formamid.
Chloralhydrat *n*: chloral hydrate.
Chloralose *f*: chloralose.
Chlorambucil *n*: chlorambucil.
Chloramphenicol *n*: chloramphenicol.
Chloranämie *f*: chloroanemia, achlorhydric anemia, achylic anemia.
Chlorazanil *n*: chlorazanil.
Chlorazol *n*: chlorazol.
Chlorbenzoxamin *n*: chlorbenzoxamine.
Chlorbetamid *n*: chlorbetamide.
Chloressigsäure *f*: chloracetic acid, monochloracetic acid.
Chlorid *n*: chloride.
Chlorisondamin *n*: chlorisondamine.
Chlormethin *n*: chlormethine, nitrogen mustard.
Chlormezanon *n*: chlormezanone.
Chloroform *n*: chloroform, trichloromethane.
Chloroformnarkose *f*: chloroform anesthesia.
Chlorom *n*: chloroma, green cancer.
Chloroquin *n*: chloroquine.
Chlorothiazid *n*: chlorothiazide.
Chlorotrianisen *n*: chlorotrianisene.
Chloroxylenol *n*: chloroxylenol.
Chlorphenamin *n*: chlorphenamine.
Chlorphenesin *n*: chlorphenesin, chlorophenesin.
Chlorpromazin *n*: chlorpromazine.
Chlorpropamid *n*: chlorpropamide.
Chlorprothixen *n*: chlorprothixene.
Chlorquinaldol *n*: chlorquinaldol.
Chlorsäure *f*: chloric acid.
Chlortalidon *n*: chlortalidone.
Chlortetracyclin *n*: chlortetracycline.
Choanalatresie *f*: choanal atresia.
Choanalpolyp *m*: choanal polyp.
Choanalstenose *f*: choanal stenosis.
Choane *f*: choana, postnaris.
Cholämie *f*: cholemia.
Cholagogum *n*: cholagogue.
Cholangiographie *f*: cholangiography; **endoskopische retrograde** ≈ endoscopic retrograde cholangiography; **intraoperative** ≈ operative cholangiography; **perkutane transhepatische** ≈ percutaneous transhepatic cholangiography; **retrograde** ≈ retrograde cholangiography.
Cholangiopankreatographie, endoskopische retrograde *f*: endoscopic retrograde cholangiopancreatography, ERCP.

C

Cholangitis *f*: cholangitis; **primär sklerosierende** ≈ primary sclerosing cholangitis; **sekundär sklerosierende** ≈ secondary sclerosing cholangitis.
Cholansäure *f*: cholanic acid.
Cholecalciferol *n*: cholecalciferol.
Choledocholithotomie *f*: choledocholithotomy.
Choledochotomie *f*: choledochotomy.
Choledochus *m*: choledochus, common bile duct.
Choledochussphinkter *m*: choledochal sphincter.
Choledochuszyste *f*: choledochus cyst.
Choleinsäure *f*: choleic acid.
Cholelithiasis *f*: cholelithiasis.
Cholera *f*: cholera.
Cholera infantum *f*: infantile gastroenteritis.
Cholestase *f*: cholestasis, biliary stasis.
Cholesteatom *n*: cholesteatoma.
Cholesterin *n*: cholesterol.
Cholesterinsenker *m*: hypocholesterinemic agent.
Cholezystektomie *f*: cholecystectomy.
Cholezystenterostomie *f*: cholecystenterostomy.
Cholezystitis *f*: cholecystitis.
Cholezystographie *f*: cholecystography.
Cholezystolithiasis *f*: cholecystolithiasis.
Cholezystostomie *f*: cholecystostomy.
cholinerg: cholinergic, parasympathomimetic.
Cholinesterase *f*: cholinesterase.
Cholinesterasehemmer *m*: cholinesterase inhibitor.
Cholsäure *f*: cholic acid.
Cholurie *f*: choluria.
chondral: chondral.
Chondritis *f*: chondritis.
Chondrodysplasie *f*: chondrodysplasia.
Chondrodystrophie *f*: chondrodystrophy.
Chondrofibromyxom *n*: chondromyxoid fibroma.
Chondroitinsäure *f*: chondroitic acid.
Chondroitinsulfat *n*: chondroitin sulfate.
Chondrom *n*: chondroma.
Chondromalazie *f*: chondromalacia.
Chondrosarkom *n*: chondrosarcoma.
Chondrozyt *m*: chondrocyte, cartilage cell.
Chopart-Operation *f*: Chopart's operation, mediotarsal amputation.
Chorda *f*: chorda, cord.
Chorditis *f*: chorditis.
Chorea *f*: chorea, Saint Vitus' dance.
Chorea Huntington *f*: hereditary chorea, degenerative chorea.
Chorea major *f*: jumping chorea, epidemic chorea.
Chorea minor *f*: chorea minor, Sydenham's chorea, rheumatic chorea.
Choreomanie *f*: choreomania, dancing mania, jumping chorea.
Chorioblastom *n*: chorioblastoma.
Chorioideaatrophie, zirkumpapilläre *f*: circumpapillary chorioretinal atrophy, peripapillary senile halo.
Chorioideremie *f*: choroideremia, tapetochoroidal dystrophy.
Chorioiditis *f*: chorioiditis.
Chorion *n*: chorion.
Choriongonadotropin *n*: chorionic gonadotropin, choriogonadotropin; **humanes** ≈ human chorionic gonadotropin, HCG.
Chorionkarzinom *n*: chorion carcinoma.
Chorionzotte *f*: chorionic villus.
Chorionzottenbiopsie *f*: chorionic villus biopsy.
Choroidea *f*: choroid.
Christ-Siemens-Touraine-Syndrom *n*: Christ-Siemens syndrome, anhidrotic ectodermal dysplasia.
Chromatid *n*: chromatid.
Chromatin *n*: chromatin.
Chromatinkörperchen *n*: chromatinic body.
Chromatographie *f*: chromatography.
Chromomykose *f*: chromomycosis.
chromophil: chromophil.

chromophob: chromophobe.
Chromosom *n*: chromosome.
chromosomal: chromosomal.
Chromosomenaberration *f*: chromosomal aberration.
Chromosomenanalyse *f*: chromosome analysis.
Chromosomenbruch *m*: chromosome break.
Chromosomendeletion *f*: chromosome deletion.
Chromosomeninversion *f*: chromosome inversion; **parazentrische** ≈ paracentric inversion; **perizentrische** ≈ pericentric inversion.
Chromosomenmapping *n*: chromosome mapping.
Chromsäure *f*: chromic acid.
chronisch: chronic, long.
Chronizität *f*: chronicity.
Chronobiologie *f*: chronobiology.
Churg-Strauss-Syndrom *n*: Churg-Strauss disease, allergic angiitis.
Chvostek-Zeichen *n*: Chvostek symptom, facialis phenomenon.
chylös: chylous.
Chylomikron *n*: chylomicron.
Chylus *m*: chyle.
Chylusfistel *f*: chylous fistula.
Chymopapain *n*: chymopapain.
Chymus *m*: chyme.
Ciclacillin *n*: ciclacillin.
Ciclesonid *n*: ciclesonide.
Cicletanin *n*: cicletanine.
Cicloniumbromid *n*: ciclonium bromide.
Ciclopirox *n*: ciclopirox.
Ciclosporin *n*: cyclosporine.
Cidofovir *n*: cidofovir.
Cilazapril *n*: cilazapril.
Cilexetil *n*: cilexetil.
Cimetidin *n*: cimetidine.
Cimex *m*: cimex, bedbug.
Cimex hemipterus *m*: Cimex hemipterus, oriental bedbug.
Cimex lectularius *m*: Cimex lectularius, common bedbug.
Cinacalcet *n*: cinacalcet.
Cinchocain *n*: cinchocaine.
Cinchona *f*: cinchona, quinaquina.
Cinnarizin *n*: cinnarizine.
Cinoxacin *n*: cinoxacin.
Ciprofloxacin *n*: ciprofloxacin.
Cirrhose cardiaque *f*: cardiac cirrhosis.
Cisaprid *n*: cisapride.
Cisatracuriumbesilat *n*: cisatracurium besilate.
Cisplatin *n*: cisplatin.
Citalopram *n*: citalopram.
Cladribin *n*: cladribine.
Clapotement *n*: clapotage, succusion sound.
Clarithromycin *n*: clarithromycin.
Claudicatio *f*: claudication.
Claudicatio intermittens *f*: intermittent claudication.
Clavulansäure *f*: clavulanic acid.
Clearance *f*: clearance; **endogene** ≈ endogenous clearance; **osmolale** ≈ osmolar clearance.
Clemastin *n*: clemastine.
Clemizolpenicillin *n*: clemizole penicillin.
Clenbuterol *n*: clenbuterol.
Click *m*: click; **systolischer** ≈ systolic click.
Clidiniumbromid *n*: clidinium bromide.
Clindamycin *n*: clindamycine.
Clobazam *n*: clobazam.
Clobetasol *n*: clobetasol.
Clobetason *n*: clobetasone.
Clocortolon *n*: clocortolone.
Clofazimin *n*: clofazimine.
Clofenamid *n*: clofenamide.
Clofenamsäure *f*: clofenamic acid.
Clofezon *n*: clofezone.
Clofibrat *n*: clofibrate.
Clomethiazol *n*: clomethiazole.
Clomifen *n*: clomifene.
Clomipramin *n*: clomipramine.
Clonazepam *n*: clonazepam.
Clonidin *n*: clonidine.
Clopamid *n*: clopamide.
Clopenthixol *n*: clopenthixol.
Clopidogrel *n*: clopidogrel.
Cloprednol *n*: cloprednol.
Clorexolon *n*: clorexolone.
Clorofen *n*: clorophene.
Clostebol *n*: clostebol.
Clostridium *n*: Clostridium.
Clostridium perfringens *n*: Clostridium perfringens, Welch's bacillus.

Clotrimazol *n*: clotrimazole.
Clouston-Syndrom *n*: hidrotic ectodermal dysplasia.
Cloxacillin *n*: cloxacillin.
Cloxiquin *n*: cloxiquine.
Clozapin *n*: clozapine.
Clusterkopfschmerz *m*: cluster headache.
Cobalamin *n*: cobalamin, vitamin B_{12}.
Coccus *m*: coccus.
Cochlea *f*: cochlea, acoustic labyrinth.
Code, genetischer: genetic code.
Codein *n*: codeine, methylmorphine.
Coffein *n*: caffeine.
Cogan-Syndrom *n*: Cogan's disease, oculovestibuloauditory syndrome.
Colchicin *n*: colchicine.
Colecalciferol *n*: colecalciferol.
Colesevelam *n*: colesevelam.
Colestipol *n*: colestipol.
Colestyramin *n*: colestyramine, cholestyramine.
Colistin *n*: colistin.
Colitis *f*: colitis.
Colitis regionalis *f*: regional colitis, Crohn's disease.
Colitis ulcerosa *f*: ulcerative colitis.
Colorado-Zeckenfieber *n*: Colorado tick fever, mountain tick fever.
Colpitis *f*: colpitis, vaginitis.
Colpitis granularis *f*: granular vaginitis.
Coma *n*: coma.
Coma diabeticum *n*: diabetic coma.
Coma vigile *n*: vigil coma.
Compliance *f*: compliance; **fehlende** ≈ noncompliance; **pulmonale** ≈ pulmonary compliance.
Computertomogramm *n*: computer tomography scan, CT scan.
Computertomographie *f*: computerized tomography, CT, computer tomography.
Concretio *f*: concretio, concretion.
Condyloma *n*: condyloma.
Condyloma acuminatum *n*: condyloma acuminatum, acuminate wart.
Condyloma latum *n*: condyloma latum, flat condyloma.
Coniin *n*: coniine, conicine.
Conjugata *f*: conjugate, conjugate diameter.
Conjugata anatomica *f*: anatomic conjugate, true conjugate.
Conjugata diagonalis *f*: diagonal conjugate, false conjugate.
Conjugata vera obstetrica *f*: conjugata vera obstetrica, obstetrical conjugate.
Conjunctivitis *f*: conjunctivitis.
Conjunctivitis actinica *f*: actinic conjunctivitis.
Conjunctivitis diphtherica *f*: diphtheritic conjunctivitis.
Conjunctivitis granulosa *f*: granular conjunctivitis.
Conjunctivitis phlyctaenulosa *f*: phlyctenular conjunctivitis.
Conjunctivitis pseudomembranosa *f*: pseudomembranous conjunctivitis.
Conjunctivitis trachomatosa *f*: trachomatous conjunctivitis, trachoma.
Conjunctivitis vernalis *f*: vernal conjunctivitis, spring catarrh.
Conn-Syndrom *n*: Conn syndrome, primary aldosteronism.
Cooley-Anämie *f*: Cooley's anemia, thalassemia major.
Coombs-Test *m*: Coombs test, antiglobulin test.
Cooper-Hernie *f*: Cooper's hernia.
Copingverhalten *n*: coping behavior.
Cor *n*: cor, heart.
Cor adiposum *n*: cor adiposum, fatty heart.
Cor biloculare *n*: cor biloculare, hemicardia.
Cor bovinum *n*: cor bovinum, bovine heart.
Corbus-Krankheit *f*: Corbus disease, gangrenous balanitis.
Cor pulmonale *n*: cor pulmonale, pulmonary heart disease.
Corpus *n*: corpse, body.
Corpus-callosum-Demyelinisierung *f*: callosal demyelinating encephalopathy.
Corpus-callosum-Syndrom *n*: callosal syndrome.
Corpus luteum *n*: corpus luteum, yellow body.
Corpus-spongiosum-Entzündung *f*: spongiositis.

Corrigan-Puls *m*: Corrigan's pulse, collapsing pulse.
Corticorelin *n*: corticorelin.
Corticosteroid *n*: corticosteroide.
Corticotropin *n*: corticotropin.
Corti-Organ *n*: Corti's organ, spiral organ.
Corticotropin *n*: corticotropin.
Cortisol *n*: cortisol.
Cortison *n*: cortisone.
Cor triloculare *n*: three-chambered heart.
Cor villosum *n*: hairy heart.
Coryza *f*: coryza, acute rhinitis.
Costa spuria *f*: false rib.
Costen-Syndrom *n*: Costen syndrome, temporomandibular syndrome.
Cotrimoxazol *n*: co-trimoxazole.
Cotton-Wool-Herde: cotton wool spots.
Couvelaire-Syndrom *n*: Couvelaire's uterus, uteroplacental apoplexy.
Coxsackie-Pharyngitis *f*: acute lymphonodular pharyngitis.
Cramer-Schiene *f*: Cramer splint, ladder splint.
Credé-Prophylaxe *f*: Credé's prophylaxis.
Creme *f*: cream.
Crepitatio *f*: crepitation.
Creutzfeldt-Jakob-Krankheit *f*: Creutzfeldt-Jakob disease.
Crigler-Najjar-Ikterus *m*: Crigler-Najjar icterus, congenital hyperbilirubinemia.
Crohn-Krankheit *f*: Crohn's disease, regional enteritis, regional ileitis.
Cromoglicinsäure *f*: cromoglicic acid.
Crossover *n*: crossing over, crossover.
Crush-Syndrom *n*: crush syndrome, compression syndrome.
Cuff-Kanüle *f*: cuffed tube.
Cullen-Zeichen *n*: Cullen sign, blue navel.
Cumaran *n*: coumaran.
Cumarin *n*: coumarin.
Curare *n*: curare.
curareartig: curare-like, curariform.
Curschmann-Batten-Steinert-Syndrom *n*: Steinert's disease, myotonic dystrophy.
Cushing-Gesicht *n*: cushingoid face.
Cutis *f*: cutis, skin.
Cutis elastica *f*: elastic skin.
Cutis laxa *f*: loose skin, dermachalasis.
Cyanocobalamin *n*: cyanocobalamin.
Cyclaminsäure *f*: cyclamic acid.
Cyclofenil *n*: cyclofenil.
Cyclopentamin *n*: cyclopentamine.
Cyclopenthiazid *n*: cyclopenthiazide.
Cyclopentolat *n*: cyclopentolate.
Cyclophosphamid *n*: cyclophosphamide.
Cycloserin *n*: cycloserine.
Cyclosporin *n*: cyclosporine.
Cyclothiazid *n*: cyclothiazide.
Cyproheptadin *n*: cyproheptadine.
Cyproteron *n*: cyproterone.
Cyproteronacetat *n*: cyproterone acetate.
Cystein *n*: cysteine.
Cystin *n*: cystine.
Cystinose *f*: cystinosis.
Cytarabin *n*: cytarabine, cytosine arabinoside.
Cytidin *n*: cytidine.
Cytidylsäure *f*: cytidylic acid.
Czerny-Naht *f*: Czerny suture.

D

D Abk. **1. Brechkraft** *f*; **2. Deuterium** *n*; **3. Dilutio** *f*: 1. refractive power; 2. deuterium, d; 3. dilution.
Dacarbazin *n*: dacarbazine.
Dachziegelverband *m*: imbricated bandage.
DaCosta-Syndrom *n*: DaCosta syndrome, effort syndrome.
Dactinomycin *n*: dactinomycin.
Dämmerungsamblyopie *f*: twilight blindness.
Dämmerungssehen *n*: twilight vision, scotopic vision.
Dämmerzustand *m*: trance, twilight state.
Dämpfung *f*: damping, flatness, dullness; **absolute** ≈ absolute dullness; **paravertebrale** ≈ Grocco's sign; **perkutorische** ≈ percussion dullness.
Dakryoadenitis *f*: dacryoadenitis.
Dakryolith *m*: dacryolith, lacrimal calculus.
Dakryozystitis *f*: dacryocystitis.
Dakryozystorhinostomie *f*: dacryorhinocystostomy, Toti's operation.
Daktylitis *f*: dactylitis.
Daktylogramm *n*: dactylogram, fingerprint.
Daktyloskopie *f*: dactyloscopy.
Daltonismus *m*: daltonism.
Damm *m*: perineum.
Dammriss *m*: perineal laceration.
Danaparoid *n*: danaparoid.
Danazol *n*: danazol.
Dandy-Operation *f*: retrogassserian neurotomy.
Dandy-Walker-Syndrom *n*: Dandy-Walker deformity, extra-axial leptomeningeal cyst.
Danofloxacin *n*: danofloxacin.
Dapiprazol *n*: dapiprazol.
Dapson *n*: dapsone.
Darbepoetin alfa *n*: darbepoetin alfa.
Darifenacin *n*: darifenacin.
Darm *m*: gut, intestine, bowel.
Darmanastomose *f*: intestinal anastomosis.
Darmatresie *f*: intestinal atresia.
Darmausgang, künstlicher *m*: artificial anus.
Darmbewegung *f*: peristalsis.
Darmblutung *f*: intestinal hemorrhage.
Darmerkrankung *f*: bowel disease; **entzündliche** ≈ inflammatory bowel disease.
Darmfistel *f*: intestinal fistula.
Darmgeräusch *n*: bowel sound.
Darmgrippe *f*: intestinal flu.
Darminfektion *f*: intestinal infection.
Darmmilzbrand *m*: intestinal anthrax.
Darmmotilität *f*: intestinal motility, bowel motility.
Darmparasit *m*: entozoic parasite, enterozoon.
Darmperforation *f*: intestinal perforation.
Darmperistaltik *f*: intestinal peristalsis.
Darmpolyp *m*: intestinal polyp.
Darmreinigung *f*: bowel preparation.
Darmresektion *f*: bowel resection.
Darmschlinge *f*: intestinal loop.
Darmverschluss *m*: ileus, intestinal obturation.
Darmzotte *f*: intestinal villus.
Darreichungsform *f*: dosage form.
Darunavir *n*: darunavir.
Dauer *f*: duration.
Dauerausscheider *m*: chronic carrier.
Dauergeräusch *n*: continuous sound.
Dauerkatheter *m*: indwelling catheter.

Dauerstriktur *f*: permanent stricture.
Daumen *m*: thumb; **schnappender** ≈ trigger thumb.
Daumenballen *m*: thenar.
Daumenzeichen *n*: thumb sign, newspaper sign.
Daunomycin *n*: daunomycin.
Daunorubicin *n*: daunorubicin.
Dawson-Einschlusskörperchenenzephalitis *f*: Dawson's encephalitis, inclusion body encephalitis, subacute sclerosing panencephalitis, SSPE.
Deanol *n*: deanol.
Debilität *f*: debility, mild mental retardation.
Decke *f*: blanket, cover.
Decrementum *n*: decrement, decrease.
Defäkationsreflex *m*: defecation reflex.
Defekt *m*: defect; **aortopulmonaler** ≈ aortopulmonary window.
Defektfehlbildung *f*: congenital deformity.
Defektheilung *f*: partial recovery.
Deferipron *n*: deferiprone.
Deferoxamin *n*: deferoxamine.
Defibrillation *f*: defibrillation.
Defibrillator *m*: defibrillator, cardioverter.
Defizienz *f*: deficiency.
Defizit *n*: deficit; **reversibles ischämisches neurologisches** ≈ reversible ischemic neurologic deficit.
Deflazacort *n*: deflazacort.
Deflexion *f*: deflexion, deflection.
Deformität *f*: deformity.
Degeneration *f*: degeneration; **axonale** ≈ axonal degeneration, Nissl's degeneration; **dienzephaloretinale** ≈ Laurence-Moon syndrome; **dystrophische** ≈ dystrophic degeneration; **faszikuläre** ≈ fascicular degeneration; **fettige** ≈ fatty degeneration; **granulovakuoläre** ≈ granulovacuolar degeneration; **hepatolentikuläre** ≈ hepatolenticular degeneration, Wilson syndrome; **hyaline** ≈ hyaline degeneration; **hydropische** ≈ hydropic degeneration; **körnige** ≈ granular degeneration; **myxomatöse** ≈ myxomatous degeneration; **parenchymatöse** ≈ parenchymatous degeneration; **retrograde** ≈ retrograde degeneration, axonal degeneration; **tapetoretinale** ≈ tapetoretinal degeneration; **vakuoläre** ≈ vacuolar degeneration; **zystische** ≈ cystic degeneration.
Deglutition *f*: deglutition.
Dehnsonde *f*: bougie, dilator, dilatator.
Dehnung *f*: dilatation.
Dehnungsreflex *m*: stretch reflex.
Dehydratation *f*: dehydration, exsiccation.
Dehydrocholsäure *f*: dehydrocholic acid.
Dehydroepiandrosteron *n*: dehydroepiandrosterone.
Dehydrogenase *f*: dehydrogenase.
Déjerine-Landouzy-Syndrom *n*: Déjerine-Landouzy dystrophy, facioscapulohumeral dystrophy.
Déjerine-Sottas-Syndrom *n*: Déjerine-Sottas syndrome, hereditary hypertrophic neuropathy.
dekapitieren: decapitate.
Dekapsulation *f*: decapsulation.
Dekompensation *f*: decompensation.
Dekompression *f*: decompression; **subtemporale** ≈ subtemporal decompression, Cushing's operation.
Dekompressionskammer *f*: decompression chamber.
Dekompressionskrankheit *f*: decompression sickness, caisson disease.
Dekrement *n*: decrement.
Dekubitalulkus *n*: decubital ulcer, decubitus ulcer.
Dekubitus *m*: decubitus, bedsore, pressure sore.
Delavirdin *n*: delavirdine.
Deletion *f*: deletion.
Delir *n*: delirium; **manisches** ≈ maniacal delirium; **oneiroides** ≈ oneiric delirium.
Delirium tremens *n*: delirium tremens, alcohol withdrawal delirium.
Delle *f*: dell, dent.
Delta-Aminolävulinsäure *f*: δ-aminolevulinic acid.
Delta-Rhythmus *m*: delta rhythm.
Deltoideusreflex *m*: deltoid reflex.

Demand-Schrittmacher *m*: demand pacemaker.
Demarkation *f*: demarcation.
Demeclocyclin *n*: demeclocycline.
Demelverin *n*: demelverine.
dement: demented.
Dementia paralytica *f*: paralytic dementia.
Demenz *f*: dementia; **infantile** ≈ infantile dementia, Heller's disease; **präsenile** ≈ presenile dementia; **primär degenerative** ≈ primary degenerative dementia; **senile** ≈ senile dementia; **vaskuläre** ≈ vascular dementia.
Demographie *f*: demography.
Demyelinisierung *f*: demyelinization.
Denaturierung *f*: denaturation.
Denaverin *n*: denaverine.
Dendrit *m*: dendrite.
dendritisch: dendritic.
Denervationspotential *n*: denervation potential.
Denervierung *f*: denervation.
Denguevirus *n*: dengue virus.
Denken *n*: thinking, thought; **autistisches** ≈ autistic thinking; **dereistisches** ≈ dereistic thinking.
Densitometrie *f*: densitometry.
dental: dental.
Dentikel *m*: denticle.
Dentin *n*: dentin.
Dentinom *n*: dentinoma.
Dentition *f*: dentition; **erste** ≈ primary dentition; **verzögerte** ≈ delayed dentition; **zweite** ≈ secondary dentition, permanent dentition.
Deodorant *n*: deodorant.
Deontologie *f*: deontology, professional ethics.
Dependenz *f*: dependency.
Depersonalisation *f*: depersonalization.
Depilation *f*: depilation, epilation.
Depletion *f*: depletion.
Depolarisationsblock *m*: depolarization block.
Depotinjektion *f*: repository injection.
Depotinsulin *n*: depot insulin, long-acting insulin.
Depotpenizillin *n*: repository penicillin.
Depotpräparat *n*: depot preparation.
Depravation *f*: depravation.
Depreotid *n*: depreotide.
Depression *f*: depression; **agitierte** ≈ agitated depression; **anaklitische** ≈ anaclitic depression; **bipolare** ≈ bipolar depression; **endogene** ≈ endogenous depression, melancholia; **exogene** ≈ exogenous depression; **larvierte** ≈ larvate depression; **reaktive** ≈ reactive depression, depressive reaction; **rezidivierende typische** ≈ recurrent major depression; **senile** ≈ senile depression; **unipolare** ≈ unipolar psychosis.
depressiv: depressive.
deprimiert: depressed.
Deprivation *f*: deprivation.
Derealisation *f*: derealization.
Derivat *n*: derivative.
dermal: dermal, dermatic.
Dermalsinus *m*: dermal sinus.
Dermatikum *n*: dermatic, dermatologic agent.
Dermatitis *f*: dermatitis; **allergische** ≈ allergic dermatitis; **atopische** ≈ atopic eczema; **chronische oberflächlich-schuppige** ≈ chronic superficial scaly dermatitis; **nässende** ≈ weeping dermatitis; **paraneoplastische** ≈ carcinomatous dermatitis; **seborrhoische** ≈ seborrheic dermatitis, seborrheic eczema.
Dermatitis exfoliativa Ritter von Rittershain *f*: desquamative erythroderma.
Dermatitis verrucosa *f*: verrucous eczema.
Dermatochalasis *f*: dermachalasis, cutis laxa.
Dermatofibrosarkom *n*: dermatofibrosarcoma.
Dermatoglyphen: dermatoglyphics.
Dermatologie *f*: dermatology.
Dermatom *n*: dermatome, dermatomic area.
Dermatomykose *f*: dermatomycosis.
Dermatomyositis *f*: dermatomyositis.
Dermatophyt *m*: dermatophyte.

Dermatophytid *n*: dermatophytid.
Dermatose *f*: dermatosis, skin disease; **akute febrile neutrophile** ≈ acute febrile neutrophilic dermatosis, Sweet syndrome; **eosinophile pustulöse** ≈ eosinophilic pustular dermatosis; **lichenartige** ≈ lichenoid dermatosis; **präkanzeröse** ≈ precancerous dermatosis; **subkorneale bullöse** ≈ subcorneal pustular dermatosis, Sneddon-Wilkinson disease.
Dermatrophie *f*: dermal atrophy.
Dermis *f*: skin, dermis.
Dermographie *f*: dermographia.
Dermoidzyste *f*: dermoid cyst.
Desaminierung *f*: deamination.
deSanctis-Cacchione-Syndrom *n*: deSanctis-Cacchione syndrome, xerodermic idiocy.
Desensibilisierung *f*: desensitization.
Desferrioxamin *n*: desferrioxamine.
Desfluran *n*: desflurane.
Desikkation *f*: desiccation.
Desinfektion *f*: disinfection.
Desinfektionsmittel *n*: disinfectant.
Desinfestation *f*: defaunation.
Desipramin *n*: desipramine.
Desirudin *n*: desirudin.
Desloratadin *n*: desloratadine.
desmal: desmoid.
Desmeninol *n*: desmeninol.
Desmoid *n*: desmoid.
Desmopressin *n*: desmopressin.
Desogestrel *n*: desogestrel.
Desonid *n*: desonide.
Desorientiertheit *f*: disorientation.
Desoximetason *n*: desoximetasone.
Desoxyadenylsäure *f*: deoxyadenylic acid.
Desoxycholsäure *f*: deoxycholeic acid.
Desoxycorton *n*: deoxycortone.
Desoxyribonuklease *f*: deoxyribonuclease, DNAase.
Desoxyribonukleinsäure *f*: deoxyribonucleic acid, DNA; **doppelsträngige** ≈ double-stranded deoxyribonucleic acid; **einzelsträngige** ≈ single-stranded deoxyribonucleic acid.
Desquamation *f*: desquamation, exfoliation.
Destillation *f*: distillation.
Desynchronisation *f*: desynchronization.
Detajmiumbitartrat *n*: detajmium bitartrate.
Detergens *n*: detergent.
Determinante *f*: determinant; **antigene** ≈ antigenic determinant.
Determination *f*: determination.
Detonationstrauma *n*: blasting injury.
Detoxikation *f*: detoxication.
Detritus *m*: detritus.
Detrusor *m*: detrusor.
Deuteranomalie *f*: deuteranomaly.
Deuteranopie *f*: deuteranopia, red-green blindness.
Deuteriumoxid *n*: deuterium oxide, heavy water.
Deutschländer-Fraktur *f*: stress fracture, march fracture.
Devianz *f*: deviance.
Deviation *f*: deviation; **ulnare** ≈ ulnar drift, seal-fin deformity
Dexamethason *n*: dexamethasone.
Dexibuprofen *n*: dexibuprofen.
Dexketoprofen *n*: dexketoprofen.
Dextran *n*: dextran.
Dextransulfat *n*: dextran sulfate.
Dextrokardie *f*: dextrocardia.
Dextrokardiographie *f*: dextrocardiography.
Dextrothyroxin-Natrium *n*: dextrothyroxine sodium.
Dezerebration *f*: decerebration.
Dezerebrationsstarre *f*: decerebrate rigidity.
Dezidua *f*: decidua.
Deziduaplatte *f*: decidual plate.
Deziduaplazenta *f*: deciduate placenta.
Deziduazelle *f*: decidual cell.
Deziduitis *f*: deciduitis.
Diabetes mellitus *m*: diabetes mellitus; **insulinabhängiger** ≈ insulin-dependent diabetes mellitus, type-1 diabetes; **juveniler** ≈ juvenile diabetes mellitus, early-onset diabetes mellitus; **labiler** ≈ brittle diabetes mellitus; **latenter** ≈ latent diabetes mellitus, subclinical diabetes mellitus; **manifester** ≈ overt diabetes

mellitus; **nicht-insulinabhängiger** ≈ non-insulin-dependent diabetes mellitus; **renaler** ≈ renal diabetes mellitus.
Diabetiker *m*: diabetic.
diabetisch: diabetic.
diabetogen: diabetogenic.
Diacetylmorhpin *n*: diacetylmorphine.
Diacetylnalorphin *n*: diacetylnalorphine.
Diät *f*: diet; **kochsalzarme** ≈ sodium-restricted diet; **purinarme** ≈ low-purine diet.
Diätbehandlung *f*: dietery therapy, alimentary therapy.
Diätberatung *f*: dietary counseling.
diätetisch: dietary.
Diäthylbarbitursäure *f*: diethylbarbituric acid, barbital.
Diäthylcarbamazin *n*: diethylcarbamazine.
Diäthylstilböstrol *n*: diethylstilbestrol, DES.
Diättherapie *f*: dietery therapy.
Diätverordnung *f*: regimen.
Diagnose *f*: diagnosis; **klinische** ≈ clinical diagnosis; **pränatale** ≈ prenatal diagnosis; **serologische** ≈ serological diagnosis.
Diagnostik *f*: diagnostics; **bildgebende** ≈ imaging diagnostics.
diagnostisch: diagnostic.
Diagramm *n*: diagram, chart, graph.
Dialyse *f*: dialysis.
Dialysemembran *f*: dialysis membrane.
Diameter *m*: diameter.
Diaminodiphenylsulfon *n*: diaminodiphenyl sulfone, dapsone.
α,δ-Diaminovaleriansäure *f*: α,δ-diaminovaleric acid, ornithine.
Diapedese *f*: diapedesis.
Diapedeseblutung *f*: diapedetic bleeding.
Diaphoretikum *n*: diaphoretic.
Diaphragma *n*: diaphragm.
Diaphragmapessar *n*: diaphragm pessary, contraceptive diaphragm.
Diaphyse *f*: diaphysis.
diaplazentar: diaplacental, transplacental.
Diarrhö *f*: diarrhea; **epidemische** ≈ infantile gastroenteritis; **schleimige** ≈ mucous diarrhea; **wässrige** ≈ watery diarrhea.
Diarthrose *f*: diarthrosis.
Diastase *f*: diastasis.
Diastole *f*: diastole.
Diastolikum *n*: diastolic murmur, diastolic sound.
diastolisch: diastolic.
Diathermie *f*: diathermy, diathermic therapy.
Diathese *f*: diathesis, constitution.
Diatrizoesäure *f*: diatrizoic acid.
Diazepam *n*: diazepam.
Diazobenzolsulfonsäure *f*: diazobenzenesulfonic acid.
Diazoxid *n*: diazoxide.
Dibekacin *n*: dibekacin.
Dibenzepin *n*: dibenzepin.
Dicarbonsäure *f*: dicarboxylic acid.
Dichlorethan *n*: dichlorethane.
Dichlorvos *n*: dichlorvos.
Dichte *f*: density, denseness, compactness; **optische** ≈ optical density; **spezifische** ≈ relative density.
Dickdarmpolypose *f*: intestinal polyposis.
Dicke *f*: thickness.
Diclazuril *n*: diclazuril.
Diclofenac *n*: diclofenac.
Diclofenamid *n*: diclofenamide.
Dicloxacillin *n*: dicloxacillin.
Dicoumarol *n*: dicoumarol.
Didanosin *n*: didanosine.
Dideoxycytosin *n*: dideoxycytosine.
dielektrisch: dielectric.
Dienst *m*: duty, on call, service.
dienzephal: diencephalic.
Diethylbarbitursäure *f*: diethylbarbituric acid, barbital.
Diethylstilböstrol *n*: diethylstilbestrol.
Differentialblutbild *n*: differential blood count.
Differentialdiagnose *f*: differential diagnosis, differentiation.
Diffraktion *f*: diffraction.
Diffusion *f*: diffusion.
Diffusionskapazität *f*: diffusing capacity; **pulmonale** ≈ pulmonary diffusing capacity.

Diffusionsstörung *f*: diffusion disorder.
Diflorason *n*: diflorasone.
Diflucortolon *n*: diflucortolone.
Diflunasil *n*: diflunasil.
DiGeorge-Syndrom *n*: DiGeorge syndrome, thymic-parathyreoid aplasia.
Digestion *f*: digestion.
Digitalis *m*: digitalis, foxglove.
Digitalisglykosid *n*: digitalis glycoside.
Digitoxin *n*: digitoxin.
Digitus *m*: digit, digitus, finger.
Digoxin *n*: digoxin.
Dihydralazin *n*: dihydralazine.
Dihydrocodein *n*: dihydrocodeine.
Dihydrocortison *n*: dihydrocortisone.
Dihydroergocornin *n*: dihydroergocornine.
Dihydroergocristin *n*: dihydroergocristine.
Dihydroergocryptin *n*: dihydroergocryptine.
Dihydroergotamin *n*: dihydroergotamine.
Dihydrostreptomycin *n*: dihydrostreptomycin.
Dihydrotachysterol *n*: dihydrotachysterol.
Dihydrouracil *n*: dihydrouracil.
Dihydroxybenzoesäure *f*: dihydroxybenzoic acid.
Dihydroxyphenylessigsäure *f*: 2,5-dihydroxyphenylacetic acid.
Dijodthyrosin *n*: diiodotyrosine.
Dikaliumclorazepat *n*: clorazepate dipotassium.
dikrot: dicrotic.
Dikrotie *f*: dicrotic pulse, dicrotism.
Dilatation *f*: dilatation.
Dilatator *m*: dilatator.
Dilazep *n*: dilazep.
Diltiazem *n*: diltiazem.
Dilution *f*: dilution.
Dimenhydrinat *n*: dimenhydrinate.
Dimepranol *n*: dimepranol.
Dimercaprol *n*: dimercaprol, British antilewisite, BAL.
Dimetacrin *n*: dimetacrine.
Dimethoxyphenylpenicillin *n*: dimethoxyphenyl penicillin sodium, methicillin.
Dimethoxystrychnin *n*: brucine.
Dimethylaminobenzaldehyd *m*: dimethylaminobenzaldehyde, Ehrlich's reagent.
Dimethylsulfoxid *n*: dimethyl sulfoxide.
Dimethyltryptamin *n*: dimethyltryptamine.
Dimethyltubocurariniumchlorid *n*: dimethyltubocurarinium iodide.
Dimorphismus *m*: dimorphism.
Dinoprost *n*: dinoprost.
Dioptometrie *f*: dioptometry.
Dioptrie *f*: diopter.
Dioptriestärke *f*: dioptric power.
Dioxin *n*: dioxin.
Diphenhydramin *n*: diphenhydramine.
Diphonie *f*: diphonia.
Diphosphoglycerinsäure *f*: diphosphoglyceric acid.
Diphtherie *f*: diphtheria.
Diphtherieserum *n*: diphtheria antitoxin, Behring serum
diphtherisch: diphtheric, diphtheritic.
Dipivefrin *n*: dipivefrine.
Diplegie *f*: diplegia; **spastische** ≈ spastic diplegia; **zerebelläre** ≈ cerebellar diplegia.
diploid: diploid.
Diplokokke *f*: diplococcus.
Diplopie *f*: diplopia, double vision.
Dipsomanie *f*: dipsomania, periodic drinking.
Dipyridamol *n*: dipyridamole.
Disaccharid *n*: disaccharide.
Discus *m*: disk, disc.
Disjunktion *f*: disjunction.
Diskographie *f*: diskography, nucleography.
Diskopathie *f*: diskopathy.
Diskrepanz *f*: discrepancy, disagreement.
Diskretion *f*: discretion.
Diskrimination *f*: discrimination.
Dislokation *f*: dislocation, luxation.
Dislokationsfraktur *f*: fracture-dislocation, dislocation fracture.
Disopyramid *n*: disopyramide.
Dispersion *f*: dispersion.
Disproportion *f*: disproportion.

Disruption *f*: disruption.
Dissektion *f*: dissection.
Dissemination *f*: dissemination.
Disse-Raum *m*: Disse space, perisinuosidal space.
dissezierend: dissecting.
Dissonanz *f*: dissonance; **kognitive** ≈ cognitive dissonance.
Dissoziation *f*: dissociation; **albuminozytologische** ≈ albuminocytologic dissociation of the cerebrospinal fluid; **atrioventrikuläre** ≈ atrioventricular dissociation; **tabische** ≈ tabetic dissociation.
distal: distal, remote.
Distanz *f*: distance.
Distanzton *m*: distant cardiac murmur.
Distichiasis *f*: distichiasis.
Distigmin *n*: distigmine.
Distigminbromid *n*: distigmine bromide.
Distorsion *f*: distortion.
Distorsionsfraktur *f*: avulsion fracture, sprain fracture.
Disulfiram *n*: disulfiram, tetraethylthiuram disulfide.
Dithranol *n*: dithranol, anthralin.
Diurese *f*: diuresis.
Diuretikum *n*: diuretic.
diuretisch: diuretic.
Divergenzlähmung *f*: divergence paralysis.
Diversität *f*: diversity.
Divertikel *n*: diverticulum; **falsches** ≈ false diverticulum.
Divertikelblase *f*: sacculated bladder.
Divertikulitis *f*: diverticulitis.
Divertikulose *f*: diverticulosis.
dizygot: dizygotic.
Dobutamin *n*: dobutamine.
Docetaxel *n*: docetaxel.
Dofetilid *n*: dofetilide.
Doktor *m*: physician, doctor.
Dokumentation *f*: documentation, reporting.
Dolasetron *n*: dolasetron.
dolent: painful.
dominant: dominant, predominant.
Dominanz *f*: dominance.
Domperidon *n*: domperidone.
Donath-Landsteiner-Kälteautoantikörper *m*: Donath-Landsteiner cold autoantibody, cold hemolysin.
Donepezil *n*: donepezil.
DOPA-Decarboxylase *f*: dopa decarboxylase.
Dopamin *n*: dopamine.
dopaminerg: dopaminergic.
Dopexamin *n*: dopexamine.
Doping *n*: doping.
Doppelbild *n*: double image, diplopia image.
Doppelblindstudie *f*: double-blind trial.
Doppelfehlbildung *f*: conjoined twins, Siamese twins.
Doppelhelix *f*: double helix.
Doppelkanüle *f*: double cannula.
Doppelkontrasteinlauf *m*: double contrast enema.
Doppellumenkatheter *m*: double-recurrent catheter.
Doppelnadelnaht *f*: doubly armed suture.
Doppelstimme *f*: diphonia.
doppelsträngig: double-stranded.
Doppelthören *n*: diplacusis.
Doppelton *m*: duplicated sound.
Doppeltsehen *n*: double vision, diplopia.
Dorn *m*: spike, thorn.
Dornase alfa *f*: dornase alfa.
dornförmig: spinous.
Dornfortsatz *m*: spinous process of vertebra.
dorsal: dorsal.
Dorsalflexion *f*: dorsiflexion.
Dorsalkrümmung *f*: dorsal curve.
Dorzolamid *n*: dorzolamide.
dosieren: dose.
Dosierung *f*: dosage.
Dosis *f*: dose, dosis, dosage; **effektive** ≈ effective dose; **genetisch signifikante** ≈ genetically significant dose; **infektiöse** ≈ infective dose; **kleinste infektiöse** ≈ minimal infecting dose; **kurative** ≈ curative dose; **letale** ≈ lethal dose, LD; **mittlere effektive** ≈ median effective dose; **tödliche** ≈ invariably lethal dose, LD_{100}.
dosisabhängig: dose-dependent, dose-related.

Dosiseinheit *f*: dose unit.
Dosisfindungsstudie *f*: dose-finding study.
Dossier, ärztliches *n*: medical dossier, medical file.
Dosulepin *n*: dosulepin.
Dotter *m*: yolk, vitellus.
Dottersack *m*: vitelline sac, yolk sac.
Dottersackgefäß *n*: vitilline vessel.
Dottersackmembran *f*: vitelline membrane.
Douglas-Raum *m*: Douglas space, rectovaginal pouch.
Down-Syndrom *n*: Langdon Down's syndrome, trisomy 21.
Doxapram *n*: doxapram.
Doxazosin *n*: doxazosin.
Doxepin *n*: doxepin.
Doxorubicin *n*: doxorubicin.
Doxycyclin *n*: doxycycline.
Drachenwurm *m*: dragon worm, dracunculus.
Dragée *n*: dragée, sugar-coated tablet.
Drahtextension *f*: wire extension.
Drahtfixation *f*: wire fixation.
Drahtleiterschiene *f*: ladder splint, Cramer splint.
Drahtpuls *m*: wire-like pulse.
Drahtschienung *f*: wiring, wire splinting.
Drahtumschlingung *f*: circumferential wiring, wire cerclage.
Drain *m*: drain.
Drainage *f*: drainage, tap.
drainieren: drain, tap.
Drakunkulose *f*: dracunculosis, guinea worm infection.
Dranginkontinenz *f*: urge incontinence.
Drehkrampf *m*: rotatory spasm.
Drehnystagmus *m*: rotation nystagmus.
Drehschwindel *m*: rotatory vertigo.
Drehung *f*: rotation, spin, twisting.
Drehversuch *m*: rotation test.
Dreieck *n*: triangle, trigon, trigonum; **suprapubisches** ≈ suprapubic space.
Dreiecktuch *n*: triangular bandage.
Dreifachanastomose *f*: triple anastomosis.
Dreifachimpfung *f*: triple vaccination.
Dreifachkombination *f*: triple combination.
Dreigläserprobe *f*: three-glass test.
Dreitagefieber *n*: three-day fever, pappataci fever.
Drepanozyt *m*: drepanocyte, sickle cell.
Dressler-Krankheit *f*: Dressler's disease, intermittent hemoglobinuria.
Dressler-Syndrom *n*: Dressler syndrome, postcardiotomy syndrome.
Drift *f*: drift.
Drillingsschwangerschaft *f*: triplet pregnancy.
Droge *f*: drug.
Drogengebraucher *m*: drug user.
Drogenkonsum *m*: drug use.
Dromedarfieberkurve *f*: dromedary curve.
Droperidol *n*: droperidol.
Drostanolon *n*: drostanolone.
Druck *m*: pressure, compression; **arterieller** ≈ arterial tension; **exspiratorischer** ≈ expiratory pressure; **inspiratorischer** ≈ inspiratory pressure; **intrakranieller** ≈ intracranial pressure; **intrathorakaler** ≈ intrathoracic pressure; **negativer endexspiratorischer** ≈ negative end-expiratory pressure; **normaler** ≈ normotension; **venöser** ≈ intravenous tension.
Druckbeatmung *f*: pressure ventilation.
Druckempfindung *f*: pressure sensation.
Druckfallkrankheit *f*: decompression sickness, Caisson disease.
Druckgeschwür *n*: pressure sore, decubitus, decubital ulcer.
Drucklähmung *f*: pressure paralysis.
Drucknekrose *f*: pressure necrosis, decubital necrosis.
Druckpunkt *m*: pressure point.
Druckrezeptor *m*: pressure receptor.
Druckschmerzhaftigkeit *f*: tenderness.
Drucksteigerung *f*: hypertension; **benigne intrakranielle** ≈ benign intracranial hypertension.
Druckverband *m*: pressure bandage.
Drüse *f*: gland; **apokrine** ≈ apocrine

D

gland; **ekkrine** ≈ eccrine gland; **endokrine** ≈ endocrine gland; **gemischte** ≈ mixed gland; **holokrine** ≈ holocrine gland; **merokrine** ≈ merocrine gland; **seröse** ≈ serous gland; **tubuloazinöse** ≈ tubuloacinar gland; **tubulöse** ≈ tubular gland.
Drüsenausführungsgang *m*: secretory duct.
Drüsenentzündung *f*: adenitis.
Drüsenexstirpation *f*: adenectomy.
Drüsenfieber *n*: glandular fever, infectious mononucleosis.
Drüsenpest *f*: glandular plague.
Drüsenphlegmone *f*: phlegmonous adenitis.
Dschungelgelbfieber *n*: sylvan yellow fever.
Duane-Syndrom *n*: Duane syndrome, retraction syndrome.
Dubin-Johnson-Syndrom *n*: Dubin-Johnson syndrome, idiopathic jaundice.
Dubreuilh-Hutchinson-Krankheit *f*: precancerous melanosis of Dubreuilh, malignant lentigo.
Ductus *m*: duct.
dünn: thin.
Dünndarm *m*: small intestine.
Dünnschichtchromatographie *f*: thin-layer chromatography.
Duftdrüsen: sweat glands.
Dukes-Filatow-Krankheit *f*: Filatow-Dukes disease, exanthema subitum.
Dukes-Klassifikation *f*: Dukes classification.
dumpf: dull.
Dumpingsyndrom *n*: dumping syndrome, postgastrectomy syndrome.
Dunbar-Syndrom *n*: mesenteric ischemia.
Dunkeladaptation *f*: dark adaptation.
Dunkelfeldmikroskopie *f*: dark-field microscopy.
Dunkelfelduntersuchung *f*: dark-field examination.
duodenal: duodenal.
Duodenalatresie *f*: duodenal atresia.
Duodenaldivertikel *n*: duodenal diverticulum.
Duodenalstenose *f*: duodenal stenosis.
Duodenalulkus *n*: duodenal ulcer.
Duodenitis *f*: duodenitis.
Duodenoplastik *f*: duodenoplasty.
Duodenoskopie *f*: duodenoscopy.
Duodenumverlegung *f*: duodenal obstruction.
Duplikation *f*: duplication.
Dupuytren-Kontraktur *f*: Dupuytren's contracture, palmar contraction.
Duraklemme *f*: dural forceps.
Durchblutung *f*: blood flow, blood perfusion.
Durchblutungsstörung *f*: circulation disorder; **periphere arterielle** ≈ peripheral circulatory insufficency.
Durchbruchblutung *f*: breakthrough bleeding.
Durchfall *m*: diarrhea.
Durchflusszytometrie *f*: flow cytometry.
Durchgängigkeit *f*: patency.
Durchgangsstadium *n*: transitional phase.
Durchgangssyndrom *n*: transitional psychosis.
Durchmesser *m*: diameter; **äußerer** ≈ outside diameter; **biparietaler** ≈ biparietal diameter; **bitemporaler** ≈ bitemporal diameter; **größter schräger** ≈ mento-occipital diameter; **innerer** ≈ inside diameter; **vorderer gerader** ≈ anterior sagittal diameter.
Durchschlafstörung *f*: intermittent insomnia.
Durchschnittsalter *n*: mean age.
durchsickern: ooze.
Durchstichnaht *f*: transfixion suture.
Duroziez-Doppelgeräusch *n*: Duroziez murmur, pistol-shot sound.
Durstfieber *n*: thirst fever, dehydration fever.
Dutasterid *n*: dutasteride.
Dying-back-Neuropathie *f*: dying-back neuropathy.
Dysäquilibriumsyndrom *n*: dysequilibrium syndrome, urea syndrome.
Dysästhesie *f*: dysesthesia.
Dysarthrie *f*: dysarthria; **spastische** ≈ spastic dysarthria; **zerebelläre** ≈ cerebellar dysarthria, ataxic speech.

Dysautonomie *f*: dysautonomia; **familiäre** ≈ familial dysautonomia, Riley-Day syndrome.
Dyschondroplasie *f*: dyschondroplasia.
Dysdiadochokinese *f*: dysdiadochokinesia.
Dysenterie *f*: dysentery; **bakterielle** ≈ bacillary dysentery, Japanese dysentery; **leichte** ≈ mild dysentery.
Dysfunktion *f*: dysfunction, malfunction; **erektile** ≈ erectile dysfunction; **minimale zerebrale** ≈ minimal brain dysfunction; **vegetative** ≈ vegetative dysfunction.
dysfunktionell: dysfunctional.
Dysgerminom *n*: dysgerminoma.
Dyskeratose *f*: dyskeratosis.
Dyskinesie *f*: dyskinesia.
Dyskorie *f*: dyscoria.
Dyslalie *f*: dyslalia.
Dyslexie *f*: dyslexia.
Dysmelie *f*: dysmelia, ectrogenic teratism; **atriodigitale** ≈ atriodigital dysplasia, Holt Oram syndrome, heart-hand syndrome.
Dysmenorrhö *f*: dysmenorrhea.
Dysmorphie *f*: dysmorphia; **kraniomandibulofaziale** ≈ Rubinstein-Taybi syndrome.
Dysostose *f*: dysostosis; **kraniofaziale** ≈ craniofacial dysostosis; **mandibulofaziale** ≈ mandibulofacial dysostosis, Franceschetti syndrome.
Dyspareunie *f*: dyspareunia.
Dyspepsie *f*: dyspepsia; **nichtulzeröse** ≈ non-ulcer dyspepsia.
Dysphagie *f*: dysphagia.
Dysplasia cranio-carpo-tarsalis *f*: craniocarpotarsal dysplasia, Freeman-Sheldon syndrome, whistling face-windmill vane hand syndrome.
Dysplasia encephaloophthalmica *f*: encephalo-ophthalmic dysplasia, Krause syndrome.
Dysplasie *f*: dysplasia; **chondroektodermale** ≈ chondroectodermal dysplasia; **diaphysäre** ≈ diaphyseal dysplasia; **fibröse** ≈ fibrous dysplasia, Jaffé-Lichtenstein disease; **kraniometaphysäre** ≈ craniometaphyseal dysplasia, Pyle's disease; **metaphysäre** ≈ metaphyseal dysplasia.
dysplastisch: dysplastic.
Dyspnoe *f*: dyspnea, shortness of breath; **exspiratorische** ≈ expiratory dyspnea; **inspiratorische** ≈ inspiratory dyspnea; **kardiale** ≈ cardiac dyspnea; **orthostatische** ≈ orthostatic dyspnea.
Dyspraxie *f*: dyspraxia.
Dysrhythmie *f*: dysrhythmia; **zirkadiane** ≈ jet lag.
Dyssynergia cerebellaris myoclonica *f*: dyssynergia cerebellaris myoclonica, Hunt's disease.
Dystokie *f*: dystocia.
Dystonie *f*: dystonia; **neurovegetative** ≈ autonomic dystonia, neurodystonia.
Dystrophia myotonica *f*: myotonic dystrophy.
Dystrophie *f*: dystrophy; **adiposogenitale** ≈ adiposogenital dystrophy, Fröhlich syndrome; **frühinfantile diffuse spongiöse** ≈ infantile spongy degeneration, Canavan's diffuse sclerosis; **kraniokarpotarsale** ≈ craniocarpotarsal dysplasia, Freeman-Sheldon syndrome, whistling face-windmill vane hand syndrome; **okulozerebrorenale** ≈ oculocerebrorenal syndrome.
Dysurie *f*: dysuria.

E

E Abk. **1. Emmetropie** *f*; **2. Energie** *f*; **3. Extinktion** *f*: 1. emmetropia, EM, E.; 2. energy; 3. extinction.
Ebastin *n*: ebastin.
eben: flat, even.
Ebene *f*: plane, planum.
Ebola-Virus *n*: Ebola virus.
Ebola-Viruskrankheit *f*: Ebola virus disease, African hemorrhagic fever.
Echinokokkose *f*: echinococcosis.
Echinokokkuszyste *f*: echinococcus cyst.
Echinozyt *m*: echinocyte, burr cell.
Echokardiogramm *n*: echocardiogram.
Echokardiographie *f*: echocardiography, ultrasonic cardiography.
Echolalie *f*: echolalia.
Echophrasie *f*: echophrasia.
echt: true.
Echtzeitverfahren *n*: real-time method.
Eckzahn *m*: corner tooth, cuspid tooth.
Econazol *n*: econazole.
Eculizumab *n*: eculizumab.
Edetinsäure *f*: edetic acid.
EEG-Welle *f*: electroencephalographic wave.
Efavirenz *n*: efavirenz.
Effekt *m*: effect; **kumulativer** ≈ cumulation effect; **nachteiliger** ≈ adverse effect; **parakriner** ≈ paracrine effect; **piezoelektrischer** ≈ piezoelectric effect; **zytopathischer** ≈ cytopathic effect.
effektiv: effective.
Effektivdosis *f*: effective dose.
Effektorzelle *f*: effector cell.
efferent: efferent.
Effizienz *f*: efficiency.
Effleurage *f*: effleurage.
Effloreszenz *f*: efflorescence.
Effort-Syndrom *n*: effort syndrome, daCosta syndrome.
Ego *n*: ego, self.
egozentrisch: egocentric, self-centered.
Ehrlich-Reagens *n*: Ehrlich's reagent, dimethylaminobenzaldehyde.
Ei *n*: egg, ovum; **alezitales** ≈ alecithal egg; **isolezitales** ≈ isolecithal egg; **telolezitales** ≈ telolecithal egg.
Eichel *f*: head of penis, glans.
Eierstock *m*: ovarium, ovary.
Eifersuchtswahn *m*: jealous delusion.
Eifollikel *m*: ovarian follicle.
Eigelb *n*: yolk.
Eigenbehandlung *f*: self-treatment.
Eigenbluttransfusion *f*: autologous transfusion.
Eigenfrequenz *f*: natural frequency.
Eigenreflex *f*: idioreflex, self-induced reflex.
Eigenschaft *f*: property, characteristic, feature.
Eigenserum *n*: autoserum, autologous serum.
Eignung *f*: fitness, aptitude.
Eihaut *f*: egg membrane.
Eileiter *m*: salpinx, fallopian tube.
Eileiterentzündung *f*: salpingitis.
Eileiterruptur *f*: tubal rupture.
Eileiterschwangerschaft *f*: tubal pregnancy, ampullar pregnancy.
Eindimensionalität *f*: unidimensionality.
eindringen: invade, penetrate.
Eindringen *n*: invasion, penetration.
Eindruck *m*: impression.
eineiig: monovular, uniovular.
Einengung *f*: narrowing.
Einflussstauung *f*: inflow obstruction.

Eingang *m*: entrance, portal.
eingedickt: inspissated.
eingekapselt: encapsuled, capsulated.
eingeklemmt: impacted, herniated.
eingeschlechtlich: monosexual, unisexual.
Eingeweide: viscera.
Eingeweideekstrophie *f*: visceral ectopia.
Eingeweideschmerz *m*: visceral pain, visceralgia.
Eingliederung *f*: integration, insertion, habilitation.
Eingriff *m*: surgery, operation, intervention; **elektiver** ≈ elective surgery; **explorativer** ≈ exploratory surgery; **großer** ≈ major surgery; **kleiner** ≈ minor surgery.
Einheit *f*: unit, entity.
einhüllen: coat, envelop.
Einkapselung *f*: encapsulation, encystation.
Einkeilung *f*: impaction.
Einkerbung *f*: incisure, indentation.
einkernig: mononuclear.
Einklemmung *f*: entrapment, impaction, herniation.
Einkoten *n*: encopresis.
Einlage *f*: inlay, insert.
Einlagerung *f*: inclusion.
Einlauf *m*: enema, clyster.
Einlaufreposition *f*: hydrostatic reduction.
Einmaldosis *f*: single dose.
Einmalspritze *f*: disposable syringe.
einmal täglich: once daily.
Einnässen *n*: enuresis, bedwetting.
Einnistung *f*: nidation.
Einreibemittel *n*: unction.
einreiben: rub, inunct.
Einreibung *f*: inunction.
einreißen: fissure, lacerate.
Einrenken *n*: reduction.
Einriss *m*: laceration.
einschläfernd: soporific, somniferous.
Einschlafstörung *f*: initial insomnia, disorder of initiating sleep.
Einschluss *m*: inclusion, enclosure; **intrazellulärer** ≈ cell inclusion.
Einschlusskörperchen *n*: inclusion body.
Einschlusskörperchenenzephalitis Dawson *f*: inclusion body encephalitis, Dawson's encephalitis, subacute sclerosing panencephalitis, SSPE.
Einschmelzung *f*: melting, fusion; **entzündliche** ≈ inflammatory softening.
Einschnitt *m*: incisure, notch.
Einschnürung *f*: constriction.
Einschussverletzung *f*: in-shot wound.
einseitig: unilateral, one-sided.
Einsetzen der Wehen: labor onset.
Einsichtsfähigkeit *f*: discerning ability.
Einspritzung *f*: injection.
Einstellung *f*: attitude, adjustment.
Einstellungstubus *m*: adjusting cone.
Einstich *m*: puncture, insertion.
einstrangig: single-stranded.
Eintagsfieber *n*: ephemeral fever.
Eintrittsblock *m*: entrance block.
Einwärtsbiegung *f*: inflection, introflexion
Einwärtsschielen *n*: internal strabismus, convergent strabismus.
Einwegartikel *m*: disposable.
Einwegspritze *f*: disposable syringe.
Einwilligung *f*: consent.
Einzeldosis *f*: single dose.
Einzelfallstudie *f*: case study.
Einzelkopie-Gen *n*: single-copy gene.
einzellig: monocellular, unicellular.
Einziehung *f*: retraction; **systolische** ≈ systolic retraction.
Eipol *m*: pole.
Eisen *n*: ferrum, Fe, iron; **freies** ≈ available iron; **reduziertes** ≈ reduced iron.
Eisenablagerung *f*: siderosis.
Eisenbindungskapazität *f*: iron-binding capacity.
eisenhaltig: ferrous.
Eisenhexacyanoferrat *n*: ferric hexacyanoferrate, ferric **ferrocyanide**.
Eisenhut *m*: aconite, monkshood.
Eisenjodid *n*: iron iodide, ferrous iodide.
Eisenmangelanämie *f*: iron-deficiency anemia, sideropenic anemia.
Eisenspeicherkrankheit *f*: iron storage disease.

Eisenverbindung *f*: iron compound.
Eisprung *m*: ovulation.
Eisprungbestimmung *f*: ovulation timing.
Eiter *m*: pus, matter.
Eiterbakterium *n*: pyogenic bacterium.
Eiterbläschen *n*: pustule.
Eitergeschwür *n*: suppurating ulcer.
Eiterhöhle *f*: pyorrhea pocket.
eitern: suppurate, fester.
Eitersackniere *f*: infected hydronephrosis, pyonephrosis.
eitrig: purulent, suppurative.
Eiweiß *n*: protein.
Eiweißmangel *m*: protein deficiency.
Eiweißprobe *f*: protein test.
Eiweißverlustsyndrom *n*: protein-losing enteropathy.
Eizelle *f*: egg cell, ovum.
Ejaculatio praecox *f*: premature ejaculation.
Ejakulation *f*: ejaculation; **vorzeitige** ≈ premature ejaculation.
Ejektionsfraktion *f*: ejection fraction.
Ekbom-Syndrom *n*: Ekbom syndrome, restless legs.
Ekchymose *f*: ecchymosis.
ekkrin: eccrine.
Eklampsie *f*: eclampsia.
eklamptisch: eclamptic.
Ektasie *f*: ectasia.
Ekthym *n*: ecthyma.
Ektoderm *n*: ectoderm.
ektodermal: ectodermal.
Ektodermaldysplasie *f*: ectodermal dysplasia; **anhidrotische** ≈ anhidrotic ectodermal dysplasia; **hidrotische** ≈ hidrotic ectodermal dysplasia.
ektogon: ectogenous.
Ektomie *f*: excision, surgical removal.
ektop: ectopic.
Ektoparasit *m*: ectoparasite.
Ektopie *f*: ectopia, dystopia.
Ektozoon *n*: ectozoon, ectoparasite.
Ektrodaktylie *f*: ectrodactyly, oligodactyly.
Ekzem *n*: eczema, eczematoid dermatitis; **allergisches** ≈ allergic eczema; **atopisches** ≈ atopic eczema, neurodermatitis; **dyskeratotisches** ≈ dyskeratotic eczema; **lichenförmiges** ≈ lichenoid eczema; **nummuläres** ≈ nummular eczema; **phlyktänuläres** ≈ phlyctenular eczema; **pustulöses** ≈ pustular eczema; **seborrhoisches** ≈ seborrheic dermatitis.
Elaidinsäure *f*: elaidic acid.
Elastin *n*: elastin.
elastisch: elastic.
Elastose *f*: elastosis.
Elastose der Haut, noduläre *f*: nodular elastosis of the skin, Favre-Racouchot syndrome.
Electuarium *n*: electuary.
elektiv: elective.
Elektrizität *f*: electricity.
Elektrode *f*: electrode.
Elektroenzephalogramm *n*: electroencephalogram.
Elektroenzephalographie *f*: electroencephalography.
Elektrokardiogramm *n*: electrocardiogram.
Elektrokardiographie *f*: electrocardiography.
Elektrokauterisation *f*: electrocauterization, electric cautery.
Elektrokoagulation *f*: electrocoagulation, electric coagulation.
Elektrokrampftherapie *f*: electroconvulsive treatment.
Elektrolyse *f*: electrolysis.
Elektrolyt *n*: electrolyte.
Elektrolythaushalt *m*: electrolyte balance.
elektromagnetisch: electromagnetic.
Elektromyogramm *n*: electromyogram.
Elektron *n*: electron.
Elektronenmikroskopie *f*: electron microscopy.
Elektronenspinresonanz *f*: electron spin resonance.
Elektrophorese *f*: electrophoresis.
Elektroretinogramm *n*: electroretinogram.
Elektrosonde *f*: electric probe.
Elektrostimulationsanalgesie *f*: electric analgesia.
Elektrotherapie *f*: electrotherapy.
Element *n*: element; **radioaktives** ≈ radioactive element, radioelement.

Elementarkörperchen *n*: elementary body.
Elephantiasis *f*: filarial elephantiasis.
Eletriptan *n*: eletriptan.
Elevation *f*: elevation, eminence.
Elfenbeintumor *m*: ivory osteoma.
ELISA: enzyme-linked immunosorbent assay, ELISA.
Elixir *n*: elixir.
Ellbogen *m*: elbow, ulna.
Ellbogengelenk *n*: elbow joint.
Ellbogengrube *f*: cubital fossa.
Ellenbogen *m*: elbow, ulna.
Elliptozytose *f*: elliptocytosis; **hereditäre** ≈ elliptocytic anemia, Dresbach syndrome.
Ellis-Creveld-Syndrom *n*: Ellis-van Creveld syndrome, chondroectodermal dysplasia.
Elongationsfaktor *m*: elongation factor.
Elternschaft *f*: parenthood, parentage.
Elution *f*: elution.
Elvucitabin *n*: elvucitabine.
Emaille *f*: enamel.
Embolektomie *f*: embolectomy; **pulmonale** ≈ pulmonary embolectomy, Trendelenburg's operation.
Embolie *f*: embolism; **arterielle** ≈ arterial embolism; **paradoxe** ≈ paradoxical embolism, crossed embolism; **venöse** ≈ venous embolism; **zerebrale** ≈ cerebral embolism.
Embolus *m*: embolus; **reitender** ≈ saddle embolus.
Embryo *m*: embryo.
Embryoid *n*: embryoid body.
Embryologie *f*: embryology.
embryonal: embryonal.
Embryonalentwicklung *f*: embryo development, prenatal development.
Embryonalkreislauf *m*: embryonic circulation.
Embryonalorgan *n*: embryonic organ.
Embryonentransfer *m*: embryo transfer; **intratubarer** ≈ gamete intrafallopian transfer, GIFT.
Embryopathie *f*: embryopathy.
Embryotomie *f*: embryotomy.
Emedastin *n*: emedastine.
Emepronium *n*: emepronium bromide.
Emesis *f*: emesis, vomiting.
Emetikum *n*: emetic, vomitory.
Emetin *n*: emetine.
Emissionsspektrum *n*: emission spectrum.
Emmetropie *f*: emmetropia, normal vision.
Emolliens *n*: emollient.
Emotion *f*: emotion.
emotional: emotional.
Emotionspsychose *f*: emotional psychosis.
Emotionsstupor *m*: emotional stupor.
Empathie *f*: empathy.
Empfänger *m*: receiver, receptor, recipient.
empfänglich: susceptible.
Empfänglichkeit *f*: susceptibility.
Empfängnis *f*: conception.
Empfängnisverhütung *f*: contraception.
empfehlen: recommend, advise.
empfehlenswert: advisable.
Empfehlung *f*: recommendation, guideline.
empfinden: sense, feel.
empfindlich: sensitive, susceptible.
Empfindlichkeit *f*: sensitivity, susceptibility.
Empfindung *f*: emotion, esthesia, sensation.
Empfindungsdissozation *f*: dissociated sensory loss.
Empfindungshalluzination *f*: sensory hallucination.
Empfindungsschwelle *f*: sensory threshold.
Emphysem *n*: emphysema; **interstitielles** ≈ interstitial emphysema; **kompensatorisches** ≈ compensatory emphysema; **kongenitales lobäres** ≈ infantile lobar emphysema; **obstruktives** ≈ obstructive emphysema; **panazinäres** ≈ ectatic emphysema; **panlobuläres** ≈ panacinar emphysema; **subkutanes** ≈ subcutaneous emphysema; **zentroazinäres** ≈ centriacinar emphysema.
Emphysemthorax *m*: emphysematous thorax.

empirisch: empiric.
Empyem *n*: empyema.
Emtricitabin *n*: emtricitabine.
Emulgentium *n*: emulgent.
Emulsion *f*: emulsion.
Emylcamat *n*: emylcamate.
Enalapril *n*: enalapril.
Enalaprilat *n*: enalaprilat.
Enarthrose *f*: enarthrosis, spheroidal articulation.
Encephalitis japonica *f*: Japanese B encephalitis, summer encephalitis.
Encephalitis lethargica *f*: lethargic encephalitis, Economo's disease.
Encephalomyelitis disseminata *f*: disseminated sclerosis, multiple sclerosis.
Encephalomyelitis equina *f*: equine encephalomyelitis, Venezuelan encephalitis.
Encephalon *n*: encephalon, brain.
Enchondrom *n*: enchondroma.
Endangiitis *f*: endangiitis.
Endarteriitis *f*: endarteritis.
Endarteriitis obliterans *f*: obliterating endarteritis.
Enddarm *m*: rectum.
Endemie *f*: endemic.
endemisch: endemic.
Endgruppe *f*: end group, terminal group.
Endhirn *n*: endbrain, telencephalon.
Endigung *f*: ending, terminal.
Endocarditis lenta *f*: subacute bacterial endocarditis.
Endoderm *n*: endoderm, entoderm.
endogen: endogenous.
Endokard *n*: endocardium.
Endokardfibroelastose *f*: endocardial fibroelastosis.
Endokarditis *f*: endocarditis; **akute bakterielle** ≈ septic endocarditis; **bakterielle** ≈ bacterial endocarditis; **chronische** ≈ chronic endocarditis; **fibroplastische** ≈ fibroplastic endocarditis, constrictive endocarditis; **infektiöse** ≈ infectious endocarditis; **parietale** ≈ mural endocarditis; **rheumatische** ≈ rheumatic endocarditis; **septische** ≈ acute bacterial endocarditis; **subakute bakterielle** ≈ subacute bacterial endocarditis; **verruköse** ≈ verrucous endocarditis.
endokrin: endocrine.
Endokrinium *n*: endocrine system.
Endokrinologie *f*: endocrinology.
Endolymphe *f*: endolymph, otic fluid.
Endometriose *f*: endometriosis.
Endometriosis interna *f*: endometriosis interna.
Endometritis *f*: endometritis.
Endometritis cervicis *f*: endocervicitis.
Endometritis decidualis *f*: decidual endometritis.
Endometritis puerperalis *f*: puerperal endometritis.
Endometrium *n*: endometrium.
Endometriumbiopsie *f*: endometrial biospy.
Endometriumhyperplasie *f*: endometrial hyperplasia.
Endometriumsarkom *n*: endometrial stromal sarcoma.
Endometriumzyste *f*: endometrial cyst.
Endomyokardfibrose *f*: endomyocardial fibrosis.
endonasal: intranasal.
Endoneuralscheide *f*: endoneurial sheath.
Endoneurium *n*: endoneurium.
endophytisch: endophytic.
Endoplasma *n*: endoplasm.
endoplasmatisch: endoplasmic.
Endorgan *n*: end-organ, terminal organ.
Endorphin *n*: endorphin.
Endorphinrezeptor *m*: narcotic receptor.
Endoskop *n*: endoscope.
Endoskopie *f*: endoscopy.
Endotheliom *n*: endothelioma, endothelial cancer.
Endothelzelle *f*: endothelial cell.
Endotoxin *n*: endotoxin, endogenous toxin.
Endotoxinschock *m*: endotoxin shock.
endotracheal: endotracheal.
Endotrachealtubus *m*: endotracheal tube.
Endplatte *f*: endplate, synaptic button.

Endpunkt *m*: end point.
Endstadium *n*: final stage.
endständig: next-to-end, terminal.
endsystolisch: end-systolic.
Endung *f*: ending.
End-zu-End-Anastomose *f*: end-to-end shunt, terminoterminal anastomosis.
End-zu-Seit-Anastomose *f*: end-to-side shunt.
Energie *f*: energy, power.
Energiequotient *m*: energy quotient.
Enervierung *f*: enervation, denervation.
Enfluran *n*: enflurane.
Enfuvirtid *n*: enfuvirtide.
eng: narrow, tight.
Enge *f*: narrowing, isthmus.
Engramm *n*: engram, memory trace.
Engwinkelglaukom *n*: angle-closure glaucoma.
Enkephalin *n*: enkephalin.
Enkopresis *f*: encopresis.
Enophthalmus *m*: enophthalmos.
Enostose *f*: enostosis.
Enoxacin *n*: enoxacin.
Enrofloxacin *n*: enrofloxacin.
Entacapon *n*: entacapone.
Entamöbe *f*: entameba.
entbinden: deliver.
Entbindung *f*: delivery; **natürliche** ≈ vaginal delivery; **vorzeitige** ≈ premature delivery.
Entbindungspfleger *m*: midwife.
Entdifferenzierung *f*: dedifferentiation, anaplasia.
Entecavir *n*: entecavir.
enteral: enteric, enteral.
Enteritis *f*: enteritis, intestinal infection; **diphtherische** ≈ diphtheritic enteritis; **nekrotisierende** ≈ necrotizing enteritis; **phlegmonöse** ≈ phlegmonous enteritis.
Enteritis regionalis *f*: regional enteritis, Crohn's disease, regional ileitis.
Enteroanastomose *f*: enteroanastomosis.
Enterobiasis *f*: enterobiasis, oxyuriasis.
enterohepatisch: enterohepatic.
Enterohormon *n*: intestinal hormone.
Enterokinase *f*: enterokinase.
Enterokokke *f*: enterococcus.
Enterokolitis *f*: enterocolitis; **nekrotisierende** ≈ necrotizing enterocolitis, NEC; **postantibiotische** ≈ antibiotic enterocolitis.
Enterolith *m*: enterolith.
Enteropathie *f*: enteropathy; **exsudative** ≈ protein-losing enteropathy.
Enteroptose *f*: enteroptosis.
Enterostenose *f*: enterostenosis.
Enterotomie *f*: enterotomy.
Enterovirus *n*: enterovirus, enteric virus.
Enterozele *f*: enterocele.
Entfaltung *f*: unfolding, display, development.
entfernen: remove, dispose.
Entfernung *f*: distance, removal; **chirurgische** ≈ surgical removal.
Entfremdung *f*: alienation.
Entgiftung *f*: detoxification.
Enthaarung *f*: depilation, epilation.
Enthaarungscreme *f*: depilatory cream.
Enthelminthikum *n*: helminthagogue.
Enthirnungsstarre *f*: decerebrate rigidity.
Entkonditionierung *f*: deconditioning.
Entladung *f*: discharge, burst, unloading.
Entladungsschwelle *f*: firing level.
entlassen: discharge, dismiss.
Entlassung *f*: discharge, dismissal, release.
Entlastung *f*: decompression, relief.
Entlastungsschnitt *m*: relieving incision, decompression incision.
Entlausung *f*: delousing, disinfestation.
Entleerung *f*: emptying, voiding, evacuation, depletion.
Entmarkung *f*: demyelination, demyelinization.
Entmarkungskrankheit *f*: demyelinating disease.
Entnahme *f*: withdrawal, taking.
Entoderm *n*: entoderm.
Entschädigung *f*: compensation, indemnity.
Entspannung *f*: relaxation.

Entstehung *f*: development, origin, genesis.
Entweichen *n*: escape.
Entwesung *f*: disinfestation, disinfection.
Entwicklung *f*: development, evolution, processing; **frühkindliche** ≈ infant development; **geistige** ≈ mental development; **kognitive** ≈ cognitive development; **psychomotorische** ≈ psychomotor development.
Entwicklungsalter *n*: developmental age.
Entwicklungsfehlbildung *f*: developmental malformation.
Entwicklungskrise *f*: developmental crisis.
Entwicklungsphase *f*: developmental period.
Entwicklungsrückstand, psychomotorischer *m*: psychomotor retardation.
Entwicklungsschaden *m*: developmental defect.
Entwicklungsstadium *n*: developmental stage.
Entwicklungsstillstand *m*: developmental arrest.
Entwicklungsstörung *f*: developmental disorder, impaired development, developmental disability.
entwöhnen: wean, withdraw.
Entwöhnung *f*: weaning, withdrawal.
Entziehungserscheinung *f*: withdrawal symptom, abstinence syndrome.
Entzügelungshochdruck *m*: neurogenic hypertension.
entzündlich: inflammatory.
Entzündung *f*: inflammation.
entzündungshemmend: anti-inflammatory.
Entzündungsreaktion *f*: inflammatory reaction.
Entzündungsvorgang *m*: inflammatory process.
Entzündungszeichen *n*: inflammatory symptom.
Entzündungszelle *f*: inflammatory cell.
Entzug *m*: withdrawal.
Enukleation *f*: enucleation.
Enurese *f*: enuresis.
Enzephalitis *f*: encephalitis; **akute nekrotisierende** ≈ acute necrotic encephalitis; **eitrige** ≈ suppurative encephalitis; **epidemische** ≈ epidemic encephalitis, Economo's disease; **otogene** ≈ otitic encephalitis; **postvakzinale** ≈ postvaccinal encephalitis; **venezolanische** ≈ Venezuelan encephalitis; **zentraleuropäische** ≈ Central European encephalitis.
Enzephalogramm *n*: encephalogram.
Enzephalomalazie *f*: encephalomalacia, cerebral softening.
Enzephalomeningitis *f*: encephalomeningitis.
Enzephalomyelitis *f*: encephalomyelitis; **benigne myalgische** ≈ benign myalgic encephalomyelitis, Iceland disease.
Enzephalomyelopathie *f*: encephalomyelopathy; **subakute nekrotisierende** ≈ subacute necrotizing encephalomyelopathy, Leigh's disease.
Enzephalomyokarditis *f*: encephalomyocarditis.
Enzephalon *n*: encephalon, brain.
Enzephalopathie *f*: encephalopathy; **bovine spongiforme** ≈ bovine spongiform encephalopathy; **hepatische** ≈ hepatic encephalopathy, portocaval encephalopathy; **metabolische** ≈ metabolic encephalopathy; **nekrotisierende hämorrhagische** ≈ necrotizing hemorrhagic encephalopathy; **palindromische** ≈ recurrent encephalopathy; **spongiforme** ≈ spongiform encephalopathy; **subkortikale arteriosklerotische** ≈ progressive subcortical encephalopathy; **toxische** ≈ toxic encephalopathy; **urämische** ≈ uremic encephalopathy.
Enzephalozele *f*: encephalocele.
Enzym *n*: enzyme, ferment; **allosterisches** ≈ allosteric enzyme; **induzierbares** ≈ inducible enzyme; **konstitutives** ≈ constitutive enzyme.
Enzymmangel *m*: enzymopenia, enzyme deficiency.
Enzymmuster *n*: enzyme pattern.
Enzym-Substrat-Komplex *m*: enzyme-substrate complex.
enzystieren: encyst.

Eosin *n*: eosin.
eosinophil: eosinophil.
Eosinophilenleukämie *f*: eosinophilic leukemia.
Eosinophiler *m*: eosinophil, eosinophilic leukocyte.
Eosinophilie *f*: eosinophilia; **tropische** ≈ tropical pulmonary eosinophilia, Weingarten syndrome.
Ependym *n*: ependyma.
Ependymom *n*: ependymoma, ependymal glioma.
Ependymzelle *f*: ependymal cell.
Ependymzyste *f*: ependymal cyst.
Ephedrin *n*: ephedrine.
Epheliden: ephelides, freckle.
EPH-Gestose *f*: edema-proteinuria-hypertension gestosis, EPH gestosis, preeclampsia.
Epiblepharon *n*: epiblepharon.
Epicillin *n*: epicillin.
Epidemie *f*: epidemic.
Epidemiologie *f*: epidemiology.
epidemiologisch: epidemiologic.
epidemisch: epidemic.
epidermal: epidermal.
Epidermis *f*: epidermis.
Epidermiszyste *f*: epidermal cyst.
Epidermolyse *f*: epidermolysis.
Epidermolysis acuta toxica *f*: toxic epidermal necrolysis, Lyell syndrome.
Epidermolysis bullosa hereditaria *f*: epidermolysis bullosa hereditaria, Herlitz syndrome.
Epidermolysis bullosa papuloalboidea *f*: bullous papuloalboid epidermolysis.
Epidermophytie *f*: epidermophytosis.
Epididymitis *f*: epididymitis.
Epididymoorchitis *f*: epididymo-orchitis.
epidural: epidural.
Epiduralabszess *m*: epidural abscess, extradural abscess.
Epiduralanästhesie *f*: epidural anesthesia, epidural block.
Epiduralhämatom *n*: epidural hematoma.
Epiduralraum *m*: epidural space, extradural space.
Epiduritis *f*: epiduritis.
epigastrisch: epigastric.
Epigastrium *n*: epigastrium, epigastric region.
Epiglottis *f*: epiglottis.
Epikard *n*: epicardium.
Epikondylitis *f*: epicondylitis.
Epikondylus *m*: epicondyle, epicondylus.
Epikrise *f*: epicrisis.
Epikutantest *m*: epidermal test.
Epilation *f*: epilation, depilation.
Epilationspinzette *f*: epilating forceps.
Epilepsia major *f*: major epilepsy.
Epilepsia minor *f*: minor epilepsy.
Epilepsia partialis *f*: partial epilepsy, focal epilepsy.
Epilepsia partialis continua *f*: continuous partial epilepsy, Kozhevnikov's epilepsy.
Epilepsie *f*: epilepsy, falling sickness; **abdominale** ≈ abdominal epilepsy, Moore syndrome; **adversive** ≈ adversive epilepsy; **akinetische** ≈ akinetic epilepsy, atonic epilepsy; **audiogene** ≈ audiogenic epilepsy; **bewegungsabhängige** ≈ movement-induced epilepsy; **dienzephale** ≈ diencephalic epilepsy, midbrain epilepsy; **diffuse** ≈ diffuse epilepsy; **familiäre** ≈ hereditary epilepsy; **generalisierte** ≈ generalized epilepsy; **genuine** ≈ essential epilepsy; **myoklonische** ≈ myoclonic epilepsy, Lafora body disease; **photogene** ≈ photic epilepsy; **posttraumatische** ≈ post-traumatic epilepsy; **symptomatische** ≈ symptomatic epilepsy, secondary epilepsy; **versive** ≈ versive epilepsy; **visuelle** ≈ visual epilepsy.
epileptiform: epileptiform.
epileptisch: epileptic.
epileptogen: epileptogenic.
Epinephrin *n*: epinephrine, adrenaline.
Epineurium *n*: epineurium.
Epiphyse *f*: epiphysis.
Epiphysenablösung *f*: epiphysiolysis, epiphyseal detachment.
Epiphysenfraktur *f*: epiphyseal fracture.

Epiphysenschluss *m*: fusion of epiphyses.
Epiphysitis *f*: epiphysitis.
Epirubicin *n*: epirubicin.
Episiotomie *f*: episiotomy.
Episkleralraum *m*: episcleral space, Tenon space.
Episkleritis *f*: episcleritis.
Episode *f*: episode; **manische** ≈ manic episode; **typische depressive** ≈ single episode major depression.
Epispadie *f*: epispadias.
Epispastikum *n*: epispastic.
Epistaxis *f*: epistaxis, nosebleed.
Epithel *n*: epithelium.
Epithelauskleidung *f*: epithelial lining.
Epithelgewebe *n*: epithelial tissue.
Epithelgrenze *f*: epithelial border.
epithelial: epithelial.
Epitheliom *n*: epithelioma.
Epithelkörperchen *n*: epithelial body.
Epitheloidzelle *f*: epitheloid cell.
Epithelschicht *f*: epithelial layer.
Epitheltumor *m*: epithelial tumor.
Epithelzapfen *m*: epithelial peg.
Epithelzelle *f*: epithelial cell.
Epithelzylinder *m*: epithelial cast.
Epitrochlea *f*: epitrochlea.
Epizoonose *f*: epizoonosis.
Eplerenon *n*: eplerenone.
Epoetin *n*: epoetin.
Eponym *n*: eponym.
Epoophoron *n*: epoophoron, Rosenmüller's organ.
Eprazinon *n*: eprazinone.
Eprinomectin *n*: eprinomectin.
Eprosartan *n*: eprosartan.
Epstein-Barr-Virus *n*: Epstein-Barr virus.
Eptifibatid *n*: eptifibatide.
Epulis gigantocellularis *f*: giant cell epulis.
Erbfaktor *m*: unit factor, gene.
erblich: hereditary, inheritable.
erbrechen: vomit, throw up.
Erbrechen *n*: vomiting, vomition, emesis; **kaffeesatzartiges** ≈ coffee-ground vomit, melenemesis; **unstillbares** ≈ incessant vomiting, persistent vomiting.
Erbsenbein *n*: pisiform bone.
Erb-Sklerose *f*: Erb sclerosis, primary lateral sclerosis.
Erdbeergallenblase *f*: strawberry gallbladder.
Erdbeerzunge *f*: strawberry tongue.
Erdheim-Tumor *m*: pituitary ameloblastoma, craniopharyngioma.
Ereignis *n*: event; **lebenskritisches** ≈ critical life event.
erektil: erectile.
Erektion *f*: erection.
Erektionsstörung *f*: erectile dysfunction.
Erfahrungsheilkunde *f*: empiric treatment.
Erfolgsorgan *n*: effector organ.
Erfordernishochdruck *m*: compensatory hypertension.
Erfrierung *f*: cold injury, freezing.
ergänzend: supplementary, ancillary.
Ergobasin *n*: ergabasine.
Ergocalciferol *n*: ergocalciferol, vitamin D_2.
Ergometer *n*: ergometer.
Ergometrie *f*: ergometry.
Ergonomie *f*: ergonomy, ergonomics.
Ergosterin *n*: ergosterol.
Ergotalkaloid *n*: ergot alkaloid.
Ergotamin *n*: ergotamine.
Ergotherapie *f*: ergotherapy, work therapy.
Ergotismus *m*: ergotism, Saint Anthony's fire.
Erguss *m*: effusion.
erhaben: eminent.
Erhängen *n*: hanging.
erhärten: harden.
Erhaltung *f*: maintenance, conservation.
Erhaltungsdosis *f*: maintenance dose.
Erhaltungstherapie *f*: maintenance therapy.
Erhebung *f*: elevation.
erhitzen: heat.
Erhöhung *f*: eminence.
Erholung *f*: rest, recreation, recovery, recuperation.
Erholungsphase *f*: recovery phase.
Erigierbarkeit *f*: erectility.
erinnern: remember, recall, recollect.
Erinnerung *f*: memory, recall, remembrance.

Erinnerungslücke *f*: memory loss.
Eritrityltetranitrat *n*: eritrityl tetranitrate.
Erkältung *f*: common cold, acute catarrhal rhinitis.
Erkennung *f*: recognition.
erkrankt: sick, diseased.
Erkrankung *f*: disease, disorder, illness, sickness; **AIDS-definierende** ≈ AIDS-defining disease; **ansteckende** ≈ contagious disease, communicable disease; **arteriosklerotische kardiovaskuläre** ≈ arteriosclerotic cardiovascular disease; **atopische** ≈ atopic disease; **bakterielle** ≈ bacterial disease; **chronisch-granulomatöse** ≈ chronic granulomatous disease, chronic X-linked granulomatosis; **degenerative** ≈ degenerative disease; **fibrosierende** ≈ fibrosing syndrome; **fieberhafte** ≈ febrile illness; **funktionelle** ≈ functional disease, functional illness; **genetische** ≈ genetic disease; **hämatologische** ≈ blood disease; **hereditäre** ≈ hereditary disease, hereditary disorder; **iatrogene** ≈ iatrogenic disease; **idiopathische** ≈ idiopathic disease; **kardiovaskuläre** ≈ cardiovascular disease; **manisch-depressive** ≈ manic-depressive psychosis; **meldepflichtige** ≈ notifiable disease; **multifaktoriell bedingte** ≈ multifactorial disorder; **organische** ≈ organic disease; **psychosomatische** ≈ psychosomatic disease, psychosomatic disorder; **übertragbare** ≈ communicable disease; **vorbestehende** ≈ preexisting condition.
Erleichterung *f*: relief, alleviation.
erleiden: suffer.
Erlotinib *n*: erlotinib.
Ermüdung *f*: fatigue.
Ermüdungsbruch *m*: fatigue fracture.
Ermüdungssyndrom *n*: fatigue syndrome.
ernähren: nourish, nurture.
Ernährung *f*: diet, nutrition, alimentation; **ausgeglichene** ≈ balanced diet; **eiweißarme** ≈ low-protein diet; **eiweißreiche** ≈ high-protein diet; **enterale** ≈ enteral nutrition; **falsche** ≈ malnutrition; **glutenfreie** ≈ gluten-free diet; **intravenöse** ≈ intravenous feeding; **kochsalzarme** ≈ sodium-restricted diet; **künstliche** ≈ artificial alimentation; **makrobiotische** ≈ macrobiotic diet; **parenterale** ≈ parenteral nutrition; **purinarme** ≈ low-purine diet.
Ernährungsberatung *f*: dietary counseling.
Ernährungssonde *f*: feeding tube.
Ernährungsstörung *f*: nutrition disorder.
Ernährungszustand *m*: nutritional status.
Erntefieber *n*: harvest fever.
Erntekrätze: harvest mite, Trombicula autumnalis *f*.
Eröffnung *f*: opening, incision.
Eröffnungsperiode *f*: first stage of labor.
Eröffnungswehen: dilating pains.
Erosion *f*: erosion.
erosiv: erosive.
erotisch: erotic.
erregbar: excitable, irritable.
Erregbarkeit *f*: excitability, irritability.
Erreger *m*: infectious agent.
Erregung *f*: excitation, excitement, agitation.
Erregungsablauf *m*: excitatory process.
Erregungsausbreitung, retrograde *f*: ventriculoatrial conduction.
Erregungsleitung *f*: conduction; **retrograde** ≈ retrograde conduction; **saltatorische** ≈ saltatory conduction.
Erregungszustand *m*: excitatory state.
Erröten *n*: flush.
Ersatz *m*: replacement, substitution.
Ersatzmutter *f*: surrogate mother.
Ersatzrhythmus *m*: escape rhythm; **vagaler** ≈ vagal escape.
Erscheinungsform *f*: manifestation.
Erschlaffung *f*: laxness, relaxation.
Erschöpfung *f*: exhaustion; **nervöse** ≈ neurasthenia.
Erschöpfungssyndrom *n*: burnout syndrome.

Erschütterung *f*: concussion, succussion.
ersetzen: replace, substitute.
Erste Hilfe *f*: first aid.
Ersthelfer *m*: first aider.
ersticken: suffocate, choke.
Erstickung *f*: choking, asphyxiation, suffocation.
Erstickungsanfall *m*: choke.
Erstimpfung *f*: initial vaccination.
Erstmanifestation *f*: initial manifestation.
Ertapenem *n*: ertapenem.
Ertrinken *n*: drowning.
Erucasäure *f*: erucic acid.
Eruktation *f*: eructation, belch.
Eruption *f*: eruption.
Erwachsene *m, f*: adult.
Erwachsenendiabetes *m*: adult-onset diabetes mellitus.
erwärmen: heat, warm.
Erweichung *f*: softening, malacia.
erweitert: dilated, enlarged.
Erweiterung *f*: dilatation, enlargement.
erwerben: acquire.
Erwerbsunfähigkeit *f*: disablement.
erworben: acquired.
erwürgen: strangle.
Erysipel *n*: erysipelas.
erysipelartig: erysipeloid.
Erysipeloid *n*: erysipeloid.
Erythem *n*: erythema.
Erythema arthriticum epidemicum *n*: erythema arthriticum epidemicum, streptobacillary fever.
Erythema infectiosum *n*: erythema infectiosum, fifth disease.
Erythema nodosum *n*: erythema nodosum, Bazin's ulcer.
Erythema subitum *n*: exanthem subitum, Zahorsky's disease.
erythematös: erythematous.
Erythemdosis *f*: erythema dose.
Erythroblast *m*: erythroblast.
Erythroblastenanämie *f*: erythroblastic anemia, thalassemia major.
Erythrodermie *f*: erythroderma; **bullöse** ≈ bullous ichthyosiform hyperkeratosis; **ichthyosiforme** ≈ ichthyosiform erythroderma, Sjögren-Larsson syndrome.
Erythromelalgie *f*: erythromelalgia, Weir-Mitchell's disease.
Erythromycin *n*: erythromycin.
Erythromycinethylsuccinat *n*: erythromycin ethylsuccinate.
Erythromycinpropionat *n*: erythromycin propionate.
Erythroplasie Queyrat *f*: erythroplasia of Queyrat.
Erythropoese *f*: erythropoiesis.
Erythropoietin *n*: erythropoietin, EPO.
Erythroprosopalgie *f*: erythroprosopalgia.
Erythrozyanose *f*: erythrocyanosis.
Erythrozyt *m*: erythrocyte, red blood cell; **getüpfelter** ≈ stippled cell; **stechapfelförmiger** ≈ burr erythrocyte, echinocyte.
Erythrozytenaggregation *f*: erythrocyte aggregation.
Erythrozytenschatten *m*: erythrocyte ghost, blood shadow.
Erythrozytenvolumen *n*: erythrocyte volume, mean corpuscular volume, MCV.
Erythrozytenzählung *f*: erythrocyte count, red cell count.
Erythrozytenzahl *f*: erythrocyte count, red blood count.
Erythrozytenzylinder *m*: red blood cell cast.
Erythrozytopenie *f*: erythrocytopenia.
Erythrozytose *f*: erythrocytosis.
Erythrozyturie *f*: erythrocyturia.
Eserin *n*: eserine.
Esketamin *n*: esketamine.
Esmolol *n*: esmolol.
Esomeprazol *n*: esomeprazole.
Esotropie *f*: esotropia, convergent strabismus.
essen: eat.
Essen auf Rädern: meals on wheels.
Essenz *f*: essence.
Esser-Plastik *f*: Esser's graft.
Essgewohnheiten: eating behavior, dietary habits.
Essigsäure *f*: acetic acid, ethanoic acid.
Esslöffel *m*: tablespoon.
Essstörung *f*: eating disorder.

Esssucht *f*: bulimia.
Esterase *f*: esterase.
Estradiol *n*: estradiol.
Estramustin *n*: estramustine.
Estriol *n*: estriol.
Etacrynsäure *f*: etacrynic acid.
Etafedrin *n*: etafedrine.
Etafenon *n*: etafenone.
Etagennaht *f*: layered suture.
Etamiphyllin *n*: etamiphyllin.
Etamivan *n*: etamivan.
Etanercept *n*: etanercept.
Ethambutol *n*: ethambutol.
Ethanol *n*: ethanol, ethyl alcohol.
Ethik *f*: ethics; **medizinische** ≈ medical ethics.
Ethikkommission *f*: ethics committee.
Ethinylestradiol *n*: ethynyl estradiol.
Ethinyltestosteron *n*: ethynyl testosterone.
Ethionamid *n*: ethionamide.
ethmoidal: ethmoidal.
Ethmoiditis *f*: ethmoiditis, ethmoidal sinusitis.
Ethnomedizin *f*: ethnomedicine.
Ethnopsychiatrie *f*: ethnopsychiatry, cross-cultural psychiatry.
Ethosuximid *n*: ethosuximide.
Ethylalkohol *m*: ethylalcohol.
Ethylendiamintetraessigsäure *f*: ethylenediaminetetraacetic acid, EDTA.
Ethylhydrogenfumarat *n*: ethylhydrogenfumarate.
Etidocain *n*: etidocaine.
Etidronat *n*: etidronate.
Etidronsäure *f*: etidronic acid.
Etikett *n*: label.
Etilefrin *n*: etilefrine.
Etiroxat *n*: etiroxate.
Etodroxizin *n*: etodroxizine.
Etofenamat *n*: etofenamate.
Etofibrat *n*: etofibrate.
Etofyllin *n*: etofylline.
Etofyllinclofibrat *n*: etofylline clofibrate.
Etomidat *n*: etomidate.
Etonogestrel *n*: etonogestrel.
Etoposid *n*: etoposide.
Etoricoxib *n*: etoricoxib.
Etozolin *n*: etozolin.
Etretinat *n*: etretinate.
Eugenik *f*: eugenics.
Eugenol *n*: eugenol.
Eulenaugenzelle *f*: owl's eye cell.
eunuchoidal: eunuchoid.
Eunuchoidismus *m*: eunuchoidism.
euphorisch: euphoric.
Euploidie *f*: euploidy, euploid state.
Eupnoe *f*: eupnea.
Eustachio-Röhre *f*: eustachian tube.
Euthanasie *f*: euthanasia.
Evagination *f*: evagination.
Evaporieren *n*: evaporation.
Eventeration *f*: eventration.
Everolimus *n*: everolimus.
Eversion *f*: eversion.
Eviszeration *f*: evisceration.
Evolution *f*: evolution.
evoziert: evoked.
Evulsion *f*: evulsion.
Exaltation *f*: exaltation.
Exanthem *n*: exanthema, rash; **makulopapulöses** ≈ maculopapular rash; **syphilitisches** ≈ syphilitic rash.
Exartikulation *f*: exarticulation, disarticulation.
Exazerbation *f*: exacerbation.
Exemestan *n*: exemestane.
Exenteration *f*: exenteration.
Exfoliation *f*: exfoliation.
Exfoliativzytologie *f*: exfoliative cytology.
Exhibitionismus *m*: exhibitionism.
Exhumierung *f*: exhumation.
Exitus *m*: exitus, death.
Exkavation *f*: excavation.
Exkoriation *f*: excoriation.
Exkrement *n*: excrement.
Exkretion *f*: excretion.
exkretorisch: excretory.
exogen: exogenous, exogenic.
exokrin: exocrine.
Exomphalos *m*: exomphalos.
Exophthalmus *m*: exophthalmos; **endokriner** ≈ endocrine exophthalmos; **maligner** ≈ malignant exophthalmos.
exophytisch: exophytic.
Exostose *f*: exostosis.
Exotoxin *n*: exotoxin.
Exotropie *f*: exotropia, divergent strabismus.

Expansion *f*: expansion.
Expektorans *n*: expectorant, mucolytic agent.
Expektoration *f*: expectoration.
Experiment *n*: experiment.
experimentell: experimental.
Expertise *f*: expertise, expert opinion.
Exploration *f*: exploration.
Explosionsschädigung *f*: blast injury.
Exposition *f*: exposure, challenge; **berufliche** ≈ occupational exposure.
Expositionstest *m*: allergen challenge.
Expression *f*: expression.
Expulsion *f*: expulsion.
Exsikkation *f*: exsiccation, dehydration.
Exspiration *f*: expiration.
Exstirpation *f*: extirpation, removal.
Exstirpationsbiopsie *f*: excisional biopsy.
Exsudat *n*: exudate.
Exsudation *f*: exudation, weeping.
Exsudationszyste *f*: exudation cyst.
Extension *f*: extension, traction.
Extensionsbett *n*: traction bed.
Extensionsbügel *m*: stirrup, traction bow.
Extensionstisch *m*: traction table, extension table.
Extensorenreflex *m*: extensor reflex.
extern: external.
extraartikulär: extraarticular.
extrahieren: extract.
extrakapsulär: extracapsular.
extrakorporal: extracorporeal.
Extrakt *m*: extract; **alkoholischer** ≈ alcoholic extract; **fester** ≈ solid extract; **flüssiger** ≈ liquid extract; **trockener** ≈ dry extract.
Extraktion *f*: extraction, traction.
extrapyramidal: extrapyramidal.
Extrasystole *f*: extrasystole, ectopic beat; **interponierte** ≈ interpolated extrasystole; **supraventrikuläre** ≈ supraventricular extrasystole; **ventrikuläre** ≈ ventricular extrasystole; **vorzeitig einfallende** ≈ premature systole.
extrauterin: extrauterine.
Extrauteringravidität *f*: extrauterine pregnancy, ectopic pregnancy.
Extravasat *n*: extravasate, extravascular fluid.
Extravasationszyste *f*: extravasation cyst, exudation cyst.
extravaskulär: extravascular.
extrazellulär: extracellular.
Extrazellularflüssigkeit *f*: extracellular fluid.
Extrazellularraum *m*: extracellular compartment.
Extremität *f*: extremity, limb; **obere** ≈ upper extremity; **untere** ≈ lower extremity.
Extremitätenableitungen: limb leads.
extrinsisch: extrinsic.
Extroversion *f*: extroversion.
Extubation *f*: extubation.
Exzision *f*: excision.
Exzitabilität *f*: excitability.
Exzitation *f*: excitation.
Exzitationssyndrom *n*: excitation syndrome.
Ezetimib *n*: ezetimibe.

F

F Abk. **1. Farad; 2. Fluor**: 1. farad, F; 2. fluorine, F.
Faber-Anämie *f*: Faber's anemia, achylic anemia.
Fabulieren *n*: fabulation.
Facette *f*: facet.
Facharzt *m*: specialist, consultant.
Fachgebiet *n*: specialty.
Facies *f*: face, facies, plane.
Facies adenoidea *f*: adenoid face.
Facies hippocratica *f*: hippocratic face.
Facies myopathica *f*: myopathic face, hatchet face.
Faden *m*: thread, string, cord.
Fadenpilz *m*: tinea, ringworm.
Fadenwurm *m*: nematode, pinworm, threadworm.
Fähigkeit *f*: capability, skill, ability, competence; **geistige** ≈ mental capacity; **motorische** ≈ motor skill.
fäkal: fecal.
Färbeindex *m*: color index.
Färbekoeffizient *m*: mean corpuscular hemoglobin, MCH.
färben: stain, color, dye.
Färben *n*: staining.
Färbung *f*: stain, staining.
Fäulnis *f*: decay, rot.
Fäulnisbakterium *n*: putrefactive bacterium.
Fäzes *f*: feces, stool.
fahrbar: mobile.
Fahrenheit: Fahrenheit.
Fahrlässigkeit *f*: negligence.
Faktor *m*: factor; **antihämophiler** ≈ hemophilic factor; **antinukleärer** ≈ antinuclear factor, ANF; **Kolonie-stimulierender** ≈ colony stimulating factor, CSF; **mitogener** ≈ mitogenic factor.
Fakultät *f*: faculty.
fakultativ: facultative.
Falciparium-Malaria *f*: falciparium malaria, malignant tertian malaria.
Fall *m*: case.
Fallbeschreibung *f*: case report.
fallen: fall, drop.
Fallfuß *m*: drop foot.
Fallhand *f*: drop hand.
Fallkontrollstudie *f*: case-control study.
Fallregister *n*: case register.
Fallstudie *f*: case study.
falschnegativ: false-negative.
falschpositiv: false-positive.
Falte *f*: fold, crease, wrinkle, plica.
Falx *f*: falx.
Famciclovir *n*: famciclovir.
familiär: familial, familiar.
Familie *f*: family.
Familienanamnese *f*: family history.
Familienmedizin *f*: family medicine.
Familienplanung *f*: family planning.
Familientherapie *f*: family therapy.
Famotidin *n*: famotidine.
Famprofazon *n*: famprofazone.
Fanconi-Abderhalden-Syndrom *n*: Fanconi-Abderhalden syndrome, renal amino acid diabetes mellitus.
Fanconi-Anämie *f*: Fanconi's anemia, congenital aplastic anemia.
Farady-Konstante *f*: Faraday's constant.
Faradisation *f*: faradization.
Farbe *f*: color.
Farbenblindheit *f*: color blindness, achromatognosia; **amnestische** ≈ color name aphasia; **komplette** ≈ achromatopia, achromatic vision; **partielle** ≈ dyschromatopsia; **totale** ≈ achromatopia, achromatic vision.
Farbenfehlsichtigkeit *f*: dyschromatopsia, faulty color discrimination.

Farbensehen *n*: color vision.
Farblösung *f*: dye.
farblos: colorless, achromatic.
Farbsinn *m*: chromatic sensation.
Farbstoff *m*: stain, coloring agent, dye; **basischer** ≈ basic stain; **saurer** ≈ acidic dye.
Farbtafel *f*: color perception table.
Farmerlunge *f*: farmer's lung.
Farnkrauttest *m*: fern test.
Fasciitis *f*: fasciitis, fascitis.
Faser *f*: fiber; **agyrophile** ≈ argyrophilic fiber, argentaffin fiber; **elastische** ≈ elastic fiber; **markhaltige** ≈ medullated fiber, myelinated fiber; **marklose** ≈ unmyelinated fiber, nonmedullated fiber; **präkollagene** ≈ precollagenous fiber; **retikuläre** ≈ reticular fiber.
Fasergewebe *n*: fibrous tissue.
Faserknorpel *m*: fibrous cartilage, fibrocartilage.
Fassthorax *m*: barrel-shaped chest.
Fassung *f*: frame, socket.
fasten: fast.
Fasten *n*: fasting, fast; **proteinmodifiziertes** ≈ protein-modified fasting.
Faszie *f*: fascia.
Faszienverschluss *m*: far-and-near suture.
Fasziitis *f*: fasciitis, fascitis.
Faszikel *m*: fascicle, bundle.
faszikulär: fascicular.
Faszikulation *f*: fasciculation.
fatal: fatal.
faul: foul, decayed, rotten.
Faulbrand *m*: hot gangrene.
Faust *f*: fist.
Faustschlussprobe *f*: handgrip test.
Favismus *m*: favism.
Favus *m*: favus, white-cap.
Favusalopezie *f*: favic alopecia.
fazial: facial.
Fazialiskern *m*: facial center, nucleus facial nerve.
Fazialiskrampf *m*: facial spasm.
Fazialislähmung *f*: facial nerve palsy; **angeborene** ≈ congenital falcial palsy; **beidseitige** ≈ bifacial paralysis; **einseitige** ≈ facial hemiplegia, Bell's palsy; **idiopathische** ≈ idiopathic facial paralysis; **periphere** ≈ peripheral facial paralysis; **zentrale** ≈ central facial paralysis.
Fazialisneuralgie *f*: facial neuralgia.
Fazialisparese *f*: facial nerve palsy; **beidseitige** ≈ facial diplegia; **einseitige** ≈ facial hemiplegia, Bell's palsy.
Fazialiszeichen *n*: facialis phenomenon, Chvostek sign.
Fazio-Londe-Syndrom *n*: Fazio-Londe disease, infantile progressive bulbar palsy.
Febantel *n*: febantel.
febril: febrile, feverish.
Febuprol *n*: febuprol.
Fechterstellung *f*: pugilistic attitude.
Fede-Riga-Geschwür *n*: Riga-Fede disease, frenal ulcer.
Feedback-Steuerung *f*: feedback control.
Feer-Krankheit *f*: Feer's disease, acrodynic erythema, pink disease.
Fehlanpassung *f*: maladjustment, dysadaptation.
Fehlbildung *f*: malformation, malformation sequence, deformity; **kongenitale** ≈ congenital defect.
Fehlbildungssyndrom *n*: malformation syndrome.
Fehldeutung *f*: misinterpretation.
fehldiagnostizieren: misdiagnose.
Fehlen *n*: lack, absence.
fehlend: absent, failing, missing.
Fehlentwicklung *f*: maldevelopment.
Fehler *m*: error; **absoluter** ≈ absolute error; **durchschnittlicher** ≈ mean error, average error; **mittlerer** ≈ standard error, average error; **systematischer** ≈ systematic error; **tendenzieller** ≈ biased error; **zufälliger** ≈ random error.
fehlerhaft: faulty.
Fehlgeburt *f*: spontaneous abortion.
Fehlpaarung *f*: mismatching.
Fehlsichtigkeit *f*: ametropia.
Fehlstellung *f*: malposition.
Feigwarze *f*: genital wart.
Feinmotorik *f*: minute motor activity.
Feinnadelbiopsie *f*: fine needle biopsy.
Feiung, stille *f*: occult immunization.
Felbamat *n*: felbamate.
Feld *n*: field, area.

Feldblock *m*: field block anesthesia, infiltration anesthesia.
Feldfieber *n*: field fever, harvest fever.
Feldstudie *f*: field study.
Felodipin *n*: felodipine.
Felsengebirgsfieber *n*: Rocky Mountain spotted fever.
Feminisierung *f*: feminization; **testikuläre** ≈ testicular feminization, Morris syndrome.
femoral: femoral.
Femoralislähmung *f*: femoral nerve paralysis.
Femoralispuls *m*: femoral pulse.
Femoralisreflex *m*: femoral reflex, Remak symptom.
Femoralkanal *m*: crural canal.
Femur *m*: femur, thigh bone.
Femurfraktur *f*: fracture of femur, femoral fracture.
Femurkopfnekrose *f*: femur head necrosis; **aseptische** ≈ aseptic necrosis of the femoral head, Chandler's disease.
Fenbencillin *n*: fenbencillin.
Fenbendazol *n*: fenbendazole.
Fenbufen *n*: fenbufen.
Fenbutrazat *n*: fenbutrazate.
Fencarbamid *n*: fencarbamide.
Fencheltee *m*: fennel tea.
Fenclofos *n*: fenclofos.
Fendilin *n*: fendiline.
Fenfluramin *n*: fenfluramine.
Fenofibrat *n*: fenofibrate.
Fenoprofen *n*: fenoprofen.
Fenoterol *n*: fenoterol.
Fenoxazolin *n*: fenoxazoline.
Fenpipramid *n*: fenpipramide.
Fenpiveriniumbromid *n*: fenpiverinium bromide.
Fenproporex *n*: fenproporex.
Fenprostalen *n*: fenprostalene.
Fenster *n*: window, fenestra; **aortopulmonales** ≈ aortopulmonary window.
Fenstergips *m*: fenestrated plaster.
Fenstertechnik *f*: window technique.
Fensterungsoperation *f*: windowing, fenestration operation.
Fensterverband *m*: fenestrated bandage, fenestrated compress.
Fentanyl *n*: fentanyl.
Fenthion *n*: fenthion.
Fenticonazol *n*: fenticonazole.
Fentoniumbromid *n*: fentonium bromide.
Fenyramidol *n*: fenyramidol.
Ferment *n*: ferment, enzyme.
Fermentation *f*: fermentation.
Fernmetastase *f*: distant metastasis.
Fernplastik *f*: distant flap.
Fernpunkt *m*: far-point.
Ferrocyanid *n*: ferrocyanide.
Ferse *f*: heel, talon.
Fersenbein *n*: calcaneum, heel bone.
Fertigarzneimittel *n*: medicinal product.
Fertilität *f*: fertility.
Fertirelin *n*: fertirelin.
Ferucarbotran *n*: ferucarbotran.
fest: solid, stable, fast.
Festfrequenzschrittmacher *m*: fixed-rate pacemaker.
Festigkeit *f*: stability.
fetal: fetal.
Fetalperiode *f*: fetal period.
Fetischismus *m*: fetishism.
Fetoprotein *n*: fetoprotein.
fett: adipose, fat, lipidic.
Fett *n*: fat, lipid; **braunes** ≈ brown fat; **gelbes** ≈ yellow fat; **gebundenes** ≈ bound fat.
fettähnlich: lipoid.
fettarm: low-fat.
Fettatrophie *f*: fat atrophy, fatty atrophy.
Fettembolie *f*: fat embolism.
Fettgeschwulst *n*: fat tumor, lipoma.
Fettgewebe *n*: adipose tissue, fatty tissue.
Fettgewebsnekrose *f*: fat necrosis, adiponecrosis.
Fettgewebsresektion *f*: adipectomy, lipectomy.
Fettherz *n*: fatty heart.
fettig: fatty.
Fettkörper *m*: fatty body.
Fettleber *f*: fatty liver; **alkoholische** ≈ alcoholic fatty liver.
fettlöslich: fat-soluble.
Fettnekrose *f*: fat necrosis.
Fettniere *f*: lipoid nephrosis, renal lipoidosis.

Fettsäure *f*: fatty acid; **essentielle** ≈ essential fatty acid; **freie** ≈ free fatty acid; **gesättigte** ≈ saturated fatty acid; **mehrfach ungesättigte** ≈ polyunsaturated fatty acid; **ungesättigte** ≈ unsaturated fatty acid.
Fettsalbe *f*: greasy ointment.
Fettspeicherkrankheit *f*: lipid storage disease, lipidosis.
Fettstoffwechsel *m*: lipid metabolism.
Fettstuhl *m*: steatorrhea.
Fettsucht *f*: obesity.
Fettzelle *f*: lipocyte, fat cell.
Fettzylinder *m*: fatty cast.
Fetus *m*: fetus.
feucht: wet, damp, moist, humid.
Feuchtigkeit *f*: moisture, humidity.
Feuchtigkeitscreme *f*: moisturizing cream.
Fexofenadin *n*: fexofenadine.
Fiberglasbronchoskop *n*: bronchofiberscope, fiberoptic bronchoscope.
Fibrillation *f*: fibrillation.
Fibrin *n*: fibrin.
fibrinfrei: defibrinated.
Fibringerinnsel *n*: fibrin clot.
Fibrinogen *n*: fibrinogen, factor I.
Fibrinogenopenie *f*: fibrinogenopenia, fibrinogen deficiency.
Fibrinolysin *n*: fibrinolysin.
Fibrinolytikum *n*: fibrinolytic agent.
Fibrinzylinder *m*: fibrinous cast.
Fibroadenom *n*: fibroadenoma.
Fibroadenomatose *f*: fibrosing adenomatosis.
Fibroblast *m*: fibroblast.
Fibrocartilago *f*: fibrocartilage, fibrous cartilage.
Fibrodysplasie *f*: fibrodysplasia, Jaffé-Lichtenstein disease; **polyostotische** ≈ polyostotic fibrous dysplasia of bone.
Fibroelastose *f*: fibroelastosis.
Fibroepitheliom *n*: fibroepithelioma.
fibrös: fibrous.
Fibrohistiozytom *n*: malignant fibrous histiocytoma.
Fibrolipom *n*: fibrolipoma.
Fibrom *n*: fibroma, fibrous tumor; **nichtossifizierendes** ≈ nonossifying fibroma; **odontogenes** ≈ odontogenic fibroma; **periunguales** ≈ periungual fibroma; **seniles** ≈ cutaneous tag, soft wart.
Fibroma cysticum *n*: cystic fibroma.
Fibroma durum *n*: fibroma durum, hard fibroma.
Fibroma molle *n*: fibroma molle, soft fibroma.
Fibromatose *f*: fibromatosis.
Fibromyom *n*: fibromyoma, myofibroma.
Fibromyxom *n*: fibromyxoma, myxofibroma.
Fibroosteom *n*: fibro-osteoma.
Fibroplasie *f*: fibroplasia; **retrolentale** ≈ retrolental fibroplasia, Terry syndrome.
Fibrosarkom *n*: fibrosarcoma.
Fibrose *f*: fibrosis; **idiopathische retroperitoneale** ≈ idiopathic retroperitoneal fibrosis, Ormond's disease; **zystische** ≈ cystic fibrosis, CF, mucoviscidosis.
Fibrositis *f*: fibrositis.
Fibroxanthom *n*: fibroxanthoma, fibrous histiocytoma.
fibrozystisch: fibrocystic.
Fibrozyt *m*: fibrocyte.
Fibula *f*: fibula, fibular bone.
Fibularisphänomen *n*: peroneal-nerve phenomenon, Lust's phenomenon.
Fieber *n*: fever, febris; **adynamisches** ≈ adynamic fever; **anhaltendes** ≈ prolonged fever; **biphasisches** ≈ saddleback fever; **brucelloseartiges** ≈ paramalta fever; **hämorrhagisches** ≈ hemorrhagic fever; **hohes** ≈ high temperature; **intermittierendes** ≈ intermittent fever; **künstliches** ≈ artificial fever, induced fever; **leichtes** ≈ slight temperature; **periodisches** ≈ periodic fever; **prätibiales** ≈ pretibial fever, Fort Bragg fever; **rekurrierendes** ≈ cyclic fever; **rheumatisches** ≈ rheumatic fever, inflammatory rheumatism; **Wolhynisches** ≈ Wolhynia fever, trench fever, five-day fever; **zentrales** ≈ neurogenic fever.
Fieberbläschen *n*: fever blister.
Fieberdelir *n*: febrile delirium.

Fieberkopfschmerz *m*: pyrexial headache.
Fieberkrampf *m*: febrile seizure, febrile convulsion.
Fieberkrise *f*: febrile crisis.
Fieberkurve *f*: fever curve, temperature chart.
fiebern: fever.
Fieberphase *f*: febrile phase.
Fieberproteinurie *f*: febrile proteinuria.
Fieberpuls *m*: febrile pulse.
fiebersenkend: antifebrile, antipyretic.
Fieberstadium *n*: febrile phase.
Fieberthermometer *n*: fever thermometer.
Fieber unbekannter Ursache *n*: fever of unknown origin, FUO.
fiebrig: feverish.
FIGLU-Test *m*: FIGLU test, histidine loading test.
Filament *n*: filament.
filamentös: filamentous.
Filarie *f*: filaria.
Filariose *f*: filariasis, Bancroft's disease, filarial elephantiasis.
Filgrastim *n*: filgrastim.
Filialgeneration *f*: filial generation.
filiform: filiform, threadlike.
Filter *m*: filter.
filtern: filter, filtrate.
Filtration *f*: filtration.
Filtrationsrate, glomeruläre *f*: glomerular filtration rate.
Filzlaus *f*: pubic louse, pthirus pubis.
Fimbrienbildung *f*: fimbriation.
final: final, terminal.
Finasterid *n*: finasteride.
Findelkind *n*: foundling.
Finger *m*: finger, digit, dactylus; **abgestorbener** ≈ dead finger; **schnellender** ≈ snapping finger.
Fingerabdruck *m*: fingerprint, dactylogram.
Fingeragnosie *f*: finger agnosia, digital agnosia.
Fingerhut *m*: foxglove, digitalis.
Fingerknöchel *m*: knuckle.
Fingerling *m*: finger cot, fingerstall.
Fingerreflex *m*: digital reflex.
Fingerschiene *f*: finger splint.
Fingerspitze *f*: fingertip.
Fingerstrahl *m*: digital ray.
Firocoxib *n*: firocoxib.
Fischvergiftung *f*: fish poisoning, ichthyotoxism.
Fisher-Syndrom *n*: Fisher syndrome, cranial polyneuritis.
Fissur *f*: fissure.
Fistel *f*: fistula; **äußere** ≈ external fistula; **aortoenterale** ≈ aortoenteric fistula; **aortokavale** ≈ aortocaval fistula; **arteriovenöse** ≈ arteriovenous fistula; **bronchoösophageale** ≈ bronchoesophageal fistula; **bronchopleurale** ≈ bronchopleural fistula; **endolymphatische** ≈ endolymphatic shunt; **enterovesikale** ≈ enterovesical fistula; **gastrokolische** ≈ gastrocolic fistula; **inkomplette** ≈ incomplete fistula, blind fistula; **innere** ≈ internal fistula; **kommunizierende** ≈ complete fistula; **ösophagotracheale** ≈ tracheoesophageal fistula; **vesikorektale** ≈ vesicorectal fistula.
Fixation *f*: fixation, fixing; **intraossäre** ≈ intraosseous fixation.
fixieren: fix, immobilize.
Fixierlösung *f*: fixing solution.
Fixierung *f*: fixation; **binokuläre** ≈ binocular fixation; **interne** ≈ internal fixation, **mechanische** ≈ mechanical restraint.
Fixierverband *m*: fixed dressing, immovable bandage.
flach: flat, even.
Flachrücken *m*: flat back.
Flagellation *f*: flagellation.
Flammenphotometer *n*: flame photometer.
Flaschenernährung *f*: bottle-feeding.
Flaschenherz *n*: flask-shaped heart.
Flaschenkind *n*: bottle-child, weanling.
Flatterflimmern *n*: flutter-fibrillation.
flattern: flutter.
Flattern *n*: flapping, flicker, flutter.
Flattertremor *m*: flapping tremor.
Flatulenz *f*: flatulence.
flaumig: fuzzy, fluffy.
Flecainid *n*: flecainide.

Flechsig-Zone *f*: Flechsig's field, myelinogenetic field.
Flechte *f*: itch, lichen.
Fleck *m*: spot, patch, stain, macule, dot; **blinder** ≈ blind spot; **gelber** ≈ yellow spot; **kalter** ≈ cold spot; **pigmentarmer** ≈ amelanotic macule.
Fleckfieber *n*: spotted fever, typhus fever, famine fever, mite fever; **epidemisches** ≈ epidemic louse-borne typhus; **murines** ≈ murine typhus, flea-borne typhus.
fleckig: patchy.
Flecktyphus *m*: typhus fever, epidemic louse-borne typhus.
Fleisch *n*: flesh, meat, pulp; **wildes** ≈ proud flesh.
fleischig: fleshy, sarcous.
Fleischmole *f*: fleshy mole.
Fleischner-Atelektase *f*: Fleischner line, platelike atelectasis.
Fleroxacin *n*: fleroxacin.
flexibel: flexible.
Flexion *f*: flection, flexion.
Flexor *m*: flexor.
Flexur *f*: flexure, bend.
Flexura duodenojejunalis *f*: duodenojejunal angle.
Fliege *f*: fly, mosquito.
fließen: flow, stream.
Fließgleichgewicht *n*: steady state.
Flimmerbewegung *f*: ciliary action.
Flimmerflattern *n*: flutter-fibrillation.
Flimmern *n*: flicker, fibrillation.
Flimmerskotom *n*: scintillating scotoma, flittering scotoma, teichopsia.
Flimmerwelle *f*: fibrillation wave.
Flimmerzelle *f*: ciliated cell.
flockig: floccular, flocculent.
Flötenschnabelkatheter *m*: whistletip catheter.
Floh *m*: flea.
Flohfleckfieber *n*: flea-borne typhus, murine typhus.
Flohstich *m*: fleabite.
Flomoxef *n*: flomoxef.
Floppy-Infant-Syndrom *n*: floppy infant, infantile hypotonia.
Floppy-Valve-Syndrom *n*: floppy-valve syndrome.
Florfenicol *n*: florfenicol.
Flossenhand *f*: seal-fin deformity.
Floxuridin *n*: floxuridine.
Fluanison *n*: fluanisone.
Flubendazol *n*: flubendazole.
Fluchtreflex *m*: flight reflex, escape reflex, fight-or-flight reflex.
Flucloxaxillin *n*: flucloxacillin.
Fluconazol *n*: fluconazole.
Flucytosin *n*: flucytosine.
Fludarabin *n*: fludarabine.
Fludeoxyglucose *n*: fludeoxyglucose.
Fludrocortison *n*: fludrocortisone.
Fludrocortisonacetat *n*: fludrocortisone acetate.
Fludroxycortid *n*: fludroxycortide.
flügelartig: winglike, pterygoid.
Flügelfell *n*: pterygium.
Flügelschlagen *n*: flapping tremor.
flüssig: fluid, liquid.
Flüssigextrakt *m*: liquid extract, fluid extract.
Flüssigkeit *f*: fluid, liquid.
Flüssigkeitsaufnahme *f*: fluid intake.
Flüssigkeitshaushalt *m*: fluid balance.
Flüssigkeitslunge *f*: fluid lung.
Flüsterprobe *f*: whisper test.
Flüsterschall *m*: whispering resonance.
Flüsterstimme *f*: whispering voice.
Flufenaminsäure *f*: flufenamic acid.
Fluktuation *f*: fluctuation.
fluktuierend: fluctuant, floating.
Flumazenil *n*: flumazenil.
Flumetason *n*: flumetasone.
Flumethrin *n*: flumethrin.
Flunarizin *n*: flunarizine.
Flunisolid *n*: flunisolide.
Flunitrazepam *n*: flunitrazepam.
Flunixin *n*: flunixin.
Fluocinolonacetonid *n*: fluocinolone acetonide.
Fluocinonid *n*: fluocinonide.
Fluocortin-Butyl *n*: fluocortin butyl.
Fluocortolon *n*: fluocortolone.
Fluor *m*: fluor, fluorine, F.
Fluor albus *m*: fluor albus, whites, leukorrhea.
Fluorescein *n*: fluorescein.
Fluoressigsäure *f*: fluoroacetic acid.
Fluoreszenzstrahlung *f*: fluorescent radiation.

Fluoreszenz-Treponema-Antikörper-Absorptionstest *m*: fluorescent treponemal antibody absorption test, FTA-ABS test.
fluoreszierend: fluorescent.
Fluorid *n*: fluoride.
Fluoridprophylaxe *f*: fluoridation, fluoridization.
Fluorometholon *n*: fluorometholone.
Fluoroskopie *f*: fluoroscopy.
Fluorouracil *n*: fluorouracil.
Fluor vaginalis *m*: discharge.
Fluorwasserstoff *m*: hydrogen fluoride.
Fluorwasserstoffsäure *f*: hydrofluoric acid.
Fluoxetin *n*: fluoxetine.
Fluoxymesteron *n*: fluoxymesterone.
Flupentixol *n*: flupentixol.
Fluphenazin *n*: fluphenazine.
Flupirtin *n*: flupirtine.
Flupredniden *n*: fluprednidene.
Fluprednisolon *n*: fluprednisolone.
Flupropion *n*: flupropione.
Flurazepam *n*: flurazepam.
Flurbiprofen *n*: flurbiprofen.
Flush-Phänomen *n*: flush phenomenon.
Fluspirilen *n*: fluspirilene.
Fluss *m*: stream, flow, current.
Flusssäure *f*: fluoric acid.
Flutamid *n*: flutamide.
Fluticason *n*: fluticasone.
Fluvastatin *n*: fluvastatin.
Fluvoxamin *n*: fluvoxamine.
Fölling-Krankheit *f*: Fölling's disease, phenylketonuria.
Foerster-Diplegie *f*: Foerster syndrome, atonic astatic encephalopathy.
Foerster-Lähmung *f*: hypotonic cerebral palsy.
Foerster-Operation *f*: Foerster's operation, posterior rhizotomy.
Foetor *m*: fetor.
Foetor ex ore *m*: halitosis, fetor oris, foul breath.
Fötus *m*: fetus.
Foix-Alajouanine-Syndrom *n*: Foix-Alajouanine syndrome, spinal varicosis.
fokal: focal.
Fokalepilepsie *f*: focal epilepsy.
Fokalinfektion *f*: focal infection.
Fokus *m*: focus.
Fokus-Haut-Abstand *m*: focal-skin distance.
fokussieren: focus.
Folat *n*: folate.
Folgekrankheit *f*: secondary sickness.
Folinsäure *f*: folinic acid, leucovorin.
Follikel *m*: follicle.
Follikelatresie *f*: follicular atresia.
Follikelhormon *n*: follicular hormone.
Follikelhyperplasie *f*: follicular hyperplasia.
Follikelreifung *f*: follicular maturation.
Follikelzyste *f*: follicular cyst.
follikulär: follicular.
Follikularkatarrh *m*: follicular conjunctivitis.
Follitropin *n*: follitropin.
Folsäure *f*: folic acid.
Folsäuremangelanämie *f*: folic acid deficiency anemia.
Fomepizol *n*: fomepizole.
Fominoben *n*: fominoben.
Fomivirsen *n*: fomivirsen.
Fomocain *n*: fomocaine.
Fondaparinuxnatrium *n*: fondaparinux sodium.
Fontanelle *f*: fontanel, fontanelle.
Foramen *n*: foramen, opening.
Forbes-Albright-Syndrom *n*: Forbes-Albright syndrome, Akumada-del Castillo syndrome, galactorrhea-amenorrhea syndrome.
Forceps *m*: forceps, pair of tongs.
forensisch: forensic, medicolegal.
Form *f*: figure, form, shape.
Formaldehyd *m*: formaldehyde.
Formalin *n*: formalin, formaldehyde solution.
Formel *f*: formula.
Formelnbuch *n*: formulary.
Formen *n*: molding, modeling, shaping.
Formestan *n*: formestane.
Formicatio *f*: formication.
Formiminoglutaminsäure *f*: formiminoglutamic acid.
formlos: amorphic, amorphous, unformed.

Formocortal *n*: formocortal.
Formoterol *n*: formoterol.
Formula *f*: formula.
Formwahrnehmung *f*: form perception.
Forschung *f*: research; **klinische** ≈ clinical research.
Forssel-Syndrom *n*: nephrogenic polycythemia.
Fort-Bragg-Fieber *n*: Fort Bragg fever, pretibial fever.
fortgeschritten: advanced.
Fortpflanzung *f*: reproduction, generation; **eingeschlechtliche** ≈ unisexual reproduction, parthenogenesis; **geschlechtliche** ≈ sexual reproduction, gamogenesis; **ungeschlechtliche** ≈ asexual reproduction, agamogony.
Fortpflanzungsperiode *f*: reproductive period.
Fortsatz *m*: process, appendage.
fortschreitend: progressive.
Fortschritt *m*: progress, advance.
Fosamprenavir *n*: fosamprenavir.
Foscarnet *n*: foscarnet.
Fosfestrol *n*: fosfestrol.
Fosfomycin *n*: fosfomycin.
Fosinopril *n*: fosinoprilat.
Fossa *f*: fossa, trench, pit.
foudroyant: foudroyant, fulminant.
Fragebogen *m*: questionary, questionnaire.
fragen: ask, question, demand.
Fragile-X-Syndrom *n*: fragile X syndrome, Martin-Bell syndrome.
Fragilität *f*: fragility.
Fraktion *f*: fraction.
Fraktur *f*: fracture; **bimalleoläre** ≈ Dupuytren's fracture; **direkte** ≈ direct fracture; **dislozierte** ≈ dislocation fracture, fracture-dislocation, displaced fracture; **extrakapsuläre** ≈ extracapsular fracture; **geschlossene** ≈ closed fracture; **indirekte** ≈ indirect fracture; **inkomplette** ≈ incomplete fracture; **intertrochantäre** ≈ intertrochanteric fracture; **intraartikuläre** ≈ intraarticular fracture; **komplizierte** ≈ complicated fracture; **offene** ≈ compound fracture; **okkulte** ≈ occult fracture; **pathologische** ≈ spontaneous fracture, pathologic fracture; **schleichende** ≈ fatigue fracture; **subperiostale** ≈ subperiosteal fracture, intraperiosteal fracture; **subtrochantäre** ≈ subtrochanteric fracture; **suprakondyläre** ≈ supracondylar fracture; **unvollständige** ≈ incomplete fracture; **vollständige** ≈ complete fracture.
Fraktureinrichtung *f*: redressement.
Frakturfehlstellung *f*: malalignment.
Frakturheilung in Fehlstellung: malunion.
Frambösie *f*: yaws, frambesia, Breda's disease.
Framycetin *n*: framycetin.
Frau *f*: female, woman.
Frauenheilkunde *f*: gynecology.
Freeman-Sheldon-Syndrom *n*: Freeman-Sheldon syndrome, whistling face-windmill vane hand syndrome.
frei flottierend: free-floating, unattached.
Freilegung *f*: exposure, disclosing.
Freiname *m*: nonproprietary name, generic name; **internationaler** ≈ international nonproprietary name, INN.
freisetzen: liberate, release.
Freisetzung *f*: liberation, release.
Freitod *m*: suicide.
freiverkäuflich: over the counter, OTC.
Freiwilliger: volunteer.
Fremdanamnese *f*: indirect anamnesis.
Fremdenfurcht *f*: xenophobia.
Fremdgen *n*: heterologous gene.
Fremdkörper *m*: foreign body.
Fremdkörperentfernung *f*: foreign-body removal.
Fremdserum *n*: foreign serum.
Fremitus *m*: fremitus.
Frenulum *n*: frenulum, small bridle.
frequent: frequent.
Frequenz *f*: frequency.
Frequenzstimulation *f*: pacing.
Fresszelle *f*: phagocyte, scavenger cell.
Freud-Theorie *f*: Freudian theory.
Friedreich-Ataxie *f*: Friedreich's ataxia, spinocerebellar ataxia.

Frigidität *f*: frigidity, sexual anesthesia.
Friktion *f*: friction.
frisch: fresh.
Frischblut *n*: fresh blood.
Frischzellentherapie *f*: cellular therapeutics, Niehaus therapy.
Fröhlich-Obrinski-Syndrom *n*: Eagle-Barrett syndrome, prune-belly syndrome.
Fröhlich-Syndrom *n*: Fröhlich syndrome, adiposogenital dystrophy.
Froment-Zeichen *n*: Froment's sign, newspaper sign.
Front *f*: front.
Frontalebene *f*: frontal plane, coronal plane.
Frontalhirnsyndrom *n*: frontal lobe syndrome.
Frontallappen *m*: frontal lobe.
Frontallappenataxie *f*: frontal ataxia, Bruns ataxia.
Froschgeschwulst *f*: ranula, ranine tumor.
Frostbeule *f*: frostbite, chilblain.
Frottage *f*: frottage.
Frovatriptan *n*: frovatriptan.
Fruchtbarkeit *f*: fertility, fecundity.
Fruchtblase *f*: amniotic bag.
Fruchttod *m*: fetal death; **intrauteriner** ≈ intrauterine death.
Fruchtwasser *n*: amniotic fluid.
Fruchtwasserdiagnostik *f*: amniotic fluid tests.
Fruchtwasserspiegelung *f*: amnioscopy.
früh: early.
Frühabort *m*: early abortion.
Frühbehandlung *f*: early treatment.
Frühchen *n*: preterm infant, immature infant.
Frühdiagnose *f*: early diagnosis.
Frühform *f*: early manifestation.
Frühgeborenes *n*: preterm infant, immature infant.
Frühgeburt *f*: premature birth, premature delivery.
Frühjahrsheuschnupfen *m*: vernal catarrh, spring catarrh.
Frühjahrskonjunktivitis *f*: vernal conjunctivitis, spring conjunctivitis.
Frühkarzinom *n*: early cancer.
Frühmobilisation *f*: early mobilization.
Frühoperation *f*: early operation.
Frühphase *f*: early phase.
Frühreife *f*: precocity, prematurity.
Frühschwangerschaft *f*: early pregnancy.
Frühsommerenzephalitis *f*: spring-summer encephalitis.
Frühstadium *n*: early stage.
Fruktose *f*: fructose, fruit sugar.
Fruktoseintoleranz *f*: fructose intolerance.
Fruktosurie *f*: fructosuria.
Fuchs-Heterochromie *f*: Fuchs syndrome, heterochromic cyclitis.
fühlen: feel.
Führungslinie des Beckens *f*: pelvic axis.
Führungstrokar *m*: piloting trocar.
Füllung *f*: filling, stuffing, packing.
Füllungsdefekt *m*: filling defect.
Füllungszeit *f*: filling time.
Fünf-Jahres Überlebensrate *f*: five-year survival.
Fünfling *m*: quintuple.
Fünftagefieber *n*: five-day fever, Wolhynia fever, trench fever.
Fünfte Krankheit *f*: fifth disease.
Fürsorge *f*: welfare, welfare care.
Füttern *n*: feeding.
fulminant: fulminant, foudroyant.
Fulvestrant *n*: fulvestrant.
Fumarat *n*: fumarate.
Fumarsäure *f*: fumaric acid.
Fundamentalfunktion *f*: fundamental function.
Fundoskopie *f*: fundoscopy.
Fundus *m*: fundus, eyeground; **gesprenkelter** ≈ tigroid fundus.
Fungizid *n*: fungicide, mycocide.
Funikulitis *f*: funiculitis, spermatitis.
Funktion *f*: function; **lebenswichtige** ≈ vital function.
funktionell: functional.
funktionieren: function.
Funktionseinschränkung *f*: function impairment.
Funktionsfähigkeit *f*: functioning, functional ability.
Funktionsminderung *f*: decreased function.

Funktionsprobe *f*: function test.
Funktionspsychose *f*: functional psychosis.
Funktionsstörung *f*: functional disorder, dysfunction; **sexuelle** ≈ sexual dysfunction.
Furacin *n*: furacin.
Furaltadon *n*: furaltadone.
Furazolidon *n*: furazolidone.
Furche *f*: furrow, groove, fissure, sulcus.
Furcht *f*: fear.
Furchung *f*: cleavage, crenation.
Furosemid *n*: furosemide.
Furunkel *m*: furuncle, boil.
Furunkulose *f*: furunculosis.
Fusidinsäure *f*: fusidic acid.
fusimotorisch: fusimotor.
Fusion *f*: fusion; **binaurale** ≈ binaural fusion; **binokuläre** ≈ binocular fusion; **zentrische** ≈ centric fusion.
Fusionsinhibitor *m*: fusion inhibitor.
Fusionskonvergenz *f*: fusional convergence.
Fusionsniere *f*: fused kidney, renal fusion.
Fuß *m*: foot, pes.
Fußdeformität *f*: foot deformity, talipes.
Fußklonus *m*: foot clonus, ankle clonus.
Fußknöchel *m*: ankle.
Fußkrampf *m*: spasm of the foot, pedal spasm.
Fußlage *f*: foot presentation.
Fußpapel *f*: pedal papule; **piezogene** ≈ piezogenic pedal papule.
Fußpflege *f*: podiatry, podology, chiropody.
Fußpilz *m*: tinea pedis.
Fußsohle *f*: sole.
Fußsohlenreflex *m*: plantar reflex.

G

g Abk. **Gravitation** *f*: gravity, gravitational constant, G.
G Abk. **Guanin** *n*: guanine, Gua.
Gabapentin *n*: gabapentin.
gabeln: bifurcate.
Gabelung *f*: furcation.
gähnen: yawn.
Gähnen *n*: yawning.
Gänsehaut *f*: goose pimples, gooseflesh.
Gärung *f*: fermentation.
Galaktagogum *n*: galactagogue, lactagogue.
Galaktorrhö *f*: galactorrhea.
Galaktorrhö-Amenorrhö-Syndrom *n*: galactorrhea-amenorrhea syndrome, Akumada-del Castillo syndrome.
Galaktosämie *f*: galactosemia.
Galaktose *f*: galactose.
Galaktosurie *f*: galactosuria.
Galaktozele *f*: galactocele, milk cyst.
Galakturonsäure *f*: galacturonic acid.
Galantamin *n*: galantamine.
Galenikum *n*: galenical.
galenisch: galenic.
Gallamin *n*: gallamine.
Galle *f*: bile, gall.
Gallenblase *f*: gallbladder, cholecystis; **flottierende** ≈ floating gallbladder, mobile gallbladder; **septierte** ≈ septate gallbladder; **wandernde** ≈ floating gallbladder, mobile gallbladder.
Gallengang *m*: bile duct, choledochus.
Gallengangabszess *m*: bile duct abscess, cholangitic abscess.
Gallengangatresie *f*: biliary atresia, bile duct atresia.
Gallengangsverschluss *m*: biliary obstruction.
Gallenkolik *f*: biliary colic, gall colic.
Gallensäure *f*: bile acid.
Gallensäuresalz *n*: bile salt.
Gallenstein *m*: gallstone, cholelith.
Gallensteinlithotripsie *f*: gallbladder lithotripsy.
Gallentrakt *m*: biliary system.
Gallereflux *m*: bile reflux.
gallertartig: gelatinous, jellylike.
Gallertkarzinom *n*: mucinous carcinoma, mucous carcinoma.
Gallertkrebs *m*: gelatiniform carcinoma, colloid carcinoma.
gallig: biliary, bilious.
Galli-Mainini-Test *m*: Galli-Mainini's test, frog test.
Galliumszintigraphie *f*: gallium scanning.
Gallopamil *n*: gallopamil.
Gallussäure *f*: gallic acid.
Galopprhythmus *m*: gallop rhythm.
Galvanismus *m*: galvanism, galvanotherapy.
Galvanokaustik *f*: galvanocautery.
Gamet *m*: gamete, sex cell.
Gammaaminobuttersäure *f*: gamma-aminobutyric acid, GABA.
Gammaglobulin *n*: gamma globulin.
Gammopathie *f*: gammopathy, gammaglobulinopathy.
Gamstorp-Krankheit *f*: Gamstorp's disease, familial hyperkalemic periodic paralysis.
Ganciclovir *n*: ganciclovir.
Gandy-Gamna-Milz *f*: Gandy-Gamna disease, siderotic splenomegaly.
Gang *m*: gait, walk, duct, meatus; **ataktischer** ≈ ataxic gait, staggering gait; **hemiplegischer** ≈ hemiplegic gait; **myopathischer** ≈ myopathic gait, waddling gait; **nachziehender** ≈ drag to gait; **paretischer** ≈ paraparetic gait; **schwankender** ≈ reel-

ing gait, staggering gait; **spastischer** ≈ spastic gait; **stampfender** ≈ stamping gait; **tabischer** ≈ tabetic gait; **zerebellärer** ≈ cerebellar gait.
Gangektasie *f*: ductectasia.
Ganglienblock *m*: ganglionic block.
Ganglienblocker *m*: ganglionic blocking agent.
Gangliogliom *n*: ganglionic glioma.
Ganglion *n*: ganglion, neuroganglion.
Ganglionektomie *f*: ganglionectomy.
Ganglioneurom *n*: ganglioneuroma.
Ganglionitis *f*: ganglionitis.
Gangliosidose *f*: gangliosidosis; **generalisierte** ≈ G_{M1} gangliosidosis, general gangliosidosis; **juvenile** ≈ juvenile gangliosidosis, Tay-Sachs disease.
Gangrän *f*: gangrene; **diabetische** ≈ diabetic gangrene; **embolische** ≈ embolic gangrene; **feuchte** ≈ moist gangrene, wet gangrene; **ischämische** ≈ ischemic gangrene; **thrombotische** ≈ thrombotic gangrene; **toxische** ≈ chemical gangrene; **trockene** ≈ dry gangrene.
gangränös: gangrenous.
Gangstörung *f*: gait disorder; **myopathische** ≈ myopathic gait, duck gait.
Ganirelix *n*: ganirelix.
Ganser-Syndrom *n*: Ganser syndrome, nonsense syndrome.
Ganzantwort *f*: whole answer.
ganzheitlich: holistic.
Ganzkörperbestrahlung *f*: whole-body irradiation.
Ganzkörperhyperthermie *f*: whole-body hyperthermia.
Gargoylismus *m*: gargoylism, Hurler's syndrome.
Gasaustausch *m*: gas exchange.
Gasaustauschquotient *m*: respiratory exchange ratio.
gasbildend: gas-forming, aerogenic.
Gasbildner *m*: aerogenic.
Gasbrandbazillus *m*: gas gangrene bacillus.
gasförmig: gaseous, volatile.
Gasgangrän *f*: gas gangrene, gaseous gangrene.
Gasödem *n*: gaseous edema.
Gasser-Ganglion *n*: Gasser's ganglion.
Gasser-Syndrom *n*: Gasser syndrome, hemolytic-uremic syndrome.
Gastrektomie *f*: gastrectomy; **antekolische** ≈ antecolic gastrectomy; **subtotale** ≈ subtotal gastrectomy.
Gastrin *n*: gastrin.
gastrisch: gastric.
Gastritis *f*: gastritis; **akute** ≈ acute gastritis; **atrophische** ≈ atrophic gastritis, Fenwick's disease; **chronisch-atrophische** ≈ chronic atrophic gastritis; **erosive** ≈ erosive gastritis; **granulomatöse** ≈ granulomatous gastritis; **lymphozytäre** ≈ lymphocytic gastritis; **phlegmonöse** ≈ phlegmonous gastritis.
gastritisch: gastritic.
Gastroduodenoenterostomie *f*: gastroduodenoenterostomy.
gastroenteral: gastroenteric.
Gastroenteritis *f*: gastroenteritis; **akute infektiöse** ≈ acute infectious gastroenteritis; **epidemische** ≈ infectious gastroenteritis.
Gastroenterologie *f*: gastroenterology.
Gastroenteropathie *f*: gastroenteropathy; **eiweißverlierende** ≈ protein-losing gastroenteropathy.
Gastroenterostomie *f*: gastroenterostomy.
gastrointestinal: gastrointestinal.
Gastrointestinaltrakt *m*: gastrointestinal tract.
Gastrojejunostomie *f*: gastrojejunostomy.
gastrokolisch: gastrocolic.
Gastrolyse *f*: gastrolysis.
gastroösophageal: gastroesophageal.
Gastropexie *f*: gastropexy.
Gastroptose *f*: gastroptosis.
Gastroskopie *f*: gastroscopy, stomach endoscopy.
Gastrostomie *f*: gastrostomy.
Gastrulation *f*: gastrulation.
Gasvolumenbestimmung *f*: gasometry.
Gate-Control-Theorie *f*: gate-control theory.
Gatifloxacin *n*: gatifloxacin.
Gattung *f*: class, strain.
Gaucher-Krankheit *f*: Gaucher's dis-

ease, glucocerebrosidase deficiency.
Gaumen *m*: palate.
Gaumenhaken *m*: palate hook, palate retractor.
Gaumenmandel *f*: palatine tonsil.
Gaumenplastik *f*: palatoplasty.
Gaumensegelinsuffizienz *f*: velopharyngeal insufficiency.
Gaumensegellähmung *f*: palatoplegia.
Gaumenspalte *f*: cleft palate, palatoschisis.
Gaze *f*: gauze.
gebärfähig: childbearing, fertile.
Gebärmutter *f*: womb, uterus.
Gebärmutterhals *m*: cervix, neck of the womb.
Gebärmutterhöhle *f*: uterine cavity.
Gebärmutterverlagerung *f*: uterine displacement.
Gebärmuttervorfall *m*: uterine prolapse.
Gebärstuhl *m*: birthing chair.
Gebirgszeckenfieber *n*: mountain tick fever.
Gebiss *n*: denture, dentition; **künstliches** ≈ dental plate; **permanentes** ≈ permanent dentition, secondary dentition.
Gebissformel *f*: dental formula.
gebläht: distended.
gebogen: bent, curved.
geboren: born.
Geburt *f*: birth, delivery; **induzierte** ≈ induced delivery; **komplizierte** ≈ complicated labor; **prolongierte** ≈ prolonged labor; **programmierte** ≈ induced delivery; **sanfte** ≈ gentle delivery.
Geburtenkontrolle *f*: birth control.
Geburtenplanung *f*: birth planning.
Geburtenrate *f*: natality rate.
Geburtenregelung *f*: birth control.
Geburtenstatistik *f*: natality statistics.
Geburtenziffer *f*: birth-rate, natality.
Geburtsdatum *n*: date of birth.
Geburtsgewicht *n*: birth weight.
Geburtshelfer *m*: obstetrician.
Geburtshilfe *f*: obstetrics, OB, midwifery.
Geburtshindernis *n*: obstructed labor.
Geburtsjahr *n*: year of birth.
Geburtskanal *m*: birth canal.
Geburtskomplikation *f*: obstetric complication.
Geburtslähmung *f*: birth paralysis.
Geburtslöffel *m*: obstetrical lever.
Geburtstermin *m*: delivery date; **errechneter** ≈ due date.
Geburtsverletzung *f*: birth injury, birth trauma.
Geburtszange *f*: delivery forceps, obstetrical forceps.
Gedächtnis *n*: memory.
Gedächtnislücke *f*: memory gap.
Gedächtnisstörung *f*: memory disorder, memory impairment.
Gedächtnisverlust *m*: loss of memory.
Gedankenhören *n*: thought audition.
Gedankenlesen *n*: thought reading, telepathy.
gefährlich: dangerous, hazardous.
Gefängniskrankenhaus *n*: prison hospital.
Gefäß *n*: vessel; **afferentes** ≈ afferent vessel; **efferentes** ≈ efferent vessel.
Gefäßband *n*: vascular band.
Gefäßbett *n*: vascular bed.
Gefäßchirurgie *f*: vascular surgery.
Gefäßentzündung *f*: angiitis, vasculitis.
Gefäßfüllung *f*: vascular filling.
Gefäßgeflecht *n*: vascular plexus.
Gefäßklemme *f*: vascular clamp.
Gefäßkrankheit *f*: angiopathy, vasculopathy.
Gefäßläsion *f*: vascular lesion.
Gefäßligatur *f*: blood vessel ligation, vasoligature.
Gefäßlumen *n*: lumen.
Gefäßprothese *f*: vascular prosthesis.
Gefäßprothesenimplantat *n*: prosthetic vascular graft.
Gefäßresektion *f*: vascular resection, vasoresection.
Gefäßruptur *f*: angiorrhexis.
Gefäßsystem *n*: vascular system.
Gefäßtransplantation *f*: vascular transplantation.
Gefäßverödung *f*: vascular obliteration.

Gefäßverschluss *m*: vascular occlusion.
Gefäßwand *f*: vessel wall.
Gefäßwiderstand *m*: vascular resistance.
Geflecht *n*: plexus, reticulum.
gefleckt: macular, spotted.
Gefrierätztechnik *f*: freeze etching technique.
Gefühl *n*: feeling, emotion, sensation.
gefühllos: insensible, numb.
Gefühllosigkeit *f*: insensibility, anesthesia, numbness.
gegabelt: furcate, bifurcate.
Gegenanzeige *f*: contraindication.
Gegengift *n*: antitoxin, antidote.
Gegenreizmassage *f*: counterirritation.
Gegenwirkung *f*: counteraction.
gehen: walk, step.
Gehen *n*: walking.
Gehgips *m*: walking cast.
Gehirn *n*: brain, cerebrum, encephalon.
Gehirnerschütterung *f*: brain concussion.
Gehörgang *m*: acoustic meatus; **äußerer** ≈ external acoustic canal; **innerer** ≈ internal acoustic canal.
Gehörgangfurunkel *m*: furuncular otitis.
Gehörknöchelchen *n*: auditory ossicle.
Gehstock *m*: cane, walking stick.
Gehstütze *f*: walker.
Geißeltier *n*: flagellate.
Geist *m*: spirit, mind.
Geisterheilung *f*: spiritual healing.
geisteskrank: lunatic, mad, insane.
Geisteskrankheit *f*: mental illness.
geistig behindert: mentally handicapped.
Gekröse *n*: mesentery, mesenterium.
Gel *n*: gel.
Gelächter *n*: laughter.
gelartig: gelatinous, jellylike.
Gelatinenährboden *m*: gelatin agar.
Gelbfieber *n*: yellow fever.
Gelbkörper *m*: yellow body.
Gelbsehen *n*: yellow vision, xanthopia.
Gelbsucht *f*: jaundice, icterus.
Geldiffusionstest *m*: gel diffusion test.
Geldrollenbildung *f*: rouleau formation, sludge phenomenon, nummulation.
Gelenk *n*: joint, articulation.
Gelenkentzündung *f*: arthritis.
Gelenkerkrankung *f*: arthropathy.
Gelenkeröffnung *f*: arthrotomy, arthrostomy.
Gelenkfacette *f*: articular facet.
Gelenkflüssigkeit *f*: synovial fluid.
Gelenkfortsatz *m*: articular process.
Gelenkkapsel *f*: joint capsule, articular capsule.
Gelenkknorpel *m*: articular cartilage.
Gelenkkörper *m*: articular calculus.
Gelenkkopf *m*: articular head.
Gelenkmaus *f*: joint mouse.
Gelenkpfanne *f*: socket, acetabulum.
Gelenkplastik *f*: arthroplasty.
Gelenkresektion *f*: arthrectomy.
Gelenkrheumatismus *m*: synovial rheumatism.
Gelenkschmerz *m*: arthralgia, joint pain.
Gelenksensibilität *f*: articular sensibility.
Gelenksperre *f*: articular block.
Gelenkverbindung *f*: articulation.
Gelenkversteifung *f*: ankylosis.
Gélineau-Syndrom *n*: Gélineau syndrome, narcolepsy.
Gemcitabin *n*: gemcitabine.
Gemeindepsychiatrie *f*: community psychiatry.
Gemeprost *n*: gemeprost.
Gemfibrozil *n*: gemfibrozil.
Gemisch *n*: mixture, mash.
Gen *n*: gene; **alleles** ≈ allelic gene; **autosomales** ≈ autosomal gene; **dominantes** ≈ dominant gene; **hemizygotes** ≈ hemizygous gene; **holandrisches** ≈ holandric gene, Y-linked gene; **rezessives** ≈ recessive gene; **X-chromosomal gebundenes** ≈ X-linked gene; **Y-chromosomal gebundenes** ≈ Y-linked gene.
Genaktivierung *f*: gene activation.
Gendiagnostik *f*: genetic diagnosis.
Gendrift *f*: genetic drift.
Geneinbau *m*: gene insertion.

Generalisierung *f*: generalization, spread.
Generation *f*: generation.
Generikum *n*: generic.
generisch: generic.
Genese *f*: genesis.
genesen: recover.
Genesung *f*: recovery, convalescence.
Genetik *f*: genetics.
genetisch: genetic.
Genick *n*: neck, nape.
Genikulatumneuralgie *f*: geniculate neuralgia.
Genikulatumotalgie *f*: geniculate otalgia.
genital: genital.
Genitaltrakt *m*: genital tract.
Genitaltuberkulose *f*: genital tuberculosis.
Genitalulkus *n*: venereal sore.
Genitalverstümmelung *f*: genital mutilation.
Genkartierung *f*: gene mapping.
Genlokus *m*: gene locus.
Genom *n*: genome.
Genotyp *m*: genotype.
Genprodukt *n*: gene product.
Gentamicin *n*: gentamicin.
Gentechnologie *f*: genetic engineering.
Gentherapie *f*: gene therapy.
Gentianaviolett *n*: gentian violet.
Gentisinsäure *f*: gentisic acid.
Genus *n*: genus, gender, sex.
Genu valgum *n*: genu valgum, knock-knee.
Genu varum *n*: genu varum, bowleg.
Geomedizin *f*: geomedicine.
Gepefrin *n*: gepefrine.
Geradlage *f*: longitudinal presentation.
Gerät *n*: apparatus, appliance, equipment; **medizintechnisches** ≈ medical device.
Geräusch *n*: murmur, sound, noise; **amphorisches** ≈ cavernous resonance; **atriosystolisches** ≈ atriosystolic murmur; **blasendes** ≈ souffle, puff; **diastolisches** ≈ diastolic murmur; **dumpfes** ≈ dull sound; **exspiratorisches** ≈ expiratory murmur; **extrakardiales** ≈ extracardiac murmur; **fauchendes** ≈ blowing sound; **fortgeleitetes** ≈ transmitted murmur; **holodiastolisches** ≈ holodiastolic murmur; **holosystolisches** ≈ holosystolic murmur; **mesodiastolisches** ≈ mid-diastolic murmur; **musikalisches** ≈ musical murmur; **spätsystolisches** ≈ late systolic murmur; **systolisches** ≈ systolic murmur; **tympanitisches** ≈ tympanitic resonance; **vesikuläres** ≈ vesicular resonance.
Geräusch des gesprungenen Topfes *n*: cracked-pot sound, cracked-pot resonance, Macewen sign.
Gerbsäure *f*: tannic acid.
Geriatrie *f*: geriatrics, geriatric medicine.
Gerichtsmedizin *f*: forensic medicine, legal medicine.
gerichtsmedizinisch: medicolegal.
Gerichtspsychiatrie *f*: forensic psychiatry.
geringgradig: low-grade, mild.
Gerinnung *f*: coagulation, clotting; **disseminierte intravasale** ≈ disseminated intravascular coagulation, DIC.
Gerinnungsfaktor *m*: coagulation factor, clotting factor.
Gerinnungsfaktorvorstufe *f*: procoagulant.
gerinnungshemmend: anticoagulative.
Gerinnungskaskade *f*: coagulation cascade.
Gerinnungsstörung *f*: coagulation disorder, coagulopathy.
Gerinnungszeit *f*: clotting time, coagulation time.
Germinoblastom *n*: germinoblastoma.
Germizid *n*: germicide.
Gerontologie *f*: gerontology, geriatrics.
Gerontopsychiatrie *f*: geropsychiatry.
Gerstenkorn *n*: hordeolum, stye.
Geruch *m*: smell, odor.
Geruchsaura *f*: olfactory aura.
Geruchshalluzination *f*: olfactive hallucination.

Geruchsschwelle *f*: olfactory threshold.
Geruchssinn *m*: olfaction.
Gerüst *n*: frame, scaffold.
Gesäß *n*: buttocks, clunes.
gesättigt: saturated, satiated.
Gesamtbilirubin *n*: total bilirubin.
Gesamtdosis *f*: integral dose, volume dose.
Gesamtfilterung *f*: total filtration.
Gesamtmenge *f*: total volume.
Gesamtumsatz *m*: total metabolism.
Gesamtzufuhr, tägliche *f*: total daily intake.
geschichtet: layered, laminated.
Geschicklichkeit *f*: skill, dexterity.
Geschlecht *n*: sex, gender.
Geschlechtschromatin *n*: sex chromatin.
Geschlechtschromosom *n*: sex chromosome.
Geschlechtsdifferenzierung *f*: sexual differentiation.
Geschlechtshormon *n*: sex hormone.
Geschlechtsidentität *f*: gender identity.
Geschlechtskrankheit *f*: venereal disease, sexually transmitted disease, STD.
Geschlechtsorgane: genital organs.
geschlechtsspezifisch: gender-specific, sex-specific.
Geschlechtstrieb *m*: sexual drive.
Geschlechtsumwandlung, operative *f*: transsexual surgery.
Geschlechtsverhältnis *n*: sex ratio, male/female ratio.
Geschlechtsverkehr *m*: sexual intercourse.
Geschlechtsverteilung *f*: sex ratio.
Geschlechtszyklus *m*: sexual cycle.
Geschmackshaar *n*: gustatory hair.
Geschmacksknospe *f*: taste bulb, gustatory bud.
Geschmacksrezeptor *m*: taste receptor, gustatory receptor.
Geschmackssinn *m*: gustatory sensation.
Geschmackswahrnehmung *f*: taste sensation.
Geschmackszentrum *n*: gustatory center, taste center.
Geschrei *n*: screaming.
Geschwätzigkeit *f*: garrulity.
Geschwindigkeit *f*: velocity, speed.
Geschwister *f*: siblings.
geschwollen: swollen, tumid.
Geschwür *n*: ulcer, sore.
geschwürig: ulcerous.
Geschwulst *f*: swelling, neoplasm.
Gesetz *n*: law, rule; **psychophysisches** ≈ psychophysical law.
Gesicht *n*: face.
Gesichtsfeld *n*: visual field.
Gesichtsfelddefekt *m*: visual-field defect, scotoma.
Gesichtslage *f*: face presentation.
Gesichtsmuskel *m*: facial muscle.
Gesichtsneuralgie *f*: facial neuralgia.
Gesichtsröte *f*: flush.
Gesichtsschmerz *m*: facial pain, face ache.
Gesichtsspalte *f*: facial cleft, schistoprosopia.
Gesichtsverletzung *f*: facial injury.
gesplittert: comminuted.
gesprenkelt: mottled, tesselated.
Gestagen *n*: gestagen.
Gestagentest *m*: gestagen test.
Gestaltpsychologie *f*: gestalt psychology.
Gestation *f*: gestation.
Gestationsalter *n*: gestational age.
Gestationshochdruck *m*: gestational hypertension.
Gestose *f*: gestosis.
gestreift: striated, striate, striped.
gesund: healthy, sane, fit.
Gesundbeten *n*: faith healing.
Gesundheit *f*: health, sanity, wholesomeness.
Gesundheitsaufklärung *f*: health information.
Gesundheitsbehörden: health authorities.
Gesundheitserziehung *f*: health education.
Gesundheitsförderung *f*: health promotion.
Gesundheitsgefährdung *f*: danger to health, health endangerment.
Gesundheitspolitik *f*: health policy.
Gesundheitsrisiko *n*: health risk, health hazard.

gesundheitsschädlich: unhealthy, unwholesome.
Gesundheitssystem *n*: health system, health care system.
Gesundheitswesen *n*: public health.
Gesundheitszustand *m*: health condition, health status.
getrübt: clouded.
getüpfelt: punctate, stippled.
Gewalt *f*: violence; **körperliche** ≈ physical violence; **sexuelle** ≈ sexual violence.
Gewalteinwirkung *f*: violence.
Gewebe *n*: tissue, web, textus.
Gewebeatmung *f*: tissue respiration, internal respiration.
Gewebebank *f*: tissue bank.
Gewebelappen *m*: surgical flap.
Gewebeprotein *n*: tissue protein.
Gewebeschädigung *f*: tissue damage.
Gewebetypisierung *f*: tissue typing, tissue crossmatching.
Gewebsblutung *f*: parenchymatous hemorrhage.
Gewebsimmunität *f*: local immunity.
Gewicht *n*: weight.
Gewichtskontrolle *f*: weight control.
Gewichtsverlust *m*: weight loss.
Gewichtszunahme *f*: weight gain.
Gewöhnung *f*: habituation, acquirement of tolerance.
Gewohnheit *f*: habit, practice.
Gewölbe *n*: vault, fornix.
gewölbt: domed, arched, fornicate.
Gewohnheit *f*: habit, habitude.
gewohnheitsmäßig: habitual.
Giannuzzi-Halbmonde: demilunes of Giannuzzi.
Giardiasis *f*: giardiasis.
Gicht *f*: gout, gouty arthritis, uratic arthritis; **tophische** ≈ tophaceous gout.
Gichtanfall *m*: gout attack.
Gichtknoten *m*: gouty node, tophus.
Gichtniere *f*: gout kidney, gouty nephropathy.
Giemen *n*: wheezing.
Gift *n*: poison, toxin.
Gigantismus *m*: gigantism.
Gigli-Säge *f*: wire saw.
Gilbert-Meulengracht-Syndrom *n*: Gilbert's disease, constitutional jaundice, benign familial icterus.
Gilchrist-Krankheit *f*: Gilchrist's mycosis, North American blastomycosis.
Gingivahyperplasie *f*: gingival hyperplasia.
gingival: gingival.
Gingivasaum *m*: gingival line.
Gingivitis *f*: gingivitis; **nekrotisierende ulzerierende** ≈ necrotizing ulcerative gingivitis, NUG, ulceromembranous gingivitis.
Ginglymus *m*: ginglymus, hinge joint.
Gips *m*: plaster of Paris, plaster cast.
Gipslonguette *f*: plaster body cast.
Gipsverband *m*: plaster.
Gitoformat *n*: gitoformate.
Gitter *n*: grid, lattice.
Gitterfaser *f*: reticular fiber.
Glabella *f*: glabella.
glänzend: lucid, lucent.
gläsern: vitreous.
Glafenin *n*: glafenine.
Glandula *f*: gland.
glandulär: glandular.
glasartig: hyaline.
Glasauge *n*: glass eye.
Glasfaseroptik *f*: glass fibre optics.
Glaskörper *m*: vitreous body.
Glaskörperhämorrhagie *f*: vitreous hemorrhage.
Glaskörperretraktion *f*: massive vitreous retraction.
Glaskörpertraktion *f*: vitreous traction.
Glaskörpertrübungen: floaters.
Glatiramer *n*: glatiramer.
Glatze *f*: bald spot, bald head.
glatzköpfig: bald-headed.
Glaubersalz *n*: Glauber salt.
Glaukom *n*: glaucoma, green cataract.
Glaukomanfall *m*: acute congestive glaucoma.
Glaukomkatarakt *f*: glaucomatous cataract.
Glaukomoperation *f*: glaucoma operation.
gleichartig: homogenous, uniform.
gleichbleibend: steady, stationary, constant, continuous.
gleichförmig: uniform, homeomorphous.
gleichgeschlechtlich: homosexual, isosexual.

G

Gleichgewicht *n*: balance, equilibrium; **kalorisches** ≈ energy balance; **metabolisches** ≈ metabolic balance.
Gleichgewichtssinn *m*: equilibrium sense, vestibular sense.
Gleichgewichtsstörung *f*: equilibratory disorder, imbalance.
Gleitbruch *m*: sliding hernia.
gleiten: glide, slide.
Gleiten *n*: slide, gliding.
Gleitfähigkeit *f*: lubrication.
Gleitgelenk *n*: gliding articulation.
Gleitmittel *n*: lubricant.
glenoidal: glenoid.
Glia *f*: glia, neuroglia.
Glibenclamid *n*: glibenclamide.
Glibornurid *n*: glibornuride.
Glicazid *n*: glicazide.
Gliedmaße *f*: member, limb.
Glimepirid *n*: glimepiride.
Glinid *n*: glinide.
Glioblastom *n*: glioblastoma.
Gliom *n*: glioma; **gemischtes** ≈ mixed glioma; **heterotopes** ≈ heterotopic glioma.
Glioneuroblastom *n*: glioneuroblastoma.
Gliosarkom *n*: gliosarcoma.
Glipizid *n*: glipizide.
Gliquidon *n*: gliquidone.
Glisoxepid *n*: glisoxepide.
Glisson-Schlinge *f*: Glisson sling.
Globalamnesie *f*: global amnesia.
Globalaphasie *f*: global aphasia.
Globoidzellen-Leukodystrophie *f*: acute diffuse familial infantile cerebral sclerosis, Krabbe's disease.
Globulin *n*: globulin.
Globus *m*: globe, globus.
Globusgefühl *n*: globus sensation.
glomerulär: glomerular.
Glomerulitis *f*: glomerulitis.
Glomerulonephritis *f*: glomerulonephritis, glomerular nephritis; **abszedierende fokale** ≈ suppurative nephritis; **extrakapilläre** ≈ extracapillary glomerulonephritis; **fokale** ≈ focal glomerulosclerosis; **hämorrhagische** ≈ hemorrhagic glomerulonephritis; **membranoproliferative** ≈ membranoproliferative glomerulonephritis; **mesangiale** ≈ mesangial nephropathy, Berger's disease.
Glomerulosklerose *f*: glomerulosclerosis; **diabetische** ≈ diabetic glomerulosclerosis, Kimmelstiel-Wilson syndrome; **fokale** ≈ focal sclerosing glomerulonephritis; **kongenitale** ≈ congenital chronic glomerulonephritis.
Glomerulumfibrose *f*: glomerular fibrosis.
Glomerulumzyste *f*: glomerular cyst.
Glomerulus *m*: glomerulus, glomerule.
Glomusorgan *n*: glomus body.
Glossodynie *f*: glossodynia.
glossopharyngeal: glossopharyngeal.
Glossopharyngeusneuralgie *f*: glossopharyngeal neuralgia, Legal's disease.
Glossoplegie *f*: glossoplegia.
Glossoptose *f*: glossoptosis.
Glossotrichie *f*: glossotrichia, hairy tongue.
Glottiskarzinom *n*: glottic carcinoma.
Glottisödem *n*: glottis edema.
Glucametacin *n*: glucametacin.
Glucuronsäure *f*: glucuronic acid.
Glukagon *n*: glucagon.
Glukagonom *n*: glucagonoma.
Glukogenese *f*: glucogenesis.
Glukokortikoid *n*: glucocorticoid.
Glukoneogenese *f*: gluconeogenesis.
Glukonsäure *f*: gluconic acid.
Glukosamin *n*: glucosamine.
Glukose *f*: glucose.
Glukoseintoleranz *f*: glucose intolerance.
Glukosetoleranztest *m*: glucose tolerance test, GTT.
Glukosurie *f*: glycosuria, glucosuria.
Glukuronsäure *f*: glucuronic acid.
Glutamin *n*: glutamine.
Glutaminsäure *f*: glutamic acid.
Glutarsäure *f*: glutaric acid.
Glutathion *n*: glutathione.
gluteal: gluteal.
Glutealreflex *m*: gluteal reflex.
Gluten *n*: gluten.
Glutenenteropathie *f*: gluten enteropathy.
glutenfrei: gluten-free.
Glycerin *n*: glycerin.

Glycerinsäure *f*: glyceric acid.
Glycerintinktur *f*: glycerinated tincture.
Glycerol *n*: glycerol.
Glyceroltrinitrat *n*: glyceroltrinitrat.
Glycin *n*: glycine, glycocoll, aminoacetic acid.
Glycopyrroniumbromid *n*: glycopyrronium bromide.
Glykämie *f*: glycemia.
Glykocholsäure *f*: glycocholic acid.
Glykogen *n*: glycogen.
Glykogenese *f*: glycogenesis.
Glykogenolyse *f*: glycogenolysis.
Glykogenose *f*: glycogenosis, glycogen storage disease.
Glykogenspeicherkrankheit *f*: glycogen storage disease, glycogenosis.
Glykolsäure *f*: glycolic acid, hydroxyacetic acid.
Glykosurie *f*: glycosuria.
Glymidin *n*: glymidine.
Glyoxylsäure *f*: glyoxylic acid.
Goethe-Knochen *m*: Goethe's bone, os incisivum.
Gold *n*: gold, Au; **radioaktives** ≈ radioactive gold, radiogold.
Goldenhar-Syndrom *n*: Goldenhar syndrome, oculoauriculovertebral syndrome.
Goldstandard *m*: gold standard.
Goldstein-Reichmann-Syndrom *n*: Goldstein-Reichmann syndrome, acquired cerebellar syndrome.
Goldthioglukose *f*: gold thioglucose.
Golgi-Sehnenorgan *n*: Golgi tendon organ, tendon spindle.
Gonade *f*: gonad.
Gonadenagenesie *f*: gonadal agenesis.
Gonadenaplasie *f*: gonadal aplasia.
Gonadendosis *f*: gonadal dose.
Gonadengeschlecht *n*: gonadal sex.
Gonadorelin *n*: gonadorelin.
gonadotrop: gonadotropic.
Gonadotropin *n*: gonadotropin.
Gonadotropin-Releasing-Hormon *n*: gonadotropin-releasing hormone, GnRH.
Gonadotropintest *m*: gonadotropin test, GnRH stimulation test.
Gonoblennorrhö *f*: gonoblennorrhea, gonococcal conjunctivitis.
Gonokokke *f*: gonococcus.
Gonokokkenkonjunktivitis *f*: gonococcal conjunctivitis, gonoblennorrhea.
Gonokokkensalpingitis *f*: gonorrheal salpingitis.
Gonorrhö *f*: gonorrhea.
Gonosom *n*: gonosome.
Goodpasture-Syndrom *n*: Goodpasture syndrome, pulmonary-renal syndrome.
Gorlin-Syndrom *n*: Gorlin syndrome, basal-cell nevus syndrome.
Goserelin *n*: gosereline.
Graaf-Follikel *m*: Graaf's follicle, tertiary follicle.
Gradeinteilung *f*: grading.
Gradenigo-Syndrom *n*: Gradenigo syndrome, temporal pyramid apex syndrome.
Gradient *m*: gradient.
Gradientenelektrophorese *f*: gradient electrophoresis.
Gradientenzentrifugation *f*: density gradient centrifugation.
Grading *n*: grading.
Graefe-Moebius-Syndrom *n*: nuclear ophthalmoplegia, nuclear paralysis.
Graefe-Syndrom *n*: progressive ophthalmoplegia.
Gram-Färbung *f*: Gram staining.
Grand-mal-Epilepsie *f*: grand mal, major epilepsy.
Granisetron *n*: granisetron.
granulär: granular, granulose.
Granulation *f*: granulation.
Granulationsgewebe *n*: granulation tissue, granulation.
Granulom *n*: granuloma; **eosinophiles** ≈ eosinophilic granuloma; **lipophages** ≈ lipogranuloma; **rheumatisches** ≈ Aschoff's body; **venerisches** ≈ venereal granuloma.
Granuloma inguinale *n*: venereal granuloma.
granulomatös: granulomatous.
Granulomatose *f*: granulomatosis.
Granulosazelltumor *m*: granulosa cell tumor.
Granulozyt *f*: granulocyte.
Granulum *n*: granule; **amphophiles** ≈ amphophilic granule; **azurophiles** ≈

azurophil granule; **keratohyalines** ≈ keratohyaline granule; **spezifisches** ≈ specific granule; **toxisches** ≈ toxic granule.
Grausyndrom *n*: gray syndrome.
Graves-Krankheit *f*: Graves disease, exopthalmic goiter.
gravid: gravid.
Gravidität *f*: gravidity, pregnancy.
Gregg-Syndrom *n*: rubella embryopathy, congenital rubella syndrome.
Greifen *n*: grasping.
Greifreflex *m*: gripping reflex, grasp reflex.
Grenze *f*: limit, border, boundary.
Grenzflächennävus *m*: junction nevus.
Grenzlinieninfarkt *m*: watershed infarction.
Grenzstrang *m*: truncus sympathicus, sympathetic chain.
Grepafloxacin *n*: grepafloxacin.
Grey-Syndrom *n*: grey syndrome, gray syndrome.
Griff *m*: grip, handle.
Grippe *f*: flu, influenza, grip; **asiatische** ≈ Asian influenza.
Grippeenzephalitis *f*: influenzal encephalitis.
Grippeschutzimpfung *f*: influenza vaccination.
Griseofulvin *n*: griseofulvin.
Grobmotorik *f*: gross motor activity.
Grocco-Zeichen *n*: Grocco sign.
Groenouw-Syndrom *n*: Groenouw syndrome, granular corneal dystrophy.
Größe *f*: size, dimension.
Größenwahn *m*: megalomania.
Größenzunahme *f*: growth.
Großhirn *n*: cerebrum.
Großhirnhemisphäre *f*: cerebral hemisphere.
Großhirnrinde *f*: cerebral cortex.
Großzehe *f*: great toe, hallux.
Grube *f*: fossa, pit, fovea, lacune.
Grübchen *n*: dimple, lacuna.
Grübchenbildung *f*: pitting.
Grübchennagel *m*: pitted nail.
Grünblindheit *f*: deuteranopia.
Grünholzfraktur *f*: greenstick fracture, willow fracture.
Grundbedarf *m*: basal requirement.
Grundbedürfnis *n*: basic need.
Grundimmunisierung *f*: basic immunization.
Grundkrankheit *f*: underlying disease.
Grundoperation *f*: unit operation.
Grundumsatz *m*: basal metabolic rate.
Grundversorgung *f*: primary care, basic care.
Gruppenpflege *f*: team care, team nursing.
Gruppenpsychotherapie *f*: group psychotherapy.
Grypose *f*: gryposis.
Gryposis penis: gryposis penis, chordee.
Guanabenz *n*: guanabenz.
Guanaclin *n*: guanacline.
Guanethidin *n*: guanethidine.
Guanfacin *n*: guanfacine.
Guanidin *n*: guanidine.
Guanosin *n*: guanosine.
Guanoxan *n*: guanoxan.
Guanylsäure *f*: guanylic acid, guanosine monophosphate.
Gürtelanästhesie *f*: girdle anesthesia.
gürtelförmig: zonular, cingulate.
Guillain-Barré-Syndrom *n*: Barré syndrome, Guillain syndrome, ascending neuritis.
Guineawurm-Infektion *f*: guinea worm infection.
Gulonsäure *f*: gulonic acid.
Gumma *n*: gumma, gummy tumor; **syphilitisches** ≈ syphilitic gumma.
Gummihandschuh *m*: rubber glove.
Gummistrumpf *m*: elastic stocking.
Gurgel *f*: throat, gullet, pharynx.
gurgeln: gurgle.
gustatorisch: gustatory.
Gutachten *n*: expert report, expertise.
gutartig: benign, mild.
Gynäkologie *f*: gynecology.
Gynäkomastie *f*: gynecomastia.
Gynatresie *f*: gynatresia.
Gyrasehemmer *m*: gyrase inhibitor.

H

H Abk. **1. Histamin** *n*; **2. Hyoscin** *n*; **3. Wasserstoff** *m*: 1. histamine; 2. hyoscine; 3. hydrogen, H.
Haab-Reflex *m*: Haab's reflex, corticopupillary reflex.
Haar *n*: hair, pilus.
Haarausfall *m*: alopecia, baldness.
Haarball *m*: hairball, bezoar.
Haarentfernung *f*: hair removal, epilation.
Haarerkrankung *f*: disease of the hair, trichopathy.
Haarfollikel *m*: hair follicle.
haarig: hairy, pilary.
Haarkegel *m*: hair cone, pilar cone.
Haarleukoplakie *f*: hairy leukoplakia; **orale** ≈ oral hairy leukoplakia.
Haarzelle *f*: hairy cell.
Haarzellenleukämie *f*: hairy-cell leukemia.
Haarzunge *f*: hairy tongue.
habituell: habitual.
Häm *n*: heme.
Hämadsorption *f*: hemadsorption.
Hämagglutination *f*: hemagglutination.
Hämagglutinin *n*: hemagglutinin.
Hämangiom *n*: hemangioma; **blastomatöses** ≈ raspberry mark; **kapilläres** ≈ capillary hemangioma; **kavernöses** ≈ cavernous hemangioma; **rankenförmiges** ≈ cirsoid hemangioma, racemose hemangioma; **sklerosierendes** ≈ sclerosing hemangioma; **venöses** ≈ venous hemangioma.
Hämangioperizytom *n*: hemangiopericytoma.
Hämarthrose *f*: hemarthrosis.
Hämaskos *m*: hemorrhagic ascites, bloody ascites.
Hämatemesis *f*: hematemesis, vomiting of blood.
Hämatin *n*: hematin.
hämatogen: hematogenic.
Hämatokolpos *m*: hematocolpos.
Hämatokrit *m*: hematocrit, HCT.
Hämatologie *f*: hematology.
Hämatom *n*: hematoma; **epidurales** ≈ epidural hematoma; **intrazerebrales** ≈ intracerebral hematoma; **subdurales** ≈ subdural hematoma; **subkutanes** ≈ subcutaneous hematoma; **subunguales** ≈ subungual hematoma.
Hämatometra *f*: hematometra.
Hämatopoese *f*: hematopoiesis; **extramedulläre** ≈ extramedullary hematopoiesis.
Hämatoporphyrin *n*: hematoporphyrin.
Hämatosalpinx *f*: hematosalpinx.
Hämatospermie *f*: hematospermia.
Hämatothorax *m*: hemothorax.
Hämatotoxin *n*: hematotoxin.
Hämatozele *f*: hematocele.
Hämaturie *f*: hematuria; **falsche** ≈ false hematuria; **renale** ≈ renal hematuria; **urethrale** ≈ urethral hematuria.
Hämiglobin *n*: methemoglobin.
Hämodialyse *f*: hemodialysis.
Hämofiltration *f*: hemofiltration.
Hämoglobin *n*: hemoglobin, Hb; **fetales** ≈ fetal hemoglobin; **glykosyliertes** ≈ glycosylated hemoglobin; **oxygeniertes** ≈ oxidized hemoglobin, oxyhemoglobin; **reduziertes** ≈ reduced hemoglobin, deoxyhemoglobin.
Hämoglobingehalt, mittlerer absoluter *m*: mean corpuscular hemoglobin, MCH.
Hämoglobinopathie *f*: hemoglobinopathy.

Hämoglobinurie *f*: hemoglobinuria; **intermittierende** ≈ intermittent hemoglobinuria, Dressler's disease; **paroxysmale nächtliche** ≈ paroxysmal nocturnal hemoglobinuria, PNH, Marchiafava-Micheli syndrome.
Hämokonzentration *f*: hemoconcentration.
Hämolyse *f*: hemolysis.
Hämolysin *n*: hemolysin.
hämolytisch: hemolytic.
Hämoperikard *n*: hemopericardium.
hämophil: hemophil.
Hämophilie *f*: hemophilia; **vaskuläre** ≈ vascular hemophilia, von Willebrand's disease.
Hämophilie A: hemophilia A, classical hemophilia.
Hämophilie B: hemophilia B, Christmas disease, factor IX deficiency.
Hämophilie C: hemophilia C, factor XI deficiency.
Hämoptyse *f*: hemoptysis; **parasitäre** ≈ parasitic hemoptysis; **vikariierende** ≈ vicarious hemoptysis.
Hämorrhagie *f*: hemorrhage; **punktförmige** ≈ punctate hemorrhage; **splitterförmige** ≈ splinter hemorrhage.
hämorrhagisch: hemorrhagic.
hämorrhoidal: hemorrhoidal.
Hämorrhoidalknoten *m*: hemorrhoidal node, hemorrhoidal nodule.
Hämorrhoiden *f*: hemorrhoids; **äußere** ≈ external hemorrhoids; **innere** ≈ internal hemorrhoids; **intermediäre** ≈ mixed hemorrhoids; **thrombosierte** ≈ thrombosed hemorrhoids.
Hämorrhoidektomie *f*: hemorrhoidectomy.
Hämostase *f*: hemostasis.
Hämostatikum *n*: hemostatic, hemostyptic.
hämostatisch: hemostatic.
Hämostyptikum *n*: hemostyptic, hemostatic.
Hämothorax *m*: hematothorax.
Hämozyt *m*: hemocyte.
Hämozytometer *n*: hemocytometer.
Händedesinfektion *f*: hand disinfection.
Händewaschen *n*: handwashing.
Hängegips *m*: hanging cast.
Häufigkeit *f*: frequency.
Häutchen *n*: membrane, pellicle.
Haftfähigkeit *f*: adhesion, tenacity.
Haftpsychose *f*: prison psychosis.
Haftung *f*: liability.
Hailey-Hailey-Krankheit *f*: Hailey-Hailey disease, benign familial pemphigus.
Haken *m*: hook, clasp; **stumpfer** ≈ blunt hook.
hakenförmig: hooklike, hamular, uncinate.
Hakenwurm *m*: hookworm, necator.
Hakenwurmbefall *m*: hookworm disease, ancylostomiasis, necatoriasis.
Halbbrille *f*: half-glass spectacles.
Halbmond *m*: demilune, half-moon, demilune body.
halbmondförmig: semilunar, crescent.
Halbmondzelle *f*: demilune cell, crescent cell.
Halbseitenataxie *f*: cerebellar hemiplegia.
Halbseitenlähmung *f*: hemiplegia, hemiparalysis.
Halbseitenlage *f*: semiprone position.
Halbseitenskotom *n*: hemianopic scotoma.
Halbwertszeit *f*: half-life, half-time.
Halcinonid *n*: halcinonide.
Hallermann-Streiff-François-Syndrom *n*: Hallermann-Streiff syndrome, François syndrome, mandibulo-oculofacial syndrome.
Hallervorden-Spatz-Krankheit *f*: Hallervorden-Spatz syndrome, pigmentary degeneration of the globus pallidus.
Hallux *m*: hallux, great toe.
Halluzination *f*: hallucination; **akustische** ≈ auditory hallucination; **epileptische** ≈ epileptic hallucination, hallucinatory aura; **haptische** ≈ tactile hallucination; **hirnorganisch bedingte** ≈ organic hallucinosis; **hypnagoge** ≈ hypnagogic hallucination; **hypnopompe** ≈ hypnopompic hallucination; **psychomotorische** ≈ psychomotor hallucination.

Halluzinogen *n*: hallucinogen.
Halo *m*: halo, rainbow syndrome.
Halofantrin *n*: halofantrine.
Halofuginon *n*: halofuginone.
Halogen *n*: halogen.
Halo glaucomatosus *m*: glaucomatous halo, glaucomatous ring.
Halometason *n*: halometasone.
Haloperidol *n*: haloperidol.
Halo senilis *m*: senile halo.
Halothan *n*: halothane.
Haloxon *n*: haloxon.
Hals *m*: neck, cervix.
Halsband der Venus *n*: venereal collar.
Halsfistel *f*: cervical fissure, cervical fistula.
Halslymphknoten *m*: cervical lymph node.
Hals-Nasen-Ohren-Heilkunde *f*: otorhinolaryngology.
Halsregion *f*: cervical region.
Halsted-Radikaloperation *f*: Halsted radical mastectomy.
Halswirbelsäule *f*: cervical spine.
Halswirbelsäulensyndrom, posttraumatisches *n*: post-traumatic cervical syndrome.
Halszyste *f*: cervical cyst.
Haltbarkeitsdauer *f*: shelf life.
Haltetonus *m*: postural tonus, orthotonus.
Haltung *f*: pose, posture.
Haltungsreflex *m*: attitudinal reflex, statotonic reflex.
Haltungsschaden *m*: positional failure.
Hamman-Rich-Syndrom *n*: Hamman-Rich syndrome, diffuse interstitial pulmonary fibrosis.
Hammer *m*: hammer, malleus.
Hammerfinger *m*: mallet finger, hammer finger.
hammerförmig: hamate, malleiform.
Hammerzehe *f*: hammer toe, mallet toe.
Hammond-Krankheit *f*: Hammond syndrome, double athetosis.
Hand *f*: hand, manus.
Handbeatmungsbeutel *m*: resuscitator bag.
Handfurche *f*: palmar crease.
Hand-Fuß-Syndrom *n*: hand-foot syndrome, atriodigital dysplasia.
Handgelenk *n*: wrist joint.
Handgriff *m*: maneuver, handle, grip.
Handschiene *f*: hand splint.
Hand-Schüller-Christian-Krankheit *f*: Hand-Schüller-Christian syndrome, chronic idiopathic xanthomatosis.
Handschuh *m*: glove; **chirurgischer** ≈ surgical glove.
Handschuhverband *m*: gauntlet bandage.
Handstück *n*: handpiece.
Hand-Vorderarm-Zeichen *n*: Léri sign, forearm sign.
Handwurzel *f*: wrist, carpus.
Hantavirus *n*: hantavirus.
haploid: haploid.
Hapten *n*: hapten, partial antigen.
haptisch: haptic.
Haptoglobin *n*: haptoglobin.
Harada-Syndrom *n*: Harada's disease, uveomeningoencephalitic syndrome.
harmlos: harmless.
Harn *m*: urine.
Harnabflussbehinderung *f*: urinary obstruction.
Harnausscheidung *f*: excretion of urine.
Harnblase *f*: urinary bladder.
Harnblasenentzündung *f*: cystitis.
Harndrang *m*: urgency.
Harngrieß *m*: gravel.
Harninkontinenz *f*: urinary incontinence.
Harnkonkrement *n*: urinary calculus.
harnleitend: uriniferous.
Harnleiter *m*: ureter; **doppelter** ≈ double ureter; **fehlmündender** ≈ aberrant ureter.
Harnretention *f*: urinary retention.
Harnröhre *f*: urethra.
Harnröhrenausfluss *m*: urethral discharge.
Harnröhrenobstruktion *f*: urethral obstruction.
Harnröhrenstenose *f*: urethrostenosis.
Harnröhrenstriktur *f*: urethral stricture.

Harnsäure *f*: uric acid.
Harnsediment *n*: urinary sediment.
Harnsperre *f*: obstructive anuria.
Harnstein *m*: urinary calculus, urolith.
Harnstickstoff *m*: urinary nitrogen.
Harnstoff *m*: urea.
Harnstoff-Clearance *f*: urea clearance.
Harnstoffzyklus *m*: urea cycle, Henseleit cycle.
Harnstottern *n*: urinary stuttering.
Harntrakt *m*: urinary tract.
Harnverhaltung *f*: anuria, urinary retention.
Harnwegsinfekt *m*: urinary tract infection.
Harnzylinder *m*: urinary cast, renal cast.
Hartspann, muskulärer *m*: hardening in a muscle.
Haschisch *n*: hashish, cannabis.
Hasenfieber *n*: rabbit fever, tularemia.
Hasenscharte *f*: harelip, stomoschisis.
Hashimoto-Thyreoiditis *f*: Hashimoto's disease, chronic lymphadenoid thyroiditis.
Hassall-Körperchen *n*: Hassall's corpuscle, thymic corpuscle.
Hauptachse *f*: main axis.
Hauptbronchus *m*: main bronchus.
Hauptbündel *n*: main bundle.
Hauptgen *n*: major gene.
Haupthistokompatibilitätskomplex *m*: major histocompatibility complex.
Hauptsymptom *n*: main symptom, cardinal sign.
Hauptwirt *m*: primary host.
Hausarzt *m*: family doctor, family physician.
Hausgeburt *f*: home childbirth.
Haushaltsunfall *m*: domestic accident.
Hauskrankenpflege *f*: home care.
Hausstauballergie *f*: house dust allergy.
Haustra coli: haustra of colon, sacculations of colon.
Haustrierung *f*: haustration.
Haut *f*: skin, dermis, cutis.
Hautamyloidose *f*: cutaneous amyloidosis.
Hautanhangsgebilde *n*: skin appendage.
Hautatrophie *f*: skin atrophy.
Hautausschlag *m*: rash, exanthem, eruption.
Hautbiopsie *f*: skin biopsy.
Hautblase *f*: blister.
Hautblutung *f*: cutaneous hemorrhage; **petechiale** ≈ petechial rash.
Hautcandidiasis *f*: cutaneous candidiasis.
Hautdosis *f*: skin dose.
Hautemphysem *n*: cutaneous emphysema.
Hautfaltenmessung *f*: skinfold measurement.
Hautjucken *n*: pruritus, itching.
Hautkrankheit *f*: skin disease, dermopathy.
Hautkrebs *m*: skin cancer, cutaneous carcinoma.
Hautläsion *f*: cutaneous lesion, skin lesion.
Hautlappen *m*: skin flap, patch.
Hautleishmaniase *f*: cutaneous leishmaniasis.
Hautleisten: dermoglyphics, dermal ridges.
Hautmilzbrand *m*: cutaneous anthrax, malignant carbuncle.
Hautmuskellappen *m*: myocutaneous flap.
Hautnaht *f*: dermal suture.
Hautpilzerkrankung *f*: dermatomycosis, mycosis of skin.
Hautprobe *f*: skin test, dermal test.
Hautreaktion *f*: cutaneous reaction, skin response.
Hautreflex *m*: cutaneous reflex, skin reflex; **galvanischer** ≈ galvanic skin reflex; **oberflächlicher** ≈ superficial reflex.
Hautschrunde *f*: crack, chap.
Hautschuppe *f*: squama, dandruff.
Hautsinn *m*: skin sense, cutaneous sensibility.
Hautspaltungslinien: cleavage lines, Langer's lines.
Hautsymptom *n*: cutaneous sign.
Hauttest *m*: skin test.

Hauttuberkulose *f*: cutaneous tuberculosis, tuberculosis of skin.
Hauttumor *m*: tumor of the skin.
Hautveränderung *f*: skin alteration.
Haverhill-Fieber *n*: Haverhill fever, streptobacillary fever.
Havers-Kanal *m*: haversian canal.
Hebamme *f*: midwife, nurse-midwife.
heben: lift.
Hebephrenie *f*: hebephrenia.
Heber *m*: lever, elevator.
Heberden-Knötchen: Heberden's nodes.
Hecht-Pneumonie *f*: Hecht's pneumonia, giant-cell pneumonia.
Heerfordt-Syndrom *n*: Heerfordt's disease, uveoparotid fever.
Hefe *f*: yeast.
Hefepilz *m*: saccharomycete, yeast-like fungus.
Hefeplasmid *n*: yeast plasmid.
heftig: severe, intense.
Heftmaschine *f*: sewer.
Heftpflaster *n*: adhesive tape, adhesive plaster.
Heftpflasterverband *m*: adhesive bandage.
Heftstich *m*: tack.
Hegar-Stift *m*: Hegar's dilator.
heilbar: curable.
Heilberuf *m*: health profession.
heilen: heal, cure.
Heiler *m*: healer.
Heilkunde *f*: medical science.
Heilmittel *n*: remedy, curative, therapeutic agent.
heilsam: healing, curative.
Heilung *f*: cure, healing; **vollständige** ≈ complete recovery.
Heimbewohner *m*: home inmate.
Heimdialyse *f*: home dialysis.
Heimtest *m*: home test.
Heinz-Innenkörper *n*: Heinz body.
heiser: hoarse, raucous.
Heiserkeit *f*: hoarseness.
Heißhunger *m*: hyperorexia, abnormally increased appetite.
Heißluft *f*: hot air.
helfen: help, assist.
Helferzelle *f*: helper cell, inducer cell.
Helikase *f*: helicase.
Heliotherapie *f*: heliotherapy, solar treatment.
Helix *f*: helix.
hell: bright, light.
Helladaptation *f*: light adaptation, photopic adaptation.
Heller-Syndrom *n*: Heller's disease, infantile dementia.
Helle-Zellen-Tumor *m*: clear cell tumor.
Helminthe *f*: helminth.
Helminthendysenterie *f*: helminthic dysentery.
Helminthiasis *f*: helminthiasis.
Helvellasäure *f*: helvellic acid.
Hemeralopie *f*: hemeralopia, day blindness.
Hemiagnosie *f*: hemiagnosia.
Hemianästhesie *f*: hemianesthesia; **alternierende** ≈ alternate hemianesthesia; **bulbäre** ≈ bulbar hemianesthesia; **gekreuzte** ≈ crossed hemianesthesia.
Hemianopsie *f*: hemianopia, hemianopsia; **bilaterale** ≈ bilateral hemianopia; **binasale** ≈ binasal hemianopia; **bitemporale** ≈ bitemporal hemianopia; **gekreuzte** ≈ crossed hemianopia; **gleichsinnige** ≈ congrous hemianopia; **heteronyme** ≈ heteronymous hemianopia; **homonyme** ≈ homonymous hemianopia; **nasale** ≈ nasal hemianopia; **obere** ≈ altitudinal hemianopia; **temporale** ≈ temporal hemianopia.
Hemiataxie *f*: unilateral ataxia, cerebellar hemiplegia.
Hemiathetose *f*: unilateral athetosis.
Hemiatrophia facialis progressiva *f*: facial hemiatrophy, Romberg's progressive facial hemiatrophy.
Hemiatrophie *f*: hemiatrophy.
Hemiballismus *m*: hemiballismus.
Hemichorea *f*: hemichorea, one-sided chorea.
Hemikolektomie *f*: hemicolectomy; **linksseitige** ≈ left hemicolectomy; **rechtsseitige** ≈ right hemicolectomy.
Hemikranie *f*: hemicrania.
Hemiparese *f*: hemiparesis.
Hemiparkinsonismus *m*: hemiparkinsonism.

Hemipelvektomie *f*: hemipelvectomy, Jaboulay's amputation.
Hemiplegia alternans *f*: alternate hemiplegia, crossed hemiplegia.
Hemiplegia alternans inferior *f*: inferior alternate paralysis, Millard-Gubler syndrome.
Hemiplegia alternans oculomotoria *f*: alternating oculomotor hemiplegia, Weber's paralysis.
Hemiplegie *f*: hemiplegia, hemiparalysis; **akute infantile** ≈ hemiconvulsive-hemiplegic syndrome; **alternierende** ≈ alternate hemiplegia, crossed hemiplegia; **homolaterale** ≈ collateral hemiplegia; **schlaffe** ≈ flaccid hemiplegia; **spastische** ≈ spastic hemiplegia; **spinale** ≈ spinal hemiplegia.
Hemisphäre *f*: hemisphere; **dominante** ≈ dominant hemisphere; **inferiore** ≈ nondominant hemisphere.
hemizygot: hemizygous.
Hemmkonzentration *f*: inhibitory concentration; **minimale** ≈ minimal inhibiting concentration.
Hemmmechanismus *m*: inhibiting mechanism.
Hemmung *f*: inhibition, blockage; **kompetitive** ≈ competitive inhibition; **nichtkompetitive** ≈ noncompetitive inhibition; **postsynaptische** ≈ postsynaptic inhibition; **präsynaptische** ≈ presynaptic inhibition; **reziproke** ≈ reciprocal inhibition.
Hemmwirkung *f*: inhibitory effect.
Hemmzone *f*: zone of inhibition.
Henle-Schleife *f*: loop of Henle, nephronic loop.
Heparin *n*: heparin.
Hepatektomie *f*: hepatectomy.
Hepatikocholangiojejunostomie *f*: hepaticocholangiojejunostomy.
Hepatisation *f*: hepatization; **gelbe** ≈ yellow hepatization; **graue** ≈ gray hepatization; **rote** ≈ red hepatization.
hepatisch: hepatic.
hepatisiert: hepatized.
Hepatitis *f*: hepatitis; **akute** ≈ acute hepatitis; **anikterische** ≈ anicteric hepatitis; **cholestatische** ≈ cholestatic hepatitis; **fulminante** ≈ fulminant hepatitis; **infektiöse** ≈ infectious hepatitis; **lupoide** ≈ lupoid hepatitis, Kunkel syndrome; **toxische** ≈ toxic hepatitis; **virale** ≈ viral hepatitis.
Hepatitis A: hepatitis A, infectious hepatitis.
Hepatitis B: hepatitis B, serum hepatitis.
Hepatitis C: hepatitis C.
Hepatitisimpfstoff *m*: hepatitis vaccine.
hepatobiliär: hepatobiliary.
hepatoduodenal: hepatoduodenal.
hepatolentikulär: hepatolenticular.
Hepatologie *f*: hepatology.
Hepatom *n*: hepatoma.
Hepatomegalie *f*: hepatomegaly.
Hepatosplenomegalie *f*: hepatosplenomegaly.
Hepatotoxizität *f*: hepatotoxicity.
hepatozellulär: hepatocellular.
Herd *m*: focus, center; **epileptischer** ≈ epileptic focus.
Herdepilepsie *f*: focal epilepsy.
Herdläsion *f*: focal lesion.
Herdnekrose *f*: focal necrosis.
Herdnephritis *f*: focal nephritis.
Herdreaktion *f*: focal reaction, local reaction.
Herdsymptom *n*: focal symptom, local symptom.
hereditär: hereditary, inborn.
Heredoataxia cerebellaris *f*: hereditary cerebellar ataxia, Marie's sclerosis.
Heredoataxie *f*: heredoataxia.
Hering-Nachbild *n*: Hering effect.
Hermaphroditismus *m*: hermaphroditism; **echter** ≈ true hermaphroditism.
Hernia femoralis *f*: femoral hernia.
Hernia synovialis *f*: synovial hernia, Birkett's hernia.
Hernie *f*: hernia; **inkarzerierte** ≈ incarcerated hernia; **irreponible** ≈ irreducible hernia; **reponierbare** ≈ reducible hernia; **retroperitoneale** ≈ retroperitoneal hernia, Treitz's hernia; **strangulierte** ≈ strangulated hernia.

Hernioplastik *f*: hernioplasty.
Herniorrhaphie *f*: herniorrhaphy.
Herniotomie *f*: herniotomy.
Heroin *n*: heroin, diacetylmorphine.
Herpesbläschen *n*: fever blister.
Herpesenzephalitis *f*: herpesvirus encephalitis.
Herpes genitalis: genital herpes.
Herpes labialis: Herpes labialis, cold sore.
Herpes simplex: herpes simplex.
Herpes-simplex-Paronychie *f*: herpetic paronychia.
Herpes zoster: herpes zoster, shingles.
herpetisch: herpetic.
Hertwig-Magendie-Syndrom *n*: Hertwig-Magendie syndrome, skew deviation.
Herunterregulation *f*: downregulation.
Herz *n*: heart, cor; **hypoplastisches** ≈ hypoplastic heart; **linkes** ≈ left heart; **rechtes** ≈ right heart.
Herzaneurysma *n*: cardiac aneurysm.
Herzanfall *m*: heart attack.
Herzasthma *n*: cardiac asthma, Rostan's asthma.
Herzatrophie *f*: cardiac atrophy, atrophic heart.
Herzauswurfvolumen *n*: cardiac output.
Herzautomatismus *m*: automatic beat.
Herzbeutel *m*: heart sac, pericardium.
Herzbeutelentzündung *f*: pericarditis.
Herzbeutelflüssigkeit *f*: pericardial fluid.
Herzblock *m*: heart block; **unvollständiger** ≈ incomplete heart block; **vollständiger** ≈ complete heart block.
Herzchirurgie *f*: cardiac surgery, heart surgery.
Herzdruckmassage *f*: heart massage, cardiac massage.
Herzerkrankung *f*: heart disease, heart condition; **angeborene** ≈ congenital heart disease; **ischämische** ≈ ischemic heart disease; **koronare** ≈ coronary heart disease; **rheumatische** ≈ rheumatic heart disease, Bouillaud's disease.
Herzfehler *m*: cardiac defect, cardiac anomaly.
Herzfrequenz *f*: heart rate, cardiac rate.
Herzfrequenzsteuerung *f*: cardiac pacing.
Herzgeräusch *n*: cardiac sound, cardiac murmur; **funktionelles** ≈ functional murmur; **weiches** ≈ cardiac souffle.
Herzindex *m*: cardiac index.
Herzinfarkt *m*: cardiac infarction, myocardial infarction; **apikaler** ≈ apical myocardial infarction; **stummer** ≈ silent myocardial infarction; **subendokardialer** ≈ subendocardial infarction, non-Q-wave infarction; **transmuraler** ≈ transmural myocardial infarction, Q-wave infarction.
Herzinsuffizienz *f*: heart failure, cardiac insufficiency, myocardial failure.
Herzkammer *f*: heart ventricle.
Herzkammerschrittmacher *m*: ventricular assist device.
Herzklappe *f*: heart valve, cardiac valve.
Herzklappeninsuffizienz *f*: valvular insufficiency, valvular incompetence.
Herzklappenprolaps *m*: valve prolapse.
Herzklappenprothese *f*: heart valve prosthesis.
Herzklappenverkalkung *f*: valvular calcification.
Herzklopfen *n*: palpitation.
Herzkompression *f*: cardiac compression.
Herzkrankheit *f*: heart disease, heart condition; **ischämische** ≈ ischemic heart disease; **koronare** ≈ coronary heart disease.
Herzkranzgefäß *n*: coronary vessel.
Herz-Kreislauf-Erkrankung *f*: cardiovascular disease.
Herz-Kreislauf-Kollaps *m*: cardiovascular collapse.
Herz-Kreislauf-System *n*: cardiovascular system.
Herz-Lungen-Maschine *f*: heart-lung machine.

Herz-Lungen-Wiederbelebung *f*: cardiopulmonary resuscitation.
Herzmassage *f*: heart massage, cardiac compression.
Herzminutenvolumen *n*: cardiac output.
Herzmittel *n*: cardiac.
Herzmuskelentzündung *f*: myocarditis.
Herzmuskelverkalkung *f*: myocardial calcification.
Herzneurose *f*: heart neurosis, cardiac neurosis.
Herzreizleitung *f*: cardiac conduction.
Herzrhythmus *m*: cardiac rhythm.
Herzruptur *f*: heart rupture, cardiac rupture.
Herzschlag *m*: heartbeat, beat.
Herzschrittmacher *m*: cardiac pacemaker, heart pacemaker; **implantierter** ≈ implanted pacemaker.
Herzschrittmacher-Pass *m*: pacemaker registration card.
Herzseptumdefekt *m*: heart septal defect.
Herzspitze *f*: apex of the heart.
Herzspitzenstoß *m*: apex beat, apical impulse; **hebender** ≈ heaving apex beat.
Herzstillstand *m*: cardiac arrest; **ventrikulärer** ≈ ventricular standstill.
Herztamponade *f*: cardiac tamponade.
Herz-Thorax-Verhältnis *n*: cardiothoracic ratio.
Herztod, plötzlicher *m*: sudden cardiac death.
Herztöne, kindliche: fetal heart tones, fetal heartbeats.
Herzton *m*: heart sound, heart tone; **dritter** ≈ third sound; **erster** ≈ first heart sound; **gespaltener** ≈ split sound; **verdoppelter** ≈ duplicated sound; **zusätzlicher** ≈ additional sound; **zweiter** ≈ second heart sound.
Herztransplantation *f*: heart transplantation.
Herzverfettung *f*: fatty cardiomyopathy.
Herzvergrößerung *f*: heart enlargement.
Herzversagen *n*: heart failure, cardiac failure.
Hetacillin *n*: hetacillin.
Heterochromiestar *m*: heterochromic cataract.
Heterochromosom *n*: heterochromosome, allosome.
heterogen: heterogenous, heterogenic.
heterolog: heterologous.
Heterophorie *f*: heterophoria.
Heteroplasie *f*: heteroplasia.
Heterosexualität *f*: heterosexuality.
Heterotopie *f*: heterotopia.
Heterotransplantat *n*: heterograft, xenograft, allogeneic graft.
Heterotropie *f*: heterotropia, concomitant strabismus.
heterozygot: heterozygous, allozygote.
Heterozygot *m*: heterozygote, genetic carrier.
Heubner-Herter-Krankheit *f*: Heubner-Herter disease, infantile celiac disease.
Heufieber *n*: hay fever.
Heuschnupfen *m*: hay fever, seasonal nasal allergy.
Hexachlorethan *n*: hexachlorethane.
Hexachlorophen *n*: hexachlorophene.
Hexamethoniumbromid *n*: hexamethonium bromide.
Hexan *n*: hexane.
Hexcarbacholinbromid *n*: hexcarbacholine bromide.
Hexenschuss *m*: crick in the back, sciatic.
Hexobarbital *n*: hexobarbital.
Hexobendin *n*: hexobendine.
Hexonsäure *f*: hexonic acid.
Hexoprenalin *n*: hexoprenaline.
Hiatus *m*: hiatus, cleft.
Hiatushernie *f*: hiatal hernia.
Hidradenitis *f*: hidradenitis.
Hidradenitis suppurativa *f*: apocrine acne.
hilär: hilar.
Hilfe *f*: help, aid, assistance; **Erste** ≈ first aid.
Hilfeleistung *f*: assistance, help, rescue work.

Hilflosigkeit *f*: helplessness.
Hilfsbedürftigkeit *f*: neediness.
Hilfsmittel *n*: device, vehicle.
Hilfsschwester *f*: auxiliary nurse.
Hilfsstoff *m*: inactive ingredient.
Hiluslymphknoten *m*: hilar lymph node.
Hiluslymphknotenschwellung *f*: hilar lymphadenopathy.
Hiluslymphknotentuberkulose *f*: hilus tuberculosis.
Hinfälligkeit *f*: decrepitude, infirmity.
hinken: limp, go lame.
Hinken *n*: claudication, limp.
Hintergrundstrahlung *f*: background radiation.
Hinterhauptlage *f*: occiput presentation.
Hinterhornzelle *f*: posterior horn cell.
Hinterlappen *m*: posterior lobe.
Hinterscheitelbeineinstellung *f*: posterior asynclitism, Litzmann's obliquity.
Hinterwurzel *f*: dorsal root, posterior root.
Hiob Syndrom *n*: Job syndrome.
hippokratisch: hippocratic.
Hippokratischer Eid *m*: hippocratic oath.
Hippotherapie *f*: hippotherapy.
Hippursäure *f*: hippuric acid.
Hippus *m*: pupil unrest, athetosis pupillaris.
Hirn *n*: brain, cerebrum.
Hirnabszess *m*: cerebral abscess, brain abscess.
Hirnanhangsdrüse *f*: hypophysis, pituitary gland.
Hirnarterienaneurysma *n*: cerebrovascular aneurysm.
Hirnarteriensklerose *f*: cerebral arteriosclerosis.
Hirnatrophie *f*: cerebral atrophy.
Hirnbiopsie *f*: brain biopsy.
Hirnblutung *f*: intracerebral hemorrhage.
Hirndruck *m*: brain pressure, cerebral compression.
Hirndrucksteigerung *f*: intracranial hypertension.
Hirndurchblutung *f*: cerebral perfusion.
Hirnembolie *f*: cerebral embolism.
Hirnfunktion *f*: brain function, cerebral function.
Hirninfarkt *m*: cerebral infarction.
Hirnleistungsschwäche *f*: impaired cerebral function.
Hirnnerv *m*: cranial nerve.
Hirnnervenpolyneuritis *f*: cranial polyneuropathy, Fisher syndrome.
Hirnödem *n*: cerebral edema.
Hirnschlag *m*: stroke, cerebral apoplexy.
Hirnsinus *m*: cerebral sinus.
Hirnsklerose *f*: cerebral sclerosis; **diffuse sudanophile** ≈ sudanophilic diffuse sclerosis; **tuberöse** ≈ tuberous sclerosis, Pringle-Bourneville syndrome.
Hirnstamm *m*: brain stem.
Hirnstammsyndrom *n*: brain stem syndrome.
Hirnstromwellen: brain waves.
Hirntätigkeit *f*: brain function.
Hirntod *m*: brain death, cerebral death.
Hirntumor *m*: brain tumor, cerebral neoplasm.
Hirnverletzung *f*: brain injury.
Hirsutismus *m*: hirsutism.
His-Bündel *n*: His band, atrioventricular bundle.
His-Bündel-Elektrokardiogramm *n*: His bundle electrogram.
Histamin *n*: histamine.
Histaminkopfschmerz *m*: histamine headache, cluster headache.
Histaminrezeptorenblocker *m*: histamine receptor blockader.
Histidin *n*: histidine.
Histiozyt *m*: histiocyte.
Histiozytom *n*: histiocytoma, xanthofibroma; **malignes fibröses** ≈ malignant fibrous histiocytoma, xanthosarcoma.
Histiozytose *f*: histiocytosis; **maligne** ≈ malignant histiocytosis; **medulläre** ≈ histiocytic medullary reticulosis.
Histochemie *f*: histochemistry, histologic chemistry.

H

Histogenese *f*: histogenesis.
Histoinkompatibilität *f*: histoincompatibility.
Histokompatibilität *f*: histocompatibility.
Histokompatibilitätsantigen *n*: histocompatibility antigen.
Histologie *f*: histology.
Histopathologie *f*: histopathology, pathologic histology.
Histoplasmose *f*: histoplasmosis.
Hitze *f*: heat.
Hitzekollaps *m*: heat collapse.
Hitzekrampf *m*: heat cramp.
Hitzeschock *m*: heat shock.
Hitzschlag *m*: heatstroke.
HIV-Infektion *f*: HIV infection.
Hochdruck *m*: hypertension, high pressure; **arterieller** ≈ arterial hypertension; **essentieller** ≈ essential hypertension; **hypophysärer** ≈ pituitary hypertension; **labiler** ≈ labile hypertension; **neurogener** ≈ neurogenic hypertension; **renaler** ≈ renal hypertension; **renovaskulärer** ≈ renovascular hypertension; **zentraler** ≈ neurogenic hypertension.
Hochdruckherz *n*: hypertensive heart.
hochkalorisch: high-caloric.
Hochvolttherapie *f*: high-voltage therapy.
Hochwuchs *m*: gigantism.
Hockerstellung *f*: squatting position.
Hoden *m*: testis, orchis; **ektoper** ≈ ectopic testis; **invertierter** ≈ inverted testis.
Hodendystopie *f*: testicular ectopia.
Hodenentzündung *f*: orchitis.
Hodenkrebs *m*: testicular cancer.
Hodensack *m*: scrotum.
Hodentorsion *f*: testicular torsion.
Höchstdosis *f*: maximum dose.
Höchstmenge *f*: maximum amount.
Höcker *m*: tuberculum, bump.
Höhenkrankheit *f*: altitude sickness, Acosta's disease.
Höhenlungenödem *n*: high-altitude pulmonary edema.
Höhepunkt *f*: summit, peak, acme.
Höhle *f*: cavity, pocket, niche, cave.
hören: hear.
Hören *n*: hearing, audition.
Hörgerät *n*: hearing aid.
Hörhaar *n*: auditory hair.
Hörkurve *f*: audiometric curve.
Hörprüfung *f*: hearing test.
Hörschärfe *f*: hearing acuity.
Hörschwelle *f*: auditory threshold.
Hörstörung *f*: hearing disorder.
Hörsturz *m*: sudden hearing loss.
Hörtest *m*: auditory test.
Hörverlust *m*: hearing loss, hearing impairment; **lärmbedingter** ≈ noise-induced hearing loss; **partieller** ≈ partial hearing loss; **sensorineuraler** ≈ sensorineural hearing loss.
Hörzelle *f*: auditory cell.
Hörzentrum *n*: auditory area, acoustic center.
hohl: hollow.
Hohlfuß *m*: pes cavus, hollow foot.
Hohlhand *f*: palm of hand.
Hohlhandphlegmone *f*: palmar phlegmon.
Hohlkreuz *n*: hollow-back.
Hohlnägel: koilonychia.
Hohlraum *m*: hollow space, cavity.
Hohlwarze *f*: sunken nipple.
Holt-Oram-Syndrom *n*: Holt-Oram syndrome, heart-hand syndrome, atriodigital dysplasia.
Holzknecht-Raum *m*: Holzknecht space, retrocardiac space.
Holzschuhherz *n*: wooden-shoe heart, sabot heart.
Homatropin *n*: homatropine.
Homöopathie *f*: homeopathy.
Homöostase *f*: homeostasis, homeostatic equilibrium.
homogen: homogenous.
Homogentisinsäure *f*: homogentisic acid.
Homogentisinurie *f*: homogentisuria.
homolateral: homolateral.
homolog: homologous.
Homosexualität *f*: homosexuality.
Homovanillinsäure *f*: homovanillic acid.
homozygot: homozygous.
Hordeolum *n*: hordeolum, sty.
Hordeolum externum *n*: zeisian stye.

Hordeolum internum *n*: meibomian stye.
Horizontalebene *f*: horizontal plane.
Horizontallage *f*: horizontal position.
Horizontalschwindel *m*: horizontal vertigo.
Horizontaltyp *m*: horizontal heart.
Hormon *n*: hormone; **adrenokortikotropes** ≈ adrenocorticotropic hormone, ACTH; **antidiuretisches** ≈ antidiuretic hormone, ADH, vasopressin; **atriales natriuretisches** ≈ atrial natriuretic factor; **follikelstimulierendes** ≈ follicle-stimulating hormone, FSH; **gonadotropes** ≈ gonadotropic hormone, gonadotropin; **luteinisierendes** ≈ luteinizing hormone, LH; **melanozytenstimulierendes** ≈ melanocyte stimulating hormone, MSH; **somatotropes** ≈ somatotropic hormone, STH, growth hormone; **wachstumshormonfreisetzendes** ≈ growth hormone releasing hormone, GHRH; **wachstumshormonhemmendes** ≈ growth hormone inhibiting hormone, GHIH.
hormonabhängig: hormone-dependent.
hormonal: hormonal.
Hormonentzugsblutung *f*: withdrawal bleeding.
Hormonrezeptor *m*: hormone receptor.
Hormontherapie *f*: hormone therapy.
Horn *n*: horn, cone.
Hornhaut *f*: hornskin, cornea.
Hornhautastigmatismus *m*: corneal astigmatism.
Hornhautdystrophie *f*: corneal dystrophy; **körnige** ≈ granular corneal dystrophy, Groenouw syndrome.
Hornhautfissur *f*: corneal cleft.
Hornhautgeschwür *n*: corneal ulcer; **serpiginöses** ≈ serpiginous corneal ulcer, Saemisch's ulcer.
Hornhautkrümmung *f*: corneal curvature.
Hornhautnarbe *f*: corneal scar.
Hornhautschuppe *f*: horny scale.
Hornhauttransplantation *f*: corneal transplantation.
Hornhauttrübung *f*: corneal opacity; **gitterartige** ≈ lattice dystrophy of cornea, Biber-Haab-Dimmer dystrophy.
Hornperle *f*: pearly body.
Hornschwiele *f*: callosity.
Hortega-Zelle *f*: Hortega cell, perivascular glial cell.
Horton-Arteriitis *f*: Horton's arteritis, temporal arteritis.
Horton-Syndrom *n*: histamine headache, cluster headache.
Hospital *n*: hospital.
Hospitalismus *m*: hospitalism, hospital infection, nosocomial infection.
Hospiz *n*: hospice.
Howell-Jolly-Körperchen *n*: Jolly's body, nuclear particle.
Hüfte *f*: hip; **schnappende** ≈ snapping hip, Perrin-Ferraton disease.
Hüftgelenk *n*: hip joint.
Hüftgelenkarthrose *f*: arthrosis of the hip, coxarthrosis.
Hüfthinken *n*: gluteal gait, Trendelenburg gait.
Hüftluxation *f*: hip dislocation.
Hühnerauge *n*: hard corn, clavus.
Hühneraugenpflaster *n*: corn-plaster.
Hühnerbrust *f*: chicken breast, keeled chest.
Hülle *f*: envelope, coat, theca, tunic.
Hürthle Zelladenom *n*: Hürthle cell adenoma, oncocytoma.
Hürthle-Zellkarzinom *n*: malignant Hürthle cell tumor.
Hufeisenniere *f*: horseshoe kidney.
Hufeisenplazenta *f*: horseshoe placenta.
Huhner-Sims-Test *m*: Huhner's test, Sims test.
human: human.
Humanalbumin *n*: human albumin.
Humangenetik *f*: human genetics.
Humaninsulin *n*: human insulin.
Humerus *m*: humerus, upper arm.
humoral: humoral.
Humoralpathologie *f*: humoralism, humoral theory.
Hunger *m*: hunger.
hungern: starve.
Hungerödem *n*: hunger edema, nutritional dropsy.

H

Hunner-Zystitis *f*: chronic interstitial cystitis.
Hunter-Addison-Anämie *f*: addisonian anemia, pernicious anemia.
Husten *m*: cough, tussis; **bellender** ≈ barking cough; **metallischer** ≈ brassy cough; **produktiver** ≈ productive cough; **trockener** ≈ dry cough.
Hustenparoxysmus *m*: paroxysmal cough.
Hustenreflex *m*: cough reflex.
Hustensynkope *f*: cough syncope, cough seizure.
Hustenzentrum *n*: coughing center.
Hutchinson-Gilford-Syndrom *n*: Hutchinson-Gilford syndrome, progeria.
hyalin: hyaline.
Hyalin *n*: hyaline.
Hyaluronsäure *f*: hyaluronic acid.
Hybrid *n*: hybrid, crossbreed.
Hybridzelle *f*: hybrid cell, hybridoma.
Hydantoin *n*: hydantoin.
Hydantoinsäure *f*: hydantoic acid.
Hydatidenschwirren *n*: hydatid thrill, Blatin sign.
hydatidiform: hydatidiform.
Hydatidzyste *f*: hydatid cyst.
Hydralazin *n*: hydralazine.
Hydramnion *n*: hydramnios.
Hydrastinin *n*: hydrastinine.
Hydratation *f*: hydration.
Hydrocephalus *m*: hydrocephalus.
Hydrocephalus internus *m*: internal hydrocephalus.
Hydrocephalus occlusus *m*: noncommunicating hydrocephalus.
Hydrochlorid *n*: hydrochloride.
Hydrochlorothiazid *n*: hydrochlorothiazide.
Hydrocortison *n*: hydrocortisone.
Hydrocortisonacetat *n*: hydrocortisone acetate.
Hydroflumethiazid *n*: hydroflumethiazide.
Hydrolyse *f*: hydrolysis; **alkalische** ≈ alkaline hydrolysis; **saure** ≈ acid hydrolysis.
Hydrometra *f*: hydrometra.
Hydronephrose *f*: hydronephrosis.
Hydroperikard *n*: hydropericardium.
Hydrophilie *f*: hydrophilicity.
Hydrophobie *f*: hydrophobia.
Hydrops *m*: hydrops, edema.
Hydrosalpinx *f*: hydrosalpinx, salpingian dropsy.
Hydrotherapie *f*: hydrotherapy.
Hydrothorax *m*: hydrothorax.
Hydroxybuttersäure *f*: hydroxybutyric acid.
Hydroxycarbamid *n*: hydroxycarbamide.
Hydroxychloroquin *n*: hydroxychloroquine.
Hydroxycolecalciferol *n*: hydroxycolecalciferol.
Hydroxydion *n*: hydroxydione.
25-Hydroxyergocalciferol *n*: 25-hydroxyergocalciferol.
Hydroxyessigsäure *f*: hydroxyacetic acid, glycolic acid.
Hydroxyglutaminsäure *f*: hydroxyglutamic acid.
5-Hydroxyindolessigsäure *f*: 5-hydroxyindoleacetic acid.
17-Hydroxykortikosteroid *n*: 17-hydroxycorticosteroid.
17-Hydroxykortikosteron *n*: 17-hydroxycorticosterone.
Hydroxyphenylessigsäure *f*: hydroxyphenylacetic acid.
Hydroxyprogesteron *n*: hydroxyprogesterone.
Hydroxysäure *f*: hydroxy acid.
Hydroxystilbamidin *n*: hydroxystilbamidine.
Hydroxytetracyclin *n*: hydroxytetracycline, oxytetracycline.
5-Hydroxytryptamin *n*: 5-hydroxytryptamine.
Hydroxyzin *n*: hydroxyzine.
Hydrozele *f*: hydrocele.
Hydrozephalus *m*: hydrocephalus; **hypertensiver** ≈ hypertonic hydrocephalus; **kommunizierender** ≈ communicating hydrocephalus, Cairns syndrome; **nicht kommunizierender** ≈ noncommunicating hydrocephalus; **normotensiver** ≈ normal-pressure hydrocephalus.
Hygiene *f*: hygiene.
Hygienebinde *f*: sanitary napkin.
Hygienemaßnahme *f*: sanitary regimen.

hygienisch: hygienic, sanitary.
Hygrom *n*: hygroma; **zystisches** ≈ cystic hygroma.
Hygrometer *n*: hygrometer.
Hygromycin *n*: hygromycin.
hygroskopisch: hygroscopic.
Hymen *m*: hymen, hymenal membrane.
Hymenalatresie *f*: hymenal atresia.
Hymen imperforatus *m*: imperforate hymen.
Hymeninzision *f*: hymenotomy.
Hymenoptera *f*: hymenoptera.
Hymen septus *m*: septate hymen.
Hyoscin *n*: hyoscine.
Hyoscyamin *n*: hyoscyamine.
Hypästhesie *f*: hypoesthesia, hypesthesia.
Hypakusis *f*: hypoacusis.
Hypalbuminämie *f*: hypoalbuminemia.
Hypalgesie *f*: hypalgesia, hypoalgesia.
Hyperämie *f*: hyperemia; **reaktive** ≈ reactive hyperemia.
Hyperästhesie *f*: hyperesthesia.
hyperaktiv: hyperactive, overactive.
Hyperaldosteronismus *m*: hyperaldosteronism, Bartter's disease.
Hyperalgesie *f*: hyperalgesia.
Hyperalimentation *f*: hyperalimentation.
Hyperazidität *f*: hyperacidity.
hyperbar: hyperbaric.
Hyperbilirubinämie *f*: hyperbilirubinemia; **familiäre** ≈ hereditary hyperbilirubinemia, Crigler-Najjar icterus.
Hyperbolgläser: hyperbolic glasses.
Hyperchlorhydrie *f*: hyperchlorhydria.
Hypercholesterinämie *f*: hypercholesterolemia; **familiäre** ≈ familial hypercholesterolemia, familial hyperlipoproteinemia type IIa.
Hyperchromasie *f*: hyperchromasia, hyperchromatism.
Hyperchromatopsie *f*: hyperchromatopsia.
hyperelastisch: hyperelastic.
Hyperemesis *f*: hyperemesis.
Hyperemesis gravidarum *f*: hyperemesis gravidarum, vomiting of pregnancy.
Hypereosinophiliesyndrom *n*: hypereosinophilic syndrome.
Hyperextension *f*: hyperextension.
Hyperextension-Hyperflexionstrauma *n*: hyperextension-hyperflexion injury.
Hyperflexion *f*: hyperflexion.
Hyperglykämie *f*: hyperglycemia.
Hypergonadismus *m*: hypergonadism.
Hyperhidrose *f*: hyperhidrosis.
Hypericin *n*: hypericin.
Hyperimmunisierung *f*: hyperimmunization.
Hyperimmunserum *n*: hyperimmune serum.
Hyperkaliämie *f*: hyperkalemia.
Hyperkalzämie *f*: hypercalcemia.
Hyperkapnie *f*: hypercapnia.
Hyperkeratose *f*: hyperkeratosis.
Hyperkeratosis congenita *f*: diffuse congenital hyperkeratosis.
Hyperkeratosis follicularis *f*: follicular hyperkeratosis.
Hyperkinese *f*: hyperkinesis.
Hyperlipidämie *f*: hyperlipidemia.
Hyperlipoproteinämie *f*: hyperlipoproteinemia.
Hypermenorrhö *f*: hypermenorrhea.
Hypermetropie *f*: hypermetropia, hyperopia.
Hypermnesie *f*: hypermnesia.
Hypermotilität *f*: hypermotility.
Hypernatriämie *f*: hypernatremia.
Hypernephrom *n*: hypernephroma, Grawitz tumor.
Hyperonychie *f*: hyperonychia.
Hyperopie *f*: hyperopia, farsightedness.
hyperosmolar: hyperosmolar.
Hyperostose *f*: hyperostosis.
Hyperoxalurie *f*: hyperoxaluria.
Hyperparathyreoidismus *m*: hyperparathyroidism.
Hyperphagie *f*: hyperphagia.
Hyperphalangie *f*: hyperphalangia.
Hyperpigmentierung *f*: hyperpigmentation.
Hyperpituitarismus *m*: hyperpituitarism.
Hyperplasie *f*: hyperplasia.

Hyperplasie der Leber, fokal-noduläre *f*: focal nodular hyperplasia of the liver.
Hyperpyrexie *f*: hyperpyrexia.
hyperreaktiv: hyperreactive.
Hypersalivation *f*: hypersalivation.
Hypersekretion *f*: hypersecretion.
Hypersensibilität *f*: hypersensibility, hypersensitivity.
Hypersensitivität *f*: hypersensitivity, hypersensibility.
Hypertension *f*: hypertension, high pressure; **portale** ≈ portal hypertension; **pulmonale** ≈ pulmonary hypertension.
Hyperthermie *f*: hyperthermia.
Hyperthrombinämie *f*: hyperthrombinemia.
Hyperthymie *f*: hyperthymism.
Hyperthyreoidismus *m*: hyperthyroidism.
Hyperthyreose *f*: hyperthyroidism; **jodinduzierte** ≈ iodine-induced hyperthyroidism, iod-Basedow; **maskierte** ≈ masked hyperthyroidism.
Hypertonie *f*: hypertonia, hypertension; **essentielle** ≈ essential hypertension; **maligne** ≈ malignant hypertension; **portale** ≈ portal hypertension; **pulmonale** ≈ pulmonary hypertension; **renale** ≈ renal hypertension; **renovaskuläre** ≈ renovascular hypertension.
Hypertonus *m*: hypertonus, high blood pressure.
Hypertrichose *f*: hypertrichosis, excessive hairiness.
Hypertriglyzeridämie *f*: hypertriglyceridemia.
hypertroph: hypertrophic.
Hypertrophie *f*: hypertrophy; **echte** ≈ true hypertrophy; **einfache** ≈ simple hypertrophy; **exzentrische** ≈ eccentric hypertrophy; **konzentrische** ≈ concentric hypertrophy; **pseudoödematöse hypoderme** ≈ Nonne-Milroy syndrome, congenital lymphedema.
Hypertyrosinämie *f*: hypertyrosinemia.
Hyperventilation *f*: hyperventilation, increased respiration.
Hypervolämie *f*: hypervolemia.
Hypnose *f*: hypnosis.
Hypnotherapie *f*: hypnotherapy.
Hypnotikum *n*: hypnotic.
Hypoaldosteronismus *m*: hypoaldosteronism.
hypoallergen: hypoallergenic.
Hypochlorämie *f*: hypochloremia.
Hypochlorhydrie *f*: hypochlorhydria.
Hypochondrie *f*: hypochondriasis.
Hypochromasie *f*: hypochromatism.
Hypodermis *f*: hypodermis.
Hypofibrinogenämie *f*: hypofibrinogenemia.
Hypogammaglobulinämie *f*: hypogammaglobulinemia.
hypogastrisch: hypogastric.
Hypoglossuslähmung *f*: hypoglossal paralysis.
Hypoglykämie *f*: hypoglycemia.
hypoglykämisch: hypoglycemic.
Hypogonadismus *m*: hypogonadism; **hypergonadotroper** ≈ hypergonadotropic hypogonadism, primary hypogonadism; **hypogonadotroper** ≈ familial hypogonadotropic hypogonadism, secondary hypogonadism.
Hypoinsulinismus *m*: hypoinsulinism.
Hypokaliämie *f*: hypokalemia.
Hypokalzämie *f*: hypocalcemia.
Hypomanie *f*: hypomania.
Hypometrie *f*: hypometria.
Hyponatriämie *f*: hyponatremia.
Hypoosmolaritätssyndrom *n*: hypoosmolar syndrome.
Hypoparathyreoidismus *m*: hypoparathyroidism, parathyroid insufficiency.
Hypopharyngoskopie *f*: hypopharyngoscopy.
Hypophorie *f*: hypophoria.
Hypophosphatämie *f*: hypophosphatemia; **familiäre** ≈ familial hypophosphatemic rickets.
Hypophosphatasie *f*: hypophosphatasia.
Hypophosphaturie *f*: hypophosphaturia.
hypophysär: hypophyseal, pituitary.
Hypophyse *f*: hypophysis, pituitary gland.

Hypophysektomie *f*: hypophysectomy.
Hypophysenadenom *n*: pituitary adenoma.
Hypophysenextrakt *m*: pituitary.
Hypophysenhormon *n*: hypophysial hormone, pituitary hormone.
Hypophyseninfarkt *m*: pituitary infarction.
Hypophyseninsuffizienz *f*: pituitary insufficiency.
Hypophysennekrose *f*: postpartal pituitary necrosis, Sheehan syndrome.
Hypophysentumor *m*: hypophyseal tumor.
Hypophysenüberfunktion *f*: hyperpituitarism.
Hypophysenunterfunktion *f*: hypopituitarism.
Hypopituitarismus *m*: hypopituitarism, anterior pituitary insufficiency.
Hypoplasie *f*: hypoplasia; **ektodermale** ≈ ectodermal hypoplasia; **fokale dermale** ≈ focal dermal hypoplasia, Goltz syndrome; **kraniofaziale** ≈ craniofacial hypoplasia.
Hypoproteinämie *f*: hypoproteinemia.
Hypoprothrombinämie *f*: hypoprothrombinemia.
Hypopyon *n*: hypopyon.
Hyposekretion *f*: hyposecretion.
Hyposensibilisierung *f*: hyposensitization.
Hyposensitivität *f*: hyposensitivity.
Hyposmie *f*: hyposmia.
Hypospadie *f*: hypospadias.
Hypostase *f*: hypostasis.
Hyposthenie *f*: hyposthenia.
Hypotension *f*: hypotension, low blood pressure.
Hypothalamus *m*: hypothalamus.
Hypothalamushormon *n*: hypothalamic hormone.
Hypothalamuskern *m*: hypothalamic center.
Hypothalamussyndrom *n*: infundibular syndrome, Claude-Lhermitte syndrome.
Hypothermie *f*: hypothermia; **künstliche** ≈ induced hypothermia.
Hypothyreose *f*: hypothyroidism, thyroid insufficiency.
hypoton: hypotonic, hypotensive.
Hypotonie *f*: hypotonia, hypotension; **arterielle** ≈ arterial hypotension; **orthostatische** ≈ orthostatic hypotension, postural hypotension.
Hypoventilation *f*: hypoventilation.
Hypovitaminose *f*: hypovitaminosis.
Hypoxie *f*: hypoxia; **anämische** ≈ anemic hypoxia; **hypoxische** ≈ hypoxic hypoxia; **respiratorische** ≈ respiratory hypoxia.
Hysterektomie *f*: hysterectomy; **radikale** ≈ radical hysterectomy; **subtotale** ≈ subtotal hysterectomy.
Hysterie *f*: hysteria.
hysterisch: hysteric, hysterical.
Hysteropexie *f*: hysteropexy.
Hysterosalpingektomie *f*: hysterosalpingectomy.
Hysterosalpingographie *f*: hysterosalpingography.
Hysteroskopie *f*: hysteroscopy.
Hysterotomie *f*: hysterotomy.
Hysterozystokleisis *f*: hysterocystocleisis.

H

I

I Abk. **Iod** *n*: iodine, I.
iatrogen: iatrogenic.
Ibafloxacin *n*: ibafloxacin.
Ibandronsäure *f*: ibandronate.
Ibogain *n*: ibogaine.
Ibufenac *n*: ibufenac.
Ibuprofen *n*: ibuprofen.
ICD Abk. **Internationale Klassifikation der Krankheiten** *f*: International Classification of Diseases, ICD.
ICF Abk. **Internationale Klassifikation der Funktionsfähigkeit, Behinderung und Gesundheit** *f*: International Classification of Functioning, Disability and Health, ICF.
Ich-Bewusstsein *n*: self-consciousness, self-awareness.
Ich-Spaltung *f*: splitting of the ego.
Ichthyose *f*: ichthyosis; **bullöse** ≈ epidermolytic hyperkeratosis; **geschlechtsgebunden-rezessive** ≈ sex-linked recessive ichthyosis.
Ichthyosis congenita *f*: sex-linked recessive ichthyosis, diffuse congenital hyperkeratosis.
Ichthyosis senilis *f*: senile ichthyosis.
Icterus *m*: icterus, jaundice.
Icterus gravidarum *m*: jaundice of pregnancy.
Icterus neonatorum *m*: newborn jaundice, neonatal jaundice.
Idarubicin *n*: idarubicin.
Idealgewicht *n*: ideal weight.
Idee *f*: idea; **fixe** ≈ fixed idea, insistent idea; **überwertige** ≈ overcharged idea.
identifizieren: identify.
Identifizierung *f*: identification.
identisch: identical.
Identitätsstörung *f*: identity disorder.
ideokinetisch: ideokinetic.
ideomotorisch: ideomotor.
idiopathisch: idiopathic, essential.
Idiosynkrasie *f*: idiosyncrasy.
Idiotie *f*: idiocy; **adulte** ≈ adult ceroid lipofuscinosis, Kufs' disease; **amaurotische** ≈ amaurotic idiocy; **amaurotische familiäre** ≈ amaurotic familial idiocy; **infantile amaurotische** ≈ infantile amaurotic familial idiocy, Tay-Sachs disease; **juvenile amaurotische** ≈ juvenile amaurotic idiocy, juvenile ceroid lipofuscinosis, Vogt-Spielmeyer syndrome; **kongenitale amaurotische** ≈ Norman-Wood syndrome; **spätinfantile amaurotische** ≈ late infantile ceroid lipofuscinosis, Jansky-Bielschowsky cerebroretinal degeneration.
Idoxuridin *n*: idoxuridine.
Id-Reaktion *f*: id reaction.
Iduronsäure *f*: iduronic acid.
Ifosfamid *n*: ifosfamide.
ikterisch: icteric.
Ikterus *m*: icterus, jaundice; **cholestatischer** ≈ cholestatic jaundice; **extrahepatischer cholestatischer** ≈ extrahepatic cholestatic jaundice; **familiärer** ≈ familial jaundice; **hämolytischer** ≈ hemolytic jaundice; **hepatozellulärer** ≈ hepatocellular jaundice; **kongenitaler hämolytischer** ≈ chronic congenital hemolytic jaundice; **physiologischer** ≈ physiologic icterus.
Ileitis *f*: ileitis.
Ileitis terminalis *f*: terminal ileitis.
Ileokolitis *f*: ileocolitis.
Ileokolostomie *f*: ileocolostomy.
Ileokolotomie *f*: ileocolotomy.
Ileopexie *f*: ileopexy.
Ileoproktostomie *f*: ileoproctostomy.
Ileostomie *f*: ileostomy.

ileozäkal: ileocecal.
Iliozäkalklappe *f*: ileocecal valve, Bauhin's valve.
Ileozäkalklappeninsuffizienz *f*: ileocecal insufficiency, ileocecal incompetence.
Ileum *n*: ileum.
Ileum-Conduit *n*: ileal conduit.
Ileus *m*: ileus; **dynamischer** ≈ dynamic ileus; **funktioneller** ≈ dynamic ileus; **mechanischer** ≈ mechanical ileus; **paralytischer** ≈ paralytic ileus, adynamic ileus; **spastischer** ≈ spastic ileus.
iliakal: iliac.
iliokokzygeal: iliococcygeal.
Ilium *n*: ilium, iliac bone.
Illusion *f*: illusion; **autokinetische** ≈ autokinetic illusion.
Iloprost *n*: iloprost.
i. m. Abk. **intramuskulär**: intramuscularly, IM.
Imatinib *n*: imatinib.
Imbezillität *f*: imbecility.
Imiclopazin *n*: imiclopazine.
Imidapril *n*: imidapril.
Imidazol *n*: imidazole.
Imidol *n*: imidole, pyrrole.
Imiglucerase *n*: imiglucerase.
Imipenem *n*: imipenem.
Imipramin *n*: imipramine.
Imiquimod *n*: imiquimod.
immatur: immature.
Immobilisierung *f*: immobilization.
immun: immune, insusceptible.
Immunabwehr *f*: immune defense.
Immunantwort *f*: immune response, immune reaction; **humorale** ≈ humoral immune response; **zelluläre** ≈ cellular immune response.
Immunbiologie *f*: immunobiology.
Immundefekt *m*: immunodeficiency, immune defect; **erworbener** ≈ acquired immunodeficiency; **humoraler** ≈ humoral immunodeficiency; **kombinierter** ≈ combined immunodeficiency; **schwerer kombinierter** ≈ severe combined immunodeficiency, SCID; **sekundärer** ≈ acquired immunodeficiency; **thymusabhängiger** ≈ thymus-dependent deficiency; **zellulärer** ≈ cellular immunodeficiency.
Immundefektsyndrom *n*: immunodeficiency syndrome; **erworbenes** ≈ acquired immunodeficiency syndrome, AIDS.
Immundefizienz *f*: immunodeficiency.
Immundepression *f*: immunodepression, immunosuppression.
Immunelektrophorese *f*: immunoelectrophoresis.
Immunfluoreszenztest *m*: immunofluorescence test.
Immungenetik *f*: immunogenetics.
Immunglobulin *n*: immunoglobulin, Ig, immune globulin.
Immunhämolysin *n*: immune hemolysin.
Immunhistochemie *f*: immunohistochemistry.
immunisieren: immunize.
Immunisierung *f*: immunization; **aktive** ≈ active immunization; **passive** ≈ passive immunization.
Immunität *f*: immunity, insusceptibility; **aktive** ≈ active immunity; **angeborene** ≈ congenital immunity, innate immunity; **erworbene** ≈ acquired immunity; **fetale** ≈ intrauterine immunity; **humorale** ≈ humoral immunity; **künstliche** ≈ artificial immunity; **mütterliche** ≈ maternal immunity; **natürliche** ≈ natural immunity; **passive** ≈ passive immunity; **spezifische** ≈ specific immunity; **unspezifische** ≈ nonspecific immunity; **zelluläre** ≈ cellular immunity, cell-mediated immunity, CMI.
Immunkomplex *m*: immune complex, immunocomplex; **zirkulierender** ≈ circulating immune complex.
Immunkomplexglomerulonephritis *f*: circulating immune-complex glomerulonephritis.
Immunkomplexkrankheit *f*: immune-complex disease.
Immunmangelsyndrom *n*: immunodeficiency syndrome, immunologic deficiency.
Immunmodulator *m*: immunomodulator.

Immunoassay *m*: immunoassay; **enzymgekoppelter** ≈ enzyme-linked immunosorbent assay, ELISA.
Immunologie *f*: immunology.
Immunozyt *m*: immunocyte, immunocompetent cell.
Immunreaktion *f*: immune response, immunoreaction.
Immunserum *n*: immune serum.
Immunstimulans *n*: immunostimulant.
Immunsuppressivum *n*: immunosuppressant.
Immunsystem *n*: immune system.
Imolamin *n*: imolamine.
impaktiert: impacted.
Impedanz *f*: impedance; **akustische** ≈ acoustic impedance, ear impedance.
Impedanzaudiometrie *f*: impedance audiometry.
Impermeabilität *f*: impermeability.
impfen: vaccinate.
Impfenzephalitis *f*: postvaccinal encephalitis.
Impffieber *n*: vaccinal fever.
Impfkalender *m*: immunization schedule.
Impfnachweis *m*: vaccination certificate.
Impfpass *m*: immunization register.
Impfstoff *m*: vaccine; **attenuierter** ≈ attenuated vaccine; **inaktivierter** ≈ inactivated vaccine; **polyvalenter** ≈ polyvalent vaccine; **univalenter** ≈ univalent vaccine.
Impfung *f*: vaccination.
Impfzwang *m*: mandatory vaccination, compulsary vaccination.
Implantat *n*: implant.
Implantation *f*: implantation.
implantieren: implant.
Impotenz *f*: impotence, impotency; **funktionelle** ≈ functional impotence, psychic impotence; **medikamentös bedingte** ≈ drug-induced impotence; **psychogene** ≈ psychic impotence, functional impotence; **symptomatische** ≈ symptomatic impotence, secondary impotence.
Imprägnation *f*: impregnation.
Impression *f*: impression.
Impressionsfraktur *f*: depressed fracture.
Impuls *m*: impulse.
Impulsleitungsverzögerung *f*: impulse conduction delay.
inaktiv: inactive, inert.
inaktivieren: inactivate.
Inaktivitätsatrophie *f*: inactivity atrophy, disuse atrophy.
Indapamid *n*: indapamide.
Index *m*: index; **optischer** ≈ optical index; **leukopenischer** ≈ chemotherapeutic index; **therapeutischer** ≈ therapeutic index.
Indexpatient *m*: index case.
Indifferenztyp *m*: indifferent type.
Indikation *f*: indication; **diagnostische** ≈ diagnostic indication; **therapeutische** ≈ therapeutic indication; **zusätzliche** ≈ second indication.
Indikator *m*: indicator.
Indinavir *n*: indinavir.
individuell: individual.
Individuum *n*: individual.
indolent: indolent, painless.
Indolessigsäure *f*: indolacetic acid.
Indometacin *n*: indomethacin.
Indophenazin *n*: indophenazine.
Indoramin *n*: indoramin.
Indoxyl *n*: indoxyl.
Induktion *f*: induction; **magnetische** ≈ magnetic induction.
Induktionsphase *f*: induction period, inductive phase.
Induktor *m*: inductor, inducer.
Induration *f*: induration; **braune** ≈ brown induration; **graue** ≈ gray induration; **rote** ≈ red induration; **schwarze** ≈ black induration.
Induratio penis plastica *f*: plastic induration of penis, Peyronie's disease.
induzieren: induce.
inert: inert.
Inertie *f*: inertia.
infantil: infantile.
Infantilismus *m*: infantilism.
Infarkt *m*: infarct, infarction; **anämischer** ≈ anemic infarct; **blander** ≈ bland infarct; **hämorrhagischer** ≈ hemorrhagic infarct; **ischämischer** ≈ anemic infarct; **lakunärer** ≈ lacunar infarction; **roter** ≈ red infarct;

septischer ≈ septic infarct; **steriler** ≈ aseptic infarct; **thrombotischer** ≈ thrombotic infarct; **transmuraler** ≈ transmural myocardial infarction; **weißer** ≈ white infarct.
Infarktembolie *f*: embolic infarct.
Infarzierung *f*: infarction.
infaust: infaust, unfavorable.
Infekt *m*: infection; **grippaler** ≈ endemic influenza.
infektiös: infectious, contagious.
Infektion *f*: infection; **abortive** ≈ abortive infection, incomplete infection; **aerogene** ≈ air-borne infection; **aszendierende** ≈ ascending infection, retrograde infection; **diaplazentare** ≈ diaplacental infection; **eitrige** ≈ pyogenic infection; **fokale** ≈ focal infection; **fortgeleitete** ≈ metastatic infection; **indirekte** ≈ indirect infection; **nosokomiale** ≈ nosocomial infection, hospital infection; **opportunistische** ≈ opportunistic infection; **stumme** ≈ inapparent infection, subclinical infection; **unspezifische** ≈ nonspecific infection.
Infektion der oberen Atemwege: upper respiratory tract infection.
Infektionsbekämpfung *f*: infection control.
Infektionsdosis *f*: infective dose.
Infektionskrankheit *f*: infectious disease, communicable disease.
Infektionsweg *m*: route of infection.
Infektiosität *f*: infectiosity, infectiousness.
Infertilität *f*: infertility.
Infestation *f*: infestation.
Infiltration *f*: infiltration; **entzündliche** ≈ inflammatory infiltration; **fettige** ≈ fatty infiltration; **tuberkulöse** ≈ tuberculous infiltration.
Infiltrationsanästhesie *f*: infiltration anesthesia.
infiltrierend: infiltrative.
Infirmität *f*: infirmity.
infizieren: infect, contaminate.
Inflammation *f*: inflammation.
Infliximab *n*: infliximab.
Influenza *f*: influenza, flu; **aviäre** ≈ avian influenza, bird flu.
Infraorbitalneuralgie *f*: infraorbital neuralgia.
Infrarotlicht *n*: infrared light.
Infrarotthermographie *f*: infrared thermography.
infundibulär: infundibular.
Infundibulektomie *f*: infundibulectomy; **transventrikuläre** ≈ Brock's infundibulectomy, transventricular closed valvulotomy.
Infusion *f*: infusion.
Infusionspumpe *f*: infusion pump, intravenous drug delivery system.
Infusionsurographie *f*: intravenous urography.
Ingestion *f*: ingestion.
Ingredienz *f*: ingredient, nutrient.
inguinal: inguinal.
inhärent: inherent.
Inhalation *f*: inhalation.
Inhalationspneumonie *f*: inhalation pneumonia, aspiration pneumonia.
Inhibition *f*: inhibition.
inhibitorisch: inhibitory.
initial: initial, incipient
Initialdosis *f*: initial dose, loading dose.
Initialsymptom *n*: initial symptom, first sign.
Injektion *f*: injection, shot.
Injektionsort *m*: injection site.
injizieren: inject.
Inkarzerierung *f*. incarceration.
Inklination *f*: inclination, trend.
Inkohärenz *f*: incoherence.
inkompatibel: incompatible.
Inkompatibilität *f*: incompatibility.
Inkontinenz *f*: incontinence.
Inkoordination *f*: incoordination.
Inkrement *n*: increment.
Inkrustation *f*: incrustation.
Inkubation *f*: incubation.
Inkubationszeit *f*: incubation period.
Inkubator *m*: incubator.
inkurable: incurable, uncurable.
Innenband *n*: intraarticular ligament, medial ligament.
Innenohr *n*: inner ear, internal ear.
Innenohrotosklerose *f*: cochlear otosclerosis.
Innenohrschwerhörigkeit *f*: labyrinthine hearing loss.
Innenrotation *f*: internal rotation.

Innere Medizin *f*: internal medicine.
innerlich: internal.
Innervation *f*: innervation; **reziproke** ≈ reciprocal innervation; **segmentale** ≈ segmental innervation.
Innervationsmuster *n*: innervation pattern.
Inokulation *f*: inoculation.
Inosin *n*: inosine.
Inosinmonophosphat *n*: inosine monophosphate.
Inosinpranobex *n*: inosine pranobex.
Inosinsäure *f*: inosinic acid, inosine monophosphate.
Inosit *n*: inosite, inositol.
Inositol *n*: inositol, inosite.
Inotropie des Herzens *f*: cardiac inotropism.
Insekt *n*: insect.
Insektenstich *m*: insect bite, insect sting.
Insel *f*: islet, island, insula.
Inselzelladenom *n*: islet cell adenoma.
Insemination *f*: insemination; **extrakorporale** ≈ extrauterine insemination; **heterologe** ≈ heterologous insemination; **homologe** ≈ homologous insemination; **künstliche** ≈ artificial insemination.
Insensibilität *f*: insensibility.
Insertion *f*: insertion.
Insertionsaponeurose *f*: aponeurosis of insertion.
Insomnie *f*: insomnia, sleeplessness.
Inspiration *f*: inspiration.
Inspirationskapazität *f*: inspiratory capacity.
inspiratorisch: inspiratory.
instabil: unstable, instable.
Instabilität *f*: instability.
Instillation *f*: instillation.
Instinkt *m*: instinct, instinctual drive.
Instinktverhalten *n*: instinctive behavior, inborn behavior.
insuffizient: insufficient, incompetent.
Insuffizienz *f*: insufficiency, incompetence; **arterielle** ≈ arterial insufficiency; **posttraumatische pulmonale** ≈ adult respiratory distress syndrome, ARDS; **pulmonale** ≈ pulmonary insufficiency; **respiratorische** ≈ pulmonary insufficiency, respiratory failure; **venöse** ≈ venous insufficiency.
Insufflationsnarkose *f*: insufflation anesthesia.
Insulin *n*: insulin.
Insulinallergie *f*: insulin allergy.
insulinartig: insulin-like.
Insulinaspart *n*: insulin aspart.
Insulinausschüttung *f*: insulin secretion.
Insulinbelastungstest *m*: insulin tolerance test.
Insulindetemir *n*: insulin detemir.
Insulineinheit *f*: insulin unit.
Insulinglargin *n*: insulin glargine.
Insulinglulisin *n*: insulin glulisine.
Insulinlispro *n*: insulin lispro.
Insulinom *n*: insulinoma.
Insulinpumpe *f*: insulin pump.
Insulinresistenz *f*: insulin resistance.
Insulinrezeptor *m*: insulin receptor.
Insulinschock *m*: insulin shock.
Insulin-Zink-Suspension *f*: insulin zinc suspension.
Insulitis *f*: insulitis.
Insult *m*: insult, attack; **hämorrhagischer** ≈ hemorrhagic stroke; **ischämischer zerebraler** ≈ cerebral infarction; **zerebrovaskulärer** ≈ stroke.
Integraldosis *f*: integral dose, volume dose.
Integrase *f*: integrase.
Integument *n*: integument, integumentum.
Intellekt *m*: intellect.
Intelligenzabbau *m*: intellectual deterioration.
Intelligenzquotient *m*: intelligence quotient.
Intelligenztest *m*: intelligence test.
Intensität *f*: intensity.
intensiv: intensive, intense.
Intensivpflege *f*: intensive care, critical care.
Intensivstation *f*: intensive care unit.
Intentionsbewegung *f*: intention movement.
Intentionstremor *m*: intention tremor, action tremor.

Interaktion *f*: interaction.
interartikulär: interarticular.
Interdentalraum *m*: interdental space.
Interferon *n*: interferon, IF; **pegyliertes** ≈ pegylated interferon, peginterferon.
interkostal: intercostal.
Interkostalanästhesie *f*: intercostal anesthesia, intercostal block.
Interkostalneuralgie *f*: intercostal neuralgia.
Interkostalraum *m*: intercostal space.
interkurrent: intercurrent.
Interleukin *n*: interleukin, IL.
intermediär: intermediary, intermediate.
Intermediärinsulin *n*: intermediate-acting insulin.
Intermediärstadium *n*: intermediate state.
Intermediärzellkarzinom *n*: intermediary carcinoma.
Intermediat *n*: intermediate.
intermittierend: intermittent.
Internationale Klassifikation der Funktionsfähigkeit, Behinderung und Gesundheit *f*: International Classification of Functioning, Disability and Health, ICF.
Internationale Klassifikation der Krankheiten *f*: International Classification of Diseases, ICD.
interossär: interosseal, interosseous.
Interphase *f*: interphase.
Intersexualität *f*: intersexuality.
Interskapularlinie *f*: scapular line.
Interspinallinie *f*: interspinal line.
Interstitialflüssigkeit *f*: intercellular lymph.
Interstitialraum *m*: interstitial space.
interstitiell: interstitial.
Intertrigo *f*: intertrigo, intertriginous eczema.
Intervall *n*: interval; **freies** ≈ lucid interval; **stummes** ≈ silent period.
Intervention *f*: intervention.
interventionell: interventional.
interventrikulär: interventricular.
intervertebral: intervertebral.
interzellulär: intercellular.
Interzellularraum *m*: intercellular space.
intestinal: intestinal.
Intestinum *n*: intestine.
Intoleranz *f*: intolerance.
Intoxikation *f*: intoxication, toxication.
Intoxikationskopfschmerz *m*: toxic headache.
Intoxikationspsychose *f*: toxic psychosis.
intraabdominell: intra-abdominal.
intraartikulär: intra-articular.
intradermal: intradermal.
intradural: intradural, endodural.
intragastral: intragastric.
intrahepatisch: intrahepatic.
intrakraniell: intracranial.
Intrakutanprobe *f*: intradermal test.
intramuskulär: intramuscular.
intranasal: intranasal.
intraokular: intraocular.
intraoperativ: intraoperative.
intrapleural: intrapleural.
intraspinal: intraspinal.
intrathekal: intrathecal.
intrathorakal: intrathoracic.
intratracheal: endotracheal.
intrauterin: intrauterine.
Intrauterinfraktur *f*: intrauterine fracture.
Intrauteringravidität *f*: intrauterine pregnancy.
Intrauterinpessar *n*: intrauterine device, IUD.
intravaginal: intravaginal.
intravaskulär: intravascular.
intravenös: intravenous, IV.
intrazellulär: intracellular, endocellular.
Intrazellulärflüssigkeit *f*: intracellular fluid.
Intrazellulärraum *m*: intracellular space, intracellular compartment.
intrazerebral: intracerebral.
intrinsisch: intrinsic.
Introspektion *f*: introspection.
Introversion *f*: introversion.
introvertieren: introvert.
Intubation *f*: intubation; **endonasale** ≈ nasal intubation; **endotracheale** ≈ endotracheal intubation; **nasotracheale** ≈ nasotracheal intubation;

orotracheale ≈ orotracheal intubation; **perorale** ≈ oral intubation.
Intumeszenz *f*: intumescence, tumescence.
Intussuszeption *f*: intussusception.
Inulin *n*: inulin.
Inulinausscheidung *f*: inulin clearance.
Inunktion *f*: inunction, inunctum.
Invagination *f*: invagination, intussusception.
Invalidität *f*: invalidity, disablement.
Invarianz *f*: invariance, invariability.
Invasion *f*: invasion.
invasiv: invasive.
invers: inverse.
In-vitro-Fertilisation *f*: in vitro fertilization.
Involucrum *n*: involucrum.
Involution *f*: involution.
Involutionsdepression *f*: involutional depression.
Involutionsmelancholie *f*: involutional melancholia.
Involutionsosteoporose *f*: postmenopausal osteoporosis.
Involutionsparanoia *f*: involutional paranoia.
Inzest *m*: incest.
Inzesttabu *n*: incest tabu.
Inzidenz *f*: incidence.
Inzision *f*: incision, cut; **retroaurikuläre** ≈ postauricular incision; **seitliche** ≈ lateral incision.
Inzisur *f*: incisure, notch.
Iobenzaminsäure *f*: iobenzamic acid.
Iocetaminsäure *f*: iocetamic acid.
Iod *n*: iodine, I.
Iodipamid *n*: iodipamic acid.
Iodohippurat *n*: iodohippurate.
Iodopansäure *f*: iodopanoic acid, iopanoic acid.
Ion *n*: ion.
Ionenaustausch *m*: ion exchange.
Ionenkanal *m*: ion channel.
Ionenpumpe *f*: ion pump.
Iopamidol *n*: iopamidol.
Iopansäure *f*: iopanic acid.
Iopromid *n*: iopromide.
Iosarcol *n*: iosarcol.
Iotalaminsäure *f*: iotalamic acid.
Iothiouracil *n*: iothiouracil.
Iotrol *n*: iotrol.
Iotrolan *n*: iotrolan.
Ioxaglinsäure *f*: ioxaglic acid.
Ioxitalaminsäure *f*: ioxitalamic acid, ioxitalamate.
Ipecacuanha *f*: ipecac.
Ipecacuanhasirup *m*: ipecac syrup.
Ipratropiumbromid *n*: ipratropium bromide.
Iprazochrom *n*: iprazochrome.
Iproclozid *n*: iproclozide.
Iproniazid *n*: iproniazid.
Ipronidazol *n*: ipronidazole.
ipsilateral: ipsilateral, homolateral.
Irbesartan *n*: irbesartan.
Iridektomie *f*: iridectomy.
Iridokornealwinkel *m*: iridocorneal angle.
Iridoplegie *f*: iridoplegia.
Iridotomie *f*: iridotomy.
Iridozyklitis *f*: iridocyclitis, anterior uveitis.
Irinotecan *n*: irinotecan.
Iris *f*: iris.
Iriserkrankung *f*: iridopathy.
Irisschlottern *n*: iridodonesis.
Irradiation *f*: irradiation.
irregulär: irregular.
Irresein *n*: insanity; **induziertes** ≈ imposed insanity, shared delusion; **moralisches** ≈ moral insanity.
Irrigation *f*: irrigation.
irritabel: irritable.
Irritabilität *f*: irritability.
Irritans *n*: irritant, irritating substance.
Irritation *f*: irritation.
Irritationsotalgie *f*: secondary otalgia.
Ischämie *f*: ischemia.
ischämisch: ischemic.
Ischiadikus *m*: sciatic nerve.
Ischialgie *f*: sciatic neuralgia.
Ischiassyndrom *n*: sciatic neuralgia, Cotugno's disease.
Isethionsäure *f*: isethionic acid.
Isoallel *n*: isoallele.
Isoaminil *n*: isoaminile.
Isoantigen *n*: isoantigen.
Isoantikörper *m*: isoantibody.
Isocarboxazid *n*: isocarboxazid.
Isoconazol *n*: isoconazole.

Isoetarin *n*: isoetarine.
Isofluran *n*: isoflurane.
isogen: isogenic, isogeneic.
Isograft *n*: isograft, isogeneic graft.
Isokorie *f*: isocoria.
isolateral: isolateral.
Isolation *f*: isolation.
isolieren: isolate, quarantine.
Isolierstation *f*: isolation unit.
Isolysergsäure *f*: isolysergic acid.
Isomer *n*: isomer.
isometrisch: isometric.
isomorph: isomorphic, isomorphous.
Isoniazid *n*: isoniazid.
Isoniazidpolyneuropathie *f*: isoniazid polyneuropathy.
Isonikotinsäure *f*: isonicotinic acid.
Isonikotinsäurehydrazid *n*: isonicotinoylhydrazine, isoniazid.
Isophaninsulin *n*: isophane insulin.
Isoprenalin *n*: isoprenaline, isoproterenol.
Isopropamidiodid *n*: isopropamide iodide.
Isopropanol *n*: isopropanol.
Isopropylalkohol *m*: isopropyl alcohol.
Isoproterenol *n*: isoproterenol, isoprenaline.
isopyknisch: isopyknic.
Isoriboflavin *n*: isoriboflacin.
Isosorbid *n*: isosorbide.
isoton: isotone, isotonic.
Isotop *n*: isotope.
Isotretinoin *n*: isotretinoin.
Isovaleriansäure *f*: isovaleric acid.
Isoxacillinpenicillin *n*: isoxazolyl penicillin.
Isozitronensäure *f*: isocitric acid.
Isradipin *n*: isradipine.
Isthmus *m*: isthmus.
Isthmusstenose *f*: stenosis of aortic isthmus.
Itai-Itai-Krankheit *f*: itai-itai disease, ouch-ouch disease.
Iteration *f*: iteration.
Itraconazol *n*: itraconazole.
Ivermectin *n*: ivermectin.
Ixodiasis *f*: ixodism, ixodism.
Ixon *n*: ixone.

J

J Abk. **1. Jod** *n*; **2. Joule**: 1. iodine, I; 2. joule, J.
Jaboulay-Amputation *f*: Jaboulay's amputation, interpelvicoabdominal amputation.
Jackson-Epilepsie *f*: jacksonian epilepsy, localized epilepsy.
Jackson-Syndrom *n*: Jackson syndrome, vagoaccessory hypoglossal paralysis.
Jacobson-Organ *n*: Jacobson's organ, vomeronasal organ.
Jaffé-Lichtenstein-Krankheit *f*: Jaffé-Lichtenstein disease, polyostotic fibrous dysplasia.
jahreszeitabhängig: seasonal.
Jaktation *f*: jactation.
Jalapenwurzel *f*: jalap.
Jansky-Bielschowsky-Syndrom *n*: Bielschowsky-Jansky disease, Bielschowsky-Dollinger syndrome, late infantile ceroid lipofuscinosis.
Jargonaphasie *f*: jargon aphasia, jumbled speech.
Jasminwurzel *f*: jasmine root.
jejunal: jejunal.
Jejunostomie *f*: jejunostomy.
Jejunum *n*: jejunum, empty intestine.
Jejunumfistel *f*: jejunostomy, nestiostomy.
Jejunumresektion *f*: jejunectomy.
Jenner-Pockenimpfung *f*: jennerian vaccination.
Jervell-Lange-Nielsen-Syndrom *n*: Jervell-Lange-Nielsen syndrome, cardioauditory syndrome.
Jetlag *m*: jet lag, jet fatigue.
Jeune-Krankheit *f*: Jeune syndrome, asphyxating thoracic dystrophy.
Jochbein *n*: zygomatic bone, yoke bone.
Jochbogen *m*: zygomatic arch.
Jod *n*: iodine, I; **butanolextrahierbares** ≈ butanol-extractable iodine; **kristallines** ≈ iodine crystal; **proteingebundenes** ≈ protein-bound iodine.
Jodbehandlung *f*: iodotherapy.
Jodbenzoesäure *f*: iodoxybenzoic acid.
Jodid *n*: iodide.
jodieren: iodize, iodinate.
Jodismus *m*: iodism.
Jodisotop *n*: iodine isotope.
Jodmangel *m*: iodine deficiency.
Jodöl *n*: iodized oil.
Jodoform *n*: iodoform.
Jodopsin *n*: iodopsin, visual violet.
Jodsäure *f*: iodic acid.
Jodsalbe *f*: iodine ointment.
Jodsalz *n*: iodized salt.
Jodstruma *f*: iodide goiter.
Jodvergiftung *f*: iodism.
Jogging *n*: jogging.
Johanniskraut *n*: St. John's wort, hypericin.
Josamycin *n*: josamycin.
Joule-Äquivalent *n*: Joule's equivalent, J.
jucken: itch.
Jucken *n*: itch, pruritus.
juckend: itching.
Juckreiz *m*: itching, pruritus.
Jugend *f*: youth.
jugendlich: juvenile, adolescent.
Jugendlicher *m*: juvenile, adolescent.
Jugendmedizin *f*: adolescent medicine.
jugulär: jugular, jugal.
Jugularisdruck *m*: jugular venous pressure.
Jugularisdruckversuch *m*: jugular compression.
Jugularispuls *m*: jugular pulse.

jung: young.
Junge *m*: boy.
Jungfräulichkeit *f*: virginity.
Junin-Fieber *n*: Junin fever, Argentinian hemorrhagic fever.
Junktionsnävus *m*: junctional nevus, marginal nevus.
juvenil: juvenile.
juxtaartikulär: juxta-articular.
juxtaglomerulär: juxtaglomerular.
Juxtaglomerularapparat *m*: juxtaglomerular apparatus.
juxtamedullär: juxtamedullary.
Juxtaposition *f*: juxtaposition.

K

K Abk. **1. Kalium** *n*; **2. Kelvin** *n*: 1. potassium, K; 2. Kelvin, k.

kachektisch: cachectic.

Kachexie *f*: cachexia; **hypothalamisch-hypophysäre** ≈ hypothalamic pituitary cachexia; **kardiale** ≈ cardiac cachexia; **psychogene** ≈ psychogenic cachexia, neurogenic cachexia; **tropische** ≈ tropical cachexia.

Kadaverstellung *f*: cadaveric position.

Kälte *f*: cold.

Kälteagglutination *f*: cold agglutination.

Kälteagglutinin *n*: cold agglutinin.

Kälteallergie *f*: cold allergy.

Kälteanästhesie *f*: cryogenic block, cryoanesthesia.

Kältechirurgie *f*: cryosurgery.

Kälteempfindung *f*: cold sensation, cryesthesia.

Kältegefühl *n*: chill.

Kältehämagglutinationskrankheit *f*: cold agglutinin disease.

Kältehämoglobinurie, paroxysmale *f*: paroxysmal cold hemoglobinuria, Donath-Landsteiner syndrome.

Kälteschaden *m*: cold injury, perniosis.

Käseschmiere *f*: vernix caseosa.

käsig: caseous, tyroid.

kahl: bald, bare.

Kahler-Krankheit *f*: Kahler's disease, plasmocytoma, multiple myeloma.

kahlköpfig: bald, bald-headed.

Kahlköpfigkeit *f*: baldness.

Kahnbauch *m*: navicular abdomen, scaphoid abdomen.

Kahnbeinbruch *m*: scaphoid fracture.

kahnförmig: navicular, scaphoid.

Kahnthorax *m*: scaphoid thorax.

Kaiserschnitt *m*: cesarean section, CS.

Kala-Azar *f*: kala-azar, visceral leishmaniasis, black fever.

Kalabarbeulen: Calabar swellings, fugitive swelling.

Kalabarbohne *f*: Calabar bean.

Kalendermethode *f*: Ogino-Knaus method.

kalibrieren: calibrate.

Kalibrierung *f*: calibration.

Kalium *n*: potassium, K.

Kaliumbromid *n*: potassium bromide.

Kaliumdichromat *n*: potassium dichromate.

Kaliummangel *m*: potassium deficiency.

Kaliumpermanganat *n*: potassium permanganate.

Kaliumverlustnephritis *f*: potassium-losing nephritis.

Kalkablagerung *f*: calcific deposit, calcification; **intrakranielle** ≈ intracranial calcification; **periartikuläre** ≈ periarticular calcification.

Kalkaneusfraktur *f*: calcaneal fracture.

kalkhaltig: calciferous, calcareous.

Kallidin *n*: kallidin, lysyl bradykinin.

Kallmann-Syndrom *n*: Kallmann syndrome, hypogonadism with anosmia.

Kallus *m*: callus; **äußerer** ≈ external callus; **bleibender** ≈ permanent callus, definitive callus; **temporärer** ≈ provisional callus.

Kallusbildung *f*: callus formation.

Kalorie *f*: calorie, C, calory.

kalorienarm: low-caloric.

Kalorienaufnahme *f*: caloric intake.

Kalorienbedarf *m*: caloric requirement.

kalorienreich: high-caloric.
Kalorimeter *n*: calorimeter.
kalorisch: caloric.
Kalotte *f*: roof of skull, calvaria.
kalt: cold, cool.
Kalzifikation *f*: calcification.
Kalzifizierung *f*: calcification.
Kalzinose *f*: calcinosis, calcium thesaurismosis; **metabolische interstitielle** ≈ Thibièrge-Weissenbach syndrome; **tumoröse** ≈ tumoral calcinosis.
Kalzium *n*: calcium, Ca.
Kalziumblocker *m*: calcium antagonist.
Kalziumkanalblocker *m*: calcium channel blocker.
Kalziumoxid *n*: calcium oxide, lime.
Kalziurie *f*: calciuria.
Kamille *f*: chamomile.
Kamm *m*: ridge, crest, crista.
Kammer *f*: ventricle, chamber.
Kammeraneurysma *n*: ventricular aneurysm.
Kammerarrhythmie *f*: ventricular arrhythmia.
Kammerasystolie *f*: ventricular standstill.
Kammerautomatie *f*: ventricular automatism.
Kammerbigeminie *f*: ventricular bigeminy.
Kammerblock *m*: ventricular block.
Kammerbradykardie *f*: ventricular bradycardia.
Kammerdruck *m*: intraventricular pressure.
Kammereigenrhythmus *m*: idioventricular rhythm.
Kammerersatzrhythmus *m*: ventricular escape.
Kammerextrasystole *f*: ventricular extrasystole.
Kammerflattern *n*: ventricular flutter.
Kammerflimmern *n*: ventricular fibrillation.
Kammerfrequenz *f*: ventricular rate.
Kammerkomplex *m*: ventricular complex.
Kammerleitung *f*: ventricular conduction.
Kammerrhythmus *m*: ventricular rhythm.
Kammerscheidewand *f*: interventricular septum.
Kammerschrittmacher *m*: ventricular pacemaker.
Kammerstimulation *f*: ventricular pacing.
Kammersystole *f*: ventricular systole.
Kammertachykardie *f*: ventricular tachycardia.
Kammerwinkel *m*: iridocorneal angle.
Kampfer *m*: camphor.
Kampferliniment *n*: camphor liniment.
Kampferöl *n*: camphor oil.
Kampfgas *n*: war gas.
Kamptomelie *f*: camptomelia.
Kanal *m*: canal, channel, tunnel, tubule; **aortolinksventrikulärer** ≈ aortico-left ventricular tunnel; **unnatürlicher** ≈ false passage.
Kanamycin *n*: kanamycin.
Kandidamykose *f*: candidiasis, candidosis.
Kankroid *n*: cancroid.
Kannabis *m*: cannabis.
Kanner-Syndrom *n*: Kanner syndrome, early infantile autism.
Kante *f*: edge, margin.
Kanüle *f*: syringe, cannula, drain.
kanzerogen: cancerogenic, carcinogenic.
Kapazität *f*: capacity.
kapillär: capillary.
Kapillarangiom *n*: capillary hemangioma.
Kapillarbett *n*: capillary bed.
Kapillarblutung *f*: punctate bleeding.
Kapillardruck *m*: capillary pressure.
Kapillare *f*: capillary.
Kapillarembolie *f*: capillary embolism.
Kapillarfragilität *f*: capillary fragility.
Kapillarhämangiom *n*: capillary hemangioma.
Kapillarpermeabilität *f*: capillary permeability.
Kapillarpuls *m*: capillary pulse, nail pulse, Quincke's pulse.

Kapillarschenkel *m*: capillary loop.
Kapillarschleife *f*: capillary loop.
Kapillarwiderstand *m*: capillary resistance.
Kaposi-Sarkom *n*: Kaposi sarcoma, KS, multiple idiopathic hemorrhagic sarcoma.
Kappe *f*: cap; **phrygische** ≈ phrygian cap.
Kapsel *f*: capsule, capsula.
Kapselantigen *n*: capsular antigen, K antigen.
Kapselblutung *f*: capsular hemorrhage.
Kapselentfernung *f*: capsulectomy, decapsulation.
Kapselentzündung *f*: capsulitis, inflammation of a capsule.
Kapseleröffnung *f*: capsulotomy.
Kapsellähmung *f*: capsular hemiplegia.
Kapselphlegmone *f*: capsular phlegmon.
Kapselpolstar *m*: capsulolenticular cataract.
Kapselstar *m*: capsular cataract.
Karbolsäure *f*: carbolic acid, phenol.
Karbunkel *m*: carbuncle.
Kardia *f*: cardia.
Kardiakarzinom *n*: carcinoma of the cardia.
kardial: cardiac, cardial.
Kardiogramm *n*: cardiogram.
Kardiologie *f*: cardiology.
Kardiomyopathie *f*: cardiomyopathy, heart muscle disease; **alkoholische** ≈ alcoholic cardiomyopathy; **diabetische** ≈ diabetic cardiomyopathy; **hereditäre** ≈ familial cardiomyopathy; **hypertrophe** ≈ hypertrophic cardiomyopathy; **hypertrophe obstruktive** ≈ hypertrophic obstructive cardiomyopathy, HOCM; **nichtobstruktive** ≈ nonobstructive hypertrophic cardiomyopathy; **obstruktive hypertrophe** ≈ obstructive hypertrophic cardiomyopathy; **thyreotoxische** ≈ thyrotoxic cardiomyopathy; **toxische** ≈ toxic cardiomyopathy.
Kardiopathie *f*: cardiopathy, heart disease.
kardiopulmonal: cardiopulmonary.
Kardiotomie *f*: cardiotomy.
Kardiotonikum *n*: cardiotonic.
kardiovaskulär: cardiovascular.
Karditis *f*: carditis; **akute rheumatische** ≈ acute rheumatic carditis.
Karies *f*: caries, tooth decay.
Karlsbader Salz *n*: Carlsbad salt.
Karnofsky-Aktivitätsindex *m*: Karnofsky performance index.
Karotis *f*: carotid artery.
Karotisangiographie *f*: carotid arteriography, carotid angiography.
Karotiskörper *m*: carotid body.
Karotissinussyndrom *n*: carotid sinus syndrome, Charcot-Weiss-Baker syndrome.
Karotisstenose *f*: carotid stenosis.
Karpalgelenk *n*: mediocarpal joint.
Karpaltunnelsyndrom *n*: carpal tunnel syndrome.
Karpometakarpalreflex *m*: carpometacarpal reflex.
Karpopedalspasmus *m*: carpopedal spasm.
Karpophalangealreflex *m*: carpophalangeal reflex.
Karpus *m*: carpus, wrist.
Kartenherzbecken *n*: cordiform pelvis, cordate pelvis.
Kartoffelnase *f*: potato nose, rhinophyma.
Karunkel *f*: caruncle.
Karyoblast *m*: karyoblast.
Karyogramm *n*: karyogram.
Karyon *n*: karyon.
Karyotyp *m*: karyotype.
karzinogen: carcinogenic.
Karzinogenese *f*: carcinogenesis.
Karzinoid *n*: carcinoid.
Karzinom *n*: carcinoma, cancer; **argentaffines** ≈ argentaffin carcinoma; **branchiogenes** ≈ branchiogenic carcinoma, branchioma; **embryonales** ≈ embryonal carcinoma, undifferentiated malignant teratoma; **entdifferenziertes** ≈ anaplastic carcinoma; **exophytisch wachsendes** ≈ exophytic carcinoma; **follikuläres** ≈ follicular carcinoma; **fungusartiges** ≈ fungating carcinoma; **inzidentes** ≈ incidental cancer; **kleinzel-**

liges ≈ small-cell carcinoma; **latentes** ≈ latent cancer; **medulläres** ≈ cerebriform carcinoma; **multizentrisches** ≈ multicentric cancer; **muzinöses** ≈ colloma; **okkultes** ≈ occult carcinoma; **polypoides** ≈ polypoid carcinoma; **präinvasives** ≈ preinvasive carcinoma, carcinoma in situ; **szirrhöses** ≈ scirrhous carcinoma; **trabekuläres** ≈ trabecular carcinoma; **undifferenziertes** ≈ undifferentiated carcinoma.

Kasein *n*: casein.

Kaskadenmagen *m*: cascade stomach.

Kastration *f*: castration; **chirurgische** ≈ surgical castration; **medikamentöse** ≈ pharmacological castration.

Kasugamycin *n*: kasugamycin.

Kasuistik *f*: case report.

Katabolismus *m*: catabolism.

Katadikrotie *f*: catadicrotic pulse.

Katalase *f*: catalase.

Katalepsie *f*: catalepsy.

Katalysator *m*: catalyzer, catalyst.

Kataphylaxie *f*: cataphylaxis.

Kataplexie *f*: cataplexy.

Katarakt *f*: cataract; **angeborene** ≈ congenital cataract; **berufsbedingte** ≈ occupational cataract; **diabetische** ≈ diabetic cataract; **infantile** ≈ infantile cataract; **periphere** ≈ peripheral cataract; **reife** ≈ mature cataract; **sonnenblumenartige** ≈ sunflower cataract; **sternförmige** ≈ stellate cataract; **unreife** ≈ immature cataract.

Katarrh *m*: catarrh, catarrhal inflammation.

Katatonie *f*: catatonia, catatonic schizophrenia.

Katechin *n*: catechin, catechol.

Katecholamin *n*: catecholamine.

Katharsis *f*: catharsis.

Kathartikum *n*: cathartic.

Katheter *m*: catheter; **doppellumiger** ≈ double-current catheter; **flexibler** ≈ flexible catheter, soft catheter; **gekrümmter** ≈ bent catheter.

Katheterangioplastie *f*: catheter angioplasty.

Katheterisierung *f*: catheterization.

Kathetersepsis *f*: catheter fever.

Kationenaustauscherharz *n*: cation exchange resin.

Katzenkratzkrankheit *f*: cat-scratch fever, benign lymphoreticulosis.

Kaubewegung *f*: chewing motion, mastication.

Kaudakompression *f*: compression of the cauda equina.

kaudal: caudal.

Kaudalanästhesie *f*: caudal anesthesia, caudal block.

Kaudasyndrom *n*: cauda equina syndrome.

kauen: chew, bite.

Kaumuskellähmung *f*: masticatory paralysis.

kausal: causal, causative.

Kaustikum *n*: caustic, cauterant.

Kautablette *f*: chewing tablet.

Kauter *m*: cautery knife.

Kauterisation *f*: cauterization, cautery.

Kavaclip *m*: caval clip.

Kavain *n*: kawain.

Kavaschirm *m*: caval umbrella.

Kava-Syndrom *n*: vena cava syndrome.

Kaverne *f*: cavern.

kavernös: cavernous.

Kavographie *f*: cavography, venacavography.

Kawa *f*: kava.

Kebuzon *n*: kebuzone.

Kehldeckel *m*: epiglottis.

Kehle *f*: throat, guttur.

Kehlkopf *m*: larynx; **künstlicher** ≈ laryngeal prosthesis, voice prosthesis.

Kehlkopfdiphtherie *f*: laryngeal diphtheria, diphtheritic laryngitis.

Kehlkopfdivertikel *n*: laryngeal diverticulum.

Kehlkopflähmung *f*: laryngeal paralysis, laryngoparalysis.

Kehlkopfreflex *m*: laryngeal reflex.

Kehlkopfschwindel *m*: laryngeal vertigo.

Kehlkopfspiegelung *f*: laryngoscopy.

Kehlkopfstenose *f*: laryngeal stenosis.

Kehlkopftuberkulose *f*: laryngeal tuberculosis, tuberculous laryngitis.

Kehlkopftumor *m*: laryngeal neoplasm.
Keilbein *n*: sphenoid, wedge bone.
Keilbeinhöhle *f*: sphenoidal sinus.
keilförmig: sphenoid, wedge-shaped, cuneiform.
Keilosteotomie *f*: wedge osteotomy, cuneiform osteotomy.
Keim *m*: infectious agent, germ, bud.
Keimblatt *n*: germ layer, blastodermic layer; **äußeres** ≈ ectoderm; **inneres** ≈ endoderm; **mittleres** ≈ mesoderm; **viszerales** ≈ visceral layer.
Keimdrüse *f*: gonad.
Keimdrüsenhormon *n*: gonadal hormone.
Keimfaktor *m*: germinal factor.
Keimfreiheit *f*: sterility, asepsis.
Keimschädigung *f*: embryopathy.
Keimzahlbestimmung *f*: bacterial count, germ count.
Keith-Flack-Knoten *m*: Keith-Flack node, sinus node.
Kelchdivertikel *n*: caliceal diverticulum.
Keloid *n*: keloid; **falsches** ≈ false keloid, cicatricial keloid.
Kelvin-Temperaturskala *f*: Kelvin scale.
Kephalgie *f*: cephalgia, headache.
Kephalhämatom *n*: cephalhematoma, cephalohematoma.
Kephalometrie *f*: cephalometry.
Kephalozele *f*: cephalocele.
Kerasinspeicherkrankheit *f*: kerasin thesaurismosis.
Keratektasie *f*: keratectasia.
Keratektomie *f*: keratectomy.
Keratin *n*: keratin.
Keratinozyt *m*: keratinocyte.
Keratitis *f*: keratitis; **herpetische** ≈ herpetic keratitis; **neuroparalytische** ≈ neuroparalytic keratitis; **sklerosierende** ≈ sclerosing keratitis, sclerophthalmia.
Keratoakanthom *n*: keratoacanthoma.
Keratokonjunktivitis *f*: keratoconjunctivitis; **allergische** ≈ vernal keratoconjunctivitis; **epidemische** ≈ epidemic keratoconjunctivitis, Sander's disease.
Keratolytikum *n*: keratolytic agent.
Keratom *n*: keratoma, keratoderma.
Keratopathie *f*: keratopathy.
Keratoplastik *f*: keratoplasty.
Keratose *f*: keratosis; **aktinische** ≈ actinic keratosis, senile keratosis; **dysplastische** ≈ epidermodysplasia; **spreitende pigmentierte aktinische** ≈ spreading pigmented actinic keratosis.
Keratosis senilis *f*: senile keratosis, actinic keratosis.
Keratoskopie *f*: keratoscopy.
Kerckring-Falten: Kerckring's folds, valves of Kerckring.
Kern *m*: nucleus, core.
Kernaplasie *f*: nuclear aplasia, nuclear agenesis.
Kerndysplasie *f*: nuclear dysplasia.
Kerneinschluss *m*: intranuclear inclusion.
Kernhülle *f*: nuclear membrane.
Kernig-Zeichen *n*: Kernig sign.
Kernikterus *m*: kernicterus, nuclear jaundice.
Kernkatarakt *f*: nuclear cataract.
Kernkörperchen *n*: nucleolus.
Kernlähmung *f*: nuclear paralysis, nuclear ophthalmoplegia.
Kernresonanz *f*: nuclear resonance.
Kernspinmagnetresonanz *f*: nuclear magnetic spin resonance.
Kernspinresonanzspektroskopie *f*: nuclear magnetic resonance spectroscopy.
Kernspinresonanztomographie *f*: nuclear magnetic resonance tomography, NMR tomography
Kernstar *m*: nuclear cataract.
Kernteilung *f*: nuclear division.
Kerntemperatur *f*: core temperature.
Kernverschiebung *f*: nuclear shift.
Ketamin *n*: ketamine.
Ketazolam *n*: ketazolam.
Ketoazidose *f*: ketoacidosis; **diabetische** ≈ diabetic acidosis.
Ketoazidurie *f*: ketoaciduria.
Ketoconazol *n*: ketoconazole.
ketogen: ketogenic.
Ketoglutarsäure *f*: ketoglutaric acid.
Ketonämie *f*: ketonemia.
Ketonkörper *m*: ketone body.

Ketonsäure *f*: keto acid.
Ketonurie *f*: ketonuria.
ketoplastisch: ketoplastic.
Ketoprofen *n*: ketoprofen.
Ketorolac *n*: ketorolac.
Ketose *f*: ketosis.
Ketosteroid *n*: ketosteroid.
Ketotifen *n*: ketotifen.
Kette *f*: chain; **leichte** ≈ light chain; **schwere** ≈ heavy chain; **verzweigte** ≈ branched chain.
keuchen: whoop, wheeze, gasp.
Keuchhusten *m*: whooping cough, pertussis.
Kiefer *m*: jaw, jowl.
Kieferchirurgie *f*: dental surgery, maxillofacial surgery.
Kieferfixation *f*: intermaxillary fixation, maxillomandibular fixation.
Kieferfraktur *f*: jaw fracture.
Kiefer-Gaumen-Spalte *f*: gnathopalatoschisis.
Kiefergelenk *n*: mandibular joint.
Kieferhöhle *f*: maxillary sinus.
Kieferhöhlenentzündung *f*: maxillary sinusitis.
Kieferhöhlenradikaloperation *f*: radical maxillary antrostomy, Caldwell-Luc operation.
Kieferklemme *f*: lockjaw, trismus.
Kieferknochen *m*: jawbone.
Kieferorthopädie *f*: orthodontics, orthodontology.
Kieferspalte *f*: gnathoschisis, cleft jaw.
Kielbauch *m*: carinate abdomen.
Kielbrust *f*: keeled chest, pectus carinatum.
kielförmig: keel-shaped, carinate.
Kiemenbogen *m*: branchial arch, pharyngeal arch.
Kiemenbogenspalte *f*: branchial cleft.
Kiemengangfistel *f*: branchial fistula.
Kiemengangzyste *f*: branchial cyst.
Kiemenspalte *f*: branchial fissure.
Kienböck-Zeichen *n*: Kienböck's phenomenon, paradoxical diaphragmatic contraction.
Kies *m*: gravel.
Kieselsäure *f*: silicic acid.
Killerzelle *f*: killer cell, killer lymphocyte; **natürliche** ≈ natural killer cell.
Kimmelstiel-Wilson-Syndrom *n*: Kimmelstiel-Wilson syndrome, diabetic glomerulosclerosis.
Kinästhesie *f*: kinesthesia, kinesthetic sensibility.
Kinase *f*: kinase.
Kind *n*: child, infant.
Kindbett *n*: childbed, puerperium.
Kindbettfieber *n*: childbed fever, puerperal sepsis.
Kindbettmastitis *f*: puerperal mastitis.
Kinderheilkunde *f*: pediatrics.
Kinderkrankenhaus *n*: children's hospital, pediatric hospital.
Kinderkrankheit *f*: children's disease.
Kinderlähmung *f*: infantile paralysis, paralytic poliomyelitis; **zerebrale** ≈ cerebral spastic infantile paralysis, infantile cerebral palsy.
kindersicher: childproof.
Kinder- und Jugendpsychiatrie *f*: child and adolescent psychiatry.
Kindesmissbrauch, sexueller *m*: childhood sexual abuse.
Kindesmisshandlung *f*: child abuse, battered-child syndrome.
Kindheit *f*: childhood.
kindisch: childish, puerile.
Kindsbewegung *f*: fetal movement.
Kindseinstellung *f*: presentation, fetal attitude.
Kindslage *f*: position, presentation.
Kindspech *n*: meconium.
Kindsteile: fetal parts.
Kindstod, plötzlicher *m*: sudden infant death syndrome, SIDS.
Kineplastik *f*: kineplasty.
Kinese *f*: kinesis.
Kinesiotherapie *f*: kinesiotherapy, kinesitherapy.
Kinetik *f*: kinetics.
Kinetose *f*: kinetosis, motion sickness.
Kinking *n*: kinking.
Kinky-Hair-Syndrom *n*: kinky hair syndrome, Menkes syndrome.
Kinn *n*: chin, mentum.
Kinnlage *f*: chin presentation.
Kinnregion *f*: chin region.

Kissen *n*: pillow, cushion, pad.
Kitasamycin *n*: kitasamycin, leucomycin.
Kitzelgefühl *n*: tickle, titillation, gargalesthesia.
Kitzeln *n*: tickling, titillation.
klagen: complain.
Klammer *f*: clamp, clasp.
Klammerhalter *m*: clamp holder.
Klammernaht *f*: clip suture.
Klammernahtgerät *n*: surgical stapler.
Klang *m*: sound, tone.
Klappe *f*: valve; **kleine** ≈ small valve, valvula.
Klappendehiszenz *f*: valve dehiscence.
Klappeninsuffizienz *f*: valve insufficiency, valvular insufficiency.
Klappensegel *n*: valve leaflet.
Klappenstenose *f*: valve stenosis, valvular stenosis.
klar: clear, bright, lucid.
Klarzellenadenom *n*: clear cell adenoma.
Klarzelltumor *m*: clear cell tumor.
Klassifikation *f*: classification.
Klatschmassage *f*: clapping.
Klauenfuß *m*: clawfoot.
Klauenhand *f*: clawhand.
Klaustrophobie *f*: claustrophobia.
Klavikula *f*: clavicle, collar bone.
Klavikulafraktur *f*: clavicular fracture.
Klavikularlinie, mittlere *f*: midclavicular line.
Klavus *m*: clavus, corn.
Klebsiellenpneumonie *f*: Klebsiella pneumonia, Friedländer's pneumonia.
Kleidotomie *f*: cleidotomy.
Kleienflechte *f*: pityriasis versicolor.
Kleinhirn *n*: cerebellum.
Kleinhirnabszess *m*: cerebellar abscess.
Kleinhirnanfall *m*: cerebellar fit.
Kleinhirnatrophie *f*: cerebellar atrophy.
Kleinhirnblutung *f*: cerebellar hemorrhage.
Kleinhirnbrückenwinkel *m*: cerebellopontine angle.
Kleinhirnbrückenwinkelsyndrom *n*: pontocerebellar angle syndrome, Cushing syndrome.
Kleinhirnbrückenwinkeltumor *m*: angle tumor.
Kleinhirndegeneration *f*: cerebellar degeneration.
Kleinhirnepilepsie *f*: cerebellar epilepsy.
Kleinhirnfunktionsstörung *f*: cerebellar dysfunction.
Kleinhirngrube *f*: cerebellar fossa.
Kleinhirnhemisphäre *f*: cerebellar hemisphere.
Kleinhirninfarkt *m*: cerebellar infarct.
Kleinhirnlappen *m*: cerebellar lobe.
Kleinhirnschwindel *m*: cerebellar vertigo.
Kleinhirnsyndrom *n*: cerebellar syndrome, cerebelloparenchymal disorder; **erworbenes** ≈ acquired cerebellar syndrome, Goldstein-Reichmann syndrome.
Kleinhirntumor *m*: cerebellar neoplasm.
Kleinkind *n*: infant, toddler.
Kleinkindalter *n*: infancy.
kleinzellig: parvicellular, small-cell.
Klemme *f*: clip, clamp.
Kletterpuls *m*: rapidly increasing pulse rate.
klientenzentriert: client-centered.
Klima *n*: climate.
Klimafaktor *m*: climatic factor.
klimakterisch: climacteric.
Klimakterium *n*: climacterium.
Klimakur *f*: climatic cure.
Klimax *f*: climax.
Klinefelter-Syndrom *n*: Klinefelter syndrome, XXY syndrome.
Klinge *f*: blade.
klingen: sound, tingle.
Klinik *f*: clinic, hospital.
klinisch: clinical.
Klippel-Trénaunay-Syndrom *n*: Klippel-Trénaunay syndrome, angioosteohypertrophy.
Klistier *n*: clyster, enema.
Klitoris *f*: clitoris.
Klitorisvergrößerung *f*: clitoromegaly.

Kloakenmembran *f*: cloacal membrane.
Klon *m*: clone.
klonen: clone.
klonisch: clonic.
Klonus *m*: clonus.
klopfen: percuss, tap.
Klopfen *n*: percussion, tapping.
klopfend: pulsatory.
Klopfschall *m*: percussion sound.
Klopfschalldämpfung *f*: dullness on percussion.
Klumpen *m*: clot, plug, lump.
Klumpfuß *m*: clubfoot, talipes, equinovarus, supination of the foot.
Klumphand *f*: clubhand, talipomanus.
Klumpke-Lähmung *f*: Klumpke's paralysis, lower brachial plexus paralysis.
Knäuel *n*: coil, convolution.
Knäueldrüse *f*: convoluted gland.
Knapp-Schieloperation *f*: Knapp's operation.
Knaus-Ogino-Methode *f*: Ogino-Knaus method.
Kneipp-Kur *f*: Kneipp cure, hydropathic treatment.
Knetmassage *f*: kneading massage, pétrissage.
Knickbruch *m*: greenstick fracture, willow fracture.
Knickfuß *m*: pes valgus, skewfoot.
Knie *n*: knee, genu.
Knie-Brust-Lage *f*: knee-chest position.
Knie-Ellbogen-Lage *f*: knee-elbow position.
Kniegelenk *n*: knee joint.
Kniegelenkerguss *m*: knee joint effusion.
Knie-Gesicht-Lage *f*: genufacial position.
Knie-Hacken-Versuch *m*: heel-knee test.
Kniekehle *f*: popliteal cavity.
Kniekussphänomen *n*: spine sign.
Knielage *f*: knee position, knee presentation.
Kniescheibe *f*: kneecap, patella.
Knistergeräusch *n*: crackling sound, crunching sound.
Knisterrasseln *n*: crepitation, crepitant rale.
Knochen *m*: bone, os; **akzessorischer** ≈ accessory bone, supernumerary bone; **heterotoper** ≈ heterotopic bone; **kurzer** ≈ short bone; **langer** ≈ long bone; **periostaler** ≈ periosteal bone; **planer** ≈ plane bone; **subperiostaler** ≈ subperiosteal bone.
Knochenalter *n*: bone age, skeletal age.
Knochenbildung *f*: ossification, bone formation.
Knochenbiopsie *f*: bone biopsy.
Knochenbruch *m*: bone fracture; **gesplitterter** ≈ comminuted fracture; **pathologischer** ≈ pathologic fracture; **spontaner** ≈ pathologic fracture; **verkeilter** ≈ impacted fracture.
Knochenbrucheinrichtung *f*: reduction, redressement.
Knochendichte *f*: bone density.
Knochenentwicklung *f*: bone development, osteogenesis.
Knochenhämangiom *n*: intraosseous hemangioma.
Knochenkern *m*: ossification center.
Knochenlamelle *f*: osseous lamella.
Knochenleiste *f*: crest, ridge, crista.
Knochenleitung *f*: bone conduction, osteotympanic conduction.
Knochenmark *n*: bone marrow; **gelbes** ≈ yellow marrow, fat marrow; **rotes** ≈ red marrow.
Knochenmarkaplasie *f*: bone marrow aplasia.
Knochenmarkpunktion *f*: bone marrow puncture.
Knochenmarktransplantation *f*: bone marrow transplantation.
Knochennekrose *f*: osteonecrosis, necrosis of the bone; **aseptische** ≈ aseptic necrosis of bone.
Knochenresektion *f*: osteoectomy, ostectomy.
Knochensarkom *n*: osteosarcoma.
Knochenschallleitung *f*: osteoacousis, osteophony.
Knochenschmerz *m*: bone pain.
Knochenspan *m*: bone onlay.
Knochenszintigramm *n*: bone scintigram.

K

Knochentuberkulose *f*: tuberculosis of the bones, skeletal tuberculosis.
Knochentumor *m*: bone tumor.
Knochenverschmelzung *f*: diaphyseal-epiphyseal fusion.
Knochenzacke *f*: spur.
Knochenzange *f*: bone-cutting forceps, rongeur, vulsellum.
Knochenzement *m*: bone cement.
Knochenzyste *f*: bone cyst, osteocystoma.
Knöchel *m*: knuckle, malleolus, ankle.
Knöchelchen *n*: ossicle, bonelet.
Knöchelödem *n*: ankle edema.
knöchern: osseous, bony.
Knötchen *n*: nodule, nodulus, tubercle.
Knötchenleber *f*: nodular liver.
knollenartig: bulbiform, bulbous.
Knopflochabszess *m*: shirt-stud abscess.
Knopflochdeformität *f*: buttonhole deformity, boutonnière deformity.
Knopflochnaht *f*: double-button suture.
Knopfsonde *f*: blunt probe.
Knorpel *m*: cartilage; **elastischer** ≈ elastic cartilage; **faseriger** ≈ fibrocartilage; **hyaliner** ≈ hyaline cartilage; **ossifizierender** ≈ ossifying cartilage.
Knorpelgewebe *n*: cartilaginous tissue.
Knospe *f*: bud.
knospen: bud, germinate.
Knoten *m*: node, nodule, notch, knot; **chirurgischer** ≈ surgeon's knot; **dikroter** ≈ dicrotic notch; **falscher** ≈ false knot; **heißer** ≈ hot nodule, warm nodule; **kalter** ≈ cold nodule; **metastatischer** ≈ metastatic nodule; **sinuatrialer** ≈ sinoatrial node, S-A node.
Knotenersatzrhythmus *m*: nodal escape.
Knotenrhythmus *m*: nodal rhythm.
Knotenstruma *f*: nodular goitre, adenomatous struma.
Koagulation *f*: coagulation.
koagulieren: coagulate, clot.
Koagulopathie *f*: coagulopathy.
Koagulum *n*: blood clot.
Koarktation *f*: coarctation.
Koaxialkatheter *m*: coaxial catheter.
Kobalamin *n*: cobalamin, vitamin B_{12}.
Kobalt *n*: cobalt, Co; **radioaktives** ≈ radioactive cobalt, radiocobalt.
kochleär: cochlear.
Kochleopupillarreflex *m*: cochleopupillary reflex.
Kochsalz *n*: sodium chloride, common salt; **jodiertes** ≈ iodized salt.
Kochsalzlösung *f*: sodium chloride solution; **gepufferte** ≈ buffered saline solution; **isotone** ≈ isotonic saline solution; **physiologische** ≈ physiologic sodium chloride solution.
Koch-Weeks-Konjunktivitis *f*: Koch-Weeks conjunctivitis, acute contagious conjunctivitis.
Kode *m*: code; **genetischer** ≈ genetic code.
Kodein *n*: codeine.
Kodominanz *f*: codominance.
Kodon *n*: codon.
Köbner-Phänomen *n*: Köbner's phenomenon, isomorphic effect.
Koenen-Tumor *m*: Koenen's tumor, periungual fibroma.
Koenzym *n*: coenzyme.
Körnchen *n*: granule.
körnig: granular.
Körper *m*: body, corps, corpus.
Körperachse *f*: axis of the body.
Körperbau *m*: body constitution, physique; **athletischer** ≈ athletic constitution; **leptosomer** ≈ leptosomia.
Körperbehaarung *f*: hairiness; **abnorm starke** ≈ excessive hairiness, polytrichia.
Körperbeherrschung *f*: body control.
Körperbehinderung *f*: physical disability, physical handicap.
Körperchen *n*: corpuscle, small body; **metachromatische** ≈ metachromatic particles, volutin granules; **sichelförmiges** ≈ demilune body; **zytoides** ≈ cytoid body.
Körperebene *f*: plane, planum.
körpereigen: autogenous.
Körperempfinden *n*: body sense, somesthesia.
Körperflüssigkeit *f*: body fluid.
Körpergewicht *n*: body weight.

Körpergröße *f*: body size.
Körperhaltung *f*: body posture.
Körperhygiene *f*: personal hygiene.
Körperkreislauf *m*: systemic circulation, greater circulation.
Körperlänge *f*: body length.
körperlich: physical, somatic.
Körperoberfläche *f*: body surface.
Körperöffnung *f*: orifice, opening.
Körperpflege *f*: personal hygiene.
Körperschema *n*: body scheme, body image.
Körperstellreflex *m*: body-righting reflex.
Körperstellung *f*: body position, posture.
Körpertemperatur *f*: body temperature.
Körperzelle *f*: body cell, somatic cell.
Kofaktor *m*: cofactor.
Koffein *n*: caffeine.
Kognition *f*: cognition.
kognitiv: cognitive.
Kohle *f*: coal, carbon.
Kohlendioxid *n*: carbon dioxide.
Kohlenhydrat *n*: carbohydrate.
Kohlenmonoxid *n*: carbon monoxide.
Kohlenmonoxidhämoglobin *n*: carboxyhemoglobin.
Kohlenmonoxidvergiftung *f*: carbon monoxide poisoning.
Kohlensäure *f*: carbonic acid.
Kohlenstaublunge *f*: coal-worker's lung, anthracosis.
Kohlenstoff *m*: carbon.
Kohlenwasserstoff *m*: hydrocarbon.
Kohortenstudie *f*: cohort study.
Koilonychie *f*: koilonychia, spoon nail.
Koinfektion *f*: coinfection.
Koitus *m*: coitus, intercourse.
Kokain *n*: cocaine.
Kokarzinogen *n*: cocarcinogen.
Kokke *f*: coccus.
Kokkzidioidomykose *f*: coccidioidomycosis.
Kokzygodynie *f*: coccygodynia, coccyalgia.
Kolben *m*: flask, ampulla.
Kolbenfinger *m*: clubbed finger, drumstick finger.
Kolektomie *f*: colectomy.
Kolibakterie *f*: colibacillus.
koliform: coliform.
Kolik *f*: colic, gripe.
Kolitis *f*: colitis; **granulomatöse** ≈ granulomatous colitis; **mukomembranöse** ≈ mucous colitis, mucomembranous enteritis; **pseudomembranöse** ≈ pseudomembranous enterocolitis.
kollabieren: collapse.
Kollagen *n*: collagen.
Kollagenfaser *f*: collagen fiber.
Kollaps *m*: collapse.
kollateral: collateral.
Kollaterale *f*: collateral.
Kollateralkreislauf *m*: compensatory circulation.
Kollektiv *n*: collective, population.
Kollektivdosis *f*: collective dose.
Kolliquationsnekrose *f*: colliquative necrosis.
Kollodiaphysenwinkel *m*: collodiaphyseal angle.
Kollodium *n*: collodion.
Kolloid *n*: colloid; **hydrophiles** ≈ lyophilic colloid; **lyophobes** ≈ lyophobic colloid; **radioaktives** ≈ radiocolloid.
Kolloidstruma *f*: colloid goiter, follicular goiter.
Kolloidzyste *f*: colloid cyst.
Kolobom *n*: coloboma.
Kolon *n*: colon; **irritables** ≈ irritable colon; **starres** ≈ lead-pipe colon.
Kolonblutung *f*: colonic bleeding.
Kolondivertikel *n*: colonic diverticulum.
Kolondivertikulitis *f*: colonic diverticulitis.
Koloneinlauf *m*: colonic enema.
Kolonfistel *f*: colonic fistula.
koloniebildend: colony-forming.
Kolonlavage *f*: colonic lavage.
kolorektal: colorectal.
Kolostomie *f*: colostomy; **endständige** ≈ end colostomy; **feuchte** ≈ wet colostomy; **ileotransversale** ≈ ileotransverse colostomy; **trockene** ≈ dry colostomy.
Kolostrum *n*: colostrum, foremilk.
Kolotomie *f*: colotomy.
Kolpitis *f*: colpitis, vaginitis.
Kolpoplastik *f*: colpoplasty.

Kolporrhagie *f*: colporrhagia, vaginal bleeding.
Kolporrhaphie *f*: colporrhaphy.
Kolposkop *n*: colposcope, vaginoscope.
Kolposkopie *f*: colposcopy, vaginoscopy.
Kolpotomie *f*: colpotomy, vaginotomy.
Kolpozele *f*: colpocele.
Kolpozytologie *f*: colpocytology, vaginal cytology.
Koma *n*: coma; **diabetisches** ≈ diabetic coma; **hepatisches** ≈ hepatic coma; **hypoglykämisches** ≈ hypoglycemic coma; **hypophysäres** ≈ hypopituitary coma; **ketoazidotisches** ≈ diabetic coma; **thyreotoxisches** ≈ thyrotoxic coma; **tiefes** ≈ deep coma; **urämisches** ≈ uremic coma; **vigiles** ≈ vigil coma.
komatös: comatose.
Komazylinder *m*: coma cast.
Kombinationsimpfstoff *m*: combined vaccine.
Kombinationstherapie *f*: combination therapy.
Komedo *m*: comedo; **reifer** ≈ open comedo, blackhead.
Komminutivfraktur *f*: comminuted fracture.
Kommissur *f*: commissure.
Kommissurensyndrom, hypothalamisches *n*: hypothalamic chiasmal syndrome.
Kommunikationsstörung *f*: communication disorder.
Kompakta *f*: compact tissue, solid bone.
Kompartiment *n*: compartment.
Kompatibilität *f*: compatibility.
Kompensation *f*: compensation.
Komplement *n*: complement, C.
Komplementärmedizin *f*: complementary medicine.
Komplementbindungsreaktion *f*: complement fixation test, CFT.
Komplex *m*: complex; **immunstimulierender** ≈ immune-stimulating complex; **inerter** ≈ inert complex.
Komplikation *f*: complication.
kompliziert: complicated.
Kompresse *f*: compress.
Kompression *f*: compression.
Kompressionsatelektase *f*: compression atelectasis.
Kompressionsfraktur *f*: compression fracture, crush fracture.
Kompressionsklemme *f*: crushing clamp.
Kompressionslähmung *f*: pressure paralysis.
Kompressionsverband *m*: compression bandage, compression dressing.
Konchektomie *f*: conchectomy, turbinectomy.
Konditionierung *f*: conditioning; **klassische** ≈ classical conditioning, Pavlovian conditioning; **operante** ≈ operant conditioning; **retrograde** ≈ backward conditioning; **verbale** ≈ verbal conditioning.
Kondom *n*: condom.
Konduktor *m*: conductor.
Kondylenfraktur *f*: condylar fracture.
Kondylom *n*: condyloma, genital wart; **spitzes** ≈ condyloma acuminatum, acuminate wart; **flaches** ≈ condyloma latum, flat condyloma.
Kondylus *m*: condyle, condylus.
Konfabulation *f*: confabulation.
Konfidenzintervall *n*: confidence interval.
konfluierend: confluent.
kongenital: congenital, inborn, innate.
Kongestion *f*: congestion.
Kongestionsabszess *m*: congestive abscess, wandering abscess.
Kongestionskopfschmerz *m*: congestive headache.
Koniometrie *f*: konimetry.
Konisation *f*: conization.
konisch: conical.
Konjunktivalreflex *m*: conjunctival reflex.
Konjunktivaltest *m*: conjunctival test.
Konjunktiveneinblutung *f*: subconjunctival hemorrhage.
Konjunktivitis *f*: conjunctivitis; **aktinische** ≈ actinic conjunctivitis, ultraviolet ophthalmia; **akute hämor-**

rhagische ≈ acute hemorrhagic conjunctivitis; **akute kontagiöse** ≈ Koch-Weeks conjunctivitis; **allergische** ≈ atopic conjunctivitis; **diphtherische** ≈ diphtheritic conjunctivitis; **gonorrhoische** ≈ gonococcal conjunctivitis; **kruppöse** ≈ croupous conjunctivitis; **membranöse** ≈ membranous conjunctivitis; **proliferative** ≈ hypertrophic conjunctivitis; **pseudomembranöse** ≈ pseudomembranous conjunctivitis.

Konkavlinse *f*: concave lens.

konkavokonvex: concavoconvex.

konkomittierend: concomitant.

Konkrement *n*: concrement, calculus, concretion; **intrazerebrales** ≈ intracerebral concretion.

konnatal: connate.

Konsanguinität *f*: consanguinity.

konservativ: conservative, nonsurgical.

Konsiliararzt *m*: consultant.

Konstitution *f*: body constitution.

konstitutionell: constitutional.

Konstriktion *f*: constriction.

Konsultation *f*: consultation.

konsultieren: consult.

Konsum *m*: consumption.

konsumierend: consumptive.

kontagiös: contagious.

Kontagiosität *f*: contagiosity.

Kontaktallergen *n*: contact allergen.

Kontaktinfektion *f*: direct infection.

Kontaktlinse *f*: contact lens.

Kontaktstörung *f*: contact disorder.

Kontamination *f*: contamination.

Kontinenz *f*: continence.

Kontinuum *n*: continuous murmur.

kontrahieren: contract.

Kontraindikation *f*: contraindication.

Kontraktilität *f*: contractility.

Kontraktion *f*: contraction.

Kontraktionsstriktur *f*: contractile stricture.

Kontraktur *f*: contracture; **ischämische** ≈ ischemic contracture, Volkmann's ischemic contracture.

kontralateral: contralateral, heterolateral.

Kontralateralreflex *m*: contralateral reflex.

Kontrast *m*: contrast.

Kontrastaussparung *f*: filling defect.

Kontrasteinlauf *m*: contrast enema.

Kontrastmittel *n*: contrast medium, radiopaque medium; **bariumhaltiges** ≈ barium contrast medium; **hochosmolares** ≈ high osmolar contrast medium; **niederosmolares** ≈ low osmolar contrast medium.

Kontrastverminderung *f*: diminution of contrast.

Kontrazeption *f*: contraception; **chemische** ≈ chemical contraception; **hormonelle** ≈ hormonal contraception; **natürliche** ≈ natural contraception; **postkoitale** ≈ postcoital contraception.

Kontrazeptivum *n*: contraceptive, contraceptive device; **orales** ≈ oral contraceptive.

Kontrolle *f*: control, check.

Kontrollgruppe *f*: control group.

Kontusion *f*: contusion, concussion, bruise.

Kontusionspneumonie *f*: contusion pneumonia.

Kontusionsverletzung *f*: concussion injury.

Kontusionswunde *f*: contused wound.

Konusbiopsie *f*: conization.

Konussyndrom *n*: conus syndrome.

Konvergenz *f*: convergence.

Konvergenzlähmung *f*: convergent paralysis.

Konvergenzlinse *f*: converging lens.

Konvergenzschielen *n*: convergent strabismus, internal strabismus.

Konversion *f*: conversion, somatization.

Konversionshysterie *f*: conversion hysteria.

konvex: convex.

Konvexlinse *f*: convex lens.

Konvulsion *f*: convulsion.

Konzentration *f*: concentration.

konzentrisch: concentric.

Konzeption *f*: conception.

Konzeptionsverhütung *f*: contraception.

Koordination *f*: coordination; **motorische** ≈ motor coordination.

K

Kopf *m*: head, caput; **frei beweglicher** ≈ floating head; **reitender** ≈ overriding head.
Kopfeinstellung *f*: engaged head.
kopfförmig: capitate.
Kopfgrind *m*: favus, white-cap, favic alopecia.
Kopflage *f*: head presentation.
Kopflaus *f*: head louse.
kopflos: acephalic, headless.
Kopfschmerz *m*: headache, cephalgia; **gewöhnlicher** ≈ common everyday headache; **meningitischer** ≈ meningeal headache; **neuralgischer** ≈ neuralgic headache; **postpunktioneller** ≈ leakage headache, lumbar puncture headache; **posttraumatischer** ≈ traumatic headache; **prämenstrueller** ≈ premenstrual headache; **symptomatischer** ≈ symptomatic headache, reflex headache; **vasomotorischer** ≈ vasomotor headache.
Kopfschuppen: scurf, dandruff.
Kopfverletzung *f*: head injury.
Kopfwackeln *n*: nutation.
kopieren: replicate, copy.
Koplik-Flecken: Koplik spots.
Koprolalie *f*: coprolalia.
Koprolith *m*: coprolith.
Kopulation *f*: copulation.
Korakoidfortsatz *m*: coracoid.
Korbhenkelriss *m*: basket handle tear.
Korkstaublunge *f*: cork dust pneumoconiosis, suberosis.
Kornährenverband *m*: spica bandage, capistrum.
Kornealreflex *m*: corneal reflex, eyelid closure reflex.
Koro *n*: koro.
koronar: coronary.
Koronarangiographie *f*: coronary angiography.
Koronarangioplastie *f*: coronary angioplasty.
Koronararterie *f*: coronary artery.
Koronararteriensklerose *f*: coronary arteriosclerosis.
Koronararterienstenose *f*: coronary stenosis.
Koronarebene *f*: coronal plane, frontal plane.
Koronarembolie *f*: coronary embolism.
Koronarkreislauf *m*: coronary circulation.
Koronarreserve *f*: coronary reserve.
Koronarsklerose *f*: coronary sclerosis.
koronoid: coronoid.
Korotkow-Geräusche: Korotkoff sounds.
Korpulenz *f*: corpulency.
Korpus *m*: corpus, body.
Korpuskarzinom *n*: uterus carcinoma.
Korpuskel *n*: corpuscle.
Korrekturosteotomie *f*: corrective osteotomy.
Korsakoff-Psychose *f*: Korsakoff's psychosis, amnestic-confabulatory syndrome.
Korsett *n*: corset.
Kortex *m*: cortex, cortical layer; **akustischer** ≈ auditory cortex; **limbischer** ≈ limbic cortex; **motorischer** ≈ motor cortex; **olfaktorischer** ≈ olfactory cortex; **prämotorischer** ≈ premotor cortex; **präzentraler motorischer** ≈ precentral motor cortex; **somatosensibler** ≈ somatosensory cortex.
kortikal: cortical.
Kortikalisdefekt *m*: cortical defect.
Kortikosteroid *n*: corticosteroid.
kortikotrop: corticotropic.
Kortikotropin *n*: corticotropin.
Kortisol *n*: cortisol.
Kortison *n*: cortisone.
Kosmetik *f*: cosmetics.
Kost *f*: diet; **ausgeglichene** ≈ balanced diet; **leichte** ≈ light diet; **purinarme** ≈ low-purine diet.
Kostalatmung *f*: costal respiration, thoracic respiration.
Kostensenkung *f*: cost reduction.
Kostochondritis *f*: costochondritis, Tietze's disease.
Kot *m*: stool, feces, excrement.
Koterbrechen *n*: fecal vomiting, copremesis.
Kotfistel *f*: fecal fistula, stercoral fistula.

Kotstein *m*: coprolith, fecalith.
Koxalgie *f*: coxalgia, hip pain.
Koxarthrose *f*: coxarthrosis, arthrosis of the hip.
Kozhevnikov-Epilepsie *f*: Kozhevnikov's epilepsy, continuous partial epilepsy.
Krabbe-Syndrom *n*: Krabbe's disease, globoid leukodystrophy.
kräftigen: strengthen, revigorate.
kräftigend: roborant.
kränkeln: sicken.
kränklich: unhealthy, sickish.
Krätze *f*: scabies, itch.
Krätzmilbe *f*: itch mite, sarcoptic mite.
Krätzmilbenkrankheit *f*: sarcoptic scabies, sarcoptic itch.
Kräutermedizin *f*: herbal medicine.
Kraft *f*: force, power, strength.
kraftlos: feeble, weak.
Kragenschnitt *m*: collar incision.
Krallenfuß *m*: clawfoot.
Krallenhand *f*: clawhand.
Krampf *m*: cramp, tonic spasm.
Krampfaderleiden *n*: varicosity.
Krampfanfall *m*: convulsion, seizure; **epileptischer** ≈ epileptic seizure; **hysterischer** ≈ hysterical convulsion; **posttraumatischer** ≈ immediate post-traumatic convulsion; **toxischer** ≈ toxic spasm.
krampfauslösend: convulsant.
Krampfschwelle *f*: convulsant threshold.
Kranialnerv *m*: cranial nerve.
Kraniometrie *f*: craniometry.
Kraniopharyngeom *n*: craniopharyngioma, Rathke's pouch tumor.
Kraniosklerose *f*: craniosclerosis, Virchow's disease.
Kraniostenose *f*: craniostenosis.
Kraniosynostose *f*: craniosynostosis.
Kraniotabes *f*: craniotabes.
Kraniotomie *f*: craniotomy.
krank: sick, ill.
Krankenbericht *m*: medical record.
Krankenbett *n*: sick-bed.
Krankengeschichte *f*: patient's history.
Krankenhaus *n*: hospital; **allgemeines** ≈ general hospital; **psychiatrisches** ≈ mental hospital; **städtisches** ≈ city hospital, urban hospital.
Krankenhausapotheke *f*: hospital pharmacy.
Krankenhausaufenthalt *m*: hospital stay.
Krankenhausaufenthaltsdauer *f*: length of stay.
Krankenhauseinweisung *f*: hospitalization, hospital referral.
Krankenhausinfektion *f*: hospital infection.
Krankenpflege *f*: nursing care.
Krankenpfleger *m*: male nurse, attendant.
Krankenpflegeversicherung *f*: health care insurance.
Krankenschwester *f*: nurse.
Krankentrage *f*: stretcher.
Krankentransport *m*: transportation of patients.
Krankenversicherung *f*: health insurance.
Krankenwagen *m*: ambulance.
Kranker *m*: sick, patient.
krankhaft: unhealthy, sickly, pathologic.
Krankheit *f*: disease, disorder, sickness, illness, morbus; **AIDS-definierende** ≈ AIDS-defining disease, **ansteckende** ≈ infectious disease, communicable disease; **auszehrende** ≈ wasting disease; **chronische** ≈ chronic disease; **erbliche** ≈ inheritable disease; **genetische** ≈ genetic disease; **iatrogene** ≈ iatrogenic disease; **konstitutionell bedingte** ≈ constitutional disease; **meldepflichtige** ≈ notifiable disease; **psychosomatische** ≈ psychosomatic disease; **schleichende** ≈ lingering illness; **sexuell übertragbare** ≈ sexually transmitted disease, STD; **terminale** ≈ terminal illness, final illness; **übertragbare** ≈ communicable disease, infectious disease.
Krankheitsausbruch *m*: disease outbreak.
Krankheitsbild *n*: clinical picture, clinical presentation.
Krankheitslehre *f*: nosology.

Krankheitsstadium *n*: disease stage.
Krankheitsursache *f*: cause of disease.
Krankheitsverhalten *n*: illness behavior, behavior of the ill.
Krankheitsverhütung *f*: disease prevention, prophylaxis.
Krankheitsverlauf *m*: course.
Krankheitszeichen *n*: symptom.
Krankschreibung *f*: sick leave.
Kranzstar *m*: coronary cataract.
Krasenlehre *f*: humoralism.
Kratzen *n*: itch, scratch, scraping, scrape.
Kraurose *f*: kraurosis.
Kreatin *n*: creatine.
Kreatinin *n*: creatinine.
Kreatininclearance *f*: creatinine clearance.
Kreatinkinase *f*: creatine kinase.
Krebs *m*: cancer.
Krebsangst *f*: cancerophobia.
Krebs-Henseleit-Zyklus *m*: Krebs-Henseleit cycle, urea cycle.
Krebsregister *n*: cancer register.
Krebszelle *f*: cancer cell.
Krebs-Zyklus *m*: Krebs cycle, ornithine cycle.
Kreisbogenschnitt *m*: radial incision.
kreischen: scream.
kreisförmig: circular, circinate.
Kreislauf *m*: circulation, cardiovascular system; **embryonaler** ≈ embryonic circulation; **enterohepatischer** ≈ enterohepatic circulation; **extrahepatischer** ≈ extrahepatic blood flow; **extrakorporaler** ≈ extracorporeal circulation; **fetaler** ≈ fetal circulation; **großer** ≈ greater circulation, systemic circulation; **kleiner** ≈ lesser circulation, pulmonary circulation.
Kreislauffunktion *f*: circulatory function.
Kreislaufmittel *n*: cardiovascular agent.
Kreislaufschwäche *f*: circulatory insufficiency.
Kreislaufstillstand *m*: circulatory arrest.
Kreislaufstörung *f*: circulatory disorder.
Kreislaufsystem *n*: circulatory system.
Kreislaufversagen *n*: circulatory failure.
kreißen: be in labor.
Kreißsaal *m*: birthing room, delivery room.
Kremasterreflex *m*: cremasteric reflex.
Kreosot *n*: kreosot, creosote.
Krepitation *f*: crepitation, crepitus, crepitance.
Kresorcin *n*: cresorcinol.
Kretinismus *m*: cretinism, congenital myxedema.
Kreuzband *n*: cruciate ligament; **hinteres** ≈ posterior cruciate ligament; **vorderes** ≈ anterior cruciate ligament.
Kreuzbandriss *m*: rupture of cruciate ligament.
Kreuzbein *n*: sacrum, resurrection bone.
Kreuzblut *n*: matched blood.
Kreuzimmunität *f*: cross immunity.
Kreuzprobe *f*: cross-matching, X-matching.
Kreuzresistenz *f*: cross-resistance.
Kreuzschmerz *m*: low-back pain, lumbar pain, lumbago.
Kreuzschnitt *m*: cruciate incision.
Kreuzstich *m*: cross-stitch.
Kribbelgefühl *n*: formication, prickle.
Krikothyreotomie *f*: cricothyreotomy, inferior laryngotomy.
Krim-Kongo-Fieber, hämorrhagisches *n*: Crimean-Congo hemorrhagic fever.
Krippentod *m*: crib death, cot death, sudden infant death syndrome, SIDS.
Krise *f*: crisis; **akinetische** ≈ akinetic crisis; **cholinerge** ≈ cholinergic crisis; **gastrische** ≈ gastric crisis; **hämolytische** ≈ hemolytic crisis; **hypertensive** ≈ hypertensive crisis; **katathyme** ≈ catathymic crisis; **myasthenische** ≈ myasthenic crisis; **okulogyre** ≈ oculogyric crisis; **tabische** ≈ tabetic crisis; **thyreotoxische** ≈ thyrotoxic crisis.

Krisenintervention *f*: crisis intervention.
Kristallarthropathie *f*: crystall arthritis.
Kristallpenicillin *n*: crystalline penicillin.
Kristallurie *f*: crystalluria.
kritisch: critical, crucial.
Krötentest *m*: frog test, toad test.
Krokodilstränenphänomen *n*: crocodile tears syndrome.
Kropf *m*: crop, goiter.
Krotonöl *n*: croton oil.
Krückenlähmung *f*: crutch paralysis.
Krümmung *f*: curvature, curve, bend.
Krumendrehertremor *m*: breadcrumbling tremor, pill-rolling tremor.
Krupp *m*: croup, laryngostasis; **diphtherischer** ≈ diphtheritic croup.
kruppös: croupous, croupy.
Kruppsyndrom *n*: croup.
krural: crural.
Kruste *f*: crust, scab.
Krustenbildung *f*: incrustation.
Kryästhesie *f*: cryesthesia.
Kryoanästhesie *f*: cryoanesthesia, cryogenic block.
Kryochirurgie *f*: cryosurgery, cryogenic surgery.
Kryoglobulinämie *f*: cryoglobulinemia.
Kryokonservierung *f*: cryopreservation.
Kryotherapie *f*: cryotherapy.
Kryptantigen *n*: minor antigen.
Kryptitis *f*: cryptitis.
Kryptokokkenmeningitis *f*: cryptococcal meningitis.
Kryptokokkose *f*: cryptococcosis, Busse-Buschke disease.
Kryptorchismus *m*: cryptorchism, cryptorchidism.
Kubitalvene *f*: cubital vein.
Kügelchen *n*: spherule, bead, pellet.
kühlen: cool, refrigerate.
Kühlsalbe *f*: soothing ointment.
künstlich: artificial.
Kürettage *f*: curettage; **fraktionierte** ≈ fractionated curettage.
Kürette *f*: curet.
kürettieren: curette.
Kürschnernaht *f*: glover's suture, lock-stitch suture.
Kufs-Hallervorden-Krankheit *f*: Kufs' disease, adult ceroid lipofuscinosis.
Kugelgelenk *n*: ball-and-socket joint.
Kugelventilthrombus *m*: ball-valve thrombosis.
Kugelzelle *f*: globe cell, spherocyte.
Kugelzellenanämie *f*: hereditary spherocytosis, Minkowski-Chauffard syndrome.
Kuhmilchallergie *f*: cow milk allergy.
Kuhnt-Junius-Krankheit *f*: Kuhnt-Junius disease, disciform macular degeneration.
Kuhpocken *f*: cowpox, bovine smallpox.
Kuhpockenlymphe *f*: bovine lymph, Jenner's vaccine.
Kuldoskopie *f*: culdoscopy.
Kulissenphänomen *n*: curtain sign, curtain moment.
Kulturmedium *n*: culture medium.
Kumarin *n*: coumarin.
Kummer *m*: sorrow, grief, pain.
Kumulativdosis *f*: accumulated dose.
Kunstfehler, ärztlicher *m*: medical malpractice.
Kupferspeicherkrankheit *f*: copper storage disease, Wilson's disease.
Kur *f*: cure, spa treatment.
kurativ: curative.
kuren: cure.
Kurpfuscherei *f*: quackery, charlatanism.
Kuru *n*: kuru.
Kurvatur *f*: curvature.
kurzatmig: dyspneic.
Kurzatmigkeit *f*: shortness of breath, short-windedness.
Kurzschädel *m*: brachycephaly.
kurzsichtig: shortsighted, nearsighted, myopic.
Kurzsichtigkeit *f*: shortsightedness, nearsightedness, myopia.
Kurzwellendiathermie *f*: short-wave diathermy.
Kurzzeitbestrahlung *f*: brachyradiotherapy.
Kurzzeitgedächtnis *n*: short-term memory.

Kussmaul-Atmung *f*: Kussmaul breathing, air hunger.
kutan: cutaneous.
Kutikularsaum *m*: cuticular layer.
Kutisfissur *f*: cutis fissure, cutaneous fissure.
Kwashiorkor *m*: kwashiorkor, protein malnutrition.
Kyphose *f*: kyphosis, round back deformity, hunchback; **juvenile** ≈ juvenile kyphosis, Scheuermann's disease.
Kyphoskoliose *f*: kyphoscoliosis.
kyphotisch: kyphotic.
Kystadenolymphoma papilliferum: papillary adenocystoma lymphomatosum, Warthin's tumor.
Kystadenom *n*: cystadenoma.
Kystom *n*: cystoma.
K-Zelle *f*: killer lymphocyte.

L

L Abk. **Liquor** *m*: liquor, cerebrospinal fluid.

Labetalol *n*: labetalol.

labial: labial.

Labialbügel *m*: labial bar.

labil: labile, unstable, brittle.

Labor *n*: laboratory.

Laborbefunde: laboratory findings.

Labormedizin *f*: laboratory medicine.

Laboruntersuchung *f*: laboratory test.

Labyrinth *n*: labyrinth; **akustisches** ≈ acoustic labyrinth; **häutiges** ≈ membranous labyrinth; **knöchernes** ≈ bony labyrinth.

Labyrinthfunktionsprüfung *f*: labyrinthine test.

Labyrinthitis *f*: labyrinthitis.

Labyrinthnystagmus *m*: labyrinthine nystagmus.

Labyrinthschwindel *m*: labyrinthine vertigo.

Labyrinthsystem *n*: labyrinthine system.

Lachen *n*: laugh, laughing; **sardonisches** ≈ sardonic laugh, risus sardonicus.

Lachgas *n*: laughing gas.

Lachkrampf *m*: spasmodic laughter.

Lacidipin *n*: lacidipine.

Lackmusprobe *f*: litmus test.

Ladung *f*: charge, loading.

lähmen: paralyze.

Lähmung *f*: paralysis, palsy; **alternierende** ≈ alternating paralysis; **episodische** ≈ periodic paralysis; **gekreuzte** ≈ crossed paralysis; **halbseitige** ≈ hemiplegia; **hereditäre hyperkaliämische periodische** ≈ familial periodic paralysis; **hereditäre hypokaliämische periodische** ≈ familial hypokalemic periodic paralysis; **hysterische** ≈ hysterical paralysis; **idiopathische** ≈ essential paralysis; **infranukleäre** ≈ infranuclear paralysis; **motorische** ≈ motor paralysis; **myogene** ≈ myogenic paralysis; **neurogene** ≈ neurogenic paralysis, neuroparalysis; **normokaliämische periodische** ≈ normokalemic periodic paralysis; **periodische** ≈ periodic paralysis, Gamstorp's disease; **postiktale** ≈ postepileptic paralysis; **schlaffe** ≈ flaccid paralysis; **spastische** ≈ spastic paralysis; **supranukleäre** ≈ supranuclear paralysis, supranuclear palsy; **zentrale** ≈ central paralysis, cerebral palsy.

Lähmungsschielen *n*: paralytic strabismus.

Länge *f*: length.

Längenbreitenindex *m*: length-breadth index.

Längenhöhenindex *m*: length-height index.

Längenwachstum *n*: growth in length.

Längsbruch *m*: longitudinal fracture, linear fracture.

Längslage *f*: longitudinal presentation.

Längsschnitt *m*: longitudinal section.

Laennec-Leberzirrhose *f*: Laennec's cirrhosis, alcoholic cirrhosis.

Läppchen *n*: lobule.

Läppchentest *m*: patch test.

Lärm *m*: noise.

Lärmaudiogramm *n*: noise audiogram, masking audiogram.

Lärmbelastung *f*: noise pollution.

Lärmschwerhörigkeit *f*: noise-induced hearing loss.

Lärmtrauma *n*: auditory trauma, acoustic trauma.

Läsion *f*: lesion, damage; **diskrete** ≈ discrete lesion; **erhabene** ≈ elevated lesion; **flache** ≈ flat lesion; **fleckförmige** ≈ patchy lesion; **makroskopische** ≈ gross lesion; **raumfordernde** ≈ mass lesion.
Läusebefall *m*: pediculosis.
Läusefleckfieber *n*: epidemic louse-borne typhus.
Läusemittel *n*: pediculicide.
Läuserückfallfieber *n*: louse-borne relapsing fever.
Lävokardie *f*: levocardia.
Lävulose *f*: levulose, fructose.
Lafora-Epilepsie *f*: Lafora's disease, progressive myoclonic epilepsy.
Lage *f*: position, situation, situs.
Lageanomalie *f*: abnormal position.
Lagedrainage *f*: postural drainage.
Lagenystagmus *m*: positional nystagmus.
Lagerdauer *f*: shelf life.
Lagereflex *m*: postural reflex.
Lageschwindel *m*: positional vertigo.
Lagetyp *m*: electrical heart position.
Lahmheit *f*: lameness.
Laken *n*: sheet.
Lakritze *f*: licorice.
Laktagogum *n*: lactagogue.
Laktalbumin *n*: lactalbumin.
Laktamase *f*: lactamase.
Laktase *f*: lactase.
Laktasemangel *m*: lactase deficiency.
Laktatazidose *f*: lactic acidosis.
Laktatdehydrogenase *f*: lactate dehydrogenase.
Laktation *f*: lactation, galactosis.
Laktationsamenorrhö *f*: lactation amenorrhea.
laktifer: lactiferous.
Laktifugum *n*: lactifuge.
laktogen: lactogenic.
Laktorrhö *f*: galactorrhea.
Laktose *f*: lactose, milk sugar.
Laktoseintoleranz *f*: lactose intolerance.
lakunär: lacunar.
lallen: babble, stammer.
Lambdanaht *f*: lambdoid suture.
Lambert-Eaton-Syndrom *n*: Lambert-Eaton syndrome, carcinomatous myasthenia.
Lambliasis *f*: lambliasis, giardiasis.
Lamelle *f*: lamella.
Lamellenknochen *m*: lamellar bone.
Lamellenzwischenraum *m*: interlamellar space.
Lamina *f*: layer, lamina.
Laminektomie *f*: laminectomy.
Lamivudin *n*: lamivudine.
Lamotrigin *n*: lamotrigine.
Landkartenschädel *m*: maplike skull.
Landouzy-Déjerine-Atrophie *f*: Landouzy-Déjerine atrophy, facioscapulohumeral atrophy.
Landry-Paralyse *f*: Landry's paralysis, ascending neuropathy.
Langerhans-Inseln *f*: islets of Langerhans, pancreatic islets.
Langlebigkeit *f*: longevity.
langsam: slow.
lang wirkend: long-acting.
Langzeitbetreuung *f*: long-term care.
Langzeitgedächtnis *n*: long-term memory.
Lanolin *n*: lanolin.
Lanreotid *n*: lanreotide.
Lansoprazol *n*: lansoprazole.
Lanzette *f*: lancet.
lanzinierend: lancinating.
Laparogastrotomie *f*: laparogastrotomy.
Laparoskopie *f*: laparoscopy.
Laparotomie *f*: laparotomy.
Laparozele *f*: laparocele, abdominal hernia.
Lappen *m*: lobe, flap, patch; **freier** ≈ free flap; **gestielter** ≈ pedicle flap; **mukoperiostaler** ≈ mucoperiosteal flap; **zungenförmiger** ≈ tongue flap.
Lappenaplasie *f*: lobular aplasia.
Lappenatelektase *f*: lobular atelectasis.
Lappenresektion *f*: lobe resection.
Laronidase *f*: laronidase.
Larvenkonjunktivitis *f*: larval conjunctivitis.
Larvenzyste *f*: larval cyst.
larviert: larvate, masked.
laryngeal: laryngeal.
Laryngektomie *f*: laryngectomy.
Laryngismus *m*: laryngismus.
Laryngismus stridulus *m*: laryngismus stridulus, false croup.

Laryngitis *f*: laryngitis; **akute katarrhalische** ≈ acute catarrhal laryngitis; **chronische** ≈ chronic laryngitis; **diphtherische** ≈ diphtheritic laryngitis; **kruppöse** ≈ croupous laryngitis; **membranöse** ≈ membranous laryngitis.
laryngopharyngeal: laryngopharyngeal.
Laryngopharyngitis *f*: laryngopharyngitis.
Laryngoskopie *f*: laryngoscopy.
Laryngospasmus *m*: laryngospasm, glottic spasm.
Laryngotomie *f*: laryngotomy.
Laryngotracheitis *f*: laryngotracheitis.
Laryngotracheobronchitis *f*: laryngotracheobronchitis.
Larynx *m*: larynx.
Larynxkarzinom *n*: laryngeal cancer.
Larynxstenose *f*: laryngostenosis, laryngeal obstruction.
Larynxzyste *f*: laryngeal cyst, laryngocele.
Lasègue-Zeichen *n*: Lasègue sign; **kontralaterales** ≈ Lasègue's contralateral sign.
Laser *m*. laser; **gepulster** ≈ pulsed laser.
Laserbehandlung *f*: laser therapy.
Laserkoagulation *f*: laser coagulation.
Lassa-Fieber *n*: Lassa fever.
Latamoxef *n*: latamoxef.
Latanoprost *n*: latanoprost.
latent: latent.
Latenzperiode *f*: latency period.
Latenzstadium *n*: stage of latency.
lateral: lateral.
Lateralität *f*: laterality.
Lateralsklerose *f*: lateral sclerosis; **amyotrophe** ≈ amyotrophic lateral sclerosis.
Latexagglutinationstest *m*: latex agglutination test.
Laudanum *n*: laudanum, opium tincture.
Laufmilbe *f*: bug, trombicula.
Laune *f*: mood.
Laurinsäure *f*: lauric acid.
Laus *f*: louse.
Laut *m*: sound, tone.
Lautagnosie *f*: auditory agnosia, acoustic agnosia.
Lautgesetz *n*: phonetic law.
Lautstärke *f*: loudness.
Lavage *f*: lavage; **bronchoalveoläre** ≈ bronchoalveolar lavage.
Laxans *n*: laxative.
Laxheit *f*: laxity.
laxierend: laxative.
Lazarett *n*: military hospital.
Lazeration *f*: laceration.
L-Carnitin *n*: L-carnitine.
L-Dopa *n*: levodopa, L-dopa.
leben: live.
Leben *n*: life.
lebend: living, vital.
Lebendgeborenes *n*: live-born infant.
Lebendgeburt *f*: live birth.
lebendig: alive, vital.
Lebendimpfstoff *m*: live vaccine.
Lebensabschnitt *m*: period of life.
lebensbedrohlich: life threatening.
Lebensdauer *f*: life time, life span.
Lebenserwartung *f*: life expectancy.
lebensfähig: viable.
Lebensgefahr *f*: danger to life.
Lebenskraft *f*: vital energy.
Lebensmittel *n*: food.
Lebensmittelallergie *f*: food allergy.
Lebensmittelvergiftung *f*: food poisoning.
lebensmüde: tired of life.
lebensnotwendig: essential.
Lebensqualität *f*: quality of life.
lebensrettend: life-saving.
Lebensversicherung *f*: life insurance.
Lebensweise *f*: lifestyle, way of life.
lebenswichtig: vital, existential.
Lebenszeichen *n*: vital signs.
Lebenszeit *f*: lifetime.
Leber *f*: liver, hepar; **biliär-zirrhotische** ≈ biliary cirrhotic liver; **zirrhotische** ≈ cirrhotic liver.
Leberabszess *m*: liver abscess, hepatic abscess.
Leberatrophie *f*: atrophy of the liver; **akute gelbe** ≈ acute yellow atrophy of the liver, Budd's jaundice.
Leberbiopsie *f*: liver biopsy.
Leberdämpfung *f*: hepatic dullness.
Leberentzündung *f*: hepatitis.

Lebererkrankung *f*: disease of the liver, hepatopathy.
Leberfibrose *f*: hepatic fibrosis.
Leberfunktionsprobe *f*: liver function test.
Lebergalle *f*: hepatic bile.
Lebergift *n*: hepatotoxic agent.
Leberinsuffizienz *f*: hepatic insufficiency.
Leberkapsel *f*: liver capsule.
Leberkarzinom *n*: liver carcinoma.
Leberlappen *m*: hepatic lobe.
Lebermetastase *f*: intrahepatic metastasis.
Leber-Optikusatrophie *f*: Leber's optic atrophy, hereditary optic atrophy.
Leberperfusion, extrakorporale *f*: extracorporeal hepatic perfusion.
Leberpforte *f*: hepatic portal.
Leberpuls *m*: hepatic pulse.
Leberresektion *f*: hepatectomy.
Leberruptur *f*: rupture of the liver.
Lebersarkoidose *f*: hepatic sarcoidosis.
Lebertran *m*: cod liver oil.
Lebertransplantation *f*: liver transplantation.
Lebervenenverschluss *m*: hepatic vein occlusion.
Lebervergrößerung *f*: hepatomegaly, enlarged liver.
Leberversagen *n*: liver failure.
Leberzelladenom *n*: hepatocellular adenoma.
Leberzelle *f*: liver cell, hepatocyte.
Leberzellkarzinom *n*: liver cell carcinoma, hepatocellular carcinoma.
Leberzirrhose *f*: liver cirrhosis; **alkoholische** ≈ alcoholic cirrhosis; **atrophische** ≈ Laennec's cirrhosis; **biliäre** ≈ biliary liver cirrhosis; **grobknotige** ≈ macronodular cirrhosis; **kardiale** ≈ cardiac cirrhosis; **kleinknotige** ≈ micronodular cirrhosis; **kongenitale** ≈ congenital hepatic fibrosis; **noduläre** ≈ nodular liver cirrhosis; **periportale** ≈ periportal liver cirrhosis; **posthepatitische** ≈ posthepatitic cirrhosis; **postnekrotische** ≈ postnecrotic cirrhosis; **syphilitische** ≈ syphilitic cirrhosis.
Leberzyste *f*: hepatic cyst.
leblos: lifeless, nonvital.
Leckage *f*: leakage.
Lecksaft *m*: lincture.
Lederzecke *f*: soft tick.
leeren: empty, void.
Leflunomid *n*: leflunomid.
LeFort-Fraktur *f*: LeFort's fracture.
Legionärskrankheit *f*: legionnaires' disease, legionellosis.
Leib *m*: body.
Leibschmerz *m*: abdominal pain.
Leiche *f*: cadaver, corpse, dead body.
Leichenbeschauer *m*: coroner.
Leichenschau *f*: necropsy, autopsy; **gerichtliche** ≈ medicolegal necropsy.
Leichenstarre *f*: rigor mortis, cadaveric rigidity.
Leichentuberkel *n*: dissection tubercle, necrogenic wart.
Leichnam *m*: dead body, corpse.
Leichte-Ketten-Krankheit *f*: light-chain disease, plasmocytoma.
leiden: suffer.
Leiden *n*: suffering, ailment.
Leigh-Enzephalomyelopathie *f*: Leigh's disease, subacute necrotizing encephalopathy.
Leihmutter *f*: surrogate mother.
Leinsamen *m*: linseed.
Leiomyom *n*: leiomyoma.
Leiomyosarkom *n*: leiomyosarcoma.
Leishmaniase *f*: leishmaniasis; **kutane** ≈ cutaneous leishmaniasis; **mukokutane** ≈ mucocutaneous leishmaniasis; **viszerale** ≈ visceral leishmaniasis, kala-azar.
Leistenband *n*: inguinal ligament.
Leistenbeuge *f*: groin.
Leistenhernie *f*: inguinal hernia; **direkte** ≈ direct inguinal hernia; **indirekte** ≈ indirect inguinal hernia; **kongenitale** ≈ infantile hernia.
Leistenhoden *m*: inguinal testis.
Leistenkanal *m*: inguinal canal, abdominal canal.
Leistenlymphknoten *m*: inguinal lymph node.
Leistenregion *f*: inguinal region.
Leistenring *m*: inguinal ring.
Leitfähigkeit *f*: conductivity.
Leitlinie *f*: guideline.

Leitsymptom *n*: characteristic symptom, guiding symptom, direct symptom.
Leitungsanästhesie *f*: nerve block anesthesia.
Leitungsaphasie *f*: conduction aphasia.
Leitungsbahn *f*: conduction path.
Leitungsschwerhörigkeit *f*: conductive hearing impairment.
Leitungsverzögerung *f*: conduction delay.
Lende *f*: loin, lumbar region.
Lendenbruch *m*: lumbar hernia.
Lendenschmerz *m*: lumbar pain.
Lendenwirbelsäule *f*: lumbar spine.
Lenograstim *n*: lenograstim.
Lentigo *f*: lentigo.
Lentigo maligna *f*: malignant lentigo, Hutchinson's melanotic freckle.
Lentigopolyposis *f*: intestinal polyposis-cutaneous pigmentation syndrome, Peutz-Jeghers syndrome.
Leontiasis *f*: leontiasis.
Lepirudin *n*: lepirudin.
Lepra *f*: leprosy; **dimorphe** ≈ dimorphous leprosy; **fleckige** ≈ macular leprosy; **lepromatöse** ≈ lepromatous leprosy; **tuberkuloide** ≈ tuberculoid leprosy.
Leprafieber *n*: leprotic fever.
Leprafleck *m*: leprotic macule.
Lepraknoten *m*: leprous nodule, leproma.
Leprostatikum *n*: leprostatic.
Leptomeningitis *f*: leptomeningitis.
Leptospirose *f*: leptospirosis, Weil's disease.
Lercanidipin *n*: lercanidipine.
Leriche-Syndrom *n*: Leriche syndrome, aortoiliac occlusive disease.
Léri-Zeichen *n*: Léri forearm sign.
Lernschwierigkeit *f*: learning difficulty.
Lesebrille *f*: reading spectacles.
Lesestörung *f*: reading disability.
Lesezentrum *n*: visual-word center.
letal: lethal, fatal.
Letaldosis *f*: lethal dose.
Letalfaktor *m*: lethal factor.
Letalgen *n*: lethal gene.
Letalität *f*: lethality.
Letalitätsrate *f*: lethality rate.
Lethargie *f*: lethargy.
Letrozol *n*: letrozole.
Leucin *n*: leucine.
Leucomycin *n*: leucomycin.
Leukämie *f*: leukemia; **akute lymphatische** ≈ acute lymphatic leukemia; **akute myeloische** ≈ acute myeloid leukemia; **aleukämische** ≈ aleukemic leukemia; **chronische lymphatische** ≈ chronic lymphatic leukemia; **chronische myeloische** ≈ chronic myelogenous leukemia.
Leukin *n*: leukin.
Leukoderm *n*: leukoderma.
Leukodystrophie *f*: leukodystrophy; **metachromatische** ≈ metachromatic leukodystrophy; **spongiforme** ≈ spongiform leukodystrophy, Canavan spongy degeneration.
Leukoenzephalitis *f*: leukoencephalitis; **akute hämorrhagische** ≈ acute hemorrhagic leukoencephalitis; **subakute sklerosierende** ≈ subacute sclerosing leukoencephalitis.
Leukoenzephalopathie *f*: leukoencephalopathy; **progressive multifokale** ≈ progressive multifocal leukoencephalopathy.
Leukonychie *f*: leukonychia.
Leukopathie *f*: leukopathy.
Leukopenie *f*: leukopenia, leukocytopenia.
Leukoplakie *f*: leukoplakia; **orale haarförmige** ≈ hairy leukoplakia.
Leukorrhö *f*: leukorrhea, whites.
Leukotomie *f*: leukotomy.
Leukozyt *m*: leukocyte, white blood cell; **basophiler** ≈ basophilic leukocyte; **eosinophiler** ≈ eosinophilic leukocyte; **neutrophiler** ≈ neutrophilic leukocyte, neutrophil.
Leukozytenantigen, humanes *n*: human leukocyte antigen, HLA.
Leukozytenmanschette *f*: buffy coat.
Leukozytenzählung *f*: leukocyte count, white blood count.
Leukozytenzahl *f*: leukocyte count.
Leukozytopenie *f*: leukocytopenia, leukopenia.
Leukozytose *f*: leukocytosis.
Leuprorelin *n*: leuprorelin.

Leuzin *n*: leucine.
Leuzinose *f*: leucinosis.
Levallorphan *n*: levallorphan.
Levamisol *n*: levamisole.
Levarterenol *n*: levarterenol.
Levatorzeichen *n*: levator sign.
Levetiracetam *n*: levetiracetam.
Levobunolol *n*: levobunolol.
Levobupivacain *n*: levobupivacaine.
Levocetirizin *n*: levocetirizine.
Levodopa *n*: levodopa, L-dopa.
Levodropropizin *n*: levodropropizine.
Levofloxacin *n*: levofloxacin.
Levomethadon *n*: levomethadone.
Levonorgestrel *n*: levonorgestrel.
Leydig-Zwischenzelle *f*: Leydig cell.
Lezithin *n*: lecithin.
Lhermitte-Lähmung *f*: anterior internuclear ophthalmoplegia.
Lhermitte-Zeichen *n*: Lhermitte sign, neck phenomenon.
LHRH-Agonist *m*: luteinizing hormone-releasing hormone agonist, LHRH agonist.
libidinös: libidinal.
Libido *f*: libido.
Libido sexualis *f*: sexual libido.
Libman-Sacks-Endokarditis *f*: Libman-Sacks disease, atypical bacterial endocarditis.
Lichen *m*: lichen.
Lichen amyloidosus *m*: lichen amyloidosus, lichenoid amyloidosis.
Licht *n*: light.
Lichtallergie *f*: photoallergy.
Lichtbehandlung *f*: phototherapy.
Lichtexposition *f*: light exposure.
Lichtheim-Aphasie *f*: Lichtheim's aphasia, transcortical aphasia.
Lichtkasten *m*: electric cradle, heat cradle.
Lichtreflex *m*: light reflex, pupillary reflex.
Lichtscheu *f*: photophobia.
Lichtsehen *n*: photopsia.
Lichturtikaria *f*: photogenic urticaria.
Lidfalte *f*: palpebronasal fold, epicanthus.
Lidkrampf *m*: blepharospasm.
Lidlähmung *f*: lid paralysis.
Lidocain *n*: lidocaine.
Lidödem *n*: eyelid edema.
Lidoflazin *n*: lidoflazine.
Lidrandentzündung *f*: marginal blepharitis.
Lidreflex *m*: lid reflex.
Lidschlussreaktion *f*: eyelid closure reflex.
L-Iduronsäure *f*: L-iduronic acid.
liegen: lie, rest.
lienal: lienal, splenic.
Lifting *n*: lifting.
Ligament *n*: ligament, band.
Ligation *f*: ligation.
Ligatur *f*: ligature.
Lightwood-Albright-Syndrom *n*: Lightwood-Albright syndrome, idiopathic renal acidosis.
Lignac-Fanconi-Krankheit *f*: Lignac-Fanconi disease, cystinosis.
Lila-Krankheit *f*: dermatomyositis.
limbisch: limbic.
Limen *n*: limen, threshold, boundary.
Lincomycin *n*: lincomycin.
Lindan *n*: lindane.
lindern: alleviate, palliate, allay.
Linderung *f*: ease, alleviation, palliation.
Linezolid *n*: linezolid.
Linie *f*: line.
Liniment *n*: liniment, linimentum.
Linitis plastica *f*: linitis plastica, gastric sclerosis.
Linksbypass *m*: left heart bypass.
linksdrehend: levorotatory.
Linksherzhypertrophie *f*: left ventricular hypertrophy.
Linksherzinsuffizienz *f*: left heart failure.
Links-Rechts-Shunt *m*: left-to-right shunt.
Linksschenkelblock *m*: left bundle branch block.
Linksseitenlage, stabile *f*: semiprone position, Sims position.
linksventrikulär: left ventricular.
Linksverspätung *f*: incomplete left bundle branch block.
Linolensäure *f*: linolenic acid.
Linolsäure *f*: linoleic acid, linolic acid.
Linse *f*: lens; **achromatische** ≈ achromatic lens; **bifokale** ≈ bifocal lens;

bikonkave ≈ biconcave lens; **bikonvexe** ≈ biconvex lens; **torische** ≈ toric lens; **zylindrische** ≈ cylindric lens.
Linsenastigmatismus *m*: lenticular astigmatism.
Linsendegeneration *f*: lenticular degeneration.
linsenförmig: lentiform, lenticular.
Linsenkapsel *f*: lens capsule.
Linsenkern *m*: lentiform nucleus.
Linsenkernschlinge *f*: lenticular loop.
Linsenkrümmung *f*: lens curvature.
Linsenstar *m*: lens star.
Lipämie *f*: lipemia; **postprandiale** ≈ postprandial lipemia.
Lipase *f*: lipase.
Lipid *n*: lipid, fat.
Lipidmembran *f*: lipid membrane.
Lipidsenker *m*: antilipemic, lipid-lowering agent.
Lipidspeicherkrankheit *f*: lipid storage disease, lipidosis.
Lipidstoffwechsel *m*: lipid metabolism.
Lipoadenom *n*: lipoadenoma.
Lipoatrophie *f*: lipoatrophy.
Lipochondrodystrophie *f*: lipochondrodystrophy.
Lipodystrophia progressiva *f*: progressive partial lipodystrophy.
Lipodystrophie *f*: lipodystrophy; **intestinale** ≈ intestinal lipodystrophy, Whipple's disease; **kongenitale generalisierte** ≈ congenital generalized lipodystrophy, Seip-Lawrence syndrome.
Lipofuszinspeicherkrankheit *f*: lipofuscinosis.
Lipogranulomatose *f*: lipogranulomatosis.
Lipoid *n*: lipoid.
Lipoidnephrose *f*: lipoid nephrosis.
Lipoidose *f*: lipoidosis, lipid storage disease.
Lipolyse *f*: lipolysis.
Lipom *n*: lipoma, fat tumor.
Lipomatose *f*: lipomatosis.
Lipoprotein *n*: lipoprotein.
Lipoproteine hoher Dichte: high-density lipoproteins, HDL.
Lipoproteine niedriger Dichte: low-density lipoproteins, LDL.
Lipoproteine sehr niedriger Dichte: very-low-density lipoproteins, VLDL.
Lipozyt *m*: lipocyte, fat cell.
Lippe *f*: lip, labium.
Lippenentzündung *f*: cheilitis.
Lippen-Kiefer-Gaumen-Spalte *f*: cheilognathopalatoschisis.
Lippenplastik *f*: labioplasty.
Lippenspalte *f*: cleft lip.
Liquor *m*: liquor, cerebrospinal fluid, CSF.
Liquorblock *m*: cerebrospinal-fluid block, Nonne-Froin syndrome.
Liquordruck *m*: cerebrospinal pressure.
Liquorrhö *f*: liquorrhea.
Lisinopril *n*: lisinopril.
Lispeln *n*: lisping.
Listeriose *f*: listeriosis.
Lisurid *n*: lisuride.
Lithagogum *n*: lithagogue.
Lithiasis *f*: lithiasis.
Lithium *n*: lithium, Li.
Lithiumsalz *n*: lithium salt.
Lithocholsäure *f*: lithocholic acid.
Litholapaxie *f*: litholapaxy.
Litholyse *f*: litholysis.
Lithotomie *f*: lithotomy; **perineale** ≈ celsian operation.
Lithotomieposition *f*: lithotomy position.
Lithotripsie *f*: lithotripsy.
Little-Krankheit *f*: Little's disease, spastic diplegia.
livid: livid.
Lobärpneumonie *f*: lobar pneumonia.
Lobärsklerose *f*: lobar sclerosis.
Lobektomie *f*: lobectomy.
Lobelin *n*: lobeline.
Lobo-Krankheit *f*: Lobo's disease.
Lobotomie *f*: lobotomy.
Lobucavir *n*: lobucavir.
Loch *n*: hole, foramen.
Lochien: lochia.
Lochienstauung *f*: retained lochia.
Lochklemme *f*: fenestrated clamp.
Locked-in-Syndrom *n*: locked-in syndrome.
Lockerung *f*: loosening, looseness.
Löffel *m*: spoon; **scharfer** ≈ curet.

Löffelnagel *m*: spoon nail, koilonychia.
Löffler-Endokarditis *f*: Löffler's parietal fibroplastic endocarditis.
Löffler-Syndrom *n*: Löffler syndrome, pulmonary infiltration with eosinophilia.
lösend: lytic, solvent.
löslich: soluble, solvable.
Lösung *f*: lotion, solution.
Lösungsblutung *f*: separation bleeding.
Lösungsmittel *n*: solvent, resolvent, dissolvent.
Löwengesicht *n*: leonine face.
Lofepramin *n*: lofepramine.
Logopädie *f*: logopedics.
Logorrhö *f*: logorrhea.
Logotherapie *f*: logotherapy.
lokal: local, topical.
Lokalanästhesie *f*: local anesthesia, regional anesthesia.
Lokalanästhetikum *n*: local anesthetic.
Lokalinfektion *f*: local infection.
Lokalisation *f*: localization, site.
Lokalreaktion *f*: local reaction.
Lokalzeichen *n*: local sign.
lokomotorisch: locomotor.
Lomefloxacin *n*: lomefloxacin.
Lomustin *n*: lomustine.
Lonazolac *n*: lonazolac.
longitudinal: longitudinal.
Longitudinalfurche *f*: longitudinal crease.
Looser-Umbauzonen: Looser's transformation zones.
Loperamid *n*: loperamide.
Lopinavir *n*: lopinavir.
Loracarbef *n*: loracarbef.
Lorazepam *n*: lorazepam.
Lorcainid *n*: lorcainide.
Lordose *f*: lordosis, hollowback.
Lormetazepam *n*: lormetazepam.
Lornoxicam *n*: lornoxicam.
Losartan *n*: losartan.
Loteprednol *n*: loteprednol.
Lotio alba: white lotion.
Lotion *f*: lotion, lotio.
Lovastatin *n*: lovastatin.
Lovirid *n*: loviride.
Lowe-Syndrom *n*: Lowe syndrome, oculocerebrorenal dystrophy.
Lubricans *n*: lubricant.
Lücke *f*: gap, void; **auskultatorische** ≈ auscultatory gap.
Lückenschädel *m*: lacuna skull.
Lues *f*: lues, syphilis.
Luft *f*: air.
Luftembolie *f*: air embolism, aeroembolism.
Luftfistel *f*: aerial fistula.
Luftkrankheit *f*: air sickness.
Luftröhre *f*: trachea, windpipe.
Luftröhrenschnitt *m*: tracheotomy.
Luftschlucken *n*: aerophagia.
Luftwege: respiratory tract, airways.
Lumbago *f*: lumbago, lumbar pain.
lumbal: lumbar.
Lumbalanästhesie *f*: spinal anesthesia.
Lumbalkanal *m*: lumbar canal.
Lumbalpunktion *f*: lumbar puncture, spinal tap.
Lumen *n*: lumen.
Lumichrom *n*: lumichrome.
Lunatummalazie *f*: lunatomalacia, Kienböck's disease.
Lunge *f*: lung, pulmo; **eiserne** ≈ iron lung; **freie** ≈ clear lung; **helle** ≈ hyperlucent lung.
Lungenabszess *m*: lung abscess, pulmonary abscess.
Lungenalveole *f*: alveolus.
Lungenaspergillose *f*: pulmonary aspergillosis.
Lungenbiopsie *f*: lung biopsy, pulmonary biopsy; **transbronchiale** ≈ transbronchial biopsy.
Lungenblutung *f*: pulmonary hemorrhage.
Lungencompliance *f*: pulmonary compliance.
Lungendurchblutung *f*: pulmonary perfusion.
Lungenembolie *f*: pulmonary embolism.
Lungenemphysem *n*: pulmonary emphysema; **bullöses** ≈ bullous emphysema; **panazinäres** ≈ panacinar emphysema.
Lungenentzündung *f*: pneumonia.
Lungenerkrankung *f*: lung disease, pulmonary disease; **chronisch-obstruktive** ≈ chronic obstructive pul-

monary disease, COPD; **interstitielle** ≈ interstitial lung disease; **obstruktive** ≈ obstructive ventilatory defect; **restriktive** ≈ restrictive ventilatory defect; **spontane interstitielle** ≈ Hamman-Rich disease.
Lungenfibrose *f*: lung fibrosis, pulmonary fibrosis.
Lungenfunktionsprobe *f*: lung function test, pulmonary function test.
Lungengangrän *f*: pulmonary gangrene.
Lungeninduration *f*: induration of lung.
Lungeninfarkt *m*: pulmonary infarction.
Lungeninfiltrat *n*: pulmonary infiltration; **eosinophiles** ≈ pulmonary infiltration with eosinophilia, Löffler syndrome.
Lungenkapazität *f*: lung capacity; **totale** ≈ total lung capacity; **vitale** ≈ vital capacity.
Lungenkreislauf *m*: pulmonary circulation.
Lungenmilzbrand *m*: pulmonary anthrax.
Lungenödem *n*: pulmonary edema.
Lungenperfusion *f*: pulmonary perfusion.
Lungenperfusionszintigraphie *f*: pulmonary perfusion scintigraph.
Lungenresektion *f*: pulmonary resection.
Lungenrundherd *m*: lung nodule; **isolierter** ≈ solitary pulmonary nodule.
Lungensarkoidose *f*: pulmonary sarcoidosis.
Lungenschichtaufnahme *f*: pulmonary tomography.
Lungensegment *n*: bronchopulmonary segment.
Lungenspitze *f*: apex of the lung.
Lungenstauung *f*: pulmonary congestion.
Lungensurfactant *m*: lung alveolar surfactant.
Lungentransplantation *f*: lung transplantation.
Lungentuberkulose *f*: pulmonary tuberculosis.
Lungenvolumen *n*: lung volume.
Lungenzyste *f*: pulmonary cyst.
Lupus erythematodes *m*: lupus erythematosus, LE; **systemischer** ≈ systemic lupus erythematosus, SLE.
Lust-Zeichen *n*: Lust's phenomenon, peroneal-nerve phenomenon.
Lutealphase *f*: luteal phase.
Lutealzelle *f*: luteal cell.
Luteinisierungshormon freisetzendes Hormon *n*: luteinizing hormone-releasing hormone, LHRH.
Lutropin alfa *n*: lutropin alfa.
Luxation *f*: dislocation, luxation; **habituelle** ≈ habitual dislocation; **offene** ≈ open dislocation.
Luxationsfraktur *f*: dislocation fracture, fracture-dislocation.
Lyell-Syndrom *n*: Lyell syndrome, toxic epidermal necrolysis.
Lymphadenitis *f*: lymphadenitis.
Lymphadenopathie *f*: lymphadenopathy.
Lymphadenosis cutis benigna *f*: benign lymphocytic reticulosis.
Lymphangiektasie *f*: lymphangiectasia.
Lymphangiom *n*: lymphangioma.
Lymphangiosarkom *n*: lymphangiosarcoma.
Lymphangitis *f*: lymphangitis.
lymphatisch: lymphatic.
Lymphdrainage *f*: lymphatic drainage.
Lymphe *f*: lymph.
Lymphfistel *f*: lymphatic fistula.
Lymphfollikel *m*: lymphoid follicle.
Lymphgefäß *n*: lymphatic vessel.
Lymphknoten *m*: lymph node; **vergrößerter** ≈ enlarged lymph node; **verschieblicher** ≈ movable lymph node.
Lymphknotenhyperplasie *f*: lymphoid hyperplasia; **gutartige hyalinisierende** ≈ giant follicular hyperplasia; **noduläre** ≈ nodular lymphoid hyperplasia.
Lymphknotensinus *m*: lymphatic sinus.
Lymphknotentuberkulose *f*: tuberculosis of lymph nodes.
Lymphknotenvergrößerung *f*: lymph node enlargement.

L

Lymphoblast *m*: lymphoblast.
Lymphoblastenleukämie *f*: lymphoblastic leukemia.
Lymphoblastom *n*: lymphoblastoma.
Lymphödem *n*: lymphedema; **hereditäres** ≈ congenital lymphedema, Nonne-Milroy syndrome.
Lymphoepitheliom *n*: lymphoepithelioma, Schmincke tumor.
Lymphogramm *n*: lymphogram.
Lymphogranulom *n*: lymphogranuloma.
Lymphogranuloma venereum *n*: lymphogranuloma venereum, Durand-Nicolas-Favre disease.
Lymphographie *f*: lymphography.
lymphohistioplasmozytär: lymphohistioplasmacytic.
Lymphom *n*: lymphoma; **histiozytäres** ≈ histiocytic lymphoma; **lymphoblastisches** ≈ lymphoblastic lymphoma; **lymphozytisches** ≈ lymphocytic lymphoma; **malignes** ≈ malignant lymphoma; **zentroblastisch-zentrozytisches** ≈ centrocytic lymphoma.
lymphoproliferativ: lymphoproliferative.
Lymphosarkom *n*: lymphosarcoma, lymphocytic lymphoma.
Lymphozele *f*: lymphocele.
Lymphozyt *m*: lymphocyte.
Lymphozytom *n*: lymphocytoma.
Lymphozytopenie *f*: lymphocytopenia.
Lymphsystem *n*: lymphatic system.
Lypressin *n*: lypressin, lysine vasopressin.
Lyse *f*: lysis.
Lysehof *m*: lysis area.
Lysergsäure *f*: lysergic acid.
Lysin *n*: lysin, diaminocaproic acid.
8-Lysinvasopressin *n*: lysine vasopressin, lypressin.
Lysis *f*: lysis.
Lysozym *n*: lysozyme.
Lyssa *f*: lyssa, rabies.
Lyster-Beutel *m*: Lyster tube.

M

M. Abk. **Musculus** *m*: muscle, M.
Mach-Syndrom *n*: idiopathic aldosteronism.
Macrogol *n*: macrogol.
Macula lutea *f*: macula lutea, yellow spot.
Madelung-Fetthals *m*: Madelung's neck, nodular circumscribed lipomatosis.
Madenwurm *m*: human pinworm, seatworm.
Madurabeule *f*: mycetoma.
männlich: male.
Mafenid *n*: mafenide.
Magen *m*: stomach, gaster.
Magen-Darm-Katarrh *m*: infectious gastroenteritis.
Magen-Darm-Passage *f*: gastrointestinal passage, gastrointestinal examination.
Magen-Darm-Trakt *m*: gastrointestinal tract.
Magendilatation *f*: stomach dilatation.
Magendivertikel *n*: gastric diverticulum, stomach diverticulum.
Magenfalte *f*: gastric fold.
Magenfistel *f*: gastric fistula, gastrostoma.
Magenfrühkarzinom *n*: early gastric cancer.
Magengeschwür *n*: gastric ulcer, ventricular ulcer.
Magengrube *f*: gastric pit, pit of the stomach.
Magenhernie *f*: gastrocele.
Magen-Ileum-Fistel *f*: gastroileal fistula.
Magenkarzinom *n*: gastric carcinoma, stomach carcinoma.
Magenkrebs *m*: gastric cancer.
Magenoperation *f*: gastric surgery.
Magenperforation *f*: perforation of the stomach, gastric perforation.
Magenpförtner *m*: pylorus.
Magenplastik *f*: gastroplasty.
Magenpolyp *m*: gastric polyp.
Magenpumpe *f*: stomach pump.
Magenreizung *f*: gastric irritation.
Magenresektion *f*: gastric resection.
Magenruptur *f*: stomach rupture, gastrorrhexis.
Magensäure *f*: gastric acid.
Magensaft *m*: gastric juice.
Magensaftmangel *m*: achylia gastrica.
Magenschleimhaut *f*: gastric mucosa.
Magenschleimhautentzündung *f*: gastritis.
Magenschleimhautschranke *f*: gastric mucosal barrier.
Magenschmerz *m*: gastric pain.
Magensonde *f*: stomach tube, feeding tube.
Magenspiegelung *f*: gastroscopy.
Magenspülung *f*: gastric lavage, gastric irrigation.
Magenulkus *n*: stomach ulcer, gastric ulcer.
Magenwand *f*: gastric wall.
mager: thin, lean.
Magermilch *f*: low-fat milk, skimmed milk.
Magersucht *f*: anorexia.
Magnesium *n*: magnesium.
Magnet *m*: magnet.
Magnetfeld *n*: magnetic field.
Magnetismus *m*: magnetism.
Mahlzeit *f*: meal.
Major Tranquilizer *m*: major tranquilizer.
Makakenaffe *m*: macaque.
Makrobiotik *f*: macrobiotics.
Makrocheilie *f*: macrocheilia.

Makrodaktylie *f*: macrodactyly.
Makroglobulinämie *f*: macroglobulinemia, Waldenström's macroglobulinemia.
Makroglossie *f*: macroglossia.
Makrolidantibiotikum *n*: macrolide antibiotic.
Makromastie *f*: macromastia, gigantomastia, megalomastia.
Makromelie *f*: macromelia.
Makromolekül *n*: macromolecule.
Makrophage *m*: macrophage.
makroskopisch: macroscopic.
Makrostomie *f*: macrostomia.
Makrozephalie *f*: macrocephaly.
Makrozyt *m*: macrocyte.
makrozytär: macrocytic.
Makrozytose *f*: macrocytosis.
Makula *f*: macula, macule, Tay spot; **kirschrote** ≈ cherry-red spot.
Makulaaussparung *f*: macular sparing.
Makulabündel *n*: papillomacular bundle.
Makuladegeneration *f*: macular degeneration; **juvenile** ≈ juvenile macular degeneration, Stargardt's disease; **scheibenförmige** ≈ disciform macular degeneration, Kuhnt-Junius disease.
Makulaerkrankung *f*: maculopathy, macular retinopathy.
Makulaödem *n*: macular edema; **passageres** ≈ transient macular edema, Berlin's disease; **zystisches** ≈ cystoid macular edema, Irvine syndrome.
makulopapulös: maculopapular, maculopapulous.
Mal *n*: stigma, mark.
Malabsorptionssyndrom *n*: malabsorption syndrome.
Maladaptation *f*: maladaptation.
malar: malar.
Malaria *f*: malaria, paludal fever, paludism; **akute** ≈ acute malaria; **benigne tertianaähnliche** ≈ benign tertian malaria; **chronische** ≈ chronic malaria; **intermittierende** ≈ intermittent malaria; **rekurrierende** ≈ relapsing malaria.
Malariabekämpfung *f*: malaria control.
Malariafieber *n*: malarial fever.
Malariamittel *n*: antimalarial, malaricidal.
Malaria quartana *f*: quartan malaria, quartana.
Malaria tertiana *f*: tertian malaria.
Malaria tropica *f*: malignant tertian malaria, falciparum malaria.
Malazie *f*: malacia.
Maldigestion *f*: maldigestion.
Maleinsäure *f*: maleic acid.
Malformation *f*: malformation.
maligne: malignant.
Malignität *f*: malignancy.
Malignom *n*: malignant tumor.
Malleolus *m*: malleolus.
Malleus *m*: malleus, glanders.
Malnutrition *f*: malnutrition.
Malokklusion *f*: malocclusion.
Malonsäure *f*: malonic acid.
Maltafieber *n*: Malta fever.
Maltase *f*: maltase.
Maltose *f*: maltose, malt sugar.
Malz *n*: malt.
Mamilla *f*: mamilla, nipple.
Mamillarlinie *f*: mamillary line.
Mamille *f*: mamilla, nipple.
Mamillenfissur *f*: cracked nipple.
Mamma *f*: mamma, mammary gland, breast; **akzessorische** ≈ accessory mamma, supernumerary mamma.
Mammaabszess *m*: mammary abscess, intramammary abscess.
Mammahypertrophie *f*: mammary hypertrophy.
Mammakarzinom *n*: breast carcinoma; **intradermales** ≈ Paget's disease of nipple; **medulläres** ≈ medullary breast carcinoma.
Mammaplastik *f*: mammoplasty, mammaplasty.
Mammareduktionsplastik *f*: reduction mammoplasty.
Mammavergrößerung *f*: augmentation mammoplasty.
Mammographie *f*: mammography, senography.
Mandel *f*: tonsil, almond.
Mandelentzündung *f*: tonsillitis, quinsy.
Mandelsäure *f*: mandelic acid.
mandibulär: mandibular.

Mandibularesektion *f*: mandibular resection.
Mandrin *m*: mandrin, mandrel, stylet.
Mangafodipir *n*: mangafodipir.
Manganvergiftung *f*: manganism, manganese poisoning.
Mangel *m*: deficiency, shortage, privation, lack; **ernährungsbedingter** ≈ nutritional deficiency; **emotioneller** ≈ emotional deprivation.
Mangelernährung *f*: malnutrition, undernourishment.
Mangelkrankheit *f*: deficiency disease.
Manie *f*: mania, manic psychosis; **akinetische** ≈ akinetic mania; **delirante** ≈ delirious mania, Bell's delirium; **depressive** ≈ depressive mania; **endogene** ≈ endogenous mania; **epileptische** ≈ epileptic mania; **symptomatische** ≈ symptomatic mania.
manifest: overt, present.
Manifestation *f*: manifestation, presentation.
Manipulation *f*: manipulation.
manisch: manic, maniacal.
manisch-depressiv: manic-depressive.
Mann *m*: male, man.
Mannitolhexanitrat *n*: mannitol hexanitrate.
Mannomustin *n*: mannomustine.
Mannstollheit *f*: nymphomania.
Manöver *n*: maneuver.
Manometer *n*: manometer.
Manschette *f*: cuff.
Manschettenaufhängung *f*: cuff suspension.
Manschettentubus *m*: cuff tubus.
Mantel *m*: mantle, coat, jacket.
Mantelatelektase *f*: subpleural collapse.
Manubrium *n*: manubrium, handle.
manuell: manual.
Mapping *n*: mapping.
Maprotilin *n*: maprotiline.
Marasmus *m*: marasmus, wasting, Parrot's atrophy of the newborn.
Marchiafava-Bignami-Syndrom *n*: Bignami's disease, Marchiafava's disease, central degeneration of the corpus callosum.
Marchiafava-Micheli-Syndrom *n*: Marchiafava-Micheli syndrome, paroxysmal nocturnal hemoglobinuria.
Marfan-Syndrom *n*: Marfan syndrome, arachnodactyly.
Marginalsinus *m*: marginal sinus.
Marie-Bamberger-Krankheit *f*: Marie-Bamberger disease, hypertrophic pulmonary osteoarthropathy.
Marie-Krankheit *f*: Marie's hereditary cerebellar ataxia, acromegaly.
Mariendistel *f*: milk thistle.
Marie-Strümpell-Krankheit *f*: Marie-Strümpell disease, ankylosing spondylitis.
Marihuana *n*: marijuana, marihuana.
Mark *n*: marrow, medulla.
Markenpräparat *n*: patent medicine.
Marker *m*: marker; **biologischer** ≈ biological marker; **immunologischer** ≈ immunologic marker; **klinischer** ≈ clinical marker.
Markersubstanz *f*: marker.
markhaltig: myelinated, medullated.
Markhöhle *f*: marrow space.
markieren: tag, label.
Markierung *f*: labeling, tag, tagging, marking; **immunhistochemische** ≈ immunolabeling; **radioaktive** ≈ radioactive label.
Markierungsprotein *n*: marker protein.
Markierungssubstanz *f*: tracer.
Markkallus *m*: central callus.
Marklager *n*: medullary layer.
marklos: unmedullated, unmyelinated.
Marknagelung *f*: marrow nailing, intramedullary nailing.
Markraum *m*: medullary space.
Markscheidensegment *n*: medullary segment.
Markschwammkarzinom *n*: medullary carcinoma.
Markschwammniere *f*: medullary sponge kidney.
Marmorknochenkrankheit *f*: marble bone disease, osteopetrosis, Albers-Schönberg disease.
Marschalbuminurie *f*: march albuminuria.

Marschhämoglobinurie *f*: march hemoglobinuria.
Marsupialisation *f*: marsupialization.
Maschinengeräusch *n*: machinelike murmur, continuous sound.
Masern *f*: measles, morbilli.
Maskengesicht *n*: mask face, parkinsonian face.
maskieren: mask.
maskulin: masculine, virile.
Masochismus *m*: masochism.
Maß *n*: measure, gauge, standard.
Massage *f*: massage.
Masse *f*: mass, compound, matter, pulp.
Maßeinheit *f*: unit of measure.
Massenblutung *f*: massive hemorrhage.
Massenneurose *f*: collective neurosis.
Massenpsychologie *f*: mass psychology.
Masseterreflex *m*: masseter reflex, jaw jerk.
massiv: massive, heavy.
Maßnahme *f*: measure.
Maßstab *m*: gauge, gage, scale.
Mastektomie *f*: mastectomy, mammectomy, Tansini's operation; **einfache** ≈ simple mastectomy; **erweiterte radikale** ≈ extended radical mastectomy; **modifizierte radikale** ≈ modified radical mastectomy; **partielle** ≈ partial mastectomy, segmental mastectomy; **radikale** ≈ radical mastectomy, Meyer's operation; **subkutane** ≈ subcutaneous mastectomy; **subtotale** ≈ subradical mastectomy.
Mastikation *f*: mastication.
Mastitis *f*: mastitis; **akute** ≈ acute mastitis; **chronische** ≈ chronic mastitis; **eitrige** ≈ suppurative mastitis; **interstitielle** ≈ interstitial mastitis, phlegmonous mastitis; **parenchymatöse** ≈ parenchymatous mastitis, glandular mastitis; **periduktale** ≈ periductal mastitis; **puerperale** ≈ puerperal mastitis; **zystische** ≈ chronic cystic mastitis.
Mastodynie *f*: mastodynia, mastalgia, Cooper's disease.
Mastoidektomie *f*: mastoidectomy, mastoid operation; **einfache** ≈ simple mastoidectomy, conservative mastoidectomy; **radikale** ≈ radical mastoidectomy, mastoidotympanectomy.
Mastoiditis *f*: mastoiditis; **einschmelzende** ≈ coalescent mastoiditis; **okkulte** ≈ silent mastoiditis, masked mastoiditis; **tuberkulöse** ≈ tuberculous mastoiditis.
Mastopathie *f*: mastopathy, mastopathia; **proliferierende** ≈ proliferative mastopathy; **zystische** ≈ cystic mastopathy, Schimmelbusch disease.
Mastozyt *m*: mastocyte, mast cell.
Mastozytom *n*: mastocytoma.
Masturbation *f*: masturbation.
Mastzelle *f*: mast cell, mastocyte.
Matching *n*: matching.
Material *n*: material.
maternal: maternal.
Maternität *f*: maternity.
Matratze *f*: mattress.
Matratzennaht *f*: mattress suture, quilted suture.
Matrix *f*: matrix.
Matrize *f*: template, die.
Maturation *f*: maturation.
Maul- und Klauenseuche *f*: foot-and-mouth disease, aphthous fever, contagious aphtha, epizootic aphtha, malignant aphtha.
maxillär: maxillary.
Maxillaresektion *f*: maxillary resection.
maximal: maximal, maximum.
Maximum *n*: maximum.
Mazeration *f*: maceration.
Mazipredon *n*: mazipredone.
McArdle-Krankheit *f*: McArdle's disease, glycogen storage disease V.
McBurney-Appendizitiszeichen *n*: McBurney sign.
McBurney-Punkt *m*: McBurney's point.
McDonald-Handgriff *m*: McDonald's maneuver.
McKusick-Syndrom *n*: cartilage-hair hypoplasia, metaphyseal chondrodysplasia.
McLean-Zange *f*: McLean forceps.
McMurray-Außenrotationsversuch

m: McMurray's circumduction maneuver.
Meatusstenose *f*: meatal stenosis.
Mebendazol *n*: mebendazole.
Mebeverin *n*: mebeverine.
Mecamylamin *n*: mecamylamine.
Mechanismus *m*: mechanism.
Meckel-Divertikel *n*: Meckel's diverticulum.
Meclocyclin *n*: meclocycline.
Meclofenaminsäure *f*: meclofenamic acid.
Meclofenoxat *n*: meclofenoxate.
Mecloxamin *n*: mecloxamine.
Meclozin *n*: meclozine.
Medazepam *n*: medazepam.
Mediafibrose *f*: medial fibroplasia.
medial: medial.
Median *m*: median.
Medianebene *f*: median plane.
Medianlinie *f*: median line, median.
Mediansagittalebene *f*: median sagittal plane.
Medianschnitt *m*: median incision.
Medianuslähmung *f*: median paralysis, milker's paralysis.
mediastinal: mediastinal.
Mediastinalemphysem *n*: mediastinal emphysema.
Mediastinalflattern *n*: mediastinal flutter.
Mediastinalverdrängung *f*: mediastinal displacement.
Mediastinalzyste *f*: mediastinal cyst.
Mediastinum *n*: mediastinum, interpleural space.
Mediator *m*: mediator, transmitter.
Medigoxin *n*: methyldigoxin.
Medikament *n*: drug, medicament, medicinal agent, remedy; **frei verkäufliches** ≈ over the counter drug, OTC drug; **geschütztes** ≈ proprietary drug; **verschreibungspflichtiges** ≈ prescription drug.
Medikamentenverzeichnis *n*: formulary.
medikamentös bedingt: drug-induced.
Medikation *f*: medication.
Medinawurm *m*: Dracunculus medinensis, serpent worm.
Medium *n*: medium; **brechendes** ≈ refracting medium, dioptric medium.
Medizin *f*: medicine; **biologische** ≈ biomedicine; **chinesische** ≈ Chinese medicine; **evidenzbasierte** ≈ evidence-based medicine; **ganzheitliche** ≈ holistic medicine; **innere** ≈ internal medicine; **klinische** ≈ clinical medicine; **orthomolekulare** ≈ orthomolecular medicine; **physikalische** ≈ physical medicine; **präventive** ≈ preventive medicine; **praktische** ≈ medical practice; **psychosomatische** ≈ psychosomatic medicine; **traditionelle** ≈ traditional medicine; **unkonventionelle** ≈ unconventional medicine.
medizinal: medicinal.
Medizinalfläschchen *n*: vial, phial.
Medizinalpflanze *f*: medicinal herb.
Medizinalsirup *m*: medicated syrup.
Medizinball *m*: medical ball.
Medizinethik *f*: medical ethics.
Medizingeschichte *f*: history of medicine.
medizinisch: medical.
Medizinmann *m*: medicine man, indigenous practitioner.
Medizinpsychologie *f*: medical psychology.
Medizinsoziologie *f*: medical sociology.
Medizintechnik *f*: medical technology.
Medrogeston *n*: medrogestone.
Medroxyprogesteron *n*: medroxyprogesterone.
Medryson *n*: medrysone.
Medulla *f*: medulla, marrow.
medullär: medullary.
Medulla-oblongata-Syndrom, laterales *n*: lateral medullary syndrome.
Medulloblastom *n*: medulloblastoma.
Medusenhaupt *n*: medusa's head.
Meerschweinchen *n*: guinea pig.
Mefenaminsäure *f*: mefenamic acid.
Mefloquin *n*: mefloquine.
Mefrusid *n*: mefruside.
Megakaryoblast *m*: megakaryoblast.
Megakaryozyt *m*: megalokaryocyte.
Megakaryozytenleukämie *f*: mega-

karyocytic leukemia.

Megakolon *n*: megacolon, giant colon; **aganglionäres** ≈ aganglionic megacolon; **idiopathisches** ≈ idiopathic constitutional megacolon; **kongenitales** ≈ congenital megacolon, Hirschsprung's disease; **toxisches** ≈ toxic megacolon.

Megaloblast *m*: megaloblast.

Megaloblastenanämie *f*: megaloblastic anemia.

Megalomanie *f*: megalomania.

Megalozyt *m*: megalocyte.

Megazephalus *m*: megacephaly.

Megestrolacetat *n*: megestrol acetate.

mehrfach: multiple.

Mehrfachbruch *m*: multiple fracture.

Mehrfachgeburt *f*: multiple birth.

Mehrfachresistenz *f*: multiple resistance.

mehrgipfelig: polycrotic.

mehrkammerig: multilocular, plurilocular.

mehrkernig: polynuclear.

Mehrlingsschwangerschaft *f*: multiple pregnancy.

Mehrphasenpille *f*: sequential oral pill.

Meibom-Drüse *f*: meibomian gland.

Meibom-Zyste *f*: meibomian cyst.

Meiose *f*: meiosis.

Meissner-Plexus *m*: Meissner's plexus, submucous plexus.

Meissner-Tastkörperchen: Meissner's corpuscles.

Mekonium *n*: meconium.

Mekonsäure *f*: meconic acid.

Melagatran *n*: melagatran.

Melancholie *f*: melancholia, melancholy, major depressive episode with melancholia.

Melanin *n*: melanin.

Melanom *n*: melanoma; **akrolentiginöses** ≈ acral lentiginous melanoma; **amelanotisches** ≈ amelanotic melanoma; **benignes juveniles** ≈ benign juvenile melanoma; **malignes** ≈ malignant melanoma; **noduläres** ≈ nodular melanoma; **oberflächlich spreitendes** ≈ superficial spreading melanoma; **subunguales** ≈ subungual melanoma; **superfiziell spreitendes** ≈ superficial spreading melanoma.

Melanose *f*: melanosis.

Melanosis circumscripta praeblastomatosa Dubreuilh *f*: precancerous melanosis of Dubreilh, Hutchinson's melanotic freckle.

melanotisch: melanotic.

Melasma *n*: melasma.

Melasse *f*: molasses, treacle.

melden: report, notify.

meldepflichtig: notifiable, certifiable.

Meldung *f*: notification, registration.

Meleney-Syndrom *n*: progressive bacterial synergistic gangrene.

Melisse *f*: melissa.

Melitracen *n*: melitracen.

Melkersson-Rosenthal-Syndrom *n*: Melkersson syndrome, Rosenthal syndrome, progressive lingual hemiatrophy.

Meloxicam *n*: meloxicam.

Melperon *n*: melperone.

Melphalan *n*: melphalan.

Memantin *n*: memantine.

Membran *f*: membrane, diaphragm; **diphtheritische** ≈ diphtheritic membrane; **hyaline** ≈ hyaline membrane; **komplexe** ≈ compound membrane; **postsynaptische** ≈ postsynaptic membrane; **präsynaptische** ≈ presynaptic membrane; **semipermeable** ≈ semipermeable membrane; **synaptische** ≈ synaptic membrane.

membranös: membranous, membranaceous.

membranoproliferativ: membranoproliferative.

Membranpotential *n*: membrane potential.

Menarche *f*: menarche.

Mendel-Mantoux-Test *m*: intradermal tuberculin skin testing, Mendel's test, Mantoux' test.

Mendel-Vererbungstheorie *f*: mendelian theory.

Ménétrier-Krankheit *f*: Ménétrier's disease, giant hypertrophic gastritis.

Menge *f*: amount, quantity, volume, bulk; **empfohlene tägliche** ≈ recom-

manded daily allowance.
Menière-Krankheit *f*: Menière syndrome, auditory vertigo.
meningeal: meningeal.
Meningiom *n*: meningioma; **entdifferenziertes** ≈ anaplastic meningioma; **fibröses** ≈ fibrous meningioma; **gemischtes** ≈ mixed meningioma; **hämangioblastomatöses** ≈ hemangioblastic meningioma; **hämangioperizytisches** ≈ hemangiopericytic meningioma; **parasagittales** ≈ parasagittal meningioma.
Meningismus *m*: meningism, Dupré's disease.
Meningitis *f*: meningitis; **abakterielle** ≈ aseptic meningitis; **akute septische** ≈ acute septic meningitis; **bakterielle** ≈ bacterial meningitis; **eitrige** ≈ purulent meningitis, suppurative meningitis; **granulomatöse** ≈ granulomatous meningitis; **lymphozytäre** ≈ benign lymphocytic meningitis; **otogene** ≈ otogenic meningitis; **syphilitische** ≈ syphilitic meningitis; **tuberkulöse** ≈ tuberculous meningitis, Whytt's disease.
meningitisch: meningitic.
Meningoenzephalitis *f*: meningoencephalitis, encephalomeningitis; **eosinophile** ≈ eosinophilic meningitis; **syphilitische** ≈ syphilitic meningoencephalitis.
Meningoenzephalozele *f*: meningoencephalocele.
Meningokokkeninfektion *f*: meningococcal infection.
Meningokokkenmeningitis *f*: meningococcal meningitis.
Meningokokkensepsis *f*: meningococcemia; **akute fulminante** ≈ acute fulminating meningococcal septicemia.
Meningomyelozele *f*: meningomyelocele.
Meningozele *f*: meningocele; **traumatische** ≈ traumatic meningocele, Billroth's disease.
Meniscus *m*: meniscus.
Meniskektomie *f*: meniscectomy.
Meniskusverletzung *f*: meniscus injury.
Menkes-Syndrom *n*: Menkes syndrome, kinky hair syndrome.
menopausal: menopausal.
Menopause *f*: menopause.
Menorrhagie *f*: menorrhagia.
Mensch *m*: human, man.
Menschenaffe *m*: man ape, anthropoid ape.
Menschenfloh *m*: human flea, Pulex irritans.
menschlich: human.
Menstruation *f*: menstruation, menstrual period; **vikariierende** ≈ vicarious menstruation.
Menstruationspsychose *f*: menstrual psychosis.
Menstruationsschmerz *m*: menstrual pain.
Menstruationsstörung *f*: menstruation disorder.
Menstruationszyklus *m*: menstrual cycle.
mental: mental.
Menthol *n*: menthol.
mentolabial: labiomental.
Mepacrin *n*: mepacrine.
Mepazin *n*: mepazine.
Mephenesin *n*: mephenesin.
Mephentermin *n*: mephentermine.
Mepindolol *n*: mepindolol.
Meproscillarin *n*: meproscillarin.
Mercaptamin *n*: mercaptamine.
Mercaptopurin *n*: mercaptopurine.
Meridian *m*: meridian.
Merkaptursäure *f*: mercapturic acid.
Merkfähigkeit *f*: recent memory.
merklich: noticeable, perceptible.
merokrin: merocrine.
Mesalazin *n*: mesalazine.
mesangiokapillär: mesangiocapillary.
Mesangiumzelle *f*: mesangial cell.
Mesarteriitis *f*: mesarteritis.
Mesencephalon *n*: mesencephalon, midbrain.
Mesenchym *n*: mesenchyme, mesenchymal tissue.
Mesenchymzelle *f*: mesenchymal cell.
mesenterial: mesenteric.
Mesenterialarterienthrombose *f*: mesenteric thrombosis.

M

Mesenterialinfarkt *m*: mesenteric infarct.
Mesenterialzyste *f*: mesenteric cyst.
Mesenterium *n*: mesentery, mesenterium.
Mesialbiss *m*: mesial occlusion, mesioclusion.
Mesitylensäure *f*: mesitylenic acid.
Mesmerismus *m*: mesmerism.
Mesna *n*: mesna.
Mesoappendix *f*: mesoappendix.
Mesoderm *n*: mesoderm.
mesodiastolisch: mesodiastolic, mid-diastolic.
Mesokolon *n*: mesocolon.
Mesonephrom *n*: mesonephroma.
Mesosalpinx *m*: mesosalpinx.
Mesothel *n*: mesothelium.
Mesotheliom *n*: mesothelioma.
messen: measure.
Messenger-Ribonukleinsäure *f*: messenger ribonucleic acid, messenger RNA, mRNA.
Messer *n*: knife.
Messung *f*: measurement, measuring; **axilläre** ≈ axillary measurement; **rektale** ≈ rectal measurement.
Mesterolon *n*: mesterolone.
Mestranol *n*: mestranol.
Mesulfen *n*: mesulfen.
Mesuximid *n*: mesuximide.
metabolisch: metabolic.
Metabolismus *m*: metabolism.
Metabolit *m*: metabolite.
metachromatisch: metachromatic.
metakarpal: metacarpal.
metakarpophalangeal: metacarpophalangeal.
Metall *n*: metal.
Metallchelatkomplex *m*: metal chelate complex.
metallisch: metallic.
Metamfepramon *n*: metamfepramone.
Metamizol *n*: metamizole.
Metamorphose *f*: metamorphosis.
Metanephros *m*: metanephros.
Metaphase *f*: metaphase.
Metaphosphorsäure *f*: metaphosphoric acid.
metaphysär: metaphyseal.
Metaphyse *f*: metaphysis.
Metaplasie *f*: metaplasia.
metapneumonisch: metapneumonic, postpneumonic.
Metaraminol *n*: metaraminol.
Metastase *f*: metastasis, metastatic tumor; **osteolytische** ≈ osteolytic metastasis; **osteoplastische** ≈ osteoplastic metastasis.
Metastasierung *f*: metastasis, spread; **hämatogene** ≈ hematogenous metastasis; **lymphogene** ≈ lymphogenous metastasis; **septische** ≈ metastasizing septicemia.
metastatisch: metastatic.
metatarsal: metatarsal.
Metempsychose *f*: metempsychosis.
Metenolon *n*: metenolone.
Meteorismus *m*: meteorism.
Meter *m*: meter.
Methacholinchlorid *n*: methacholine chloride.
Methadon *n*: methadone.
Methadonsubstitution *f*: methadone maintenance.
Methämoglobin *n*: methemoglobin, methaemoglobin.
Methämoglobinämie *f*: methemoglobinemia.
Methandriol *n*: methandriol.
Methanol *n*: methanol, methyl alcohol.
Methantheliniumbromid *n*: methanthelinium bromide.
Methionin *n*: methionine.
Methocarbomal *n*: methocarbomal.
Methode *f*: method, technique.
Methotrexat *n*: methotrexate.
Methoxaminhydrochlorid *n*: methoxamine hydrochloride.
Methoxyfluran *n*: methoxyflurane.
8-Methoxypsoralen *n*: 8-methoxypsoralen.
Methylalkohol *m*: methyl alcohol.
Methyldigoxin *n*: metildigoxin.
Methyldopa *n*: methyldopa.
Methylergometrin *n*: methylergometrine.
Methylhydantoinsäure *f*: methylhydantoic acid.
Methylmalonazidurie *f*: methylmalonicaciduria.
Methylmalonsäure *f*: methylmalonic acid.

Methylorange *n*: methyl orange.
Methylpentynol *n*: methylpentynol.
Methyl-phenyl-tetrahydropyridin n: methyl-phenyl-tetrahydropyridine.
Methylprednisolon *n*: methylprednisolone.
Methylsulfonal *n*: methylsulfonal.
Methyltestosteron *n*: methyltestosterone.
Methysergid *n*: methysergide.
Meticillin *n*: meticillin.
Metildigoxin *n*: metildigoxin.
Metipranolol *n*: metipranolol.
Metoclopramid *n*: metoclopramide.
Metolazon *n*: metolazone.
Metoprolol *n*: metoprolol.
metrisch: metric.
Metritis *f*: metritis.
Metronidazol *n*: metronidazole.
Metropathie *f*: metropathy, hysteropathy.
Metrorrhagie *f*: metrorrhagia.
Metyrapon *n*: metyrapone.
Mexiletin *n*: mexiletine.
Meyer-Operation *f*: Meyer's operation.
Mezlocillin *n*: mezlocillin.
Mianserin *n*: mianserin.
Miconazol *n*: miconazole.
Midodrin *n*: midodrine.
Mifepriston *n*: mifepristone.
Miglitol *n*: miglitol.
Miglustat *n*: miglustat.
Migräne *f*: migraine; **ophthalmoplegische** ≈ ophthalmoplegic migraine, Charcot's disease.
Migraine accompagnée *f*: complicated migraine.
Migraine cervicale *f*: cervical migraine, Barré-Lieou syndrome.
Migraine ophtalmoplégique *f*: ophthalmoplegic migraine, Charcot's disease.
Mikroangiopathie *f*: microangiopathy; **diabetische** ≈ diabetic microangiopathy; **nierenbezogene diabetische** ≈ diabetic renal microangiopathy; **thrombotische** ≈ thrombotic microangiopathy.
Mikrobe *f*: microbe, microorganism.
mikrobiell: microbial.
Mikrobiologie *f*: microbiology.
mikrobizid: microbicide.
Mikrobizid *n*: microbicide.
Mikrochirurgie *f*: microsurgery.
Mikroglia *f*: microglia.
Mikrogliazelle *f*: microglial cell, Hortega cell.
Mikrognathie *f*: micrognathia.
Mikroläsion *f*: microlesion.
Mikromelie *f*: micromelia.
Mikrometrie *f*: micrometry.
Mikroorganismus *m*: microorganism, microbe.
Mikrophthalmus *m*: microphthalmos.
Mikropsie *f*: micropsia, micropia.
Mikroskop *n*: microscope.
Mikroskopie *f*: microscopy.
mikroskopisch: microscopic.
Mikrosom *n*: microsome.
Mikrosporidiose *f*: microsporidiosis.
Mikrotom *n*: microtome, section cutter.
Mikrozephalie *f*: microcephaly.
Mikrozytose *f*: microcytosis.
Miktion *f*: micturation, urination.
Miktionshäufigkeit *f*: micturition frequency.
Miktionsreflex *m*: urinary reflex, renoureteral reflex.
Miktionszystographie *f*: voiding cystography.
Miktionszysturethrogramm *n*: voiding cysturethrogram.
Milbe *f*: mite.
Milch *f*: milk; **adaptierte** ≈ adapted milk; **angereicherte** ≈ fortified milk; **homogenisierte** ≈ homogenized milk; **kondensierte** ≈ condensed milk; **pasteurisierte** ≈ pasteurized milk; **sterilisierte** ≈ sterilized milk.
Milchfertignahrung *f*: infant formula.
Milchfleck *m*: milk spot, white patch.
milchführend: galactophorous, lactiferous.
Milchgang *m*: milk duct.
Milchgangfistel *f*: lacteal fistula.
Milchgebiss *n*: primary dentition.
milchig: milky, lactic, galactic.
Milchpumpe *f*: breast pump.
Milchretention *f*: milk retention.
Milchsäure *f*: lactic acid.

Milchsaft *m*: chyle.
Milchschorf *m*: milk crust, cradle cap.
Milchsekretion *f*: milk secretion, lactation.
Milchstar *m*: milky cataract, fluid cataract.
Milchstau *m*: milk retention.
Milchzahn *m*: milk tooth, primary tooth.
Milchzyste *f*: lacteal cyst, galactocele.
mild: bland, mild, slight.
mildern: allay, relieve.
Milderung *f*: relief.
miliar: miliary.
Miliarabszess *m*: miliary abscess.
Miliartuberkulose *f*: miliary tuberculosis.
Milieu *n*: milieu, environment.
Milieutherapie *f*: milieu therapy, socioenvironmental therapy.
Militärhospital *n*: military hospital.
Millard-Gubler-Syndrom *n*: Millard-Gubler syndrome, inferior alternate paralysis.
Milrinon *n*: milrinone.
Miltefosin *n*: miltefosine.
Milz *f*: spleen.
Milzamyloidose *f*: amyloid spleen.
Milzbrand *m*: anthrax, carbuncular fever.
Milzexstirpation *f*: splenectomy.
Milzruptur *f*: splenic rupture.
Milzvenenthrombose *f*: thrombophlebitic splenomegaly, Opitz disease.
Milzvergrößerung *f*: enlarged spleen, splenomegaly.
Mimetikum *n*: mimetic.
mimetisch: mimetic.
Mimikry *f*: mimicry.
mimisch: mimic.
Minderwuchs *m*: dwarfism, nanosomia; **hypophysärer** ≈ hypophysial dwarfism, pituitary dwarfism; **myxödematöser** ≈ myxedematous dwarfism; **thanatophorer** ≈ thanatophoric dysplasia.
Mineral *n*: mineral.
Mineralwasser *n*: mineral water.
minimal: minimal.
Minimaldosis *f*: minimum dose.
Minipille *f*: minipill.
Minocyclin *n*: minocycline.
Minor Tranquilizer *m*: minor tranquilizer.
Minoxidil *n*: minoxidil.
Minuslinse *f*: minus lens.
Minutenvolumen *n*: minute ventilation.
Miosis *f*: miosis.
Mirtazapin *n*: mirtazapine.
Mischinfektion *f*: mixed infection, complex infection.
Mischinsulin *n*: combination insulin.
Mischplasma *n*: pooled plasma.
Mischpsychose *f*: mixed psychosis.
Mischtumor *m*: mixed tumor.
Misoprostol *n*: misoprostol.
Missbildung *f*: malformation, deformity.
Missbrauch *m*: abuse; **sexueller** ≈ sexual abuse.
missbrauchen: abuse.
Missempfindung *f*: paresthesia.
Misshandlung *f*: maltreatment, battery.
Mistel *f*: mistletoe.
Mitbewegung *f*: associated movement, synkinesis; **kontralaterale** ≈ contralateral synkinesis; **spastische** ≈ spasmodic synkinesis.
Mitesser *m*: blackhead, comedo.
Mithramycin *n*: mithramycin.
Mitochondrium *n*: mitochondrion.
Mitogen *n*: mitogen.
Mitoguazon *n*: mitoguazone.
Mitomycin *n*: mitomycin.
Mitose *f*: mitosis.
Mitosegift *n*: mitotic poison.
Mitotan *n*: mitotane.
Mitoxantron *n*: mitoxantrone.
mitral: mitral.
Mitralklappe *f*: mitral valve, bicuspidal valve.
Mitralklappengeräusch *n*: mitral murmur.
Mitralklappeninsuffizienz *f*: mitral insufficiency.
Mitralklappenprolaps *m*: mitral valve prolapse.
Mitralklappenstenose *f*: mitral stenosis; **kongenitale** ≈ congenital mitral stenosis, Duroziez disease.
Mitralöffnungston *m*: mitral click, opening snap.

Mittel *n*: mean, medium, agent; **appetitanregendes** ≈ appetizer; **blutstillendes** ≈ styptic; **fiebersenkendes** ≈ febricide, defervescent; **gerinnungshemmendes** ≈ anticoagulant; **herzstärkendes** ≈ cardiotonic; **prophylaktisches** ≈ prophylactic; **sekretionsförderndes** ≈ secretagogue; **verdauungsförderndes** ≈ digestant.
mittelbar: mediate.
Mittelblutung *f*: midcycle bleeding.
Mittelfinger *m*: middle finger.
Mittelhand *f*: metacarpus.
Mittelhirn *n*: midbrain, mesencephalon.
Mittelhirnsyndrom *n*: mesencephalic paralysis.
Mittellappen *m*: middle lobe.
Mittellinie *f*: midline.
Mittelliniengranulom *n*: midline granuloma.
Mittelmeerfieber *n*: Mediterranean fever, Malta fever.
Mittelohr *n*: middle ear.
Mittelohrentzündung *f*: otitis media.
Mittelschmerz *m*: mittelschmerz, intermenstrual pain.
Mittelstrahlurin *m*: midstream urine.
Mittelwert *m*: mean value.
Mivacuriumchlorid *n*: mivacurium chloride.
Mixtur *f*: mixture.
Mizolastin *n*: mizolastine.
MMN-Syndrom *n*: mucosal neuroma syndrome, multiple endocrine neoplasia type 2B.
mnestisch: mnestic, mnemic.
Mobilisation *f*: mobilization.
Mobilität *f*: mobility.
Mobitz-Block *m*: Mobitz block, Mobitz-type atrioventricular dissociation.
Moclobemid *n*: moclobemide.
moderat: moderate.
Modifikatorgen *n*: modifying gene, modification allel.
modifizieren: modify.
Moebius-Syndrom *n*: Moebius syndrome, nuclear agenesis, congenital facial diplegia.
Moeller-Barlow-Syndrom *n*: Moeller-Barlow syndrome, infantile scurvy, Barlow's disease.
Möller-Hunter-Glossitis *f*: Möller's glossitis, chronic lingual papillitis.
Mönckeberg-Sklerose *f*: Mönckeberg's medial sclerosis, medial arteriosclerosis.
Moexipril *n*: moexipril.
Mofebutazon *n*: mofebutazone.
Mogigraphie *f*: mogigraphia, writer's cramp.
Molalität *f*: molality.
molar: molar.
Molar *m*: molar, multicuspid tooth.
Molarität *f*: molarity.
Mole *f*: mole.
Molekül *n*: molecule.
molekular: molecular.
Molekularbiologie *f*: molecular biology.
Molekulargenetik *f*: molecular genetics.
Molekularpathologie *f*: molecular pathology.
Molenschwangerschaft *f*: molar pregnancy.
Molgramostim *n*: molgramostim.
Molsidomin *n*: molsidomine.
Molybdänsäure *f*: molybdenic acid.
Mometasonfuroat *n*: mometasone furoate.
monaural: monaural.
Mondbein *n*: lunate bone.
Mondbeinnekrose *f*: Kienböck's disease.
Mondonesi-Reflex *m*: facial reflex, bulbomimic reflex.
Mongolenfleck *m*: mongolian spot, dermal melanocytoma.
monilial: monilial.
Monitor *m*: monitor.
Monitoring *n*: monitoring.
Monoaminoxidasehemmer *m*: monoamine oxidase inhibitor, MAO inhibitor.
Monobenzon *n*: monobenzone.
Monoblast *m*: monoblast.
Monogamie *f*: monogamy.
monoklonal: monoclonal.
Monokularschielen *n*: monocular strabismus, unilateral strabismus.
Monomanie *f*: monomania.
Mononeuritis *f*: mononeuritis.

Mononucleosis infectiosa *f*: infectious mononucleosis, Pfeiffer's disease.
mononukleär: mononuclear.
Mononukleose *f*: mononucleosis; **infektiöse** ≈ infectious mononucleosis, Pfeiffer's disease.
monophasisch: monophasic.
Monoplegie *f*: monoplegia.
monoploid: monoploid.
Monorchidie *f*: monorchidism.
Monosaccharid *n*: monosaccharide.
Monosom *n*: monosome.
Monotherapie *f*: monotherapy.
monovalent: monovalent.
monozentrisch: monocentric.
Monozyt *m*: monocyte.
monozytär: monocytoid.
Monozytenleukämie *f*: monocytic leukemia, Naegeli's leukemia.
Monstrezellensarkom *n*: monstrocellular sarcoma.
Monteggia-Fraktur *f*: Monteggia's fracture, parry fracture.
Montelukast *n*: montelukast.
Moore-Syndrom *n*: Moore syndrome, abdominal migraine.
Moorpackung *f*: mudpack.
moosartig: mossy.
Moperon *n*: moperone.
Mopidamol *n*: mopidamol.
Morazon *n*: morazone.
morbid: morbid.
Morbidität *f*: morbidity.
morbilliform: morbilliform.
Mord *m*: murder, homicide.
Morgagni-Hernie *f*: diaphragmatic hernia.
Morgagni-Katarakt *f*: morgagnian cataract, fluid cataract.
Morgagni-Papille *f*: anal papilla.
Morgagni-Zyste *f*: morgagnian cyst.
moribund: moribund.
Moroxydin *n*: moroxydine.
Morphaea *f*: morphea, circumscribed scleroderma.
Morphin *n*: morphine, morphium.
Morphinderivat *n*: morphine derivative.
Morphinrezeptor *m*: morphine receptor.
Morphium *n*: morphium, morphine.
Morphogenese *f*: morphogenesis.
Morphologie *f*: morphology.
morphologisch: morphological.
Mortalität *f*: mortality, death rate.
Mortalitätsrisiko *n*: mortality risk.
Morula *f*: morula.
Mosaik *n*: mosaic, mosaicism.
Moschcowitz-Syndrom *n*: Moschcowitz disease, thrombotic thrombocytopenic purpura.
Moskito *m*: mosquito, gnat.
Motilität *f*: motility.
Motoneuron *n*: motoneuron, motor cell.
Motorik *f*: motoricity, motor activity.
motorisch: motor.
Moutard-Martin-Zeichen *n*: Moutard-Martin sign, Lasègue's contralateral sign.
Moxaverin *n*: moxaverine.
Moxibustion *f*: moxibustion.
Moxidectin *n*: moxidectin.
Moxifloxacin *n*: moxifloxacin.
Moxonidin *n*: moxonidin.
Müdigkeit *f*: fatigue, tiredness, exhaustion.
Müdigkeitssyndrom *n*: fatigue syndrome.
Münzenklirren *n*: coin sound, bell-metal resonance.
mukoid: mucoid.
Mukoid *n*: mucoid.
Mukoitinschwefelsäure *f*: mucoitinsulfuric acid.
Mukolipidose *f*: mucolipidosis.
Mukolytikum *n*: mucolytic agent.
mukolytisch: mucolytic.
mukomembranös: mucomembranous.
Mukoperiost *n*: mucoperiosteum.
Mukopolysaccharidose I-H *f*: mucopolysaccharidosis IH, Hurler syndrome.
mukopurulent: mucopurulent.
Mukormykose *f*: mucormycosis, zygomycosis.
Mukosa *f*: mucosa.
Mukoviszidose *f*: mucoviscidosis, cystic fibrosis.
Mukozele *f*: mucocele.
Mukus *m*: mucus.
Mulde *f*: hollow, cradle.

Multidetermination *f*: multidetermination.
multifaktoriell: multifactorial.
multifokal: multifocal, plurifocal.
Multiinfarktdemenz *f*: multi-infarct dementia, vascular dementia.
multipel: multiple.
multipolar: multipolar.
Multisystemerkrankung *f*: multiple-system illness.
Multivariatanalyse *f*: multivariate analysis.
multizentrisch: multicentric.
Mumifizierung *f*: mummification.
Mumps *m*: mumps, epidemic parotitis.
Mund *m*: mouth, os, stoma.
Mundgeruch *m*: bad breath, halitosis.
Mundhöhle *f*: oral cavity, buccal cavity.
Mundhygiene *f*: oral hygiene.
Mundpflege *f*: oral hygiene.
Mundsoor *m*: thrush, oral candidiasis.
Mundspülung *f*: mouthwash, mouth rinsing.
Mundtrockenheit *f*: mouth dryness, xerostomia.
Mundwasser *n*: gargle, collutory.
Mund-zu-Mund-Beatmung *f*: mouth-to-mouth respiration, mouth-to-mouth resuscitation, kiss of life.
Mund-zu-Nase-Beatmung *f*: mouth-to-nose respiration.
Muraminsäure *f*: muramic acid.
murin: murine.
Murmeln *n*: mumbling, mussitation.
Murmeltier *n*: woodchuck.
Muschelknorpel *m*: conchal cartilage.
Muschelvergiftung *f*: mussel poisoning, shellfish poisoning.
Musculus *m*: muscle.
Musiktherapie *f*: music therapy.
Muskarin *n*: muscarine.
muskarinartig: muscarinic.
Muskarinvergiftung *f*: muscarinism.
Muskel *m*: muscle; **glatter** ≈ smooth muscle, unstriated muscle; **quergestreifter** ≈ striated muscle.
Muskelaktionspotential *n*: muscle action potential.
Muskelatrophie *f*: muscular atrophy, amyotrophy; **ischämische** ≈ ischemic muscular atrophy; **neurogene** ≈ neurogenic atrophy, Werdnig-Hoffmann paralysis, Kugelberg-Welander disease; **progressive** ≈ wasting paralysis, creeping paralysis, Cruveilhier's atrophy; **progressive nukleäre** ≈ progressive nuclear amyotrophy; **spinale** ≈ spinal muscular atrophy; **spinale progressive** ≈ progressive spinal muscular atrophy, Aran-Duchenne dystrophy.
Muskelbauch *m*: muscle belly.
Muskeldegeneration *f*: muscular degeneration, myodegeneration; **wachsige** ≈ waxy degeneration, Zenker's degeneration.
Muskeldystrophie *f*: muscular dystrophy, myodystrophia, Erb's disease; **distale** ≈ distal muscular dystrophy; **erbliche neurale** ≈ Charcot-Marie-Tooth syndrome; **fazioskapulohumerale** ≈ facioscapulohumeral dystrophy, Landouzy-Déjerine disease; **kongenitale** ≈ congenital muscular dystrophy; **neurale** ≈ Hoffmann syndrome; **progressive** ≈ progressive muscular dystrophy, Simmerlin's disease; **pseudohypertrophe** ≈ pseudohypertrophic muscular dystrophy.
Muskeleigenreflex *m*: deep tendon reflex, muscular proprioceptive reflex.
Muskelentzündung *f*: myositis.
Muskelerkrankung *f*: muscle disease, myopathy.
Muskelermüdung *f*: muscular fatigue.
Muskelfaser *f*: muscle fiber, myofiber.
Muskelgewebe *n*: muscle tissue.
Muskelhartspann *m*: myosclerosis.
Muskelhypertonie *f*: muscle hypertonia.
Muskelkontraktion *f*: contraction of muscle; **isokinetische** ≈ isokinetic contraction; **isometrische** ≈ isometric contraction; **isotonische** ≈ isotonic contraction; **tetanische** ≈ tonic muscular contraction.
Muskelkontraktur *f*: muscle contracture.

Muskelkraft *f*: muscle power.
Muskelkrampf *m*: muscle cramp, muscle spasm.
Muskelmilchsäure *f*: sarcolactic acid.
Muskelplastik *f*: myoplasty.
Muskelpropriozeptivität *f*: myostatic sensibility.
Muskelrelaxation *f*: muscle relaxation.
Muskelschmerz *m*: muscular pain.
Muskelschwäche *f*: muscle weakness.
Muskelsensibilität *f*: muscular sensibility, muscle sense.
Muskelspannung *f*: muscle tension, muscular tension.
Muskelsteife *f*: muscle rigidity.
Muskelton *m*: muscle sound, muscular murmur.
Muskeltonus *m*: muscular tonus, muscle tone; **erniedrigter** ≈ muscle hypotonia; **gesteigerter** ≈ muscle hypertonia.
Muskelzuckung *f*: muscle twitch, jerk.
muskulär: muscular.
Muskulatur *f*: musculature.
muskulös: muscular.
muskuloskeletal: musculoskeletal.
Mussitation *f*: mussitation.
Muster *n*: specimen, pattern.
mutagen: mutagen.
Mutagen *n*: mutagen.
Mutagenese *f*: mutagenesis.
Mutante *f*: mutant, variant.
Mutation *f*: mutation; **induzierte** ≈ induced mutation; **silente** ≈ silent mutation; **somatische** ≈ somatic mutation; **sprunghafte** ≈ saltatory mutation.
Mutilation *f*: mutilation; **genitale** ≈ genital mutilation.
Mutismus *m*: mutism; **akinetischer** ≈ akinetic mutism; **elektiver** ≈ elective mutism; **neurotischer** ≈ hysterical mutism; **schizophrener** ≈ schizophrenic mutism.
Mutter *f*: mother.
Mutter-Kind-Übertragung *f*: maternofetal transmission.
Mutterkornalkaloid *n*: ergot alkaloid.
Muttermal *n*: birthmark, nevus.
Muttermilch *f*: mother milk, breast milk.
Mutterschaft *f*: motherhood, maternity.
Mutterschutz *m*: maternity protection.
Muzilago *f*: mucilago, mucilage.
Muzin *n*: mucin.
muzinolytisch: mucinolytic.
Myalgia acuta epidemica *f*: epidemic myalgia, Bornholm disease.
Myalgie *f*: myalgia.
Myasthenia gravis *f*: myasthenia gravis, Erb-Goldflam disease.
Myasthenia gravis pseudoparalytica *f*: myasthenia gravis pseudoparalytica, Hoppe-Goldflam syndrome.
Myasthenie *f*: myasthenia, Erb-Goldflam disease.
myasthenisch: myasthenic.
Mycolsäure *f*: mycolic acid.
Mycoplasma *n*: Mycoplasma.
Mydriasis *f*: mydriasis.
myelinhaltig: myelinated.
Myelitis *f*: myelitis; **akute syphilitische** ≈ acute syphilitic myelitis; **aszendierende** ≈ ascending myelitis; **deszendierende** ≈ descending myelitis; **disseminierte** ≈ disseminated myelitis; **fokale** ≈ focal myelitis; **metastatische** ≈ metastatic myelitis; **parenchymatöse** ≈ parenchymatous myelitis; **posttraumatische** ≈ traumatic myelitis; **subakute nekrotisierende** ≈ subacute necrotic myelitis, Foix-Alajouanine syndrome; **tuberkulöse** ≈ tuberculous myelitis; **zentrale** ≈ central myelitis.
Myeloblast *m*: myeloblast.
Myelofibrose *f*: myelofibrosis.
Myelom *n*: myeloma, plasmacytoma; **multiples** ≈ multiple myeloma, Kahler's disease.
Myelomalazie *f*: myelomalacia.
Myelopathie *f*: myelopathy; **aszendierende** ≈ ascending myelopathy; **deszendierende** ≈ descending myelopathy; **diabetische** ≈ diabetic myelopathy; **fokale** ≈ focal myelopathy; **ischämische** ≈ ischemic myelopathy; **subakute nekrotisierende** ≈ necrotic myelopathy, Foix-Alajoua-

nine syndrome; **toxische** ≈ toxic myelopathy; **vakuoläre** ≈ vacuolar myelopathy; **zervikale** ≈ cervical myelopathy.

myeloproliferativ: myeloproliferative.

Myelosarkom *n*: myelosarcoma.

Myiasis *f*: myiasis.

Mykologie *f*: mycology.

Mykoplasma *n*: mycoplasma.

Mykoplasmenpneumonie *f*: mycoplasmal pneumonia, Eaton agent pneumonia.

Mykose *f*: mycosis; **systemische** ≈ systemic mycosis.

Mykotoxin *n*: mycotoxin, fungal toxin.

Myoblast *m*: myoblast.

Myoblastenmyom *n*: myoblastic myoma, Abrikosov's tumor.

Myofibrille *f*: myofibril, muscle fibril.

myogen: myogenic.

Myoglobin *n*: myoglobin.

Myoglobinurie *f*: myoglobinuria; **familiäre** ≈ familial myoglobinuria, Meyer-Betz disease; **paroxysmale** ≈ paroxysmal myoglobinuria, idiopathic rhabdomyolysis.

Myokard *n*: myocardium.

myokardial: myocardial.

Myokardinfarkt *m*: myocardial infarction; **akuter** ≈ acute myocardial infarction; **apikaler** ≈ apical myocardial infarction; **stummer** ≈ silent myocardial infarction; **subendokardialer** ≈ subendocardial infarction; **transmuraler** ≈ transmural myocardial infarction.

Myokardinsuffizienz *f*: myocardial insufficiency, cardiac insufficiency.

Myokardiopathie *f*: myocardiopathy.

Myokarditis *f*: myocarditis; **akute bakterielle** ≈ acute bacterial myocarditis; **akute rheumatische** ≈ acute rheumatic myocarditis; **chronische** ≈ chronic myocarditis; **chronisch-interstitielle** ≈ fibrous myocarditis; **diphtherische** ≈ diphtheritic myocarditis; **eitrige** ≈ suppurative myocarditis; **ernährungsbedingte** ≈ nutritional myocarditis; **idiopathische** ≈ idiopathic myocarditis; **interstitielle** ≈ interstitial myocarditis, Fiedler's myocarditis; **parenchymatöse** ≈ parenchymatous myocarditis; **rheumatische** ≈ rheumatic myocarditis.

Myokardruptur *f*: heart rupture.

Myokardsarkoidose *f*: myocardial sarcoidosis.

Myoklonie *f*: myoclonia.

Myoklonus *m*: myoclonus, myoclonic attack; **fokaler** ≈ focal myoclonus; **lichtinduzierter** ≈ photomyoclonus; **massiver** ≈ massive myoclonus; **massiver bilateraler epileptischer** ≈ myoclonic epilepsy; **nächtlicher** ≈ nocturnal myoclonus; **postenzephalitischer** ≈ encephalitic myoclonus.

Myoklonusepilepsie *f*: myoclonia epilepsy, Unverricht syndrome.

Myom *n*: myoma.

Myomalazie *f*: myomalacia.

Myomektomie *f*: myomectomy.

Myometritis *f*: myometritis.

Myometrium *n*: myometrium.

Myopathia distalis hereditaria *f*: slow distal hereditary myopathy.

Myopathie *f*: myopathy; **alkoholische** ≈ alcoholic myopathy; **diabetische** ≈ diabetic myopathy; **distale** ≈ distal myopathy; **metabolische** ≈ hypermetabolic myopathy; **multifokale** ≈ multicore disease; **myotonische** ≈ myotonic myopathy; **myotubuläre** ≈ centronuclear myopathy; **myxödematöse** ≈ hypothyroid myopathy; **okuläre** ≈ ocular myopathy; **paraneoplastische** ≈ carcinomatous myopathy; **thyreotoxische** ≈ thyrotoxic myopathy.

myopathisch: myopathic.

Myoperikarditis *f*: myopericarditis.

Myopie *f*: myopia, nearsightedness.

Myoplastik *f*: myoplasty.

Myosarkom *n*: myosarcoma.

Myosin *n*: myosin.

Myositis *f*: myositis.

Myositis epidemica *f*: epidemic myositis.

myostatisch: myostatic.

Myotomie *f*: myotomy.

Myotonia congenita: myotonic myopathy, Thomsen's disease.
Myotonie *f*: myotonia; **chondrodystrophische** ≈ chondrodystrophic myotonia, Schwartz-Jampel syndrome.
myotonisch: myotonic.
myotrop: myotropic.
Myringitis *f*: myringitis.
Myringoplastik *f*: myringoplasty.
Myringotomie *f*: myringotomy, tympanotomy.
Myristinsäure *f*: myristic acid.
Myxödem *n*: myxedema, mucous edema; **postoperatives** ≈ postoperative myxedema, surgical myxedema; **prätibiales** ≈ pretibial myxedema; **tuberöses** ≈ nodular myxedema.
myxödematös: myxedematous.
Myxom *n*: myxoma.
Myxomyzet *m*: myxomycete, slime mold.
Myxosarkom *n*: myxosarcoma.
Myzet *m*: mycete.
Myzetom *n*: mycetoma, Madura foot, maduromycosis.

N

N. Abk. **Nervus** *m*: nervus, nerve.
Na Abk. **Natrium** *n*: natrium, Na, sodium.
Nabel *m*: navel, umbilicus, omphalos; **blauer** ≈ blue navel; **nässender** ≈ draining umbilicus.
Nabelblutung *f*: umbilical hemorrhage, omphalorrhagia.
Nabelbruch *m*: umbilical hernia.
Nabeldiphtherie *f*: umbilical diphtheria.
Nabelentzündung *f*: omphalitis.
Nabelfistel *f*: umbilical fistula.
Nabelgranulom *n*: umbilical granuloma.
Nabelhernie *f*: umbilical hernia.
Nabelschnur *f*: umbilical cord.
Nabelschnurblut *n*: cord blood.
Nabelschnurumschlingung *f*: twisted cord.
Nabelschnurvorfall *m*: prolapse of cord, presentation of the cord.
Nabelschnurzyste *f*: umbilical cyst.
Naboth-Zysten: nabothian cysts.
Nabumeton *n*: nabumetone.
Nachahmungsverhalten *n*: mimetic behavior.
Nachbestrahlung *f*: postoperative irradiation.
Nachbild *n*: afterimage.
Nachblutung *f*: secondary hemorrhage.
Nachgeburt *f*: afterbirth.
Nachgeburtsperiode *f*: postpartum period.
Nachgeschmack *m*: aftertaste.
Nachkommenschaft *f*: progeny, offspring.
Nachkontrolle *f*: follow-up.
Nachlast *f*: afterload.
Nachsorge *f*: aftercare.
Nachstar *m*: secondary cataract.
Nachtangst *f*: pavor nocturnus, night terrors.
Nachtblindheit *f*: night blindness, nyctanopia.
Nachtklinik *f*: night clinic, night hospital.
Nachtruhe *f*: night rest.
Nachtschweiß *m*: night sweat.
Nachuntersuchung *f*: follow-up.
Nachwehen: afterpains.
Nachweisgrenze *f*: detection limit.
Nachwirkung *f*: aftereffect.
Nacken *m*: neck, nape.
Nackenregion *f*: nuchal region.
Nackensteife *f*: neck stiffness, nuchal rigidity.
Nackenzeichen *n*: neck sign, Brudzinski sign.
nackt: nude, naked.
Nadel *f*: needle, pin; **atraumatische** ≈ atraumatic needle; **gebogene** ≈ curved needle, **runde** ≈ round needle; **scharfe** ≈ cutting needle.
Nadelaspirationsbiopsie *f*: needle aspiration biopsy.
Nadelaustausch *m*: needle exchange.
Nadelhalter *m*: needle holder.
Nadelstichverletzung *f*: needlestick injury.
Nadifloxacin *n*: nadifloxacin.
Nadolol *n*: nadolol.
Naegele-Regel *f*: Naegele's rule, delivery date rule.
Nägelkauen *n*: nail biting, onychophagia.
nähen: sew, stitch, suture.
Nährboden *m*: culture medium.
Nährstoff *m*: nutrient.
Nährstoffbestandteil *m*: nutritional component.
Nährwert *m*: nutritional value.
nässen: weep.

Nävus *m*: nevus; **blauer** ≈ blue nevus; **intradermaler** ≈ intradermal nevus; **junktionaler** ≈ junctional nevus, marginal nevus; **nichtpigmentierter** ≈ amelanotic nevus; **pigmentierter** ≈ pigmented nevus; **warzenförmiger** ≈ warty mole; **weißer** ≈ nevus albus.
Naevus araneus *m*: nevus araneus, spider nevus.
Nävus Pringle *m*: sebaceous adenoma.
Nävuszellnävus *m*: nevus-cell nevus.
Nafarelinacetat *n*: nafarelin acetate.
Nafcillin *n*: nafcillin.
Nafoxidin *n*: nafoxidine.
Naftalofos *n*: naftalofos.
Naftidrofuryl *n*: naftidrofuryl.
Nagel *m*: nail; **eingewachsener** ≈ ingrown nail; **hippokratischer** ≈ hippocratic nail, watch-glass nail.
Nagelbett *n*: nail bed.
Nagelfehlbildung *f*: malformed nail.
Nagelgeschwür *n*: whitlow.
Nagelhämatom *n*: subungual hematoma.
Nagelhaut *f*: nail skin, cuticle.
Nagelmykose *f*: onychomycosis.
nageln: nail.
Nageln *n*: nailing.
Nagelplatte *f*: nail plate.
Nagelpuls *m*: nail pulse.
Nagelung *f*: nailing, pinning.
Nagelweiß *n*: lunula, moon.
Nager-Reynier-Syndrom *n*: Nager's acrofacial dysostosis.
Nahfeld *n*: near field.
Nahplastik *f*: direct flap, local flap.
Nahpunkt *m*: near point.
Nahrung *f*: food, nourishment.
Nahrungsbedarf *m*: nutrition requirements.
Nahrungseiweiß *n*: dietary protein.
Nahrungsfett *n*: dietary fat.
Nahrungskette *f*: food chain.
Nahrungsmittel *n*: food, nutriment.
Nahrungsmittelallergie *f*: food allergy.
Nahrungsmittelaufnahme *f*: food intake.
Nahrungsstoff *m*: nutrient.
Naht *f*: suture, stitch; **atraumatische** ≈ atraumatic suture; **aufgeschobene** ≈ delayed suture; **diskontinuierliche** ≈ interrupted suture; **evertierende** ≈ everting suture; **fortlaufende** ≈ continuous suture; **invertierende** ≈ infolding suture; **knöcherne** ≈ bony suture; **resorbierbare** ≈ absorbable suture; **sekundäre** ≈ secondary suture; **seroseröse** ≈ seroserous suture; **transmurale** ≈ through-and-through suture; **versenkte** ≈ implanted suture; **verzögerte** ≈ delayed suture; **zirkuläre** ≈ circular suture.
Nahtapparat *m*: sewer.
Nahtdehiszenz *f*: dehiscence of a suture.
Nahtmaterial *n*: suture material; **nichtresorbierbares** ≈ nonabsorbable suture; **resorbierbares** ≈ absorbable suture.
Nahtstar *m*: sutural cataract.
Nalbuphin *n*: nalbuphine.
Nalidixinsäure *f*: nalidixic acid.
N-Allylnormorphin *n*: N-allylnormorphine.
Nalorphin *n*: nalorphine.
Naloxon *n*: naloxone.
Naltrexon *n*: naltrexone.
Name *m*: name.
Nanismus *m*: nanism, nanosomia.
Nanukayami *n*: nanukayami, seven-day fever, autumn fever.
Naphazolin *n*: naphazoline.
β-Naphthalensulfonsäure *f*: beta-naphtholsulfonic acid.
Naphthalin *n*: naphthalin, naphthalene.
Naphthochinon *n*: naphthoquinone.
Naphthol *n*: naphthol.
Naphtholsulfonsäure *f*: naphtholsulfonic acid.
Naphthylaminosulfonsäure *f*: naphthylaminosulfonic acid.
Naproxen *n*: naproxen.
Naratriptan *n*: naratriptan.
Narbe *f*: scar, cicatrix.
Narbengewebe *n*: scar tissue, cicatricial tissue.
Narbenhernie *f*: incisional hernia.
Narbenhypertrophie *f*: cicatricial hypertrophy.

Narbenkeloid *n*: cicatricial keloid, keloma.
Narbenkontraktur *f*: scar contracture.
Narbenstriktur *f*: bridle scar.
Narcotin *n*: narcotine, noscapine.
Narkoanalyse *f*: narcoanalysis, narcosynthesis.
Narkolepsie *f*: narcolepsy, Friedmann's disease, Gélineau syndrome.
Narkose *f*: anesthesia, narcosis.
Narkosearzt *m*: anesthesist.
Narkoserisiko *n*: anesthetic risk.
Narkotikum *n*: anesthetic, narcotic.
Narkotin *n*: narcotine, noscapine.
Narzissmus *m*: narcissism.
nasal: nasal.
Nase *f*: nose.
Nasenatmung *f*: nasal respiration.
Nasenbluten *n*: nosebleed, epistaxis.
Nasenfalte *f*: nasal fold.
Nasenfurunkel *m*: nasal furuncle.
Nasenhöhle *f*: nasal cavity.
Nasenloch *n*: nostril, naris.
Nasenmuschel *f*: nasal turbinate.
Nasennebenhöhle *f*: paranasal sinus.
Nasennebenhöhlenentzündung *f*: sinusitis.
Nasenpolyp *m*: nasal polyp.
Nasenrachenraum *m*: nasopharynx.
Nasenscheidewand *f*: nasal septum, nose septum.
Nasenscheidewanddefekt *m*: septal defect.
Nasenscheidewanddeviation *f*: septal deviation.
Nasenschleimhaut *f*: nasal mucosa.
Nasenschleimhautentzündung *f*: rhinitis.
Nasensondenernährung *f*: nasal feeding.
Nasenspekulum *n*: nose speculum, rhinoscope.
Nasenspiegelung *f*: nasoscopy, rhinoscopy.
Nasenstein *m*: rhinolith, nasal calculus.
Nasentropfen: nose drops.
Nasenvorhof *m*: nasal vestibule.
nasogastrisch: nasogastric.
Nasolabialreflex *m*: nasolabial reflex.
nasolakrimal: nasolacrimal.
nasopharyngeal: nasopharyngeal.
Nasopharyngealspekulum *n*: nasopharyngeal speculum.
Nasopharyngoskopie *f*: nasopharyngoscopy.
Nasopharynx *m*: nasopharynx.
Nasopharynxkarzinom *n*: nasopharyngeal carcinoma.
Nasotrachealtubus *m*: nasotracheal tube.
nasoziliar: nasociliary.
Natalität *f*: natality.
Natalizumab *n*: natalizumab.
Natamycin *n*: natamycin.
Nateglinid *n*: nateglinide.
nativ: native, natural.
Nativaufnahme *f*: plain film, scout film.
Natriämie *f*: natremia.
Natrium *n*: sodium.
Natriumaurothiomalat *n*: sodium aurothiomalate.
Natriumchlorid *n*: sodium chloride.
Natriumkanal *m*: sodium channel.
Natriumnitrat *n*: sodium nitrate.
Natriumnitrit *n*: sodium nitrite.
Natriumnitroprussid *n*: sodium nitroprusside.
Natriumspeichersyndrom *n*: hypernatremia.
Natriumvalproat *n*: valproate sodium.
natürlich: natural, native.
Natur *f*: nature.
Naturheilkunde *f*: naturopathy.
Nausea *f*: nausea.
navikulär: navicular.
Nebelfleck *m*: nebula.
Nebenhodenentzündung *f*: epididymitis.
Nebenhöhle *f*: paranasal sinus.
Nebenkern *m*: accessory nucleus.
Nebenniere *f*: adrenal body, epinephros.
Nebennierenapoplexie *f*: adrenal apoplexy, Waterhouse-Friderichsen syndrome.
Nebennierenentfernung *f*: adrenalectomy.
Nebennierenmark *n*: adrenal medulla.
Nebennierenrinde *f*: adrenal cortex.

Nebennierenrindenadenom *n*: adrenocortical adenoma.
Nebennierenrindenhyperplasie *f*: adrenal hyperplasia.
Nebennierenrindeninfarkt *m*: adrenal apoplexy.
Nebennierenrindeninsuffizienz *f*: adrenocortical insufficiency.
Nebennierensteroid *n*: adrenal steroid.
Nebennierenzyste *f*: adrenal cyst.
Nebenplazenta *f*: accessory placenta.
Nebenschilddrüse *f*: parathyroid, accessory thyroid.
Nebenschilddrüsenadenom *n*: parathyroid adenoma.
Nebenschilddrüseninsuffizienz *f*: hypoparathyroidism.
Nebenstoffwechselweg *m*: accessory pathway.
Nebenstruma *f*: aberrant goiter.
Nebensymptom *n*: accessory sign.
Nebenwirkung *f*: side effect, adverse effect.
Nebivolol *n*: nebivolol.
Nebramycin *n*: nebramycin.
Nedocromil *n*: nedocromil.
Nefazodon *n*: nefazodone.
Nefopam *n*: nefopam.
Negation *f*: negation.
negativ: negative.
Neigungswinkel *m*: angle of inclination.
Neisseria gonorrhoeae *f*: Neisseria gonorrhoeae, gonococcus.
Nekrobiose *f*: necrobiosis, bionecrosis.
Nekrolyse *f*: necrolysis; **toxische epidermische** ≈ toxic epidermal necrolysis, Lyell syndrome.
Nekrose *f*: necrosis; **fibrinoide** ≈ fibrinous degeneration; **hyaline** ≈ hyaline necrosis; **verkäsende** ≈ cheesy necrosis.
nekrotisch: necrotic.
Nelfinavir *n*: nelfinavir.
Nematode *f*: nematode, pinworm.
Neodym *n*: neodymium, Nd.
Neomycin *n*: neomycin.
neonatal: neonatal.
Neonatologie *f*: neonatology, neonatal medicine.
Neoplasie *f*: neoplasia; **multiple endokrine** ≈ multiple endocrine adenomatosis, Wermer syndrome; **zervikale intraepitheliale** ≈ cervical intraepithelial neoplasia.
Neoplasma *n*: neoplasm, true tumor.
Neostigmin *n*: neostigmine.
neovaskulär: neovascular.
Nephrektomie *f*: nephrectomy.
Nephritis *f*: nephritis; **familiäre** ≈ hereditary nephritis, familial nephritis; **hereditäre chronische** ≈ hereditary nephritis and nerve deafness, Alport syndrome; **interstitielle** ≈ interstitial nephritis, Balkan nephropathy; **lupoide** ≈ lupus nephritis.
nephritisch: nephritic.
Nephroblastom *n*: nephroblastoma, Wilms' tumor.
Nephrokalzinose *f*: nephrocalcinosis.
Nephrolithotomie *f*: nephrolithotomy.
Nephrom *n*: nephroma.
Nephron *n*: nephron.
Nephropathia epidemica *f*: epidemic nephropathy, epidemic hemorrhagic fever.
Nephropathie *f*: nephropathy, kidney disease; **autosomal-dominante polyzystische** ≈ polycystic renal disease, adult type; **autosomal-rezessive** ≈ polycystic renal disease, childhood type; **diabetische** ≈ diabetic nephropathy; **hypertonische** ≈ hypertensive renal disease; **obstruktive** ≈ obstructive nephropathy; **polyzystische** ≈ polycystic renal disease; **toxische** ≈ toxic nephropathy; **tubuläre** ≈ tubular nephropathy; **zystische** ≈ polycystic kidneys.
Nephropexie *f*: nephropexy.
Nephrophthisis *f*: nephrophthisis, renal tuberculosis.
Nephroptose *f*: nephroptosis.
Nephrorrhagie *f*: nephrorrhagia, renal hemorrhage.
Nephrosklerose *f*: nephrosclerosis.
Nephrosonephritis *f*: nephrosonephritis; **fernöstliche hämorrhagische** ≈ Far Eastern hemorrhagic fever.

Nephrostomie *f*: nephrostomy.
nephrotisch: nephrotic.
Nephrotomie *f*: nephrotomy.
Nephrotomographie *f*: nephrotomography.
Nephrotoxizität *f*: nephrotoxicity.
Nephroureterektomie *f*: nephroureterectomy.
Nerv *m*: nerve, nervus, N; **afferenter** ≈ afferent nerve; **efferenter** ≈ efferent nerve; **gemischter** ≈ mixed nerve; **motorischer** ≈ motor nerve; **peripherer** ≈ peripheral nerve; **sensorischer** ≈ sensory nerve; **sympathischer** ≈ sympathetic nerve.
Nervenaktionspotential *n*: nerve action potential.
Nervenbahn *f*: nerve tract.
Nervenendigung *f*: nerve ending.
Nervenentzündung *f*: neuritis.
Nervenfaser *f*: nerve fiber.
Nervengift *n*: neurotoxin.
Nervenkanal *m*: nerve canal.
Nervenkompressionssyndrom *n*: nerve compression syndrome.
Nervenläsion *f*: nerve lesion.
Nervenleitung *f*: nerve conduction.
Nervenleitungsgeschwindigkeit *f*: nerve conduction velocity.
Nervennaht *f*: nerve suture.
Nervenplastik *f*: neuroplasty.
Nervenscheidenentzündung *f*: adventitial neuritis.
Nervenschmerz *m*: nerve pain.
Nervenstimulation *f*: nerve stimulation; **transkutane elektrische** ≈ transcutaneous electric stimulation.
Nervensystem *n*: nervous system; **autonomes** ≈ autonomic nervous system; **parasympathisches** ≈ parasympathetic system; **peripheres** ≈ peripheral nervous system; **sensibles** ≈ sensory system; **sympathisches** ≈ sympathetic nervous system; **vegetatives** ≈ vegetative nervous system; **zentrales** ≈ central nervous system, CNS.
Nervenverletzung *f*: nerve injury.
Nervenwurzelstimulation *f*: root stimulation.
Nervenzelle *f*: nerve cell, neuron.
Nervenzusammenbruch *m*: nervous breakdown.
nervös: nervous, jittery, jumpy.
Nervonsäure *f*: nervonic acid.
Nervus Abk. **N.**: nervus, nerve.
Nesselsucht *f*: nettle rash, urticaria.
Netilmycin *n*: netilmycin.
Netz *n*: net, omentum, web.
Netzhaut *f*: retina.
Netzhautablösung *f*: retinal detachment.
Netzhautadaptation *f*: retinal adaptation.
Netzhautarteriosklerose *f*: retinal arteriosclerosis.
Netzhautastigmatismus *m*: retinal astigmatism.
Netzhautbezirk *m*: retinal area.
Netzhautbild *n*: retinal image.
Netzhautblutung *f*: retinal hemorrhage.
Netzhautdysplasie *f*: retinal dysplasia.
Netzhauteinriss *m*: retinal tear.
Netzhautembolie *f*: retinal embolism.
Netzhautentzündung *f*: retinitis.
Netzhauterkrankung *f*: retinopathy.
Netzhautkorrespondenz *f*: retinal correspondence.
Netzhautpigment *n*: retinal pigment.
Netzhautruptur *f*: retinal rupture.
Netzhautwahrnehmung *f*: retinal perception.
Netzhautzapfen *m*: retinal cone, visual cone.
Netztransplantat *n*: meshgraft.
Neubildung *f*: neoformation, neoplasm.
neugeboren: newborn, neonatal.
Neugeborenenatemnotsyndrom *n*: idiopathic respiratory distress of the newborn.
Neugeborenenhyperbilirubinämie *f*: neonatal hyperbilirubinemia; **passagere familiäre** ≈ Lucey-Driscoll syndrome.
Neugeborenenikterus *m*: neonatal jaundice.
Neugeborenenperiode *f*: neonatal period.
Neugeborenen-Screening *n*: neonatal screening.
Neugeborenensterblichkeit *f*: post-

natal mortality, neonatal mortality.
Neugeborenes *n*: newborn, neonate; **reifes** ≈ term infant; **unreifes** ≈ preterm infant.
neural: neural.
Neuralgie *f*: neuralgia, nerve pain.
Neuralrinne *f*: neural canal, medullary canal.
Neuralrohr *n*: neural tube, medullary tube.
Neuralrohrdefekt *m*: neural-tube defect.
Neuraltherapie *f*: neural therapy.
Neuraminidase *f*: neuraminidase.
Neuraminidasehemmer *m*: neuraminidase inhibitor.
Neuraminsäure *f*: neuraminic acid.
Neurapraxie *f*: neurapraxia.
Neurasthenie *f*: neurasthenia, Beard's disease.
Neurektomie *f*: neurectomy.
Neurilemm *n*: neurilemma, neurilemmal sheath.
Neurilemmom *n*: nerve sheath tumor, Schwann cell tumor.
Neurinom *n*: neurinoma.
Neuritis *f*: neuritis; **diphtherische** ≈ diphtheritic neuritis; **interstitielle** ≈ interstitial neuritis; **periaxiale** ≈ periaxial neuritis; **retrobulbäre** ≈ retrobulbar neuritis, optic neuritis; **segmentale** ≈ segmental neuritis; **zentrale** ≈ central neuritis.
Neuritis nervi optici *f*: optic neuritis, retrobulbar neuritis.
Neuroanatomie *f*: neuroanatomy.
Neuroblast *m*: neuroblast.
Neuroblastom *n*: neuroblastoma.
Neurochirurgie *f*: neurosurgery.
Neurodermitis *f*: neurodermatitis.
Neurodermitis atopica *f*: neurodermatitis, atopic dermatitis.
Neuroepithel *n*: nerve epithelium, neuroepithelium.
Neuroepitheliom *n*: neuroepithelioma.
Neurofibrom *n*: neurofibroma; **hantelförmiges** ≈ dumbbell neurofibroma.
Neurofibromatose *f*: neurofibromatosis, Recklinghausen's disease.
Neurofibrosarkom *n*: neurofibrosarcoma.
neurogen: neurogenic.
Neuroglia *f*: neuroglia, glia.
Neurogliom *n*: neuroglioma.
Neurohormon *n*: neurohormone.
Neuroleptikasyndrom, malignes *n*: neuroleptic malignant syndrome.
Neuroleptikum *n*: neuroleptic, major tranquilizer.
Neurolinguistik *f*: neurolinguistics.
Neurolipid *n*: neurolipid.
Neurologie *f*: neurology.
neurologisch: neurological.
Neurolysin *n*: neurolysin.
Neurom *n*: neuroma; **rankenförmiges** ≈ plexiform neuroma.
neuromuskulär: neuromuscular.
Neuromyelitis optica *f*: neuromyelitis optica, Devic's disease.
Neuron *n*: neuron.
Neuronitis vestibularis *f*: vestibular neuronitis.
neuroparalytisch: neuroparalytic.
Neuropathie *f*: neuropathy, neuropathia; **alkoholische** ≈ alcoholic neuropathy; **autonome** ≈ autonomic neuropathy; **diabetische** ≈ diabetic neuropathy; **genetisch bedingte** ≈ genetically determined neuropathy; **ischämische** ≈ ischemic neuropathy; **medikamentenbedingte** ≈ drug-induced neuropathy; **migrierende sensible** ≈ migrant sensory neuropathy; **motorische** ≈ motor neuropathy; **paraneoplastische** ≈ carcinomatous neuropathy; **periphere** ≈ peripheral neuropathy; **proximale** ≈ proximal neuropathy; **sensomotorische** ≈ sensimotor neuropathy; **sensorische** ≈ sensory neuropathy; **toxische** ≈ toxic neuropathy; **urämische** ≈ uremic neuropathy.
neuropathisch: neuropathic.
Neuropathologie *f*: neuropathology.
Neuropsychiatrie *f*: neuropsychiatry.
Neuropsychologie *f*: neuropsychology.
Neuroradiologie *f*: neuroradiology.
Neurose *f*: neurosis; **hypochondrische** ≈ hypochondriacal neurosis; **traumatische** ≈ traumatic neurosis.

neurosekretorisch: neurosecretory.
neurosensorisch: neurosensory, neurosensorial.
Neurosyphilis *f*: neurosyphilis, neurolues.
neurotisch: neurotic.
Neurotomie *f*: neurotomy.
Neurotransmitter *m*: neurotransmitter.
neuroviszeral: neurovisceral.
neurozirkulatorisch: neurocirulatory.
Neutralbiss *m*: balanced occlusion, balanced bite.
Neutralinsulin *n*: neutral insulin.
Neutropenie *f*: neutropenia, neutrocytopenia.
neutrophil: neutrophilic.
Neutrophiler *m*: neutrophil, neutrophil granulocyte.
Neutrophilie *f*: neutrophilia.
Neutrozytopenie *f*: neutrocytopenia, neutropenia.
Nevirapin *n*: nevirapine.
Newton: newton, N.
Nexus *m*: nexus, linkage, tie.
Niacin *n*: niacin.
Niacinamid *n*: niacinamide, nicotinamide.
Nicardipin *n*: nicardipine.
Nicergolin *n*: nicergoline.
nichtinvasiv: noninvasive.
Nickkrampf *m*: nodding spasm, saltatory tic.
Niclofolan *n*: niclofolan.
Nicofuranose *f*: nicofuranose.
Nicotin *n*: nicotine.
Nicotinamid *n*: nicotinamide.
Nicotinsäure *f*: nicotinic acid, niacin.
Nidation *f*: nidation.
Niednagel *m*: hangnail.
niedrig dosiert: low-dose.
Niere *f*: kidney; **künstliche** ≈ artificial kidney; **stumme** ≈ silent kidney, inactive kidney.
Nierenabszess *m*: renal carbuncle.
Nierenamyloidose *f*: renal amyloidosis.
Nierenangiographie *f*: intravenous renal angiography.
Nierenarteriographie *f*: renal arteriography.
Nierenarteriolosklerose *f*: arteriolar nephrosclerosis.
Nierenbecken *n*: renal pelvis.
Nierenblutung *f*: renal hemorrhage.
Nierenclearance *f*: renal clearance.
Nierendekapsulation *f*: renal capsulectomy, nephrocapsectomy.
Nierendurchblutung *f*: renal blood flow.
Nierendysplasie *f*: renal dysplasia.
Nierendystopie *f*: renal ectopia.
Nierenembolie *f*: renal embolism.
Nierenentzündung *f*: nephritis.
Nierenerkrankung *f*: kidney disease, nephropathy.
Nierenfibrose *f*: renal fibrosis.
Nierenfistel *f*: renal fistula.
Nierenfunktion *f*: renal function.
Niereninfarkt *m*: renal infarction, kidney infarct.
Niereninsuffizienz *f*: renal insufficiency.
Nierenkarbunkel *m*: renal carbuncle.
Nierenkarzinom *n*: carcinoma of the kidney.
Nierenkolik *f*: renal colic.
Nierenrindenabszess *m*: renal abscess.
Nierenschwelle *f*: renal threshold.
Nierensklerose *f*: nephrosclerosis.
Nierenstauung *f*: renal congestion.
Nierenstein *m*: kidney stone, nephrolith.
Nierentransplantation *f*: kidney transplantation.
Nierentuberkulose *f*: renal tuberculosis; **verkäsende** ≈ cheesy nephritis.
Nierentumor *m*: nephroma.
Nierenverletzung *f*: kidney trauma, renal injury.
Nierenversagen *n*: renal failure, kidney failure; **akutes** ≈ acute renal failure; **prärenales** ≈ prerenal failure; **terminales** ≈ end-stage renal failure.
Nierenzellkarzinom *n*: renal cell carcinoma.
Nierenzyste *f*: renal cyst.
niesen: sneeze.
Nieswurz *f*: veratrum.
Nifedipin *n*: nifedipine.

N

Nifenalol *n*: nifenalol.
Nifenazon *n*: nifenazone.
Nifluminsäure *f*: niflumid acid.
Nifuratel *n*: nifuratel.
Nifuroxazid *n*: niforoxazide.
Nifurprazin *n*: nifurprazin.
Nikotin *n*: nicotine.
Nikotinamid *n*: nicotinamide.
nikotinartig: nicotinic, nicotinomimetic.
Nikotinsäure *f*: nicotinic acid, niacin.
Niktation *f*: nictation.
Nilutamid *n*: nilutamide.
Nilvadipin *n*: nilvadipine.
Nimodipin *n*: nimodipine.
Nimorazol *n*: nimorazole.
Nimustin *n*: nimustine.
Niridazol *n*: niridazole.
Nisbuterol *n*: nisbuterol.
Nische *f*: niche, recess.
Nisoldipin *n*: nisoldipine.
Nisse *f*: nit.
Nitisinon *n*: nitisinone.
Nitrat *n*: nitrate.
Nitratbildner *m*: nitrifier.
Nitratzyanose *f*: enterogenous cyanosis.
Nitrefazol *n*: nitrefazole.
Nitrendipin *n*: nitrendipine.
Nitrofural *n*: nitrofural, nitrofurazone.
Nitrofuran *n*: nitrofuran.
Nitrofurantoin *n*: nitrofurantoin.
Nitrofurazon *n*: nitrofurazone, nitrofural.
Nitroglycerin *n*: nitroglycerin, nitroglycerol.
Nitroprussid *n*: nitroprusside.
Nitroprussidnatrium *n*: sodium nitroprusside.
Nitroxinil *n*: nitroxinile.
Nitroxolin *n*: nitroxoline.
Niveau *n*: level, standard.
Nizatidin *n*: nizatidine.
nodulär: nodular.
Nodus *m*: node, nodus.
Noma *f*: noma, gangrenous stomatitis.
Nomifensin *n*: nomifensine.
Non-Hodgkin-Lymphom *n*: non-Hodgkin lymphoma.
Nonne-Milroy-Syndrom *n*: Nonne-Milroy syndrome, congenital lymphedema.
Nonoxinol 9 *n*: nonoxynol-9.
Non-REM-Schlaf *m*: NREM sleep, dreamless sleep.
Noradrenalin *n*: noradrenaline, norepinephrine.
Norepinephrin *n*: norepinephrine, noradrenaline.
Norethisteron *n*: norethisterone.
Norfenefrin *n*: norfenefrine.
Norfloxacin *n*: norfloxacin.
Norfluoxetin *n*: norfluoxetine.
Norgesteron *n*: norgesterone.
Norgestrel *n*: norgestrel.
Norlevorphanol *n*: norlevorphanol.
Norm *f*: norm, standard.
normal: normal, regular.
Normalatmung *f*: normal breathing, normal respiration.
Normalbereich *m*: normal range.
Normalinsulin *n*: regular insulin.
Normalisierung *f*: normalization.
Normalsichtigkeit *f*: normal vision, emmetropia.
Normalwert *m*: normal value.
Normalzustand *m*: ground state.
Normazidität *f*: normal acidity.
Normoblast *m*: normoblast.
normochrom: normochromic.
Normorhythmie *f*: normal rhythm.
Normozyt *m*: normocyte.
Nortestosteron *n*: nortestosterone.
Nortriptylin *n*: nortriptyline.
Noscapin *n*: noscapine, narcotine.
Nosokomialinfektion *f*: nosocomial infection.
Nosologie *f*: nosology.
Nosophobie *f*: nosophobia.
Notaufnahme *f*: emergency admission.
Notfall *m*: emergency.
Notfallmedizin *f*: emergency medicine.
Notfallversorgung *f*: emergency care.
Notwendigkeit *f*: necessity.
Novobiocin *n*: novobiocin.
Noxe *f*: noxa, noxious agent.
Noxiptilin *n*: noxiptiline.
Nozizeption *f*: nociception.
nüchtern: fasting, sober.
Nüchternschmerz *m*: hunger pain, fasting pain.

Nüchternwert *m*: fasting value.
Nuklearmedizin *f*: nuclear medicine.
Nukleinsäure *f*: nucleic acid.
Nukleokapsid *n*: nucleocapsid.
Nukleoprotein *n*: nucleoprotein.
Nukleosid *n*: nucleoside.
Nukleosidanalogon *n*: nucleoside analogue.
Nukleotid *n*: nucleotide.
Nukleotidanalogon *n*: nucleotide analogue.
Nukleus *m*: nucleus, karyon.
Nuklid *n*: nuclide.
Nullpunkt *m*: zero point, zero.
Nullstellung *f*: off-position.
numerisch: numeric.
nummulär: nummular.
Nutrition *f*: nutrition.
Nyktalopie *f*: nyctalopia, night blindness.
Nykturie *f*: nycturia.
Nymphomanie *f*: nymphomania.
Nystagmographie *f*: nystagmography.
Nystagmus *m*: nystagmus; **abwärtsgerichteter** ≈ downbeat nystagmus; **ataktischer** ≈ Harris sign; **dissoziierter** ≈ dissociated nystagmus; **horizontaler** ≈ horizontal nystagmus; **kalorischer** ≈ caloric nystagmus; **konjugierter** ≈ conjugate nystagmus; **okulärer** ≈ ocular nystagmus; **optokinetischer** ≈ optokinetic nystagmus; **physiologischer** ≈ physiologic nystagmus; **vertikaler** ≈ vertical nystagmus; **vestibulärer** ≈ vestibular nystagmus, labyrinthine nystagmus; **zentralnervöser** ≈ central nystagmus.
Nystagmusbrille *f*: nystagmus goggles.
Nystatin *n*: nystatin.

O

O Abk. **Sauerstoff** *m*: oxygen, O.
Oat-cell-Karzinom *n*: oat cell carcinoma.
Obduktion *f*: obduction, autopsy, necropsy.
O-Bein *n*: genu varum, bowleg.
Oberarm *m*: upperarm, humerus.
Oberbauchschmerz *m*: epigastric abdominal pain.
Oberfläche *f*: surface.
oberflächenaktiv: surface-active, detergent.
Oberflächenanästhesie *f*: surface anesthesia.
Oberflächenantigen *n*: surface antigen.
Oberflächenfaktor *m*: surfactant, contact factor.
oberflächlich: superficial.
Oberhaut *f*: epidermis, cuticle.
Oberkiefer *m*: maxilla, upper jawbone.
Oberkieferosteom *n*: maxillary osteoma.
Oberlappen *m*: upper lobe; **linker** ≈ left upper lobe; **rechter** ≈ right upper lobe.
Oberlippe *f*: upper lip.
Oberschenkel *m*: femur, femoral bone.
Oberschenkelfraktur *f*: femoral fracture.
Oberschenkelhals *m*: femur neck, neck of femur.
Oberschenkelhalsfraktur *f*: femoral neck fracture.
Oberschwester *f*: head nurse, chief nurse.
Obesitas *f*: obesity; **endokrine** ≈ endocrine obesity.
Objekt *n*: object.
objektiv: objective.
Objektiv *n*: objective, object-lens.
Objektträger *m*: slide.
obligat: obligate.
obligatorisch: obligatory, mandatory.
Obliteration *f*: obliteration.
Oblongatasyndrom, dorsolaterales *n*: Babinski-Nageotte syndrome.
Oblongatasyndrom, medianes *n*: lateral medullary syndrome, Wallenberg syndrome.
Oblongatasyndrom, paramedianes *n*: Jackson paralysis, vagoaccessory hypoglossal paralysis.
Obsession *f*: obsession.
Obstetrik *f*: obstetrics.
Obstgeruch *m*: fruity odor.
Obstipation *f*: constipation, obstipation.
Obstruktion *f*: obstruction.
Obstruktionsatelektase *f*: obstructive atelectasis.
Obstruktionsikterus *m*: obstructive jaundice.
Obstruktionspneumonie *f*: obstructive pneumonia.
obstruktiv: obstructive, obstruent.
Obturatoriushernie *f*: obturator hernia.
Octadekansäure *f*: octadecanoic acid, stearic acid.
Octreotid *n*: octreotide.
ODD-Syndrom *n*: ODD syndrome, oculodentodigital dysplasia.
Odontalgie *f*: odontalgia, toothache.
Odontoameloblastom *n*: odontoameloblastoma.
Odontologie *f*: odontology, dentistry.
Odontom *n*: odontoma; **kalzifiziertes** ≈ calcified odontoma.
Odor *m*: odor, smell.
Ödem *n*: edema, dropsy; **angioneurotisches** ≈ angioneurotic edema,

Quincke's disease; **entzündliches** ≈ inflammatory edema; **idiopathisches** ≈ idiopathic edema; **interstitielles** ≈ interstitial edema; **kardiales** ≈ cardiac edema; **lageabhängiges** ≈ dependent edema; **malignes** ≈ malignant edema, gaseous edema; **nicht wegdrückbares** ≈ pitting edema; **renales** ≈ renal edema; **toxisches** ≈ toxic edema; **umschriebenes** ≈ localized edema; **wegdrückbares** ≈ nonpitting edema.
ödematös: edematous.
Öffnung *f*: opening, ostium, outlet, aperture; **fehlende** ≈ imperforation.
Öffnungsverhältnis *n*: relative aperture.
Öl *n*: oil, oleum; **ätherisches** ≈ ethereal oil; **aromatisches** ≈ aromatic oil.
Ölimmersion *f*: oil immersion.
Ölpneumonie *f*: oil-aspiration pneumonia.
Ölsäure *f*: oleic acid.
Ölsäuretriglyzerid *n*: olein.
örtlich: local.
Öse *f*: eyelet.
ösophageal: esophageal.
Ösophagektomie *f*: esophagectomy.
Ösophagitis *f*: esophagitis; **eosinophile** ≈ eosinophilic esophagitis.
Ösophagogastrektomie *f*: esophagogastrectomy.
Ösophagogastroskopie *f*: esophagogastroscopy.
Ösophagoskopie *f*: esophagoscopy, oesophagoscopy.
Ösophagospasmus *m*: esophageal spasm.
Ösophagotrachealfistel *f*: tracheoesophageal fistula.
Ösophagus *m*: esophagus, gullet.
Ösophagusachalasie *f*: esophageal achalasia.
Ösophagusatresie *f*: esophageal atresia.
Ösophagusdivertikel *n*: esophageal diverticulum.
Ösophagus-Elektrokardiographie *f*: esophageal electrocardiography.
Ösophagusmotilitätsstörung *f*: esophageal paralysis.
Ösophagusperforation *f*: esophageal perforation.
Ösophagusruptur *f*: esophageal rupture.
Ösophagussonde *f*: esophageal probe, esophageal tube.
Ösophagussoor *m*: esophageal candidiasis.
Ösophagussphinkter *m*: esophageal sphincter.
Ösophagussprache *f*: esophageal speech.
Ösophagusstriktur *f*: esophageal stricture.
Ösophagusvarizen: esophageal varices.
Ösophagusverätzung *f*: corrosive esophagitis.
Östradiol *n*: estradiol.
Östriol *n*: estriol.
Östrogen *n*: estrogen.
Östrus *m*: estrus, estrous cycle.
offen: open, patent.
offizinell: officinal.
Ofloxacin *n*: ofloxacin.
Ogilvie-Syndrom *n*: Ogilvie syndrome, false colonic obstruction.
Ohnmacht *f*: blackout, fainting.
ohnmächtig: faint.
Ohr *n*: ear; **abstehendes** ≈ prominent ear; **äußeres** ≈ external ear; **inneres** ≈ inner ear.
Ohrenheilkunde *f*: otology.
Ohrensausen *n*: buzzing.
Ohrenschmalz *m*: earwax.
Ohrenschmerz *m*: otalgia, earache.
Ohrenspiegelung *f*: otoscopy.
Ohrfehlbildung *f*: ear deformity, ear malformation.
Ohrgeräusch *n*: ear noise, tinnitus.
Ohrläppchen *n*: lobule of auricle, earlobe.
Ohrmuschel *f*: auricle.
Ohrspeicheldrüse *f*: parotid gland.
okklusal: occlusal.
Okklusion *f*: occlusion, bite; **anatomische** ≈ ideal occlusion; **exzentrische** ≈ eccentric occlusion; **lingualisierte** ≈ linguoclusion; **mittige** ≈ centric occlusion; **physiologische** ≈ occlusal harmony; **zentrische** ≈ centric contact.
Okklusionsileus *m*: occlusive ileus.

Okklusionskraft *f*: occlusion force.
Okklusivverband *m*: occlusive bandage, occlusive dressing.
okkult: occult, hidden.
Okkupanz *f*: occupancy.
okulär: ocular.
Okular *n*: ocular, eyepiece.
okulogyr: oculogyric.
okulokardial: oculocardiac.
Okulomotoriuslähmung, periodische *f*: ophthalmoplegic migraine.
Okulovestibularisreflex *m*: oculovestibular reflex.
okzipital: occipital.
Okzipitalpunkt *m*: occipital point.
Olanzapin *n*: olanzapine.
Oleandomycin *n*: oleandomycin.
Olefinsäure *f*: olefinic acid.
Olekranon *n*: olecranon.
Olfaktometrie *f*: olfactometry.
olfaktorisch: olfactory.
Oligodendrogliom *n*: oligodendroglioma.
Oligomenorrhö *f*: oligomenorrhea.
Oligonukleotid *n*: oligonucleotide.
Oligophrenie *f*: oligophrenia, mental retardation.
Oligospermie *f*: oligospermia.
Oligotrichie *f*: oligotrichy, oligotrichia, hypotrichosis.
Oligozoospermie *f*: oligozoospermia.
Oligurie *f*: oliguria.
Olmesartan *n*: olmesartan.
Olopatadin *n*: olopatadine.
Olsalazin *n*: olsalazine.
Omalizumab *n*: omalizumab.
Omentitis *f*: omentitis.
Omentopexie *f*: omentopexy, omentofixation.
Omentumzyste *f*: omental cyst.
Omeprazol *n*: omeprazole.
Omphalitis *f*: omphalitis.
Omphalozele *f*: omphalocele.
Onchozerkose *f*: onchocerciasis; **kutane** ≈ onchocercal dermatitis, filarial itch; **okuläre** ≈ river blindness.
Ondansetron *n*: ondansetron.
Onkogen *n*: oncogene, cancer gene.
Onkologie *f*: oncology.
Onkovirus *n*: oncovirus, tumor virus.
Onkozytom *n*: oncocytoma.
Ontogenese *f*: ontogenesis.
Onychie *f*: onychia, onychitis.
Onychodystrophie *f*: onychodystrophy.
Onychogrypose *f*: onychogryposis.
Onychomykose *f*: onychomycosis.
Onychophagie *f*: onychophagia, nail biting.
Oogenese *f*: oogenesis.
Oophorektomie *f*: oophorectomy.
Oophoritis *f*: oophoritis.
Oophoron *n*: oophoron.
Oophorosalpingektomie *f*: oophorosalpingectomy.
Ootomie *f*: ootomy.
Oozyste *f*: oocyst.
Oozyt *m*: oocyte.
opak: opaque.
Opazität *f*: opacity.
operabel: operable.
Operation *f*: operation, surgical procedure.
Operationsfeld *n*: field of operation.
Operationshandschuh *m*: surgical glove.
Operationsmikroskop *n*: surgical microscope.
Operationssaal *m*: operating room.
Operationsteam *n*: surgical team.
Operationsverfahren *n*: surgical procedure.
Operationsvorbereitung *f*: surgical preparation, preoperative preparation.
Operationswunde *f*: surgical wound.
operativ: surgical, operative.
operieren: operate.
Ophthalmie *f*: ophthalmia.
Ophthalmographie *f*: ophthalmography.
Ophthalmologie *f*: ophthalmology.
Ophthalmopathie *f*: ophthalmopathy; **endokrine** ≈ endocrine ophthalmopathy.
Ophthalmoplegia externa *f*: external ophthalmoplegia, Ballett's disease.
Ophthalmoplegia interna *f*: internal ophthalmoplegia.
Ophthalmoplegie *f*: ophthalmoplegia; **angeborene** ≈ congenital ophthalmoplegia; **diabetische** ≈ diabetic ophthalmoplegia; **internukleäre** ≈ internuclear ophthalmople-

gia, internuclear paralysis; **internukleäre vordere** ≈ anterior internuclear ophthalmoplegia; **supranukleäre** ≈ Parinaud's ophthalmoplegia.
Ophthalmoskopie *f*: ophthalmoscopy, funduscopy.
Opiat *n*: opiate.
Opiatabhängigkeit *f*: opiate dependency.
opiatartig: opiate-like.
Opioid *n*: opioid.
Opipramol *n*: opipramol.
Opisthorchiasis *f*: opisthorchiasis.
Opisthotonus *m*: opisthotonus, neck stiffness.
Opisthotonusepilepsie *f*: opisthotonic epilepsy.
Opitz-Krankheit *f*: Opitz disease, thrombophlebitic splenomegaly.
Opium *n*: opium; **eingestelltes** ≈ standardized opium.
Opiumtinktur *f*: opium tincture, laudanum.
opportunistisch: opportunistic.
OPSI-Syndrom *n*: overwhelming postsplenectomy infection syndrome, OPSI syndrome.
Opsonin *n*: opsonin.
Optik *f*: optics.
Optiker *m*: optician.
Optikusatrophie *f*: optic atrophy.
Optikusgliom *n*: optic glioma.
Optikusneuropathie *f*: optic neuropathy.
Optimaldosis *f*: optimal dose.
optisch: optic, optical.
Optometrie *f*: optometry.
oral: oral.
Orangenhautzeichen *n*: orange-peel sign.
Orazamid *n*: orazamide.
Orbikularisphänomen *n*: orbicularis phenomenon, Westphal-Piltz sign.
Orbikularisreaktion *f*: eyelid closure reflex, blink reflex.
Orbita *f*: orbit, orbita.
Orbitarand *m*: supraorbital arch.
Orbitaspitzensyndrom *n*: orbital apex syndrome.
Orbitatumor *m*: orbital neoplasm.
Orchidektomie *f*: orchiectomy.
Orchidopexie *f*: orchidopexy.
Orchiektomie *f*: orchiectomy.
Orchiepididymitis *f*: orchidoepididymitis.
Orchitis *f*: orchitis; **akute eitrige** ≈ acute pyogenic orchitis; **metastatische** ≈ metastatic orchitis; **traumatische** ≈ traumatic orchitis.
Orciprenalin *n*: orciprenaline.
Ordinate *f*: ordinate, y-axis.
Ordination *f*: surgery hours, consulting hours.
Organ *n*: organ, organum.
Organbank *f*: transplant bank.
Organdosis *f*: organ dose.
Organempfänger *m*: organ recipient.
organisch: organic.
Organismus *m*: organism.
Organneurose *f*: organ neurosis.
organspezifisch: organ-specific.
Organstumpf *m*: stump.
Organversagen *n*: organ failure.
Orgasmus *m*: orgasm.
Orgasmusstörung *f*: orgasmic dysfunction.
Orgotein *n*: orgotein.
Orientbeule *f*: oriental boil, oriental sore.
Orientierung *f*: orientation; **örtliche** ≈ orientation of place; **räumliche** ≈ spatial orientation.
Orientierungspunkt *m*: landmark.
Orientierungsreaktion *f*: orienting reaction.
Orientierungsstörung *f*: disorientation.
Orificium *n*: orifice, opening.
Orlistat *n*: orlistat.
Ormond-Syndrom *n*: Ormond's disease, idiopathic retroperitoneal fibrosis.
Ornidazol *n*: ornidazole.
Ornithin *n*: ornithine.
Ornithose *f*: ornithosis.
orofazial: orofacial.
orofaziodigital: orofaciodigital.
oropharyngeal: oropharyngeal.
Oropharyngealtubus *m*: oropharyngeal airway.
Orotazidurie *f*: oroticaciduria, orotic aciduria.
Orotrachealtubus *m*: orotracheal tube.

Orotsäure *f*: orotic acid.
Orphenadrin *n*: orphenadrine.
Orthese *f*: orthesis, orthosis.
Orthetik *f*: orthetics, orthotics.
Orthocain *n*: orthocaine.
Orthodontie *f*: orthodontics, orthodontia.
Orthomolekularmedizin *f*: orthomolecular medicine.
Orthopädie *f*: orthopedics, orthopedic surgery.
Orthophosphorsäure *f*: orthophosphoric acid.
Orthoptik *f*: orthoptics.
Orthoskopie *f*: orthoscopy.
Orthostase *f*: orthostasis.
orthotop: orthotopic.
Oseltamivir *n*: oseltamivir.
Osgood-Schlatter-Syndrom *n*: Osgood-Schlatter disease, rugby knee.
Osler-Rendu-Weber-Syndrom *n*: Osler-Rendu-Weber syndrome, familial telangiectasis.
Osler-Vaquez-Krankheit *f*: Osler-Vaquez disease, chronic splenomegalic polycythemia.
Osmodiuretikum *n*: osmotic diuretic.
Osmolalität *f*: osmolality.
Osmolarität *f*: osmolarity.
Osmometrie *f*: osmometry.
Osmotherapie *f*: osmotherapy.
Ossifikation *f*: ossification; **desmale** ≈ intramembraneous ossification; **enchondrale** ≈ enchondral ossification, cartilaginous ossification; **endesmale** ≈ intramembraneous ossification; **heterotope** ≈ heterotopic ossification; **perichondrale** ≈ perichondral ossification.
Osteitis *f*: osteitis.
Osteitis deformans *f*: Paget's disease of bone.
Osteitis fibrosa cystica *f*: osteitis fibrosa.
Osteoarthritis *f*: osteoarthritis, degenerative joint disease.
Osteoarthropathie *f*: osteoarthropathy; **hypertrophe pulmonale** ≈ hypertrophic pulmonary osteoarthropathy, Bamberger-Marie disease; **tabische** ≈ tabetic osteoarthropathy.
Osteoarthrose *f*: osteoarthrosis.
Osteoblast *m*: osteoblast.
Osteoblastom *n*: osteoblastoma, giant osteoid osteoma.
osteochondral: osteochondral.
Osteochondritis *f*: osteochondritis.
Osteochondritis syphilitica *f*: syphilitic osteochondritis, Wegner's disease.
Osteochondrodysplasie *f*: osteochondrodysplasia.
Osteochondrom *n*: osteochondroma.
Osteodystrophie *f*: osteodystrophy; **hereditäre** ≈ Albright's hereditary osteodystrophy; **hyperparathyreoide** ≈ parathyroid osteodystrophy; **infantile renale** ≈ renal osteodystrophy; **pankreatische** ≈ celiac rickets; **renale** ≈ renal osteodystrophy, osteoporosis with renal diabetes.
Osteofibrom *n*: osteofibroma.
osteogen: osteogenic.
Osteogenese *f*: osteogenesis, bone development.
Osteogenesis imperfecta *f*: osteogenesis imperfecta, Eddowes disease.
Osteoid *n*: osteoid.
Osteoidosteom *n*: osteoid osteoma.
Osteoklast *m*: osteoclast.
Osteolyse *f*: osteolysis.
Osteom *n*: osteoma.
Osteomalazie *f*: osteomalacia.
Osteomyelitis *f*: osteomyelitis, bone inflammation.
Osteomyelofibrose *f*: bone marrow fibrosis, osteomyelofibrotic syndrome.
Osteopathia hyperostotica multiplex infantilis *f*: osteopathia hyperostotica multiplex infantilis, diaphyseal dysplasia.
Osteopathie *f*: osteopathy, osteopathia.
Osteopetrose *f*: osteopetrosis, Albers-Schönberg disease.
Osteophyt *m*: osteophyte.
Osteoplast *m*: osteoplast, osteoblast.
Osteopoikilie *f*: osteopoikilosis.
Osteoporose *f*: osteoporosis.
Osteosarkom *n*: osteosarcoma, osteogenic sarcoma.
Osteosklerose *f*: osteosclerosis.

Osteosynthese *f*: osteosynthesis.
Osteotom *n*: osteotome.
Osteotomie *f*: osteotomy; **gerade** ≈ linear osteotomy; **intertrochantäre** ≈ transtrochanteric osteotomy; **subtrochantäre** ≈ subtrochanteric osteotomy.
Osteozyt *m*: osteocyte, osseous cell.
Ostitis *f*: ostitis, osteitis; **chronische** ≈ chronic osteitis; **hämatogene** ≈ hematogenous osteitis; **sklerosierende** ≈ sclerosing osteitis; **syphilitische** ≈ gummatous osteitis.
Ostitis condensans *f*: condensing osteitis.
Ostitis deformans *f*: pagetoid osteitis.
Ostitis fibrosa cystica *f*: fibrocystic osteitis, Engel-Recklinghausen disease.
Otalgie *f*: otalgia, earache; **reflektorische** ≈ referred otalgia.
Otitis *f*: otitis; **adhäsive** ≈ adhesive otitis; **seröse** ≈ serous otitis; **traumatische** ≈ traumatic otitis.
Otitis media *f*: otitis media; **eitrige** ≈ purulent otitis media, suppurative otitis media; **nekrotisierende** ≈ necrotizing otitis; **sekretorische** ≈ hydrotympanum; **seromuköse** ≈ serous otitis media.
otogen: otogenous, otogenic.
Otolith *m*: otolith.
Otologie *f*: otology.
Otomyiasis *f*: otomyiasis.
Otomykose *f*: otomycosis.
Otoneurologie *f*: neuro-otology.
Otoplastik *f*: otoplasty.
Otorhinolaryngologie *f*: otorhinolaryngology.
Otorrhö *f*: otorrhea.
Otosklerose *f*: otosclerosis.
Otoskopie *f*: otoscopy.
Ototoxizität *f*: ototoxicity.
Ovalärschnitt *m*: elliptic amputation.
Ovar *n*: ovary, ovarium.
ovarial: ovarian.
Ovarialabszess *m*: ovary abscess.
Ovarialgravidität *f*: ovarian pregnancy.
Ovarialkarzinom *n*: ovarian cancer.
Ovarialsyndrom, polyzystisches *n*: polycystic ovary syndrome, Stein-Leventhal syndrome.
Ovarialtorsion *f*: ovary torsion.
Ovarialtumor *m*: ovarian tumor.
Ovarialzyste *f*: ovarian cyst.
Ovariektomie *f*: ovarectomy.
Ovariotomie *f*: ovariotomy.
Oversuppression-Syndrom *n*: oversuppression syndrome.
Ovozyt *m*: ovocyte, oocyte.
Ovulation *f*: ovulation.
Ovulationsblutung *f*: midcyclical bleeding.
Ovulationshemmer *m*: ovulation inhibitor, anovulant.
Ovulationsinduktion *f*: ovulation induction.
Ovulationsmethode *f*: ovulation method.
Oxaboloncipionat *n*: oxabolone cipionate.
Oxaceprol *n*: oxaceprol.
Oxacillin *n*: oxacillin.
Oxacillinnatrium *n*: sodium oxacillin.
Oxalatblut *n*: oxalated blood.
Oxalatstein *m*: oxalate calculus.
Oxalbernsteinsäure *f*: oxalosuccinic acid.
Oxalessigsäure *f*: oxaloacetic acid.
Oxaliplatin *n*: oxaliplatin.
Oxalsäure *f*: oxalic acid.
Oxalurie *f*: oxaluria.
Oxalursäure *f*: oxaluric acid.
Oxaminsäure *f*: oxamic acid.
Oxamycin *n*: oxamycin.
Oxanamid *n*: oxanamide.
Oxandrolon *n*: oxandrolone.
Oxaprozin *n*: oxaprozin.
Oxatomid *n*: oxatomide.
Oxazepam *n*: oxazepam.
Oxazolam *n*: oxazolam.
Oxcarbazepin *n*: oxcarbazepine.
Oxetacain *n*: oxetacaine, oxetazaine.
Oxiconazol *n*: oxiconazole.
Oxidant *m*: oxidant.
Oxidation *f*: oxidation.
Oxidationsmittel *n*: oxidant, oxidizer.
Oximetrie *f*: oximetry, oxymetry.
Oxitriptan *n*: oxitriptan.
Oxitropiumbromid *n*: oxitropium bromide.
Oxolin *n*: oxoline.

Oxolinsäure *f*: oxolinic acid.
5-Oxoprolin *n*: pyroglutamic acid.
Oxprenolol *n*: oxprenolol.
β-Oxybuttersäure *f*: beta-oxybutyric acid.
Oxybutynin *n*: oxybutynin.
Oxyclozanid *n*: oxyclozanide.
Oxygenisation *f*: oxygenation; **extrakorporale** ≈ extracorporeal oxygenation.
Oxyhämoglobin *n*: oxyhemoglobin, oxidized hemoglobin.
Oxymesteron *n*: oxymesterone.
Oxymetholon *n*: oxymetholone.
Oxymetrie *f*: oximetry, oxymetry.
Oxynervonsäure *f*: oxynervonic acid.
Oxypertin *n*: oxypertine.
Oxyphenbutazon *n*: oxyphenbutazone.
Oxyphencyclimin *n*: oxyphencyclimine.
Oxyphenisatin *n*: oxyphenisatin.
oxyphil: oxyphil, oxyphilic.
Oxytetracyclin *n*: oxytetracycline.
Oxytocicum *n*: oxytocic.
Oxytocin *n*: oxytocin, ocytocin.
Oxyuriasis *f*: oxyuriasis.
Ozäna *f*: ozena.
Ozonkrankheit *f*: ozone sickness.
Ozytocin *n*: ocytocin.

P

P Abk. **1. Perzentile** *f*; **2. Phosphor** *m*; **3. Puls** *m*: 1. percentile; 2. phosphorus, P; 3. pulse.
Paartherapie *f*: couple therapy.
Paarung *f*: pairing, mating.
Paarungsverhalten *n*: mating behavior.
Pacchioni-Granulationen: Pacchioni's granulations, meningeal granules.
Pachydermie *f*: pachyderma.
Pachydermitis spinalis externa *f*: acute spinal pachymeningitis.
Pachymeningitis *f*: pachymeningitis.
Pachymeningitis cervicalis hypertrophica *f*: hypertrophic cervical pachymeningitis.
Packung *f*: pack, package; **feuchte** ≈ wet pack; **kalte** ≈ cold pack; **warme** ≈ hot pack.
Packungsbeilage *f*: package insert.
Paclitaxel *n*: paclitaxel.
Pädiatrie *f*: pediatrics.
pädiatrisch: pediatric.
Paget-Krankheit *f*: Paget's disease of bone, pagetoid osteitis.
Paget-Schroetter-Syndrom *n*: Paget-von Schroetter syndrome, effort thrombosis.
Palatoplastik *f*: palatoplasty.
Pallästhesie *f*: pallesthesia, vibratory sensibility.
palliativ: palliative, alleviative.
Palliativbehandlung *f*: palliative treatment.
Palliativmedizin *f*: palliative medicine.
Palliativversorgung *f*: palliative care.
Pallidumsyndrom *n*: pallidal syndrome, pallidal rigidity.
palmar: palmar.
Palmarabdruck *m*: palmprint.
Palmarerythem *n*: palmar erythema.
Palmarkontraktion *f*: palmar contraction.
Palmarreflex *m*: palmar reflex.
Palmitinsäure *f*: palmitic acid.
Palmitoleinsäure *f*: palmitoleic acid.
Palmomentalreflex *m*: palmomental reflex, Marinesco-Radovic reflex.
Palonosetron *n*: palonosetron.
Palpation *f*: palpation.
Palpitation *f*: palpitation.
Paludismus *m*: paludism, malaria.
Pamaquin *n*: pamaquine.
Pamidronsäure *f*: pamidronate.
Panaritium *n*: felon, whitlow.
Panarteriitis *f*: panarteritis.
Panarteriitis nodosa *f*: polyarteritis nodosa, necrotizing arteritis.
Panarthritis *f*: panarthritis.
Pancreas annulare *n*: annular pancreas.
Pancreas divisum *n*: divided pancreas.
Pancuroniumbromid *n*: pancuronium bromide.
Pandemie *f*: pandemic.
pandemisch: pandemic.
Panenzephalitis *f*: panencephalitis; **subakute sklerosierende** ≈ subacute sclerosing panencephalitis, SSPE, Dawson's encephalitis.
Panhypopituitarismus *m*: panhypopituitarism.
Panik *f*: panic.
Panikattacke *f*: panic attack.
panisch: panic.
Pankarditis *f*: pancarditis.
Pankreas *n*: pancreas.
Pankreasabszess *m*: pancreatic abscess.
Pankreasamylase *f*: pancreatic amylase.

Pankreasfibrose *f*: fibrosis of pancreas; **zystische** ≈ cystic fibrosis of pancreas.
Pankreasinsuffizienz *f*: pancreatic insufficiency.
Pankreaskarzinom *n*: pancreatic cancer.
Pankreaskolik *f*: pancreatic colic.
Pankreaslipase *f*: pancreatic lipase.
Pankreastransplantation *f*: pancreatic transplantation.
Pankreastumor *m*: pancreatic neoplasm.
Pankreatektomie *f*: pancreatectomy.
Pankreatin *n*: pancreatin.
pankreatisch: pancreatic.
Pankreatitis *f*: pancreatitis; **akute hämorrhagische** ≈ acute hemorrhagic pancreatitis; **chronische** ≈ chronic pancreatitis; **fulminante** ≈ fulminant pancreatitis; **medikamenteninduzierte** ≈ drug-induced pancreatitis; **ödematöse** ≈ edematous pancreatitis.
Pankreatoduodenostomie *f*: pancreaticoduodenostomy.
Pankreatographie *f*: pancreatography.
Pankreozymin *n*: pancreozymin.
Panmyelopathie *f*: panmyelopathy.
Pannikulitis *f*: panniculitis; **rekurrierende nichteitrige** ≈ relapsing febrile non-suppurative panniculitis, Christian-Weber disease; **subakute noduläre** ≈ subacute nodular migratory panniculitis.
Panophthalmitis *f*: panophthalmitis.
Panoramaschichtverfahren *n*: panorama panographic system.
Pantokain *n*: pantocaine.
Pantoprazol *n*: pantoprazole.
Pantothensäure *f*: pantothenic acid.
Panzerherz *n*: armored heart.
Panzerkrebs *m*: cancer en cuirasse, corset cancer.
Papageienkrankheit *f*: parrot fever, psittacosis.
Papanicolaou-Abstrich *m*: Papanicolaou smear, Pap test.
Papaverin *n*: papaverine.
Papaverinsulfat *n*: papaverine sulfate.
Papel *f*: papule, pimple; **flache** ≈ flat papule; **nässende** ≈ moist papule.
Papilla duodenalis major *f*: major duodenal papilla.
Papilla duodenalis minor *f*: minor duodenal papilla.
Papille *f*: papilla.
Papillenabblassung, temporale *f*: temporal pallor.
Papillengangkarzinom *n*: ductal papillary carcinoma.
Papillenkarzinom *n*: papillary carcinoma.
Papillenödem *n*: papilledema, choked disk.
Papillitis *f*: papillitis.
Papillo-: papillo-.
Papillom *n*: papilloma; **endophytisches** ≈ endophytic papilloma, inverted papilloma; **exophytisches** ≈ exophytic papilloma; **fibroepitheliales** ≈ fibroepithelial papilloma; **intraduktales** ≈ intraductal papilloma; **intrakanalikuläres** ≈ intracanalicular papilloma.
Papillosphinkterotomie *f*: papillosphincterotomy; **endoskopische** ≈ endoscopic papillosphincterotomy.
Pappataci-Fieber *n*: pappataci fever, sandfly fever.
papulös: papular.
papulopustulös: papulopustular.
Para-Aminobenzoesäure *f*: para-aminobenzoic acid.
Para-Aminohippursäure *f*: para-aminohippuric acid.
Para-Aminosalicylsäure *f*: para-aminosalicylic acid.
paraaortal: para-aortic.
Paracetamol *n*: paracetamol, acetaminophen.
paradontal: parodontal, periodontal.
Parästhesie *f*: paresthesia; **schmerzhafte** ≈ paralgesia.
Paraffin *n*: paraffin.
Paraffinkrebs *m*: paraffin cancer.
Paraflutizid *n*: paraflutizide.
Paraganglion *n*: paraganglion, chromaffin body.
Paragonimiasis *f*: paragonimiasis.
Paragonimus *m*: paragonimus.
Parainfluenza *f*: parainfluenza.

Parakokzidioidomykose *f*: paracoccidioidomycosis.
Parakusis *f*: paracusia, paracusis.
Paraldehyd *m*: paraldehyde.
Paralyse *f*: paralysis, palsy; **juvenile** ≈ juvenile paralysis; **progressive** ≈ progressive paralysis, general paralysis, GP.
Paralysis acuta ascendens spinalis *f*: acute ascending paralysis.
Paralysis agitans *f*: paralysis agitans, Parkinson's disease.
Paralysis agitans juvenilis *f*: juvenile paralysis agitans, Ramsey-Hunt paralysis.
Paralysis spinalis ascendens acuta *f*: acute ascending paralysis, Landry's paralysis.
paralytisch: paralytic.
Paramedianebene *f*: paramedian plane.
Paramedianschnitt *m*: paramedian incision.
paramedizinisch: paramedical.
Paramethadion *n*: paramethadione.
Paramethason *n*: paramethasone.
Paramethasonacetat *n*: paramethasone acetate.
Parametritis *f*: parametritis.
Parametrium *n*: parametrium.
Paramnesie *f*: paramnesia.
Paramyxovirus *n*: paramyxovirus.
paraneoplastisch: paraneoplastic.
Paranoia *f*: paranoia, paranoid disorder; **alkoholische** ≈ alcoholic paranoid state.
paranoid: paranoid.
Paraoxon *n*: paraoxon.
Paraparese *f*: paraparesis.
Paraphimose *f*: paraphimosis.
Paraplegie *f*: paraplegia; **ataktische** ≈ ataxic paraplegia; **infantile spastische** ≈ congenital spastic paraplegia; **hereditäre spastische** ≈ familial spastic paraplegia; **hysterische** ≈ hysterical paraplegia; **schlaffe** ≈ flaccid paraplegia; **senile myopathische** ≈ senile myopathic paraplegia; **spastische** ≈ spastic paraplegia.
Parapsoriasis *f*: parapsoriasis.
Pararektalschnitt *m*: pararectal incision.
Parasit *m*: parasite; **autochthoner** ≈ autochthonous parasite; **eurytropher** ≈ eurytrophic parasite; **euryxener** ≈ euroxenous parasite; **fakultativer** ≈ facultative parasite; **heteroxener** ≈ digenetic parasite; **inchoativer** ≈ periodic parasite; **obligater** ≈ obligate parasite; **stenoxener** ≈ stenoxenous parasite; **wirtspezifischer** ≈ specific parasite.
Parasitenbefall *m*: parasitization, infestation.
Parasitizid *n*: parasiticide.
Parasomnie *f*: parasomnia.
Parastellung *f*: para-position.
Parasympatholytikum *n*: parasympatholytic.
Parasystole *f*: parasystole.
Parasystolie *f*: parasystolic rhythm.
Parathion *n*: parathion.
Parathormon *n*: parathormone, parathyroid hormone.
Parathyreoidea *f*: parathyroid, parathyroid body.
Paratyphus *m*: paratyphoid, parenteric fever.
paraumbilikal: paraumbilical, parumbilical.
Paraurethraldrüse *f*: paraurethral gland.
Paravaginalschnitt *m*: paravaginal incision.
paravenös: paravenous.
Paravertebralanästhesie *f*: paravertebral block.
Parazentese *f*: paracentesis.
Parecoxib *n*: parecoxib.
Parenchym *n*: parenchyma.
parenchymatös: parenchymatous, parenchymal.
parenteral: parenteral.
Parese *f*: paresis, incomplete paralysis.
Pargylin *n*: pargyline.
Paricalcitol *n*: paricalcitol.
parietal: parietal.
Parietallappen *m*: parietal lobe.
Parietalzelle *f*: parietal cell, acid cell.
Parinaud-Konjunktivitis *f*: Parinaud's oculoglandular syndrome.
Parkinsonismus *m*: parkinsonism, Parkinson's disease.

Parkinson-Syndrom *n*: Parkinson's disease, parkinsonism; **arteriosklerotisches** ≈ atherosclerotic parkinsonism; **medikamentös bedingtes** ≈ drug-induced parkinsonism; **postenzephalitisches** ≈ postencephalitic parkinsonism; **symptomatisches** ≈ symptomatic parkinsonism; **traumatisches** ≈ traumatic parkinsonism.

Parodontitis *f*: periodontitis.

Paromomycin *n*: paromomycin.

Paronychie *f*: paronychia, perionychia.

Paroophoritis *f*: paroophoritis.

Parosmie *f*: parosmia.

Parotidektomie *f*: parotidectomy.

Parotis *f*: parotid gland.

Parotitis *f*: parotitis.

Parotitis epidemica *f*: epidemic parotitis, mumps.

Paroxetin *n*: paroxetin.

Paroxysmus *m*: paroxysm.

Parthenogenese *f*: parthenogenesis.

Partialblock *m*: partial block.

Partialdruck *m*: partial pressure.

Partialvolumen *n*: partial volume.

Partikelgröße *f*: particle size.

Partnertherapie *f*: partner therapy.

Partus *m*: partus, parturition.

PAS-Färbung *f*: PAS stain.

Pasini-Syndrom *n*: bullous papuloalboid epidermolysis.

Passage *f*: passage, transit.

passiv: passive, inactive.

Paste *f*: paste.

Pasteurisation *f*: pasteurization.

Pastille *f*: pastille.

pastös: pasty.

Patau-Syndrom *n*: Patau syndrome, trisomy 13 syndrome.

Patchtest *m*: patch test.

Patella *f*: patella, kneecap; **tanzende** ≈ floating patella.

Patellarsehnenreflex *m*: patellar tendon reflex, knee jerk.

Patent *n*: patent.

pathogen: pathogenic.

Pathogenese *f*: pathogenesis.

Pathogenität *f*: pathogenicity.

pathognomonisch: pathognomonic.

Pathologie *f*: pathology; **allgemeine** ≈ general pathology; **experimentelle** ≈ experimental pathology; **forensische** ≈ forensic pathology.

pathologisch: pathologic, pathological.

pathologisch-anatomisch: anatomicopathologic.

Pathomechanismus *m*: pathogenetic mechanism.

Pathophysiologie *f*: pathophysiology.

Patient *m*: patient.

Patientenanwalt *m*: patient advocacy.

Patientendosis *f*: patient dose.

Patientenheber *m*: patient lift.

Paukengang *m*: tympanic canal.

Paukenhöhle *f*: tympanic cavity.

Paukenröhrchen *n*: ventilation tube, grommet.

Paukensklerose *f*: tympanosclerosis.

Pause *f*: pause, silent period; **diastolische** ≈ diastolic pause; **kompensatorische** ≈ compensatory pause; **postextrasystolische** ≈ post-extrasystolic pause; **präautomatische** ≈ preautomatic pause.

Pavor diurnus *m*: pavor diurnus, day terrors.

Pavor nocturnus *m*: pavor nocturnus, night terrors.

Pectus carinatum *n*: pectus carinatum, keeled chest.

Pectus excavatum *n*: pectus excavatum, funnel chest.

Pedikulizid *n*: pediculicide.

Pedikulose *f*: pediculosis.

Pefloxacin *n*: pefloxacin.

Pegaspargase *f*: pegaspargase.

Pegfilgrastim *n*: pegfilgrastim.

Peginterferon *n*: peginterferon, pegylated interferon.

Pegvisomant *n*: pegvisomant.

pegyliert: pegylated.

Peiper-Lichtreflex *m*: Peiper's reflex, dazzle reflex.

Peitschenkatheter *m*: whip catheter, filiform-tipped catheter.

Peitschenschlagphänomen *n*: whiplash injury, whiplash syndrome.

Peitschenwurm *m*: whipworm.

pektanginös: anginose.

Pellagra *f*: pellagra.

Pellet *n*: pellet.
Pelvigraphie *f*: pelviography.
Pelvimetrie *f*: pelvimetry.
Pemphigoid *n*: pemphigoid; **bullöses** ≈ bullous pemphigoid; **umschriebenes chronisches** ≈ chronic localized pemphigoid.
Pemphigus *m*: pemphigus.
Pemphigus chronicus benignus familiaris *m*: benign familial pemphigus, Hailey-Hailey disease.
Pemphigus erythematosus *m*: pemphigus erythematosus, Senear-Usher syndrome.
Pemphigus vulgaris *m*: pemphigus vulgaris, pemphigus.
Penbutolol *n*: penbutolol.
Penciclovir *n*: penciclovir.
Pendelgang *m*: swing-through gait.
Pendelnystagmus *m*: pendular nystagmus.
Penetration *f*: penetration, sperm penetration.
Penetrationswunde *f*: penetration wound, penetrating wound.
Penfluridol *n*: penfluridol.
Penflutizid *n*: penflutizide.
Penicillamin *n*: penicillamine.
Penicillansäure *f*: penicillanic acid.
Penicillin *n*: penicillin.
Penicillinallergie *f*: penicillin allergy.
Penicillinase *f*: penicillinase.
Penicillinresistenz *f*: penicillin resistance.
Penicillinsäure *f*: penicillic acid.
Penicilloinsäure *f*: penicilloic acid.
Penicillsäure *f*: penicillic acid.
penil: penile.
Penis *m*: penis, phallus.
Penisdeviation *f*: penile deviation.
Penisneid *m*: penis envy.
Penisschaft *m*: penile root.
Pentaerithrityltetranitrat *n*: pentaerythrityl tetranitrate.
Pentafusid *n*: pentafuside.
Pentagastrin *n*: pentagastrin.
Pentamethonium *n*: pentamethonium.
Pentamidin *n*: pentamidine.
Pentansäure *f*: pentanoic acid, valerianic acid.
Pentazocin *n*: pentazocine.
Pentetreotid *n*: pentetreotide.
Pentobarbital *n*: pentobarbital.
Pentose *f*: pentose.
Pentosurie *f*: pentosuria.
Pentoxifyllin *n*: pentoxifylline.
Pepsin *n*: pepsin.
Peptid *n*: peptide; **vasoaktives intestinales** ≈ vasoactive intestinal peptide, VIP.
peptisch: peptic, pepsic.
perakut: superacute, hyperacute.
Perchlorsäure *f*: perchloric acid.
Peressigsäure *f*: peracetic acid.
Perforation *f*: perforation.
Perfusion *f*: perfusion.
Pergamenthaut *f*: paper skin, parchment skin.
Pergolid *n*: pergolide.
Perhexilin *n*: perhexiline.
Periarteriitis *f*: periarteritis.
Periarteriitis nodosa *f*: disseminated necrotising periarteritis.
Periarthritis *f*: periarthritis.
periartikulär: periarticular.
Pericarditis *f*: pericarditis.
Pericarditis carcinomatosa *f*: carcinomatous pericarditis.
Pericarditis constrictiva *f*: constrictive pericarditis.
Pericarditis serofibrinosa *f*: serofibrinous pericarditis.
Periduralanästhesie *f*: peridural anesthesia, epidural block.
Periektomie *f*: peridectomy, peritomy.
Perifollikulitis *f*: perifolliculitis.
Perihepatitis *f*: perihepatitis, parahepatitis.
Perikard *n*: pericardium, pericardial sac.
Perikarderguss *m*: pericardial effusion.
perikardial: pericardiac, pericardial.
Perikarditis *f*: pericarditis; **adhäsive** ≈ adhesive pericarditis; **akute benigne** ≈ acute benign pericarditis; **akute exsudative** ≈ acute exudative pericarditis; **eitrige** ≈ purulent pericarditis; **fibrinöse** ≈ fibrinous pericarditis; **hämorrhagische** ≈ hemorrhagic pericarditis; **leukämische** ≈ leukemic pericarditis; **maligne** ≈

malignant pericarditis; **rheumatische** ≈ rheumatic pericarditis; **septische** ≈ septic pericarditis; **tuberkulöse** ≈ tuberculous pericarditis; **urämische** ≈ uremic pericarditis.
Perikardreiben *n*: pericardial murmur, pericardial friction.
Perikardsynechie *f*: adhesive pericarditis.
Perikardverkalkung *f*: pericardial calcification.
Perikolitis *f*: pericolitis.
perikorneal: pericorneal.
Perilymphe *f*: perilymph.
Perimetrie *f*: perimetry.
perinatal: perinatal.
Perinatalmedizin *f*: perinatal medicine.
Perinatalsterblichkeit *f*: perinatal mortality.
Perinatalzeit *f*: perinatal period, early neonatal period.
perineal: perineal.
Perineorrhaphie *f*: perineorrhaphy.
perinephritisch: perinephric, perirenal.
Perineum *n*: perineum.
Perineurium *n*: perineurium.
Perineuriumzelle *f*: perineurial cell.
Periode *f*: period, phase; **monatliche** ≈ monthly period, menstruation.
periodisch: periodic.
perioperativ: paraoperative.
periorbital: periorbital.
Periorchitis *f*: periorchitis.
Periost *n*: periost, periosteum.
Periosthaken *m*: periosteal retractor.
Periostitis *f*: periostitis.
Periostreflex *m*: periosteal reflex.
peripher: peripheral.
Periproktitis *f*: periproctitis; **abszedierende** ≈ periproctic abscess.
perirenal: perirenal, pararenal.
Peristaltik *f*: peristalsis, peristaltic movement; **retrograde** ≈ retrograde peristalsis, retroperistalsis; **verlangsamte** ≈ slow bowel movement.
Peritomie *f*: peritomy.
peritoneal: peritoneal.
Peritonealdialyse *f*: peritoneal dialysis.
Peritonealkarzinose *f*: peritoneal carcinomatosis.
Peritoneallavage *f*: peritoneal irrigation.
Peritoneum *n*: peritoneum.
Peritonitis *f*: peritonitis; **adhäsive** ≈ adhesive peritonitis; **akute abakterielle** ≈ acute sterile peritonitis; **chylöse** ≈ chyle peritonitis; **gallige** ≈ biliary peritonitis, bile peritonitis; **perforierende** ≈ perforating peritonitis; **rekurrierende** ≈ benign paroxysmal peritonitis; **septische** ≈ septic peritonitis; **seröse** ≈ serous peritonitis.
peritonsillär: peritonsillar, paratonsillar.
Peritonsillarabszess *m*: peritonsillar abscess, quinsy.
Periurethritis *f*: periurethritis.
Perivaskulärraum *m*: perivascular space.
Perizyt *m*: pericyte, perivascular cell, adventitial cell.
Perjodsäure *f*: periodic acid.
Perkussion *f*: percussion; **direkte** ≈ direct percussion; **indirekte** ≈ indirect percussion; **vergleichende** ≈ comparative percussion.
Perkussion des Abdomens: abdominal percussion.
Perkussionswelle *f*: percussion wave.
perkutan: percutaneous, transcutaneous.
perkutieren: percuss, tap.
Permangansäure *f*: permanganic acid.
Permeabilität *f*: permeability.
Permethrin *n*: permethrin.
Pernio *m*: pernio, chilblain.
Perniose *f*: perniosis, cold injury.
perniziös: pernicious.
peroneal: peroneal.
Peroneuslähmung *f*: peroneal paralysis.
Perphenazin *n*: perphenazine.
Perschwefelsäure *f*: persulfuric acid.
Perseveration *f*: perseveration.
Persistenz *f*: persistence.
Persönlichkeit *f*: personality, character; **antisoziale** ≈ antisocial personality; **multiple** ≈ multiple personality; **psychopathische** ≈ psycho-

pathic personality; **zyklothyme** ≈ cycloid type, affective personality.
Persönlichkeitsstörung *f*: personality disorder, character disorder; **dependente** ≈ dependent personality disorder; **histrionische** ≈ histrionic personality disorder; **paranoide** ≈ paranoid personality disorder; **schizoide** ≈ schizoid personality disorder; **schizotypische** ≈ schizotypical personality disorder; **transitorische** ≈ acute situational reaction, crisis reaction; **zwanghafte** ≈ compulsive personality disorder.
Person *f*: person, subject.
Personal *n*: personnel, staff; **medizinisches** ≈ medical personnel, medical staff.
Perspiration *f*: perspiration, sweating.
Pertussis *f*: pertussis, whooping cough.
Peru-Warze *f*: peruvian wart, verruga peruviana.
Perzentile *f*: percentile.
Perzeption *f*: perception.
Pessar *n*: pessary.
Pest *f*: plague, pest.
petechial: petechial.
Petit mal *n*: petit mal, minor epilepsy; **atonisches** ≈ atonic petit mal; **myoklonisches** ≈ myoclonic petit mal, myoclonic epilepsy, myoclonic seizure.
Petrifikation *f*: petrifaction.
Pétrissage *f*: pétrissage, kneading.
Peutz-Jeghers-Syndrom *n*: Peutz-Jeghers syndrome, intestinal polyposis-cutaneous pigmentation syndrome.
Peyronie-Krankheit *f*: Peyronie's disease, plastic induration of penis.
Pfaundler-Hurler-Syndrom *n*: Hurler syndrome, lipochondrodystrophy, gargoylism.
Pfeifen *n*: sibilant rale.
pfeifend: sibilant, whistling.
Pfeifengesicht *n*: whistling deformity.
Pfeifer-Weber-Christian-Syndrom *n*: Weber-Christian syndrome, relapsing febrile non-suppurative panniculitis.
Pfeiffer-Drüsenfieber *n*: Pfeiffer's disease, infectious mononucleosis.
Pfeifgeräusch *n*: whistling sound.
Pferdeenzephalitis *f*: equine encephalitis.
Pferdefuß *m*: tip foot.
Pferderotz *m*: glanders.
Pflanzenextrakt *m*: vegetable extract.
Pflanzenheilkunde *f*: phytotherapy.
Pflaster *n*: tape, plaster.
Pflege *f*: nursing, nursing care.
Pflegebedürftigkeit *f*: need for care.
Pflegeberuf *m*: nursing profession.
Pflegedienst *m*: nursing service.
Pflegefamilie *f*: foster-family.
Pflegeheim *n*: nursing home.
Pflegepersonal *n*: nursing staff.
Pflegestandard *m*: standard of nursing care.
Pflichtimpfung *f*: mandatory vaccination, compulsary vaccination.
Pfötchenstellung *f*: obstetrician's hand, Trousseau's phenomenon.
Pfortaderblock *m*: portal block.
Pfortaderdruck *m*: portal venous pressure.
Pforte *f*: portal, entrance.
Pfropf *m*: plug, ball.
Phänomen der paroxysmalen Tränen *n*: paroxysmal lacrimation, crocodile tears syndrome.
Phänotyp *m*: phenotype.
phänotypisch: phenotypic.
Phage *m*: phage, bacteriophage.
Phagedaena gangraenosa *f*: phagedaena gangraenosa, sloughing phagedena.
Phagozyt *m*: phagocyte.
Phagozytose *f*: phagocytosis.
Phalanx *f*: phalanx.
Phallus *m*: phallus, penis.
Phantasie *f*: phantasy, fantasy.
Phantomglied *n*: phantom limb.
Phantomschmerz *m*: phantom limb pain.
Pharmakoepidemiologie *f*: pharmacoepidemiology.
Pharmakogenetik *f*: pharmacogenetics.
Pharmakognosie *f*: pharmacognosy, pharmacognostics.

Pharmakokinetik *f*: pharmacokinetics.
Pharmakologie *f*: pharmacology.
pharmakologisch: pharmacologic.
Pharmakon *n*: pharmaceutical, medicinal agent.
Pharmakopoe *f*: pharmacopeia.
Pharmakotherapie *f*: pharmacotherapy, drug therapy.
Pharmakovigilanz *f*: pharmacovigilance.
pharmazeutisch: pharmaceutical, pharmaceutic.
Pharmazie *f*: pharmacy, pharmaceutics.
Pharmazietechnik *f*: pharmaceutical technology.
pharyngeal: pharyngeal.
Pharyngektomie *f*: pharyngectomy.
Pharyngismus *m*: pharyngismus.
Pharyngitis *f*: pharyngitis; **akute** ≈ acute pharyngitis; **chronische** ≈ chronic pharyngitis; **gangränöse** ≈ gangrenous pharyngitis, necrotic angina; **hypertrophe** ≈ hypertrophic pharyngitis; **ulzeromembranöse** ≈ ulceromembranous pharyngitis, ulcerated sore throat.
Pharyngitis atrophicans *f*: atrophic pharyngitis.
Pharyngitis herpetica *f*: herpetic pharyngitis.
Pharyngokonjunktivalfieber *n*: pharyngoconjunctival fever.
Pharyngolaryngektomie *f*: pharyngolaryngectomy.
Pharyngoplastik *f*: pharyngoplasty.
Pharyngoskopie *f*: pharyngoscopy.
Pharyngotomie *f*: pharyngotomy.
Pharyngozele *f*: pharyngocele.
Pharynxdivertikel *n*: pharyngeal diverticulum.
Pharynxlähmung *f*: pharyngeal paralysis.
Pharynxstenose *f*: pharyngostenosis.
Phase *f*: phase, period.
Phasenkontrastmikroskop *n*: phase-contrast microscope.
Phenacemid *n*: phenacemide.
Phenacetin *n*: phenacetin.
Phenacetinniere *f*: phenacetin nephropathy.
Phenamacid *n*: phenamacide.
Phenbenicillin *n*: phenbenicillin, fenbencillin.
Phenbenzamin *n*: phenbenzamine.
Phenelzin *n*: phenelzine.
Phenethicillin *n*: phenethicillin.
Pheniprazin *n*: pheniprazine.
Pheniramin *n*: pheniramine.
Phenobarbital *n*: phenobarbital, phenylethylbarbituric acid.
Phenolkampfer *m*: camphorated phenol.
Phenolsulfonphthalein *n*: phenolsulfonphthalein, phenol red.
Phenothiazin *n*: phenothiazine.
Phenoxybenzamin *n*: phenoxybenzamine.
Phenoxymethylpenicillin *n*: phenoxymethylpenicillin.
Phenprobamat *n*: phenprobamate.
Phenprocoumon *n*: phenprocoumon.
Phensuximid *n*: phensuximide.
Phentolamin *n*: phentolamine.
Phenyl *n*: phenyl.
Phenyläthylbarbitursäure *f*: phenylethylbarbituric acid, phenobarbital.
Phenylalanin *n*: phenylalanine, Phe.
Phenylbrenztraubensäure *f*: phenylpyruvic acid.
Phenylbutazon *n*: phenylbutazone.
Phenylephrin *n*: phenylephrine.
Phenylessigsäure *f*: phenylacetic acid.
Phenylindandion *n*: 2-phenyl-1,3-indandione, phenindione.
Phenylketonurie *f*: phenylketonuria, PKU.
Phenylketonuriedemenz *f*: phenylpyruvic amentia.
Phenylmercuriborat *n*: phenylmercuric borate.
Phenylpropanolamin *n*: phenylpropanolamine.
Phenyltoloxamin *n*: phenyltoloxamine.
Phenytoin *n*: phenytoin, diphenylhydantoin.
Phimose *f*: phimosis.
Phlebektomie *f*: phlebectomy.
Phlebitis *f*: phlebitis.
Phlebitis migrans *f*: migrating phlebitis.

Phlebosklerose *f*: phlebosclerosis.
Phlebothrombose *f*: phlebothrombosis.
Phlebotomie *f*: phlebotomy, venesection.
Phlebotomusfieber *n*: phlebotomus fever, sandfly fever.
Phlegmasia *f*: phlegmasia, phlegmonosis.
Phlegmone *f*: phlegmon.
Phlyktäne *f*: phlyctena, burn blister.
phlyktänulär: phlyctenular.
Phobie *f*: phobia.
Phokomelie *f*: phocomelia.
Phonation *f*: phonation.
Phoniatrie *f*: phoniatrics.
Phonokardiogramm *n*: phonocardiogram.
Phosphat *n*: phosphate.
Phosphatämie *f*: phosphatemia.
Phosphatase *f*: phosphatase; **alkalische** ≈ alkaline phosphatase; **saure** ≈ acid phosphatase.
Phosphatdiabetes *m*: phosphate diabetes.
Phosphaturie *f*: phosphaturia.
Phosphoglycerinsäure *f*: phosphoglyceric acid.
Phospholipid *n*: phospholipid.
Phosphomolybdänsäure *f*: phosphomolybdic acid.
Phosphornekrose *f*: phosphonecrosis, phosphorus necrosis.
Phosphorsäure *f*: phosphoric acid.
Phosphorwolframsäure *f*: phosphotungstic acid.
Phosphorylierung *f*: phosphorylation.
Photochemotherapie *f*: photochemotherapy.
Photodermatitis *f*: photodermatitis.
Photodermatose *f*: photodermatosis.
Photographie *f*: photography.
Photokoagulation *f*: photocoagulation, photocauterization.
Photophobie *f*: photophobia.
photopisch: photopic.
Photoretinitis *f*: photoretinitis, sun blindness.
Photosensibilisierung *f*: photosensitization.
Phrenikuslähmung *f*: phrenic paralysis.
Phrenikusresektion *f*: phrenicectomy.
Phrenosin *n*: phrenosin.
Phthalsäure *f*: phthalic acid.
Phykomykose *f*: phycomycosis, phycomycetosis.
Phylogenese *f*: phylogenesis, phylogeny.
Physiatrik *f*: physiatrics.
Physik *f*: physics.
physikalisch: physical.
Physiologie *f*: physiology.
physiologisch: physiologic, physiological.
Physiotherapie *f*: physiotherapy.
physisch: physical, bodily.
Physostigmin *n*: physostigmine.
Phytagglutinin *n*: phytagglutinin, plant agglutinin.
Phytinsäure *f*: phytic acid.
Phytosterin *n*: phytosterol, plant sterol.
Phytotherapie *f*: phytotherapy.
Pick-Atrophie *f*: Pick's convolutional atrophy, Pick syndrome.
Pickel *m*: pimple, whelk.
Pickwick-Syndrom *n*: pickwickian syndrome.
Pigment *n*: pigment.
Pigmentablagerung *f*: pigment deposition.
Pigmentanomalie *f*: pigmentation disorder.
Pigmentdermatose *f*: pigmentary dermatosis; **progressive** ≈ progressive pigmented purpuric dermatosis, Schamberg's dermatosis.
Pigmentfleck *m*: pigmental spot.
Pigmentierung *f*: pigmentation.
Pigmentleber *f*: pigmented liver.
Pigmentsaum *m*: pigment border.
Pigmentzylinder *m*: pigmented cast.
Pikrinsäure *f*: picric acid.
Pikrinsäuredermatitis *f*: picric itch.
Pikrotoxin *n*: picrotoxin.
pilar: pilar, pilary.
Pille *f*: pill.
Pillendrehertremor *m*: pill-rolling tremor, lenticulostriate tremor.
Pillenmasse *f*: pill mass, pillular mass.
Piloarrektion *f*: piloerection.

Pilocarpin *n*: pilocarpine.
Pilonidalsinus *m*: pilonidal sinus.
Pilotstudie *f*: pilot study.
Pilz *m*: mushroom, fungus, mycete; **pathogener** ≈ mycopathogen.
Pilzflechte *f*: fungal eczema.
Pilzinfektion *f*: fungal infection.
Pilzstomatitis *f*: mycotic stomatitis.
Pilzvergiftung *f*: mushroom poisoning.
Pimecrolimus *n*: pimecrolimus.
Pimozid *n*: pimozide.
Pindolol *n*: pindolol.
Pinealdrüse *f*: pineal gland, pineal organ.
Pinealom *n*: pinealoma.
Pinguecula *f*: pinguecula.
Pinozytose *f*: pinocytosis.
Pinzette *f*: pincers, tweezers.
Pioglitazon *n*: pioglitazone.
Pipamazin *n*: pipamazine.
Pipamperon *n*: pipamperone.
Pipazetat *n*: pipazethate.
Pipemidsäure *f*: pipemedic acid.
Pipenzolatbromid *n*: pipenzolate bromide.
Piperacillin *n*: piperacillin.
Piperazin *n*: piperazine.
Piperazinhexahydrat *n*: piperazine hexahydrate.
Piperidin *n*: piperidine.
Piperidolat *n*: piperidolate.
Piperidyl *n*: piperidyl.
Piperocain *n*: piperocaine.
Piperonylbutoxid *n*: piperonyl butoxide.
Pipette *f*: pipette.
Pipoxolan *n*: pipoxolan.
Piracetam *n*: piracetam.
Pirbuterol *n*: pirbuterol.
Pirenzepin *n*: pirenzepine.
Piretanid *n*: piretanide.
Piribedil *n*: piribedil.
Piridoxilat *n*: piridoxilate.
Piritramid *n*: piritramide.
Piroplasmose *f*: piroplasmosis, babesiasis.
Piroxicam *n*: piroxicam.
Pirprofen *n*: pirprofen.
Pistolenschussphänomen *n*: pistol-shot sound.
Pitofenon *n*: pitofenone.
pituitär: pituitary.
Pituitarismus *m*: pituitarism, pituitary dysfunction.
Pityriasis *f*: pityriasis.
Pivampicillin *n*: pivampicillin.
Pizotifen *n*: pizotifen.
Placebo *n*: placebo.
Placeboeffekt *m*: placebo effect.
Placenta *f*: placenta.
Placenta accessoria *f*: accessory placenta.
Placenta adhaerens *f*: adherent placenta.
Placenta marginata *f*: marginal placenta, battledore placenta.
Placenta praevia *f*: placental presentation.
Plätschergeräusch *n*: succusion sound, hippocratic sound.
Plättchen *n*: platelet, thrombocyte.
Plage *f*: plague, pest.
Plagiozephalie *f*: plagiocephaly.
Plakode *f*: placode.
plantar: plantar.
Plaque *f*: plaque, patch; **atheromatöse** ≈ atheromatous plaque; **senile** ≈ senile plaque.
Plaque muqueuse *f*: mucous plaque.
Plaque opaline *f*: opaline patch.
Plasma *n*: plasma, blood plasma; **frisch eingefrorenes** ≈ fresh frozen plasma, FFP; **gepooltes** ≈ pooled plasma.
Plasmaaustausch *m*: plasma exchange.
Plasmaexpander *m*: plasma volume expander.
Plasmahalbwertszeit *f*: plasma half-life.
Plasmapherese *f*: plasmapheresis.
plasmatisch: plasmatic.
Plasmazelle *f*: plasma cell.
Plasmid *n*: plasmid.
Plasmozytom *n*: plasmocytoma.
Plasmozytose *f*: plasmocytosis.
Plastik *n*: plastic.
plastisch: plastic.
Plathelminthe *f*: platyhelminth, flatworm.
Platte *f*: plate, plaque.
Plattenatelektase *f*: platelike atelectasis, Fleischner line.

Plattenepithelkarzinom *n*: squamous cell carcinoma.
Plattenepithelmetaplasie *f*: squamous metaplasia.
Plattenepithelzelle *f*: pavement cell, prickle cell.
Plattfuß *m*: flatfoot, planovalgus.
Plattwurm *m*: flatworm, platyhelminth.
Platybasie *f*: platybasia.
Platzangst *f*: agoraphobia.
Platzbauch *m*: burst abdomen.
platzen: burst, break.
Plazenta *f*: placenta; **gelappte** ≈ lobed placenta; **kindliche** ≈ fetal placenta; **mütterliche** ≈ maternal placenta; **ringförmige** ≈ annular placenta, zonular placenta; **zweilappige** ≈ bilobate placenta.
Plazentaaustreibung *f*: expulsion of placenta.
Plazentahormon *n*: placental hormone.
Plazentainsuffizienz *f*: placental insufficiency.
Plazentalaktogen, humanes *n*: human placental lactogen, HPL.
plazentar: placental.
Plazentaretention *f*: retained placenta, trapped placenta.
Plazentaschranke *f*: placental barrier.
Plazentazeichen *n*: placental sign.
Pleomorphismus *m*: pleomorphism.
Plessimeterperkussion *f*: mediate percussion.
Plethora *f*: plethora.
Plethysmographie *f*: plethysmography.
Pleura *f*: pleura.
Pleuradrainage *f*: pleural drainage.
Pleuradruck *m*: pleural pressure.
Pleuraempyem *n*: pleural empyema.
Pleuraerguss *m*: pleural effusion, pleurorhea; **seröser** ≈ serothorax.
Pleurafibrose *f*: pleural fibrosis.
Pleurahöhle *f*: pleural space.
pleural: pleural.
Pleuramesotheliom *n*: pleural mesothelioma.
Pleurapunktion *f*: pleurocentesis, thoracocentesis.
Pleurareiben *n*: pleural friction, pleural rub.
Pleurareizung *f*: pleurisy.
Pleuraspülung *f*: pleural lavage.
Pleuritis *f*: pleurisy, pleuritis; **adhäsive** ≈ adhesive pleurisy; **basale** ≈ basal pleurisy; **chylöse** ≈ chylous pleurisy; **exsudative** ≈ exudative pleurisy, wet pleurisy; **fibrinöse** ≈ fibrinous pleurisy; **metapneumonische** ≈ metapneumonic pleurisy; **seröse** ≈ serous pleurisy; **serofibrinöse** ≈ serofibrinous pleurisy; **trockene** ≈ dry pleurisy.
Pleuritis sicca *f*: dry pleurisy.
Pleurodynie *f*: pleurodynia; **epidemische** ≈ epidemic benign dry pleurisy.
Pleuroperikardialreiben *n*: pleuropericardial rub.
Plexus *m*: plexus; **submuköser** ≈ submucous plexus, Meissner's plexus.
Plexusblockade *f*: plexus anesthesia.
Plexuslähmung *f*: plexus paralysis; **obere** ≈ upper brachial plexus paralysis, Erb paralysis; **untere** ≈ lower brachial plexus paralysis, Déjerine-Klumpke paralysis.
Plica *f*: plica, fold.
Plummer-Vinson-Syndrom *n*: Plummer-Vinson syndrome, sideropenic syndrome.
pluriglandulär: pluriglandular.
pneumatisch: pneumatic.
Pneumatozele *f*: pneumatocele.
Pneumaturie *f*: pneumaturia.
Pneumektomie *f*: pneumectomy, pulmonectomy.
Pneumocystis-jirovecii-Pneumonie *f*: pneumocystis jirovecii pneumonia.
Pneumographie *f*: pneumography.
Pneumokokkenmeningitis *f*: pneumococcal meningitis.
Pneumokokkennephritis *f*: pneumococcal nephritis.
Pneumokokkenpneumonie *f*: pneumococcal pneumonia.
Pneumokoniose *f*: pneumokoniosis, coal-worker's lung.
Pneumolipidose *f*: oil-aspiration pneumonia.
Pneumonia alba *f*: white pneumonia.

Pneumonie *f*: pneumonia; **apikale** ≈ apical pneumonia; **atypische** ≈ atypical pneumonia; **bakterielle** ≈ bacterial pneumonia; **chronisch-fibröse** ≈ chronic fibrous pneumonia; **fibrinöse** ≈ fibrous pneumonia; **gangränöse** ≈ gangrenous pneumonia; **interstitielle** ≈ interstitial pneumonia; **interstitielle plasmazelluläre** ≈ interstitial plasma cell pneumonia; **lobuläre** ≈ lobular pneumonia; **lymphoide interstitielle** ≈ lymphoid interstitial pneumonia, LIP; **persistierende** ≈ unresolved pneumonia; **rheumatische** ≈ rheumatic pneumonia; **tuberkulöse** ≈ tuberculous pneumonia; **tularämische** ≈ tularemic pneumonia; **wandernde** ≈ wandering pneumonia, migratory pneumonia.

Pneumonitis *f*: pneumonitis.

Pneumoperitonitis *f*: pneumoperitonitis.

Pneumoradiographie *f*: pneumoradiography.

Pneumothorax *m*: pneumothorax; **geschlossener** ≈ closed pneumothorax; **offener** ≈ open pneumothorax.

Pneumotomie *f*: pneumotomy, pneumonotomy.

Pneumozele *f*: pneumatocele.

Pneumozyt *m*: pneumocyte, alveolar cell.

Pocken *f*: variola, smallpox.

Pockenvakzine *f*: smallpox vaccine.

Podagra *f*: podagra.

Podophyllin *n*: podophyllin.

Podophyllotoxin *n*: podophyllotoxin.

Poikilozytose *f*: poikilocytosis.

Pol *m*: pole, polus.

polar: polar.

Poliklinik *f*: ambulant clinic, outpatient clinic.

Polioencephalopathia haemorrhagica superior *f*: Wernicke's encephalopathy.

Polioenzephalitis *f*: polioencephalitis.

Polioimpfstoff *m*: poliomyelitis vaccine.

Poliomyelitis *f*: poliomyelitis.

Poliomyelitis anterior acuta *f*: acute anterior poliomyelitis, Heine-Medin disease.

Politzer-Luftdusche *f*: Politzer's treatment, politzerization.

Pollakisurie *f*: pollakiuria, pollakisuria.

Pollenallergie *f*: pollen allergy.

Pollution *f*: pollution; **nächtliche** ≈ nocturnal emission.

Polresektion *f*: pole resection.

Polyacrylamid-Gelelektrophorese *f*: polyacrylamide gel electrophoresis.

Polyadenopathie *f*: polyadenopathy.

Polyarteriitis *f*: polyarteritis.

Polyarteriitis nodosa *f*: polyarteritis nodosa, necrotizing arteritis.

Polyarthritis *f*: polyarthritis; **juvenile** ≈ Still-Chauffard syndrome; **primär-chronische** ≈ chronic polyarthritis; **rheumatoide** ≈ rheumatoid polyarthritis.

Polychondritis *f*: polychondritis.

Polycythaemia vera *f*: polycythemia vera, Osler-Vaquez disease.

Polydaktylie *f*: polydactyly.

Polydipsie *f*: polydipsia.

Polyethylenglykol *n*: polyethylene glycol.

polyklonal: polyclonal.

Polymenorrhö *f*: polymenorrhea.

Polymerasekettenreaktion *f*: polymerase chain reaction, PCR.

Polymorphie *f*: polymorphism.

Polymorphkerniger *m*: polymorphonuclear granulocyte.

Polymyopathie *f*: polymyopathy.

Polymyositis *f*: polymyositis.

Polymyxin *n*: polymyxin.

Polyneuritis *f*: polyneuritis.

Polyneuritis cranialis *f*: cranial polyneuritis.

Polyneuropathie *f*: polyneuropathy; **alkoholische paraplegische** ≈ alcoholic paraplegia; **diabetische** ≈ diabetic polyneuropathy; **paraneoplastische** ≈ paraneoplastic polyneuropathy; **rezidivierende** ≈ recurrent polyneuropathy, relapsing polyneuropathy; **rezidivierende familiäre** ≈ familial recurrent polyneuropathy.

Polyopie *f*: polyopia, multiple vision.

Polyp *m*: polyp, polypus; **adenomatöser** ≈ adenomatous polyp; **breitbasig aufsitzender** ≈ sessile polyp; **fleischiger** ≈ fleshy polyp; **gestielter** ≈ pedunculated polyp.
Polypose *f*: polyposis; **adenomatöse** ≈ adenomatous polyposis; **familiäre** ≈ familial polyposis syndrome.
Polysaccharid *n*: polysaccharide.
Polysomatie *f*: polysomaty.
Polythiazid *n*: polythiazide.
Polytrauma *n*: polytrauma, multiple trauma.
Polyurie *f*: polyuria.
polyzystisch: polycystic.
Polyzythämie *f*: polycythemia; **familiäre** ≈ familial polycythemia; **kompensatorische** ≈ compensatory polycythemia; **relative** ≈ relative polycythemia.
Polzone *f*: polar zone.
Pompholyx *f*: pompholyx, dyshidrotic eczema.
pontin: pontine.
Pool-Schlesinger-Zeichen *n*: Pool-Schlesinger sign, leg sign.
Poplitealzyste *f*: politeal bursitis, Baker cyst.
Population *f*: population.
Pore *f*: pore.
Porenzephalie *f*: porencephaly.
Porfimer *n*: porfimer.
Porphobilinogen *n*: porphobilinogen.
Porphyria cutanea tarda *f*: porphyria cutanea tarda, cutaneous porphyria.
Porphyria variegata *f*: variegate porphyria, mixed porphyria.
Porphyrie *f*: porphyria; **akute intermittierende** ≈ acute intermittent porphyria; **hepatische** ≈ hepatic porphyria; **kongenitale erythropoetische** ≈ congenital erythropoietic porphyria; **photosensitive** ≈ photosensitive porphyria.
Porphyrin *n*: porphyrin.
Porphyrinogen *n*: porphyrinogen.
Porta *f*: portal, entrance.
Portalkreislauf *m*: portal circulation.
Portalvenendruck *m*: portal venous pressure.
Portalvenenkatheterdruck *m*: wedged hepatic pressure.
Portiokappe *f*: cervical cap.
Portographie *f*: portography.
portokaval: portacaval.
Porzellangallenblase *f*: porcelain gallbladder.
Posaconazol *n*: posaconazol.
positiv: positive.
Positronenemissionstomographie *f*: positron emission tomography, PET.
Posologie *f*: posology.
postabortiv: postabortal.
posterior-anterior: posteroanterior, P-A.
postexpositionell: postexposure.
Postgastrektomiesyndrom *n*: postgastrectomy syndrome, dumping syndrome.
postiktal: postictal.
Postkardiotomiesyndrom *n*: postcardiotomy syndrome.
Postkoitalpille *f*: morning-after pill.
post mortem: postmortal.
Postmyokardinfarktsyndrom *n*: post-myocardial infarction syndrome, Dressler syndrome.
postprandial: postprandial.
Poststreptokokkennephritis *f*: poststreptococcal nephritis.
Posttransfusionshepatitis *f*: transfusion-associated hepatitis.
potent: potent.
Potentia coeundi *f*: sexual potency.
Potentia generandi *f*: generative power.
Potential *n*: potential; **akustisch evoziertes** ≈ auditory evoked potential; **evoziertes kortikales** ≈ evoked cortical potential; **somatosensibel evoziertes** ≈ somatosensory evoked potential; **visuell evoziertes** ≈ visual evoked potential.
Potenz *f*: potency, power, ability.
Povidoniod *n*: povidone iodine solution.
Practolol *n*: practolol.
Präaurikulärfistel *f*: preauricular fistula.
Prädiktor *m*: predictor.
Präeklampsie *f*: preeclampsia.
präfrontal: prefrontal.
Präinfarktsyndrom *n*: preinfarction syndrome.

Präkanzerose *f*: precancerosis.
Präkapillare *f*: precapillary.
präkordial: precordial.
Präkordialschmerz *m*: precordial pain.
prämatur: premature.
Prämedikation *f*: premedication.
prämenopausal: premenopausal.
Prämenstruationsphase *f*: premenstrual phase.
prämenstruell: premenstrual.
Pränarkose *f*: preanesthesia.
pränatal: prenatal, antenatal.
Pränataldiagnostik *f*: prenatal diagnosis.
Pränatalzeit *f*: prenatal period.
Präparat *n*: preparation, compound.
Präparation *f*: preparation.
Präpubertät *f*: prepuberty, prepubescence.
Präputium *n*: prepuce, foreskin.
Präservativ *n*: prophylactic, condom.
Präsystolikum *n*: presystolic murmur.
Prävalenz *f*: prevalence.
Prävention *f*: prevention.
präventiv: preventive.
Präzipitation *f*: precipitation.
Präzipitationsreaktion *f*: precipitation test.
Präzipitatsalbe *f*: precipitate ointment, mercurial ointment.
Präzipitin *n*: precipitin.
Pragmatagnosie *f*: pragmatagnosia, apraxic agnosia.
Prajmaliumbitartrat *n*: prajmalium bitartrate.
Praktiker *m*: practitioner.
praktizieren: practice.
Pralidoxim *n*: pralidoxime.
Pramipexol *n*: pramipexol.
Pramiverin *n*: pramiverine.
Prasteron *n*: prasterone.
Pratzenhände: spade finger.
Pravastatin *n*: pravastatin.
Praxis *f*: surgery, practice.
Praziquantel *n*: praziquantel.
Prazosin *n*: prazosin.
Predigerhand *f*: preacher's hand, Charcot's hand.
Prednicarbat *n*: prednicarbate.
Prednimustin *n*: prednimustine.
Prednisolon *n*: prednisolone.
Prednisolonacetat *n*: prednisolone acetate.
Prednisolon-Natriumphosphat *n*: prednisolone sodium phosphate.
Prednison *n*: prednisone.
Prednyliden *n*: prednylidene.
Pregabalin *n*: pregabalin.
Pregnandiol *n*: pregnanediol.
Prellung *f*: contusion, bruise.
Prenylamin *n*: prenylamine.
Presbyakusis *f*: presbyacusis, senile deafness.
Presbyopie *f*: presbyopia.
pressen: press, squeeze, compress.
Priapismus *m*: priapism.
prickeln: tingle.
Pridinol *n*: pridinol.
primär: primary.
Primäraffekt *m*: primary lesion, initial syphilitic lesion.
Primärfollikel *m*: primary follicle.
Primärharn *m*: primary urine.
Primärheilung *f*: healing by first intention.
Primärkomplikation *f*: immediate complication.
Primärprävention *f*: primary prevention.
Primärtumor *m*: primary tumor; **unbekannter** ≈ unknown primary neoplasm.
Primärverschluss *m*: primary closure, primary suture.
Primaquin *n*: primaquine.
Primidon *n*: primidone.
Primitivknochen *m*: primitive bone.
Primordialfollikel *m*: primordial ovarian follicle.
Pringle-Bourneville-Syndrom *n*: Bourneville-Pringle syndrome, tuberous sclerosis.
Prion *n*: prion.
Prismenbrille *f*: prismatic spectacles.
Probarbital *n*: probarbital.
Probe *f*: specimen, sample, assay, test.
Probeexzision *f*: sample excision, incisional biopsy.
Probelaparotomie *f*: explorative laparotomy.
Probemahlzeit *f*: test meal.
Probenaufbewahrung *f*: sample sto-

rage.
Probenecid *n*: probenecid.
Probenentnahme *f*: sample collection.
Probucol *n*: probucol.
Procain *n*: procaine.
Procainamid *n*: procainamide.
Procainpenicillin G *n*: procaine penicillin G.
Procarbazin *n*: procarbazine.
Procaterol *n*: procaterol.
Procedere *n*: procedure.
Procyclidin *n*: procyclidine.
prodromal: prodromal.
Prodromalstadium *n*: prodromal stage.
Prodromalzeichen *n*: precursory symptom.
Proenzym *n*: proenzyme.
Progerie *f*: progeria, Hutchinson-Gilford syndrome.
Progesteron *n*: progesterone.
Progestin *n*: progestin.
Proglumetacin *n*: proglumetacin.
Proglumid *n*: proglumide.
Prognathie *f*: prognathism.
Prognose *f*: prognosis, forecast.
prognostisch: prognostic.
progredient: progressive.
Progredienz *f*: progression, progress.
Proguanil *n*: proguanil hydrochloride.
Projektionsbahn *f*: projection tract.
Proktalgie *f*: proctalgia.
Proktektomie *f*: proctectomy.
Proktitis *f*: proctitis.
Proktokolitis *f*: proctocolitis.
Proktoskopie *f*: proctoscopy, anoscopy.
Proktostomie *f*: proctostomy, rectostomy.
Proktozele *f*: proctocele.
prolabieren: prolapse.
Prolaktin *n*: prolactin, lactogenic hormone.
Prolaktinom *n*: prolactinoma.
Prolaps *m*: prolapse.
Proliferation *f*: proliferation.
Proliferationsphase *f*: proliferative phase.
Prolintan *n*: prolintane.
Promazinhydrochlorid *n*: promazine hydrochloride.
Promonozyt *m*: promonocyte.
Promyelozyt *m*: promyelocyte.
Promyelozytenleukämie *f*: promyelocytic leukemia.
Pronations-Supinations-Versuch *m*: pronation-supination test.
Propafenon *n*: propafenone.
Propamidin *n*: propamidine.
Propanidid *n*: propanidid.
Propanol *n*: propanol, propyl alcohol.
Propanthelinbromid *n*: propantheline bromide.
Properdin *n*: properdin, P.
Prophylaxe *f*: prophylaxis.
Propicillin *n*: propicillin.
β-Propiolacton *n*: beta-propiolactone.
Propionazidämie *f*: propionic acidemia.
Propionsäure *f*: propionic acid.
Propionyl *n*: propionyl.
Propionylsalicylsäure *f*: propionylsalicylic acid.
Propiverin *n*: propiverine.
Propofol *n*: propofol.
Propolis *n*: propolis.
Proportionalität *f*: proportionality.
Propoxycain *n*: propoxycaine.
Propranolol *n*: propranolol.
Propriorezeptor *m*: proprioceptor.
propriozeptiv: proprioceptive.
Propulsion *f*: propulsion.
Propylalkohol *m*: propyl alcohol, propanol.
Propylen *n*: propylene, propene.
Propylhexedrin *n*: propylhexedrine.
Proquazon *n*: proquazone.
Prostacyclin *n*: prostacyclin.
Prostaglandin *n*: prostaglandin.
Prostanoid *n*: prostanoid.
Prostata *f*: prostate.
Prostataadenom *n*: prostatic adenoma.
Prostatahypertrophie *f*: prostatic hypertrophy; **benigne** ≈ benign prostatic hypertrophy, BPH.
Prostatakarzinom *n*: carcinoma of prostate, prostatic cancer.
Prostatakonkrement *n*: prostatic concretion.
Prostataresektion *f*: prostatic resection; **transurethrale** ≈ transurethral resection of prostate, TURP.

Prostatektomie *f*: prostatectomy; **perineale** ≈ perineal prostatectomy; **retropubische** ≈ retropubic prostatectomy; **suprapubische transvesikale** ≈ suprapubic transvesical prostatectomy, Freyer's operation; **transurethrale** ≈ transurethral prostatectomy.
Prostatitis *f*: prostatitis.
Prostazyklin *n*: prostacyclin.
Prostration *f*: prostration.
Protamin *n*: protamine.
Protamin-Insulin *n*: protamine insulin.
Proteaseinhibitor *m*: protease inhibitor.
Protein *n*: protein; **C-reaktives** ≈ C-reactive protein.
Proteinbindungskapazität *f*: protein binding capacity.
Proteinurie *f*: proteinuria; **asymptomatische** ≈ asymptomatic proteinuria; **benigne** ≈ benign proteinuria; **essentielle** ≈ essential proteinuria; **glomeruläre** ≈ glomerular proteinuria; **lordotische** ≈ lordotic proteinuria, orthostatic proteinuria; **physiologische** ≈ physiologic proteinuria, functional proteinuria; **transitorische** ≈ transient proteinuria; **tubuläre** ≈ tubular proteinuria.
Proteolyse *f*: proteolysis.
Prothese *f*: prosthesis, prosthetic.
Prothipendyl *n*: prothipendyl.
Prothrombin *n*: prothrombin.
Prothrombintest *m*: prothrombin test, Quick's test.
Prothromboplastinzeit *f*: prothromboplastin time.
Protionamid *n*: protionamide.
Protirelin *n*: protirelin.
Protokatechusäure *f*: protocatechuic acid.
Protonenpumpenhemmer *m*: proton pump inhibitor.
Protoplasma *n*: protoplasm.
Protozoon *n*: protozoon.
Protrahierung *f*: protraction.
Protrusion *f*: protrusion.
Protuberanz *f*: protuberance.
proviral: proviral.
Provitamin *n*: provitamin.
Provokationstest *m*: provocation test.
proximal: proximal.
Prozess *m*: process.
prüfen: examine, assay.
Prüfung *f*: examination, test, assessment.
Prune-Belly-Syndrom *n*: prune-belly syndrome, abdominal muscle deficiency syndrome.
Prurigo Besnier *f*: Besnier's prurigo, atopic dermatitis.
Pruritus *m*: pruritus, itching.
Pseudästhesie *f*: pseudesthesia.
Pseudarthrose *f*: pseudarthrosis, false articulation.
pseudobulbär: pseudobulbar.
Pseudobulbärparalyse *f*: pseudobulbar paralysis, Henneberg's disease.
Pseudodivertikel *n*: false diverticulum.
Pseudoencephalitis haemorrhagica superior *f*: superior hemorrhagic polioencephalitis, Wernicke's encephalopathy.
Pseudoganglion *n*: pseudoganglion.
Pseudohermaphroditismus *m*: pseudohermaphroditism, spurious hermaphroditism; **hereditärer männlicher** ≈ Reifenstein syndrome.
Pseudokrise *f*: pseudocrisis, false crisis.
Pseudokrupp *m*: pseudocroup.
Pseudomonas *f*: pseudomonas.
Pseudomyxoma peritonei *n*: pseudomyxoma peritonei, Werth's tumor.
Pseudomyzel *f*: pseudomycelium.
Pseudoobstruktion *f*: pseudo-obstruction; **akute intestinale** ≈ false colonic obstruction, Ogilvie syndrome.
Pseudoparalyse *f*: pseudoparalysis.
Pseudoparasit *m*: pseudoparasite.
Pseudopelade Brocq *f*: pseudopelade of Brocq, patchy alopecia.
Pseudophakie *f*: pseudophakia; **fibröse** ≈ pseudophakia fibrosa, fibroid cataract.
Pseudoproteinurie *f*: false proteinuria.
Pseudorotz *m*: melioidosis.
Pseudoschwangerschaft *f*: pseudopregnancy, phantom pregnancy.

Pseudotabes *f*: pseudotabes.
Pseudotumor *m*: pseudotumor, tumorlike lesion.
Pseudotumor cerebri *m*: pseudotumor cerebri, benign intracranial hypertension.
Pseudozyanose *f*: false cyanosis.
Pseudozylinder *m*: pseudocast, false cast.
Pseudozyste *f*: pseudocyst, cystoid.
Psittakose *f*: psittacosis, parrot fever.
Psoaszeichen *n*: psoas sign.
Psoriasis *f*: psoriasis.
Psoriasis pustulosa *f*: pustular psoriasis.
Psychasthenie *f*: psychasthenia, Janet's disease.
Psyche *f*: psyche, soul, spirit, mind.
psychedelisch: psychedelic.
Psychiatrie *f*: psychiatry; **dynamische** ≈ dynamic psychiatry; **existentialistische** ≈ existential psychiatry; **forensische** ≈ forensic psychiatry; **interkulturelle** ≈ cross-cultural psychiatry, transcultural psychiatry; **phänomenologische** ≈ phenomenological psychiatry.
psychisch: psychic, mental.
Psychoanalyse *f*: psychoanalysis.
Psychobiologie *f*: psychobiology, biopsychology.
psychogen: psychogenic.
Psychologie *f*: psychology; **analytische** ≈ analytic psychology, jungian psychology; **angewandte** ≈ applied psychology; **humanistische** ≈ humanistic psychology; **klinische** ≈ clinical psychology; **kognitive** ≈ cognitive psychology; **medizinische** ≈ medical psychology; **pädagogische** ≈ educational psychology; **physiologische** ≈ physiologic psychology.
psychologisch: psychologic, psychological.
psychomotorisch: psychomotor.
Psychoneuroimmunologie *f*: psychoneuroimmunology.
Psychoneurose *f*: psychoneurosis, actual neurosis.
Psychoonkologie *f*: psychooncology.
Psychopathie *f*: psychopathy, sociopathy.
Psychopathologie *f*: psychopathology, pathological psychology.
Psychose *f*: psychosis, psychotic disorder; **affektive** ≈ affective psychosis; **atypische** ≈ atypical psychosis; **bipolare** ≈ bipolar disorder; **bipolare affektive** ≈ bipolar affective psychosis; **depressive** ≈ depressive psychosis, major depression; **induzierte** ≈ induced psychosis; **infantile** ≈ childhood psychosis; **juvenile** ≈ juvenile psychosis; **kurze reaktive** ≈ brief reactive psychosis; **manisch-depressive** ≈ bipolar disorder, manic-depressive psychosis; **manische** ≈ manic psychosis; **organische** ≈ organic psychosis; **paranoide** ≈ paranoid psychosis; **periodische** ≈ periodic psychosis; **präsenile** ≈ presenile psychosis; **reaktive** ≈ reactive psychosis; **schizoaffektive** ≈ schizoaffective psychosis; **schizophreniforme** ≈ schizophreniform psychosis; **substanzbedingte** ≈ substance-induced psychosis; **symbiotische** ≈ symbiotic psychosis; **unipolare** ≈ unipolar depression.
psychosexuell: psychosexual.
Psychosomatik *f*: psychosomatics, psychosomatic medicine.
Psychosyndrom *n*: psychosyndrome; **hirnorganisches** ≈ organic mental disorder, organic brain syndrome.
Psychotherapie *f*: psychotherapy; **analytische** ≈ analytic therapy; **direktive** ≈ directive psychotherapy; **gerichtete** ≈ active therapy; **psychoanalytische** ≈ psychoanalytic psychotherapy; **unterstützende** ≈ supportive psychotherapy.
psychotisch: psychotic.
Pteroinsäure *f*: pteroic acid.
Pteroylglutaminsäure *f*: pteroylglutamic acid.
Pterygium *n*: pterygium, web-eye.
Pterygium colli *n*: pterygium of the neck, congenital webbing of the neck.
Ptose *f*: ptosis.
Ptyalismus *m*: ptyalism, hypersalivation.
Pubertät *f*: puberty.

Pubertätsepilepsie *f*: pubertal epilepsy.
Pubertätsphase *f*: pubescence, puberty.
Pubertas praecox *f*: precocious puberty.
Pubertas tarda *f*: delayed puberty.
Pudendusanästhesie *f*: pudendal anesthesia.
Pudendusneuralgie *f*: pudendal neuralgia.
Puder *m*: powder.
Puerilismus *m*: childishness.
puerperal: puerperal.
Puerperalfieber *n*: puerperal fever, puerperal septicemia.
Puerperalperiode *f*: puerperal period, puerperium.
Puffer *m*: buffer.
Pulex *m*: pulex, flea.
Pulex irritans *m*: Pulex irritans, common human flea.
Pulmologie *f*: pulmonology.
pulmonal: pulmonary, pulmonic.
Pulmonalarterienstenose *f*: pulmonary artery stenosis.
Pulmonalarterienverschlussdruck *m*: pulmonary artery wedge pressure.
Pulmonalgeräusch *n*: pulmonic murmur.
Pulmonalisdruck *m*: pulmonary pressure.
Pulmonaliston *m*: pulmonic second sound.
Pulmonalklappe *f*: pulmonary valve.
Pulmonalklappeninsuffizienz *f*: pulmonary insufficiency.
Pulmonalstenose *f*: pulmonary stenosis; **infundibuläre** ≈ infundibular pulmonary stenosis.
Pulpa *f*: pulp.
Pulpitis *f*: pulpitis, endodontitis.
Puls *m*: pulse; **anadikroter** ≈ anadicrotic pulse; **atriovenöser** ≈ atrial venous pulse; **beschleunigter** ≈ frequent pulse; **fadenförmiger** ≈ filiform pulse, thready pulse; **hüpfender** ≈ jerky pulse; **kräftiger** ≈ strong pulse; **schnellender** ≈ abrupt pulse; **schneller** ≈ quick pulse; **schwacher** ≈ weak pulse; **ungleicher** ≈ unequal pulse; **unregelmäßiger** ≈ irregular pulse; **voller** ≈ full pulse; **weicher** ≈ soft pulse, low-tension pulse.
Pulsation *f*: pulsation; **epigastrische** ≈ epigastric pulse; **palpable** ≈ palpable pulsation; **sichtbare** ≈ visible pulsation.
Pulsfrequenz *f*: pulse rate.
pulsieren: pulsate.
Pulsionsdivertikel *n*: pulsion diverticulum.
pulslos: pulseless.
Pulsus *m*: pulse.
Pulsus alternans *m*: alternating pulse.
Pulsus celer et altus *m*: collapsing pulse, Corrigan's pulse.
Pulsus durus *m*: hard pulse.
Pulsus intermittens *m*: intermittent pulse.
Pulsus paradoxus *m*: paradoxical pulse.
Pulsus parvus *m*: small weak pulse.
Pulsus plenus *m*: full pulse.
Pulver *n*: powder.
Pumpe *f*: pump, aspirator.
Punctum *n*: point.
Punktat *n*: punctate.
punktförmig: punctate.
punktieren: puncture, tap.
Punktion *f*: puncture, tap.
Punktionsnadel *f*: puncture needle.
Punktmutation *f*: point mutation.
Punktprävalenz *f*: point prevalence.
Pupille *f*: pupil; **springende** ≈ bounding pupil; **starre** ≈ fixed pupil.
Pupillenerweiterung *f*: pupil dilatation, mydriasis.
Pupillenreaktion *f*: pupillary reflex, light reflex; **hemianopische** ≈ hemiopic pupillary reaction; **indirekte** ≈ indirect pupillary reaction; **konsensuelle** ≈ consensual light reflex; **myotone** ≈ myotonic pupillary reaction; **paradoxe** ≈ paradoxical pupillary reaction; **vagotone** ≈ vagal pupillary reflex.
Pupillenreflex *m*: pupillary reflex, light reflex.
Pupillenstarre *f*: fixed pupil.
Pupillotonie *f*: pupillotonia, tonic pupil.

Puppenaugenphänomen *n*: doll's head phenomenon.
Purgativum *n*: purgative.
Purin *n*: purine.
purinarm: low-purine.
Purkinje-Fasern: Purkinje's fibers, impulse-conducting fibers.
Purpura *f*: purpura; **allergische** ≈ allergic purpura; **thrombozytopenische** ≈ thrombocytopenic purpura, Werlhof's disease.
Purpura hyperglobulinaemica *f*: benign hyperglobulinemic purpura, Waldenström's macroglobulinemia.
Purpura Schoenlein-Henoch *f*: Schoenlein-Henoch purpura, allergic purpura.
Purpursäure *f*: purpuric acid.
purulent: purulent.
Pustel *f*: pustule, pimple.
Putrefaktion *f*: putrefaction.
Puusepp-Reflex *m*: Puusepp's reflex, little-toe reflex.
Pyämie *f*: pyemia.
Pyelitis *f*: pyelitis.
Pyelographie *f*: pyelography.
Pyelolithotomie *f*: pyelolithotomy.
Pyelonephritis *f*: pyelonephritis.
pyelonephritisch: nephropyelitic.
pyknisch: pyknic.
Pyknose *f*: pyknosis.
Pyknozytose *f*: pyknocytosis.
Pyle-Syndrom *n*: Pyle's disease, metaphyseal dysplasia.
pylorisch: pyloric.
Pylorogastrektomie *f*: pylorogastrectomy.
Pyloroplastik *f*: pyloroplasty.
Pylorus *m*: pylorus, pyloric stomach.
Pylorusinsuffizienz *f*: pyloric insufficiency.
Pylorusstenose *f*: pyloric stenosis.
Pyodermie *f*: pyodermia.
pyogen: pyogenic, pyogenous.
Pyometra *f*: pyometra.
Pyometritis *f*: pyometritis.
Pyonephrose *f*: pyonephrosis.
Pyopneumothorax *m*: pyopneumothorax.
Pyorrhö *f*: pyorrhea, periodontitis.
Pyosalpinx *f*: pyosalpinx.
pyramidal: pyramidal.
Pyramide *f*: pyramid.
Pyramidenbahn *f*: pyramidal tract.
Pyramidenfraktur *f*: pyramidal fracture.
Pyramidenstar *m*: pyramidal cataract.
Pyrantel *n*: pyrantel.
Pyrazinamid *n*: pyrazinamide.
pyretisch: pyretic, febrile.
Pyrexie *f*: pyrexia, fever.
Pyridin *n*: pyridine.
Pyridostigminbromid *n*: pyridostigmine bromide.
Pyridoxin *n*: pyridoxine.
Pyridoxinsäure *f*: pyridoxic acid.
Pyrimethamin *n*: pyrimethamine.
Pyrimidin *n*: pyrimidine.
Pyrithion-Zink *n*: pyrithione zinc.
Pyrogen *n*: pyrogen.
Pyroglutaminsäure *f*: pyroglutamic acid
Pyrophosphorsäure *f*: pyrophosphoric acid.
Pyrosis *f*: pyrosis, heartburn.
Pyrrol *n*: pyrrole.
Pyrrolidin *n*: pyrrolidine.
Pyruvatdehydrogenase-Komplex *m*: pyruvate dehydrogenase complex.
Pyurie *f*: pyuria.

Q

Q-Fieber *n*: Q fever, Nine Mile fever.
QRS-Komplex *m*: QRS complex.
QT-Syndrom *n*: QT syndrome; **familiäres** ≈ long QT syndrome, Romano-Ward syndrome.
Quacksalberei *f*: quackery.
Quaddel *f*: wheal, hive.
Quadrant *m*: quadrant.
Quadrantenhemianopsie *f*: quadrantic hemianopia.
Quadrantenresektion *f*: quadrantectomy.
Quadrat *n*: quadrate, square.
quadratisch: quadrate, square.
Quadrizepssehnenreflex *m*: patellar reflex, patellar tendon reflex, knee jerk.
Qual *f*: distress.
Qualität *f*: quality.
Qualitätskontrolle *f*: quality control.
Qualitätssicherung *f*: quality assurance.
qualitativ: qualitative.
Quallengift *n*: jellyfish poison.
Quantität *f*: quantity, amount.
quantitativ: quantitative.
Quantum *n*: quantum.
Quarantäne *f*: quarantine.
Quarantänezeit *f*: quarantine period.
quartär: quaternary.
Quartana *f*: quartan, quartana.
Quartilbereich *m*: quartile range.
Quarzlampe *f*: quartz lamp.
Quecksilber *n*: hydrargyrum, Hg, mercury.
Quecksilberstomatitis *f*: mercurial stomatitis.
Quelle *f*: source, well, resource, spring; **heiße** ≈ hot spring.
Quellung *f*: swelling, bulking.
Quellungskatarakt *f*: intumescent cataract.
quer: transverse, diagonal.
Querbruch *m*: oblique fracture, transverse fracture.
Querdurchmesser *m*: transverse diameter.
Querfraktur *f*: transverse fracture, oblique fracture.
Querlage *f*: transverse position, transverse presentation; **dorsoposteriore** ≈ right dorsoposterior position; **rechte hintere** ≈ right occipitotransverse position; **rechte vordere** ≈ right frontotransverse position; **tiefe** ≈ deep transverse presentation; **vordere** ≈ frontotransverse position.
Querschnitt *m*: transverse section, transsection, cross section.
Querschnittmyelitis *f*: transverse myelitis.
Querschnittuntersuchung *f*: cross-sectional study.
Querstand *m*: transverse presentation; **tiefer** ≈ deep transverse arrest.
Quervain-Thyreoiditis *f*: de Quervain's thyroiditis, subacute granulomatous thyroiditis.
Quetiapin *n*: quetiapine.
quetschen: bruise, contuse, crush, squeeze.
Quetschpräparat *n*: crush preparation.
Quetschung *f*: contusion, crush injury.
Quetschwunde *f*: contused wound, crushed wound.
Queyrat-Erythroplasie *f*: erythroplasia of Queyrat.
Quick-Test *m*: Quick's test, prothrombin-time test.
Quillaja *f*: quillaja, soapbark.
Quinagolid *n*: quinagolide.

Quinapril *n*: quinapril.
Quinaprilat *n*: quinaprilat.
Quincke-Kapillarpuls *m*: Quincke's pulse, capillary pulse.
Quincke-Ödem *n*: Quincke's disease, angioedema; **hereditäres** ≈ hereditary angioneurotic edema.
Quinethazone *n*: quinethazone.
Quintiofos *n*: quintiofos.
Quinupristin *n*: quinupristine.
Quotidiana *f*: quotidian malaria, double tertian malaria.
Quotient *m*: quotient, ratio.
Q-Zacke *f*: Q wave.

R

r Abk. **rekombinant**: recombinant, r.
R Abk. **1. Radikal** *n*; **2. Ribose** *f*; **3. Röntgen**: 1. radical; 2. ribose; 3. roentgen, R.
Rabenschnabelfortsatz *m*: coracoid process of scapula.
Rabeprazol *n*: rabeprazole.
Rabies *f*: rabies, lyssa.
Racecadotril *n*: racecadotril.
Racefemin *n*: racefemine.
Rachenabstrich *m*: throat swab.
Rachendiphtherie *f*: pharyngeal diphtheria, Brettoneau's disease.
Rachenentzündung *f*: pharyngitis.
Rachenmandel *f*: pharyngeal tonsil, adenoid.
Rachenmandelentzündung *f*: adenoiditis.
Rachenmandelhyperplasie *f*: adenoids, adenoid vegetation.
Rachenraum *m*: pharyngeal space.
Rachenreflex *m*: pharyngeal reflex, gag reflex, faucial reflex.
Rachentubus *m*: pharyngeal tube.
Rachitis *f*: rickets, rachitis; **angeborene** ≈ fetal rickets; **familiäre hypophosphatämische** ≈ familial hypophosphatemic rickets; **fetale** ≈ fetal rickets; **hämorrhagische** ≈ hemorrhagic rickets, scurvy rickets; **hepatische** ≈ hepatic rickets; **Vitamin-D-resistente** ≈ vitamin D-resistant rickets.
Rachitis renalis *f*: renal rickets, renal osteodystrophy.
radial: radial.
Radialislähmung *f*: radial nerve paralysis, radial palsy.
Radialispuls *m*: radial pulse.
Radiatio *f*: radiation, radiatio.
Radiator *m*: radiator.
radikal: radical.
Radikal *n*: radical; **freies** ≈ free radical.
Radikalentfernung *f*: radical excision.
Radikalfänger *m*: radical scavenger.
Radikaloperation *f*: radical surgery.
Radikaloperation der Mamma: radical mastectomy, Halsted's operation.
Radikaloperation des Mittelohrs: radical mastoidectomy.
Radikotomie *f*: radicotomy, rhizotomy.
radikulär: radicular.
Radikulitis *f*: radiculitis, radicular neuritis.
Radikuloneuritis *f*: radiculoneuritis, Guillain-Barré-Strohl syndrome.
Radikulotomie *f*: rhizotomy, radicotomy; **hintere** ≈ posterior rhizotomy, Dana's operation; **vordere** ≈ anterior rhizotomy.
radioaktiv: radioactive.
Radioaktivität *f*: radioactivity.
Radioallergosorbenttest *m*: radioallergosorbent test, RAST.
Radiobiologie *f*: radiobiology.
Radiogold *n*: radiogold.
Radioimmunoassay *m*: radioimmunoassay, RIA.
Radioimmunpräzipitationstest *m*: radioimmunoprecipitation assay, RIPA.
Radioindikator *m*: radioindicator, radiotracer, radioactive tracer.
Radioisotop *n*: radioisotope, radioactive isotope.
Radiokarpalgelenk *n*: radiocarpal joint.
Radiologie *f*: radiology, roentgenology; **diagnostische** ≈ diagnostic radiology; **interventionelle** ≈ interventional radiology.

radiologisch: radiologic.
Radionuklid *n*: radionuclide, radioactive nuclide.
Radius *m*: radius.
Radiusaplasie *f*: radial aplasia.
Radiusfraktur *f*: fracture of the radius.
Radiusköpfchen *n*: head of radius.
Radiusperiostreflex *m*: radioperiosteal reflex.
Radix *f*: radix, root.
Räudemilbe *f*: mange mite.
Raloxifen *n*: raloxifene.
Ramipril *n*: ramipril.
Ramstedt-Weber-Operation *f*: Ramstedt's operation, pyloromyotomy.
Rand *m*: border, boundary, margin, edge.
Randatelektase *f*: marginal atelectasis.
Randkeratitis *f*: marginal keratitis.
Randomisierung *f*: randomization.
Randpsychose *f*: marginal psychosis; **zykloide** ≈ cycloid psychosis, atypical psychosis.
Randsaumzelle *f*: lining cell.
Randsinus *m*: marginal sinus.
Randulkus *n*: marginal ulcer.
Randzone *f*: marginal zone, Lissauer's marginal zone.
Ranibizumab *n*: ranibizumab.
Ranitidin *n*: ranitidine.
Rankenhämangiom *n*: racemose hemangioma, cirsoid hemangioma.
Ranula *f*: ranula, sublingual cyst.
Rarefizierung *f*: rarefaction.
Rasagilin *n*: rasagiline.
Rasburicase *f*: rasburicase.
Raspatorium *n*: raspatory, rugine.
Rasselgeräusch *n*: rale, rhonchus; **feuchtes** ≈ moist rale; **giemendes** ≈ whistling rale, sibilant rale; **klingendes** ≈ consonating rale, consonation; **knisterndes** ≈ vesicular rale; **metallisches** ≈ metallic rale; **pfeifendes** ≈ whistling rale, sibilant rhonchus; **trockenes** ≈ dry rale.
Rastelli-Operation *f*: Rastelli's operation.
Rasterverschiebungsmutation *f*: frame-shift mutation.
Rathbun-Syndrom *n*: hypophosphatasia.
Rathke-Tasche *f*: Rathke's pouch, craniobuccal cyst.
Ratschow-Lagerungsprobe *f*: Ratschow's test.
Rattenbissfieber *n*: rat-bite fever.
Rattenfloh *m*: rat flea.
Rattenpest *f*: urban plague, domestic plague.
Raubwanze *f*: cone-nose bug, kissing bug, reduviid.
rau: hoarse, raucous, rough.
Rauchen *n*: smoking; **passives** ≈ passive smoking.
Rauchvergiftung *f*: smoke poisoning.
R-auf-T-Phänomen *n*: R-on-T phenomenon.
Rauheit *f*: roughness, hoarseness.
Raum *m*: room, space, spatium.
Raumdesinfektion *f*: room disinfection.
Raumforderung *f*: mass lesion, space-occupying lesion; **intrakranielle** ≈ intracerebral mass.
Raumorientierung *f*: space orientation.
Raupenhaarkonjunktivitis *f*: caterpillar conjunctivitis.
Rausch *m*: intoxication, inebriation, drunken fit; **pathologischer** ≈ pathologic intoxication.
Rauschgift *n*: drug, narcotic.
Rauschmittel *n*: inebriant, intoxicant.
Rautenhirn *n*: rhombencephalon, hindbrain.
Rauwolfia-Alkaloid *n*: rauwolfia alkaloid.
Raymond-Syndrom *n*: Raymond syndrome, inferior pontine syndrome.
Reagenz *n*: reagent, reactant.
Reagenzglas *n*: test tube.
Reaktion *f*: reaction, response; **allergische** ≈ allergic reaction; **anamnestische** ≈ anamnestic response, booster response; **anaphylaktische** ≈ anaphylactic reaction, anaphylaxis; **antizipatorische** ≈ anticipatory reaction; **argentaffine** ≈ argentaffin reaction; **biphasische** ≈ biphasic reaction; **disjunktive** ≈ disjunctive reaction; **generalisierte anaphylaktische** ≈ systemic anaphylaxis, generalized anaphylaxis;

heterologe anaphylaktische ≈ heterocytologic anaphylaxis; **konditionierte** ≈ conditioned response; **lokale anaphylaktische** ≈ local anaphylaxis; **myasthenische** ≈ myasthenic reaction; **myotonische** ≈ myotonic reaction; **neurotonische** ≈ neurotonic reaction; **orthostatische** ≈ orthostatic reaction; **pseudomyotonische** ≈ pseudomyotonic reaction; **tuberkulinartige** ≈ tuberculin-like reaction; **verzögerte allergische** ≈ delayed allergy; **zytotoxische** ≈ cytotoxic reaction.

Reaktionsfähigkeit *f*: reactivity, responsiveness.

Reaktionspartner *m*: reactant.

Reaktion vom Soforttyp, allergische *f*: immediate allergy.

Reaktion vom verzögerten Typ *f*: delayed reaction, late reaction.

reaktiv: reactive.

Reaktivität *f*: reactivity.

Realangst *f*: real anxiety.

Realitätsbezug *m*: reality orientation.

Reanastomisierung *f*: reanastomosis.

Reanimation *f*: reanimation, resuscitation; **kardiale** ≈ cardiac resuscitation; **kardiopulmonale** ≈ cardiopulmonary resuscitation.

Reboxetin *n*: reboxetine.

Recht auf Behandlung *n*: right to treatment.

rechtshändig: right-handed.

Rechtsherzhypertrophie *f*: right ventricular hypertrophy.

Rechtsherzinsuffizienz *f*: right heart failure.

Rechtsherzversagen *n*: right heart failure.

Rechts-links-Shunt *m*: right-to-left shunt.

Rechts-links-Störung *f*: right-left disorientation.

Rechtsmedizin *f*: forensic medicine, legal medicine.

Rechtsschenkelblock *m*: right bundle branch block.

Recklinghausen-Krankheit *f*: von Recklinghausen's disease, neurofibromatosis.

Redoxreaktion *f*: redox reaction, oxidation-reduction reaction.

Redressement *n*: surgical correction.

Reduktion *f*: reduction.

Reduktionsdiät *f*: reducing diet.

Reduktionskost *f*: weight reduction diet.

Reduktionsteilung *f*: reduction division.

Reentryleitungsweg *m*: reentrant pathway.

Reentrymechanismus *m*: reentry mechanism.

Reentrytachykardie *f*: reentry tachycardia.

Reese-Syndrom *n*: encephalo-ophthalmic dysplasia, Krause syndrome.

Referenzbereich *m*: reference range, normal range.

Reflex *m*: reflex; **alternierender** ≈ antagonistic reflex; **angeborener** ≈ inborn reflex; **bedingter** ≈ conditioned reflex, Pavlov's reflex; **enterozeptiver** ≈ enteroceptive reflex; **exterozeptiver** ≈ exteroceptive reflex; **frühkindlicher** ≈ primitive reflex; **gekreuzter** ≈ crossed reflex; **homolateraler** ≈ direct reflex; **okulokardialer** ≈ oculocardiac reflex, Aschner's phenomenon; **okulozephaler** ≈ oculocephalic reflex, doll's head phenomenon; **pathologischer** ≈ pathologic reflex; **primitiver** ≈ primitive reflex; **propriozeptiver** ≈ proprioceptive reflex; **spinaler** ≈ spinal reflex; **statokinetischer** ≈ statokinetic reaction; **tonischer** ≈ tonic reflex; **unkonditionierter** ≈ unconditioned reflex, unconditioned response; **vasovagaler** ≈ vasovagal reflex; **vestibulospinaler** ≈ vestibulospinal reflex.

Reflexautomatie *f*: reflex automatism.

Reflexbahnung *f*: facilitation of reflexes.

Reflexhammer *m*: reflex hammer.

Reflexion *f*: reflexion, reflection.

Reflextherapie *f*: reflex therapy.

Reflexzonentherapie *f*: zone therapy.

Reflux *m*: reflux, backflow; **duodenogastrischer** ≈ duodenogastric reflux; **gastroösophagealer** ≈ gastroesophageal reflux; **hepatojugulärer** ≈ hepatojugular reflux; **ösophagealer** ≈ esophageal reflux; **pyelorenaler** ≈ pyelorenal reflux; **pyelotubulärer** ≈ pyelotubular reflux; **vesikoureteraler** ≈ vesicoureteral reflux.

Refluxösophagitis *f*: reflux esophagitis.

refraktär: refractory, refractive.

Refraktärperiode *f*: refractory period.

Refraktion *f*: refraction.

Refraktionsanomalie *f*: refractive ametropia, refractive error.

Regelblutung *f*: menstruation, monthly period.

Regenbogenhaut *f*: iris.

Regeneration *f*: regeneration.

Regenerationsvorgang *m*: regenerative process.

Regime *n*: regimen.

Regimen sanitatis *n*: sanitary regimen.

Region *f*: region, area, site; **aktive** ≈ active site; **flexible** ≈ hinge region; **hypervariable** ≈ hypervariable region; **motorische** ≈ motor region.

Regionalanästhesie *f*: regional anesthesia.

Regionalperfusion *f*: regional perfusion, selective perfusion.

Register *n*: registry, register.

registrieren: register, record.

Regression *f*: regression.

Regressionsanalyse *f*: regression analysis.

Regressionskoeffizient *m*: regression coefficient.

Regurgitation *f*: regurgitation.

Regurgitationsgeräusch *n*: regurgitant murmur.

Rehabilitation *f*: rehabilitation; **berufliche** ≈ vocational rehabilitation; **funktionelle** ≈ functional rehabilitation.

Reibegeräusch *n*: friction sound, friction rub.

Reiben *n*: rub, friction; **extraperikardiales** ≈ pleuropericardial rub.

Reibung *f*: friction, rubbing.

reif: ripe, mature, adult.

Reife *f*: maturity, adulthood.

Reifebestimmung, intrauterine *f*: intrauterine maturity test.

Reifezeichen: maturity signs.

Reifung *f*: maturation, postnatal development, ripening.

Reifungsteilung *f*: maturation division.

Reihenimpfung *f*: mass immunization.

Reihentest *m*: screening test.

Reihenuntersuchung *f*: screening, mass examination.

Reil-Finger *m*: dead finger, white finger.

Reil-Insel *f*: island of Reil.

Reinfarkt *m*: reinfarction.

Reinfektion *f*: reinfection.

Reinigungseinlauf *m*: intestinal lavage.

Reisediarrhö *f*: traveller's diarrhea.

Reisekrankheit *f*: travel sickness.

Reisemedizin *f*: travel medicine.

reissen: rupture, tear.

Reiter-Arthritis *f*: Reiter's syndrome, venereal arthritis.

Reiterknochen *m*: rider's bone, cavalry bone.

Reithosenanästhesie *f*: saddle block anesthesia.

Reittherapie *f*: hippotherapy.

Reiz *m*: stimulus, stimulation, impulse; **adäquater** ≈ adequate stimulus; **akustischer** ≈ auditory stimulus; **ektoper** ≈ ectopic impulse; **elektrischer** ≈ electric stimulation, electric excitation; **inadäquater** ≈ inadequate stimulus; **mechanischer** ≈ mechanical stimulus; **überschwelliger** ≈ supraliminal stimulus; **unterschwelliger** ≈ subthreshold stimulus.

reizbar: irritable.

Reizbarkeit *f*: irritability, excitability.

Reizblase *f*: irritable bladder, nervous bladder.

Reizeffekt, isomorpher *m*: isomorphic effect, Köbner's phenomenon.

Reizgelenk *n*: irritable joint.

Reizgeneralisierung *f*: stimulus generalization.

Reizgift *n*: irritant poison.
Reizhusten *m*: tickling cough.
Reizkolon *n*: irritable colon, irritable bowel syndrome.
Reizleitung *f*: stimulus conduction; **intraatriale** ≈ intra-atrial conduction.
Reizperitonitis *f*: chemical peritonitis.
Reizpunkt *m*: trigger point.
Reizschwelle *f*: stimulus threshold.
Reizstoff *m*: irritating substance, irritant.
Reiztherapie *f*: irritation therapy, stimulation therapy.
Reizüberflutung *f*: overstimulation, flooding.
Reizüberleitung *f*: conduction; **abnorme** ≈ aberrant conduction; **beschleunigte** ≈ accelerated conduction.
Reizung *f*: irritation.
Reklination *f*: reclination.
rekliniert: recumbent.
rekombinant: recombinant.
Rekombinante *f*: recombinant.
Rekombination *f*: recombination; **genetische** ≈ genetic recombination; **intrachromosomale** ≈ intrachromosomal recombination.
rekonstruktiv: reconstructive.
Rekonvaleszenz *f*: convalescence, recuperation, recovery.
Rekrudeszenz *f*: recrudescence.
Rekrutierung *f*: recruitment.
rektal: rectal.
Rektalfistel *f*: rectal fistula.
Rektalspekulum *n*: rectal speculum.
Rektaltemperatur *f*: rectal temperature.
Rektosigmoideoskopie *f*: rectosigmoidoscopy.
Rektoskopie *f*: rectoscopy.
Rektovaginalfistel *f*: rectovaginal fistula.
Rektovesikalfistel *f*: rectovesical fistula.
Rektozele *f*: rectocele.
Rektum *n*: rectum.
Rektumabstrich *m*: rectal swab.
Rektumexstirpation *f*: resection of rectum.
Rektumkarzinom *n*: rectal carcinoma.
Rektumprolaps *m*: rectal prolapse, prolapse of rectum.
Rektum-Sigmoid-Anastomose *f*: rectosigmoid anastomosis.
Rektumspreizer *m*: rectal retractor.
Rektumstriktur *f*: rectal stricture.
Rektusscheide *f*: rectus sheath.
Relaiszelle *f*: relay cell.
relativ: relative.
Relaxans *n*: relaxant.
Relaxation *f*: relaxation.
relaxierend: relaxant.
Relaxin *n*: relaxin.
Releasingfaktor *m*: releasing factor.
Releasinghormon *n*: releasing hormone, RH; **hypothalamisches** ≈ hypothalamic releasing hormone.
Reliabilität *f*: reliability.
Remedium *n*: remedy.
Remission *f*: remission, remittence.
remittierend: remittent.
REM-Schlaf *m*: REM sleep, desynchronized sleep, paradoxical sleep.
renal: renal, nephric.
Rendu-Fiessinger-Syndrom *n*: Rendu-Fiessinger syndrome, Stevens-Johnson syndrome.
Rendu-Osler-Weber-Syndrom *n*: Rendu-Osler-Weber syndrome, hereditary hemorrhagic teleangiectasia.
Renin *n*: renin.
Renovasographie *f*: intravenous renal angiography.
Renshaw-Hemmung *f*: Renshaw inhibition, recurrent inhibition.
Rentenneurose *f*: pension neurosis.
Repaglinid *n*: repaglinide.
Reparaturmechanismus *m*: repair mechanism.
Repellent *n*: repellent.
Replikation *f*: replication.
reponieren: reduce, reset.
Reposition *f*: reposition, reduction.
Repressorgen *n*: repressor gene.
Reproduktion *f*: reproduction.
Reproduktionsbiologie *f*: reproductive biology.
Reproterol *n*: reproterol.
Reptilase *f*: reptilase.

Resektion *f*: resection; **submuköse** ≈ submucous resection; **transurethrale** ≈ transurethral resection.
Resektoskop *n*: resectoscope.
Reserpin *n*: reserpine.
Reservekapazität, funktionelle *f*: functional residual capacity.
Reservekraft des Herzens *f*: cardiac reserve.
Reservevolumen *n*: reserve volume, respiratory reserve; **exspiratorisches** ≈ expiratory reserve volume; **inspiratorisches** ≈ inspiratory reserve capacity.
Reservoir *n*: reservoir.
resezieren: resect.
residual: residual.
Residualkapazität *f*: residual capacity; **funktionelle** ≈ functional residual capacity.
Residualkörperchen *n*: residual body.
Residualschizophrenie *f*: residual schizophrenia.
Residualvolumen *n*: residual volume.
Residuum *n*: residue, residuum.
resistent: resistant.
Resistenz *f*: resistance, fastness; **genotypische** ≈ genotypic resistance; **phänotypische** ≈ phenotypic resistance.
Resistenzbestimmung *f*: resistance screening.
Resorcortol *n*: resocortol.
Resolvens *n*: resolvent.
Resonanz *f*: resonance; **nuklearmagnetische** ≈ nuclear magnetic resonance.
Resorption *f*: resorption, absorption.
Resorptionsatelektase *f*: resorption atelectasis.
Respiration *f*: respiration, breathing.
Respirationstrakt *m*: respiratory tract.
Respirator *m*: respirator, ventilator.
respiratorisch: respiratory.
Rest *m*: rest, residue.
Restharn *m*: residual urine.
Restriktion *f*: restriction.
Restriktionsallel *n*: restriction allele.
Restvolumen *n*: end-systolic volume.
Retardierung *f*: retardation; **geistige** ≈ mental retardation.
Retardpräparat *n*: delayed-action preparation, time-release preparation.
Retention *f*: retention.
Retentionszyste *f*: retention cyst.
Reteplase *f*: reteplase.
retikulär: reticular.
Retikulärzelle *f*: reticular cell.
Retikulin *n*: reticulin.
Retikulinfaser *f*: reticular fiber.
Retikuloendothel *n*: reticuloendothelium, reticuloendothelial tissue.
Retikulose *f*: reticulosis; **familiäre histiozytäre** ≈ familial histiocytic reticulosis; **histiozytäre medulläre** ≈ histiocytic medullary reticulosis; **lipomelanotische** ≈ lipomelanotic reticulosis; **maligne** ≈ malignant histiocytosis; **mastozytäre** ≈ malignant mast cell reticulosis; **pagetoide** ≈ pagetoid reticulosis.
Retikulozyt *m*: reticulocyte.
Retikulozytose *f*: reticulocytosis.
Retikulum *n*: reticulum.
Retikulumzelle *f*: reticulum cell; **aktivierte** ≈ activated reticular cell; **primitive** ≈ primitive reticular cell.
Retikulumzellsarkom *n*: reticulum cell sarcoma, malignant histiocytic lymphoma.
Retina *f*: retina.
retinal: retinal.
Retinal *n*: retinal.
Retinaödem *n*: macular edema, Berlin's disease.
Retinitis *f*: retinitis.
Retinitis exsudativa *f*: exudative retinitis, Coats disease.
Retinitis pigmentosa *f*: retinitis pigmentosa, pigmentary retinopathy.
Retinitis punctata *f*: punctate retinitis.
Retinoblastom *n*: retinoblastoma.
Retinol *n*: retinol.
Retinopathia diabetica *f*: diabetic retinopathy.
Retinopathia hypertonica *f*: hypertensive retinopathy.
Retinopathie *f*: retinopathy, retinal disease; **aktinische** ≈ actinic retinopathy; **diabetische** ≈ diabetic retino-

pathy; **eklamptische** ≈ eclamptic retinopathy; **leukämische** ≈ leukemic retinopathy; **präproliferative** ≈ preproliferative retinopathy; **proliferative** ≈ proliferative retinopathy; **septische** ≈ septic retinopathy.
Retinsäure *f*: retinoic acid, vitamin A acid.
Retorte *f*: retort.
retrahieren: retract.
Retraktion *f*: retraction.
Retraktionssyndrom *n*: retraction syndrome.
retroaktiv: retroactive.
retroaurikulär: retroauricular.
retrobulbär: retrobulbar.
Retrobulbärneuritis *f*: retrobulbar neuritis, optic neuritis.
Retrobulbärraum *m*: retrobulbar space.
Retroflexion *f*: retroflexion.
Retroflexio uteri *f*: retroflexion of uterus.
retrograd: retrograde.
Retrokardialraum *m*: retrocardiac space, Holzknecht space.
retrokochlear: retrocochlear.
retroperitoneal: retroperitoneal.
Retroperitonealhämatom *n*: retroperitoneal hematoma.
Retroperitonealraum *m*: retroperitoneal space.
retropharyngeal: retropharyngeal.
Retropharyngealabszess *m*: retropharyngeal abscess.
retrospektiv: retrospective.
retrosternal: retrosternal.
Retrosternalschmerz *m*: retrosternal pain.
Retrosternalstruma *f*: substernal goiter.
Retrotonsillarabszess *m*: retrotonsillar abscess, peritonsillar abscess.
retten: rescue, salvage.
Rettung *f*: rescue, salvage.
Rettungssanitäter *m*: ambulanceman.
Reverse-Transkriptase-Inhibitor *m*: reverse transcriptase inhibitor.
reversibel: reversible.
Revitalisierung *f*: revitalization.
Reye-Syndrom *n*: Reye syndrome, encephalopathy and fatty degeneration of viscera.
rezent: recent.
Rezept *n*: prescription, recipe.
Rezeptgebühr *f*: prescription fee.
rezeptiv: receptive.
Rezeptor *m*: receptor; **adrenerger** ≈ adrenergic receptor; **cholinerger** ≈ cholinergic receptor; **dopaminerger** ≈ dopaminergic receptor; **muskarinartiger** ≈ muscarinic receptor; **nikotinartiger** ≈ nicotinic receptor.
Rezeptorenblocker *m*: blocker, alpha blocker, beta blocker.
rezessiv: recessive.
Rezidiv *n*: relapse, recurrence.
rezidivieren: relapse, recur.
Reziprozität *f*: reciprocation.
Rezirkularisation *f*: recircularization.
Rhabdomyolyse *f*: rhabdomyolysis.
Rhabdomyosarkom *n*: rhabdomyosarcoma.
Rhagade *f*: crack, fissure.
Rh-Blutgruppe *f*: Rh blood groop.
Rhesusinkompatibilität *f*: rhesus incompatibility, Rh incompatibility.
Rheuma *n*: rheumatism.
Rheumafaktor *m*: rheumatoid factor.
Rheumaknötchen *n*: rheumatic nodule, rheumatoid nodule.
rheumatisch: rheumatic.
Rheumatismus *m*: rheumatism; **extraartikulärer** ≈ nonarticular rheumatism; **palindromischer** ≈ palindromic rheumatism.
Rheumatismus nodosus *m*: nodose rheumatism.
rheumatoid: rheumatoid.
Rheumatologie *f*: rheumatology.
Rhinitis *f*: rhinitis, nasitis; **akute** ≈ acute rhinitis, coryza; **allergische** ≈ allergic rhinitis, atopic rhinitis; **atrophische** ≈ atrophic rhinitis; **infektiöse** ≈ infective rhinitis.
Rhinitis acuta *f*: acute rhinitis, coryza.
Rhinitis atrophicans *f*: atrophic rhinitis, ozena.
Rhinitis vasomotorica *f*: vasomotor rhinitis.
Rhinolith *m*: rhinolith, nasal calculus.

Rhinopathie *f*: rhinopathy; **allergische** ≈ allergic rhinitis, atopic rhinitis.
Rhinopharyngitis *f*: rhinopharyngitis.
Rhinopharyngoskopie *f*: nasopharyngoscopy, posterior rhinoscopy.
Rhinophym *n*: rhinophyma.
Rhinoplastik *f*: rhinoplasty; **indische** ≈ Indian rhinoplasty, Carpue's rhinoplasty; **italienische** ≈ Italian rhinoplasty, Tagliacozzi rhinoplasty.
Rhinorrhö *f*: rhinorrhea.
Rhinosklerom *n*: rhinoscleroma.
Rhinoskopie *f*: rhinoscopy, nasoscopy.
Rhizotomie *f*: rhizotomy, radicotomy; **hintere** ≈ posterior rhizotomy, Dana's operation; **vordere** ≈ anterior rhizotomy.
Rhodanin *n*: rhodanic acid.
Rhonchus *m*: rhonchus.
Rhythmus *m*: rhythm; **ektoper** ≈ ectopic rhythm; **gekoppelter** ≈ coupled rhythm; **regelmäßiger** ≈ regular rhythm; **reziproker** ≈ reciprocal rhythm; **sinusartiger** ≈ sinusoidal rhythm; **zirkadianer** ≈ circadian rhythm.
Rhythmusmethode *f*: rhythm contraception, periodic abstinence.
Rhythmusstörung *f*: rhythm disturbance, dysrhythmia.
Ribavirin *n*: ribavirin.
Riboflavin *n*: riboflavin.
Ribonukleinsäure *f*: ribonucleic acid, RNA; **ribosomale** ≈ ribosomal ribonucleic acid, rRNA.
Ribosom *n*: ribosome.
Ribostamycin *n*: ribostamycin.
Ribothymidin *n*: ribothymidine.
Ribozym *n*: ribozyme.
Richtlinie *f*: guideline.
Rickettsie *f*: rickettsia.
Riechbahn *f*: olfactory bundle, olfactory pathway.
riechen: smell.
Riechepithel *n*: olfactory epithelium.
Riechnerv *m*: olfactory nerve.
Riechvermögen *n*: olfactory perception, olfaction.
Riechzentrum *n*: olfactory center, olfactory area.
Riedel-Lappen *m*: Riedel's lobe, appendicular lobe.
Riedel-Struma *f*: Riedel's thyroiditis, ligneous thyroiditis, chronic fibrous thyroiditis.
Riesenbaby *n*: large-for-date baby.
Riesenfaltengastritis *f*: giant hypertrophic gastritis, Ménétrier's disease.
Riesenkondylom *n*: giant condyloma, Buschke-Loewenstein tumor.
Riesenwuchs *m*: gigantism; **akromegaler** ≈ acromegalic gigantism; **angiektatischer** ≈ hemangiectatic hypertrophy; **halbseitiger** ≈ hemigigantism; **hypophysärer** ≈ hypopituitary gigantism; **hypothalamischer** ≈ hypothalamic gigantism; **konstitutioneller** ≈ constitutional gigantism.
Riesenzellarteriitis *f*: giant-cell arteritis, temporal arteritis, Horton's arteritis.
Riesenzelle *f*: giant cell.
Riesenzellgeschwulst *f*: giant-cell tumor; **kalzifizierende** ≈ calcifying giant-cell tumor, Codman's tumor.
Riesenzellgranulom *n*: central giant-cell reparative granuloma.
Riesenzellhepatitis *f*: giant cell hepatitis.
Riesenzellkarzinom *n*: giant-cell carcinoma.
Riesenzellpneumonie *f*: giant-cell pneumonia, Hecht's pneumonia.
Riesenzellthyreoiditis *f*: giant-cell thyroiditis.
Rifabutin *n*: rifabutin.
Rifampicin *n*: rifampicin, rifampin.
Rifamycin *n*: rifamycin.
Riga-Fede-Geschwür *n*: Riga-Fede disease, frenal ulcer.
Rigidität *f*: rigidity, rigor.
Rigor *m*: rigor, rigidity; **extrapyramidaler** ≈ extrapyramidal rigidity; **psychogener** ≈ hysterical rigidity.
Rigor mortis *m*: rigor mortis, cadaveric rigidity.
Riluzol *n*: riluzole.
Rimantadin *n*: rimantadine.
Rimexolon *n*: rimexolone.

Rimonabant *n*: rimonabant.
Rinde *f*: cortex, cortical layer.
Rindenatrophie *f*: cortical atrophy.
Rindenblindheit *f*: cortical blindness.
Rindenepilepsie *f*: cortical epilepsy.
Rindenfeld *n*: cortical area.
Rindenstar *m*: cortical cataract.
Rindentaubheit *f*: cortical deafness, central deafness.
Rinderalbumin *n*: bovine albumin.
Rinderinsulin *n*: bovine insulin.
Rindertuberkulose *f*: bovine tuberculosis.
Rinderwahnsinn *m*: mad cow disease, bovine spongioform encephalopathy, BSE.
Ring *m*: ring, annulus.
Ringelröteln *f*: erythema infectiosum, fifth disease.
ringen nach Luft: gasp.
ringförmig: ring-shaped, annular, cricoid.
Ringknorpel *m*: cricoid cartilage.
Ringskotom *n*: ring scotoma, annular scotoma.
Ringstriktur *f*: annular stricture.
Ringthrombus *m*: annular thrombus.
Rinne *f*: groove, furrow, sulcus.
Riolan-Anastomose *f*: Riolan's arc, intermesenteric arterial anastomosis.
Rippe *f*: rib, cost.
Rippenbogen *m*: costal arch.
Rippenbogenrandschnitt *m*: subcostal incision.
Rippenfell *n*: pleura.
Rippenfellentzündung *f*: pleurisy.
Rippenfortsatz *m*: costal process.
Rippenfraktur *f*: rib fracture.
Rippenknorpel *m*: costal cartilage.
Rippenknorpelentzündung *f*: costochondritis.
Rippenwinkel *m*: costal angle.
Rippenzange *f*: rib-cutting forceps.
Risedronsäure *n*: risedronate.
Risiko *n*: risk; **kumulatives** ≈ cumulative risk; **relatives** ≈ relative risk, risk ratio.
Risikoabschätzung *f*: risk assessment.
Risikofaktor *m*: risk factor.
Risikogeburt *f*: high-risk delivery.
Risikogruppe *f*: risk group.
risikoreich: high-risk.
Risikoverhalten *n*: risk behavior, risk-taking behavior.
riskieren: risk.
Risperidon *n*: risperidone.
Riss *m*: tear, laceration, rupture.
Risswunde *f*: lacerated wound, laceration.
Risus sardonicus: risus sardonicus, sardonic laugh.
Ritodrin *n*: ritodrine.
Ritonavir *n*: ritonavir.
Rituximab *n*: rituximab.
ritzen: scratch, lance.
Ritztest *m*: scratch test.
Rivastigmin *n*: rivastigmine.
Rizatriptan *n*: rizatriptan.
Rizin *n*: ricin.
Rizinolsäure *f*: ricinoleic acid.
Rizinusöl *n*: castor oil, ricinus oil.
Robbengliedrigkeit *f*: phocomelia.
Robb-Smith-Krankheit *f*: histiocytic medullary reticulosis.
Roborans *n*: roborant, strengthening agent.
Rocky-Mountain-Fieber *n*: Rocky Mountain spotted fever.
Rocuroniumbromid *n*: rocuronium bromide.
Röhrchen *n*: tubule, tubulus.
Röhre *f*: tuba, tube, tubus.
Röhrenknochen *m*: long bone, tubular bone.
röntgen: x-ray.
Röntgen *n*: roentgen.
Röntgenaufnahme *f*: radiography, x-ray, radiograph.
Röntgenbefund *m*: roentgenographic finding.
Röntgenbild *n*: x-ray image, radiographic picture.
Röntgendiagnostik *f*: radiodiagnostics, diagnostic radiology.
röntgendicht: roentgenopaque.
Röntgengerät *n*: x-ray equipment, x-ray apparatus.
Röntgenkastration *f*: x-ray castration.
Röntgenstrahlen: x-rays, roentgen rays; **charakteristische** ≈ characteristic x-rays; **harte** ≈ hard x-rays; **sehr weiche** ≈ supersoft x-rays; **ultraharte** ≈ ultrahard x-rays; **weiche** ≈ soft x-rays.

Röntgenstrahlenschutz *m*: x-ray protection.
Röntgenstrahlung *f*: x-radiation, x-ray scattering.
Röntgentherapie *f*: x-ray therapy, radiotherapy.
Röntgenthoraxaufnahme *f*: chest radiograph, chest film.
Röntgenuntersuchung *f*: radiographic examination.
Röteln *f*: rubella, German measles.
Rötelnembryopathie *f*: rubella embryopathy.
Rötung *f*: redness, rubor.
Roger-Syndrom *n*: Roger's disease, ventricular septal defect.
Rohdroge *f*: crude drug.
Rokitansky-Becken *n*: Rokitansky's pelvis, spondylolisthetic pelvis.
Rolitetracyclin *n*: rolitetracycline.
Rollstuhl *m*: wheelchair.
Romano-Ward-Syndrom *n*: Romano-Ward syndrome.
Romberg-Syndrom *n*: Romberg's disease, facial hemiatrophy.
Romberg-Versuch *m*: Romberg's test, station test.
Ropinirol *n*: ropinirole.
Ropivacain *n*: ropivacaine.
Rosakrankheit *f*: pink disease, Feer's disease, acrodynic erythema.
Rosazea *f*: rosacea, acne rosacea.
Rosenholzöl *n*: rosewood oil.
Rosenkranz, rachitischer *m*: rachitic bead.
Rosiglitazon *n*: rosiglitazone.
Rosoxacin *n*: rosoxacin.
rostral: rostral.
Rotation *f*: rotation; **manuelle** ≈ manual rotation.
Rotationsbestrahlung *f*: rotating irradiation.
Rotationslappen *m*: rotation flap.
Rotationsnystagmus *m*: rotation nystagmus, rotatory nystagmus.
Rotatorenmanschette *f*: rotator cuff.
Rotatorenzerrung *f*: high-jumpers' strain.
Rotblindheit *f*: red blindness.
Rotes Kreuz *n*: Red cross.
Rotgrünblindheit *f*: red-green blindness.
Rotlauf *m*: erysipeloid.
Rouleaubildung *f*: rouleaux formation, nummulation.
Routinediagnostik *f*: routine diagnosis.
Routineuntersuchung *f*: routine diagnostic test, routine examination.
Roxithromycin *n*: roxithromycin.
Rubefaziens *n*: rubefacient.
Rubella *f*: rubella, rubeola, German measles.
Rubeola *f*: rubeola, rubella, German measles.
Rubor *m*: rubor, redness.
Rucknystagmus *m*: jerk nystagmus.
rudimentär: rudimentary.
Rückabsorption *f*: reabsorption.
Rückatmungsbeutel *m*: rebreathing bag.
Rückbildung *f*: regression, recession, remission.
Rücken *m*: back, dorsum.
Rückenlage *f*: dorsal position, supine position.
Rückenlagerung *f*: supination.
Rückenmark *n*: spinal marrow, spinal cord.
Rückenmarkblutung *f*: spinal hemorrhage.
Rückenmarkkompression *f*: spinal compression.
Rückenmarkreflex *m*: spinal reflex.
Rückenmarkschädigung *f*: spinal cord lesion.
Rückenmarksegment *n*: spinal segment.
Rückenmarktumor *m*: spinal tumor.
Rückenmarkverletzung *f*: spinal trauma.
Rückenmarkwurzel *f*: spinal root.
Rückenmarkzentrum *n*: spinal center.
Rückenschmerzen: backache, back pain, dorsalgia.
Rückenstütze *f*: backrest.
Rückfall *m*: relapse.
Rückfallfieber *n*: recurrent fever, relapsing fever.
Rückfluss *m*: reflux, backflow, regurgitation; **venöser** ≈ venous return.
Rückgang *m*: recession.
Rückgrat *n*: spine.

R

Rückkopplung *f*: feedback.
Rückresorption *f*: reabsorption; **intestinale** ≈ intestinal reabsorption; **tubuläre** ≈ tubular reabsorption.
Rückstand *m*: remainder, residue, residuum.
Rückstoßphänomen *n*: rebound phenomenon, Holmes sign.
Rückwärtsversagen *n*: backward heart failure.
Rufbereitschaft *f*: call, on call.
Ruhe *f*: silence, rest, calm.
ruhelos: restless.
ruhend: resting, dormant, quiescent.
Ruhephase *f*: rest period, resting state.
Ruheschmerz *m*: rest pain.
Ruhestellung *f*: rest position.
Ruhetremor *m*: resting tremor, passive tremor.
Ruhezelle *f*: resting cell.
Ruhigstellung *f*: restraint.
Ruhr *f*: dysentery.
Rumination *f*: rumination, regurgitation of food.
Rumpf *m*: trunk.
Rumpfataxie *f*: trunk apraxia.
Rumpfmuskulatur *f*: muscles of the trunk.
Rundherd *m*: round lesion, coin lesion.
Rundrücken *m*: round back, kyphosis.
Rundschatten *m*: round lesion, coin lesion.
Rundstiellappen *m*: gauntlet flap, tubed flap.
Runt-Krankheit *f*: runt disease.
Runzel *f*: rugosity.
Ruptur *f*: rupture, laceration, tear.
rupturieren: rupture, tear.
Russell-Syndrom *n*: Russell syndrome, diencephalic syndrome of infancy.
Rußkrebs *m*: soot cancer, chimney sweepers' cancer.
R-Zacke *f*: R wave.

S

S Abk. **Schwefel** *m*: sulfur, S.
SA-Block Abk. **sinuatrialer Block** *m*: sinoatrial block.
Saccharid *n*: saccharide.
Saccharin *n*: saccharin.
Sachverständigengutachten *n*: expert evidence.
Sack *m*: sac, bag, pouch.
Sackbildung *f*: sacculation.
Sackniere *f*: sacciform kidney.
Sadismus *m*: sadism.
Sadomasochismus *m*: sadomasochism.
Säbelscheidentibia *f*: saber shin, saber-shaped tibia.
Säge *f*: saw.
Sägezahnpalme *f*: saw palmetto.
Sängerknötchen *n*: singers' nodules, vocal nodule.
Sättigung *f*: saturation, satisfaction.
Säugen *n*: nursing, suckling.
Säugling *m*: baby, nursling.
Säuglingsalter *n*: infancy, postneonatal period.
Säuglingsnahrung *f*: baby food.
Säuglingssterblichkeit *f*: infant mortality.
Säule *f*: column, pillar.
Säulenepithel *n*: columnar epithelium.
Säure *f*: acid; **aliphatische** ≈ aliphatic acid; **anorganische** ≈ inorganic acid; **aromatische** ≈ aromatic acid; **chlorige** ≈ chlorous acid; **phosphorige** ≈ phosphorous acid; **salpetrige** ≈ nitrous acid; **schweflige** ≈ sulfurous acid; **unterbromige** ≈ hypobromous acid; **unterchlorige** ≈ hypochlorous acid; **unterphosphorige** ≈ hypophosphorous acid.
Säure-Basen-Gleichgewicht *n*: acid-base balance.
Säure-Basen-Stoffwechsel *m*: acid-base metabolism.
Säurebeständigkeit *f*: acid resistance.
Säureempfindlichkeit *f*: acid susceptibility.
säurefest: acid-fast, acid-proof.
Säuresekretion *f*: acid output.
Saft *m*: juice, sap.
sagittal: sagittal.
Sagittalebene *f*: sagittal plane.
saisonal: seasonal.
Sakkade *f*: saccade.
Sakkulation *f*: sacculation.
sakral: sacral.
Sakralanästhesie *f*: sacral anesthesia.
Sakralisation *f*: sacralization.
Sakralkanal *m*: sacral canal.
Sakroiliakalgelenk *n*: scaroiliac articulation.
Sakrum *n*: sacrum, sacral bone.
Salbe *f*: ointment, unction.
Salbengesicht *n*: hatchet face.
Salbutamol *n*: salbutamol.
Salicylat *n*: salicylate.
Salicylsäure *f*: salicylic acid.
Salicylsäure *f*: salicylic acid.
Salicylursäure *f*: salicyluric acid.
Salivation *f*: salivation.
Salmeterol *n*: salmeterol.
Salmiak *m*: ammonium chloride.
Salmonellose *f*: salmonellosis, salmonella infection, enteric fever.
Salpeter *m*: saltpeter, nitre, potassium nitrate, sodium nitrate.
Salpetersäure *f*: nitric acid.
Salpingektomie *f*: salpingectomy.
Salpingitis *f*: salpingitis; **chronische interstitielle** ≈ chronic interstitial salpingitis; **eitrige** ≈ pyosalpingitis; **noduläre** ≈ nodular salpingitis; **pseudofollikuläre** ≈ pseudofollicular salpingitis; **tuberkulöse** ≈ tuberculous salpingitis.
Salpingographie *f*: salpingography.

Salpingoophorektomie *f*: salpingo-oophorectomy.
Salpingostomie *f*: salpingostomy.
Salpingotomie *f*: salpingotomy; **abdominale** ≈ laparosalpingotomy.
Salpinx *f*: salpinx, tube.
Saluretikum *n*: saluretic.
saluretisch: saluretic.
Salvarsan *n*: salvarsan, arsphenamine.
Salverin *n*: salverine.
Salz *n*: salt; **jodiertes** ≈ iodized salt; **Karlsbader** ≈ Carlsbad salt.
salzarm: low-sodium.
salzig: salty, saline.
Salzlösung *f*: saline solution; **hypertone** ≈ hypertonic saline; **hypotone** ≈ hypotonic saline.
Salzsäure *f*: hydrochloric acid.
Salzverlustnephritis *f*: salt-losing nephritis.
Salzverlustsyndrom *n*: salt-depletion syndrome, Thorn syndrome.
Samen *m*: semen, sperm.
Samenbank *f*: sperm bank.
Samenblase *f*: seminal vesicle.
Samenblasenentzündung *f*: seminal vesiculitis.
Samenflüssigkeit *f*: semen.
Samengang *m*: seminal duct.
Samenspender *m*: sperm donor.
Samenstrang *m*: spermatic cord, testicular cord.
Samenstranghernie *f*: funicular hernia.
Sammelrohr *n*: collecting tubule.
Sanatorium *n*: sanatorium.
Sandfliegenfieber *n*: sandfly fever, phlebotomus fever, pappataci fever.
Sanduhrmagen *m*: hourglass stomach.
sanft: bland, mild, soft.
sanitär: sanitary.
Sanitation *f*: sanitation.
Sankt-Antons-Feuer *n*: Saint Anthony's fire, ergotism.
S-Antigen *n*: soluble antigen.
Saphenaresektion *f*: saphenectomy.
Saponifikation *f*: saponification.
Saponin *n*: saponin.
Saprophyt *m*: saprophyte.
Sapropterin *n*: sapropterin.
Saquinavir *n*: saquinavir.
Saralasin *n*: saralasin.
Sarcoma botryoides *n*: botryoid sarcoma.
Sarcoma idiopathicum multiplex haemorrhagicum *n*: multiple idiopathic hemorrhagic sarcoma, Kaposi sarcoma, KS.
Sarkoid *n*: sarcoid.
sarkoidartig: sarcoid.
Sarkoidose *f*: sarcoidosis, Besnier-Boeck disease; **hyperkalzämische** ≈ hypercalcemic sarcoidosis; **pulmonale** ≈ pulmonary sarcoidosis; **thorakale** ≈ intrathoracic sarcoidosis.
Sarkolemm *n*: sarcolemma.
Sarkom *n*: sarcoma; **osteogenes** ≈ osteogenic sarcoma; **periostales** ≈ parosteal sarcoma.
SARS: severe acute respiratory syndrome, SARS.
Satellitenvirus *n*: satellite virus.
Sattelblockanästhesie *f*: saddle-block anesthesia.
Sattelgelenk *n*: saddle joint.
Sattelnase *f*: saddle nose.
Sattheit *f*: satiety.
Saturnismus *m*: saturnism, lead poisoning.
sauer: sour, acid.
Sauerstoff *m*: oxygen, O; **reiner** ≈ pure oxygen.
Sauerstoffaufnahme *f*: oxygen uptake.
Sauerstoffbedarf *m*: oxygen requirement.
Sauerstoffbehandlung *f*: oxygen therapy; **hyperbare** ≈ hyperbaric oxygen therapy, HOT.
Sauerstoffgradient *m*: oxygen gradient.
Sauerstoffkapazität *f*: oxygen capacity.
Sauerstoffmangel *m*: oxygen deficiency, hypoxia.
Sauerstoffmaske *f*: oxygen mask.
Sauerstoffmessung *f*: oximetry; **perkutane** ≈ transcutaneous oximetry.
Sauerstoffüberdrucktherapie *f*: hyperbaric oxygenation.
Sauerstoffutilisation *f*: oxygen utilization.

Sauerstoffzelt *n*: oxygen tent.
Sauerstoffzufuhr *f*: oxygenation.
Saugdrainage *f*: suction drainage.
saugen: suck.
Saugen *n*: suction.
Sauger *m*: aspirator, suction apparatus.
Saugkürettage *f*: suction curettage, vacuum curettage.
Saugpolster *n*: sucking cushion.
Saugreflex *m*: suck reflex, lip reflex.
Saugwurm *m*: trematode.
Sauna *f*: sauna bath, Finnish bath.
Scabies *f*: scabies.
Scabies norvegica *f*: Norwegian scabies, Norway itch.
Scan *m*: scan.
scannen: scan.
Scanner *m*: scanner.
Scapula *f*: scapula, shoulder blade.
Scapula alata *f*: alar scapula, winged scapula.
schaben: scrape.
Schaber *m*: scraper, xyster.
schaden: harm, damage, injure.
Schaden *m*: harm, damage, injury.
Schadenersatz *m*: compensation, indemnity.
Schadenersatzanspruch *m*: damage claim, claim for compensation.
Schädel *m*: skull, cranium.
Schädelbasis *f*: skull base.
Schädelbasisfraktur *f*: basal skull fracture.
Schädelbruch *m*: skull fracture.
Schädeldach *n*: roof of skull, calvaria.
Schädeldurchmesser, parietaler *m*: parietal diameter.
Schädelhirntrauma *n*: craniocerebral trauma.
Schädelhöhle *f*: cranial cavity.
Schädelimpressionsfraktur *f*: depressed skull fracture.
Schädellage *f*: cephalic presentation.
Schädelregion *f*: cranial region.
Schädelsynostose *f*: cranial synostosis.
Schädeltrauma *n*: cranial trauma.
Schädelumfangsbestimmung, sonographische *f*: ultrasonic cephalometry.
schädigen: damage, injure, impair.
Schädigung *f*: damage, injury, lesion.
schädlich: noxious, harmful, detrimental.
Schädling *m*: parasite.
Schälblase *f*: pemphigus, bullous pemphigoid.
schälen: peel.
Schärfe *f*: acuity, acuteness.
schäumend: effervescent, frothy.
Schaft *m*: shaft.
Schafzellagglutination *f*: sheep cell agglutination.
schalenähnlich: dishlike, cotyloid.
Schall *m*: sound, resonance; **amphorischer** ≈ amphoric resonance.
schalten: switch.
Schaltgen *n*: switch gene.
Schaltkern *m*: intercalated nucleus.
Schaltlamelle *f*: intermediate lamella.
Schambein *n*: pubic bone.
Schamberg-Dermatose *f*: Schamberg's dermatosis, progressive pigmented purpuric dermatosis.
Schamlaus *f*: pubic louse.
Schanker *m*: chancre, chancroidal ulcer; **harter** ≈ hard chancre, hard sore; **weicher** ≈ soft chancre, chancroid, soft sore.
Schankroid *n*: chancroid, soft chancre, soft sore.
Scharfeinstellung *f*: focusing.
Scharlach *m*: scarlet fever, scarlatina.
Scharlachexanthem *n*: scarlatinous eruption, scarlet rash.
Scharlachnephritis *f*: scarlatinal nephritis.
Scharlatan *m*: charlatan.
Scharniergelenk *n*: hinge joint, ginglymus.
Schatten *m*: shadow, shade.
Schaukelbett *n*: rocking bed.
schaumig: foamy.
Schaumleber *f*: foamy liver.
Schaumzelle *f*: foam cell.
Scheibe *f*: disk, disc.
Scheide *f*: sheath, vagina.
Scheidenabstrich *m*: vaginal smear.
Scheidenblutung *f*: vaginal bleeding, colporrhagia.
Scheidenentzündung *f*: colpitis, vaginitis.
Scheidenflora *f*: vaginal flora.

Scheidengwölbe *n*: vaginal vault, vaginal fornix.
Scheidenkrampf *m*: vaginal spasm, vaginism.
Scheidenpessar *n*: vaginal pessary.
Scheidenplastik *f*: vaginoplasty, colpoplasty.
Scheidenprolaps *m*: vaginal prolapse.
Scheidenspekulum *n*: vaginal speculum, vaginoscope.
Scheidenspülung *f*: vaginal douche.
Scheidentampon *m*: vaginal tampon.
Scheidenvorfall *m*: vaginal prolapse.
Scheidenwand *f*: vaginal wall.
Scheidewand *f*: septum.
Scheinblödsinn *m*: nonsense syndrome, Ganser syndrome.
Scheinschwangerschaft *f*: pseudopregnancy, phantom pregnancy.
Scheintod *m*: apparent death.
Scheitel *m*: vertex.
Scheitelbein *n*: parietal bone.
Scheitelbeineinstellung *f*: asynclitism.
Scheitel-Fersen-Länge *f*: heel-to-crown measurement.
Scheitellage *f*: vertex presentation.
Schema *n*: scheme, schedule, pattern.
Schenkel *m*: limb, shank.
Schenkelblock *m*: bundle branch block; **inkompletter** ≈ incomplete bundle branch block; **kompletter** ≈ complete bundle branch block.
Schenkelfraktur *f*: femoral fracture.
Schenkelhernie *f*: femoral hernia.
Scherengang *m*: scissor gait, cross-legged gait.
Scherfraktur *f*: shear fracture.
Scherkraft *f*: shearing force.
Scheuerdesinfektion *f*: scrub disinfection.
Scheuermann-Krankheit *f*: Scheuermann's disease, juvenile kyphosis.
Scheuklappenhemianopsie *f*: bitemporal hemianopsia.
Schicht *f*: layer, slice.
Schichtaufnahme *f*: section roentgenography, tomography.
Schichtstar *m*: lamellar cataract, zonular cataract.
Schichtthrombus *m*: stratified thrombus, laminated thrombus.
Schiefhals *m*: torticollis, wryneck; **angeborener** ≈ congenital torticollis; **atlantoepistrophealer** ≈ nasopharyngeal torticollis; **labyrinthärer** ≈ labyrinthine torticollis; **muskulärer** ≈ myogenic torticollis; **okulärer** ≈ ocular torticollis; **reflektorischer** ≈ reflex torticollis; **spastischer** ≈ spastic torticollis.
Schielamblyopie *f*: strabismic amblyopia.
schielen: squint.
Schielen *n*: squint, strabismus; **alternierendes** ≈ binocular strabismus; **intermittierendes** ≈ intermittent strabismus; **latentes** ≈ latent strabismus.
Schieloperation *f*: strabismus operation.
Schielwinkel *m*: squint deviation, strabismic deviation, deviation angle.
Schienbein *n*: shin, tibia.
Schiene *f*: splint, cradle.
schienen: splint.
Schild *m*: shield.
Schilddrüse *f*: thyroid gland.
Schilddrüsenadenom *n*: thyroid adenoma; **toxisches** ≈ toxic thyroid adenoma, Plummer's disease.
Schilddrüsenhormon *n*: thyroid hormone.
Schilddrüsenkarzinom *n*: thyroid carcinoma; **anaplastisches** ≈ anaplastic thyroid carcinoma; **papilläres** ≈ papillary thyroid carcinoma; **sklerosierendes** ≈ nonencapsulated sclerosing carcinoma of thyroid gland.
Schildzecke *f*: hard-bodied tick.
Schimmelpilzmykose *f*: mold mycosis.
Schinkenmilz *f*: lardaceous spleen, waxy spleen.
Schistosoma *n*: schistosoma.
Schistosomas-Dysenterie *f*: schistosomal dysentery.
Schistosomendermatitis *f*: schistosome dermatitis, swimmers' itch.
Schistosomiasis *f*: schistosomiasis, bilharziosis.
Schistosomiasis japonica *f*: schistoso-

miasis japonica, Katayama disease.
Schistosomiasis pulmonalis *f*: pulmonary schistosomiasis.
Schistozyt *m*: schistocyte.
schizoaffektiv: schizoaffective.
Schizophrenia simplex *f*: simple schizophrenia.
Schizophrenie *f*: schizophrenia, schizophrenic psychosis; **beginnende** ≈ incipient schizophrenia; **einfache** ≈ simple schizophrenia; **hebephrene** ≈ hebephrenic schizophrenia; **katatone** ≈ catatonic schizophrenia; **latente** ≈ latent schizophrenia; **paranoide** ≈ paranoid schizophrenia; **periodische** ≈ periodic schizophrenia; **pseudoneurotische** ≈ pseudopsychopathic schizophrenia; **traumatische** ≈ traumatic schizophrenia; **zönästhetische** ≈ coenesthetic schizophrenia.
schizophreniform: schizophreniform.
Schläfe *f*: temple.
Schläfenlappen *m*: temporal lobe.
schläfrig: sleepy, drowsy.
Schläfrigkeit *f*: sleepiness, drowsiness.
Schlaf *m*: sleep; **desynchronisierter** ≈ desynchronized sleep, REM sleep; **künstlicher** ≈ artificial sleep; **orthodoxer** ≈ slow wave sleep; **paradoxer** ≈ paradoxic sleep, REM sleep; **postepileptischer** ≈ postictal sleep; **synchronisierter** ≈ synchronized sleep.
Schlafanfall *m*: paroxysmal sleep.
Schlafapnoesyndrom *n*: sleep apnea syndrome.
Schlafbehandlung *f*: sleep therapy.
schlafen: sleep.
Schlafentzugsbehandlung *f*: sleep deprivation treatment.
Schlafepilepsie *f*: nocturnal epilepsy.
schlaff: floppy, flabby.
Schlafkrankheit *f*: sleeping sickness, trypanosomiasis; **afrikanische** ≈ African trypanosomiasis, acute sleeping sickness.
Schlaflosigkeit *f*: sleeplessness, insomnia.
Schlafmittel *n*: sleeping pill, somnifacient.
Schlafstörung *f*: sleep disorder.
Schlaftherapie *f*: sleep therapy, hypnotherapy.
Schlafwandeln *n*: sleepwalking, somnambulism.
Schlag *m*: beat, knock, stroke.
Schlagader *f*: artery.
Schlaganfall *m*: apoplexy, stroke; **progredienter** ≈ progressive stroke; **zerebraler** ≈ cerebral apoplexy.
schlagen: beat, throb, pulse.
Schlagvolumen des Herzens *n*: systolic volume, cardiac output.
Schlangenbissserum *n*: antisnakebite serum.
Schlangengift *n*: snake venom.
schlank: slender, slim.
schleichend: creeping, lingering.
Schleifendiuretikum *n*: loop diuretic.
Schleim *f*: mucus, slime.
Schleimbeutelentzündung *f*: bursitis, bursal synovitis.
Schleimbeutelzyste *f*: bursal cyst
Schleimdrüse *f*: mucous gland.
Schleimfäden. mucous threads.
Schleimhaut *f*: mucous membrane, mucosa.
Schleimhautanästhesie *f*: surface anesthesia.
Schleimhautimmunität *f*: mucosal immunity.
Schleimhautpemphigoid *n*: mucosal pemphigoid.
schleimig: mucic, mucilaginous.
Schleimpfropf *m*: mucous plug, cervical plug.
Schleimpilz *m*: myxomyces.
Schleimzyste *f*: mucous cyst.
Schleudertrauma *n*: whiplash injury.
Schleuse *f*: baffle, gate.
Schließmuskel *m*: sphincter muscle.
Schlinge *f*: sling, loop; **afferente** ≈ afferent loop; **blinde** ≈ blind loop.
Schlitzsonde *f*: eyed probe.
Schlottergelenk *n*: loose joint.
schlottern: wobble.
Schluckakt *m*: swallowing, deglutition.
Schluckauf *m*: hiccup, singultus.
Schluckbeschwerden: dysphagia.
schlucken: swallow.
Schlucken *n*: swallowing.

Schluckimpfung *f*: oral vaccination.
Schluckreflex *m*: swallowing reflex.
Schluckschmerz *m*: painful swallowing.
Schlüsselbein *n*: clavicle, collar bone.
Schlüsselbeinfraktur *f*: clavicle fracture.
Schlund *m*: gullet, pharynx.
Schlundlähmung *f*: pharyngoparalysis, pharyngeal palsy.
schlurfen: shuffle, slouch.
Schlussbiss *m*: occlusion.
Schlussdesinfektion *f*: final disinfection.
Schmalspektrum-Antibiotikum *n*: narrow-spectrum antibiotic.
schmecken: taste, savor.
Schmelz *m*: enamel.
Schmerz *m*: pain, ache; **akuter** ≈ acute pain; **bohrender** ≈ nagging pain; **brennender** ≈ burning pain; **chronischer** ≈ chronic pain; **einschießender** ≈ shooting pain; **fortgeleiteter** ≈ referred pain; **klopfender** ≈ throbbing pain; **kneifender** ≈ griping pain; **krampfartiger** ≈ spasmodic pain, colic; **lanzinierender** ≈ lancinating pain; **nagender** ≈ nagging pain; **radikulärer** ≈ radicular pain; **somatischer** ≈ somatic pain; **stechender** ≈ terebrant pain; **umschriebener** ≈ localized pain.
Schmerzbehandlung *f*: pain management.
Schmerzbeurteilungsbogen *m*: pain assessment card.
Schmerzensgeld *n*: compensation for pain and suffering.
schmerzerzeugend: algogenic.
schmerzfrei: painfree.
schmerzhaft: painful, aching.
Schmerzleitung *f*: pain conduction.
schmerzlindernd: pain-relieving.
schmerzlos: painless.
Schmerzmittel *n*: painkiller, analgesic.
Schmerzreflex *m*: pain reflex, nociceptive reflex.
Schmerzsyndrom *n*: pain disorder.
Schmerztherapie *f*: analgesic therapy.
Schmerzwahrnehmung *f*: nociception, pain sense.
Schmierblutung *f*: spotting.
Schmierinfektion *f*: smear infection.
Schnabelbecken *n*: beaked pelvis.
Schnabeltasse *f*: feeding cup.
Schnake *f*: gnat.
Schnappatmung *f*: gasping breathing.
Schnappdaumen *m*: jerk thumb.
schnarchen: snore.
Schnarchen *n*: snoring.
schnaufen: snort, snuffle, wheeze.
Schneckenlabyrinth *n*: acoustic labyrinth.
Schneeblindheit *f*: snow blindness.
schneiden: cut, incise, intersect, snip.
Schneiden *n*: cutting, section.
Schneidermuskel *m*: tailor's muscle.
Schneidezahn *m*: incisor tooth.
Schnelldesensibilisierung *f*: rapid desensitization.
Schnelldiagnose *f*: rapid diagnosis.
schnellend: snapping, jerking.
Schnellentbindung *f*: forced delivery.
Schnellschnitt *m*: rapid section.
Schnelltest *m*: rapid test.
Schnitt *m*: cut, incision, section.
Schnittanatomie *f*: cross-sectional anatomy.
Schnittentbindung *f*: operative delivery, cesarean section.
Schnittverletzung *f*: cut.
Schnittwunde *f*: incised wound.
Schnüffelsucht *f*: glue sniffing.
Schnuller *m*: comforter, pacifier.
Schnupfen *m*: acute rhinitis, coryza.
Schnupfen-Virus *n*: rhinovirus, common cold virus.
Schnur *f*: cord.
schnurren: thrill, purr.
Schock *m*: shock; **allergischer** ≈ anaphylactic shock; **anaphylaktischer** ≈ anaphylactic shock; **hämorrhagischer** ≈ hemorrhagic shock; **hypoglykämischer** ≈ hypoglycemic shock; **hypovolämischer** ≈ hypovolemic shock; **kardiogener** ≈ cardiogenic shock, heart shock; **neurogener** ≈ neurogenic shock; **osmotischer** ≈ osmotic shock; **septischer** ≈ septic shock; **spinaler** ≈ spinal shock, neural shock; **toxischer** ≈ toxic shock; **traumatischer** ≈ trau-

matic shock; **zerebraler** ≈ cerebral shock.
Schocklunge *f*: shock lung.
Schocksyndrom, toxisches *n*: toxic shock syndrome.
Schönheitsoperation *f*: cosmetic operation, cosmetic surgery.
Schoenlein-Henoch-Purpura *f*: Schoenlein-Henoch purpura, acute vascular purpura.
Scholz-Bielschowsky-Henneberg-Sklerose *f*: Scholz metachromatic leukoencephalitis, metachromatic leukodystrophy.
Schonatmung *f*: suppressed breathing.
Schonhaltung *f*: relieving posture.
Schonkost *f*: smooth diet, bland diet.
Schorf *m*: eschar, crust, scab.
Schornsteinfegerkrebs *m*: chimney sweeps' cancer, soot cancer.
schräg: oblique, skew, slant.
Schräglage *f*: oblique presentation.
Schrägverband *m*: oblique bandage.
Schramme *f*: scratch, abrasion.
Schranke *f*: barrier, bar.
Schreckmyoklonus *m*: startle myoclonus.
Schreckreaktion *f*: startle response.
Schreibkrampf *m*: writer's cramp, graphospasm.
Schreib-Lese-Schwäche *f*: writing and reading disability.
Schreitphänomen *n*: stepping.
Schreitreflex *m*: walking reflex.
Schritt *m*: step, pace.
Schrittmacher *m*: pacemaker; **ektoper** ≈ ectopic pacemaker; **externer** ≈ external pacemaker; **frequenzstabiler** ≈ fixed-rate pacemaker; **starrfrequenter** ≈ fixed-rate pacemaker; **synchroner** ≈ synchronous pacemaker; **temporärer** ≈ temporary pacing; **wandernder** ≈ wandering pacemaker.
Schröpfbecher *m*: cupping glass.
Schröpfen *n*: leeching, cupping.
Schröpfkopf *m*: artificial leech.
Schrumpfblase *f*: contracted bladder.
schrumpfen: shrink.
Schrumpfniere *f*: atrophic kidney.
Schubladenphänomen *n*: drawer sign, Rocher sign.
Schürfwunde *f*: abrasion, crease.
Schüssel *f*: dish, basin, bowl.
Schüttelfrost *m*: shivers, shaking ague, chill.
Schüttellähmung *f*: shaking palsy, Parkinson's disease.
Schüttelmixtur *f*: shaking mixture, lotion.
Schuh *m*: shoe; **orthopädischer** ≈ orthopedic shoe.
Schulalter *n*: school age.
Schulschwester *f*: teaching nurse.
Schulter *f*: shoulder.
Schulteramyotrophie, neuralgische *f*: neuralgic amyotrophy, Parsonage-Turner syndrome.
Schulterblatt *n*: shoulder blade, scapula.
Schultergelenk *n*: shoulder joint, articulation of humerus.
Schultergürtel *m*: shoulder girdle, pectoral girdle.
Schulterlage *f*: shoulder presentation.
Schultervorfall *m*: shoulder presentation.
Schuppe *f*: scale, squama, dandruff.
Schuppenflechte *f*: psoriasis.
Schuppenkrankheit *f*: ichthyosis.
Schuppenzelle *f*: squamous cell.
Schusswunde *f*: shotgun wound.
Schutz *m*: protection, guard.
Schutzbrille *f*: protective spectacles.
Schutzfunktion *f*: protective function.
Schutzimpfung *f*: protective vaccination.
Schutzkleidung *f*: protective clothing.
Schutzreflex *m*: protective reflex, defense reflex.
Schutzsalbe *f*: protective ointment.
Schutzschranke *f*: protective barrier.
Schutzverband *m*: protective bandage.
Schutzvorrichtung *f*: protective device, defender.
Schutzwirkung *f*: protective effect.
schwach: weak, feeble, faint.
Schwäche *f*: weakness, tenderness, faintness, feebleness.

Schwächezustand *m*: weakness; **hyperästhetisch-emotionaler** ≈ emotional hyperesthetic hyposthenia.
Schwammbiopsie *f*: sponge biopsy.
Schwammniere *f*: sponge kidney.
Schwanenhalsdeformität *f*: swan-neck deformity.
schwanger: pregnant, gravid.
Schwangere *f*: pregnant woman.
Schwangerenbetreuung *f*: prenatal care.
Schwangerschaft *f*: pregnancy, gravidity, gestation.
Schwangerschaftsabbruch *m*: abortion, termination of pregnancy.
Schwangerschaftsanämie *f*: anemia of pregnancy.
Schwangerschaftsdauer *f*: gestational period.
Schwangerschaftsdauer post conceptionem *f*: postconceptional gestational period.
Schwangerschaftsdauer post menstruationem *f*: postmenstrual gestational period, menstrual age.
Schwangerschaftsdepression *f*: depression of pregnancy.
Schwangerschaftsdiabetes *m*: pregnancy diabetes, gestational diabetes mellitus.
Schwangerschaftserbrechen *n*: vomiting of pregnancy.
Schwangerschaftskomplikation *f*: pregnancy complication.
Schwangerschaftsödem *n*: gestational edema.
Schwangerschaftsproteinurie *f*: gestational proteinuria.
Schwangerschaftspsychose *f*: gestational psychosis.
Schwangerschaftstest *m*: pregnancy test.
Schwangerschaftstoxikose *f*: gestosis, toxicosis of pregnancy.
Schwangerschaftstrimenon *m*: pregnancy trimester.
Schwann-Scheide *f*: Schwann sheath.
Schwanz *m*: tail, cauda.
Schwartz-Bartter-Syndrom *n*: Schwartz-Bartter syndrome, syndrome of inappropriate antidiuretic hormone secretion, SIADH.
Schwarzwasserfieber *n*: blackwater fever, hemoglobinuric fever, hemolytic malaria.
Schwefelbad *n*: sulfur bath.
Schwefelmilch *f*: milk of sulfur, precipitated sulfur.
Schwefelsäure *f*: sulfuric acid.
Schwefelwasserstoff *m*: hydrogen sulfide.
Schwefelzyanwasserstoffsäure *f*: sulfocyanic acid.
Schweigepflicht *f*: professional discretion, confidentiality.
Schweinehüterkrankheit *f*: swineherds' disease, leptospirosis.
Schweineinsulin *n*: porcine insulin.
Schweiß *m*: sweat, sudor.
Schweißdrüse *f*: sweat gland.
Schweißdrüsenabszess *m*: sweat gland abscess.
Schweißdrüsenentzündung *f*: hidradenitis.
Schweißsekretion *f*: hidrosis, perspiration.
schweißtreibend: sudorific, diaphoretic.
Schwelle *f*: threshold, limen.
schwellen: swell, engorge.
Schwellendosis *f*: threshold dose.
Schwellenreiz *m*: threshold stimulus, liminal stimulus.
Schwellkörper *m*: cavernous body.
Schwellung *f*: swelling, tumescence, engorgement; **prämenstruelle** ≈ premenstrual swelling; **trübe** ≈ cloudy swelling; **variköse** ≈ varicose tumor.
Schwellungsdegeneration *f*: ballooning degeneration.
Schwenklappen *m*: rotation flap.
Schwerbehinderung *f*: severe disability, major disability.
schwerhörig: hard-of-hearing, deaf.
Schwerhörigkeit *f*: hearing impairment, deafness.
schwer krank: severely ill.
schwermütig: melancholic.
Schwertfortsatz *m*: xiphoid process.
schwer verletzt: seriously injured.
Schwester *f*: sister, nurse.
Schwesternhelferin *f*: nursing auxiliary.

Schwimmbadkonjunktivitis *f*: epidemic conjunctivitis.
Schwimmbadotitis *f*: swimmers' ear.
Schwindel *m*: vertigo, dizziness; **arteriosklerotischer** ≈ angiopathic vertigo; **aurikulärer** ≈ aural vertigo; **epileptischer** ≈ epileptic vertigo; **objektiver** ≈ objective vertigo; **paralytischer** ≈ paralytic vertigo; **subjektiver** ≈ subjective vertigo; **vestibulärer** ≈ vestibular vertigo.
schwinden: vanish, waste.
Schwindsucht *f*: phthisis, tuberculosis.
schwingen: swing, vibrate, undulate.
Schwingung *f*: oscillation, vibration.
Schwirren *n*: thrill, whirr; **arterielles** ≈ arterial thrill; **arteriovenöses** ≈ arteriovenous thrill; **venöses** ≈ humming-top murmur.
Schwitzen *n*: sweating, perspiration; **gustatorisches** ≈ gustatory sweating, auriculotemporal syndrome.
Schwund *m*: wasting, shrinkage, atrophy.
Scilla-Glykosid *n*: squill glycoside.
Scopolamin *n*: scopolamine.
Scratch-Test *m*: scratch test.
Screening *n*: screening; **genetisches** ≈ genetic screening; **pränatales** ≈ prenatal screening.
Scrub-Typhus *m*: scrub typhus, tsutsugamushi disease, chigger-borne typhus.
Seagull-Geräusch *n*: seagull murmur.
Seborrhö *f*: seborrhea.
Secale-Alkaloid *n*: ergot alkaloid.
Secnidazol *n*: secnidazole.
Secobarbitalnatrium *n*: sodium secobarbital.
Second-Look-Operation *f*: second-look procedure.
Sectio *f*: sectio, section.
Sedativum *n*: sedative.
sedierend: sedative.
Sedierung *f*: sedation.
Sediment *n*: sediment, deposit.
Sedimentationsrate *f*: sedimentation rate.
Seebad *n*: seaside resort.
Seekrankheit *f*: seasickness.
Seele *f*: soul, spirit, psyche.
Seelenblindheit *f*: visual agnosia, psychic blindness.
Seemöwengeräusch *n*: seagull murmur.
Segelklappen: atrioventricular valves.
Segment *n*: segment.
segmental: segmental, segmentary.
Segmentatelektase *f*: segmental atelectasis.
Segmentbronchus *m*: segmental bronchus.
Segmentkerniger *m*: segmented neutrophil.
Segmentresektion *f*: segmentectomy.
Segregation *f*: segregation.
Sehen *n*: vision, sight, visus; **binokulares** ≈ binocular vision; **photopisches** ≈ photopic vision, daylight vision; **skotopisches** ≈ scotopic vision; **stereoskopisches** ≈ stereoscopic vision.
Sehfeld *n*: visual field.
Sehgelb *n*: visual yellow.
Sehkraft *f*: visual power, eyesight.
Sehne *f*: tendon, sinew; **schnappende** ≈ snapping tendon.
Sehnenansatz *m*: insertion.
Sehnenorgan *n*: tendon organ, neurotendinous organ.
Sehnenplastik *f*: tendoplasty, tendinoplasty.
Sehnenreflex *m*: tendon reflex, periosteal reflex.
Sehnenscheide *f*: tendon sheath, vagina.
Sehnenscheidenentzündung *f*: tendovaginitis, peritendinitis.
Sehnenxanthom *n*: tendinous xanthoma.
Sehnerv *m*: optic nerve.
Sehnervenatrophie *f*: optic atrophy.
Sehnervenentzündung *f*: optic neuritis, ophthalmoneuritis.
Sehnervenkreuzung *f*: optic chiasma.
Sehnervenpapille *f*: optic disk, optic papilla.
Sehpigment *n*: visual pigment.
Sehpurpur *m*: visual purple, rhodopsin.
Sehrinde *f*: visual cortex.
Sehschärfe *f*: visual acuity, visus.

Sehschwäche *f*: amblyopia, asthenopia.
Sehstörung *f*: visual defect, vision disorder.
Sehtest *m*: vision test, sight test.
Sehverlust *m*: loss of vision.
Sehvermögen *n*: sight, vision.
Sehwinkel *m*: visual angle.
Sehzelle *f*: visual cell.
Sehzentrum *n*: visual center, optical center.
Seife *f*: soap, sapo.
Seitbiss *m*: eccentric occlusion.
Seite *f*: side.
Seitenaufnahme *f*: lateral view.
Seitenbetonung *f*: laterality.
Seitenlage *f*: lateral position.
Seitenstechen *n*: stitch, pleurodynia.
Seitenstrang *m*: lateral column.
Seitenventrikel *m*: lateral ventricle.
Seit-zu-Seit-Anastomose *f*: side-to-side anastomosis.
Sekret *n*: secretion.
Sekretagogum *n*: secretagogue.
Sekretin *n*: secretin.
Sekretion *f*: secretion.
sekretionsfördernd: secretagogue.
sekretionshemmend: antisecretory, secretoinhibitory.
Sekretionsphase *f*: secretory phase, luteal phase.
Sektion *f*: section, autopsy.
Sektionsbericht *m*: autopsy report.
sekundär: secondary.
Sekundärfollikel *m*: secondary follicle.
Sekundärheilung *f*: healing by second intention.
Sekundärinfektion *f*: secondary infection.
Sekundärnaht *f*: secondary suture.
Sekundärprävention *f*: secondary prevention.
Sekundärtumor *m*: secondary tumor.
Sekundenkapazität *f*: forced expiratory volume, timed vital capacity.
Selamectin *n*: selamectin.
Selbst *n*: self.
Selbstbeobachtung *f*: self-observation.
Selbstbeschädigung *f*: self-mutilation, self-inflicted injury.
Selbstentwicklung *f*: spontaneous evolution.
Selbsthilfegruppe *f*: self-help group.
Selbstkontrolle *f*: self-control, self-monitoring.
Selbstmedikation *f*: self medication.
Selbsttötung *f*: suicide.
Selbstuntersuchung der Brust *f*: breast self-examination.
Selegilin *n*: selegiline.
Selektion *f*: selection.
Selektionsdruck *m*: selection pressure.
Selektivnährboden *m*: selective culture medium.
Semilunarklappe *f*: semilunar valve.
Seminom *n*: seminoma, seminal carcinoma.
semipermeabel: semipermeable.
Seneszenz *f*: senescence.
Senfwickel *m*: mustard poultice.
senil: senile, aged.
Senilität *f*: senility, old age.
Senium *n*: senium, old age.
Senkfuß *m*: weak foot.
Senkmagen *m*: gastroptosis.
Senkung *f*: lowering, ptosis, descent.
Senkungsabszess *m*: gravitation abscess, wandering abscess.
Sensation *f*: sensation.
sensibel: sensible.
sensibilisiert: sensitized, primed.
Sensibilisierung *f*: sensibilization, sensitization.
Sensibilität *f*: sensibility; **epikritische** ≈ epicritic sensibility; **gnostische** ≈ gnostic sensibility; **protopathische** ≈ protopathic sensibility; **somatische** ≈ somatognosis, somesthesia.
Sensibilitätsstörung *f*: sensory disorder; **dissoziierte** ≈ dissociated sensory loss.
Sensibilitätsverlust *m*: sensory loss.
sensitiv: sensitive.
Sensitivität *f*: sensitivity.
Sensor *m*: sensor.
sensorisch: sensory, sensorial.
Sepsis *f*: sepsis.
septiert: septate.
Septikämie *f*: septicemia.
septisch: septic.

Septum *n*: septum, partition.
Septumdefekt *m*: septal defect.
Septumdeviation *f*: septal deviation.
Septum-pellucidum-Zyste *f*: pellucid cyst.
Septumperforation *f*: septal perforation.
sequentiell: sequential.
Sequenz *f*: sequence.
Sequenzierung *f*: sequencing.
Sequesterbildung *f*: sequestration.
Sequestrotomie *f*: sequestrotomy.
Serienfraktur *f*: serial fracture.
Serienschnitt *m*: serial section.
Serin *n*: serine.
serös: serous.
Serologie *f*: serology.
serologisch: serologic.
Serom *n*: seroma.
Seromukotympanon *n*: secretory otitis media, middle-ear effusion.
Serositis *f*: serositis.
Serotonin *n*: serotonin, 5-hydroxytryptamine.
serpiginös: serpiginous.
Serrapeptase *f*: serrapeptase.
Sertindol *n*: sertindole.
Sertralin *n*: sertraline.
Serum *n*: serum; **antiretikuloendotheliales** ≈ antireticular cytotoxic serum, Bogomolez serum; **gepooltes** ≈ pooled serum; **inaktiviertes** ≈ inactivated serum; **normales menschliches** ≈ normal human serum; **polyvalentes** ≈ polyvalent serum.
Serumkrankheit *f*: serum disease, serum sickness.
Serumnarbe *f*: serum mark.
Serumspiegel *m*: serum level.
Serumtherapie *f*: serum therapy.
Sesambein *n*: sesamoid bone.
sessil: sessile.
Seuche *f*: plague, epidemic.
Seuchenbekämpfung *f*: epidemics control.
Seufzeratmung *f*: sigh respiration.
Sevelamer *n*: sevelamer.
Sever-Krankheit *f*: Sever's disease, calcaneal osteochondritis.
Sevofluran *n*: sevoflurane.
Sexualaufklärung *f*: sex education.
Sexualberatung *f*: sexual counseling.
Sexualdelikt *n*: sex offense.
Sexualhormon *n*: sex hormone.
Sexualität *f*: sexuality, sexual life.
Sexualkontakt *m*: sexual contact.
Sexualmedizin *f*: sexual medicine.
Sexualverhalten *n*: sexual behavior; **abweichendes** ≈ paraphilia.
sexuell: sexual.
Sézary-Syndrom *n*: Sézary syndrome, lymphoblastic erythroderma.
Sezierpinzette *f*: dissecting forceps.
Sheehan-Syndrom *n*: Sheehan syndrome, postpartum panhypopituitary syndrome.
Shigellose *f*: shigellosis, bacillary dysentery.
Shunt *m*: shunt; **arteriovenöser** ≈ arteriovenous shunt; **lymphatikovenöser** ≈ lymphaticovenous anastomosis; **mesenterikokavaler** ≈ cavomesenteric shunt; **peritoneothekaler** ≈ peritoneosubarachnoid shunt; **peritoneovenöser** ≈ LeVeen shunt; **portokavaler** ≈ portacaval shunt; **portorenaler** ≈ portarenal shunt; **portosystemischer** ≈ portasystemic shunt; **pulmonaler** ≈ pulmonary shunt; **splenorenaler** ≈ splenorenal shunt; **subdural-pleuroperitonealer** ≈ subduropleural shunt; **ureterothekaler** ≈ ureterothecal shunt; **ventrikuloatrialer** ≈ ventriculoatrial shunt; **ventrikulojugulärer** ≈ ventriculojugular shunt; **ventrikuloperitonealer** ≈ ventriculoperitoneal shunt; **ventrikulovenöser** ≈ ventriculovenous shunt.
Shuntzyanose *f*: shunt cyanosis.
Shy-Drager-Syndrom *n*: Shy-Drager syndrome, chronic orthostatic hypotension.
Sialadenitis *f*: sialadenitis.
Sialagogum *n*: sialagogue.
Sialinsäure *f*: sialic acid.
Sialographie *f*: sialography.
Sialolith *m*: salivary calculus.
Sialolithiasis *f*: sialolithiasis.
Sialorrhö *f*: sialorrhea, ptyalism.
Sibutramin *n*: sibutramine.
Sicard-Ostitis *f*: Sicard's posterior condylar syndrome, glossopharyngeal neuralgia.

Sichelzelle *f*: sickle cell, drepanocyte.
Sichelzellenanämie *f*: sickle-cell anemia, hemoglobin SC disease.
Sichelzellenhämoglobin *n*: sickle-cell hemoglobin.
Sicherheit *f*: safety, security; **biologische** ≈ biosafety.
Sicherheitsgurtsyndrom *n*: seat-belt syndrome.
Sicherheitsrand *m*: margin of safety.
Sicht *f*: sight, view, visibility.
Sichtgerät *n*: monitor.
Sickerblutung *f*: oozing hemorrhage.
sickern: seep, ooze.
Sick-Sinus-Syndrom *n*: sick sinus syndrome.
Sideroblast *m*: sideroblast.
Sideroblastenanämie *f*: sideroblastic anemia.
Siderose *f*: siderosis, siderotic pneumoconiosis.
Siderozytose *f*: siderocytosis.
Siebbein *n*: ethmoid bone.
Siebbeinhöhle *f*: ethmoidal labyrinth.
Siebentagefieber *n*: seven-day fever.
Siegelringzellkarzinom *n*: signet ring cell carcinoma.
Sigmablase *f*: sigmoid bladder.
Sigmadivertikel *n*: sigmoid diverticulum.
Sigmakarzinom *n*: sigmoid carcinoma.
Sigmatismus *m*: sigmatism, lisping.
Sigmoid *n*: sigmoid.
Sigmoidoskopie *f*: sigmoidoscopy.
Sigmoidostomie *f*: sigmoidostomy.
Signallymphknoten *m*: signal node.
Signatura *f*: signature.
Signifikanz *f*: significance; **statistische** ≈ statistical significance.
Silbernitrat *n*: silver nitrate.
Sildenafil *n*: sildenafil.
Silibinin *n*: silibinin.
Silikonbrustimplantat *n*: silicone breast implant.
Silikose *f*: silicosis.
Simons-Syndrom *n*: Simons disease, progressive lipodystrophy.
Sims-Lage *f*: Sims position, semiprone position.
Sims-Spekulum *n*: duck-billed speculum.
Simulation *f*: simulation, malingering.
Simulator *m*: simulator.
simulieren: simulate, malinger.
Simvastatin *n*: simvastatin.
Sincalid *n*: sincalide.
Single-Photon-Emissions-Computertomographie *f*: single photon emission computed tomography, SPECT.
Singultus *m*: singultus, hiccup.
Sinistrokardie *f*: sinistrocardia.
Sinn *m*: sense, sensation.
Sinnesempfindung *f*: sensation, sensory perception.
Sinneshaar *n*: sensory hair.
Sinnesorgan *n*: sense organ.
Sinnestäuschung *f*: illusion.
Sinneswahrnehmung *f*: sensory perception, sensibility.
Sinneszelle *f*: sensory cell.
Sinneszentrum *n*: sensory center.
Sinus *m*: sinus.
Sinusarrhythmie *f*: sinus arrhythmia.
Sinusbradykardie *f*: sinus bradycardia.
sinusförmig: sinusoid.
Sinus frontalis *m*: frontal sinus.
Sinusitis *f*: sinusitis.
Sinusitis frontalis *f*: frontal sinusitis.
Sinusitis maxillaris *f*: maxillary sinusitis.
Sinusitis sphenoidalis *f*: sphenoidal sinusitis.
Sinusknoten *m*: sinus node, sinoatrial node.
Sinusknotensyndrom *n*: sick sinus syndrome.
Sinusoid *n*: sinusoid.
Sinusrhythmus *m*: sinus rhythm.
Siomycin *n*: siomycin.
Sirolimus *n*: sirolimus.
Sirup *m*: sirup, syrup.
Sisomicin *n*: sisomicin.
Sitosterin *n*: sitosterol.
Situation *f*: situation.
situativ: situational.
Situs inversus *m*: visceral inversion.
Sitzbein *n*: ischiatic bone.
Sitzhaltung *f*: sitting posture.
Sjögren-Larsson-Syndrom *n*: Sjögren-Larsson syndrome, ichthyosiforme erythroderma.

Skabies *f*: scabies, sarcoptic itch.
Skala *f*: scale.
Skalenus-anterior-Syndrom *n*: scalenus anterior syndrome, Haven syndrome.
Skalpell *n*: scalpel, surgical knife.
Skaphoidfraktur *f*: scaphoid fracture.
Skaphokephalie *f*: scaphocephaly.
Skapulakonkavität *f*: scaphoid scapula.
Skarifikation *f*: scarification.
Skarifikationstest *m*: scratch test.
Skelett *n*: skeleton.
Skelettdeformität *f*: skelton deformity.
Skelettmuskel *m*: sceletal muscle.
Sklera *f*: sclera; **blaue** ≈ blue sclera; **gelbe** ≈ yellow sclera.
Skleritis *f*: scleritis.
Sklerodaktylie *f*: sclerodactyly.
Skleroderm *n*: scleroderma.
Sklerodermie *f*: scleroderma; **diffuse** ≈ diffuse scleroderma; **generalisierte** ≈ generalized scleroderma; **progressive** ≈ progressive scleroderma; **systemische** ≈ systemic sclerosis; **umschriebene** ≈ localized scleroderma; **zirkumskripte** ≈ circumscribed scleroderma.
Sklerödem *n*: scleredema.
Sklerose *f*: sclerosis; **bulbäre multiple** ≈ bulbar multiple sclerosis; **konzentrische** ≈ concentric sclerosis, Baló's disease; **multiple** ≈ multiple sclerosis, MS, disseminated sclerosis; **progressive systemische** ≈ progressive scleroderma; **tuberöse** ≈ tuberous sclerosis, Bourneville-Pringle syndrome.
Sklerosierung *f*: sclerosing, sclerotherapy.
Sklerotinsäure *f*: sclerotic acid.
sklerotisch: sclerotic.
Sklerotomie *f*: sclerotomy.
Skolex *m*: scolex.
Skoliose *f*: scoliosis, lateral curvature; **fixierte** ≈ fixed scoliosis; **korrigierbare** ≈ mobile scoliosis; **osteopathische** ≈ osteopathic scoliosis; **unkorrigierbare** ≈ structural scoliosis.
Skoliosebecken *n*: scoliotic pelvis.
Skopophilie *f*: scopophilia, voyeurism.
Skorbut *m*: scurvy; **asymptomatischer** ≈ subscurvy state; **infantiler** ≈ infantile scurvy, Barlow syndrome.
Skotom *n*: scotoma.
skrotal: scrotal.
Skrotalhernie *f*: scrotal hernia.
Skrotalreflex *m*: scrotal reflex, Mooser's reaction.
Skrotumhydrozele *f*: scrotal hydrocele.
Skutulum *n*: scutulum, favus cup.
Skybalon *n*: scybalum.
Sludge-Phänomen *n*: sludge phenomenon, blood sludge.
Smegma *n*: smegma.
Smegmolith *m*: smegmolith.
Sodbrennen *n*: heartburn, water brash.
Sodoku *n*: sodoku, spirillar fever.
Sofortreaktion *f*: immediate reaction, immediate response.
Soforttransfusion *f*: direct transfusion.
Sofortwirkung *f*: immediate effect.
Solarplexus *m*: solar plexus, celiac plexus.
Soldatenherz *n*: soldier's heart, neurocirculatory asthenia.
Solifenacin *n*: solifenacin.
solitär: solitary.
Solitärfollikel *m*: solitary follicle.
Solitärzyste *f*: solitary cyst.
Sollgewicht *n*: ideal weight.
Solvens *n*: solvent.
somatisch: somatic.
somatisieren: somatize.
Somatisierung *f*: somatization.
Somatisierungssyndrom *n*: somatization disorder.
Somatoliberin *n*: somatotropin releasing hormone, SRH.
Somatologie *f*: somatology.
Somatorelin *n*: somatorelin.
Somatostatin *n*: somatostatin, growth hormone inhibiting hormone, GHIH.
Somatotropin *n*: somatotropin, human growth hormone, HGH.
Sommerdiarrhö *f*: summer diarrhea.

Sommerenzephalitis *f*: summer encephalitis.
Sommersprossen: freckles, sunspots.
Somnambulismus *m*: somnambulism, sleepwalking.
somnolent: somnolent.
Somnolenz *f*: somnolence, drowsiness.
Sonde *f*: sound, tube, probe; **stumpfe** ≈ blunt probe.
Sondenernährung *f*: tube feeding.
Sondierung *f*: sounding, probing.
Sonnenbrand *m*: sunburn.
Sonnenfleck *m*: sunspot.
Sonnenschutz *m*: sun protection.
Sonnenstich *m*: sunstroke.
Sonnenuntergangsphänomen *n*: sunset phenomenon.
Sonographie *f*: sonography, ultrasound examination.
Soor *m*: thrush.
Soorkolpitis *f*: candidal vaginitis, monilial vaginitis.
Sorbinsäure *f*: sorbic acid.
Sorbit *n*: sorbitol.
Sorbitol *n*: sorbitol.
Sotalol *n*: sotalol.
Sotos-Syndrom *n*: Sotos syndrome, cerebral gigantism.
sozial: social.
Sozialdienst *m*: social services.
Sozialmedizin *f*: social medicine.
Sozialpsychiatrie *f*: social psychiatry.
Sozialversicherung *f*: social insurance, social security.
Soziologie *f*: sociology.
Spätabort *m*: late abortion.
Spätepilepsie *f*: late epilepsy.
Spätgeburt *f*: post-term birth.
Spätreaktion *f*: delayed reaction, delayed hypersensitivity.
Spätschizophrenie *f*: late schizophrenia.
Spätsyphilis *f*: late syphilis.
Spalt *m*: cleft, fissure; **synaptischer** ≈ synaptic gap.
spalten: split, fissure, cleave.
Spaltfraktur *f*: split fracture.
Spaltfuß *m*: cleft foot, split foot.
Spalthand *f*: cleft hand, split hand.
Spaltlampe *f*: slit lamp.
Spaltung *f*: division, splitting, cleavage; **operative** ≈ surgical division.
Spaltung der Herztöne *f*: splitting of heart sounds.
Spaltungsirresein *n*: schizophrenia.
Spanner *m*: tensor muscle.
Spannung *f*: tension, stretch.
Spannungskopfschmerz *m*: tension headache.
Spannungspneumothorax *m*: tension pneumothorax.
Spannungssyndrom, prämenstruelles *n*: premenstrual tension syndrome.
Sparfloxacin *n*: sparfloxacin.
Spartein *n*: sparteine.
spasmodisch: spasmodic, spastic.
Spasmolytikum *n*: spasmolysant, antispasmodic.
spasmolytisch: spasmolytic, antispasmodic.
Spasmophilie *f*: spasmophilia, infantile tetany.
Spasmus *m*: spasmus, spasm.
Spasmus nictitans *m*: nictitating spasm, blepharospasm.
Spasmus nutans *m*: spasmus nutans, nodding spasm.
Spasmus rotatorius *m*: rotatory spasm.
Spastik *f*: spasticity.
spastisch: spastic, spasmodic.
Spastizität *f*: spasticity, spastic rigidity.
Spatel *m*: spatula.
Speckleber *f*: lardaceous liver, waxy liver.
Speckmilz *f*: lardaceous spleen, waxy spleen.
Spectinomycin *n*: spectinomycin.
Speiche *f*: radius, spoke bone.
Speichel *m*: saliva, spit.
Speicheldrüse *f*: salivary gland.
Speicheldrüsenfistel *f*: salivary fistula.
Speicheldrüsenstein *m*: salivary gland calculus.
Speicheldrüsentumor *m*: salivary gland tumor.
Speichelfluss *m*: salivation.
Speichelsekretion *f*: salivary secretion, salivation.
Speichelstein *m*: salivary calculus.

Speicherkrankheit *f*: storage disease, thesaurismosis.
Speicherung *f*: storage, accumulation.
Speiseröhre *f*: esophagus, gullet.
Spektrometrie *f*: spectrometry.
Spektrophotometrie *f*: spectrophotometry.
Spektroskopie *f*: spectroscopy.
Spektrum *n*: spectrum.
Spekulum *n*: speculum.
Spender *m*: donor.
Spenderorgan *n*: donor organ.
Spenderselbstausschluss *m*: donor self-exclusion.
Sperma *n*: sperm.
spermatisch: spermatic.
Spermatoblast *m*: sperm cell.
Spermatogenese *f*: spermatogenesis.
Spermatozele *f*: spermatocele.
Spermatozoon *n*: spermatozoon, sperm.
Spermatozyt *m*: spermatocyte.
Spermauntersuchung *f*: sperm analysis.
Spermie *f*: sperm cell.
Spermienmotilität *f*: sperm motility.
Spermientransport *m*: sperm transport.
spermizid: spermicidal, spermatocidal.
Spermizid *n*: spermicide, spermicidal agent.
Spezies *f*: species.
Spezifikum *n*. specific.
spezifisch: specific.
Spezifität *f*: specificity.
sphäroidal: spheroid.
Sphärozyt *m*: spherocyte, globe cell.
Sphärozytose *f*: spherocytosis; **hereditäre** ≈ hereditary spherocytosis, Chauffard syndrome.
sphenoidal: sphenoidal.
Sphenoiditis *f*: sphenoiditis.
Sphenokephalie *f*: sphenocephaly.
Sphingolipid *n*: sphingolipid.
Sphingolipidose *f*: sphingolipidosis.
Sphinkter *m*: sphincter muscle.
Sphinkterinkontinenz *f*: paralytic incontinence.
Sphinkterotomie *f*: sphincterotomy.
Sphinkterschwäche *f*: sphincter weakness.
Sphinxgesicht *n*: myopathic face.
Sphygmographie *f*: sphygmography.
Sphygmomanometrie *f*: sphygmomanometry.
Spider-Nävus *m*: spider nevus.
Spiegel *m*: mirror, speculum.
Spiegelung *f*: reflection.
Spieltherapie *f*: play therapy.
Spike-Entladung *f*: spike discharge.
Spina *f*: spina, spine.
Spina bifida *f*: spina bifida, cleft spine.
spinal: spinal.
Spinalanästhesie *f*: spinal anesthesia, spinal block.
Spinalerkrankung, funikuläre *f*: funicular myelitis, Lichtheim's disease.
Spinalganglion *n*: spinal ganglion.
Spinalkanal *m*: spinal canal.
Spinalkanalabszess *m*: intraspinal abscess.
Spinalkanalstenose *f*: spinal stenosis.
Spinalnerv *m*: spinal nerve.
Spinalparalyse *f*: spinal paralysis; **epidurale aszendierende** ≈ epidural ascending spinal paralysis; **spastische** ≈ spastic spinal paralysis.
Spinapunktion *f*: spinal puncture.
Spinatstuhl *m*: spinach stool.
Spindel *f*: spindle, coil.
Spindelfaser *f*: spindle fiber, interzonal fiber.
spindelförmig: spindle-shaped, fusiform.
Spindelgift *n*: spindle poison, mitotic poison.
Spindelkatarakt *f*: fusiform cataract.
Spindelzelle *f*: spindle cell.
Spindelzellkarzinom *n*: spindle cell carcinoma.
Spirale *f*: spiral, coil, helix.
Spiralfraktur *f*: spiral fracture.
spiralisieren: coil.
Spiralkatheter *m*: spiral-tip catheter.
Spiramycin *n*: spiramycin.
Spirapril *n*: spirapril.
Sprillum-minus-Krankheit *f*: spirillary fever, sodoku.
Spiritus *m*: spirit.
Spirochätose *f*: spirochetosis, spirochetal infection.

Spirogramm *n*: spirogram.
Spirograph *m*: spirograph, pneumatograph.
Spirographie *f*: spirography.
Spirometrie *f*: spirometry.
Spironolacton *n*: spironolactone.
Spital *n*: hospital, clinic.
Spitze *f*: spike, peak, point, spicule, tip.
Spitzenpotential *n*: spike potential.
Spitzenstoß *m*: apex beat; **hebender** ≈ heaving apex beat.
Spitzfuß *m*: tip foot, equinovalgus.
Spitzschädel *m*: oxycephaly.
Splanchnikektomie *f*: splanchnicectomy.
Splanchnikus *m*: splanchnic nerve.
Splanchnikusblock *m*: splanchnic block.
Spleißen *n*: splicing.
Splenektomie *f*: splenectomy.
Splenographie *f*: splenography.
Splenomegalie *f*: splenomegaly, enlarged spleen; **siderotische** ≈ siderotic splenomegaly, Gamna-Gandy spleen; **tropische** ≈ tropical splenomegaly, visceral leishmaniasis, kala-azar.
Splenoportographie *f*: splenoportography.
Split-Brain-Syndrom *n*: split-brain state.
Splitter *m*: splinter, sliver.
Splitterfraktur *f*: comminuted fracture, splintered fracture.
Spondylarthritis ankylopoetica *f*: ankylosing spondylitis, Bekhterev's arthritis.
Spondylarthrose *f*: spondylarthrosis.
Spondylitis *f*: spondylitis; **ankylosierende** ≈ ankylosing spondylitis, Bechterew's disease, Marie-Strümpell disease; **hypertrophe** ≈ hypertrophic spondylitis; **tuberkulöse** ≈ tuberculous spondylitis.
Spondylolisthesisbecken *n*: spondylolisthetic pelvis, Rokitansky's pelvis.
Spondylolyse *f*: spondylolysis.
Spondylose *f*: spondylosis; **degenerative** ≈ degenerative spondylosis, degenerative vertebral arthropathy; **hyperostotische** ≈ hyperostotic spondylosis, senile ankylosing hyperostosis of spine.
Spongioblast *m*: spongioblast.
spongiös: spongy, spongiose, cancellous.
Spongiosa *f*: spongiosa, spongy bone.
spontan: spontaneous.
Spontanabort *m*: spontaneous abortion.
Spontanatmung *f*: spontaneous respiration.
Spontanbewegung *f*: spontaneous movement.
Spontanblutung *f*: spontaneous hemorrhage.
Spontanepilepsie *f*: spontaneous epilepsy.
Spontanfraktur *f*: spontaneous fracture, pathologic fracture.
Spontangeburt *f*: spontaneous delivery, spontaneous labor.
Spontanheilung *f*: spontaneous recovery.
Spontanluxation *f*: spontaneous luxation.
Spontanpneumothorax *m*: spontaneous pneumothorax.
Spontanremission *f*: spontaneous remission.
Spontanrückbildung *f*: spontaneous regression.
Spontanruptur *f*: incidental rupture.
Spontanwendung *f*: spontaneous inversion.
sporadisch: sporadic.
Spore *f*: spore.
Sporenbildung *f*: spore formation, sporulation.
Sporn *m*: spur, calcar.
spornförmig: spicular.
Sporotrichose *f*: sporotrichosis.
Sporozoit *m*: sporozoite.
Sportarzt *m*: sports physician.
Sportlerherz *n*: athlete's heart.
Sportmedizin *f*: sports medicine.
Sportverletzung *f*: athletic injury.
Sprachaudiogramm *n*: speech audiogram.
Sprache *f*: speech; **abgehackte** ≈ staccato speech; **skandierende** ≈ scanning speech; **verwaschene** ≈ slurred

speech, clipped speech.
Sprachentwicklungsstörung *f*: disorder of speech development.
Sprachtherapie *f*: speech therapy.
Sprachvermögen *n*: verbal ability.
Sprachzentrum *n*: speech center, language center; **motorisches** ≈ motor speech area; **sensorisches** ≈ sensory speech area, auditory speech area.
Sprechhilfe *f*: speaking aid.
Sprechkanüle *f*: speaking tube.
Sprechstimme *f*: speaking voice.
Sprechzeiten: surgery hours.
spreitend: spreading.
Spreizfuß *m*: splayfoot, spread foot.
Spreizgips *m*: expanding cast.
Spreizhaken *m*: retractor.
Sprenkelung *f*: mottling, stippling.
Spritze *f*: syringe.
spröde: brittle.
Sprossmyzel *f*: yeast-like mycel.
Sprossung *f*: gemmation.
sprudeln: bubble.
Sprue *f*: sprue, catarrhal dysentery; **einheimische** ≈ nontropical sprue, celiac disease; **tropische** ≈ tropical sprue.
Sprungbein *n*: ankle bone, talus.
Sprunggelenk *n*: ankle joint; **oberes** ≈ talocrural joint; **unteres** ≈ talocalcaneonavicular joint.
Sprungmutation *f*: saltatory mutation.
spucken: spit.
spülen: irrigate, wash, flush, lavage, rinse.
Spülflüssigkeit *f*: lavage fluid, rinsing fluid.
Spülsubstanz *f*: irrigant.
Spülung *f*: lavage, rinsing, irrigation, douche.
Spur *f*: track, trace.
Spurenelement *n*: trace element.
Sputum *n*: sputum; **blutig tingiertes** ≈ blood-tinged sputum; **eitriges** ≈ purulent sputum; **grünliches** ≈ green sputum; **rostbraunes** ≈ rusty sputum.
squamös: squamous.
Stab *m*: rod.
stabil: stable.
Stabilisation *f*: stabilization.
Stabilität *f*: stability.
Stabkerniger *m*: stab cell, rod neutrophil.
Stachel *m*: spike, spine, spina.
Stachelzelle *f*: spine cell.
Stacke-Mittelohrradikaloperation *f*: Stacke's meatoplasty.
Stadieneinteilung *f*: staging.
Stadium *n*: stage, stadium.
Stäbchen *n*: rod, visual receptor.
Stängel *m*: stalk, stem.
Stärke *f*: power, strength, starch.
stärken: strengthen.
Stärkeprobe *f*: starch test.
Stakkatohusten *m*: hacking cough.
Stamm *m*: stem, strain, line, truncus.
stammeln: babble, stammer.
Stammhirn *n*: brain stem.
Stammhirnsyndrom *n*: brain stem syndrome.
Stammzelle *f*: stem cell; **aplastische** ≈ aplastic stem cell; **pluripotente** ≈ pluripotent stem cell.
Stammzellenleukämie *f*: stem-cell leukemia.
Stand *m*: standing position.
Standard *m*: standard, norm.
Standardableitungen: standard leads.
Standardabweichung *f*: standard deviation.
Standardbikarbonat *n*: standard bicarbonate.
Standbildverfahren *n*: static imaging.
Stand-by-Schrittmacher *m*: stand-by pacemaker.
Stanger-Bad *n*: hydroelectric bath.
Stanozolol *n*: stanozolol.
Stanzbiopsie *f*: punch biopsy.
Stapedektomie *f*: stapedectomy.
Stapediotenotomie *f*: stapediotenotomy, stapedial tenotomy.
Stapediusreflex *m*: acoustic stapedial reflex.
Staphylektomie *f*: staphylectomy, uvulectomy.
Staphylokokkeninfektion *f*: stapohylococcal infection.
Staphylokokkenpneumonie *f*: staphylococcal pneumonia.
Staphylokokkensepsis *f*: staphylococcemia.

Staphylokokkus *m*: staphylococcus.
Staphylom *n*: staphyloma.
Staphylorrhaphie *f*: staphylorrhaphy.
Staphylotomie *f*: staphylotomy, uvulotomy.
Star *m*: cataract; **grauer** ≈ grey cataract; **grüner** ≈ green cataract, glaucoma; **reifer** ≈ ripe cataract.
Stargardt-Syndrom *n*: Stargardt's disease, juvenile macular degeneration.
stark: vigorous, intense, strong.
Starre *f*: rigidity.
Starrkrampf *m*: tetanus.
Stase *f*: stasis.
Statin *n*: statin.
Station *f*: department, ward, station.
stationär: hospitalized, stationary.
statisch: static.
Statistik *f*: statistics.
statistisch: statistical.
Statur *f*: stature.
Status *m*: status, state, condition.
Status epilepticus *m*: status epilepticus, epileptic state.
Status lacunaris *m*: status lacunaris, lacunar state.
Status praesens *m*: present condition.
Staublungenkrankheit *f*: dust disease, pneumoconiosis.
Stauschlauch *m*: tourniquet.
Stauung *f*: congestion, stasis.
Stauungsaszites *m*: mechanical ascites.
Stauungsekzem *n*: stasis eczema, varicose eczema.
Stauungsgastritis *f*: congestive gastritis.
Stauungslunge *f*: cardiac lung, pulmonary congestion.
Stauungsniere *f*: engorged kidney.
Stauungspapille *f*: choked disk, papillary stasis.
Stavudin *n*: stavudine.
Steal-Effekt *m*: steal.
Stearinsäure *f*: stearic acid.
Steatom *n*: steatoma.
Steatorrhö *f*: steatorrhea; **idiopathische** ≈ idiopathic steatorrhea, celiac disease.
Steatose *f*: steatosis.
Stechapfelform *f*: crenated erythrocyte.
stechen: stitch, stab, prick.
Stechen *n*: stitch, stinging.
stechend: stinging, stabbing, terebrating.
Stechmücke *f*: mosquito, culex.
Steckbecken *n*: bedpan.
Stecker *m*: plug.
Steele-Richardson-Olszewski-Syndrom *n*: Steele-Richardson-Olszewski syndrome, progressive supranuclear palsy.
steif: stiff.
Steife *f*: rigidity, rigor.
Steigungswinkel *m*: angle of elevation.
Steiltyp *m*: vertical heart.
Stein *m*: stone, calculus.
Steinauflösung *f*: litholysis.
Steinleiden *n*: lithiasis.
Stein-Leventhal-Syndrom *n*: Stein-Leventhal syndrome, polycystic ovary syndrome.
Steinschnitt *m*: lithotomy, cystotomy.
Steinschnittlage *f*: lithotomy position.
Steißbein *n*: coccygeal bone.
Steißbeinfistel *f*: sacrococcygeal fistula.
Steißbeinzyste *f*: sacral cyst.
Steißlage *f*: breech presentation.
Steißwirbel *m*: coccygeal vertebra.
Stellreaktion *f*: placing reflex, equilibrium reaction.
Stellreflex *m*: static reflex, postural reflex.
Stellung *f*: position.
Stellungsnystagmus *m*: positional nystagmus, postural nystagmus.
Stenose *f*: stenosis, narrowing.
Stenoseatmung *f*: stenotic respiration, wheezing.
Stenosegeräusch *n*: stenotic murmur.
stenotisch: stenotic.
Stent *m*: stent; **urologischer** ≈ prostatic stent.
Stent-Abdruckmasse *f*: Stent's mass, Stent's dressing.
Steppergang *m*: steppage gait, footdrop gait.
Sterbebegleitung *f*: terminal care.
Sterbehilfe *f*: euthanasia.

sterben: die.
Sterberate *f*: mortality rate.
Sterbetafel *f*: life table.
Sterbeziffer *f*: death rate.
sterblich: mortal.
Sterblichkeit *f*: mortality.
Stereoagnosie *f*: stereoagnosis.
Stereoanästhesie *f*: stereoanesthesia.
Stereognosie *f*: stereognosis.
stereotaktisch: stereotactic.
steril: sterile, germ-free.
Sterilisation *f*: sterilization.
Sterilisator *m*: sterilizer.
Sterilität *f*: sterility.
Sterin *n*: sterol.
Sterkobilin *n*: stercobilin.
Sterkobilinogen *n*: stercobilinogen.
Sterkolith *m*: stercolith.
Sterkoralabszess *m*: stercoral abscess, fecal abscess.
Stern *m*: star.
sternal: sternal.
Sternalpunktion *f*: sternal puncture, sternal biopsy.
sternförmig: star shaped, stellate.
Sternum *n*: sternum, breast bone.
Sternzelle *f*: stellate cell, astrocyte.
Steroid *n*: steroid; **anaboles** ≈ anabolic steroid; **heterozyklisches** ≈ heterocyclic steroid; **ovarielles** ≈ ovarian steroid; **semisynthetisches** ≈ semisynthetic steroid; **testikuläres** ≈ testicular steroid.
Steroidakne *f*: steroid acne.
Steroidmyopathie *f*: steroid myopathy.
Sterol *n*: sterol.
Stethoskop *n*: stethoscope.
steuern: control, regulate.
Steuerung *f*: regulation, control.
Stibium *n*: antimony.
Stich *m*: stitch, sting.
Stichinzision *f*: stab incision, stab wound.
Stichprobe *f*: sample, quota sample.
Stichprobenerhebung *f*: sampling.
Stichwunde *f*: stab wound.
Stickoxidul *n*: nitrous oxide.
Stickstoff *m*: nitrogen, N.
Stickstoffmonoxid *n*: nitric oxide.
Stiel *m*: stalk, footplate, peduncle.
Stiellappen *m*: pedicle flap.
Stift *m*: pin, pen, stylus.
Stigma *n*: stigma.
Stigmatisierung *f*: stigmatization.
Stilbamidin *n*: stilbamidine.
Stilböstrol-Syndrom *n*: diethylstilbesterol syndrome, DES syndrome.
Stilett *n*: stilet, stylet.
Stillen *n*: breast-feeding.
Stillen nach Bedarf *n*: demand feeding.
Stilling-Türk-Duane-Syndrom *n*: Stilling-Türk-Duane syndrome, massive vitreous retraction.
Stillperiode *f*: lactation period.
Stillstand *m*: standstill, stagnancy, arrest.
Stimmband *n*: vocal cord.
Stimmbandknötchen: vocal nodules, Singer's nodes.
Stimme *f*: voice.
Stimmfremitus *m*: vocal fremitus.
Stimmlosigkeit *f*: voicelessness, aphonia.
Stimmritze *f*: glottis.
Stimmritzenkrampf *m*: laryngospasm, glottic spasm.
Stimmschall *m*: vocal resonance.
Stimmtraining *n*: voice training.
Stimmung *f*: mood, temper.
Stimmungslabilität *f*: lability of mood.
Stimulans *n*: stimulant, stimulator.
Stimulation *f*: stimulation, pacing.
Stimulator *m*: stimulator.
stimulieren: stimulate, excite.
Stimulus *m*: stimulus.
Stippchenepiphyse *f*: stippled epiphysis.
Stippchengallenblase *f*: stippled gallbladder.
Stirn *f*: forehead, brow.
Stirnhirnsyndrom *n*: frontal lobe syndrome.
Stirnhöhle *f*: frontal sinus.
Stirnhöhlenentzündung *f*: frontal sinusitis.
Stirnlage *f*: brow presentation.
St.-Louis-Enzephalitis *f*: St. Louis encephalitis.
Stock-Spielmeyer-Vogt-Krankheit *f*: Spielmeyer-Vogt disease, juvenile amaurotic idiocy.

Störung *f*: disorder, disturbance, dysfunction; **affektive** ≈ affective disorder, mood disorder; **akute paranoische** ≈ acute paranoic disorder; **atypische somatoforme** ≈ atypical somatoform disorder; **atypische vorgetäuschte** ≈ atypical factitious disorder; **dysthyme** ≈ depressive neurosis; **emotionale** ≈ emotional disturbance; **gnostische** ≈ gnostic disorder; **körperliche** ≈ physical disorder; **multifaktorielle** ≈ multifactorial disorder; **phobische** ≈ phobic disorder; **psychische** ≈ mental disorder; **psychosomatische** ≈ psychosomatic disorder; **schizoaffektive** ≈ schizoaffective disorder; **schizophrene** ≈ schizophrenic disorder; **somatoforme** ≈ somatoform disorder.

Stoff *m*: material, substance, matter.

Stoffabhängigkeit *f*: substance dependancy.

Stoffwechsel *m*: metabolism.

Stoffwechselgleichgewicht *n*: metabolic equilibrium.

Stoffwechselkoma *n*: metabolic coma.

Stoffwechselkrankheit *f*: metabolic disease.

Stoffwechselpsychose *f*: metabolic psychosis.

Stoffwechselstörung *f*: metabolic disorder.

Stoffwechselweg *m*: metabolic pathway.

Stokvis-Talma-Syndrom *n*: toxic cyanosis, enterogenous cyanosis.

Stomabeutel *m*: ileostomy bag.

Stomatitis *f*: stomatitis; **akute nekrotisierende** ≈ acute necrotizing stomatitis; **aphthöse** ≈ aphthous stomatitis; **vesikuläre** ≈ vesicular stomatitis.

Stomatitis gangraenosa *f*: gangrenous stomatitis.

Stomatitis scorbutica *f*: scorbutic stomatitis.

Stomatologie *f*: stomatology.

Stoßwellenlithotripsie, extrakorporale *f*: extracorporeal shock-wave lithotripsy.

stottern: stutter, stammer.

Stottern *n*: balbuties, stuttering.

Strabismus *m*: strabismus, squint.

Strabismus alternans *m*: binocular strabismus.

Strabismus concomitans *m*: concomitant strabismus.

Strabismus convergens *m*: convergent strabismus, esotropia.

Strabismus divergens *m*: divergent strabismus, exotropia.

Strabismus externus *m*: external strabismus, exotropia.

Strabismus non-concomitans *m*: noncomitant strabismus.

straff: tense, tight.

Strahl *m*: ray, beam.

Strahlen: rays; **aktinische** ≈ actinic rays; **harte** ≈ hard radiation; **ultraviolette** ≈ ultraviolet rays.

Strahlenbelastung *f*: radiation exposure, exposure dose.

Strahlenbiologie *f*: radiation biology, radiobiology.

Strahlendermatitis *f*: radiation dermatitis, x-ray dermatitis.

Strahlendosis *f*: radiation dose.

strahlendurchlässig: radiotransparent.

Strahlenexposition *f*: radiation exposure.

Strahlenfibrose *f*: radiation fibrosis.

strahleninduziert: radiation-induced.

Strahlenkarzinom *n*: radioepithelioma.

Strahlenkastration *f*: radiologic castration.

Strahlenkatarakt *f*: irradiation cataract.

Strahlenkörper *m*: ciliary body.

Strahlenkrankheit *f*: radiation sickness.

Strahlenschutz *m*: radiation protection.

Strahlentherapie *f*: radiation therapy, radiotherapy; **intrakavitäre** ≈ intracavitary radiation therapy; **lokale** ≈ local irradiation.

Strahlung *f*: radiation, radiatio; **elektromagnetische** ≈ electromagnetic radiation; **ionisierende** ≈ ionizing radiation; **kosmische** ≈ cosmic ra-

diation; **natürliche** ≈ natural radiation; **nichtionisierende** ≈ non-ionizing radiation.
Strang *m*: strand, cord.
Strangulierung *f*: strangulation.
Stratifikation *f*: stratification.
Stratum *n*: stratum, layer.
Streckapparat *m*: traction apparatus.
Streckbett *n*: orthopedic bed.
strecken: stretch, extend.
Strecken *n*: stretch, traction, extension.
Streckmittel *n*: adulterant, extender.
Streckmuskel *m*: extensor.
Streichmassage *f*: effleurage.
Streifen *m*: stripe, strip, stria, streak.
Streptokinase *f*: streptokinase.
Streptokokke *f*: streptococcus.
Streptokokkenangina *f*: streptoangina, septic sore throat.
Streptokokkeninfektion *f*: streptococcal infection.
Streptokokkenkarditis *f*: streptococcal carditis.
Streptolysin *n*: streptolysin.
Streptomycin *n*: streptomycin.
Streptomycinsulfat *n*: streptomycin sulfate.
Stress *m*: stress; **psychischer** ≈ mental stress.
Stressbewältigung *f*: stress management.
Stressinkontinenz *f*: urinary stress incontinence.
Streulinse *f*: dispersion lens.
Streustrahlung *f*: scatter radiation.
Streuung *f*: dispersion, scattering.
Stria *f*: stria, streak, stripe.
Stridor *m*: stridor; **exspiratorischer** ≈ expiratory stridor; **inspiratorischer** ≈ inspiratory stridor.
Stridor laryngealis *m*: laryngeal stridor.
Striktur *f*: stricture.
strömen: stream.
Strömung *f*: streaming, flow.
Strömungswiderstand *m*: circulatory resistance.
Strom *m*: current, electric power, stream.
Stromazelle *f*: stroma cell.
Strophanthidin *n*: strophanthidin.
Strophanthin *n*: strophanthin.
Strümpell-Leichtenstern-Enzephalitis *f*: Strümpell-Leichtenstern encephalitis, acute infantile hemiplegia.
Strümpell-Zeichen *n*: Strümpell sign, anterior tibial sign.
Struktur *f*: structure.
Strukturgen *n*: structural gene.
Struma *f*: struma, goiter; **diffuse toxische** ≈ toxic diffuse goiter; **eisenharte** ≈ iron-hard tumor; **endemische** ≈ endemic goiter; **familiäre** ≈ familial goiter; **kongenitale** ≈ congenital goiter; **myxödematöse** ≈ myxedematous goiter; **retrosternale** ≈ retrosternal goiter, retrosternal struma.
Strumektomie *f*: strumectomy.
Strychnin *n*: strychnine.
Studie *f*: study, trial; **klinische** ≈ clinical trial; **offene randomisierte** ≈ randomized open study; **prospektive** ≈ prospective study; **retrospektive** ≈ retrospective study, case-control study.
Studiendesign *n*: study design.
stützen: support.
Stützfaser *f*: sustentacular fiber.
Stützgewebe *n*: sustentacular tissue, supporting tissue.
Stützkorsett *n*: brace.
Stützmechanismus *m*: suspensory mechanism.
Stützreflex *m*: supporting reflex.
Stützstrumpf *m*: support stocking.
Stufenleiter der Analgetika *f*: analgesic ladder.
Stuhl *m*: stool, feces.
Stuhlgang *m*: bowel movement.
Stuhlinkontinenz *f*: fecal incontinence.
stumm: mute, silent.
stumpf: blunt, dull, obtuse.
Stumpf *m*: stump.
Stupidität *f*: stupidity.
Stupor *m*: stupor.
Sturge-Weber-Krabbe-Syndrom *n*: Sturge-Weber syndrome, cephalooculocutaneous telangiectasia.
Sturz *m*: fall, drop.
Sturzentleerung des Magens *f*: dumping syndrome.

Styptikum *n*: styptic.
subakut: subacute.
Subarachnoidalblutung *f*: subarachnoid hemorrhage.
Subarachnoidalraum *m*: subarachnoid space, meningeal space.
Subclavia *f*: subclavian artery.
subdural: subdural.
Subduralabszess *m*: subdural abscess.
Subduralblutung *f*: subdural hemorrhage, subdural bleeding.
Subduralhämatom *n*: subdural hematoma.
Subduralraum *m*: subdural space.
Suberose *f*: suberosis.
subfebril: subfebrile.
subikterisch: subicteric.
Subjekt *n*: subject.
subjektiv: subjective.
Subklaviaarteriitis *f*: Takayasu's arteritis, aortic arch syndrome.
Subklavikulargeräusch *n*: subclavicular murmur.
subklinisch: subclinical.
subkutan: subcutaneous, hypodermic.
Subkutannaht *f*: intradermal suture.
Subkutis *f*: subcutis, hypodermis.
sublingual: sublingual.
Sublingualtablette *f*: sublingual tablet.
Subluxation *f*: subluxation, incomplete dislocation.
submaxillar: submaxillary.
submeningeal: submeningeal.
submukös: submucosal.
Subokzipitalpunktion *f*: suboccipital puncture.
Subscriptio *f*: subscription.
Substantia *f*: substantia, substance.
Substanz *f*: substance, substantia, material, matter, agent; **basophile** ≈ basophil substance; **graue** ≈ grey substance, grey matter; **hyaline** ≈ hyaline substance; **interstitielle** ≈ interstitial substance; **mitogene** ≈ mitogen; **muskarinartige** ≈ muscarinic agent; **oberflächenaktive** ≈ surface-active agent; **positiv inotrop wirkende** ≈ positive cardiac inotropic agent; **weiße** ≈ white substance, white matter.
Substanzabhängigkeit *f*: substance dependency.
substituieren: substitute, replace.
Substitution *f*: substitution, repletion.
Substitutionsbehandlung *f*: substitution therapy.
Substrat *n*: substrate.
Subtraktionsangiographie *f*: subtraction angiography.
Subunit-Vakzine *f*: subunit vaccine.
Subvitalfaktor *m*: subvital factor.
Succubus *m*: succubus.
Succussio Hippocratis *f*: hippocratic succussion.
Sucht *f*: addiction, dependency.
Sucralfat *n*: sucralfate.
Sudeck-Syndrom *n*: Sudeck-Leriche syndrome, post-traumatic osteoporosis.
Süßstoff *m*: sweetener.
Suffizienz *f*: sufficiency.
Suggestibilität *f*: suggestibility.
Suggestionstherapie *f*: suggestion therapy.
Suizid *m*: suicide; **erweiterter** ≈ collective suicide.
Suizidalität *f*: suicidal potential.
Suizidversuch *m*: attempted suicide.
Sulbactam *n*: sulbactam.
Sulfacarbamid *n*: sulfacarbamide.
Sulfaguanidin *n*: sulfaguanidine.
Sulfamoxol *n*: sulfamoxole.
Sulfanblau *n*: sulfan blue.
Sulfanilamid *n*: sulfanilamide.
Sulfanilsäure *f*: sulfanilic acid.
Sulfasalazin *n*: sulfasalazine.
Sulfatid *n*: sulfatide.
Sulfid *n*: sulfide.
Sulfinpyrazon *n*: sulfinpyrazone.
Sulfinsäure *f*: sulfinic acid.
Sulfonamid *n*: sulfonamide.
Sulfonsäure *f*: sulfonic acid.
Sulfosalicylsäure *f*: sulfosalicylic acid.
Sulindac *n*: sulindac.
Suloctidil *n*: suloctidil.
Sulpirid *n*: sulpiride.
Sulproston *n*: sulprostone.
Sultamicillin *n*: sultamicillin.
Sultiam *n*: sultiame.
Sumatriptan *n*: sumatriptan.

Summationspotential *n*: summation potential.
Summen *n*: hum.
Superfekundation *f*: superfecundation.
Supination *f*: supination.
Suppositorium *n*: suppository.
Suppression *f*: suppression.
supprimieren: suppress.
Supraklavikulargrube *f*: supraclavicular fossa.
supranukleär: supranuclear.
supraorbital: supraorbital.
suprapontin: suprapontine.
Suramin *n*: suramin.
Suraminnatrium *n*: suramin sodium.
Surfactantfaktor *m*: pulmonary surfactant.
Suspension *f*: suspension.
Suspensorium *n*: suspensory.
Suxamethonium *n*: suxamethonium.
Suxamethoniumchlorid *n*: suxamethonium chloride.
Suxibuzon *n*: suxibuzone.
Sweet-Syndrom *n*: Sweet syndrome, acute febrile neutrophilic dermatosis.
Sydenham-Chorea *f*: Sydenham's chorea, infective chorea, juvenile chorea.
Sykose *f*: sycosis.
Symbiose *f*: symbiosis.
Sympathektomie *f*: sympathectomy.
Sympathikusausschaltung *f*: sympathetic block.
Sympathikuslähmung *f*: sympathetic paralysis.
sympathisch: sympathic, sympathetic.
Sympatholytikum *n*: sympatholytic.
Sympathomimetikum *n*: sympathomimetic.
Symphyse *f*: symphysis.
Symphysensprengung *f*: fracture-seperation of symphysis.
Symptom *n*: symptom, sign, phenomenon; **akzessorisches** ≈ accessory sign; **charakteristisches** ≈ characteristic symptom; **indirektes** ≈ indirect symptom; **klinisches** ≈ clinical sign; **körperliches** ≈ objective sign; **lokales** ≈ local sign; **neurologisches** ≈ neurological symptom, neurological manifestation; **objektives** ≈ objective sign; **pathognomonisches** ≈ pathognomonic symptom; **subjektives** ≈ subjective sign.
Symptomatik *f*: symptoms and signs; **klinische** ≈ clinical signs.
symptomatisch: symptomatic.
Symptomenkomplex *m*: symptom complex, syndrome.
Symptothermalmethode *f*: symptothermal method.
Synapse *f*: synapse.
Synarthrose *f*: synarthrosis.
Synchondrose *f*: synchondrosis.
Synchronie *f*: synchrony, synchronism.
Synchronisation *f*: synchronization.
Syndaktylie *f*: syndactyly, webbed fingers.
Syndrom *n*: syndrome; **adiposogenitales** ≈ adiposogenital syndrome; **adrenogenitales** ≈ adrenogenital syndrome; **akinetisch-abulisches** ≈ akinetic-abulic syndrome; **angio-osteo-hypertrophisches** ≈ angio-osteohypertrophy, Klippel-Trénaunay syndrome; **aplastisches** ≈ malignant thrombocytopenia; **atonisch-astatisches** ≈ atonia-astasia; **aurikulotemporales** ≈ auriculotemporal syndrome, Baillarger syndrome; **amentielles** ≈ acute hallucinatory confusion; **aurikulotemporales** ≈ gustatory hyperhidrosis, Frey syndrome; **depressives** ≈ depressive syndrome; **dienzephales** ≈ diencephalic syndrome; **extrapyramidales** ≈ extrapyramidal syndrome; **hepatorenales** ≈ hepatorenal syndrome; **hepatozerebrales** ≈ cerebrohepatorenal syndrome, Reye syndrome; **hirnorganisches** ≈ organic brain syndrome; **hyperkinetisches** ≈ hyperkinetic syndrome of childhood; **kardioauditives** ≈ cardioauditory syndrome, Jervell-Lange-Nielsen syndrome; **myelodysplastisches** ≈ dysmyelopoietic syndrome; **neuroleptisches** ≈ neuroleptic malignant syndrome; **mandibulo-okulo-faziales** ≈ Hallermann-Streiff syndrome;

S

nephrotisches ≈ nephrotic syndrome; **okuloaurikuläres** ≈ oculoauriculovertebral syndrome, Goldenhar syndrome; **okulodentodigitales** ≈ oculodentidigital syndrome, ODD syndrome; **okuloglanduläres** ≈ Parinaud's oculoglandular syndrome; **okulopupilläres** ≈ Horner syndrome; **okulovertebrales** ≈ oculovertebral syndrome, Weyers-Thier syndrome; **okulozerebrorenales** ≈ oculocerebrorenal syndrome, Lowe syndrome; **olfaktogenitales** ≈ olfactory genital dysplasia, Kallmann syndrome; **paraneoplastisches** ≈ paraneoplastic syndrome; **prämenstruelles** ≈ premenstrual syndrome; **pseudomyasthenisches** ≈ Lambert-Eaton syndrome; **schweres akutes respiratorisches** ≈ severe acute respiratory syndrom, SARS; **surdokardiales** ≈ surdocardiac syndrome, Jervell-Lange-Nielsen syndrome; **zentrales anticholinerges** ≈ central anticholinergic syndrome; **zerebrohepatorenales** ≈ cerebrohepatorenal syndrome, Zellweger syndrome.

Syndrom der blauen Skleren *n*: blue sclera syndrome, Lobstein syndrome.

Syndrom der blinden Schlinge *n*: blind loop syndrome.

Syndrom der eingedickten Galle *n*: inspissated bile syndrome.

Syndrom der fetofetalen Bluttransfusion *n*: placental transfusion syndrome.

Syndrom der inappropriaten ADH-Sekretion *n*: syndrome of inappropriate antidiuretic hormone secretion, SIADH.

Syndrom der kaudalen Regression *n*: caudal dysplasia syndrome.

Syndrom der leeren Sella *n*: empty sella syndrome.

Syndrom der zuführenden Schlinge *n*: afferent loop syndrome.

Syndrom des irritablen Darms *n*: irritable bowel syndrome, irritable colon syndrome.

Syndrom des plötzlichen Kindstods *n*: sudden infant death syndrome, SIDS.

Syndrom des toxischen Schocks *n*: toxic shock syndrome.

Synechie *f*: synechia.

Synergie *f*: synergy.

Synergist *m*: synergist.

Synklitismus *m*: synclitism.

Synkope *f*: syncope; **orthostatische** ≈ orthostatic syncope, postural syncope; **vasovagale** ≈ vasovagal syncope.

Synophthalmie *f*: synophthalmia.

Synostose *f*: synostosis.

Synovektomie *f*: synovectomy.

Synovia *f*: synovia, synovial fluid.

synovial: synovial.

Synovialmembran *f*: synovial membrane.

Synovialzotte *f*: synovial villus.

Synovialzyste *f*: synovial cyst.

Synovitis *f*: synovitis; **seröse** ≈ serous synovitis.

Synovitis sicca *f*: synovitis sicca, dry synovitis.

Synthese *f*: synthesis.

synthetisch: synthetic.

Synzym *n*: synzyme.

Synzytienbildung *f*: syncytia formation.

Synzytiumzelle *f*: syncytial cell.

Syphilid *n*: syphilid.

Syphilis *f*: syphilis, lues; **endemische** ≈ endemic syphilis, bejel; **kongenitale** ≈ congenital syphilis; **primäre** ≈ primary syphilis; **sekundäre** ≈ secondary syphilis; **tertiäre** ≈ tertiary syphilis; **zerebrospinale** ≈ cerebrospinal syphilis.

syphilitisch: syphilitic, luetic.

Syringomyelie *f*: syringomyelia.

Syringotomie *f*: syringotomy.

Syrosingopin *n*: syrosingopine.

System *n*: system; **aufsteigendes retikuläres aktivierendes** ≈ ascending reticular activating system, ARAS; **gastrointestinales therapeutisches** ≈ enteric-coated tablet; **hämatopoetisches** ≈ hematopoietic system; **limbisches** ≈ limbic system; **lymphatisches** ≈ lymphatic system; **metrisches** ≈ metric system; **retikuloendotheliales** ≈ reticuloendothelial system.

Systematik *f*: systematics.
Systemerkrankung *f*: systemic disease.
systemisch: systemic.
Systemmykose *f*: systemic mycosis.
Systole *f*: systole.
Systolikum *n*: systolic murmur.
systolisch: systolic.
Syzygiologie *f*: syzygiology.
Szintigraphie *f*: scintigraphy.
Szintillationsaudioradiographie *f*: scintillation autoradiography.
szirrhös: scirrhous.
Szirrhus *m*: scirrhus.

T

T Abk. 1. **Temperatur** *f*; 2. **Translokation** *f*; 3. **Tritium** *n*: 1. temperature, temp, T; 2. translocation; 3. tritium, T.
Tabakbeutelnaht *f*: tobacco bag suture.
Tabakmosaikvirus *n*: tabac mosaic virus.
Tabelle *f*: chart, table.
Tabes *f*: tabes.
Tabes dorsalis *f*: tabes dorsalis, tabetic neurosyphilis.
tabisch: tabetic, tabic.
Tablette *f*: tablet.
Tacalcitol *n*: tacalcitol.
Tachyarrhythmie *f*: tachyarrhythmia.
Tachykardie *f*: tachycardia, tachyrhythmia; **digitalisinduzierte** ≈ digitalis-induced tachycardia; **ektope** ≈ ectopic tachycardia; **heterotope** ≈ supranodal tachycardia; **orthostatische** ≈ orthostatic tachycardia; **paroxysmale** ≈ paroxysmal tachycardia, Bouveret's disease; **supraventrikuläre** ≈ supraventricular tachycardia; **ventrikuläre** ≈ ventricular tachycardia.
Tacrin *n*: tacrine.
Tacrolimus *m*: tacrolimus.
Tadalafil *n*: tadalafil.
täglich: daily, quotidian.
Tänie *f*: taenia.
Tätowierung *f*: tattoo, tattooing.
Täuschung *f*: delusion, illusion; **optische** ≈ optical illusion.
Tag *m*: day.
Tagesbedarf *m*: daily requirement.
Tagesdosis *f*: daily dose.
Tagesklinik *f*: day hospital, day-care clinic.
Tagespflege *f*: day care.
Tagesschwankung *f*: diurnal variation.
Tagessehen *n*: photopic vision.
Taille *f*: waist.
Takahara-Krankheit *f*: Takahara's disease, acatalasia.
Takayasu-Krankheit *f*: Takayasu's arteritis, aortic arch syndrome.
taktil: tactile.
Talgdrüse *f*: sebaceous gland.
Talgdrüsenadenom *n*: sebaceous adenoma.
Talgdrüsenkarzinom *n*: sebaceous carcinoma.
Talgdrüsenzyste *f*: sebaceous cyst.
talgig: sebaceous.
Talgzyste *f*: sebaceous cyst.
Talinolol *n*: talinolol.
Talus *m*: talus, ankle bone.
Tamoxifen *n*: tamoxifen.
Tampon *m*: tampon.
Tamponade *f*: tamponade.
tamponieren: tamponade.
Tamponsyndrom *n*: toxic shock syndrome.
Tamsulosin *n*: tamsulosin.
Tanner-Stadien: Tanner stages.
Tannin *n*: tannin.
Tanninsäure *f*: tannic acid.
Tapetenschichtzelle *f*: tapetal cell.
tapetoretinal: tapetoretinal.
Tapirlippenzeichen *n*: tapir snout sign.
tarsal: tarsal.
Tarsalgie *f*: tarsalgia.
Tarsaltunnelsyndrom *n*: tarsal tunnel syndrome.
Tarsorrhaphie *f*: tarsorrhaphy, blepharorrhaphy.
Tarsus *m*: tarsus.
Tarsusresektion *f*: tarsectomy.
Tartrat *n*: tartrate.

Tasche *f*: pocket, recess, pouch, bursa, sac.
Taschenmesserphänomen *n*: clasp-knife phenomenon.
Tasonermin *n*: tasonermin.
Tastblindheit *f*: tactile agnosia, astereognosis.
Tasteindruck *m*: tactile image.
Tastfeld *n*: tactile field.
Tastkörperchen *n*: tactile corpuscle.
Tastpunkt *m*: touch spot.
Tastrezeptor *m*: tactile receptor.
Tastsinn *m*: touch sensibility, tactile sensation; **stereognostischer** ≈ stereognostic sense.
Tastunterscheidung *f*: tactile discrimination.
Tastwahrnehmung *f*: touch perception, tactile perception.
taub: deaf, numb.
Taubheit *f*: deafness, surdity; **heredodegenerative** ≈ heredodegenerative deafness; **kochleäre** ≈ cochlear deafness; **kongenitale** ≈ congenital deafness; **sensorineuronale** ≈ sensorineural hearing loss; **zentrale** ≈ central deafness, cortical deafness.
Taubheitsgefühl *n*: numbness.
taubstumm: deaf-mute, deaf and dumb.
Taubstummensprache *f*: deaf-and-dumb language.
Taucherohr *n*: divers' ear.
taumeln: stagger, reel.
Taurocholat *n*: taurocholate.
Taurocholsäure *f*: taurocholic acid.
Tawara-Knoten *m*: His-Tawara node.
Taxonomie *f*: taxonomy.
Tay-Sachs-Syndrom *n*: Tay-Sachs disease, infantile amaurotic familial idiocy.
Tazaroten *n*: tazarotene.
Tazobactam *n*: tazobactam.
Technik *f*: technique, technology.
Teelöffel *m*: teaspoon.
Teerakne *f*: tar acne.
Teerstuhl *m*: tarry stool.
Tegafur *n*: tegafur.
Tegaserod *n*: tegaserod.
Teichoinsäure *f*: teichoic acid.
Teichopsie *f*: teichopsia.
Teicoplanin *n*: teicoplanin.
Teil *m*: part, portion.
Teilamputation *f*: partial amputation.
Teilchen *n*: particle.
Teilganzes *n*: sub-whole.
Teilnahmslosigkeit *f*: listlessness.
Teilung *f*: division, fission, partition, cleavage; **enzymatische** ≈ enzymatic cleavage; **meroblastische** ≈ meroblastic cleavage; **ungleiche** ≈ unequal cleavage; **unvollständige** ≈ partial segmentation; **vollständige** ≈ complete segmentation.
Telbivudin *n*: telbivudine.
Teleangiektasie *f*: telangiectasia; **hereditäre** ≈ hereditary hemorrhagic telangiectasia, Osler-Rendu-Weber syndrome.
Telekobalttherapie *f*: telecobalt therapy.
Telepathie *f*: telepathy.
Telephonberatung *f*: telephone counseling.
Telithromycin *n*: telithromycin.
Tellurschädigung *f*: tellurism.
Telmisartan *n*: telmisartan.
Temazepam *n*: temazepam.
Temocapril *n*: temocapril.
Temozolomid *n*: temozolomide.
Temperament *n*: temperament.
Temperatur *f*: temperature, fever; **erhöhte** ≈ elevated temperature; **rektale** ≈ rectal temperature; **septische** ≈ septic fever.
temperaturabhängig: temperature-dependent.
Temperaturanstieg *m*: temperature increase.
Temperaturmethode *f*: temperature method.
Temperatursinn *m*: temperature sense.
temperent: temperate.
temporär: temporary.
temporal: temporal.
Temporalarterienarteriitis *f*: temporal arteritis, Horton's arteritis.
Temporallappen *m*: temporal lobe.
Temporallappenepilepsie *f*: temporal epilepsy, psychomotor epilepsy.
Temporomandibularsyndrom *n*: temporomandibular syndrome.
Tenalgie *f*: tendon pain.

Tendenz *f*: tendency, bias.
Tendinitis *f*: tendinitis, tendonitis.
Tendoplastik *f*: tendoplasty, tenoplasty.
Tendovaginitis *f*: tendovaginitis, tenosynovitis; **stenosierende** ≈ stenosing tenosynovitis, Quervain syndrome.
Tenecteplase *f*: tenecteplase.
Tenesmus *m*: tenesmus.
Teniposid *n*: teniposide.
Tennisellenbogen *m*: tennis elbow.
Tenofovirdisoproxil *n*: tenofovir disoproxil.
Tenorrhaphie *f*: tenorrhaphy, tenosuture.
Tenosynovitis *f*: tenosynovitis, tendovaginitis.
Tenotomie *f*: tenotomy; **offene** ≈ open tenotomy; **Z-förmige** ≈ graduated tenotomy.
Tentoriumshernie *f*: tentorial hernia.
Teratoblastom *n*: teratoblastoma.
teratogen: teratogenic.
Teratokarzinom *n*: teratocarcinoma.
Teratom *n*: teratoma, teratoid tumor.
Terazosin *n*: terazosin.
Terbinafin *n*: terbinafine.
Terbutalin *n*: terbutaline.
Terconazol *n*: terconazole.
Terfenadin *n*: terfenadine.
Terizidon *n*: terizidone.
Termin *m*: term, date.
terminal: terminal, terminad.
Terminalhaar *n*: terminal hair.
Terminologie *f*: terminology.
Tertatolol *n*: tertatolol.
tertiär: tertiary.
Tertiärfollikel *m*: tertiary follicle.
Tertiärprävention *f*: tertiary prevention.
Tertiärsyphilis *f*: tertiary syphilis, late syphilis.
Tertiana *f*: tertian.
Test *m*: test; **diagnostischer** ≈ diagnostic test; **psychometrischer** ≈ psychometric test; **psychomotorischer** ≈ psychomotor test.
Testen *n*: testing.
Testergebnis *n*: test result.
testikulär: testicular.
Testlösung *f*: test solution.
Testolacton *n*: testolactone.
Testosteron *n*: testosterone.
Testosteronphenylpropionat *n*: testosterone phenylpropionate.
Teststreifen *m*: test strip, dipstick.
Testwert *m*: test value.
Tetanie *f*: tetany; **hypokalzämische** ≈ hypocalcemic tetany; **parathyreogene** ≈ parathyroid tetany, hypoparathyroid tetany.
Tetanisierung *f*: tetanization.
Tetanus *m*: tetanus.
Tetanusantitoxin *n*: tetanus antitoxin, antitetanus serum.
Tetanusbazillus *m*: tetanus bacillus, Clostridium tetani.
Tetanusimpfstoff *m*: tetanus vaccine.
Tetraamelie *f*: tetra-amelia, complete amelia.
Tetrabenazin *n*: tetrabenazine.
Tetraborsäure *f*: tetraboric acid, pyroboric acid.
Tetracain *n*: tetracaine.
Tetrachlorethylen *n*: tetrachloroethylene.
Tetrachlorkohlenstoff *m*: carbon tetrachloride.
Tetracosansäure *f*: tetracosanic acid.
Tetracyclin *n*: tetracycline.
Tetradaktylie *f*: tetradactyly.
Tetrahydrofolsäure *f*: tetrahydrofolic acid.
Tetraplegie *f*: quadriplegia, tetraplegia.
Tetrofosmin *n*: tetrofosmin.
Tetroxoprim *n*: tetroxoprim.
Thalamotomie *f*: thalamotomy.
Thalamus *m*: thalamus.
Thalamusausschaltung *f*: thalamectomy.
Thalamusschmerz *m*: thalamic pain.
Thalamussyndrom *n*: thalamic syndrome, Déjerine-Roussy syndrome.
Thalassaemia major *f*: thalassemia major, homozygous thalassemia, Cooley's anemia.
Thalassaemia minor *f*: thalassemia minor, heterozygous thalassemia, Greppi-Micheli anemia.
Thalassämie *f*: thalassemia.
α-Thalassämie *f*: α-thalassemia, hemoglobin H disease.

β-Thalassämie *f*: β-thalassemia, Mediterranean disease.
Thalassotherapie *f*: thalassotherapy.
Thalidomid *n*: thalidomide.
Thalidomidembryopathie *f*: thalidomide syndrome.
Thallium *n*: thallium.
Thekazelltumor *m*: theca cell tumor, thecoma.
Theobromin *n*: theobromine.
Theophyllin *n*: theophylline.
Theophyllin-Ethylendiamin *n*: theophylline ethylendiamine.
Therapeut *m*: therapist.
therapeutisch: therapeutic, therapeutical.
Therapie *f*: therapy, treatment; **adjuvante** ≈ adjuvant therapy, supportive therapy; **immunsuppressive** ≈ immunosuppressive therapy; **kausale** ≈ causal treatment; **klientenzentrierte** ≈ client-centered therapy; **kognitive** ≈ cognitive therapy; **konservative** ≈ conservative treatment; **medikamentöse** ≈ drug therapy; **physikalische** ≈ physical therapy, physiatrics; **psychoanalytische** ≈ psychoanalytic therapy; **symptomatische** ≈ symptomatic treatment; **unkonventionelle** ≈ unconventional therapy.
Therapieplan *m*: regimen.
Thermästhesie *f*: thermesthesia, temperature perception.
Thermodilutionsverfahren *n*: thermodilution technique.
Thermographie *f*: thermography.
Thermokaustik *f*: thermocautery.
thermolabil: thermolabile.
Thermometer *n*: thermometer.
thermophil: thermophilic.
Thermoregulation *f*: thermoregulation.
thermostabil: thermostable.
Thermostat *m*: thermostat.
Thesaurismose *f*: thesaurismosis, storage disease.
Thevetin *n*: thevetin.
Thiabendazol *n*: thiabendazole.
Thiamazol *n*: thiamazole, methimazole.
Thiambutosin *n*: thiambutosine.
Thiamin *n*: thiamin, vitamin B_1.
Thiamphenicol *n*: thiamphenicol.
Thiobarbitursäure *f*: thiobarbituric acid.
Thioctansäure *f*: thioctic acid, lipoic acid.
Thiomilchsäure *f*: thiolactic acid.
Thiopental-Natrium *n*: thiopental sodium.
Thioschwefelsäure *f*: thiosulfuric acid.
Thiotepa *n*: thiotepa.
Thiouracil *n*: thiouracil.
Thiozyansäure *f*: thiocyanic acid.
thorakal: thoracic, thoracal.
Thorakalatmung *f*: thoracic respiration.
thorakoabdominal: thoracoabdominal.
Thorakoplastik *f*: thoracoplasty.
Thorakoskopie *f*: thoracoscopy.
Thorakotomie *f*: thoracotomy.
Thorakozentese *f*: thoracocentesis.
Thorax *m*: thorax, chest; **abgeflachter** ≈ flat chest; **fassförmiger** ≈ barrel-shaped thorax; **instabiler** ≈ flail chest, stove-in chest; **knöcherner** ≈ bony thorax.
Thoraxapertur *f*: thoracic outlet.
Thoraxaufnahme *f*: thoracic radiography.
Thoraxchirurgie *f*: thoracic surgery.
Thoraxdystrophie, asphyxierende *f*: asphyxating thoracic dystrophy, Jeune syndrome.
Thoraxkontusion *f*: chest contusion.
Thorn-Syndrom *n*: Thorn syndrome, salt-depletion syndrome.
Threonin *n*: threonine.
Thrombangitis obliterans *f*: thromboangiitis obliterans, Buerger's disease.
Thrombangitis *f*: thromboangiitis.
Thrombarteriitis *f*: thromboarteritis.
Thrombektomie *f*: thrombectomy.
Thrombelastographie *f*: thrombelastography.
Thrombin *n*: thrombin.
Thromboembolie *f*: thromboembolism.
Thrombokinase *f*: thrombokinase.
thrombolytisch: thrombolytic.

Thrombopenie *f*: thrombopenia, thrombocytopenia.
Thrombophlebitis *f*: thrombophlebitis.
Thrombophlebitis migrans *f*: migratory thrombophlebitis.
Thrombophlebitis obliterans *f*: obliterating endarteritis.
Thrombophlebitis profunda *f*: deep thrombophlebitis.
Thromboplastin *n*: thromboplastin.
Thromboplastinzeit *f*: thromboplastin time; **partielle** ≈ partial thromboplastin time, PTT.
Thrombose *f*: thrombosis; **tiefe** ≈ deep thrombosis.
Thrombosis migrans *f*: migrating thrombosis.
Thrombozyt *m*: thrombocyte, blood platelet.
Thrombozytenaggregation *f*: thrombocyte aggregation.
Thrombozytenzählung *f*: platelet count.
Thrombozytenzahl *f*: thrombocyte count, platelet count.
Thrombozythämie *f*: thrombocythemia.
Thrombozytopenie *f*: thrombocytopenia, thrombopeny.
Thrombozytose *f*: thrombocytosis; **essentielle** ≈ essential thrombocytosis; **idiopathische** ≈ idiopathic thrombocythemia.
Thrombus *m*: thrombus, blood clot; **gemischter** ≈ mixed thrombus; **hyaliner** ≈ hyaline thrombus; **infizierter** ≈ infected thrombus; **kanalisierter** ≈ canalized thrombus; **organisierter** ≈ organized thrombus; **roter** ≈ red thrombus; **septischer** ≈ septic thrombus; **wandständiger** ≈ lateral thrombus; **weißer** ≈ white thrombus.
Thymektomie *f*: thymectomy.
Thymianöl *n*: thyme oil.
Thymidin *n*: thymidine.
Thymin *n*: thymine, Thy.
Thyminsäure *f*: thyminic acid.
Thymol *n*: thymol.
Thymom *n*: thymoma.
Thymozyt *m*: thymocyte.
Thymus *m*: thymus, thymus gland.
Thymusaplasie *f*: thymic aplasia.
Thymusfaktor *m*: thymic hormone.
Thymushormon *n*: thymic hormone.
Thymushyperplasie *f*: thymic hyperplasia.
Thymuszyste *f*: thymic cyst.
Thyreoglobulin *n*: thyroglobulin.
thyreoglossal: thyroglossal.
Thyreoglossuszyste *f*: thyroglossal cyst.
thyreoidal: thyroidal.
Thyreoidea *f*: thyroid, thyroid gland.
Thyreoidektomie *f*: thyroidectomy.
Thyreoiditis *f*: thyroiditis; **akute eitrige** ≈ acute suppurative thyroiditis; **chronisch-atrophische** ≈ chronic atrophic thyroiditis; **fokale lymphozytäre** ≈ focal lymphocytic thyroiditis.
thyreostatisch: antithyroid.
Thyreotoxikose *f*: thyrotoxicosis.
thyreotrop: thyrotropic.
Thyronin *n*: thyronine.
Thyrotrophin *n*: thyrotrophin.
Thyrotropin *n*: thyrotropin.
Thyroxin *n*: thyroxine, T_4.
Tiabendazol *n*: tiabendazole.
Tiagabin *n*: tiagabine.
Tiaprid *n*: tiapride.
Tiaprofensäure *f*: tiaprofenic acid.
Tibia *f*: tibia, shinbone.
Tibiafraktur *f*: shinbone fracture.
Tibia-Kompartment-Syndrom *n*: anterior tibial syndrome.
Tibiakopfnekrose, aseptische *f*: Osgood Schlatter disease, rugby knee.
tibial: tibial.
Tibialisphänomen *n*: tibialis sign, Strümpell sign.
Tibiofibulargelenk *n*: tibiofibular joint.
Tibolon *n*: tibolone.
Tic *m*: tic, mimic convulsion.
Ticarcillin *n*: ticarcillin.
Ticlopidin *n*: ticlopidine.
Ticstörung *f*: tic disorder.
Tiefendosis *f*: depth dose.
Tiefenreflex *m*: deep reflex.
Tiefenschärfe *f*: focal depth.
Tiefensensibilität *f*: depth sensibility, deep sensitivity.
Tiefschlaf *m*: deep sleep.

Tierfellnävus *m*: hairy nevus.
Tiermodell *n*: animal model.
Tierphobie *f*: zoophobia.
Tietze-Syndrom *n*: Tietze's disease, costochondritis.
Tigerherz *n*: tiger heart.
Tiglinsäure *f*: tiglic acid.
Tigrolyse *f*: tigrolysis.
Tiludronsäure *f*: tiludronic acid.
Timolol *n*: timolol.
Tinidazol *n*: tinidazole.
Tinktur *f*: tincture; **aromatische** ≈ aromatic tincture; **wässrige** ≈ aqueous tincture.
Tinnitus *m*: tinnitus.
Tinzaparin *n*: tinzaparin.
Tioconazol *n*: tioconazole.
Tioguanin *n*: tioguanine.
Tiopronin *n*: tiopronin.
Tiotixen *n*: tiotixene.
Tiotropiumbromid *n*: tiotropium bromide.
Tioxolon *n*: tioxolone.
Tipranavir *n*: tipranavir.
Tiracizin *n*: tiracizine.
Tirofiban *n*: tirofiban.
Titer *m*: titer.
Titration *f*: titration.
Tixocortol *n*: tixocortol.
Tizanidin *n*: tizanidine.
T-Lymphozyt *m*: thymus-derived lymphocyte, T lymphocyte.
Tobramycin *n*: tobramycin.
Tobsucht *f*: frenzy, mania.
Tocainid *n*: tocainide.
Tochterzelle *f*: daughter cell.
Tochterzyste *f*: secondary cyst.
Tocopherol *n*: tocopherol.
Tod *m*: death, exitus; **gewaltsamer** ≈ violent death; **plötzlicher** ≈ sudden death; **schwarzer** ≈ black death, black plague; **sofortiger** ≈ instantaneous death.
Todd-Paralyse *f*: Todd's paralysis, postepileptic paralysis.
Todesbescheinigung *f*: death certificate.
Todesursache *f*: cause of death.
Todeszeichen: signs of death.
tödlich: deadly.
töten: kill.
Toilettentraining *n*: toilet training.
Tokographie *f*: tocography.
Tokolyse *f*: tocolysis.
Tolazamid *n*: tolazamide.
Tolbutamid *n*: tolbutamide.
Tolcapon *n*: tolcapone.
Tolciclat *n*: tolciclate.
tolerabel: tolerable.
Toleranz *f*: tolerance, allowable variation.
Toleranzbereich *m*: tolerance range.
Toleranzdosis *f*: tolerance dose.
Toleranztest *m*: tolerance test.
tolerieren: tolerate.
Toliprolol *n*: toliprolol.
Tollkirsche *f*: belladonna, deadly nightshade.
Tollwut *f*: rabies, lyssa; **paralytische** ≈ paralytic rabies.
Tollwutimpfstoff *m*: antirabies vaccine.
Tollwutschutzimpfung *f*: antirabies vaccination.
Tollwutserum *n*: antirabies serum.
Tolmetin *n*: tolmetin.
Tolosa-Hunt-Syndrom *n*: Tolosa-Hunt syndrome, painful ophthalmoplegia.
Tolterodin *n*: tolterodine.
Tomographie *f*: tomography.
Ton *m*: tone, sound, murmur.
Tonhöhenunterscheidung *f*: tonal discrimination.
tonisch: tonic.
tonisch-klonisch: tonic-clonic.
Tonographie *f*: tonography.
Tonometrie *f*: tonometry.
Tonsille *f*: tonsil, tonsilla.
Tonsillektomie *f*: tonsillectomy.
Tonsillenabszess *m*: abscessed tonsil.
Tonsillitis *f*: tonsillitis; **diphtherische** ≈ diphtheritic tonsillitis; **eitrige** ≈ suppurative tonsillitis; **follikuläre** ≈ follicular tonsillitis; **phlegmonöse** ≈ parenchymatous tonsillitis; **ulzeromembranöse** ≈ ulceromembraneous tonsillitis.
Tonsillitis lacunaris *f*: lacunar tonsillitis.
Tonsillotomie *f*: tonsillotomy.
Tonus *m*: tone, tonus; **erhöhter** ≈ hypertonus, hypertonia; **erniedrigter** ≈ hypotonia.

Tonverschmelzung *f*: tonal fusion.
Tophus *m*: tophus, gouty node.
Topiramat *n*: topiramate.
topisch: topical.
Topographie *f*: topography.
Topotecan *n*: topothecan.
Torasemid *n*: torasemide.
Toremifen *n*: toremifene.
Tornisterlähmung *f*: knapsack paralysis.
Torpidität *f*: torpidity.
Torpor *m*: torpor.
Torsion *f*: torsion.
Torsionsdeformität *f*: torsional deformity.
Torsionsdystonie *f*: torsion dystonia, Oppenheim-Ziehen syndrome.
Torsionsfraktur *f*: torsion fracture.
Tortikollis *m*: torticollis, wryneck.
tot: dead.
Totalendoprothese *f*: total prosthetic replacement.
Totalexstirpation *f*: total removal, complete removal.
Totalkapazität *f*: total lung capacity.
Totenschein *m*: death certificate.
Totenstarre *f*: cadaveric rigidity.
totgeboren: stillborn.
Totgeburt *f*: stillbirth, dead birth.
Totraum *m*: dead space.
Tourette-Syndrom *n*: Gilles de la Tourette syndrome, compulsive tic.
Tourniquet *m*: tourniquet.
Tourniquet-Presse *f*: Spanish windlass, torcular tourniquet.
Toxämie *f*: toxemia; **präeklamptische** ≈ preeclamptic toxemia.
Toxikologie *f*: toxicology.
Toxikose *f*: toxicosis.
Toxin *n*: toxin.
toxisch: toxic.
Toxizität *f*: toxicity.
Toxoid *n*: toxoid.
Toxoplasmose *f*: toxoplasmosis.
Toxoplasmose-Enzephalitis *f*: toxoplasmic encephalitis.
Toxoplasmosezyste *f*: toxoplasmic cyst.
Trabekelbildung *f*: trabeculation.
Trabekelblase *f*: trabeculated bladder.
Trachea *f*: trachea, windpipe.
Trachealkanüle *f*: tracheostomy tube.
Trachealstenose *f*: tracheal stenosis.
Trachealtubus *m*: tracheal tube.
Tracheitis *f*: tracheitis.
Tracheobronchitis *f*: tracheobronchitis.
Tracheostomie *f*: tracheostomy.
Tracheotomie *f*: tracheotomy.
Trachom *n*: trachoma, trachomatous conjunctivitis, Egyptian conjunctivitis.
Trachomeinschlusskörperchen-Konjunktivitis *f*: trachoma inclusion conjunctivitis, TRIC.
Tractus *m*: tractus, tract.
träge: inert, slow.
Träger *m*: carrier, vector, vehicle; **gesunder** ≈ healthy carrier.
Trägheit *f*: inaction, inertia, slowness.
Tränenbein *n*: lacrimal bone.
Tränenbildung *f*: lacrimation, production of tears.
Tränendrüse *f*: lacrimal gland.
Tränengang *m*: lacrimal duct, tear duct.
Tränengangsfistel *f*: lacrimal fistula.
Tränengangsonde *f*: lacrimal probe.
Tränensack *m*: lacrimal sac.
Trage *f*: litter, stretcher.
Tragusdruckschmerz *m*: tragus pain.
Tragzeit *f*: gestational period.
Training *n*: training; **autogenes** ≈ autogenic training.
Trakt *m*: tract, tractus.
Traktion *f*: traction.
Traktotomie *f*: tractotomy.
Tramadol *n*: tramadol.
Tramazolin *n*: tramazoline.
Trance *f*: trance.
Trandolapril *n*: trandolapril.
Tranexamsäure *f*: tranexamic acid.
Tranquilizer *m*: tranquilizer.
transabdominal: transabdominal.
Transaktionsanalyse *f*: transactional analysis.
Transaminase *f*: transaminase.
transdermal: transdermic, transdermal.
Transfektion *f*: transfection.
Transformationszone *f*: transformation zone.
Transfusion *f*: transfusion, blood

transfusion; **autologe** ≈ autologous blood transfusion; **fetofetale** ≈ fetofetal transfusion; **fetomaternale** ≈ fetomaternal transfusion; **gerichtete** ≈ directed transfusion; **indirekte** ≈ indirect transfusion; **intraarterielle** ≈ intra-arterial transfusion.
Transfusionshepatitis *f*: transfusion hepatitis, post-transfusion hepatitis.
transgen: transgenic.
transitorisch: transitory, transitional.
trans-Konfiguration *f*: trans configuration.
Transkriptase *f*: transcriptase; **reverse** ≈ reverse transcriptase, RT.
Transkription *f*: transcription.
Translokation *f*: translocation.
Transmission *f*: transmission; **maternofetale** ≈ maternofetal transmission.
Transmissionselektronenmikroskopie *f*: transmission electron microscopy.
transmural: transmural.
transnasal: transnasal.
Transpiration *f*: transpiration.
Transplantat *n*: transplant, graft; **allogenes** ≈ allogeneic graft; **alloplastisches** ≈ alloplast graft; **autogenes** ≈ autogenous graft; **autologes** ≈ autograft; **heterotopes** ≈ heterotopic graft; **orthotopes** ≈ orthotopic graft; **syngenes** ≈ syngeneic graft; **xenogenes** ≈ xenogeneic graft.
Transplantatempfänger *m*: transplant recepient.
Transplantation *f*: transplantation.
transplantieren: graft, transplant.
transplazentar: transplacental.
Transposition *f*: transposition.
Transposition der großen Arterien *f*: transposition of the arterial trunk.
Transsexualismus *m*: transsexualism.
Transsudat *n*: transudate.
transversal: transverse, transversal.
Transversalbruch *m*: transverse fracture.
Transversalebene *f*: transverse plane.
Transversalwelle *f*: transverse wave.
Transvestismus *m*: transvestism.
Tranylcypromin *n*: tranylcypromine.
trapezförmig: trapeziform, trapezoid.
Trapezius *m*: trapezius muscle.
Traubenaneurysma *n*: cirsoid aneurysm, racemose aneurysm.
traubenartig: cirsoid, racemose, grapelike.
Trauer *f*: grief.
Trauerarbeit *f*: work of grief, process of mourning.
Trauerreaktion *f*: grief reaction.
Traum *m*: dream.
Trauma *n*: trauma, injury; **psychisches** ≈ psychic trauma; **spinales** ≈ spinal trauma; **stumpfes** ≈ blunt injury.
traumatisch: traumatic.
Traumzustand *m*: dreamy state.
Travoprost *n*: travoprost.
Trazodon *n*: trazodone.
Treibmittel *n*: purgative, propellant.
Treitz-Hernie *f*: Treitz's hernia, retroperitoneal hernia.
Trematode *f*: trematode, fluke.
Tremor *m*: tremor, trembling; **alternierender** ≈ alternating tremor; **bewegungsunabhängiger** ≈ nonintention tremor; **essentieller** ≈ essential tremor; **feinschlägiger** ≈ fine tremor; **grober** ≈ gross tremor; **hepatischer** ≈ liver flap; **physiologischer** ≈ physiologic tremor.
Trendelenburg-Gang *m*: Trendelenburg gait, gluteal gait.
Trendelenburg-Lagerung *f*: Trendelenburg's position, high pelvic position.
Trendelenburg-Operation *f*: Trendelenburg's operation, pulmonary embolectomy.
Treosulfan *n*: treosulfan.
Trepanation *f*: trepanation, trephination.
Treponema-pallidum-Hämagglutinationstest *m*: treponema pallidum hemagglutination test, TPHA test.
Treppeneffekt *m*: staircase phenomenon, Bowditch phenomenon.
Tretamin : tretamine.
Tretinoin *n*: tretinoin.
Triage *f*: triage.
Triamcinolon *n*: triamcinolone.
Triamcinolonacetonid *n*: triamcinolone acetonide.

Triamteren *n*: triamterene.
Triazolam *n*: triazolam.
Tribenosid *n*: tribenoside.
Tribrommethan *n*: tribromomethane.
Trichiasis *f*: trichiasis.
Trichine *f*: trichina, porkworm.
Trichinose *f*: trichinosis.
Trichloräthylen *n*: trichloroethylene.
Trichloräthylensucht *f*: glue sniffing.
Trichloressigsäure *f*: trichloracetic acid.
Trichlormethiazid *n*: trichlormethiazide.
Trichobezoar *m*: trichobezoar, hairball.
Trichoglossie *f*: trichoglossia, hair tongue.
Trichophytose *f*: trichophytosis.
Trichterbrust *f*: funnel chest, pectus excavatum.
trichterförmig: funnel-shaped, infundibular.
Trichuriasis *f*: trichuriasis.
Trieb *m*: drive, instinct.
Triebhandlung *f*: impulsive action.
Trifluperidol *n*: trifluperidol.
Trifluridin *n*: trifluridine.
Trifokalgläser: trifocal glasses.
Trigeminie *f*: trigeminy, trigeminal pulse.
Trigeminus *m*: trigeminus, nervus trigeminus.
Trigeminusdekompression *f*: trigeminal decompression.
Trigeminusneuralgie *f*: trigeminal neuralgia.
Triggerpunkt *m*: trigger point.
Trihexyphenidyl *n*: trihexyphenidyl.
Trikuspidalgeräusch *n*: tricuspid murmur.
Trikuspidalklappe *f*: right atrioventricular valve.
Trikuspidalklappeninsuffizienz *f*: tricuspid insufficiency.
Trikuspidalklappenstenose *f*: tricuspid stenosis.
Trikuspidalton *m*: tricuspid murmur.
Trimetaphancamsilat *n*: trimetaphan camsylate.
Trimethadion *n*: trimethadione.
Trimethoprim *n*: trimethoprim.
Trimetozin *n*: trimetozine.
Trimipramin *n*: trimipramine.
Trinitrophenol *n*: trinitrophenol.
Trinken *n*: drinking; **episodisches** ≈ episodic excessive drinking.
Trinkverhalten *n*: drinking behavior.
Triparanol *n*: triparanol.
Triplegie *f*: triplegia.
Triple-X-Syndrom *n*: triple-X syndrome.
triploid: triploid.
Trippelgang *m*: festinating gait, festination.
Tripper *m*: gonorrhea, clap.
Triptan *n*: triptan.
Trismus *m*: trismus, lockjaw.
Trisomie *f*: trisomy.
Trisomiesyndrom *n*: trisomy syndrome.
Trivialname *m*: trivial name.
Trizeps *m*: triceps.
Trizepsreflex *m*: triceps reflex, elbow reflex.
Trochanter *m*: trochanter.
trochlear: trochlear.
Trochlearislähmung *f*: trochlear paralysis.
trocken: dry, xerotic.
Trockenextrakt *m*: dry extract.
Trockenmilch *f*: dried milk.
Trockenplasma, humanes *n*: dried human plasma.
Tröpfchen *n*: droplet, bead.
Tröpfcheninfektion *f*: droplet infection.
tröpfeln: drip, dribble.
Trofosfamid *n*: trofosfamide.
Trokar *m*: trocar.
Trokarbiopsie *f*: trephine biopsy.
Tromantadin *n*: tromantadine.
Trombiculamilbe *f*: trombicular mite, harvest mite.
Trommelfell *n*: tympanic membrane, eardrum, myrinx.
Trommelfellentzündung *f*: myringitis.
Trommelfellperforation *f*: eardrum perforation.
Trommelgeräusch *n*: drumming noise.
Trommelschlägelfinger *m*: drumstick finger, clubbed finger.

Tropalpin *n*: 2-dimethylaminoethyl benzilate.
Tropasäure *f*: tropic acid.
Tropenkrankheit *f*: tropical disease.
Tropenmedizin *f*: tropical medicine.
Tropf *m*: drip, drip infusion.
Tropfen *m*: drop; **hängender** ≈ hanging-drop preparation.
Tropfenherz *n*: drop heart.
Trophik *f*: nutritional state.
trophisch: trophic.
Trophoblast *m*: trophoblast.
Trophödem *n*: trophedema.
Tropicamid *n*: tropicamide.
Tropin *n*: tropine.
tropisch: tropical.
Tropisetron *n*: tropisetron.
Trospiumchlorid *n*: trospium chloride.
Trovafloxacin *n*: trovafloxacin.
Trümmerfraktur *f*: complicated fracture, comminuted fracture.
Trugbild *n*: hallucinatory image.
Truncus *m*: truncus, trunk.
Trunkenheit *f*: drunkenness.
Trunksucht *f*: alcoholism, inebriety.
trunkulär: truncal.
Trypanosomiasis *f*: trypanosomiasis, sleeping sickness; **afrikanische** ≈ African trypanosomiasis, acute sleeping sickness; **amerikanische** ≈ American trypanosomiasis, Chagas-Cruz disease; **südamerikanische** ≈ South American trypanosomiasis, Chagas-Cruz disease.
Trypsin *n*: trypsin.
Trypsinogen *n*: trypsinogen.
Tryptophan *n*: tryptophan.
Tsutsugamushi-Krankheit *f*: tsutsugamushi disease, scrub typhus, chigger-borne typhus.
Tuba *f*: tuba, tube, tubus.
Tuba auditiva *f*: auditory tube, eustachian tube.
tubar: tubal.
Tubarabort *m*: tubal abortion.
Tubargravidität *f*: tubal pregnancy.
Tuba uterina *f*: uterine tube, fallopian tube.
Tube *f*: uterine tube, auditory tube.
Tubendurchgängigkeit *f*: tube patency.
Tubenkatheter *m*: eustachian catheter.
Tubenligatur *f*: tubal ligature.
Tuben-Mittelohrkatarrh *m*: catarrhal otitis.
Tubentransport *m*: tubal transport.
Tuberkel *n*: tubercle, tuber.
Tuberkelbazillus *m*: tubercle bacillus, Mycobacterium tuberculosis.
Tuberkulid *n*: tuberculid.
Tuberkulin *n*: tuberculin.
Tuberkulinprobe *f*: tuberculin testing; **intrakutane** ≈ intradermal tuberculin skin testing.
Tuberkulinreaktion *f*: tuberculin reaction.
tuberkulös: tuberculous, tubercular.
Tuberkulose *f*: tuberculosis, TB; **aerogene** ≈ aerogenic tuberculosis; **aktive** ≈ active tuberculosis; **disseminierte** ≈ disseminated tuberculosis; **extrapulmonale** ≈ extrapulmonary tuberculosis; **fibrös-käsige** ≈ fibrocaseous tuberculosis; **hämatogene** ≈ hematogenous tuberculosis; **inaktive** ≈ latent tuberculosis, quiescent tuberculosis; **offene** ≈ open tuberculosis; **verkäsende** ≈ caseous tuberculosis.
Tuberkulostatikum *n*: tuberculostatic, antituberculotic, tuberculostatic agent.
tuberkulostatisch: tuberculostatic.
tuberös: tuberous.
Tuberositas *f*: tuberosity.
Tubocurarin *n*: tubocurarine.
Tuboovarialabszess *m*: tubo-ovarian abscess.
tubulär: tubular.
Tubulus *m*: tubule, tubulus.
Tubulustransport *m*: tubular transport; **aktiver** ≈ active renal tubular transport; **kompetitiver** ≈ competitive renal tubular transport.
Tubuluszyste *f*: tubular cyst, tubulocyst.
Tubus *m*: cone, tubus, tube.
Tüpfelnagel *m*: pitted nail.
Tüpfelung *f*: stippling; **basophile** ≈ basophil stippling.
Tüpfelzelle *f*: stipple cell.
Tularämie *f*: tularemia, rabbit fever.

Tulathromycin *n*: tulathromycin.
Tulobuterol *n*: tulobuterol.
Tumeszenz *f*: tumescence, tumefaction.
Tumor *m*: tumor, neoplasm; **benigner** ≈ benign neoplasm, benign tumor; **embryonaler** ≈ embryonal tumor, dysontogenetic tumor; **gemischter** ≈ mixed tumor; **infiltrierender** ≈ infiltrating tumor; **maligner** ≈ malignant neoplasm, malignant tumor, cancer; **metastasierender** ≈ metastatic neoplasm.
Tumor albus *m*: tumor albus, white swelling.
Tumoranämie *f*: tumor anemia.
Tumorantigen *n*: tumor-specific antigen.
Tumorantikörper *m*: tumor antibody.
Tumorklassifikation *f*: classification of tumors.
Tumor-Nekrose-Faktor *m*: tumor necrosis factor, TNF.
Tumorstadieneinteilung *f*: tumor staging.
Tumorvirus *n*: tumor virus.
Tumorwachstum *n*: tumor growth.
Tupfer *m*: swab, sponge, gauze pad.
Turgor *m*: turgor.
Turmschädel *m*: tower head, turricephaly.
Tylosin *n*: tylosin.
Tympanektomie *f*: tympanectomy.
Tympanie *f*: tympany, tympanic resonance.
Tympanoplastik *f*: tympanoplasty.
Typ *m*: type, typus.
Typhoid *n*: typhoid.
Typhus *m*: typhoid fever.
Typhus abdominalis *m*: abdominal typhus, enterotyphus.
typhusähnlich: typhuslike, typhoid.
Typhuspneumonie *f*: typhoid pneumonia.
Typhusroseola *f*: rose spot, typhoid spot.
typisch: typical.
Typisierung *f*: typing.
Tyrosin *n*: tyrosine.
Tyrosinurie *f*: tyrosinuria.

U

U Abk. 1. **Umwandlungszone** *f*; 2. **Uracil** *n*; 3. **Uran** *n*: 1. transformation zone; 2. uracil, U; 3. uranium, U.

Ubichinon *n*: ubiquinone.

ubiquitär: ubiquitous.

Übelkeit *f*: nausea, queasiness.

üben: exercise.

Überalterung *f*: overaging.

Überanstrengung *f*: overstrain, overexertion.

Überanstrengungsthrombose *f*: effort thrombosis, Paget-von Schroetter syndrome.

Überbein *n*: ganglion, weeping sinew.

Überbiss *m*: overbite, supraocclusion.

Überdosis *f*: overdose.

Überdruck *m*: positive pressure, hyperbaric pressure.

Überdruckbeatmung *f*: positive pressure ventilation.

Überdruckkammer *f*: hyperbaric chamber.

Übereinkommen *n*: agreement.

überempfindlich: hypersensitive, allergic, hypersusceptible.

Überempfindlichkeit *f*: hypersensibility, hypersensitivity, hypersusceptibility.

Überempfindlichkeitsreaktion *f*: hypersensitivity reaction, allergic reaction.

Überernährung *f*: overnutrition, hyperalimentation.

Übererregbarkeit *f*: hyperexcitability.

Überflutungstherapie *f*: flooding.

Übergangsepithel *n*: transitional epithelium.

Übergangsepithelkarzinom *n*: transitional cell carcinoma.

Übergangsphase *f*: transitional phase.

Übergangsstadium *n*: transitional stage.

Übergewicht *n*: obesity, overweight.

übergewichtig: obese.

Übergröße *f*: oversize.

Überkompensation *f*: overcompensation.

Überladung *f*: overload.

Überlagerung *f*: overlapping, superimposition.

Überlastung *f*: overload, overstrain; **linksventrikuläre** ≈ aortic overload.

Überlaufblase *f*: overflow incontinence.

Überlaufdrainage *f*: tidal drainage.

Überlaufinkontinenz *f*: overflow incontinence, paradoxical incontinence.

überleben: survive.

Überlebensdauer *f*: survival time.

Überlegenheit *f*: superiority.

Überleitung *f*: conduction; **anterograde** ≈ anterograde conduction; **antidrome** ≈ antidromic conduction; **atrioventrikuläre** ≈ atrioventricular conduction; **synaptische** ≈ synaptic conduction.

Überleitungsblock *m*: conduction block.

Überleitungsstörung *f*: conduction disturbance.

Überleitungsverzögerung *f*: delayed conduction.

Überprüfung *f*: check, review.

überreif: hypermature, postmature.

Überrest *m*: remnant, rest.

Übersäuerung *f*: hyperacidity.

überschichten: overlay.

Überschuss *m*: excess, surplus.

Überschwingung *f*: overoscillation.

Übersichtigkeit *f*: longsightedness, hyperopia.

Übersichtsaufnahme *f*: scout film, radiographic survey.
Überträger *m*: transmitter, transvector.
übertragbar: communicable, transmissible.
übertragen: transmit, transfer, communicate.
Übertragung *f*: transmission, transfer, communication; **diaplazentare** ≈ placental transmission; **gegenseitige** ≈ bilateral transfer; **horizontale** ≈ horizontal transmission; **humorale** ≈ humoral transmission; **kochleäre** ≈ cochlear transmission; **maternofetale** ≈ maternofetal transmission; **neurale** ≈ nerval transmission; **sexuelle** ≈ sexual transmission; **vertikale** ≈ vertical transmission.
überwachen: monitor.
Überwachung *f*: monitoring, surveillance.
überweisen: refer.
Überweisung *f*: referral.
überzählig: supernumerary, redundant, accessory.
Übung *f*: training, exercise; **körperliche** ≈ physical training.
Uhr *f*: clock; **biologische** ≈ biological clock.
Uhrglasmagen *m*: hourglass stomach.
Uhrglasnagel *m*: watch-glass nail, hippocratic nail.
Ulcus *n*: ulcer, sore.
Ulcus cruris *n*: ulcus cruris, venous stasis ulcer.
Ulcus duodeni *n*: duodenal ulcer.
Ulcus durum *n*: ulcus durum, hard sore.
Ulcus molle *n*: ulcus molle, soft chancre, chancroid.
Ulcus serpens *n*: serpiginous ulcer, creeping ulcer.
Ulkus *n*: ulcer, sore; **gastroduodenales** ≈ gastroduodenal ulcer; **hyperkeratotisches** ≈ hyperkeratotic ulcer; **penetrierendes** ≈ penetrating ulcer; **peptisches** ≈ peptic ulcer; **phagedänisches** ≈ phagedenic ulcer, Malabar ulcer; **trophisches** ≈ trophic ulcer.
Ulkusnische *f*: ulcer niche.
Ulkusperforation *f*: perforated ulcer.
Ullrich-Turner-Syndrom *n*: Ullrich-Turner syndrome, X zero syndrome.
Ulnafraktur *f*: ulnar fracture.
Ulnaköpfchen *n*: ulnar head.
ulnar: ulnar.
Ulnardeviation *f*: ulnar drift, seal-fin deformity.
Ulnarislähmung *f*: ulnar nerve paralysis.
Ulnarreflex *m*: ulnar reflex.
Ultimobranchialkörper *m*: ultimobranchial body.
Ultrafiltration *f*: ultrafiltration.
Ultraschall *m*: ultrasound.
Ultraschallfrequenz *f*: ultrasonic frequency.
Ultraschall-Kardiographie *f*: ultrasonic cardiography, echocardiograph.
Ultraschall-Schädelumfangsbestimmung *f*: ultrasonic cephalometry.
Ultraschallsonographie *f*: ultrasonography, sonography.
Ultraschalluntersuchung *f*: ultrasound examination.
Ultrastruktur *f*: ultrastructure.
ultraviolett: ultraviolet.
Ultraviolettfilter *m*: ultraviolet filter.
Ultraviolettstrahlung *f*: ultraviolet radiation.
Ultrazentrifuge *f*: ultracentrifuge.
Ulzeration *f*: ulceration.
ulzerieren: ulcerate.
ulzerös: ulcerous.
ulzeromembranös: ulceromembranous.
Umbilicus *m*: umbilicus, navel.
umbilikal: umbilical, omphalic.
Umdrehung *f*: rotation, turn.
Umfang *m*: circumference, volume.
Umfeld *n*: context, environment.
Umgebung *f*: environment, milieu, surroundings.
Umgebungstemperatur *f*: environmental temperature.
umgehen: bypass.
Umgehungskreislauf *m*: collateral circulation.
umgekehrt: reverse, inverse.
umhüllen: wrap, jacket.
Umkehr *f*: reversal, reversion.

Umkehrplastik *f*: subvolution.
Umklammerungsreflex *m*: embrace reflex, Moro's reflex.
Umlauf *m*: runaround, whitlow.
Ummantelung *f*: coating, jacket.
Umsatz *m*: turnover.
Umschlag *m*: compress, poultice; **feuchter** ≈ wet compress; **heißer** ≈ hot compress.
umschrieben: localized, circumscribed.
Umstand *m*: circumstance, condition, situation.
umstellen: switch, change.
Umwandlung *f*: transformation, conversion.
Umwelt *f*: environment.
Umweltkrankheit *f*: environmental disease.
Umweltmedizin *f*: environmental medicine.
unartikuliert: inarticulate.
Unausgeglichenheit *f*: imbalance.
unbehaart: hairless.
unbeständig: variable, unstable.
Unbeweglichkeit *f*: immobility.
Uncinariasis *f*: uncinariasis.
Undecylensäure *f*: undecylenic acid.
undifferenziert: undifferentiated.
undulierend: undulant.
undurchgängig: obstructed, imperforate.
Undurchsichtigkeit *f*: opacity.
uneben: uneven.
unecht: spurious, false.
unempfindlich: insensible, insusceptible.
Unempfindlichkeit *f*: insensitivity.
unerträglich: intolerable, unbearable.
Unfähigkeit *f*: incapability, disability, incompetence.
Unfall *m*: accident.
Unfallkrankenhaus *n*: accident hospital.
Unfallneurose *f*: traumatic neurosis.
Unfallopfer *n*: casualty.
Unfalltod *m*: accidental death.
Unfallverhütung *f*: accident prevention.
Unfallversicherung *f*: accident insurance.
unfruchtbar: infertile, sterile.
Unfruchtbarkeit *f*: infertility, infecundity.
ungesättigt: unsaturated.
ungeschlechtlich: asexual, nonsexual, vegetative.
ungesund: unhealthy.
ungewollt: unwanted.
Ungezieferbekämpfung *f*: vermin control.
ungezuckert: sugarless, sugar-free.
Ungleichgewicht *n*: imbalance, dysequilibrium.
Unguentum *n*: unguentum, ointment.
Unguentum hydrargyri flavum *n*: unguentum hydrargyri flavum, golden ointment.
Unguentum hydrophilicum *n*: unguentum hydrophilicum, hydrophilic ointment.
unheilbar: incurable, uncurable.
unhygienisch: unhygienic.
unidirektional: unidirectional.
unifokal: unifocal.
uniform: uniform.
unilateral: unilateral.
unipolar: unipolar, monopolar.
Universalempfänger *m*: universal recipient.
Universalspender *m*: universal donor.
Universitätsklinik *f*: university hospital.
unkompliziert: uncomplicated, simple.
Unktion *f*: unction, ointment.
unlöslich: insoluble.
unmerklich: insensible.
Unna-Nävus *m*: Unna's nevus.
Unoproston *n*: unoprostone.
unpässlich: unwell.
Unpässlichkeit *f*: malaise, ailment.
unregelmäßig: irregular, aperiodic.
unreif: immature, premature.
Unreife *f*: immaturity, prematurity.
Unruhe *f*: restlessness.
unschädlich: harmless, innocent.
Unschärfe *f*: unsharpness, blurring, vagueness.
unscharf: blurred, out of focus, vague.

Unterarm *m*: underarm, forearm.
Unterbauch *m*: lower abdomen.
Unterbelichtung *f*: underexposure.
Unterbewusstsein *n*: subconsciousness.
unterbinden: ligate.
Unterbindung *f*: ligation, ligature.
Unterbrechung *f*: interruption, disconnection.
Unterdosierung *f*: underdosage.
Unterdruck *m*: negative pressure.
unterdrücken: suppress.
Unterdrückung *f*: suppression, repression.
Untereinheit *f*: subunit.
Unterentwicklung *f*: underdevelopment.
Untererfassung *f*: underreporting.
Unterernährung *f*: undernourishment, undernutrition.
Unterfunktion *f*: underfunction, impaired function; **endokrine** ≈ hypoendocrinism; **ovarielle** ≈ hypoovarianism.
Untergewicht *n*: underweight.
Untergruppe *f*: subgroup.
Unterhautgewebe *n*: subcutaneous tissue.
Unterkiefer *m*: mandible, lower jawbone.
Unterkieferfistel *f*: submental fistula.
Unterkieferresektion *f*: mandibulectomy.
Unterkühlungskoma *n*: hypothermic coma.
Unterlappen *m*: lower lobe.
Unterlippe *f*: lower lip.
Unterricht *m*: teaching.
Unterricht am Krankenbett *m*: bedside teaching.
Unterscheidung *f*: discrimination, differentiation.
Unterscheidungsvermögen *n*: discriminatory power.
Unterschenkel *m*: lower leg, foreleg.
Unterschied *m*: difference.
unterschwellig: subliminal, subthreshold.
Unterstützung *f*: support, help.
untersuchen: examine, investigate, study.
Untersuchung *f*: examination, inspection, study, investigation, analysis; **ärztliche** ≈ physician's examination; **bimanuelle** ≈ bimanual examination; **digitale** ≈ digital examination; **klinische** ≈ clinical examination; **körperliche** ≈ physical examination; **neurologische** ≈ neurologic examination; **rektale** ≈ rectal examination; **spektroskopische** ≈ spectroscopic test; **vaginale** ≈ vaginal examination.
Untersuchungsbefund *m*: findings; **körperlicher** ≈ physical findings.
Untersuchungsmaterial *n*: specimen.
Untersuchungsverfahren *n*: examination technique.
Unterteilung *f*: partition, segmentation.
Untertemperatur *f*: temperature below normal, hypothermia.
Untertisch-Bildverstärker *m*: undertable image intensifier.
Unterwassermassage *f*: underwater massage, hydromassage.
Unterzungendrüse *f*: sublingual gland.
unverdaulich: indigestible, undigestible.
Unverträglichkeit *f*: intolerance, incompatibility.
Unverträglichkeitsreaktion *f*: intolerance reaction, adverse reaction.
unvollständig: incomplete.
unwirksam: ineffective, noneffective.
Unwirksamkeit *f*: ineffectivity.
unwohl: unwell.
Unwohlsein *n*: discomfort, queasiness, malaise.
Unzinatusanfall *m*: uncinate epilepsy, uncinate attack.
Unzurechnungsfähigkeit *f*: lack of criminal responsibility.
unzuverlässig: unreliable.
Urachus *m*: urachus.
Urachusfistel *f*: urachal fistula.
Uracil *n*: uracil.
Uracil-Lost *n*: uracil mustard.
Urämie *f*: uremia.
Uranoplastik *f*: uranoplasty, palatoplasty.

Urapidil *n*: urapidil.
Urat *n*: urate.
Uratablagerung *f*: urate deposition.
Uratkonjunktivitis *f*: uratic conjunctivitis.
Uratnephropathie *f*: urate kidney.
Urdarm *m*: primitive gut.
Urea *n*: urea, carbamide.
Ureter *m*: ureter, renal duct.
Ureterdilatation *f*: dilated ureter.
Ureter duplex *m*: double ureter.
Ureterektomie *f*: ureterectomy.
Ureterfistel *f*: ureteral fistula.
Ureteritis *f*: ureteritis.
Ureterkolik *f*: ureteral colic.
Ureterographie *f*: ureterography.
Ureterolithotomie *f*: ureterolithotomy.
Ureterostomie *f*: ureterostomy.
Ureterotomie *f*: ureterotomy.
ureterovesikal: ureterovesical.
Ureterozele *f*: ureterocele.
Ureterresektion *f*: resection of ureter.
Ureterstein *m*: ureteral calculus.
Ureterstenose *f*: ureteral stenosis.
Ureterverschluss *m*: ureteral obstruction.
Urethan *n*: urethane.
Urethra *f*: urethra.
urethral: urethral.
Urethralabstrich *m*: urethral smear
Urethraldrüse *f*: urethral gland.
Urethralfieber *n*: urethral fever.
Urethritis *f*: urethritis; **gonorrhoische** ≈ gonococcal urethritis, specific urethritis; **nichtgonorrhoische** ≈ nongonococcal urethritis, nonspecific urethritis; **unspezifische** ≈ nonspecific urethritis, simple urethritis.
Urethrographie *f*: urethrography.
Urethroplastik *f*: urethroplasty.
Urethroskopie *f*: urethroscopy.
Urethrostomie *f*: urethrostomy.
Urethrotomie *f*: urethrotomy.
urethrovaginal: urethrovaginal.
Urethrozystitis *f*: urethrocystitis.
Urge-Inkontinenz *f*: urge incontinence.
Urhirn *n*: archencephalon, old brain.
Uridin *n*: uridine.
Uridylsäure *f*: uridylic acid.
Urin *m*: urine; **dunkler** ≈ black urine; **flockiger** ≈ cloudy urine; **trüber** ≈ milky urine, turbid urine.
Urinfistel *f*: urinary fistula.
Urinflasche *f*: urinal.
Urinkonzentration *f*: urinary concentration.
Urinphlegmone *f*: urinary phlegmon.
Urinstatus *m*: urine analysis.
Urinstick *m*: dipstick.
Urinuntersuchung *f*: urine analysis.
Urinzyste *f*: urinary cyst.
Urkeimzelle *f*: primordial germ cell.
Urobilin *n*: urobilin.
Urobilinogen *n*: urobilinogen.
Urochrom *n*: urochrome.
Uroflowmetrie *f*: uroflowmetry.
urogenital: genitourinary.
Urogenitalfistel *f*: genitourinary fistula.
Urogenitalspalte *f*: genital cleft.
Urogenitaltrakt *m*: genitourinary tract.
Urogenitaltuberkulose *f*: urogenital tuberculosis, genitourinary tuberculosis.
Urographie *f*: urography; **retrograde** ≈ ascending urography.
Urokaninsäure *f*: urocanic acid.
Urokinase *f*: urokinase.
Urolith *m*: urolith, urinary calculus.
Urolithiasis *f*: urolithiasis.
Urologie *f*: urology.
Urometrie *f*: urometry.
Uronsäure *f*: uronic acid
Urorgan *n*: primitive organ.
Urothelkarzinom *n*: transitional cell carcinoma.
Urozele *f*: urocele.
Ursache *f*: causative agent, cause, origin.
ursächlich: causative.
Ursodeoxycholsäure *f*: ursodeoxycholic acid.
Ursprung *m*: origin, source.
Ursprungsaponeurose *f*: aponeurosis of origin.
Urtica *f*: nettle.
Urtikaria *f*: urticaria, angioedema.
uterin: uterine.
Uterovesikalfistel *f*: uterovesical fistula.

Uterus *m*: uterus, womb.
Uterusagenesie *f*: agenesis of the uterus.
Uterusaplasie *f*: uterine aplasia.
Uterus arcuatus *m*: arcuate uterus.
Uterusatrophie *f*: uterine atrophy.
Uterus bicornis *m*: bicornate uterus.
Uterus biforis *m*: double-mouthed uterus.
Uterusblutung *f*: uterine bleeding.
Uterus didelphys *m*: double uterus, didelphia.
Uterus duplex *m*: double uterus, didelphia.
Uterus infantilis *m*: infantile uterus.
Uterusperforation *f*: uterine perforation.
Uterusplastik *f*: uteroplasty, hysteroplasty.
Uterusprolaps *m*: uterine prolapse.
Uterusruptur *f*: uterine rupture.
Uterus septus *m*: uterus septus, bipartite uterus.
Uterussonde *f*: uterine probe, uterine sound.
Uteruswandaussackung *f*: uterine sacculation.
Uteruszange *f*: uterine forceps.
Utriculus *m*: utricle.
UV-Blindheit *f*: solar blindness.
Uvea *f*: uvea.
Uveitis *f*: uveitis, iridochoroiditis.
UV-Strahlung *f*: ultraviolet radiation, UV radiation.
Uvula *f*: uvula, staphyle.
Uvulektomie *f*: uvulectomy, staphylectomy.
U-Welle *f*: U wave.

V

V Abk. **1. Vanadium** *n*; **2. Vene** *f*; **3. Visus** *m*: 1. vanadium, V; 2. vein; 3. visus, vision.
Vaccinia *f*: vaccinia.
Vacciniavirus *n*: vaccinia virus, cowpox virus.
vagal: vagal.
Vagantenhaut *f*: vagabond's disease, parasitic melanoderma.
Vagina *f*: vagina, sheath; **septierte** ≈ septate vagina.
Vaginalabstrich *m*: vaginal smear.
Vaginalaplasie *f*: vaginal aplasia.
Vaginalatresie *f*: vaginal atresia.
Vaginalblutung *f*: vaginal hemorrhage.
Vaginalmykose *f*: vaginal mycosis.
Vaginalprolaps *m*: colpoptosis.
Vaginalstenose *f*: vaginal stenosis.
Vaginalzyste *f*: vaginal cyst.
Vaginalzytologie *f*: vaginal cytology.
Vaginaplastik *f*: vaginoplasty, colpoplasty.
Vaginismus *m*: vaginism, vaginal spasm.
Vaginitis *f*: vaginitis, colpitis; **gonorrhoische** ≈ gonococcal vaginitis.
Vaginographie *f*: vaginography.
Vaginozele *f*: vaginocele, colpocele.
Vagolyse *f*: vagolysis.
Vagotomie *f*: vagotomy; **selektive proximale** ≈ selective proximal vagotomy; **trunkuläre** ≈ truncular vagotomy, Dragstedt's operation.
vagovagal: vagovagal.
Vagovagalreflex *m*: vagovagal reflex.
Vagus *m*: vagus nerve, depressor.
Vagusarrhythmie *f*: vagal arrhythmia.
Vaguskrise *f*: vagus crisis, vagal crisis.
Vaguslähmung *f*: vagal paralysis.
Vaguspuls *m*: vagal pulse.
Vakanz *f*: vacancy.
Vakatwucherung *f*: fatty atrophy.
vakuolär: vacuolar.
Vakuole *f*: vacuole; **sekretorische** ≈ secretory granule.
Vakuum *n*: vacuum.
Vakuumaspiration *f*: vacuum aspiration.
Vakzination *f*: vaccination.
Vakzine *f*: vaccine.
Valaciclovir *n*: valaciclovir.
Valdecoxib *n*: valdecoxib.
Valeriansäure *f*: valerianic acid, pentanoic acid.
Valganciclovir *n*: valganciclovir.
Valgusstellung *f*: valgus position.
Validierung *f*: validation.
Valin *n*: valine, 2-aminoisovaleric acid.
Valinomycin *n*: valinomycin.
Valnemulin *n*: valnemulin.
Valproat *n*: valproate.
Valproinsäure *f*: valproic acid.
Valsalva-Versuch *m*: Valsalva maneuver.
Valsartan *n*: valsartan.
Valvula *f*: valvula, valve.
valvulär: valvular.
Valvulotomie *f*: valvulotomy.
Vanadinsäure *f*: vanadic acid.
Vanadium *n*: vanadium.
Vancomycin *n*: vancomycin.
Vanillinmandelsäure *f*: vanillylmandelic acid.
Vanillinsäure *f*: vanillic acid.
Vaquez-Osler-Krankheit *f*: Vaquez's disease, polycythemia vera.
Vardenafil *n*: vardenafil.
Vareniclin *n*: varenicline.
variabel: variable.
Variabilität *f*: variability.
Variable *f*: variable.

Variante *f*: variant, variation.
Varianzanalyse *f*: variance analysis.
Variation *f*: variation.
Variationsbreite *f*: range.
Varicella *f*: varicella, chickenpox.
Varicella-Zoster-Virus *n*: varicella-zoster virus.
Varietät *f*: variety.
variieren: vary.
varikös: varicose, variceal.
Varikose *f*: varicosis; **spinale** ≈ spinal varicosis, Foix-Alajouanine syndrome.
Varikozele *f*: varicocele.
Variola *f*: variola, smallpox.
Variolavirus *n*: variola virus.
Variolois *f*: varioloid, modified smallpox.
Varize *f*: varix, varicose vein.
Varizellen: varicella, chickenpox.
Varizenblutung *f*: variceal hemorrhage.
Varusstellung *f*: varus position.
Vasektomie *f*: vasectomy.
Vaselin *n*: vaseline.
vaskulär: vascular.
Vaskularisierung *f*: vascularization.
Vaskulitis *f*: vasculitis.
vasoaktiv: vasoactive.
Vasodilatation *f*: vasodilatation.
Vasokonstriktion *f*: vasoconstriction.
Vasomotor *m*: vasomotor.
Vasomotorenkopfschmerz *m*: vasomotor headache.
Vasomotorenlähmung *f*: vasomotor paralysis.
Vasomotorenspasmus *m*: vasomotor spasm.
vasomotorisch: vasomotor.
Vasopressin *n*: vasopressin, antidiuretic hormone.
Vasopressor *m*: vasopressor.
Vasospasmus *m*: vasospasm, angiospasm.
Vasotomie *f*: vasotomy, Belfield's operation.
vasotonisch: vasotonic.
vasovagal: vasovagal.
Vasovagalsyndrom *n*: vasovagal syncope.
Vaterkomplex *m*: father complex.
Vater-Papille *f*: papilla of Vater, major duodenal papilla.
Vaterschaftstest *m*: paternity test.
VDRL-Test *m*: venereal disease research laboratory test, VDRL test.
Vecuroniumbromid *n*: vecuronium bromide.
Vedaprofen *n*: vedaprofen.
Vegetation *f*: vegetation; **adenoide** ≈ adenoid vegetation; **verruköse** ≈ verrucous vegetation.
vegetativ: vegetative, vegetal.
Vehikel *n*: vehicle.
Veitstanz *m*: Saint Vitus' dance, epidemic chorea.
Vektor *m*: vector.
Vektorkardiogramm *n*: vectorcardiogram.
Vena-cava-inferior-Syndrom *n*: inferior vena cava syndrome.
Vena-cava-superior-Syndrom *n*: superior vena cava syndrome.
Venaesectio *f*: venesection, phlebotomy.
Vene *f*: vein; **variköse** ≈ varicose vein.
Venenbypass *m*: venous bypass.
Venendruck, zentraler *m*: central venous pressure.
Venenentzündung *f*: phlebitis.
Venenerkrankung *f*: venous disorder, venopathy.
Veneninsuffizienz *f*: venous insufficiency.
Venenklappe *f*: venous valve.
Venenpuls *m*: venous pulse.
Venenthrombose *f*: venous thrombosis; **tiefe** ≈ deep venous thrombosis.
Venenwinkel *m*: venous angle.
venerisch: venereal.
Venerologie *f*: venerology.
Venlafaxin *n*: venlafaxine.
venös: venous.
Venostase *f*: venous stasis.
Ventilation *f*: ventilation.
Ventilpneumothorax *m*: valvular pneumothorax.
Ventilstenose *f*: valvular stenosis.
ventral: ventral.
Ventrikel *m*: ventricle.
Ventrikelaneurysma *n*: ventricular aneurysm.
Ventrikelblutung *f*: intraventricular hemorrhage.

Ventrikeldrainage *f*: drainage of ventricular fluid.
Ventrikeldruck *m*: ventricular pressure.
Ventrikelfüllung *f*: ventricle filling.
Ventrikelpunktion *f*: ventricular puncture.
Ventrikelseptumdefekt *m*: ventricular septal defect.
Ventrikelvolumen *n*: ventricular volume.
ventrikulär: ventricular.
Ventrikulographie *f*: ventriculography.
Ventrikulozisternostomie *f*: ventriculocisternostomy.
Venushalsband *n*: venereal collar.
veränderlich: variable, changeable.
verändern: alter, vary.
Veränderung *f*: change, alteration, variation; **krankhafte** ≈ pathologic change; **psychische** ≈ mental change.
Verästelung *f*: ramification, branching.
Verankerung *f*: anchorage, bracing.
Verantwortung *f*: responsibility, liability.
Verapamil *n*: verapamil.
Veratramin *n*: veratramine.
Verband *m*: bandage, dressing.
Verbandmull *m*: absorbent gauze.
Verbandskasten *m*: first-aid kit.
Verbandswechsel *m*: redressement.
verbinden: dress, link, unite, articulate, bind, connect.
Verbindung *f*: connection, coupling, junction, joint, union, linkage, association, nexus, interface; **alkylierende** ≈ alkylating compound; **neuromuskuläre** ≈ nerve-muscle junction; **offene** ≈ gap junction.
verblassen: fade.
Verblockung *f*: blocking operation.
Verbrauch *m*: consumption.
Verbraucherschutz *m*: consumer's protection.
Verbrauchskoagulopathie *f*: consumption coagulopathy.
Verbreiterung *f*: widening.
Verbreitung *f*: dissemination, spreading.
verbrennen: burn.
Verbrennung *f*: burn, combustion.
Verbrennungsschock *m*: burn shock.
Verbrennungszentrum *n*: burn center.
Verbrühung *f*: scald.
Verdachtsdiagnose *f*: tentative diagnosis.
Verdamycin *n*: verdamycin.
verdauen: digest.
Verdauung *f*: digestion.
Verdauungsenzym *n*: digestive enzyme.
Verdauungstrakt *m*: digestive system, alimentary canal, gastrointestinal canal.
Verdickung *f*: thickening.
Verdrängung *f*: repression, displacement, suppression.
Verdünnung *f*: dilution, attenuation, rarefaction.
Verdünnungsanämie *f*: dilution anemia.
Vereinheitlichung *f*: standardization.
vereinigen: unite, join.
Vereinigung *f*: fusion, union, coalition, association.
vereisen: ice, freeze.
Verengung *f*: narrowing, tighting, phimosis, stricture.
Vererbung *f*: heredity, inheritance.
Verfärbung *f*: discoloration, color change.
Verfahren *n*: method, technique, procedure, process; **bildgebendes** ≈ imaging technique.
Verfall *m*: decline, rot.
verfaulen: rot, decay.
Verfettung *f*: fatty change, steatosis.
Verfolgungswahn *m*: delusion of persecution.
Verformung *f*: deformity, distortion.
Verfügbarkeit *f*: availability; **biologische** ≈ bioavailability.
Vergewaltigung *f*: rape.
Vergiftung *f*: poisoning, intoxication, toxicosis.
Vergrößerung *f*: enlargement, magnification, increase.
Verhältnis *n*: relation, relationship, rate, index, ratio.
Verhärtung *f*: hardening, induration.

Verhalten *n*: behavior, attitude; **abweichendes** ≈ deviant behavior; **gesundheitsbezogenes** ≈ health-related behavior; **gesundheitsorientiertes** ≈ health-directed behavior; **impulsives** ≈ impulsive behavior; **instinktives** ≈ instinctive behavior; **kognitives** ≈ cognitive behavior.
Verhaltensänderung *f*: behavior modification.
Verhaltensstörung *f*: behavior disorder, habit disorder.
Verhaltenstherapie *f*: behavior therapy.
verheilen: heal.
Verhornung *f*: keratinization.
Verhornungsstörung *f*: abnormality of keratinization.
Verhütungsmittel *n*: contraceptive, contraceptive device.
Verhungern *n*: starvation.
Verifikation *f*: verification.
verkäsend: caseous.
verkalkt: calcified.
Verkalkung *f*: calcification.
Verkehrsunfall *m*: traffic accident, road accident.
Verklumpung *f*: clumping, caking.
Verknöcherung *f*: ossification.
Verknorpelung *f*: chondrification.
Verkürzung *f*: shortening.
Verlängerung *f*: lengthening, elongation, extension.
Verlagerung *f*: displacement, transposition.
Verlangen *n*: appetite, desire, demand.
Verlauf *m*: course; **natürlicher** ≈ natural history; **zeitlicher** ≈ time course.
Verlaufskontrolle *f*: follow-up.
verletzen: injure, violate, traumatize.
Verletzter *m*: casualty.
Verletzung *f*: injury, trauma.
Verleugnung *f*: disavowal, denial.
Verlust *m*: loss, wastage, decrement.
Vermännlichung *f*: virilization.
Vermehrung *f*: multiplication, reproduction.
vermeidbar: preventable, avoidable.
Vermeidung *f*: avoidance, prevention.
Vermeidungsverhalten *n*: avoidance behavior.
Vermifugum *n*: vermifuge.
Verminderung *f*: diminution, lessening, decline.
Vermizid *n*: vermicide.
vernarben: scar, cicatrize.
Vernebler *m*: nebulizer, atomizer.
Verneinung *f*: negation.
Verödung *f*: obliteration, scarification, sclerotherapy.
verordnen: prescribe.
Verordnung *f*: prescription.
Verordnungstreue *f*: compliance.
verpflegen: care, nurse.
Verrenkung *f*: dislocation, luxation, sprain.
Verruca *f*: verruca, wart.
versagen: fail.
Versagen *n*: failure.
Versagerquote *f*: failure rate.
Verschattung *f*: shadow, overshadowing.
Verschiebelappen *m*: advancement flap, sliding flap.
Verschiebung *f*: shift, advancement, displacement.
Verschiedenheit *f*: diversity, disparity, variety.
verschlechtern: worsen, deteriorate.
Verschlechterung *m*: worsening, deterioration.
verschließen: close, seal, occlude.
verschlimmern: worsen, aggravate, progress.
Verschlimmerung *f*: aggravation.
verschlossen: impatent.
Verschluss *m*: occlusion, obturation, closure, sealing.
Verschlussikterus *m*: mechanical jaundice, obstructive jaundice.
Verschlusskrankheit *f*: occlusive disease; **aortoiliakale** ≈ aortoiliac occlusive disease; **periphere arterielle** ≈ peripheral arterial occlusive disease; **venöse** ≈ veno-occlusive disease.
Verschlussthrombus *m*: occlusive thrombus.
verschmelzen: amalgamate, fuse.
Verschmelzungsniere *f*: fused kidney.

verschreiben: prescribe.
Verschreibung *f*: prescription.
Verschwommenheit *f*: vagueness.
Versicherung *f*: insurance, assurance.
Versivanfall *m*: versive epilepsy.
versorgen: manage, care, supply.
Versorgung *f*: management, supply; **ambulante** ≈ outpatient service, ambulatory care; **medizinische** ≈ medical care; **palliative** ≈ palliative care; **stationäre** ≈ hospital care.
Verständnis *n*: understanding, comprehension, apprehension.
Verständnistest *m*: comprehension test.
verstärken: amplify, intensify, boost.
Verstärkung *f*: enhancement, reinforcement, intensification.
Verstärkung der Immunantwort: immunologic enhancement.
Verstand *m*: reason.
Verstauchung *f*: sprain, wrench.
Verstehen *n*: understanding, comprehension, apprehension.
Versteifung *f*: stiffening
Versteinerung *f*: petrifaction.
Verstopfung *f*: constipation.
Verstümmelung *f*: mutilation; **genitale** ≈ genital mutilation.
Versuch *m*: attempt, experiment, trial.
Versuchsperson *f*: proband, test subject
vertebral: vertebral.
Vertebralarterienstenose *f*: vertebral stenosis.
Vertebralisangiographie *f*: vertebral angiography.
vertebrobasilär: vertebrobasilar.
Verteilung *f*: distribution, dispersal, allocation.
Verteporfin *n*: verteporfin.
Vertigo *f*: vertigo, dizziness.
vertikal: vertical.
Vertikalebene *f*: vertical plane.
Verträglichkeit *f*: tolerance, compatibility.
Vertrauensintervall *n*: confidence interval.
Vertraulichkeit *f*: confidentiality.
Verunreinigung *f*: contamination, pollution, impurity.
verursachen: cause.
Verwachsung *f*: concretion, adherence, accretion, fusion.
verwandt: related.
Verwandtschaft *f*: relationship, kinship.
Verweiblichung *f*: feminization.
Verweilkatheter *m*: indwelling catheter.
Verwendung *f*: use, utilization, application.
Verwertung *f*: utilization.
Verwesung *f*: putrefaction, decomposition.
Verwirrtheit *f*: confusion.
Verwischung *f*: blurring, unsharpness.
verwunden: wound, injure.
verwundet: wounded, injured.
Verzerrtsehen *n*: metamorphopsia.
Verzerrung *f*: distortion, bias.
verzögert: delayed, tardive.
Verzögerung *f*: delay, lag, retardation.
Verzögerungspräparat *n*: delayed-action preparation, time-release preparation.
Verzweigung *f*: branching, ramification.
Verzweigungsblock *m*: arborization block.
vesikal: vesical.
Vesikel *f*: vesicle.
Vesikoabdominalfistel *f*: vesicoabdominal fistula.
vesikovaginal: vesicovaginal.
Vesikovaginalfistel *f*: vesicovaginal fistula.
Vesikozele *f*: vesicocele.
vesikulär: vesicular.
Vesikulitis *f*: vesiculitis.
vestibulär: vestibular.
Vestibularapparat *m*: vestibular apparatus.
Vestibularisausfall *m*: vestibular neuronitis, Gerlier's disease.
Vestibularislähmung *f*: vestibular paralysis.
Vestibularisschwindel *m*: vestibular vertigo.
Vestibularnystagmus *m*: vestibular nystagmus.

Vestibulum *n*: vestibule, vestibulum.
Veterinärmedizin *f*: veterinary medicine.
Vibrationsempfinden *n*: vibration sense, vibratory sensation.
Vicriviroc *n*: vicriviroc.
Vidarabin *n*: vidarabine.
vielkernig: multinucleate.
Vierfingerfurche *f*: simian crease.
Vierhügelsyndrom *n*: Parinaud syndrome.
Vierpunktgang *m*: four-point gait.
Viertagefieber *n*: quartan fever.
Vigabatrin *n*: vigabatrin.
Vigilambulismus *m*: vigilambulism, vigil ambulatory automatism.
Vigilanz *f*: vigilance, alertness.
vikariierend: vicarious.
villös: villous.
Viloxazin *n*: viloxazine.
Vinblastin *n*: vinblastine, vincaleukoblastine.
Vincain *n*: vincaine.
Vincamin *n*: vincamine.
Vincristin *n*: vincristine, leurocristine.
Vindesin *n*: vindesine.
Vinorelbin *n*: vinorelbine.
Vinpocetin *n*: vinpocetine.
Viomycin *n*: viomycin.
Viquidil *n*: viquidil.
Virämie *f*: viremia.
viral: viral, viroid.
Virchow-Robin-Raum *m*: Virchow-Robin space, perivascular space.
Virginiamycin *n*: virginiamycin.
Virilisierung *f*: virilization, masculinization.
Virion *n*: virion, viral particle.
Virologie *f*: virology.
Virostatikum *n*: virostatic.
virostatisch: virostatic.
virulent: virulent.
Virulenz *f*: virulence.
Virus *n*: virus; **adeno-assoziierter** ≈ adenoassociated virus; **hämagglutinierender** ≈ hemagglutinating virus; **onkogener** ≈ oncogenic virus.
Virusenteritis *f*: viral enteritis.
Virusenzephalitis *f*: viral encephalitis.
Viruserkrankung *f*: viral disease.
Virusgrippe *f*: influenza.
Virushepatitis *f*: viral hepatitis.
Virusinfektion *f*: viral infection.
Viruslast *f*: viral load.
Viruspartikel *n*: viral particle, virion.
Virusstamm *m*: viral strain.
viruzid: virucidal.
Visierlappenplastik *f*: bipedicle flap, hinged flap.
Vision *f*: vision, visus.
Visite *f*: visit.
viskös: viscous.
Viskosimeter *n*: viscosimeter.
Viskosität *f*: viscosity.
visuell: visual.
Visus *m*: visus, vision.
Visusverlust *m*: visual loss.
viszeral: visceral, splanchnic.
Viszeralbogen *m*: visceral arch.
Viszeropleura *f*: visceral wall.
Viszerosensibilität *f*: visceral sense, interoceptive sensibility, splanchnesthesia.
Viszerozeptor *m*: visceroceptor.
vital: vital.
Vitalindikation *f*: vital indication.
Vitalität *f*: vitality.
Vitalkapazität *f*: vital capacity.
Vitamin *n*: vitamin, vitamine.
Vitamingehalt *m*: vitamin content.
Vitaminmangel *m*: vitamin deficiency.
Vitellin *n*: vitellin.
Vitiligo *f*: vitiligo, acquired leukopathia.
Vitriol *n*: vitriol.
Viviparie *f*: viviparity.
Vivisektion *f*: vivisection.
Vogelgesicht *n*: birdlike face.
Vogelgrippe *f*: bird flu, avian influenza.
Vogt-Koyanagi-Syndrom *n*: Vogt-Koyanagi syndrome, oculocutaneous syndrome.
vokal: vocal.
Volarflexion *f*: volar flection.
volatil: volatile.
Volkmann-Kontraktur *f*: ischemic muscular atrophy.
Vollbad, hydroelektrisches *n*: hydroelectric bath.
Vollbild *n*: complete picture.

Vollblut *n*: whole blood.
Vollhautlappen *m*: composite flap.
Vollmondgesicht *n*: moon face.
Vollnarkose *f*: general anesthesia.
Vollwirkdosis *f*: effective dose.
Volumen *n*: volume; **endsystolisches** ≈ end-systolic volume; **forciertes exspiratorisches** ≈ forced expiratory volume.
Volumendehnbarkeit *f*: compliance.
Volumenersatz *m*: volume replacement.
Volumenüberfüllung *f*: plethora.
Volvulus *m*: volvulus.
Vomitus *m*: vomiting, emesis.
vorbehandelt: pretreated, previously treated.
Vorbereitung *f*: preparation.
Vorbeugung *f*: prophylaxis, prevention.
Vorderarmzeichen *n*: forearm sign, Léri sign.
Vorderhauptlage *f*: deflexed vertex presentation.
Vorderhornzelle *f*: anterior horn cell, root cell.
Vorderscheitelbeineinstellung *f*: anterior asynclitism.
Vorderseitenstrang *m*: anterolateral tract, Gowers' tract.
Vorderseitenstrang-Syndrom *n*: anterolateral syndrome.
Vorderwandinfarkt *m*: anterior myocardial infarction.
Vorderwurzel *f*: ventral root, anterior root.
Vorerkrankung *f*: previous disease.
Vorfall *m*: prolapse.
Vorfilterung *f*: primary filtration.
Vorfußgangrän *f*: forefoot gangrene.
Vorgeschichte *f*: history.
Vorhaut *f*: foreskin, prepuce.
Vorhautkonkrement *n*: preputial calculus.
Vorhersage *f*: prognosis, forecast.
Vorhof *m*: atrium, auricle, vestibule.
Vorhofbigeminie *f*: atrial bigeminy.
Vorhofdissoziation *f*: atrial dissociation.
Vorhofflattern *n*: atrial flutter.
Vorhofflimmern *n*: atrial fibrillation.
Vorhofgalopp *m*: atrial gallop.
Vorhofgeräusch *n*: atrial sound.
Vorhofkammerseptumdefekt *m*: atrioventricular septal defect.
Vorhofkomplex *m*: atrial complex.
Vorhofkontraktion *f*: atrial contraction.
Vorhofmyxom *n*: atrial myxoma.
Vorhofscheidewand *f*: atrial septum.
Vorhofseptum *n*: atrial septum.
Vorhofseptumdefekt *m*: atrial septal defect.
Vorhofstillstand *m*: atrial standstill.
Vorhofstimulation *f*: atrial pacing.
Vorhofsystole *f*: atrial systole.
Vorhoftachykardie *f*: atrial tachycardia.
Vorhofthrombose *f*: atrial thrombosis.
Vorhofwelle *f*: atrial beat.
Voriconazol *n*: voriconazole.
Vorkommen *n*: occurrence.
Vorkrankheit *f*: preexisting condition.
Vormilch *f*: foremilk, colostrum.
Vormundschaft *f*: guardianship.
Vorrat *m*: stock, supply, reserve.
Vorsatzlinse *f*: front lens.
Vorschulalter *n*: preschool age.
Vorsichtsmaßnahme *f*: precaution.
Vorsorge *f*: care, precaution, foresight.
Vorsorgemedizin *f*: preventive medicine.
Vorsorgeuntersuchung *f*: checkup.
Vorsprung *m*: prominence, eminence.
Vorsteherdrüse *f*: prostate gland.
Vorstellung *f*: imagination, idea, presentation.
Vorstufe *f*: precursor stage.
vorteilhaft: beneficial, favorable.
vorübergehend: transient, momentary.
Vorversuch *m*: pilot study, preliminary experiment.
Vorwärtsbewegung *f*: forward movement, progression.
Vorwärtsmutation *f*: forward mutation.
Vorwärtsversagen *n*: forward heart failure.
Vorwasser *n*: forewaters, false waters.

Vorwehen: premonitory pains, false pains.
Vorwölbung *f*: protrusion.
Vorzeichen *n*: antecedent sign, prognostic.
vorzeitig: premature, preterm.
Voyeurismus *m*: voyeurism.
Vulnerabilität *f*: vulnerability.
Vulva *f*: vulva.
Vulvakarzinom *n*: carcinoma of vulva.
Vulvaspreizer *m*: vulva retractor.
Vulvektomie *f*: vulvectomy.
Vulvitis *f*: vulvitis.

W

W Abk. **1. Watt; 2. Wolfram** *n*: 1. watt, W; 2. tungsten, W.
Wabenlunge *f*: honeycomb lung.
Wachepilepsie *f*: diurnal epilepsy.
Wachkoma *n*: vigil coma.
Wacholderöl *n*: juniper oil.
Wachs *n*: wax.
Wachsabdruck *m*: waxy cast.
wachsam: alert, vigilant.
Wach-Schlaf-Rhythmus *m*: wake-sleep cycle.
wachsen: grow, increase.
Wachsleber *f*: waxy liver.
Wachsmilz *f*: waxy spleen.
Wachsniere *f*: waxy kidney.
Wachstation *f*: recovery room.
Wachstum *n*: growth; **appositionelles** ≈ appositional growth; **exzessives** ≈ excessive growth; **infiltrierendes** ≈ infiltrative growth; **invasives** ≈ invasive growth; **konfluierendes** ≈ confluent growth; **nichtinvasives** ≈ non-invasive growth; **radiales** ≈ radial growth.
Wachstumsfaktor *m*: growth factor; **epidermaler** ≈ epidermal growth factor; **insulinartiger** ≈ insulin-like growth factor.
Wachstumshormon *n*: growth hormone, GH, somatotropic hormone, STH; **menschliches** ≈ human growth hormone, hGH.
Wachstumskurve *f*: growth chart.
Wachstumsrate *f*: growth rate.
Wachstumsverzögerung *f*: growth retardation.
Wachszylinder *m*: waxy cast.
Wachtraum *m*: waking dream.
Wackelgelenk *n*: loose joint.
Wade *f*: sura, calf.
Wadenbein *n*: fibula, calf bone.
Wärme *f*: warm, warmth, heat, calor.
Wärmeagglutinin *n*: warm agglutinin.
Wärmehaushalt *m*: thermal balance.
Wärmerauschen *n*: white noise, white sound.
Wärmeregulation *f*: thermoregulation.
Wärmeverlust *m*: heat loss.
Wäscherkrätze *f*: dhobie itch.
wässrig: watery, aqueous.
Wahl *f*: choice, option.
Wahn *m*: delusion; **messianischer** ≈ messianic delusion; **nihilistischer** ≈ nihilistic delusion; **primärer** ≈ primary delusion; **sekundärer** ≈ secondary delusion; **somatischer** ≈ somatic delusion; **systematisierter** ≈ systematized delusion, paranoid psychosis.
wahnhaft: delusional.
Wahnidee *f*: delusional idea.
Wahnsyndrom *n*: delusional syndrome.
Wahnsystem *n*: systematized delusion.
wahrnehmbar: perceptible, noticeable.
Wahrnehmung *f*: perception, sensation; **akustische** ≈ auditory perception; **entoptische** ≈ entoptic vision; **kinästhetische** ≈ kinesthetic sensation, kinesthetic sensibility; **optische** ≈ visual perception; **räumliche** ≈ space perception; **unterschwellige** ≈ subliminal perception.
Wahrnehmungsfeld *n*: perceptual field.
Wahrnehmungstäuschung *f*: perceptual illusion.
Wahrscheinlichkeit *f*: probability, likelihood.
Waise *m*: orphan.

Waldenström-Krankheit *f*: Waldenström's macroglobulinemia, benign hyperglobulinemic purpura.
Waldeyer-Rachenring *m*: Waldeyer's tonsillar ring.
Wall *m*: wall, vallum.
Wallenberg-Syndrom *n*: Wallenberg syndrome, lateral medullary syndrome.
Waller-Degeneration *f*: wallerian degeneration, ascending degeneration.
Wand *f*: wall, paries.
Wandaneurysma *n*: mural aneurysm.
Wanddruck *m*: transmural pressure.
Wandel *m*: change.
Wanderleber *f*: wandering liver.
Wandermilz *f*: wandering spleen.
wandernd: wandering, migrating, floating.
Wanderniere *f*: wandering kidney, nephroptosis.
Wandhämatom *n*: intramural hematoma.
Wandspannung *f*: wall stress, wall tension.
Wandthrombus *m*: mural thrombus.
Wandzelle *f*: mural cell.
Wange *f*: cheek; **eingefallene** ≈ hollow cheek.
Wangenfettpfropf *m*: fatty body of the cheek, fatty ball of Bichat.
Wangenlappen *m*: cheek flap, buccal flap.
Wangenschleimhaut *f*: buccal mucosa.
Wangenschleimhautabstrich *m*: buccal smear.
Wangenspalte *f*: cleft cheek.
wanken: stagger.
Wanze *f*: cimex, bug.
Warfarin *n*: warfarin.
warm: warm.
Warnzeichen *n*: signal symptom.
Wartezimmer *n*: waiting room.
Warthin-Tumor *m*: Warthin's tumor, adenolymphoma.
Warze *f*: wart, verruca; **flüchtige** ≈ fugitive wart.
warzenförmig: warty, verrucous, mastoidal.
Warzenhütchen *n*: nipple shield, nipple protector.
Warzenvirus *n*: wart virus, human papillomavirus.
Waschzwang *m*: washing compulsion.
Wasser *n*: water; **destilliertes** ≈ distilled water; **kohlensäurehaltiges** ≈ carbonated water.
Wasserbad *n*: water bath.
Wasserbett *n*: water bed.
Wassereinlagerung *f*: water retention.
Wasserhammerpuls *m*: water-hammer pulse.
Wasserkopf *m*: hydrocephalus.
Wasserkrebs *m*: water cancer, noma.
Wasserlassen *n*: urination, micturition.
wasserlöslich: water-soluble.
Wassersackniere *f*: hydronephrosis.
Wasserscheu *f*: hydrophobia.
Wasserstoff *m*: hydrogen, H.
Wasserstoffperoxid *n*: hydrogen peroxide.
Wassersucht *f*: edema, dropsy.
Wasserverlust *m*: water loss.
Waterhouse-Friderichsen-Syndrom *n*: Waterhouse-Friderichsen syndrome, acute fulminating meningococcal septicemia.
Watschelgang *m*: waddling gait, myopathic gait.
watscheln: waddle, toddle.
Watte *f*: wadding, cotton wool.
Watteträger *m*: cotton applicator.
Weberhusten *m*: weaver's cough, woolsorter's disease.
Weber-Syndrom *n*: Weber-Dubler syndrome, alternating oculomotor hemiplegia.
Wechseldruckbeatmung *f*: positive-negative pressure ventilation.
Wechselfieber *n*: malarial fever.
wechselnd: alternating.
Wechselwirkung *f*: reciprocal action, interaction.
Weckamin *n*: sympathomimetic amine.
Weck-Effekt *m*: arousal effect.
Wehen: contractions, labor, pains; **frustrane** ≈ missed labor; **künstliche** ≈ artificial labor, induced labor; **vorzeitige** ≈ immature labor.

wehenauslösend: oxytocic.
Wehenbeginn *m*: labor onset.
Wehendystokie *f*: dystocia.
Wehenmittel *n*: oxytocic.
Wehenschwäche *f*: uterine insufficiency.
Wehrmedizin *f*: military medicine.
Weiberknoten *m*: false knot, granny knot.
weiblich: female, feminine.
weich: soft, flaccid, tender.
Weichteilrheumatismus *f*: muscular rheumatism.
Weichteilsarkom *n*: soft-tissue sarcoma.
Weichteiltumor *m*: soft-tissue tumor.
Weil-Krankheit *f*: Weil's disease, acute infectious jaundice, leptospirosis.
Weinsäure *f*: tartaric acid.
Weisheitszahn *m*: wisdom tooth, third molar.
Weißfleck *m*: white macule.
weißlich: whitish, albugineous.
weitlumig: large-bore.
Weitsichtigkeit *f*: farsightedness, longsightedness.
weitverbreitet: widespread.
Weitwinkelglaukom *n*: wide-angle glaucoma, open-angle glaucoma.
Welander-Myopathie *f*: Kugelberg Welander syndrome, slow distal hereditary myopathy.
Welle *f*: wave; **anakrote** ≈ anacrotic wave; **dikrote** ≈ dicrotic wave; **katakrote** ≈ catacrotic wave; **kontinuierliche** ≈ continuous wave; **peristaltische** ≈ peristaltic wave; **polymorphe** ≈ polymorphic wave; **spitze** ≈ sharp wave; **stehende** ≈ standing wave.
wellenförmig: undulatory.
Wellenlänge *f*: wavelength.
Weltgesundheitsorganisation *f*: World Health Organization, WHO.
Wendung *f*: version, rotation, inversion; **äußere** ≈ external version; **bimanuelle** ≈ bimanual version; **innere** ≈ internal version; **kombinierte** ≈ combined version; **spontane** ≈ spontaneous version.
Werdnig-Hoffmann-Krankheit *f*: Werdnig-Hoffmann paralysis, acute infantile spinal muscular atrophy.
Werner-His-Krankheit *f*: Werner-His disease, trench fever, Wolhynia fever.
Wernicke-Aphasie *f*: Wernicke's aphasia, sensory aphasia.
Wernicke-Enzephalopathie *f*: Wernicke's encephalopathy, necrotizing hemorrhagic encephalopathy.
Wernicke-Korsakoff-Psychose *f*: Wernicke-Korsakoff psychosis, alcoholic polyneuritic psychosis.
Wertheim-Schauta-Operation *f*: Wertheim-Schauta operation, interposition operation.
Wesensänderung *f*: personality change.
Wespengift *n*: wasp venom.
Westphal-Pilcz-Zeichen *n*: Westphal-Piltz sign, Gifford's reflex, orbiculopupillary reflex.
Whipple-Krankheit *f*: Whipple's disease, intestinal lipodystrophy.
Wickel *m*: compress; **feuchter** ≈ wet compress; **kalter** ≈ cold compress.
Widerstand *m*: resistance; **arterieller** ≈ artery resistance; **exspiratorischer** ≈ expiratory resistance; **peripherer** ≈ peripheral resistance.
Wiederaufnahme *f*: readmission, (biochemistry) re-uptake.
Wiederauftreten *n*: reappearance, recurrence.
wiederbeleben: resuscitate, revive, revitalize.
Wiederbelebung *f*: resuscitation, revival.
Wiederbelebungszeit *f*: resuscitation time.
Wiedereingliederung *f*: rehabilitation; **berufliche** ≈ vocational rehabilitation.
Wiederherstellungschirurgie *f*: reconstructive surgery, surgical reconstruction.
Wiederholungsimpfung *f*: revaccination, booster inoculation.
Wiederholungszwang *m*: compulsive repetition.
Wiederkäuen *n*: rumination.

Wiege *f*: cradle.
wiegen: weigh.
Wildtyp *m*: wild type.
Willkürbewegung *f*: voluntary movement, active movement.
Wilms-Tumor *m*: Wilms' tumor, nephroblastoma.
Wilson-Ableitungen: precordial leads.
Wilson-Krankheit *f*: Wilson syndrome, hepatolenticular degeneration, copper storage disease.
Wimper *f*: eyelash.
Windel *f*: diaper, napkin.
Windeldermatitis *f*: diaper dermatitis.
Windkolik *f*: flatulent colic.
Windpocken *f*: varicella, chickenpox.
Winkel *m*: angle, angulus; **epigastrischer** ≈ epigastric angle.
Wirbel *m*: vertebra, vortex, whirl, whorl.
Wirbelblock *m*: vertebral block.
Wirbelfortsatz *m*: vertebral process.
Wirbelfraktur *f*: vertebral fracture.
Wirbelfusion *f*: vertebral fusion.
Wirbelsäule *f*: spine, spinal column, vertebral column.
Wirbelsäulengelenkerkrankung *f*: spondylosis; **degenerative** ≈ degenerative spondylosis.
Wirbelsäulenverletzung *f*: spinal injury.
Wirbelsäulenversteifung *f*: rigid spine, stiff spine.
Wirbeltuberkulose *f*: tuberculous spondylitis.
Wirbelverschmelzung *f*: vertebral fusion.
Wirkdauer *f*: action time.
Wirkdosis *f*: effective dose.
Wirkkomponente *f*: active component.
Wirkmechanismus *m*: mode of action.
wirksam: effective, operative.
Wirksamkeit *f*: efficacy, activity.
Wirkspektrum, antibiotisches *n*: antibiotic spectrum.
Wirkung *f*: effect, action; **additive** ≈ additive effect; **anhaltende** ≈ lasting effect; **auslösende** ≈ trigger action; **insulinartige** ≈ insulin-like activity; **kumulative** ≈ accumulative effect; **lokale** ≈ local effect; **muskarinartige** ≈ muscarinic effect; **nikotinartige** ≈ nicotinic action; **relative biologische** ≈ relative biologic effect; **synergistische** ≈ synergistic action; **unerwünschte** ≈ side effect.
wirkungslos: uneffective.
wirkungsvoll: efficacious.
Wirt *m*: host.
wirtspezifisch: host-specific.
Wirtswechsel *m*: change of host.
Wirtszelle *f*: host cell.
Witterungseinfluss *m*: weather factor.
Wittmaack-Ekbom-Syndrom *n*: Ekbom syndrome, restless legs.
Wochenbett *n*: childbed, puerperal period.
Wochenbettdepression *f*: puerperal depression.
Wochenbettendometritis *f*: puerperal endometritis.
Wochenbettfieber *n*: puerperal fever.
Wochenbettpsychose *f*: puerperal psychosis.
Wochenbettthrombose *f*: puerperal thrombosis.
Wochenfluss *m*: lochia.
Wohlbefinden *n*: wellness.
Wohlfahrtsverband *m*: welfare organization.
Wolff-Parkinson-White-Syndrom *n*: Wolff-Parkinson-White syndrome, anomalous atrioventricular excitation.
Wolff-Zyste *f*: wolffian cyst.
Wolframsäure *f*: tungstic acid.
Wolhynisches Fieber *n*: Wolhynia fever, trench fever, Werner-His disease.
Wollarbeiterkrankheit *f*: woolsorter's disease.
Wollen *n*: volition.
Wolman-Krankheit *f*: Wolman's disease, familial xanthomatosis.
Wortblindheit *f*: word blindness, verbal alexia.
Wortfindungsstörung *f*: amnestic aphasia, anomia.

Wortflüssigkeit *f*: word fluency, verbal fluency.
Worttaubheit *f*: word deafness, auditory aphasia.
Worttest *m*: vocabulary test.
WPW-Syndrom *n*: Wolff-Parkinson-White syndrome, WPW syndrome, anomalous atrioventricular excitation.
Wuchereriasis *f*: wuchereriasis.
wuchernd: proliferative, luxuriant.
Würgen *n*: regurgitation, retching.
Würgreflex *m*: vomiting reflex, pharyngeal reflex.
Wunde *f*: wound.
Wundermittel *n*: panacea, remedy for all ills.
Wundexzision *f*: wound excision.
Wundhaken *m*: surgical hook.
Wundheilung *f*: wound healing.
Wundklemme *f*: clip, wound clamp.
Wundstarrkrampf *m*: tetanus.
Wundverband *m*: wound dressing.
Wundversorgung *f*: wound management, wound care.
Wurm *m*: worm.
Wurmbefall *m*: worm infestation.
wurmförmig: wormlike, vermiform.
Wurzel *f*: root.
Wurzelirritationssyndrom *n*: nerve root irritation.
Wurzelkompressionssyndrom *n*: compression of nerve roots, motor radicular syndrome.
Wurzelneuralgie *f*: radicular neuralgia.
Wurzelresektion *f*: root resection, radectomy.
Wurzelscheide *f*: root sheath.
Wurzelsyndrom *n*: radicular syndrome, radiculopathy; **lumbales** ≈ lumbar radicular syndrome; **zervikales** ≈ cervical radicular syndrome.
Wutreaktion *f*: rage reaction.

X

X-Achse *f*: x-axis.
Xanthen *n*: xanthene.
Xanthin *n*: xanthine.
Xanthinurie *f*: xanthinuria.
xanthochrom: xanthochromic.
Xanthochromie *f*: xanthochromia.
Xanthocillin *n*: xanthocillin.
Xanthofibrom *n*: xanthofibroma.
Xanthogranulom *n*: xanthogranuloma; **juveniles** ≈ juvenile xanthogranuloma.
xanthogranulomatös: xanthogranulomatous.
Xanthom *n*: xanthoma; **diabetisches** ≈ diabetic xanthoma; **eruptives** ≈ eruptive xanthoma; **generalisiertes** ≈ generalized xanthoma, xanthomatosis; **tendinöses** ≈ tendinous xanthoma.
xanthomatös: xanthomatous.
Xanthomatose *f*: xanthomatosis, generalized xanthoma; **biliäre hypercholesterinämische** ≈ biliary hypercholesterolemic xanthomatosis; **normocholesterinämische** ≈ normocholesterolemic xanthomatosis; **zerebrotendinöse** ≈ cerebrotendinous xanthomatosis.
Xanthomzelle *f*: xanthoma cell, foam cell.
Xanthoproteinsäure *f*: xanthoproteic acid.
Xanthopsie *f*: xanthopsia, yellow vision.
Xanthopsin *n*: xanthopsin, visual yellow.
Xanthosin *n*: xanthosine.
Xanthurensäure *f*: xanthurenic acid.
Xanthylsäure *f*: xanthylic acid.
Xantocillin *n*: xantocillin.
Xantorubin *n*: xantorubin.
X-Bein *n*: genu valgum, knock-knee.
X-Chromosom *n*: X chromosome.
Xenobiotikum *n*: xenobiotic.
xenobiotisch: xenobiotic.
xenogen: xenogeneic, xenogenous.
Xenophobie *f*: xenophobia.
Xenotransplantat *n*: xenograft, heterograft.
Xeroderma *n*: xeroderma.
Xeroderma pigmentosum *n*: xeroderma pigmentosum.
Xerodermie *n*: xeroderma.
Xerophthalmie *f*: xerophthalmia.
Xeroradiographie *f*: xeroradiography.
Xerose *f*: xerosis.
Xerostomie *f*: xerostomia, mouth dryness.
Xibornol *n*: xibornol.
Ximelagatran *n*: ximelagatran.
Ximoprofen *n*: ximoprofen.
Xinomilin *n*: xinomiline.
Xipamid *n*: xipamide.
Xiphoiditis *f*: xiphoiditis.
Xipranolol *n*: xipranolol.
X0-Syndrom *n*: Turner syndrome.
X-Strahlen: x-rays.
XXX-Frau *f*: XXX syndrome, triple-X syndrome.
XXY-Syndrom *n*: XXY syndrome, Klinefelter syndrome.
Xylamidin *n*: xylamidine.
Xylazin *n*: xylazine.
Xylenol *n*: xylenol.
Xylidin *n*: xylidine.
Xylidinrot *n*: xylidine red.
Xylocain *n*: xylocaine.
Xyloflavin *n*: xyloflavine.
Xylokumarol *n*: xylocoumarol.
Xylometazolin *n*: xylometazoline.
Xylose *f*: xylose.
Xylosurie *f*: xylosuria.
Xysma *n*: xysma.
Xyster *m*: xyster.

Y

Y Abk. **Yttrium** *n*: yttrium, Y.
Y-Achse *f*: y-axis.
Yamswurzel *f*: yam.
Y-Chromosom *n*: Y chromosome.
Yersinia *f*: yersinia.
Yersinia-Arthritis *f*: yersinial arthritis.
Yersiniose *f*: yersiniosis, yersinia infection.
Y-förmig: y-shaped.
Yoga *m*: yoga.
Yoghurt *m*: yogurt, yoghurt.
Yohimbin *n*: yohimbine.
Yohimbinsäure *f*: yohimbic acid.
Y-Plastik *f*: Y-plasty.
Y-Schlinge *f*: Roux-en-Y gastroenterostomy.
Yvon-Reaktion *f*: Yvon's test.

Z

Zacke *f*: spike, wave.
zäh: tough, sticky.
zähflüssig: viscous.
zählen: count.
Zähler *m*: counter.
Zählkammer *f*: counting chamber.
Zählung *f*: count, counting.
Zähneknirschen *n*: gnashing, grinding.
Zähnung *f*: dentation, serration.
Zäkum *n*: cecum, blindgut.
Zäpfchen *n*: uvula, suppository.
Zäruloplasmin *n*: ceruloplasmin.
Zahl *f*: number, figure, digit.
zahlreich: numerous.
Zahn *m*: tooth, dens.
Zahnabdruck *m*: dental cast.
Zahnabszess *m*: tooth abscess, dental abscess.
Zahnamalgam *n*: dental amalgam.
Zahnarzt *m*: dentist.
Zahnbehandlung *f*: dental treatment.
Zahnbelag *m*: dental plaque.
Zahnen *n*: teething, dentition.
Zahnersatz *m*: denture; **partieller** ≈ partial denture; **vollständiger** ≈ complete denture, full denture.
Zahnfistel *f*: dental fistula, alveolar fistula.
Zahnfleisch *n*: gingiva, gum.
Zahnfleischblutung *f*: gingival hemorrhage.
Zahnfleischfistel *f*: gingival fistula.
Zahnfleischrand *m*: gingival margin.
Zahnformel *f*: dental formula.
Zahnfüllung *f*: filling, inlay.
Zahngranulom *n*: dental granuloma.
Zahnhals *m*: neck of the tooth.
Zahnheilkunde *f*: dentistry, odontology.
Zahnkaries *f*: dental caries, tooth decay.
Zahnkrone *f*: crown, cap.
zahnlos: toothless.
Zahnpasta *f*: toothpaste.
Zahnpflege *f*: dental hygiene, dental care.
Zahnprothese *f*: dental prosthesis, denture.
Zahnradphänomen *n*: cogwheel sign, Negro sign.
Zahnschema *n*: dental formula.
Zahnschmerz *m*: toothache, odontalgia.
Zahnspitzenostitis *f*: apical osteitis.
Zahnstein *m*: dental calculus, dental stone.
Zahntasche *f*: periodontal pocket.
Zahnung *f*: serration.
Zahnverfärbung *f*: tooth discoloration.
Zahnwurzelzyste *f*: radiculodental cyst.
Zalcitabin *n*: zalcitabine.
Zaleplon *n*: zaleplon.
Zanamivir *n*: zanamivir.
Zange *f*: forceps, pliers, pair of tongs.
Zangengeburt *f*: forceps delivery.
Zapfen *m*: peg, cone, visual receptor
Zapfennaht *f*: clavate suture, quilled suture.
Zapizolam *n*: zapizolam.
Z-Diagramm *n*: z chart.
Zecke *f*: tick.
Zeckenbissfieber *n*: tick-bite fever.
Zeckenenzephalitis *f*: tick-borne encephalitis; **russische** ≈ Russian spring-summer encephalitis; **zentraleuropäische** ≈ Central European encephalitis.
Zeckenlähmung *f*: tick paralysis, ixodiasis.
Zeckenrückfallfieber *n*: tick-borne relapsing fever; **afrikanisches** ≈

African tick fever, Dutton's relapsing fever; **amerikanisches** ≈ Rocky Mountain spotted fever.
Zehe *f*: toe, dactyl.
Zeichen *n*: sign, symptom, mark, phenomenon; **pathognomonisches** ≈ pathognomonic sign.
Zeichensprache *f*: sign language.
Zeichentest *m*: design test.
Zeichnung *f*: drawing.
Zeigefinger *m*: index finger, forefinger.
Zeinagar *m*: zein agar.
Zeitintervall *n*: time interval, span.
Zeitwahrnehmung *f*: time perception.
Zellatmung *f*: cellular respiration, cell respiration.
Zelle *f*: cell; **amakrine** ≈ amacrine cell; **amöboide** ≈ ameboid cell; **antigenpräsentierende** ≈ antigen-presenting cell; **apokrine** ≈ apocrine cell; **ballonierte** ≈ balloon cell; **basalgekörnte** ≈ basal granular cell; **begeißelte** ≈ flagellate cell; **bewegliche** ≈ motile cell; **dendritische** ≈ dendritic cell; **embryonale** ≈ embryonic cell; **enterochromaffine** ≈ enterochromaffin cell; **hämatopoetische** ≈ hematopoietic cell; **halbmondförmige** ≈ cellular crescent; **helle** ≈ clear cell; **hyperchrome** ≈ hyperchromatic cell; **immunkompetente** ≈ immunologically competent cell, immunocyte; **juxtaglomeruläre** ≈ juxtaglomerular cell, Goormaghtigh cell; **kernhaltige** ≈ nucleated cell; **kernlose** ≈ akaryocyte, akaryote; **mesenchymale** ≈ mesenchymal cell, human fibroblastoid cell; **myeloische** ≈ myeloid cell; **neurosekretorische** ≈ neurosecretory cell; **neurosensorische** ≈ neurosensory cell; **omnipotente** ≈ totipotential cell; **phäochrome** ≈ pheochrome cell; **pluripotente** ≈ pluripotent cell; **pneumatische** ≈ air cell; **polyploide** ≈ polyploid; **pyknotische** ≈ pyknotic cell; **ungekörnte** ≈ agranular cell; **vakuolisierte** ≈ vacuolated cell; **wasserhelle** ≈ water-clear cell.
Zellgift *n*: cell poison, cytotoxin.
Zellkern *m*: cell nucleus, karyon.
Zellkompartiment *n*: cellular compartment.
Zellkultur *f*: cell culture.
Zellmembran *f*: cell membrane.
Zellplasma *n*: cytoplasma, cell plasma.
Zellstoff *m*: cellulose.
Zellteilung *f*: cell division.
zellulär: cellular.
Zellularpathologie *f*: cellular pathology.
Zellulitis *f*: cellulitis.
Zelluntergang *m*: cellular decay.
Zellvolumen *n*: cell volume; **mittleres** ≈ mean corpuscular volume, MCV.
Zellwand *f*: cell wall.
Zellweger-Syndrom *n*: Zellweger syndrome, cerebrohepatorenal syndrome.
Zellzählung *f*: cell count.
Zellzahl *f*: cell count.
Zenith *m*: zenith.
Zenker-Divertikel *n*: Zenker's diverticulum, pharyngoesophageal diverticulum.
zentral: central.
Zentralisation *f*: centralization.
Zentralnervensystem *n*: central nervous system, CNS.
Zentralskotom *n*: central scotoma.
Zentralstar *m*: central cataract.
Zentralvenenthrombose *f*: central venous thrombosis.
Zentralzelle *f*: central cell.
zentrieren: centre.
zentrifugal: centrifugal.
Zentrifuge *f*: centrifuge.
Zentriole *f*: centriole.
zentripetal: centripetal.
Zentroblastom *n*: centroblastic lymphoma.
Zentromer *n*: centromere.
Zentrosom *n*: centrosome.
Zentrum *n*: centre, core.
Zepastin *n*: zepastine.
Zephalgie *f*: cephalgia, headache.
Zeranol *n*: zeranol.
zerbrechlich: fragile, brittle.
zerebellär: cerebellar.
zerebral: cerebral.

Zerebralparese *f*: cerebral palsy; **spastische** ≈ infantile spastic paralysis, Little's disease.
zerebrospinal: cerebrospinal.
zerebrovaskulär: cerebrovascular.
Zerfall *m*: decay, decomposition, lysis; **radioaktiver** ≈ radioactive decay.
Zerfallskonstante *f*: decay constant.
Zerkarie *f*: cercaria.
Zeroidlipofuszinose *f*: ceroid lipofuscinosis; **adulte** ≈ adult ceroid lipofuscinosis, Kufs' disease; **infantile** ≈ infantile ceroid lipofuscinosis, Tay-Sachs disease; **juvenile** ≈ juvenile ceroid lipofuscinosis, Spielmeyer-Vogt disease; **spätinfantile** ≈ late infantile ceroid lipofuscinosis, Bielschowsky-Jansky disease.
zerquetschen: crush, mash.
Zerrung *f*: strain, distorsion.
Zersetzung *f*: decomposition, dissolution.
zersplittern: splinter, comminute.
zersprengen: burst, break.
Zerstreuungslinse *f*: dispersing lens.
Zerstückelung *f*: dismemberment, dissection.
zertrümmern: shatter, crush.
Zerumen *n*: cerumen, earwax.
Zeruminalpfropf *m*: impacted cerumen.
zervikal: cervical.
Zervikalabstrich *m*: cervical smear.
Zervikalganglien: cervical ganglia.
Zervikalkanal *m*: cervical canal.
zervikobrachial: cervicobrachial.
Zervikobrachialgie *f*: cervicobrachialgia.
Zervikobrachialsyndrom *n*: cervicobrachial syndrome.
Zervix *f*: cervix, nape, neck.
Zervixabstrich *m*: cervical smear.
Zervixdilatation *f*: cervical dilatation.
Zervixdystokie *f*: cervical dystocia.
Zervixektopie *f*: cervical ectopia.
Zervixfaktor *m*: cervical factor.
Zervixkarzinom *n*: cervix carcinoma, cervical cancer.
Zervixleukoplakie *f*: cervical leukoplakia.
Zervixnaht *f*: trachelorrhaphy.
Zervixpolyp *m*: cervical polyp.
Zervixresektion *f*: cervicectomy.
Zervizitis *f*: cervicitis.
Zetidolin *n*: zetidoline.
Zeugungsfähigkeit *f*: procreative capacity.
Zeugungsunfähigkeit *f*: impotency, sterility.
Ziconotid *n*: ziconotide.
Zidovudin *n*: zidovudine.
Zielbewegung *f*: directed movement.
ziliar: ciliary.
Ziliardrüsen: ciliary glands.
Ziliarisreflex *m*: ciliary reflex.
Ziliarneuralgie *f*: ciliar neuralgia.
Zimelidin *n*: zimelidine.
Zinkmangel *m*: zinc deficiency.
Zinkoxid *n*: zinc oxide.
Zinksalbe *f*: zinc ointment.
Zinnsäure *f*: stannic acid.
Zinstatin *n*: zinstatin.
Zinterol *n*: zinterol.
Zinviroxim *n*: zinviroxime.
Zipeprol *n*: zipeprol.
Ziprasidon *n*: ziprasidone.
Zirbeldrüse *f*: pineal gland, pineal body.
zirkadian: circadian.
Zirkelschnitt *m*: circular amputation.
Zirkulation *f*: circulation; **extrakorporale** ≈ extracorporeal circulation.
zirkumskript: circumscribed.
Zirkumzision *f*: circumcision.
Zirrhose *f*: cirrhosis; **biliäre** ≈ biliary cirrhosis; **metabolische** ≈ metabolic cirrhosis; **periportale** ≈ periportal cirrhosis; **posthepatitische** ≈ posthepatitic cirrhosis; **primäre biliäre** ≈ primary biliary cirrhosis, PBC; **sekundäre biliäre** ≈ secondary biliary cirrhosis.
zirrhotisch: cirrhotic.
zirzinär: circinate.
Zisterne *f*: cistern.
Zisternenpunktion *f*: cisternal puncture.
Zitratblut *n*: citrated blood.
Zitraturie *f*: citruria.
Zitratzyklus *m*: tricarboxylic acid cycle, Krebs cycle.
Zitronensäure *f*: citric acid.
Zittern *n*: shivering, trembling, tre-

mor; **fibrilläres** ≈ fibrillation.
Z-Lappen *m*: Z-flap.
Zocainon *n*: zocainone.
zöliakal: celiac.
Zöliakie *f*: celiac disease, nontropical sprue; **infantile** ≈ infantile celiac disease, Gee-Herter-Heubner disease.
Zöliakiekrise *f*: celiac crisis.
Zölikographie *f*: celiac arteriography.
Zöliokolpotomie *f*: celiocolpotomy.
Zofenopril *n*: zofenopril.
Zoficonazol *n*: zoficonazole.
Zolamin *n*: zolamine.
Zolazepam *n*: zolazepam.
Zoledronsäure *n*: zoledronic acid.
Zolertin *n*: zolertine.
Zollinger-Ellison-Syndrom *n*: Zollinger-Ellison syndrome.
Zolmitriptan *n*: zolmitriptan.
Zoloperon *n*: zoloperone.
Zolpidem *n*: zolpidem.
Zomepirac *n*: zomepirac.
zonal: zonal.
Zone *f*: zone, zonule; **erogene** ≈ erogenous zone; **hyperästhetische** ≈ hyperesthetic zone.
Zonisamid *n*: zonisamide.
Zonula *f*: zonula, zonule.
Zooanthroponose *f*: zooanthroponosis.
Zoom-Optik *f*: zoom lens.
Zoonose *f*: zoonosis.
Zooparasit *m*: zooparasite, animal parasite.
Zoophilie *f*: zoophilia.
Zoospermie *f*: zoospermia.
Zoospore *f*: zoospore.
Zoosterin *n*: zoosterol.
Zopiclon *n*: zopiclone.
Zorubicin *n*: zorubicin.
Zoster *m*: zoster, herpes zoster, shingles; **neuralgischer** ≈ neuralgic herpes; **symptomatischer** ≈ symptomatic zoster.
zosterartig: zosteriform.
Zotepin *n*: zotepine.
Zotte *f*: villus.
Zottenadenom *n*: villous adenoma.
Zottenatrophie *f*: villous atrophy.
Zottenherz *n*: hairy heart.
Zottenkrebs *m*: villous carcinoma.
Zottenplazenta *f*: villous placenta.
zottig: villous.
Zoxazolamin *n*: zoxazolamine.
Z-Plastik *f*: Z-plasty.
Z-Streifen *m*: Z line, Z band.
Zubereitungsanweisung *f*: subscription.
Zubereitungsform *f*: formulation.
zucken: twitch, jerk, quiver.
Zuckeraustauschstoff *m*: sugar substitute.
Zuckergussleber *f*: icing liver.
Zuckergussmilz *f*: iced spleen.
Zuckerkandl-Organ *n*: Zuckerkandl's organ.
Zuckerkrankheit *f*: sugar diabetes, diabetes mellitus.
Zuckung *f*: twitching, convulsion, spasm; **choreatiforme** ≈ choreic convulsion; **faszikuläre** ≈ fascicular twitching, fasciculation; **fibrilläre** ≈ fibrillar twitching; **mimische** ≈ tic; **tetanische** ≈ tetanic contraction, tetanic convulsion.
Zuclopenthixol *n*: zuclopenthixol.
züchten: breed.
Zufall *m*: accident, random.
Zufallsbefund *m*: incidental finding.
Zufallsparasit *m*: accidental parasite, incidental parasite.
Zufallsstichprobe *f*: random sample.
Zufluss *m*: inflow, afflux.
zuführend: afferent.
Zufuhr *f*: supply.
Zug *m*: traction, tension.
Zugang *m*: approach, access, entrance.
Zugangsweg *m*: route.
Zulassung *f*: admission, approval.
Zunahme *f*: increase, gain.
zunehmen: gain, increase.
Zunge *f*: tongue, lingua; **belegte** ≈ coated tongue; **pelzige** ≈ furred tongue.
Zungenatrophie *f*: lingual atrophy.
Zungengrundstruma *f*: lingual goiter.
Zungenlähmung *f*: glossoplegia.
Zungenlappen *m*: lingual flap, tongue flap.
Zungenspatel *m*: tongue blade, tongue spatula.
Zungentonsille *f*: lingual tonsil.

Zungenwurm *m*: tongue worm, pentastomid.
Zuordnungstest *m*: matching test.
zurückhalten: retain.
Zurückhalten *n*: retention.
Zurückweisung *f*: rejection.
Zusammenbruch *m*: breakdown.
Zusammenfluss *m*: confluence.
Zusammenhang *m*: relationship, context, association, link; **kausaler** ≈ causal relationship.
Zusammenklumpung *f*: clotting.
Zusatzmedikation *f*: additional medication.
Zustand *m*: condition, state, status.
Zustimmung *f*: consent, approval.
Zuträglichkeit *f*: conduciveness, wholesomeness, salubrity.
Zuverlässigkeit *f*: reliability.
Zuwachs *m*: increment, increase.
Zwang *m*: compulsion, obsession, force.
zwanghaft: compulsory, obsessive.
Zwangsbehandlung *f*: compulsory treatment.
Zwangscharakter *m*: obsessive-compulsive personality, compulsive personality.
Zwangserbrechen *n*: forced vomiting.
Zwangsernährung *f*: forced alimentation.
Zwangshandlung *f*: compulsive action, imperious act.
Zwangsidee *f*: compulsive idea, persistent idea.
Zwangsjacke *f*: straitjacket, camisole.
Zwangslachen *n*: compulsive laughter.
Zwangsmaßnahme *f*: restraint.
Zwangsneurose *f*: compulsive neurosis.
Zwangsvorstellung *f*: obsession, compulsive idea.
Zwangsweinen *n*: compulsive crying.
zweieiig: binovular.
Zweifachkombination *f*: double combination.
Zweigläserprobe *f*: two-glass test.
zweihörnig: bicornate.
zweikammerig: biventricular, bilocular.
Zweikammerstimulation *f*: dual-chamber pacing.
Zweipunktediskrimination *f*: two-point discrimination.
Zweistärkenbrille *f*: bifocal spectacles, bifocal glasses.
Zweitgutachten *n*: second opinion.
Zweittumor *m*: secondary tumor.
Zweiwegkatheter *m*: two-way catheter.
Zwerchfell *n*: diaphragma.
Zwerchfellatmung *f*: diaphragmatic breathing.
Zwerchfellhernie *f*: diaphragmatic hernia.
Zwerchfellhochstand *m*: elevation of diaphragm.
Zwerchfelllähmung *f*: diaphragmatic paralysis.
Zwerchfellzuckung *f*: diaphragmatic flutter.
Zwergenkrankheit *f*: runt disease.
Zwergwuchs *m*: dwarfism, nanosomia; **greisenhafter** ≈ progeria, Hutchinson-Gilford syndrome; **hypophysärer** ≈ hypophyseal dwarfism, Lorain's disease; **thanatophorer** ≈ thanatophoric dysplasia.
Zwicken *n*: pinch, twinge.
Zwieback *m*: rusk.
Zwillinge: twins; **eineiige** ≈ uniovular twins, homozygotic twins; **monochoriale** ≈ monochorionic twins; **monozygote** ≈ monozygotic twins, true twins; **siamesische** ≈ Siamese twins, conjoined twins; **zweieiige** ≈ binovular twins, dichorial twins.
Zwillingsschwangerschaft *f*: twin pregnancy.
Zwischenblutung *f*: spotting, intermenstrual bleeding.
Zwischenhirnsyndrom *n*: diencephalic syndrome, Berardinelli syndrome.
Zwischenkiefer *m*: intermaxillary bone.
Zwischenlappen *m*: intercalated flap.
Zwischenraum *m*: interspace, interstice.
Zwischenwirt *m*: intermediate host, transfer host.
Zwölffingerdarmgeschwür *n*: duodenal ulcer.

Zyanose *f*: cyanosis; **autotoxische** ≈ toxic cyanosis, enterogenous cyanosis; **kardiale** ≈ shunt cyanosis; **periphere** ≈ peripheral cyanosis; **pulmonale** ≈ pulmonary cyanosis; **zentrale** ≈ central cyanosis.
Zyansäure *f*: cyanic acid.
Zyanursäure *f*: cyanuric acid.
Zyanwasserstoffsäure *f*: hydrocyanic acid.
zygomatikofazial: zygomaticofacial.
Zygomatizitis *f*: inflammation of the os zygomaticum.
Zygomykose *f*: zygomycosis.
Zygote *f*: zygote.
zyklisch: cyclic.
Zyklitis *f*: cyclitis; **heterochrome** ≈ heterochromic cyclitis.
Zyklodialyse *f*: cyclodialysis.
Zyklopie *f*: cyclopia.
Zyklothymie *f*: cyclothymia.
Zyklotomie *f*: cyclotomy.
Zyklozephalie *f*: cyclopean brain.
Zyklus *m*: cycle; **anovulatorischer** ≈ anovulatory cycle, monophasic cycle; **biphasischer** ≈ biphasic cycle; **monophasischer** ≈ monophasic cycle, anovulatory menstruation; **ovarieller** ≈ ovarian cycle.
Zylinder *m*: cylinder, cast; **hyaliner** ≈ hyaline cast.
Zylinderlinse *f*: cylindric lens.
Zylinderzellkarzinom *n*: cylindrical carcinoma.
Zylinderzellsarkom *n*: cylindromatous sarcoma.
Zylindrom *n*: cylindroma, adenoid cystic carcinoma.
Zymogen *n*: zymogen.
Zymogengranula: zymogen granules.
zymotisch: zymotic.
Zystadenom *n*: cystadenoma.
Zyste *f*: cyst; **bronchogene** ≈ bronchogenic cyst; **hämorrhagische** ≈ hemorrhagic cyst; **intestinale** ≈ enteric cyst; **paraösophageale** ≈ paraesophageal cyst; **perirenale** ≈ paranephric cyst; **präaurikuläre** ≈ preauricular cyst; **seröse** ≈ serous cyst.
Zystein *n*: cysteine.
Zystektomie *f*: cystectomy.
Zystenlunge *f*: honeycomb lung.
Zystenniere *f*: cystic kidney, nephrocystosis.
Zystin *n*: cystine.
Zystinose *f*: cystinosis, Lignac-Fanconi disease.
Zystinurie *f*: cystinuria.
zystisch: cystic.
Zystische Fibrose *f*: cystic fibrosis, CF, mucoviscidosis.
Zystitis *f*: cystitis; **diphtherische** ≈ diphtheric cystitis; **gangränöse** ≈ gangrenous cystitis; **interstitielle** ≈ interstitial cystitis; **mechanische** ≈ mechanical cystitis; **transmurale** ≈ panmural cystitis; **ulzerierende** ≈ ulcerative cystitis.
Zystizerkose *f*: cysticercosis.
Zystographie *f*: cystography.
Zystolithiasis *f*: cystolithiasis.
Zystometrie *f*: cystometry.
Zystometrogramm *n*: cystometrogram.
Zystopyelonephritis *f*: cystopyelonephritis.
Zystoskopie *f*: cystoscopy.
Zystostomie *f*: cystostomy, vesicostomy.
Zystotomie *f*: cystotomy, vesicotomy; **suprapubische** ≈ suprapubic cystotomy.
Zystourethrographie *f*: cystourethrography.
Zystozele *f*: cystocele.
Zytisin *n*: cytisine.
Zytochrom *n*: cytochrome.
Zytogenetik *f*: cytogenetics.
Zytokin *n*: cytokine.
Zytologie *f*: cytology.
Zytolyse *f*: cytolysis.
zytolytisch: cytolytic.
Zytomegalie *f*: cytomegaly.
Zytomegalievirus *n*: cytomegalovirus, CMV.
zytopathisch: cytopathic.
zytophil: cytophilic.
Zytoplasma *n*: cytoplasma.
zytoplasmatisch: cytoplasmic.
zytotoxisch: cytotoxic.
zytotrop: cytotropic.
Zytotrophoblast *m*: cytotrophoblast, Langhans layer.
Zytozym *n*: cytozyme.

Appendix I: Abbreviations in Medicine
Anhang I: Medizinische Abkürzungen

A

a <*abbr*> **1. about; 2. absent; 3. absolute; 4. absorbent; 5. accommodation; 6. acid; 7. actin; 8. active; 9. adenine; 10. allergy; 11. ampere; 12. ante; 13. artery; 14. asymmetry**: 1. ungefähr; 2. abwesend; 3. absolut; 4. Absorbens *n*; 5. Akkomodation *f*, A; 6. Säure *f*; 7. Aktin *n*; 8. aktiv; 9. Adenin *n*, A; 10. Allergie *f*; 11. Ampere *n*, A; 12. ante; 13. Arteria *f*, A., Arterie *f*; 14. Asymmetrie *f*.

aa <*abbr*> **arteries**: Arterien, Arteriae, Aa.

AA <*abbr*> **1. achievement age; 2. Alcoholics Anonymous**: 1. Leistungsalter *n*; 2. Anonyme Alkoholiker, AA.

AAV <*abbr*> **adenoassociated virus**: adenoassoziiertes Virus *n*.

ab <*abbr*> **1. abort, abortion; 2. about; 3. antibody**: 1. Abort *m*, Schwangerschaftsunterbrechung *f*; 2. ungefähr; 3. Antikörper *m*, Ak.

ABC <*abbr*> **antigen binding capacity**: Antigenbindungskapazität *f*.

ABLC <*abbr*> **amphotericin B lipid complex**: liposomales Amphotericin B *n*.

ABMT <*abbr*> **autologous bone marrow transplantation**: autologe Knochenmarktransplantation *f*.

ABP <*abbr*> **arterial blood pressure**: arterieller Blutdruck *m*.

abs <*abbr*> **1. absolute; 2. absent**: 1. absolut; 2. fehlend.

ABS <*abbr*> **acute brain syndrome**: akutes hirnlokales Syndrom *n*.

AC <*abbr*> **1. adrenal cortex; 2. alternating current**: 1. Nebennierenrinde *f*, NNR; 2. Wechselstrom *m*.

ACC <*abbr*> **1. alveolar cell carcinoma; 2. anodal closure contraction**: 1. Alveolarzellkarzinom *n*; 2. Anodenschlusszuckung *f*.

acc <*abbr*> **accommodation**: Akkommodation *f*.

ACCl <*abbr*> **anodal closure clonus**: Anodenschlusszuckung *f*.

ACE <*abbr*> **angiotensin converting enzyme**: Angiotensin umwandelndes Enzym *n*, ACE.

AcG <*abbr*> **accelerator globulin**: Akzeleratorglobulin *n*, Faktor V *m*.

ACG <*abbr*> **1. angiocardiography; 2. apexcardiogram**: 1. Angiokardiographie *f*; 2. Apexkardiogramm *n*.

ACh <*abbr*> **acetylcholin**: Acetylcholin *n*, ACh.

AChE <*abbr*> **acetylcholinesterase**: Acetylcholinesterase *f*, AChE.

ACTH <*abbr*> **adrenocorticotropic hormone**: adrenokortikotropes Hormon *n*, ACTH.

ADA <*abbr*> **adenosine deaminase**: Adenosindesaminase *f*, ADA.

ADD <*abbr*> **attention deficit disorder**: Aufmerksamkeits-Hyperaktivitätsstörung *f*, ADHS.

Ade <*abbr*> **adenine**: Adenin *n*, A.

ADH <*abbr*> **1. alcohol dehydrogenase; 2. antidiuretic hormone**: 1. Alkoholdehydrogenase *f*; 2. antidiuretisches Hormon *n*, ADH, Adiuretin *n*.

ADP <*abbr*> **adenosine diphosphate**: Adenosindiphosphat *n*, ADP.

AF <*abbr*> **amniotic fluid**: Amnionflüssigkeit *f*.

AFB <*abbr*> **acid-fast bacterium**: säurefestes Bakterium *n*.

AFO <*abbr*> **ankle-foot orthosis**: Berliner Schuh *m*.

AFP <*abbr*> **alpha-fetoprotein**: Alphafetoprotein *n*, AFP.

AGS <*abbr*> **adrenogenital syndrome**: adrenogenitales Syndrom *n*, AGS.

AHF *<abbr>* **antihemophilic factor**: Antihämophiliefaktor *m*, AHF, Faktor VIII *m*.

AHG *<abbr>* **antiglobulin test**: Antiglobulintest *m*, Coombs-Test *m*.

AI *<abbr>* **1. aortic insufficiency; 2. artificial insemination**: 1. Aorteninsuffizienz *f*; 2. artifizielle Insemination *f*, künstliche Befruchtung *f*.

AID *<abbr>* **artificial insemination by donor**: heterologe künstliche Insemination *f*.

AIDS *<abbr>* **Acquired Immune Deficiency Syndrome**: erworbenes Immundefektsyndrom *n*, AIDS.

AIH *<abbr>* **artificial insemination by husband**: homologe Insemination *f*.

AIN *<abbr>* **anal intraepithelial neoplasia**: anale intraepitheliale Neoplasie *f*.

AIP *<abbr>* **acute intermittent porphyria**: akute intermittierende Porphyrie *f*.

ALA *<abbr>* **δ-aminolevulinic acid**: δ-Aminolävulinsäure *f*, ALS.

Ala *<abbr>* **alanine**: Alanin *n*.

alb *<abbr>* **albumin**: Albumin *n*.

ALG *<abbr>* **antilymphocyte globulin**: Antilymphozytenglobulin *n*.

ALI *<abbr>* **annual limit of intake**: Jahresgrenzwert für die Aufnahme von Radionukliden *m*.

ALL *<abbr>* **acute lymphoblastic leukemia**: akute lymphatische Leukämie *f*, ALL.

ALS *<abbr>* **1. amyotrophic lateral sclerosis; 2. antilymphocyte serum**: 1. amyotrophe Lateralsklerose *f*, ALS; 2. antilymphozytäres Serum *n*.

ALT *<abbr>* **alanine transaminase**: Alanintransaminase *f*.

AMA *<abbr>* **against medical advice**: gegen medizinischen Rat.

amb *<abbr>* **1. ambulance; 2. ambulatory**: 1. Krankenwagen *m*; 2. ambulant.

AMI *<abbr>* **acute myocardial infarction**: akuter Myokardinfarkt *m*.

AMP *<abbr>* **adenosine monophosphate**: Adenosinmonophosphat *n*, AMP.

amp *<abbr>* **1. ampere; 2. amperage; 3. ampule; 4. amputation**: 1. Ampere *n*; 2. Amperezahl *f*, Stromstärke *f*; 3. Ampulle *f*; 4. Amputation *f*.

amt *<abbr>* **amount**: Menge *f*.

ANA *<abbr>* **antinuclear antibody**: antinukleärer Antikörper *m*, ANA.

anat *<abbr>* **anatomy**: Anatomie *f*.

AnCC *<abbr>* **anodal closure contraction**: Anodenschlusszuckung *f*.

ANF *<abbr>* **antinuclear factor**: antinukleärer Faktor *m*, ANF.

ANS *<abbr>* **autonomic nervous system**: autonomes Nervensystem *n*.

ANUG *<abbr>* **acute necrotizing ulcerative gingivitis**: akute nekrotisierende ulzerierende Gingivitis *f*.

AP *<abbr>* **1. action potential; 2. alkaline phosphatase; 3. anterior pituitary; 4. anteroposterior; 5. aortic pressure; 6. arterial pressure**: 1. Aktionspotential *n*; 2. alkalische Phosphatase *f*; 3. Adenohypophyse *f*; 4. anteroposterior, a-p; 5. Aortendruck *m*; 6. arterieller Blutdruck *m*.

A-P *<abbr>* **anterior-posterior**: anterior-posterior, a-p.

APC *<abbr>* **1. acetysalicylic acid, phenacetin, and caffeine; 2. antigen-presenting cell**: 1. Acetylsalicylsäure, Phenazetin und Koffein; 2. antigenpräsentierende Zelle *f*.

appl *<abbr>* **application**: Applikation *f*, Anwendung *f*.

approx *<abbr>* **approximate**: annähernd, ungefähr.

APPT *<abbr>* **activated partial thromboplastin time**: partielle Thromboplastinzeit *f*, PTT.

AR *<abbr>* **1. aortic regurgitation; 2. artificial respiration**: 1. Aortenregurgitation *f*; 2. künstliche Beatmung *f*.

ara-A *<abbr>* **vidarabine**: Vidarabin *n*.

ARAS *<abbr>* **ascending reticular activating system**: aufsteigendes retikuläres aktivierendes System *n*, ARAS.

ARC *<abbr>* **1. AIDS-related complex; 2. abnormal retinal corre-**

spondance: 1. AIDS-related Komplex *m*, ARC; 2. abnorme Netzhautkorrespondenz *f*.

ARD *<abbr>* **acute respiratory distress**: akutes Atemnotsyndrom *n*.

ARDS *<abbr>* **adult respiratory distress syndrome**: posttraumatische pulmonale Insuffizienz *f*, Schocklunge *f*, ARDS.

Arg *<abbr>* **arginine**: Arginin *n*, Arg.

ARM *<abbr>* **artificial rupture of the membranes**: Amniotomie *f*, künstliche Blasensprengung *f*.

ARS *<abbr>* **autonomously replicating sequence**: autonom replizierende Sequenz *f*, ARS.

AS *<abbr>* **1. aortic stenosis; 2. arteriosclerosis**: 1. Aortenstenose *f*; 2. Arteriosklerose *f*.

ASCVD *<abbr>* **arteriosclerotic cardiovascular disease**: arteriosklerotische kardiovaskuläre Erkrankung *f*.

ASD *<abbr>* **atrial septal defect**: Vorhofseptumdefekt *m*, Atriumseptumdefekt *m*, ASD.

ASHD *<abbr>* **arteriosclerotic heart disease**: arteriosklerotische Herzerkrankung *f*.

ASO *<abbr>* **allele-specific oligonucleotide**: allelspezifisches Oligonukleotid *n*, ASO.

assn *<abbr>* **association**: Assoziation *f*, Vereinigung *f*.

AT *<abbr>* **atrial tachycardia**: Vorhoftachykardie *f*.

ATA *<abbr>* **alimentary toxic aleukia**: alimentär-toxische Leukopenie *f*, alimentär-toxische Aleukie *f*.

ATP *<abbr>* **adenosine triphosphate**: Adenosintriphosphat *n*, ATP.

ATPase *<abbr>* **adenosine triphosphatase**: Adenosintriphosphatase *f*.

ATS *<abbr>* **antitetanus serum**: Tetanusserum *n*, Antitetanusserum *n*.

av *<abbr>* **1. average; 2. arteriovenous; 3. atrioventricular**: 1. Durchschnitt *m*; 2. arteriovenös; 3. atrioventrikulär, AV-.

ax. *<abbr>* **axis**: Axis *m*, Achse *f*.

AZT *<abbr>* **1. Aschheim-Zondek test; 2. azidothymidine**: 1. Aschheim-Zondek-Schwangerschaftstest *m*; 2. Azidothymidin *n*, AZT, Zidovudin *n*, ZDV.

B

B *<abbr>* **1. magnetic induction; 2. bacillus**: 1. magnetische Induktion *f*; 2. Bazillus *m*.

BA *<abbr>* **bronchial asthma**: Bronchialasthma *n*.

BAL *<abbr>* **1. British antilewisite; 2. bronchoalveolar lavage**: 1. Dimercaprol *n*, BAL; 2. bronchoalveoläre Lavage *f*, BAL.

BAO *<abbr>* **basal acid output**: BAO, basale Säuresekretion *f*.

BBB *<abbr>* **1. blood-brain barrier; 2. bundle branch block**: 1. Blut-Hirn-Schranke *f*; 2. Schenkelblock *m*.

BBBB *<abbr>* **bilateral bundle branch block**: beidseitiger Schenkelblock *m*, trifaszikulärer Block *m*.

BBT *<abbr>* **basal body temperature**: Basaltemperatur *f*, BT.

BC *<abbr>* **1. birth control; 2. bone conduction**: 1. Geburtenkontrolle *f*; 2. Knochenleitung *f*.

BCAA *<abbr>* **branched-chain amino acid**: verzweigtkettige Aminosäure *f*.

BCG *<abbr>* **bacille Calmette-Guérin**: Bacille Calmette-Guérin *m*.

BCGF *<abbr>* **B-cell growth factor**: B-Zell-Wachstumsfaktor *m*.

b. d. *<abbr>* **bis die**: bis die, zweimal täglich.

BE *<abbr>* **1. barium enema; 2. base excess**: 1. Bariumkontrasteinlauf *m*; 2. Basenüberschuss *m*.

BFP *<abbr>* **biologic false-positive**: biologisch falsch-positiv.

BLS *<abbr>* **basic life support**: Herz-Lungen-Wiederbelebung *f*, HLW.

BM *<abbr>* **bowel movement**: Stuhlgang *m*.

BMG *<abbr>* **benign monoclonal gammopathy**: benigne monoklonale Gammopathie *f*.

BMI *<abbr>* **body mass index**: Body-Mass-Index *m*, BMI.

BMR <*abbr*> **basal metabolic rate**: Grundumsatz *m*.

BNA <*abbr*> **Basle Nomina Anatomica**: Basler Nomina Anatomica.

BP <*abbr*> **1. blood pressure; 2. British Pharmacopoeia**: 1. Blutdruck *m*, RR; 2. Britische Pharmakopoe *f*.

bp <*abbr*> **1. base pair; 2. boiling point**: 1. Basenpaar *n*; 2. Siedepunkt *m*.

BPH <*abbr*> **benign prostatic hypertrophy**: benigne Prostatahypertrophie *f*, BPH.

BPL <*abbr*> **β-propiolactone**: β-Propiolacton *n*.

BS <*abbr*> **1. blood sugar; 2. bowel sound; 3. breath sounds**: 1. Blutzucker *m*, BZ; 2. Darmgeräusch *n*; 3. Atemgeräusche.

BSA <*abbr*> **bovine serum albumin**: Rinderserumalbumin *n*.

BSE <*abbr*> **1. bovine spongiform encephalopathy; 2. breast self-examination**: 1. bovine spongiforme Enzephalopathie *f*, BSE; 2. Selbstuntersuchung der Brust *f*.

BSER <*abbr*> **brainstem evoked response audiometry**: Brainstem-evoked-response-Audiometrie *f*, BERA.

BSP <*abbr*> **bromsulphalein**: Bromsulfalein *n*.

BSS <*abbr*> **buffered saline solution**: gepufferte Kochsalzlösung *f*.

BST <*abbr*> **blood serological test**: Blutserumprobe *f*.

BUDR <*abbr*> **5-bromodeoxyuridine**: Bromodesoxyuridin *n*.

BUN <*abbr*> **blood urea nitrogen**: Harnstoffstickstoff *m*.

C

C <*abbr*> **1. calorie; 2. cathode; 3. clonus; 4. closure; 5. color sense; 6. complement; 7. compliance; 8. contraction**: 1. Kalorie *f*; 2. Kathode *f*; 3. Klonus *m*; 4. Verschluss *m*; 5. Farbensinn *m*; 6. Komplement *n*; 7. Compliance *f*, Volumendehnbarkeit *f*; 8. Kontraktion *f*.

CA <*abbr*> **1. cardiac arrest; 2. chronological age; 3. coronary artery; 4. cancer**: 1. Herzstillstand *m*; 2. chronologisches Alter *n*; 3. Koronararterie *f*; 4. Krebs *m*.

CABG <*abbr*> **coronary artery bypass graft**: Koronararterienbypasstransplantat *n*.

CaCC <*abbr*> **cathodal closure contraction**: Kathodenschlusszuckung *f*.

CAD <*abbr*> **coronary artery disease**: Koronararterienerkrankung *f*.

CaDTe <*abbr*> **cathodal duration tetanus**: Kathodendauerzuckung *f*.

cAMP <*abbr*> **cyclic adenosine monophosphate**: zyklisches Adenosinmonophosphat *n*, cAMP.

CAP <*abbr*> **catabolite activator protein**: katabolitisches Aktivatorprotein *n*, CAP.

CAT <*abbr*> **computerized axial tomography**: Computertomographie *f*, CT.

CATEEM <*abbr*> **computer aided topographical electroencephalometry**: computergestützte topographische EEG-Analyse *f*.

cath <*abbr*> **1. cathartic; 2. catheter**: 1. Abführmittel *n*; 2. Katheter *m*.

CBC <*abbr*> **complete blood count**: vollständiges Blutbild *n*.

CBF <*abbr*> **cerebral blood flow**: zerebrale Durchblutung *f*.

CBG <*abbr*> **coricosteroid-binding globulin**: kortikosteroidbindendes Globulin *n*.

CCC <*abbr*> **cathodal closure contraction**: Kathodenschlusszuckung *f*.

CCHF <*abbr*> **Crimean-Congo hemorrhagic fever**: hämorrhagisches Krim-Kongo-Fieber *n*.

CCK <*abbr*> **cholecystokinin**: Cholezystokinin *n*.

CCU <*abbr*> **coronary care unit**: kardiologische Intensivstation *f*.

CD <*abbr*> **cardiovascular disease**: Herz-Kreislauf-Erkrankung *f*.

CD_{50} <*abbr*> **mean curative dose**: mittlere kurative Dosis *f*.

CDA <*abbr*> **congenital dyserythro-**

poietic anemia: kongenitale dyserythropoetische Anämie *f*.

CDP <*abbr*> **cytidine diphosphate**: Cytidindiphosphat *n*, CDP.

CEA <*abbr*> **carcinoembryonic antigen**: karzinoembryonales Antigen *n*, CEA.

CES <*abbr*> **central excitatory state**: zentralnervöser Erregungszustand *m*.

CF <*abbr*> **1. cardiac failure; 2. Christmas factor; 3. citrovorum factor; 4. complement fixation; 5. cystic fibrosis**: 1. Herzversagen *n*; 2. Christmas-Faktor *m*, Faktor IX *m*; 3. Citrovorumfaktor *m*; 4. Komplementbindung *f*; 5. zystische Fibrose *f*, Mukoviszidose *f*.

CFA <*abbr*> **complete Freund's adjuvant**: komplettes Freund-Adjuvans *n*.

CFF <*abbr*> **critical fusion frequency**: kritische Flimmerfusionsfrequenz *f*.

CFT <*abbr*> **complement fixation test**: Komplementbindungsreaktion *f*, KBR.

cgs <*abbr*> **centimeter-gram-second system**: CGS-System *n*.

CH <*abbr*> **crown-heel**: Scheitel-Steiß-Länge *f*, SSL.

CHAD <*abbr*> **cold hemolytic antibody disease**: Kälteantikörperkrankheit *f*.

CHD <*abbr*> **1. congenital heart disease; 2. coronary heart disease**: 1. kongenitale Herzerkrankung *f*; 2. koronare Herzkrankheit *f*, KHK.

ChE <*abbr*> **cholinesterase**: Cholinesterase *f*, ChE.

CHF <*abbr*> **congestive heart failure**: kongestives Herzversagen *n*.

CI <*abbr*> **1. color index; 2. coronary insufficiency**: 1. Färbeindex *m*; 2. Koronarinsuffizienz *f*.

CIC <*abbr*> **circulating immune complex**: zirkulierender Immunkomplex *m*.

CID <*abbr*> **cytomegalic inclusion disease**: Zytomegalie-Einschlusskörperchenkrankheit *f*.

CIDP <*abbr*> **chronic inflammatory demyelinating polyneuropathy**: chronisch entzündliche demyelinisierende Polyneuropathie *f*.

CIE <*abbr*> **counterimmunoelectrophoresis**: Counterimmunelektrophorese *f*.

CIN <*abbr*> **cervical intraepithelial neoplasia**: zervikale intraepitheliale Neoplasie *f*.

CK <*abbr*> **creatine kinase**: Kreatinkinase *f*.

CLL <*abbr*> **chronic lymphatic leukemia**: chronische lymphatische Leukämie *f*, CLL.

CLO <*abbr*> **campylobacter-like organism**: Campylobacter-ähnlicher Organismus *m*.

CMD <*abbr*> **cerebromacular degeneration**: zerebromakuläre Degeneration *f*, juvenile Ceroidlipofuscinose *f*.

CME <*abbr*> **Continuing Medical Education**: Continuing Medical Education, CME, zertifizierte Medizin-Fortbildung *f*.

CMI <*abbr*> **cell-mediated immunity**: zellvermittelte Immunität *f*.

CML <*abbr*> **chronic myelogenous leukemia**: chronisch-myeloische Leukämie *f*, CML.

CMP <*abbr*> **cytidine monophosphate**: Cytidinmonophosphat *n*.

CMV <*abbr*> **cytomegalovirus**: Cytomegalie-Virus *n*, CMV.

CNS <*abbr*> **central nervous system**: Zentralnervensystem *n*, ZNS.

CoA <*abbr*> **coenzyme A**: Coenzym A *n*, CoA.

COD <*abbr*> **cause of death**: Todesursache *f*.

con A <*abbr*> **concanavalin A**: Concanavalin A *n*, Con A.

COPD <*abbr*> **chronic obstructive pulmonary disease**: chronisch-obstruktive Lungenerkrankung *f*, COLE.

COTe <*abbr*> **cathodal opening tetanus**: Kathodenöffnungszuckung *f*.

CPAP <*abbr*> **continuous positive airway pressure**: kontinuierlicher positiver Atemwegdruck, CPAP.

CPC <*abbr*> **clinicopathological**

conference: klinisch-pathologische Konferenz *f*.

CPE <*abbr*> **cytopathic effect**: zytopathischer Effekt *m*.

CPK <*abbr*> **creatine kinase**: Kreatinphosphokinase *f*.

cpm <*abbr*> **1. counts per minute; 2. cycles per minute**: 1. counts per minute, cpm, Anzahl pro Minute; 2. Zyklen pro Minute.

CPR <*abbr*> **cardiopulmonary resuscitation**: kardiopulmonale Reanimation *f*.

CR <*abbr*> **1. complement receptor; 2. conditioned response**: 1. Komplementrezeptor *m*; 2. konditionierte Reaktion *f*.

CRD <*abbr*> **chronic respiratory disease**: chronische Atemwegserkrankung *f*.

CRF <*abbr*> **1. chronic renal failure; 2. corticotropin-releasing hormone**: 1. chronische Niereninsuffizienz *f*; 2. Kortikotropin-Releasing-Faktor *m*.

CRH <*abbr*> **corticotropin-releasing hormone**: Kortikotropin-Releasing-Hormon *n*.

CRI <*abbr*> **chronic respiratory insufficency**: chronische Ateminsuffizienz *f*.

CRM <*abbr*> **cross-reacting material**: kreuzreagierende Substanz *f*.

CRP <*abbr*> **C-reactive protein**: C-reaktives Protein *n*.

CRS <*abbr*> **Chinese restaurant syndrome**: China-Restaurant-Syndrom *n*.

CS <*abbr*> **1. cesarean section; 2. conditioned stimulus; 3. coronary sinus**: 1. Sectio caesarea *f*, Kaiserschnitt *m*, Schnittentbindung *f*; 2. konditionierter Stimulus *m*; 3. Sinus coronarius *m*.

CSA <*abbr*> **childhood sexual abuse**: sexueller Kindesmissbrauch *m*.

CSF <*abbr*> **1. cerebrospinal fluid; 2. colony-stimulating factor**: 1. Liquor cerebrospinalis *m*; 2. colony-stimulating factor *m*, koloniestimulierender Faktor *m*, CSF.

CSM <*abbr*> **cerebrospinal meningitis**: zerebrospinale Meningitis *f*.

CT <*abbr*> **computerized tomography**: Computertomographie *f*, CT.

CTL <*abbr*> **cytotoxic T lymphocytes**: zytotoxische T-Lymphozyten.

CTP <*abbr*> **cytidine triphosphate**: Cytidintriphosphat *n*, CTP.

cu <*abbr*> **cubic**: kubisch.

CV <*abbr*> **1. cardiovascular; 2. coefficient of variability; 3. conjugate vera**: 1. kardiovaskulär; 2. Variabilitätskoeffizient *m*; 3. Conjugata vera *f*.

CVA <*abbr*> **1. cerebrovascular accident; 2. costovertebral angle**: 1. Apoplexie *f*; 2. Kostovertebralwinkel *m*.

CVD <*abbr*> **cardiovascular disease**: Herz-Kreislauf-Erkrankung *f*, kardiovaskuläre Erkrankung *f*.

CVO <*abbr*> **conjugata vera obstetrica**: Conjugata vera obstetrica *f*.

CVP <*abbr*> **central venous pressure**: zentraler Venendruck *m*, ZVD.

CVS <*abbr*> **cardiovascular system**: Kreislauf *m*.

CW <*abbr*> **continuous wave**: kontinuierliche Welle *f*.

Cx <*abbr*> **1. cervix; 2. convex**: 1. Zervix *f*; 2. konvex.

Cys <*abbr*> **cysteine**: Cystein *n*, Cys, Zystein *n*.

D

d <*abbr*> **1. day; 2. density; 3. deoxyribose**: 1. Tag *m*; 2. Dichte *f*; 3. Desoxyribose *f*.

D <*abbr*> **1. dioptry; 2. duration; 3. dorsal; 4. dose; 5. duration**: 1. Dioptrie *f*, dpt; 2. Dauer *f*; 3. dorsal; 4. Dosis *f*; 5. Dauer *f*.

DA <*abbr*> **developmental age**: Entwicklungsalter *n*.

DAG <*abbr*> **direct antiglobulin test**: direkter Antiglobulintest *m*.

D and C <*abbr*> **dilatation and curettage**: Dilatation und Kürettage *f*.

DAT <*abbr*> **direct antiglobulin test**: direkter Antiglobulintest *m*.

DBP <*abbr*> **diastolic blood pressure**: diastolischer Blutdruck *m*.

dc <*abbr*> **direct current**: Gleichstrom *m*.

dC <*abbr*> **deoxycytidine**: Desoxycytidin *n*, dC.

DCIS <*abbr*> **ductal carcinoma in situ**: duktales Carcinoma in situ *n*.

DCT <*abbr*> **direct Coombs test**: direkter Coombs-Test *m*.

DDA <*abbr*> **dideoxyadenosine**: Dideoxyadenosin *n*, DDA.

DDC <*abbr*> **dideoxycytosine**: Dideoxycytosin *n*, DDC.

DDI <*abbr*> **dideoxyinosine**: Dideoxyinosin *n*, DDI.

DDS <*abbr*> **diaminodiphenyl sulfone**: Diaminodiphenylsulfon *n*, DDS.

DDT <*abbr*> **dichlorodiphenyltrichloroethane**: Dichlordiphenyltrichloräthan *n*, DDT, Chlorophenotan *n*.

DEACE <*abbr*> **diethylaminochloroethane**: Diäthylaminochloräthan *n*.

DEAE <*abbr*> **diethylaminoethanol**: Diäthylaminäthanol *n*.

dept <*abbr*> **department**: Abteilung *f*, Station *f*.

DES <*abbr*> **diethylstilbestrol**: Diäthylstilböstrol *n*.

DFDT <*abbr*> **difluorodiphenyl trichloroethane**: Difluordiphenyltrichloräthan *n*, DFDT.

DFP <*abbr*> **diisopropyl fluorophosphate**: Diisopropylfluorphosphat *n*.

DHEA <*abbr*> **dehydroepiandrosterone**: Dehydroepiandrosteron *n*, DHEA.

DHEAS <*abbr*> **dehydroepiandrosterone sulfate**: Dehydroepiandrosteronsulfat *n*, DHEAS.

DIC <*abbr*> **disseminated intravascular coagulation**: disseminierte intravasale Gerinnung *f*, akute Verbrauchskoagulopathie *f*, DIC.

diff <*abbr*> **difference**: Differenz *f*, Unterschied *m*.

DM <*abbr*> **diabetes mellitus**: Diabetes mellitus *m*.

DMGT <*abbr*> **DNA-mediated gene transfer**: DNA-vermittelter Gentransfer *m*.

dMM <*abbr*> **1-deoxymannojirimycin**: 1-Deoxymannojirimycin *n*, dNM.

DMSO <*abbr*> **dimethyl sulfoxide**: Dimethylsulfoxid *n*, DMSO.

DN <*abbr*> **dicrotic notch**: dikroter Knoten *m*.

DNA <*abbr*> **deoxyribonucleic acid**: Desoxyribonukleinsäure *f*, DNS, DNA.

DNase <*abbr*> **deoxyribonuclease**: Desoxyribonuklease *f*, DNase.

DNB <*abbr*> **dinitrobenzene**: Dinitrobenzol *n*.

DNCB <*abbr*> **dinitrochlorobenzene**: Dinitrochlorbenzol *n*.

DNFB <*abbr*> **dinitrofluorobenzene**: Dinitrofluorbenzol *n*.

DNJ <*abbr*> **1-deoxynojirimycin**: 1-Deoxynojirimycin *n*, DNJ.

dNM <*abbr*> **1-deoxynojirimycin**: 1-Deoxynojirimycin *n*, DNJ.

DNP <*abbr*> **2,4,-dinitrophenol**: Dinitrophenol *n*.

DOA <*abbr*> **dead on arrival**: tot bei Einlieferung.

DOB <*abbr*> **date of birth**: Geburtsdatum *n*.

DOC <*abbr*> **deoxycholate**: Desoxycholat *n*, DOC.

DOE <*abbr*> **dyspnea on exertion**: Belastungsdyspnoe *f*.

dopa <*abbr*> **3,4-dihydroxyphenylalanine**: 3,4-Dihydroxyphenylalanin *n*, DOPA *n*.

DR <*abbr*> **doctor**: Doktor *m*, Dr.

DSM <*abbr*> **Diagnostic and Statistical Manual of Mental Disorders**: Diagnostisches und statistisches Manual psychischer Störungen *n*, DSM.

DT <*abbr*> **duration tetany**: Dauertetanus *m*.

DTH <*abbr*> **delayed-type hypersensitivity**: Hypersensitivität vom verzögerten Typ *f*.

DTP <*abbr*> **distal tingling on percussion**: Tinel-Zeichen *n*, Hoffmann-Tinel-Klopfzeichen *n*.

DW *<abbr>* **distilled water**: destilliertes Wasser *n*, Aqua destillata *f*, Aq. dest.

E

E. *<abbr>* **1. emmetropia; 2. enzyme; 3. eye**: 1. Emmetropie *f*; 2. Enzym *n*, 3. Auge *n*.

EA *<abbr>* **erythrocyte antibody**: Erythrozytenantikörper *m*.

EAC *<abbr>* **erythrocyte antibody complement**: Erythrozytenantikörperkomplement *n*.

EACA *<abbr>* **epsilon aminocaproic acid**: Epsilon-Aminocapronsäure *f*, EACA.

EAE *<abbr>* **experimental allergic encephalomyelitis**: experimentelle allergische Enzephalomyelitis *f*.

EAHF complex *<abbr>* **eczema, asthma, and hay fever complex**: Ekzem-Asthma-Heuschnupfen-Komplex *m*.

EAP *<abbr>* **1. epiallopregnanolone; 2. expanded access program**: 1. Epiallopregnanolon *n*; 2. Expanded-Access-Programm *n*.

EB *<abbr>* **elementary body**: Elementarkörperchen *n*.

EBV *<abbr>* **Epstein-Barr virus**: Epstein-Barr-Virus *n*, EBV.

EC *<abbr>* **enzyme commission**: Enzymkommission der International Union of Biochemistry *f*.

ECF *<abbr>* **1. eosinophil chemotactic factor; 2. extracellular fluid**: 1. Eosinophilen-Chemotaxisfaktor *m*; 2. Extrazellularflüssigkeit *f*, EZF.

ECG *<abbr>* **electrocardiography**: Elektrokardiographie *f*, EKG.

E. Coch. G. *<abbr>* **electrocochleography**: Elektrokochleographie *f*.

ECS *<abbr>* **electroconvulsive shock**: Elektrokrampftherapie *f*, EKT.

ECT *<abbr>* **electroconvulsive treatment**: Elektrokrampftherapie *f*, EKT.

ED *<abbr>* **1. effective dose; 2. erythema dose**: 1. Wirkdosis *f*; 2. Erythemdosis *f*.

EDC *<abbr>* **expected date of confinement**: erwarteter Geburtstermin *m*.

EDR *<abbr>* **electrodermal response**: psychogalvanische Hautreaktion *f*.

EDTA *<abbr>* **ethylenediaminetetraacetic acid**: Ethylendiamintetraessigsäure *f*, EDTA, Editinsäure *f*.

EEE *<abbr>* **eastern equine encephalomyelitis**: östliche Pferdeenzephalitis *f*.

EEG *<abbr>* **1. electroencephalogram; 2. electroencephalography**: 1. Elektroenzephalogramm *n*; 2. Elektroenzephalographie *f*.

EENT *<abbr>* **eye, ear, nose and throat**: Augen, Ohren, Nase und Hals.

EF *<abbr>* **1. elongation factor**; **2. eosinophilic folliculitis**: 1. Elongationsfaktor *m*, EF; 2. eosinophile Follikulitis *f*.

EFA *<abbr>* **essential fatty acid**: essentielle Fettsäure *f*.

EGF *<abbr>* **epidermal growth factor**: epidermal growth factor, epidermaler Wachstumsfaktor *m*.

EHBF *<abbr>* **extrahepatic blood flow**: extrahepatischer Kreislauf *m*.

EHEC *<abbr>* **enterohemorrhagic Escherichia coli**: enterohämorrhagische Escherichia coli, EHEC.

EIEC *<abbr>* **enteroinvasive Escherichia coli**: enteroinvasive Escherichia coli.

EKY *<abbr>* **electrokymogram**: Elektrokymogramm *n*, EKyG.

ELC *<abbr>* **expression-linked copy**: expressionsgebundene Kopie *f*.

ELISA *<abbr>* **enzyme-linked immunosorbent assay**: enzymgekoppelter Immunoassay *m*, ELISA.

EM *<abbr>* **emmetropia**: Emmetropie *f*.

EMB agar *<abbr>* **eosin methylene blue agar**: Eosin-Methylenblauagar *m*.

embryol *<abbr>* **embryology**: Embryologie *f*.

EMC *<abbr>* **encephalomyocarditis**: Enzephalomyokarditis *f*, EMC.

EMF *<abbr>* **1. electromotive force; 2. erythrocyte maturation factor**: 1. elektromotorische Kraft *f*; 2. Erythrozytenreifungsfaktor *m*.

EMG *<abbr>* **electromyogram**: Elektromyogramm *n*, EMG.

EMI *<abbr>* **electromagnetic interference**: elektromagnetische Interferenz *f*.

EMIT *<abbr>* **enzyme-multiplied immunoassay technique**: homologer Enzym-Immunoassay *m*, EMIT.

EMS *<abbr>* **emergency medical service**: Notarztdienst *m*, schnelle medizinische Hilfe *f*.

ENG *<abbr>* **electronystagmography**: Elektronystagmographie *f*, ENG.

ENT *<abbr>* **ear, nose and throat**: Hals-, Nasen-, Ohren-, HNO.

EP *<abbr>* **evoked potential**: evoziertes Potential *n*.

EPH gestosis *<abbr>* **edema-proteinuria-hypertension gestosis**: EPH-Gestose *f*, Gestose mit Ödemen, Proteinurie und Hypertonus *f*.

EPO *<abbr>* **erythropoietin**: Erythropoetin *n*, EPO.

EPR *<abbr>* **electrophrenic respiration**: elektrophrenische Atmung *f*.

EPSP *<abbr>* **excitatory postsynaptic potential**: exzitatorisches postsynaptisches Potential *n*, EPSP.

ER *<abbr>* **1. emergency room; 2. estrogen receptor; 3. evoked response**: 1. Notfallbehandlungsraum *m*; 2. Östrogenrezeptor *m*; 3. evoziertes Potential *n*.

ERA *<abbr>* **electric response audiometry**: Electric-Response-Audiometrie *f*, ERA.

ERCP *<abbr>* **endoscopic retrograde cholangiopancreatography**: endoskopische retrograde Cholangiopankreatikographie *f*, ERCP.

ERG *<abbr>* **electroretinogram**: Elektroretinogramm *n*, ERG.

ERPF *<abbr>* **effective renal plasma flow**: effektiver Nierenplasmastrom *m*.

ERV *<abbr>* **expiratory reserve volume**: exspiratorisches Reservevolumen *n*.

ESF *<abbr>* **erythropoietic stimulating factor**: erythropoiesestimulierender Faktor *m*.

ESP *<abbr>* **extrasensory perception**: außersinnliche Wahrnehmung *f*.

ESR *<abbr>* **1. erythrocyte sedimentation rate; 2. electron spin resonance**: 1. Blutkörperchensenkungsgeschwindigkeit *f*, BSG; 2. Elektronenspinresonanz *f*.

EST *<abbr>* **electroshock therapy**: Elektrokrampftherapie *f*, EKT.

ETEC *<abbr>* **enterotoxic Escherichia coli**: enterotoxische Escherichia coli.

F

F. *<abbr>* **1. Fahrenheit; 2. visual field; 3. French; 4. formula**: 1. Fahrenheit; 2. Gesichtsfeld *n*; 3. French; 4. Rezept *n*.

FA *<abbr>* **1. Fanconi's anemia; 2. fatty acid; 3. fluorescent antibody; 4. femoral artery**: 1. Fanconi-Anämie *f*; 2. Fettsäure *f*; 3. fluoreszierender Antikörper *m*; 4. Arteria femoralis *f*.

Fab *<abbr>* **fragment, antigen binding**: antigenbindendes Fragment *n*, Fab-Fragment *n*.

FAB classification *<abbr>* **French-American-British classification**: Französisch-Amerikanisch-Britische Klassifikation *f*, FAB-Klassifikation *f*.

FAD *<abbr>* **flavin adenine dinucleotide**: Flavin-Adenin-Dinukleotid *n*, FAD.

F. B. *<abbr>* **foreign body**: Fremdkörper *m*.

FCA *<abbr>* **Freund's complete adjuvant**: Freund's komplettes Adjuvans *n*.

FCS *<abbr>* **fetal calf serum**: fetales Kälberserum *n*, FKS.

FD *<abbr>* **1. focal distance; 2. fatal dose**: 1. Fokusabstand *m*; 2. Letaldosis *f*, letale Dosis, LD.

FDNB *<abbr>* **fluoro-2,4-dinitro-**

benzene: 2,4-Dinitro-1-fluorbenzol *n*.

FDP <*abbr*> **fibrin degradation products**: Fibrinabbauprodukte.

FES <*abbr*> **functional electric stimulation**: funktionelle Elektrostimulation *f*.

FEV <*abbr*> **forced expiratory volume**: forciertes expiratorisches Volumen *n*, Sekundenkapazität *f*.

FF <*abbr*> **filtration fraction**: Filtrationsfraktion *f*.

FFA <*abbr*> **free fatty acid**: freie Fettsäure *f*.

F factor <*abbr*> **fertility factor**: Fertilitätsfaktor *m*, F-Faktor *m*.

FFP <*abbr*> **fresh frozen plasma**: Fresh-frozen-Plasma *n*, FFP, frisch eingefrorenes Plasma *n*.

FFT <*abbr*> **flicker fusion threshold**: Flimmerfusionsschwelle *f*.

FGF <*abbr*> **fibroblast growth factor**: Fibroblastenwachstumsfaktor *m*.

FHT <*abbr*> **fetal heart tone**: kindliche Herztöne.

FIA <*abbr*> **Freund's incomplete adjuvant**: Freund's inkomplettes Adjuvans *n*.

fig <*abbr*> **figure**: Figur *f*, Zahl *f*, Abbildung *f*.

FIGLU <*abbr*> **formiminoglutamic acid**: Formiminoglutaminsäure *f*, FIGLU.

fl. <*abbr*> **fluid**: Flüssigkeit *f*, flüssig.

fld. <*abbr*> **fluid**: Flüssigkeit *f*, flüssig.

FLT <*abbr*> **fluorothymidine**: Fluorothymidin *n*, FLT.

FMN <*abbr*> **flavin mononucleotide**: Flavinmononukleotid *n*.

FNH <*abbr*> **focal nodular hyperplasia**: fokal noduläre Hyperplasie der Leber *f*, FNH.

f. p. <*abbr*> **freezing point**: Gefrierpunkt *m*.

FR <*abbr*> **flocculation reaction**: Flockungsreaktion *f*.

FRC <*abbr*> **functional residual capacity**: funktionelle Residualkapazität *f*.

FRF <*abbr*> **follicle-releasing factor**: Follikel-Releasing-Faktor *m*, follikelfreisetzender Faktor *m*.

FSH <*abbr*> **follicle-stimulating hormone**: follikelstimulierendes Hormon *n*, FSH.

FSH-RH <*abbr*> **follicle-stimulating hormone releasing hormone**: follikelstimulierendes Hormon-Releasing-Hormon *n*, FSH-RH.

FTA-ABS test <*abbr*> **fluorescent treponemal antibody absorption test**: Fluoreszenz-Treponema-Antikörper-Absorptionstest *m*, FTA-ABS-Test *m*.

FTI <*abbr*> **free thyroxine index**: freier Thyroxinindex *m*.

FUO <*abbr*> **fever of undetermined origin**: Fieber unbekannter Ursache *n*.

FVC <*abbr*> **forced vital capacity**: maximales Atemsekundenvolumen *n*, Sekundenkapazität *f*.

G

G <*abbr*> **1. glycine; 2. guanosine; 3. gonidial**: 1. Glycin *n*; 2. Guanosin *n*; 3. Konidien-.

GA <*abbr*> **glutaric aciduria**: Glutarsäureausscheidung im Urin *f*.

GABA <*abbr*> **gamma-aminobutyric acid**: Gamma-Amino-Buttersäure *f*, GABA.

GAG <*abbr*> **glycosaminoglycan**: Glykosaminoglykan *n*, GAG.

gal <*abbr*> **1. galactose; 2. gallon**: 1. Galaktose *f*, Gal; 2. Gallon *f*.

GALT <*abbr*> **gut-associated lymphoid tissue**: Darm-assoziiertes lymphatisches Gewebe *n*.

GAS <*abbr*> **general adaptation syndrome**: allgemeines Anpassungssyndrom *n*, Adaptationssyndrom *n*.

GBM <*abbr*> **glomerulal basement membrane**: glomeruläre Basalmembran *f*.

GC <*abbr*> **gas chromatography**: Gaschromatographie *f*.

G-CSF <*abbr*> **granulocyte colony-**

stimulating factor: Granulozytenkoloniestimulierender Faktor *m*.

GDH <*abbr*> **1. glucose dehydrogenase; 2. glutamate dehydrogenase; 3. glycerol-3-phosphate dehydrogenase**: 1. Glukosedehydrogenase *f*; 2. Glutamatdehydrogenase *f*; 3. Glyzerin-3-phosphat-dehydrogenase *f*, GDH.

GDP <*abbr*> **guanosine diphosphate**: Guanosindiphosphat *n*, GDP.

GFR <*abbr*> **glomerular filtration rate**: glomeruläre Filtrationsrate *f*, GFR.

GH <*abbr*> **growth hormone**: Wachstumshormon *n*, Somatotropin *n*.

GH-IH <*abbr*> **growth hormone inhibiting hormone**: wachstumshormonhemmendes Hormon *n*, Somatostatin *n*.

GH-RH <*abbr*> **growth hormone releasing hormone**: wachstumshormonfreisetzendes Hormon *n*, Somatotropin-Releasing-Faktor *m*.

GI <*abbr*> **gastrointestinal**: gastrointestinal.

GIFT <*abbr*> **gamete intrafallopian transfer**: intratubarer Embryonentransfer *m*.

GIP <*abbr*> **gastric inhibitory polypeptide**: gastrisches inhibitorisches Polypeptid *n*, GIP.

Glc <*abbr*> **glucose**: Glukose *f*.

GLC <*abbr*> **gas-liquid chromatography**: Gas-Flüssigkeits-Chromatographie *f*.

GlcA <*abbr*> **1. glucuronic acid; 2. gluconic acid**: 1. Glukuronsäure *f*; 2. Glukonsäure *f*.

GlcN <*abbr*> **glucosamine**: Glucosamin *n*, GlcN, Glukosamin *n*.

GlcNAc <*abbr*> **N-acetylglucosamine**: N-Acetylglukosamin *n*.

GLI <*abbr*> **gastrointestinal glucagonlike immunoreaction**: gastrointestinale glukagonähnliche Immunreaktion *f*.

Gln <*abbr*> **glutamine**: Glutamin *n*, Gln.

Glu <*abbr*> **glutamic acid**: Glutaminsäure *f*, Glu.

Gly <*abbr*> **glycine**: Glycin *n*, Gly.

Gm allotype <*abbr*> **gamma chain marker-allotype**: Gm-Allotyp *m*.

GM-CSF <*abbr*> **granulocyte macrophage colony-stimulating factor**: Granulozyten-Makrophagenkoloniestimulierender Faktor *m*.

GMP <*abbr*> **guanosine monophosphate**: Guanosinmonophosphat *n*, GMP.

GnRH <*abbr*> **gonadotropin-releasing hormone**: Gonadotropin-Releasing-Hormon *n*.

GOT <*abbr*> **glutamate oxalacetate transaminase**: Glutamat-Oxalacetat-Transaminase *f*, GOT.

gp <*abbr*> **glycoprotein**: Glykoprotein *n*, gp.

GP <*abbr*> **1. general paresis; 2. general practitioner**: 1. progressive Paralyse *f*; 2. Arzt für Allgemeinmedizin *m*, praktischer Arzt *m*.

GPT <*abbr*> **glutamate pyruvate transaminase**: Glutamat-Pyruvat-Transaminase *f*, GPT.

GSH <*abbr*> **reduced glutathione**: reduziertes Glutathion *n*, GSH.

G-spot <*abbr*> **Gräfenberg spot**: Gräfenberg-Zone *f*.

GSR <*abbr*> **galvanic skin reflex**: galvanischer Hautreflex *m*.

GSSG <*abbr*> **oxidized glutathione**: oxidiertes Glutathion *n*, Glutathiondisulfid *n*, GSSG.

GTN <*abbr*> **glyceryl trinitrate**: Glycerintrinitrat *n*.

GTO <*abbr*> **Golgi tendon organ**: Golgi-Sehnenorgan *n*.

GTP <*abbr*> **guanosine triphosphate**: Guanosintriphosphat *n*, GTP.

GTT <*abbr*> **glucose tolerance test**: Glukosetoleranztest *m*, GTT.

GU <*abbr*> **1. genitourinary; 2. gastric ulcer**: 1. urogenital; 2. Magenulkus *n*.

Gua <*abbr*> **guanine**: Guanin *n*, Gua.

GUM <*abbr*> **genito-urinary medicine**: Urologie *f*.

Guo <*abbr*> **guanosine**: Guanosin *n*, Guo.

GVH <*abbr*> **graft-versus-host**: Graft-versus-host-Reaktion *f*, Transplantat-Wirt-Reaktion *f*.

H

H <*abbr*> **1. hydrogen; 2. histidine**: 1. Wasserstoff *m*, H; 2. Histidin *n*.

HACS <*abbr*> **hyperactive child syndrome**: Hyperaktivitätssyndrom *n*.

HAV <*abbr*> **hepatitis A virus**: Hepatitis-A-Virus *n*, HAV.

Hb <*abbr*> **hemoglobin**: Hämoglobin *n*, Hb.

HBD <*abbr*> **hydroxybutyrate dehydrogenase**: Hydroxybutyrat-Dehydrogenase *f*, HBDH.

HBE <*abbr*> **His bundle electrogram**: His-Bündel Elektrokardiogramm *n*.

HBsAg <*abbr*> **hepatitis B surface antigen**: Hepatitis-B-Oberflächenantigen *n*.

HBV <*abbr*> **hepatitis B virus**: Hepatitis-B-Virus *n*, HBV.

HCG <*abbr*> **human chorionic gonadotropin**: humanes Choriongonadotropin *n*, HCG.

H chain <*abbr*> **heavy chain**: schwere Kette *f*.

HCM <*abbr*> **hypertrophic cardiomyopathy**: hypertrophe Kardiomyopathie *f*.

HCP <*abbr*> **hereditary coproporphyria**: hereditäre Koproporphyrie *f*.

HCS <*abbr*> **human chorionic somatotropin**: Plazentalaktogen *n*, HPL.

HCT <*abbr*> **hematocrit**: Hämatokrit *m*, HK.

HCV <*abbr*> **hepatitis C virus**: Hepatitis-C-Virus *n*, HCV.

HDC <*abbr*> **human diploid cell**: menschliche diploide Zelle *f*.

HDL <*abbr*> **high-density lipoprotein**: High-Density-Lipoprotein *n*, Lipoprotein hoher Dichte *n*, HDL.

HDN <*abbr*> **hemolytic disease of the newborn**: Morbus haemolyticus neonatorum *m*.

HEMPAS <*abbr*> **hereditary erythroblastic multinuclearity with positive acid serum test**: kongenitale dyserythropoetische Anämie *f*.

HF <*abbr*> **Hageman factor**: Hageman-Faktor *m*, Faktor XII *m*.

HFT <*abbr*> **high-frequency transduction**: hohe Transduktionsfrequenz *f*.

Hgb <*abbr*> **hemoglobin**: Hämoglobin *n*, Hb.

hGH <*abbr*> **human growth hormone**: menschliches Wachstumshormon *n*, Somatotropin *n*.

HGPRT <*abbr*> **hypoxanthine-guanine phosphoribosyltransferase**: Hypoaxanthin-Guanin-Phosphoribosyltransferase *f*, HGPRT.

HI <*abbr*> **hemagglutination inhibition**: Hämagglutinations-Hemmtest *m*.

HIG <*abbr*> **hyperimmunglobulin**: Hyperimmunglobulin *n*, HIG.

HIV <*abbr*> **human immunodeficiency virus**: humanes Immunodefizienz-Virus *n*, HIV.

HLA <*abbr*> **human leukocyte antigene**: humanes Leukozytenantigen *n*, HLA.

HLHS <*abbr*> **hypoplastic left heart syndrome**: Linksherzhypoplasiesyndrom *n*, HPLS.

Hm <*abbr*> **manifest hyperopia**: manifeste Hyperopie *f*.

HMG <*abbr*> **human menopausal gonadotropin**: Menopausengonadotropin *n*.

HMG CoA <*abbr*> **hydroxymethylglutamyl CoA**: Hydroxymethylglutaryl-CoA *n*, HMG-CoA.

HMSN <*abbr*> **hereditary motor and sensory neuropathy**: hereditäre sensomotorische Neuropathie *f*.

HOCM <*abbr*> **1. high osmolar contrast medium; 2. hypertrophic obstructive cardiomyopathy**: 1. Kontrastmittel hoher Osmolarität *n*; 2. hypertrophe obstruktive Kardiomyopathie *f*.

HOT <*abbr*> **human old tuberculin**: humanes Alt-Tuberkulin *n*.

Hp <*abbr*> **haptoglobin**: Haptoglobin *n*.

HPI <*abbr*> **history of present illness**: jetzige Anamnese *f*.

HPL <*abbr*> **human placental lactogen**: humanes Plazentalaktogen *n*.

HPV <*abbr*> **human papillomavirus**: humanes Papillomavirus *n*, HPV.

HSA <*abbr*> **human serum albumin**: humanes Serumalbumin *n*.

HSV <*abbr*> **highly selective vagotomy**: hochselektive Vagotomie *f*.

5-HT <*abbr*> **5-hydroxytryptamine**: 5-Hydroxytryptamin *n*, 5-HT, Serotonin *n*.

HTLV <*abbr*> **1. human T-cell leukemia virus; 2. human T-lymphotropic virus**: 1. humanes T-Zell-Leukämievirus *n*; 2. humanes T-lymphotropes Virus *n*.

HTP <*abbr*> **5-hydroxytryptophan**: 5-Hydroxytryptophan *n*.

HV <*abbr*> **1. herpes virus; 2. hyperventilation**: 1. Herpes-Virus *n*; 2. Hyperventilation *f*.

HVL <*abbr*> **half-value layer**: Halbwertschichtdicke *f*, HWS.

Hyl <*abbr*> **hydroxylysine**: Hydroxylysin *n*.

I

I <*abbr*> **1. isoleucine; 2. inosine**: 1. Isoleucin *n*; 2. Inosin *n*.

IABP <*abbr*> **intra-aortic balloon pump**: intraaortale Ballonpumpe *f*.

IAG <*abbr*> **indirect antiglobulin test**: indirekter Antiglobulintest *m*, indirekter Coombs-Test *m*.

IAS <*abbr*> **intraatrial septum**: Vorhofseptum *n*.

IB <*abbr*> **1. immune body; 2. inclusion body**: 1. Immunkörper *m*; 2. Einschlusskörperchen *n*.

IBC <*abbr*> **iron-binding capacity**: Eisenbindungskapazität *f*.

IC <*abbr*> **1. inspiratory capacity; 2. intermittent claudication; 3. irritable colon**: 1. Inspirationskapazität *f*; 2. Claudicatio intermittens *f*; 3. irritables Kolon *n*.

ICA <*abbr*> **islet cell antibody**: Inselzellantikörper *m*.

ICC <*abbr*> **intensive coronary care**: kardiologische Intensivstation *f*.

ICD <*abbr*> **1. International Classification of Diseases; 2. intrauterine contraceptive device; 3. ischemic coronary disease**: 1. Internationale Klassifikation der Krankheiten *f*, ICD; 2. Intrauterinpessar *n*; 3. ischämische koronare Herzkrankheit *f*.

ICF <*abbr*> **International Classification of Functioning, Disability and Health**: Internationale Klassifikation der Funktionsfähigkeit, Behinderung und Gesundheit *f*, ICF.

ICL <*abbr*> **idiopathic chronic lymphocytopenia**: idiopathische chronische Lymphozytopenie *f*, ICL.

ICM <*abbr*> **inner cell mass**: innere Zellmasse *f*.

ICP <*abbr*> **intracranial pressure**: intrakranieller Druck *m*.

ICSH <*abbr*> **interstitial cell-stimulating hormone**: interstitielle Zellen stimulierendes Hormon *n*, ICSH.

ICT <*abbr*> **1. insulin coma therapy; 2. inflammation of connective tissue**: 1. Insulinkomabehandlung *f*; 2. Bindegewebsentzündung *f*.

ICU <*abbr*> **intensive care unit**: Intensivstation *f*.

ID <*abbr*> **1. infective dose; 2. intradermal; 3. infectious disease; 4. inside diameter**: 1. infektiöse Dosis *f*; 2. intradermal; 3. Infektionskrankheit *f*; 4. Innendurchmesser *m*.

ID_{50} <*abbr*> **1. minimal infecting dose; 2. median infective dose**: 1. kleinste infektiöse Dosis *f*; 2. mittlere infektiöse Dosis *f*.

IDDM <*abbr*> **insulin-dependent diabetes mellitus**: insulinabhängiger Diabetes mellitus *m*, IDDM.

IDP <*abbr*> **inosine diphosphate**: Inosin-5'-diphosphat *n*, IDP.

IDU <*abbr*> **1. idoxuridine; 2. injecting drug user**: 1. Idoxuridin *n*, IDU; 2. injizierender Drogengebraucher *m*.

IE <*abbr*> **immunoelectrophoresis**: Immunelektrophorese *f*.

IEM <*abbr*> **1. immune electron microscopy; 2. inborn error of metab-**

olism: 1. Immunelektronenmikroskopie *f*; 2. Inborn Error of Metabolism *m*, angeborene Stoffwechselstörung *f*.

IEP <*abbr*> **isoelectric point**: isoelektrischer Punkt *m*, IEP.

IF <*abbr*> **1. interferon; 2. interstitial fluid; 3. intrinsic factor**: 1. Interferon *n*, IF; 2. interstitielle Flüssigkeit *f*; 3. intrinsischer Faktor *m*, IF.

Ig <*abbr*> **immunoglobulin**: Immunglobulin *n*, Ig.

IGF <*abbr*> **insulin-like growth factor**: insulinartiger Wachstumsfaktor *m*.

IH <*abbr*> **infectious hepatitis**: epidemische Hepatitis *f*, Hepatitis A *f*.

IL <*abbr*> **interleukin**: Interleukin *n*, IL.

ILA <*abbr*> **insulin-like activity**: insulinartige Wirkung *f*.

Ile <*abbr*> **isoleucine**: Isoleucin *n*, Ile.

IM <*abbr*> **1. infectious mononucleosis; 2. internal medicine; 3. intramuscular**: 1. infektiöse Mononukleose *f*, Pfeiffer-Drüsenfieber *n*; 2. innere Medizin *f*; 3. intramuskulär, i.m.

IMP <*abbr*> **inosine monophosphate**: Inosinmonophosphat *n*, IMP.

IMV <*abbr*> **intermittent mandatory ventilation**: intermittierende assistierte Beatmung *f*.

INN <*abbr*> **international nonproprietary name**: internationaler Freiname *m*, INN.

intrakine <*abbr*> **intracellular chemokine**: intrazelluläres Chemokin *n*.

IOP <*abbr*> **intraocular pressure**: Augeninnendruck *m*.

IP <*abbr*> **1. intraperitoneal; 2. isoelectric point**: 1. intraperitoneal; 2. isoelektrischer Punkt *m*, IEP.

IPPB <*abbr*> **intermittent positive pressure breathing**: intermittierende Überdruckbeatmung *f*.

IPPV <*abbr*> **intermittent positive pressure ventilation**: intermittierende Überdruckbeatmung *f*.

IPSID <*abbr*> **immunoproliferative small intestine disease**: immunproliferative Dünndarmerkrankung *f*.

IPSP <*abbr*> **inhibitory postsynaptic potential**: inhibitorisches postsynaptisches Potential *n*, IPSP.

IPV <*abbr*> **inactivated poliovirus vaccine**: inaktivierter Poliovirusimpfstoff *m*.

IQ <*abbr*> **intelligence quotient**: Intelligenzquotient *m*, IQ.

IRC <*abbr*> **inspiratory reserve capacity**: inspiratorisches Reservevolumen *n*.

IRI <*abbr*> **immunoreactive insulin**: immunreaktives Insulin *n*.

IRMA <*abbr*> **immunoradiometric assay**: immunradiometrischer Assay *m*.

IS <*abbr*> **1. intercostal space; 2. intraspinal; 3. immune serum**: 1. Interkostalraum *m*, ICR; 2. intraspinal; 3. Immunserum *n*, Antiserum *n*.

ISCOM <*abbr*> **immune-stimulating complex**: immunstimulierender Komplex *m*, ISCOM.

ITP <*abbr*> **1. idiopathic thrombocytopenic purpura; 2. inosine triphosphate**: 1. idiopathische thrombozytopenische Purpura *f*, ITP; 2. Inosintriphosphat *n*, ITP.

IU <*abbr*> **1. immunizing unit; 2. international unit; 3. intrauterine**: 1. Immunisierungseinheit *f*, IE; 2. internationale Einheit *f*, SI-Einheit *f*; 3. intrauterin.

IUCD <*abbr*> **intrauterine contraceptive device**: Intrauterinpessar *n*, IUP.

IUD <*abbr*> **1. intrauterine death; 2. intrauterine device**: 1. intrauteriner Fruchttod *m*; 2. Intrauterinpessar *n*, IUP.

IUGR <*abbr*> **intrauterine growth retardation**: intrauterine Wachstumsverzögerung *f*.

IV <*abbr*> **intravenous**: intravenös, i.v.

IVC <*abbr*> **inferior vena cava**: Vena cava inferior *f*.

IVDU <*abbr*> **intravenous drug user**: i.v. Drogengebraucher *m*.

IVF <*abbr*> **in vitro fertilization**: In-vitro-Fertilisation *f*, IVF.

IVP <*abbr*> **1. intravenous pyelogram; 2. intraventricular pressure**: 1. intravenöses Pyelogramm *n*; 2. intraventrikulärer Druck *m*.

IVRT <*abbr*> **isovolumetric relaxation time**: isovolumetrische Entspannungszeit *f*.

J

J <*abbr*> **1. joule; 2. Joule's equivalent**: 1. Joule; 2. Joule-Äquivalent *n*.

JBE virus <*abbr*> **Japanese B encephalitis virus**: japanisches B-Enzephalitis-Virus *n*, JBE-Virus *n*.

J-chain <*abbr*> **joining chain**: J-Kette *f*, Verbindungskette *f*.

jct. <*abbr*> **junction**: Verbindung *f*.

JCV <*abbr*> **JC virus**: JC-Virus *n*.

JEE <*abbr*> **Japanese E encephalitis virus**: japanisches E-Enzephalitis-Virus *n*, JEE-Virus *n*.

JNA <*abbr*> **Jena Nomina Anatomica**: Jenaer Nomina Anatomica, JNA.

JND <*abbr*> **just noticeable difference**: eben merklicher Unterschied *m*.

J point <*abbr*> **junctional point**: J-Punkt *m*, Junctional Point *m*.

K

K <*abbr*> **1. kalium, potassium; 2. Kelvin**: 1. Kalium *n*, K; 2. Kelvin *n*.

kerma <*abbr*> **kinetic energy released in matter**: Kerma *n*.

KFD <*abbr*> **Kyasanur forest disease**: Kyasanur-Wald-Krankheit *f*.

KJ <*abbr*> **knee jerk**: Patellarsehnenreflex *m*, Quadrizepssehnenreflex *m*, QSR.

Km allotype <*abbr*> **kappa chain marker-allotype**: Km-Allotyp *m*.

KP <*abbr*> **keratitic precipitate**: Hornhautpräzipitat *n*.

KS <*abbr*> **Kaposi sarcoma**: Kaposi-Sarkom *n*, KS.

17-KS <*abbr*> **17-ketosteroids**: 17-Ketosteroide, 17-KS.

KUB <*abbr*> **kidney, ureter, and bladder**: Niere, Harnleiter und Harnblase.

L

L <*abbr*> **1. Lactobacillus; 2. left; 3. levorotatory; 4. light sense; 5. length; 6. lumbar**: 1. Lactobacillus; 2. links; 3. linksdrehend; 4. Gesichtssinn *m*; 5. Länge *f*; 6. lumbal.

LAE <*abbr*> **left atrial enlargement**: Vergrößerung des linken Vorhofs *f*.

LAP <*abbr*> **1. leukocyte alkaline phosphatase; 2. lyophilized anterior pituitary**: 1. alkalische Leukozytenphosphatase *f*; 2. lyophilisiertes Hypophysenvorderlappengewebe *n*.

laser <*abbr*> **light amplification by stimulated emission of radiation**: Laser *m*.

LATS <*abbr*> **long-acting thyroid stimulator**: Long-acting-Thyroid-Stimulator *m*, LATS.

LAV <*abbr*> **lymphadenopathy-associated virus**: Lymphadenopathie-assoziiertes Virus *n*, LAV.

LBBB <*abbr*> **left bundle branch block**: Linksschenkelblock *m*.

LBF <*abbr*> **Lactobacillus bulgaricus factor**: Pantethein *n*.

LBW <*abbr*> **low birth weight**: niedriges Geburtsgewicht *n*.

LC <*abbr*> **liquid chromatography**: Flüssigkeitschromatographie *f*.

LCA <*abbr*> **left coronary artery**: Arteria coronaria sinistra *m*.

LCAT <*abbr*> **lecithin-cholesterol acyl transferase**: Lezithin-Cholesterin-Azyltransferase *f*.

L chain <*abbr*> **light chain**: leichte Kette *f*, L-Kette *f*.

LCIS <*abbr*> **lobular carcinoma in situ**: lobuläres Carcinoma in situ *n*.

LCM <*abbr*> **lymphocytic choriomeningitis**: lymphozytäre Choriomeningitis *f*, LCM.

LCMV <*abbr*> **lymphocytic choriomeningitis virus**: LCM-Virus *n*.

LD <*abbr*> **lethal dose**: Letaldosis *f*, letale Dosis *f*, LD.
LD$_{50}$ <*abbr*> **lethal dose fifty percent**: mittlere letale Dosis *f*.
LDH <*abbr*> **lactate dehydrogenase**: Laktatdehydrogenase *f*.
LDL <*abbr*> **low-density lipoprotein**: Low-Density-Lipoprotein *n*, Lipoprotein niedriger Dichte *n*, LDL.
L-dopa <*abbr*> **levodopa**: Levodopa *n*, L-Dopa *n*.
LE <*abbr*> **lupus erythematosus**: Lupus erythematodes *m*, LE.
LET <*abbr*> **linear energy transfer**: lineare Energieübertragung *f*.
Leu <*abbr*> **leucine**: Leucin *n*.
LFD <*abbr*> **least fatal dose**: kleinste letale Dosis *f*.
LFT <*abbr*> **liver function test**: Leberfunktionsprobe *f*.
LGH <*abbr*> **lactogenic hormone**: Prolaktin *n*.
LGL <*abbr*> **large granular lymphocyte**: großer granulärer Lymphozyt *m*, GGL.
LH <*abbr*> **luteinizing hormone**: luteinisierendes Hormon *n*, LH.
LHRH <*abbr*> **luteinizing hormone-releasing hormone**: Luteinisierungshormon-Releasing-Hormon *n*, LHRH.
LHRH agonist <*abbr*> **luteinizing hormone-releasing hormone agonist**: LHRH-Agonist *m*.
LIF <*abbr*> **1. left iliac fossa; 2. leukocyte inhibitory factor; 3. leukocytosis inducing factor**: 1. linke Fossa iliaca *f*; 2. Leukozytenhemmfaktor *m*; 3. Leukozytose-induzierender Faktor *m*.
LIP <*abbr*> **lymphoid interstitial pneumonia**: lymphoide interstitielle Pneumonie *f*, LIP.
Liq. <*abbr*> **1. liquid; 2. liquor**: 1. flüssig; 2. Liquor *m*.
LNPF <*abbr*> **lymph node permeability factor**: Lymph-node permeability factor *m*, LNPF.
LOCM <*abbr*> **low osmolar contrast medium**: niederosmolares Kontrastmittel *n*.
L-PAM <*abbr*> **melphalan**: Melphalan *n*, L-Pam.
LPF <*abbr*> **leukocytosis-promoting factor**: leukozytosefördernder Faktor *m*.
LPH <*abbr*> **1. left posterior hemiblock; 2. lipotropic hormone**: 1. linker hinterer Hemiblock *m*; 2. lipotropes Hormon *n*, LPH.
LRF <*abbr*> **luteinizing hormone-releasing factor**: Gonadorelin *n*.
LSD <*abbr*> **lysergic acid diethylamide**: D-Lysergsäurediäthylamid *n*, LSD.
L-S ratio <*abbr*> **lecithin-sphingomylin ratio**: L/S-Quotient *m*, Lezithin-Sphingomyelin-Quotient *m*.
LT <*abbr*> **lymphotoxin**: Lymphotoxin *n*.
LTF <*abbr*> **lymphocyte transforming factor**: Lymphozytentransformationsfaktor *m*, LTF.
LTH <*abbr*> **luteotropic hormone**: luteotropes Hormon *n*, LTH.
LVH <*abbr*> **left ventricular hypertrophy**: linksventrikuläre Hypertrophie *f*, LVH.
Lys <*abbr*> **lysin**: Lysin *n*, Lys, Diaminocapronsäure *f*.

M

m <*abbr*> **mmedian**: Median *m*.
M <*abbr*> **1. male; 2. methionine; 3. muscle; 4. myopia**: 1. männlich; 2. Methionin *n*; 3. Muskel *m*, Musculus, M.; 4. Myopie *f*.
MA <*abbr*> **1. mental age; 2. meter angle**: 1. Intelligenzalter *n*; 2. metrischer Winkel *m*.
MAC <*abbr*> **1. maximum allowable concentration; 2. membrane attack complex; 3. minimum alveolar concentration**: 1. maximale Arbeitsplatzkonzentration *f*, MAK; 2. Membranangriffskomplex *m*; 3. minimale alveoläre Konzentration *f*.
MAF <*abbr*> **macrophage activating factor**: Migrationsaktivierungsfaktor *m*, MAF.
MALT <*abbr*> **mucosa-associated lymphoid tissue**: Mukosa-assoziier-

tes lymphatisches Gewebe *n*, MALT.

MAO <*abbr*> **monoamine oxidase**: Monoaminoxidase *f*, MAO.

MAOI <*abbr*> **monoamine oxidase inhibitor**: Monoaminoxidasehemmer *m*, MAO-Hemmer *m*.

max <*abbr*> **maximum**: 1. Maximum *n*; 2. maximal.

MBC <*abbr*> **1. maximum breathing capacity; 2. minimum bactericidal concentration**: 1. Atemgrenzwert *m*; 2. minimale bakterizide Konzentration *f*, MBK.

MBD <*abbr*> **mimimal brain dysfunction**: minimale zerebrale Dysfunktion *f*.

MCF <*abbr*> **macrophage chemotaxis factor**: Makrophagenchemotaxin *n*.

MCH <*abbr*> **mean corpuscular hemoglobin**: mittlerer absoluter Hämoglobinkoeffizient *m*, Färbekoeffizient *m*, MCH.

MCHC <*abbr*> **mean corpuscular hemoglobin concentration**: Sättigungsindex *m*, MCHC.

MCHg <*abbr*> **mean corpuscular hemoglobin**: mittlerer absoluter Hämoglobinkoeffizient *m*, Färbekoeffizient *m*, MCH.

MCL <*abbr*> **midclavicular line**: mittlere Klavikularlinie *f*, MCL.

MCS <*abbr*> **multiple chemical sensitivity**: multiple Chemikaliensensitivität *f*.

M-CSF <*abbr*> **macrophage colony-stimulating factor**: Makrophagenkoloniestimulierender Faktor *m*, CSF.

MCT <*abbr*> **mean circulation time**: mittlere Kreislaufzeit *f*.

MCTD <*abbr*> **mixed connective tissue disease**: Mixed connective tissue disease, Kollagenmischkrankheit *f*, MCTD.

MCV <*abbr*> **mean corpuscular volume**: Erythrozytenvolumen *n*, MCV.

MDA <*abbr*> **mentum dexter anterior**: rechte vordere Kinnlage *f*.

MDD <*abbr*> **mean daily dose**: mittlere Tagesdosis *f*.

MDR <*abbr*> **minimum daily requirement**: täglicher Mindestbedarf *m*.

MEA <*abbr*> **multiple endocrine adenomatosis**: multiple endokrine Neoplasie *f*.

MED <*abbr*> **1. minimum effective dose; 2. minimal erythema dose**: 1. geringste wirksame Dosis *f*; 2. minimale Erythemdosis *f*.

MEG <*abbr*> **magnetoencephalograph**: Magnetenzephalograph *m*.

MEN <*abbr*> **multiple endocrine neoplasia**: multiple endokrine Neoplasie *f*.

Met <*abbr*> **methionine**: Methionin *n*.

MetHb <*abbr*> **methemoglobin**: Methämoglobin *n*, Met-Hb.

MF <*abbr*> **mitotic figure**: Mitosefigur *f*.

MFD <*abbr*> **minimal fatal dose**: minimale letale Dosis *f*, LD_{min}.

MGT <*abbr*> **mean generation time**: mittlere Verdopplungszeit *f*.

MGUS <*abbr*> **monoclonal gammopathy of undetermined significance**: benigne monoklonale Gammopathie *f*.

MHC <*abbr*> **major histocompatibility complex**: Major Histocompatibility Complex *m*, Haupthistokompatibilitätskomplex *m*, MHC.

MHD <*abbr*> **minimal hemolytic dose**: minimale hämolytische Dosis *f*.

MID <*abbr*> **1. minimal infective dose; 2. minimal inhibiting dose**: 1. minimale infektiöse Dosis *f*; 2. minimale Hemmkonzentration *f*, MHK.

MIF <*abbr*> **1. migration inhibiting factor; 2. melanocyte stimulating hormone inhibiting factor**: 1. Migrationsinhibitionsfaktor *m*, MIF; 2. MSH-Inhibiting-Faktor *m*, Melatonin *n*.

ML <*abbr*> **midline**: Mittellinie *f*.

MLC <*abbr*> **mixed lymphocyte culture**: gemischte Lymphozytenkultur *f*.

MLD <*abbr*> **1. median lethal dose; 2. minimum lethal dose**: 1. mittlere letale Dosis *f*, LD_{50}; 2. minimale letale Dosis *f*, LD_{min}.

MLR <*abbr*> **mixed lymphcyte reaction**: gemischte Lymphozytenkultur *f*.

MM <*abbr*> **1. mucous membrane; 2. myeloid metaplasia**: 1. Schleimhaut *f*; 2. myeloische Metaplasie *f*.

MMPI <*abbr*> **Minnesota multiphasic personality inventory**: Minnesota Multiphasic Personality Inventory, MMPI.

mmpp <*abbr*> **millimeters partial pressure**: mm Partialdruck *m*.

MMR vaccine <*abbr*> **measles-mumps-rubella vaccine**: Mumps-Masern-Röteln-Impfstoff *m*.

MO <*abbr*> **mesio-occlusal**: mesiookklusal.

mp <*abbr*> **melting point**: Schmelzpunkt *m*.

MP <*abbr*> **mercaptopurine**: Mercaptopurin *n*.

MPA <*abbr*> **mycophenolic acid**: Mycophenolsäure *f*.

MPD <*abbr*> **maximum permissible dose**: maximal zulässige Dosis *f*.

MPGN <*abbr*> **membranoproliferative glomerulonephritis**: membranoproliferative Glomerulonephritis *f*.

MPS <*abbr*> **mucopolysaccharidosis**: Mukopolysaccharidose *f*.

MPTP <*abbr*> **methyl-phenyl-tetrahydropyridine**: Methyl-phenyl-tetrahydropyridin *n*, MPTP.

MPV <*abbr*> **mean platelet volume**: mittleres Thrombozytenvolumen *n*.

MR <*abbr*> **mitral regurgitation**: Mitralklappeninsuffizienz *f*.

MRD <*abbr*> **minimal reacting dose**: kleinste wirksame Dosis *f*.

MRI <*abbr*> **magnetic resonance imaging**: Kernspinresonanztomographie *f*.

mRNA <*abbr*> **messenger ribonucleic acid**: Boten-RNS *f*, Messenger-Ribonukleinsäure *f*, mRNA.

MR tomography <*abbr*> **magnetic resonance tomography**: Kernspinresonanztomographie *f*.

MS <*abbr*> **1. mitral stenosis; 2. multiple sclerosis**: 1. Mitralklappenstenose *f*; 2. multiple Sklerose *f*, MS.

MSH <*abbr*> **melanocyte stimulating hormone**: melanozytenstimulierendes Hormon *n*, MSH.

MSHRF <*abbr*> **melanocyte stimulating hormone releasing factor**: MSH-Releasing-Faktor *m*, MSH-RF.

MSL <*abbr*> **midsternal line**: mittlere Sternallinie *f*.

MT <*abbr*> **1. empty; 2. membrana tympani; 3. metatarsal**: 1. leer; 2. Membrana tympani *f*; 3. metatarsal.

MTU <*abbr*> **methylthiouracil**: Methylthiouracil *n*, MTU.

MTX <*abbr*> **methotrexate**: Methotrexat *n*, MTX.

MU <*abbr*> **mouse unit**: Mäuseeinheit *f*.

MVP <*abbr*> **mitral prolapse**: Mitralklappenprolaps *m*.

MVV <*abbr*> **maximum voluntary ventilation**: Atemgrenzwert *m*.

MW <*abbr*> **molecular weight**: Molekulargewicht *n*, MG.

My. <*abbr*> **myopia**: Myopie *f*.

N

n <*abbr*> **normal**: normal.

n. <*abbr*> **nervus**: Nervus *m*, n, Nerv *m*.

N <*abbr*> **1. nasal; 2. newton; 3. nitrogen**: 1. nasal; 2. Newton, N; 3. Stickstoff *m*.

NA <*abbr*> **1. Nomina Anatomica; 2. numerical aperture; 3. nurses' aide**: 1. Nomina Anatomica, NA; 2. numerische Apertur *f*; 3. Krankenpflegehelfer *m*, Krankenpflegehelferin *f*.

NAD <*abbr*> **1. nicotinamide adenine dinucleotide; 2. no agglutination discovered; 3. no antibodies discovered; 4. no appreciable disease; 5. nothing abnormal detected**: 1. Nicotinamid-Adenin-Dinucleotid *n*, NAD; 2. keine Agglutination nachweisbar; 3. keine Antikörper nachweisbar; 4. ohne pathologischen Befund, o.B.; 5. ohne pathologischen Befund, o.B.

NADH <*abbr*> **reduced nicotinamide adenine dinucleotide**: reduziertes Nicotinamid-Adenin-Dinucleotid *n*, NADH.

NADP <*abbr*> **nicotinamide-adenine dinucleotide phosphate**: Nicotinamid-Adenin-Dinucleotid-Phosphat *n*, NADP.

NADPH <*abbr*> **reduced nicotinamide-adenine dinucleotide phosphate**: reduziertes Nicotinamid-Adenin-Dinucleotid-Phosphat *n*, NADPH.

NANB hepatitis <*abbr*> **non-A, non-B-Hepatitis**: Non-A, Non-B-Hepatitis *f*.

NB <*abbr*> **newborn**: Neugeborenes *n*.

NBT <*abbr*> **nitroblue tetrazolium test**: Nitroblautetrazolium-Test *m*, NBT-Test *m*.

NCA <*abbr*> **neurocirculatory asthenia**: neurozirkulatorische Asthenie *f*, DaCosta-Syndrom *n*.

NCL <*abbr*> **neuronal ceroid lipofuscinosis**: neuronale Ceroidlipofuscinose *f*.

NCV <*abbr*> **nerve conduction velocity**: Nervenleitungsgeschwindigkeit *f*, NLG.

NDV <*abbr*> **Newcastle disease virus**: Newcastle-Virus *n*.

Nd:YAG <*abbr*> **neodymium:yttrium-aluminium-garnet**: Neodym-Yttrium-Aluminium-Granat *n*, Neodym-YAG *n*.

NEC <*abbr*> **necrotizing enterocolitis**: nekrotisierende Enterokolitis *f*.

NED <*abbr*> **no evidence of disease**: kein Nachweis einer Erkrankung.

NEEP <*abbr*> **negative end-expiratory pressure**: negativer endexspiratorischer Druck *m*.

NEFA <*abbr*> **nonesterified fatty acid**: freie Fettsäure *f*, FFS.

neurol <*abbr*> **1. neurology; 2. neurologic**: 1. Neurologie *f*; 2. neurologisch.

NF <*abbr*> **1. National Formulary; 2. neurofibromatosis**: 1. Nationale Pharmakopoe *f*; 2. Neurofibromatose *f*, Recklinghausen-Krankheit *f*.

NG <*abbr*> **nasogastric**: nasogastrisch.

NGF <*abbr*> **nerve growth factor**: Nervenwachstumsfaktor *m*.

NGU <*abbr*> **nongonococcal urethritis**: nicht-gonorrhoische Urethritis *f*, NGU.

NHL <*abbr*> **non-Hodgkin lymphoma**: Non-Hodgkin-Lymphom *n*.

NHS <*abbr*> **1. normal human serum; 2. National Health Service**: 1. normales menschliches Serum; 2. National Health Service *m*, Nationaler Gesundheitsdienst *m*.

NIDDM <*abbr*> **non-insulin-dependent diabetes mellitus**: nicht-insulinabhängiger Diabetes mellitus *m*.

NIS <*abbr*> **near-normoglycemic insulin substitution**: nahe-normoglykämische Insulin-Substitution *f*.

NK cell <*abbr*> **natural killer cell**: Natural-Killer-Zelle *f*, natürliche Killerzelle, NK-Zelle *f*.

NM <*abbr*> **1. nanometer; 2. neuromuscular; 3. nicotinamide mononucleotide; 4. non-motile; 5. nuclear medicine**: 1. Nanometer; 2. neuromuskulär; 3. Nicotinamid-Mononucleotid *n*; 4. unbeweglich; 5. Nuklearmedizin *f*.

nml <*abbr*> **normal**: normal.

NMN <*abbr*> **nicotinamide mononucleotide**: Nicotinamidmononukleotid *n*.

NMP <*abbr*> **nucleoside monophosphate**: Nukleosidmonophosphat *n*.

NMR <*abbr*> **nuclear magnetic resonance**: Kernspinresonanz *f*, NMR.

NMS <*abbr*> **neuroleptic malignant syndrome**: malignes neuroleptisches Syndrom *n*.

Nn <*abbr*> **nerves**: Nerven, Nervi, Nn.

NNN culture medium <*abbr*> **Novy-Nicolle-McNeal culture medium**: Novy-Nicolle-McNeal-Agar m, NNN-Medium s.

no <*abbr*> **number**: Zahl *f*, Nummer *f*.

NOEL <*abbr*> **no observed effect level**: kein Effekt nachweisbar.

NP <*abbr*> **neuropsychiatry**: Neuropsychiatrie *f*.

NPO <*abbr*> **nil per os, nothing per mouth**: nichts peroral.

NPT <*abbr*> **noctile penile tumescence**: nächtliche Penistumeszenz *f*.

nr <*abbr*> **1. near; 2. no refill**: 1. nahe; 2. nicht nachfüllen.

NRC <*abbr*> **normal retinal correspondence**: normale Netzhautkorrespondenz *f*.

NREM <*abbr*> **non rapid eye movement**: Phase der langsamen Augenbewegungen *f*, Non-REM-Schlafphase *f*.

NREM sleep <*abbr*> **non-rapid eye movement sleep**: Non-REM-Schlaf *m*.

n. s. <*abbr*> **not significant**: nicht signifikant.

NSAIA <*abbr*> **nonsteroidal anti-inflammatory agents**: nichtsteroidale Antiphlogistika, nichtsteroidale antiinflammatorische Antirheumatika, NSAIR.

NSR <*abbr*> **normal sinus rhythm**: normaler Sinusrhythmus *m*.

NTP <*abbr*> **normal temperature and pressure**: Körpertemperatur und Blutdruck normal.

NUG <*abbr*> **necrotizing ulcerative gingivitis**: nekrotisierende ulzerierende Gingivitis *f*.

NYD <*abbr*> **not yet diagnosed**: noch nicht diagnostiziert.

O

OAF <*abbr*> **osteoclast activating factor**: Osteoklastenaktivierungsfaktor *m*.

OB <*abbr*> **obstetrics**: Geburtshilfe *f*.

OB-GYN <*abbr*> **obstetrics-gynecology**: Gynäkologie und Geburtshilfe.

OBS <*abbr*> **obstetrics**: Obstetrik *f*, Geburtshilfe *f*, Tokologie *f*.

OCA <*abbr*> **oculocutaneous albinism**: okulokutaner Albinismus *m*.

OD <*abbr*> **1. optical density; 2. outside diameter; 3. overdose**: 1. optische Dichte *f*; 2. äußerer Durchmesser *m*; 3. Überdosis *f*.

OER <*abbr*> **oxygen enhancement ratio**: Sauerstoffverstärkungsverhältnis *n*.

OFD <*abbr*> **orofaciodigital syndrome**: orofaziodigitales Syndrom *n*.

OI <*abbr*> **1. opportunistic infection; 2. osteogenesis imperfecta**: 1. opportunistische Infektion *f*; 2. Osteogenesis imperfecta *f*.

Ol <*abbr*> **oleum, oil**: Oleum *n*, Öl *n*.

OM <*abbr*> **1. otitis media; 2. outer membrane**: 1. Otitis media *f*; 2. äußere Membran *f*.

OPD <*abbr*> **outpatient department**: Ambulanz *f*, Poliklinik *f*.

OPSI syndrome <*abbr*> **overwhelming postsplenectomy infection syndrome**: OPSI-Syndrom *n*, Pneumokokkensepsis nach Splenektomie *f*.

OPV <*abbr*> **poliovirus vaccine live oral**: oraler Poliovirus-Lebendimpfstoff *m*.

OR <*abbr*> **operating room**: Operationssaal *m*, OP.

ORD <*abbr*> **optical rotatory dispersion**: optische Rotationsdispersion *f*.

Orn <*abbr*> **ornithine**: Ornithin *n*, Diaminovaleriansäure *f*.

OSAS <*abbr*> **obstructive sleep-apnea syndrome**: obstruktives Schlafapnoesyndrom *n*, OSAS.

OT <*abbr*> **1. old tuberculin; 2. original tuberculin; 3. occupational therapy**: 1. Alttuberkulin *n*; 2. Alttuberkulin *n*; 3. Beschäftigungstherapie *f*.

OTC drug <*abbr*> **over the counter drug**: frei verkäufliches Medikament *n*, rezeptfreies Arzneimittel *n*.

OTD <*abbr*> **organ tolerance dosis**: Organtoleranzdosis *f*, OTD.

P

P <*abbr*> **1. phosphorus; 2. plasma; 3. proline; 4. properdin; 5. pupil**: 1.

Phosphor *m*, P; 2. Plasma *n*; 3. Prolin *n*; 4. Properdin *n*; 5. Pupille *f*.

P. <*abbr*> **1. position; 2. presbyopia**: 1. Position *f*, Lage *f*; 2. Presbyopie *f*.

p- <*abbr*> **para-**: p-, para-.

PA <*abbr*> **1. paralysis agitans; 2. pernicious anemia; 3. physician assistant; 4. pulmonary artery**: 1. Paralysis agitans *f*; 2. perniziöse Anämie *f*; 3. Arzthelferin *f*; 4. Arteria pulmonalis *f*.

P-A <*abbr*> **posteroanterior**: posterior-anterior, p.a.

P & A <*abbr*> **percussion and auscultation**: Perkussion und Auskultation.

PABA <*abbr*> **para-aminobenzoic acid**: Para-Aminobenzoesäure *f*, PABA.

PAC <*abbr*> **premature atrial contraction**: vorzeitige Vorhofkontraktion *f*.

PACS <*abbr*> **Picture Archiving and Communication System**: Bild-Archiv-Kommunikations-System *n*.

PAF <*abbr*> **platelet activating factor**: Platelet activating Factor, thrombozytenaktivierender Faktor *m*, PAF.

PAGE <*abbr*> **polyacrylamide gel electrophoresis**: Polyacrylamid-Gelelektrophorese *f*, PAGE.

PAHA <*abbr*> **p-aminohippuric acid**: Paraaminohippursäure *f*, PAH.

PAI <*abbr*> **plasminogen activator inhibitor**: Plasminogenaktivator-Inhibitor *m*, PAI.

PALS <*abbr*> **periarterial lymphatic sheath, periarterial lymphoid sheath**: periarterielle Lymphscheide *f*, PALS, Vagina periarterialis lymphatica *f*.

PAO <*abbr*> **peak acid output**: Peak Acid Output *m*, maximale Säuresekretion *f*.

PAS reaction <*abbr*> **periodic acid Schiff reaction**: PAS-Reaktion *f*.

PAT <*abbr*> **paroxysmal atrial tachycardia**: paroxysmale Vorhoftachykardie *f*.

PAT-SED <*abbr*> **pseudoachondroplastic dysplasia**: pseudoachondroplastische Dysplasie *f*, Pseudoachondroplasie *f*.

PAWP <*abbr*> **pulmonary artery wedge pressure**: Pulmonalarterienverschlussdruck *m*.

PB <*abbr*> **1. Pharmacopoeia Britannica; 2. pressure breathing**: 1. Britische Pharmakopoe *f*; 2. Druckbeatmung *f*.

PBC <*abbr*> **primary biliary cirrhosis**: primär biliäre Zirrhose *f*, PBZ.

PBG <*abbr*> **porphobilinogen**: Porphobilinogen *n*, PBG.

PBI <*abbr*> **protein-bound iodine**: proteingebundenes Jod *n*.

PCA <*abbr*> **passive cutaneous anaphylaxis**: passive kutane Anaphylaxie *f*.

PCB <*abbr*> **polychlorinated biphenyl**: polychloriertes Biphenyl *n*, PCB.

PCE <*abbr*> **pseudocholinesterase**: Pseudocholinesterase *f*, PCHE.

PCG <*abbr*> **phonocardiogram**: Phonokardiogramm *n*, PKG.

PCM <*abbr*> **protein-calorie malnutrition**: Eiweiß-Kalorien-Unterernährung *f*.

PCO syndrome <*abbr*> **polycystic ovary syndrome**: polyzystisches Ovarialsyndrom *n*, PCO-Syndrom *n*.

PCP <*abbr*> **1. phencyclidine hydrochloride; 2. Pneumocystis carinii pneumonia**: 1. Phencyclidinhydrochlorid *n*, PCP; 2. Pneumocystis-carinii-Pneumonie *f*, PcP, Pneumocystis-jirovecii-Pneumonie *f*.

PCR <*abbr*> **polymerase chain reaction**: Polymerasekettenreaktion *f*, PCR.

PCV <*abbr*> **packed cell volume**: Hämatokrit *m*, Hk.

PCWP <*abbr*> **pulmonary capillary wedge pressure**: Wedge-Druck *m*, pulmonal-kapillärer Verschlussdruck *m*.

PD <*abbr*> **1. prism diopter; 2. interpupillary distance; 3. peritoneal dialysis**: 1. Prismendioptrie *f*; 2. Pupillenabstand *m*; 3. Peritonealdialyse *f*.

pd <*abbr*> **1. potential difference; 2.**

prism diopter; 3. pupillary distance: 1. Potentialdifferenz *f*; 2. Prismendioptrie *f*; 3. Pupillenabstand *m*.

PDA <*abbr*> **patent ductus arteriosus**: persistierender Ductus arteriosus Botalli *m*.

PDGF <*abbr*> **platelet derived growth factor**: platelet-derived growth factor, PDGF.

PDLL <*abbr*> **poorly differentiated lymphocytic lymphoma**: schlecht differenziertes lymphozytisches Lymphom *n*.

PE <*abbr*> **1. phosphatidylethanolamine; 2. physical examination; 3. potential energy; 4. pulmonary edema; 5. pulmonary embolism**: 1. Phosphatidyläthanolamin *n*; 2. körperliche Untersuchung *f*; 3. Potentialenergie *f*; 4. Lungenödem *n*; 5. Lungenembolie *f*.

PEEP <*abbr*> **positive end-expiratory pressure**: PEEP, positiver endexspiratorischer Beatmungsdruck *m*.

PEFR <*abbr*> **peak expiratory flow rate**: maximaler Exspirationsstoß *m*.

PEG <*abbr*> **1. pneumencephalography; 2. polyethylene glycol**: 1. Pneumenzephalographie *f*, PEG; 2. Polyäthylenglykol *n*, PEG.

PEP <*abbr*> **1. phosphoenolpyruvate; 2. preejection period**: 1. Phosphoenolpyruvat *n*, PEP; 2. Präejektionsperiode des Herzens *f*, Anspannungszeit *f*.

perna <*abbr*> **perchloronaphthalene**: Perchlornaphthalin *n*, Perna *n*.

PERRLA <*abbr*> **pupils equal, round, and react to light and accommodation**: seitengleiche runde Pupillen, Lichtreaktion und Akkommodationsreaktion.

PET <*abbr*> **1. positron emission tomography; 2. preeclamptic toxemia**: 1. Positronenemissionstomographie *f*, PET; 2. präeklamptische Toxämie *f*, Präeklampsie *f*.

PETT <*abbr*> **positron emission transaxial tomography**: transaxiale Positronenemissionstomographie *f*, PET.

Pf <*abbr*> **platelet factor**: Plättchenfaktor *m*, PF.

PFC <*abbr*> **1. persistent fetal circulation; 2. plaque-forming cells**: 1. persistierender fetaler Kreislauf *m*; 2. plaquebildende Zellen.

PFO <*abbr*> **patent foramen ovale**: offenes Foramen ovale *n*.

PFU <*abbr*> **plaque-forming unit**: plaquebildende Einheit *f*.

PG <*abbr*> **prostaglandin**: Prostaglandin *n*, PG.

PGR <*abbr*> **psychogalvanic reflex**: psychogalvanische Hautreaktion *f*.

Ph <*abbr*> **1. phenyl; 2. pharmacopeia**: 1. Phenyl *n*; 2. Pharmakopoe *f*.

pH <*abbr*> **potential of hydrogen ions**: Wasserstoffionenpotential *n*, pH.

PHA <*abbr*> **phytohemagglutinin**: Phytohämagglutinin *n*, PHA.

phar <*abbr*> **1. pharmaceutical; 2. pharmacopeia; 3. pharmacy**: 1. pharmazeutisch; 2. Pharmakopoe *f*; 3. Apotheke *f*, Pharmazie *f*, Arzneimittelherstellung *f*.

pharm <*abbr*> **1. pharmaceutical; 2. pharmacopeia; 3. pharmacy**: 1. pharmazeutisch; 2. Pharmakopoe *f*; 3. Apotheke *f*, Pharmazie *f*, Arzneimittelherstellung *f*.

Phe <*abbr*> **phenylalanine**: Phenylalanin *n*, Phe.

PI <*abbr*> **1. present illness; 2. protamine insulin; 3. protease inhibitor**: 1. derzeitige Erkrankung *f*; 2. Protamin-Insulin *n*; 3. Proteaseinhibitor *m*, Proteasehemmer *m*.

PID <*abbr*> **pelvic inflammatory disease**: entzündliche Beckenerkrankung *f*, PID.

PIE <*abbr*> **1. pulmonary infiltration with eosinophilia; 2. pulmonary interstitial emphysema**: 1. eosinophiles Lungeninfiltrat *n*, PIE-Syndrom *n*, Löffler-Syndrom *n*; 2. interstitielles Lungenemphysem *n*.

PIF <*abbr*> **1. prolactin inhibiting factor; 2. proliferation inhibiting factor**: 1. Prolaktin-Inhibiting-Faktor *m*, PIF; 2. Proliferationsinhibitorfaktor *m*, proliferationshemmender Faktor *m*.

PIH <*abbr*> **prolactin inhibiting hormone**: Prolaktin-Inhibiting-Hormon *n*, PIH.

PJT <*abbr*> **paroxysmal junctional taxhycardia**: paroxysmale AV-Knoten-Tachykardie *f*.

PK <*abbr*> **1. pharmacokinetics; 2. pyruvate kinase**: 1. Pharmakokinetik *f*; 2. Pyruvatkinase *f*.

PKC <*abbr*> **protein kinase C**: Proteinkinase C *f*.

PKU <*abbr*> **phenylketonuria**: Phenylketonurie *f*, PKU.

PLE <*abbr*> **protein-losing enteropathy**: Eiweißverlustsyndrom *n*, exsudative Enteropathie *f*.

PMB <*abbr*> **1. polymorphonuclear basophil leukocyte; 2. postmenopausal bleeding**: 1. polymorphkerniger basophiler Leukozyt *m*; 2. postmenopausale Blutung *f*.

PME <*abbr*> **polymorphonuclear eosinophil leukocyte**: polymorphkerniger eosinophiler Leukozyt *m*.

PMI <*abbr*> **point of maximum impulse**: Punctum maximum *n*, PM.

PML <*abbr*> **progressive multifocal leukoencephalopathy**: progressive multifokale Leukenzephalopathie *f*, PML.

PMN <*abbr*> **polymorphonuclear neutrophil leukocyte**: polymorphkerniger neutrophiler Leukozyt *m*.

PMS <*abbr*> **pregnant mare serum**: Serum trächtiger Stuten *n*.

PMT <*abbr*> **premenstrual tension**: prämenstruelle Verspannung *f*.

PN <*abbr*> **1. percussion note; 2. peripheral nerve; 3. peripheral neuropathy; 4. polyneuritis**: 1. Perkussionsschall *m*, Klopfschall *m*; 2. peripherer Nerv *m*; 3. periphere Neuropathie *f*; 4. Polyneuritis *f*.

PNA <*abbr*> **peanut agglutinin**: Erdnussagglutinin *n*.

PND <*abbr*> **paroxysmal nocturnal dyspnea**: paroxysmale nächtliche Dyspnoe *f*.

PNH <*abbr*> **paroxysmal nocturnal hemoglobinuria**: paroxysmale nächtliche Hämoglobinurie *f*, PNH.

PNPB <*abbr*> **positive-negative pressure breathing**: positiv-negative Druckbeatmung *f*, PNPB.

PNS <*abbr*> **peripheral nervous system**: peripheres Nervensystem *n*.

PO <*abbr*> **per os**: per os, peroral.

PPCF <*abbr*> **proserum prothrombin conversion accelerator**: Faktor V *m*, PPCF.

PPD <*abbr*> **purified protein derivative of tuberculin**: gereinigtes Tuberkulin *n*, PPD.

PPDS <*abbr*> **purified protein derivative of tuberculin Seibert**: PPD-Seibert *n*, PPDS.

PPLO <*abbr*> **pleuropneumonialike organism**: Mykoplasma *n*, PPLO.

PR <*abbr*> **1. partial remission; 2. production rate**: 1. partielle Rückbildung *f*, teilweise Remission *f*; 2. Produktionsrate *f*.

PRA <*abbr*> **plasma renin activity**: Plasmareninaktivität *f*.

PrEP <*abbr*> **preexposure prophylaxis**: Präexpositionsprophylaxe *f*, PrEP.

PRF <*abbr*> **prolactin releasing factor**: Prolaktin-Releasing-Faktor *m*, PRF.

prl <*abbr*> **prolactin**: Prolaktin *n*.

Pro <*abbr*> **proline**: Prolin *n*, Pro.

PRU <*abbr*> **peripheral resistance unit**: Einheit des peripheren Widerstands *f*.

PS <*abbr*> **1. phosphatidylserine; 2. pulmonary stenosis**: 1. Phosphatidylserin *n*; 2. Pulmonalstenose *f*.

PSA <*abbr*> **prostate specific antigen**: Prostata-spezifisches Antigen *n*, PSA.

PSM <*abbr*> **presystolic murmur**: Präsystolikum *n*.

PSVT <*abbr*> **paroxysmal supraventricular tachycardia**: paroxysmale supraventrikuläre Tachykardie *f*, PST.

pt <*abbr*> **point**: Punkt *m*.

PT <*abbr*> **prothrombin time**: Prothrombinzeit *f*.

PTA <*abbr*> **plasma thromboplastin antecedent**: Plasma-Thromboplastin-Antecedent *m*, PTA, Faktor XI *m*.

PTC <*abbr*> **plasma thromboplastin component**: Plasma-Thromboplastin-Component *f*, PTC, Faktor IX *m*, Christmas-Faktor *m*.

PTF <*abbr*> **plasma thromboplastin factor**: Plasmathromboplastinfaktor *m*.

PTH <*abbr*> **1. parathormone; 2. parathyroid hormone**: 1. Parathormon *n*, PTH; 2. Parathyrin *n*.

PTHC <*abbr*> **percutaneous transhepatic cholangiogram**: perkutanes transhepatisches Cholangiogramm *n*.

PTLD <*abbr*> **posttransplant lymphoproliferative disorder**: transplantationsassoziierte lymphoproliferative Erkrankung *f*.

PTT <*abbr*> **partial thromboplastin time**: partielle Thromboplastinzeit *f*, PTZ.

PUBS <*abbr*> **percutaneous umbilical blood sampling**: perkutane Nabelschnurblutentnahme *f*.

PUO <*abbr*> **pyrexia of unknown origin**: Fieber unbekannter Ursache *n*.

pur <*abbr*> **purine**: Purin *n*.

PUVA <*abbr*> **psoralens and longwave ultraviolet light**: Psoralen plus UV-A, PUVA.

PV <*abbr*> **1. polycythemia vera; 2. plasma volume; 3. peripheral vascular; 4. portal vein**: 1. Polycythaemia vera *f*; 2. Plasmavolumen *n*, PV; 3. peripher vaskulär; 4. Pfortader *f*.

PVC <*abbr*> **1. premature ventricular contraction; 2. polyvinylchloride; 3. premature ventricular contraction**: 1. vorzeitige Kammerkontraktion *f*; 2. Polyvinylchlorid *n*, PVC; 3. ventrikuläre Extrasystole *f*.

PVP <*abbr*> **polyvinylpyrrolidone**: Polyvinylpyrrolidon *n*, PVP.

PVP-I <*abbr*> **povidone iodine**: Povidon-Iod *n*, PVP-Jodlösung *f*.

PYLL <*abbr*> **potential years of life lost**: potentielle Lebensverkürzung *f*.

PZI <*abbr*> **protamine zinc insulin**: Protamin-Zink-Insulin *n*.

Q

q.d. <*abbr*> **quaque die**: quaque die, täglich.

qns <*abbr*> **quantity not sufficient**: Menge nicht ausreichend *f*.

QOL <*abbr*> **quality of life**: Lebensqualität *f*.

q.v. <*abbr*> **quantum vis**: quantum vis, beliebig viel.

R

r <*abbr*> **recombinant**: rekombinant, r.

R <*abbr*> **1. roentgen; 2. gas constant; 3. rough; 4. respiratory exchange ratio; 5. arginine**: 1. Röntgen *n*; 2. Gaskonstante *f*; 3. roh; 4. Gasaustauschquotient *m*; 5. Arginin *n*.

-R <*abbr*> **Rinne's test negative**: negativer Rinne-Test *m*.

+R <*abbr*> **Rinne's test positive**: positiver Rinne-Test *m*.

RAS <*abbr*> **reticular activating system**: retikuläres aktivierendes System *n*.

RAST <*abbr*> **radioallergosorbent test**: Radioallergosorbenttest *m*, RAST.

RAV <*abbr*> **Rous-associated virus**: Rous-assoziiertes Virus *n*.

RBBB <*abbr*> **right bundle branch block**: Rechtsschenkelblock *m*.

RBC <*abbr*> **1. red blood cell; 2. red blood count**: 1. rotes BLutkörperchen *n*, Erythrozyt *m*; 2. Erythrozytenzahl *f*.

RBE <*abbr*> **relative biologic effectiveness**: relative biologische Wirksamkeit *f*, RBW.

RBF <*abbr*> **renal blood flow**: Nierendurchblutung *f*.

RD <*abbr*> **1. reaction of degeneration; 2. retinal detachment**: 1. Entartungsreaktion *f*, EaR; 2. Netzhautablösung *f*.

RDA <*abbr*> **recommended daily allowance**: empfohlene tägliche Menge *f*.

RDP <*abbr*> **right dorsoposterior**

position: dorsoposteriore Querlage *f*.

RDS <*abbr*> **respiratory distress syndrome**: Atemnotsyndrom *n*.

redox <*abbr*> **reduction and oxidation**: Redox *n*.

REM <*abbr*> **rapid eye movement**: schnelle Augenbewegung *f*, REM-Bewegung *f*.

RES <*abbr*> **reticuloendothelial system**: retikuloendotheliales System *n*, RES.

RF <*abbr*> **1. releasing factor; 2. rheumatoid factor**: 1. Releasing-Faktor *m*; 2. Rheumafaktor *m*, RF.

RFA <*abbr*> **right frontoanterior position**: rechte vordere Vorderhauptlage *f*.

R-factor <*abbr*> **resistance factor**: Resistenzfaktor *m*, R-Faktor *m*.

RFP <*abbr*> **right frontoposterior position**: rechte hintere Vorderhauptlage *f*.

RFT <*abbr*> **right frontotransverse position**: rechte vordere Querlage *f*.

RH <*abbr*> **releasing hormone**: Releasing-Hormon *n*.

rh <*abbr*> **rhesus**: Rhesusantigen *n*, Rh.

RHD <*abbr*> **rheumatic heart disease**: rheumatische Herzerkrankung *f*.

rhGH <*abbr*> **recombinant human growth hormone**: rekombinantes menschliches Wachstumshormon *n*.

RIA <*abbr*> **radioimmunoassay**: Radioimmunoassay *m*, RIA.

RID <*abbr*> **radioimmunodiffusion**: Radioimmunodiffusion *f*, RID.

RIF <*abbr*> **right iliac fossa**: rechte Fossa iliaca *f*.

RIND <*abbr*> **reversible ischemic neurologic deficit**: reversibles ischämisches neurologisches Defizit *n*, RIND.

RIPA <*abbr*> **radioimmunoprecipitation assay**: Radioimmunpräzipitationstest *m*.

RISA <*abbr*> **radioiodinated serum albumin**: radioaktiv markiertes Serumalbumin *n*.

RIST <*abbr*> **radioimmunosorbent test**: Radioimmunosorbenttest *m*, RIST.

RLF <*abbr*> **retrolental fibroplasia**: retrolentale Fibroplasie *f*.

RLL <*abbr*> **right lower lobe**: rechter Unterlappen *m*.

RLQ <*abbr*> **right lower quadrant**: rechter unterer Quadrant *m*.

RMA <*abbr*> **right mentoanterior position**: rechte vordere Gesichtslage *f*.

RML <*abbr*> **right middle lobe**: rechter Mittellappen *m*.

RMP <*abbr*> **right mentoposterior position**: rechte hintere Gesichtslage *f*.

RMSF <*abbr*> **Rocky Mountain spotted fever**: Rocky-Mountain-Fieber *n*, amerikanisches Zeckenfieber *n*.

RN <*abbr*> **registered nurse**: examinierte Krankenschwester *f*.

RNA <*abbr*> **ribonucleic acid**: Ribonukleinsäure *f*, RNS.

RNase <*abbr*> **ribonuclease**: Ribonuklease *f*, RNase *f*.

ROA <*abbr*> **right occipitoanterior position**: rechte vordere Hinterhauptlage *f*.

ROC curve <*abbr*> **receiver operating characteristic curve**: ROC-Kurve *f*.

ROI <*abbr*> **region of interest**: Region of Interest *f*, Objektbereich *m*.

ROM <*abbr*> **rupture of membranes**: Blasensprung *m*.

ROP <*abbr*> **right occipitoposterior position**: rechte hintere Hinterhauptlage *f*.

ROT <*abbr*> **right occipitotransverse position**: rechte hintere Querlage *f*.

RPF <*abbr*> **renal plasma flow**: Nierenplasmastrom *m*, renaler Plasmafluss *m*, RPF.

rpm <*abbr*> **revolutions per minute**: Umdrehungen pro Minute.

RPR test <*abbr*> **rapid plasma reagin test**: RPR-Test *m*, Plasmareaginschnelltest *m*.

RQ <*abbr*> **1. recovery quotient; 2. respiratory quotient**: 1. Erholungsquotient *m*; 2. respiratorischer Quotient *m*, RQ.

rRNA <*abbr*> **ribosomal ribonucleic acid**: ribosomale Ribonukleinsäure *f*, rRNA.

RSA <*abbr*> **right sacroanterior position**: rechte vordere Steißlage *f*.

RSI <*abbr*> **repetitive strain injury**: repetitive strain injury, RSI, Verletzung nach wiederholter Belastung *f*.

RSP <*abbr*> **right sacroposterior position**: rechte hintere Steißlage *f*.

RST <*abbr*> **right sacrotransverse position**: rechte transversale Steißlage *f*.

RSV <*abbr*> **Rous sarcoma virus**: Rous-Sarkomvirus *n*, RSV.

RS virus <*abbr*> **respiratory syncytial virus**: RS-Virus *n*.

RT <*abbr*> **1. reverse transcriptase; 2. room temperature**: 1. reverse Transkriptase *f*, RT; 2. Raumtemperatur *f*, RT.

RTA <*abbr*> **renal tubular acidosis**: renal-tubuläre Azidose *f*.

RTF <*abbr*> **resistance transfer factor**: Resistenztransferfaktor *m*, RTF.

RU <*abbr*> **rat unit**: Ratteneinheit *f*.

RUL <*abbr*> **right upper lobe**: rechter Oberlappen *m*.

RUQ <*abbr*> **right upper quadrant**: rechter oberer Quadrant *m*.

RUV <*abbr*> **residual urine volume**: Restharnvolumen *n*.

RV <*abbr*> **residual volume**: Residualvolumen *n*, RV.

RVH <*abbr*> **right ventricular hypertrophy**: Hypertrophie des rechten Ventrikels, Rechtsherzhypertrophie *f*.

Rx <*abbr*> **medical prescription**: Rezept *n*.

S

S <*abbr*> **1. siemens; 2. serum**: 1. Siemens *n*; 2. Serum *n*.

S_1 <*abbr*> **first heart sound**: erster Herzton *m*.

S_2 <*abbr*> **second heart sound**: zweiter Herzton *m*.

SAA <*abbr*> **severe aplastic anemia**: schwere aplastische Anämie *f*.

SARS <*abbr*> **severe acute respiratory syndrome**: SARS, schweres akutes Atemwegssyndrom *n*, schweres akutes respiratorisches Syndrom *n*.

SBE <*abbr*> **subacute bacterial endocarditis**: subakute bakterielle Endokarditis *f*, SBE.

SC <*abbr*> **closure of semilunar valves**: Semilunarklappenschluss *m*.

SCAT <*abbr*> **sheep cell agglutination test**: Rose-Waaler-Test *m*, Paul-Bunnell-Reaktion *f*.

SCF <*abbr*> **stem-cell factor**: Stammzellfaktor *m*.

SCID <*abbr*> **severe combined immunodeficiency**: schwerer kombinierter Immundefekt *m*.

SD <*abbr*> **1. standard deviation; 2. streptodornase; 3. skin dose; 4. sudden death**: 1. Standardabweichung *f*; 2. Streptodornase *f*; 3. Hautdosis *f*; 4. plötzlicher Herztod *m*.

SDA <*abbr*> **1. sacrodextra anterior; 2. specific dynamic action**: 1. rechte vordere Steißlage *f*; 2. spezifisch-dynamische Wirkung *f*.

SDE <*abbr*> **specific dynamic effect**: spezifisch-dynamische Wirkung *f*.

SDS <*abbr*> **sodium dodecyl sulfate**: Natriumdodecylsulfat *n*, SDS.

SE <*abbr*> **standard error**: Standardfehler *m*.

SED <*abbr*> **skin erythema dose**: Hauterythemdosis *f*.

SEM <*abbr*> **1. scanning electron microscope; 2. slow eye movement**: 1. Rasterelektronenmikroskop *n*, REM; 2. langsame Augenbewegung *f*, non-REM-Bewegung *f*.

SER <*abbr*> **1. sensory-evoked response; 2. smooth endoplasmic reticulum**: 1. sensibel evozierte Response; 2. glattes endoplasmatisches Retikulum *n*.

Ser <*abbr*> **serine**: Serin *n*, Ser.

SF <*abbr*> **1. spinal fluid; 2. synovial fluid**: 1. Liquor *m*; 2. Synovia *f*, Gelenkflüssigkeit *f*.

SGOT <*abbr*> **serum glutamic oxaloacetic transaminase**: Serum-Glutamat-Oxalat-Transaminase *f*, SGOT.

SGPT <*abbr*> **serum glutamic pyruvic transaminase**: Serum-Glutamat-Pyruvat-Transaminase *f*, SGPT.

SHBG <*abbr*> **sex-hormone binding globulin**: Sexualhormon bindendes Globulin *n*, SHBG.

SI <*abbr*> **1. soluble insulin; 2. Système International d'Unités**: 1. Altinsulin *n*; 2. Système International d'Unités, SI-System *n*.

SIAD <*abbr*> **syndrome of inappropriate ADH secretion**: Syndrom der inappropriaten ADH-Sekretion *f*, SIADH, Schwartz-Bartter-Syndrom *n*.

SIADH <*abbr*> **syndrome of inappropriate antidiuretic hormone secretion**: Syndrom der inappropriaten ADH-Sekretion, SIADH, Schwartz-Bartter-Syndrom *n*.

SID <*abbr*> **sudden infant death**: plötzlicher Kindstod *m*.

SIDS <*abbr*> **sudden infant death syndrome**: plötzlicher Kindstod *m*.

SIg <*abbr*> **surface immunoglobulin**: Oberflächenimmunglobulin *n*.

SISI <*abbr*> **short increment sensitivity index**: SISI, Erkennbarkeit kurzer Lautstärken *f*.

SLE <*abbr*> **systemic lupus erythematosus**: systemischer Lupus erythematodes *m*, SLE.

SLEDA <*abbr*> **systemic lupus erythematosus disease activity**: Krankheitsaktivität bei systemischem Lupus erythematodes *f*, SLEDA.

SMON <*abbr*> **subacute myeloopticoneuropathy**: subakute Myelooptikoneuropathie *f*, SMON.

SMR <*abbr*> **submucous resection**: submuköse Resektion *f*.

SNS <*abbr*> **sympathic nervous system**: sympathisches Nervensystem *n*.

SOB <*abbr*> **shortness of breath**: Kurzatmigkeit *f*, Dyspnoe *f*.

sp. <*abbr*> **1. species; 2. specific**: 1. Spezies *f*, Sp.; 2. spezifisch.

SPCA <*abbr*> **serum prothrombin conversion accelerator**: Proconvertin *n*, Faktor VII *m*.

spec. <*abbr*> **1. special; 2. specific; 3. specimen**: 1. speziell; 2. spezifisch; 3. Probe *f*, Untersuchungsmaterial *n*.

SPECT <*abbr*> **single photon emission computed tomography**: Single-Photon-Emissions-Computertomographie *f*, SPECT.

SQ <*abbr*> **subcutaneous**: subkutan.

sq <*abbr*> **square**: Quadrat *n*.

SRBC <*abbr*> **sheep red blood cells**: Schaferythrozyten.

SRF <*abbr*> **somatotropin releasing factor**: Somatotropin-Releasing-Faktor *m*.

SRH <*abbr*> **somatotropin releasing hormone**: Somatotropin-Releasing-Hormon *n*, SRH.

sRNA <*abbr*> **soluble ribonucleic acid**: lösliche Ribonukleinsäure *f*, sRNA.

SRS <*abbr*> **slow-reacting substance**: Slow-reacting Substance *f*, langsam reagierende Substanz *f*, SRS.

SRT <*abbr*> **1. sedimentation rate test; 2. speech reception threshold**: 1. Blutkörperchensenkungsreaktion *f*, BSG; 2. Sprachwahrnehmungsschwelle *f*.

SSPE <*abbr*> **subacute sclerosing panencephalitis**: subakute sklerosierende Panenzephalitis *f*, SSPE.

SSRI <*abbr*> **selective serotonin reuptake inhibitor**: selektiver Serotonin-Wiederaufnahmehemmer *m*.

SSS <*abbr*> **sick sinus syndrome**: Sick-Sinus-Syndrom *n*, SS-Syndrom *n*.

ST <*abbr*> **1. stable toxin; 2. survival time; 3. standardized test; 4. skin test**: 1. stabiles Toxin *n*; 2. Überlebensdauer *f*; 3. standardisierter Test *m*; 4. Hautprobe *f*, Hauttest *m*.

STD <*abbr*> **1. sexually transmitted disease; 2. skin test dose; 3. standard test dose**: 1. sexuell übertragbare Krankheit *f*; 2. Hauttestdosis *f*; 3. definierte Testdosis *f*.

STH <*abbr*> **somatotropic hormone**: somatotropes Hormon *n*, Somatotropin *n*, Wachstumshormon *n*.

STI <*abbr*> **sexually transmitted infection**: sexuell übertragbare Infektion *f*.

STP <*abbr*> **standard temperature and pressure**: Normaltemperatur und Normaldruck.

STS <*abbr*> **serologic test for syphilis**: Syphilisserologie *f*.

STU <*abbr*> **skin test unit**: Haut-test-Einheit *f*.

SV <*abbr*> **simian virus**: Simian-Virus *n*, SV-Virus *n*.

SWS <*abbr*> **slow wave sleep**: non-REM-Schlaf *m*.

T

T <*abbr*> **1. temperature; 2. threonine**: 1. Temperatur *f*; 2. Threonin *n*, Thr.

T_3 <*abbr*> **triiodothyronine**: Trijodthyronin *n*, T_3.

T_4 <*abbr*> **thyroxine**: Tetrajodthyronin *n*, Thyroxin *n*, T_4.

TAR syndrome <*abbr*> **thrombocytopenia absent-radius syndrome**: TAR-Syndrom *n*, Hand-Herz-Syndrom *n*.

TAT <*abbr*> **thematic apperception test**: thematischer Apperzeptionstest *m*, TAT.

TB <*abbr*> **1. tubercle bacillus; 2. tuberculosis**: 1. Tuberkelbazillus *m*; 2. Tuberkulose *f*, TB, Tbk.

TBG <*abbr*> **thyroxine-binding globulin**: thyroxinbindendes Globulin *n*, TBG.

TBPA <*abbr*> **thyroxine-binding prealbumin**: thyroxinbindendes Präalbumin *n*, TBPA.

TCA <*abbr*> **1. tricarboxylic acid; 2. trichloracetic acid**: 1. Trikarboxylsäure *f*; 2. Trichloressigsäure *f*.

TCD <*abbr*> **transcranial Doppler**: transkranielle Doppler-Ultraschalluntersuchung *f*.

T cell <*abbr*> **thymus-derived cell**: T-Zelle *f*, T-Lymphozyt *m*.

TCR <*abbr*> **T-cell receptor**: T-Zell-Rezeptor *m*.

tDNA <*abbr*> **transfer deoxyribonucleic acid**: Transfer-Desoxyribonukleinsäure *f*, tDNS.

TED <*abbr*> **threshold erythema dose**: Erythemschwellendosis *f*.

temp <*abbr*> **temperature**: Temperatur *f*, T.

TENS <*abbr*> **transcutaneous electric nerve stimulation**: transkutane elektrische Nervenstimulation *f*, TENS.

TEPA <*abbr*> **triethylenephosphoramide**: Triäthylenphosphoramid *n*, TEPA.

TF <*abbr*> **1. tetralogy of Fallot; 2. transfer factor**: 1. Fallot-Tetralogie *f*; 2. Transferfaktor *m*, T-Faktor *m*.

TG <*abbr*> **thyroglobulin**: Thyreoglobulin *n*.

TGF <*abbr*> **T-cell growth factor**: T-Zell-Wachstumsfaktor *m*, Interleukin-2 *n*.

TGT <*abbr*> **thromboplastin generation test**: Thromboplastinbindungstest *m*, TGT.

THF <*abbr*> **tetrahydrofolate**: Tetrahydrofolat *n*.

Thr <*abbr*> **threonine**: Threonin *n*, Thr.

Thy <*abbr*> **thymine**: Thymin *n*, Thy.

TIA <*abbr*> **transient ischemic attack**: transitorische ischämische Attacke *f*, TIA.

TIBO <*abbr*> **tetrahydroimidazobenzodiazepine**: Tetrahydroimidazobenzodiazepin *n*, TIBO.

tinct <*abbr*> **tincture**: Tinktur *f*.

TKD <*abbr*> **tokodynamometer**: Tokodynamometer *n*.

TKG <*abbr*> **tokodynagraph**: Tokodynamograph *m*.

TL <*abbr*> **1. temporal lobe; 2. tubal ligature; 3. total lipids**: 1. Temporallappen *m*; 2. Tubenligatur *f*; 3. Gesamtlipide.

TLC <*abbr*> **1. thin-layer chromatography; 2. total lung capacity**: 1. Dünnschichtchromatographie *f*; 2. totale Lungenkapazität *f*.

TLE <*abbr*> **thin-layer electrophoresis**: Dünnschichtelektrophorese *f*.

TLV *<abbr>* **total lung volume**: Gesamtvolumen *n*.

T lymphocyte *<abbr>* **thymus-derived lymphocyte**: T-Lymphozyt *m*, Thymuslymphozyt *m*, thymusabhängiger Lymphozyt *m*.

Tm *<abbr>* **transport maximum**: Transportmaximum *n*.

TMV *<abbr>* **tabac mosaic virus**: Tabakmosaikvirus *n*.

Tn *<abbr>* **normal intraocular tension**: normaler Augeninnendruck *m*.

TNF *<abbr>* **tumor necrosis factor**: Tumor-Nekrose-Faktor *m*, TNF.

TNM *<abbr>* **tumor, node, metastasis**: Tumor, Nodus, Metastase, TNM.

TP *<abbr>* **1. threshold potential; 2. tuberculin precipitation**: 1. Schwellenpotential *n*; 2. Calmette-Tuberkulin *n*.

TP5 *<abbr>* **thymopentin**: Thymopentin *n*.

tPA *<abbr>* **tissue plasminogen activator**: Gewebeplasminogenaktivator *m*

TPHA test *<abbr>* **treponema pallidum hemagglutination test**: Treponema-pallidum-Hämagglutinationstest *m*, TPHA-Test *m*.

TPI test *<abbr>* **treponema pallidum immobilization test**: Treponema-pallidum-Immobilisationstest *m*, TPI-Test *m*.

TPN *<abbr>* **triphosphopyridine nucleotide**: Triphosphopyridinnukleotid *n*, TPN,

TR *<abbr>* **1. tricuspid regurgitation; 2. tuberculine residue**: 1. Trikuspidalklappeninsuffizienz *f*; 2. Neutuberkulin *n*.

TRBF *<abbr>* **total renal blood flow**: gesamte Nierendurchblutung *f*.

TRF *<abbr>* **thyrotropin releasing factor**: Thyreotropin-Releasing-Faktor *m*, TRF.

TRH *<abbr>* **thyrotropin releasing hormone**: Thyreotropin-Releasing-Hormon *n*, TRH.

TRIAC *<abbr>* **triiodothyroacetic acid**: Trijodthyroessigsäure *f*.

TRIC *<abbr>* **trachoma inclusion conjunctivitis**: Trachomeinschlusskörperchen-Konjunktivitis *f*, TRIC.

TRIS *<abbr>* **trishydroxymethylaminomethane**: Tris-Hydroxymethyl-Aminomethan *n*, THAM *n*.

tRNA *<abbr>* **transfer ribonucleic acid**: Transfer-Ribonukleinsäure *f*, Transfer-RNA *f*, tRNA.

Trp *<abbr>* **tryptophan**: Tryptophan *n*, Trp.

TS *<abbr>* **1. test solution; 2. tricuspid stenosis**: 1. Testlösung *f*; 2. Trikuspidalklappenstenose *f*.

TSH *<abbr>* **thyroid-stimulating hormone**: Thyreotropin *n*, TSH.

TSH-RF *<abbr>* **thyroid-stimulating hormone-releasing factor**: Thyreotropin-Releasing-Faktor *m*, TSHRF.

tsp *<abbr>* **teaspoon**: Teelöffel *m*.

TTP *<abbr>* **1. thymidine triphosphate; 2. thrombotic thrombocytopenic purpura**: 1. Thymidintriphosphat *n*; 2. thrombotisch-thrombozytopenische Purpura *f*, TTP.

TUIP *<abbr>* **transurethral incision of the prostate**: transurethrale Inzision der Prostata *f*, TUIP.

TUR *<abbr>* **transurethral resection**: transurethrale Resektion *f*, TUR.

TURP *<abbr>* **transurethral resection of prostate**: transurethrale Resektion der Prostata, TURP.

Tyr *<abbr>* **tyrosine**: Tyrosin *n*, Tyr.

U

U *<abbr>* **1. uracil; 2. uridine**: 1. Uracil *n*; 2. Uridin *n*.

U. *<abbr>* **unit**: Einheit *f*.

UARS *<abbr>* **upper airway resistance syndrome**: Widerstandssyndrom der oberen Atemwege *n*.

UBO *<abbr>* **unidentified bright objects**: unklare hyperintense Herde, UBO-Syndrom *n*.

UDP *<abbr>* **uridine 5'-diphosphate**: Uridindiphosphat *n*.

UDPG *<abbr>* **uridine 5'-diphosphate glucose**: Uridindiphosphatglukose *f*.

UFA *<abbr>* **unesterified fatty acid**: freie Fettsäure *f*.

UGI *<abbr>* **upper gastrointestinal tract**: oberer Gastrointestinaltrakt *m*.

UMP *<abbr>* **uridine 5'-monophosphate**: Uridinmonophosphat *n*, UMP.

URI *<abbr>* **upper respiratory infection**: Infektion der oberen Atemwege *f*.

U.S.P. *<abbr>* **United States Pharmacopeia**: Pharmakopoe der USA *f*.

UTI *<abbr>* **urinary tract infection**: Harnwegsinfekt *m*, HWI.

UTP *<abbr>* **uridine 5'-triphosphate**: Uridintriphosphat *n*, UTP.

UV *<abbr>* **ultraviolet**: ultraviolett, UV.

UVR *<abbr>* **ultraviolet radiation**: Ultraviolettstrahlung *f*, UV-Strahlung *f*.

V

V *<abbr>* **vision**: Sehvermögen *n*.

VA *<abbr>* **1. viral antigen; 2. visual acuity**: 1. Virusantigen *n*; 2. Sehschärfe *f*.

VAD *<abbr>* **ventricular assist device**: Herzkammerschrittmacher *m*.

var. *<abbr>* **variety**: Varietät *f*, Varietas *f*, var.

VC *<abbr>* **vital capacity**: Vitalkapazität *f*, VK.

VCG *<abbr>* **vectorcardiography**: Vektorkardiographie *f*, VKG.

VD *<abbr>* **venereal disease**: Geschlechtskrankheit *f*, sexuell übertragbare Krankheit *f*.

VDBP *<abbr>* **vitamin-D-binding protein**: Vitamin-D-bindendes Protein *n*.

VDRL test *<abbr>* **venereal disease research laboratory test**: VDRL-Test *m*.

VE *<abbr>* **ventricular extrasystoles**: ventrikuläre Extrasystolen, VES.

VEE *<abbr>* **Venezuelan equine encephalomyelitis**: venezuelanische Pferdeenzephalomyelitis *f*.

VF *<abbr>* **1. ventricular fibrillation; 2. visual field**: 1. Kammerflimmern *n*; 2. Sehfeld *n*.

VHD *<abbr>* **ventricular heart disease**: ventrikuläre Herzkrankheit *f*.

VIC *<abbr>* **vaso-inhibitory center**: Vasomotorenhemmzentrum *n*.

vif *<abbr>* **viral infectivity factor**: viraler Infektionsfaktor *m*.

VIP *<abbr>* **vasoactive intestinal peptide**: vasoaktives intestinales Peptid *n*, VIP.

VIP stain *<abbr>* **vaginal identification of pathogens stain**: VIP-Färbung *f*.

VLDL *<abbr>* **very-low-density lipoprotein**: Lipoprotein sehr niedriger Dichte *n*, VLDL.

VMA *<abbr>* **vanillylmandelic acid**: Vanillinmandelsäure *f*.

vol *<abbr>* **volume**: Volumen *n*, Menge *f*.

VP *<abbr>* **venous pressure**: venöser Blutdruck *m*.

VPC *<abbr>* **volume packed cells**: Hämatokrit *m*, Hk.

VP test *<abbr>* **Voges-Proskauer test**: Voges-Proskauer-Reaktion *f*.

VS *<abbr>* **1. ventricular septum; 2. vesicular sound; 3. vesicular stomatitis**: 1. Ventrikelseptum *n*; 2. vesikuläres Atemgeräusch *n*; 3. vesikuläre Stomatitis *f*.

VSA *<abbr>* **variant surface antigen**: variantes Oberflächenantigen *n*.

VSD *<abbr>* **ventricular septal defect**: Ventrikelseptumdefekt *m*, VSD.

VSG *<abbr>* **variant surface glycoprotein**: variantes Oberflächenglykoprotein *n*.

Vv *<abbr>* **venae**: Venae, Vv., Venen.

Vx *<abbr>* **vertex**: Vertex *m*, Scheitel *m*.

VZV *<abbr>* **varicella-zoster virus**: Varicella-Zoster-Virus *n*, VZV.

W

W *<abbr>* **1. watt; 2. wolfram, tungsten**: 1. Watt; 2. Wolfram *n*, W, Tungsten *n*.
WAIS *<abbr>* **Wechsler Adult Intelligence Scale**: Wechsler-Erwachsenen-Intelligenz-Skala *f*.
WB *<abbr>* **whole blood**: Vollblut *n*.
WBC *<abbr>* **1. white blood cell; 2. white blood count**: 1. weißes Blutkörperchen *n*, Leukozyt *m*; 2. Leukozytenzählung *f*.
WDHA syndrome *<abbr>* **water diarrhea hypokalemia achlorhydria syndrome**: wässrige Diarrhoe, Hypokaliämie, Anazidität-Syndrom *n*, WDHA-Syndrom *n*, Verner-Morrison-Syndrom *n*.
WDLL *<abbr>* **well-differentiated lymphocytic lymphoma**: lymphozytäres Lymphosarkom *n*.
WEE *<abbr>* **western equine encephalomyelitis**: Westliche Pferdeenzephalitis *f*.
WHO *<abbr>* **World Health Organization**: Weltgesundheitsorganisation *f*.
WISC *<abbr>* **Wechsler Intelligence Scale for Children**: Wechsler-Intelligenzskala für Kinder *f*.
WNL *<abbr>* **within normal limits**: innerhalb normaler Grenzen.
WPW syndrome *<abbr>* **Wolff-Parkinson-White syndrome**: Wolff-Parkinson-White-Syndrom *n*, WPW-Syndrom *n*.
WR *<abbr>* **Wassermann reaction**: Wassermann-Reaktion *f*, WaR.
ws *<abbr>* **water-soluble**: wasserlöslich.
wt *<abbr>* **weight**: Gewicht *n*.

X, Y, Z

X *<abbr>* **1. xanthine; 2. xanthosine**: 1. Xanthin *n*, X; 2. Xanthosin *n*.
Xao *<abbr>* **xanthosine**: Xanthosin *n*.
X-bite *<abbr>* **crossbite**: Kreuzbiss *m*.
XDH *<abbr>* **xanthine dehydrogenase**: Xanthindehydrogenase *f*.
XDR-TB *<abbr>* **extensively drug-resistant tuberculosis**: extrem medikamentenresistente Tuberkulose *f*.
XZ syndrome *<abbr>* **X zero syndrome**: X0-Syndrom *n*, Ullrich-Turner-Syndrom *n*.

y *<abbr>* **1. yellow; 2. young**: 1. gelb; 2. jung.
YF *<abbr>* **yellow fever**: Gelbfieber *n*.
YOB *<abbr>* **year of birth**: Geburtsjahr *n*.
yr *<abbr>* **year**: Jahr *n*.
yrs *<abbr>* **years**: Jahre.
ys *<abbr>* **yellow spot**: gelber Fleck *m*, Macula lutea *f*.

Z *<abbr>* **1. atomic number; 2. proton number**: 1. Ordnungszahl *f*, OZ; 2. Protonenzahl *f*.
ZDV *<abbr>* **zidovudine**: Zidovudin *n*, ZDV, Azidothymidin *n*, AZT.
ZE syndrome *<abbr>* **Zollinger-Ellison syndrome**: Zollinger-Ellison-Syndrom *n*.
zpg *<abbr>* **zero population growth**: Bevölkerungsnullwachstum *n*.
ZSR *<abbr>* **zeta sedimentation rate**: Zeta-Sedimentationsrate *f*.

Appendix II: SI Units in Medicine
Anhang II: SI-Einheiten in der Medizin

SI-Einheiten: Übersicht der Maßeinheiten.

Messgröße	Einheit (Kurzzeichen)
Länge	Meter (m)
Fläche	Quadratmeter (m^2)
Volumen	Kubikmeter (m^3)
ebener Winkel (Winkel)	Radiant (rad)
räuml. Winkel (Raumwinkel)	Steradiant (sr)
Masse	Kilogramm (kg)
Dichte	Kilogramm durch Kubikmeter (kg/m^3)
Zeit	Sekunde (s)
Frequenz	Hertz (Hz)
Geschwindigkeit	Meter durch Sekunde (m/s)
Beschleunigung	Meter/Sekundenquadrat (m/s^2)
Winkelgeschwindigkeit	Radiant durch Sekunde (rad/s)
Winkelbeschleunigung	Radiant/Sekundenquadrat (rad/s^2)
Kraft	Newton (N)
Druck, mechanische Spannung	Pascal (Pa), Bar (bar)
dynamische Viskosität	Pascalsekunde ($Pa \cdot s$)
kinematische Viskosität	Quadratmeter durch Sekunde (m^2/s)
Energie, Arbeit, Wärmemenge	Joule (J)
Leistung, Energie, Wärmestrom	Watt (W)
elektr. Spannung (Potentialdifferenz)	Volt (V)
elektr. Widerstand	Ohm (Ω)
elektr. Stromstärke	Ampere (A)
elektr. Leitwert	Siemens (S)

SI-Einheiten: Übersicht der Maßeinheiten.

Messgröße	Einheit (Kurzzeichen)
Elektrizitätsmenge, elektr. Ladung	Coulomb (C)
elektr. Kapazität	Farad (F)
elektr. Flussdichte	Coulomb durch Quadratmeter (C/m^2)
elektr. Feldstärke	Volt durch Meter (V/m)
magnet. Fluss	Weber (Wb)
magnet. Flussdichte oder Induktion	Tesla (T)
Induktivität	Henry (H)
magnet. Feldstärke	Ampere durch Meter (A/m)
thermodynam. Temperatur	Kelvin (K), Grad Celsius (°C)
Lichtstärke	Candela (cd)
Leuchtdichte	Candela durch Quadratmeter (cd/m^2)
Lichtstrom	Lumen (lm)
Beleuchtungsstärke	Lux (lx)
Aktivität einer radioaktiven Substanz	Becquerel (Bq), reziproke Sekunde (s^{-1})
Energiedosis	Gray (Gy)
Äquivalentdosis	Joule durch Kilogramm (J/kg)
Energiedosisrate, -leistung	Gray durch Sekunde (Gy/s)
Äquivalentdosisrate, -leistung	Watt durch Kilogramm (W/kg)
Ionendosis	Coulomb durch Kilogramm (C/kg)
Ionendosisrate, -leistung	Ampere durch Kilogramm (A/kg)
Stoffmenge	Mol (mol)
stoffmengenbezogene Masse, molare Masse	Kilogramm durch Mol (kg/mol)
Stoffmengenkonzentration, Molarität	Mol durch Kubikmeter (mol/m^3)
Brechkraft optischer Systeme	Dioptrie (dpt)
Radioaktivität	reziproke Sekunde (s^{-1})
katalyt. Aktivität	Katal (kat)

SI-Einheiten: Vorsätze für dezimale Vielfache u. Teile von Einheiten.

Vorsatz*	Kurzzeichen	Bedeutung			
Tera	T	Billionenfaches	$= 10^{12}$	=	1 000 000 000 000
Giga	G	Milliardenfaches	$= 10^{9}$	=	1 000 000 000
Mega	M	Millionenfaches	$= 10^{6}$	=	1 000 000
Kilo	k	Tausendfaches	$= 10^{3}$	=	1 000
Hekto	h	Hundertfaches	$= 10^{2}$	=	100
Deka	da	Zehnfaches	$= 10^{1}$	=	10
Dezi	d	Zehntel	$= 10^{-1}$	=	0,1
Zenti	c	Hundertstel	$= 10^{-2}$	=	0,01
Milli	m	Tausendstel	$= 10^{-3}$	=	0,001
Mikro	μ	Millionstel	$= 10^{-6}$	=	0,000 001
Nano	n	Milliardstel	$= 10^{-9}$	=	0,000 000 001
Piko	p	Billionstel	$= 10^{-12}$	=	0,000 000 000 001
Femto	f	Billiardstel	$= 10^{-15}$	=	0,000 000 000 000 001
Atto	a	Trillionstel	$= 10^{-18}$	=	0,000 000 000 000 000 001

* *zulässig ist jeweils nur 1 Vorsatzzeichen, das mit dem (ohne Zwischenraum nachstehenden) Einheitenzeichen ein Ganzes bildet (DIN 1301)*